STUDIES IN CHRISTIAN HISTORY

Hinterland Theology

A Stimulus to Theological Construction

Alan P. F. Sell

STUDIES IN CHRISTIAN HISTORY AND THOUGHT

A full listing of all titles in this series
appears at the close of this book

STUDIES IN CHRISTIAN HISTORY AND THOUGHT

Hinterland Theology

A Stimulus to Theological Construction

Paternoster:
thinking faith

MILTON KEYNES · COLORADO SPRINGS · HYDERABAD

First published 2008 by Paternoster

Paternoster is an imprint of Authentic Media
9 Holdom Avenue, Bletchley, Milton Keynes, MK1 1QR, UK
1820 Jet Stream Drive, Colorado Springs, CO 80921, USA
OM Authentic Media, Medchal Road, Jeedimetla Village,
Secunderabad 500 055, A.P., India

www.authenticmedia.co.uk
Authentic Media is a Division of IBS-STL UK, a company limited by guarantee
(registered charity no. 270162)

14 13 12 11 10 09 08   7 6 5 4 3 2 1

British Library Cataloguing in Publication Data
A catalogue record for this book is available from the British Library

ISBN 978–1–84227–331–9

Typeset by A.R. Cross
Printed and bound in Great Britain
for Paternoster
by AlphaGraphics Nottingham

STUDIES IN CHRISTIAN HISTORY AND THOUGHT

Series Preface

This series complements the specialist series of *Studies in Evangelical History and Thought* and *Studies in Baptist History and Thought* for which Paternoster is becoming increasingly well known by offering works that cover the wider field of Christian history and thought. It encompasses accounts of Christian witness at various periods, studies of individual Christians and movements, and works which concern the relations of church and society through history, and the history of Christian thought.

The series includes monographs, revised dissertations and theses, and collections of papers by individuals and groups. As well as 'free standing' volumes, works on particular running themes are being commissioned; authors will be engaged for these from around the world and from a variety of Christian traditions.

A high academic standard combined with lively writing will commend the volumes in this series both to scholars and to a wider readership.

To my friends in the Reformed faculties and churches of
Hungary, Romania and Slovakia,
with gratitude for their kindness to my wife and myself over a quarter of a century,
and in memory of
Professors Czeglédy Sándor and Pásztor János

Contents

Preface

My purpose in this Preface is simply to express my thanks to those who have assisted me during the writing of this book: Rachel Hart, Archivist, University of St. Andrews; Richard Temple and Zoë Browne, Archivists, Senate House Library, London; Alma Jenner, Librarian, Mansfield College, Oxford; Richard Kidd, Principal, Northern Baptist College; Margaret Thompson, Westminster College, Cambridge; William D. McNaughton of Kirkcaldy; Peter Nockles and John Hodgson of The John Rylands University Library of Manchester; the staffs of the British Library and Dr. Williams's Library and The Congregational Library, London, and in particular Dr David L. Wykes, Director of Dr. Williams's Trust, for supplying the images of Chandler, Payne, Alliott, Adeney and Duthie and granting permission to publish them; Julian Lock, Archivist of Regent's Park College, Oxford, for supplying the image of Tymms, which may never have been published and concerning which the search for copyright holders has been in vain; and those former students of Charles Duthie who answered my queries about him. I was privileged to receive papers from the late Charles and Nancy Duthie in the expectation that I would in due course write an account of Charles's life and thought. I trust that Chapter 11 represents a not altogether unworthy attempt to discharge this happy task.

Thanks are also due to Jeremy Mudditt, Robin Parry and Anthony R. Cross of Paternoster Press, not only for their assistance to me – and in particular for Dr. Cross's expert typesetting of my text, but also for their commitment to the publishing of scholarly works through their burgeoning series. I am grateful, too, to Lyn Sneddon, who designed the front cover image which suggests that conversation between the Bible, the heritage of Christian testimony and the world in which I believe constructive and systematic theology to consist. The church depicted is Sedbergh United Reformed (formerly Congregational) Church, where I was ordained and inducted to my first pastorate. It was photographed by my late father, Arthur Philip Sell, who, together with my late mother, Freda Marion Sell, I remember with much gratitude and affection.

My oft-expressed thanks to Karen, my wife, for her never-failing support is utterly sincere and never a matter of form. We are just distinguishable, standing together in the Sedbergh church porch, as we have stood by one another through the years.

Alan P. F. Sell
Milton Keynes
August 2008

Abbreviations

BH	*The Baptist Handbook*
CCPD	*Calendar of the Correspondence of Philip Doddridge*, ed. G. F. Nuttall
CHST	*Transactions of the Congregational Historical Society*
CQ	*The Congregational Quarterly*
CR	*Calamy Revised*, ed. A. G. Matthews
CYB	*The Congregational Year Book*
CUEW	*The Congregational Union of England and Wales*
DBI	*Dictionary of Biblical Interpretation*, ed. John H. Hayes
DEB	*Dictionary of Evangelical Biography*, ed. D. M. Lewis
DECBP	*Dictionary of Eighteenth-Century British Philosophers*, eds J. W. Yolton, J. V. Price, and J. Stephens
DHT	*Dictionary of Historical Theology*, ed. T. Hart
DMBI	A *Dictionary of Methodism in Britain and Ireland*, ed. J. A. Vickers
DNB	*Dictionary of National Biography*
DNCBP	*Dictionary of Nineteenth-Century British Philosophers*, eds W. J. Mander and A. P. F. Sell
DSCHT	*Dictionary of Scottish Church History and Theology*, ed. N. M. deS. Cameron
DSCBP	*Dictionary of Seventeenth-Century British Philosophers*, ed. A. Pyle
DTCBP	*Dictionary of Twentieth-Century British Philosophers*, ed. S. Brown
DWB	*Dictionary of Welsh Biography*
EEUTA	*English Education Under the Test Acts*, H. McLachlan
EM	*The Evangelical Magazine*
ET	*The Expository Times*
FAE	*Freedom After Ejection*, A. Gordon
GEE	G. E. Evans, *Vestiges of Protestant Dissent*
JEREMY	W. D. Jeremy, *The Presbyterian Fund, etc.*
JURCHS	*The Journal of the United Reformed Church History Society*
MURCH	J. Murch, *A History of the Presbyterian and General Baptist Churches in the West of England*
ODNB	*Oxford Dictionary of National Biography*
PNT	*Protestant Nonconformist Texts*, series editor, A. P. F. Sell
SCM	W. D. McNaughton, *The Scottish Congregational Ministry*
TSJ	T. S. James, *Presbyterian Chapels and Charities*
URCYB	*The United Reformed Church Year Book*
UHST	*Transactions of the Unitarian Historical Society*
WTW	*Who They Were*, eds J. Taylor and C. Binfield
WWW	*Who Was Who*
WW	W. Wilson, *History and Antiquities of Dissenting Churches and Meeting-houses in London, Westminster and Southwark*

Hinterland Theology
A Stimulus to Theological Construction

The fundamental needs of men undergo little serious change from age to age—not even those of the body, still less those of the mind. Nor does the environment from which the supply of human needs has to be drawn really change. And if God through Christ has veritably been discharging for the last two thousand years the environmental functions which He imposed on Himself, is it likely that any great belief, any great fact, and great truth which has ministered in the past to human redemption, invigoration, illumination and blessedness can ever be out of date?

D. W. Simon, *The Making of a Preacher*, 1907, 40-41.

CHAPTER 1

Introduction

> In short, although it consists largely of criticism, the interest of the book is neither critical not historical, but constructive throughout. This method of construction through criticism is the one which I have instinctively followed in everything I have written.[1]

Thus wrote the philosopher, A. S. Pringle-Pattison, in the Preface to his published Gifford Lectures of 1912 and 1913. By adjusting myself to his words I can explain what is intended in this book in a way that will, I trust, be clear to all but postmodernists of the kind who deny that we can never know what an author's intention is even if it be proclaimed in block capitals. Where Pringle-Pattison describes his method as being that of 'construction through criticism', my method—'the one which I have followed in *much* that I have written'—is best thought of as construction through conversation. Although criticism may be both positive and negative, the word is often construed negatively only, and I wish to guard against this. But this does not sufficiently explain my preference for 'conversation' over 'criticism'. The main point is that I understand theology to be the product of a conversation with the Bible, the heritage of Christian thought, and the current socio-political-intellectual environment. Thus, for example, there can be little doubt that the ecclesiology of the sixteenth-century English Separatists was formed as they brought the Bible to bear upon the political circumstances in which they found themselves, or that the liberation theology of twentieth-century Latin America was prompted by a fresh reading of the Bible in relation to adverse social conditions then prevailing in many parts of that region On the assumption that inconsistency is not the objective, it is difficult to see how the product of any particular theologian's conversation could exclude either positive or negative criticism, for the participants in the conversation so frequently disagree with one another.

Some may deem it a perverse characteristic of one whose roots lie in the Dissenting tradition of Reformed thought that I have never been greatly impressed by mere size, status or fame. I have found that some of the most faithful churches are

---

[1] A. S. Pringle-Pattison, *The Idea of God in the Light of Recent Philosophy*, vi-vii. For Pringle-Pattison (1856-1931) see DNCBP; DCBP; ODNB; Alan P. F. Sell, *Philosophical Idealism and Christian Belief.*

small ones; that the largest centres of theological education are not necessarily the liveliest; that some of the most stimulating scholars are not in the most prestigious centres of learning; that those who hold high ecclesiastical office are not necessarily the worthiest—as Columbanus said to Pope Boniface, 'It is not a man's station but his principles that matter'[2]; and that some of the best pastors are among the humble in the land. Where matters of the intellect are concerned, it has been borne in upon me that some of the most interesting thinkers are those who might be classed as 'hinterland' persons. They are seldom dignified, or fossilized, in lists of 'set texts', but their writings sometimes stimulated those of their better-known contemporaries and successors either positively or negatively. Even when they did not, the ways in which the hinterland people adjusted to, or the reasons why they ignored, what better-known authors were saying is in itself interesting. It may even be argued that we have not fully understood the Lockes and Barths of this world until we have investigated what the hinterland people made of them. For these reasons I have devoted a not inconsiderable amount of time over the years to inviting hinterland persons back into the theological conversation.

I am, of course, aware that the term 'hinterland theologian' is imprecise, and may even be thought to be rough and ready. Where courses in higher education are concerned, it is also a relative term. Thus, for example, I have written on Locke, Mill and P. T. Forsyth, and I do not regard them as hinterland persons because I should expect graduates in philosophy to have some knowledge of the first two, and graduates in theology to have some knowledge of the third. But where more specialized courses are concerned some of the hinterland people are, as it were, promoted *pro tem*, so that, for example, in a course on English Dissenting Thought in the Eighteenth Century, I should expect students to become acquainted with Isaac Watts, Henry Grove, John Taylor, John Gill, Andrew Fuller, Richard Price, Joseph Priestley and others. These, however, remain hinterland persons in the sense that their writings are not the staple of general undergraduate courses.

While the theologians I have selected for study may be said to be representative, as hinterland persons, of many other such divines within and beyond the Dissenting traditions, I am not concerned to argue that they are fully representative of their own traditions as such. It is not simply that several shades of theological opinion may be found within every Christian tradition; it is that, especially until the nineteenth-century 'invention' of denominations as we have come to know them, the borders between the several Dissenting 'tendencies' were porous so that, for example, a minister might serve now a Presbyterian, now a Congregational church, and one trained by the Baptists might end among the Unitarians. The ten theologians have been selected because they are interesting in themselves, and because they can stimulate the ongoing theological conversation. Not, indeed, that they can contribute to every item on the current theological agenda. The most recent of them, Charles Duthie, who discussed numerous then current theological trends before his death in 1981, made his contribution before the voices of 'postmodernists', feminists and

[2] Columbanus, *Sancti Columbani Opera*, trans. G. S. M. Walker, 49.

people of other faiths were as clearly hear in British theological circles as they are thirty years on.

All of which is to say that the theological conversation always takes place in changing times. When constructive and systematic theologians[3] fail to respond to intellectual challenges, time-lags result; when they 'go with the flow' dramatic oscillations can occur between the stance of one generation and its immediate predecessor. In this book I do not deal at length with the factors which prompted significant intellectual shifts from the seventeenth century to the twentieth: the Enlightenment, the Evangelical Revival, modern biblical criticism, and liberal theology, Barth and the two World Wars. These have been much discussed and enormous bibliographies exist regarding each of them. Rather, I have selected some hinterland people from the English Dissenting traditions, who responded in one way or another to these significant movements of thought. They are the Congregationalists Thomas Ridgley and Abraham Taylor and the Presbyterian Samuel Chandler who wrote in the wake of the Toleration Act of 1689 which gave liberty of worship to Protestant trinitarians, and gave the Dissenting academies greater (if at times still precarious) freedom than they had previously enjoyed; George Payne and Richard Alliott, also Congregationalists, who, in the wake of the Enlightenment and the Evangelical Revival, were among those who adjusted the received Reformed tradition in the light of the moral critique of doctrine and the call to preach the Gospel to every creature; David Worthington Simon, Thomas Vincent Tymms and Frederic W. Adeney—two further Congregationalists and Tymms the Baptist—whose writings could not overlook the advent of modern biblical criticism and the need for a fresh approach in apologetics; and Robert Sleightholme Franks and Charles Sim Duthie, both of whom were Congregationalists, the latter of whom—a Scot serving in English Congregationalism—aligned himself with The United Reformed Church on its formation in 1972. It fell to Franks and Duthie to take account of modern liberal theology and its aftermath, not least as this was influenced by the intellectual, emotional and physical upheavals of two World Wars. It may at first sight seem odd that Franks, born in 1871, should appear in the section of this book headed, 'In the wake of theological liberalism,' for he was over fifty when Barth's theology of the Word broke upon English shores. The choice of Franks is, however, quite deliberate for, owing to his long life, his ability to publish to an advanced age, and his adverse reaction to Barth, he exemplifies those continuities of thought which could easily be overlooked by those too eager to parcel up the history of thought into over-tidy, chronologically distinct, bundles. Clearly, I have provided samples only from the four periods (and, to repeat, because ideas know no calendrical boundaries the term 'period' is not to be understood in any way which would preclude the time-lags which occur in intellectual history); but these samples will

---

[3] The position is rather different with biblical and historical theologians who, on grounds of pure scholarship, must be permitted to devote themselves, respectively, to, for example, the concept of 'covenant' or the *filioque* while the whole world collapses around them.

suffice to enable at least tentative judgments to be made concerning continuities and discontinuities over time in Dissenting thought.

It is right to observe that although I am here concerned with English Dissenters and with one Scot who sojourned among them on two occasions, I am not unaware of the importance of Scotland in the story of English Dissent, nor or the permeability of the Scottish-English border in both directions. Thus, for example, at a time when English Dissenters were excluded from Oxford and Cambridge universities, their ancient Scottish counterparts were open to them, and such relations have continued down to our own time, notwithstanding the open doors of Oxbridge and the establishment of religious-test-free English and Welsh universities from the nineteenth century onwards. Both Payne and Alliott studied in Glasgow, and all but one of the ten theologians studied in this book were honoured by Scottish universities thus: Ridgley, Taylor and Chandler were DDs of Aberdeen, while Chandler was also a DD of Edinburgh, as was Simon. Payne and Alliott were alumni and LLDs of Glasgow, and Tymms and Adeney were DDs of St. Andrews. Duthie was a DD of Aberdeen, of which University he was an alumnus. Duthie is included here partly by way of demonstrating the contribution Scots have made to English Dissenting education. Among others in this category to whom passing reference will be made are W. Lindsay Alexander, A. M. Fairbairn, P. T. Forsyth, Robert Mackintosh and A. E. Garvie. But that the traffic was not in one direction only is evidenced by the fact that Payne ministered in Scotland and Simon taught there, as did Duthie, and as did other Englishmen such as J. M. Hodgson and H. F. Lovell Cocks, and the Welshman, T. Hywel Hughes.

Why am I concerned in this book only with Dissenters? It is patently obvious that Anglicans and others have also had theological adjustments to make over the centuries. My answer is in two parts. First, I have understood it to be an aspect of my mission over the years to bring the diverse English Dissenting theological traditions more clearly to the fore in theological and ecumenical discussion. Intelligence gathered during my academic and ecclesiastical peregrinations has persuaded me that much of it is scarcely remembered in England, it is relatively little known in America,[4] and it is almost entirely unknown in parts of Europe and

---

[4] Hence, for example, a gracious American reviewer of my book, *Nonconformist Theology in the Twentieth Century*, suggested that a better title would have been *British Nonconformity in the Twentieth Century*. See Stephen M. Garrett, *Reviews in Religion and Theology*, XIV no. 4, September 2007, 605. I beg to differ because, for the following reasons very briefly stated, I did not cover Scottish Nonconformity: (a) the Scottish and English establishments are significantly different, and hence the Nonconformities are different. (b) The Scottish Nonconformists do not have the Separatist martyrs, the Pilgrims, or the Great Ejectment of 1662 in their heritage. (c) Whereas the *raison d'être* of the English and Welsh Dissenters was ecclesiological (the true Church, they thought, was something other than the Anglican establishment), the bulk of the Scottish Nonconformists maintained the Presbyterian order and, indeed, the Free Church of 1843, regarding itself as the Church of Scotland (Free), upheld the establishment principle. (d) While the Scottish Baptists and Congregationalists have tenuous pre-histories, they are

elsewhere.[5] To say no more than this would, however, leave the incorrect impression that mine is a gap-filling exercise only. Hence, secondly, if, as I believe, constructive theologizing entails heeding the Bible, conversing with the heritage of Christian thought, and being alive to requirements of contemporary proclamation,[6] then the best theology, not least the best ecumenical theology, will be thoroughly researched theology (something of which, one is sometimes tempted to think, there is too little at the present time[7]); and, as every botanist knows, interesting specimens are to be found in the byways. Thirdly, by concentrating upon one particular tradition (or cluster of traditions) it is possible to demonstrate the considerable variety of theological thinking within it. Thus, this contribution to the wider theological debate comprises soundings taken in English Dissent, in the hope that they will refresh the memories of those who belong to that tradition, stimulate interest in that tradition in other parts of the Christian family and, above all, contribute some building-blocks for theological construction in our time.

As I proceed I shall offer reflections on the writings of the ten theologians, but I shall also refer a number of discussions to the Conclusion, in which I shall be able

---

largely the product of evangelical movements from the end of the eighteenth century onwards (cf. the Calvinistic Methodists/Presbyterian Church of Wales).

[5] I speak as I have found, and I do not imply an adverse judgment. I am well aware that while most theological students trained in Britain will not have been able to avoid Barth, Bonhoeffer, Pannenberg and others, their acquaintance with the Dutch, Scandinavian and other European traditions may be slight, and their knowledge of the New England theology, or of such authors as Thornwell, Park, Nevin and Van Ruler may, to put it mildly, be less than intimate (though I observe that B. B. Warfield, Cornelius Van Til and Herman Dooyeweerd are meat and drink in certain evangelical coteries. I suspect, however, that this is not normally attributable to the influence of British university departments of theology). On the general point: in his review of my *Nonconformist Theology in the Twentieth Century* Keith Clements has properly pointed out that 'observers from outside the British Isles, especially on the European continent, never cease needing to be reminded that in Britain the free churches have always claimed and occupied a much more central place in both the religious and political life of the nation than their minority co-denominationalists elsewhere.' See *The Ecumenical Review*, LIX no. 4, October 2007, 564.

[6] See further, Alan P. F. Sell, *Testimony and Tradition*, ch. 1.

[7] While competent specialist work in historical theology proliferates, I fear that some of the 'big names' of systematic and constructive theology are not always as careful in scholarship as they might be: one-sided interpretations of the Cappadocian Fathers in relation to the Trinity, and undiscriminating assaults upon the Enlightenment(s) come immediately to mind. Of course, research into the historic witness and alertness to the world as it is are not the only criteria of satisfactory constructive and systematic theology. I do not think that all theologians have benefited as much as they might have done from the rigour and clarity which follow upon the skilful application of the techniques of analytical philosophy—a wonderful purgative of that internal incoherence that is sometimes offloaded onto the unsuspecting, perhaps in the hope that it will be mistaken for depth.

to treat the divines together, and fasten in a thematic way upon matters of continuing importance to which they draw our attention.

It might be said that my chosen subjects are accurately placed in the hinterland because they are second rank thinkers, and hence they may justifiably be left on one side. No doubt they did not gather schools of disciples around them; they did not hit the headlines with sensational new theories; their published offerings would not sit easily alongside the inconsequential imaginations, mystical musings or ideological idolatries of some of the religious authors who are sufficiently marketable to grace the shelves of our major book chains. On account of none of these 'deficiencies' need they be denied a fresh hearing. Each is stimulating in his own way and, as I shall hope to show in the Conclusion, they have questions to pose to, and gauntlets to thrown down before, present-day toilers in the theological field.

Part I

In the Wake of Toleration

Thomas Ridgley (1667–1734)

Samuel Chandler (1693–1766)

CHAPTER 2

Thomas Ridgley (1667–1734): Doctrinal Zeal and Personal Humility

Very little is known about Thomas Ridgley's early life and family circumstances. He was born in London and educated at a Dissenting academy in Wiltshire. Walter Wilson speculates that he may have studied under 'Mr. Davidson' of Trowbridge.[1] This would seem to be a reference to John Davisson, a General Baptist whose academy was senior and rival to that of the Particular Baptists at Bristol. Since 1670, Davisson had been a lay leader at the churches at Southwick and Conigre, Trowbridge, where Thomas Collier had ministered until his death in 1691. Collier was born *circa* 1613, and raised among the Particular Baptists. But his published *Body of Divinity* of 1674 makes it abundantly clear that he had by that date forsaken the doctrine of particular election for that of general election. Indeed, he went so far as to argue that because God foresaw that human beings would be so lost in sin that few would willingly respond to the gospel, he provided for two elections: one from eternity, so that some would certainly be saved and that Christ's honour would not be impugned, and a 'second special election' of those who would respond to the gospel during their lifetimes. Whereas the former could not fall away during their lifetimes, the latter might do so, he declared. None of this appealed to the Bristol Baptists under the leadership of Andrew Gifford, Sr. Following Collier's death in 1691, the Western Association recommended that Davisson should serve as elder at Southwick and Trowbridge. In 1697, as a result of dissention, the Southwick-Trowbridge pastorate was divided, and Davisson ministered at the latter only until his death in 1721, by which time it was said that he had adopted Socinian views.[2] From all of this is would seem that if Ridgley had initial sympathy with the general position of his teacher, he subsequently reacted against it—if, indeed, he was at Trowbridge at all.

---

[1] WW, II,72. For Ridgley see also EEUTA; ODNB; J. A. Jones, ed., *Bunhill Memorials*, 230-232; A. W. Light, *Bunhill Fields*, II, 24-7. For Ridgley in his intellectual context see Alan P. F. Sell, *Philosophy, Dissent and Nonconformity*, ch. 2.

[2] For the Trowbridge situation see Roger Hayden, *Continuity and Change*, 1-28. For Collier see MURCH, 192-3; ODNB.

'It is said' that Ridgley also studied under Thomas Doolittle, a protégé of Richard Baxter's, at Islington.[3] Doolittle's academy was deemed to be the leading Presbyterian institution of its kind in London. Edmund Calamy, Matthew Henry, Thomas Emlyn, and the academy tutors John Ker and Thomas Rowe were among its alumni. There is no hard evidence that Ridgley was of their number. We need to move to firmer ground. As we do so, I should explain that my plan is to introduce some of the incidents of Ridgley's life in this introductory section and in section I, but I shall reserve incidents of particular doctrinal import to subsequent sections, when I shall relate them to Ridgley's writings.

In 1695 Ridgley became assistant minister to Thomas Gouge at the Independent church at Three Cranes, Fruiterers' Alley, Thames Street, London.[4] Gouge had made a name for himself as a popular preacher. In the estimation of the young Isaac Watts he ranked with John Howe and Joseph Stennett as one of the three greatest preachers of the day. In 1694 he was appointed to succeed Daniel Williams as a Merchants' lecturer at Pinners' Hall. On Gouge's death on 8 January 1700 Ridgley succeeded him as pastor at Three Cranes. Owing to strife within the fellowship—a matter to which I shall return, the church was at a low ebb, but under Ridgley it revived, though the congregation was never large.

Ridgley followed in the footsteps of Gouge in becoming a Tuesday morning Merchants' Lecturer at the Pinners' Hall. He was also appointed a Thursday evening lecturer at Jewin Street chapel, and on Sunday evenings he gave lectures designed for male catechumens at the Old Jewry meeting house. Of these venues the first was home to a Congregational church, the latter two to Presbyterian congregations.

We may catch something of the flavour of his preaching to the young men at the Old Jewry from his sermon on *The Abuse of Feasting and Recreations.* Appropriately enough, he delivered this on 26 December, 1717. His text was Exodus 32:6, concerning the disobedient Hebrews who, during Moses's period of communion with God on the mountain, 'rose up early ... and offered burnt offerings, and brought peace offerings' to the golden calf that Aaron had made; and then 'the people sat down to eat and to drink, and rose up to play.'

Ridgley begins with the slighting of Moses:

> When Sin abounds, it not only breaks the Bonds of Friendship; but renders a People unmindful of the Laws of Gratitude. They who have been made publick Blessings to them; to whom, under God, they owe their Lives, their Liberties, yea, all that's dear to them in this World, these shall not have common Justice from Them, by whom God and his true Worship are abandoned. ... When a People forget the Mercies of

---

[3] EEATA, 118; cf. 10. The supposition is repeated in ODNB, though not by Alexander Gordon in DNB. For Doolittle (1630/1633?-1707) see CR; FAE, 254; JEREMY, 7, 12, 30, 32; ODNB; TSJ, 84; J. A. Jones, *Bunhill Memorials*, 37-9; A. W. Light, *Bunhill Fields*, II, 46-52.

[4] For Gouge (c.1665-1700) see FAE, 273; WW, II, 69-72; ODNB.

> God and depart from out of his holy ways, they are oftentimes given up to all manner of licentiousness.[5]

He considers the abuse of eating and drinking, and of recreation that, 'if rightly us'd, is not only allowable but necessary.'[6] However, 'all Games which depend upon Lot are unlawful.'[7] 'Let me conclude,' he says, 'with an earnest Request to you, to take heed of falling by Things which seem harmless, and commit your selves into his Hand, who is able to keep you safe in the Hour of Temptation, and to sweeten all outward Enjoyments with a sense of his Love.'[8]

In the appended *Discourse* Ridgley traces the history of religious festivals through the Bible and on to Constantine, and comes to the realization that every age has added new festivals. As to Christmas, 'the exact time of Christ's Nativity remains uncertain', but even if it were not, to celebrate it with 'Revellings, Masquerades, Gluttony, Drunkenness, and Gaming ... [would be] very unbecoming a Christian, who professes Subjection to him, who was manifest that he might destroy the Works of the Devil.'[9]

Meanwhile, on 3 June 1712, Ridgley had married Emlin Norris, and one daughter is mentioned in his will. In 1721 he was among those who signed the Preface, and subscribed, to John Asty's edition of John Owen's *Sermons*.[10] On 25 September 1727 he was present at the first meeting of the London Congregational Board, but he does not appear to have continued in membership.[11] In 1731, Emlin having died, he married Phoebe Brockatt.

In the following year Ridgley preached at the funeral of the Reverend John Hurrion, who died at the age of 56. From his ordination in 1701 to 1724, Hurrion had ministered at Denton, Norfolk, and in the latter year he removed to Hare Court, London.[12] Ridgley's text was John 5: 35, 'He was a burning and a shining light.' During that section of his sermon in which he offers an appreciation of Hurrion's life, Ridgley begins conventionally enough: 'When it pleases God to take away from churches, ministers that have obtain'd mercy to be faithful, it ought to be laid to

---

[5] T. Ridgley, *The Abuse of Feastings and Recreations Consider'd*, 4, 7.

[6] Ibid., 16.

[7] Ibid., 23.

[8] Ibid., 30.

[9] Ibid., 48.

[10] The other signatories were John Nesbitt (FAE, 316; ODNB; WW, III, 282-7), Matthew Clarke (ODNB; WW, I, 474-491, III, 287), John Asty (FAE, 313; ODNB; WW, II, 537-545) and Thomas Bradbury (ODNB; TSJ, 45; WW, III, 450-452, 504-535). They were all Congregationalists and Calvinists, albeit Clarke's tolerance of ministers who did not subscribe at Salters' Hall in 1719 (for which matter see below) prompted some to view him with suspicion. The ODNB article on Asty incorrectly gives 1712 as the year of publication of Owen's *Sermons*.

[11] Anon., 'London Congregational Board,' 50.

[12] For Hurrion (1676-1731) see ODNB; WW, III, 288-96; John B. Marsh, *The Story of Harecourt*, 240-241; John Browne, *History of Congregationalism ... in Norfolk and Suffolk*, 336-7.

heart by all, as a very afflictive stroke.'[13] But then he speaks with a candour which is not always shown by those delivering funeral orations:

> [F]or some years before he came to London, he very much affected a reclusive and sedentary life, in which he shut himself up from the world, unless, when he appeared in publick, on the Lord's days; and hardly convers'd with his own family, excepting in what respects the necessary duties respecting it; but addicted himself to close Study, by which means he gained a great stock of knowledge, tho' hereby he prejudiced his health, the declining state whereof soon appeared after this, and, for want of exercise, subjected himself to a confluence of humours, which afterwards made him a burden to himself.[14]

Ridgley further observes that while some thought Hurrion foolish to contemplate a London pastorate, he wants the world to know that the deceased 'kept between twenty and thirty private fasts to seek direction from God concerning this matter, before he determined to do it.'[15]

Ridgley was equally to the point the following year, when delivering the funeral oration for the Reverend John Sladen.[16] Sladen had studied under Timothy Jollie at Attercliffe academy, where his 'vivacity and gaiety of temper ... procured him frequent reproofs from his tutor',[17] and he was ordained at Dockhead, Surrey in 1711, the church removing to Back Street, Horsleydown in 1729. He died on 19 October 1733. Ridgley says that in his youth Sladen was greatly influenced by Richard Taylor, Abraham Taylor's father; that he was a stalwart defender of the doctrines of the Christian faith; but, since all the congregation knew it, there was no point in hiding the fact that he had a fiery temper. This is not quite the impression left later by John Waddington, who remarked of Sladen that, 'With all his unflinching fidelity, he was, however, a man of genial disposition and lively wit.'[18] This last was on one occasion at least directed at Ridgley himself. He and Sladen were out walking one day and the Doctor, 'a very careless man, and as heedless in his manner of walking, as he was negligent in his person,' slipped and fell into a ditch. As he helped him out, Sladen remarked, 'What a pity it was to see so orthodox a body of divinity in a ditch.'[19]

---

[13] T. Ridgley, *A Sermon Occasioned by the Death of the Reverend Mr. John Hurrion*, 35.

[14] Ibid., 36.

[15] Ibid., 37.

[16] Idem, *A Sermon Occasion'd by the Death of the Reverend Mr. John Sladen*, 43.

[17] WW, IV, 265.

[18] J. Waddington, *Surrey Congregational History*, 159. See also Edward E. Cleal, *The Story of Congregationalism in Surrey*, 48-9.

[19] WW, IV, 267-8.

I

Earnest preacher and faithful pastor though he was, without question Ridgley's greatest contribution lay in the field of theological education. On the death of Isaac Chauncy in 1712,[20] Ridgley succeeded to the post of theological tutor at the prominent academy in Tenter Alley, Moorfields, where his colleague was the distinguished lay scientist John Eames, who taught languages, natural and moral philosophy, and mathematics. A former student, Richard Densham,[21] assumed responsibility for these subjects when, on Ridgley's death, Eames transferred his attention to divinity.[22] It would seem that this outcome brought to an end a period of uncertainty in the academy's affairs, for during the vacancy, on 6 April 1734, David Jennings wrote to Philip Doddridge in these terms: 'I hear that not A[braham] T[aylor] but Alexander is the man which a certain powerful Party have their Eye upon.'[23]

Of Ridgley it was said that

> his qualifications for this office were very considerable. To solid learning, he united an accurate judgment, conciliating manners, and great aptitude at communicating instruction. In this station he was extremely useful, and had the honour of furnishing the Dissenting churches with many ministers, who distinguished themselves by their talents, and proved great blessings in their day and generation.[24]

The University of Aberdeen conferred its Doctorate of Divinity upon Ridgley in December 1728.[25]

David Jennings was probably Ridgley's most scholarly pupil.[26] He was born at Kibworth, Leicestershire, on 18 May 1691, and his education spanned the last period of Chauncy's tutorship and the first of Ridgley's. Of particular interest is a

---

[20] For Chauncy (1632-1712) see FAE, 234; JEREMY, 55; ODNB; WW, I, 289-291. He served as tutor from 1701 until his death.

[21] For whom see WW, II, 74 n; though WW, II, 73 has Joseph, and EEUTA p. 119 has James Densham

[22] For Eames (1686-1744) see ODNB; WW, II, 73-4 n.

[23] CCPD, no. 407. The Alexander referred to is John (1686-1743), an orientalist and patristics scholar, who had conducted an academy at Stratford-upon-Avon, but had become minister of Plunket Street Presbyterian Church, Dublin, in 1730. See EEUTA, 13; ODNB. He exemplifies those ministers who moved between ecclesiological 'persuasions' ('denominations' as we have inherited them from the nineteenth century is too institutional a term for those fluid times), because for some ten years from 1713 he had been a Congregational minister in Gloucester.

[24] WW, II, 74-5.

[25] Ridgley's editor, J. M. Wilson, probably following WW, II, 76, implies that the DD was awarded in recognition of Ridgley's *A Body of Divinity*. See ibid., xxi. But the work was not published until 1731.

[26] For Jennings, whose older brother, John, conducted an academy at Kibworth, see EEUTA, 119-122; ODNB; WW, III, 174-5;

testimonial dated 13 August 1715, signed by Ridgley, John Nesbitt, Matthew Clarke and Daniel Neal:[27]

> Whereas Mr. David Jennings, hath spent several Years in those Studies, more especially which tend to qualify him for the work of the Ministry; and in order to his more regular entrance upon and comfortable progress in that Service, has desired us to make Trial of his Gifts & Fitness for it.
>
> We do hereby Testify, That upon his examination, it appears to us, he has made a good Improvement of his Time, and his endeavours have been bless'd with a very considerable Degree of learning; so that in this Respect we esteem him, wel furnished for that great work unto which he devotes himself.
>
> And since he hath also the Testimony of a good Conversation, in the Church, to which he stands related, and from the Tutors under which he studied, we recomend him to others as One, that we verily believe will approve himself an able Minister of the New Testament, and hope God will make of eminent service in his Church.[28]

Jennings served as assistant at Haberdashers' Hall from 1716; from 1718 until his death in 1762 he was pastor at Old Gravel Lane, Wapping and, from 1744, he taught alongside Eames, his former tutor, at the academy. He published *An Introduction to the use of the Globes and the Orrery: With the application of Astronomy to Chronology* in 1739. This work contains an appendix in which Jennings discusses the first and fourth days of creation as described in Genesis 1. In 1749 he was awarded the degree of Doctor of Divinity by the University of St. Andrews. His *Jewish Antiquities*, posthumously published in 1766, was edited by his former student, Philip Furneaux.

John Hurrion's sons, John and Samuel, studied under Ridgley. They were born during their father's Denton ministry, the former probably in 1705, the latter in 1710. Following his training, John Jr. served as assistant to Ridgley at Three Cranes Court (1731/2). He proceeded to Gosport, where he was ordained on 3 May 1732, Abraham Taylor delivering the charge.[29] There he remained until his death in 1750. Of him it was said that 'He was celebrated as a preacher, both for the excellence of the matter, and the agreeableness of his delivery.'[30] Samuel Hurrion was ordained at Guestwick, Norfolk, on 26 September 1733. He resigned in 1754 owing to ill

---

[27] For Nesbitt (1661-1727) see FAE, 316; ODNB; WW, III, 382-7; John B. Marsh, *The Story of Harecourt*, 208-235. Nesbitt preceded Hurrion at Harecourt, the latter preaching his funeral sermon on 29 October 1727. He married Elizabeth, the daughter of Isaac Chauncy. For Neal (1678-1743), historian of New England and of the Puritans, see JEREMY, 28, 112, 140; ODNB; TSJ, 709, 717; WW, III, 92-102. He was educated at Thomas Rowe's academy at Newington Green, and also studied for two years in Utrecht and one year in Leiden.

[28] Dr. Williams's Library MS. 38.97.1.

[29] WW, II, 81.

[30] Ibid.

health, lived for a period in Bungay and Beccles, died on 25 October 1763, and was buried at Denton. His son, John, to whom he wrote a letter concerning his 'remarkably pious ancestors', became a Congregational minister at Southwold, Suffolk.[31]

Samuel Bruce, was born *circa* 1711. He studied first under John Wadsworth, Timothy Jollie's successor at Attercliffe academy, and then proceeded to Moorfields under Ridgley. He served as assistant to Daniel Mayo at Kingston, and was then called to succeed John Hurrion at Harecourt, where he was ordained in 1732. He proved himself a popular minister.

> His composures were very exact, his reasoning solid and convincing, and his delivery grave and serious. ... He had a very successful way of addressing persons under temptation and distress of mind, and possessed a happy skill in answering and removing the doubts and fears of discouraged Christians. He greatly lamented the growing errors and corruptions of the times, and manifested a just and commendable zeal for the great and important truths of the gospel. ... Few were more diligent in watching over their flocks ...[32]

Sadly, this promising young man became ill and died on 5 December 1737, aged twenty-seven.

It is to be feared that not all of Ridgley's pupils brought distinction to the ministry. One such was Thomas Tingey, a child of the manse who bore his father's name.[33] He had begun his studies under John Fleming at the Stratford-on-Avon academy, and then transferred to Moorfields. He served at Lower Rotherhithe, London from 1729 or 1730 to 1736, when he removed to Beccles, where he remained until his death in 1748/9. Walter Wilson records two adverse comments upon him: he was 'a young man of good pulpit talents, but of too good an opinion of himself, and of a very unsociable disposition.' Again, 'Mr. Tingey was generally reckoned a good preacher; but latterly he unhappily involved himself in secular business of various kinds, and this with some improprieties of conduct which naturally followed, sunk him very much in the esteem of the professing world.'[34] The lack of detail, together with those sensitivities of conscience to which the godly are prone, makes it difficult to know where precisely Tingey stood on the continuum from 'Jack the lad' to 'criminal'.

John Lavington (1715-1764) was among Ridgley's last students.[35] The Presbyterian son of a staunchly Presbyterian father, also John, and with the notable

---

[31] See J. Browne, *History of Congregationalism ... in Norfolk and Suffolk*, 326-7, 336; WW, III, 296; [A. F. Thorpe], *Guestwick-Briston 1652-1952*, privately printed, [1952].

[32] WW, III, 297-8. See also John B. Marsh, *The Story of Harecourt*, 240-241.

[33] Reference will be made to Thomas Tingey, Sr., below.

[34] WW, IV, 369. The briefest reference is made to Tingey, Jr., in J. Browne, *A History of Congregationalism and Memorials of the Churches in Norfolk and Suffolk*, 464-5.

[35] For Lavington see EEUTA, 12; ODNB; Alan P. F. Sell, *Dissenting Thought and the Life of the Churches*, 357, 360, 364.

John Ball of Honiton as his maternal grandfather, it is not surprising that Lavington continued in their line. He held a number of positions in the West-country before settling at Ottery St. Mary in 1751. He remained there until his death, and conducted an academy from 1752 to 1764. This was the first in a succession of western academies. He published *An Humble Enquiry into the Nature of the Gospel-Offer, Faith, and Assurance* (1759). When Lavington died, Thomas Rooker of Bridport, to whom Lavington was distantly related by marriage, assumed responsibility for the academy,[36] and continued to use Lavington's lectures which were based on Johannes Marck's *Christianae theologiae medulla*.

The lasting memorial to Ridgley's teaching is his book, *A Body of Divinity*. First published in 1731, the work comprises his lectures on the *Westminster Larger Catechism*.[37] It went through a number of editions, and was used by Bernard Foskett at Bristol Baptist College.[38] Of the importance of catechetical teaching Ridgley was in no doubt. In 1719, the year of the Salters' Hall proceedings concerning the Trinity and subscription (to which further reference shall be made), he delivered a funeral sermon following the death of a young person entitled, *The Advantage of Falling into the Hand of God rather than Man*. His text was I Chronicles 21: 13, and he cautioned his hearers that it would not do to say, 'we will embrace Religion when we can pursue our Lusts no longer.'[39] Of particular interest is the Epistle Dedicatory, addressed to 'the society of Catechumens who attend on the Lecture in the Old-Jewry.' In it he writes,

> We live in a day wherein the most Important Doctrines of Christianity are not only Opposed, but treated with Contempt; many deny the only Lord God, and our Lord Jesus Christ; and the Work and Glory of the Holy Ghost is traduced, or deem'd unnecessary to the promoting of practical Godliness. A Flood of Atheism and Irreligion rushes in upon us with a threatening Violence, and many who boast their Sprightly Parts, pretending to be Masters of Reason, are by the Arts of those who lie in wait to deceive, turn'd aside from the Simplicity of the Gospel.
>
> I need not infer from hence, how necessary it is for you to be well Established in the first Principles of the Oracles of God. And, that you esteem the Excellent Composure of the Reverend Assembly of Divines at Westminster, adapted to answer

---

[36] See further, Alan P. F. Sell, *Dissenting Thought and the Life of the Churches*, ch. 11.

[37] In what follows I use the two-volume edition of 1855. It was edited by John M. Wilson, who made slight cosmetic amendments to the language, and appended his own notes to the several sections as appropriate. To a few of Wilson's comments I wish to refer.

[38] See Alan P. F. Sell, *Philosophy, Dissent and Nonconformity*, 42-3. For Foskett (1685-1758) see EEUTA, 92; ODNB; *Bristol Baptist College. 250 Years 1679-1929*; Norman Moon, *Education for Ministry. Bristol Baptist College 1679-1979*; Roger Hayden, 'The contribution of Bernard Foskett'; idem, *Continuity and Change*, *passim*.

[39] T. Ridgley, *The Advantage of Falling into the Hand of God rather than Man*, 31.

this valuable End, your Practice in attending the Explication thereof sufficiently declares.[40]

In the opening sentence of the Preface to his *Body of Divinity* Ridgley provides a telling characterisation of the theological environment within which he went to work:

The influence which the different sentiments of men, in matters of religion, have, for the most part, on their temper and behaviour towards one another, affords very little ground to expect that any attempt to explain or defend the most important doctrines of Christianity, should not be treated with dislike and opposition by some, how much soever it may afford matter of conviction to others.[41]

As he later put it, 'men's sentiments in divinity differ as much as their faces, and some are not disposed to weigh those arguments that are brought to support any scheme of doctrine, which differs from what they have before received.'[42]

This circumstance, he continues, would have 'put a stop to my pen' but for the 'call of providence' which has prompted him to enter the lists against those who contend that fundamental doctrines—election, particular redemption and efficacious grace among them, are 'inconsistent with the moral perfections of the divine nature.'[43] These doctrines

are now traduced by many, as though they were new and strange doctrines, not founded on scripture, nor to be maintained by any just methods of reasoning deduced from it; or as if the duties of practical religion could not be inculcated consistently therewith. If this insinuation were true, our preaching would be vain, our hope also vain, and we should be found false witnesses for God, and have no solid ground whereon to set our feet. ... And if this be not sufficient to justify my present undertaking, I have nothing to allege of equal weight.[44]

Ridgley resolves that he will pursue his expository objective in the conviction that the 'inspired writings' are the only 'infallible rule of faith', and says that if any of his interpretations differ from those commonly received this is not because he has affected 'singularity, or taken pleasure in going out of the beaten path.'[45] It is noticeable that time and again when venturing an opinion he does so humbly, acknowledging that 'liberty of thinking and reasoning which we are allowed to use', but always open to the ineradicable element of mystery at the heart of the Christian faith, to the place of reverent agnosticism, and to the possibility that he may be mistaken. Of all dogmaticians, Ridgley is the least dogmatic.

---

[40] Ibid., 4-5.

[41] Idem, *A Body of Divinity*, I, vii.

[42] Ibid., I, ix.

[43] Ibid., I, vii.

[44] Ibid.

[45] Ibid., I, viii.

Before discussing a selection of issues raised by Ridgley's writings there is one further matter to be considered: his method. It has already become clear that his intention is to pay supreme regard to the witness of Scripture, and any temptations I may feel to dismantle his biblical proofs by reference to latter day biblical criticism shall resolutely be shunned. But he was also working in a general intellectual environment that was undergoing significant change. This is a long and complicated story. Suffice it to say that there flowed down from the Middle Ages a codified Aristotelianism the linchpin of which was the syllogism. Peter Ramus (1515-1572) did as much as any to break the stranglehold which this mode of argument had placed upon much intellectual life. For it he substituted the adumbration of self-evidently true maxims. Concurrently, there was the influence of the new science as represented in the works of Bacon and Newton, which turned the method of argumentation in an empirical direction. Henceforth the quest of reasonableness in religion as elsewhere would no longer be a matter of reason abstracted from experience—a methodological departure to which Locke gave significant impetus.[46]

What all of this means for Ridgley's writings is that unlike many of his predecessors and some of his contemporaries, there is an experimental—even a pastoral—thread running through is work. We are not for the most part in the realm of logic-chopping. He does not normally appeal to the more technical intricacies of scholastic terminology. On the contrary, he declares that 'Terms of art ... used by metaphysicians and schoolmen, have done little service to the cause of Christ.'[47] Again, while he refers to other writers as necessary, he does not indulge in the habit of piling authority upon authority, as if the appeal to antiquity alone sufficed to sustain an argument. Finally, his work is plainly written and 'less embarrassed with scholastic terms than some controversial writings are', because it is designed to be read in families and by private Christians. This is consistent with his view that

> it is a duty incumbent on all who profess the Christian name, to be well acquainted with those great doctrines on which our faith, hope, and worship are founded; for, without the knowledge of these, we must necessarily be at a loss as to the way of salvation ... This knowledge of divine truth must be derived from the holy scriptures ... It will be of singular use for us not only to know the doctrines which are contained in scripture, but to observe their connection and dependence on one another, and to digest them into such a method that subsequent truths may give

[46] See further, Alan P. F. Sell, *Philosophy, Dissent and Nonconformity*, 21-5. For the position of Isaac Watts on the matter see ibid., 38-9. See also idem, *John Locke and the Eighteenth-Century Divines*.

[47] T. Ridgley, *A Body of Divinity*, viii. Although his editor declares that Ridgley in general 'strives to write as if Aristotle's dialectics had never been enthroned in the schools of theology, and the philosophy of the heathens never empowered to communicate its aspirings and its diction to ministers of the Christian faith,' at times he shows that 'he still wears, if not the full uniform, at least the badge and the collar of scholasticism.' Wilson finds it odd that while Ridgley does not apply technical distinctions to the doctrine of the Trinity, he does so when discussing God's everlasting purpose. Ibid., I, xii, xiv.

light to those which went before; or to lay them down in such a way that the whole scheme of religion may be comprised in a narrow compass, and, as it were, beheld with one view.[48]

II

I shall now select, largely in the order of their appearance, some matters of particular interest from Ridgley's *Body*, relating them to the theological circumstances of the time and to his other writings as appropriate.

The eighteenth century has been called the age of the cosmological argument for God's existence, and as we read Ridgley on the being of God, we can be in no doubt as to the century we are in. First, he justifies the attempt to prove God's existence because of the necessity of our giving a reason for our belief. The doctrine of God is 'the foundation of all natural and revealed religion,' and it is not to be received 'merely by tradition, as though there were no other reason for our believing it than that others do so, or that we have been instructed in it from our childhood.' Furthermore, we need to answer the atheism which arises both within our own hearts and in the world around us.[49]

The being of God can be proved by the light of nature, notwithstanding that our reasoning powers are 'very much sullied, depraved, and weakened, by our apostacy from God; but they are not wholly obliterated.'[50] Hence, quite apart from revelation, we may know that there is a God. He then launches into the arguments to, and from, a first cause. He introduces an argument from design, anticipating Paley's watch, adverting to the organization of nature, to human bodies as 'fearfully and wonderfully made', and then cites the provision of human souls and consciences. Indeed (and here is an example of Ridgley's reverent agnosticism), 'since we cannot fully describe what [souls] are, and know little of them but by their effects, certainly we could not form them;—and therefore there is a God, who is "the Father of spirits".'[51] For its part, conscience implies a superior being before whom human beings are responsible. There follows the argument from universal assent. In this connection Ridgley grants that there have been instances of persons who have been deemed atheists, 'yet their number has been very inconsiderable', and (in circular fashion) if there are people anywhere in the world who are so stupid as not to worship God, that simply shows that they are not acting like reasonable creatures.[52] Both special providences (miracles) which run 'contrary to the common course of nature' and the 'common dispensations of providence' attest to the fact of God's being. So, too,

---

[48] Ibid.,I, 1.

[49] Ibid.,I, 9.

[50] Ibid., I, 10.

[51] Ibid., I, 13.

[52] As in with biblical criticism, so with Ridgley's theistic arguments: I bite my tongue, Hume and Kant not having arrived as yet.

does the fulfilment of prophecy—prophecy being understood as the foretelling of future events.

All of the above notwithstanding, 'The scriptures of the Old and New Testaments contain a revelation of the whole mind and will of God, and therefore are justly styled a perfect rule of faith and obedience.'[53] As if arrested by the adjective 'whole', Ridgley immediately qualifies his assertion. We do not have in the Bible an account of everything that God has done, or will do, still less of his secret counsels and purposes. Again, God's perfections are not perfectly revealed to human beings, for 'That which is in itself incomprehensible, cannot be so revealed that we should be able fully to comprehend it; though that which is possible, or at least necessary, to be known of God, is clearly revealed to us.'[54] Nor is 'every doctrine which is to be assented to as an article of faith ... revealed in express words in scripture; since many truths are to be deduced from it by just and necessary consequences, and thereby become a rule of faith.'[55] With this Ridgley leaves open the door to interpretations of biblical material ranging from the sober to the fantastic, which are defensible only upon the most elastic construction of the scholastic phrase, 'just and necessary consequences.'

While Scripture is, positively, a rule of faith and obedience, it is also, negatively, a bulwark against 'the popish doctrine of human traditions, which are pretended to be of equal authority with the word of God.'[56] Further, the Scripture has been given by divine inspiration, as is shown internally by harmony of all its parts, and externally by miracles which confirmed the message of the apostles, and subsequently by the efficacy of scripture in converting sinners and edifying believers.

His foundations in reason and revelation thus laid, Ridgley proceeds to discuss the attributes of God. For an example of his treatment of these we may turn to God's omnipotence. Ridgley makes it clear that there are some things that God cannot do because he has willed not to do them. He cannot save reprobates, for example. He cannot do what is contrary to the nature of things. He cannot make an independent creature, for 'independence is contrary to the idea of a creature. Nor can he make a creature equal to himself, for then it would not be a creature.'[57] God cannot deny himself: he cannot lie, or act in a manner contrary to any of his perfections. He cannot repent or change his mind, or do anything 'which would argue him not to be a holy God.'[58]

Many divines would have agreed with Ridgley thus far. But when we turn to the doctrine of the Trinity, especially as that doctrine concerns the Son of God and confessional subscription, we find ourselves confronted by the most doctrinally neuralgic, not to say explosive, theological issue of Ridgley's day.

---

[53] T. Ridgley, *A Body of Divinity*, I, 28.

[54] Ibid. It would therefore seem that, *pace* the first clause here, the perfections of God are not absolutely incomprehensible, or we could not know anything about them at all.

[55] Ibid.

[56] Ibid., I 30.

[57] Ibid., I. 93.

[58] Ibid.

III

The Trinity had been under discussion since the closing decades of the seventeenth century, and added impetus to the debate was provided by the publication in 1712 of the Anglican Samuel Clarke's book, *The Scripture Doctrine of the Trinity*.[59] Clarke argued that while there were three divine persons in the Trinity, the Father alone enjoyed independent existence and was underived, whereas the Son existed by derivation from the Father, and the Spirit by derivation from the Son. This became the principle doctrinal platform of the eighteenth-century Arians.

In Dissenting circles this position was adopted by a number of Presbyterians, by a few Congregationalists, and by rather more General Baptists. Strife over the issue arose with particular intensity in 1719, and the Exeter Presbyterian minister, James Peirce, an erstwhile Calvinist, was at the heart of it.[60] Peirce's views had been causing concern to some at least since 1716, but in 1719 he published *Plain Christianity Defended* in reply to the charge of Arianism. From this work it becomes abundantly clear that if the question of the derivation of the Son were the catalyst, the question of the manner of deriving any doctrine from Scripture was the underlying issue. For Peirce writes, 'We are sure that there is but one God the Father, because the Scriptures are express in saying so, but we cannot be so certain that the Father, Son and Holy Ghost are one God, because the Scripture never so much as once says so.'[61] Clearly, the appeal here is to the principle of the sufficiency of Scripture over against the doctrinal tradition of the Church. In a sermon preached on 18 March 1719, the Sunday following his ejectment from the Exeter pastorate, Peirce denied that he was indebted to Arius for his views: 'Why should we I pray, be denominated from Arius? Did we ever propose any particular veneration for him? Do we pretend, nay, do we not most positively deny, that we have received our opinions from him?'[62] Peirce did not contend for the subordination of the Son in so many words. He argued that the God and Father of Jesus Christ is the one God, and that it is not the case that Father, Son and Spirit together constitute the one God; but the subordinationist implication was not lost upon his 'Athanasian' peers.

In the broader world of Dissent, matters came to a head at the Salters' Hall conference of 1719. The Arians appealed to the principle of Scripture sufficiency, but they refused to subscribe to a human form of words affirming the Trinity. The orthodox party did subscribe, and they lost the vote by four. Twenty-nine Presbyterians and twenty-eight Congregationalists subscribed, and of the seventy-three non-subscribers, forty-seven were Presbyterians. Benjamin Avery and Nathaniel

---

[59] For Clarke (1675-1729) see DECBP; ODNB; J. P. Ferguson, *An Eighteenth Century Heretic*; T. C. Pfizenmaier, *The Trinitarian Theology of Samuel Clarke*, and cf. the review of this book by Alan P. F. Sell in *Enlightenment and Dissent*.

[60] For Peirce (1674?-1726) see GEE, 83, 84, 180; MURCH, *passim*; ODNB; TSJ, *passim*.

[61] J. Peirce, *Plain Christianity Defended*, 1719, 29.

[62] Idem, *The Evil and Cure of Divisions*,

Lardner were the only professed Arians among the non-subscribers, while Luke Langdon and Martin Tomkins were tending in that direction. With hindsight, Edmund Calamy accurately reflected that at Salters' Hall the Trinity was 'not the point in question,'[63] but subscription was. Indeed, following the debate, the non-subscribers, with the exception of Avery, Lardner, Langdon and Tomkins, singed a statement signifying their commitment to the doctrine of the Trinity, and explaining that their refusal formally to subscribe was, among other things, owing to their conviction that undue deference should not be paid to the *Westminster Confession*, or, indeed, to any attempt to permit 'the Words of *Men*' to 'determine the Sense of *Scripture*.'[64] It is interesting to note that most subscribers were over forty years of age, while most non-subscribers were under forty.

That Thomas Ridgley was firmly on the side of the subscribers is clear from the fact that he thus recorded his name at Salters' Hall.[65] He did more than sign his name, he rose in defence of the subscribers in a pamphlet entitled, *The Unreasonableness of the Charge of Imposition exhibited against several Dissenting Ministers in and about London* (1719). His purpose is to answer the charge that those ministers who voted on, and signed their names to trinitarian formulae at Salters' Hall, were guilty of a desire to impose a particular interpretation of Scripture upon others. Ridgley in no way denies that creeds are fallible, nor may they be deemed to be on a par with Scripture. Further, assent to creeds cannot legitimately be made a condition of a persons' obtaining things to which they have a natural or a civil right. However, a church has the right to expect that its members will adhere to the rules in its constitution, and it may properly require a profession of faith as a term of communion. Anticipating a rebuttal, he continues, 'If it be objected that we ought not to make Terms of communion which Christ has not made, and that to assert him to be God equal with the Father is one of those Terms, I answer, this is to suppose that the Doctrine of the Trinity is not a fundamental Article of Faith ...'[66] The necessity of ensuring that ministers are secure in the fundamental articles is, he continues, the reason why we hear ministers preach before they are called to a pastorate. As to the precise matter of formal subscription: 'subscribing to what we

---

[63] E. Calamy, *An Historical Account of my Own Life*, II, 414.

[64] See *An Authentick Account of Several Things Done and agreed upon by the Dissenting Ministers*, paras. vi, vii. For the general doctrinal context see further, Alan P. F. Sell, DTLC, ch. 5. For the texts of the subscribers and non-subscribers see PNT, 66-70. For the Salters' Hall controversy see A. Gordon, *Addresses Biographical and Historical*, ch. 5; F. J. Powicke, 'The Salters' Hall controversy'; Roger Thomas in C. G. Bolam, *et al.*, *The English Presbyterians*, ch. 4; idem, 'The non-subscription controversy amongst Dissenters in 1719.'

[65] See *A True Relation of some Proceedings at Salters-Hall*. The lists of subscribers and non-subscribers are reproduced by T. S. James, *The History of the Litigation and Legislation respecting Presbyterian Chapels and Charities*, 705-9. Ridgley's name appears on p. 707.

[66] T. Ridgley, *The Unreasonableness of the Charge of Imposition*, 24.

believe, differs but in a very small circumstance from a verbal declaration thereof.'[67] Moreover, it is not enough tell the non-subscribers that we are not Arians, or that we 'utterly disown the Arian doctrine', because even Socinians can declare belief in the Trinity in their own understanding of the term, and can say that Christ is 'God by nature' over against idols, which are not gods.[68] He concludes by affirming that 'the Father, Son, and Holy Ghost are the one and only God blessed for evermore.'[69]

There can be little doubt that Ridgley urgently impressed the importance of trinitarian doctrine upon his students, and in his *Body of Divinity* he certainly paid full attention to it, and treated it in such a way that his pastoral concern shines through. Thus he declares that we are to assent to the doctrine of the Trinity, 'and to use our utmost endeavours to defend it,' but human explications of it are not on the same level of importance, and

> Every private Christian ... is not to be censured as a stranger to this doctrine, who cannot define personality in a scholastic way, or understand all the terms used in explaining it, or several modes of speaking which some writers tenaciously adhere to,—such as "hypostasis", "subsistence", "consubstantiality", "the model distinction of the Persons in the Godhead", "filiation", "the communication of the divine essence by generation", "the communication of it by procession". ... When we consider how far the doctrine of the Trinity is to be known and believed to salvation, we must not exclude the weakest Christian from a possibility of knowing it, by supposing it necessary for him to understand some hard words, which he doth not find in the Bible, and which, if he meet them elsewhere, will not add much to his edification.'[70]

Since God does not make 'the comprehensive knowledge of mysterious doctrines a term of salvation', it follows that

> When we affirm that there is one God, that the Father, Son, and Spirit, have all the perfections of the Godhead, and that these perfections, and the personality of each of them, are infinitely greater than what can be found in the creature, we state what we yield our assent to. But if it be inquired how far God herein exceeds all the ideas which we have of finite perfections, or personality, our understandings are at a loss. So far, however, as this does not contain the form of a proposition, it cannot,

---

[67] Ibid., 33.

[68] Ibid., 47.

[69] Ibid., 48.

[70] Idem, *A Body of Divinity*, I, 137. The Arian Presbyterian of the following generation, John Taylor (1694-1761), was equally averse to such no-scriptural terminology, but in his case the motive was not pastoral, but a concern to maintain the sufficiency of Scripture. See his *A Narrative of Mr. Joseph Rawson's Case*, 13. For Taylor see Alan P. F. Sell, *Dissenting Thought and the Life of the Churches*, ch. 7; idem, *Philosophy, Dissent and Nonconformity*, *passim*; G. T. Eddy, *Dr. Taylor of Norwich. Wesley's Arch-heretic*, Peterborough: Epworth Press, 3003.

according to our common acceptation of the word, be said to be the object of faith.[71]

If anti-trinitarians, who in this matter take their cue from the deists, object that the doctrine of the Trinity is utterly unintelligible, it may be replied that 'the discovery of the glories of God by the light of nature [to which deists and anti-trinitarians pay heed], are, in some respects, as incomprehensible as the doctrine of the Trinity,' but 'we are not, for that reason, obliged to disbelieve or reject them.'[72] While fully to comprehend the doctrine of the Trinity is beyond our reasoning powers, the doctrine is not contrary to reason.

Staunch trinitarian though he was, Ridgley caused a fluttering in the Calvinistic dovecotes concerning the eternal generation of the Son and the procession of the Holy Spirit. Ridgley opposes those who speak of the Father as communicating the divine essence, or the divine personality, to the Son. The problem is that Arians can use such phrases without meaning what should be meant by them, namely, that the divine essence or personality are communicated necessarily and from all eternity to the Son. The Arians construe the phrases as indicative of the subordination of the Son to the Father; similarly with the procession of the Holy Spirit from the Father and the Son. In his determination to deny the Arians this foothold in trinitarian doctrine, Ridgley declines to assent to the doctrines of the eternal generation of the Son and the procession of the Holy Spirit. Positively, 'I assert that the divine essence is not communicated by the Father to the Son and Holy Ghost, as imparting or conveying it to them. I take the word "communicate" in another sense, and say that all the perfections of the divine nature are communicated, that is, equally distributed to, or predicated of, the Father, Son, and Spirit. ... I cannot but conclude that the divine personality, not only of the Father, but of the Son and Spirit, is as much independent and underived, as the divine essence.'[73]

It is difficult at this late hour not to be nonplussed by the sometimes strident opposition which Ridgley's exposition engendered. There is no question that he staunchly upheld the doctrine of the Trinity. He was equally concerned that Arianism should be vanquished, and to that end he proposed the curtailment of language hitherto used by the orthodox that could be hijacked by Arians to their own subordinationist ends.[74] Positively, he was contending that the Son's generation and the Spirit's procession were necessary, eternal and perpetual, not physical. He was referring to what Richard A. Muller has described as 'an eternal and perpetual relation in the Godhead, an unchanging activity or motion that is in the divine essence according to its very nature.'[75] None of which prevented the agitated twitching of

[71] T. Ridgley, *A Body of* Divinity, I, 141.

[72] Ibid., I, 143.

[73] Ibid., I, 158, 159. His editor regretted that Ridgley had used the term 'communicated' at all. See ibid., I, 241; cf. xv, where Wilson wrongly supposes that Ridgley took talk of eternal generation for a scholastic invention.

[74] See his defence of his policy in *A Body of Divinity*, I, viii.

[75] R. A. Muller, *Dictionary of Greek and Latin Theological Terms*, 127.

Calvinist doctrinal antennae, especially when Ridgley went on to say that 'When we read of the Son of God as dependent on the Father, inferior and obedient to him, and yet as being equal with him, and having the same divine nature, we cannot conceive of any character which answers to all these ideas of sonship, except that of Mediator.'[76]

David Millar was among those who, some time after Ridgley's death, took him to task at this point. Millar contends that the title 'Son of God' was a title of nature, but Ridgley and others have construed it only as a title of office: Christ is Son of God as Mediator.[77] The redoubtable high Calvinist Baptist, John Gill, went so far as to express puzzlement that Ridgley, a trinitarian, could veer so far in a Socinian direction as to adopt the notion of Sonship by office.[78] Neither of these notes Ridgley's strong statement to the effect that his reference to Christ's mediatorial Sonship 'does not take away any argument by which we prove his deity. When we consider him as Mediator, or speak of the person of Christ as such, we always suppose him to be both God and man.'[79] Again, they quite fail to heed Ridgley's criticism of the Socinians in this connection:

> the Socinians suppose that [Christ's] being called the Son of God, refers only to some dignities conferred upon one whom they suppose to be no more than a man. This is infinitely below the glory which we ascribe to him as Mediator. Their idea of him, as the Son of God, how extraordinary soever his conception was, argues him to be no more than a creature; but ours ... proves him to be a divine Person, since we never speak of him as Mediator, without including both natures.[80]

Finally, Ridgley's opponents do not trouble to weigh his anti-Arian grounds for suggesting terminological caution, or his exposition of the important term 'communication',[81] and they completely fail to address his claim that

> the principal thing in which I am obliged, till I receive farther conviction, to differ from many others, is, whether the Son and Spirit have a communicated or derived

---

[76] T. Ridgley, *A Body of Divinity*, I, 162.

[77] See D. Millar, *Useful and Important Answers*, 53.

[78] See J. Gill, *A Body of Divinity*, I, 206-7; *A Dissertation on the Eternal Sonship of Christ*, 219.

[79] J. Ridgley, *A Body of Divinity*, I, 162-3.

[80] Ibid., I, 163.

[81] It is to be feared that Tom Nettles swallows Gill too uncritically at this point. See his paper, 'John Gill and the Evangelical Awakening,' 143-4. A. W. Light was equally uncritical on the matter. See his *Bunhill Memorials* II, 26-7. Walter Wilson seems to reiterate second-hand opinions on the matter; see WW, II, 78. More recently, Alexander Gordon, in an uncharacteristic missing of the mark, declared that Ridgley 'denuded' his system of the doctrines of eternal generation and the procession of the Spirit, and was 'essentially Sabellian.' See his article on Ridgley in the original *Dictionary of National Biography*. Alan Ruston, who revised Gordon's article for ODNB, wisely did not repeat the charge.

> personality. This many assert, but, I think, without sufficient proof; for I cannot but conclude that the divine personality, not only of the Father, but of the Son and the Spirit, is as much independent and underived, as the divine essence.[82]

It would seem that Ridgley's gravest 'sin' was to leave himself open to misunderstanding by those who were intent upon misunderstanding him.

IV

Underlying Ridgley's teaching on sin, election and predestination is his view of God's discriminating grace. Grace is free and sovereign. Hence, 'That is given to one which [God] denies to another: and only because it is his pleasure.'[83] The discriminating nature of grace is shown in God's determination to save human beings, not fallen angels; in conversion; and in the comparison between what the recipients of grace become, with what they were before. To the objection that the afflictions of God's people argue against the glory of God's grace and mercy, Ridgley replies that such afflictions actually illustrate the glory of God's perfections because they are 'an expedient to humble us for sin, and to prevent it in the future.'[84] Ridgley's question to those who protest that the doctrine of free grace leads to licentiousness because recipients of it consider themselves secure and freed from the claims of God's law is, '[D]oes it follow, that because the doctrine of grace is abused by some, as an occasion of licentiousness, through the corruption of their nature, it therefore leads to it? The greatest blessings may be the occasion of the greatest evils; but yet they do not lead to them.'[85]

Ridgley holds that 'The doctrine of discriminating grace cannot well be maintained, without asserting a discrimination in God's purpose relating to it, which is what we call election.'[86] As he prepares to expound the doctrine of the decrees of God Ridgley sets out his stall with great care. He is well aware of the prejudices against the doctrine, and says that he shall

> endeavour to vindicate it from the reproach which is generally cast on it, by those who suppose that it cannot be defended without asserting God to be the Author of sin, or supposing him to be severe, cruel, and unjust to his creatures ... We are far

---

[82] T. Ridgley, *A Body of Divinity*, I, 159. It is interesting to note in passing that the doctrine of the eternal generation of the Son subsequently troubled Wesleyan, Strict Baptist and Brethren waters. For the first see W. B. Pope's quotation from A. M. Fairbairn in his *The Person of Christ: Dogmatic, Scriptural, Historical*, 282-3. For the second see J. C. Philpot, *The True, Proper, and Eternal Sonship of the Lord Jesus Christ*, S. F. Paul, *Historical Sketch of the Gospel Standard Baptists*, 44-5, Alan P. F. Sell, *Alfred Dye*, 33-4, and Kenneth Dix, *Strict and Particular*, 93-5. For the third see Tim Grass, *Gathering to His Name*, 294-5.

[83] T. Ridgley, *A Body of Divinity*, I, 109.

[84] Ibid., I, 111.

[85] Ibid., I, 112.

[86] Ibid., I, 303.

> from asserting ... that God, from all eternity, purposed to damn a great part of the world, as a result of his mere sovereign will, without foresight of sin, which would render them liable to condemnation. Moreover, we shall endeavour to make it appear, ... that the decree of God does not destroy, or take away, the liberty of man's will, with respect to things within its own sphere ... [W]e shall maintain, that the decree of God does not lay any force on the will of man,—that it does not preclude the means of grace, as ordained by him, for the salvation of them that do or shall believe unto life everlasting,—and that it does not obstruct the preaching of the gospel, or the proclaiming of the glad tidings of salvation, to those who sit under the Christian ministry as an ordinance for their faith.[87]

In these few sentences Ridgley carefully marks out the doctrinal slalom course which all high Calvinists have to negotiate as best they can, and he ends the paragraph by reiterating his view that far from its being the case that the elect may 'live as they please', the doctrine of the decrees 'is consistent with practical godliness, and ... a very great motive and inducement to it.'[88]

With this we come to Ridgley's opposition to antinomianism, which surfaces on a number of occasions in his writings. The memory was still fresh of the way in which the Happy Union of Presbyterians and Congregationalists in London had foundered in 1691, when the former suspected the latter of antinomianism, while the latter suspected the former of Arian tendencies.[89] Closer to home, it appears that when Philip Doddridge visited London in 1733 he sustained a 'very furious and severe attack' from some 'high orthodox people.' The apparent ringleaders were some of Ridgley's students, but Doddridge thought that 'a party of Antinomians' was the real culprit.[90] Ridgley's abhorrence of antinomianism was absolutely clear: 'I want words to express the wickedness of those who pervert the gospel of Christ, so as to make it appear to exempt them from the obligation which all are under to universal obedience.'[91] He knew full well that as well as practical antinomians there were writers, Crisp, Eaton, Saltmarsh, and Towne among them, who sometimes incautiously made assertions which could be construed as theoretical antinomianism. Such 'do great disservice to the truth, and, it may be, give occasion to some to be licentious. ...'[92] His most all-embracing remark on the matter appears in his discussion of sanctification: 'Since holiness is required of all persons, as what is absolutely necessary to salvation, and is also recommended as that which God works in those in whom the gospel is made effectual to salvation; we may infer that no gospel doctrine has the least tendency to lead to licentiousness.'[93]

---

87 Ibid., I, 254.

88 Ibid.; cf. ibid., I, ix.

89 See further, Alan P. F. Sell, *The Great Debate*, 42-52.

90 CCPD, no. 390; letter of Doddridge to John Barker dated August 1733.

91 T. Ridgley, *A Body of Divinity*, II, 305.

92 Ibid., 306. For Tobias Crisp (1601-1643), John Eaton (1594/5-1630/31), and John Saltmarsh (d. 1647) see ODNB.

93 T. Ridgley, *A Body of Divinity*, II, 144.

Ridgley is well aware that the doctrines of predestination and election have been the subjects of 'nice metaphysical speculations', and that divines have divided into supralapsarians and sublapsarians. As to the former, he declares, 'I cannot approve of any thing advanced by them, which seems to represent God as purposing to create man, and then to suffer him to fall, as a means by which he designed to demonstrate the glory of his vindictive justice.'[94] For their part the sublapsarians 'distinguish between God's purpose to create and suffer man to fall, and his purpose considered as a means to advance his sovereignty, grace, and justice.'[95] Ridgley takes neither side, and simply concludes that whatever may be said about God's eternal purpose, when choosing some for salvation God could not consider them as simply 'created, or as created but not fallen, but as sinners.'[96] He is concerned that in all of these matters we carefully distinguish between God's secret will and his revealed will, and that we affirm that 'The purpose of God relating to election, is free and sovereign, or absolute and unconditional.'[97] Similarly with reprobation, which includes the idea of preterition—the foreordained passing by of those who shall not be saved, and the punishment of those whom God wills not to save, it being clearly understood that the reprobate suffer no more than their just deserts. 'God forbid,' Ridgley expostulates, 'that any one should think that there is a positive act affirmed [in preterition], as though God infused hardness into the hearts of any. The meaning only is this, that he determined to deny heart-softening grace to that part of mankind whom he had not foreordained to eternal life.'[98] The 'only' in the last sentence quoted is more than ordinarily forbidding. But, as I have suggested elsewhere,[99] it does appear that Ridgley was well aware of the bad press which scholastic Calvinism could attract, and he took such steps as he felt he consistently could to ameliorate matters.

Turning to the subject of sin, Ridgley follows the confessional line in asserting that by an act of God's sovereign will Adam was constituted the federal head of the race. His sin is imputed to his posterity. To those who contend that this is a slur upon God's love and justice, Ridgley replies,

> when we speak of persons being punished for a crime committed by another as being imputed to them, we understand the word 'imputation' in a forensic sense; and we do not suppose that there is a wrong judgment passed on persons or things, as though the crime were reckoned to have been committed by them. Accordingly, we do not say that we committed that sin which was more immediately committed by Adam. In him it was an actual sin; it is ours as it is imputed to us, or as we are

---

[94] Ibid., I, 269.

[95] Ibid., I, 270.

[96] Ibid.

[97] Ibid., I, 288.

[98] Ibid., I, 269.

[99] See Alan P. F. Sell, *Enlightenment, Ecumenism, Evangel*, 150-151.

punished for it, according to the demerit of the offence, and the tenor of the covenant in which we were included.[100]

Ridgley insists on the distinction between Adam's guilt as imputed to us, and our guilt for the sins we have committed. The punishment meted out on account of the latter is proportionate to the actual offences because we sinned against the light, whereas the punishment for the sin that is imputed to us is less. Awkward though this explanation appears to be (unless we may translate it into terms of our suffering the consequences of the sins of others) it is clear that Ridgley will not allow us to invoke the imputation of Adam's sin as a full explanation of, still less as an excuse for, our own sins.

In two of his Pinners' Hall sermons Ridgley discusses original sin at some length. In the Preface to the published texts he says that he has been charged with denying the imputation of both Adam's sin and Christ's righteousness, as well as the universal depravity and corruption of human nature, and the propensity of all human beings to sin from infancy onwards. He insists that, on the contrary, he has sought to establish these doctrines. The two sermons are on Romans 5: 18: 'Therefore as by the offences of one judgment came upon all men to condemnation, so by the righteousness of one the free gift came upon all men unto justification of life.'

Ridgley's case is that 'All Mankind are under a Sentence of Condemnation for the Sin of our first parents. By the Offence of One Judgment came upon all Men to Condemnation.'[101] God could not create humanity in a state of moral evil, for this would make him the author of sin. Rather, Adam, the 'Head and Representative of all his Posterity' broke the covenant God had made with him, and Christ came into the world to deliver us from the resulting curse.[102] Adam lost the supernatural image of God, and endured 'a total Separation from him who is the Fountain of all Blessedness.'[103] He was left to his own vile conduct, and was incapable of doing any good. Confronted by the difficulty posed by the fact that God does not create people in a state of moral evil on the one hand, and on the other with the fact that those to whom Adam's guilt is imputed sometimes die as infants, Ridgley argues (less than satisfactorily) that the punishment which is meted out to such infants is 'comparatively small', for they are not conscious of sin, and have not committed any actual sin. Infants are born guilty yet non-culpable, and without a bias towards sin. Were it otherwise, God would be the author of sin. If we ask, Whence comes this propensity to sin? Ridgley can only reply, 'This is justly esteemed the most difficult Question in the whole Scheme of Divinity.'[104] Some have said that if a pregnant woman has a sinful thought, this is impressed on the soul of the unborn infant. Ridgley, however, rejects this theory. He thinks that the 'Bias to Sin enters into the

---

[100] T. Ridgley, *A Body of Divinity*, I, 403.
[101] Idem, *The Doctrine of Original Sin Considered*, 4.
[102] Ibid., 14.
[103] Ibid., 60.
[104] Ibid., 51.

Soul at the Door of Temptation',[105] and he concludes: 'If Original Sin needs a Pardon to remove its Guilt, what need have we of pardoning Mercy, who add Iniquity to Iniquity?'[106]

In the Postscript to his sermons Ridgley acknowledges a debt to Locke's reasoning on the subject of ideas.[107] Locke encourages him to think of the soul as a thinking, reasoning entity, whose power is not always 'deduc'd into Act'—as it is not, he supposes, in the womb. He cannot see that God would 'reveal those things to Infants, which without special Revelation they could not know, meerly that they may have a tormenting sense of their Loss.'[108] As for the heathen, they are punished 'in proportion to the Light they have rebelled against; or the corrupt Habits of Sin they have contracted. And therefore, as God was not obliged to save any, he is not to be charged with Injustice or Severity for punishing any according to the Demerit of their Sin.'[109]

Salvation comprises numerous blessings. We are saved from the guilt of sin in justification, and from the dominion of it in sanctification. We are saved from that bondage which held us in perpetual fear of God's wrath. Salvation is bestowed solely because of God's love and mercy.[110] Many divines have held that in sovereign freedom, the Father enters into a covenant of redemption with the Son, and inaugurates a covenant of grace with humanity. While Ridgley does not wish to dispute with those who think in terms of two covenants, he prefers to regard the alleged two covenants as branches of the one covenant, and that 'the covenant of grace was made with Christ as the head, and, in him, with the elect as his seed ...'[111] Of this covenant, Christ is the sole Mediator,[112] and in him alone is salvation to be found.[113] His righteousness is the ground of our justification, for 'Christ was a surety for us, or substituted in our room, with a design to pay the debt which was due to the justice of God from us.'[114]

Grace is not an acquisition, but is infused into those who are effectually called, and this calling is the special work of the Holy Spirit. God's power and grace are irresistible in the sense that they are not subject to any control, so that when God calls effectually that call cannot go unanswered. The grace of faith accompanies the grace of salvation, and faith is wrought in us 'by the power of the Spirit, and by the instrumentality of the word.'[115] As Ridgley put it in a sermon on the death of Mrs. Gertrud [*sic*] Clarkson, 'As the most Cogent Argument cannot convict an

---

[105] Ibid., 52.
[106] Ibid., 57.
[107] See John Locke, *An Essay concerning Human Understanding*, I.1 and II.2.
[108] T. Ridgley, *The Doctrine of Original Sin Considered*, 62-3.
[109] Ibid., 67.
[110] See further, T. Ridgley, *A Body of Divinity*, I, 436-7.
[111] Ibid., I, 448.
[112] Ibid., I, 472.
[113] See ibid.,I, 641-7.
[114] Ibid., II, 88-9.
[115] Ibid., II, 114.

Unregenerate Person, unless, by Supernatural Power, God works a Change in the Soul: So the strongest Reasons, and clearest Evidences cannot comfort; 'tis Sovereign Grace that refreshes, as well as quickens and enlivens.'[116]

Ridgley strongly affirms the doctrine of the perseverance of the saints: 'The purpose of God, in choosing men to eternal life, renders their salvation necessary, so that nothing shall defeat or disannul it.'[117] The union of believers with Christ is inseparable, and his intercession for them is continuous.[118] This was the main theme of the sermon preached on the death of Mrs. Clarkson. In his Dedication 'To the much respected, Mrs. Elizabeth Clarkson' he offers the consolation that the deceased's 'Soul was fit for better Entertainment, than those can have, who lodge in Houses of Clay. ... [T]here is a Sufficiency of Comfort and Salvation in that Everlasting Covenant, which is order'd in all things and sure.' The sermon is entitled, *Saints kept from Falling and presented Faultless*, and the text is Jude verse 24. He expounds the verse, and then draws out the doctrine:

> That the consideration, that the Lord Jesus is engaged, as well as able, to keep his People from Falling, and to present them Faultless before the Presence of the Divine Glory with exceeding Joy; redounds much to the Honour of God, and the Support of Believers. ... A Believer cannot fall from his Interest in the Blessings and Promises of the Covenant of Grace, or those things which are given him in Christ his Head.[119]

He proceeds to argue that grace does not 'destroy Corruption as to is Residence', but it overcomes it. Then, with the confidence of one not entirely immune to scholastic inferences, he roundly declares that although Christ could have prevented the Fall of humanity, he did not do so, 'For he had a Design to get Honour thereby, as the Second Adam, and Restorer of his People.'[120] Jesus is the fit person to treat with God from eternity, for he is God's equal, and he cannot fail in his task. He is 'In one Nature too High to Suffer: In the other, not too Low to merit.'[121] 'Christ,' he says, 'is Sent by the Father to redeem, and Sends his Spirit to apply what he has purchased. ... Who is so fit to be the head of God's Adopted Sons; as his Only Begotten Son?'[122]

Over and above the saint's standing at the last day, there is 'Matter of Great Encouragement to him in this Life. 'Tis the most refreshing Cordial to support his

---

[116] Idem, *A Funeral Sermon Preached ... on the Decease of Mrs. Gertrud Clarkson*, 99. Mrs. Clarkson was the daughter of the Reverend David Clarkson (bap. 1621/2, d. 1686), one of the ministers ejected following the Restoration of the monarchy. He became co-pastor with John Owen in 1682, and pastor on Owen's death in 1683, until he himself died. See CR; ODNB; WW, I, 285-8.

[117] T. Ridgley, *A Body of Divinity*, I, 294.

[118] Ibid., II, 172-3.

[119] Idem, *A Funeral Sermon ... on the Death of Mrs. Gertrud Clarkson*, 9, 12.

[120] Ibid., 20.

[121] Ibid., 58.

[122] Ibid., 59.

Fainting Spirits, when he seen Sin abounding, Conscience reproving, and finding Innumerable Faults in the best he can do; to Consider, at the same time, that he shall be presented Faultless before God hereafter.'[123]

Suffice it to say that the other side of the coin is the eternal punishment in store for the wicked.[124] As for believers, although they are 'habitually prepared for Christ's second coming, yet they should endeavour after an actual meetness for it; and ought always so to walk, as that they may not be afraid to receive the summons, though it may be given on a sudden.'[125]

V

What of Ridgley's teaching on the Church, ministry and sacraments? The Church, he declares, comprises those who are called. However, there is an external call 'whereby some are made partakers of the external privileges of the gospel and its ordinances' and thus belong to the Church visible; and there is an internal call which has saving effect. Those who are called in the latter sense 'are made partakers of those special and distinguishing blessings which God bestows on the heirs of salvation.'[126] They belong to the invisible Church. Members of the Church visible are so by profession; members of the Church invisible are so because they are 'united to Christ as their Head and husband, and made partakers of spiritual life from him, and shall live for ever with him.'[127]

In one sense the visible Church is one, though not in such a way that there is one body of men who may rule over the one Church as a whole; in another sense there are particular churches bound together by mutual consent, each with its pastor. The visible Church includes not only professed believers, but also their children. In Ridgley's opinion some of the patristic writers went too far in connection with the churchly rights of children, for they 'not only considered them as members of the church, but brought them to the Lord's table, and gave them the bread dipped in the wine, in the same way as food is applied to infants when they are too young to discover anything of its design. In doing this they misconstrued the words of Jesus, 'Except ye eat the flesh of the Son of man, and drink his blood, ye have no life in you' by referring them to the Lord's Supper. In fact since these words were spoken before the institution of the Lord's Supper they could not refer to it. Furthermore, when the Supper was instituted, there is no suggestion that those who did not partake of it should for that reason be excluded from salvation. When children are spoken of as members of the Church together with their parents, what is meant is that 'children being the property of their parents, the latter are obliged to dedicate them, together with themselves, to God, and, pursuant to their doing so, to

---

[123] Ibid., 65.

[124] See *A Body of Divinity*, II, 281-5.

[125] T. Ridgley, *A Sermon Occasioned by the Death of the Reverend Mr. Thomas Tingey*, 38.

[126] Idem, *A Body of Divinity*, II, 4.

[127] Ibid., II, 5.

endeavour to bring them up in the nurture and admonition of the Lord, hoping that, through his blessing on education, they may, in his own time and way, be qualified for church-communion, and then admitted to it, that hereby the churches of Christ may have an addition of members to fill up the places of those who are called off the stage.'[128]

As to the governance of the Church visible, Ridgley, good Congregationalist that he was, eschews Erastianism, remarking that 'It is a great dishonour to Christ, the King and Head of his church, to suppose that he has left them without a rule to direct them in what respects the communion of saints.'[129] Moreover, 'If a church which styles itself national, exclude persons from its communion, whether it be for real or supposed crimes, it takes away a right which it had no power to confer, but which is founded on the laws of men, which are very distinct from those which Christ has given to his churches.'[130]

What are the qualifications for church communion? Ridgley fully understands that members will not have perfect unanimity on all doctrinal points (living when he did he could hardly have denied this). But they must not deny any of the fundamental articles of the faith. This was a theme to which Ridgley paid special attention in his pamphlet of 1721, *An Essay concerning Truth and Charity*. He here argues that Scripture is the foundation and rule of truth; that every part of Scripture has one determining sense; that every assertion which is contrary to the general sense of Scripture is an error (though not all error is sinful, for there are matters which are beyond the grasp of human reason). Anyone who denies the fundamental truths of the faith is to be refused church communion. However, following in the wake of John Owen and others, Ridgley at once explains that such exclusion is 'design'd to reclaim him who is thus dealt with, as well as to assert the honour of Christ. ... Such dealings ought to proceed with the greatest tenderness and Compassion ... [not] with Malice and Revenge, as tho' 'twas not the Cause of God that was herein pleaded; but with a Spirit of Love and Meekness.'[131] Those who propagate doctrines subversive of the faith on which the Church is founded are to be excluded. In such a case 'the church ought to express their public resentment' against the misdemeanour.[132] On other occasions and on other matters private admonition may suffice. But in either case sincere repentance is the prerequisite of resumption of fellowship. When members are excluded from fellowship, 'There ought to be a zeal expressed for the glory of God, and, at the same time, compassion to the souls of those who have rendered themselves obnoxious to it; without the least degree of hatred being felt towards their persons.'[133]

---

[128] Ibid., II, 9.

[129] Ibid., II, 17.

[130] Ibid., II, 25.

[131] Idem, *An Essay concerning Truth and Charity*, 30-31. Cf. John Owen, *The True Nature of a Gospel Church*, in his *Works*, ed. William H. Goold, (1850-1853), London: The Banner of Truth Trust, 1968, XVI, 171.

[132] T. Ridgley, *A Body of Divinity*, II, 23.

[133] Ibid.

That Ridgley had practical experience of church discipline cannot be gainsaid. During the closing years of his ministry at Three Cranes, Thomas Gouge was distressed by strife within the church, and by now Ridgley was his assistant. In 1679 Joseph Jacob, who preached a weekly lecture at the church, delighted to find fault 'with his betters.' This caused dissention, and he was dismissed from the fellowship, taking others with him.[134] It is said that this sorry episode hastened Gouge's death. Two years later, Ridgley by now being in pastoral charge, a Mrs. Sarah Peirce alleged that the church at Three Cranes had called her a liar and an hypocrite, and of being in love with Thomas Ridgley. She believed that Ridgley was preaching sermons about her, and that he was guilty of blasphemy. All of this was brought to the Church Meeting, and she denied having entertained these views. She produced a number of testimonials to her good character. Despite this, it would seem that the church members concluded that she was of unstable character. She did not go quietly, however, for in 2 January 1700 a pamphlet 'Printed for the Sufferer' was published under her name. Its title sufficiently explains its contents: *An Account of Mr. Thomas Ridgley, an Independent Minister and Preacher at the Three Cranes in Thames Street, [his] wilful and malicious blaspheming the Work of the Spirit of God in a Member of that Church; and how he and Mr. Peter Pindar, and Mr. Robert Hancock, have labour'd to drive her to Distraction or Despair ... and also how the Sufferer declar'd all this to his Face at Pinners-Hall, before the Ministers, and he did not contradict one word she said.*[135]

Because God alone knows the heart, Ridgley says, we cannot pronounce upon whether a person's heart is right with God; we can judge only by external appearances, but 'we are bound, by a judgment of charity, to conclude, that [church members] are what they profess themselves to be, till their conduct plainly gives the lie to their profession. The visible church is compared to the net, which had good and bad fish in it.'[136] Profession of faith and godly conduct are not by themselves enough to constitute a person a member of a church: 'there must be a mutual consent to walk together, or to have communion with one another in all the ordinances which Christ has established.'[137] Further, 'the terms of Christian communion are fixed by Christ, the Head of his church; and therefore no society of men have a right to make the door of admission into their own communion straiter or wider than Christ has made it.'[138] A person's qualifications for membership must be made known to the church to which application is made, though Ridgley does not make a public confession the necessary condition of membership.

---

[134] See WW, II, 70.

[135] I have found no reference to this incident in any of the lives of Ridgley I have been able to discover.

[136] T. Ridgley, *A Body of Divinity*, II, 18.

[137] Ibid.

[138] Ibid., II, 19. Ridgley is here in the line of John Howe, who was of the opinion that 'the main inlet of all the distractions, confusions and divisions of the Christian world, hath been by adding other conditions of Church communion than Christ hath done.' In Howe's reply to Bishop Stillingfleet's sermon 'Of Schism' in *Works*, V, 226.

Pastors are called to serve by a particular church. This is clearly taught in Scripture, and it was the practice during the first three Christian centuries. Pastors are publicly ordained—that is, they are set apart with fasting and prayer, and with the imposition of hands. Pastors are not to act or rule independently of the church, but in its name and with its consent. In particular, 'a pastor, or other elders with him, have no power to act without the consent of the church, in receiving members into or excluding them from its communion.'[139] Among those obligations of the pastoral office which may be undertaken without the immediate consent of the church are preaching, the administration of the sacraments, and pastoral visitation. There is a place for wider churchly councils of an advisory nature only.

Since Ridgley devoted so many years to the education of ministers, it will be instructive to pursue his thoughts on the ministry by reference to two funeral sermons that he delivered on the death of ministerial colleagues. In his oration following the death of John Hurrion, Ridgley took John 5: 35 as his text: '[John the Baptist] was a burning and a shining light: and ye were willing for a season to rejoice in his light.' Ridgley presents John the Baptist as a prophet who shunned worldly applause, had great faith and integrity, and was humble and steadfast. He then relates these themes to the idea of a Gospel minister. Such should consider their personal obligations to Christ and promote his interest in the world. They should serve him without reserve; have due regard to the difficulties and blessings of ministerial work; and be qualified for the task. They must be instructed 'in the great doctrines of the gospel, otherwise it is impossible for them rightly to divide the word of truth.'[140] When preaching, 'Whatever sense we give of scripture, must have a tendency to promote practical godliness. Therefore no doctrine is to be reckoned true that leads to licentiousness.'[141] Ministers must declare the whole counsel of God, and have 'a zeal for the glory of God, and compassion to the souls of men.'[142]

For his funeral sermon for Thomas Tingey, Sr., Ridgley preached on Philippians 3: 9, 'And be found in him, not having mine own righteousness, which is of the law, but that which is through the faith of Christ, the righteousness which is of God by faith.' In this discourse the innermost condition and motives of the minister come to the fore: 'It is possible for a person to preach Christ, and not to experience his special and distinguishing grace: I am not safe because I am a minister, but my safety consists in my relation to the blessed Jesus; therefore may I be found living and dying in him.'[143] Ridgley imagines Paul encouraging ministerial self-examination with reference to the following formidable check-list:

---

[139] T. Ridgley, *A Body of Divinity*, II, 31.

[140] Idem, *A Sermon Occasioned by the Death of the Reverend Mr. John Hurrion*, 25.

[141] Ibid., 27.

[142] Ibid., 29.

[143] Idem, *A Sermon Occasioned by the Death of the Reverend Mr. Thomas Tingey*, 4. Thomas Tingey (d. 1 November 1729), was trained under Thomas Goodwin at Pinner, and ministered at Newport Pagnell (1699/1700-1709), Castle Hill, Northampton, (1709-1729) and at Fetter Lane, London, from February 1729 until his death. See WW, III, 453-4.

> God has employ'd me in a great work; how shall I be found? Shall I be among those who walk in craftiness, or handle the word of God deceitfully? Shall I be found among the number of those who preach not Christ, but themselves? Shall I be found among those who shun to declare the whole counsel of God, and are not much concern'd whether they do good to souls or no, provided they may have their good opinion? This supposes a person enquiring; What doctrines have I deliver'd? Are they such as tend to advance the glory of Jesus Christ, and how have I deliver'd them? Has it been with a becoming zeal for his honour? And have I always been sensible of my need of assistance from him? And have I experienced much of his presence in all my ministrations? Have I reckon'd my self as his servant, to be employ'd by him at his pleasure, and accounted this my glory? And have I had any secret testimonies from his hand, that though with many infirmities, yet I have obtained mercy from him to be faithful?[144]

Turning now to the sacraments, we find that in Ridgley's view baptism and the Lord's Supper share the following features: God is the author of both; the benefits of Christ are signified by both; both are to be 'dispensed' only by ministers of the Gospel;[145] and both are to continue until Christ comes again. They differ in that baptism is to be administered once only, while the Lord's Supper is to be observed frequently. While the candidates for baptism may be believing adults or children of believing parents, the Lord's Supper is not for children, but for those only 'who have such a degree of knowledge that they are able to discern the Lord's body' and undertake preparatory self-examination.[146]

As we might expect, Ridgley denies that the sacraments have any power in themselves to effect salvation, and their efficacy is 'not derived from the piety or intention of those by whom they are administered.'[147] Nor do the sacraments have grace-conferring powers as the Papists wrongly believe; and the 'absurd notion', espoused by Roman Catholics and some Protestants, that in paedobaptism the guilt of original sin is washed away and that infants are thus entitled to heaven if they die before they commit actual sin, 'is absurd to the last degree; for it puts a sanctifying and saving virtue into that which is no more than an outward and ordinary means of grace.'[148] Positively, 'The sacraments become effectual means of salvation only by

[144] Ibid., 6-7.

[145] It was not until the middle of the nineteenth century that 'lay' persons began to conduct the Lord's Supper in Congregational circles. If, as the liturgiologists tell us, Word and sacrament belong together as testifying to the one gospel, is not a wedge driven between them if 'lay' preaching but not 'lay' 'presidency' (Christ is the President) is permitted. And is not a wedge driven between the sacraments if any may baptize in the name of the Trinity and with water, but the ordained only may officiate at the Lord's table?

[146] Idem, *A Body of Divinity*, II, 550-552.

[147] Ibid., II, 487.

[148] Ibid., II, 487-8.

the working of the Holy Ghost, and the blessing of Christ, by whom they were instituted.'[149]

As we saw when discussing membership of the church, Ridgley made some general remarks concerning the proper recipients of baptism, whether infant or believer. Now, in his section on baptism he explains that when we say that baptism is administered in the name of the divine Trinity, we do not mean, as some ant-trinitarians do, that it is simply performed on the authority of the divine persons. Rather, in baptism persons are dedicated to the Father, Son and Holy Ghost: 'a solemn profession is made that these divine persons have a right to all religious worship, which we are obliged to perform, as well as that all our hope of salvation is from them.'[150] He then adds a problematic comment concerning the 'validity' of baptism: if, when baptizing, the minister omits to mention the Son and the Holy Spirit because he denies them to be divine persons, the baptism is invalid; if he thinks that we need not be tied to a particular form of words, so that on occasion baptism in the name of Jesus alone is in order, the sacrament is not invalid, but this procedure 'will be highly offensive to many serious Christians, and can hardly be reckoned an instance of faithfulness to Christ; who has, by express command, intimated what words are to be used.'[151] Ridgley was, of course, undisturbed by those who have subsequently questioned the authenticity of Matthew 28: 19, and he does not reflect on the propriety of speaking of the 'validity' of sacraments at all. In the latter connection one might quote the twentieth-century Congregationalist, Bernard Lord Manning, whose words apply equally to baptism as to the Lord's Supper: 'The grace of God ... needs no legal machinery to protect it ... The Supper of the Lord is either celebrated or not celebrated. ... We simply do not know what an irregular or an invalid sacrament is. We do not deal in percentages with the grace of God. When we can botanise about the Burning Bush, either it has ceased to burn or else it has been consumed ...'[152]

Ridgley proceeds to dwell on the fact that baptism is 'a sign and seal of the covenant of grace.' It does not confer the grace of the covenant, 'as the Papists pretend; for it is, at most, but a significant sign or seal of the covenant, while the grace of the covenant is the thing signified by it.'[153] It remains only to add that Ridgley strongly opposes the provision of 'sureties' (godparents) for infant baptismal candidates, on the ground that the role of the parents is thereby diminished, and the godparents make vows which they cannot adequately, and sometimes do not at all, fulfil. He does not invoke the argument that the covenanted

---

[149] Ibid., II, 188.

[150] Ibid., II, 493.

[151] Ibid., II, 494.

[152] Bernard Lord Manning, *Essays in Orthodox Dissent*, (1939), London: Independent Press, 1953, 114, 116-17. For further reflections on this theme see Alan P. F. Sell, *Enlightenment, Ecumenism, Evangel*, ch. 11.

[153] T. Ridgley, *A Body of Divinity*, II, 495.

church membership stands by the family and the infant, though he does assume that the service of baptism will be performed in the presence of the church.[154]

Not surprisingly, Ridgley's teaching on infant baptism did not find favour in Baptist circles. David Rees, for example, charged that Ridgley grounded paedobaptism in natural, not revealed, religion, and defended immersion as the proper mode of baptism, except in cases when the candidate's health would be threatened.[155] This substantial study, replete with citations of authors ancient and modern, appeared in 1734, any possible reply from Ridgley being forestalled by his death.

Concerning the Lord's Supper, Ridgley marshals the New Testament references to it, and refers to the 'outward elements of bread and wine' which are to be used. These should be set apart with prayer and thanksgiving. This leads him at once into a stern repudiation of the way in which

> the Papists pervert this ordinance in the manner of consecrating the bread. ... They ... advance the absurd doctrine of transubstantiation ... This they assert contrary to all sense and reason, as well as the end and design of the ordinance. For from this opinion it will follow, that man has a power to make the body and blood of Christ. Another consequence of it will be that the human nature of Christ is omnipresent; an idea which is inconsistent with a finite nature, and with those properties which belong to it as such, and from which it is to be concluded that his human nature is nowhere but in heaven. ... This opinion also supposes that Christ has as many bodies as there are consecrated wafers in the world; which is a monstrous absurdity.[156]

The fact is that Jesus's words, 'This is my body', 'imply no more than that the bread, which is the same in itself, after the words of consecration that it was before, is an external symbol of Christ's body, that is, of the sufferings which he endured in it for his people.'[157]

Although the Lord's Supper focuses upon Christ's sacrificial death, we should remember that in the Bible the death of Christ is often a synecdoche denoting the whole course of his obedience. In reflecting upon this, we are not simply to be moved as we might be when pondering any tragic story. Rather we are to recall that Christ's death is

> the result of an eternal agreement between the Father and the Son, and of that covenant which he came into the world to fulfil, and of his being made sin for us, to take away our sins by atonement. We may add, that the highest and most affecting consideration in Christ's sufferings, ought to include the idea of his being a divine

---

[154] See ibid., II, 511, 514.

[155] See David Rees, *Infant Baptism no Institution of Christ.*

[156] T. Ridgley, *A Body of Divinity*, II, 520.

[157] Ibid. Note the particularist restriction in the two concluding words.

person; which is the only thing that argued them sufficient to answer the great ends designed by them ...'[158]

At the Lord's Supper we are to confess our sins, plead for forgiveness, and rededicate ourselves to Christ; and at the same time, express our mutual love for those who share the sacrament with us. While the wicked are to be excluded from the table until they repent, we must not erect the barrier too low for doubting Christians to pass under; and it is not necessary for us to know the date and time of our conversion before we approach the table. What is required is a visible profession of faith and a desire to adhere to Christ and worship him in all his ordinances. With reference to the law that permitted Dissenters to hold civic positions if they occasionally received communion at the parish church, Ridgley declares that such behaviour is an abuse of the terms of communion.

Finally, a footnote on other parts of worship. Ridgley opposes instrumental music on the ground that there is no New Testament precedent for it;[159] imprecatory psalms are to be construed not as expressing individual or personal vindictiveness, but as the 'sentiments of the church of God in general, as acquiescing in his righteous judgments, which should be poured forth against those that hate him and persecute his people;[160] and hymns, as well as psalms, may be sung provided that their sentiments are in harmony with Scripture.[161]

VI

Although it has been possible in this paper to touch upon only a few of the discussions which are to be found in Ridgley's substantial work, *A Body of Divinity*, I trust that enough has been said to indicate his approach to a number of significant doctrinal matters. It has been illuminating, too, to relate the doctrinal material to his more pastoral concerns by reference to his sermons and pamphlets, and to place the whole in the context of the doctrinal debates of his day.

What emerges is a picture of a theologian who was a child of his time. This is only to be expected, but the expectation is not always realised, for some theologians are adept at being children of times earlier than their own. Ridgley was not of this kind. He expounded doctrines with a view to the controversies of his day. He delivered sermons with a view to the needs of the hearers before him. He educated students on the basis of a clear understanding of the nature of the Christian ministry. He could be forthright against what he conceived to be error, but when advancing his own ideas, he did so with a certain caution, and in a humble manner. A person of great integrity, he could speak with candour—not least when delivering funeral

---

[158] Ibid., II, 523.

[159] See ibid., II, 437. One shudders to think how Ridgley would have reacted to those drum kits and overhead projectors in the absence of which worship in some quarters cannot, in these latter days, get under way.

[160] See ibid., II, 439.

[161] See ibid., II, 442-3.

orations, where that quality was sometimes at a premium. ''Tis to [*sic*] well known,' he declared on one such occasion, 'that Funeral Discourses have been much abused, by Expatiating in the Praise of those whose Name deserved rather to be buried with them in Silence; or with a Design to Flatter their Surviving Friends, rather than advance the glory of God.'[162] How we should like to know what was said of Ridgley following his death on 27 March 1734. Sadly, no funeral oration in memory of him is extant. He was, however, subsequently recalled in the following terms:

> He was a man of extensive and sound learning, of remarkable diligence, and a strict oeconomist of his time. His skilful knowledge of the learned languages, large acquaintance with ancient and modern writers, and critical knowledge of the sacred writings, rendered him well qualified for theological controversy; and he was accounted one of the most considerable divines of his day.[163]

[162] Idem, *A Funeral Sermon Preached ... on the death of Mrs. Gertrud Clarkson*, 82.
[163] WW, II, 78.

CHAPTER 3

Abraham Taylor (fl. 1721–1740): A Volatile Theological Meteor

Even less is known about Abraham Taylor than about Thomas Ridgley. Both he and Ridgley subscribed to John Asty's 1721 edition of John Owen's *Sermons*,[1] and this is the earliest reference I have found to Taylor. He faded from the scene in 1740, as we shall see. For about twenty years, his entry and his exit undetected, he shot across the London sky like a volatile theological meteor.

It is known that Abraham was the son of the Reverend Richard Taylor (d. 1717), the Congregational minister at Little Moorfields, London. He it was who had encouraged Timothy Jollie of Attercliffe academy to take the somewhat boisterous John Sladen as a student.[2] Ebenezer Chandler, a paedobaptist who had been a member at Little Moorfields during Richard's ministry, succeeded John Bunyan in the Bedford pastorate, where served from 1690 to 1746, and was ordained on 3 November 1691.[3] Richard Taylor published a number of works including, *A History of the Union between the Presbyterian and Congregational Ministers in and about London, and the Causes of the Breach of it*, (1698), and *A Discourse of Christ as He is a Rock of Salvation*, (1701). John Nesbitt of Harecourt preached his funeral sermon.[4]

Taylor was a member of the Harecourt church during the ministry of John Nesbitt, and when Nesbitt became too ill to continue in the work Taylor approved of the appointment of John Hurrion as his successor. 'As I was a member of that Society,' he wrote to Hurrion's sons, 'I thought [their father] was a very fit man to succeed my friend, who was laid aside.'[5] If John Gill's invective is to be believed, Taylor began as a schoolmaster,[6] but he became the third minister of the

---

[1] See ch. 2, n. 10 above. For Taylor see EEUTA, 175-7, 276, 287; ODNB; T. Timpson, *Church History in Kent*, 348; Alan P. F. Sell, *Philosophy, Dissent and Nonconformity*, 43-4.

[2] See ch. 2, ns. 16-19 above.

[3] WW, I, 178; H. J. Tibbutt, *Bunyan Meeting Bedford*, 24-6.

[4] WW, III, 287.

[5] A. Taylor in his Letter to John and Samuel Hurrion, printed with Taylor's *Of the Difficult Work and Happy End of Faithful Ministers*, 14.

[6] See John Gill, *The Necessity of Good Works unto Salvation considered*, 38. The full quotation is given below.

Congregational church at High Street, Deptford. The first settled pastor there was Henry Godman, who had been ejected from Rodmell, Sussex, in 1660. He began his Deptford ministry in 1672, retired in 1696, and died on 29 January 1701/2, aged 72.[7] His successor, John Beaumont, served from 1696 to 1728, when Taylor assumed pastoral charge. On 4 November 1730 Taylor preached a funeral sermon for 'that old disciple', Beaumont, which contained a sketch of the latter's life, which I shall slightly embellish. Beaumont was born in London in 1663 and died on 31 October 1730. He attended Dean Colet's School under Thomas Gale, and was formed under the ministry of Richard Steele (1629-1692), an ejected minister who was preaching at Armourers' Hall, Coleman Street, London from about 1667.[8] Beaumont's Nonconformist scruples prevented his taking the advice of those who would have sent him to Cambridge University, Steele's *alma mater*. Instead, the Reverend Dr. Thomas Jarcombe placed him in Charles Morton's academy at Newington Green,[9] where Thomas Reynolds and Joseph Hill were among his fellow-students.[10] In 1686, when Morton, 'infested with processes from the Bishops Court', sailed for New England, his remaining students received lectures from Francis Glasscock, Stephen Lobb and William Wickins.[11] Beaumont was ordained 'after the Presbyterian model' on 1 July 1689, Dr. Samuel Annesley, John Reynolds, Robert Franklyn and John Quick—all of them ministers who had been ejected—taking part in the service.[12] Beaumont 'had well studied the body of divinity, and was acquainted with the controversies which have disturbed the Christian church, occasion'd by the opposition made to the truth by Arians, Socinians, and Arminians.'[13] In conclusion, we learn that Beaumont was of a lenient disposition, and, as the discreet veil is drawn, that he was not to be blamed 'for not keeping too close a restraint over his family, as might have been wish'd.'[14]

---

[7] For Godman see CR; FAE, 272; T. Timpson, *Church History in Kent*, 347.

[8] For Steele see CR; ODNB; WW, II, 448-457. Both Steele and Beaumont were Presbyterians. That they were succeeded by the Congregationalist Taylor is further evidence of the fluidity of Dissent at that period.

[9] For Morton (bap. 1627/7, d. 1698) see CR; EEUTA, 76-80; FAE, 315; JEREMY, 116; ODNB; TSJ, 82; WW, I, 158; II, 309, 332.

[10] For Reynolds (c.1667-1727) see FAE, 339; JEREMY, 4, 5, 114-15; ODNB; WW, I, 157-169). He was prominent among the subscribers at Salters' Hall. For Hill (1667-1729) see ODNB.

[11] For Lobb (d. 1699) see FAE, 304; JEREMY, 12, 28, 31; ODNB; WW, III, 436-446. For Wickins (d. 1699) see CR; FAE, 383. For Glasscock (d. 1706?) see FAE, 271.

[12] For Annesley (bap. 1620, d. 1696) see CR; FAE, 200-201; JEREMY, 23, 109; ODNB; WW, I, 365-70. For Reynolds (d. 1691) see CR; TSJ, 209; WW, I, 343. For Franklyn (1630-1690/91) see CR; ODNB; WW, III, 219. For Quick (bap. 1636, d. 1706) see CR; FAE, 337; ODNB; WW, III, 372-7.

[13] A. Taylor, *Of the Happiness of Believers in their Death*, 48.

[14] Ibid., 49. There is a brief reference to Beaumont in T. Timpson, *Church History in Kent*, 347.

Although he began his Deptford ministry in 1728, Taylor was not ordained until 1 January 1731.[15] A sampling of the confession of faith which Taylor delivered on that occasion will indicate something of the tenor of his thought. That his statement was comprehensive is clear from its 'heads': God, Scripture, Trinity, election, the covenant of grace, creation and providence, the primitive state of man, and his fall, Christ the Redeemer, justification by faith and adoption, efficacious grace and free will, effectual calling and sanctification, repentance and good works, the privilege of believers, the Church and instituted worship, the resurrection and the last judgment. He begins in the cosmological vein typical of his time: 'The light of nature assures us, that there is a God ...'[16] As to election, he assures us that some angels and people are 'appointed to eternal life ... without any foresight of faith and good works,' while 'the rest ... [God], in his sovereign pleasure, has left to feel the consequences of their transgressions.'[17] Adam broke the covenant of works, and 'The guilt of [his] first sin is imputed to his posterity.'[18] Although Christ's death is sufficient for all, 'the saving benefits of it are extended no farther than to the elect.'[19] Human beings are not forced to do good or evil; they have free will; but, as fallen, they cannot will what is spiritually good, for they are dead in sin. Converts are freed from bondage, and by grace are enabled to will and to do the good. In the state of glory believers will be perfectly free to do God's will. Baptism and the Lord's Supper are seals of the new covenant in Christ. Baptism is a privilege which 'belongs to the children of believing parents, otherwise we under the new testament, must, as to outward privileges, be inferior to believers under the old.'[20] In the Lord's Supper,

> Christ is not offered up to his Father, nor is any real sacrifice made, but there is a memorial of his once offering up himself, and a spiritual oblation of praise to God for the same; neither are the elements used turn'd into the body and blood of Christ, but they remain bread and wine, tho' they are symbols of his body broke, and his blood shed, for the sins of men. Such as by receive these symbols of Christ's death, spiritually feed on Christ crucified; and as this is the design of the ordinance, all unregenerate men are to be kept from it.[21]

After death, bodies return to dust, but souls 'immediately return to God as judge.'[22]

The ordination sermon was delivered by John Hurrion. The text is I Thessalonians 5: 12, 13: 'And we beseech you, brethren, to know them which labour among you, and are over you in the Lord, and admonish you; And to esteem them very highly in

---

[15] Churches sometimes had ministers 'on trial' for a number of years prior to ordination, the longest period I have come across being seventeen years.

[16] A. Taylor, 'Confession of faith' in *Of the Work of Ministers*, 1.

[17] Ibid., 9-10.

[18] Ibid., 15.

[19] Ibid., 19.

[20] Ibid., 31.

[21] Ibid., 32.

[22] Ibid., 33.

love for their work's sake. And be at peace among yourselves.' Hurrion (possibly because he is well aware of Taylor's temperament) emphasizes the fact that 'The power which Christ has given to his ministers is not magisterial, but ministerial.'[23] In the Charge to Taylor that he delivered on the same occasion Hurrion sets out from II Timothy 4: 1, urging Taylor to take heed to himself, to his doctrine, and to all the flock. The motives for thus doing his duty were the coming judgment, the glory of God and the welfare of the people, and the 'all-sufficient grace, and faithful promises of Christ.'[24] Thus John Hurrion on the first day of 1731. On the last day of that year Taylor preached a funeral sermon on the death of his friend. He found his text in the same chapter of II Timothy from which Hurrion had drawn his Charge to Taylor: 'I have fought a good fight ...' (II Timothy 4: 7-8).

This sermon, expanded to 194 pages, was published under the title, *Of the Difficult Work and Happy End of Faithful Ministers* (1733). The sermon itself is a standard exposition of the text, but the volume is the more interesting because it contains three other documents. The first is a dedication to Thomas Ridgley who, as we saw, also preached a funeral sermon on Hurrion's death. Taylor says that he is delighted to find that Ridgley and he are in agreement as to Hurrion's character and worth; and he also thanks Ridgley for that part of his *Body of Divinity* which has so far been published: 'you have shew'd, that the ancient faith is not left without an able and judicious advocate.'[25] Following the sermon there is a *Letter* from Taylor to the brothers John and Samuel Hurrion, written on the occasion of their father's death. He reminds them what a stalwart for doctrinal truth their father was and says that in his early years Hurrion had engaged in 'private controversy' concerning the divinity of Christ with Thomas Emlyn.[26] Indeed,

> He was exceedingly well acquainted with the controversies with the Arminians, and Antinomians, and knew how to oppose the first, without weakening mens obligations to duty, and running into the dream of justification from eternity, and how to avoid the phrensies of the latter, without entrenching on the sovereignty of God, or detracting from the glory of free grace.[27]

Taylor's ordination charge to John Hurrion, Jr. follows the *Letter*, and I shall refer to it in due course.

In the following year Taylor wrote the 'Advertisment' to a collection of sixteen of Hurrion's sermons, which were published under the title, *The Scripture Doctrine of the proper Divinity, real Personality, and the external and extraordinary Works of the Holy Spirit* (1734). Included in the collection are Hurrion's four Lime Street lectures on 'The Scripture-Doctrine of Particular Redemption, Stated and Vindicated.' For

---

[23] Ibid., (independently paginated), 16.

[24] Ibid., 52.

[25] Idem, *Of the Difficult Work and Happy End of Faithful Ministers*, xlvii.

[26] Ibid., Letter, 7. For Emlyn (1663-1741) see GEE, 288; ODNB; TSJ, 32, 39, 57, 70, 92, 163, 445.

[27] Ibid., Letter, 10-11.

these Hurrion took Titus 2: 14 as his text: 'Who gave himself for us, that he might redeem us from all iniquity, and purify unto himself a peculiar people, zealous of good works.' Taylor remarks upon the struggle Hurrion endured in order to complete the last two sermons for the press before his death and then, combining pious aspiration with a thumping broadside, he writes, 'I heartily wish, that [the sermons] may be, by the divine blessing, made beneficial and useful to such as may read them, and may be of service to guard Christians against the absurd notion of universal redemption, the evident tendency of which is to represent Christ as dying in vain.'[28]

The funeral sermon for Hurrion was by no means Taylor's first appearance in print. On the contrary, he had burst onto the authorial scene in 1726 with *The Scripture Doctrine of the Trinity Vindicated.* He swiftly followed this up with a hammering of the Arians in two volumes: *The True Scripture-Doctrine of the Holy and Ever-Blessed Trinity, Stated and Defended, in Opposition to the Arian Scheme* (1727). I shall return to these works in due course, and wish now only to show that from the outset Taylor plunged straight into the neuralgic doctrinal issues of the day. But if Taylor were a pugilistic controversialist by nature, he could also be a thoughtfully pastoral preacher by grace. For evidence of this I shall refer to two sermons and one substantial book. The first is his sermon, *Of Assurance of God's Love*, preached at Deptford and published in 1728, in the wake of his belabouring of the Arians.

Taylor introduces his theme as follows:

> When Christ ... looks on any of the unhappy seed of Adam, who are cast out to the loathing of their persons ... he knocks off their fetters, and girds them with gladness. ... However, by reason of sin remaining in the best of Christians, their joys will often be damp'd, and their evidences of heaven clouded. ... It is only by the holy Spirit, witnessing with the spirits of Christians, that they can be assured of their interest in the joys and pleasures of the upper world.[29]

Christian assurance, he continues, presupposes faith, but it is not essential to faith at all times. He feels that those Reformers were mistaken who spoke of faith as always carrying assurance with it. 'The prime work of justifying faith is to look to Christ, and to close with him; but assurance is ... faith looking back to a mystical union with Christ, and our justification by him.'[30] Assurance is 'principally founded in the witness of the holy Spirit'; it is 'to be judged by the fruits it produces'; and it 'is afforded to Christians more at some seasons, than at others.'[31]

In applying the foregoing, Taylor cautions that we are not to judge the reality of our faith in terms of our feelings of assurance. True assurance involves our valuing Christ. By contrast, 'They are wretchedly infatuated, who pretend to elevated

---

[28] A. Taylor in J. Hurrion, *The Scripture-Doctrine of Particular Redemption, Stated and Vindicated*, 198.

[29] A. Taylor, *Of Assurance of God's Love*, 3, 4.

[30] Ibid., 13.

[31] Ibid., 18, 25, 29. Cf. A. Taylor, *An Address to Young Students of Divinity*, 26.

communion with God, in the perfection of a contemplative life, or in internal prayer, or inward martyrdom, or whatever swelling words of vanity they invent, and at the same time neglect Christ, by whom, only we can have communion with God.'[32] If we desire assurance, we must not provoke the Spirit; we must frequently examine ourselves, depend utterly on Christ, 'labour after higher degrees of holiness and purity, in heart and life', and grow in humility.[33]

For the second example of Taylor in pastoral mode I return to his funeral sermon for John Beaumont. The title is, *Of the Happiness of Believers in their Death*, and the text is Revelation 14: 13: 'And I heard a voice from heaven saying unto me, Write, Blessed are the dead which die in the Lord from henceforth: Yea, saith the Spirit, that they may rest from their labours; and their works do follow them.' Taylor's points are:

> None can be happy in death who die out of Christ.
> They only who have Christ for their life, or who live in him, by him, and to him, can be blessed in their death.
> They who live in Christ, die in the Lord, and so are blessed.
> They who die in the Lord are blessed, because they rest from their labours.
> They who die in the Lord will be blessed, because of the happiness they will enjoy.[34]

Coming to his application, Taylor declares that if those only are happy who die in the Lord, the misery of all others is thrown into relief. Christ's faithful labourers should 'bear up under all the difficulties they meet with' as they contemplate what is to come. Real rest awaits the happy dead, and meanwhile the saints should be patient. We should not despair if we are taken young, and 'aged saints' should not 'be uneasy under weakness of body.' If there is work to be done here, we should not be impatient to leave this world. He then exhorts his hearers to impress the truth of the blessed state of those who die in the Lord upon their hearts.[35]

Thirdly, in *A Practical Treatise of Saving Faith in Three Parts* (1730) Taylor sustains pastoral sensitivity over 362 pages. God, we learn, is the principal and fundamental object of saving faith, while Christ is the immediate object of saving faith in his person and mediatorial offices. Since sinners cannot work saving faith in themselves, the Holy Spirit does this by the instrumentality of the Word. Faith assents to what Scripture has revealed about Christ. It empties sinners of all conceit concerning their own worth. We are to look to Christ by faith, by faith fly to him for refuge, and by faith receive him. Believers rely upon Christ by faith for pardon, justification, strength to perform their duties, sanctification, and for the ability to resist spiritual enemies. They rely upon Christ for admission to God's presence, and for eternal life. He then discusses the evidences of saving faith, namely, the fruits of

[32] Ibid., 40-41.
[33] Ibid., 45.
[34] Idem, *Of the Happiness of Believers in their Death*, 7, 9, 18, 21, 24.
[35] Ibid., 31-41.

holiness. Finally, he recognizes that true saving faith 'may flag and falter.'[36] On such occasions, we should look to Christ and 'beg him to increase' our faith.[37]

I

It was Taylor's reply of 1730 to Strickland Gough, an erstwhile Presbyterian who had conformed to the Church of England, which altered the course of Taylor's life.[38] His tract was entitled, *A Letter to the Author of an Enquiry into the Causes of the Decay of the Dissenting Interest. Containing an Apology for some of his Inconsistencies; with a Plea for the Dissenters and the Liberty of the People* (1730). This *Letter* brought him to the attention of the city merchant and Congregational benefactor, William Coward.[39]

Coward, a stalwart Calvinist who funded lectures in defence of his favoured theological position, engaged Taylor in 1730 to deliver four lectures at the meeting house in the Paved Alley, Lime Street. Also on the panel of lecturers was the formidable high Calvinist Baptist, John Gill, with whom Taylor entered into controversy, as we shall see. Coward organized twenty-six lectures on the Lime Street foundation, and nine ministers, including John Sladen, John Hurrion and Thomas Bradbury, constituted the panel.[40]

Another of Coward's interests was the funding of ministerial students educated under the auspices of the King's Head Society.[41] This body was constituted in 1730. It took its name from its meeting place, the King's Head, Sweeting's Alley, a hostelry run by Edmund Munday, who himself was admitted to the Society on 21 February 1727. The Society's members were, of set purpose, non-ministerial: Joseph Lloyd, Jonathan Rowle, Daniel Booth, Nathaniel and William Field, Dr. Beerman, and Messrs. Hargrave, Rutt, Hitchen, Sharp, Towell, Rolleston, Stratton, and Crouch. Hitherto the Congregational Fund Board had supported students at its academy at Moorfields,[42] but there was disquiet on the part of the King's Head men that under Ridgley insufficient attention was paid to the spiritual development of the students. In the opinion of Thomas Conder, 'Many young men ... were .. introduced into the ministry, whose subsequent conduct gave too much reason to fear that they never experienced the grace of God in truth. Instead of their edifying and building up the Churches over which they presided, many once flourishing congregations were

---

36 Idem, *A Practical Treatise of Saving Faith*, 349.

37 Ibid., 360.

38 For Gough (d. 1752) see FAE, 273; GEE, 35; MURCH, 106; ODNB. He was a student of Henry Grove at Taunton academy, did some preaching in London, but was never in pastoral charge. There is no evidence that he was ordained.

39 For Coward (1647/8-1738) see ODNB; John Handby Thompson, *A History of the Coward Trust*.

40 See WW, I, 212.

41 For information on this Society I draw upon John Waddington, *Congregational History 1700-1800*, London: Longmans Green, 1876, 263-268.

42 For the history of the Board see John H. Taylor, *The Congregational Fund Board*.

suffered to crumble away under their hands. In several instances divisions took place ...'[43] There were theological concerns too. The distinguished scientist and Moorfields tutor, John Eames, was an Arminian, whereas the King's Head men were staunch Calvinists. Indeed, in 1732 Abraham Taylor devised 'A Declaration as to some controverted points of Christian Doctrine' for them to which all their students and recognized tutors were required to assent. It was also felt that whereas students went to Ridgley and Eames following their classical education, it would be preferable if two years of such education were given under the auspices of the Society, to be followed by four years of divinity.[44] To this end, Samuel Parsons of the Congregational church, Basingstoke, was appointed to teach the arts courses. For this purpose, Parsons removed to Clerkenwell, where he boarded his students in his own house. He joined Thomas Bradbury's church at New Court, Carey Street, but when John Hurrion, Jr. left Three Cranes for Gosport, Parsons followed him as Ridgley's assistant[45]—a move which suggests that Ridgley bore no ill will to the King's Head enterprise. Nineteen students had passed through Parsons's hands by 24 December 1734. In 1735 he removed to the pastorate of Witham, Essex, where he remained until his death.

Abraham Taylor was appointed King's Head theological tutor, and began his duties in May 1735.[46] Students were sent to him at Deptford, and classes were held in 'the Great House', Union Street.[47] Lectures were given on natural and revealed theology. In these Taylor, like some other academy tutors, followed Johannes Marck's *Christianae theologiae medulla.* While the gift of reason is not to be slighted, he argues, in theological matters 'it must be subject to the obedience of faith.'[48] As to the fundamental purpose of theology, 'The end to which all theology tends is to being glory to God; and to further the compleating the salvation of all those who are redeemed by Christ ...'[49] There are lectures on the revelation of God's mind and will in the Old and New Testaments,[50] and a manuscript entitled *An Introduction to Logick, with a few Lectures, on Perception, the first part of that Science* (1739). In the *Logick* Taylor agrees with the 'wise man of old' that 'man is born like the wild asses colt', and that without instruction he does not exercise his intellect.[51] At the root of the problem are the noetic effects of sin, to which Taylor refers in a delightfully quaint (and *ad hominem*) way: 'If we consider matters justly

---

[43] Quoted by J. Waddington, *Congregational History 1700-1800*, 263.

[44] See EEUTA, 175.

[45] WW, II, 82.

[46] WW, II, 530 wrongly implies that Taylor ('Tayler' *ad loc.*) was appointed on the formation of the King's Head Society.

[47] So T. Timpson, *Church History in Kent*, 348.

[48] A. Taylor, *Lectures on Natural and Revealed Theology*, 286-7. Congregational Library at Dr. Williams's Library, London, MS 1.d.24

[49] Ibid., 302.

[50] Congregational Library MS 1.d.25

[51] A. Taylor, *An Introduction to Logick*, Dr. Williams's Library, London, MS 69.24. Also in the Congregational Library MSS, 1.d.25.

and impartially, we must conclude; that Adam our common parent, impair'd his intellectuals greatly by his fall ...'[52]

For a final sounding in his *Logick* we may turn to a paragraph in which trounces some of his foes in a characteristically 'Aunt Sally' way, concluding with a typically English 'put down' of one of England's greatest philosophers:

> The Popish writers have run into great confusion in endeavouring to make free thinking consistent with implicit faith in the dictates of their church; and Mr. Locke, who let his admirers say what they will of him, was no better than a Socinian in principle, and but a mean Divine of that sort, and no great friend of revelation, has interlarded his work with a great many subtleties, which tend to bring persons to have a mean and low view of what is properly mysterious. These men were certainly persons of deep thought, and penetrating genius, but their learning was very inconsiderable, and their reading was not large. This, in a particular manner, was true of Mr. Locke. Those that knew him personally were satisfied, that, as to ancient literature he was but very superficial.[53]

We may place these remarks in context by observing that Taylor held Aristotle in high esteem, and, unlike Ridgley, he larded his writings with authorities and was enamoured of the scholastic method. That Taylor's reputation as a scholar had spread beyond London and even England is evidenced by the fact that in 1736 Marischal College, Aberdeen, conferred its Doctor of Divinity degree upon him. The staunch Calvinist, Alexander Cruden of biblical concordance fame, an *alumnus* of the College who was by now living in London, was instrumental in securing this honour for Taylor. Taylor, he wrote, 'exceeds all the Dissenting ministers of my acquaintance for learning.'[54]

We may gain at least a partial insight into Taylor's understanding of the Christian ministry from two ordination charges that he delivered. On 3 May 1732 he exhorted John Hurrion, the son of Taylor's great friend of the same name, on the occasion of his ordination at Gosport. Hurrion had studied under Ridgley at Moorfields, and had been his assistant at Three Cranes Court (1731/2). He remained at Gosport until his death in 1750. 'The preaching of the glorious gospel of the blessed Jesus,' Taylor declared, 'is committed to your trust, and as you have consented to serve the chief shepherd, in this part of his fold, you are in a particular manner to take care and feed this church, and to act the part of a spiritual guide, to direct the members of it, from

---

[52] Ibid., 12.

[53] Ibid., 43, 44. For a more balanced view of Locke's alleged Socinianism, and of the place he accorded to revelation, see Alan P. F. Sell, *John Locke and the Eighteenth-Century Divines*, ch. 6. Taylor's concluding sentence calls to mind a similar remark of Bishop George Horne *contra* Joseph Priestley who, declared Horne, 'is defying all the world, and cannot construe a common piece of Greek or Latin.' See William Jones, *Memoirs of ... George Horne*, 148.

[54] P. J. Anderson, *Fasti academiae Mariscallanae Aberdonensis*, 2.82. For Cruden (1699-1770) see ODNB; DSCHT.

the word, in all things which are necessary for them to know.'[55] Hurrion must take heed of doctrine, and vindicate the truth of the Christian religion. In this latter connection Taylor unloads a formidable set of tasks upon the young man. I set them down in full because they comprise a check-list of Taylor's major doctrinal concerns, some of which will concern us shortly:

> You are called to defend the being of God against the atheists, and his supreme authority, as a lawgiver against such as set up moral fitnesses, rising from the nature of things, as the grounds of his will and determination; you are to plead for the truth of divine revelation, against deists, and for its necessity and perfection, against such betrayers of the christian cause, as make natural religion a sufficient rule; you are to stand up for the distinct personality and supreme Deity of the Son, and the Holy Spirit, against such as make them powers of God, or creatures, and for the reality of Christ's human nature, against such as pretend, he had a super-angelic Spirit, to supply the place of a human soul; you are to contend for the free election of believers to glory, against such as make it to be for foreseen faith; for the infinite perfection of Christ's satisfaction, against them who would join something of their own to it; for the certain efficacy of his death, against such as will have it, that he died for all men, and yet rendered salvation sure to no one man; for justification by his righteousness, against the abettors of the notion of our being accepted with God, for our sincerity; for the irresistible power and the efficacious grace of the Spirit, in regenerating us, against the patrons of free will; for the perseverance of the saints in holiness, against such as assert, they may fall from grace; for the perfection of God's law, against those who would weaken the obligations we lie under to it; for the activity of the soul after death, against those who make the sameness of it line in self-consciousness; and for the general judgment and the eternity of hell torments, against such as would not think themselves to be accountable to God, and are not for sin being punished in the other world. These points at proper seasons you ought, as far as you are able, to clear and vindicate, and to confute the opposite errors.[56]

As if this were not enough, Taylor immediately adds, 'You must not, in your public administrations, confine yourself wholly to these.'[57] Hurrion must declare the whole counsel of God. He must not preach up the necessity of good works in such a way as to disparage God's sovereign grace or Christ's imputed righteousness. He must speak a word in season to the weary, and 'Receive nothing as truth, without you find it is revealed in scripture.'[58] He must be a good student, and when in the pulpit, he must 'use plainness and perspicacity of speech.'[59] He must lead a holy and blameless life, and administer the gospel ordinances to the people, remembering that 'you are tied to them, in a near and close relation, bear them much on your heart, and

---

[55] A. Taylor, *Exhortation* to Hurrion in *Of the Difficult Work and Happy End of Faithful Ministers*, 3.

[56] Ibid., 14-16.

[57] Ibid., 16.

[58] Ibid., 23.

[59] Ibid., 29.

frequently remember them in your private addresses to the throne of grace.'[60] Hurrion must 'shew a true Christian temper to all', but 'have as little intimate conversation with such as pervert the doctrines of Christ, as possible.'[61] He must trust in Christ and be much in prayer. Taylor concludes by wishing him well in the great work he has undertaken.

William Johnson was ordained at Reigate Congregational Church on 6 October 1736. He had begun his studies under John Eames, and completed them under Taylor. He was born near Skeyton, Norfolk, in 1710. Following a brief ministry at Reigate (1736-1738)[62] he removed to Romsey, Hampshire (1738-1763), and thence in 1763 to Paul's Meeting, Taunton, where he died on 4 December 1768.[63] Taylor begins his ordination charge by acknowledging the fact that Johnson has undertaken what will be an arduous task, but Christ will assist him. There follows a series of exhortations: search the Scriptures continually; exalt 'the sacred Three' and do not 'set up one perfection of God to the injury of another;'[64] he must in particular teach the people the roles of the three persons of the Trinity in salvation. Taylor cautions Johnson against antinomianism, warning him not to be misled by that 'corrupt herd' who preach 'electing love, and free rich grace, but cannot bear any thing to be said about duty.'[65] 'Suit your preaching to the different states and frames of those who hear you,'[66] he continues. Johnson is then urged to take care in sermon preparation, and the injunction to search the scriptures' is repeated, this time with the addition: 'especially in the original languages.'[67] As to the manner of his preaching, Johnson is advised not to 'mistake rattling bombast for true sublime.'[68] In addition to all of this, the new pastor must take care over his conduct in the world and the church, avoiding intemperance and shunning evil. He must be humble, practice Christian love, honour Christ in all things and show Christian courage. Finally, he must care for the flock. Since none of this can be done in his own strength, he must pray daily

---

[60] Ibid., 37.

[61] Ibid., 41, 44.

[62] For which see J. Waddington, *Surrey Congregational History*, 283; E. E. Cleal, *The Story of Congregationalism in Surrey*, 378. Johnson thus arrived in Reigate one hundred and twenty years before G. J. Adeney, for whom see ch. 10 below.

[63] It is possible that Johnson preached the sermon at Newport, Isle of Wight on 7 August 1756, on the occasion of the ordination of John Chater, who began in Congregationalism and ended in Sandemanianism. See WW, III, 112. Wilson says that the sermon was published, but it has not come to light. For Chater see Alan P. F. Sell, *Dissenting Thought and the Life of the Churches*, ch. 14.

[64] Idem, in *A Sermon preach'd at the ordination of the Reverend Mr. William Johnson*, 61.

[65] Ibid., 64.

[66] Ibid.

[67] Ibid., 65.

[68] Ibid., 67.

to the Holy Spirit for light and help. Taylor wishes him all success, commends him to Christ, and concludes with a Trinitarian ascription.[69]

The highly regarded Thomas Towle (1724-1806) was another of Taylor's students. He also attended Eames's classes at Moorfields, and finished his training under Zephaniah Marryatt at Plasterers' Hall, the successor academy to Taylor's.[70] He was ordained in 1747/8 at the Congregational church meeting in Ropemakers' Alley, which in 1765 removed to a new meeting house in Aldermanbury Postern. There he remained until his death, having served his pastorate for almost fifty-nine years.[71]

Taylor's best known student was Thomas Gibbons (1720-1785).[72] The son of Thomas Gibbons, erstwhile minister at Olney and Royston, he was born at Reach, Swaffham Prior. He seems to have attended three grammar schools, and then entered Taylor's academy at the age of fifteen, finishing his studies under Eames at Moorfields. Wilson opines that 'Dr. Gibbons must have suffered considerable disadvantages in his education, owing to his being obliged so often to shift his tutors.'[73] It is not impossible that this remark gives the impression that Gibbons was more at the mercy of events than in fact he was. For on 3 January 1737 he wrote to the King's Head Society, informing the members of his 'design of leaving Dr. Taylor.' A Committee chaired by Mr. Hill interviewed Gibbons, and reported to the Society on 10 January. Gibbons complained about the lack of logic, the over-lengthy introduction to divinity, and the undue concentration upon classical literature. The committee dismissed these complaints and asked Gibbons if he had any other points to raise. He said that he 'thought himself under too great a confinement' in having to ask Taylor's permission to leave the premises at other than stated times. The committee was apparently unmoved by this. Mr. Booth then asked Gibbons 'whether he had any objection to the temper and behaviour of the Doctor, or if he found any inconveniences in the family that rendered him uneasie? To which he readily answered, "No, not in the least."'[74] It was then 'Agreed that Thomas Gibbons be discharged from the care of this Society.'[75]

The committee did not allow the matter to rest there. Mr. Hitchen and Mr. Nathaniel Field met all the students under Taylor's care. The students 'gave a very satisfactory account of themselves and that they had comfortable hopes that they

---

[69] Taylor also gave the Exhortation to Benjamin Vowell at Colchester on 19 April 1738, where he served until 1745. See *A Sermon preached at the Ordination of the Reverend Mr. Benjamin* Vowell. Vowell was highly regarded, but 'in the latter part of life a period was put to his usefulness and his ministry by a total derangement of mind.' See E. A. Blaxill, *History of Lion Walk Congregational Church*, 16.

[70] For Marryatt (1684?-1754) see EEUTA, 176-9; WW, IV, 199-203.

[71] For Towle see WW, II, 547-554.

[72] For Gibbons see EEUTA, 177; ODNB; WW, III, 178-183; Alan P. F. Sell, *Philosophy, Dissent and Nonconformity*, 44-5. Extracts from Gibbons's Diary are to be found in CHST I, beginning on 328, 384 and 480

[73] WW, III, 178.

[74] J. Waddington, *Congregational History 1700-1800*, 266-7.

[75] Ibid., 267.

made progress in experimental religion', 'declared their satisfaction as to the Doctor's conduct and economy of the house', and 'express'd their inclination and desire to go through [their studies] with the Doctor.'[76] These comments are of some importance, as we shall see.

Gibbons completed his studies under Eames, became an assistant to Thomas Bures in Silver Street, and on 27 October 1743 was ordained at Haberdashers' Hall, where he remained until his death. From 1754, on the death of Zephaniah Marryatt, he also taught logic, metaphysics, ethics and rhetoric at the Mile End academy. In 1764 Gibbons, like Taylor and Ridgley before him, became a Doctor of Divinity of Aberdeen.[77] Of Gibbons it was said that

> In his ministry he was truly *evangelical*, and bore an unambiguous testimony to the grace of God and the atonement of Christ, as the grand and sole foundation of the sinner's hope. And in connection with this, he maintained the absolute necessity of genuine *holiness* and *piety* as an essential part of the great salvation, and the evidence of our title to life and blessedness.[78]

If Gibbons did not complain about Taylor, another student, Joseph Griggs, most certainly did, in a letter of 30 May 1738. The Society found his words 'insolent, injurious, and ungrateful,' and he was discharged from the Society's care.[79]

Was it the case that there was no smoke without fire? Did the fact that 'The Gentlemen that are advocates for Moderation seem to sink in [Coward's] esteem' and the fact that Coward 'begins to think Dr. Watts a Baxterian & is almost come to open Rupture with him'[80] work against Taylor? Did the fears of those, like Doddridge, that Coward, having 'grown cold to' Jennings, Watts and Guyse, would leave his money to Taylor with the prospect of 'Bigotry intailed on the rising Generation'[81] work their way into the minds of those who were to become Coward Trustees? Did the manner in which Taylor laid into Isaac Watts over the latter's view of the Trinity (to which I shall return) sow seeds of discord among the Coward Trustees, of whom Watts was one? The fact remains that on Coward's death in 1738 the Coward Trust, which first met on 16 May 1738, disendowed the seven of Taylor's students whom Coward had been financing, ostensibly on the ground that Coward's will would leave insufficient funds to continue supporting so many students. In the event the funds available were so large that the Trustees could not

---

[76] Ibid.

[77] So, too did Zephaniah Marryatt, Philip Doddridge, Samuel Morton Savage, and others. Indeed, Aberdeen was particularly open towards those of the Congregational Way, no least to its own *alumnus*, P. T. Forsyth. Hence my decision some years ago to 'reward' the University with a copy of all of my own published books.

[78] Benjamin Davies, *Israel's Testament*, 22.

[79] J. Waddington, *Congregational History 1700-1800*, 267.

[80] CCPD no. 465; letter of 14 July 1737 from Hugh Farmer and Celia Snell to Doddridge.

[81] CCPD no. 467; letter of 20 July 1737 from Doddridge to Samuel Clark of St. Albans.

imagine how they could exhaust them. Even so, while they agreed to fund three of Taylor's students elsewhere, they sent no more to him.[82]

Not surprisingly, on 4 March 1739/40 the King's Head Society

> Agreed that the students with Dr. Taylor at Deptford, under the care of this Society, have a month's vacation at present on account of the unhappy circumstances of the tutor. That a committee be appointed to get all the intelligence they can of the situation of Dr. Taylor's affairs, to be laid before the Society at the next meeting.[83]

This was duly done, and at the following General Meeting on 18 March 1739/40 Mr. Booth reported that ''tis the opinion of this committee that Dr. Taylor's circumstances are such as to render him incapable of serving the Society any longer in the capacity of a tutor.'[84] The loss of Coward funding cannot have helped Taylor's situation. On the contrary, it had been the financial life-blood of his academy.

With this Taylor fades from the scene. Nothing is known of his death. No funeral sermon preached in his memory is extant. What happened to him? He did not continue in the Deptford pastorate, being succeeded by the Revd Thomas Pickersgill.[85] I wonder whether, seeing the writing on the wall, he opened a bookshop in Deptford? If he did, any success was short lived, for, according to the *Sherborne Mercury*,[86] in 1740 one Abraham Taylor, bookseller of Deptford, was declared bankrupt. Would it be too much of a coincidence to suppose that there were two Abraham Taylors in Deptford, both of whom were in financial straits in 1740?

II

It is now time to introduce themes of particular concern to Taylor and his intellectual opponents. I shall consider in turn Taylor's rebuttal of the deists, his views on doctrinal and spiritual declension, and his confidence in the final triumph of Christ's kingdom.

It would seem that few eighteenth-century orthodox divines managed to resist at least a few broadsides against the deists. As we might expect, Taylor was no exception. Before rehearsing his position on the matter, however, and without wishing to call down the wrath of the godly upon my head, something must be said concerning the context in which that diverse collection of writers (they were too disparate to be a group or a school) labelled 'deist' lived. They embarked upon the path of reasonableness in the wake of the seventeenth century's record of sectarian strife and civil unrest, some of it fuelled by idiosyncratic appeals to special revelations. In the wake of the Toleration Act of 1689 there was no longer one authority to which appeals on religious questions could be lodged. The question

---

82 See J. H. Thompson, *A History of the Coward Trust*, 12-13.

83 J. Waddington, *Congregational History 1700-1800*, 267.

84 Ibid., 268.

85 T. Timpson, *Church History in Kent*, 348.

86 See www.devon.gov.uk/etched?_IXP_=1&_IXR=100159.

therefore arose as to whether societal harmony could be achieved on the basis of an appeal to natural religion in a way analogous to that in which the new science was drawing tenable generalizations from observation of the phenomena of the natural order.[87]

By none of the foregoing considerations was Taylor moved. On the contrary, he contented himself with rebutting the claims of natural religion. Two of his Lime Street lectures will demonstrate the point. In the first, *The Insufficience of Natural Religion*, he declares that whereas Christ is the Saviour from sin, the deists elevate natural religion, and while they pretend to esteem Christianity, they concurrently declare that natural religion is sufficient and needs nothing added to it. Sadly, their task has been made easier 'by many treacherous professors of the religion of Jesus'[88] who attack such doctrines as the Trinity, election and original sin. Christianity has also been weakened by those who elevate systems of morality above the doctrines of the faith. Those who uphold human reason argue fallaciously, because they speak of reason in the abstract, whereas the question to be answered is 'whether reason, as it now is in men, ... is not in a state of degeneracy.'[89] Underlying all the opposition to God's revelation is human pride. Natural man counts as foolish the great things of God; indeed, 'the man of mere rational attainments will never know [them], because they are spiritually discerned.'[90]

For his second sermon on the theme[91] Taylor took the sufficiently provocative text, 'Professing themselves to be wise, they became fools' (Romans 1: 22). He sets out from the claim that while the works of creation do indeed proclaim their great Original, defenders of natural religion take no account of the Fall. Furthermore, they offer no consistent scheme of practical religion on the basis of which the social and other duties on which they insist might be carried out. Some proponents of natural religion have ideas of immortality, but they have no secure ground for them. By contrast Christians have the revelation of the triune God, and this alone suffices.

III

If Taylor was concerned by ideas advanced, as it were, from without the boundaries of 'standard' Christianity, he was no less concerned by spiritual and doctrinal declension within the Christian fold. On 6 January 1731/2 he delivered a sermon, *Of Spiritual Declensions, and the Danger of being Insensible under them*, at Harecourt church. His text was Isaiah 1: 2-4:

> Hear, O heavens, and give ear, O earth: for the Lord hath spoken. I have nourished and brought up children, and they have rebelled against me. The ox knoweth his owner, and the ass his master's crib: but Israel doth no know, my people doth not

---

[87] See further, Alan P. F. Sell, *Enlightenment, Ecumenism, Evangel*, ch. 4.

[88] A. Taylor, *The Insufficience of Natural Religion*, 5.

[89] Ibid., 15.

[90] Ibid., 33.

[91] For which see [A. Taylor], *A Defence of some Important Doctrines of the Gospel.*

> consider. Ah sinful nation, a people laden with iniquity, a seed of evildoers, children that are corrupters: they have forsaken the Lord, they have provoked the holy One of Israel unto anger, they are gone away backward.

Taylor begins by observing that when God has favoured a religious people, they have too often abused his mercies. He copiously illustrates this point from Adam onwards. The Christian Church is caught up in this guilt, for declensions in both doctrine and practice are observable. There was, first, the 'attempt to obscure the great and glorious doctrine of justification by Christ's imputed righteousness.'[92] Then came the challenge to the doctrines of election and the imputation of Adam's sin. This was followed by denial of the 'supreme Deity of our blessed Lord and Redeemer Jesus Christ, and of the Holy Spirit, the Comforter of the elect people of God.'[93] However, the greatest depth was plumbed by 'the Socinians who skulked in Poland.'[94] On the heels of doctrinal declension came the corruption of manners. The Sabbath became a day of pleasure, and natural religion was made the supreme rule. Professors who abuse God's mercies are often unaware of their spiritual declensions, and 'this insensibility is an aggravated sin ... and it is often followed with severe rebukes'[95]—a further point illustrated at some length from the Bible. Turning to exhortation, Taylor declares that in a time of religious declension, those who 'have the interest of God at heart' should not be indolent.[96] They should carefully practice the duties that others neglect, and they should pray God to revive his work—something which history shows he can do.

Turning to more specific examples of doctrinal declension, we may first note Taylor's diatribe entitled, *A Letter to a Friend: Occasioned by a Rhapsody, Delivered in Old Jewry; by A Reverend Bookseller in London; At the shutting-up of his Evening Entertainment, for the last Winter Season* (1729). The 'Reverend Bookseller' was the Presbyterian Samuel Chandler, who had opened a bookshop to augment his income following the ill-advised investment of his wife's fortune;[97] Chandler's 'Rhapsody' was his sermon entitled, *Knowledge and Practice necessary to Happiness* (1729); and the 'shutting up of his Evening Entertainment' refers to the last of a series of evening sermons delivered at Old Jewry meeting house.

Taylor quotes Chandler as saying that 'Religion does not so much consist in knowing that God is, and that he is an infinitely wise, and good, and just, and powerful Being ... but in adoring, loving, and praising him as such.' Taylor retorts that this is 'Nonsense dropping from him unawares', for the first principle of religion is to know that God is, for we cannot worship one of whose existence we are uncertain.[98] There is, of course, a kinder interpretation of Chandler's words and,

---

[92] A. Taylor, *Of Spiritual Declensions*, 24.

[93] Ibid., 27.

[94] Ibid., 28.

[95] Ibid., 33.

[96] Ibid., 45.

[97] See further ch. 4 below.

[98] A. Taylor, *A Letter to a Friend*, 10.

indeed, Taylor himself later grants that 'it signifies nothing to a man's self, if he understands the Theory of Religion, and does not practise according to his Knowledge.'[99] This, it would seem, is what Chandler was contending for. But Chandler is otherwise guilty, according to Taylor: he has opposed the doctrines of election and particular redemption, and he says that he is obliged to believe 'Whatever can be proved to be a genuine doctrine' of God, 'so far as I can understand it.' This means, Taylor retorts, that 'according to him, his Understanding is the mighty Thing, at the Bar of which, every Revealed Truth must be arraigned'[100]—a reply which overlooks the willingness of the more liberal divines to agree that there were aspects of revealed truths which were above reason; their concern was not to believe what was against reason.

Taylor proceeds to accuse Chandler of injustice to other writers, though 'for him to rail at Persons, is the greatest Honour which he had in his power to confer upon them.'[101] Against any suggestion that those who value creeds and confessions are blinkered, he declares that such formulations are valued only to the extent that they accord with Scripture. He grants that there is some plausibility in Chandler's assertion that 'the Words of divine Revelation are the best,' but he immediately points out that 'it has been the constant bellow of the Anti-trinitarian Party, *The Bible, the Bible, is the Religion of Protestants*! To which senseless Noise, I am sorry others have returned an Eccho.'[102] In other words, Taylor is objecting to the way in which more liberal divines appealed to the principle of the sufficiency of Scripture, and objected to what they regarded as 'Protestant Popery'—the attempt on the part of the orthodox to secure adherence to particular confessional formulations of doctrine, or particular understandings of the *ordo salutis*.[103] Taylor concludes that Chandler's sermon is 'the boldest Attack on the Doctrines of the Reformation, that ever was made by a Dissenter.'[104]

IV

As far as Taylor was concerned, there was more than one route by which doctrinal declensions travel to afflict the Church. That he was no less concerned by antinomian tendencies within the Calvinist fold is clear from a letter dated 25 December 1738 which he addressed to the King's Head Society, and printed with *An Address to Young Students in Divinity, By way of a Caution against some Paradoxes, Which lead to Doctrinal Antinomianism* (1739). He addresses his letter 'To the Society of Ministers and Gentlemen, Engaged in the Design of encouraging

---

99 Ibid., 15.

100 Ibid., 26.

101 Ibid., 34.

102 Ibid., 35.

103 For some latter day reflections on this point see Alan P. F. Sell, 'Confessing the Faith and confessions of faith,' forthcoming in Eduardus Van der Borght, ed., *Christian Identity*.

104 A Taylor, *A Letter to a Friend*, 38.

young men in their studies for the Ministry, Whose hearts God has inclined to that Sacred Work.' He makes it clear that he intends to hold in balance the doctrine of salvation by free grace alone, and the obligation of duty and holiness. Hence his critique of doctrinal antinomianism. He asks for the prayers of those who 'have call'd me to a very difficult and laborious work.'[105] There follows an 'Advertisment' in which Taylor points out that he has not dealt with specific authors by whose inclinations to doctrinal antinomianism he is concerned. Rather,

> I would charitably hope, that the hearts of these men are better than their heads, but I confess I should never care to enter the lists with such botchers in divinity, as they are, who make the decree of God, and his execution of it, the same thing, and cannot tack together truths so consistent as these, Salvation is all of free grace, and good works the fruit of holiness, a part of salvation, are absolutely necessary to complete salvation; or as these, It is the duty of sinners to believe in Christ, or they must perish, and, Faith is not of ourselves, it is the gift of God in particular.[106]

In this one paragraph Taylor offered hostages to fortune at two doctrinally neuralgic points: by making good works a necessary part of salvation, was he, in his desire to shun antinomianism, tending in an Arminian direction? (Yes, answered John Gill). In declaring that unconverted sinners are duty bound to believe or perish, was he imposing upon the unregenerate a duty impossible of fulfilment? (Yes, answered John Brine).

At the opening of his *Address* Taylor throws down the gauntlet by countering those who say that it is not the duty of unconverted sinners to believe in the Saviour. He addresses those who, rightly, do not make God's sovereignty inconsistent with his holiness and justice; who hold to the Trinity and to particular redemption; but who have wrongly inferred from these that the penitent sinner contributes nothing to his salvation. While the danger from Arianism and Arminianism is great, he continues, it is now the case that antinomianism is 'making a progress, among such as profess themselves friends to free and sovereign grace.'[107] He denies the charge of antinomianism which has been levelled against those of his persuasion, and insists that people who deny the necessity of good works to salvation must be rebuffed. He then adduces evidence from the New Testament regarding the importance of good works. By contrast, some, 'who set up for the only pure gospel-preachers, and who for the generality are raw, and illiterate men, to deny that Christ is to be offer'd to sinners ... This odd fancy was started above thirty years since, by a gentleman of a great deal of rambling learning, but of a confused head, as appears from his writings, some parts of which, I will venture to say, no person ever really understood.'[108] This person had 'a tincture of

---

[105] Idem, *An Address to Young Students in Divinity*, v.
[106] Ibid., unpaginated.
[107] Ibid., 4.
[108] Ibid., 14.

Enthusiasm'[109]—by which Taylor, with 'Dictionary' Johnson, means 'a vain confidence of divine favour or communication'—and those persuaded by him believe that sinners cannot be exhorted to repent and believe because they have no power to do so. Taylor agrees that sinners cannot contribute towards their saving faith and repentance, but it is their duty to cast themselves on Christ. Some preachers, apparently recognizing that they are out of accord with Scripture, say that faith and repentance may be preached to sinners, but only as moral virtues, not as evangelical graces. Taylor dismisses this approach on the ground that it is no more than a call for moral reformation. The claim that the law is not to be preached because grace now prevails is to be resisted, for it is the very foundation of the antinomian heresy. Among those who peddle the false doctrine there are not three 'who have so much as a little smattering of learning.'[110] Taylor exhorts his students not to fall for antinomian theory, and concludes with a trinitarian ascription.

Taylor returned to his anti-antinomianism crusade on other occasions. In a sermon entitled, *A Vindication of the Evangelical Doctrine of Man's Salvation by the Free Grace of God from the Charge of promoting Licentiousness*, he sets out from Romans 5: 20-21 and 6:1-2, where Paul sternly rebukes those who might think it appropriate to sin that grace may abound. Taylor affirms, citing Ridgley with approval, that election is free and sovereign, but it entails the call to holiness. Indeed, he continues, none of the great evangelical doctrines conduce to licentiousness—on the contrary. Sin is therefore to be shunned, moral duties are to be fulfilled, and Christ is to be relied upon for assistance.

As already indicated, John Gill sallied forth against Taylor's address to his students with a tract entitled, *The Necessity of Good Works unto Salvation considered: Occasion'd by some Reflections and Misrepresentations of Mr. (alias Dr.) Abraham Taylor* (1739). In passing we may note the nasty 'Mr. (alias Dr.)' that Gill inserts into his title. It might be taken as implying that the Aberdeen authorities did not know what they were doing when they honoured Taylor with their DD, yet they were the very authorities who were similarly to honour Gill in 1743. All of which dents any sympathy we might feel towards Gill, who feels aggrieved that Taylor continually renders 'my character odious among men.'[111] Despite this, and despite also the fact that 'notwithstanding [Taylor's] ill-natured reflections in his noisy and bombast charges at several ordinations of ministers; and notwithstanding his wrathful prayers pursed out before the Most High in monthly exercises, which must be shocking to pious minds, and abominable in the sight of God,'[112] Gill (piously) does not wish to engender further controversy (!).

Coming to the point, Gill argues that good works must be performed, but not with a view to attaining salvation. He denies the charge of antinomianism and

---

[109] Ibid.

[110] Ibid., 36.

[111] J. Gill, *The Necessity of Good Works unto Salvation considered*, 4. I do not think there is a theological term for this. There is, however, the homely adage about the pot's calling the kettle black.

[112] Ibid., 4.

complains that in his *Address* to his students Taylor nowhere defines 'doctrinal antinomianism'. Gill will therefore do it for him: 'Doctrinal Antinomianism, properly speaking, is a denying, or setting aside the law of God, as a rule of life, action, or conversation.'[113] Gill insists that he is not guilty of this. He then takes the *ad hominem* line:

> Who is this man that looks with such disdain and contempt upon all around him? The other day he was an ordinary school-master, a teacher of babes, as best became him. Who called this proud, haughty, wrathful man, to be a tutor and director of young men, in their studies for the Ministry? Did the ministers and messengers concerned in the Fund for the Independent Denomination, of which denomination he is? No; they did not: They put their youth under the care of the very learned Mr. Eames ... Who called this man to this work, I ask again? A society of men that meet in a tavern, commonly call'd the King's Head Society; to whom he had dedicated this performance, and who seem to have put him upon writing it.[114]

Gill does not expect that Taylor will reply to him, for 'the most blustering fellows are the greatest cowards.'[115] This is Gill at his most bilious.

Gill had earlier, and more temperately, taken Taylor to task over one paragraph in his sermon *Of the Insufficience of Natural Religion*, and he now regrets that Taylor had never replied to him.[116] Interestingly, in this earlier work Gill had cited Richard Taylor against his son. In his book, *The Scripture Doctrine of Justification, Explained and Vindicated*—posthumously edited by Abraham, Richard, following Thomas Goodwin, Witsius and others, had argued that 'all elect sinners had a representative union with Christ from eternity.'[117] Gill correctly quotes Abraham Taylor as saying that this doctrine is to be 'abhorred' as 'an immoral conceit'.[118] Gill's point is that our faith is not the cause of union with Christ, but the effect of it. If we are not first united to Christ, we cannot believe in him. In short, 'The everlasting love of God, the Father, Son, and Spirit, is the bond of the elect's union to the sacred Three.'[119] To think otherwise would, in Gill's opinion, be an assault upon God's eternal decrees. Taylor's point is that some 'ignorant and enthusiastic preachers' of the antinomian sort have wrongly inferred from such propositions as this that because of this eternal union, 'sin could do a believer no harm',[120] and

---

[113] Ibid., 33.

[114] Ibid., 38-9.

[115] Ibid., 40. It is interesting to note that Gill's letter has been 'cleaned up' by those responsible for the 1814 edition of his *Sermons and Tracts*. See vol. 6, 157-177.

[116] Ibid., 4. See J. Gill, *The Doctrines of God's Everlasting Love to his Elect, and their Eternal Union with Christ.*

[117] J. Gill, *The Doctrines of God's Everlasting Love to his Elect, and their Eternal Union with Christ*, in *Sermons and Tracts*, V, 18, quoting R. Taylor, *The True Scripture Doctrine of Justification*, 14-15.

[118] J. Gill, ibid., 2.

[119] Ibid., 25.

[120] Ibid., 2.

hence licence was thought to be legitimated. Gill can find no responsible authors who teach this in so many words, but, of course, Taylor did not have responsible authors in mind when he wrote. Again, Gill takes issue with Taylor's objection to those who say that God sees no sin in his people. This does not mean, Gill replies, that believers are sinless. On the contrary, the work of sanctification is never completed in this life. Rather, it means that for the sake of Christ, who has borne their sins, and because of the forgiveness he has bestowed, God sees no sin in his people. He does, however, wish, notwithstanding Tobias Crisp's desire to encourage distressed believers, that Crisp had been more circumspect in his language on this point.[121] Finally, Gill takes exception to Taylor's anti-antinomian insistence that good works are in any sense necessary to salvation. Gill contends that good works are not the causes or conditions of salvation (something with which Taylor was in full accord), but this is not to say that they are not necessary to anything else. They are necessary under God's law; as evidence of the genuineness of our election; as laying neighbourly obligations upon us; and as a witness against the enemies of the Christian religion. Taylor might well have replied that all of these necessities comprise the fruit of faith, and in so far as they are necessary, they are required. It is difficult to resist the feeling that Gill here protests too much. Can it be that the threat of doctrinal antinomianism was sufficiently close to home to cause him a pang of discomfort? Certainly Taylor is as far as a theologian could be from works righteousness, and his strictures against Arminianism are no less sincere that his strictures against numerous other perceived attenuations of what he regarded as true Christian doctrine.[122]

V

A related doctrinal issue which prompted some Calvinists to accuse other Calvinists of Arminianism concerned the Modern Question, namely, whether sinners have a duty to repent and turn to God in faith. Abraham Taylor answered the question in the affirmative, thereby prompting the charge of Arminianism from some quarters, while his opponent, the high Calvinist Baptist John Brine answered it in the negative, thereby opening himself to the charge of limiting the free offer of the Gospel.[123] Taylor's work on this specific subject appeared in 1742 under the self-explanatory

---

[121] Ibid., 10. For Crisp (1600-1643) see ODNB. For a brief account of antinomianism see Alan P. F. Sell, *The Great Debate*, 42-50. See also, Curt Daniel, 'John Gill and Calvinistic Antinomianism.'

[122] Gill also pursued the Arminianism of Daniel Whitby in his book, *The Cause of God and Truth* (1735-8). See further, Alan P. F. Sell, *The Great Debate*, 79-80. His gracious references to this book notwithstanding, I do not see how George Ella can justifiably associate me with the view of 'modern research' that Taylor took the 'wrong' (that is, the Arminian) side in the Arminian Calvinist controversy.' See his *John Gill and the Cause of God and Truth*, 147, 308 n. 18.

[123] For the rise of this debate see Alan P. F. Sell, *The Great Debate*, 52-7, 78-9. For Brine (1703-1765) see ODNB; WW, II, 574-9.

title, *The Modern Question concerning Repentance and Faith, Examined with Candour. In Four Dialogues; between Zelotes and Bathynous on one Side, and Purodoxus and Sophronius on the other. In which the Arguments on both Sides are fairly stated and discussed; and Repentance unto Life, and Faith unto Salvation, are proved at large to be the Duties of Sinners*. Into the intricacies of the debate we need not enter. Suffice it to say that, in Taylor's opinion, among the many hurtful consequences of the denial of duty faith is that sinners are not condemned for neglecting or abusing the Gospel means of salvation, but only for original sin and offences against God's moral law; and this is contrary to the Gospel. It also follows that those parents and ministers who cry to heaven for the salvation of those in their charge, are in error. In fact, however, the Gospel enjoins us to call all people to repentance and faith. The way in which in this pamphlet Taylor develops his case with reference to biblical citations subsequently exercised a formative influence upon Andrew Fuller (1754-1815), a leading evangelical Calvinistic Baptist and mission advocate of the latter part of the eighteenth-century.[124]

John Brine's reply to Taylor, *A Refutation of Arminian Principles* (note the already loaded title) appeared in 1743. According to Brine, the controversy over duty faith arose at Brigstock, Northamptonshire, in connection with a successful lecture series there. Some lecturers took one side of the argument, others the other. The former made 'Special Faith the immediate Duty of unregenerate Persons, who hear the Gospel.' The others disagreed, but nevertheless assumed 'the Necessity of Faith in Christ.'[125] Those on the affirmative side established an anti-antinomian lecture series, the first lecture of which was given by Philip Doddridge, 'who is well known for his remarkable Candour of Temper, and Catholic Sentiments.'[126] The Arminians say that the will can choose good or evil 'without the Infusion of spiritual Principles.'[127] Taylor is accused of saying this, and Brine disagrees with it. 'If the Scriptures speak of an external Call to the Duties of natural Repentance and historical Faith, to interpret them of evangelical Repentance and Special Faith, is

---

[124] A fact which did nothing to commend Taylor to George Ella, who informs us that Fuller published his 'notorious book, *The Gospel Worthy of all Acceptation*' in 1785, and explains that 'Answering the Modern Question in the affirmative is a true form of Arminianism as it leaves the onus of salvation to man's awareness of his spiritual duties which the Reformed Faith declares have been extinct since the Fall.' See his *John Gill and the Cause of God and Truth*, 169, 316. Even Tobias Crisp appealed to his congregation in the following terms: 'Beloved, will you starve in a cook's shop, as they say? Is there such plenty in Christ, and will you perish for hunger?' See his *Christ's Pre-eminence*, reprinted Sheffield: Zoar Publications, c. 1974, 13-14. For a short list of similar appeals by Calvinists see Alan P. F. Sell, *Commemorations*, 168-9. For Fuller see ODNB; Peter J. Morden, *Offering Christ to the World*; Gerald L. Priest, 'Andrew Fuller, hyper-Calvinism and the Modern Question'; Alan P. F. Sell, *Enlightenment, Ecumenism, Evangel*, ch. 4; idem, *Testimony and Tradition*, ch. 6.

[125] J. Brine, *A Refutation of Arminian Principles*, 3.

[126] Ibid., 4. Praising with faint damns?

[127] Ibid., 16.

applying to them a Sense far beyond what they Design, and therefore it cannot be true, which is what this person [Taylor] does.'[128]

Even if it is said that repentance and faith are conditions of life 'as an Effect of divine Grace,' Brine continues, we are still in the realm of salvation by law; and even if duty is performed with the strength of God's grace, life results from the performance, not from grace, but of debt. Brine agrees with Taylor that sinners certainly ought to pray, read their Bibles, hear sermons, and consider the dreadful effects of sin; and that ministers ought to warn them of their danger and tell them of the necessity of an interest in Christ and of faith in him. Hence, the unhappy consequences that Taylor supposes to follow from the anti-duty-faith position 'are entirely false, and far from being justly drawn.'[129]

As with eternal generation, so here: echoes of this dispute can be heard to this day. It seems to me, however, that Brine's concluding list of injunctions encourages sinners to do everything except fulfil the Gospel injunction to repent and believe. No doubt they do not do it unaided, but the fact that they do it at all is testimony not to the truth of 'Arminian' free-willism, or to 'natural man's' innate ability, but to God's prevenient grace. Taylor, it would seem, grasped this point. To put the point in homely fashion, if any sinner anywhere is at all inclined to repent, God has already been busy.

VI

The drift away from trinitarian doctrine on the part of Dissenters no less than Anglicans, was, to Taylor, a further sorry sign of doctrinal declension and, as we might expect, he took up his pen against it. Indeed, as I noted at the outset, Taylor's plunge into trinitarian controversy yielded his first published work, and it was one adversely critical of the position of his fellow Congregationalist, Isaac Watts: *The Scripture Doctrine of the Trinity Vindicated in Opposition to Mr. Watts's Scheme of One Divine Person and Two Divine Powers* (1726).[130] Taylor says that while he was pleased to see Watts's work, *The Christian Doctrine of the Trinity* (1722), he regrets that Watts has made too many concessions 'to the adversaries of the truth.'[131] He is especially concerned that trinitarians in the Church of England should think that Dissenters would let pass the errors of one of their most prominent ministers. What, in brief was Watts's position?

When Watts published his book the memory of the Salters' Hall conference was still fresh in many minds. His intention was to provide a biblically-grounded account of the Trinity without recourse to 'human schemes', in the hope that this would make for peace and reconciliation. He argues that the term 'person' need not be taken

---

[128] Ibid., 31.

[129] Ibid., 45.

[130] For Watts (1674-1748) see DECBP; FAE, 377-8; JEREMY, 28, 122; ODNB; TSJ, 36, 717; Arthur Paul Davis, *Isaac Watts, His Life and Works*, London: Independent Press, 1943; Alan P. F. Sell, *Philosophy, Dissent and Nonconformity*, *passim*.

[131] Idem, *The Scripture Doctrine of the Trinity Vindicated*, 5.

literally and, deeply concerned to maintain the divine unity, that the Holy Spirit may properly be understood as a personified attribute of the Godhead. The Son, though with the Father in eternity, was nevertheless derived from the Father, whilst being fully united with him. To the end of his days, and after a number of other publications on the theme, in some of which, following criticism, he altered his opinion on particular points, Watts wrestled with this theme to the point of weariness, and was never finally satisfied with his attempts to expound the doctrine.[132] It is noticeable that Taylor never accused him of denying the Trinity, and Watts never did this, despite what has been said by some later Unitarians.[133] His difficulty lay not so much in believing the doctrine as in stating it satisfactorily, and this is testimony to his intellectual integrity.

Taylor faults Watts for seeking clear and distinct ideas of something that will for ever be mysterious to human beings. He is thus led beyond the biblical witness to the denial of the real personality of the Son and the Spirit who are, says Watts, called persons only figuratively. In fact, Taylor retorts, they are divine powers which proceed from the divine essence in Watts's view. Taylor cannot understand how Watts can consistently deny that 'person' when used of the Father is also merely a figurative term. He strongly objects to Watts's account of Christ's human soul as being a super-angelic spirit, and rebuts Watts's 'groundless Arian claim' that Scripture is silent as to the worship of the Holy Spirit, and his opinion that some prominent followers of Athanasius, including Bishops Pearson and Bull and John Howe, have landed in tritheism. He refers Watts to Bishop Stillingfleet's vindication of Athanasius against this charge. Taylor's disappointment at Watts's performance comes out in his remark that 'It has been the glory of the Dissenters of the Congregational denomination, that no one pretending to be of their persuasion, had ever printed any thing erroneous relating to the Trinity, till Mr. Watts published his books.'[134]

Taylor brings his book to a close by specifying six tasks that Watts ought to undertake, and twelve points regarding which he should seek the pardon of the Church of Christ.[135] Among the tasks are to show that his scheme 'differs from the Sabellian scheme, or the Socinian, except in words, and his adding the fancy of Christ's having a super-angelic Spirit, to supply the place of the human soul'; to adduce scriptural evidence to show that 'the one God is properly one person', that the Son and Spirit are 'properties, faculties, or powers of the divine nature', and that Scripture cautions us not to ascribe personhood to the Spirit and the Son in the same sense in which we ascribe it to the Father.[136] Watts should seek pardon for, *inter alia*, producing a scheme 'full of thick darkness'; for 'obtruding upon us the Socinian

---

[132] For a careful account of this, though one which, somewhat surprisingly, makes no mention of Abraham Taylor, see A. P. Davis, *Isaac Watts*, 111-121.

[133] For example, Watts appears in the volume of *Memorable Unitarians*, 80-86.

[134] A. Taylor, *The Scripture Doctrine of the Trinity Vindicated*, 107.

[135] The tasks and points are reprinted in Alan P. F. Sell, David J. Hall and Ian Sellers, eds, *Protestant Nonconformist Texts II. The Eighteenth Century*, 71-3.

[136] A. Taylor, *The Scripture Doctrine of the Trinity Vindicated*, 114.

scheme, in a new dress, yet not knowing he does so'; and 'for representing the doctrine of the eternal generation of the Son, and the procession of the Spirit, to be a popish and scholastic hypothesis.'[137] There follows a paragraph of rhetorical questions, one of which is as follows: 'Mr. Watts ... bears the character of a person of great devotion; have his devotions, all the past years of his life, been directed to wrong objects?'[138] Watts, disinclined to polemics, did not directly reply to Taylor on this point, or on any other.

However, in 1727 an author wrote a *Letter* in Watts's defence. Since Taylor had published his *Vindication* anonymously under the guise of a Dissenting country gentleman, the equally anonymous respondent begins by objecting to the subterfuge, since Taylor was neither a countryman nor a gentleman, but a well known preacher in London. (Taylor's name appears on the cover of the second edition of the *Vindication*, 1728). The respondent objects to Taylor's 'fiery zeal', despite his profession of temperateness, and wonders why, since Watts 'allows the Sacred Three to be the greatest Distinctions possible in one infinite Spirit,' he is guilty of a crime? It can be only because Watts 'supposes we may arrive at some clear Ideas of these Distinctions, by way of Analogy and resemblance to created things.'[139] He notes that Watts has pointed out that the Bible never calls the Trinity a mystery, though Taylor does; and he denies that Watts telescoped the Son and the Spirit into the Father. He wishes that Watts would publish what he has written in defence of the Trinity, but he has no love of controversy.

In 1727 Taylor's two-volume defence of the Trinity appeared under the precise title, *The True Scripture-Doctrine of the Holy and Ever-Blessed Trinity, Stated and Defended, in Opposition to the Arian Scheme*. He dedicates the work to the Anglican divine, Daniel Waterland,[140] of whose anti-Arian arguments Taylor approves, and says that his objective is to 'throw together the scripture proofs of the catholic doctrine of the Trinity.'[141] He attributes the growth of atheism and deism to Arianism: 'we have no reason to wonder at this, for when once men make their imperfect reason the standard, according to which matters of pure revelation must be interpreted, they have but a short step to take, to deny, that the scriptures have any divine authority at all.'[142] In his Preface he declares that Sabellianism and Socinianism are 'almost the same', and that they and Arianism 'have taken their rise, from mens confounding being and person, and resolving that nothing shall be a person, but what is a separate being.'[143] Whereas the Sabellians deny the real personality of the three persons, the Arians reduce the Son and Spirit to the status of creatures. While it is true that the Son is economically subordinate to the Father, whose commissioned servant he is, and to whom he prays, the Arians 'countenance

---

[137] Ibid., 115.

[138] Ibid., 116.

[139] Anon., *A Letter to the Author of The Doctrine of the Trinity Vindicated*, 10-11.

[140] For Waterland (1683-1740) see DECBP; ODNB; R. T. Holtby, *Daniel Waterland*.

[141] A. Taylor, *The True Scripture Doctrine of the ... Trinity*, A3.

[142] Ibid., A5.

[143] Ibid., i.

the notion of an inferiority of nature,' and in all ages they have been remarkable for 'tricking and disguise, for insincerity and double dealing.'[144] He applauds Bishop Bull's treatise against Arianism, and finds Whitby's reply to it 'more the effect of dotage than anything else.'[145]

In setting out his stall, Taylor accepts both that there are depths in what is revealed to us which we can never fathom, and that we are not to believe anything that our reason tells us is plainly false on the ground that it is a mystery, because this is the tactic of 'the papists who impose that monstrous absurdity of transubstantiation.'[146] No mystery revealed by God is contrary to right reason, and of all such mysteries, the most important is the Trinity. The kernel of his claim against the Arians is that 'The great mystery of the Trinity in unity, or that the Father, the Son, and the holy Spirit, tho' three real persons, are the one infinitely blessed God, while yet the Father is not the Son, nor the Son the Father, nor the Spirit either the Father or the Son.'[147] All other revealed mysteries depend upon this one. He cites the Church of England's *Articles* I, II and V, and the *Westminster Confession* and the *Savoy Declaration of Faith and Order* in support, noting that in the Congregational statement 'the following clause is with great judgment added; "The doctrine of the Trinity is the foundation of all our communion with God, and comfortable dependence on him."'[148] Against the Anglican, Samuel Clarke,[149] he argues that the three persons are one in nature and substance, and that all equally to be worshipped by us. He then traces the doctrine through history, with ample reference to biblical and patristic writers, and concludes Part I in the confidence, rhapsodically expressed, that faith in the Trinity will prevail universally

> till all the chosen people are gather'd in, and united in one general assembly and church, in the pure realms of blessedness above. In that happy country, the noise of controversies will cease; and none inhabiting that desirable and pleasant land, will ever have diminishing thoughts of the Son and the holy Spirit rise up in their breasts. All who are brought to stand in the presence of God, dress'd in the umblemish'd robes of innocence and immortality, will know, that all the three divine persons were concerned in bringing them, thither.[150]

A trinitarian ascription terminates the first part of his discussion.

In Part II Taylor endeavours to prove Christ's divinity from his consubstantiality with the Father. He rebuts those who suggest that when the Bible says that Christ is in the form of God it means that he impersonates him, and upholds the eternal

---

[144] Ibid., ii.

[145] Ibid., xxi. For George Bull (1634-1710) and Daniel Whitby (1628-1736) see ODNB.

[146] Ibid., 8. The pages are numbered consecutively from the beginning of vol. I to the end of vol. II.

[147] Ibid., 12.

[148] Ibid., 13 n.

[149] For whom see the references at ch. 2 n. 59.

[150] A. Taylor, *The True Scripture Doctrine of the ... Trinity*, 153-4.

generation of the Son. He believes (in circular fashion) that Christ's divinity is proved from his equality with the Father, and he stretches exegesis to breaking-point by anachronistically reading Jesus back into the Old Testament so that, for example, it was God the Son who appeared to Moses at the burning bush. Pausing only to rebuke Clarke and Emlyn, he then 'proves' Christ's divinity from his being called God; his supremacy; his attributes; his being the creator of all things; his behaviour on earth; and his accomplishing the work of redemption. In this last connection he refers to Christ's cry from the Cross, asking, 'What could be more miraculous, than to hear the Lord of thunders groan, and sigh, and cry? What could be more surprizing, than to see the Almighty maker of heaven and earth hang on a cross?'[151] He goes on to prove Christ's divinity from his universal Lordship, from his being judge of the world, and from the religious worship which is paid to him.

In Part III Taylor proves Christ's divinity from his names and titles, his attributes, his works, and the worship paid to him. He concludes that

> When we worship God the Father, as the author and spring of all our happiness, and God the Son as the redeemer of our souls from guilt, and the purchaser of all blessedness for us; we must not omit to worship God the holy Spirit, the sanctifier and renewed of our hearts, and the comforter, who must conduct us safe to the purchased inheritance. These we must worship, not as three Gods, but as the one God, of whom, and by whom, and from whom, are all the blessings we can enjoy here, or hereafter.[152]

A further trinitarian ascription completes the work.

In 3 March 1733/4 Taylor, who says that the author was not known personally to him, wrote a commendatory Preface to Charles Mastertown's book, *The Doctrine of the Holy Trinity*. He cannot understand how any who claim to hold the catholic faith can say that the doctrine of the Trinity is of no importance, for it is the fundamental article of faith. If we do not believe in Christ's true and supreme Deity, we cannot believe in him as Saviour. As for the Holy Spirit, his work is 'to renew and sanctify Christians, and to conduct them safe to heaven.'[153] In short, the Trinity is 'a doctrine on which the hope and comfort of the church of Christ is founded.'[154] This was a position from which Taylor never moved. Latter-day Christians may find it easier to assent to the doctrine than to swallow some of Taylor's arguments in favour of it.

VII

That Taylor was greatly concerned by doctrinal declension has become abundantly clear. But he was no less concerned by the general decline of religion, especially among the Dissenters. Indeed, to him the latter was to a large extent the result of the

---

[151] Ibid., 382-4.

[152] Ibid., 517.

[153] A. Taylor, Preface to C. Mastertown, *The Doctrine of the Holy Trinity*, ix.

[154] Idem., xi.

former. It was Strickland Gough's anonymous pamphlet, *An Enquiry into the Causes of the Decay of the Dissenting Interest* (1730) that provoked Taylor and others to reply to the erstwhile ministerial candidate. Gough contended that 'the grand causes of the present decay of the dissenting interest are *ignorance* of their own principles, and *ill conduct* and management of their own interests.'[155] As if anticipating the question, 'What is the fundamental principle of Dissent?' Gough declares that it is 'a *liberty* for every man to form his own sentiments ...'[156] Dissenters are also committed to the view that 'The Church of Christ is not *national*, but private.'[157] After opining that the 'unhappy difference' at Salters' Hall 'injur'd the dissenting interest more than all their enemies together,'[158] he finds two faults in Dissenting worship: 'your prayers are too short, and your sermons too long. The one has little of reverence towards God, and the other is too tedious to ourselves.'[159] He ends with some recommendations concerning the training of ministers, one of which is that candidates should be drawn only from genteel families, and that in each academy there should be a tutor appointed to ensure that ordinands are graceful and well-mannered.

Taylor was quick off the mark with his *Letter* to Gough, which also appeared in 1730. He says that Dissent is not in universal decline, for in some places it flourishes. Dissenting ministers are 'of as respectable families as their neighbours, the Clergy of the Church of England,'[160] and they are esteemed for the piety of their lives. He points out that Dissenters chose to resign their livings rather than compromise their principles. He claims that Gough seems to favour liberal over orthodox Dissenters, the latter of whom he says are full of spiritual pride. Gough is further partial in applauding those Dissenters who stand for liberty and conscience, but not those who oppose the anti-scriptural establishment principle; yet the latter act on the principle of liberty no less than the former. Taylor observes that Dissenters express their liberty in questioning a prospective minister before addressing a call to him. Indeed, that is why some Arminians have found their way into the ministry of the Church of England: they could not affirm the Calvinistic doctrines that were freely put to them by Dissenters. Taylor holds that 'The cause of truth and the cause of liberty are both to be served; but we should not prejudice the one under the pretence of serving the other.'[161] A further letter, dated 2 December 1730, is appended to Taylor's text. In it he returns to the question of integrity in the matter of subscription. He points out that many Dissenting ministers could obtain preferment in the Church of England if only they subscribed to the Articles, but their integrity forbids it. By contrast, some in the Church of England ministry have

155 S. Gough, *An Enquiry into the Causes of the Decay of the Dissenting Interest*, 4-5.
156 Ibid., 6.
157 Ibid., 7.
158 Ibid., 28.
159 Ibid., 39.
160 A. Taylor, *A Letter to the Author of an Enquiry*, 4.
161 Ibid., 34.

subscribed to the Articles whilst believing that some of them are untrue, or whilst entertaining contrary opinions on certain points.

Alongside Taylor's response to Gough we may set that of Philip Doddridge. He makes it clear that any prospective minister who would be generally acceptable to Dissenters 'must be an evangelical, an experimental, a plain and affectionate preacher.'[162] Towards the end of his letter he would seem to take liberty further than Taylor, and certainly adumbrates a method which was foreign to Taylor when in controversial mode: 'if a man desires to do good by what he says, he must oppose and contradict as little as possible.'[163] Where fundamental doctrines and questions of practical religion were concerned, Taylor's linguistic armoury did not include the injunction, 'Live and let live.'

When Taylor turned on his own account to the real causes of religious declension, he took as his text Revelation 3: 1-3—the letter to the church at Sardis, whose members are cautioned to 'be watchful and strengthen the things that remain, that are ready to die, for I have not found thy works perfect before God. Remember therefore how thou hast received and heard, and hold fast, and repent.' Taylor is convinced that the Dissenters have fallen from their first love. Almost all the biblical doctrines are struck out of the list of articles of faith, and practice is wanting too. There is contempt for Gospel doctrines, a neglect of preaching Christ, the ascription of too much power to fallen man, failure to instruct the young, and contempt for the work of the Holy Spirit, who is omitted from sermons on duty, so that moral suasion is deemed sufficient. Taylor appeals to Christians to attend to these matters, to contend for the truth, never to be weary in well doing: 'Let us always fight under the banner of the great Captain of our salvation',[164] for then we shall come 'to the deathless realms of joy',[165] we shall see Christ as he is and praise and adore him for ever.

Casting his net wider, Taylor turns to the state in a November 5th sermon. He contrasts the instability of earthly monarchies with the stability of Christ's kingdom. His text is Daniel 2: 44: 'And in the days of these kings shall the God of heaven set up a kingdom, which shall never be destroyed ...' The printed version of the sermon is dedicated to the Congregational stalwart Thomas Bradbury and his brother Peter.[166] Taylor's theme is that while Christ's kingdom is an everlasting kingdom that cannot fail, the strongest of earthly governments can fall. By way of evidence he refers to a variety of kingdoms—Babylon and Persia among them. He then makes a number of points concerning Christ's kingdom: 'Christ could not manage his mediatorial kingdom were he not God as well as man.'[167] Christ manages his kingdom 'according to the oeconomy agreed upon between the divine

---

[162] [P. Doddridge], *Free Thoughts on the Most Probable Means of Reviving the Dissenting Interest*, 21.

[163] Ibid., 38.

[164] A. Taylor, *A Humble and Impartial Enquiry*, 410.

[165] Ibid., 411.

[166] For Thomas Bradbury (1676/7-1759) see ODNB; WW, III, 504-535. For Peter Bradbury see WW, III, 452-3, 535-6.

[167] A. Taylor, *Of the Instability of Earthly Monarchies*, 22.

persons ... as the reward of his sufferings.'[168] His government is supreme, spiritual and universal. He displays his kingly power in the spread of the Gospel throughout the world, and in raising up witnesses to his truth. The present dispensation of Christ's kingdom will terminate at the last day, or final judgment, and then there will be a far more glorious manifestation of it, and Christ will continue as King for ever. By way of applying the doctrines thus enumerated to his hearers, Taylor says that when we look at the state of religion today, we 'cannot but tremble for the ark of God.'[169] But Christ still has the government on his shoulder, and we should look to him to revive his work.

VIII

In publishing as in ministerial terms, Abraham Taylor burned brightly and briefly. He caught the attention of friends and enemies alike. He was a stout defender of classical trinitarian doctrine, and of Reformed doctrine as promulgated in the *Westminster Confession* and the *Savoy Declaration*. He was firm in his beliefs and tenacious in opposing those who differed from him. He pulled no punches against Arminianism, atheism, antinomianism, Arianism and (to spoil the alliteration) deism. On occasion his argumentative instruments were as blunt as his language, and he has come down to us as being of an irascible temperament. But this is not all there was to him. With one exception, none of his students expressed a personal grievance against him, and the one who did so was expelled. In his funeral sermons he could speak in the most gracious pastoral terms, and in his ordination charges he displayed deep of knowledge the Christian ministry and regarded it as a high calling. On the face of it, and in the absence of explanatory considerations, it seems a tragedy that he should have ended his days in obscurity, denied even a published memorial sermon.

---

[168] Ibid., 23-4.
[169] Ibid., 55.

CHAPTER 4

Samuel Chandler (1693–1766): Conscience, Controversy, Circumspection

To a greater degree than either Ridgley or Taylor, Samuel Chandler was a man of affairs.[1] A Presbyterian rather than a Congregationalist, he was the most theologically liberal of the three. Like Taylor, Chandler was a son of the manse. His father, Henry (d. 1717), the son of a Taunton tradesman who had suffered financial loss under the 'persecutions' of Charles II, was, like Ridgley, educated under Thomas Doolittle in London, where he was contemporary with Matthew Henry.[2] Henry Chandler's wife's maiden name was Bridgman, and his pastorates were Malmesbury, Hungerford, Coleford, and, finally, Frog Lane, Bath, whither he went *circa* 1700, and where he died.

The Chandlers' first child was Mary (1687-1745). She loved to read the classics in translation, her favourite being Horace. She was deformed as a result of a childhood accident, and felt debarred from marriage, a country gentleman's proposal notwithstanding. She became a milliner and had her own shop in Bath. She published a number of poems, that on Bath being her best known.[3] John Chandler (1699/1700-1780), the youngest child, became an apothecary, and in between was Samuel, born at Hungerford on 20 September 1693.

---

[1] For Chandler see JEREMY, 4, 39, 136-8; ODNB; TSJ, 35, 97-8, 668, 680, 697, 717, 723, 822; WW, II, 360-384; T. Amory, Preface to Chandler's *Sermons*, I; J. A. Jones, *Bunhill Memorials*, 24; A. W. Light, *Bunhill Fields*,I, 62-3; J. Waddington, *Surrey Congregational History*, 263-4; E. E. Cleal, *The Story of Congregationalism in Surrey*, 19-20.

[2] For Henry Chandler see FA, 233; MURCH, 152-3; W. H. Summers, *History of the Congregational Churches in ... Berks*, 127. Summers, himself minister at Hungerford, wrongly says that Chandler came to Hungerford from Marlborough. John Stephens, in his ODNB article on Samuel Chandler, correctly says that Henry had previously been in Malmesbury. DNB incorrectly gives the father's name as Samuel.

[3] See Mary Chandler, *A Description of Bath. A Poem. With Several other Poems*; Caryn Chaden, 'The rhetoric of landscape in Mary Chandler's "A Description of Bath"', at http://condor.depaul.edu/~cchaden/bath/Chandler.html. For M. Chandler see ODNB; Charles Atmore in his edition of S. Chandler, *The History of Persecution*, 21-23.

Samuel was educated first under John Moore at Bridgewater.[4] This John Moore had, in 1693, succeeded his father of the same name, both as pastor in Bridgewater and as head of the academy there. On his adoption of Arian views the number of students declined, though there is no hard evidence that this explains the removal of Chandler to Gloucester/Tewkesbury under the 'very learned and ingenious Mr. Samuel Jones,'[5] where Joseph Butler and Thomas Secker, both of whom subsequently conformed to the Church of England, were among his contemporaries.[6]

Chandler began to preach in 1714, and was called to Hanover (Presbyterian) Chapel, Peckham, in 1716. A series of letters published in *The Monthly Repository* are of interest at this point. On 28 July 1716 Secker wrote to Mr. John Fox in the following terms: 'Sam. Chandler is married; his wife's fortune is tolerably good; what her humour will prove, time only can shew; he likes her well at present, ... , but if she proves barren or froward, resolves to divorce her.' The editor adds the note, 'This letter was signed by Mr. Secker, and afterwards by Mr. Chandler, who was probably present when it was written.'[7] In a further letter to Fox of 1 December 1716, Secker explains, 'I must give you to understand ... that Mr. Chandler's wife is no other than his church at Peckham, to which he has been contracted for some time, and the public ceremony is to be performed upon his return, the 19th inst.'[8]

More significant is Chandler's own letter to Fox of 7 July 1716, in which he writes, 'As for religion, I profess I scarce know where to fix, or what to believe ... [Christianity is] founded upon a religion that I can scarce allow to be divine.' If the Scriptures are the foundation of faith, he continues, 'I cannot help saying, I could have wished them a little more certain. ... I am in a perfect wandering an maze.'[9] In a Preface to this letter, the editor, with hindsight, and clearly wishing to leave a highly regarded personage untarnished, declares that Chandler's doubts 'were the random impulses of the moment ... patient enquiry and diligent research not only confirmed [Chandler] in the belief of Christianity, but enabled him to take his rank amongst the most eminent and successful advocates of the gospel which his age produced, though no age abounded more in able and satisfactory defences of divine revelation.'[10]

---

[4] For Moore (1673-1747) see EEUTA, 7;FAE, 314; GEE, 31; MURCH, 178-9; ODNB, see at 'John Moore (1642-1717); H. McLachlan, 'Bridgwater Academy, 1688-1756?', UHST, III, 1945, 93-6.

[5] So Thomas Amory, Preface to Chandler's *Sermons*, vii. For Jones (1681/2-1719) see DECBP; DWB; EEUTA, 126-31; JEREMY, 39-40; William Davies, *The Tewkesbury Academy*, 5-16; [Walter Wilson], 'Some account of Mr. Samuel Jones'; Alan P. F. Sell, *Philosophy, Dissent and Nonconformity*, 48-9.

[6] Some authorities, among them DNB (but not ODNB) and Jeremy Goring, 'The break-up of the Old Dissent', 181, say that Chandler completed his education in Leiden. I have found no hard evidence that this was so.

[7] *The Monthly Repository*, XVI, October 1821, 570.

[8] Ibid., 572.

[9] Ibid., 698.

[10] Ibid., 697-8.

Any lingering doubts notwithstanding, Chandler was ordained, alongside James and Henry Read, Richard Briscoe and George Smyth, on 19 December 1716.[11] The Read brothers had studied under Dr. John Ker at Highgate.[12] Smyth also studied under Ker there and at Clerkenwell, then under Drs. Spademan, Oldfield and Lorimer at Hoxton Square.[13] He then graduated in Scotland and pursued further studies in Holland. He had been a member of Dr. Daniel Williams's church at New Broad Street, Petty France.[14] Richard Briscoe had studied at Newington Green academy. All of the ordinands were found among the non-subscribers at Salters' Hall in the following year,[15] and shortly after that gathering Briscoe conformed to the Church of England.

On the occasion of the ordination, the charge was delivered by Edmund Calamy[16] from Acts 20: 28, 'Take heed therefore unto yourselves, and to all the flock, over the which the Holy Ghost hath made you overseers, to feed the church of God, which he hath purchased with his own blood.' Calamy welcomes the newly ordained to the ranks, and wishes them well in their ministries. He hopes that his words will encourage them at a time when it is necessary to show that 'we that are excluded the publick Establishment, are no such Persons, as some have industriously represented

---

[11] For J. Read (1684-1755) see JEREMY, 2, 115-16;TSJ, 668, 722; WW, I, 169, II, 222-5. After preaching in Worcestershire he became assistant to Thomas Reynolds (c.1667-1727) at the Weigh House (1707-20), for whom see FAE, 339; ODNB; JEREMY, 4, 5, 114-15; WW, I, 157-69. Finding himself on the opposite side to Reynolds at Salters' Hall, Read was required to resign. He then became assistant to Dr. John Evans (c.1680-1730), for whom see FAE, 260; ODNB; TSJ, 668; WW, II,212-19, at Hand Alley (1720-30), and in 1730 succeeded him as pastor until his own death. For H. Read (1686-1774) see JEREMY, 5, 135-6; TSJ, 129, 670, 722; WW, III, 207-8, IV, 312-14. He served at Ratcliffe Cross, Middlesex as assistant to John Mottershead (1662-1728), for whom see FAE, 315. Read next ministered at Monkwell Street (1718-23) under Daniel Wilcox (c.1676-1733), for whom see WW, III, 203-7. To the annoyance of some of the church members, Wilcox dismissed Read on his own authority because of suspected Arminianism, thereby causing a secession (see WW, III, 204). Read then moved to St. Thomas Street, Southwark as assistant to John Sheffield (1654?-1725/6), for whom see FAE, 350, succeeding him as pastor from 1726 until his death in 1774. For Smyth (d. 1746, aet. 57) see JEREMY 6, 121; TSJ, 680; WW, II, 215, 225. He was assistant at Kingston-upon-Thames until 1716, when he removed to Gravel Pit meeting, Hackney.

[12] For Ker (1639-1723) see EEUTA, 10, 15, 82, 85-6, 305; FAE, 296; JEREMY, 12, 23-4.

[13] For John Spademan (d. 1708) see EEUTA, 9, 18; JEREMY, 35, 102, 103; For Joshua Oldfield (1656-1729) see DSCBP; EEUTA, 8, 9, 14; FAE, 322; GEE, 57; JEREMY, 102-4; ODNB; J. A. Jones, *Bunhill Memorials*, 195-6; A. W. Light, *Bunhill Fields*, I, 184-6; Alan P. F. Sell, *Philosophy, Dissent and Nonconformity*, 25-6. For William Lorimer (1640/1-1722) see EEUTA, 9;FAE, 305; JEREMY, 95-102.

[14] For Williams (1643?-1716) see CR; FAE, 384; GEE, 287; JEREMY, 81-94; ODNB; J. A. Jones, *Bunhill Memorials*, 322-5; A. W. Light, *Bunhill Fields*, I, 240.

[15] See TSJ, 705-6.

[16] For Calamy (1671-1732) see FAE, 228; JEREMY, 1, 17, 18, 104-5; ODNB; TSJ, *passim*; WW, IV, 69-89.

us.'[17] Lest it be thought that an ordination charge was not the most appropriate occasion for such a demonstration, we should remember that the Sacheverell riots were fresh in people's minds;[18] that the Schism Bill of 1714, which would seriously have disadvantaged Dissenters and especially the Dissenting academies had failed to pass into law only because Queen Anne died on 1 August, the day she was to have signed the Act; and that throughout the eighteenth century there were those who wished to turn back the clock of toleration.[19] In the Preface to the ordination proceedings there is the strong affirmation, 'we think ourselves oblig'd to Dissent from the national Church Establishment, tho' none go beyond us in Zeal for the State.' These were not rabid republicans.

Turning more directly to the matter in hand, Calamy urges the newly ordained to take heed to doctrine, to be faithful teachers, and to 'convince Gainsayers.'[20] 'Be prudent in your general Carriage,' he continues; 'Have Regard to young Ones as well as elder Persons'; work hard to bring the unconverted 'to a hearty Subjection to the Lord Jesus Christ'; and take particular care of 'such as are under Spiritual Trouble.'[21] Further advice follows:

> In your Sermons, aim at edifying your Hearers, rather than gratifying their Curiosity. ... To Preaching, add Catechizing, the want of which keeps many all their Days in ignorance, and is the Cause that they never rightly understand the Sermons they hear, nor profit by them. ... Be serious and solemn in Administring both the Sacraments, which in the Age we live in are so much slighted. ... When you baptize Infants, take the Opportunity of making the Parents sensible of their Neglect, if they come not to the Lord's Table. ... Stick not at taking Pains with such as are passing out of the State of Infant into that of Adult Church Members, that so you may bring 'em to renew their Baptismal Covenant, in the holy Eucharist, understandingly, deliberately, and sincerely. Make not the Terms of Admission to the table of the Lord either more lax, or more strait, than God has done in his Word. ... Be not negligent of Christian Discipline, and yet affect not Dominion. ... Visit the Sick. Deal freely with them about everlasting Matters, but with all possible Prudence. ... Give attendance to reading, and close Thought, and strict Observation. Particularly study the holy Scriptures, with great Application.[22]

As he works towards his conclusion, Calamy reminds the newly ordained ministers to take heed of snares and temptations: 'You are ingag'd in a Warfare, not only as Christians, but as Ministers also. ... You set out in a difficult Season. Real Religion is at a very low ebb among us. The Ministerial Office is much slighted. ...

---

[17] E. Calamy, *The Principles and Practice of Moderate Nonconformists*, 25.

[18] For examples see Alan P. F. Sell, *Dissenting Thought and the life of the Churches*, 326-332.

[19] See Alan P. F. Sell, *Commemorations*, 140-141.

[20] E. Calamy, *The Principles and Practice of Moderate Nonconformists*, 27.

[21] Ibid., 27-32.

[22] Ibid., 33-5.

Do your Duty, and leave Events to God. ... And depend upon it, if you are but diligent and faithful, your reward will be great.'[23]

Also in 1716, Chandler married Elizabeth. They had three sons and three daughters. Financial disaster struck when he invested his wife's fortune in the South Sea Bubble, whereupon, with a view to supplementing his church stipend, he set up as a bookseller and publisher. An anonymous biographer, clearly thinking that booksellers were not among the higher orders of society, remarked, 'it must be confessed rather surprising, that he should not have preferred taking pupils to educate.'[24] In 1726 Chandler added the assistantship to Thomas Leavesly at the Old Jewry Chapel to his duties, still continuing to preach at Peckham on Sunday mornings.[25] Leavesly, with whom Chandler enjoyed good relations, had been a non-subscriber at Salters' Hall. He had come to Old Jewry from a rural ministry at Little Baddow, Essex. The Old Jewry church had suffered a two-year vacancy following the resignation through ill health of Simon Browne in 1723.[26] According to the church's local constitution, a two-thirds majority was required when a minister was to be called to the pastorate. John Warren of Coventry would not move, while the Presbyterian Dr. Samuel Wright of Carter Lane, Blackfriars,[27] twice failed to secure the required number of votes. Eventually, 'being tired out with disappointments,' the church 'unanimously chose Mr. Thomas Leavesly.'[28] It may be that Wright, who enjoyed great success at Blackfriars, was too lively for the respectable souls of Old Jewry. There is reason to think that Leavesly, apparently called by default, was too rustic: 'by his living long in the country, amongst a plain people, he used himself to such latitude in his composures, that he could not bring himself to a correct and methodical way of preaching, such as is expected in London, especially in such a congregation as that at the Old Jewry: on this account he was not popular.'[29]

While still at Peckham, Chandler was appointed to contribute lectures on the evidences of revealed religion to the series based at the Old Jewry chapel. In the first instance he shared this task with Nathaniel Lardner,[30] but shortly continued alone. His lectures became the substance of his reply to the deist Anthony Collins, *A Vindication of the Christian Religion* (1725). Among those impressed by this

[23] Ibid., 36-8. In the appended Letter to the German divine, Calamy provides 'An Account of the Protestant Dissenters in England,' in which he declares that 'besides private Seminaries, where Philosophical and Theological Lectures are read, they send their Children to North Britain and Holland for Academical Education. They are zealous for a Learned Ministry.' Ibid., 44.

[24] Anon, 'Biography of the Life of the Rev. Samuel Chandler,' 219.

[25] For Leavesly (d. 1737), see JEREMY, 4, 132; WW, II, 358-60.

[26] For Browne (c.1680-1732) see ODNB; TSJ, 116; WW, II, 338-357.

[27] For Wright (1683-1746) see GEE, 149; JEREMY, 5, 6, 125; ODNB; TSJ, 116, 169, 717, 721-2; WW, II, 139-147. He was a non-subscriber at Salters' Hall.

[28] So WW, II, 359. Yet ODNB says that the church regretted Browne's departure so much that they did not take steps to replace him for two years.

[29] WW, II, 359.

[30] For Lardner (1684-1768) see DECBP; ODNB.

performance, to which I shall return, were Archbishop William Wake,[31] to whom Chandler had sent a copy of his book, the anti-deist writer John Leland,[32] and the congregation at Old Jewry. In 1729 this latter body invited Chandler to become co-pastor, and promised him an additional £100/0/0 per annum if he surrendered his bookselling; and so it was. Chandler remained at Old Jewry until his death.

During the course of his ministry Chandler served a number of worthy causes. In 1730 he became a member of the Presbyterian [Fund] Board and, in 1744, of Dr. Williams's Trust (1744). The former body, founded in 1689,[33] was devoted to the support of ministerial candidates; the latter, constituted in 1716, embraced that concern, but was also involved in the assistance of ministers and their widows, in distributing books, instructing children, and establishing a public library. He was involved in the distribution of government grants to German Dissenters in Pennsylvania, and in the *Regium Donum*—the government body founded in 1722 for the support of poor Dissenting ministers and their widows.[34] Indeed, Chandler became the administrator of the latter fund in 1761, something that prompted some Dissenters to query his sincerity regarding his general anti-Establishment stance, for he was administering (modest) state funds. Not, indeed, that Chandler was simply content to rely upon government funds. On the contrary, he was to the fore in 1733 in founding the Society for the Relief of Necessitous Widows and Fatherless Children of Protestant Dissenting Ministers, and on 3 March 1735/6 we find him delivering a powerful sermon at the Old Jewry chapel on their behalf.

The text is James 1:27, 'Pure religion and undefiled before God and the Father is this, To visit the fatherless and widows in their affliction, and to keep himself unspotted from the world.' Chandler first sketches the plight of widows and the fatherless:

> [A]s to the State of *Widowhood*, how many are the Inconveniences and Afflictions that attend it, from the natural Weakness of the Sex it self, and from the prevailing Laws and Customs of Nations. ... So that when the Husband, and Father of the Family is removed by Death, the Means of Subsistence generally die with him, the disconsolate *Widow* loses the proper Source of her Maintenance and Support, and hath oftentimes no future Dependence for the very Necessaries of Life, but the cold and uncertain Affections of this World, and the immediate Compassions and Care of providence. Afflictions of this Kind are extremely moving, and the Fears, Distresses, and Straits of a destitute *Widowhood* too tender for me to describe.[35]

---

[31] For Wake (1657-1737) see ODNB.

[32] See J. Leland, *A View of the Principal Deistical Writers*, 1766, I, 95. For Leland (1691-1766) see DECBP; GEE, 288; ODNB.

[33] Until 1693, when the Congregationalists seceded to establish the Congregational Fund Board, the organization had embraced both Presbyterians and Congregationalists. See the Introduction to JEREMY.

[34] See John Stephens, 'Samuel Chandler and the *Regium Donum*.'

[35] S. Chandler, *Benevolence and Integrity Essentials of Christianity*, 6.

As he nears the end of his sermon Chandler (save the marketing-speak) makes his pitch in a passionate way, and at the same time forestalls any who might have refrained from giving on the grounds that the Society was of the partisan sort:

> 'tis in behalf of the Orphans and Widows of the Ministers of our Lord Jesus that I stand here as an Intercessor; Men, who contented themselves with Poverty that they might fill others with the *unsearchable riches of Christ*; and chose Usefulness with a good Conscience and a due Regard to Liberty, rather than any worldly Advantages with the Want of either; Men, whom God made instrumental to beget others to Salvation and Happiness through the Gospel, living themselves in many Necessities, and leaving their Widows and Children, after death, wholly destitute and unprovided. Send not away therefore the Widows of such men empty, nor despise the Cry of their fatherless Children.
>
> The Charity itself is built upon the most extensive and generous Foundation: 'Twas never begun with a Party Spirit, and I trust in God, will never be managed with Partiality. The Widows and Children of the Ministers of all our Denominations, without Exception, are entitled to Assistance; and the Preference that will be made will be only of such whose Necessities are most pressing, and first deserve Compassion and Regard.[36]

Concurrently, from 1732 to 1739 Chandler was a prime advocate of the repeal of the Test and Corporation Acts that precluded Dissenters from holding state or civic office.[37] Chandler entered the fray with the publication in 1732 of his answer to Edmund Gibson, Bishop of London, entitled, *The Dispute better adjusted about the Proper Time of applying for a Repeal of the Corporation and Test Acts*. In 1736 he followed up with *The Case of the Protestant Dissenters with Reference to the Corporation and Test Acts*, and William Plumer, Member of Parliament for Hertfordshire, moved the repeal of the Acts. Robert Walpole, having urged patience, the motion was defeated by 251 votes to 123. Two years later Chandler addressed John Barnard in *A Letter to the Right Hon. the Lord Mayor, occasioned by his Lordship's nomination of five Persons, disqualified by Act of Parliament, as fit and proper Persons to serve the Office of Sherrifs, in which the Nature and Design of the Corporation Act is impartially considered and stated*; and in 1739 he led a deputation to Walpole, who continued to insist that 'The time has not yet arrived.' To this Chandler retorted, 'You have so repeatedly given this answer, that I trust you will give me leave to ask when the time will come.'' If you require a specific answer,' Walpole replied, 'I will give it to you in one word—never.'[38] There for the time being the matter rested. The Acts were not repealed until 1828.

During the period just reviewed, Chandler came to the aid of Philip Doddridge in relation to the ecclesiastical courts. It appears that one of Doddridge's students had preached in a barn at Kingsthorpe, Northamptonshire—an event that the incumbent

---

[36] Ibid., 19.

[37] They were not finally repealed until 1828.

[38] See Bernard Lord Manning, *The Protestant Dissenting Deputies*, 29-30.

of the parish, Wills, reported to Reynolds, the diocesan chancellor. The latter threatened legal recourse unless Doddridge obtained bishop's licence—something that he refused to do. On 6 November 1733 Doddridge was required to appear in the consistory court. In the following month his house was attacked by a mob, and this elicited the sympathy of Lord Halifax and other notables. On 5 December he wrote to Samuel Chandler, thanking him for his willingness 'to assist me under the prosecution which is commencing against me in the Ecclesiastical Court.'[39] On 31 January 1734 the trial took place in Westminster Hall, where the judges found in his favour. In the following June, Reynolds protested that this decision was illegal, but a missive from George II terminated the proceedings.

In 1741 Chandler was appointed to give the Tuesday morning Merchants' lecture at Salters' Hall, and the Friday evening lecture at the Weigh House. In the same year he delivered a funeral sermon on the death of Dr. Thomas Hadfield. Hadfield had been ordained as Chandler's assistant at Peckham in 1726, and had succeeded him there on Chandler's departure to the Old Jewry in 1729. He had been educated under the open-minded tutelage of Dr. Ebenezer Latham at Findern academy. What is of particular interest is Chandler's observation that during the course of his relatively short ministry, Hadfield had changed his opinion on 'some of the abstruser Points of Religion.' This, in Chandler's eyes was no sin. On the contrary,

> I am well assured this alteration did not proceed from Fickleness and Levity of Temper, or of a Love of Novelty, but from the full Persuasion and maturest Conviction of his Judgment and Conscience. ... An alteration of Sentiments in such Circumstances, must I think create a real Esteem for his memory, even amongst such of you, should there be any such, to whom such Alteration might no be altogether so agreeable.[40]

From this we may gather that Harwood tended in an Arian direction, that Chandler did not chide him for this, and that on the contrary he respected his younger colleague's intellectual integrity. We shall do well to bear this attitude in mind as we proceed.

In 1744 Richard Price came to the Old Jury as Chandler's afternoon preacher, though the budding philosopher and actuary's sojourn there was brief.[41] As his nephew put it, Price

---

[39] CCPD no. 395.

[40] S. Chandler, *Death the Wages of Sin*, 60-61. For Hadfield (bap. 1701, d. 1741) see Alan P. F. Sell, *Dissenting Thought and the Life of the* Churches, 37-9, 45-6; idem, *Enlightenment, Ecumenism, Evangel*, 80-81; J. Waddington, *Surrey Congregational History*, 264; E. E. Cleal, *The Story of Congregationalism in Surrey*, 20. For Latham (1688-1754) see EEUTA, 132, 133 and *passim*; ODNB; H. McLachlan, *Essays and Addresses*, ch. 7; Alan P. F. Sell, *Philosophy, Dissent and Nonconformity*, 27, 28, 30.

[41] For Price (1723-91) see DECBP; DWB; GEE, 145, 154; JEREMY, 150-2; ODNB; WW, I, 126, III, 384; William Morgan (Price's nephew), *Memoirs of the Life of the Rev.Richard Price,* (1815), now reprinted, edited and introduced by D. O. Thomas in *Enlightenment and Dissent*; D. O. Thomas, *Richard* Price; idem, *The Honest Mind*; W. B.

> seemed to acquire considerable popularity, but Dr. Chandler, for reasons best known to himself, advised him to be less energetic in his manner, and to deliver his discourses with more diffidence and modesty. This rebuke had its natural effect on the mild and unassuming temper of Mr. Price. To avoid an extreme into which he was in no danger of falling, he ran into the opposite extreme of a cold and lifeless delivery, which, by rendering him less popular with the congregation, disposed them to feel less regret when their minister had no further occasion for his services.[42]

Walter Wilson, clearly reluctant to have the reputation of a distinguished personage needlessly tarnished, remarks,

> The occasion of [Price's] removal is said to have been a specious of jealousy on the part of Dr. Chandler, on account of the rising talents and growing popularity of Mr. Price. As the indulgence of such a temper was wholly unnecessary, and reflects some reproach upon the character of so great a man, we are backward in giving it full credit; nevertheless, the source from whence we have derived our information is of that credible nature as to warrant brief mention of the circumstance.[43]

It was not until 1759 that Chandler had another assistant at the Old Jewry, Thomas Amory, his future memorialist.[44] Since 1725 Amory had been a tutor at Taunton academy, first under his uncle, Henry Grove,[45] with whom he had studied before completing his studies under Dr. Eames at Moorfields. After Grove's death in 1738 he was placed in charge of the academy. On Chandler's death, Amory succeeded him at the Old Jewry.

In 1748, while visiting a friend in Norwich, Chandler heard a charge of the bishop, Thomas Gooch, during the course of which Gooch declared that the leaders of the Jacobite rebellion of 1745 were Presbyterians. His ground for this assertion was that their imprisoned leaders in the Tower of London asked for Presbyterian confessors. This was too much for Chandler, who wrote a letter to Gooch. The latter requested a meeting with Chandler when he was in London, and this took place. At a subsequent meeting Thomas Sherlock, Bishop of Salisbury, was also present.

Peach and D. O. Thomas, eds, *The Correspondence of Richard* Price; D. O. Thomas, J. Stephens and P. A. L. Jones, *A Bibliography of the Works of Richard* Price; Roland Thomas, *Richard* Price; Carl B. Cone, *Torchbearer of Freedom*.

[42] W. Morgan, *Memoirs*, 11-12; D. O. Thomas, ed, Morgan's *Memoirs*, 6.

[43] WW, II, 384.

[44] For Amory (1700/01-1774) see DECBP; GEE, 154; JEREMY, 163; MURCH, 198, 200, 208, 235; ODNB; WW, II, 385-393, IV, 311-12; J. A. Jones, *Bunhill Memorials*, 6; Alan P. F. Sell, *Dissenting Thought and the Life of the Churches*, *passim*; idem, *Philosophy, Dissent and Nonconformity*, *passim*; Brian Kirk, *The Taunton Dissenting Academy*.

[45] For Grove (1684-1738) see DECBP; EEUTA, 72-4; ODNB; Amory's Memoir prefixed to Grove's posthumous *Works*; Alan P. F. Sell, *Dissenting Thought and the Life of the Churches*, ch. 6; idem, *Philosophy, Dissent and Nonconformity*, *passim*; idem, *Testimony and Tradition*, ch. 5; B. Kirk, *The Taunton Dissenting Academy*.

Sherlock explained to Chandler that the Church of England consisted of doctrines, discipline and ceremonies, and that the last were by general consent regarded as indifferent. What, then, was Chandler's objection to their doctrines? Chandler said that the Articles should be expressed in biblical words, and the Athanasian Creed should be discarded. The bishops had no problem with either of these suggestions, but then raised the question of ordination. Chandler made it clear that Presbyterians would not renounce their ordination, though they might submit to the laying on of hands, this being understood as recommending them 'to public service in their society.'[46] The bishops then suggested that Chandler meet Archbishop Thomas Herring, and this he duly did, Gooch also being present, and again there was a considerable degree of accord.[47] However, Chandler's remark at the second meeting that articles in biblical terms would be for the benefit of others, since he, as a 'moderate Calvinist', was content with the existing ones, was 'leaked' to the great annoyance of 'several persons', and thus the discussion of possible comprehension ceased.[48]

By now Chandler was becoming widely known for his writings on a variety of subjects. I shall outline his principal ethical and doctrinal positions shortly, but we should not overlook his voluminous biblical works. In 1735 he published *A Paraphrase and Critical Commentary on the Prophecy of Joel*, while his last major work was a massive *Critical History of the Life of David* (1760). This two-volume account had its origin in controversy. On 9 November 1760 Chandler preached a memorial sermon on the death of George II entitled, *The Character of a great and good King Full of Days, Riches and Honour*. His text was I Chronicles 29: 28, where the reference is to David's dying 'full of days, riches and honour.' Chandler extols the virtues of David: he held religion is high esteem, he was temperate, charitable, had a concern for the welfare of his people, notwithstanding that on occasion he had to 'cut off incorrigible offenders' and behave as a 'terrour to evil doers.'[49] The late King is likened to David. King George was rich, both materially and in the esteem of his people, and he died at a good old age. Chandler thanks God for him, and wishes his successor a long and prosperous reign.

This sermon spawned a satirical tract, *The History of a Man after God's own Heart* (1761), in which the author, John Noorthouck,[50] drew attention to Uriah the Hittite and Bathsheba—persons omitted from Chandler's sermon—and argued that

---

[46] WW, II, 373.

[47] For Gooch (1675-1754), Sherlock (1677-1761) and Herring (1693-1757) see ODNB. Gooch was Bishop of Norwich (1738-48) and of Ely (1748-54); Sherlock was Bishop of Bangor (1728), Salisbury (1734) and London (1748); Herring was Bishop of Bangor (1737), York (1743) and (reluctantly) Archbishop of Canterbury (1747-57).

[48] WW, II, 374. For a full account of the proceedings see the Presbyterian minister John Barker's letter to Doddridge of 2 February 174[7]/8, CCPD, no. 1314. See also CCPD, 1281, 1315, 1321, 1481. For Barker (1682-1762) see JEREMY, 127-8; ODNB; WW, II, 39-54. See G. F. Nuttall, 'Chandler, Doddridge, and the Archbishop'.

[49] S. Chandler, *The Character of a great and good King*, 32.

[50] For Noorthouck (1732-1816) see ODNB.

David's character faults classed him with Nero or Caligula. Chandler dashed off a somewhat ill-tempered, exhaustive (and exhausting) reply of 302 pages, *A Review of the History of the Man after God's own Heart* (1762), in which he conceded that David was not without faults, but brought Hebrew learning to bear upon the misrepresentations of his opponent. More soberly, there followed his major work on David, published in the year of Chandler's death. He had earlier begun a substantial work on the prophecy [sic] of Isaiah, but the technical philological studies of the Dutch Arabist, Albertus Schultens (1686-1750), prompted him to think that he ought to study Hebrew-Arabic comparisons in greater detail. As it turned out, owing to the pressure of other concerns he never completed either this work or a projected life of Moses. At his death it was found that his interleaved Bible was replete with his notes in Latin. It was hoped that these might be published. This hope being disappointed, it was decided to deposit the notes at Dr. Williams's Library, London. It is not known whether this was ever done; it is known that they are not now at the Library.[51]

On a number of occasions Chandler was called upon to deliver funeral orations. Among these is the one preached at Hackney on 18 May 1746, ten days after his friend and fellow-ordinand, George Smyth died at the age of fifty-seven. Smyth, we learn, was a devoted student, who could read Greek before the age of nine. His religious convictions

> were not the Effect of Party Attachment, not drawn from narrow and contracted Systems. ... [H]e never servilely courted the Reputation and Character of *what is called Orthodoxy*, though he honoured and loved the Thing, whether with the Name, without it, or with a contrary one. ... He thought it a *sordid Thing*, to disguise or dissemble his Sentiments, or to express himself in such an ambiguous Manner, that he might appear to be what some call *Sound*, when conscious to himself that he was not so.[52]

There can be no question that for these characteristics Smyth is warmly commended by Chandler.

Two years later Chandler spoke at the interment of Isaac Watts. I shall refer to the doctrinal content to this sermon in due course, but for the present I simply record the concluding exhortation:

> Remember therefore those faithful Guides, who have had the Rule over you, who have spoken to you the Word of God, whose Faith follow, considering the End of

---

[51] I am grateful to Dr. David L. Wykes, the Director of the Library, for confirming this latter point.

[52] S. Chandler, *Christ the Pattern of the Christian's Future Glory*, 27.

> their Conversation; that you may be their Hope, their Joy, and their Crown of rejoycing, in the Presence of our Lord Jesus Christ at his Coming.[53]

Four years on, we find Chandler preaching at Clapham on the occasion of the death of the Reverend Moses Lowman, who had ministered there from 1710 until his death on 3 May 1752.[54] Lowman, a Congregationalist, had studied in Utrecht and Leiden, and had published on Jewish antiquities. A non-subscriber at Salters' Hall, he was a Dr. Williams Trustee, and was clearly not averse to mingling with more liberal divines. Chandler finds that Lowman exemplifies the minister of integrity. Returning to one of his familiar themes he says,

> If [a minister] preaches what he doth not believe, he deals falsely with God and man, and deserves to be doubly abhorred for his hypocrisy, and vice. He forfeits all claim to respect and honour from men, and hath a double condemnation to expect from God.[55]

Lowman was not of this sort—though one cannot suppress the thought that even if he were, some of his members might have been none the wiser, for an intelligent member of his church confessed that he could never understand him.[56] Be that as it may, 'His principles in religion were moderate, and clear of all extremes. He thought that truth generally lay in the golden mean. ... [T]his impartiality ... rendered him benevolent and *catholic* in his disposition to all others.'[57]

In the very different context of an ordination service, Chandler's stance on pulpit integrity emerges once more. On 16 October 1765 his son-in-law, Edward Harwood, of Bristol, and Benjamin Davis, of Marlborough, were ordained at the Old Jewry chapel. Thomas Amory delivered the sermon, and Chandler gave the charge.[58] In two sentences, the first of which would have found the approval of an Abraham Taylor or a John Gill, while the second would have flashed warning lights at them, Chandler's 'moderatism' becomes clear: 'Our principal business is to preach the gospel of the grace of God, to represent to our hearers the great truths relative to God the father, our Lord Jesus Christ, the holy Spirit of God, and the nature and method of that

---

[53] Idem, the Funeral Oration appended to David Jennings, *A Sermon Occasioned by the Death of the late Reverend Isaac Watts, D.D.*, 45. Jennings and Chandler each received two guineas for their services on this occasion. See Arthur Paul Davis, *Isaac Watts*, 71.

[54] For Lowman (bap. 1679, d. 1752) see JEREMY, 134; ODNB; TSJ, 116, 705, 713, 716-17; J. Waddington, *Surrey Congregational History*, 185; E. E. Cleal, *The Story of Congregationalism in Surrey*, 175-6.

[55] S. Chandler, *The Character and Reward of a Christian Bishop*, 19.

[56] See E. E. Cleal, *The Story of Congregationalism in Surrey*, 176.

[57] S. Chandler, *The Character and Reward of a Christian Bishop*, 43.

[58] For Harwood (1729-1794) see EEUTA, 124, 224; ODNB; Alan P. F. Sell, *Dissenting Thought and the Life of the Churches*, 39, 199, 252; W. Wilson MSS at Dr. Williams's Library, A8.61.62, where he is described as 'An eminent scholar but a poor theologian.' He had studied at Hoxton academy

redemption, which is the great and comprehensive blessing of the gospel.'[59] Then, after saying that gainsayers are to be convinced, and error is to be rebuked, he says that they must distinguish 'between the plain simple Gospel doctrine, and the metaphysical and philosophical additions to it, that have been made by systematical and polemical divines.'[60]

Seven months later, on 18 May 1766, we find Amory in Chandler's pulpit at the Old Jewry, this time to preach at his friend's funeral, for Chandler had died on 8 May. Amory's text is Hebrews 11: 13, 'These all died in faith, not having received the promises, but having seen them afar off, and were persuaded of them, and embraced them, and confessed that they were strangers and pilgrims on the earth.' Amory first outlines the faith in which good Christians die. In the cosmological vein typical of so may eighteenth-century sermons, he begins by declaring that the world cannot be attributed to blind chance or necessity, and then speaks of Jesus, sent by God to be the light of the world and the redeemer from death. The Holy Spirit, poured out upon the apostles, qualified them 'to teach and confirm the Gospel of Salvation thro' the world.'[61] Those who die in faith are those who are firmly persuaded of the truth during their lives, their conduct is animated by their beliefs, and they have 'a rational and full Persuasion of the Reality of the promised Blessedness.'[62]

We are clearly intended to conclude that all of these characteristics were exemplified in Chandler's life. However, Amory says that he is precluded by the terms of Chandler's will from speaking of his friend's 'uncommon Greatness and Strength of his Genius, etc. etc.' (!)[63] He does, however, speak of the 'animated' way in which Chandler defended the doctrines of natural and revealed religion; his commitment to 'the cause of rational piety and Christian liberty'; and the esteem in which Chandler was held, not least by senior clerics of the Church of England. He reassures Chandler's congregation that their minister bore his last painful illness with his eye on the felicity to come.

In his 'Account' of Chandler, Amory allows himself greater scope. He speaks of Chandler's quick apprehension and penetrating judgment; of his instructive and animating sermons; of his strong, clear, voice and rapid pronunciation; of the grand and just ideas that he communicated; and of his prayers which were extempore, varied, and free of preaching. He reiterates the point that

> the high reputation which he had gained, by his defences of the Christian religion, procured him from some of the governors of the established church, the offers of considerable preferment, which he nobly declined. He valued more than these the liberty and integrity of his conscience, and scorned for any worldly considerations

---

[59] S. Chandler in T. Amory, *The Motives and Obligations to Love and good Works*, 27.

[60] Ibid., 37.

[61] T. Amory, *Dying in Faith explained*, 6.

[62] Ibid., 17.

[63] Ibid., 22.

> to profess as divine truths, doctrines which he did not really believe, and to practice in religion, what he did not inwardly approve. An honourable sacrifice to truth and honesty, and well compensated by the affection and generosity of his people; as far as such sacrifices are recompenced on this side of the grave.[64]

It is pleasant to note the consistency of Chandler's attitude as here expressed with what he had said in his ordination charge to Thomas Wright at Lewin's Mead, Bristol on 31 May, 1759:

> Let us, who are engaged in this sacred service of preaching the doctrines of the gospel, be chearful and diligent in the discharge of our duty, nor ever be persuaded to desert it, by any worldly or lucrative considerations whatsoever. It is a good and honourable office, and when executed with care, fidelity, and prudence, will be useful to society, comfortable to ourselves, and acceptable to God.[65]

Recognition came in other ways, however, for 'while [Chandler] was ... employed in advancing the interests of religion, learning and liberty, he received the highest literary honour from two universities, *Edinburgh* and *Aberdeen*; who each of them sent him, unasked, the diploma of *Doctor* in *Divinity*.'[66] The degrees were conferred in 1755 and 1756, respectively, though Chandler had previously declined such offers on the ground that 'so many blockheads had been made Doctors.'[67] He was also elected a Fellow of the Royal Society and of the Society of Antiquaries of London. That Chandler was held in high esteem not only by his contemporaries, but also by one of the younger generation of ministers is clear from a sermon preached on his death by the Unitarian minister, William Hazlitt (1737-1820). Chandler's he declares, is 'A death, that must be long lamented, by every lover of liberty and truth, by every friend to the Dissenting interest, and the cause of primitive and uncorrupted Christianity.'[68] Chandler 'was a most strenuous and unanswerable advocate in the Christian cause.' He was 'governed by the most diffusive charity.' He was a diligent scholar, 'almost buried in books.' But 'it was in the pulpit that his talents most conspicuously shone forth.'[69]

Having thus introduced Samuel Chandler, I shall now turn in more detail to his generally lively, frequently controversial, and sometimes elusive thought. I shall consider in turn the themes of liberty of conscience and freedom of thought, morality, deism, and Christian doctrine.

---

[64] T. Amory, Preface to Chandler's *Sermons*, xii.

[65] S. Chandler, *Preaching the Gospel*, 54. For Wright see GEE, 35; MURCH, 114-15. He ministered at Lewin's Mead, first as assistant, from 1751 to 1797.

[66] T. Amory, Preface to Chandler's *Sermons*, xi.

[67] WW, II, 372.

[68] W. Hazlitt, *A Sermon on Human Immortality*, 20.

[69] Ibid., 21, 22.

I

Chandler, as we saw, described himself as a 'moderate Calvinist' in a context in which the adjective presumably meant 'doctrinally discriminating', though high Calvinists would, no doubt, have construed it to mean 'lukewarm'. But 'moderate' may also refer to a divine's attitude. In this sense was may say that Chandler was the last person to wish to tie any Christian's conscience to particular doctrinal formulations, and he stands forth as an apostle of liberty of conscience and freedom of thought.

We recall that as a young man Chandler had been on the side of those opposed to confessional subscription at Salters' Hall. In the Introduction to his translation of Limborch's *The History of the Inquisition* (1731), he contends that the doctrines of the Gospel should be defended with meekness and charity, that novel terms of church communion should not be introduced, and that the Church was not to be encumbered with metaphysical subtleties and abstruse questions. This drew him into controversy with William Berriman.[70] Berriman, the Rector of St. Andrew's Undershaft, had earlier entered into the Trinitarian controversy, and had also delivered a sermon the title of which sufficiently explains its theme: *The Authority of the Civil Powers in Matters of Religion asserted and vindicated* (1722). He now published *Some Brief Remarks on Mr. Chandler's Introduction to the History of the Inquisition* (1733), in which he objected to Chandler's account of the cause of Arianism, and replied to his 'calumnies' against Archbishop Laud. In the same year Chandler published *An Answer to the Brief Remarks of William* Berriman. However, the latter was not satisfied, and swiftly responded with *A Review of the Remarks on Mr. Chandler's Introduction to the History of the Inquisition* (1733), in which he charged Chandler with misrepresentations of fact and prevarication. Back came Chandler with *A Second Letter to William Berriman* (1733). In 1734 Chandler again went into print against Berriman, this time by way of *A Vindication of a Passage of the Right Reverend the Lord Bishop of London, in his Second Pastoral Letter, against the misrepresentation of William Berriman, D.D. In a Letter to his Lordship.*[71] It would appear that by now Berriman's zeal had waned or his ammunition had been depleted, for he wrote no more to, or about, Chandler.

In his substantial *History of Persecution* (1736) Chandler laid it down that 'the imposing subscription to creeds and articles of faith, as tests of orthodoxy, is a thing unreasonable in itself, as it hath proved of infinite ill consequence in the church of God.'[72] Subscription 'is a great hindrance to that freedom and impartiality of inquiry which is the unalterable duty of every man, and necessary to render his religion reasonable and acceptable.'[73] With his 1748 pamphlet, *The Case of Subscription to*

---

[70] For Berriman (1688-1750) see ODNB.

[71] The bishop was Edmund Gibson (bap. 1669, d. 1748). His *Second Pastoral Letter* contained an anti-deist denial of the view that reason sufficed and that revelation was redundant.

[72] S. Chandler, *The History of Persecution*, 377.

[73] Ibid., 384.

Explanatory Articles of Faith, Chandler entered a wide-ranging controversy. He was here concerned in part to answer the Reverend John White's *Third Letter to a Gentleman Dissenting from the Church of England* (namely, the Presbyterian high Arian, Micaijah Towgood[74]).

White, the Church of England parson, wrote in defence of subscription to articles of faith. Chandler points out that the Bible says nothing on this subject, and challenges White to show where Scripture sanctions the imposition of extra-canonical words and explications. For his own part, Chandler loftily declares, 'Proper Authority I hope I shall never oppose, but in Matters of Religion I own no human Authority to be proper, and will bend, no not to the greatest. 'Tis my Honour as a Christian, that in these I submit only to the most high God.'[75] There follows a concise, powerfully expressed, summary of Chandler's view of the matter:

> I have but one Lord, even Christ. ... The Scriptures I receive as a Divine Revelation: By these I humbly endeavour to form my own Sentiments of Christianity. ... All who receive these as the Rule of their Faith, and live by them as the Rule of their Morals, I own so far as sound Members of Christ's Body, I embrace them as my Brethren, I will gladly communicate with them, and will never debar them from my Communion. I will, if other Qualifications are not wanting, willingly receive them into the Ministry, I hope to die in full Friendship with them, and to be happy with them as my Companions in a better State: And thus I declare, without Exception of any Denomination or Party of Christians whatsoever, or whatever be the external Disadvantages they are under, or opprobrious Names that are given to them. Hard Names and Party Reproaches terrify me not at all. Without this Latitude of principle I can see no possible End to the Divisions of the Church; and if I should mark or avoid any Christians who thus adhere to the only Rule of Christianity, I transgress this apostolical Canon, and am myself chargeable with a schismatical and unchristian spirit.[76]

Chandler proceeds to cite patristic authors and General Councils in support of his position, and explains that he denounces the Church of England's arbitrary subscription, not because it constricts the liberty of Englishmen, but because it encroaches upon 'that liberty wherewith Christ hath made them free.'[77]

To the Presbyterian minister, John Barker—a Calvinist, Chandler's discussion of subscription was 'a very good Defence of Us & a fine performance.'[78] Others

---

[74] For White (1685-1755) see *Alumni Cantabrigienses*, I, iv. Ordained at Peterborough on 22 September 1706, he served at Kettering, Stoke Nayland and Ospringe. For Towgood (1700-1792) see ODNB; Alan P. F. Sell, *Dissenting Thought and the Life of the Churches*, ch. 7. I describe Towgood a high Arian because unlike Richard Price, for example, he did not object to the offering of worship to Christ.

[75] S. Chandler, *The Case of Subscription*, 39.

[76] Ibid., 40.

[77] Ibid., 148. Cf. idem, *Reflections on the Conduct of the Modern Deists*, xxiv-xxix, xlix-liii.

[78] J. Barker, Letter to Philip Doddridge of 5 May 1748. See CCPD, no. 1337.

disagreed, and replies to Chandler quickly followed. George Harvest, a Fellow of Magdalen College, Cambridge, argues for the necessity of subscription to articles by ordinands, for the objective of subscription is 'that the Ministers and teachers of the Gospel do themselves hold the Faith of the Gospel.'[79] Since the propositions of Scripture are open to interpretation, he continues, creeds make clear the sense in which they are to be taken, and what ministers are to believe. To this Joseph Clark, formerly a fellow of Magdalen, added the consideration that Chandler uses the word 'imposition' tendentiously, for 'the Church of England does not lay any necessity upon men to profess their belief in the articles ... against their judgment and their conscience.'[80] On the contrary, the requirement of subscription enables men to discover whether they believe the articles or not. For his part, 'Philochristus' seeks to turn Chandler's argument against him: Presbyterian ordinands, no less than Anglican ones, are required to profess their faith in their own words, and their governors, pastors and congregations can deem such professions inadequate—hence the ejectment of 'those two great and good Men, Mr. Emlyn and Mr. Peirce.'[81] In other words, personal confessions and formal subscription to creeds can have the same consequences, and neither can unite the Protestants.

Chandler's opposition to confessional subscription was but one sphere in which he appealed for liberty of conscience and the right of recourse to Scripture. We recall his praise of his friend George Smyth for the latter's insistence upon forming his own mind on religious matters in general. Indeed, as he elsewhere put it, religion 'is a purely personal matter, and every man ought to be persuaded in his own mind of the nature of its proofs, and doctrines, and principles, and to dissent from the publick conscience if he finds it erroneous, in any or every article of its publick belief, since no man is to be saved or damned hereafter for the faith or practice of his superior in Church or State ...'[82] The alternative paths lead to servile obedience or superstition. The general principle is that

> nothing can or ought to be believed, but under the direction of the understanding, nor any scheme of religion and worship to be received but what appears reasonable in itself, and worthy of God; the necessary consequence if, that every man is bound in interest and duty to make the best use he can of his reasonable powers, and to examine, without fear, all principles before he receives them, and all rites and means of religion and worship before he submits to and complies with them.[83]

Nor is it sufficient that a person arrive at his or her opinions; it must be possible for those opinions to be published freely. Moreover, the irreligious have the same right:

---

[79] G. Harvest, *A Letter to Mr. Samuel Chandler*, 9.

[80] J. Clark, *A Full and Particular Reply to Mr. Chandler's Case*, 7.

[81] 'Philochristus', *A Letter to Mr. Samuel Chandler*, 7.

[82] S. Chandler, *Reflections on the Conduct of the Modern Deists*, xlvii-xlviii.

[83] Idem, *The History of Persecution*, 28.

> not only dissenters from the publick establishment are tolerated, and secured in many of their rights as men and Christians, but even dissenters from Christianity it self have been suffer'd to enjoy and publish their sentiments, without any other opposition but that of reason and argument. And why should they not? If Christianity be true, it will stand firm against their attacks, as an house founded on a rock ... If it be not true, ... 'tis not a religion for wise and good men, who would be glad to discard it for a better system of principles and morals.[84]

Consistently with the foregoing, Chandler resolutely opposes the propagation of religion by persecutory means. The following is typical of his many strong statements on the matter:

> I would have all church Regiments for the propagating religion by dint of authority and tying up mens hands, disbanded, broken, and scattered as dust before the wind. The business of Christian stewards is to feed the people, i.e. to teach and preach the genuine doctrines of Christianity; and if medicines and antidotes must come in, they ought to administer such as are most gentle and easy, that they may be looked on not only as faithful stewards, but as kind and compassionate physicians too. ... Other antidotes you'll not find in the gospel of Christ, and to use others is a certain sign of Quackery and Imposture.[85]

As he later adds, 'If Jesus Christ designed that his religious should be defended by civil terrors and punishments, why did he not at first propagate it by the same means?'[86] Furthermore,

> The sole claim [Christianity] hath on the consciences of men is, that it is a religion worthy of God, and published to the world by his authority. And therefore the civil magistrate can have no right to enforce the belief of any particular opinions, said to be Christian, no nor of real Christianity itself, except they can convince the consciences of men by the evidence of truth; and if they can do this, men will believe it, without any secular motives or methods of persuasion.[87]

Chandler's *The History of Persecution* is a chronicle of events designed to show that his convictions as just stated have, through the course of history, been repudiated by Church and state alike and, indeed, not within the Christian realm alone, in which connection he refers, among others, to 'Antiochus, the Egyptian heretic eaters, and the Roman emperors.'[88] He goes so far as to declare that Christians learned their persecutory ways from the heathen. Nor does he hesitate to remind his readers of what is 'well known', namely, that the 'avowed method' whereby the Mahometans propagate religion 'is by the sword.'[89] As we might

---

[84] Idem, *Reflections on the Conduct of the Modern Deists*, 14-15.

[85] S. Chandler, *Reflections on the Conduct of the Modern Deists*, xlviii-xlix.

[86] Ibid., 15.

[87] Ibid., 16.

[88] Idem, *The History of Persecution*, 53.

[89] Ibid., 54.

expect, Chandler is pleased to note that Tertullian, Cyprian and Lactantius insisted that all people had a right to their own religious convictions, and that these should be voluntarily embraced and not compelled; but such persons were in the minority among the Christian leaders. Where physical persecution was not employed, bribery and offers of preferment frequently were. Chandler faults both Bishop Alexander and Arius 'for leaving the plain account of scripture, introducing terms of their own invention into a doctrine of pure revelation, and at last censuring and writing one against another, and dividing the whole church of Christ upon account of them.'[90] There followed the dictation of belief and the anathematization of those who could not assent to agreed formulae. Still worse, 'the orthodox first brought in the punishment of heresy with death, and persuaded the emperor to destroy those whom they could not easily convert.'[91] Athanasius himself was not guiltless: 'To speak plainly, I think that Athanasius was a man of a haughty and inflexible temper, and more concerned for victory and power, than for truth, religion, or peace.'[92]

Turning to the Middle Ages, Chandler catalogues the crimes committed by the Western Church in the cause of punishing heretics. He has particularly stern things to say against the Spanish Inquisition, where stripping and binding, the rack, and squassation were the methods used. He concludes this part of his work by recommending that God alone, the searcher of hearts, is able and competent to judge a person's religion, and he will do so. 'Let us in the mean while detest the tyranny of the papists; and strive to reduce those who, in our judgment, hold errors, into the way of truth, by the good offices of charity and benevolence, without arrogating to ourselves a judgment over the consciences of others.'[93]

Chandler does not find much to cheer him, as far as methods are concerned, when he turns to the Reformers, who 'were angry with the papists, not for persecuting, but for persecuting themselves and their followers; being really of opinion that heretics might be persecuted, and, in some cases, persecuted to death.[94] Thus, for example, Luther, 'that otherwise great and good man', although he did not approve of the execution of heretics, nevertheless recommended that Jewish synagogues be razed to the ground and their rabbis subjected to forced labour; while Calvin's record in the cases of Castillio and Servetus was dismal in the extreme, his hope that while put to death, Servetus would not be burned alive doing nothing to dissipate Chandler's repugnance of Calvin's actions. An account of the treatment of Arminians by Calvinists in the Netherlands follows, and then the scene changes to England.

The English Reformers were by no means immune to the persecuting tendency, declares Chandler: even 'Cranmer's hands were stained with the blood of several. He had a share in the prosecution and condemnation of that pious and excellent martyr John Lambert, and consented to the death of Ann Askew, who were burnt to death

---

90 Ibid., 69.
91 Ibid., 85.
92 Ibid., 92.
93 Ibid., 263.
94 Ibid, 285.

for denying the corporeal presence; which, though Cranmer then believed, he saw afterwards reason to deny.'[95] We proceed through the inquisitorial methods of Archbishops Whitgift and Laud, arriving at the Great Ejectment of 1662, when, by 24 August of that year, almost two thousand ministers who could not conscientiously give their 'unfeigned assent and consent' to the *Book of Common Prayer* had lost their livings. Chandler pronounces upon the incident thus:

> The consequence of this act was, that between two and three thousand excellent divines were turned out of their churches; many of them, to say the least, as eminent for learning and piety as the bishops, who were the great promoters of this barbarous act; and themselves and families, many of them, exposed to the greatest distress and poverty.[96]

The Ejectment, he continues, 'occasioned such a division from the established church, as will, I hope, ever remain, to witness against the tyranny of those times, and the reverend authors and promoters of that act ...'[97] The upshot of the Act of Uniformity and of subsequent legislation is that despite the Toleration Act of 1689, while Dissenters have 'zeal for his majesty's person and family' and 'the inclination to serve him, ... by law we are denied the opportunity and power.'[98]

The Dissenters themselves have known quarrels and strife among themselves, which they have managed 'with great warmth and eagerness of temper.'[99] Thus the 'high flown orthodox party' dealt most unfairly with the moderate Daniel Williams on account of his opposition to antinomianism, and then came the Trinitarian controversy, during which James Peirce was dismissed from his Exeter pastorate on the grounds of heresy; and the Salters' Hall subscription controversy caused further bitterness. Chandler finally turns his attention briefly to New England, where erstwhile English Dissenters acted on occasion with inquisitorial cruelty, as when four Quakers were hanged in Boston.

Chandler concludes that in all the Christian ages the clergy have been to the fore in persecutory zeal. By contrast Jesus was meek and lowly and, far from giving his followers permission to persecute, he said that they must suffer persecution for his sake. Chandler does not wish to blacken the episcopal office as such, but some of its representatives, far from being overseers of Christ's flock, have torn and devoured it. The situation is rendered even less tolerable because 'the things for which christians have persecuted each other, have been generally "matters of no importance in

---

[95] Ibid., 312.

[96] Ibid., 343. In the text, 'almost two thousand ministers' is my statement; in the quotation Chandler over-estimates. See further Alan P. F. Sell, *Commemorations*, 124-30, 332.

[97] Ibid., 344.

[98] Ibid., 349.

[99] Ibid., 350.

religion," and oftentimes such as have been "directly contrary" to the nature of it.'[100] The sad truth is that

> hard words, technical terms, and inexplicable phrases, points of mere speculation, abstruse questions, and metaphysical notions; rites and ceremonies, forms of human invention, and certain institutions, that have their rise and foundation only in superstition: these have been the great engines of division; these the sad occasions of persecution.[101]

Salt is rubbed into Calvinist wounds when Chandler goes on to repeat his view that 'Arius ... expressly allowed the son to be "before all times and ages, perfect God, unchangeable", and begotten after the most perfect likeness of the unbegotten father. This, to me, appears to bid very fair for orthodoxy.'[102] This should have sufficed to reconcile Arius and Alexander; but new, complicated, terms were introduced which gave the controversy a fresh lease of life:

> Arius knew not how to reconcile the bishop's words, 'ever begotten', with the assertion, that the Son, co-exists 'unbegottenly with God'; and thought it little less than a contradiction to affirm, that he was 'unbegottenly begotten.' And as to the word 'consubstantial', Arius seems to have thought that it destroyed the personal subsistence of the Son, and brought in the doctrine of Sabellius; or else that it implied that the Son was a 'part of the Father'; and for this reason declined to use it.[103]

At the root of the problem was the metaphysical question: Could God generate a person as eternal as himself? Did not God's generating necessarily imply the Father's precedence over the Son—something which Arius believed, and which the bishop denied?

As if recognizing that he is he is skating on thin ice, Chandler refers to the General Councils, rises to the heights of oratory and, in a paragraph which must be quoted in full, enters an impassioned plea which summarizes the stance he consistently maintained throughout his ministry:

> If I know my own heart, I would be far from giving up any plain and important doctrine of the gospel. But will any man coolly and soberly affirm, that nice and intricate questions, that depend upon metaphysical distinctions, and run so high as the most minute supposable atom or point of time, can be either plain or important doctrines of the gospel? Oh Jesus! if thou be 'the Son of the everlasting God, the brightness of thy Father's glory, and the express image of his person'; if thou art the most perfect resemblance of his all-perfect goodness, that kind benefactor, that God-like friend to the human race, which the faithful records of thy life declare thee to be; how can I believe the essential doctrines of thy gospel to be thus wrapped up

---

[100] Ibid., 363.
[101] Ibid., 363-4.
[102] Ibid., 364.
[103] Ibid., 364-5.

in darkness? or, that the salvation of that church, 'which thou hast purchased with thy blood', depends on such mysterious and inexplicable conditions? If thy gospel represents thee right, surely thou must be better pleased with the humble, peaceable christian, who when honestly searching into the glories of thy nature, and willing to give thee all the adoration thy great father hath ordered him to pay thee, falls into some errors, as the consequence of human weakness; than with that imperious and tyrannical disciple, who divides thy members, tears the bowels of thy church, and spreads confusion and strife throughout thy followers and friends, even for the sake of truths that lie remote from men's understanding, and in which thou hast not thought proper to make the full, the plain decision. If truth is not to be given up for the sake of peace, I am sure peace is not to be sacrificed for the sake of such truths; and if the gospel is a rule worthy our regard, the clergy of those times can never be excused for the contentions they raised, and the miseries they occasioned in the christian world, upon account of them.[104]

Chandler opines that it was their love of power and riches which prompted most of the persecuting clergy to act as they did, and he denies that the deliverances of General Councils have any authority. Indeed, 'Their very meeting to pronounce damnation on their adversaries, and to form creeds for the consciences of others, is no less than a demonstration that they had no concurrence of the Son of God, no influence of the Holy Spirit of God.'[105] Moreover, if one prescribed creed can be deemed legitimate, so can many: 'Upon this foot the doctrines of the council of Trent, the thirty-nine articles of the church of England, and the assemblies confession of faith, are all of them equally true, christian and sacred ...'[106] The comes the pressing question,

What security then shall we have left us for truth and orthodoxy, when our subscriptions are gone? Why, the sacred scriptures, those oracles of the great God, and freedom and liberty to interpret and understand them as we can; the consequence of this would be great integrity and peace of conscience, in the enjoyment of our religious principles, union and friendship amongst christians, notwithstanding all their differences in judgment, and great respect and honour to those faithful pastors, that carefully feed the flock of God and lead them into pastures of righteousness and peace. We shall lose only the incumbrances of religion ...[107]

While Chandler would say that he stands for the sufficiency of Scripture, his remarks do seem to overlook the sad fact that divergent interpretations of Scripture can be, and too often have been, as divisive as creeds themselves; indeed, some of his controversial writings themselves illustrate the fact. Be that as it may, he concludes with a repetition of his view that the Bible in nowhere countenances persecution on account of religious belief.

---

[104] Ibid., 366.
[105] Ibid., 375.
[106] Ibid., 383.
[107] Ibid., 388.

After the textual dissections of Berriman and others, it is refreshing to read the knock-about tracts of the swashbuckling Church of England parson, Zachary Grey.[108] He wrote a number of pamphlets in which he denounces Presbyterian principles and practice, staunchly upholds episcopacy, and extols Charles I as a fine monarch. In *English Presbyterian Eloquence* he writes to Chandler, in the wake of the latter's *The History of Persecution*, under the name of 'an Admirer of Monarchy, and Episcopacy'. We need travel no further than his Dedication in order to catch something of his spirit:

> to His Reverend, the Worshipful Mr. Samuel Chandler, Bookmaker, and Bookseller, Presbyterian-Teacher, famed orator, and Prize-fighter at Salter's [*sic*] Hall, Patron General of Schismaticks, and Great Friend to Liberty of Writing and Speaking (*alias* Licentiousness). But Mauler of Hereticks. (*Haereticorum Malleus*). The following Collection of curious Fanatical Flowers is humbly subscribed ...[109]

That Chandler's differences with Rome extended beyond the question of persecution and into doctrine and politics is manifest in his writings. On 16 January 1734/5 he preached at Salters' Hall on *The Notes of the Church Considered.* None who were present could have mistaken his theme, which he announced in the forthright manner he adopted throughout:

> You have already been informed, that the design of this lecture is to represent and expose the absurdity, and antichristian nature of the corruptions and errors of the apostate church of Rome, and to confirm and establish you in the belief of those doctrines of the Reformation, which have the sacred writings, and all the valuable remains of antiquity to support them; that you may always be upon your guard, against the attempts of those who lye in wait to seduce you from the simplicity of the Christian faith, to enslave your consciences to the tyrannical impositions of imperious and cruel deceivers, and to bring you back to those impious idolatries, which are a reproach to the Christian name, and contrary to the plainest dictates of natural and revealed Religion.[110]

His particular focus is upon the question of power and authority in the Church, and his argumentative weapons are trained upon tyrannical bishops and clergy 'who have appropriated the name of the Church to themselves, and under that venerable character have erected themselves an empire, upon the ruins of primitive Christianity, and the civil and religious liberties of mankind.'[111]

Positively, Chandler is concerned to display the true nature of the Church. In order to discern what a true church is we must have recourse to Scripture, 'the infallible word of God.'[112] The problem is that some cede to the Church the right to

---

[108] For Grey (1688-1766) see ODNB.

[109] [Z. Grey], *English Presbyterian Eloquence*, Dedication.

[110] S. Chandler, *The Notes of the Church Considered*, 1-2.

[111] Ibid., 2.

[112] Ibid., 3.

pronounce upon the true sense of Scripture, and elevate unwritten churchly traditions to the same level as the Bible. But this would place us in the impossible situation that

> if the Scriptures are to determine the marks of the church, the Scriptures must be known and understood, before we can form any judgment from them. But if the church is to judge for us what is Scripture, and what the sense of it, then we must know what the church is, and what her distinguishing marks are, before we can pretend to judge what the sense of Scripture is. The consequence of which is, that 'tis impossible to form any judgment of either.[113]

Similarly,

> if the Scripture be the rule whereby we are to judge of the marks of the church, the authority of Scripture must be superior to that of the church; and if the church is to determine what is Scripture, the authority of the church is superior to that of Scripture; and consequently, they are each of them of superior and inferior authority to the other ... To these shameful absurdities are the Papists reduced ...[114]

Chandler's objective is to set down the biblical marks or notes of the Church and to show that what the Roman Catholics say are marks of the Church are either no marks at all or, if they are, that the Roman Church does not manifest them. He shows from the Bible that the church is the *ecclesia*, a company of called-out people, and that the clergy as a group do not on their own comprise the Church. He strongly objects to the way in which the clergy appropriate the title 'Church' to themselves. In this and in what follows, Bellarmine[115] is firmly within his sights.

First, however, Chandler presents his own account of what the true marks of the Church are: the adherence of all members to Jesus Christ 'as the common head and Lord and Saviour of Christians, and the submitting themselves wholly and intirely to his influence and direction';[116] and the holy lives of its members. He then proceeds to contrast with these a number of notes of the Church proposed by Bellarmine.[117]

The cardinal's first note is that the Roman Church is catholic, to which Chandler retorts, 'I think this is direct nonsense; because the catholick church is nothing but the collection of all true Christians and particular churches thro' the world.'[118] Bellarmine's second note, antiquity, fares no better, for antiquity is no guarantor of truth. With some zest Chandler contrasts Rome's errors with the Protestants' grasp of biblical truth: Protestants acknowledge the one Lord, Jesus Christ, not the Pope.

---

[113] Ibid., 4.

[114] Ibid., 5.

[115] For the Jesuit scholar, Bellarmine (1542-1621) see James Brodrick, *The Life and Work of ... Bellarmine*; idem, *Robert Bellarmine, Saint and Scholar*.

[116] S. Chandler, *The Notes of the Church Considered*, 11.

[117] In his text we have notes 1-5 and 7-8; note 6 is not present.

[118] Ibid., 18.

They hold that Christ is the sole mediator, and hence saints and angels cannot be mediators. Contrary to what Rome teaches, the bread and wine at the Lord's Supper undergo no change, and the sacrament is 'only a memorial of Christ's death, and not a propitiatory sacrifice either for the living or dead.'[119] The Protestants worship in the language of the people, not in a tongue unintelligible to most of them. Particularly galling is the fact that the Roman Church has persecuted those who have stood for the biblical principles—and Chandler proceeds to illustrate this point from history.

Bellarmine's third note is the Church's perpetual and uninterrupted duration. Chandler denies that this is a mark of the Church. On the contrary, 'Idolatry and Paganism may lay a better claim to this note than the Church of Rome.'[120] As for the cardinal's fourth note, the amplitude and size of the Church, Chandler counters that pagans, 'Mahometans' and Christians who renounce Rome vastly outnumber it. The following note, apostolic succession, is likewise dismissed by Chandler on the ground that, independently of any such succession, 'the terms of salvation and communion are fix'd by God in the gospel of Christ',[121] and compliance with them suffices for salvation. He then adverts to the ambiguities that the alleged succession has displayed in history. Bellarmine's seventh note, the union of all members into one body, brings the retort that mere union does not necessarily imply union in truth and righteousness; and this there clearly is not, in the Roman Church, as the manifold disagreements among 'Papists' clearly show. Bellarmine's final note here considered is the sanctity of doctrine. But, says Chandler, to profess holiness is not the same as manifesting it.

As far as Chandler is concerned, the upshot is that

> nothing is more evident, than that the church of Rome cannot be, in any sense, the true Church of Christ, because she hath forsaken both the doctrines and worship of that church. Her doctrine is impure, and her worship idolatrous. The gospel she believes and preaches is a quite different one from what was taught by Christ and his apostles, and she hath made void the commandments of God by her traditions.[122]

Chandler appeals to any hearers who may be inclined to favour Rome to examine the evidence. He cannot say that Roman Catholics who are invincibly ignorant are excluded from the range of God's tender mercies, but he does insist that 'Popery is not the religion of Christ,'[123] and he concludes by calling upon the nation to renounce it.[124]

---

[119] Ibid., 23.
[120] Ibid., 32.
[121] Ibid., 34.
[122] Ibid., 44.
[123] Ibid., p. 48.
[124] For a curious reply to Chandler's sermon see, *A Letter from a Friend to Samuel Chandler ... by a Countryman, and a lover of Truth.*

In a supplement to his sermon Chandler mops up Bellarmine's remaining notes of the Church. The ninth concerns the efficacy of doctrine. Chandler protests that doctrines are efficacious not because they are professed by the true Church alone, but because they are agreeable to truth and reason. Conversely, some beliefs professed by the Roman Church are absurd and contradictory. For example, 'The doctrine of Transubstantiation is an insult upon common sense,'[125] and the worship of images and relics is against truth and reason. Roman practice is indefensible too: priests tell people that there is no salvation outside their Church, and if that does not work, they have recourse to force in the name of eradicating heresy. Moreover, they will not allow the people to read the Bible. As for Bellarmine's elevating the glory of miracles into a mark of the Church, Chandler declares that miracles can never prove contradictory doctrines to be true, or that idolatry is an acceptable form of worship. Nor can prophecy—another of Bellarmine's notes—prove false doctrines true. As for the contention that even Protestants speak up in Rome's favour, Chandler attributes this to the fact that 'Protestants have more charity, or less prejudice than the Papists.'[126]

Bellarmine next posits the unhappy deaths of Rome's enemies as a sign that his Church is the true one. He cites the sudden deaths of Luther and Oecolampadius; the death on the battlefield of Zwingli; Carlostadius's death at the hands of the devil; and Calvin's death by worms. Chandler replies that Bellarmine has his facts wrong; and in any case, from the mode of a man's death we may not legitimately infer the goodness or badness of his principles or cause. Finally, in response to Bellarmine's note concerning the temporal felicity of those who have defended the Catholic Church, Chandler points out that, for example, 'Mary Queen of Scots lost her head upon the block.'[127] His not unexpected conclusion is that the Roman is the false Church, the Protestant, the true.

On 7 and 13 February 1734/5 discussions took place in Nicholas Lane, London, between two Roman Catholic priests and some Protestant divines. Chandler was present at the second of the two meetings, and afterwards published a report of it. Among the topics discussed was the assertion by the Presbyterian John Barker and the Congregationalist Daniel Neal in their Salters' Hall sermons that 'the Papists had sometimes given the Title of *our Lord God* to the Pope.'[128] It appears that Barker had failed to bring his evidence to the meeting, but John Eames made out the case that the title had on occasion been applied to the Pope, and that if this were not authorized by Rome, it had certainly not been condemned.

The doctrine of transubstantiation was also discussed at the meeting. The Congregationalist, Dr. Jeremiah Hunt, of Pinners' Hall, conceded that while the literal sense of Scripture should normally be taken, unless 'it conveyed to us an improper or absurd meaning', the words, 'This is my body' conveyed precisely such

[125] S. Chandler, *A Second Treatise on the Notes of the Church*, 5.
[126] Ibid., 45.
[127] Ibid., 57.
[128] Idem, *An Account of the Conference held in Nicholas-Lane*, 4-5.

a meaning if taken literally.[129] Chandler contended that even a child could see that Jesus's words, 'This do in remembrance of me' meant that the bread and wine were to be consumed in memory of Christ, not that the elements were to be consecrated into his body and blood. He challenged the Roman Catholic priests to show that their view was current during the first five Christian centuries. One of them, Mr. Morgan, undertook to investigate the matter and said that he would let Chandler know when he was ready to present his findings; but he never did. At the end of the discussion Chandler remained convinced that 'the Protestant Doctrine of the Sacrament still remains firm and unshaken; and the Popish Tenet, of the real Presence, or Transubstantiation, will be found an Absurdity and Falsehood, if there be any such thing as Truth in the World; or if we allow either our Senses, or reason, the Scriptures, or the primitive Fathers, to judge concerning it, or finally to determine it.'[130]

Chandler summed up his anti-Roman case in an undated pamphlet entitled, *Plain Reasons for being a Protestant.* We should not speak of the Protestant religion, he says, as if the Protestants had a religion distinct from that of all other Christians. Rather, we should speak of the religion of Protestants, which means 'simple Christianity, as it lies in the writings of the New Testament, and is common to all Christians, only purged from the errors and corruption which the Church of Rome had gradually introduced and mingled with it, and which several princes and states agreed together to protest against at the time of the Reformation.'[131] He proceeds to discuss the distinguishing features of Protestantism: Christ alone is head of the Church; the Scriptures are the rule of faith and duty; and the right of private judgment is maintained. Protestants oppose the supremacy of the Pope, the denial of the right of private judgment, the unwritten traditions and the licentious casuistry of Rome, the doctrine of transubstantiation, worship in an unknown tongue, idolatry in worship, cruelty and persecution.

Hovering over the anti-Roman polemics of the first half of the eighteenth century, and stimulating controversy and tractarian polemics, was the genuine fear on the part of many Protestants that the English throne would fall into Roman Catholic hands once more, and that the nation would become subject to a foreign power, namely, the Pope. Hence the political impetus to anti-Roman pamphleteering. This activity was at its height in the 1740s, when the possible usurpation of the English throne by the Young Pretender was the focus of attention. Samuel Chandler, as we might by now expect, took up his quill in the cause of the Protestantism of England. In 1745 he published *Great-Britain's Memorial against the Pretender and Popery.* The Pretender, he declares, is supported by the Pope, and were he to succeed in taking the English crown, all subjects deemed heretical by Rome would be exterminated. Once again he plunders history for examples of Rome's persecutory zeal. The doctrines of Roman Catholics are abominable, and their practice matches

---

129 Ibid., 21. For Hunt (1678-1744) see ODNB; WW, II, 262-270.

130 Ibid., 76-7.

131 Idem, *Plain Reasons for being a Protestant*, 10.

it—for example, 'that truly hellish Design of the Gun-Powder-Plot.'[132] He reminds his readers of the cruel sufferings which Hungarian Christians have suffered at the hands of Rome, and ends with a plea to all citizens to defend England to the death rather than succumb to Popish tyranny.

On 29 September 1745 Chandler returned to the theme in a sermon at the Old Jewry meeting house. Even the pious tremble in times of public danger, he says; but Christians should not fear like others, for however dark the hour, God is, and his providence is over all. If the present invasion were to succeed, endless calamities would fall on the land, and would do so by God's will, and because of the nation's sins. We may take heart from the fact that other persecuting empires—the Egyptian and Syrian among them—have been destroyed, and from the fact that God will be a sanctuary to those who fear him. There is no circumstance in which the principles of true religion are not our best support. Let us therefore amend our ways and discharge the duties essential to the Christian character, being ready to die 'when soever, and by what Means soever, it may please God to call us hence.'[133]

Thirteen months later, Chandler was able to preach in more cheerful vein. On 9 October 1746, the nation's day of thanksgiving for deliverance, his theme was, *National Deliverances just Reasons for Publick Gratitude and Joy*. His text was Isaiah 25: 9, 'And it shall be said in that day, Lo, this is our God; we have waited for him, and he will save us: this is the Lord; we have waited for him, we will rejoice and be glad in his salvation.' The grounds for rejoicing were abundantly clear to Chandler: 'Our Houses and Substance we began to look on as almost relinquished to the Plunder of insulting Barbarians, and our Places of Worship as destined to the Flames, or, which was much worse, to be turned into Temples of Idols, and devoted to the foulest and most abject Superstitions and Idolatries.'[134] Happily the worst had been avoided. Had it been otherwise, spiritual and temporal disasters would have followed. We should be warned by past evils to 'improve the Mercy of God as becomes a people marvellously saved by his Hand.'[135]

II

It cannot be denied that the passion—extending on occasion to intemperance—that Chandler injected into his more polemical writings was the product of a strong, undergirding, sense of right and wrong, justice and injustice. Not surprisingly, therefore, we find him in more placid mood reflecting upon the principles of morality.

For the foundations of his moral theory we may turn to his pamphlet, *Benevolence and Integrity Essentials of Christianity* (1736). This was Chandler's Old Jury sermon of 3 March 1735/6 on behalf of the Society for Relief of the Widows and Children of Dissenting Ministers, to which brief reference has already been made.

[132] Idem, *Great-Britain's Memorial against the Pretender and Popery*, 15.
[133] Idem, *The Danger and Duty of Good Men, under the Present Unnatural Invasion*, 46.
[134] Idem, *National Deliverances just Reasons for Publick Gratitude and Joy*, 22.
[135] Ibid., 41.

Expounding James 1: 22, 'Be ye doers of the word, and not hearers only', he insists that it is not enough to profess belief in the Gospel doctrine: 'the belief of it should lead you to universal Virtue and Goodness; and unless this be the Effect of it, your Profession is vain.'[136] Chandler proceeds to delineate the close relationship between religion and morality. Religion

> implies that Regard which reasonable Creatures shew and express towards [God], upon the Account of his Perfections and Benefits, and in Obedience to his Will, whether discovered by reason of Revelation, either in the inward Affections of their Minds, the Words of their Mouths, or the Actions of their Lives, upon the Views, and with the Hopes of a Reward in a future State. ... [N]othing can deserve the honourable Character of Religion that is not founded in Truth, and directed by Reason and Understanding.[137]

How, then, is religion related to morality? Chandler answers,

> When the Rule [persons] act by is the Truth and Fitness of Things; Reason, and the natural Obligation which results from it; this is strictly Morality and Virtue. When to this they add the Authority of God, the Consideration of his Will, the Desire of Conformity to him, and the expectation of a Reward from him, as the Motives of their Actions; this is properly Religion and Piety.[138]

He further explains that

> If by Religion we mean those Expression of our Homage and Duty to God, which are founded upon his express Command, and inculcated immediately and directly by his Authority, Benevolence, and Integrity of heart and Life, will come under this Denomination equally with any other Influences of Duty whatsoever. For though their primary Obligation flows from the unchangeable Nature of Things, and our Character and Relation as reasonable Beings, and must therefore be so far antecedent to, and independent of all positive Will and Command; yet this natural Obligation is strengthen'd by the express Authority of God himself ...[139]

It would seem that Chandler is here indebted to widespread and longstanding convictions regarding natural law, of which divine revelation is the endorsement. He returned to the theme two years later when, on 25 September 1738, he addressed the Societies for Reformation of Manners on *The Necessary and Immutable Difference between Moral Good and Evil*. At the outset he insists upon the fact that 'the Difference between moral Good and Evil is certain, necessary, and immutable.'[140] Furthermore, this distinction is as eternal as that which proclaims that light cannot be the same thing as darkness, or *vice versa*. It follows, he continues, that not even

---

[136] Idem, *Benevolence and Integrity Essentials of Christianity*, 4.

[137] Ibid., 9.

[138] Ibid., 10.

[139] Ibid., 13.

[140] Idem, *The Necessary and Immutable Difference between Moral Good and Evil*, 5.

God is 'capable of altering or confounding the Nature of these things. ... [H]is Will can never make the one to be the other, because the very Ideas of them imply an essential Opposition to each other.'[141] It is not derogating to God's being and honour to say that he cannot do what would be utterly contradictory and absurd. The fact is that the eternal difference between moral good and evil is 'intirely independent of the Will of God.'[142]

To John Gill this was tantamount to wresting God from his position as the fount of all morality, so he plunged in the polemical knife in a tract entitled, *The Moral Nature and Fitness of things considered* (1738). The nub of his case is as follows: if it be true that the distinction between moral good and evil is grounded in the nature of things and not in the will of God, then

> all laws of God and men are to be disregarded; and, indeed, they are plainly superseded by it; for if this is the supreme, original, and universal rule to all reasonable beings, then all inferior, subordinate, and particular laws, as all the after-laws of God and men must be thought to be, merit no regard; at least are no further to be regarded than as they be thought to agree with, and are reducible to, this grand one; and if it is the most perfect rule, then certainly there is no need of another.[143]

Gathering steam as he approaches his terminus, Gill warns that Chandler's view of the independence of morality from the will of God opens the gates to polytheism, deism, antinomianism and libertinism.

It must be said that this is not Gill at his argumentative best. His selection of quotations from Chandler's sermon is partial and biased. One would never think from reading Gill that Chandler had granted that the independence of the distinction between moral good and evil from God's will 'may seem a little harsh, at first View,'[144] or that he had taken pains to clarify it. The meaning, Chandler explains, is not 'that the Mind of God had not, from all Eternity, a full Discernment of this Distinction,' but rather,

> The true and only Meaning of it is, That the Distinction between moral Good and Evil doth so arise out of the Nature of the Things themselves, as not to be originally and properly the mere Effect of the divine Order and Will, so as that it never would have been, had God not willed and commanded it to be; but that this Difference did originally and eternally subsist in the Mind or God, as certainly as the Difference between Light and Darkness, and was, in Idea, ever present with him,

---

[141] Ibid., 9.

[142] Ibid.

[143] J. Gill, *The Moral Nature and Fitness of Things considered*, in *Sermons and Tracts*, VI, 142.

[144] S. Chandler, *The Necessary and Immutable Difference between Moral Good and Evil*, 9-10.

before ever it became the Law of his Creatures, and appeared to them as the Matter of his Command and Will ...[145]

By stopping his quotation of these words at the phrase, 'commanded it to be', Gill entirely omits Chandler's balancing assertion.[146] It does not appear that Chandler rose in his own defence on this occasion, or that he needed to. His claim that 'The Reason of every good and wise Law is antecedent to the Law itself'[147] seems unexceptionable, and it is all that he wishes to assert. Happily, Gill would seem to have no quarrel with Chandler's statement that 'The great Design of our blessed Saviour's coming into the World, was its Reformation from that Ignorance, Idolatry and Vice that universally abounded amongst mankind, to recover to their Minds the lost Principles of Religion and Virtue ...'[148]

III

Since an emphasis upon the moral order was characteristic of more liberal divines such as Chandler, it is perhaps not surprising that in those theologically pugilistic days ultra-conservative divines would charge them with deism. No doubt partly for this reason, but also on principle, Chandler and others came out strongly in opposition to deism albeit, consistently with his views on freedom of conscience and expression, he defended the right of deists not only to think but to publish their thoughts.[149] Not, indeed, that he always approved of their manner of writing. On the contrary, he objected to the way in which Anthony Collins, the author of *The Scheme of Literal Prophecy Considered* (1726), represented 'most of our divines' as a 'perjured and abandoned crew ... as preaching one thing and believing another; as professing a religion they deny the truth of ...'[150] Chandler wishes that all such remarks had been excluded, for 'principles are in themselves independent of the conduct of any persons whatsoever.'[151]

Turning to substantive questions, Chandler was intent upon answering the charges which Collins had levelled against Christianity in his deistic *Discourse of*

---

[145] Ibid., 10-11.

[146] See J. Gill, *Sermons and Tracts*, 132. By not offering a single direct reference to Chandler's to Chandler's sermon, Tom Nettles leaves his readers in ignorance of Gill's partiality, is tendentious in his reference to 'The glib naturalistic moralism of the early eighteenth century', and ill-advisedly describes Gill's performance as 'succinct and lucid', when it is in fact wordy and selective. See his 'John Gill and the Evangelical Awakening,' 133-5.

[147] S. Chandler, *The Necessary and Immutable Difference between Moral Good and Evil*, 31.

[148] Ibid., 41.

[149] See, for example, Chandler's *Reflections on the Conduct of the Modern Deists*, vi.

[150] Ibid., 31.

[151] Ibid., 34.

the Grounds and Reasons of the Christian Religion (1724).[152] I describe Collins's book as 'deistic' because that is how it was widely regarded. In fairness, however, it must be remembered that Collins's self-description was 'freethinker'—a term which a number of divines had no difficulty in construing as synonymous with 'deist'. Again, as we proceed we shall do well to remember that, as I have elsewhere pointed out,

> the deists did not constitute anything so precise as a school of thought, or even a clearly-defined movement. Rather, they were writers who in a general way imbibed prevalent scepticism regarding some of the claims of orthodox Christianity, revelation, Christian 'evidences' as generally conceived, the authority of the Church, and the probity of the priesthood, whilst being unlike one another on many points of detail.[153]

The nub of Collins's case is that if the facts alleged in the Bible are unreliable, apologetic arguments based upon the appeal to prophecy are seriously weakened. He argues that the Old Testament prophecies were not fulfilled by Christ, 'these proofs taken out of the Old, and urg'd in the New Testament, being sometimes, either not to be found in the Old, or not urg'd in the New, according to the literal and obvious sense, and therefore not proofs according to scholastick rules ...'[154] In the second part of his work he argues that the Arian divine William Whiston (by now deposed from his Cambridge chair), who wished to show that the text of the Old Testament had never undergone corruption, undercut his own position by specifying textual corruptions in, and inconsistencies between, the Old and New Testaments.[155]

In 1725 Chandler responded with a substantial discussion of miracles. His title was *A Vindication of the Christian Religion*. The book comprises a preface and two parts. Although Chandler does not turn directly to Collins's *Discourse* until Part II, we shall do well to catch the general drift of the whole. In his Preface Chandler outlines his method. He does not rely upon testimonies, but rather has tried 'to vindicate our Saviour and his Apostles, upon the plain ground of reason.'[156] He welcomes Collins's prefatory 'defence of that liberty of every one's judging for himself, and of proposing his opinions to others, and of defending them with the best reasons he can, which every one hath a right to, as a Man and a Christian.'[157] He declares that while the civil magistrate has the right to 'keep men from violating the publick peace', he cannot stop free enquiry into 'matters of religion and speculation.'[158] Those who would convert the deists by invoking the civil magistrate

---

[152] For Collins (1676-1729) see DSCBP; DECBP; ODNB; James O'Higgins, *Anthony Collins*.

[153] Alan P. F. Sell, *Enlightenment, Ecumenism, Evangel*, 113.

[154] A. Collins, *Discourse of the Grounds and Reasons of the Christian Religion*, 43.

[155] For Whiston (1667-1752) see DSCBP; DECBP; ODNB. Whiston left the Church of England for the General (Arminian) Baptists in 1747.

[156] S. Chandler, *A Vindication of the Christian Religion*, vii.

[157] Ibid., ix.

[158] Ibid., xi.

should first vindicate their method—the very thing that has prejudiced deists against the religion of Christ. 'If the scheme of our modern deists be founded in truth,' he generously declares, 'I cannot help wishing it all success.'[159] Indeed, 'I am perswaded that nothing could be of greater service to Christianity, than to suffer, and even invite the enemies of it to speak out their difficulties with freedom',[160] for then people would become Christians on ground not of education or custom, but of reasoned conviction. As for the enemies of religion, they need to 'disprove the being of a God, and his providence, and the necessary distinction and difference between moral good and evil.'[161]

Chandler begins Part I by taking Locke to task. Locke had defined 'miracle' as 'a sensible operation, which, being above the comprehension of the spectator, and in his opinion contrary to the established course of nature, is taken by him to be divine.' The problem is, says Chandler, that Locke later says that a miracle 'must be that, which surpasses the force of nature, in the established steady laws of causes and effects.' But this means that whether or not an event is miraculous is not, after all, a matter of the judgment of one who deems it miraculous.[162] Chandler grants that there may be counterfeit miracles, and proposes that Jesus laid the greatest emphasis, not upon his miracles but upon the word he received from his Father. The purpose of miracles is to confirm that those who perform them are indeed sent by God. Chandler finds it incongruous that deists should laud Jesus as a teacher of morals, whilst finding him an impostor in other aspects of his life and ministry.

A miracle, Chandler continues, must be possible and probable; it must reveal something of God's power; it must be done openly; and it must be possible to prove that it was actually performed. Furthermore, those who perform miracles must be in possession of their reason and senses, and the ends for which miracles are performed must be reasonable. Where divine power and a responsible performer of miracles coincide, one has proof of the performer's divine mission. There follows a discussion of Jesus's miracles which leads to the claim that 'none of the New Testament writers have ever been convicted of forgery and imposture.'[163]

Against this background Chandler proceeds in Part II to deal with Collins under the title, *An Answer to a Late Book entituled, A Discourse of the Grounds and reasons, &c*. Chandler says that the deist's objective was to show that Christianity had only the Old Testament prophecies to base itself upon; that these are typical or allegorical only; and that they are not invoked as proofs in the New Testament. He replies to the effect that miracles do not comprise the sole foundation of Christianity, and that Jesus never urged them as being such. *Pace* Collins, Christianity is more than Judaism set in a new light. There are many points of contrast between the two religions. For example, Judaism is for the Jews, Christianity is for the world. While agreeing with Collins that the Old Testament

---

[159] Ibid., xiv.
[160] Ibid., xv.
[161] Ibid., xx1.
[162] Ibid., 7-8.
[163] Ibid., 105.

prophecies have reference to those who first heard them, Chandler denies that the significance of prophecies is restricted to first hearers. On the contrary, the Old Testament prophecies are fulfilled in Christ.

In his *Vindication* we find Chandler discussing textual questions. He concedes that while there may be some insignificant errors in the Old Testament texts, in general those texts are uncorrupted and reliable. He then shows that the apostles had recourse to Old Testament prophecies and construed them in relation to Christ as Messiah. As he works towards his conclusion he claims that even if the difficulties pertaining to Old Testament citations were greater than they are, Christianity would not be discredited, for the apostles, when in conversation with Gentiles, argued from facts alone, not from Old Testament prophecies, while when approaching Jews they referred to facts and prophecies together. Certain it is that 'eleven or twelve poor mean illiterate Jews' could not have invented the story of the life, death and resurrection of Jesus, while the conduct of the apostles is explicable only on the basis of their being 'under a divine assistance and influence.'[164] Those who deny this must 'disprove the truth of the gospel history, and tell us upon what other views and principles the apostles acted, that could be supposed, either to inspire them with courage sufficient to prosecute their design, or with wisdom to render them successful in it.'[165]

Chandler sent a copy of his book to William Wake, Archbishop of Canterbury who, in a letter of 14 February 1725, said that he 'found it very good, and such as I hope will be of service to the end for which you designed it.' Presumably, and apparently unfamiliar with Chandler's dual role as minister and bookseller, Wake continues, 'I cannot but own myself to be surprised, to see so much good learning and just reasoning, in a person of your profession; and do think it a pity you should not spend your time in writing books, rather than in selling them. But I am glad, since your circumstances oblige you to the latter, yet you do not wholly omit the former.'[166] Among others who 'greatly admir'd' Chandler's book was Philip Doddridge.[167]

Undaunted, Anthony Collins came forth with *The Scheme of Literal Prophecy* in 1726. Here his focus was on the book of Daniel, and his contention was that the prophecies contained therein related only to those in whose presence they were uttered, and not to Jesus Christ. This, in turn, drew from Chandler, *A Vindication of the Antiquity and Authority of Daniel's Prophecies, and their application to Jesus Christ: in Answer to the Objections of the Author of the Scheme of Literal Prophecy Considered* (1728). In the meantime, in his tract on deistic literary method, and with reference to *The Scheme of Literal Prophecy*, Chandler had expressed what was for him the heart of the matter:

---

[164] Ibid., 403.

[165] Ibid.

[166] WW, II, 363-3 n., where the full text is reproduced.

[167] CCPD, no. 203; a letter of 26 April 1726 to Samuel Clark (1684-1750) of St. Albans, for whom see ODNB.

> The argument from prophecies, as stated by the most judicious Christian writers, stands thus. That there are certain passages in the prophetick writings that do relate to future things and events; that there is a particular person spoken of throughout most of those writings, and described by particular marks and characters; that the several prophets do agree in their descriptions of him; that those descriptions did not literally agree to any person or persons living at the time when those predictions were delivered; that these predictions do generally agree to Jesus Christ; that he did declare himself to be the person spoken of under those descriptions; that he wrought miracles to confirm his divine mission; and that therefore he was the person whom those descriptions did point out. Now I apprehend if this argument be fairly overthrown, it must be proved, either that there are no prophecies of such a person in the old testament; or that those descriptions contradict one another; or that they were accomplished in some person or persons before Christ; or that they were not accomplished in him.[168]

Collins, Chandler ruefully observes, repeatedly declares that the deists do not 'think themselves obliged to shew, how any prophecy in the old testament was ever fulfilled.'[169] Furthermore, he thinks that 'as friends to the common interests and welfare of mankind, [the deists should] endeavour to advance a nobler and truer scheme in the room of that they are labouring to destroy.'[170] But they do no such thing. Indeed, Collins's 'opposition to the religion of the gospel, without telling us whether we must turn Mahometans, Pagans, Jews, or other sort of religionist; his endeavouring to confound and destroy Christianity, and at the same time concealing and palliating his own sentiments as to God and religion, is neither an argument of his own integrity, nor of his regard to the peace and welfare of societies.'[171] Chandler concludes with an aspiration: 'I heartily wish that for the future the writers on both sides of the question may keep wholly to the point, since Christianity can gain no ground by our abusing the adversaries of it, nor lose any ground by their abusing and misrepresenting it.'[172]

In 1740 Chandler turned his attention to another deist, Thomas Morgan.[173] An Independent minister at Burton, Somerset, he was nevertheless ordained by the Presbyterian, John Bowder at Frome in 1716. He became heterodox and was dismissed by his church in 1720. He practised medicine, became a freethinker, and described himself as a Christian deist. In *The Moral Philosopher* (1737) he argues that whether doctrines were conveyed by reason, revelation or authentic testimony, the proof of religion turns upon 'the moral Truth, Reasonableness and Fitness of the Doctrines themselves, as appearing to the Understanding, upon a fair, impartial

[168] S. Chandler, *Reflections on the Conduct of the Modern Deists*, 89-90.

[169] Ibid., 90.

[170] Ibid., 104.

[171] Ibid., 107-8.

[172] Ibid., 110.

[173] For Morgan (d. 1743) see DECBP; ODNB; Alan P. F. Sell, *Enlightenment, Ecumenism, Evangel*, 123.

Consideration and Judgment of Reason.'[174] He is severely critical of the Old Testament, which he disjoins from the New, and he repudiates the doctrine of the atonement as being a corruption of Jewish sacrificial ideas. In short, 'None of the Doctrines of Revelation ... can be fundamental or necessary' because they are 'delivered in ambiguous Terms, and cloth'd with Expressions capable of very different Constructions.'[175]

Chandler's response to Morgan's book is entitled, *A Vindication of the History of the Old Testament* (1720). He took Morgan to task on a number of points of fact and interpretation, with special reference to Abraham, but Morgan was not to be silenced. He returned to the fray in 1741 with *A Vindication of the Moral Philosopher; against the False Accusations, Insults, and Personal Abuses, of Samuel Chandler, Late Bookseller and Minister of the Gospel.* He explains that he had once embraced orthodox Christianity's 'sacrificial Scheme of Redemption,' but does so no longer.[176] He points out that Chandler argues on the basis of a supposition which he knows Morgan will not accept, namely, that 'the Hebrew History is of positive Divine Authority, and immediate Inspiration, or that those Historians, in their Account of Things, were all along under the unerring Guidance and infallible Direction of the Holy Ghost.'[177] Chandler cannot, however, prove this, whereas Morgan's own approach to the subject is to discuss it in a manner 'consistent with Nature, Reason, and human Probability.'[178] The upshot is that Chandler and Morgan succeed only in talking past one another. This did not prevent Chandler from returning to the fray in 1743 with a second instalment of his work, this one focusing on Joseph; but by the time the work appeared, Morgan had died.

IV

It is now time to see how, in the light of his convictions regarding freedom of conscience, morality and the inadequacies of deism, Chandler dealt with particular Christian doctrines. The short answer is that he dealt with some of them only cursorily, and with some of them not at all. Unlike Ridgley, he was not given to the systematic exposition of the broad range of Christian teaching. On the contrary, the emphasis of his lecturing, preaching and writing was upon morality and the Christian life—an Arminian tendency in a self-confessed moderate Calvinist; and upon particular aspects of the life of Christ, notably his resurrection.

One way of approaching Chandler's doctrinal emphases, and of detecting those lacunae which were meat and drink to polemical orthodox Calvinists, is to examine *A Short and Plain Catechism*, which he published in 1741. Significantly, this is based not upon the *Westminster Confession*, but upon the Apostles Creed, the Decalogue and the Lord's Prayer. Of the importance of catechizing Chandler is in no

[174] T. Morgan, *The Moral Philosopher*, x.
[175] Ibid., 17-18.
[176] Idem, *A Vindication of the Moral philosopher*, 12.
[177] Ibid., 16.
[178] Ibid., 17.

doubt. In the Preface he contends that the neglect of it has weakened the Dissenting cause, and has 'been one occasion of that growing Disregard to real Piety and Virtue, that is too visible among many of them';[179] hence his urgent attention to the matter. Announcing a policy intended to make for harmony, but clearly interpretable by those so inclined as 'trimming', he says of his *Catechism* that he has 'endeavoured to make it *unexceptionable* to all Parties.'[180] As if aware that this could be construed as 'fighting talk' he proceeds to justify his avoidance of the *Westminster Catechism*: 'I Perswade no Person to lay aside that Composure, who thinks he can profitably explain it, so as to make children capable of understanding it,' but he has chosen the method which he deems most appropriate to his intended learners. After all, the *Westminster* is 'Meat for strong Men, and not Food for Children.'[181] The following extracts from his *Catechism* will sufficiently indicate Chandler's approach:

> 8. Qu. What do you mean by the Gospel of Christ?
>
> An. That good news, relating to the Salvation of Sinners, that God hath sent them, by Jesus Christ.
>
> 15. Qu. Why do you call God, the Father?
>
> An. I call God the father, because he is in an especial manner the God and Father of our Lord Jesus Christ, and because in and through him he is the gracious God and Father of all sincere Christians.
>
> 34. Qu. What do you mean by Christ's descending into hell?
>
> An. I mean by Christ's descending into hell, that his Body was put into the Grave, and that he went into that State which is appointed for the Reception of the Dead.
>
> 43. Qu. What do you intend by this Profession, that you believe in the Catholick Church?
>
> An. My meaning is, that I believe that the Church, or the Kingdom of Christ, consists not of any particular Number, Denomination, or Party of Christians; but of all without exception, in every Nation, and of every Sect and Party, who profess their faith in him, and are obedient to the Laws of his Gospel.
>
> 45. Qu. What is the particular Duty of all the members of Christ's Catholick Church towards one another?
>
> An. Their particular Duty towards one another, is, to maintain the Communion of Saints.

---

179 S. Chandler, *A Short and Plain Catechism*, iii.

180 Ibid., iv.

181 Ibid., v.

> 99. Qu. Why are those, who are to be baptised, to be baptised into the Name of the Father, Son and Holy Spirit?
>
> An. They are to be baptised into the Name of the Father, Son and Holy Spirit, as a standing Memorial in the Christian Church, of that Relation which all Christians have to the Father as their Creator, the Son as their Redeemer, and the Holy Spirit of God as their Sanctifier and Comforter.[182]

If we place Chandler's *Catechism* alongside the check-list of doctrines said to be characteristic of Arminians in *An Account of the Presbyterian and Independent Ministers in London about the year 1730*, we have an indication of the grounds on which Chandler's catechetical performance would be deemed inadequate by the orthodox. In the *Account* Chandler is listed among those ministers who

> are accounted Arminians, or such as have gone far that way, by which are meant such as are against particular redemption and election, original sin, at least the imputation of it, for the power of man's will, in opposition to efficacious grace, and for justification by sincere obedience in the room of Christ's righteousness, &c.[183]

Against Chandler's name are the remarks:

> A minister of good parts and abilities, as well as pulpit talents, and for a treatise he wrote against deism, &c., he was much caressed by some of the Church of England clergy, and of whom it shall only be further said that the matter, as well as the manner of his sermons, is more suited to bring people to church than to make serious Christians, or to promote the Dissenting interest.[184]

Chandler had earlier published some *Plain Reasons for being a Christian* (1730), and here, too, we can readily detect his emphasis upon reason and moral character, and his avoidance of such high Calvinist concerns as the *ordo salutis*. Although he is grateful for the way in which his parents raised him, Chandler knows that 'Religion ought to be my own free and rational choice.'[185] It is reason that tells him that there is a God on whom we depend and whom we should worship. While the religion of nature is 'prior to and distinct from revealed religion,' it is not sufficient owing to the ignorance of God and duty that flows from the degeneracy of humanity.[186] Hence we need, and we have, an 'immediate revelation from God himself.'[187] Christians find this in the New Testament, and there is 'the highest reason to believe' that the books therein are 'authentick and genuine.'[188] What is said of God in revelation

---

[182] Ibid., 2, 4, 9, 11, 12, 26.
[183] TSJ, 696.
[184] Ibid., 697.
[185] Idem, *Plain Reasons for being a Christian*, 1.
[186] Ibid., 3.
[187] Ibid., 6.
[188] Ibid., 8.

accords with the deliverances of reason on the matter. Christianity requires 'the most rational and excellent Worship of God.'[189] Furthermore, it provides weighty and sufficient motives to duty, namely, 'The assurance of pardon thro' the Blood of Christ, and of the assistance of his good spirit under all the difficulties of our present duty.' These 'carry in them the noblest encouragement to obnoxious and disabled sinners, when they entertain the Thoughts of returning to God their sovereign and happiness.'[190] Christ's heavenly intercession on behalf of believers is a further encouragement, as is the challenge of his coming return and judgment.

Jesus, Chandler continues, holds the highest place among the founders of religions, and he proceeds to recount his life and to assert his divinity. The apostles are credible witnesses, for they received the Holy Spirit and spoke by the authority of Jesus. With a certain godly defiance, Chandler routs possible opposition thus: 'Notwithstanding all the objections that can be urged, I still find that the directions to serve God, and obey Christ, and secure my eternal salvation, are very obvious and plain, and therefore I am not under any pain or fear upon account of things I do not understand, or cannot explain.'[191] Nobody has been able to prove Christian doctrines irrational or absurd, and while reason apart from revelation may be able to grasp the duties of religion, it cannot 'certainly discover what the rewards of being religious and virtuous shall be.'[192]

According to the New Testament, salvation depends upon some plain and intelligible doctrines, namely, 'the existence of one God, the resurrection of Christ from the dead, and there being one mediator between God and man ...'[193] By contrast with Christianity, paganism is impious and false; Mahometanism 'hath all the evident marks of a real imposture'[194]; and Judaism is confined to one people. Hence Chandler is and remains a Christian. He concludes by quoting John 3: 16, 'God so loved the world...'

Turning to the doctrine of God, we find that Chandler regularly appeals to the providence of God, as may be seen in a sermon entitled, *The Scripture Account of the Causes and Intention of Earthquakes* (1750). For his text he takes the striking words of Job 9:5-6, which refer to the God 'Which removeth the mountains, and they know not: which overturneth them in his anger. Which shaketh the earth out of her place, and the pillars thereof tremble.' He sets out boldly with the claim that 'To such who believe the universal Providence of God, and that nothing happens without his Knowledge, or contrary to his Permission, the Improvement of extraordinary and surprising Events to religious and moral Purposes, will not be unacceptable ...'[195] Just as we daily receive providences from God, and attribute the succession of the seasons of the year to his providential care, so

---

[189] Ibid., 12.
[190] Ibid., 15.
[191] Ibid., 33-4.
[192] Ibid., 41.
[193] Ibid., 46.
[194] Ibid., 49.
[195] Idem, *The Scripture Account of the Cause and Intention of Earthquakes*, 1.

> It cannot ... be contrary to the Dictates of Reason, as I am sure it is perfectly consistent with the Spirit of genuine Piety, seriously to take notice of those more uncommon Effects that happen in the Course of Providence, which are in their Nature astonishing, that create an inward terror, which have been frequently attended with the most dreadful Calamities, and owned by all civilized Nations, as signal Marks of the Displeasure of god, and the awful Punishments of his Justice for the Impieties and Vices of mankind.[196]

Chandler does not deny that extraordinary events may be naturalistically explained, but this does not rule out the fact that they are also intended by God, whose 'Providence over-rules all the Events of Good and Evil ...'[197] The events themselves call us 'to immediate Repentance and Reformation,' and at the same time they remind us 'how sure a Refuge have good Men in God.'[198]

It would not be difficult to find sermons by orthodox Calvinists who took a similar line in face of natural disasters. But when we come to the question of sin and the Fall, the matter is far otherwise. In a sermon on *The Original State and Fall of Man* Chandler forthrightly declares that the guilt of Adam and Eve is not imputed to their heirs. Rather, their action depicts what all their human successors have actually done, namely, they have sinned. This would not, of course meet with the approval of a Thomas Ridgley or an Abraham Taylor, who stoutly affirmed the imputation of Adams guilt to his heirs. But there were possibilities of disquiet in other quarters too. Thus by 1768, Thomas Amory, the Arian Presbyterian editor of Chandler's sermons, found it prudent to offer readers even more liberal than Chandler the following explanation in his Preface:

> Should any Readers be less pleased with some Sermons in the fourth volume, on a controverted subject, and think the account therein given of the corruption of human nature to be aggravated above fact and experience; we beg them to consider,—that the Doctor allows this disorder, as far as it is natural, to be in no sense our fault, or imputed to us as such by God our creator; but to be merely a trial of our virtue, and obedience to our heavenly Father, who will, as becomes his equity and goodness, make every reasonable allowance for it, and grant answerable assistance to those who ask it, and who hath provided a suitable remedy. That the honour of God as our Creator and Moral Governor is thus vindicated; and persons may amicably differ as to the more or less of this natural disorder and weakness, and be left to determine their sentiments by impartial observation and experience.[199]

Few issues were more sensitive during the first half of the eighteenth century than those surrounding the person of Christ. We may find our way into this thicket by recounting the quite angry dispute between the Congregationalist John Guyse and Chandler on what it means to preach Christ. Guyse, of New Broad Street meeting

[196] Ibid., 2.
[197] Ibid., 12.
[198] Ibid., 38, 43.
[199] T. Amory, Preface to Chandler's *Sermons*, iv-v.

house, was on William Coward's panel of lecturers at Little St. Helens. In 1729 two sermons that he had delivered there on the subject, *Christ the Son of God the great Subject of a Gospel Ministry*, were published. Guyse, a member of the King's Head Society, was hot against Arianism and an ardent exponent of Calvinistic orthodoxy.[200]

Chandler initiated the controversy by publishing a *Letter* to Guyse in response to the latter's two sermons. He begins by making it clear that it is not his intention to speculate on the precise distinctions of the Father, Son and Spirit within the divine nature, for such a thing is 'of very little importance for us to know, because 'tis incomprehensible and cannot be understood and known by us. And I am more persuaded of this, because you gentlemen, who set up for the direct preachers of Christ, and to be the only sound men in the doctrine of the Trinity, differ greatly yourselves about it.'[201] One of the points at issue was Guyse's complaint concerning preachers who deny the eternal generation of the Son. Chandler challenges him to adduce biblical evidence for the doctrine. Guarding his flank, he insists that he is not 'arguing against the proper Deity of our Lord Jesus Christ',[202] but he does think that 'a plain practical sermon that tends to make men fear, and love, and serve God and Christ, is infinitely more useful, than to preach about niceties, that the preacher can scarce explain, and not one in a thousand of his hearers can understand.'[203]

Chandler expresses the hope that

> your congregation and good Mr. Coward will take notice of this, that when Mr. Guyse talks about preaching Christ, he means just the same thing as I do, viz. preaching the gospel; and this may be done without entring into your stiffness and peculiarity of stile, and set forms of speech, many of which need explication, and seem to be so much insisted on for no other purpose, but to support the reputation of orthodoxy, and to be the Shibboleth of a party.[204]

Chandler demands proof of Guyse's serious charges that 'the greatest number of preachers seem contented to lay [Christ] aside', and that 'The religion of nature makes up the darling topicks of our age.'[205] In Chandler's opinion, 'the religion of Jesus' is in 'perfect harmony and agreement with the principles of natural religion, or those principles of religion which the reason and nature of mankind point out, and which are demonstrable by reason to have their foundation in truth.'[206]

When Guyse charges that some preachers elevate moral duties instead of Christ, Chandler says that he could retort that some preachers 'harangue so on the righteousness of Christ, and attribute so much to faith, as to vacate the necessity,

---

[200] For Guyse (d. 1761) see ODNB; WW, II, 232-243. He succeeded Thomas Ridgley as a Tuesday morning Merchants' lecturer at Pinners' Hall.

[201] S. Chandler, *A Letter to the Reverend Mr. John Guyse*, 28.

[202] Ibid., 33.

[203] Ibid., 34.

[204] Ibid., 47.

[205] Ibid., 60, 67.

[206] Ibid., 69.

and weaken the obligation of moral duties'—but he will not (!).[207] In response to Guyse's lament that instances of conversion-work are rare, and the state of religion is low, Chandler thunders,

> the bringing of party-differences into our pulpits, the mixing them with our prayers and sermons, the venting personal resentment instead of preaching the gospel of Christ, the inflaming the passions of our hearers against others that differ from them, the insisting on nice and curious speculations instead of plain and practical truths, the depreciating good works and moral duties, and the leading men to, and encouraging them in false dependences for salvation and happiness; I should think these and the like things, when and where ever they obtain, very probable causes of the cold, low, and withering state of religion.[208]

Chandler concludes by declaring that he, no less than Guyse, laments the parlous condition of religion. What he stoutly rebuts is the charge that the majority of ministers have caused the decline by 'their abandoning the peculiars of Christianity.'[209]

Chandler's tract drew a prompt reply from Guyse, who complains that on many points he has been misrepresented. He does not discount the principles of natural religion, but he refuses to let them take precedence over Christ, or displace him. Neither does he think that moral duties are 'indifferent things.'[210] What riles him is Chandler's latitudinarian approach to preaching Christ: 'I am free to own,' says Guyse, 'that according to your notion of preaching Christ, it is certainly wrong to say that there are but few that preach him: For, as you have stretch'd that notion, it seems almost impossible for any man to preach at all upon any text of the Bible, and not preach Christ ...'[211] Guyse will not accept such a wide definition of 'preaching Christ', and says that it is clear that when he says many fail to preach Christ he means that they fail to preach Christ in his own sense of the term. He then turns 'pious', and declares that whereas Chandler claims that his purpose is to reproach his brethren, his objective in fact is to honour Christ. He proceeds to cite examples of Anglican and Dissenting divines, including John Owen, to show that he is not alone in finding the preaching of morality insufficient; and, for good measure, he turns Howe and Watts against Chandler—two writers whom the latter had cited with approval.

Chandler returned to the fray with *A Second Letter to the Reverend Mr. John Guyse* (1730), in which he recapitulated numerous points, and arrived at an instructive conclusion:

---

207 Ibid., 78.

208 Ibid., 88.

209 Ibid., 92.

210 J. Guyse, *The Scripture-Notion of Preaching Christ further Clear'd and Vindicated*, 49.

211 Ibid., 113.

> But, Sir, my temper is naturally chearful, and all your solemnity hath not spoiled it, and I hope never will. My orthodoxy consists in believing as well as I can, from the best knowledge I can gather from Scripture; and I think that every honest man will form his principles according to the best of his understanding, and according to what he apprehends to be the mind of God in Christ. And if any man so believes the gospel, as to be influenced by it, to live the christian life, I hope I shall ever have the courage to own and receive him as a Christian, whatever character he may be distinguished by. Calvinist, Arminian, Baxterian, Athanasian, Arian, Sabellian, Socinian, all are the distinguishing names of a party. I doubt not but there have been good men, and acceptable Christians amongst them all; and tho' they differ many of them from me in opinion, as I shall take the liberty to support and defend my own sentiments, I hope I shall ever do it, with the spirit which the gospel recommends.[212]

Guyse was not again drawn into full-scale rebuttal, but he did offer some final remarks in an appendix to his funeral sermon for John Asty.[213] Walter Wilson takes obvious comfort in reflecting that 'notwithstanding the ill temper with which the debate was conducted, the combatants afterwards met at a friend's house, and were cordially reconciled; a circumstance which reflects the highest honour on the memory of both these gentlemen.'[214]

Although Chandler's name was among those who were alleged to have laid the foundation for Arianism in Somerset prior to 1720,[215] and although his agnostic humility before such doctrines as that of the eternal generation of the Son laid him open to attack from the orthodox side, he was also capable of quite 'high' statements concerning Christ:

> He, as the eldest Son, and Heir of all Things, is the most perfect Image and Resemblance of his Father, whose essential Glory is expressed in him, and in whom all the treasures of Divine Perfection unite, and the Fulness of Deity bodily, i.e. substantially resides.[216]

Again, in connection with Christ's atoning work, Chandler can on occasion sound quite evangelical. Thus he can say of Christ that

> His Life of Obedience was for an Example to us, how to live so as to please God. His Death was to put an end to Sin by the Sacrifice of himself, and to introduce everlasting Righteousness, and establish our Hopes in the Mercy of God. His

---

212 Ibid., 97.

213 For Asty (1672-1729/30) see FAE; ODNB; WW, II, 537-45; J. Browne, *History of Congregationalism in Norfolk and Suffolk*, 328-9, 615-16.

214 WW, II, 235. It also invites the speculation that some of these performances may not have been entirely innocent of a degree of posturing; in which connection the unsanctified analogy comes to mind of those professional wrestlers, sworn enemies in public, who after the match enjoy a calm pint together in a pub.

215 TSJ, 97.

216 S. Chandler, *Christ the Pattern of the Christian's Future Glory*, 18.

> Resurrection from the Dead was not merely to secure himself of his promised Reward, but to be a sensible Proof of a future State, to inspire us with the Hope of Triumph over death; and to be the Pledge of our resurrection by his Almighty Power. His Ascension into Heaven was to engage us to have our Conversation there, and to prepare those mansions of Bliss for our final Reception into them.[217]

However, there is no extended treatment of Christ's atoning work in Chandler's writings (though he does insist that Christ was not punished by God, but bore the punishment due for our sins[218]) and, in a manner reminiscent of Clement of Alexandria, he quite frequently refers to Christ's work as that of teacher rather than saviour:

> Now this salvation consists, in mens being delivered from that gross ignorance, and those destructive prejudices and errors, in matters of the greatest importance and concern, under which they had for many ages lain, and for which human wisdom had never been able to find our and apply any competent remedy. This God effected, by causing the light of the glorious gospel of his Son, to shine in upon their hearts, and carry such full conviction of the truth of the principles it revealed, as rendered them sincere converts to the belief of them. ... [God] first sent his Son into the world, as a teacher of divine truth, and a preacher of righteousness; and afterwards commissioned the Apostles of Christ to the same sacred employment, sending them amongst mankind, as his messengers and heralds ...to proclaim his will, to instruct men in his truth, to recover them from their sins, to raise them to a spiritual and divine life, and call them to the inheritance of everlasting blessedness.[219]

As intimated earlier, Chandler is firmly persuaded of the reality of the resurrection of Jesus, and he is equally aware of the scepticism with which the topic in general is greeted in some quarters:

> The Philosophy indeed of the present, as well as ancient Times, would fain persuade us, that the Resurrection of a dead Body is a Thing impossible, to which even the Power of God cannot extend. But why should it be judged impossible for that to be effected a second Time, which indisputably hath been done once, or more difficult to raise from Death a Body that hath once lived, than to give Life to a dead Body that hath never before lived at all?[220]

The allusion here is to the conviction that 'originally, the Human Body, when first animated, was really a dead Body raised up to Life.'[221]

On resurrection of Jesus in particular, Chandler published *The Witnesess of the Resurrection of Jesus Christ re-examined: and their Testimony proved entirely Consistent*. He argues that the prophets foretold the sufferings and glory of Christ;

---

[217] Ibid.

[218] See idem, *Sermons*, IV, 390-391.

[219] Idem, *Preaching the Gospel a more effectual Method of Salvation*, 24, 33.

[220] Idem, *Christ the Pattern of the Christian's Future Glory*, 8.

[221] Ibid.

that Christ declared that he would suffer and be raised from the dead. He notes that the Jewish priests set a guard at Jesus's sepulchre, and discusses the resurrection appearances of Christ. He finds that on all major points the evangelists agree, and contends that inconsistencies in the resurrection narratives show that they did not set out to deceive others. The number of those who saw the risen Jesus is significant, as is the changed post-resurrection conduct of the apostles. They proclaimed the resurrection at a time where there were many around who could have confuted it had it been possible to do so. Many believed in Jesus, and the gift of the Spirit came to many. The speedy and widespread progress of the Gospel is, he thinks, a further testimony to the fact of the resurrection, for all the teaching given was in the name of the risen Christ.

The resurrection must be seen as integrally related to the ascension, and both must be viewed in relation to 'the grand scheme of Christianity', otherwise 'they will appear as incredible as any of the enemies of Christianity can present them.'[222] When understood as part of God's plan, they cohere and are credible. They are to be attributed to 'the immediate power of God,' which is exercised for good reason.[223]

Since Chandler's views on the Church and the Lord's Supper have been treated in connection with his anti-Roman Catholic polemic,[224] we may turn finally to eschatology. In Chandler's day a number of the more liberal divines,[225] repelled by the doctrine of eternal punishment, were becoming attracted to the idea of the annihilation of the wicked at death. Among these was the Arian Presbyterian, Samuel Bourn of Norwich.[226] In *A Letter to the Reverend Samuel Chandler* (1759), he says that he has heard Chandler repudiate the idea of annihilation, and invites him to provide the grounds of his denial. His own view is that everlasting punishment reflects badly on the Father of mercies, and that 'Nothing is of greater importance to religion, than to preserve the character of the Supreme Being inviolate.'[227] Equally,

> Nothing ... can be more becoming those, who are appointed to be Ministers of Religion ... than to vindicate God's Government of the World, and to rescue that most sublime and sacred Character ... from those unworthy Notions, which Men are apt to intermix with their Belief of a Deity; and especially, from those black

[222] Idem, *Sermons*, I, 311.

[223] Ibid., 310-311.

[224] Many of his sacramental points are resumed in two sermons on the Lord's Supper. See *Sermons*, IV. xv and xvi, where his emphasis is strongly on the Supper as a memorial, and hardly at all upon the believer's union with Christ.

[225] For some of the winds fanning the debate see Alan P. F. Sell, *John Locke*, 262-7.

[226] For Bourn (1714-1796) see ODNB.

[227] S. Bourn, *A Letter to the Revd. Samuel Chandler*, 11. Bourn exemplifies those divines who advanced the characteristically Enlightenment critique of doctrine from the ethical point of view. See further on this subject Alan P. F. Sell, *Enlightenment, Ecumenism, Evangel*, ch. 3.

> Calumnies, by which he is represented as no better, in effect, than the greatest Tyrant, instead of being the most just, beneficent and merciful Governor.[228]

Bourn thinks that eternal punishment 'is certainly a Mahometan if not a Heathen doctrine,'[229] but the question whether is it a Jewish or a Christian one is still subject to debate. He encourages Chandler to turn his mind to the question and to publish his thoughts on it.

Chandler does not seem to have replied directly to Bourn, but there is in his writings an occasional allusion to the difficulty adumbrated by his younger colleague. Thus, for example, in his funeral sermon for George Smyth, Chandler lists the ability to 'reconcile the Condemnation and final Destruction of those that perish, with all the acknowledged Attributes of the Father of Mercy'[230] as one of the joys of heaven. It was, in fact, upon the joys of heaven that Chandler most delighted to dwell, and in his sermon delivered on the occasion of Isaac Watts's death, as if to counter all who suppose that the preaching of liberal divines was uniformly and irredeemably cold, dry and formal,[231] he rises to the heights of lyricism:

> though at last [faithful ministers] must lye down in the Corruption of the Grave, and these earthly Houses of their Tabernacles be intirely dissolved; yet, as they sleep in Jesus, and enter into that Rest which remains for the People of God; that Rest which puts an End to all their Trials, Pains and Services, to them sweet and refreshing, as the calm and gentle slumbers of the Night, to those who are wearied and worn our with the long Labours of the Day; Death shall not have a perpetual Dominion over them. God will redeem their Souls from the Power of the Grave. He will receive them. In the Morning they shall awake, and triumph over the grand Destroyer. Their special Relation to and Interest in the great Shepherd and Bishop of souls, is the firm Security of their Resurrection. His Power shall command them into a new Life. His Hand form them for an immortal duration.
>
> How joyful, how happy will the Circumstances of that Revival be! ... What Heart can conceive, what Imagination paint out the lively solid Joys resulting from the blessed Reunion of the faithful Pastor and his believing Flock![232]

V

Of Chandler's prominence among the Dissenting ministers of his day there can be no doubt. He had dealings with Church of England dignitaries and Roman Catholic priests; he was involved in societies concerned to support the poor and ameliorate

---

[228] Ibid., 12.

[229] Ibid., 16.

[230] S. Chandler, *Christ the Pattern of the Christian's Future Glory*, 16.

[231] See on the manner of eighteenth-century preaching, Alan P. F. Sell, *Dissenting Thought and the Life of the Churches*, 152-6.

[232] S. Chandler, *A Sermon Occasioned by the Death of ... Isaac Watts*, 43, 45.

society; he was active in controversy, notably against the deists; and he stood publicly for religious liberty, and against persecution or restriction on ground of religious belief and practice.

For all that, some found themselves ill at ease with Chandler, especially on points of doctrine. They did not hear from him their favoured 'language of Canaan', and their suspicions were aroused. What to him was the circumspection of one who would not probe the divine mysteries further than his reason would take him, was to them caginess on cardinal points of doctrine. The John Gills among them would certainly have queried his passing self-description, 'moderate Calvinist'; indeed, Gill feared that Chandler's emphasis upon the nature and fitness of things was, whatever his intentions, an encouragement to the deists.[233] On the other hand Walter Wilson concluded that 'though Dr. Chandler was not a Calvinist, yet we are told that he often insisted on those topics which are usually esteemed evangelical, and that in a manner highly acceptable to many whose doctrinal sentiments were more Calvinistical than his own.'[234] In this connection we may note Philip Doddridge's remark that that he had heard Chandler preach 'one of the finest Sermons that ever was delivered.'[235] To Bogue and Bennett we are indebted for recounting the teasing observation that Chandler always preached more evangelically after an illness.[236]

Ministers of religion, no less than others, are known by the company they keep. From this standpoint it is clear that Chandler was among the liberals: a non-subscriber at Salters' Hall; Arminian in his elevation of natural morality, but with tilts towards evangelicalism. His education under Samuel Jones, the lectureships he held, the friends whose funeral sermons he preached and whose ordination charges he delivered, were all of the moderate sort; and the sermon on the occasion of his own death was delivered by Thomas Amory, his successor at the Old Jewry, and a leading Arian of his generation. Conversely, the high Calvinists Gill and Guyse were in his controversial firing line. Skeats and Miall were right to say that 'Chandler was one of the few eminent Presbyterian ministers who were not either Arians or Socinians,'[237] but there is something to be said for Drysdale's judgment that 'The lack of the distinctive features of the Gospel, rather than any antagonism to Gospel doctrine, is the characteristic of [his] position.'[238] Thus, for example, in Chandler's writings we find more passing references to the doctrine of the Cross than explications of it. For all that, John Waddington goes too far in saying that, 'As a pastor ... [Chandler] cannot be reckoned amongst the most exemplary and evangelical. His printed discourses are wanting in the explicit statement of Christian doctrine, and in unction and practical fidelity.'[239] While the first clause of the second sentence is acceptable if qualified by the phrase 'at some points', I have provided

---

[233] J. Gill, *Sermons and Tracts*, VI, 152-4.

[234] TSJ, 723; cf. 'Biography of the Life of ... Chandler,' 223.

[235] CCPD no. 1516; Letter of 3 August 1749 to Mercy Doddridge.

[236] D. Bogue and J. Bennett, *History of Dissenters*, II, 593 n.

[237] H. S. Skeats and C. S. Miall, *History of the Free Churches of England*, 364.

[238] A. H. Drysdale, *History of the Presbyterians in England*, 530 n.

[239] J. Waddington, *Surrey Congregational History*, 263.

examples of Chandler's homiletic unction, while his sermons are so full of practical fidelity that one wonders how Waddington could have missed it.

Let us, in fairness, hear Chandler's own account of his method:

> [A]s preachers of the doctrine of the cross, we should be extremely careful to avoid every thing, that may expose our ministry to contempt, and the doctrine we preach to the deserved charge of foolishness. If indeed men will be offended, because we preach what we apprehend to be the necessary and peculiar doctrines of christianity, in this I think we should not gratify them, nor omit to insist on these things, with moderation and prudence, merely to escape their censures and reproach on this account. Christ the wisdom and power of God, should be the motto of a christian pastor, the sentiment of his heart, and the governing subject of his preaching. But if we preach ourselves, our own speculations, our philosophical subtleties, or our secular interests; if leaving the plain practical doctrines of Christ, we preach unintelligible, abstruse, mysterious points; especially if we preach them with a dogmatical positiveness and assurance, or with a censorious, bitter spirit; if we press any particular party-explication of them, as necessary to communion and salvation, and thereby create disturbances and schisms in the church, and spread a spirit of contention and strife amongst the members of it; if we enter into political debates, and the low spirit of faction; if we preach up our own divine prerogatives and powers, our authority over the flock, our being lords of the heritage; if we preach up pomp and ceremony, instead of pure and spiritual religion; or if in preaching the truth, we make use of unintelligible terms, quaint phrases, swelling words, false rhetorick, odd gestures, ridiculous actions, violent agitations, distortions of face, and the like unnatural peculiarities; or if we condescend to low expressions, vulgar and mean comparisons, forced and unnatural similitudes, or spin natural ones into indecent lengths and applications; if we abuse and pervert scripture, fetch doctrines from texts that God never put into them, and endeavour to prove points by strained and tortures applications of scripture, or forced by unnatural criticisms; these and the like methods will expose us to contempt, and justly fix on us the charge of the foolishness of preaching.[240]

If we apply this lengthy statement as a check-list to Chandler's own sermons, I think we shall find that he took his own medicine. There are homiletic principles here that are as pertinent in our own time as they were when Chandler first uttered them. More broadly, there is integrity here, both with respect to the Bible and to doctrine, and also a catholicity of spirit, which, even in our own enlightened times are not as prevalent as one could wish. As to integrity, we recall Chandler's words on the occasion of Lowman's death:

> If [a minister] preaches what he doth not believe, he deals falsely with God and man, and deserves to be doubly abhorred for his hypocrisy and vice. He forfeits all claim

---

[240] S. Chandler, *Preaching the Gospel a more effectual Method of Salvation, that human Wisdom and Philosophy*, 57-8; cf. 44.

> to respect and honour from me, and hath a double condemnation to expect from God.[241]

As to catholicity of spirit, Chandler declares that

> tho' the choice with whom we will statedly worship, must be left to every particular person's judgment and conscience, yet, where-ever there is that faith in Christ, which purifies the heart, recovers men from the corruptions of life, and enables them to keep God's commandments; there is the sincerity of religion, and there will finally be the reward of it, whatever be the particular name by which we may be distinguished.[242]

---

[241] Idem, *The Character and Reward of a Christian Bishop*, 19.
[242] Ibid., 47-8.

Part II

In the Wake of Enlightenment and Revival

George Payne (1781–1848)

Richard Alliott (1804–1863)

CHAPTER 5

George Payne (1781–1848): Usefulness from a Dangerous Eminence

According to his biographer, John Pyer,[1] 'To be brilliant, to dazzle, to surprise men, was not [Payne's] ambition; but to be holy, and devout, and useful.'[2] I turn the last word here into a noun and deploy it in the subtitle of this chapter. For the other words in the subtitle I turn to that Scottish Independent-turned-Baptist evangelical entrepreneur, James A. Haldane, who declared of Payne that he

> seems to court the title of a Philosophical Divine. It is a dangerous eminence. The man who aspires to it trespasses on forbidden ground. 'Stop, traveller!' is inscribed on the entrance gate. Paul, the ambassador of Jesus Christ, with all the authority of his apostolic character, and under the infallible guidance of inspiration, warns us of the danger of blending our philosophy with the doctrine of Jesus. (Col. ii.8). It is impossible to neglect the warning without becoming dupes of our own subtleties.[3]

Any thinker who set out to be 'useful' but was perceived as 'dangerous' is worthy of some attention. I shall therefore outline Payne's life and then present the kernel of his thought under the headings, metaphysics and ethics, moderate Calvinism, the Church, and the Trinity.

Payne's career, we are informed, 'presented no extraordinary incidents, no strange, uncommon occurrences; nor was there anything in his position or circumstances to

---

[1] For Pyer (1790-1859) see K. P. Russell (his daughter), *Memoirs of the Rev. John Pyer*. Pyer sold his chemist's business and for nine years was a preacher among the Tent Methodists. He then became a Town Missionary in Manchester, during which time the church at Canal Street, Ancoats, became Congregational with him. From 1830 to 1834 he was an agent for the Christian Instruction Society, London, and then held pastorates at South Molton (1834-8), Cork (1838-9) and Mount Street (Wycliffe), Devonport (1839-59). On 7 April 1759 he was found dead in his study.

[2] J. Pyer, 'Memoir of the Rev. George Payne, LL.D. with notices of his writings,' prefixed to Payne's *Lectures on Christian Theology*, I. For Payne see also DNCBP; ODNB; SCM; Alan P. F. Sell, *Philosophy, Dissent and Nonconformity*, *passim*; idem, *Testimony and Tradition*, ch. 9; E. Kaye, *For the Work of Ministry*.

[3] J. A. Haldane, *The Doctrine of the Atonement*, 366. For Haldane (1768-1851) see DSCHT; ODNB; Alexander Haldane, *The Lives of Robert and James Haldane*.

startle, or dazzle, or astonish mankind.'[4] He was born in the Costwold wool town of Stow-on-the-Wold on 17 September 1781. His father was Alexander Payne, a cooper, his mother was Mary Dyer of Bampton, and George was their youngest son. Married in October 1769, Alexander and Mary had eleven children of whom seven died in infancy. At some time after their wedding the couple left the Church of England for the Baptists of Bengeworth, a village east of the river Avon in Worcestershire. Formed in 1732 the current minister was Lawrence Butterworth, M.A. He enjoyed a ministry there of sixty years, and was by all accounts someone to be reckoned with. In 1788 a new chapel was erected over the river in Evesham, and in it is a memorial of 1828 to Butterworth, 'under whose direction and by whose active exertions this chapel was erected.'[5]

Alexander Payne became an enthusiastic Baptist. He began to pray and exhort publicly, and in due course undertook lay preaching in the villages around Evesham. John Ryland of Northampton[6] commended him to the members of the Baptist Church at Walgrave, Northamptonshire, and, at the invitation of the church, Alexander and his family moved there in 1783. He supplied the Walgrave pulpit for two years, and on 29 May 1785, as the Church Book records, he was, 'By an honourable Letter of Dismission ... received as a member in Church fellowship with us.'[7] His wife was baptized and admitted to church membership on 20 June 1785. Three weeks later, having received and accepted a call to the pastorate, he was ordained on 6 July. The participants in the two services, John Sutcliff of Olney, John Ryland of Northampton, and the preacher for the occasion, Andrew Fuller of Kettering, comprised a roll-call of evangelical Calvinist, missionary-minded Baptists, all of whom had been influenced by Jonathan Edwards's evangelistic Calvinism.[8] In all twenty-two ministers were present. That the greatly-esteemed Alexander Payne was of that ilk is amply suggested by the evidences of revival that accompanied his ministry, and by the fact that during the year following his ordination a new chapel, in the cause of which Alexander had tramped many miles raising funds, was erected and opened on 3 August 1786. Ryland and Fuller preached the opening sermons.

The early enthusiasm of the Walgrave saints seems to have died down, for in 1791, dismayed by the lack of spiritual life and conversions, Alexander called for days of humiliation, fasting and prayer, whereupon a 'glorious revival' ensued.[9] During his ministry nine men, not counting his son George, were sent into the ministry, and George, having preached acceptably in three villages, was invited to

---

[4] J. Pyer, 'Memoir,' xv.

[5] See Christopher Stell, *An Inventory of Nonconformist Chapels and Meeting-houses in Central England*, 249.

[6] For Ryland (1753-1825) see DEB; ODNB.

[7] Quoted by F. C. Lusty, *Walgrave Baptist Church 1700-1950*, 9.

[8] For Sutcliff (1752-1814) and Fuller (1754-1815) see DEB; ODNB; Michael A. G. Haykin, *At the Pure Fountain of Thy Word*; Alan P. F. Sell, *Testimony and Tradition*, ch. 6; idem, *Enlightenment, Ecumenism, Evangel*, ch. 4.

[9] So F. C. Lusty, *Walgrave Baptist Church*, 11.

preach in his father's chapel. This he did, taking as his text the words, 'He that endureth to the end shall be saved.' The Walgrave church supported the infant Baptist Missionary Society, and one of the members, Hannah Smith, married John Chamberlain, with whom she sailed to India in 1802. After a ministry of almost thirty-three years, Alexander Payne died on 13 February 1819 at the age of seventy-seven, Mary having predeceased him on 5 January 1814, aged seventy-one. Alexander was interred by the pulpit steps on 19 February. At his request Thomas Berridge of Moulton, Northamptonshire, delivered the funeral sermon, taking as his text the words, 'I have finished the course' (1 Tim. 4: 7). The church sent a letter to the ministers and messengers due to meet in association at Dunstable on 2nd and 3rd June, reporting the death of Alexander Payne, and stating that the church membership stood at fifty-one. A memorial tablet to Alexander and Mary adorns a wall in Walgrave Baptist Chapel.

George Payne was not a robust child, but he was intelligent and amiable. He set his heart on the ministry from an early age, and would conduct services in the house with his sisters, at which he preached and the youngest sister led the singing. He went to school in Walgrave, where the headmaster was 'a man who exhibited some oddities', but who 'taught his young ideas to shoot.'[10] By the age of fourteen Payne had read all of the books in his father's library. A fellow pupil at Mr Comfield's school in Northampton, to which Payne proceeded, remembered that George 'was always fonder of amusing himself by reading than by joining with the other boys in their juvenile games and sports.'[11] His upbringing, his father's allegiance—and Comfield's—notwithstanding, Payne thought his way out of the Baptist tradition and into the Congregational, and in 1801 he came to the notice of Thomas Wilson, the treasurer of Hoxton academy in London. Wilson advised George to apply for admission there, and this he did in a letter of 7 December 1801. He referred to his experience, especially to a conversation on the duty of prayer he had had with his father at the age of fourteen. The latter 'represented to me that a prayerless soul was a Christless soul ... and represented the awful state and condition of all those who leave the world without an interest in the Redeemer.' He reflected on his own state, and was much impressed by a young friend's prayer; all of which 'eventually issued, I trust, in real conversion.'[12] He then set down his doctrinal convictions:

> My sentiments are Calvinistic. I believe that there are three equal persons in the Godhead;—that, in consequence of the fall of Adam, we bring into the world with us a disposition prone to everything that is bad, and averse to everything that is good;—that sovereign, efficacious grace is manifested in regeneration;—that we are justified by the imputed righteousness of Christ;—that salvation is of grace, not of works;—[and] that God has, from all eternity, predestinated a certain number to be saved. I believe in the final perseverance of all true believers;—[in] a future state of retribution,—the eternal happiness of the righteous, and everlasting misery of

[10] So Pyer, 'Memoir,' xx, xxi.
[11] Ibid., xxiii.
[12] Ibid., xxv.

> the finally impenitent. Concerning baptism—I am decidedly of opinion that baptism by sprinkling, or pouring, and administered to the infant offspring of Christian parents, is true, scriptural baptism; and though I do not think immersion essentially wrong, I am led by several considerations to prefer baptism by sprinkling or pouring.[13]

The Committee satisfied, Payne entered Hoxton academy at the beginning of 1802.

Whilst in London he attended the Weigh-House Chapel, where he was baptized by the minister, John Clayton, Sr.[14] The following year Joseph Fletcher, also a Hoxton student, joined the Chapel, and the two students became life-long friends.[15] During one of their vacations, Payne and Fletcher went to Walgrave together, and whilst there they visited Comfield in Northampton. They were delighted to find that Robert Hall was there, and he entranced them by the way in which he 'discanted with wonderful clearness and fluency' on a number of metaphysical subjects. 'It was at that house,' Payne later recalled, 'that my attention was first directed to metaphysics. On that evening my bent toward the study became more fixed; and since then metaphysical subjects have been among my favourite pursuits.'[16]

It does not seem that Hoxton was well placed to foster metaphysical interests, for no philosophical subjects appear in its curriculum until Logic makes an entry in 1803. The principal Hoxton tutor, Robert Simpson was otherwise gifted. Born at Orwell, Kinross-shire, he had come to England as a cloth dresser, been converted in County Durham, and had trained for the ministry by James Scott of Heckmondwike academy. Following Lancashire pastorates at Haslingden, Elswick and Bolton, he was appointed tutor at Hoxton in 1791, remaining there until his death in 1817. When he arrived four students were on the roll; when he died there were forty. He was a systematic (and alliterative) theologian. He taught the 'three R's': 'Ruin, Redemption and Regeneration,' and he expected his students to preach with 'Animation, Affection and Application.'[17] In short, he was 'distinguished for his

---

[13] Ibid.

[14] For Clayton (1753-1843) see ODNB; WW, I, 201-204. Following medical training in Manchester and London, he studied at Trevecca, and itinerated under the auspices of the Countess of Huntingdon's Connexion. On leaving the Connexion he was briefly assistant to Sir Harry Trelawney at Looe

(c. 1777), whence he was called to King's Weigh House, London, in 1778. He was ordained on 25 November in that year, and remained in that pastorate until he retired to Upminster in 1826.

[15] For Fletcher (1784-1843) see CYB, 1846, 188; ODNB; Joseph Fletcher, Jr., *The Select Works ... of ... Joseph Fletcher*; E. Kaye, *For the Work of Ministry*. Fletcher served at Chapel Street, Blackburn (1807-23); as first President of Blackburn academy (1816-23); and then at Stepney Meeting, London (1823-1843). He was an Ancient Merchant's Lecturer (1829-1843) and Chairman of the CUEW (1837).

[16] J. Pyer, 'Memoir,' xxvii. For Hall (1764-1831) then Baptist minister in Cambridge, see DEB; ODNB.

[17] So his entry in DEB. For Simpson (1746-1817) and Scott (1710-1783) see K. W. Wadsworth, *Yorkshire United Independent College*; E. Kaye, *For the Work of Ministry*.

consistent and systematic theology which was in every particular Calvinistic.'[18] In 1801 John Atkinson[19] arrived as assistant tutor, and the course was extended from two to three years.

In 1804, prompted by Thomas Wilson who hoped that study in a Scottish university would equip able Hoxton students to 'defend the truth against the attacks of learned infidels and sceptics',[20] the Hoxton tutors recommended Payne and Fletcher to the Dr Williams's Trustees as the most suitable candidates for the first two scholarships awarded to Hoxton students. They would read classical and philosophical studies at the University of Glasgow. The application was successful, so the two friends, together with their fellow Hoxton student, Henry Forster Burder,[21] whose father, George Burder, sent him to Glasgow with the approval of the Hoxton Committee, made their way to Glasgow in 1804, where they were welcomed by the Revd Greville and Mrs Ewing.[22] They became particularly friendly with Ralph Wardlaw[23] of West George Street Congregational Church, Glasgow, as he himself recalled:

> I had not then been two years in the ministry, and not much more than one under my own connubial roof. Under that roof, all the three were very soon as familiarly intimate as if they had been brothers to each other, and brothers to myself and the 'wife of my youth.' We somehow took mightily to each other. ... [Many] were the happy evenings ... which we spent together ... conversing on every variety of topic ... and blending and relieving conversation with interludes of music, in which they were all adepts in their respective parts, and formed a first-rate trio in singing 'the songs of Zion.' ... On Lord's-day evenings, when the public services were over, frequently they would come and take part in domestic devotions and our closing meal, and talk over the texts and sermons of the day ... with a buoyant yet

---

Simpson is said to have studied at St. Andrews University; he certainly was at Heckmondwike academy (1776-1780).

[18] *The Monthly Repository*, XIII, 1818, 66.

[19] For Atkinson (d. 1821) see EEUTA, 172, 174, 238, 239. He ministered at Ulverston (1794-1801), when he removed to Hoxton. He left 1807 to become the first headmaster of Mill Hill School, and from 1819 until his death he was tutor at Wymondley academy.

[20] J. Waddington, *Congregational History 1800 to 1850*, 149.

[21] For Burder (1783-1864) see CYB, 1866, 239; ODNB. He was Classical Tutor at Wymondley academy (1807-1808); Professor of Philosophy and Mathematics at Hoxton and Highbury academies (1809-1829/30); assistant pastor at St. Thomas's Square, Hackney (1811-1814) and pastor there from 1814 to 1852, when he retired. He was Chairman of the CUEW in 1844. For his father, George Burder (1752-1832) see DEB; ODNB; WW, III, 467-71; H. F. Burder, *Memoir*; Alan P. F. Sell, *Dissenting Thought and the Life of the Churches*, ch. 10.

[22] For Ewing (1767-1841) see DEB; DSCHT; ODNB; SCM, 43. He left the Church of Scotland for the Haldanes, but when in 1808 they adopted believer-baptist restorationism he became a Congregationalist. Together with Ralph Wardlaw he founded the Glasgow Theological Academy (1809) and the Congregational Union of Scotland (1812).

[23] For Wardlaw (1779-1853) see DEB; DSCHT; ODNB; SCM; W. L. Alexander, *Memoir of the Life and Writings of Ralph Wardlaw*.

> hallowed cheerfulness. ... The attendance [at Glasgow University] of evangelical students from any of the dissenting theological colleges of the South was a new thing ...[24]

Payne was received as a member of the West George Street church.

The three pioneers from the South shared the same lodgings and attended the same classes. In the latter connection they sat under the Professor of Moral Philosophy, James Mylne,[25] who pitted Condillac's sensationalism against the common sense philosophy of Dugald Stewart, Mylne's opposite number in Edinburgh, and Thomas Reid, Mylne's predecessor at Glasgow, who had pioneered the approach deemed suspect. The English students graduated M.A. in 1807; Payne received the Glasgow LL.D. in 1829 in recognition of his *Elements of Mental and Moral Science* (1828), while Fletcher and Burder were awarded Glasgow's D.D. in 1830.[26]

Before completing his M.A. course Payne was invited to preach from time to time at the Tabernacle, where Ewing was pastor,[27] with a possible view to becoming the assistant there. Payne, however, felt it right not to proceed. In a letter to Thomas Wilson he explained that he felt called to England, and noted that his parents did not wish him to remain in Scotland.[28] His degree secured, Payne returned home and, on a visit to London, he proposed to Eleanor Gibbs, daughter of Alexander Gibbs, a Scottish corn factor who had come to London, but who had died while his daughter was a child. She lived with her widowed mother, and they worshipped with the church which met in the Hoxton academy chapel. The proposal accepted, they were married on 30 October 1807. Shortly afterwards they removed to Leeds where Payne became assistant to Edward Parsons of Salem church.[29] The chapel had been erected during Parsons's pastorate of forty-one years, and he was regarded as an energetic preacher of the evangelical sort. He had been trained at Trevecca, and had preached in many of Lady Huntingdon's chapels before coming to Leeds. Payne's sojourn at Salem was, however, brief. He proceeded to Fish Street Congregational Chapel,

---

[24] R. Wardlaw, 'Reminiscences,' cxxxiii-cxxxiv. Cf W. L Alexander, *Memoir*, 83-6.

[25] For Mylne (1757-1839) see DNCBP.

[26] Fletcher had previously declined offers of honorary doctorates from Aberdeen and America 'on the ground that having graduated from Glasgow as Master of Arts, it would not become him to receive such an honour from any other source than his own *alma mater*.' See J. Fletcher, Jr., ed., *The Select Works and Memoirs of the late Rev. Joseph Fletcher, D.D.*, I, 392. That not all shared Fletcher's scruple is clear from T. Larsen, 'Honorary doctorates and the Nonconformist ministry.' For an account of one of Fletcher's essays which impressed Mylne, see ibid., 97.

[27] For this prominent pastorate see W. D. McNaughton, *Early Congregational Independency in Lowland Scotland*, II, forthcoming.

[28] J. Pyer, 'Memoir,' xxxi.

[29] For Parsons (1760-1833) see ODNB; J. G. Miall, *Congregationalism in Yorkshire*, 306-7. Parsons preached on the occasion of Lambert's death. So highly regarded was the latter, that no fewer that seven memorial sermons were preached in Hull alone by Anglican clergymen and Dissenting ministers alike. See Anon., 'Memoir of the late Rev. George Lambert,' 637.

Hull, first as a supply preacher alongside the minister, George Lambert, and then as the latter's assistant.[30] In the course of his written reply of 28 August 1808 to the call to the latter position Payne declared,

> I think I am obeying the leadings of Providence, when I signify, as this letter is intended to do, my compliance with your invitation.
>
> May the God of all grace render our connexion a mutual blessing.
>
> I trust it will be my aim, in all my public ministrations, to lead sinners to the Lord Jesus Christ, and to establish his people in the faith, comfort, and obedience of the gospel; to preach the truth as it is in Jesus; and, as far as I know it, to declare unto you the whole counsel of God.[31]

When Lambert, a student from Heckmondwike academy, was ordained at Blanket Row, Hull, on 14 March 1770 the church had eleven members. Two years later the chapel had to be enlarged and then, in 1782, a still larger building was opened in Fish Street. In turn, that building was enlarged in 1802 to accommodate 1047 persons. By the time Payne and his wife arrived there the church was thriving indeed, and it continued strong throughout the forty-six years of Lambert's ministry there.

Payne was well liked by the church, and in his diary Lambert frequently praised his preaching. According to one of Fish Street's historians, 'The portrait of Mr. Payne explodes the idea that doctors of divinity are the grim ogres they are supposed to be. It shows us a dapper little man, bubbling over with kindness and fun, a thoroughly loveable, yet shrewd face.'[32] That Payne was kind no one doubted; and he could enjoy bouts of hilarity. But the balancing assertion is that of John Pyer, who wrote that with Payne 'all was solid and judicious, but withal quiet and retiring.'[33]

On 8 January 1809 Payne preached a sermon that became his first published work: *Youth Admonished to Submit to the Guidance of God*. The text is Jeremiah 3: 4, 'Wilt thou not from this time cry unto me, My father, thou art the guide of my youth?' Payne insists, first, upon the importance—especially to young people—of having a guide for the journey of life on which they are embarked. Secondly, he cautions his hearers against false guides: their own passions, which need to be subjected to rational scrutiny; their own reasoning, which needs to be measured against God's revelation; and ungodly companions. Thirdly, he declares that God is the supremely competent guide for he has perfect knowledge of the road ahead: 'He will conduct you, not only in a *right* and *secure* path, but in a pleasant one'[34]—indeed, he will lead them to everlasting bliss. Young people must accordingly be aware of the folly of submitting to any guide other than God. They

---

[30] For Lambert see J. G. Miall, *Congregationalism in Yorkshire*, 292; G. T. Coster, *Pastors and People*; C. E. Darwent, *The Story of Fish Street Church, Hull*.

[31] Quoted by J. Pyer, 'Memoir,' xxxii-xxxiii.

[32] C. E. Darwent, *The Story of Fish Street Church, Hull*, 38.

[33] J. Pyer, 'Memoir,' cvi.

[34] G. Payne, *Youth Admonished to Submit to the Guidance of God*, 25.

must conform all their sentiments, feelings and conduct 'to the decisions of his word.'[35] They must earnestly pray that God will direct them by his providence and grant them the influences of his spirit. Payne concludes with an exhortation to those who have, and those who have not, taken God for their guide. God forbid, he warns, that the latter should be separated from their believing parents 'at the great day ... which is to determine the eternal state of all mankind.'[36]

That Payne had a lively interest in public affairs is clear from a report of 25 May 1811 in the *Hull Rockingham*. He had made a speech at a well-attended meeting called to discuss Lord Sidmouth's Bill. This ill-judged proposal was rightly perceived as meddling with the discipline of Dissenting churches by requiring the registration of preachers by magistrates who would have power to decline to register some or all who applied to them. According to the Hull newspaper, Payne's speech on the subject was 'ingenious and impressive.' The Bill failed.

In the following year Payne cast his eye over the troubled scene at home and abroad, and published a sermon entitled, *Britain's Danger and Security, or the Conduct of Jehosophat Considered and Recommended*. His text was II Chronicles 20: 3, 'And Jehosophat feared, and set himself to seek the Lord, and proclaimed a fast throughout all Judah.' The Moabites, Ammonites and others are advancing upon Judah, and Jehosophat wisely reflects upon the danger which faces him, and considers ways of averting it. Similarly, Britain has much to fear. The King is ill, commerce is all but annihilated, and the nation has hardly any friends abroad. Many in the land face beggary and starvation. The iniquity which everywhere abounds is further reason to be afraid. Worship is neglected, vice flourishes, and religion must either retire or be openly insulted. Alarm is also prompted by the open hostility towards evangelical truth. Although 'The gospel is God's best gift, to a lost and ruined world,'[37] multitudes reject it, and there are renewed assaults on religious liberty. What can be done to avert the fear? Like Jehosophat we must seek the Lord; we must reform our conduct, and play our part in those societies which are 'designed to promote the glory of God by ministering to the temporal and spiritual wants of our fellow-creatures. ... We have molopolized the blessings of the gospel.'[38] The Bible Society is 'pre-eminently calculated to promote the glory of God.'[39] We must send forth the gospel to humanize, civilize, sanctify and save our fellow-countrymen; and may God prompt in all the inhabitants of Britain the desire to seek him.

A few months later, on 14 June, Payne tendered his resignation to the Hull church, having accepted the call from a church meeting in Bernard's Rooms, West Thistle Street, Edinburgh. This church originally comprised about one hundred members who seceded from J. A. Haldane's Tabernacle on 26 March 1808 as a consequence of Haldane's having adopted believer baptist views. In October of that year William Innes was inducted to the pastorate, but he also turned Baptist and left

[35] Ibid., 28.
[36] Ibid., 32.
[37] Idem, *Britain's Danger and Security*, 12.
[38] Ibid., 26, 29.
[39] Ibid., 30.

in 1810, taking the majority of members with him.[40] About forty remained, and they called Payne in 1812: 'Their invitation was earnest, cordial, unanimous.'[41] The Fish Street church was saddened by Payne's departure—by Lambert above all, for he 'entertained a strong affection for him, and could hardly have felt more, at the time of their separation, had he been his own son.'[42]

Payne was inducted in Edinburgh on 2 July 1812, and there he remained for nine years. He was diligent in preaching, constant in pastoral visitation, and in his Sunday evening Bible classes for young people he nurtured a considerable number who became stalwart Christians. The church grew, and in 1816 a new building was begun in Albany Street at a cost of £4500/0/0. The first services in Albany Chapel were held on 2 May 1817, with Greville Ewing presiding.

Payne contributed to the *Christian Herald*; from its formation in 1812 until 1816 he was joint-secretary of the Congregational Union of Scotland;[43] and in 1814 he and Ewing published *A Collection of Hymns from the best Authors, Adapted both for Public and Family Worship*. The hymns are classified under Christian Doctrines, Christian Experience, Christian Duties, and Family and Public Worship. There are indices of subjects, first lines and biblical texts, but the authors of the hymns are neither indexed nor named. Among hymns still sung are the following: 'When I survey the wondrous cross' (no. 552; Watts); 'I'm not ashamed to own my Lord,' (no. 318, Watts); 'Give to our God immortal praise' (no. 58, Watts); 'Amazing grace! (no. 306, Newton); 'Begone, unbelief; My Saviour is near,' (no. 424, Newton); and 'Christ, the Lord, is ris'n today,' (no. 131, C. Wesley). There are some metrical psalms and paraphrases, among the latter, 'Behold the amazing gift of love' (no. 203, *Scottish Paraphrases*, 1781), though the well-known hymns, 'All people that on earth do dwell' and 'Now thank we all our God' are omitted. Many of the hymns are less familiar. The following, by Newton, exemplifies many which I have never head sung (still less seen projected) in any church during my lifetime.[44] I cite it as an example of doctrinal density verging upon godly doggerel. It is headed, 'God glorious and sinners saved.'

Salvation! what a glorious plan
  How suited to our need!
The grace that raises fallen man
  Is wonderful indeed!

---

[40] The ecclesiastical pilgrimage of William Innes (1770-1855) took him from the Church of Scotland, from whose ministry he was deposed by the General Assembly in 1799, *via* Congregationalism to the Baptists, whose Dublin Street Church, Edinburgh, he served from 1811 to 1855. See SCM, 71.

[41] J. Pyer, 'Memoir,' xlix.

[42] Anon, 'Memoir' of Lambert, 637.

[43] For Payne's Edinburgh pastorate see Pyer's 'Memoir' and W. D. McNaughton, *Early Congregational Independency in Lowland Scotland*, I, 318.

[44] One of my ambitions is to gather a collection of old hymns which still *ought* to be sung.

'Twas wisdom form'd the vast design,
  To ransom us when lost:
And love's unfathomable mine
  Provided all the cost.

Strict justice, with approving look,
  The holy cov'nant sealed;
And truth and power undertook
  The whole should be fulfilled.

Truth, wisdom, justice, pow'r and love
  In all their glory shone,
When Jesus left the courts above,
  And dy'd to save his own.

Truth, wisdom, justice, pow'r and love
  Are equally display'd,
Now Jesus reigns enthron'd above
  Our advocate and head.

Now sin appears deserving death,
  Most hateful and abhorr'd;
And yet the sinner lives by faith,
  And dares approach the Lord.

Hymn no. 83,[45] on 'Corrupt nature from Adam', makes no bones about the fact that

From Adam flows our tainted blood,
  The poison reigns within,
Makes us averse to all that's good,
  And willing slaves of sin;

while no. 59 by Watts, on 'The necessity of divine revelation' does not balk at drawing an unfavourable contrast between the Bible and the other literature:

Let all the heathen writers join
  To form a perfect book,
Great God, if once compared with thine
  How mean their writings look!

There are hymns on the attributes of God, the titles of Christ, and the Holy Spirit; and a considerable section on the Christian life and character. 'See Israel's gentle

[45] Thus far the writer of this chilling gem eludes me.

Shepherd stands' (no. 542, Doddridge) is among three baptismal hymns; there are hymns for the Lord's Supper, for church meetings, and for times and seasons.

In 1818 Payne followed up with *A Collection of Psalm and Hymn Tunes*. In the Preface, Payne insists that proper preparation of music is required lest we become as guilty of impropriety as a minister who 'entertains his hearers with what cost him no thought and labour.'[46] There are 90 tunes in all, and no composers are acknowledged. 27 tunes are in CM; 21 in LM; and 11 in SM. Some of the tunes are still in common use, among them, Abridge, Cary's, French, Hanover, Miles Lane, Old 100th and Sicilian Mariners. Tune no. 32, marked 'Lively' (66688), is clearly a new composition entitled Albany Street Chapel. It is intended to be sung to the words, 'Join all the glorious names' (Watts).

Meanwhile in 1816 Payne published *An Exposition of Romans chap. ix. 6-24, Designed to Illustrate the Doctrine of Divine Sovereignty*. This pamphlet grew out of lectures delivered at Albany Chapel and published as a series in the *Christian Herald*. Twenty years later Payne published his full-scale work, *Lectures on Divine Sovereignty, Election, the Atonement, Justification, and Regeneration*, and I shall return to this in due course. In 1820 a further pamphlet appeared, *Remarks on the Moral Influence of the Gospel upon Believers; and on the Scriptural Manner of ascertaining our State before God: occasioned by Mr. Walker's Letters on Primitive Christianity:- to which are added, Observations on the Radical Error of the Glassite or Sandemanian System; and on the Doctrine of Divine Influence*. To all of these themes he subsequently returned in greater detail, as he did to the doctrine of sanctification, the subject of his published sermon of 1823, *The Instrumentality of Divine Truth, in the Sanctification of the Souls of Men*.

In 1822 Payne's great friend, Joseph Fletcher, resigned from the presidency and theological tutorship at Blackburn Independent Academy, and Payne was invited to succeed him. The Committee of that Academy met in Mosley Street vestry, Manchester, on 7 November and

> Resolved unanimously on the motion of Mr. Harbottle seconded by Mr. Roberts, That the chairman be instructed to invite the Rev. George Payne, A.M. of Edinburgh, (with the consent of the churches concerned) to supply the vacant pulpits of Blackburn & Darwen, as soon as convenient; and to intimate to him that this is done with the ultimate view of his being invited to fill the Theological Chair vacated by the resignation of the Rev. Jos. Fletcher, A.M.[47]

On 27th November the Committee heard that Payne had replied favourably in a letter of 22nd, and on 19 December the Committee agreed to offer him a removal grant of £50/0/0 in the event of his acceptance of the call. It would seem that Payne visited the Committee on 19th, for on 22nd his name appears in the baptismal register of Mount Street chapel, Blackburn—the church that gave him an unanimous call to its

---

[46] G. Payne, *A Collection of Psalm and Hymn Tunes*, iv.

[47] Congregational College Archives at John Rylands University Library of Manchester: Lancashire Independent College Box 32, item 2.

pastorate.[48] Sundry other practicalities having been satisfactorily attended to over the next few weeks, Payne's letter of acceptance of the call to the pastorate and of the theological post was received by the Committee.

Payne's biographer notes that 'it was not without painful struggles, and unfeigned reluctance, he surrendered his pastoral charge in Edinburgh.'[49] The young people and church members were equally reluctant that he should leave. The Paynes received many gifts of appreciation, among them a handsome Polyglot Bible for George and a beautifully bound Family Bible for Eleanor. The Albany Street church was not bereft for long. Gilbert Wardlaw, Ralph's nephew, who had served for three years as classical tutor at Blackburn accepted the call to Edinburgh, and began his ministry there on 20 November 1823. He remained there until 1830, when he returned to Blackburn following Payne's departure in 1829 for Western College, Exeter.[50]

While Payne never lost personal contact with the churches, it is clear that he was in his element as a president and theological tutor. Before outlining his service at Blackburn and Exeter/Plymouth it may be appropriate to refer to his remarks on education. These make it clear that he was deeply concerned for the education of the churches at large; and from this we may infer that he regarded the education of Christ's flock as a primary responsibility of ministers in pastoral charge. Thus, in the preface to the first edition of his *Lectures on Divine Sovereignty, etc.* (1836), he wrote that he

> has not been able to escape the conviction, that, in the present day, there does not exist, among the members of the church of Christ at large, a sufficiently correct and comprehensive knowledge of first principles in religion—of the leading doctrines of the gospel. He is not without his fears, that even many Christians hold rather a form of sound words—though even the form held by some is not a very accurate one—than possess an acquaintance with things; nor can he altogether divest himself of he apprehension, that, if a moral deluge were to sweep away our accustomed words and phraseology on religious subject, it would not, in very numerous instances, leave many ideas behind it. It is at least certain that we have less of extensive reading, of vigorous thinking, and of profound meditation, upon the great principles of theological science, in all its branches, than in the 'olden times.' The days of John Owen and John Howe, in this respect, are gone by. ... It is truth, not words, that constitutes the food of the soul. If the orthodoxy of an individual, or of a body of Christians, be a mere orthodoxy of phraseology ... there can be no spiritual growth.[51]

We may also note that Payne's educational concerns were not restricted to the churchly sphere. On the contrary, in 1843 he published a pamphlet on *The Question:*

---

[48] See B. Nightingale, *Lancashire Nonconformity*, II, 70. On p. 71 Nightingale wrongly states that Payne was born at Walgrave.

[49] J. Pyer, 'Memoir,' lvi.

[50] For Gilbert Wardlaw (1798-1873) see CYB, 1874, 359; SCM, 166; Alan P. F. Sell, *Philosophy, Dissent and Nonconformity*, 173.

[51] G. Payne, *Lectures on Divine Sovereignty*, v-vi.

'Is it the Duty of the Government to Provide the Means of Education for the People?' Examined. He here construes Sir James Graham's Bill respecting popular education as a plot 'to recover for the [Established] Church its lost ground in the country by taking the young under its fostering care ... Its object is to close the doors of all the dissenting schools,—to extinguish dissent itself,—and to force back again, by indirect and Jesuitical means, those wanderers from the fold of the Establishment who would never voluntarily return!'[52]—and all of this in violation of the law of the land which permits and sanctions dissent. He accuses the prime movers of the legislation of having 'stedfastly resisted the education of the operative classes as long as it was possible to do so.'[53] In that education the Dissenters had taken the initiative. Payne's case is that education must be supplied to all, but that this is not the task of the Government: 'Statesmen have yet to learn the lesson, "Do not intermeddle."'[54] He fears that state-supported schools may 'Church-of-Englandize the country, and pervade the masses with High Church and Tory leaven.'[55] In answer to those who claim that all education must be religiously grounded, he asks, How can reading, writing and arithmetic, or the knowledge of them, be based upon religion? As for the teaching of religion itself, he is convinced that religious persons only are competent to undertake the task. He concedes that to many the Established Church may be a blessing; but it would be better to have no such Church than to enforce the support of the multitudes for 'a religious faith they deem unscriptural.'[56] No one can be morally bound to support the 'ism' of another. He concludes that the Government should give aid to voluntary schools for their secular and general, but not for their religious, education. Such aid should be given to the schools of all denominations, and all schools in receipt of aid should be subject to inspection. His parting shot is a challenge to the Establishment to allow Dissenters to inspect Establishment schools, and *vice versa*.

In the same year, presumably as a contribution to mass education, Payne published *Elements of Language, and General Grammar*. This book, though thorough and discriminating, is utterly devoid of exercises, and cannot be said to be an easy read for those for whom it was intended. There are some written illustrations intended to illuminate the text, though one cannot help wondering what the children of the 'operative classes' made of the contradictions of the American divine, Moses Stuart, regarding the definite article. A college and school foolscap edition of the work followed in 1845, and it is not inconceivable that concessions to the condition of the pupils were made therein.

On 20 March 1823, at an adjourned meeting of the Blackburn Independent Academy Committee, meeting at the Academy House, Blackburn, the chairman, the Revd Dr. Clunie, delivered an address 'on occasion of the Introduction of the Rev.

---

[52] Ibid., *The Question*, 4.

[53] Ibid., 5.

[54] Ibid., 9.

[55] Ibid., 15.

[56] Ibid., 28.

Geo. Payne A.M. to the Office of Theological Tutor.'[57] Without question the principal motivation in establishing the Blackburn academy was the supply of adequately trained ministers of the Gospel. But by reading between the lines of the records we may detect a subsidiary doctrinal motive: the desire to hold back Unitarianism in Lancashire. James Scott had come down from Scotland as long ago as 1739 with a view to countering Socinianism, and had presided over the academy at Heckmondwike, Yorkshire since 1754. In April 1763 thirty-one similarly motivated orthodox Dissenters in Kendal, Westmorland, had appealed to Scotland for ministers.[58] Reporting upon the Lancashire situation seventy years later, the Committee of the Blackburn academy noted that whereas Yorkshire boasted three Congregational academies and until recently no Unitarian academy, Lancashire had not been home to an orthodox Dissenting academy since 1712. To this circumstance was attributed the fact that while in Yorkshire there were but 20 Unitarian chapels, in Lancashire there were 39. Indeed,

> no fewer than 32 chapels originally belonging to orthodox Dissenters of the Independent and Presbyterian denominations, have, with their endowments, fallen into the hands of Unitarians. This circumstance speaks volumes as to the efficiency of Academical Institutions, in diffusing the principles of those communities by which they are established.[59]

While this argument may smack of the fallacy of incomplete enumeration, there can be no doubt that the Lancastrians were genuinely concerned by the losses sustained by defections to Unitarianism (and more than likely peeved by the fact that Yorkshire's record was better than theirs); and it is certainly the case that in his major writings Payne lost no opportunity of routing the Unitarians who were, to him, as the Roman Catholics had been to Samuel Chandler a century before.

Every candidate for entry to the Blackburn academy was

> required to bring before the Committee, from the church to which he belonged, a testimonial to the suitableness of his character and qualifications, and that he present in writing a brief account of his views of Divine truth, of his religious experience, and of the motives which induce him to enter into the Christian Ministry; that he then deliver a short address; after which, and subsequent conversation, if he be approved, he shall be received for six months; and if he

---

[57] As n. 47 above.

[58] See Alan P. F. Sell, *Church Planting. A Study of Westmorland Nonconformity*, 39-46.

[59] Quoted by R. Slate, *A Brief History of ... Blackburn Independent Academy*, 130. For the doctrinal transition from Presbyterianism to Unitarianism see Alan P. F. Sell, *Dissenting Thought and the Life of the Churches*, ch. 5.

continue to give satisfaction, at the expiration of that period he shall be fully admitted.[60]

During Payne's tenure the curriculum was expanded and now included the following subjects: 'Latin, Greek and the Biblical Oriental Languages; History; Geography; Mathematics; Natural Philosophy; the Theory of Languages and General Grammar; Mental Philosophy; Theology, and Ecclesiastical History.'[61] Two classical tutors served with Payne: Ebenezer Millar (1823-7), who also held the pastorate at Belthorn;[62] and W. Lindsay Alexander (1827-31).[63] Both were graduates of Glasgow University; Millar had also studied at Edinburgh University, and Alexander at Edinburgh and St. Andrews.

Owing to the pressure of work, and to the regret of the church members, Payne resigned his Mount Street pastorate during his third year in Blackburn, but his pen remained busy, most notably in the writing of his *Elements of Mental and Moral Science*. Of this work a reviewer in the *Eclectic Review* wrote that 'It contains more valuable information, more correct sentiment, more clear, condensed, and conclusive reasoning, on the subjects of Mental and Moral Science, than any single volume we ever perused.'[64] The fourth edition of this work appeared in 1856. Payne played his part in the affairs of the Lancashire Congregational Union, not least in connection with public affairs. Thus at the Annual Meeting of the Union in April 1827 he seconded the following successful motion proposed by Thomas Raffles[65] of Liverpool:

> That in the opinion of this meeting it is desirable that the congregations in this county should stand prepared to support petitions to Parliament for the repeal of the Corporation and Test Acts whenever the Societies in London shall think it a suitable time to express the sense of the Protestant Dissenters throughout the kingdom on that subject.[66]

---

[60] Ibid., 120; cf. p. 123 for William Roby's views on the objectives of the Academy and the requirements of its candidates. For Roby (1766-1830) see DEB; ODNB; W. Gordon Robinson, *William Roby*. Roby had preached on the theme during Fletcher's Presidency.

[61] R. Slate, *A Brief History*, 123.

[62] For Millar (1779-1857) see SCM. He went on to Old Gravel Lane Church, London (1828-31), then became Headmaster of Silcoats School (1831-9). He was minister of the English Reformed Church in Amsterdam (1839-46), and finally served as a missionary in Cape Town (1846-50) and Bengal (1850-57).

[63] For Alexander (1808-84) see SCM..

[64] Quoted by J. Pyer, 'Memoir,' lxiv.

[65] For Raffles (1788-1863) see CYB, 1864, 238-9; ODNB; T. S. Raffles, *Memoirs of the Life and Ministry of ... Thomas Raffles*. Educated at Homerton, he served at Hammersmith (1809-12), and at Great George Street, Liverpool (1812-1861). He was Chairman of the CUEW in 1839.

[66] See B. Nightingale, *The Story of the Lancashire Congregational Union*, 113.

In 1825 and 1826 Lancashire had suffered a period of economic depression. Even prior to that the academy had been running a deficit, and more than one financial appeal to the churches had been launched. What is quite clear is that the tutors' stipends were set at £180/0/0 *per annum*, and this could not be met. There was also uncertainty prompted by the possibility that the academy might be removed to more populous Manchester (as, indeed, happened in 1843). With reference to Fletcher and Payne, Slate speculates that 'The removal of a Theological Tutor who had been so long resident in the county, and the succession of one, who, however admirably his abilities were adapted to the office, was comparatively a stranger'[67] may have been among the causes of financial decline. Against this, when the academy Committee met on 7 January 1829, the hope was expressed that the removal of the enterprise to Manchester would be 'a probable means of securing [Payne's] valuable Presidency.' Following an interlude during which the Chairman, Raffles, and two others met with Payne, it was resolved that the Academy remove to Manchester, and 'that Mr. Payne's salary be increased to such an amount as shall render his situation comfortable and respectable.' But it was not to be. At an adjourned meeting on 14 January 1829 Payne's letter of resignation was read to the Committee. It was

> Resolved, That the Committee accept with unfeigned regret the resignation of Mr. Payne, & are desirous of assuring him of their deep sense of obligation for the services which, during the last six years, he has rendered to the Institution—their cordial attachment to him—& their earnest desire & fervent prayer for his comfort and usefulness, in the sphere of labour to which he may shortly be removed.

A deputation headed by Raffles conveyed these sentiments to Payne, who 'fully reciprocated every fraternal & friendly expression.' Presumably Payne was to have left at the end of the academic session, but on 16 February he wrote to the Committee to say that he could not continue after the end of March. This was agreed with more felicitations and gratitude for his consideration 'in their extremely embarrassed circumstances.' The source of the embarrassment became quite clear in Payne's letter of 1 April. He requested the £300/0/0 owing to him, and the Committee asked Dr. Clunie to write around for loans from friends and supporters, to be repaid when 'the affairs of the Academy shall be finally settled.'[68]

Providentially from the point of view of the Paynes a call came from the Western Academy, which was on the point of removing from Axminster to Exeter, and in the latter city Payne began his duties at President and Theological Tutor on 1 July 1829. With him came James Gregory and John Edwards, two Blackburn students who wished to complete their studies under his tutelage. In addition there were three other students, and soon the total student body numbered twelve. The last in a succession

---

[67] R. Slate, *A Brief History*, 127. See further on the finances, Joseph Thompson, *Lancashire Independent College*, 22-3.

[68] For the quotations in this paragraph from the Committee Minutes see n. 47 above. For John Clunie, M.A., LL.D (Glasgow) see CYB, 1859, 194-5. Like Payne, he was educated at Hoxton and then went to Glasgow as a Dr. Williams scholar.

of tutorial assistants to Payne was Samuel Newth (1821-1898). He had studied at Coward College, London, where he graduated M.A. (London). He had held pastorates at Broseley, Shropshire, and Stonehouse, Devonshire, before becoming tutor in the Western College (1845-1854). He went on to become Professor of Mathematics and Ecclesiastical History at New College, London (1854-1872), adding Classics to his duties from 1867. He assumed the Principalship of New College in 1872 and served in that capacity until 1889. He was Chairman of the Congregational Union of England and Wales in 1880 and he was awarded the Honorary Degree of D.D. (Glasgow).[69]

The Congregational Fund Board, which had earlier supported the predecessor academies of Exeter, now known as Western, resumed funding of £150/0/0 per annum in 1837, and in the following year the College building was enlarged. The College moved yet again in 1845, to Plymouth, and there Payne served for three years until his death, when he was succeeded by Richard Alliott.[70] Thirty-four students had been educated under him at Exeter. By no means confined to the West Country, they served across the land, and no fewer than eight of them went overseas with the London Missionary Society.[71]

Payne preached in churches across the West Country, not only on Sundays but at ordinations and chapel openings, and in the winter of 1829-30 he gave a series of lectures on The Evidences of Christianity' to 'the Members of the Exeter Tradesmen and Mechanics' Institution.' These lectures were much appreciated, and Payne valued such work as catching the attention of those who would not feel inclined to peruse a formidable volume on the same subject. Among other topics covered was the argument from miracles, and to this, as subsequently published, I shall return. In 1834 Payne published a pamphlet on *The Separation of Church and State calmly considered*. This was followed by the *Lectures on Divine Sovereignty* (1836), which ran to three editions, and was hailed by the reviewer in *The Eclectic Review* for July 1837 in the following terms: 'In no other volume can be found so much clear statement, sifting investigation, and sound reasoning, on subjects which form the burden of Divine revelation, and have become some of the most important and perplexing objects of human thought.'[72] In the following year Payne published two funeral sermons. The first was for his late friend Mr. Thomas Heudebourck of Taunton,[73] the second for a former student of Western College, Joseph Buck, minister at Wiveliscombe.[74] In the same year *The Church of Christ Considered*

---

[69] For Newth see CYB, 1899, 62-3, 195-7; ODNB. He worked on the New Testament for the Revised Version of the Bible (1881-85).

[70] For whom see ch. 6 below.

[71] For the Western College details see J. Charteris Johnstone, 'The Story of the Western College,' CHST, VII, 1916-1918, 103-4.

[72] See the commendations appended to the 1846 edition of the book.

[73] G. Payne, *The Response of the Church to the Promise of the Second Coming of our Lord.*

[74] Idem, *A Funeral Discourse occasioned by the Death of the late Rev. Joseph Buck.* Buck had trained at Axminster.

appeared. An abridged version this, *A Manual explanatory of Congregational Principles*, was published in 1842. Meanwhile in 1835 Payne had held the Chair of the Congregational Union of England and Wales. Ever socially concerned, he attended the Manchester conference on the Corn Laws in 1841, and in the same year he published a pamphlet entitled, *Facts and Statements in Reference to the Bible-Printing Monopoly*. Also in 1841 he paid his last visit to Walgrave, where he preached in his father's church John 17: 15, 'I pray not that thou shouldst take them out of the world, but that thou shouldst keep them from the evil.' In 1845 he gave the eleventh series of Congregational Lectures on *The Doctrine of Original Sin*, a work that ran to a second edition, and of which a reviewer in the *Congregational Magazine* declared that 'A place will unquestionably be assigned to it among the very first productions of the age in the department of theological literature.'[75]

The Western College opened in Plymouth in January 1846. There were eight students, of whom three had come from Exeter. On 28 April 1846 Payne was in Stonehouse to address the Assembly of the South Devon Congregational Union on *The Nature and Means of Religious Revivals*.[76] The text of the address is Psalm 85: 6, 'Wilt thou not revive us again: that thy people may rejoice in thee?' That Payne believed that holy churches were a key to the reception of God's blessing in revival is clear. He advocates

> the acting out of holy principles, and desires, and affections, in holy conduct,—an embodying of what we feel in what we do, so that the inner man may appear in the outer man, and the grace of God in the heart may become visible to the eye of sense. ... The spectacle is singularly beautiful, when a church, with the deacons and pastor, feel that they have something more to do than to secure their own edification,—that God has placed them in the position they occupy that they may become the source of light, and life, and joy, to all within the reach of their influence;—the sight is singularly beautiful, where the whole body, under the direction of the head of the body, are, as we familiarly say, up and doing,—where everyone has something to do, and is doing it,—something calculated to promote the prosperity of the church, and its usefulness, by turning sinners from the errors of their ways, and bringing them into the fold of Christ.'

On September 29 1846 Payne delivered the 'Introductory Address' at the ordination of the Rev. Hugh M'Kay at Liskeard, Cornwall.[77] Hopes were high, there having been no ordination at Liskeard for many years, and M'Kay was one from whom much was expected. He had been a student at Aberdeen University, and had

---

[75] See the commendations at the end of the 1846 edn of *Lectures on Divine Sovereignty*.

[76] I am reliant upon J. Pyer's account of this scarce pamphlet in his 'Memoir', xciv-xcv.

[77] See *Discourses delivered at the Ordination of the Rev. Hugh M'Kay*. M'Kay's ordination is noted in CYB, 1846, 183.

trained for the ministry at Cotton End under John Frost.[78] Sadly, he contracted a 'pulmonary disease', and died on 6 April 1849. In 1847 Western College became affiliated to London University, thereby opening the degrees of B.A. and M.A. in classics, mathematics and philosophy to its students.

As a family, the Paynes had known both happiness and loss. Two children had died in Edinburgh; one daughter went with her missionary husband to the East Indies, another with her husband to Jamaica. In 1838 their oldest son died. Their daughter, Fanny, married Richard Perry Clarke, who had been a Western (Exeter/Plymouth) College student from 1844 to 1848.[79] For some years Eleanor Payne's health had been precarious, and she died on 25 October 1847. On the day after her funeral Payne preached in George Street Chapel, Plymouth on I Thessalonians 4: 8, 'Wherefore comfort one another with these words.' The sermon is headed, 'Consolation for Christian mourners.' Our friends, he declared, are fallen asleep in Jesus. Their sleep is but temporary, for they will awake again. Then will come a union of the Saviour with all his redeemed, 'which eternity itself will not be able to dissolve.'[80] He closed as follows:

> We shall go to them, though they shall not return to us.
> A few short years of evil past,
> We touch the happy shore,
> Where death-divided friends, at last
> Shall meet to part no more.
> 'Wherefore let us comfort one another with these words.'[81]

Accompanied by his daughter, Sarah, he paid a final visit to Scotland as a delegate to the Scottish Congregational Union assembly. He saw Ralph Wardlaw for the last time,[82] and preached in Albany Chapel. On returning home past and present students presented him with his portrait and a purse of gold. He then completed what was to be his last published work, his article on 'Assurance of salvation;'[83] and preached his last sermon in John Pyer's church at Mount Street, Devonport, on I John 6: 8, 'God is love.' He died on 19 June 1848. The next day the Executive Committee was summoned, and their memorial minute includes the following statement: 'The Executive Committee deeply feel that, personally, they have lost a most sincere and affectionate friend—the Western College a most learned and devoted professor—and

---

78 For Frost (1808-1878) see CYB, 1879, 312-313. Educated at Turvey under Richard Cecil, he served the Cotton End, Bedfordshire, church (1832-1878), and was tutor of the academy there (1840-1874), during which time some 127 students were trained for the ministry.

79 For Clarke (1821-1878) see CYB, 1879, 306-7.

80 G. Payne, 'Consolation for Christian mourners,' *Evangelical Magazine*, 1846, 685.

81 Ibid., 686.

82 For Wardlaw's account of the visit see 'Reminiscences,' cl-cli.

83 Ibid., 1848, 398-402.

the church of Christ a most laborious and useful minister ...'[84] The funeral took place on 27 June, the interment address being given by his old friend, H. F. Burder, the last survivor of the three pioneer Hoxton and Glasgow contemporaries; and on the following evening, one week after Payne's last sermon there, Burder delivered a funeral sermon in John Pyer's church.[85] 'Who can doubt,' he asked, 'that [Payne] ranks, and ranks high, among the faithful servants of his Lord?'[86]

I

In the Preface to the second edition of his *Elements of Mental and Moral Science* George Payne told nothing less than the truth when he wrote of himself that 'Every doctrine to which he has given such sanction as his name can bestow has passed through the crucible of his own mind.' In evidence he adverts to his attitude towards the writings of a then prominent Edinburgh philosopher: 'his frequent differences from Dr. Thomas Brown, even on several important points in the department of Mental Science, and his entire departure from him in that of Ethics, will show that he does not "slavishly follow any leader, nor consent to hold his mind in bondage to any system, or any man."'[87] So much for his authorial practice. As to his general intellectual stance:

> The writer has long been of the opinion that ethical and theological systems are modified to a greater degree than is frequently imagined, by the views which those who advocate them take of the nature and laws of the mind. ... He thinks he can trace certain false conceptions in theology to false views in mental science.[88]

Payne makes it clear that in the present work he cannot pursue 'the practical bearing of psychological doctrines upon theological tenets,' though he subsequently offers suggestions along this line, as when he observes that while our emotions are not under the direct control of the will, they are subject indirectly to it, for if volition 'cannot directly produce the emotion of gratitude to God, it can lead our contemplations to the amazing exhibitions of his kindness and love, and these contemplations will kindle the emotion.'[89] His primary objective here, however, is to make good his claim that 'Mental philosophy is the anatomy of the human mind. How is it, then, possible to exhibit the rationale of morals, if we are ignorant of this species of anatomy?' Mental philosophy, after all, is concerned with such states of

---

[84] J. Pyer, 'Memoir,' cv.

[85] For the funeral address see J. Pyer, 'Memoir', cxxv-cxxix.

[86] See notes of Burder's funeral sermon prefaced to J. Pyer's 'Memoir' of Payne in *Evangelical Magazine*, 1848, 395.

[87] From the Preface to the second edition of G. Payne, *Elements of Mental and Moral Science* (hereinafter EMMS) prefixed to the fourth edition, iv. For Brown (1778-1820) see DNCBP; ODNB.

[88] Ibid., v.

[89] Ibid., 226.

mind as hatred, love, gratitude, anger, desire. These are improperly called moral affections, and 'To possess an intimate acquaintance with the nature, causes, and results of these emotions, must be of incalculable importance to the Christian moralist.'[90]

Payne proceeds to a discussion of mind and matter:

> We give the name of mind to that mysterious principle within us, which constitutes "the permanent subject" of certain phenomena differing essentially from those which matter exhibits. Matter is that which is extended, divisible, impenetrable, &c.; mind is that which perceives, remembers, compares, judges, &c.

There follows immediately a cautionary word: 'the reader is especially requested to observe, that the object of the present enquiry is to ascertain what are the phenomena, or properties, and not what is the essence, of mind. Indeed, of the essence both of matter and of mind, we are profoundly ignorant.'[91] We do not know the essence of either; we know them relatively, not absolutely.

Payne proceeds to argue that the faculties or powers of the mind are not distinguishable from the mind itself. Rather, they 'denote the constitution [the mind] has received from its Creator, by which it is capable of existing in all those different stated which form the consciousness of life.'[92] Feeling, thinking, conceiving and judging are states of the mind itself, not phenomena distinguishable from it. On the related issue whether consciousness is a distinct power of the mind or a general term encompassing all our feelings, Payne concurs with Brown holding the latter view against Thomas Reid and Dugald Stewart, who held that our feelings are objects of consciousness.[93] The sensation produced by the scent of a rose is not one thing and the consciousness of it another. On the contrary, 'all sensation is in the mind,'[94] and particular sensations are mental states occasioned by 'the action of some material cause upon some one or other of the organs of sense.'[95] However, 'we know nothing of the nature of the connexion between external objects, or the impressions made by them upon the organs of sense, and the percipient mind.'[96] I note in passing that whether in his philosophical or theological writings, Payne knows when the time is ripe for humble agnosticism.

Next, Payne explains that 'what we call perception is the reference we make of our sensations to something external as the cause of them. ... Perception of the rose is ... the belief that these visual and nasal feelings are produced by a certain external

---

[90] Ibid., 6.

[91] Ibid., 9.

[92] Ibid., 26.

[93] For Reid (1710-1796) see DECBP; ODNB; A. Campbell Fraser, *Thomas Reid*; Melvin T. Dalgarno and Eric Matthews, eds, *The Philosophy of Thomas Reid*; K. Lehrer, *Thomas Reid*; S. A. Grave, *The Scottish Philosophy of Common Sense*. For Stewart (1753-1828) see DECBP; DNCBP; ODNB.

[94] EMMS, 63.

[95] Ibid., 68.

[96] Ibid., 71.

body, to which we give the name of rose.'[97] There follows a lengthy rebuttal of ' the absurd doctrine of perception by images',[98] that is, that the objects around us continually throw off ideas or impressions and these, not the objects themselves, are what we perceive. In this connection Reid is applauded because he 'demolished the crazy fabric altogether.'[99] There is no evidence of an image in the brain even of those objects which might be supposed to form one. The theory, which was supposed to relate mind and external objects only succeeds in interposing a class of images between them.

Payne proceeds to discuss the sensations of smell, taste, hearing, touch and sight, and then considers the internal affections of the mind. These do not depend directly upon the body, for one state of mind is the direct cause of the succeeding one. Thus the sensation of hunger, itself a mental state, prompts the desire for food, a succeeding mental state. We cannot prove conclusively that there are such internal affections, but we cannot doubt that we experience them. Payne is quick to note the theological significance of this internal-external distinction between sensations: if all sensation were of external origin, the mind would not be able to exist independently the body; yet this is required by the doctrine concerning the state between death and resurrection. There follow discussions of such topics as conception, memory, imagination, habit, resemblance, judging and emotions.

Payne classifies the emotions under three headings. In the first category are those emotions which are immediate. Among these are cheerfulness and melancholy, beauty and sublimity, deformity and ludicrousness among them. In this class Payne includes moral approbation and disapprobation. He suggests that while many writers on ethical subjects discuss moral judgments, 'some appear to forget that we have moral emotions, as well as moral judgments: or, in other words, that the mind possesses an original susceptibility of moral emotion, in consequence of which actions of a moral character are regarded with powerful feelings of approval or condemnation.'[100] These emotions distinguish us from the brute creation and inanimate objects, which can be governed only by instinct or physical power; and 'They are part of the necessary qualifications of a moral agent.'[101] But if some overlook moral emotions, Brown plays down moral judgment, being misled, Payne contends, by his ideas concerning beauty. He wrongly 'supposes that, as we do not first *pronounce* an object beautiful, and then *feel* the emotion of beauty, so we do not first judge an action to be right, and then feel the emotion of moral approbation.' Against this Payne urges that 'a conception or notion of an action, as right or wrong, invariably precedes an emotion of approbation or disapprobation.'[102] Thus, 'Let an action be ever so praiseworthy, it excites no feeling of approbation, if we do not *regard* it as a *right* action. And, on the contrary, let is be ever so flagitious, it

---

[97] Ibid., 86, 87.
[98] ibid., 90.
[99] Ibid., 93.
[100] Ibid., 259.
[101] Ibid., 260.
[102] Ibid., 261.

awakens no feeling of condemnation, if it be not *considered* an *improper* action.'[103] If one person feels moral approbation concerning a particular course of action, while another feels moral disapprobation of the same action, this can only be because they have taken contrary views of the action's moral character. The remaining emotions discussed under the first heading are love and hate, sympathy, and pride and humility.

The second category comprises retrospective emotions, namely, those which involve the conception of an object of former pleasure or pain. They are anger, gratitude, regret and gladness, remorse and self-approbation. Conscience is 'the susceptibility of experiencing the specific emotions of remorse and self-approbation.'[104] These emotions arise when a person feels guilty or innocent, but those convictions may be well or ill-founded:

> The approval of conscience does not ... afford certain evidence that our conduct has been consistent with true rectitude; the disapprobation of conscience is not an infallible proof that our conduct has been contrary to it. The conscience of Paul applauded him while persecuting the church of God.[105]

This view of conscience neither identifies it with the moral judgment, nor renders it independent of the judgment.

The final class of emotions are designated prospective emotions. They concern desires and fears regarding future objects. There is the desire of continued existence, and the desire of society (that is, social association). In the latter connection Payne again dissents from Brown, who thinks that society is desired and therefore gives pleasure. Payne, by contrast, holds that society gives pleasure and is therefore desired. Again, there is the desire of knowledge, of power, of the esteem and love of others, and of superiority, or emulation. Whereas envy involves a malevolent affection emulation 'may exist amongst those who are united in the most cordial friendship.'[106]

With this Payne passes to the elements of moral science. He reiterates his view that 'it is impossible not merely to decide, but even to speculate rationally, concerning what man, that is, existing man, ought to be and to do, without ascertaining first what man is.' But having attempted the latter task, 'we have become prepared to enter, with greater probability of success, upon the enquiry what man ought to be—the great point which ethical science seeks to investigate and unfold.'[107] Thus emboldened, Payne divides his (shorter) ethics section into two parts: rectitude in the action and rectitude in the agent. By 'rectitude' he means 'the

---

103 Ibid.

104 Ibid., 284.

105 Ibid., 285.

106 Ibid., 323.

107 Ibid., 328. This, uttered in the confidence that few would disagree, is a very long way from P. H. Nowell-Smith's remark of a century later: 'A philosopher is not a parish priest or Universal Aunt or Citizens' Advice Bureau.' See his *Ethics*, Harmondsworth: Penguin, 1954, 12.

conformity of an action, or a state of mind, with the relations of the agent.'[108] The three questions which fall under the heading of the rectitude of the action are, 'What is the duty of man? Why is it his duty? and How may it be known to be his duty?' Payne at once rules the first question out of consideration, partly on grounds of space, but mostly because he thinks that there is general agreement regarding the duties a person owes to God, himself and others.[109]

He sets his scene by distinguishing the concerns of the moral philosopher from those of the physical scientist and the mental philosopher. A chemist analysing a piece of gold finds the constituents that ought to be in the gold, and from what he finds to be present he rightly infers what should be present. But from the phenomena exhibited by human beings we infer that they are not what they should be. There is 'sometimes a great and lamentable difference, between what is, and what ought to be.'[110] The mental philosopher has to investigate the powers and capacities of the mind. Accordingly, he will, in a way analogous to the method of the physical scientist, find that what is in the mind ought to be there. He may find the emotion of anger, which may be right or wrong—'against God, or against sin' and hence 'The rectitude of the emotion cannot ... be inferred from its being in the mind.'[111] Again, the mental philosopher may find the emotion of self-condemnation in the mind, which indicates the existence of the power of remorse. He may then infer that the power, though not the emotion, is right because it is in the mind. But 'the rectitude thus ascribed to the mental powers, in contradistinction from the mental phenomena, is not of a moral character.'[112] This distinction is of great importance in ethics and theology alike. The capacities of the mind are God-given and must be right; it is the phenomena of the mind that are wrong, sinful. Hence, 'Actual proneness to moral good or evil, in the case of a moral agent, constitutes ... his moral character, not his moral nature.'[113]

Payne further distinguishes his understanding of rectitude from that of sceptical philosophers who hold that the term 'denotes merely that conduct which happens to be sanctioned by the customs or laws of the country, or age, in which we live.'[114] This view, he contends, entails the denial of all moral distinctions and of the moral law itself—not to mention our obligation to obey God rather than man. He agrees with the sceptics that the mind is capable of perceiving moral qualities, but he strongly denies that we infallibly perceive the moral character of every action. He takes Hobbes to task for supposing that actions previously devoid of rectitude may become right when commanded by legal enactments. Payne retorts, 'The command of a multitude, of a thousand, or a million, is equally powerless with the command,

---

[108] EMMS, 329.

[109] A further suggestion here of the distance we have travelled since Payne's day.

[110] G. Payne, EMMS, 330.

[111] Ibid., 333.

[112] Ibid.

[113] Ibid., 335.

[114] Ibid., 338.

even of one, to make an action right or wrong.'[115] While human laws may make an action expedient, they cannot make it right.

What, then, does make an action right? Here Payne comes to the ethical 'chestnut', Are actions made right by God's command, or does God command what is right? Payne agrees both that there is nothing more certain than the command of God to 'make us know' that an action is right, and that 'the nature of God is the foundation of rectitude.'[116] But 'the Divine will or command, though the proximate, is not the ultimate standard, and far less the foundation or source, of rectitude.'[117] For if actions became right only because God commanded them, they would have no rectitude in themselves, and Richard Price's rhetorical question stands: 'Is it no derogation to [God's] infinite excellences, to suppose him guided by mere unintelligent inclination, without any direction from reason, or any moral approbation?'[118] Furthermore, if rectitude were founded on God's will he might have commanded what he now prohibits, and *vice versa*; and there would be no wrong acts previous to a divinely willed command, and no distinction in degrees of sinfulness following the breach of such commanded actions. Payne proceeds to detailed criticism of Hutcheson, Adam Smith[119] and Brown—from the last of whom 'it pains me to differ so materially'[120]—all of whom advance views of rectitude which ground it in the arbitrary constitution of the human mind. According to Hutcheson, approbation by the moral sense is what imparts virtue to an action: 'The action is not merely proved to be right, but rendered right, by the emotion.'[121] Payne, here following Price, deems this a fatal objection to Hutcheson's theory. Smith is faulted for supposing that the mind is so constituted as to sympathize with some actions and not with others. This 'whimsical theory', counters Payne, might have had some substance were man what he ought to be. But he is depraved, and his judgment clouded. The theory of Brown is similarly defective, but Brown faces a further difficulty. He contends that until the emotion of approbation has arisen there is no virtue in an action. But what prompts the emotion? Is it uncaused? Surely it is awakened by the rectitude in the action itself. Brown goes so far as to admit a tendency in virtuous actions to awaken the emotion of approbation, but at the same time holds that there is no virtue in the action as such. Payne pulls no punches:

> Dr. Brown's system leaves us utterly in the dark as to the manner in which the emotion arises, or rather to the source from which it springs; unless, indeed, he has

---

[115] Ibid., 342.

[116] Ibid., 342.

[117] Ibid., 344.

[118] Ibid., 345, quoting R. Price, *A Review of the Principal Questions of Morals*, 72. In the third edition of 1787, p. 49, the opening words of the sentence quoted above are, 'Is it no diminution of his perfect character ...'

[119] For Hutcheson (1694-1746) see DECBP; DSCHT; ODNB. For Smith (1723-1790) see DECBP; ODNB.

[120] G. Payne, EMMS, 347.

[121] Ibid., 349.

> identified it with the notion of relation. And as this notion depends for its existence upon the precious existence of the emotion, for the previous existence of which the system supplies no adequate cause, I cannot but regard the whole theory as baseless.[122]

More seriously still, Brown's theory 'proceeds on a practical forgetfulness of the distinction which exists, as he himself admits, between what is, and what ought to be, in human conduct;'[123] for on his view we deem certain actions virtuous the moment we contemplate them, thereby 'considering what is, an infallible measure of what ought to be.'[124]

Most serious of all is 'one of the most objectionable passages' in Brown's writings in which he declares that 'there may be virtue, where there is no regard to the Divine authority in what we do, nor, indeed, any thought of the Divine existence.'[125] At this point Payne shows himself to be towards the end of a long line of Christian writers on ethics who could not conceive that an atheist could be a moral person. Elsewhere he lamented that 'There was a time, when the rejector of Divine revelation, would have been considered, as he deserves to be considered, as being, in the highest degree, inimical to the best interests of the human race,' but now such persons frequently receive applause and public acclaim.[126] He returns to the theme in a lecture on God's existence, where he grants that while there is much practical atheism in the world, 'I very much doubt whether there is, or ever has been, such a being as a speculative atheist. An honest atheist we know there cannot be. Infidelity, in all its grades, has its origin not in the perversion of the intellect, but the moral obliquity of the heart.'[127]

Returning to more strictly ethical matters, Payne points out that on Brown's theory the most flagitious actions may be transmuted into virtuous ones when greeted with approbation, and then the performance of them would become a duty. Payne concludes that 'To maintain the guilt of a man who does wrong, when he thinks himself in the right, we must suppose that there is a moral obligation to actions which is totally independent of the state of feeling of the agent, and this the views of Dr. Brown will not allow him to admit.'[128]

With 'extreme reluctance' Payne invokes Butler[129] as one who, in some of his statements, appears to make rectitude depend upon the constitution of the mind. For him, virtue, as with the Stoics of old, consists in living in accordance with nature; and by this Butler means living in accordance with conscience. Payne's objection is

---

[122] Ibid., 358-9.
[123] Ibid., 361.
[124] Ibid., 363.
[125] Ibid., 365.
[126] Idem, *Britain's Danger and Security*, 9.
[127] Idem, LCT, I, 17-18.
[128] Idem, EMMS, 369.
[129] For Joseph Butler (1692-1752) see DECBP; ODNB; Terence Penelhum, *Butler*; Christopher Cunliffe, ed., *Joseph Butler's Moral and Religious Thought.*

that this does not tell us what makes an action right, and it leaves us devoid of a criterion of virtue apart from the approbation of conscience. Butler agrees that there are real moral distinctions, and that antecedently to the operation of conscience actions are right or wrong, but his theory can provide no account of how this is so.

Next, Payne tackles utilitarianism and here, once again, his running theme is that 'The assertion of an essential difference between right and wrong, is opposed to the sentiments of those who maintain that the consequences of actions impart to them their moral character ...'[130] He can agree that what is virtuous is also useful, but it is not approved on account of its utility. Moreover, utilitarianism cannot be reconciled with the idea that 'the practice of moral duties is enforced upon us in the Sacred Scriptures.'[131] Payne does not hesitate to brand utilitarianism 'the selfish system', for

> Let it once be conceded that virtue has its foundation in private utility, and it will necessarily follow that the man who throws away all concern about the welfare of his fellow creatures ... is the individual who is the most entitled to the approbation of his fellow men! ... Or, let it be granted that virtue is founded in public rather than private utility, and, '*mutatis mutandis,*' similar consequences will unavoidably follow.[132]

Richard Price's theory is next briefly discussed. According to Price our ideas of necessity, contingency, possibility, power, causation, right and wrong, are formed by the understanding. Thus 'ideas of right and wrong are ... necessary perceptions of the understanding, and morality is a branch of necessary truth.'[133] Payne's complaint is that while tracing our perceptions of right and wrong to what he conceives to be their source, Price 'says nothing of that which is perceived, that is, of rectitude itself.'[134] The underlying fault in Price's intellectualist approach, is that it leads him to 'make virtue depend upon the arbitrary constitution of the mind.'[135] Furthermore, he overlooks the fact that the human being's 'moral state has suffered a most fearful change since he came from the hands of his Maker,'[136] and consequently our perceptions cannot provide a reliable criterion of virtue:

> We must have a more infallible standard of rectitude than either our perceptions or our feelings. We have placed that standard in the Divine intellect, guided in its exercise by his perfectly holy nature. Virtue is conformity to relations; but the

---

[130] Idem.,EMMS, 371.

[131] Ibid., 382.

[132] Ibid., 383.

[133] Ibid., 389.

[134] Ibid., 389.

[135] Ibid., 390. It should be remembered that Price is prompted by his concern to deny that benevolence is the whole of virtue and that utilitarianism is a viable approach in ethics.

[136] Ibid., 395.

> ultimate and perfect judge of that conformity, is that great Being who, in none of his decisions, can be mistaken.[137]

Moreover God has made his will known in the Bible. His word is the standard of virtue, and by the applying our reason to its pages we arrive at knowledge of its meaning. [But is not our ability to discern God's word also influenced by that 'most fearful change' in our nature which prevents our perceptions of virtue from being wholly reliable?]

On the other hand,

> If virtue ... be the relation of an action to a certain emotion ... The rise of the emotion is the only criterion of virtue; our susceptibility of moral emotion, is that part of our nature by which we attain the knowledge of right and wrong.[138]

For thus locating virtue in the emotion of benevolence towards being in general, Jonathan Edwards is trenchantly criticized.[139]

After some eighty pages on rectitude in the action Payne concludes his treatise with seventeen pages on virtue in the agent. In a nutshell his case is that a person is virtuous if his or her action is voluntary; is right; and is performed because it is right. Payne reiterates his view that while the divine command is the paramount source of obligation, it is not the source of rectitude: 'Rectitude is the source of the command; the command is not the source of rectitude. ... Rectitude is one; obligations may be manifold.'[140] But if an action is to be performed because it is right, what of the theological argument that whatever we do should be done because God commands it? At this point Payne invokes the 'pre-eminent Christian moralist', Thomas Chalmers,[141] according to whom it is right to obey God, and that when we do what God commands because he commands it, we are doing what is right because it is right. This leads Payne to his conclusion:

Godliness is an essential part of morality; it is the highest branch of morality; so that to be destitute of godliness, and to be destitute of morality, are convertible terms. ... [A] person might fulfil all the claims of men upon him, yet, if he practically forget the claims of God upon him, in no way can he be designated, with consistency and truth, but as an immoral and a bad man.[142]

Before leaving the field of ethics we may note a lecture that Payne delivered to the Literary and Scientific Society in Exeter in 1733 on the subject *Conscience—its Nature and Claims*. He here defines conscience as follows:

> Conscience is a power or faculty or susceptibility of the mind, distinct from all others, in the sense in which any of the mental faculties can be distinct from the

---

[137] Ibid.

[138] Ibid., 441.

[139] Ibid., 396-403. For Edwards (1703-1758), on whom the literature is vast, see DEB.

[140] Ibid., 422-3.

[141] For Chalmers (1780-1847) see DEB; DNCBP; DSCHT; ODNB.

[142] G. Payne, EMMS, 428.

> rest, rendering it capable of experiencing powerful emotions of self-approbation or self-condemnation, when, on the retrospect of our actions, they are regarded by us as right or wrong.[143]

The operations of conscience, he continues, are restricted to the individual in a way that judgments are not, and are distinct from the intellect.[144] That is, it is not the role of conscience to judge our own actions or those of others as being right or wrong; conscience cannot yield knowledge of right or wrong. Rather, 'its sole office is to reward the virtuous, and punish the wicked man, and thus to enforce general rectitude by the emotions of approbation, or of self-condemnation, which it permits to arise' in us.[145] Moral judgments precede, and are not the offspring of, conscience. The moral philosopher Henry Grove is faulted for eliding reason and conscience when he defines the latter as 'reason or understanding considered in the relation it bears to [man's] actions in their moral nature, and most important consequences.'[146] For, according to Payne, 'An emotion can never be traced to the reason or judgment. The intellect can no more give us feelings, than the sensitive part of our nature can give us notions or ideas.'[147] Payne recognises a certain similarity between his position and that of Hutcheson, for we have a susceptibility to moral emotion. But whereas Hutcheson attributes our moral ideas to the moral sense, Payne insists that they are derived from the intellect. He agrees with Brown that when we regard the virtues and vices of others and ourselves the emotions are involved. But whereas 'Our hearts may be broken by the delinquencies of others, ... conscience condemns only ourselves.'[148]

Conscience is an instrument of God's moral government the purpose of which is to 'impel to the discharge of duty.'[149] There is a great practical difference, says Payne, between challenging a person to do what he or she thinks is right, and challenging someone to do what is really right. For guidance as the latter we have recourse to the Bible. He concludes by exhorting the younger members of his audience especially never to silence the voice of conscience.

It will be clear from all that has been said that Payne's view of mental and moral philosophy revolves around the then widely-followed faculty psychology which, though not entirely dormant to this day has, to put it mildly, had a chequered subsequent history.

---

143 Idem, *Lectures on Christian Theology* (hereinafter LCT) II, 336.

144 See further EMMS, Note U, 441-7.

145 G. Payne, LCT II, 337.

146 Ibid., 341. These are Payne's words. For the Presbyterian divine Henry Grove (1684-1738) see DECBP; EEUTA; ODNB; Alan P. F. Sell, *Dissenting Thought and the Life of the Churches*, ch. 6; idem, *Philosophy, Dissent and Nonconformity*, *passim*; idem, *Testimony and Tradition*, ch. 5; B. Kirk, *The Taunton Dissenting Academy*.

147 Ibid., 346.

148 Ibid., 350.

149 Ibid., 355.

II

George Payne's endeavours in the field of doctrine were motivated by the following conviction:

> Imperfect conceptions of the great system of evangelical truth—obscure notions of any of its radical principles—a defective acquaintance with the connexions of its various parts, will render the piety of an age—not much less certainly and rapidly than positive error—deformed, or stunted and dwarfish. It will give existence to all kinds of monstrosities, or produce a race of religious pigmies. The generation that has passed away were men of extensive reading and deep reflection; but they were not men of vigorous action. We have become men of action, but it is to be feared we have partially ceased to be men of research and meditation. We *do* more, but we *think* less and *know* less than our forefathers ...[150]

In rising to this challenge Payne seeks to resist denominational or sectional prejudices, claiming that 'though Calvinistic in his own views, he has tried every sentiment ... not by statements of John Calvin, but by those of Jesus Christ and his apostles.'[151]

As we now turn to particular theological and doctrinal questions we shall find that Payne's approach is, at least implicitly, a response to a two-fold pincer movement flowing down to him from the previous century. In so far as the Enlightenment and the Evangelical Revival are distinguishable (and in their individualism and experientialism they have more in common than is sometimes supposed) we may say that from the former he received the challenge to modify Calvinism in a moral direction; from the latter he received the challenge to modify it in a religious direction. That is to say, he saw the need to respond to the moral critique which eighteenth-century 'Arians' and others had levelled against what they perceived as moral objections to expressions of Calvinism then current;[152] and he also sought to articulate a Gospel for the world, albeit one that did not expose him to the pitfall of evangelical Arminianism.

Payne launches his *Lectures on Christian Theology* by asserting that since theology concerns God, it transcends all other sciences to an incalculable degree. He affirms that our theological knowledge is derived from both reason and revelation. He grants that there are truths of natural religion, that is to say, that there are theological truths which the human mind can grasp without the aid of a written revelation. Were it not so the heathen could not be without excuse when they refuse to acknowledge God. Payne does not think that natural religion can take us very far: indeed the low level of morality in those nations which have not benefited from divine revelation prompts him to conclude that natural religion cannot lead us to the 'axiomatical truth' of God's existence.[153] From one point of view Payne sees no

---

[150] G. Payne, *Lectures on Divine Sovereignty* (hereinafter LDS), vi-vii.
[151] Ibid., viii.
[152] See further, Alan P. F. Sell, *Enlightenment, Ecumenism, Evangel*, ch. 3.
[153] LCT, I, 6.

benefit in maintaining the distinction between natural and revealed religion, for the former is insufficient to prove God's existence, while the latter does not undertake this task.

Given that the Bible's purpose is practical rather than theoretical, why erect a theological system at all? Certainly, 'No conceivable good purpose would be accomplished by converting a man to the faith, and not to the spirit of Christianity,—by giving him a believing head, while he retains an infidel and depraved heart.'[154] But while the Bible's objective is to prepare the generality of humanity—not least the poor and the illiterate—for eternity, the systematic study of theology has 'important advantages' for theological students and Christian ministers. It makes for accuracy of viewpoint, it aids the communication of truth, it precludes both 'offensive dogmatism' and 'weakness and hesitation', and it yields a comprehensive grasp of Christian truth.[155]

Although the Bible does not prove God's existence, Payne thinks that systematicians need to be able to offer some thoughts on the matter: 'To prove the existence of God, we need no *postulata* but the two following: viz. that something beyond all question exists at present; and, that in the universe there are to be found unequivocal marks of contrivance and design.'[156] This leads him to present a cosmological argument for God's existence, and to contend that 'The supposition of an infinite series of derived and dependant beings is absurd, because it runs counter to what is universally admitted to be an axiom in both moral and physical science, viz. that nothing can exist without an adequate cause of its existence.'[157] He concludes his theistic chapter with an appeal to (almost) universal consent on the matter of God's existence.

It is not difficult to pick holes in Payne's theism. Clearly, a postulate is not a proof; there is the counter-evidence to (beneficent) contrivance and design supplied by the problem of evil; and universal consent, while it may be psychologically suggestive, is far from being a copper-bottomed guarantee of the truth of that to which consent is given. Here Payne lingers on one side of Enlightenment rationalism, the eighteenth century being the century of the cosmological argument; but without any reference to the other side, so devastating to the classical theistic arguments, as represented supremely by Hume.[158] (Elsewhere, in a lecture on miracles as evidence of Christianity's divine origin, Payne does take Hume to task for arguing that no amount of testimony could justify us in accepting a report of the miraculous. Payne agrees that no fact can be proved by testimony, but contends that a conviction must have a cause adequate to the effect, and if no cause can be found

---

[154] Ibid., 9.

[155] Ibid., 10-14.

[156] Ibid., 18-19.

[157] Ibid., 22.

[158] Likewise there is no reference to Kant. While is true that apart from Coleridge, few in England paid much heed to Kant before about 1830 (and Payne could not read German), in Scotland, where Payne had studied and worked, Kant was somewhat more widely, but not always more knowledgably, discussed.

other than the real occurrence of the event, then it is legitimate to allow the claim that the miraculous event occurred.[159])

Undeterred, Payne proceeds to God's self-existence and immutability. The first cause argument demonstrates the former to his satisfaction, and the Bible confirms it. As to the latter, he invokes 'the estimable Charnock'[160] in support of his view that God is 'absolutely incapable of change in any point of view, either as to his essence, attributes, knowledge, or determinations.'[161] What, then, of Genesis 6: 6 which declares that the Lord repented and grieved? Payne insists that since grief is incompatible with God's blessedness and repentance with his infallible foreknowledge, God is 'said to do both, in accommodation to the weakness of our capacities.'[162] Be that as it may (and we shall return to the doctrine of divine impassibility when we come to Robert Franks[163]), to Payne God's immutability is a great source of comfort, for it 'forbids the fear that our imperfections and sins, distressing as they are to us, will cause him to withdraw his love from us.' On the other hand, 'how awful will be the condition of those to whom this great Being is an enemy!'[164]

As the First Cause, Payne declares, 'God must be omnipresent, or infinite.'[165] He cannot agree with Brown that matter is simply a bundle of properties, for qualities must have some substance in which they inhere. He agrees with Ridgley that God's omnipresence must mean more than his knowing all that is done in heaven and on earth, though it is not easy to specify what this 'more' is. Again, Samuel Clarke rightly claims that while the self-existent being must be infinite or omnipresent, we cannot comprehend how this is so. Payne further agrees with Clarke that 'When the ground of the existence of any being is absolutely necessary, that being cannot be limited to time or space,'[166] and this is confirmed by divine revelation. God's omniscience is likewise confirmed by 'the inspired volume.'[167]

At this point Payne enters the lists against the Arminian Adam Clarke, a swashbuckling anti-Calvinist.[168] In the hope of drawing the sting of the Calvinist jibe that to admit God's foreknowledge is to admit predestination, Clarke argues that as God's omnipotence implies only his power to do all things, so his omniscience implies only his power to know all things. Payne disagrees on the ground that to say that there are some things God does not know, though he had the power to know them, is to ascribe imperfection to him. Omnipotence, he contends, means that God

---

159 See LCT, II, Lecture 6.

160 For the Puritan Stephen Charnock (1628-1680) see ODNB. His *magnum opus* is *Several Discourses on the Existence and Attributes of God.*

161 G. Payne, LCT, I, 34.

162 Ibid., 39.

163 See ch. 10 below.

164 G. Payne, LCT, I, 43-4.

165 Ibid., 45.

166 Ibid., 51.

167 Ibid., 57.

168 For Clarke (c.1760-1832) see DEB; ODNB.

has the ability to do all things; omniscience means that he actually knows all things. If Jehovah were not omnipotent and omniscient we could not expect an equitable decision on the day of judgment. Indeed, these attributes serve as a deterrent: 'How awful the thought to the ungodly!'[169]

God's omnipotence notwithstanding, there are, says Payne, some things he cannot do. He cannot cause a thing to be and not to be at the same time, and he cannot do what is inconsistent with his moral perfections. The existence and vastness of the created order witnesses to God's great power. Creation *ex nihilo* does not mean that God formed the universe out of nothing conceived as 'the materials on which the Divine power acted'; it means that God produced the original substance.[170] The laws of nature are not God's agents, they are his mode of operation, and 'Providence is God upholding and operating in every part of the immense universe, and at every moment of time.'[171] In two separate lectures Payne returns to the theme of providence. Where the conditions of human beings are concerned, he argues, 'Providence appoints the station we are to occupy in society—the rank in which we move.'[172] Everything is ordained by God and 'There is no such thing a chance.'[173] Where our voluntary actions are concerned providence does not compel, but inclines the will. Payne goes on to claim that 'There is no essential and characteristic difference between the ordinary and extraordinary operations of Providence, between every-day events and miracles.[174] In the former case God acts according to certain rules, in the latter he sets them aside; but in both cases the actor is God. But what of evil actions? Payne replies that a sinful act is one that breaks a rule, and the sin is in the breaking of the rule, not in the act. God supports a person in the evil act, but does not condone the sinfulness of it. Payne adds his customary caution: even if sinners appear to prosper here, the day of reckoning will come.

Returning to the topic of God's omnipotence, Payne's final point is that 'The power of God is displayed in renewing the depraved heart of man, in order to the enjoyment of the blessings of redemption.'[175] For this we should praise him—not that he needs our praises, but his condescension and goodness lead him to accept them. God's power should encourage us in times of trial, and his power 'in connection with the threatenings of his word, should awaken the fears of the ungodly.'[176]

Turning to God's moral perfections, Payne returns to the concept of rectitude, but now discusses it in theological terms. God's character is constituted by his moral perfections, which resolve into holiness, or rectitude, and goodness. God's holiness is displayed in his law, and in the judgments against those who have violated it, and

---

[169] G. Payne, LCT, I, 60.
[170] Ibid., 67-8.
[171] Ibid., 74.
[172] Idem, LCT, II, 270.
[173] Ibid., 272.
[174] Ibid., 282.
[175] Idem, LTC, I, 74.
[176] Ibid., 76.

above all in the work of redemption, for God refuses to pardon sin without an atonement: his holiness must be satisfied. To those who object that the fact of moral evil counts against God's rectitude Payne retorts that God is not the author of evil, and that while he did not prevent the entrance of evil into the world, this is not the same as causing it. He reiterates his view expressed in his *Elements of Mental and Moral Science* that affections and actions are not rendered good or evil by a mere act of volition on God's part. Rather, they are proved to be virtuous by their conformity to the divine nature. The thought of God's holiness should prompt our humility and self-abasement; it should make plain the need of a Mediator, and encourage us cheerfully to 'submit to the discipline which is intended to promote our holiness.'[177]

Continuing his study of God's moral perfections, Payne turns next to justice. He notes that 'justice' is sometimes used as if it were synonymous with 'rectitude'. This is an error, however, because God would have been a God of rectitude even if no one else had existed. But justice presupposes the existence of beings other than God, and an established system of moral government. God's law is enshrined in the Decalogue, wherein God's rights are placed first. Our present state is one in which character is to be developed, and the day of retribution will display the equity of God's justice by securing the salvation of the faithful and condemning the wicked to everlasting fire.

The question then arises, If justice requires that the judge punish the sinner appropriately, how can there be a place for forgiveness? Only because the Saviour stood as the guilty party's surety. In this way the spirit of the law was preserved even though its letter was set aside. It does not follow, however, that, atonement having been made, God's justice demands the believer's exemption from punishment, for 'The atonement of Christ only renders forgiveness not inconsistent with the Divine character; it does not render it necessary that God should accept the sinner on the ground of justice—at least justice to him.'[178] Sinners cannot claim any entitlement to God's mercy, they can rely only upon God's grace. This leads Payne into some reflections upon God's veracity, goodness, mercy and patience. He faces the objection from moral evil once again; he declares that individuals are not doomed except by their own sinfulness; and he contends that 'The mission and sufferings and death of the Son of God proclaim the mercy and grace of God',[179] as does the appointment of preachers of the good news. God's grace is 'favour exercised to the creature, without any merit on his part',[180] and despite his demerits. It is sovereign in its exercise: God has mercy on whom he will; and it is 'irreversible as to its communications.'[181]

Payne's list of God's moral perfections concludes with wisdom, a compound attribute encompassing the knowledge to discern what is to be done, and the wisdom to choose the appropriate means. God's wisdom is seen in his works in the material

---

[177] Ibid., 95.

[178] Ibid., 112.

[179] Ibid., 170.

[180] Ibid., 174.

[181] Ibid., 175. Payne proceeds to quote Romans 8: 35, 37-9.

realm—in the way that bodies are designed, for example; and we see it in his providential governance of all things, and in everything pertaining to the work of human redemption. The plan of salvation is 'consistent with the claims of truth, and holiness, and justice.'[182] It is accomplished in such a way as to exclude boasting on the part of the saved, and to provide for their sanctification and preparation for heaven. God's wisdom is shown also in the way in which the Gospel is to be propagated, namely, by churches gathered under the headship of Christ and made effective by the Holy Spirit. Because God is infinitely wise we may have confidence in his, and we should seek wisdom from him. Furthermore, we should 'expect perpetual progress in wisdom in the world above.'[183]

George Payne was under no illusions concerning the supreme obstacle to our arriving at 'the world above.' Indeed, as we have seen, he devoted his Congregational Lecture to *The Doctrine of Original Sin*. The entire discourse is conducted on the basis that Genesis 3 recounts actual happenings in history. Neither modern biblical criticism nor modern historical method had made their full impact when Payne was writing, and while granting that provided the fact of the Fall and it consequences are grasped, it does not matter so much whether the narrative is an allegory or a piece of literal history, Payne nevertheless thinks that the truth is more likely to be grasped if it is the latter.[184] Leaving on one side the status of the narrative, it must be said that Payne makes a valiant attempt to divest the doctrine original sin of its more objectionable aspects, and can even say the term's 'banishment from our theological nomenclature would not give him great concern.'[185] He wishes to distinguish his position from that of Socinians, but equally from that of high Calvinists. He further wishes to counter a tendency flowing down from the Evangelical Revival to identify the Holy Spirit's influence in conversion with the truth which enlightens and persuades sinners. This conflation renders impossible an answer to the question, How is it that 'a depraved mind comes to understand and believe the Gospel?'[186] It is not that the Spirit is in the truth; the Spirit is in the mind so that by regeneration the mind may receive the truth. The Spirit takes the (true) things of Christ and reveals them to us.

The nub of Payne's case is that the blessings which would have accrued to Adam as the federal head of the race, and which he forfeited by his disobedience, were chartered blessings. That is, they were blessings which God was not bound in equity to bestow or continue. Hence, 'the establishment of the Adamic dispensation was merely a suspending of the permanent enjoyment of chartered blessings upon the performance of a certain condition by the federal head of the race; and that the damage which the race sustained ... by the federal failure of its head, was the loss of chartered

---

[182] Ibid., 203.
[183] Ibid., 207.
[184] Idem, *The Doctrine of Original Sin* (hereinafter DOS), 82-4.
[185] Ibid., v.
[186] Ibid., viii.

blessings—and the loss of such blessings exclusively.'[187] As he elsewhere puts it, Adam's sin 'bore away from us invaluable blessings, and it entailed upon us that "carnal mind" which, as we know from infallible authority, "is enmity against God."'[188] It follows that the 'guilt' of Adam's heirs 'can only be exposure to the loss. Now this generic sense of guilt is found nowhere but in systematic theology. I have no desire to retain it. It never explains anything; it often misleads, by suggesting the specific instead of the generic sense.'[189] Philip Doddridge and Jonathan Edwards are faulted for employing the generic sense of 'guilt'.[190]

We can see already how Payne is attempting to chart a middle course between Socinians who contend that Adam was simply the father of the human race and that his descendants are not adversely placed by his disobedience, and the 'Arian' Presbyterian John Taylor who argued that whether we are approved or condemned by the divine law depends on our own habitual actions on the one hand;[191] and high Calvinists who insisted that Adam's guilt was imputed to his heirs on the other. Payne can accept that Adam's sin was imputed to his heirs, but not his guilt; and hence we are not deserving of punishment for what Adam did, but only for the sins we commit.[192] Both Augustine and Edwards overlook the distinction between individual responsibility and representative responsibility, he declares.[193] Payne summarizes his position thus:

> The whole of the ultra-Calvinistic, or rather Antinomian, doctrine upon this subject, rests upon the forgetfulness of the great facts that the Adamic charter promised blessings to Adam and the race, to which they had no claim—suspended their permanent enjoyment upon a certain condition to be observed by the beneficiary—and that this condition being broken, we naturally and necessarily suffer the loss of the blessings.[194]

---

[187] Ibid., 39. On this point the Scottish Calvinist, William Cunningham, did not find Payne to be a true son of Calvin. See W. Cunningham, *Historical Theology*, I, 321-7.

[188] G. Payne, DOS, 86.

[189] Ibid.,39 n.

[190] See ibid., 85. Cf. 353-5, where Watts is found wanting.

[191] See ibid., 227-8. For Taylor (1694-1751), with whom Payne conducts a running battle, see DECBP; ODNB; Alan P. F. Sell, *Dissenting Thought and the Life of the Churches*, ch. 7; idem, *Philosophy, Dissent and Nonconformity*; G. T. Eddy, *Dr. Taylor of Norwich*. It is testimony to the provocative power of Taylor's work, *The Scripture-Doctrine of Original Sin*, that Payne should feel it necessary to counter his arguments more than a century later.

[192] See ibid., 90. Payne does not shrink from agreeing with Pelagians on this precise point. See ibid., 154-5. For this he was rebuked by J. A. Haldane in *The Doctrine of the Atonement*, 320.

[193] See ibid., 65-6.

[194] Ibid., 90-91. In the course of his work Payne enters into friendly dispute with Moses Stuart (1780-1852) of the Congregational Andover Seminary, Massachusetts, for whom see DEB. He also published *A Letter to the Editor of The American Biblical*

In this sense only is Adam's sin imputed to us. But Christ's righteousness is also imputed to believers. His sufferings on the Cross were not a punishment for any offence he had committed, for there was no such offence. What would have been punishment to us was suffering to him.[195]

In the course of his argument Payne drives to the heart of the matter in the following words:

> Unless I mistake, the grand moral lesson taught by the issue of the trial of Adam in paradise, is the entire dependence of man upon the Holy Spirit of God. God says to us, by the whole of this melancholy history—may the important lesson not be given in vain!—'Without me ye can do nothing.'[196]

What, in particular, has God done for us? With this we come to Payne's account of God's sovereign grace, Christology and soteriology. On the question of the divine sovereignty Payne early realised that there was a work of rehabilitation to be undertaken. In a pamphlet of 1816 he wrote,

> It has been the aim of the writer to state the doctrine of Scripture upon this important subject, divested of those false and disgusting appendages too frequently attached to it, and which he cannot but think have operated most powerfully in preventing its general reception. The practical influence of the doctrine, also, has not been overlooked. Any statement of this branch of the Christian system which does not include its moral tendency must be extremely defective; since there is no part of the word of God more eminently calculated to promote humility, dependence upon God, gratitude for all his mercies, and, in short, to foster every grace of the Holy Spirit, than the doctrine of Divine Sovereignty, clearly understood and powerfully felt.[197]

Payne returned to the theme at greater length in his *Lectures on Divine Sovereignty* (1836). In its most general and comprehensive sense, he claims, 'sovereignty' as applied to God denotes 'his right to do whatever seems good in his sight.'[198] He cautions against our equating sovereignty with arbitrariness or capriciousness, ruefully noting that 'many have fallen into this mistake.'[199] God has sufficient reasons for all his acts, and 'His essential and infinite goodness is ever

---

Repository, containing Remarks upon a paper in that work, by Professor Stuart, on Original Sin. He here finds Stuart inconsistent in denying both inherent and imputed sin. Payne was challenged by 'R' in *A Letter in Answer to Dr. Payne's work on Original Sin.* 'R' argues that all moral agents are comparatively unworthy, and that this is what total depravity means; and that the eternal security of agents arises from their character and not from an arbitrary decree.

195 See ibid., 32, 104.

196 Ibid., 79.

197 Quoted by J. Pyer, 'Memoir', lii-liii, from Payne's pamphlet, *An Exposition of Rom. chap. ix.. 6-24: Designed to Illustrate the Doctrine of Divine Sovereignty.*

198 G. Payne, LDS, 17.

199 Ibid., 22.

developed under the guidance of infinite wisdom and perfect holiness.'[200] Whereas punishment falls within the remit of justice and equity, 'The grand and paramount display of Divine sovereignty, in reference to individuals, is ... the exertion of that holy influence upon the minds of the chosen to salvation, by which they are brought to the knowledge and belief of the gospel;—together with the Divine purpose to exert this influence ...'[201]

I shall return to the doctrine of election and other doctrines beloved of Calvinists in due course, but it will be well first to elucidate Payne's general position on the central doctrines of Christology and soteriology. In his opinion the deity of Christ is the foundational Christian doctrine,[202] and three competing systems of thought have sought to expound it. There is first the view that Jesus was merely a man, and that he had no existence prior to his birth. The second is Arianism, which exalts the Saviour above the rest of humanity (thereby differing from Socinianism, which does not do this), but denies that he is consubstantial with the Father. The third, to which Payne holds, is that Christ is Emmanuel, God with us, having two natures in one person. He writes approvingly of the Chalcedonian Formula and cites Thomas Ridgley and John Pye Smith from his own tradition as concurring with it.

In seeking to prove Christ's divinity Payne invokes both presumptive and direct arguments. As to the former, he contends that only by positing Christ's deity may we make sense of those New Testament propositions which variously call him God and man; only so can we account for the quality of his love and condescension; only so can we explain the impact he had upon the New Testament writers: Socinians cannot account for it, they can say only that the authors were mistaken concerning Christ's character. Indeed, 'Socinians have made many attempts to nibble away at those texts which directly assert the Divinity of the Saviour; but till they can, not only do this, but expunge from the book of God that numerous class of passages to which we have referred ... they will accomplish next to nothing after all.'[203]

Among the direct arguments for Christ's divinity adduced by Payne are the names and divine perfections which are applied to him; his omniscience (Rev. 2: 23), omnipresence (Matt. 28:20) and involvement in the creation of the world (John 1: 1-3). He denies the Arian claim that the attribution of creative power to Christ does not prove his divinity but simply means that he was an instrument empowered by God, and asserts that Christ is the sustainer of all things (Col. 1:17; Heb. 1:1-3). He proceeds to cite numerous texts to support his contention that universal government is ascribed to Christ, and that worship is properly offered to him.

In considering Christ's redeeming work Payne continues his running battle with the Socinians. In his view, while 'Saviour' and 'Redeemer' are terms truly descriptive of Christ's work he thinks that 'the name Mediator is the most

---

[200] Ibid.

[201] Ibid., 32.

[202] Though, as we shall see later, he also thinks that the doctrine of the Trinity is the foundation on which all else rests.

[203] G. Payne, LCT, II, 39.

comprehensive epithet that is applied to him.'[204] The several branches of his mediatorial work are signified by the titles, prophet, priest and king. Payne reminds us that by sinning 'The whole human race had exposed themselves to the inflictions of God's wrath.[205] On grounds of equity under a system of moral government there is thus an obstacle to God's bestowing favour on rebels. Hence Christ's prophetic work that, Payne surmises, was performed no less under the old dispensation than under the new. Indeed, 'Christ may have exercised his prophetical office even in the Garden of Eden'—advisedly adding, 'but on this I do not insist.'[206] Under the former dispensation Christ exercised his prophetic office through the prophets; while on earth he exercised it is person; after his death he exercised it by delegation to his apostles.

As to Christ's priestly office, his work in this connection 'is the basis of all the blessings we derive from him.'[207] With indebtedness to the Letter to the Hebrews, Payne explains that Christ's assumption of human nature enabled him to offer the necessary sacrifice to God, as did his unspotted holiness and his tender compassion and sympathy. His precise duties were to make atonement and to intercede for sinners. Payne follows John Owen in denying the Socinian view that Christ became priest only on his entrance to heaven, for this would mean that his death was not a sacrifice for sin. For their part, Payne declares, Unitarians understand Christ's heavenly intercession in a figurative sense only, whereas to Payne it is a real intercession whose direct object is God, not man, as Unitarians falsely suppose. Christ's intercession is, however, on behalf of the elect only. Whereas the atonement was made for all people and the whole human family is invited to partake of the blessings of salvation, the intercession concerns only those for whom Christ gave his life. He prays 'for everything which is necessary to secure their final enjoyment of the kingdom above.'[208] Those who come to God through Christ are thus infallibly secure, and Christ's love for his people is boundless and unchangeable. As he elsewhere put it in a critique of a pamphlet by David Thomas of Mauchline, 'In consequence of the death of Christ God can honourably show mercy to all men; he has promised to show mercy to all who *believe. Thus* faith, to adopt the not very elegant description of our author, "helps a man in the matter of salvation."'[209]

Christ's kingly office concerns his real, not figurative, dominion. It is not essentially his, but was conferred on him by his Father as a reward for his work. As king he secures the salvation of the elect and diffuses his gospel throughout the world. The Holy Spirit 'exerts his saving power under the direction of the Saviour.'[210] The saved are governed by the laws of the kingdom of God, which do not interfere with the authority of temporal powers. The saints will finally triumph

---

[204] Ibid., 154.
[205] Ibid., 156.
[206] Ibid., 167.
[207] Ibid., 186.
[208] Ibid., 236.
[209] Idem, *Remarks upon a Pamphlet*, 31.
[210] Idem, LCT, II, 253.

over all their adversaries, and 'Christ will appear as the glorified head of his body—the church—throughout eternity.'[211]

Having outlined Payne's biblically based position on the person and work of Christ, we may now turn to his more systematic treatment of the atonement. He says that 'to atone' is to reconcile two parties who were at variance; but 'when we speak of the atonement of Christ, we do not merely intend to denote the reconciliation which he effected between God and man; but to express the means, also, by which it was accomplished.' Accordingly, 'The atonement may ... be defined as that satisfaction for sin, which was rendered to God, as the moral Governor of the world, by the perfect obedience unto death of our Lord Jesus Christ: a satisfaction which has removed every obstacle, resulting from the Divine perfections and government, to the bestowment of mercy upon the guilty in any method which Divine wisdom may see fit to adopt.'[212] Payne proceeds at once to rebuke those Unitarian writers who misrepresent the nature of the atonement: 'Who is unaware of their efforts to fix upon the God of the Calvinists, as they sneeringly call him, the charge of sternness and inflexibility',[213] so that God becomes one whom it is impossible to love? What the Unitarians ignore is God's relation to humanity as moral governor; they fail to distinguish between God's public and personal character, thereby failing to take account of the fact that God is our present ruler and future judge. Furthermore, 'atonement is not only rendered to God as a public character, *but as displeased, in that character, with the conduct of men.*'[214] God is angered by sin, and by this anger is meant 'the displeasure which in his public character he bears, and must manifest, against sin.'[215] God's anger 'was that judicial and absolute necessity, under which, irrespectively of the atonement, he must have been placed, to inflict the punishment of the law upon all who had broken it, while he might feel the tenderest commiserations for the fate of the transgressors themselves.'[216] What was required was a moral, not a pecuniary satisfaction—at which point Payne invokes the support of Andrew Fuller. Sin is a crime, and only figuratively a debt; and while the repayment of a pecuniary debt justifies the demand for the debtor's discharge, there is not such right where sin is concerned.

Payne proceeds to counter the view that satisfaction for sin entails the endurance by the substitute of 'the precise amount of punishment, which must otherwise have fallen upon the elect',[217] for this is the language of pecuniary debt; it would make the deliverance of the elect a matter of justice, a position incompatible with the idea of pardoning grace. Furthermore by grounding the efficacy of atonement in a *quasi*-pecuniary transaction, the real ground, namely, the dignity of the suffering Christ as he sustains the moral law, is set on one side. Again, the pecuniary view cannot

---

[211] Ibid., 257.
[212] Idem, LDS, 132.
[213] Ibid., 133.
[214] Ibid., 135.
[215] Ibid., 136.
[216] Ibid., 137.
[217] Ibid., 143.

allow for the fact that 'Christ was a propitiation for the sins of the whole world. It necessarily limits the *sufficiency* of the atonement to the elect'[218]—a point of difference between Payne and those whom he calls 'ultra Calvinists', on whose principles, and despite their claim that Christ's atonement possessed infinite value, 'the atonement foes not save the elect because it was an infinitely meritorious act on the part of the Saviour, but because he endured the punishment which they must have sustained. In the case of those whose punishment he did not sustain, it has no value, no power: the ultra Calvinist deludes men, or deserts his principles, when he affirms that it has.'[219] Finally, to claim that Christ endured precisely the same punishment as that deserved by sinners is 'to add blasphemy to absurdity', since remorse is an aspect of the punishment and torment of sinners, and remorse cannot be transferred: 'No righteous power in the universe can kindle this flame in the bosom of innocence. It is impossible that the Saviour can have been its prey.'[220] Payne concludes that 'To make satisfaction for sin is ... to do that which shall preserve to the moral government of God that powerful control over its subjects which the entrance of sin tended to enfeeble, and which its unconditional forgiveness would have entirely destroyed.'[221]

Payne next argues that 'as far as we are able to judge [here is a further example of Payne's characteristic caution], there existed a moral necessity for the sufferings and death of Christ, in order to the forgiveness of sin.'[222] This immediately brings him into conflict with Unitarians and deists who, he says, unite in denying the necessity of a sacrifice for sin, and, *a fortiori*, that any satisfaction by Christ's death was called for. He quotes Joseph Priestley's view that 'the great object of the mission and death of Christ, was to give the fullest proof of a state of retribution, in order to supply the strongest motives to virtue'; and that 'remission of sins is consequent on reformation', pardon being 'always dispensed by the free mercy of God, upon account of men's personal virtue ... without regard to the sufferings or merit of any being whatever.'[223]

Payne's response to this is that while there was no personal reluctance on God's part to forgive sin, in his rectoral character and relation to human beings God could not pardon apart from Christ's satisfaction. Indeed it was his personal desire to forgive that led him to give his Son, 'that an honourable ground of extending pardon might be laid.'[224] The question arises, in what precisely did the atonement consist? Did it include both his conformity to the divine law (his active obedience) and his

---

[218] Ibid., 144.

[219] Ibid., 153, n.

[220] Ibid., 145.

[221] Ibid., 147.

[222] Ibid., 157.

[223] Ibid., 159-60. I find the first part of Payne's quotation from Priestley in the latter's *An History of the Corruptions of Christianity* in his *Theological and Miscellaneous Works*, V, 103, but not the whole of it. Payne does, however, present Priestley's overall position accurately. For Priestley (1733-1804) see DECBP; ODNB.

[224] G. Payne, LDS, 167, n; cf. 318-319.

endurance of the penalty to which human beings had exposed themselves (his passive obedience)? Some writers claim that by his active obedience Christ merits for us the kingdom of heaven, while by his passive obedience he redeems us from guilt. Others say that the atonement concerns only Christ's passive obedience. With such scholasticism Payne takes a short way: 'Atonement was ... made by the obedience as well as the sufferings of our Lord; but the ascription of one part of our salvation to his obedience, and of another part to his death, savours too much of the technical theology of the schools. It is a distinction unsupported by any of the representations of the word of God.'[225] On the contrary, 'the exaltation and glory of Christ are represented, not merely as the reward of his death, but of his previous humiliation and sufferings [Phil 2:5-11] ... The obedience of Christ, and the sufferings of his life ... enter ... into the very essence of the atonement; though we mainly ascribe that blessed result to his death.'[226] Throughout his discussion Payne maintains that Christ's human nature only, not his divine, could suffer, and he proceeds to adduce biblical texts to support the reality of the atonement. Christ is said to have died for our sins; to be a propitiation for sin and a ransom for humanity. Reconciliation and peace with God are declared to be the result of Christ's death. In this last connection the Unitarians, once more, are in error. They understand reconciliation to be the reconciliation of humanity to God, not *vice versa*, on the ground that Christ's sufferings could not produce a change in God's disposition towards us, and that in any case God was never at enmity with humanity. This, on the basis of biblical texts, Payne denies: 'God did need to be reconciled to man; and ... reconciliation ... was actually effected by the death of Christ.'[227]

There is sufficient reason, in Payne's opinion, to believe that when Jesus uttered the words, 'It is finished' on the Cross, 'he had done all that was necessary to render the bestowment of mercy consistent with the honour of the Divine character, and the safety of the Divine government.'[228] Among his reasons for asserting the efficacy of the atonement are that the Son of God's intention in becoming incarnate, namely, to make atonement for sin, could not be thwarted; that his atonement exhibits the excellence of the divine law and manifests the holiness and justice of God; and that the resurrection confirms the fact.

In introducing the thorny question of the extent of the atonement, Payne says, 'I need not say that no point of Scripture doctrine has given rise to more disputed, than the subject on the consideration of which we are about to enter.'[229] He advances his argument through a series of propositions:

1. All are invited to come to Christ and secure the blessings flowing to sinners from his atonement.

2. Refusal to come is the ground of present censure and the foundation or cause of condemnation hereafter.

---

[225] Ibid., 173.

[226] Ibid., 174; cf. 178.

[227] Ibid., 187.

[228] Ibid., 195.

[229] Ibid., 198.

3. Christ's sacrifice is adequate to the salvation of all, and this justifies 'the general and unlimited calls of the gospel.[230] Payne further explains that 'on the one hand, Christ did not so die instead of any as that they shall be saved without repentance and faith; and, on the other hand, he so died instead of all men, as that all men may be saved on their faith and repentance.'[231] However, while believing in 'the unlimited, universal, infinite sufficiency of the atonement of Christ ... I believe ... in the limited application of the atonement.'[232] God's intention as sovereign is general; his intention as ruler is particular.

The ultra-Calvinists, who contend that the Gospel call is directed to the elect alone, vainly attempt to escape the difficulty which confronts them because they argue from their preconceived notions to the terms used. Thus, for example, when the Bible says that 'God so loved the world', they construe this to mean that God love part of the world, namely, the elect. They will not allow terms to bear their obvious signification, and therefore they must prove that 'God in no sense loved the whole world,—that Christ was in no sense the Saviour of the world,—that in no sense did he give his flesh to be the life of the world ...'[233] This, Payne contends, they cannot do, and in passing he rebukes James Haldane who, 'with no inconsiderable degree of Haldanean infallibility, quietly [assumes], as if it were a matter of course, that his own views are right, and those of his opponents wrong. ... I desire to enter my protest against this tone and manner, in conducting a religious discussion, especially in the Protestant camp.'[234] For good measure Payne lines Calvin up against Haldane, noting that in his last will Calvin refers to the blood of Christ that was '*effuso pro humani generis peccatis*.'[235]

The fact remains, however, that all are not saved and, against the Arminians, Payne holds that this shows that is was not God's purpose actually to save all. God does what he determines to do, and what he does not do he did not determine to do:

> It was not the design of God ... to render, by special influence, the atonement effectual to the salvation of all; but, permitting the sentence of the law to overtake some, to rescue others, upon whom his sovereign choice rested for reasons of which we can form no adequate conception, from that abyss of wretchedness to which sin had reduced them. Can it be conceived, then, for a moment, that the intention of Christ, to render the atonement thus effectual, extended beyond these individuals? Must not the special purpose of Christ, in his death, coincide with the decree of election?[236]

Along these lines alone can a middle way be found between Arminianism on the one hand and ultra-Calvinism on the other. Arminianism

---

230 Ibid., 202.
231 Ibid.
232 Ibid., 203-4.
233 Ibid., 215.
234 Ibid., 217 n.
235 Ibid., 223.
236 Ibid., 227.

> rejects any speciality of intention in reference to the application of the atonement, both on the part of the Father and the Son; and, rejecting this notion, the system supplies us with no grounds of confidence that the Saviour may not have shed his blood in vain. It is right in stating that it rendered the salvation of all men possible; it is wrong in disregarding those previous engagements of the Father and the Son, and that gracious design on the part of the Son—arising out of them—to lead certain individuals, by special grace, to implore that mercy which is offered freely to all, (without which no man can obtain it;) by which the salvation of some men is rendered certain.[237]

On the other hand,

> ultra Calvinism, seems to me to consider this speciality of intention, ... as entering into the very nature of atonement, so that there can be no value, no sufficiency, in the atonement, beyond its efficiency. To taste death for every man, or for all men, so necessarily means, in the apprehension of the advocates of this system, to die instead of all men, or with the design of saving all men, that they feel themselves absolutely compelled to limit the application of the general terms, to escape the unscriptural conclusion that all men must be saved. They forget the important distinction which exists between the design of God as a Sovereign, and a moral Governor. ... [T]heir system forbids the supposition that the door of mercy was set open to all men by the death of Christ. ... On their part here is no *bonâ fide* proffer of mercy to any, but to those to whose salvation they conceive God designs to render it effectual; nor is there any such, as they conceive, on the part of God himself. The non-elect ... at the great day, ... will be condemned for not resting on that atonement which was not in itself sufficient to secure their salvation![238]

As moral Governor God exhibits mercy to all, but as Sovereign he originates a disposition on the part of many to embrace it, and hence they are saved. On the Arminian scheme no answer can be given to the question, When God offers blessings to all is he obliged to impart a disposition to seek and enjoy them? For common grace does not 'impart a disposition to repent and believe.'[239] As Payne elsewhere points out, 'It is the tendency of Arminianism to fix attention more upon what man does when a sinner is converted to God, than upon what God does in his conversion.[240] Once again Payne seeks a *via media* between Arminianism and ultra-Calvinism. Election, he declares, 'is the determination of God to impart converting grace to certain individuals; but it is not a counter-determination, to deny converting grace to the remainder; far less a determination, formed without any reference to their state and character, that they shall ultimately perish.'[241] Indeed, 'There is no election, properly so called, of any to damnation,'[242] and Arminians, Richard Watson among

[237] Ibid.
[238] Ibid., 227-8.
[239] Ibid., 229.
[240] Ibid., 35.
[241] Ibid., 37.
[242] Ibid., 38.

them, are mistaken in thinking that the doctrines of election and reprobation are necessarily conjoined.[243] He further clarifies his position in an important footnote:

> I must not be understood here to deny that, since God foresees who will finally reject the gospel, and since he will condemn them hereafter for rejecting it, there must have existed in his mind, from eternity, a determination to perform this specific act of condemnation equally with all other acts. But this determination (resting on foreseen impenitence,) is not the proper opposite of the electing decree, which is unconditional, and, therefore, it must not be identified from that reprobating decree which is said to be inseparable with predestination.[244]

On the other hand, while agreeing that the electing decree presupposes humanity's fallen state, Payne is appalled by the ultra-Calvinistic, supralapsarian, view that 'God determined to glorify his justice in the condemnation of some, as well as his mercy in the salvation of others.'[245] 'I know no term,' he declares, 'either in any living or dead language, sufficiently strong to express my abhorrence of this doctrine. ... How can anyone contrive to persuade himself that a decree, emanating from a moral governor, ... appointing a considerable number of the subjects of his government to misery—eternal misery, which is not founded on their transgressions, can be compatible with justice?'[246]

As we might expect, Payne takes Watson to task over the latter's advocacy of conditional election. He reasons that 'an election founded on faith—can make no provision for the existence of faith.'[247] It relies solely on common grace, and this has to do with physical powers, means and opportunities of believing—factors which cannot by themselves originate faith in the human heart.

The final cluster of doctrines to be considered in this section are the characteristically Reformation-cum-evangelical ones of justification, regeneration, sanctification and perseverance. In his account of justification Payne explains that sinners cannot be pronounced just or made just, but if they have faith in Christ they will be treated by God as if they were just. He follows Fuller in finding this to be the view expressed in the Bible, and he regrets that the language of the *Westminster Larger Catechism* speaks of a justifying *act* of God, for this begs the questions, Did the act take place in time or in eternity? Did it take place in heaven or on earth? From these questions have flowed numerous regrettable doctrinal squabbles. For his part Payne rules out the doctrine of eternal justification. It runs counter to the biblical witness that in the order of nature justification follows calling, repentance and faith; it involves the 'great and obvious absurdity ... that sin was pardoned before it was committed, and guilt removed before it was contracted'; and it 'mistakes the

---

[243] For Watson (1781-1833) see DEB; ODNB.

[244] G. Payne, LDS, 38 n.

[245] Ibid., 44.

[246] Ibid.

[247] Ibid., 77.

purpose of God to justify, for the accomplishment of that purpose, that is, the act of justification itself.'[248]

None, Payne continues, are accounted justified on the ground of their own works; on the contrary, 'the ground of justification is the all-sufficient and perfect work of our Lord and Saviour Jesus Christ; including, in that expression, his perfect obedience even unto death.'[249] At this point the doctrine of imputation comes into view. Both Calvin and Fuller teach that sinners must first be constituted righteous and only then can they be treated as righteous. This constituting, they agree, is not accomplished by the literal transfer of Christ's righteousness, but by regarding Christ's righteousness as if it were the sinner's own. Payne thinks that this qualification marks an improvement on the literalist position of Tobias Crisp[250] and other ultra-Calvinists. But Payne nevertheless feels that Fuller has posited two steps in what is in reality a single-step process. He carefully states his own position in the following terms:

> [Imputation] consists not in the actual transfer of [Christ's] righteousness to believers; nor yet in the legal counting of it to them as a thing distinct from, and a step previous to, treating them as righteous; but that this latter identifies itself with the former,—the scriptural sense of the phrases, to count sin, or righteousness, to an individual (whether his own, or that of someone else), being to treat that individual as a sinful or a righteous man. ... [T]his latter view of the nature of imputation assumes, that the one perfect work of the Son of God, is the ground of justification, to the total exclusion of any and every other; though it denies that his righteousness actually passes over to the believer, or literally becomes his; or, that it is legally counted to the believer, that is, if by that phraseology be meant anything distinct from, and previous to, his being treated as a just man, for the sake or in reward of the righteousness of Immanuel.[251]

This view of the matter, Payne observes, 'completely ... subverts the whole fabric of Antinomianism, removing the very foundation on which it stands, ... a literal commutation of persons in the case of Christ and his people.'[252]

Justification is by grace through faith, and by 'faith' Payne understands 'the belief of the gospel.'[253] This belief is more than mere assent to the great facts of the gospel—'the extreme to which Sandemanianism tends, if it has not exactly reached it;'[254] and 'assent' and 'belief' are not to be deemed synonymous. Payne had a

---

[248] Ibid, 237.

[249] Ibid., 248.

[250] For Crisp (1600-1643) see ODNB; Alan P. F. Sell, *The Great Debate*, ch. 2, 67, 79, 85.

[251] G. Payne, LDS, 257; cf. 314-315.

[252] Ibid., 257-8.

[253] Ibid., 269.

[254] Ibid., 274. For Sandemanianism and further references to it see Alan P. F. Sell, *Dissenting Thought and the Life of the Churches*, 406-417. Named after Robert Sandeman

personal interest in distancing himself from Sandemanianism, for during his Hull ministry some church members had suspected him of erring in that direction.[255] In the 'Advertisement' to his early pamphlet, *Remarks on the Moral Influence of the Gospel on Believers* (1820), he declared that 'Sandemanianism is, in fact, Antinomianism under another name. It may be less gross and repulsive at first view, than that which usually bears this designation; it may be adapted for men of greater intellectual refinement, but still it is Antinomianism. At least, so it must be pronounced, if we adopt the rule of judgment laid down by our Lord,—"By their fruits ye shall know them"'[256]

A second class of writers whom Payne rebukes are those 'who contend that assurance, or an unwavering confidence of personal acceptance with God, enters into the nature of faith.'[257] The teaching of the Bible is that believing sinners will be saved, not specific individuals. He further explains that 'It may, indeed, be a certain truth, that Christ died with the purpose of saving John Owen, and the knowledge of that truth may be essential to the permanent peace and happiness of John Owen; but still, it is not that truth which is emphatically denominated the good news, that is, the gospel.'[258] Accordingly, 'In the first act of faith it is utterly impossible that the subject of our faith ... can be that we are in a state of acceptance with God, because that fact, if it were a fact, is not revealed; and faith is not the belief of any proposition, even though it should be true, but the belief of some truth contained in the Scriptures.'[259] Moreover, assurance cannot enter into the nature of faith because those who are already believers are exhorted in the Bible to attain it (II Peter 1: 10, etc.); and also because many believers are destitute of it. In the latter case we must either deny that assurance is a necessary component of faith or deny that the believers in question are Christians. It is possible for Christians to believe that God will save all who repent and believe, even though they are not fully confident that they are penitents and believers. At this point I could wish that, as a guard against unduly subjective—even emotional—understandings of assurance Payne had emphasised that regardless of their feelings, which may blow hot or cold, the objective aspect of the doctrine of assurance, namely, that it concerns the One of whose love and grace we are assured, is of primary importance to believers.[260]

Finally, Payne turns to the relation between faith and justification. Once again he sets his face against antinomianism: the death of Christ has in no way relaxed the divine law; the law continues to impose obligations upon believers; and none may regard the reward promised in the Gospel as their right. The work of Christ, not the sinner's moral excellence, is the sole ground of the sinner's justification. The

---

(1718-1771), for whom see ODNB, the kernel of it is that intellectual assent to the apostolic testimony suffices for salvation.

[255] See J. Pyer, 'Memoir,' xxxiv-xxxvi.

[256] Quoted by J. Pyer, 'Memoir,' liii.

[257] G. Payne, LDS, 276.

[258] Ibid., 277.

[259] Ibid.

[260] See further Alan P. F. Sell, *Confessing and Commending the Faith*, 347-350.

believer may be said to have faith, to have or receive Christ, to be a believer, to be in Christ—all of these are different ways of expressing the same thing. It is the Holy Spirit who leads people to exercise faith, but the faith is ever that of those concerned. On the ground of their faith God the Judge will, as he has promised, bestow upon them the rewards of his kingdom. God is ever the moral Governor, and Thomas Erskine of Linlathen errs is supposing that the death of Christ was necessary 'not so much to render the exercise of forgiveness consistent with the claims of truth, justice, and holiness, but to afford a display of love so overpowering as to win back the alienated hearts of sinners to God, that is, to cure their moral disease.'[261] Indeed, 'there does not appear to me to be more than a step or two between this and Unitarianism. It overlooks, with that system, the relation which God sustains to man as his moral Governor; and where that is lost sight of, one of the most effectual barriers against that system is removed. The direct object aimed at and accomplished in the mission, and suffering, and death of Christ, was to open a way for the honourable exercise of mercy.'[262] Payne concludes his treatment of justification by concurring with his friend Ralph Wardlaw that Paul and James are not in conflict on the question of justification, because Paul addresses those who think that works may avail, while James rebukes Christians 'whose professed faith was unproductive of good works.'[263]

If justification removes the legal barrier against admission to heaven, regeneration removes the moral barrier. 'Justification', declares Payne, 'is a change of state; regeneration, a change of character.'[264] More particularly,

> Regeneration denotes that entire moral change which is effected upon men by the instrumentality of the gospel of Christ. It comprehends the spiritual illumination of the understanding, the sanctification of the affections, the renewal of the will, and the purification of the conduct. In short, it is the commencement of that spiritual cure, which will be perfected when 'mortality shall have been swallowed up in life.'[265]

In thus defining the term, Payne recognizes that he is overlooking a frequently-drawn distinction between regeneration and conversion, according to which the former concerns the direct or proximate effect of the divine influence on the mind prior to any response, while the latter denotes the actual and active turning of the soul to God. That is to say, that in regeneration the soul is passive, in conversion it is active. While Payne does not doubt that the Holy Spirit operates on the mind so that there is a change in its moral state prior to the reception of divine truth, he cannot 'describe the precise nature of the change, or even ... form any distinct conceptions

---

[261] G. Payne, LDS, 325. For Erskine (1788-1870) see ODNB; Don Horrocks, *Laws of the Spiritual World.*

[262] Ibid.

[263] Ibid., 329.

[264] Ibid., 330.

[265] Ibid., 333.

of its nature.'[266] Here is yet another example of Payne's reverent agnosticism. He does, however, think that the change of which he speaks is previous to regeneration, not regeneration itself, and those who think otherwise (Robert Sandeman among them)[267] mistakenly conflate the mind's illumination by the truth of the gospel and the influence of the Holy Spirit in their definition of regeneration. For example, some writers speak as if love of God is directly kindled in the mind by the direct influence of Holy Spirit; but in fact love to God is subsequent to knowledge of God conveyed in the Gospel. In his opinion, therefore, 'Regeneration is the whole of that change which is effected upon men by the instrumentality of the gospel,'[268] which itself illuminates the understanding, purifies the affections, subdues the stubborn will, and imparts holy joys, sorrows, hopes, fears, pursuits and prospects. In a word, 'the influence, both of the word and of the Spirit of God, are necessary to effect the renewal of a sinner in the spirit of his mind.'[269] If the truth of the Gospel is the proximate cause of regeneration, the special agency of the Spirit is the ultimate cause. The spiritual influence of the latter is without means, whereas renovation is by means, namely, the truth of the Gospel. In other words, 'that influence which leads to the conversion of the sinner is exerted immediately upon the mind, [whereas] the actual turning of the affections from sin to God, is effected by the moral influence of Divine truth.'[270] Payne recalls his earlier distinction when he identifies the divine influence as issuing from God as sovereign; it is not moral influence or suasion. It is a direct influence on the mind whereby 'the good which the gospel exhibits objectively, is made to appear good; and, consequently, to excite volition, and lead to obedience.'[271] It is not, however, necessary to accountability, for this 'would constrain us to maintain that Jehovah is bound to convert all men. It would prove that the fall of man could not have taken place ...'[272] Of one thing Payne is quite sure: regeneration is an absolute and universal necessity. Apart from regeneration 'the duties of the heavenly world would be irksome' and 'the pure and spiritual delights of the world above would yield no measure of enjoyment.'[273]

Turning now to sanctification, we find that in Payne's view this carries forward the work begun in regeneration. It extends, though not necessarily equally, to all the powers of the mind, for 'There are cases in which the understanding makes a more rapid progress than the heart.'[274] It is easier to prove that Christians ought to advance in sanctification than to prove that they actually do so. Sanctification is a process which will not be completed until 'deliverance from this body of sin and death.'[275]

---

[266] Ibid., 334.
[267] Ibid., 358.
[268] Ibid., 336.
[269] Ibid., 348.
[270] Ibid., 373.
[271] Ibid., 375.
[272] Ibid.
[273] Ibid., 384, 385.
[274] Idem, LCT, II, 293.
[275] Ibid., 294.

'Every part of divine truth is adapted to sanctify [God's] people,' he continues, and the Holy Spirit is 'the ultimate cause of sanctification; because it is his continued agency that preserves [God's] people in the knowledge and belief of divine truth.'[276] All of which facts preserve us from presumption and undue confidence in ourselves. The importance of sanctification is shown in that 'our Lord assumed the mediatorial office to secure it.'[277] Sanctification had great practical importance in that it renders us 'extensively useful in the world.' Indeed, 'It will be generally found that the most holy man is the most useful man.'[278] Sanctification is necessary to 'our ultimate reception into those mansions which Christ is gone to prepare for his people.'[279] Holiness and happiness are inextricably combined, and 'In heaven we shall be perfectly happy, because we shall then be perfectly holy, i.e. perfectly conformed to the holy image of God.[280]

In the systematic statement to which reference has just been made, Payne reiterates themes which also appear in a sermon of 1823 entitled, *On the Instrumentality of Divine Truth in the Sanctification of the Souls of Men*. His text is John 17:17, 'Sanctify them through thy truth: thy word is truth.' He argues that a spiritual and believing view of the truth 'is necessary to secure its native and proper influence upon the hearts of the people of God.'[281] Sanctification does not come apart from the truth, but *via* the truth. Accordingly, believers should study God's word attentively, and 'live in the habitual use of all the means which God has appointed for the growing sanctification of his people.'[282] Payne sums up much of his ethical approach to doctrine when he says, 'The light of intellect is far less valuable, and truly beautiful, than the light of moral purity; and it is only when the fires of the former are directed and governed by the latter, that they bring either good to man or glory to God.'[283]

By perseverance Payne understands that 'all who have been really converted to God will be kept by his mighty power through faith unto final salvation.'[284] Those who are professed Christians only may finally fall. While it is undeniable that true Christians continue to sin, this does not legitimate antinomianism. Whereas the high Calvinist John Gill holds that the nature of grace implies that none of the elect shall perish, Payne retorts, 'This I do not believe. It is in my apprehension perfect nonsense. Grace has often been called an incorruptible principle. I believe it is so; but not in its own nature,—it is rendered so by Divine decree. If it were impossible in the nature of the case for faith to sink, there would be no need for our being kept

---

[276] Ibid., 299.
[277] Ibid., 303.
[278] Ibid., 304, 305.
[279] Ibid., 306.
[280] Ibid., 309.
[281] G. Payne, *On theInstrumentality of Divine Truth*, 26.
[282] Ibid., 35.
[283] Quoted from ibid. by J. Pyer, 'Memoir,' lv.
[284] G. Payne, LCT, II, 311.

in the faith by the power of God.'[285] The saints will persevere because they are predestined to do so, and because Christ laid down his life for the sheep. Payne counters a number of points made by the Anglican-turned-Unitarian Daniel Whitby, among them Whitby's notion that the elect might perish, not because of any deficiency on Christ's part, but by their own choice to depart from Christ.[286] Even 'Mr. [John] Wesley has expressed the same sentiment, in very coarse but very emphatic terms,—"They may wriggle themselves out."'[287] By contrast Payne insists that the saints have the presence of the Holy Spirit and the intercession of Christ, which cannot fail. He cites Paul's conviction that 'he who hath begun a good work in your will perform it until the day of Christ' (Philippians 1: 6). He then considers a number of biblical texts which confirm or imply the doctrine of perseverance, and then addresses three objections to it. First, If the saints cannot finally fall away, why are all the warnings concerning that possibility addressed to them? Payne replies that falling is not impossible in itself, but is rendered so by divine decree. Secondly—the Arminian objection—If saints are kept, why the need of prayer and watchfulness? Because, says Payne, God keeps them, as moral beings, by means which secure their preservation. As to the final objection, the apostasy of the saints, Payne declares that apostates were never genuine saints. The fact remains, as Payne argued in a sermon on 'The Sealing and Earnest of the Spirit' preached in Exeter, that the sealing means that God has set his mark upon the saints, while the earnest of the Spirit in the saint's heart is 'our security that we shall finally enjoy the glory which is in reserve for [God's] people in the world above.'[288]

III

Congregational polity, Church and state, the Christian ministry, and mission—these are the subjects which come to the fore in Payne's writings on ecclesiology, and I shall introduce each in turn.

Thinking that the principles of Congregational Dissent were not as well known, even to church members, as they ought to be, Payne was prompted to write *The Church of Christ considered* (1837), of which his smaller work, *A Manual Explanatory of Congregational Principles* (2nd edn, 1842) is largely an abridgment. He surmises that this unfortunate situation may in part be attributed to increasing cooperation in missionary and Bible societies, the worthy ends of such activity taking precedence over denominational distinctives. Nevertheless Congregationalism's distinctive tenets are believed to be part of divine truth, and

---

[285] Ibid., 316. Payne refers to Gill's *The Cause of God and Truth*, in which Gill agrees that 'the new creature is imperfect', but affirms that 'such is the nature, strength, and firmness of true grace, that it [that is, the new creature] can never perish.' 1971 edn, 130(b).

[286] For Whitby (1638-1726) see ODNB.

[287] G. Payne, LCT, II, 322. The literature on John Wesley (1703-1791) is vast, but a start may be made with ODNB.

[288] Ibid., 449.

therefore they must be inculcated. No doubt, 'if we could think that the New Testament leaves it really uncertain whether a Christian church should be a heterogeneous mixture of the pious and the profane—whether it should be in a position of alliance or not, with the state—whether the liberty of approach to the Lord's table should be restricted to those who are the Lord's people, or be granted to all,—there would, in that case, be no reason why we should not hold out peace.'[289] But we are not left in such uncertainty. Not, indeed, that in repudiating latitudinarianism we should embrace bigotry.

Turning first to the definition of 'Church' Payne says that it means (a) 'the great assembly or congregation of redeemed and sanctified men which will meet at length in heaven. Strictly speaking, they will not constitute a church till they arrive in heaven; they are, however, so called now by anticipation.'[290] (b) 'A particular assembly or congregation of persons ... meeting statedly for religious purposes on earth.'[291] To use the term 'church' of a building, or of a denomination, has no divine authority.[292] The Church comprises only those 'who make a credible profession of faith in Christ.'[293] They gather, and the church is formed by a voluntary act. The members are united in faith, and by the one baptism.

The Church's objects are spiritual and eternal, not political, literary or commercial: 'The ultimate object of Christian fellowship is the promotion of the glory of the Triune God,'[294] and the Church's task is to disseminate the truth as it is in Jesus. Church members must own no authority but Christ; they must study the Scriptures, and order their lives accordingly. They must love one another, rebuke those who err and forgive them when they repent. They owe the world effort towards the promotion of its salvation, and worship, prayer, the Lord's Supper and, above all, preaching, are the means to this end.

The church's officers are pastors and deacons. Church members only may call ministers: 'The pastor must choose the flock—the flock the pastor.'[295] By 'ordination' Payne understands 'the orderly and solemn induction of an individual into the pastoral office subsequent to the election of the church, and dependent upon

---

[289] Idem, *The Church of Christ considered*, x.

[290] Ibid., 1.

[291] Ibid., 2.

[292] One hundred and thirty years on the question whether the Congregational *Union of* England and Wales should become the Congregational *Church in* England and Wales was the subject of lively debate. See Alan P. F. Sell, *Testimony and Tradition*, ch. 12. For my own attitude to the adoption of the term 'Church' see my *Saints: Visible Orderly and Catholic*, 114-115, the gist of which is that 'so long as the term "Church" was used denominationally as a temporary, irregular, expedient, Congregational catholicity was unimpaired'; but this usage should not be regarded as 'normal' by those in that tradition. I did not think that it would be ecumenically helpful if the denomination became an ever more impregnable bloc.

[293] G. Payne, *The Church of Christ considered*, 6.

[294] Ibid., 18.

[295] Ibid., 53.

it.'[296] The pastor's authority is 'chiefly, if not exclusively, confined to the application and execution of the laws of Christ, in regard to the church as an associated body.'[297] The office is ministerial, not legislative. Deacons elected by the church should be concerned with material, not spiritual, matters.

Congregationalists are distinguished from Presbyterians by their belief that 'A single congregation of visible believers ... is a complete church,' and 'every such congregation has the entire power of government within itself.'[298] Then comes a crucial cautionary word: 'Real congregationalism is not democracy.' The power is not vested in individual members. Pastors alone are the rulers, but they do not make the laws, they execute Christ's laws, and do so 'with the concurrence of the church.'[299] The members 'have a voice in, and some power over, the exclusion and restoration of offenders,'[300] and on all churchly matters the decision of pastor and people together is final.

In the concluding chapter church discipline is discussed in more detail. Two or three members should engage an offender in private conversation, and then lay all particulars before the church. The pastor's role is to expound the law of Christ as it bears upon the case and guide the church to a decision. Penitents are to be restored, impenitents excluded, but all is to be done with affection towards the offender, with impartiality, and only after prayer for divine direction. Members must 'avoid all unnecessary private intercourse with the expelled member.'[301] The results of inattention to church discipline are disastrous—among them are that the Holy Spirit withholds his influence, and sinners are not converted.

For the contents of Payne's position on Church and state I am largely dependent upon Pyer's 'Memoir', in which a full account is given of the 1834 pamphlet, *The Separation of Church and State calmly considered.* The first edition was pseudonymously attributed to a Devonshire Dissenter, the second appeared under Payne's own name. He fears that the position of the Dissenters has been misrepresented. It is said that Dissenters wish to destroy the Established Church.

> Our reply [says Payne] ... has been that we merely wish to destroy the civil establishment of that Church. ... The dissolution of the conjugal union between two individuals who ought not to have formed it, is not surely the destruction of the female, but the destruction of a relation merely in which she had stood, or had been supposed to stand, to the other party. *The* Church, as it is called by courtesy, *i.e.* the Episcopalian denomination, is now the spouse of the State (we think she ought to be the spouse of Christ only);—our anxiety is simply to obtain a writ of divorce. If our opponents will continue to represent this as a desire to put the wife to death,

---

296 Ibid., 57.
297 Ibid., 60.
298 Ibid., 77.
299 Ibid., 80.
300 Ibid., 97.
301 Ibid., 115.

the public must judge whether the defect is in our statements, or in their perceptions.[302]

In another pamphlet, *Facts and Statements in reference to the Bible-Printing Monopoly*, Payne argues that the civil magistrate steps out of his bounds in deciding which Bibles the nation shall use and who shall print them. Finally, in the preface he contributed to a reprint of an extract by Reed and Matheson on *The Operation of the Voluntary Principle in America*, he roundly declared that

> It is the duty of all who have come to a decision to avow it;—of the Churchman to show, if he can, that the alliance of Church and State is scriptural and expedient;—nor less so, that of the Dissenter to prove, if he is able, that it necessarily bring the former into vassalage to the latter,—corrupts her principles, mars her purity, defaces her glory, and paralyzes her influence. On this subject there ought to be no neutrals.[303]

Apart from passing references, I do not find that Payne published specifically on the sacraments,[304] and what he had to say about the Christian ministry is largely found in one extant ordination charge, *Counsels to a Young Minister*. He here brings two biblical texts together: 'Take heed unto thyself' (I Timothy 4: 16); 'Take heed to the ministry' (Colossians 4:17). He begins by expressing the hope that God's blessing will be upon the minister and his flock; he reminds the ordinand that he is a warrior for the Lord and must not renage upon his calling. On the contrary, 'You must ... my young friend, calculate on remaining at your post till removal from it by the King of Terrors.'[305]

Turning to the texts, Payne refers first to the minister's personal conduct: 'Even the fox-hunting, card-playing, swearing, and drunken black-coated companion of the wildest country squire in existence does less injury to the cause of God than a man of equivocal reputation ... in connection with the ministry of the gospel.'[306] Ministers must be characterized by propriety, decorum and prudence: 'Be at all times the man of God,'[307] he urges. Be kind and accessible to all your people; be ready to assist other churches: some churches are so selfish and, to Payne, this aspect of 'dissenterism' is offensive. Be brotherly, humble and unassuming: 'You will not be

---

302 J. Pyer, 'Memoir,' lxx.

303 Quoted ibid., lxxv-lxxvi. The report by Andrew Reed, the Elder, and James Matheson is entitled, *A Narrative of the Visit to the American Churches by the Deputation from the Congregational Union of England and Wales*. For Reed (1787-1862) see CYB, 1863, 255; ODNB; for Matheson (d. 1846 aged 52) see CYB, 1846, 170. They both received the Honorary DD (Yale) in 1834.

304 Though in LDS, 452-4 he savages the doctrine of baptismal regeneration—a doctrine which is 'so outrageously absurd that it might be left to perish by its own folly'; and he refers to Matthew 28: 19.

305 G. Payne, *Counsels to a Young Minister*, in LCT, II, 479.

306 Ibid., 483.

307 Ibid., 485.

suffered to remain at the bottom, if you really deserve to be at the top.'[308] With a view to all of this the minister must take heed to the state of his own soul: 'The two grand streams which feed the flame of piety are prayer and a devotional study of the word of God.'[309]

As for taking heed to the ministry, the minister's motive must be to promote the glory of Christ by 'extending the triumphs of his gospel in the world.'[310] In manner the minister must be plain, practical, evangelical, affectionate, diligent and persevering. In connection with matters evangelical Payne exhorts the young man as follows: 'Act not as some men do, who introduce [evangelical doctrines] sparingly and cautiously as if they were about to let loose some beasts of prey among the people of their charge.'[311] Man's fall in Adam and his recovery in Christ must be preached; indeed, the entire Christian system must be exhibited: 'The doctrinal and experimental and practical branches of our holy religion form one beautiful and consistent whole, of which the atonement of Christ is at once the centre and support. It would be as absurd, says an excellent writer, to affirm that there is a single lane in the country which does not lead to the metropolis, as to suppose that there is a single doctrine, promise or precept in the word of God which is not connected directly or indirectly with the cross.'[312] The charge ends with nine lines on pastoral care, the gist of which is that private instruction and encouragement are to be given to the people as the minister goes from house to house.

Payne was a great supporter of missionary work, and he has left us one sermon on this theme. The text is Luke 19: 13, 'Occupy till I come.' The means God has appointed for his mission, he declares, are the translation and circulation of the Bible and the employment of agents to call men to its truth. The Bible Society is not to be placed above the Missionary Society in the affections of Christians, for they are twin sisters. Christ does not give his commission without giving the power and means to undertake it. Payne proceeds to point out that all the property of the church and of the individual Christian has been bestowed by God; it has been loaned, not given; and it is to be used for the purpose for which the loan was made. 'Nothing,' he continues, 'appears to me so great an obstacle to the spread of the gospel as the practical inattention of the church to the precept, "Honour the Lord with thy substance."'[313] Christians ought to surpass the Jew's tithing, but in fact Jewish tithing is almost princely compared with what some Christians give. We ought to give more to the Lord's work than what we give to 'superfluities', for the task we have been given—the evangelization of the world—is enormous. We may be sure that 'the proprietor will come, and demand an account of our stewardship.' So 'Occupy till I come.'[314]

---

[308] Ibid., 489.
[309] Ibid., 491.
[310] Ibid.
[311] Ibid., 496.
[312] Ibid., 497.
[313] Ibid., 467.
[314] Ibid., 475.

IV

If, to Payne, the atonement was Christianity's central doctrine, the doctrine of the Trinity was foundational: 'The doctrine of the Trinity, or, as the word imports, of three distinct subsistences or persons in the one undivided nature or essence, lies at the foundation of the entire economy of salvation ... [It] constitutes the very basis of that wonderful scheme of mercy on which rest all our hopes of salvation.'[315] With accustomed caution Payne point out that we cannot explain the manner or mode of the unity and plurality of the persons; in fact, we are 'better able to say what it not true than what is so.'[316] The three are not separate beings, nor are Sabellians correct in saying that the persons simply exhibit the same being in different aspects. We are, he thinks, concerned with something analogous to personality, 'though what that something is we are totally unable to explain.'[317] The subordinationism of Arianism is rebutted, and the Nicene *homoousios* is affirmed.

Payne construes the Athanasian divines of the early centuries as holding that the Father was the fountain of deity, not in the sense that the he predated the Son and the Spirit, but in the philosophical sense of 'the principle from which another arises.' They did not mean that the Son and Holy Spirit each had a beginning, or that the Father, 'after existing for some time alone, brought them into being by an act of his will, and imparted to them such powers as he chose.'[318] Such as view would have been Arian—a position unavailable to those who believe in three persons in one substance. Payne surmises that the Athanasians were tempted to move from thinking that the Father and the Son were of the same nature to thinking that the latter derived his essence and perfections from the former, and this with a view to sustaining their belief in the divine unity. In Payne's view, 'To say that [the Son and the Spirit] derived this personal distinction from the Father, rather increases than diminishes the difficulty of conceiving that they are at the same time one with him.'[319] As if sensitive to the problem, the orthodox spoke of the three persons as inseparably joined together, and of the indwelling of the persons in one another.

Payne is blunt:

> That the three persons of the Sacred Trinity are, in some mysterious manner, united so as that this plurality does not impair the unity of the Godhead is a most important sentiment. But the attempt of the ancient church to explain this union ... is worse than useless. It crowds together a heap of words without any meaning. It mocks us by substituting sound for sense. It gives us ashes for bread. It is a clear display of that lack of modesty which has been too often manifested with reference

[315] G. Payne, LCT, I, 222, 223.
[316] Ibid., 223.
[317] Ibid., 224.
[318] Ibid., 242-3.
[319] Ibid., 244.

> to this ineffable subject; and it may serve as a beacon to guard us against so foolish an attempt.[320]

A further possible reason why the orthodox theologians used language as they did may derive from their understanding of such terms as 'Son' and 'only-begotten' as indicating not a distinction of office, but of essence; and Payne notes that supporters of eternal generation from patristic times to Waterland, Pearson, Bull and John Owen, have connected that doctrine with the idea that the Father, the fount of deity, has communicated the divine nature to the Son and the Spirit.[321]

Were the early theologians and their modern successors correct in their view of the essential difference of the Son and Spirit from the Father? At this point Payne comes 'to the discussion of a point which, I confess, I would on various counts rather have avoided, if I could have done it consistently, in my apprehension, with honour and conscience,—the question with reference to the Sonship of Christ.'[322] He follows many in holding that the terms 'Father, Son and Holy Spirit' are

> descriptive of the office which these Divine persons sustain in the economy of redemption; and that though they imply their true and proper Deity, they have no reference to them merely as Divine persons; and of course give no sanction to the opinion that the Father is the Fountain of Deity; and indeed leave us as much in ignorance of the nature of that connection which exists amongst the sacred three as they found us,—the object of Divine revelation being, not to show what God is in himself, but what he is in relation to us.[323]

Indeed, the position of the orthodox divines tends 'either to degrade the Lord Jesus Christ, or to throw impenetrable obscurity over all our statements concerning the Trinity.'[324] His reasoning is that the term 'son' in ordinary usage implied 'posteriority, derivation, inferiority.'[325] If the term 'Son' when used of the second person of the Trinity is used in its ordinary sense it necessarily implies the aforementioned characteristics. If it is not used in the ordinary sense nothing is revealed concerning 'the manner and order of his eternal subsistence in the Godhead.'[326] Payne's conclusion—and we recall that it was a position advocated by Thomas Ridgley—is that 'as a Divine subsistent [the second person of the Trinity] does not bear the name of Son, ... that title is given to him on account of the office

---

[320] Ibid., 245-6.

[321] For Daniel Waterland (1683-1740), John Pearson (1613-1686), George Bull (1634-1710) and John Owen (1613-1683) see ODNB.

[322] G. Payne, LCT, I, 247.

[323] Ibid., 247-8.

[324] Ibid., 249.

[325] Ibid.

[326] Ibid. On this matter Payne, 'With all my regard for Dr. [Edward] Williams—and it almost approaches to reverence', takes issue with Williams. I shall return to Williams in the conclusion to this chapter.

he assumed as Emmanuel, or God with us.'[327] He proceeds to analyse biblical texts which are alleged to show that as a subsistent of the Godhead Christ is referred to as Son, that is that the Son is eternally generate. He finds the argument wanting (though when, for example, he supposes that such Old Testament texts as Psalm 2:1: 'Thou art my Son; this day have I begotten thee', refer explicitly to Christ, I, standing on my side of modern biblical criticism, cannot endorse his method). The New Testament texts he refers to are Hebrews 1:3 and John 5:26. In his exposition of the latter he quotes at length from Ridgley to show that the verse will not support eternal generation either. Positively, like Ridgley before him, he adduces biblical evidence to show that such terms as 'Son' and 'only begotten' refer to the incarnate Christ as God-man Mediator. Thus, for example, on the passage in John's Gospel in which we learn that the Son does not know the day or the hour of judgment, Payne remarks,

> if the term Son be applied to Christ as a Divine person merely if it be intended to intimate some essential difference which exists between the first and the second person of the Trinity, it is utterly impossible to say of the Son that he knows not the hour of judgment, that he increased in wisdom and well as in stature, without surrendering the omniscience of that Saviour in whom we have put our trust; and in that case our truth must prove a vain confidence, a broken reed, which can but pierce and destroy. I conscientiously believe that the view of the Sonship of Christ which I have endeavoured to give you rescues his Divinity from certain perplexities and objections, which I at least should find it difficult to meet.[328]

Payne then seeks to meet five objections to his position, of which I shall notice two by way of giving the flavour of his whole case. The first is that if the names Father, Son and Spirit do not express relations essential to the eternal subsistence of the divine persons, they cannot reveal a Trinity of persons in the Godhead. Payne replies, 'this is a mistake; because the names are personal names, and cannot properly be applied but to persons. The relations, indeed, which they express are not essential to personality, for a person may exist without being either a father or a son; but personality is essential to these relations, for no one can be a father or a son but a person.'[329] Secondly, To those who say that Christ was called 'Son' before he became incarnate, Payne replies that 'he was so in intention and appointment, though not in act and accomplishment; ... He became actually the Son of God by his miraculous incarnation.'[330] This is not to deny the eternal pre-existence of the second person of the Trinity (with which claim Payne avoids adoptionism), but it is to claim that Christ did not eternally exist as a Son.

Payne sums up his view of the Trinity in the following terms:

[327] Ibid., 251.
[328] Ibid., 266-7.
[329] Ibid., 267.
[330] Ibid., 268.

> There are in the Godhead three distinct hypostases, subsistences, distinctions, or persons, who are strictly co-eternal, and in all respects co-equal,—the titles Father, Son, and Holy Ghost being applied to them to mark out the relation they sustain to each other in the economy of salvation, and not any essential distinction which exists amongst the sacred three as subsistents in the Godhead, and far less any subordination of one to the other. What is the precise nature of the distinction which exists between the three persons of the Godhead as Divine persons,—for we believe that there is an essential distinction between them, though not the relations suggested by the terms Father, Son, and Holy Ghost;—the Scriptures, we think, nowhere reveal; and therefore it is useless, and indeed, improper, to speculate about it. Nor do they explain in what mysterious manner the sacred three are united. They merely affirm the fact that in some ineffable way they are united, so that our Jehovah Elohim is but one Jehovah.[331] His unity does not preclude the plurality we ascribe to him, nor does his plurality destroy his unity; but what is the precise sense of the personality and the unity of God we are totally inadequate to say,—both these matters, to a very considerable extent at least, being in that *terra incognito* into which we do well not to enter.[332]

Payne sets out to justify the Trinitarian claim by reference to biblical texts, and in the course of so doing he rebuts the position of the Unitarian Thomas Belsham, and relies for linguistic guidance on his fellow Congregationalist John Pye Smith.[333] As hinted earlier, Matthew 28:19, 'Go, teach all nations, baptizing them in the name of the Father, and of the Son, and of the Holy Ghost', is among the texts to which he draws attention. His claim is that 'if in Christian baptism we are devoted or dedicated unto the name, *i.e.* the glory of the Father, and of the Son, and of the Holy Ghost, how can it be doubted that the Son and the Holy Ghost are Divine persons as well as the Father?'[334] Some have objected that the Matthean text was not intended as a formulary of the rite of baptism, to which Payne replies that the words nevertheless remain as a 'revealed description of Christian baptism, deduced from its reference, intention, and use; and it is on this revealed description that we build our confidence in the doctrine of the Trinity.'[335] Moreover, since Christ issued the command to baptize in the terms given, that is not Christian baptism which is not administered in the threefold name. In this connection the Arian Nathaniel Lardner's paraphrase of the text in such a way that the Son and the Holy Spirit are not persons 'is little less than absurd.'[336] The other texts examined by Payne confirm his general

---

[331] Following Pye Smith, Payne makes much of the fact that 'Elohim' is a plural noun. See LCT, I, 283-6.

[332] G. Payne, LCT, I, 273-4.

[333] For Belsham (1750-1829) and Smith (1774-1851) see ODNB.

[334] G. Payne, LTC, I, 296.

[335] Ibid., 297.

[336] Ibid., 299. Lardner's paraphrase is: 'Go ye therefore into all the world, and teach, or disciple, all nations; baptizing them into the profession of faith in, and an obligation to obey, the doctrine taught by Christ, with authority from God the Father, and confirmed by the Holy Ghost.' For Lardner (1684-1768) see ODNB.

position, and he ends his lectures on the Trinity by reminding his audience that the deity of the Son and of the Holy Spirit are further attested in many places in the Bible. To his Christology and pneumatology I have already paid some attention.

V

Of George Payne it was said that as a theological professor 'He sought not so much to place the truth before the mind, as to implant it in the mind; and to do this he spared no pains.'[337] He rose to this challenge at a time of shifting intellectual landmarks, when the question, What is truth? was at a premium, and when the answers to it, not least from within the ranks of Nonconformity, were diverse and frequently mutually contradictory. It was also said of Payne that 'acuteness of perception, power of analysis, and ingenuity of research, were the most striking features of Dr. Payne's mental conformation. ... [H]e was more discriminating than original—more philosophical than poetical—more analytical than profound.'[338] At a time when the finer points of doctrine could so easily become badges of sectarianism, and when more than sufficient 'pulpit poets' were abroad, a theologian of analytical skill and discriminating intelligence who was as competent in arguing his case as in fairly stating and (sometimes bluntly) rebutting that of his intellectual foes was a bonus indeed.

Payne, as we saw, wished Christians to have a firm grasp of the truths of the Gospel; he regretted that so few studied the fundamentals of the faith; and he feared that 'if a moral deluge were to sweep away our accustomed words and phraseology on religious subjects, it would not, in very numerous instances, leave many ideas behind it.'[339] It was this concern which prompted him to write his *Lectures on Divine Sovereignty* not so much for ministers, but for church members who will have to hand 'a volume which might tend, with the blessings of God, to promote generally a more correct and familiar acquaintance with the great principles on which it treats than perhaps at present prevails.'[340]

My reflections upon Payne's published works incline me to the view that he is to be commended for the part which he, along with a number of others, played in reformulating Calvinistic doctrine in the wake of the moral challenge flowing down from the Enlightenment and the call to evangelism so clamantly heard in the Evangelical Revival.[341] It also seems to me that in a variety of ways Payne stood very near the end of a philosophico-theological line which was very soon to hit the buffers of modern biblical criticism and agnosticism, with results that he could not have foreseen. We could not nowadays subscribe to his view that there is general

[337] J. Pyer, 'Memoir,' cxii.

[338] Ibid., cvii, cxiii.

[339] G. Payne, LDS, vi.

[340] Ibid., ix.

[341] See further Alan P. F. Sell, *Enlightenment, Ecumenism, Evangel*, chs 3, 5. See also John McLeod Campbell's searching analysis of 'Calvinism as recently modified,' in *The Nature of the Atonement*. Campbell makes numerous references to Payne.

agreement on the duties which persons owe to God, themselves and others; that those who forget the claims of God are necessarily immoral and bad; that godliness is an essential part of morality. Payne was still persuaded by the long-lived view that a morally good atheist is something inconceivable. Again, in the wake of Hume and Kant we cannot simply adopt Payne's theistic arguments, nor, in the wake of modern biblical criticism and historical method can we accept his approach to the Bible in its entirety. We can, however, see that in his own day he performed a valuable service—and what else can be expected of any of us?

For example, Payne sought to steer a careful course between the Scylla of evangelical Arminianism and the Charybdis of high Calvinism. Thus he agreed with the evangelical Arminians against the high Calvinists that the Gospel should be freely offered to all the world; but against the evangelical Arminians he maintained that while Christ's atonement was sufficient for all (something the high Calvinists denied) it was efficient only in respect of the elect. This, as W. F. Adeney later argued, was to circumscribe the efficiency of the atonement by predestination.[342] Again, Payne sought a middle way between those Socinians and Arians who held that Adam's descendents are not affected by his disobedience but are answerable only for their own sins, and the high Calvinists who held that Adam's guilt is imputed to us. Payne held that the consequences of Adam's sin are imputed to us, but not his guilt: we are guilty of our own misdeeds alone. Yet again, Payne was concerned that God's sovereignty be construed in moral terms. Hence, for example, Christ was not punished for the sins of others, and he himself was sinless. He bore our sins, however, and what would have been punishment for us was suffering for him. What is operative here is the view that humanity's primary need is to escape eternal punishment for sins committed—and we have seen how frequently Payne utters warnings to this effect, with the result that against Payne's better judgment a transactional view of Christ's work becomes almost inevitable. Robert Mackintosh pulled no punches in denouncing a not dissimilar view:

> To tell us that God inflicted something hardly to be called punishment upon One who had not sinned, in order subsequently to remit the punishment of those who had sinned, and that He did this because He was sure that psychologically sinners must now be convinced of the inevitable sequence of punishment upon sin—what theology is that for any place except a madhouse? ... The harsh old doctrine that Christ bore that pains of hell is dignified and beautiful compared with this contemptible scheme of administrative smartness.[343]

---

[342] W. F. Adeney, *A Century's Progress in Religious Life and Thought*, 119. More strictly, by a particular understanding of predestination which too readily identified what is a religious concept with philosophical determinism. For further reflections on this doctrine see Alan P. F. Sell, *Enlightenment, Ecumenism, Evangel*, 325-338.

[343] R. Mackintosh, *Historic Theories of Atonement*, 186-7. For Mackintosh (1858-1933) see DNCBP; DSCHT; DTCBP; ODNB; Alan P. F. Sell, *Robert Mackintosh, Theologian of Integrity*.

As to the doctrine of election, Payne insists (in agreement with the high Calvinists and against the evangelical Arminians) that while the elect are called from eternity, there is no corresponding decree of reprobation. In this connection as in others, a prominent device in Payne's modifying of scholastic Calvinism is the distinction he inherits from Edward Williams of Rotherham academy, whose book, *An Essay on the Equity of Divine Government* (1809) acted as a solvent upon rationalistic scholastic Calvinism.[344] The distinction is that between God's sovereignty conceived as personal and his moral governorship of all things. A sovereign God could choose whom he would to be saved; but in his rectoral capacity he had no option but to honour justice and punish the generality of sinners. This distinction is also said to explain why Christ's death as a satisfaction was required: there was no personal reluctance on God's part to pardon sinners, but in his rectoral character he could no do this apart from Christ's satisfaction. Vincent Tymms was later to expostulate, 'how fallacious is would be to mentally divide the Godhead into separate departments and offices which involve different principles in the treatment of men';[345] and it is, indeed, difficult to suppress the feeling that there is a certain artificiality in Payne's dualistic view of a God who, wearing one hat would pardon if he could, but wearing the other hat can pardon only on terms. To put it otherwise, there are sufficient difficulties in speaking of the personality of the Godhead without tending in the direction of speaking as if the divine personality is a split one.

The implication of my adversely critical remarks is that for all his good intentions, Payne's theological legacy, like that of other exponents of moderate Calvinism is an inherently unstable one, involving as it did the attempt to modify traditional confessional assertions when what was really required was a revision of a confessional method which had all but passed its 'sell-by' date. In other words, a fresh starting-point was needed—a point perceived by none more clearly in the mid-nineteenth century that by John McLeod Campbell.[346] The grace of God, not the sin of humanity, must be the first word of the Gospel and of the Christian 'system'. Payne's Congregational successor, P. T. Forsyth, made his pungently-expressed view the heart of his theology: 'The atonement did not procure grace, it flowed from grace.'[347] I shall return to the question of starting-points in the concluding chapter of this book.

It remains to assess Payne's ecclesiology and his doctrine of the Trinity. His published ecclesiology was not comprehensive. He did not dwell on the sacraments,

---

[344] For Williams (1750-1813) see DEB; DNCBP; ODNB; J. Gilbert, *Memoir of the Life and Writings of Edward Williams*; W. T. Owen, *Edward Williams, D.D.*

[345] T. Vincent Tymms, for whom see ch. 8 below, *The Christian Idea of Atonement*, 385.

[346] This is not to imply complete endorsement of the way in which McLeod Campbell pursued his course. For Campbell (1800-1872) see DEB; DSCHT; ODNB; J. B. Torrance, 'The contribution of McLeod Campbell to Scottish theology'; J. M. Tuttle, *So Rich a Soil*; Peter K. Stevenson, *God in Our Nature*.

[347] P. T. Forsyth, *The Cruciality of the Cross*, (1909), London: Independent Press, 1951, 41.

for example, and in his exposition of Congregationalism he, rather oddly, made little use of the concept of covenant, though it is implicit in what he writes as to the nature of the church as the gathering of the saints; in his clear declaration that the Church Meeting is not a ruling democratic assembly but that Christ alone is Lord of the Church; and in his careful discussion of church discipline which concerns the breach of the covenant by offenders. It is tempting to speculate that the reason for the inattention to baptism and the covenant concept was that in some circles following the Evangelical Revival the gathering in of sinners by conversion was the route to church membership, and that this tended to diminish the emphasis upon baptism as the entry to the Church. Certainly it is demonstrable that from about 1830 onwards there was a sharp decline in the number of local Congregational covenants, notwithstanding the increase of Congregational churches.[348] Again, Payne does not emphasise that by virtue of one's engrafting into Christ along with other saints in the church local one concurrently becomes a member of the Church catholic; and while he approves of the mutual support and concerted witness of the wider family of churches he does not dwell upon it as an ecclesiological development. His strictures against the Church of England *qua* established are standard, and his insistence that Christ alone is head of the Church is, in that connection, not redundant to this day.[349] What Payne has to say about ministry and mission does not call for comment.

The same is not true of his account of the doctrine of the Trinity. Here Payne's cautious agnosticism is at its height. Wisely, he will not make pronouncements concerning the inner recesses of the life of the triune God about which we are ignorant, for this would be to speculate beyond the revelation which God has been pleased to give. This leads Payne to deny the doctrine of the eternal generation of the Son. This denial places him in the line of Ridgley and many others who argued that while the second Person of the Trinity was eternally of the Godhead (hence *homoousion*, hence no Arian subordinationism), the terms 'Son', 'only begotten' and the like denote the incarnate Christ—that is, they refer to the mediatorial office fulfilled by the second Person (hence no adoptionism) in the economy of redemption. It should be emphasised that none of this is to deny the divinity of Christ, but those in favour of the doctrine of eternal generation would say that their view more adequately preserves the idea that God was eternally Father and hence Christ was eternally Son, and that this more readily coheres with the view that a divine Christ alone could save the world, while a human Christ alone could do for us at the Cross what we could never have done for ourselves. While concurring in the motive as just expressed, I tend, with Payne, to the side of godly agnosticism where the attempt to probe the inner life of the Godhead is concerned, and I can understand why some have felt that the doctrine of the eternal Sonship is an inference drawn the Christian experience of Father, Son and Spirit and then read back into eternity. On the other

---

[348] See Alan P. F. Sell, *Dissenting Thought and the Life of the Churches*, 61-67.

[349] See further ibid., ch. 22; idem, *Testimony and Tradition*, ch. 11; idem, *Nonconformist Theology in the Twentieth Century*, 136-145, 183-4.

hand, if, with Payne, we say that there are eternal relations in the Godhead which, because relations are impersonal, are not properly named by the terms 'Father, Son and Spirit', have we not introduced a further unbridgeable dualism, this time between God as he is in his triune self, about which we are ignorant, and God as he has made himself known to us? And does not this leave us with an alleged revelation which does not, in fact, reveal anything to us? May—indeed, ought—we not to say that while God's revelation is accommodated to our intellectual capacities—which is to say that our minds cannot grasp the whole of God—it is nevertheless the case that, being a God of truth, as he has revealed himself to be, so he is; and he has made himself known as Father, Son and Holy Spirit. Whatever conclusions are reached on this strictly mysterious matter, I do not think that those on either side of the debate can win the day by the proof-texting method which came so naturally to George Payne and his forebears in the faith, but which cannot, I believe, be utilized with integrity on our side of modern biblical criticism.

Without question George Payne's philosophical and analytical skills were put to good use within the terms of the methodologies current in his time. *Pace* James Haldane, theologians have nothing to fear from careful philosophical analysis, and the writings of some would benefit greatly from more of it. Without question also Payne was 'useful' in his time as he picked his way carefully through the available doctrinal options and sought to hold ministers and church members to the truths of the Gospel. But equally without question is the fact that he did not claim that his method and conclusions had eternal validity. Nor have ours.

CHAPTER 6

Richard Alliott (1804–1863): Inexorable Logician and Winsome Evangelist

Richard Alliott's family inheritance was staunchly Congregational and ministerial.[1] His grandfather, also Richard, was born at Kenilworth in 1738. He trained for the ministry under David Jennings at Kibworth and Samuel Morton Savage at Hoxton.[2] Following a very brief assistantship at Kenilworth, he became assistant to Patrick Simson at Vicar Lane church, Coventry, in 1759. He was well received, and three years later was called by the church to be co-pastor. He was ordained at the more capacious Old Meeting, Coventry, on 11 November 1762. We learn that 'The [Vicar Lane] chapel was crowded every Lord's day during his ministry. His preaching was eminently blessed in the conversion of sinners to God. But alas! he was cut off in the midst of his days and usefulness, being the victim of a pulmonary consumption.'[3] Simson made the following entry in the Church Book:

> The Lord thought fit to make an awful breach in this church on March 11,[4] 1769, by calling to himself our late beloved pastor, the Rev. Richard Alliott, after labouring among us in the gospel about nine years, with diligence, fidelity, and success.[5]

Alliott was thirty years of age; his wife died fifty-two years later.[6]

Their son Richard was born at Coventry on 1 February 1769, a few weeks before his father's death. He trained for the ministry at Homerton, receiving a Trotman grant in 1790. From 1792 to 1794 he was minister at Stratford upon Avon,[7] but his great ministry was at Castle Gate, Nottingham, whither he went in 1794, where he was ordained on 8 April 1795,[8] and where he served for almost forty-six years until

---

[1] For Alliott see CYB, 1865, 217-18; DNCBP; EM, 1864, 129-135; A. R. Henderson, *History of Castle Gate Congregational* Church, 170-4 and passim; Alan P. F. Sell, *Philosophy, Dissent and Nonconformity*, 115-118 and *passim*.

[2] For Jennings (1691-1762) and Savage (1721-1791) see ODNB; EEUTA.

[3] John Sibree and M. Caston, *Independency in Warwickshire*, 65.

[4] EM, 1821, 284, gives 10 March.

[5] Quoted by Sibree and Caston, op.cit, 65..

[6] EM, 1821, 284.

[7] See Sibree and Caston, op.cit., 199.

[8] So EM, 1985, 244. See also, *A Discourse on The Nature of a Christian Church, by the Rev. J. Brewer, etc.*

his death on 19 April 1840.[9] The membership of Castle Gate church stood at forty-one on Alliott's arrival. During his ministry the chapel was twice enlarged, but in October 1817 Alliott ruefully reflected that although the congregation numbered some nine hundred, the membership was less than two hundred. Under his leadership the church became an ardent supporter of the infant Missionary [later, the London Missionary] Society, and on 14 May 1828 he spoke in Surrey Chapel on the occasion of the thirty-fourth Anniversary Service of the Society. His address was published under the title, *The Nature and Obligations of Christian Liberality, and the Influence of these Obligatins on the Support of Christian Missions*. Alliott was an energetic supporter of Sunday Schools in the area—notwithstanding the fact that in 1813 the Castle Gate Sunday School Society took more than a week to decide whether to admit their pastor as a member.[10] Meanwhile in 1801 the Sunday School examinations were held in Stoney Street General Baptist Chapel, where the scholars were examined on Dan Taylor's catechism and Alliott delivered the Sunday School sermon.[11] In 1805 he again served in this capacity.[12] On 19 July 1815 we find him preaching at the formation of a Sunday School Union Society at Loughborough. His subject was *Christian Union*; his text John 17:21; and his theme, the unity of Christians despite denominational differences.

That Alliott was a force to be reckoned with in wider society is evidenced by the fact that in 1803 he was selected to preach to three united congregations of Nottingham Protestant Dissenters on the occasion of a general fast. He spoke on *The Danger and Duty of our Country*. In face of threats posed by our enemies, he declared, the nation needs to confess, pray, repent and reform. Writing as I am on the occasion of the two hundredth anniversary of the Act to abolish the slave trade, it is interesting to note Alliott's view that the nation is especially subject to God's anger because of 'the African slave trade.'[13] 1820 Alliott, together with the Quakers Fox and Gill, the Baptist J. Jarman, and the Unitarian Thomas Wakefield, comprised a committee supportive of the Framework Knitters Society whose members sought minimum prices for their work.[14] In 1834 Alliott chaired a meeting that urged the reform of the Factory Acts.

In the midst of his busy ministry, Alliott found time for polemics. His first publication of this kind was occasioned by a sermon preached on Christmas Day 1808 by David Davies of the Unitarian Chapel, Belper, Derbyshire. Davies published his sermon, using his text, John 1: 45, as the title: *Jesus of Nazareth the Son of Joseph*. The kernel of his case was that 'if Jesus was more than man, he was no

[9] See A. R. Henderson, *History of Castle Gate, passim*. For the Church Meeting's memorial tribute to him see ibid., 172-3.

[10] Ibid., 178.

[11] See F. M. W. Harrison, *The Life and Thought of the Baptists of Nottinghamshire*, II, 1731. (Pagination is consecutive through the two volumes of this thesis.)

[12] See A. R. Henderson, *History of Castle Gate*, 189.

[13] R. Alliott, Sr., *The Danger and Duty of our Country*, 10.

[14] See F. M. W. Harrison, *The Life and Thought of the Baptists of Nottinghamshire*, II, 879-80; cf. 886.

example for us.'[15] Alliott replied with *Jesus of Nazareth the Son of God* (1809), in which he presented the orthodox view of the Incarnation. Undeterred, Davies followed up with *Letters on the Miraculous Conception* (1809), in which he ransacked the Bible and came to the conclusion that

> For disbelieving in the miraculous conception; a doctrine as inconsistent with revelation as it is contrary to reason, I am branded with the name of unbeliever:- but if to believe in the existence of one supreme and Almighty God, and in Jesus Christ as the Messenger of that God, sent to lead mankind in the way of salvation, and to instruct them to aspire to a life after this: and if a firm belief in the scriptures, as a revelation from heaven, does not constitute an unbeliever, then I am not one: and let those who charge me with it, blush for their injustice.[16]

It seems unlikely that Alliott blushed; it is certain that he offered no further response.

That Alliott was polemically active on more than one ecclesiastical front is clear from the fact that when the Vicar of St. Mary, Nottingham, rebuked Calvin over the death of Servetus, Alliott addressed two published letters to him. In the first he argues that the Genevan laws, not Calvin himself, were responsible for the death of Servetus; and, invoking the 'pot and kettle' defence, he reminds the Vicar of the death of the Anabaptist Joan Bocher in 1549 where Cranmer was Archbishop. Finally, he rebuts the Vicar's charge that Calvinistic doctrine was at the root of Servetus's death, and reminds him that it was the Trinity that was at issue, that this is a doctrine of the Church of England, and that the Athanasian Creed 'excludes from salvation all who deny it.'[17] In his second letter he advances a moderate Calvinistic position on reprobation, pointing out that 'there is a great body of modern Calvinists who think that the doctrine of reprobation, as it is commonly understood, has no real countenance from scripture, and is no essential part of the system called Calvinism.'[18] Predestination and election are, however, biblical concepts, and they are asserted in the Church of England's seventeenth *Article*.

Finally, in 1827 Alliott published a pamphlet on *Jewish and Christian Controversy*, in which he replied to a letter of Rabbi Hart Symonds, arguing that the divine mission of Jesus may be established by the same kind of evidence as that which established the divine mission of Moses.

The Alliotts had two sons. The younger, William, was born at Nottingham on 22 July 1807. He matriculated in the University of Glasgow in 1827, and also studied at the academy at Wymondley. He was assistant minister at Pavement Chapel, Moorfield, London in 1832, and later that year removed to the New Meeting (later, Howard Chapel), Bedford, where he remained until his death on 12 August 1867. From 1840 to 1866 he conducted a theological academy jointly with John Jukes of

---

[15] D. Davies, *Jesus of Nazareth the Son of Joseph*, 21.

[16] Idem, *Letters on the Miraculous Conception*, 83.

[17] R. Alliott (Sr.), *An Apology for Calvin and Calvinism*, 9.

[18] Ibid., 20.

Bunyan Meeting. Until 1849 the academy prepared candidates for the home ministry, but in that year the London Missionary Society began to send intending missionaries to Bedford.[19] On 1 December 1850 Alliott gave a lecture at Howard Chapel which was subsequently published under the title, *What is Popery?* His text was Galatians 6: 1, 'Brethren, if any man be overtaken in a fault, ye which are spiritual, restore such an one in the spirit of meekness; considering thyself, lest thou also be tempted.' The 'doctrine of merit,' he declared, '[Rome's] spirit of persecution, its numberless superstitions ... are merely offshoots of the system. The power of the Priest, constitutes the soul, of Popery.'[20] He has in mind the claims that, among other things, the priest can turn the bread and wine into the body and blood of Christ, and absolve sinners. Over against this priestly power he sets the liberty wherewith Christ has made us free. His other publication is in a quite different vein. It is intensely pastoral and full of consolation. It comprises a pair of sermons published under the title, *Christianity a Religion of Consolations* (1858). The text of the first sermon is II Corinthians 1: 3-4: 'Blessed be God, even the Father of our Lord Jesus Christ, the Father of mercies, and the God of all comfort; Who comforteth us in all our tribulations, that we may be able to comfort them which are in any trouble, by the comfort wherewith we ourselves are comforted of God.' Sorrows cannot be avoided, he says, but sorrow 'is only good as it prepared the mind to receive the consolations of God.'[21] The second sermon is on I Timothy 1: 10, which speaks of 'our Saviour Jesus Christ, who hath abolished death, and hath brought life and immortality to light through the gospel.' Alliott graciously works towards his conclusion that 'In the view of a true Christian "to die is gain." It is not a loss, it is not a deprivation, but an immense increase of happiness.'[22]

William Alliott's son, yet another Richard, also became a Congregational minister. He was born at Bedford on 29 March 1839; he studied at Trinity College, Cambridge (1855-59), and then proceeded to Lancashire Independent College, Manchester (1859-1863), whose third President, the man of letters-*cum*-apologist Henry Rogers, assumed office also in 1859.[23] Alliott became minister at Knutsford, Cheshire, but made his greatest contribution as Principal of the Nonconformist Grammar School at Bishops Stortford from 1868 until his death on 28 October 1899. In 1875 he addressed the Hertfordshire Congregational Association on *The Attitude of the Church towards the Young*. He urged all concerned to take baptism and Christian nurture much more seriously than was the general custom, and he pleaded with ministers to give time to the young of their flocks. In the following year he addressed the Association on *The Supply of Christian Ministry*. He lamented

---

[19] For the academy and some of its alumni see H. G. Tibbutt, *Bunyan Meeting Bedford 1650-1950*, ch. 5.

[20] W. Alliott, *What is Popery?* 13. For William Alliott see CYB, 1868, 248-9.

[21] Idem, *Christianity a Religion of Consolations*, 7.

[22] Ibid., 18.

[23] For this Richard Alliott see CYB, 1900, 159-60. For Henry Rogers see DNCBP; ODNB; R. W. Dale, Memoir; Alan P. F. Sell, *Dissenting Thought and the Life of the Churches*, chs. 17, 18.

the paucity of ministerial candidates and their quality; he surmised that few men could really produce two competent sermons and at least one weekday address every week; and he deeply regretted that so few ministers were given adequate financial support by their churches.

But our particular concern is with Richard Alliott of Castle Gate's older son, Richard, and to him I now turn.

I

This Richard Alliott was born in Nottingham on 1 September 1804. He trained for the ministry at Homerton, where subscription to Calvinistic articles had been required of all students until 1817. John Pye Smith, who had himself studied under Edward Williams at Rotherham, began his half century of service to Homerton in 1801, and became Professor of Theology in 1806.[24] Alliott sat under him in this latter capacity. Pye Smith pioneered the introduction of German scholarship into his courses and, as we shall see, Alliott was among the first Congregationalists to notice Schleiermacher in print. From Homerton, where his course had been interrupted by ill health, Alliott, like George Payne before him, proceeded to the University of Glasgow, where James Mylne was still occupying the Chair of Moral Philosophy. During the two sessions, 1826 and 1827, of his residency, Alliott won prizes, and wrote a long-remembered essay on the *a priori* argument for the existence of God[25]—an earnest of much *a priori* argumentation to come. He graduated MA, and in 1840 Glasgow awarded him the degree of Doctor of Laws.

In 1827, initially together with his brother William, Alliott was appointed to conduct the newly-introduced evening service at Castle Gate church. In the following year, William now having left town, Richard was invited to become assistant minister to his father. On 10 August, he delivered a sermon entitled, *The Christian Ministry. A Sermon, delivered on entering into the duties of that important work.* His text was Jeremiah 1: 6-8: 'Then said I, Ah, Lord God! behold, I cannot speak: for I am a child. But the Lord said unto me, Say not, I am a child: for thou shalt go to all that I shall send thee, and whatsoever I command the thou shalt speak. Be not afraid of their faces: for I am with thee to deliver thee, saith the Lord.' Alliott enumerates the qualifications for ministry thus: 'If ... there be an ardent desire springing from holy and benevolent feelings; if there be the attainment of suitable qualifications, and an invitation from a particular Church; we may reasonably infer, that the Lord in his providence speaks to us as he spoke to Jeremiah "Before I formed

---

[24] For Pye Smith (1774-1851) see DEB; EEUTA, 180-186; ODNB; John Medway, *Memoirs*; T. H. Simms, *Homerton College*, 11-14.

[25] EM, 1864, 130; G. B. Johnson, 'Sketch', 27. George Burlingham Johnson was born at Bressingham, Norfolk, on 26 August 1819. He trained at Coward College and ministered at East Retford (1840-44), Hallgate, Doncaster (1844-9), Belgrave, Darwen (1849-57); Kings Weigh House, London (supply) (1857-8); Francis Road, Edgbaston (1858-77) and Belgrave, Torquay (1877-87). He retired through ill health and died on 17 July 1902. See CYB, 1903, 183-4.

thee in the bowels I knew thee ...''[26] He then cautions those 'called to official stations in the church' to 'feel a becoming sense of diffidence of their own qualifications and strength.'[27] This should not, however, prevent their submission to Christ's will; rather, it should prompt them to look to him for instruction and support. He offers the following encouragement: 'Our Lord Jesus will never lay on us a burden, without enabling us to bear it: the promise which he will most assuredly perform, is, that our strength shall be equal to our day.'[28] The objectives of the Christian ministry are (and we may note the post-Revival order here) 'the conversion of sinners and the edification of the Church.'[29] He next refers to high Calvinists who 'object to inviting sinners to repentance and faith on account of their inability to exercise these graces without Divine assistance.'[30] But we must place Christ's evangelical command above our own reasonings. Pastors must edify Christ's flock and tend Christ's sheep. Alliott asks his Castle Gate hearers to pray for him, and concludes with the sobering reminder that 'the effects of our Ministry will be felt in Heaven or in Hell.'[31]

In 1829 his father proposed to the church that Richard become co-pastor with himself, and on 6 January 1830 Alliott was ordained and inducted to this office. His father delivered the charge to his son, taking Deuteronomy 31: 23 as his text: 'Be strong and of a good courage: for thou shalt bring the children of Israel into the land which I sware unto them: and I will be with thee.' Among others taking part were James Gawthorne of Derby and Robert McAll of Manchester.[32] The latter delivered a charge to the church based on Revelation 3: 22, 'He that hath an ear, let his hear what the Spirit saith unto the churches.' That Alliott quickly made a name for himself is clear from the fact that on 16 March 1837 he preached to the Nottinghamshire Association of Independent Ministers and Churches in James Street Chapel. His text was Matthew 16: 27, 'For the Son of man shall come in the glory of his Father with his angels; and then he shall reward every man according to his works.' Alliott makes is clear that the last clause here refers to good and bad people alike. Sinners, he continues, cannot receive the reward of debt from God, but only the reward of grace. Moreover, 'an important design of the dispensation of the

---

[26] R. Alliott, *The Christian Ministry*, 5.

[27] Ibid.

[28] Ibid., 9. This was a recurring theme in the preaching of George Sydney Morgan, the minister of my youth.

[29] R. Alliott, *The Christian Ministry*, 12.

[30] Ibid.

[31] Ibid., 16.

[32] Gawthorne, a Hoxton alumnus, served the one pastorate at Brookside Chapel (later Victoria Street), Derby from 1801-1857, when he died aged 82. See CYB, 1882, 299-300. Robert Stephens McAll (1792-1838) ODNB. He had a distinguished ministry at Mosley Street, Manchester. Following a pastorate at Hallgate, Doncaster, his son, Samuel (1807-1888), succeeded Alliott at Castle Gate on the latter's removal to Lambeth, and then, from 1860 to 1881 was Principal of Hackney College. See A. R. Henderson, *History of Castle Gate Congregational Church*, ch. 16.

gospel, is, to render it consistent with divine justice to bestow blessing on sinners.'[33] Hence God's provision of his Son, the substitute. The degrees of happiness experienced hereafter will be relative to a believer's holiness and usefulness here. The eternal reward is utterly unmerited; it is all of grace. The works acceptable to God flow from faith and love. Alliott closes by exhorting his hearers to excel in such works.

On Easter Sunday, 19 April 1840, Richard Alliott, Sr., died, having served Castle Gate church for almost forty-six years. A memorial resolution was agreed at the Church Meeting on 17 June, the last part of which concerns the pastor's son:

> The brethren desire ... to acknowledge with thankfulness the kind providence of Almighty God in giving them a beloved son of their esteemed pastor, whose united labours with his revered father, have already, through a period of twelve years, been eminently blessed amongst them; they desire now that he had succeeded to the sole pastorship to express their great attachment and esteem for him, and their heart's desire an prayer is that a great outpouring of the Holy Spirit may rest upon him, and that his labours may be long continued, his usefulness greatly increased, and that the whole of his ministry may be crowned with the Divine blessing.[34]

Alliott thus became the sole pastor at Castle Gate.

In a sermon preached there on 23 January 1842 Alliott tested the doctrine of apostolic succession by Scripture. He sets out, provocatively enough, from Matthew 7: 15, 'Beware of false prophets, which come to you in sheep's clothing, but inwardly they are ravening wolves.' He first makes the general point that we must beware of false teachers because the natural depravity of the heart may predispose us to love darkness rather than light. He then comes directly to the point: if by 'apostolic succession' is meant 'a treading in the steps of the apostles, the preaching their doctrines, the imitation of their example', this is entirely in accordance with Scripture.[35] The problem arises when 'a party' is said to be in the apostolical succession because of a particular line of ordination. This is a ceremonial succession only, which confers authority on those concerned 'whether they preach truth or error, whether their lives are an ornament or a disgrace to their profession, whether they have been wise to win souls to Christ, or have been instrumental in leading them to perdition.'[36] It is ironic that those not in the apostolic succession as thus defined are deemed false ministers, even though they 'declare the whole counsel of God' and have been used to turn multitudes from Satan to God. The biblical tests by the application of which we may discern those who are truly in the apostolic succession are,

> 1. Is their preaching in accordance with holy writ?

---

[33] R. Alliott, *The Christian Rewarded according to his Works*, 11.

[34] Castle Gate Church Book, quoted by A. R Henderson, op.cit., 172-3.

[35] R. Alliott, *The Doctrine of Apostolical Succession*, 4.

[36] Ibid.

2. Are their lives consistent with their profession?
3. Have they been made instrumental to the salvation of souls?[37]

In a day of heresy and false doctrine, he concludes, we must try the spirits to see whether they are of God.

That Alliott took his own medicine is clear from his own post-Revival practice of pressing the claims of Christ on all possible occasions. G. B. Johnson records one such instance which occurred during Alliott's Nottingham ministry:

> One Sabbath evening, a young man who had been for two or three years on the provincial stage, and who had just obtained an appointment to London, which he was to enter upon the next week, challenged a friend to a stroll. Rain fell, an heavily. They took shelter, and observing that they were near a chapel, and that the rain continued, they entered it. It was Castle Gate. Dr. Alliott was in the pulpit: the discourse was addressed to young people, from the words, 'Come, ye children, hearken unto me, I will teach you the fear of the Lord.' The young actor was smitten to the heart. He returned to his lodgings, but not to rest. He asked for a Bible, and in great tumult of soul spent the night, reading and praying. One thing was clear to him, he could not fulfil his metropolitan engagement. He wrote to the preacher, and was at once invited to his house. He found peace in believing. But what now of his temporal prospects and future course? He was generously received into the Doctor's family. There he remained for weeks, and the issue was his study for the ministry at Rotherham College. He has for nearly twenty years preached the Gospel of Christ, and God has much blessed him in his work.[38]

The hopes of the Castle Gate members that Alliott's work among them might be 'long continued' were dashed. In 1843 he made the difficult decision to leave them for York Chapel, Lambeth. A writer of some 'Historical Notices' published on the occasion of the bicentenary of the Castle Gate church said that 'The period of Dr. Alliott's sole pastorate, was marked by a spiritual and successful movement for discharging a debt which had gradually accumulated from the cost of repairs &c.—amounting in all to nearly £800.'[39] While we may be sure that Alliott was relieved to have the debt cleared, there is strong evidence that he was more gratified by those who had found Christ during his ministry. In his letter of resignation he wrote,

> I have now held this office for more than thirteen years, and have ministered amongst you for more than fifteen; it has, through this period, been my endeavour to watch for souls, and, though my duties have been discharged with may imperfections and much weakness, God has been pleased to prosper me; a very large proportion of the Church consists of those whom God has (I believe) given me for

---

[37] Ibid., 5.
[38] G. B. Johnson, 'Sketch', 30.
[39] Anon., *Bi-Centenary of Castle Gate Meeting*, 91.

my hire; they are my epistles, known and read of all men, and I anticipate the day when they will constitute my crown of rejoicing in another world.[40]

Whereas the Castle Gate church had a long and distinguished history, that at York Road, Lambeth, was a product of nineteenth-century home missionary endeavour.[41] Noting that a small school and preaching station had been opened in 1835 in Captain's Walk in the deprived area of Vine Street, Lambeth, The Metropolitan Chapel Fund Association decided to lend its support by building a chapel and schoolroom in York Road. The Reverend Thomas Morell laid the foundation stone on 6 June 1838, and the chapel was opened on 17 January 1839 at a cost of £3465. The Revs James Sherman of Surrey Chapel, Blackfriars and George Clayton of Lock's Fields, Walworth, were present at the constitution of the church on 28 February of the same year.[42] It would seem that for the next few years the pulpit was supplied by various ministers, for on 7 April 1843 Alliott became the first settled pastor. At the time of his arrival there were 92 church members. During his ministry of six years 376 people were added to the roll, of whom '261 were received from the world, "many of them acknowledging with affection and gratitude that to him, under God, they owed their conversion."'[43]

Among those gathered in was the older son of a churchgoing Anglican family who lived near Alliott's manse. One Sunday, during a violent storm, the son attended the morning service at York Road. Impressed by Alliott's earnestness, he went again in the evening. Alliott spotted him and accompanied him home. Next, he sent the boy a letter inviting him to supper. The boy accepted, and thus began his regular attendance at York Road. He enrolled in the Sunday School and was eventually received as a member. When Alliott became President of the Western College the boy became one of his students. In due course Alliott delivered the charge when he was ordained to the ministry.[44]

Alliott did not confine his evangelistic appeals to personal approaches. For example, on Christmas Day 1843, in the course of a series of lectures on the Christian life, he preached on *The Union of the Convert with the Visible Church*. His text was Acts 2: 47(b), 'And the Lord added to the church daily such as should be saved.' He first defines the term 'church': 'A Christian church is a society of professing christians united, under the authority of Christ, for the observation of his ordinances, mutual edification, and the conversion of sinners. Of such a society Christ is the only head, and his word the only statute book.'[45] Three things are required to unite the convert with the church: a credible profession of faith; church

---

[40] Quoted by A. R. Henderson, *History of Castle Gate Congregational Church*, 173-4.

[41] See J. Waddington, *Surrey Congregational History*, 240-241; E. E. Cleal, *The Story of Congtregationalism in Surrey*, 283.

[42] For Sherman (1796-1862) see CYB, 1863, 263-6; ODNB; for Clayton (1783-1862) see CYB, 1863, 219-22.

[43] G. B. Johnson, 'Sketch', 31.

[44] For a fuller account see G. B. Johnson, 'Sketch', 31-2.

[45] R. Alliott, *The Union of the Convert with the Visible Church*, 83.

association with believers; and communion with believers at the table of the Lord. As to the last, the Lord's Supper 'ought to be celebrated for the sake of our own christian consolation and edification. Amongst the means of grace of the Divine institution, I consider none so adapted as this to gratify the spiritual appetite or to promote faith, hope, love, and every christian grace.'[46] He ends with an appeal to new converts to join themselves to the church.

Alliott's series of sermons continued into 1844, and on 28 January we find him preaching on *The Christian Working for God.* His text is I Corinthians 15: 58, 'Therefore, my beloved brethren, be ye stedfast, unmoveable, always abounding in the work of the Lord, forasmuch as ye know that your labour is not in vain in the Lord.' The objectives of Christian activity, he declares, are 'the glory of Christ and the salvation of men.'[47] Such activity is motivated by gratitude to Christ for his love; by a desire more fully to answer the end of our conversion; by a spirit of compassion for the lost; and by our hope of finding in Christian exertion a means of grace.

Two years later Alliott gave seven lectures to young men, of which the third, delivered at York Road on Sunday evening 1 February 1846, is entitled, *On the varied mental constitution of young men, and the peculiar temptations to which their mental constitutions expose them.* In this lecture we see an early indication of Alliott's interest in psychology. He begins by observing that all people have certain intellectual faculties, passions and emotions; and they all have a conscience—'an inward monitor who sits in judgment on our thoughts, feelings, words and actions. This monitor is, in some instances, almost stifled ...'[48] But although sharing all of the foregoing characteristics people also differ. Some young men are of a sceptical turn of mind, others are credulous. The sceptical may reject truth, or may be so taken with objections that they fail to examine positive evidence carefully. Some distrust their own judgment, and they may be led astray by those who are spiritually blind. Some 'are credulous through mental indolence.'[49] Some young men 'seem to be naturally grave and sedate, and others to be gay, light and trifling.'[50] Finally, some are naturally ambitious, others are selfish. Alliott has recommendations and cautions for every class of young man.

In 1848 Alliott travelled to Abbey Road chapel, Torquay, where he delivered the charge to the church on the occasion of the ordination and induction of Nicholas Hurry, a Liverpudlian who had been among the first intake of students at Lancashire Independent College.[51] On this occasion Alliott spoke from two texts: Philippians 2: 29, and II John 5, 8. He urges the church to pray that the new pastor will be holy

---

[46] Ibid., 87.

[47] Idem, *The Christian Working for God*, 185.

[48] Idem, *On the varied Mental Constitution of Young Men*, 383.

[49] Ibid., 388.

[50] Ibid., 390.

[51] For Hurry (1822-1909) see CYB, 1910, 173-4. He remained in Torquay until 1857, then proceeded to Richmond Hill, Bournemouth (1858-69), Neuchatel (1869-71), Sevenoaks (1871-3) and Wanstead (1873-82).

and full of the Holy Ghost; that he will be wise; and that the Holy Spirit will apply his words to his hearers. The members must also cooperate with the minister. They must esteem him and hold him in affection because of the truth he brings them. They must love and respect him even when he reproves sin judiciously and affectionately. They must attend his ministry regularly. If they do not profit from the ministry they must not assume that it is necessarily the pastor's fault: they must come to church in a humble, teachable and prayerful spirit. The minister must be their 'confidential spiritual friend and counsellor.'[52] They must remember that the minister is called to work for the whole church and not just for particular individuals; indeed, he must work for the unconverted too, and they must assist him in this. Having addressed the church he turned to 'the congregation at large' (thereby observing a distinction crucial to the Congregational polity). He exhorts the congregation to profess their faith if they have it, or be converted out of their 'fearful condition' if they have not.[53]

Alliott's pastoral concern tempered with warnings is evident in a sermon he preached at York Road under the title, *Mutual Recognition in Heaven*. The occasion was the death of George Wright, whose parents were church members. The text was I Thessalonians 4: 18, 'Wherefore comfort one another with these words.' 'Christian friends,' he declares, 'will be loved in heaven better than they are loved on earth, but worldly friends, being see in all their moral unloveliness, will cease to attract regard.'[54] 'O that will be joyful, when we meet to part no more,' he says, immediately posing the question, 'Have you, brethren, christian relatives or friends in heaven? There is no hope of re-union for you except you be christians.'[55]

Whilst at York Road Alliott gave lectures on the history of the Jews, and on moral philosophy and rhetoric at the college sponsored by the British Society for the Propagation of the Gospel among the Jews. For two years he edited the Society's paper, *The Jewish Herald*. Founded in 1842 by Andrew A. Bonar and Robert Murray McCheyne, the Society's objective was the conversion of Jews to Christianity.[56] Alliott was particularly encouraging to converts who proceeded to the Christian ministry, as a number of them did. During this period he prepared a course of lectures on *The History of the Children of Israel* [1849], in which he recounted the history and drew moral and spiritual lessons from it.

Alliott served some of the Congregational theological colleges as an examiner, and it became increasingly clear that a professorial appointment in one of them would be the most appropriate use of his gifts. Indeed, 'nearly every Independent College in England has at one time sought to secure him as Theological, Philosophical, or Mathematical Professor.'[57] But it was to the Presidency of the Western College in Plymouth that he went in 1849, to the great regret, but with the

---

[52] R. Alliott, *The Duty of a Church to its Pastor*, 9.
[53] Ibid., 15.
[54] Idem, *Mutual Recognition in Heaven*, 9.
[55] Ibid., 15.
[56] For Bonar (1810-1892) and McCheyne (1813-1843) see DEB; DSCHT; ODNB.
[57] G. B. Johnson, 'Sketch,' 33.

genuine support, of the church at York Road. A Valedictory Service was held at which Sherman and Clayton gave addresses. Drs Thomas Jenkyn, Principal of Coward College, and John Waddington of Union Street church, Southwark, and the Revd J. Baldwin Brown of Claylands Chapel, Clapham Road, London were among others taking part.[58] In the course of his remarks Sherman thanked Alliott on behalf of the trustees and tutors of Cheshunt College for the occasions of which he had rendered ready assistance to the College; and he rhetorically asked of Alliott, 'who ever had a quarrel with you except he began it and carried it on, and was obliged at last to seek your aid to put out the fire which he had kindled ... The churches all around love you, which of them does not regret your leaving?'[59] But leave for Plymouth he did.

II

Alliott began his duties at Western College, in succession to George Payne, on 20 June 1849. He remained there until 7 April 1857, when he left to assume the Presidency of Cheshunt College.[60] The Western College flourished under the harmonious leadership of Alliott and his colleague Samuel Newth. Student numbers rose from 12 to 29, eight non-resident lay students being admitted from 1850. A Centenary Appeal was launched with a view to providing a new building for the College.

In 1854 Alliott gave *The Congregational Lecture*. This was published during the following year under the title, *Psychology and Theology: or, Psychology applied to the Investigation of Questions relating to Religion, Natural Theology, and Revelation.* As G. B. Johnson accurately said, 'It was the very subject to absorb him: and his treatment of it is most characteristic,—simple, unaffected, clear, logical, laborious, but utterly devoid of those illustrations or digressions which minds less capable than his of abstruse reasoning seem imperatively to demand even in such discussion as he there pursues.'[61] I shall return to this, Alliott's most significant work, in due course.

Alliott maintained contact with the Castle Gate church in Nottingham, and on 7 October 1855 he preached there on the occasion of that church's bi-centenary. His subject was 'The rise of British Congregationalism with a special reference to its

---

[58] For Thomas Williams Jenkyn, DD (Middlebury) (1794-1858), an alumnus of Homerton, see CYB, 1859, 203-4; DWB; for John Waddington, DD (Williamstown) (1810-1880) the historian, an alumnus of Airedale academy, see CYB, 1881, 398; ODNB; for James Baldwin Brown (1820-1884), an alumnus of Coward College and a BA of University College, London, who was regarded by stricter Calvinists as dangerously liberal in theology, see CYB, 181-4; ODNB; Mark D. Johnson, *The Dissolution of Dissent*; Mark Hopkins, *Nonconformity's Romantic Generation*. See Bibliography for my reviews of the books by Johnson and Hopkins.

[59] G. B. Johnson, 'Sketch,' 35.

[60] See MS 'Tutors in the College at Plymouth.'

[61] G. B. Johnson, 'Sketch,' 37.

spiritual aspects and results.' He took Romans 14: 10 as his text: 'But why dost thou judge thy brother? or why dost thou set at nought thy brother? for we shall all stand before the judgment seat of Christ.' While he has no difficulty in finding the Congregational polity in the New Testament, Alliott's emphasis is upon the period from the Reformation onwards. Congregationalism, he declares, is of great spiritual value in that it fosters individual responsibility among church members, and because, to a greater degree than any other system of church government, it stands for the 'direct kingly authority of our Lord Jesus Christ over every individual members of the church.'[62] He then cautions that there is a spurious Independency which claims freedom from human control 'for some other purpose than subjection to [Christ's] Divine control.'[63] This is decidedly not Bible Independency.

Of Alliott's service at Western College it was said that he, 'along with Mr. Newth, led the College to a great height of prosperity, usefulness, and even renown.'[64] Not surprisingly, therefore, 'The Committee of the Western College greatly deprecated his leaving them, unable to see that it was possible for him to fill a position of higher influence and usefulness than that he had attained to in the West of England.'[65] But Alliott accepted the call to Cheshunt.

A clue to the reasons for his decision is found in the following observations of his friend G. B. Johnson,

> The proximity of the College to the metropolis, and the catholicity of its constitution attracted him. While firm in his Dissent and Congregationalism, and highly valuing the simplicity of its worship and the purity of its fellowship he thought he might find greater liberty for certain tastes in the conduct of Divine worship and in the development of Church principles as President of a Lady Huntingdon's College administered by Trustees who are as liberal as they are judicious.[66]

We may perhaps infer from these remarks that Alliott, who was also to serve as pastor the church which met in the Cheshunt chapel, valued the modified Church of England liturgy which was at that time still used in Lady Huntingdon's chapels.

In addition to the work within his own College, Alliott assisted Hackney College following the death of Professor Watson.[67] He gave lectures there until Samuel McAll, Alliott's successor at Castle Gate, came to replace Watson. During 1858-59 Alliott served as Chairman of the Congregational Union of England and Wales. In this capacity he gave two addresses. Between them these addresses embrace Alliott's theological and evangelistic interests, for the first was on 'The new theology'—and

---

[62] *Bi-Centenary of Castle Gate Meeting*, 30. Cf. A. R. Henderson, *History of Castle Gate Congregational Church*, 205.

[63] Ibid., 33.

[64] J. Charteris Johnstone, 'The story of the Western College,' CHST, VII, 1916-1918, 104.

[65] G. B. Johnson, 'Sketch,' 37.

[66] Ibid., 37-8.

[67] For John Watson see CYB, 1860, 210-11.

to this I shall return shortly; the second concerned the evidences of revival. In electing to speak on revivals, Alliott was following themes which John Angell James of Carrs Lane church, Birmingham, and Mr. Charles Reed of London, the staunch advocate of Sunday Schools, had introduced at a previous Union Assembly.[68]

Alliott says that there is no subject of greater importance to the Church than revival. There is widespread agreement that revival, understood as 'an increase in the life and power of religion in the heart, and in an enlarged manifestation of it in the life'[69] would be a boon to the universal church; and also that apart from the pouring out of the Holy Spirit, there will be no revival. There is not, however, general agreement as to the evidences of a revival or the means by which a revival should be sought. Some seek evidence of revival in 'an increased attendance on the means of grace, and especially at prayer meetings...Now, I can conceive of a revival of religion where there is no increase at all in the attendance on public ordinances. ... On the other hand, there may possibly be an enlarged attendance without any true revival.'[70] Again, some argue that increased church attendance proves that religion is advancing; to which Alliott replies in characteristically analytical style, 'Now, additions to the church would doubtless be a valid test, if conversion was invariably followed by outward profession, if none made a profession but true converts, and if increase of grace on the part of Christians was always proportionate to the additions made to their number.'[71] But none of these criteria are necessarily, or in practice, met. Equally, 'there may ... be the absence of conversions, and yet anything but spiritual death.'[72] Yet again, some advert to an increase of zeal and liberality on the part of professing Christian as evidence of a real revival. But such can occur from other causes, and without there being any increase of true piety. None of Alliott's cautions are intended to deny the fact that numerical increase, and increase of zeal and liberality are signs of a true revival, but they are so only if they flow from an 'increase of the life of God in the soul. ... There is no revival till we experience within stronger faith in the presence and word of our God, in the finished work of Christ, in the indwelling of the Spirit in our hearts.'[73]

The greatest difference of opinion among Christians, he continues, concerns the means to be used in the quest of revival. Some advocate the continuing use of the ordinary means of grace, while others introduce extraordinary means. The former do not wish to countenance the suggestion that the ordinary means appointed by God are inadequate, or to risk what might in these latter days be called temporary 'spiritual highs' followed by slumps into indifference. The latter believe that in a time of spiritual declension only something extraordinary will arouse the attention of those who need to be reached, and that any excitement which occurs, while not itself

[68] For James (1785-1859) and Reed (1819-1881) see ODNB.

[69] R. Alliott, 'Address' on revival, CYB, 1859, 39.

[70] Ibid., 39-40.

[71] Ibid., 40.

[72] Ibid., 41.

[73] Ibid., 42.

revival, may lead to it. On all of which Alliott reflects in a judicious, balanced way designed to cover all the bases:

> Both are, I believe, to a certain extent, right. Whenever the extraordinary means advocated are *in their nature* different from the more ordinary means, and are therefore different from what God has appointed, to resort to them would be to impugn the Divine wisdom, to set aside the Divine authority, and to deprive ourselves of any right to expect the Divine blessing. But this is not the case with all extraordinary means. Often all that is implied in extraordinary means is the extraordinary use of ordinary ones. ... The authority of God does not ... forbid the extraordinary use of ordinary means, or even of means which, though not in form ordinary, do not differ in nature. Nay more, not merely is there nothing in Scripture to forbid, there is everything to encourage it.[74]

On the other hand, he continues, there are dangers in the use of extraordinary means, against which we need to be on our guard.

> If special services do good, it will only be in the same way as ordinary services. They may excite more interest and attention, and hence may more readily reach the understanding and the heart; but whether a service is ordinary or extraordinary the understanding and the heart must be reached, or no good will be accomplished. ... If, then, we would see a revival, let us begin with ourselves, cry mightily to God in secret, and not let Him go till He excite in us the feeling which will prepare us to be a blessing to others. We must have a more thoroughly earnest, prayerful, self-sacrificing ministry, if our churches are to become earnest, prayerful and self-sacrificing.[75]

Alliott then resumes a theme dear to his heart which is already familiar to us. 'Preaching,' he declares, 'is instituted for two objects—the conversions of sinners, and the edification of the people of God.'[76] Ministers should aim at both objectives (though not in every sermon they preach), and 'if they have no talent for both ends, they are scarcely the men for a single pastorate.'[77] They must learn to speak to people not merely officially, but as having a sincere and ardent love for their souls. Above all, 'What is most needed is earnestness, simplicity, and a full prominence to the leading truths of the Gospel. By simplicity I do not mean unstudied common-places, but such an exhibition of truth as shall reach the comprehension of the bulk of our hearers.'[78] Having been reached, the church members must do more to witness to what they have heard in their lives.

Finally, Alliott adverts to the importance of the theological colleges in relation to the revival of religion. He recognizes that some think the colleges unnecessary,

---

[74] Ibid., 43-4.
[75] Ibid., 45.
[76] Ibid.
[77] Ibid., 47.
[78] Ibid., 49.

while others even think that they are 'an evil and a curse.'[79] Colleges are places where men can be formed for ministry, not simply informed about various academic disciplines. Not that the latter are unimportant. On the contrary, theology and the study of the Bible are of supreme importance but, Alliott insists, they will be best studied if students have first had their mental powers stimulated by classics, mathematics and philosophy. So many in the churches never think about the colleges until they are seeking a pastor; and it would be of great benefit if, instead of complaining that students arrive in pastorates will too little practical experience, churches took steps to cooperate with the colleges in providing opportunities of gaining such experience. Alliott ends with a plea that all will be 'more thoroughly in earnest about our own spiritual interests, and the spiritual interests of those committed to our care. And let us ... be also more prayerful. ... "Let thy priests be clothes with righteousness; and let thy saints shout for joy!"'[80]

After three years Alliott left Cheshunt for Spring Hill College, Birmingham. This move was precipitated by the state of his wife's health. He was succeeded at Cheshunt by H. R. Reynolds who spoke highly of the way in which Alliott had raised the state of the College following 'an interregnum of painful occurrence and tedious length.'[81] He noted Alliott's kindness to the students, and expressed his own gratitude for the way in which Alliott had welcomed him as his successor. He quoted a student who said, 'I consider Dr. Alliott's lectures were quite perfect of their kind,'[82] and he marvelled at the range of Alliott's teaching—indeed, he did so much that he set his successor a real challenge. Another student, Urijah R. Thomas of Redland Park church, Bristol, felt 'no lack of gratitude to our former president' recognizing that 'We had had much laborious and lucid instruction in may things from the principal who had just left us an his colleagues. But Dr. Reynold's great and gracious personality immediately threw a spell over us such as we had not known before.'[83] Reynolds was an entirely capable principal, but it does not take much imagination to surmise what Alliott might have said of a non-substantial 'spell'.

At Spring Hill College Alliott's Chair was that of Theology and Philosophy. He did not carry the responsibilities of the Principalship, and he did not live in the College. He did, however, combine his teaching with the pastorate of Acocks Green Congregational Church. On 21 September 1860, Alliott gave an Inaugural Lecture on 'Our Colleges', in which he resumed some of the points he had made towards the end of his second lecture from the Chair of the Congregational Union of England and

[79] Ibid., 50.

[80] Ibid., 51-2.

[81] G. B. Johnson, 'Sketch,' 38.

[82] Ibid., 41.

[83] *Henry Robert Reynolds, D.D.*, 171. For Reynolds (1825-1896) see CYB, 1897, 213-215; ODNB. Trained at Coward College, he served at Halstead (1846-9), East Parade, Leeds (1849-60), and retired from Cheshunt College in 1894. For Thomas (1838/9-1901) see CYB, 1902, 201-203. Redland Park (with Avonmouth from 1895) was his sole pastorate (1862-1901).

Wales. In this lecture he wastes no time in nailing his colours to the mast. Speaking at a time when some questioned the desirability of a theological college education he testifies, 'I have no sympathy with the sentiment expressed by some, that our ministry is over-educated, and that we should have better preachers if we were content to have inferior scholars.'[84] He next observes that 'True piety indeed is the first qualification of a candidate for the ministry,'[85] and he grants that education is not essential to the acquisition of piety. But piety by itself will not sustain a ministry. He further grants that some who have few literary attainments have been greatly blessed in God's service, and he agrees that natural talent and extraordinary mental power may compensate for the lack of mental culture. But would not the outcomes have been even better had natural talent and mental powers been developed together? In the latter connection he returns to his recommendation of classics, mathematics and philosophy as disciplines preparatory to the study of theology, so that subsequent theological teaching will not be passively received and students will bring independent and vigorous minds to the pursuit of truth. He further suggests that 'there is less danger of trifling with philosophy than with theology.'[86] Students need developed intellectual powers in order to approach theology, and philosophy is more apt to secure these than theology, for the latter, as revealed, is accepted on authority, whereas 'authority finds no legitimate place in philosophy,' where 'our own observation and reason are the ultimate standard of appeal.'[87] In a way which might well have made some of his more conservative peers tremble, he insists that 'If we bring out and strengthen the intellectual faculties of our students, teach them to think for themselves—fit them to investigate truth, we do far more for their future power and usefulness than if we were to store their memories with all the divinity found in the works of our most eminent theologians.'[88]

Scholarship will not by itself make a person into a good preacher, he says, and there are scholars who have no talent for public speaking. But where there is that talent, scholarship will render a preacher more effective. Alliott strongly dissents from the view, held by some, that increased attention in the curriculum to homiletics, elocution and pastoral theology at the expense of classics, mathematics and philosophy would be a better use of students' time and make them more effective ministers. He has no objection to acquainting students with the principles of

---

[84] R. Alliott, 'Our Colleges,' 17

[85] Ibid.

[86] Ibid., 4.

[87] Ibid.

[88] Ibid., 5. The regurgitation of memorized, undigested, lecture notes was not unknown in the theological colleges of Alliott's day. There is some reason to think that many present-day academics are in no position to pour scorn on their nineteenth-century forebears, such is their predilection for 'course handouts' (the bane of higher education—at least in my fields). Even H. R. Reynolds remarked with approval that Alliott's lectures were 'so arranged as to be capable of easy reproduction.' See G. B. Johnson, 'Sketch,' 39. Nothing seems further from the sentiments of Alliott himself, as just rehearsed.

rhetoric, or with impressing upon them the need to speak plainly and clearly and to attend to remediable imperfections in their speech. As to pastoralia, useful hints may be given by tutors experienced in it; but even better would be the opportunity for leaving students to spend a few months with a good pastor.[89] In Alliott's experience 'the men who have had first-rate powers for the pulpit have also had first-rate abilities for the classroom.'[90] In a rather backhanded compliment, Alliott finds a place for such 'artificial stimulants' as the examinations and honours of the University of London: 'Whether the degrees conferred are of any value or not in themselves, they are of high value as a stimulus to labour, and they are, moreover, valuable as evidence to the world of both the ability and the willingness to work.'[91] He regrets that 'We are far behind our neighbours in Scotland, who give a much longer period than we do to preparatory study, and whose ministers have in many cases a proportionately stronger hold on the people.[92]

He next meets head on the objection that learning is dangerous to orthodoxy and injurious to piety: '*Dangerous to orthodoxy!* We believe firmly in the scriptural truth of the doctrines ordinarily characterised amongst us as orthodox; but, if these doctrines are true, they will bear the most searching investigation. ... Truth ... loves light. It is error that cannot exist in light. Error is founded on ignorance, is dependent on ignorance, and hence loves darkness rather than light.'[93] As for piety, secular knowledge could only injure this if study were not accompanied by watchfulness and prayer: but the same holds for every occupation of life. Certainly 'Learning ... is compatible with unholiness of heart and aversion from God; but wherever it so exists it is not the learning that had depraved the heart and turned it away from the Creator: the heart was depraved and far off from God ere it was associated with learning.'[94] Anything may be abused and made an occasion of sin, but this is not an argument for total abstinence.

Alliott argues in a calmly defiant way that if any changes are to be made in the theological college curriculum they should be designed to make the students more thorough scholars and philosophers. On such a foundation the rudiments of theology may be laid, but theology should be so taught 'as to lead our men to think for themselves, and to fit them for pursuing the study through life, rather than merely fill their minds and their memories with the thoughts and dogmas of other men.'[95]

There are those who lament the fact that some ministerial students do not in the end enter the ministry. Alliott is convinced that it is better that those whose call has been tested and found wanting do not proceed to the pastorate. Such persons are

---

[89] Alliott was spared the burgeoning in some quarters of the clinical pastoral counselling industry of the twentieth century which in some places swamped some of the traditional theological disciplines, notably languages and philosophy.

[90] R. Alliott, 'Our colleges,' 9.

[91] Ibid., 10.

[92] Ibid., 11.

[93] Ibid., 11, 12.

[94] Ibid., 13.

[95] Ibid. An admirable sentiment!

educated for whatever service within the Church that God intends for them, and it is no loss if they devote their talents to their true end.

Alliott next specifies the courses he will teach. In view of his position on the nature of theological education we are not surprised to learn that 'I intend to take my students through a course of logic and a somewhat extended course of mental and moral philosophy.'[96] In theology his course 'will comprehend natural theology, the evidences of Christianity, the inspiration of the Scriptures, tradition, the right of private judgment, and the doctrines of Scripture. I shall also call attention to ecclesiastical history, and the history of doctrines, to the early fathers, and to the Christian Church, its officers, and its ordinances.'[97] His earlier remarks notwithstanding, he also undertakes to cover homiletics and pastoral theology, explaining that 'In homiletics it will be my object not to cramp natural talent, but to develop and direct it in such a manner as shall lead to the accomplishment of the grand end of preaching—the conversion of sinners and the increase of believers in knowledge, piety, and devotedness.'[98]

He concludes by asking for the prayers of all for the College professors; and by exhorting the students to remember that 'you are working for [God] as much when engaged in preparing for future service as when actively employed in that service.'[99] He prays that God will 'bless you with large, very large usefulness on earth, and at length give you to enter into your Saviour's joy! Amen.'[100]

On Sunday 29 July 1860 Alliott delivered a funeral sermon for the late Joseph Sortain in North Street Chapel, Brighton, where the deceased had ministered for almost twenty-nine years.[101] Sortain was an alumnus of Cheshunt College, and had served as a part-time tutor there. The prayer which Alliott offered before preaching is prefixed to the published sermon. In setting out from a slightly modified version of the collect for All Saint's Day in the Church of England's *Book of Common Prayer*, it witnesses to Alliott's concern for liturgical propriety and his sympathy with the forms used in the Countess of Huntingdon's Connexion. He then gives thanks for Sortain's life and happy death, and prays for the bereaved family and church: 'Let Thy people trust in Thee, in the darkness, as well as in the light, and may they be consoled with the thought, that thought their pastor is taken from them, their Saviour lives, the same yesterday, and to-day, and for ever.'[102] The text of the sermon is Hebrews 13: 7, 'Remember them which have the rule over you, who have spoken unto you the world of God: whose faith follow, considering the end of their conversation.' Sortain, he says was 'possessed of a philosophic mind and a polished

---

[96] R. Alliott, 'Our colleges,' 15.

[97] Ibid.

[98] Ibid.

[99] Ibid., 16.

[100] Ibid.

[101] For Sortain (1809-1860) see CYB, 1861, 239-40; DNCBP; Bridget Margaret Sortain (his wife), *Memorials of Joseph Sortain*; Alan P. F. Sell, *Philosophy, Dissent and Nonconformity*, 122, 236.

[102] R. Alliott, *The Funeral Sermon for the late Rev. Joseph Sortain, B.A.*, 2.

taste,' and 'leading men of literature and science' were to be found in his congregation.[103] He exhorts his hearers to remember Sortain's teaching, noting his facility for putting truth in new forms; to remember the life of one who resolved at the age of sixteen to devote all his powers to the ministry; and to remember his death in relation to their own forthcoming decease: 'if his earthly course had a limit which it could not pass, so will yours.'[104] Let all, therefore, prepare for this eventuality. He ends with a word of consolation:

> May the God of the departed be the God of the widow in His holy habitation, and may He impart that strength and solace, which none but He can give. To her and to all who feel that they have lost a beloved friend let me say, that he is not lost—only gone before. ...Pastors die, but Christ, whom they preach, lives; the doctrines which they preach, live; the hopes which these doctrines inspire, live. ... "[T]he word of the Lord endureth for ever, and this is the word, by which the gospel is preached unto you."[105]

By 1863 Alliott's health was deteriorating and he had no option but to resign from the College. On learning of this his students sent him a letter containing the following words:

> We cannot but feel that in your relation to us as Tutor you have ever striven with a generous earnestness to impart to us the results of your own thoughts and study. We cordially thank you for that kindness and consideration which you have ever taken in our welfare; as well as for those kindly wishes for our future usefulness and prosperity which you have now conveyed to us.[106]

On 14 June 1863 Alliott preached his last sermon to the people of the Acocks Green church, taking Hebrews 2: 10-13 as his text. In August he conducted the Lord's Supper there for the last time. During his lengthy illness he expressed his interest in who might be his successor in the College. In the event George Bubier, an *alumnus* of Homerton College and a student of Pye Smith was appointed;[107] and he was equally concerned as to who would follow him at Acocks Green: 'He charged those on whose judgment in this matter much might depend to admit no one into their pulpit who would not make Christ and Him crucified their great theme.'[108] He was greatly moved when, in the hope that he might yet be restored to them, the church refused to accept his letter of resignation. The day before he died he said, 'I

---

[103] Sortain published, *inter alia*, *The life of Francis, Lord Bacon*, and in a lecture of 1838 delivered on assuming his occasional lectureship at Cheshunt College he said that he would use the method of Bacon to discover, and the method of Aristotle to demonstrate. See his *A Lecture Introductory to the Study of Philosophy*.

[104] R. Alliott, *The Funeral Sermon*, 19.

[105] Ibid., 21, 22.

[106] G. B. Johnson, 'Sketch,' 41-2.

[107] For Bubier (1823-1869) see CYB, 1870, 279-281.

[108] G. B. Johnson, 'Sketch,' 44.

say it not unsubmissively I hope, but I should rejoice if it were God's will to rise again from this bed and preach, to tell what I have learnt and felt in this affliction.'[109] But it was not to be, and he died on 20 December 1863.

Alliott was buried in the General Cemetery, Nottingham, on Monday 28 December. Members of Acocks Green joined the cortège as far as Birmingham, while the deacons of the church and members of the Spring Hill College Committee continued to Nottingham. Three deacons from Acocks Green and three from Castle Gate church were the pall-bearers; T. R. Barker, President of Spring Hill College,[110] and F. E. Anthony, Classical Professor at Western College,[111] were in the procession. Alliott's former student at Western College, Clement Clemance, by now, on Alliott's recommendation, pastor at Castle Gate, conducted the service.[112] On 3 January 1864 G. B. Johnson preached a funeral sermon at Acocks Green. I shall return to Clemance's and Johnson's remarks in the conclusion to this chapter. For the present I turn to Alliott's most substantial writings.

III

Without question, *Psychology and Theology* was Alliott's most important publication. It throws into relief his relentlessly logical mind, his conciseness of expression, and habit of shunning both digressions and illustrations. We may set his thought in context by referring first to his address to the Congregational Union on the old and the new in theology. The new theology, he says, is known by a variety of names, among them, the negative theology, Germanism, spiritualism, and the intuitional theology. His concern is to ask in what this new theology consists, what in the older theology or the Church gave rise to it, how much of truth or error there is in it, and what may be learned from it.

Alliott suggests that the primary distinction between the old and the new theology is found in the fact that the former emphasizes the objective in religion, the latter, the subjective. He poses a number of questions to illuminate the distinction, and these may be summed up in the question, Are we to place our reliance upon truths objectively revealed by God, or upon an inward light which, it is supposed, has been given more or less fully to all by God? More particularly, Does it matter what a person's intellectual faith is, or are the feelings, or the state of the heart the only matters of importance? Alliott says that this question has been posed because people have been taught that intellectual assent to the truth alone is important, and the result has been 'a cold, lifeless valueless orthodoxy.'[113] In face of this some have

---

[109] Ibid., 45.

[110] For Thomas Richard Barker (1798/9-1870), a Homerton alumnus, see CYB, 1871, 302-4; ODNB.

[111] For Frederick E. W. Anthony (d. 1908), a Western alumnus, see CYB, 1909, 158-9.

[112] For Clemance (d. 1895 aged 66) see CYB, 1896, 203-5; A. R. Henderson, *History of Castle Gate Congregational Church*, ch. 17. He gave classes on Butler's *Analogy* to the young people of Castle Gate—verily, a chip off the old block.

[113] R. Alliott, 'Address' on the old and the new theology, 7.

rushed too swiftly in the opposite direction. They elevate the subjective and denigrate the objective. In fact, however, it is only in relation to the objective that we can evaluate the subjective. After all, 'There is a false subjective as well as a true one, for it is not all supposed religious experience that is true, valuable, or desirable.'[114] Nor is a person's religious consciousness an adequate judge of religious experience, for its decisions vary in relation to changing frames of mind. Similar variations will be found if we suppose that the individual's religious consciousness may be brought to bear upon the fruits of religious experience. Again, those who disregard the objective deprive themselves of the means of producing the true subjective. 'I admit,' he says, 'that a mere intellectual assent to objective truth will not produce it; but the case is very different with a cordial, hearty, loving reception of truth—a reception accompanied with self-application, and including trust and confidence.'[115] We need neither a dead orthodoxy nor a disregard of objective truth: 'The true way to escape spiritual deadness is not by a rejection or a neglect of truth, but by a warm, hearty, living reception of it.'[116]

If there is important truth that we must believe, Alliott continues, it must come by divine authority. But what has that authority? External evidence alone will not suffice, for there must be human powers which can appreciate and receive it: 'Thus far the subjective lies unquestionably at the foundation of all our knowledge.'[117] But such evidence may be partly objective and partly subjective. For example, we may appeal to the evidence of miracles; but miracles may be 'objective to ourselves, or may also include moral and spiritual miracles wrought in our own hearts.'[118] There are different species of evidence, and 'It is the concurrence of all these different species of evidence that gives weight to the whole.'[119]

The religious consciousness which, as Alliott has shown, is no infallible judge where religious experience is concerned is equally fallible in assessing objective truth. Thus, for example, faced by the objective truth of Christ's atonement, one person may see 'a moral beauty and glory in it', whereas to another it may be 'so revolting to his religious consciousness that he cannot possibly believe it to be of God.'[120] At this point some may object that the arguments against the religious consciousness apply equally to our ability to judge of evidence at all. To this Alliott replies,

> The two cases ... are not parallel: a man who implicitly follows the guidance of his religious consciousness as the voice of God cannot [consistently] question any of its decisions; if he did, we would practically admit that his intellectual powers are a superior authority, or at least a co-ordinate authority, and hence that his religious

---

[114] Ibid., 8.
[115] Ibid., 9.
[116] Ibid.
[117] Ibid.
[118] Ibid.
[119] Ibid., 10.
[120] Ibid., 10.

> consciousness is not an infallible or even his only leader. But a man who does not implicitly trust his religious consciousness, but believes it possible for his religious feeling to lead him astray, is led to exert all his mental powers to discover truth, instead of indolently following wherever his feeling leads him—is led to view truth in all its possible aspects, and to examine every kind of evidence by which it is supported.[121]

He does not deny that the influences of the Holy Spirit are required to lead us in the right way, 'but we have no authority for regarding these influences as leading us by a blind instinct, but rather as helping us to exercise our faculties aright.'[122]

What, then, is objective truth? Alliott discusses this question with reference to Christ's sacrifice at the Cross. According to the old theology the purpose of this was that God, as a just God and a Saviour, might pardon sinners consistently with his law and moral government. If, says Alliott, this was the immediate end of Christ's sacrifice, it was so with reference to the effect produced on the sinner's heart. 'This ultimate subjective end of the atonement', he declares, 'has been by some too lightly regarded.'[123] Others, however, bypassing the objective end have supposed that 'the first and only direct object of the atonement of Christ was to manifest Divine love, and thus draw the sinner back to God.'[124] While this theme is not to be downplayed, it will not suffice by itself, and that for two reasons:

> it is the objective end of the atonement which adapts it to produce this subjective effect; and ... this subjective effect is not the ultimate end, the ultimate end being an effect produced not simply on the sinners who are drawn back to God, but also on the universe of intelligent creation—an effect which could not be produced except by means of the objective end.[125]

Alliott then turns to those who view Jesus as the model of the whole human race, and regard his self-sacrifice as the type and pattern for every person's self-sacrifice. Alliott does not deny the fact of Jesus's self-sacrifice, nor its significance as a pattern for the self-sacrifice of us all. But this is not nearly sufficient, for along this line Christ is presented not so much as an individual, but as something generic which appeared perfectly in Jesus and appears less perfectly in everyone else: 'I admit that He dwells by His Spirit in the hearts of his people, and thus that there is an intimate union between them and himself; but this is a very different things from supposing that there is a generic Christ. In the former case we come into union with a personal Saviour; but in the latter we simply possess some of the general characteristics which the man Jesus fully possessed.'[126]

---

[121] Ibid., 11.
[122] Ibid., 12.
[123] Ibid.
[124] Ibid.
[125] Ibid., 13.
[126] Ibid., 15.

Again, it is not sufficient to say that Jesus's sufferings serve to portray the divine estimation of sin and the divine sympathy for the sinner. No doubt they do, but Jesus 'manifested His sympathy and love not simply by ... subjecting himself to the pain and anguish to which contact with sinful beings would expose Him, but by subjecting himself to other sufferings which could be more fitly regarded as the penal consequences of their guilt.'[127] His death was more than a sympathetic suffering.

Towards the end of his address Alliott draws a moral: we must give prominence both to the objective and the subjective aspects of truth; and if some lean too much towards older, stereotypical expressions of the truth, while others clothe the old truth in new dress, sometimes risking clarity and intelligibility, neither party is heterodox, and what is at stake is the most appropriate way of expressing the truth. Moreover, we may learn from those on both sides of the argument: 'from the one never to lose sight of the subjective aspect of Christianity; from the other, not to imagine terms and phrases for the expression of though as intelligible merely because they are old, nor to object to new terms and phrases, when they are intelligible, merely because they are new.'[128]

Clearly this was the address of a non-disjunctive, peace-seeking, speaker, delivered at a time when many were becoming increasingly disturbed—either that theological dinosaurs would evacuate the Gospel of its experiential consequences, or that new school subjectivists would, by attenuating the Gospel, saw off the branch on which they were sitting. To both parties Alliott, turning now from logically rigorous exposition to evangelistic concern, has a parting word: 'Those of us who are ministers of Christ have a great work committed to us—the work of saving souls. Let us ever remember that this is *our* work [well, the preaching is; the saving is God's work], and that if we would successfully accomplish it we must preach Christ crucified; that it is by this preaching that God is pleased to save those that believe.'[129]

From the foregoing we may infer that Alliott is a theologian between the times. In the wake of the Enlightenment he has a concern for epistemological objectivity and for the traditional evidences of miracle and prophecy; but he is also in the wake of the Evangelical Revival, from which he inherits not only his evangelistic thrust but also his 'inward' turn which has reference both to personal piety and to epistemology—namely, to the subjective ground of knowledge. To put it otherwise, using somewhat slippery terms, Alliott is indebted both to the older scholasticism and the newer Romanticism. This will become clearer as we turn to his major work, *Psychology and Philosophy*, in which his overall objective is to show that 'mental science is related to religion, theology, and revelation.'[130]

Alliott first discusses the relations between religion and psychology, recognizing that the science of psychology is in its infancy.[131] At first sight it seems that we

---

[127] Ibid.

[128] Ibid., 17.

[129] Ibid.

[130] Idem, *Psychology and Theology*, 33.

[131] Ibid., 38.

cannot understand the 'inward working of religion' if we do not have 'a knowledge of the mental powers on which it acts, and which it subjugates and uses for its own purposes.'[132] But to pose the question in this way presupposes that 'the religious capacity, or susceptibility, is something essentially different from every other mental capacity and susceptibility', and Alliott hopes to show that this is not the case. If he can show that the religious capacity 'arises entirely from, and is wholly dependent upon, the general powers and susceptibilities of the mind; it must be still more evident that the science of mind is essential to the science of religion.'[133] He does not, of course, argue that a person ignorant of mental science cannot have a deep religious experience, but the former is required for a scientific understanding of the latter.

If there is, then, a relation between mental science and subjective religion, there is also a relation between the science of mind and the science of God, for 'the existence of a personal God is the foundation fact of all theology. If there be no God, there cannot possibly be any true science of God; if the supposition of God is a delusion, theology, whatever be its form, is a mistake and a deception.'[134] Hence the importance of the questions, What is our idea of God? and Have we any grounds for believing that a being corresponding to that idea exists? To frame the questions is to demonstrate the intimate relation between mental science and the science of God.

Whence comes our idea of God? If it is entirely the creation of our own minds there can be no evidence that an objectively existing reality corresponds with it. This would not demonstrate God's non-existence, but it would be perfectly compatible with it. Alternatively, if the idea of God is said to originate in a supernatural communication, how can we ascertain that this is the case? Again, the supposition that the idea of God is innate in human beings raises all the questions pertaining to human nature. Or do we have an immediate or a mediate intuition of God? Alliott discusses the latter possibility at some length, and the following quotation will illustrate the care with which he dissects matters:

> [T]he question whether the lessons concerning God, derived from phenomena, are worthy of our confidence, not only depends on the question, whether our knowledge of phenomena is to be relied upon, but also on the mental power we have of drawing inferences; for if that power is not trustworthy, or if it has exceeded its proper limits, no confidence could be placed in any conclusion it may have drawn. We must, consequently, investigate this power, if we would arrive at a philosophical conviction that the lessons inferentially derived from phenomena concerning God are worthy of belief.[135]

In no matter which way we conclude our idea of God to have arisen we see that the deliverances of mental science are germane to the discussion.

---

[132] Ibid., 5.
[133] Ibid., 6.
[134] Ibid., 8.
[135] Ibid., 19.

The same is true when we ask whether a supernatural communication from God is physically and morally possible. For if God's modes of communication are adapted to human beings, we must study human nature to discern what capacities we have for receiving knowledge from him, and for communicating received knowledge to others. Thus, 'Psychology is ... seen to be necessary to judge of that species of evidence of the supernatural origin of a communication, which arises from the mode in which it is made.'[136] The results of psychological enquiry will benefit both philosophy and theology, and a true philosophy will not undermine, but will establish, a true theology. In this latter connection Alliott quotes Morell (with whose psychological and theological views he does not agree) with approval:

> All revealed religion ... rests upon the pedestal of natural religion; all natural religion ... rests upon the existence of God; and the certainty of his existence must be derived from the relation of the laws of nature to those of the human mind.[137]

Having delineated to his own satisfaction the relations between psychology and religion, Alliott turns to the two questions which principally interest him in this course of lectures. The first is 'whether religion be owing to a distinct faculty, susceptibility, or principle of the human mind.'[138] As already indicated, he returns a negative answer to this question. Preparatory to considering subjective experience he defines morality as 'that state of mind, which is the exercise of feelings due to our fellow men, and which prompts to the doing of actions due to them,' and religion as 'that state of mind, which is the exercise of the feelings, and which prompts to the doing of actions due to God.'[139] The latter arise from the fact that God is our Creator, Preserver, Benefactor, Absolute Disposer, and Moral Governor, and in response to God's nature as specified, subjective religion 'includes the exercise of dependence, gratitude, confidence, voluntary subjection, and complacency.'[140] Religion thus concerns the understanding, the will and the emotions: it concerns the whole nature of the individual.

At this point Alliott shows himself as an early Congregational disputant with Schleiermacher, whose ideas he discusses at some length. He understands Schleiermacher to teach that while knowledge, feeling and action all belong to religion, knowledge and action are not pious in and of themselves; rather the piety of both is determined by the feeling. But Alliott counters that it may also be said of the feeling that it is not pious in and of itself. Specifically, Schleiermacher's feeling of

---

[136] Ibid., 28.

[137] Ibid., 36, quoting J. D. Morell, *Historical and Critical View*, I, 28. For Morell (1816-1891) see DNCBP; ODNB; Alan P. F. Sell, *Philosophy, Dissent and Nonconformity*, 110. Morell studied at Homerton under Pye Smith and, like Payne and Alliott, proceeded to Glasgow University. He left the ministry on grounds of ill health following a brief pastorate at Gosport (1842-5).

[138] R. Alliott, *Psychology and Theology*, 37.

[139] Ibid., 39.

[140] Ibid., 40.

absolute dependence is not pious in and of itself; it is only so in relation to God. *Qua* instinct, the feeling of absolute dependence is not religious. Schleiermacher wrongly assumes that 'wherever the idea of God is present, there *must* be the feeling of absolute dependence ... [and] that that feeling can *only* exist in relation to God.'[141] Alliott does not deny that feeling is integral to piety, but he stoutly denies that it constitutes its whole essence. Developed piety, or religion, concerns feeling, knowledge, and the exercise of the will.

The second question that prompted Alliott's enquiry is whether religion derives directly or indirectly from a separate original religious power or susceptibility: in other words, whether 'after we have gained some idea of God, a special religious faculty be requisite to invest the idea with the peculiarities which render it influential, or in any other way give it power.'[142] He argues—especially against Morell—that there is no such faculty. Even if there were such a power, he says, it would not suffice to account for the effects produced; and in any case the effects can be produced without the assumption of a special power. Hence, 'If God awakens within us a religious feeling, it is not by the impartation of a new faculty, nor by awakening a faculty previously existing in a dormant state, but simply by directing anew faculties already existing and already developed.'[143]

A further related question to be considered is whether the will—by which he means 'the power which the mind has of action[144]—is self-determining or not. He concedes that the will has the physical power to act as it pleases; what he denies (against William Hamilton,[145] whom he finds inconsistent on the matter) is that it has self-determining moral power to act irrespective of motive. For support he appeals to human consciousness, to the common judgment of humanity, and to the principle that every change implies a cause. Two truths are undeniable, he declares: one that the will is determined by motive, including under motive the subjective feeling as well as the objective appeal of the mind,—the other, that man is righteously responsible for all his actions.'[146] His clinching argument is that the will can make an erroneous choice in preferring an object which is apparently but not really preferable; 'Hence it follows irrefragably, that *the state of the mind* is the true and proper source of a right and wrong choice.'[147]

Having considered the assistance afforded by psychology to the examination of religious questions, Alliott next turns directly to questions regarding our knowledge of God. In traditional theistic fashion (and begging a huge question) he treats the idea of God 'considered as prior to, and therefore independent of, any supernatural revelation.'[148] He contends that the human being's idea of God is that God is first

---

[141] Ibid., 49.
[142] Ibid., 57.
[143] Ibid., 58.
[144] Ibid., 63.
[145] For Hamilton (1788-1856) see DNCBP; DSCHT; ODNB.
[146] R. Alliott, *Psychology and Theology*, 85.
[147] Ibid., 87.
[148] Ibid., 88.

cause, necessary, eternal, independent and infinite. Whence comes this idea? He argues that it is not of our own creation, nor is it innate. Hence it is not a product exclusively of the subjective. On the other hand, it is not a matter of the rational intuition of the objective; and it is certainly not attributable to Cousin's 'spontaneous reason' that is alleged to be the voice of God within, distinct from our own personality.[149] Rather, the idea 'is attainable by the simple exercise of our reasoning faculty in reference to phenomena within the sphere of phenomenal intuition.'[150] He grants that in addition to the divine attributes already noted there are God's wisdom, holiness, goodness, justice and truth. But we form our ideas of these 'at least so far as we form any notion at all of them, from the attributes which we ourselves possess',[151] and such ideas are imperfect.

Does there exist a being corresponding to our idea of God? Alliott argues by means of a cosmological argument that our idea of God is objectively true. He is the first to admit that our grasp of God's nature, essence, and attributes is limited. 'Can the creature comprehend the Creator?' he rhetorically asks. He answers,

> How much reason have we for gratitude that, seeing we can know so little of God as he really is, and are compelled to look to our own nature as the medium whence alone we can gain the notions essential to the chief part even of what we can know, he has been pleased, with the view to bringing himself down to our capacity, to assume, in the person of his Son, our nature![152]

With this Alliott comes more directly to theology, and to the question of a supernatural revelation. There is no other question which so intimately connects theology with theological science, he thinks. The doubts and difficulties which have been expressed in the present age concerning the possibility of supernatural communication and the Bible, have inclined some to think that the study of psychology is dangerous. He would remind all such that 'if Christianity be, as we believe, really from God, true science cannot be in antagonism to it.'[153]

The preliminaries over, Alliott discusses the terms 'revelation' and 'inspiration', and finds that Morell's definitions of these are too restrictive, for he confines the subject matter of revelation to the realities of the spiritual world, and he restricts inspiration to God's production of special influences on the faculties to enable the reception of truth and does not allow for the divine infusion of truth. Alliott holds that supernatural revelation may be received immediately by intuition, or mediately. There is also an *a priori* argument in favour of supernatural revelation, for human beings desire more light than is afforded by nature. Hence, 'if Christianity be, professedly, a revelation from God, and be adapted to meet the wants, and to satisfy

---

[149] For a brief account in English of the French philosopher Victor Cousin (1792-1867), see Robert Flint, *History of the Philosophy of History*, 452-479.

[150] R. Alliott, *Psychology and Theology*, 143.

[151] Ibid., 145.

[152] Ibid., 183.

[153] Ibid., 185.

the desires, of our nature, there is, in this fact, an argument that it is what it professes to be—*Divine in its origin.*'[154] Christianity meets otherwise unmet human needs by offering a divine Mediator, through whom the human race can be delivered from its present state of intellectual and moral degradation.

Further support for the view that Christianity is a supernatural revelation from God is found in the consistency of the character and influence of the revelation with what nature and reason had previously revealed concerning God. If it be true, as Alliott claims to have demonstrated, that we can learn something of a cause from its effect, it follows that (to give an extended example of his argumentative style),

> it must be impossible for anything which is holy in its character and beneficial in its influence, to proceed from an unholy and malevolent cause. If, then, Christianity can be proved to be holy in its character and beneficial in its influence, its author cannot be unholy and malevolent, and, therefore since it professes to be from God, it must be really from him; for otherwise it would be the result either of wilful deception, or of mistake and fanaticism; but it could not be the result of wilful deception, or its author would be deceptious, and therefore (contrary to the supposition) unholy and malevolent; nor could it be the result of mistake and fanaticism, or (contrary to the supposition) it would not be beneficial in its influence.[155]

He proceeds to argue that the holiness of Christianity is shown by the facts that it reveals a holy God who seeks holiness in his creatures; it teaches the inseparable connexion between holiness and happiness here and hereafter; and its professed design is to restore human beings to perfect holiness. To this latter end it calls human beings to strive to produce the fruits of holiness in heart and life. All of which raises the question of our knowledge of right and wrong. Alliott insists that prior to the empirical acquisition of ideas of right and wrong, human beings are incapable of making immediate moral judgments. That is to say, such judgments are neither instinctive nor intuitive. Were they so, they could never be proved to be erroneous, nor could they be susceptible to correction and improvement.

But is Christianity moral in character? Some have objected that one of its central doctrines, that of the atonement, is immoral:

> The doctrine is said to be opposed to our moral intuitions; any punishment for sin, but what is corrective in its nature, is deemed, on the ground of a supposed

---

[154] Ibid., 221.

[155] Ibid., 229. Page after page of such close, patient, reasoning makes Alliott's argument very hard to summarize. Hence my recourse to reporting Alliott's conclusions with, where manageable, just a hint of his grounds for reaching them. To have attempted more would have been to reproduce extended and detailed arguments. From the point of view presenting his case in a nutshell Alliott is by far the most difficult person in this book. Happily, he is also among the most likeable.

> immediate intuition, to be contrary to the moral perfection of God; and so is any requirement of atonement in order to its forgiveness.[156]

Alliott grants that the doctrine has suffered from caricature, but he insists that properly understood it does not contradict the ideas of God's justice or goodness. On the contrary it upholds the truth that God is the Moral Governor of humanity. Sin, after all, is not a private offence requiring suffering and blood to appease God's wrath; sin is a transgression of God's law and an offence against his moral government. If God should seek some compensation when his law is violated, this is not evidence of vindictiveness on his part, 'but of a benevolent regard for the future moral welfare of his creatures.'[157] Moreover, according to the Christian doctrine of atonement, 'God ... not only manifested his love to us by requiring the compensation to which I have referred, but by himself providing it', with the result that 'with a due regard to the future authority of his moral government' he could 'exercise infinite mercy.'[158] Then, in a strong statement designed by implication to rebuke doctrinal distortions whether Calvinist or Arminian, he makes it clear that

> It is not ... taught by the doctrine of the atonement that God needed to be stirred up by his Son to exercise a mercy to which he was indisposed, much less to be bought over to exercise it. He himself was predisposed to its exercise, and, hence, of his own love provided the sacrifice whereby he could exercise it without inflicting a moral injury on the rest of his intelligent creatures. Christianity, I conceive, teaches no other doctrine in reference to the atonement than this; and this cannot be fairly represented as implying that he is cruel, vindictive, and delighting in suffering and blood.[159]

But even to the doctrine as now stated it is objected that the innocent suffers for the guilty, and that this is unjust. But the suffering and death of Christ on behalf of the guilty were voluntarily undertaken. Again, it is objected that the doctrine of the atonement elevates the inferior moral motives concerning reward and punishment, instead of promoting a morality in which love is the primary motive. But 'So far from disconnecting love and obedience, [the doctrine] represents God to an offender in such a way as to stimulate to strong affection and gratitude, thus exciting to obedience on the principle of love.'[160] Others take the opposite view and contend that the doctrine of imputation, which is closely connected to that of the atonement, destroys the effect of reward and punishment as motives, for the reward is bestowed upon those who have not earned it. In fact, Alliott retorts, the doctrine leads to morality on both principles:

---

156 Ibid., 243.
157 Ibid., 246.
158 Ibid.
159 Ibid., 246-7.
160 Ibid., 249.

> it is calculated to sustain the motives of reward and punishment in the case of sinless beings whose love is perfect ... and it is equally calculated to excite love in the case of sinful beings previously destitute of the principle, by showing a provision made for them, at a vast expense, of blessings wholly undeserved; thus inducing in them a desire to please God, not indeed with the view of purchasing his favour, but yet because the love stirred up within moves them to regard pleasing him as pleasurable, and grieving him as painful, to themselves.[161]

Turning to the general influence of Christianity, Alliott argues that the religion has had a beneficial effect in renovating the character and reforming the conduct of people. But its influence is best known to those who know experimentally what Christianity has done. He adds the rider that not all who profess the faith are true Christians, but those who are have confidence in a religion that makes them holier and happier than anything else. But there is, in addition, the external evidence supplied by miracles. By his own testimony, the miracles of Christ were a witness to his own divinity; they prove all that he said to have been of God. By contrast, the miracles of Paul, for example, prove only that what he said regarding Christ and the gospel was of God. The upshot is that occurrences which are *prima* facie supernatural 'may be possibly a sufficient evidence [note the careful qualifications here] of the Divine origin of a revelation: but, in order that this may be the case to any, except those by whom they were actually witnessed, it must be possible for testimony to be an adequate ground for believing in supernatural occurrences.'[162] But this is precisely what Hume has denied.[163]

Alliott categorizes Hume's argument as psychological, and declares that it can be met only in psychological terms. Hume argues that a miracle is contradictory of uniform experience and this undermines the force of any testimony grounded in such experience. On the other hand, miracles can never be proved if testimony is based upon variable experience. In response, Alliott first enquires whether experience supplies the only ground of reliable testimony. He thinks that those who have discussed Hume's argument have paid too much attention to the historical question of the way a person comes to believe in testimony, for this obscures the critical question which is not that of the origin of testimony but its worth. His question, therefore, is, For what reasons ought a person to believe in experience-based testimony? As a prelude to his answer he engages in some careful conceptual analysis:

> if by experience, in reference to testimony, is simply meant our observation of the conformity of testimony to fact, we have other grounds than experience for believing it; whilst if by experience we may understand all the knowledge derivable from experience, and all the inferences which such knowledge fairly warrants, we shall find in experience a two-fold ground for believing testimony; and, moreover,

---

[161] Ibid., 250.

[162] Ibid., 277.

[163] The bibliography for David Hume (1711-1776) is vast. DECBP and ONDB helpfully scratch the surface.

shall find each to be a ground which will not, like the 'experience' spoken of by Hume, equally apply to all kinds of testimony, but will point out what the particular kinds of testimony are which are worthy of our confidence, and to what extent they are so to be regarded.[164]

At this point psychology comes into play, he continues. From it we learn that people act as influenced by motives, and not because of a self-determining power of the will. Accordingly, one test of the credibility of testimony is to consider the motives which have inspired it. Psychology 'leads us to believe that testimony will be true except there be some special motive for falsehood.'[165] This implies that the evidence of testimony is of varying degrees of reliability. A further test concerns the concurrence of a number of witnesses who have not colluded in the offering of testimony. There are thus differing foundations for faith in testimony, and 'Hume is totally wrong when he builds the credibility of testimony, *in all cases*, on precisely the same foundation.'[166]

But still it will be said that miracles run counter to the ordinary experience of humanity. What can this mean? Only that humanity's experience is limited to the natural and never reaches the supernatural. In this case miracles are *ex hypothesi* ruled out. But this would not prove the impossibility of the supernatural, 'except it could be shown that possibility is *necessarily* limited to human experience; nay, it would not even prove the supernatural *improbable* under circumstances different from those in which mankind have been placed.'[167] Hence the appeal to the ordinary experience of mankind does not suffice to show that miracles as supernatural occurrences are impossible.

In his concluding lecture Alliott turns to the inspiration of Scripture. On the assumption, now deemed to have been proved, that Jesus Christ was a divine messenger and that the religion taught by him and his immediate disciples is of divine origin, the question is not whether the religion of the Bible is true, but whether the books of the Bible 'give us an inspired, or an uninspired representation of it; and if inspired, whether with or without any admixture of what is merely human.'[168] It is *a priori* possible that a communication from God could be made through a book. More than that, it is *a priori* probable that the fundamental facts and doctrines of the faith should be recorded by inspiration in a book, the inspired nature of which would render the book 'in every important point of view' infallible and authoritative [we should note the serious qualification here].[169] By inspiration is meant not merely elevated writing, or a heightening of mental powers for perceiving objective truth, but the direct supernatural communication of such truth to the mind.

---

164 R. Alliott, *Psychology and Theology*, 279.
165 Ibid., 280.
166 Ibid., 281.
167 Ibid., 282.
168 Ibid., 286.
169 Ibid., 287.

Psychology is of great assistance in supporting this *a priori* argument, for 'It is psychology which must decide the question whether we have any intuitional powers which refer to the metaphenomenal.'[170] Furthermore psychology can show us how the moral and spiritual life which is the grand end of Christianity' may be produced by means of its facts and doctrines, and how important it is that these last have been reliably and authoritatively communicated to us. But how far does this line of argument take us, he asks? Must the expected book revelation be verbally inspired in all its parts? How far must it exclude the human? Drawing upon the distinction between the content and the form of a communication, Alliott argues that

> *A priori* evidence leads us ... to anticipate not merely a divinely inspired record, but that the language may possibly be the man's own, seeing that if the substance is given the man is not only competent to frame a dress which will not materially alter or distort it, but may be known to have used his power honestly.[171]

He admits that this argument does not prove that the form must be human; it simply shows that, as far as we are able to judge, verbal inspiration is not necessary. The next question is whether the *a priori* argument can show us that the Bible must contain nothing but what is divine. He answers that the absence of the human is not a necessary accompaniment to the Bible's authority, 'except there be no evident criterion for distinguishing between the human and the divine.'[172]

Thus far the *a priori* approach. Is there any other evidence that the biblical writers were inspired, and if so, to what degree? Alliott thinks that the following considerations 'cannot fail to be satisfactory to the candid mind'[173]: the promise of Christ that the apostles (by whom all but Mark's Gospel and Luke-Acts were written, he thinks) would be guided to the truth by the Holy Spirit; the miraculous powers possessed by the apostles themselves; their testimony as reliable witnesses to their own inspiration; the fact that while they did not know all things, what they knew was 'free from the intermixture of error.'[174] There is also probable evidence that Mark and Luke were likewise inspired, and no conclusive evidence that they were not. They were not disowned by the early Christians, and their writings harmonize well with the others in the New Testament. Alliott next considers six objections which have been levelled against the theory of inspiration. The first is that the New Testament writers made mistakes in science, minor facts, logic and important doctrines. Alliott does not admit any of this; but even if it were true it would not destroy his case for inspiration because, for example, 'we have not contended that [the writers] were inspired in reference to science',[175] but only in regard to the foundational doctrines of the faith [thereby begging a question which

---

[170] Ibid., 296.
[171] Ibid., 307.
[172] Ibid., 310.
[173] Ibid., 311.
[174] Ibid., 317.
[175] Ibid., 327.

was to become increasingly clamant as the decades rolled on]. Secondly, some object that the plenary inspiration of the New Testament requires the plenary inspiration of the Old, and that the latter contains much that is immoral. Alliott retorts that it is one thing to record defects, another to inculcate them, and the Old Testament does not do the latter. The third objection is 'that an authoritative external revelation of moral and spiritual truth is essentially impossible to man,'[176] because before an external revelation could be authoritative, we should first need to establish independently that God knows the truth and wishes to communicate it to us. Even if this argument were sound, Alliott replies, it would not prove that there could not be an external authoritative revelation capable of awakening our moral and spiritual sensibilities. But the argument is not sound:

> It does not prove that there can be no authoritative external revelation *at all* in reference to moral and spiritual truth; the utmost it proves is, that such a revelation could not *authoritatively* reveal any moral and religious truth *which is in opposition to the knowledge on which the evidence of its authority is founded.* Except, then, that knowledge comprehends all moral and spiritual truth, there may be truth authoritatively revealed which is not in opposition to, but only in extension of, previous knowledge.[177]

The fourth objection is that the theory of inspiration exalts the letter above the spirit. Morell argues that the two are incommensurable, but he is mistaken. Without objective revelation there could be no subjective experience, and in that case the objective revelation would have been useless. The fifth objection is that plenary inspiration gives a low view of the spiritual and moral value of inspiration. In fact, however, inspiration as such has no influence on the moral and spiritual nature of individuals, for bad people have been inspired—Balaam among them. We believe that the apostles were holy men, but they were so not because of inspiration but because of grace. Finally, it is objected that plenary inspiration bypasses the role of the Holy Spirit in communicating God's word to people. Alliott answers that spiritual influences are not necessary to a theoretical understanding of the truths of revelation, otherwise there could be no such thing as 'a dry, barren orthodoxy.'[178] But by the Holy Spirit the heart is turned to sympathize with what is theoretically understood, so that it may be 'received into the heart, and become the living, practical experience of the soul.'[179] If the word is better understood thereafter, this is an indirect, not a direct, effect of the Spirit's agency.

Alliott concludes thus:

---

[176] Ibid., 330.
[177] Ibid., 331.
[178] Ibid., 334.
[179] Ibid.

> We do not contend for a dead orthodoxy, but we do contend for the reception, both into the intellect and into the heart, of that objective revelation which is the instrument of God for raising us up from spiritual death to a life of righteousness.[180]

Both in his Address to the Congregational Union and in *Psychology and Theology* Alliott strives to hold objective and subjective, head and heart, together, and it seems to me that to a considerable extent he succeeds. It is therefore somewhat surprising that, following a brief account of Alliott's work, Dale Johnson should say that 'in his own development of the argument, the focus fell decidedly on the understanding.'[181] I do not find that Alliott's emphasis upon the intellectual is too heavy, especially given that his concern throughout his major book is to enquire what help mental science can give to theology. Indeed, in his Preface he sets his stall out very clearly:

> Questions in reference to religion are first discussed. Some may think that, as the being and attributes of God and the Divine origin of Christianity are presupposed by religion, it would have been most natural to have deferred what related to the latter, till the former topics had been disposed of. When, however, it is remembered that the different topics are introduced *in consequence of their relation to psychology*, it will be perceived that there is a reason for beginning with what concerns the subjective experience, that having naturally a closer relation to the science of mind than what refers merely to the objective.[182]

The same consideration regarding the primary purpose of this book applies to Johnson's finding it 'notable' that Alliott's consideration of the inspiration of Scripture was subordinated to other grounds for the certainty of Christianity. While the question of the most appropriate starting-point for theological enquiry is a perfectly proper one, given Alliott's way of working from the subjective to the objective and so to the objectively authoritative, his sequence is perfectly understandable and defensible. That is to say, his ordering of topics was determined in relation to the question he posed concerning the bearing of mental science upon theology, and this is precisely what we should expect of a coherent thinker. By contrast, on another occasion, when opening a series of lectures on *The Evidences of Christianity* [1844], Alliott did, more traditionally, set out from the Bible as foundational.[183]

I shall have one further observation to offer on Johnson's opinion of Alliott in my conclusion, but now I turn to a further line of apologetic enquiry which Alliott pursued in *The Moral Evidence of Christianity*. By 'moral evidence' Alliott understands not strict demonstration, but evidence that is 'fully satisfactory to every sincere enquirer after truth.'[184] Moral evidence does not compel assent or necessarily

---

[180] Ibid., 335.
[181] Dale A. Johnson, *The Changing Shape of English Nonconformity*, 107.
[182] R. Alliott, *Psychology and Theology*, vi.
[183] See R. Alliott, *On the Evidences of Christianity*.
[184] Idem, *The Moral Evidence of Christianity*, 3.

exclude doubt. It admits of degrees of strength, and in this sense the whole of Scripture is moral. But we also speak of moral evidence as one species of Scripture evidence, and it is in this sense than he here understands the matter. First, he infers that the Bible is moral in character and tendency from the description it gives of God's character. To those who say that the Bible represents God as capricious Alliott replies that it is not given to us to know all of God's motives for action. As to the charge that God is unjust: all which needs to be rectified will be adjusted on the day of reckoning. And when God's punishments are properly understood in context it cannot justifiably be said that God is cruel. Secondly, we infer that Christianity is moral from the preceptive parts of Scripture. We are shown what is right, and powerful motives to obey are given, among them gratitude to God for the free gift of purchased salvation. No other religion, he declares, is as successful as Christianity in supplying motives to the fulfilment of obligations. Finally, the same inference may be drawn from the way in which the Bible represents the Gospel dispensation as one in which pardon leads to holiness; the atonement exhibits the tremendous evil of sin; and the Gospel call is to faith and repentance. His conclusion, expressed in godly doggerel, is,

What if we trace the globe around,
  And search from Britain to Japan,
There shall be no religion found
  So just to God, so safe for man.

IV

Enough has been said to justify my claim that Richard Alliott was a theologian between the times. In him classical theism's cosmological-causal head came together with Romanticism's heart, and the whole was undergirded by the Evangelical Revival's concern for souls, and this to a greater degree than was detectable in the writings of George Payne of a few years earlier. Thus when Dr. Johnson writes that 'Alliott's understanding of the grounds of religious certainty was neither distinctive nor especially insightful in his day,'[185] I feel I must demur. I do not claim that no other theologian contemporary with Alliott was striving to hold matters subjective and objective in balance in the way he was; but many were majoring on one aspect or the other, and some were doing neither. In his non-disjunctive, pacific, patient, way he was bringing together things too easily sundered, and doing so in a serious attempt to commend Christianity in intellectually changing times. In regard to his theory of inspiration, it is clear that his limitation of biblical authority to those matters which are foundational to the faith was a harbinger of many discussions to come, and shows him to be, yet again, between the times. For even as he proposes this limitation he is generally content with older readings of biblical texts which

[185] D. Johnson, *The Changing Shape of English Nonconformity*, 108.

would soon become subject to the challenge of modern biblical criticism. He was just on the far side—indeed, he was at the threshold—of those critical studies of which Simon and the rest of the divines to come in this book had to take account. As a child of his time his arguments will not at all points satisfy us now. For example, he manages his defence of miracles without reference to the problem posed by the definition which he casually assumes, namely, that miracles are breaches of the natural order. But much of what he says is still of value; and if asked to specify Alliott's most significant stance I should refer to his clear statement of the view that religion is not the offspring of a distinct mental faculty.

So much for the present concerning Alliott's thought. What, finally, of the man himself? 'Learned and accomplished,' writes an anonymous obituarist, 'he was gentle and unobtrusive.'[186] In the words of his former student, Clement Clemance, speaking at Alliott's funeral, 'He was not a blazing meteor that flashed in dazzling brilliance, that shot athwart the sky and speedily disappeared; but the calm steady light which constantly and gently shone, and told whence all its lustre was derived.'[187] Reynolds, his successor at Cheshunt College, said of him that 'It is not often that we meet with one whose intellect was so keen, and whose heart was so tender and whose will was so strong.'[188] In his funeral sermon for Alliott, James Gawthorne of Derby observed that although Alliott held definite views on evangelical doctrine, worship and church polity, 'he did not suffer these to alienate him from other Christians, but was a lover of all good men. Sectarianism and bigotry had no charms for him. If Christ were preached, if the honour of God and the benefit of man were promoted, he therein rejoiced.'[189]

Alliott

> was eminently successful both in the instruction of believers and the conversion of the ungodly. He was a laborious man: and it were hard to say which most testified his zeal, the study, the class room, or the pulpit. As a pastor he was tender and assiduous: very accessible, simple, humble, and loving.[190]

'Little children,' said Clemance, 'were at once at home with him.'[191]

Clemance further observed that 'As a Teacher, Preacher, and Pastor, to win souls was [Alliott's] only aim';[192] and he spoke nothing less than the truth when he said that Alliott's work, 'both as Student and Tutor, Pastor and Preacher, was remarkable rather for thoroughness and depth, than for wideness and range.'[193] The slightest acquaintance with *Psychology and Theology* will confirm the claim. His students

---

[186] CYB, 1865, 218.

[187] C. Clemance, *Funeral Services for the Rev. R. Alliott, LL.D.*, 6.

[188] Quoted by G. B. Johnson, 'Sketch,' 40.

[189] Quoted by G. B. Johnson, ibid., 26.

[190] Ibid., 28.

[191] C. Clemance, *Funeral Services*, 6.

[192] Ibid.

[193] Ibid., 6-7. Cf. G. B. Johnson, 'Sketch,' 36.

and his congregations were delighted by his 'logic so inexorable and resistless'; and 'How restless would he be under any insinuation that the Christian faith was unphilosophical ... His conviction was that that so-called philosophical system in which there was no room for a Redeeming, Incarnate God was rotten to the core.'[194] As to his own preaching, Alliott said, 'I do not remember one thing I have done which gives me entire satisfaction, yet I have one pleasant thought, that I have scarcely ever preached a sermon except about Jesus Christ.'[195] When G. B. Johnson was deputed to preach a funeral sermon for Alliott at Acocks Green, Alliott instructed him, 'Don't praise me, but use my death for others' good.'[196] More than that, he gave him the text on which he should preach: Jude 21, 'Keep yourselves in the love of God, looking for the mercy of our Lord Jesus Christ unto eternal life.' Johnson duly obliged, referring to the trust of Alliott's life; the witness of his ministry; the hope of his death; and the joy of his eternity. He closed by exhorting his hearers so to live that when God called them they could say, in the words of the last text on which Alliott had preached to them: '"Behold I and the children which God hath given me." Be that your joy and his!'[197]

[194] Ibid., 7.
[195] Ibid., 8.
[196] G. B. Johnson, *Funeral Services*, 13.
[197] Ibid., 23.

Part III

In the Wake of Modern Biblical Criticism

David Worthington Simon (1830–1909)

Thomas Vincent Tymms (1842–1921)

Walter Frederic Adeney (1849–1920)

CHAPTER 7

David Worthington Simon (1830–1909): Striving for Intellectual and Spiritual Depth

David Worthington Simon is the most spiritually anguished, the slowest-burning, and the most pioneering scholar—and hence the most highly suspect—to fall within the confines of this book. To a greater degree than any of the others here treated he homed in upon one doctrine above all others: the doctrine of our redemption. Whether writing for a learned readership or composing a sermon, his language oscillates between the homely and down-to-earth and the metaphysical-to-the-point-of-incoherence. He is the only one of our ten hinterland theologians for whom there exists a full-scale published biography. It was written by his former student, F. J. Powicke, himself no mean scholar, and I am much indebted to it as I attempt a brief sketch of Simon's life.[1]

Simon was born on 28 April 1830 at what, since 1836, had been known as Hazel Grove, near Stockport, but was always known to him by its original name, Bullock Smithy. His paternal grandfather was David Simon, a prominent farmer of Trelpool, Carmarthenshire, and a staunch Independent. His father, Samuel, who had trained under Dr. George Lewis at the academy at Llanfyllen, had become the Congregational minister at Bullock Smithy in 1827.[2] Of a scholarly disposition Samuel was said to be proficient in Hebrew, Syriac, Chaldean, Greek, Latin and French. He had no English until he entered Lewis's academy. Soon after his arrival in Bullock Smithy he met Mary, daughter of the hat manufacturer, Thomas Ryle, of the nearby parish of Bredbury, and they were married at Stockport Parish Church on 15 July 1829. David was their first child, to be followed by three further sons and two daughters. Before David was a week old the family removed to New Mills, Derbyshire, and there Samuel ministered until he retired to Levenshulme twenty-eight years later. It would appear that, though sincere, Samuel was not the most scintillating of public speakers, for on occasion, prompted from the pulpit, the church caretaker would arouse members of the small congregation who had succumbed to slumber during the sermon.

---

[1] See Frederick J. Powicke, *David Worthington Simon* (in this chapter, DWS). For Powicke (1854-1935) see Alan P. F. Sell, *Enlightenment, Ecumenism, Evangel*, ch. 1; WTW, 180-181. For Simon see also CYB, 1910, 189-191; SCM, 146-7; WTW, 203-4.

[2] For Samuel Simon (1796-1868) see CYB, 1869, 278-9. For Lewis (1763-1822) see DWB; ODNB.

The family's resources were limited, and the Sabbath was strictly observed, with family prayer preceding Sunday School and the morning service; then the afternoon Sunday School; and finally the evening service followed by a prayer meeting and more family prayers at home. The young Simon he liked to know how things were made, and spent many hours watching the village cobbler at work; but he also tried his hand a making things himself—a large hen-house being among his sturdy creations. He was happy and full of fun, and not averse to such pranks as that of raiding a nearby orchard. His father was his first teacher, as he was of other children of the village, but in 1842, at the age of thirteen, he was sent to Silcoates School near Wakefield, a school for the sons of Congregational ministers and missionaries situated a day-and-a-half's journey (then) from New Mills. The Revd J. H. Gwyther, who entered Silcoates as Simon's final year there began, remembered him 'as a rosy, round-faced, rather heavy lad of sixteen. Even then he struck me as rather silent, and perhaps a little dull. ... I think I must have considered him a little commonplace and slow. ... Remembering what he afterwards became it is hard to think of him as being the same person.'[3] In 1847 Simon left school and returned home. By then he had already preached at Marple Bridge, where one of his hearers felt that the experience was 'like listening to an angel.'[4] Any thoughts of entering the ministry were postponed by an interlude spent as a clerk in the office of the cotton manufacturers, Mellor and Robinson, of Torr Mill. Simon did not long remain there, and his subsequent movements are unclear, except that before September 1849 he seems to have been associated with Low Croft Congregational Church, Sheffield, and was employed as an usher in the school conducted by the minister, the Revd W. B. Landells.[5]

By now Simon was intent upon the Congregational ministry, and in September 1849 he appeared before the Committee of Lancashire Independent College, Manchester, was admitted on probation, and was formally enrolled in 1850. The President of the College from its inauguration in 1843 was Robert Vaughan; the Professor of Old Testament was Samuel Davidson; and Robert Halley was the Professor of General Literature. Halley's classical teaching had recently inspired a student revolt, and he had been 'rescued' by the opening of Owens College to which Congregational ordinands were thereafter directed for the classics and, later, for mathematics and science.[6]

---

[3] Quoted by F. J. Powicke, DWS, 12. For John Howe Gwyther who, after ten years at Stalybridge, served for nearly forty at Liscard, Cheshire, see CYB, 1918, 131. He also studied in Halle and Heidelberg, and at Leipzig with his Lancashire College contemporary, J. Allanson Picton.

[4] DWS, 12.

[5] Landells, trained at Idle and Airedale, became minister at mount Zion, Sheffield, in 1834. In 1837 he and his congregation exchanged buildings with John Thorpe of Lee Croft. He resigned the pastorate in 1853 and became minister at Collingwood, Melbourne, Australia. He died at Geelong, Australia, in 1871.

[6] For Robert Vaughan (1795-1868) see CYB, 1869, 288-291; DNCBP; ODNB; Anon, 'Dr. Robert Vaughan'; John Noake, *Worcester* Sects, 129-134; William Urwick,

Some of the students at Lancashire College during Simon's time went on to make a distinguished contribution to the Congregational ministry. In due course we shall meet William Urwick, who entered the College in 1848, and John Brown and James Allanson Picton, who entered in 1851. Robert Bruce, who also entered in the latter year, became a lifelong friend of Simon.[7] At the Jubilee of the College in 1893 Bruce gave an address entitled, 'Forty years ago', in which he described Vaughan as 'a brave, noble, and large-minded man, but more fitted for the rostrum and the forum than for the class-room.'[8]. A man of elevated tastes, Vaughan's great concern was to achieve for his denomination a cultured ministry and to demolish Congregationalism's reputation as comprising 'a sort of rude commonwealth.' He went out of his way to reassure distinguished laymen that 'if they take their place frankly among protestant dissenters, [they] need not be apprehensive that the respect shewn to their civil rank elsewhere, will be wanting on the part of their new friends.'[9] However effective he may have been as an ambassador for Congregational refinement and good manners, it must be lamented that Vaughan was not in his element as Professor of Dogmatics. The anonymous author of a more than ordinarily candid article published after Vaughan's death made no bones about it:

Nonconformity in Worcester, 120-121; Joseph Thompson, *Lancashire Independent College*; Elaine Kaye, *For the Work of Ministry*; Alan P. F. Sell, *Philosophy, Dissent and Nonconformity*. For Samuel Davidson (1806-1898) see ODNB; Anne J. Davidson, ed., *The Autobiography and Diary of Samuel Davidson*; R. Allen, *The Presbyterian College, Belfast 1853-195* , Belfast: Mullan, 1954, 44-6, 307-8; and other works to which I shall refer in section two of this chapter. For Halley (1827-1885) see CYB, 1886, 175-7. For the classics incident see DWS, 15, and for its aftermath see Joseph Thompson, *The Owens College*, 136-7; idem, *Lancashire Independent College*. Halley proceeded in 1856 to the principalship of Doveton College, Madras, and on his return he became first, principal of Tettenhall College, Wolverhampton, and then minister at Arundel.

[7] Bruce (1829-1908) was MA and later (1880) DD of Aberdeen University. His career began as a teacher of mathematics at a school for Nonconformists conducted in Blackburn by William Hoole (d. 1878), who had been tutor in classics at Blackburn Independent Academy from 1819 to 1821. See R. Slate, *A Brief History of the Rise and Progress of the Lancashire Congregational* Union, 123-4; W. A. Abram, *A Century of Independency in Blackburn*, 44, 46. E. Kaye gives him as Howle, see *For the Work of Ministry*, 55, 249. Among Bruce's pupils was John Morley, later a Member of Parliament. Bruce studied at Lancashire College from 1851-54, and then ministered at Highfield Congregational church, Huddersfield, until he retired in 1905. He was Chairman of the CUEW in 1888, and became a Freeman of Huddersfield in 1906. See CYB, 1909, 162-5.

[8] Quoted in DWS, 15. Privately educated in Bristol, Vaughan had been minister at Angel Street, Worcester (1819-25), and then at Horton Street, Kensington (1825-43), concurrently holding the Chair of Modern History at the University of London from 1833 to 1843, when he became President of the newly-opened Lancashire Independent College, Manchester. He founded *The British Quarterly Review* in 1845 and edited it for the next twenty years.

[9] R. Vaughan, *Congregationalism*, 197, 200.

> Dr. Vaughan identified himself so thoroughly with literary movements and was so desirous especially of securing higher intellectual culture for the Dissenting ministry, that it was generally supposed that he was a distinguished scholar himself. But this he was certainly not. ... The truth is, he never had the opportunity of regular scholastic discipline, not even of so much as the Dissenting academy of his early years would have afforded. ... What an active and powerful brain and incessant diligence could do to overcome the disadvantages arising from want of early training, was done. But everyone knows that it cannot supply deficiencies in the minutiae of scholarship.[10]

Robert Bruce allowed that 'Although he was not altogether in his right place as Professor of Theology, he made an excellent Principal, was most patient, gentlemanly, and kind, free from unworthy suspicions and mean espionage.'[11]

Bruce's last sentence is telling in view of what can only be described as the persecution on inadequate theologico-biblical grounds by College Committee to which Vaughan's colleague, Samuel Davidson, was subjected, which led to his departure from the College in 1857. To this shameful incident I shall come in the next section, but for the present I note Bruce's characterisation of Davidson as

> a very lovable, humble, childlike man, very kind, and accessible to the students; but in most of his ways and methods at the antipodes of Dr. Vaughan, utterly devoid of everything that is dramatic or rhetorical, largely a bookworm and recluse—too much so. With all his extensive learning and reading in Hebrew, Greek, and especially in German, he did not succeed in inspiring his students with a passion for biblical exegesis or for Hebrew ... But dear "old Targum", as we jocularly and lovingly named him, was a most affable and interesting man in one's study or at his hospitable table.[12]

Simon records visits of Davidson to the students' rooms, observing that the Professor would never come fully into the room, but stand between the open door and the wall, his hand on the door handle, discussing the latest developments in German biblical scholarship at some length. As he later wrote to Davidson's daughter, these conversations 'were most stimulating; indeed, I am not sure that they did not constitute the best part of the learned Doctor's instructions.'[13] As to Davidson's classroom performances, 'his lectures were undoubtedly always solid, clear, packed with learning, and we could not but feel a profound respect for the lecturer; but as a teacher of the elements of Hebrew he was not a success. He was, in fact, far too innocent for the task. He knew his subject himself, but he did not appreciate our ignorance or our need of drill.'[14] For all that, as John Brown remarked,

---

[10] Anon., 'Dr Robert Vaughan,' 135, 136.

[11] DWS, 15.

[12] Ibid., 16.

[13] A. Davidson, ed., *Autobiography and Diary*, 346.

[14] Ibid., 347.

'Simon's whole life-work may be said to have been determined in those days when he was admitted to Dr. Davidson's study and family circle as a privileged friend.'[15]

A further memory of Bruce is of the role Simon took in Halley's beneficial Logic class as 'an adroit combatant ... in the spirit of Athanasius contra mundum.'[16] This spiritedness is confirmed by the very Gwyther, now a junior student at Lancashire College, who had thought Simon slow and dull at Silcoates School. Now, 'he was full of fun and life, ever ready for discussion and controversy, not particularly docile as a pupil, especially when he thought he detected incompetency or pretentiousness in his teachers, and often propounding startling and as it seemed perilous opinions. We all felt that he was no ordinary man and used to speculate as to his future course.'[17]

Ever one to get to the bottom of things, Simon realised that where his favoured theological speculations were concerned, Vaughan was not the man to take him to the depths, and this he regretted. John Brown recalled that

> So far as the theological lectures of the College were concerned I am afraid it must be said their influence on our friend was practically nil. Or perhaps it would be truer to say that they created within him a revulsion of feeling against the system of lecturing then in vogue, which consisted largely in repeating over again to successive generations of students lectures which had never had very much contact with reality and had certainly never grown beyond their first conception. The method of evoking mind and kindling thought by Socratic questioning which Dr. Simon followed with so much effect in after-days with his own students was really a reaction from bygone experiences he had felt to be utterly wearisome and futile.[18]

As Simon afterwards wrote, 'I remember having a dread and disdain of sciolism, or would-be knowledge, burnt into my soul by ... A. J. Scott, the first Principal of The Owens College, now Victoria University, Manchester. I have never ceased to be grateful to him.'[19] Indeed, he and Allanson Picton became personal friends of Scott, and they were not the only Lancashire College students to be stimulated by Scott's lectures, in particular by his emphasis upon the authority of the conscience understood as a faculty for discerning spiritual truth. Bruce noted that as a result of Scott's teaching, and also that of Baldwin Brown, George Macdonald, F. D. Maurice

---

[15] DWS, 33.

[16] Ibid., 17.

[17] Ibid., 19.

[18] Quoted in DWS, 33. John Brown (1830-1922) was at Lancashire College from 1851-55. His first pastorate was at Park Chapel, Manchester (1855-64), whence he removed to Bunyan meeting, Bedford (1864-1903 and Emeritus, 1903-22). A BA of London and DD of Yale, he was Chairman of the CUEW in 1891, and the noted biographer of Bunyan. His daughter, Florence Ada, was the mother of the economist John Maynard Keynes, for both of whom see ODNB. For John Brown see CYB, 1923, 100-101.

[19] D. W. Simon, *The Making of a Preacher*, 12. For Scott (1805-1866) see ODNB; Joseph Thompson, *The Owens College*.

and Charles Kingsley, minds were being opened 'to wider, more rational and more merciful views of religious truth.'[20] We shall return to this point in due course.

The reference 'spiritual truth' prompts mention of Simon's striving in that area. Powicke had access to a notebook which Simon kept from November 1849 to February 1855. Two extracts will exemplify the remainder. On Sunday 24 November 1849, during his first College term, he wrote, 'Oh! the littleness of my soul! ... Sunday again has come and gone. Alas! that it should be so little a Sabbath to my heart and mind. I am oppressed, an undefinable uneasiness torments me. Oh! that God would relieve me!'[21] On 28 December we find him making the following 'determinations': '1. I will try always to do right as far as I know it; 2. I will I will endeavour to see right as far as I can; 3. I will strive to think and know right as far as maybe.'[22]

That his struggles were intellectual as well as spiritual is clear from the fact that as he entered the theological section of his course in September 1851 we find Simon listing the things he needs to do, of which the first is: 'Definitively fix my opinion on the Bible, what it is and is not; its inspiration, what and how far.'[23] On 25th of the same month he set down his dilemma in the following terms:

> I want spirituality, say people. And I do, for certain. But oh! how am I to have it? What can I do? I have to proclaim as truth—and expound as felt applicable to truth—the contents of that book as to whose true character and design I am yet undecided. ... My heart needs changing; my mind needs certifying; and to the accomplishment of these two things I am powerless.[24]

By the end of his College course he was able to articulate his principal beliefs as follows:

> I believe in one living personal God, creator of the world and all things therein, self-existent, eternal. I believe in Jesus Christ as the Saviour of Sinners, in whom I see the Father.
>
> I believe in the full personality of man and his consequent responsibility to God whose will is revealed to us. I believe in the universal need of men of a Saviour, even Christ Jesus.[25]

Perhaps the most obvious lacuna here is any direct reference to the Holy Spirit.

Simon the student was remembered as one who, as far as the College arrangements and discipline were concerned, was 'constantly in more or less open

---

[20] Quoted in DWS, 17.
[21] Quoted, ibid., 22.
[22] Ibid., 23.
[23] Ibid., 25.
[24] Ibid., 26.
[25] Ibid., 29.

rebellion.'[26] However, fifty-one years after leaving the institution, and notwithstanding the fact that 'Lancashire College did very poorly for us', he could write, more generously, 'As far as I myself am concerned, but for Silcoates and Lancashire College I should have had no educational advantages beyond what the village afforded where my father was minister on a very small salary.'[27]

Simon's course at Lancashire College ended in June 1854, and on 18 December of that year the College subscribers were informed that 'Mr. Simon is at present pursuing his studies at the University of Halle.'[28] Thither he had gone with the encouragement of Davidson, as he recalled to Anne Davidson:

> I should never have dreamt of going to Germany ... but for the information and encouragement he gave. And I owe both your father and mother a great debt for their kindness to me when I reached Halle, where they were then spending their summer holidays.[29]

Davidson, who had himself been awarded Halle's Doctorate on the recommendation of Professors Tholuck and Hupfeld, introduced his protégé to those scholars and others.[30] Tholuck became a particular friend. They went on walks together, Simon was a welcome visitor at Tholuck's home, and when he paid the fee to attend one of Tholuck's courses the latter, aware his student's genuine impecuniosity, graciously returned it. Greatly though he benefited from German scholarship, Simon was not yet as ease with himself. Shortly after arriving in Halle he confided to his notebook,

> I have struggles against forms of sin, and occasionally a victory seems to be gained; but I cannot say that through Jesus Christ I obtain the victory overcoming the world ... Why the absence of a clear conviction about Jesus Christ in one direction or another? ... I seem more and more to be drawing near to two branches of my spiritual road—one of which leads to thorough orthodoxy, the other to thorough heterodoxy.[31]

Simon seems to have returned to England in the late summer of 1855, for we learn that 'for a short time' between September and Christmas he had oversight of a newly-formed church at Oxton Road, Birkenhead. He seems next to have been based

---

[26] CYB, 1910.

[27] Letter of 24 November 1905 to the Revd R. Briggs, quoted DWS, 32, 31.

[28] DWS, 31.

[29] A. Davidson, ed., *Autobiography and Diary*, 348.

[30] Friedrich August Gottreu Tholuck (1799-1877) was a biblical scholar of wide learning, who influenced the Halle Faculty of Theology in an evangelical direction in face of the prevailing rationalism. See DBI; D. K. McKim, *Dictionary of Major Biblical* Interpreters. For an engaging pen portrait of him see Philip Schaff, *Germany; Its Universities, Theology and* Religion, ch. 26. His death was noted in *The Christian* World, 22 June 1877. Hermann Hupfeld (1796-1866) was a considerable Semitic philologist and Old Testament commentator.

[31] DWS, 47, 50.

at home in New Mills, though with a probationary excursion to Royston, whence he received a letter of 12 February 1856 calling him to the pastorate of John Street Congregational Church, Royston. 51 church members voted for him, 3 opposed him, 9 were neutral and 14 were out of town when the ballot was taken. In addition 35 subscribers were supportive of the call and none against. On 21 February Simon wrote his letter of acceptance. Less than seven months later he wrote to the church saying that

> From what I have observed myself, and what has been most kindly, and according to my express desire, communicated to me by the Deacons, I judge that it will be better both for you and myself, and for the work of God generally, that I should withdraw from the pastorate to which you invited me six months ago.[32]

The memory of older church members was communicated to Powicke when he was writing his biography of Simon, and it was to the effect that 'some of [Simon's] teaching was too broad for the people here, and that he gave offence in some quarters by attending a party at which there was dancing.'[33] More than enough there to cause the godly to rise up against a pastor, none of them, perhaps, aware that from his side the inner turmoil had not yet abated. It has also been pointed out that Royston had 'uncomfortably recent memories of heresy,' and that 'large pretentious families of flimsy financial security are quarrelsome, and the interrelated Royston dissenters were prone to lawsuits with each other ...'[34]

From the point of view of future employment Simon was not left high and dry. Indeed, he had already been invited to act as tutor to Barnard, the son of Henry Sturt of Clapham, who was about to embark upon a twelve-month sojourn in Germany. They sailed to Hamburg in September 1856, visited a number of German cities, and on 27 April 1857 saw the Easter Mass in Rome. For the last part of that year Simon was back in New Mills, but on the first Sunday of January 1858 he conducted his first service at the new minister at Moor Street, Rusholme, Manchester. On Tuesday 5th he was ordained. His father read the Bible and offered prayer; the Revd G. F. Bubier delivered an Introductory Address, the Reverend Watson Smith received the Statement of Principles and offered the ordination prayer, and Dr. Davidson delivered the charge to the minister and people. 'All these,' remarks Powicke, 'with the exception perhaps of Simon the elder, stood suspect of heresy (more or less) in those quarters which had produced the assault upon Dr. Davidson',[35] which had occasioned his departure from Lancashire College only some six months before. Here was sown that guilt by association which, in more conservative circles, was never entirely erased from Simon's reputation.

After a few months Simon felt increasingly ill at ease, and even contemplated removal to Canada where he might find the stillness in which to address his doubts

---

[32] Ibid., 56.

[33] Ibid., 57.

[34] C. Binfield, 'Chapels in crisis,' 242.

[35] DWS, 59-60.

and difficulties. At the end of 1858 he resigned his charge, but it was not to Canada that he went, but to Germany that he returned as escort once again to Barnard Sturt and another friend. Simon spent much of the time in Halle learning Modern Greek, but also paid regular visits to Dessau, where Sturt married Helene Schilling on 13 September 1859, and Simon married her older sister, Johanne Marie Franziska, in May 1860. In due course they had three sons and two daughters. Following the wedding they returned to Levenshulme, Manchester where, for the next two years Simon worked on his translation of J. A. Dorner's *History of the Development of the Doctrine of the Person of Christ.*[36] Begun in collaboration with Dr. Lindsay Alexander,[37] Simon produced the notes to the first volume and was solely responsible for the translation of the remaining four volumes.[38]

From March 1862 until 1864 the Simons lived at Darmstadt, and whilst there Simon completed his postgraduate studies. On 6 June 1863 he graduated MA and PhD in the University of Tübingen. His doctoral thesis was entitled, *The Dissenting Sects of Russia.* On removing to Berlin in 1863 or 1864 he became an agent for the British and Foreign Bible Society. He was successful in his work, happy in his family life and stimulated by numerous theological contacts, notably with 'my never-to-be-forgotten teacher and friend',[39] Dorner, of whom he wrote, 'It was my pride and joy and profit to see him pretty frequently during my six years' residence in Berlin, and I shall perhaps never know the greatness of the debt I owe him for spiritual and intellectual stimulus and aid.'[40] The conjunction 'spiritual and intellectual' should not go unnoticed: for so long Simon had been in quest of help on both fronts (assuming that they are entirely distinct). After some years in Berlin

---

[36] Isaak August Dorner (1809-1884) taught New Testament theology and exegesis and, especially, dogmatics and ethics successively at Tübingen, Bonn, Göttingen and Berlin. See DBI; P. Schaff, *Germany; Its Universities, Theology and Religion*, ch. 34.

[37] Formerly tutor at Blackburn academy, Alexander was now minister at North College Street Church (removed to Augustine Church in 1861), and in 1878 he became Principal of Edinburgh [Congregational] Theological Hall. He retired in 1883 and Simon succeeded him as Principal in 1884.

[38] Not long before Simon plunged into Dorner's volumes Philip Schaff had expressed himself thus: 'As to an English translation which has been spoken of long since, both in England and in this country [the United States], it would require a hand of unusual skill and perseverance. We think it more desirable, however, that some able divine should prepare an independent Christological work, on the basis of the labors, not only of Dorner, but also of Liebner, Thomasius, Lange, Ullmann, and Wilberforce (on the Incarnation,) and condense the biblical historical and dogmatic material into one volume. Such a book, well executed, would fill a most important place in English literature.' See his, *Germany; Its Universities, Theology and Religion*, 379. Readers of English had to wait until 1912 for the realisation of Schaff's *desideratum*. In that year H. R. Mackintosh's work, *The Doctrine of the Person of Jesus Christ* was published. In it Mackintosh referred to Dorner, Thomasius and Ullmann from Schaff's list, and to numerous others. A second edition followed in 1913, and by 1956 a further ten reprints had appeared.

[39] D. W. Simon, *Reconciliation by Incarnation*, 12.

[40] DWS, 70.

attempts were made to entice Simon to move elsewhere. Although he was very interested in the prospect, he declined oversight of the English Church in St. Petersburg on grounds of his wife's health, and he also felt unable to accept an invitation to become the minister of Keighley Congregational Church.

He continued with his Bible Society work, and also made a significant contribution to the work of Sunday Schools in Berlin, but June 1869 he received the invitation which he did feel it right to accept. The Committee of Spring Hill College, Birmingham, called him to be Resident Tutor and Professor of Theology. He accepted the position, was treated to two farewell gatherings by the Bible Society in Germany which were attended by the twenty-four colporteurs for whom he had been responsible, and by September he and his family had completed the removal and he was ready to assume his new duties. James Ward, the Senior Student at Spring Hill, and subsequently Professor of Moral Philosophy at Cambridge,[41] sent Simon a letter of welcome, in reply to which Simon declared his professorial hand: 'My wish and aim will be to stimulate and aid to independent work and thought. Our motto must be: Read, think, write, pray *hard*!'[42] In his formal letter of acceptance of the appointment Simon wrote,

> I have long yearned ... to be taking an active part in the labours and struggles which engage the attention of the Christians of England; particularly as I have been bold enough to think that my experiences in Germany—that land of the profoundest intellectual struggles—would stand me in good stead. The truths most surely believed among us, especially such cardinal points as the personality of the Holy Spirit, the Godmanhood of Christ; His atonement in its twofold relation to God and the Divine Law and to the human soul; and the authority and sufficiency of the Scriptures as the divinely ordained and inspired guide to truth and life:- I too most sincerely believe.[43]

In coming to Spring Hill, Simon was entering an institution where at least relatively open theological enquiry was the order of the day, and in which the students were encouraged to think their own thoughts and reach their own conclusions. This, as we saw, had been the objective of Richard Alliott, who had died in 1863.[44] Alliott had been succeeded by George Bubier, who, when on the Committee of Lancashire Independent College, had been a prominent supporter of Samuel Davidson, and who had given the Introductory Address at Simon's ordination.[45] If it be true that 'by their alumni ye shall know them', the names of R.

---

[41] For Ward (1843-1925) see ODNB.

[42] DWS, 73.

[43] DWS, 81.

[44] See ch. 6 above.

[45] George Burdon Bubier (1823-1869) was educated at Homerton under John Pye Smith. He ministered at Orsett and Grays (1844-6) and as co-pastor at Union Chapel, Brixton (1846-9); then at Downing Street, Cambridge (1849-54) and Hope Chapel, Salford (1854-64). He became Professor of Theology and Philosophy at Spring Hill and, like Alliott before him, pastor at Acocks Green church in 1864 He died in 1869. A man of

W. Dale, J. B. Paton and others suggest that the Professors' efforts to foster independence of thought on the part of the students had, in at least some cases, met with considerable success.[46] On occasion, it must be said, the success was too much for some church members, and in some quarters 'Simon's men' were suspect (occasionally with good reason); and for encouraging such freedom of thought, Simon was viewed by the disgruntled 'as a rather dangerous new theologian.'[47] He abominated the formal lecture, and 'fell into—I did not so much deliberately adopt—what is called the Socratic method.'[48] The result was that he 'tended rather to produce independent sowers than mere reapers or gatherers up.'[49]

In other ways Simon took what the ultra-conservative regarded as risks. He knew that some students went to hear George Dawson the minister of the recently-established Church of the Saviour, who was anti-credal and proclaimed universal grace, and, against the judgment of some members of the College Committee, Simon did not forbid this.[50] Indeed, when the students asked permission to invite Dawson to speak to them on the subject of preaching, Simon not only acceded to the request but went to the lecture 'as a learner', and welcomed the speaker warmly. His own opinion was that Dawson 'offered an excellent object-lesson in preaching, but was all that a theologian should not be—impatient, unsystematic, superficial, and rather flippant.'[51]

A certain amount of guilt by association was heaped upon Simon as a result of John Hunter's ministry in York. Hunter was an able student, but too 'advanced' for the members at Salem York, where Simon had preached the ordination sermon. Hunter's opponents faced him with the Calvinistic trust deed and a sorry dispute resulted which found its way into the columns of the press. Eventually the traditionalists seceded and Hunter, a devotee of the thought of F. D. Maurice, was left with a depleted congregation of those who valued his emphasis upon God's love at the expense of his righteousness.[52] Hunter exercised a great influence upon his fellow student, John T. Stannard. Stannard did not have the intellectual ability of

---

high culture, he was Literary Editor of *The British Quarterly Review*. See CYB, 1870, 279-281.

[46] For Robert William Dale (1829-1895) see CYB, 1896, 208-212 ; ODNB; A. W. W. Dale, *The Life of R. W. Dale of Birmingham*; Clyde Binfield, ed., *The Cross and the City*; Mark Hopkins, *Nonconformity's Romantic Generation*, ch. 3. Dale, an MA of London, DD of Yale and LL.D of Glasgow, was assistant at Carrs Lane Congregational Church, Birmingham (1853-4), co-pastor (1854-8) and pastor (1858-95); and Chairman of the CUEW in 1869. John Brown Paton (1830-1911), MA (London), DD (Glasgow) was minister at Wicker, Sheffield (1854-63) and Tutor at Cavendish College, Manchester (1860-63) and then Principal of the Nottingham Congregational Institute (later renamed Paton College) (1863-97). See CYB, 1912, 16-31; ODNB; WTW, 171-2.

[47] DWS, 85.

[48] DWS, 260.

[49] Ibid., 261.

[50] For Dawson (1821-1876) see ODNB.

[51] DWS, 87.

[52] For Hunter (1849-1917) see CYB, 1918, 135-7.

Hunter, and Simon was concerned that his theology was inadequately rooted. He spent time with Stannard during the latter's first pastorate at Ramsden Street church, Huddersfield, but to no avail. Stannard would publicly denounce Calvinism, and went so far as to say that while the new emphasis upon the Fatherhood of God was very welcome, it should be balanced by an emphasis upon the Motherhood of God. Salt was rubbed in traditionalist wounds by the fact that Hunter and Stannard—'Simon's men!'—were ringleaders of the Leicester Conference of 1877, to which I shall return in section three of this chapter. Stannard nevertheless managed to hold his pastorate until 1881, when a lawsuit resulted in a decision in favour of the Calvinistic trust deed. During the trial Simon had written a fairly non-committal letter in Stannard's defence, to the effect that like other more thoughtful students, his theology was still in the making and not altogether clear. What horrified him was that his friend Robert Bruce read out in court a private letter which Simon had written to him in which the Principal declared that Stannard's 'flabby, goody, useless theology' was an 'abomination'.[53] Following the court's judgment Stannard and others seceded to become Milton church, Huddersfield. There, in February 1880, Simon preached at his ordination alongside such luminaries as P. T. Forsyth (then in his liberal phase)[54] and J. Baldwin Brown; and there Stannard remained until his death by drowning at Blackpool on 12 September 1889.[55]

In view of Simon's personal striving after both intellectual and spiritual depth it is not at all surprising that on 21 June 1870, his first Anniversary Meeting of the College, Simon should have taken *Historical Christianity and the Spiritual Life* as the subject of his address. He sets out from a long quotation from *Broken Lights* by Frances Power Cobbe—an ultra-spiritualistic passage containing, in his opinion, half-truths, truths and errors. He counters by arguing that the historical and the spiritual are not to be divorced, and that the relation of the soul to God is not independent of biblical facts. This might be shown, he suggests, by demonstrating the historical reliability of the books of the Bible, but his case is that experience and the constitution of human nature are against those who would separate the factual from the spiritual. As to experience, Simon unearths similarities and dissimilarities between Cobbe and the deists, rationalists and Socinians, pronouncing that the 'inevitable result' of the false disjunction 'has been to empty the places of worship, to foster a separating individualism, to extinguish proselytizing zeal, and to substitute cold morality for vital godliness.'[56] As to the human constitution, it comprises 'inseparably woven' principles of dependence and independence—including

[53] See *The Nonconformist and Independent*, 3 February 1881, 109.

[54] The bibliography of works on Peter Taylor Forsyth (1848-1921) is considerable. See ODNB; the Bibliography by Leslie McCurdy in Trevor Hart, ed., *Justice the True and Only Mercy*, 303-317; and more recently, Alan P. F. Sell, *Testimony and Tradition*, chs. 7, 8; idem, ed., *P. T. Forsyth: Theologian for a New Millennium*.

[55] For Stannard see CYB, 1890, 187. For a somewhat fuller account of the incidents just noted see Mark D. Johnson, *The Dissolution of Dissent*, 143-8. See also Clyde Binfield, *So Down to Prayers*, 158-9.

[56] D. W. Simon, *Historical Christianity and the Spiritual Life*, 10.

dependence upon the inheritance flowing down from previous generations. Nevertheless, by overlooking the spiritual dimension we have been misled into thinking that the Christian faith is merely a matter of history and is grounded in probabilities, so that 'everything else has been eschewed as mysticism, enthusiasm, Rationalism, or Germanism.'[57] We should remember, he continues, that what God said in the past can still reveal him, and that the same Spirit whose 'inward influence enabled the first recipient of revelations to discern their true significance, is promised also to us. ... Viewed thus, there is nothing past in the bible; so far as it records God's presence, so far it is present, absolutely present.'[58] To the budding ministers in his audience he says, 'We must supplement and vitalize the ordinary evidences for our religion by this higher personal certainty. ... We must not simply know about God, we must be intimate with him.'[59] He concludes by declaring that our sufficiency is only in God, and only there when God is all in all to us.

Alive to the changing intellectual environment, Simon broke with a long pedagogical tradition, represented by George Payne and Richard Alliott and, up to 1858 by Henry Rogers at Spring Hill College,[60] in turning from the apologetic method of William Paley as enshrined in *A View of the Evidences of Christianity* (1794) and *Natural Theology* (1802). Consistently with his objective of holding things intellectual and spiritual together, he acquainted his students with the experiential emphasis flowing down from Schleiermacher whilst warning them against the perils of the brasher German rationalism.[61] Simon taught a considerable number of subjects[62] and in his own words, 'worked like a lion'—so much so that his health broke down in 1872. In the same year he received an invitation to the influential pastorate of Clapton Park, London, but, to the delight of those students who made representations to him, he decided to remain at the College. He suffered a further breakdown in health in 1875, and made known his feeling that professors in the Congregational colleges were expected to cover so many subjects that they could give adequate time to none, still less could they make effective contributions to their disciplines. In 1877 he and his family moved out of residence in the College to a

---

[57] Ibid., 16.

[58] Ibid., 17, 18.

[59] Ibid., 18, 19.

[60] For Henry Rogers (1806-1877) see DNCBP; ODNB; R. W. Dale, 'Memoir'; Alan P. F. Sell, *Dissenting Thought and the Life of the Churches*, chs. 17, 18; idem, *Philosophy, Dissent and Nonconformity*, *passim*. Trained at Highbury, Rogers served an assistantship at Poole, but vocal problems precluded regular ministry, hence his turn to literary work and teaching. He taught Logic and Rhetoric at his *alma mater* (1632-9); in 1836 he became Professor of English Language and Literature is what is now University College, London; and he went to Spring Hill College in 1839. On leaving Birmingham in 1858 he removed to Manchester in the wake of the Davidson episode, as President of Lancashire Independent College. He retired, following an accident, in 1871.

[61] For nineteenth-century apologetics see Alan P. F. Sell, *Philosophy, Dissent and Nonconformity*, 166-203. See also Dale A. Johnson, 'The end of the "Evidences"'; idem, *The Changing Shape of English Nonconformity*.

[62] For the list see DWS, 82.

house nearby, and a marked improvement in his health resulted. Apart from a few articles his duties did not permit much by way of publication, nor did Simon seek more public denominational office. He stuck to his last, taking only occasional preaching appointments, and giving occasional addresses.

One of his addresses, indicative of his continuing interest in the children's work of the churches, was *A New Year's Address to Sunday School Teachers and Members of Birmingham Sunday School Union* [1972]. His text is a clause from II Timothy 2: 2, 'Faithful men who shall be able to teach others.' He first explains that teaching comprises both instruction (building in) and education (drawing out). He urges Sunday School teachers to remember that they are dealing with human souls 'that are made in, and are to be restored to, the image of God.'[63] What has to be built in is the knowledge of Jesus Christ, human and divine. He does not overlook the fact that the Holy Spirit alone will open the eyes of the children, but teachers must faithfully do what they are called to do. The in-building and out-drawing are effected by the conscious imparting of knowledge, but also by the unconscious influence of such things as the teachers' dress, manners, tone of voice, patience or impatience. Teachers must not simply impart the contents of the New Testament; they must have Christ living in them. 'The greatest lesson all teachers of Christ need to learn', he declares, 'is this—they can only communicate as much of Christ as they have of him—have as life and have as intelligence.'[64]

Ever since his return from Germany in 1869 Simon had felt that 'somehow or other we ought to get out of the narrow limits imposed by our ordinary denominational institutions. The very year after my return I remember at Cambridge conspiring with a gentleman there to see if it might not be possible to purchase the Leys estate, which now belongs to the Methodist Church.'[65] It was not until 1875 that Simon suggested to the Education Board at Spring Hill College that, in the wake of the abolition of the Test Acts, the association of the College with one of the ancient universities might be beneficial in the broadening of the training of ministerial candidates. Some members of the Committee welcomed the idea, and a formal motion was moved by G. B. Johnson and seconded by Simon in April 1876. The chairman, R. W. Dale, was non-committal. Of him Simon write that 'He filled the office of Chairman of the Education Board during the whole of my tenure of office, and more fortunate in the holder of such an office no teacher could have been. Never was there the shadow of meddling. He shrank even from doing in the College what might fairly have been expected of him, for fear of seeming to interfere.'[66] Without the strong support of Dale the success of such a radical proposal as that of Simon was inconceivable.

In 1878 Simon had a further opportunity of commending thorough theological education at the gathering to celebrate the opening of the extensions to Lancashire Independent College. In the course of his paper on 'Theological training for

[63] D. W. Simon, *A New Year's Address*, 4.

[64] Ibid., 7.

[65] DWS, 108.

[66] Ibid., 107.

ministerial students' he drew a distinction between evangelistic and pastoral work, and suggested that the kind of training he was advocating was not necessary, and could be a hindrance, to the former kind of work. But sinners who have been brought to God need to be taken further on their Christian path by ministers who are theologically competent. What do such ministers need to know? 'Primarily,' he answers, that

> Christianity is Christ and the work He wrought once for all during His mission on earth; secondarily, it is the doctrine which, under the enlightening influence of the Holy Spirit, the Apostles evolved out of Christ and His work; in the third rank, it is the life of the Jewish nation ... which prepared the way for Christ ... In a word, Christianity is essentially history.[67]

Hence the importance of exegesis and biblical languages, followed by biblical criticism, introduction and archaeology. Then come biblical history, theology and ethics. On this basis the systematician goes to work. Systematic Theology is 'The scientific coordination and justification of the teachings of the Scriptures regarding the Existence, Nature, and Works of God, and specially regarding the moral relations of God and man.'[68] There immediately follows the rueful comment that 'Systematic Theology is not in high favour at the present time either with believers or unbelievers—not with the latter, because they discredit the data with which it deals; not with the former, because they think the application of scientific method to religion a thing of very doubtful utility.'[69] He advances three reasons against this position. First, that an assemblage of biblical teaching is insufficient: the Christian faith must be vindicated against its opponents. Secondly, the human mind 'needs to know the why and how of the things that come within its range of experience.'[70] Thirdly, the Christian system is correlated to a larger whole which is investigated by history and the moral and natural sciences, and it 'cannot ... be adequately appreciated unless viewed in connection therewith.'[71] This last reason justifies the sweeping into the theological curriculum of the natural sciences, psychology, ethics, the science of religion and philosophy. So considered, theology itself would be the best apology for Christianity, for 'it would give insight into the inner reasonableness and self-consistency of the teachings of the Scriptures, and into their harmony with the known cosmos.'[72]

To all of the foregoing must be added Historical Theology, to which the preliminary studies are Patristic Greek, Medieval Latin, Ancient Geography and Chronology, while auxiliary studies include General History, the History of Christian Art and Patristics. The core of the subject comprises Church History, the

---

[67] Anon., *Memorial of the Opening of the New and Enlarged Buildings*, 81.
[68] Ibid., 85.
[69] Ibid., 85-6.
[70] Ibid., 86.
[71] Ibid., 87.
[72] Ibid., 88.

History of Creeds and Confessions and the History of Doctrine. If more ministers had an adequate grasp of these subjects 'we should hear less, I believe, of vagaries, eccentricities, and novelties, for they would discover that in the domain of theological speculation, as well as in other domains, too frequently what is new is not true, and what is true is not new.'[73] Finally, special attention should be paid to the history and thought of Congregationalism in England and America.

Clearly, the ambitious curriculum he describes was such as to challenge the colleges which proposed to offer it as much as the students who worked through it. It will be noted that Simon makes no mention of homiletics and pastoral theology, though he did in fact conduct a sermon class. Students were required to choose a text, and submit a sermon plan during the evening before the class. Following the sermon, Simon would offer criticism but also share with the student his own plan for the student preacher's text.

In 1879 a consortium of Congregational theological colleges, later to be joined by Baptists and English Presbyterians, established the Senatus Academicus. This body devised externally examined courses leading to its Associate and Fellowship diplomas.[74] Simon played his part in the Senatus, but he did not surrender his hope of collegiate association with a university. On the contrary, on 13 August 1883 he gave an address at the Reform Club in Liverpool before prominent citizens, including Sir James Allanson Picton, the father of Simon's theologically 'advanced' student. His subject was, 'The university training of Congregational ministers.' Among his reasons for advocating this was that 'in the majority of cases a certain general culture, a widening of the mental horizon, a deprovincialisation could not but result, which it is hopeless to expect at present.'[75] He also thought that a higher calibre of candidate would be attracted, and that a college in proximity to an ancient university would be a 'rallying point for the Nonconformist students who now frequent the universities.'[76] Less justifiably in my opinion, he also appealed to what can only be described as the 'snob value' of even a pass degree from Oxford and Cambridge.[77]

Simon's next recourse was through his friend J. B. Paton to the Autumn Assembly of the Congregational Union in Sheffield. Paton had intended to speak about ministerial training, but Simon persuaded him to propose the establishment of two or three theological lectureships at Oxford or Cambridge which would be for the benefit of Nonconformist graduates and any others who might care to attend. The

---

[73] Ibid., 90.

[74] For the Senatus see further Alan P. F. Sell, *Philosophy, Dissent and Nonconformity*, 128-132. By 1901, the last year of its operation, the Senatus comprised representatives of seventeen colleges, including the Congregational College, Melbourne. It was disbanded as the Faculty of Theology of London University came into being, and seven of its colleges became divinity schools of that University.

[75] DWS, 111.

[76] DWS. 112.

[77] I do not deny the possibility that some of Simon's hearers may have been moved (as, to this day, some still are) by this low species of argument. It is a pity that it is so.

motion was defeated. Some Congregationalists feared that Oxbridge would give intending ministers ideas above their stations, and would divide them culturally from the bulk of the people to whom they would be ministering. Others, including Simon's colleague, John Massie,[78] argued that a Nonconformist theological hall would be shunned and its professors regarded as inferior. In due time the opponents lost, and Simon won the day, but only after he had resigned from his post at Spring Hill College. In November 1883 the College Committee was informed that Simon was resolved upon accepting the Principalship of the Scottish Congregational Theological Hall in Edinburgh. His letter of resignation was read to the Committee at its meeting on 5 December 1883, and Simon's concluding sentence was particularly revealing. He expressed the hope that 'my removal will become the occasion of some new movement that shall result in the College realizing more completely than ever before the intention of its founders to provide the most efficient possible training for candidates for the Congregational ministry.'[79]

Simon's decision to leave caused great consternation among members of the Committee, and the College treasurer, Frederick Keep, who had received a letter of 26 September 1883 from the Revd James Gregory,[80] a member of the Scottish Theological Hall Committee, enquiring as to the likelihood of Simons's removing to Edinburgh replied, 'The removal of Dr. Simon would, I think, be the utter collapse of the College.'[81] Among others to whom Gregory wrote was the Lancashire College alumnus, J. Guinness Rogers.[82] Gregory's concern was clearly theological, for Rogers replied that Simon was 'thoroughly evangelical', said that 'Dale has the highest opinion of him', and added, 'If I have any doubt about him it is not as to his own doctrine, but as to his mode of dealing with men. He has gone through serious sifting himself and come right. This makes him take not only hopeful but optimistic views of others; and his expression of this tendency has got

---

[78] For Massie (1842-1925) see ODNB; *The Christian World*, 10 December 1942, 3; J. V. Bartlet, 'Obituary', *Mansfield College Magazine*. Never ordained, Massie had studied at St. John's College, Cambridge, and began his tutorial duties at Spring Hill College in 1869. He removed with the College to Mansfield, and resigned in 1903 on becoming Liberal MP for Cricklade, a position he held until 1910. He chaired the Council of the CUEW, 1919-20.

[79] *Minute Book of the Spring Hill College Committee*, entry for 5 December 1883.

[80] For Gregory (1844-1912) see CYB, 1914, 177-8; SCM, 58. Trained at New College, London, he ministered at Belgrave, Leeds (1874-9), at Augustine, Edinburgh (1879-94), and was Chairman of the Congregational Union of Scotland in 1890.

[81] DWS, 138.

[82] For Rogers (1822-1911), see CYB, 1912, 168-70; ODNB; *J. Guinness Rogers. An Autobiography*. A graduate of Trinity College Dublin, and later DD (Edinburgh), Rogers trained under Vaughan and Davidson at Lancashire Independent College, where he was the first student to enrol in the new College on its foundation in 1843. He served at St. James Congregational Church, Newcastle-upon-Tyne (1846-51); Albion, Ashton-under-Lyne (1851-65); and Grafton Street, Clapham (1865-1900). He was prominent in political affairs and Chairman of the CUEW in 1874.

him into trouble. But I believe him very able, devoted, and trustworthy.'[83] The Edinburgh position offered, Simon accepted it, and gave a parting lecture to the students of Spring Hill on 24 June 1884. His subject was 'The authority of the Bible'. So impressed were his hearers that they unanimously requested the publication of the paper. It appeared in the October issue of *The British Quarterly Review*, and subsequently as a pamphlet. The Spring Hill Committee adopted a lengthy and gracious resolution in which they expressed deep gratitude to Simon for his fifteen years' work, and wished him well. The resolution concludes:

> The friends of the College now assembled would take this occasion to express their keen sense of this loss; their high esteem for Dr. Simon; their admiration for his character, abilities, and fidelity; and their earnest prayer and hope that, if the Lord will, he may be spared to serve Christ and His truth, that still larger opportunities of usefulness may be given to him, and that through all the years to come his service may be crowned with rich results.[84]

In the Autumn of 1884 Simon began his work in Edinburgh as successor to W. Lindsay Alexander, his former translation colleague,.

Within a month of Simon's resignation Dale came out in favour of the scheme to remove the College to a university city. A. M. Fairbairn was waiting in the wings, so to speak, at Airedale College, and Dale and he began to enlist the support of numerous people of influence in the denomination, not least the Liverpudlians whom Simon had addressed the year before.

When Mansfield College, Oxford, was opened on 14-16 October 1889 Dale gave an address on 'The History of Spring Hill College' in which he said with regard to Simon's resignation, that 'The Committee would gladly have retained his services, but he was satisfied that duty called him away.'[85] Simon's removal provided the opportunity for a fresh consideration of the College's future, and in the event his vision was realised, though without his involvement in it. In his paper on 'Mansfield College', W. B. Selbie, the first student to be enrolled at Mansfield and later to become its second Principal, acknowledged the Johnson-Simon motion of 1876,[86] and in his opening speech at a breakfast gathering Fairbairn said 'My friend, Principal Simon, while head of Spring Hill College, earnestly and variously urged that some such enterprise as this be attempted, and many still have a recollection of the words in which he pleaded for it.[87] The concluding breakfast speech was delivered by Simon himself. He acknowledged that whilst at Spring Hill 'my colleagues and some others, I fancy, sometimes regarded me as a dreamer of dreams, and as a sort of

---

[83] DWS, 140.
[84] Ibid., 145.
[85] Anon., *Mansfield College, Oxford*, 24.
[86] Ibid., 29.
[87] Ibid., 168.

volcanic agency. They never felt sure what was coming next.'[88] He went on to say that

> As far, indeed, as external features are concerned, Mansfield College far transcends any notion I ever entertained. Nor would it have been possible for me to carry a scheme like this to the splendid issue which we see today. It was not the time to do it. There were needed men like Dr. Fairbairn, Dr. Dale—whom I congratulate on his conversion to the idea—and Mr. Albert Spicer to do the work.[89]

Simon went on to show that he had not run out of visions: he appealed for a learned theological society for Britain comparable with the existing scientific societies, and he pleaded for a system of theological education by extension, for 'Until a deeper interest is taken by our people at large in the theology .. and rational justification of their faith, I can cherish but very little hope for that profound and deep revival of spiritual religion among us which, I know is the desire of men of all denominations and of all Christian views.'[90]

It is not easy to determine whether Simon's reference to Dale's conversion to the idea is intended as sarcastic or innocent—or was it sarcasm disguised by innocence? It is likewise not easy to know if Fairbairn was 'damning with faint praise' when he wrote in a letter of December 1883, 'Dr. Simon, of Birmingham, is going to Edinburgh. I hope he may be successful. He is a very fine fellow, very anxious to do well, and will do his best.'[91]

There can be no question that Fairbairn was Dale's man for the post of Principal in Oxford, and so it came to pass. Certainly Fairbairn had the public persona for the task, whereas Simon was the more retiring type.[92] Fairbairn seemed robust, whereas Simon had suffered two breakdowns of health. Fairbairn was published in his own right, whereas Simon had so far published two articles in *Bibliotheca Sacra* and three in *The British Quarterly Review*—though his diligent work as a translator should not have been underestimated. Fairbairn had administrative skills that Simon lacked. Fairbairn had not suffered the guilt by association that had befallen Simon because of the doctrinal effusions of some of 'Simon's men', some of whom had greatly

---

[88] Ibid., 191.

[89] Ibid., 192.

[90] Ibid., 193-4.

[91] Quoted in W. B. Selbie, *The Life of Andrew Martin Fairbairn*, 126. For Fairbairn (1838-1912) see also DNCBP; DSCHT; ODNB; SCM; E. J. Price, 'Dr. Fairbairn and Airedale College'; K. W. Wadsworth, *Yorkshire United Independent College*; Elaine Kaye, *Mansfield College, Oxford*; idem, *For the Work of Ministry*; R. S. Franks, 'The theology of Andrew Martin Fairbairn'; M. D. Johnson, *The Dissolution of Dissent*; Alan P. F. Sell, *Dissenting Thought and the Life of the Churches*, ch. 19. For Selbie (1862-1944) see CYB, 1945, 441; ODNB; WTW; E. Kaye, *Mansfield College*.

[92] According to his obituarist, 'Always retiring and diffident in disposition, he shrank from the thought of the principalship in Oxford.' See CYB, 1910, 190. He is, however, given credit for being the first to have had the idea of removing Spring Hill College to a university town (the University of Birmingham received its charter in 1900).

disturbed Dale (whose own views concerning the post-mortem annihilation of the wicked were suspect in some quarters). Fairbairn had held high office in Congregationalism—indeed, he was Chairman of the Union in 1883, whereas Simon shrank from such duties. But of the two Simon was the more competent scholar, Fairbairn, like Vaughan before him, having made every effort to overcome the deficiencies of his early education largely by his own industry.[93] Perhaps Simon and Fairbairn were most alike in that each had found his soul in Germany.[94]

Be all that as it may, there is no question that Powicke and other Spring Hill alumni felt that Simon had been treated badly. He took no part in the inaugural services at Mansfield, and his constant pressing for such an outcome as that which had been achieved was not formally recognized. Perhaps, surmises his biographer, this 'was an oversight; but, if so, it was an unfortunate oversight, and one which ought not to have been possible.'[95] He immediately adds that Simon 'was by no means "sensitive" about his personal claims; but that he felt the slight in this connection is certain, and his friends ... felt it more keenly than himself.'[96] For all that, Simon preached at Mansfield on 22 May 1892, and in July 1894 he delivered a course of lectures on 'Some points of an ethical theory of the redeeming work of Christ.'

Meanwhile Simon had been establishing himself in Edinburgh.[97] In 1886 he was a prime mover in the founding of the Symposium, a gathering of ministers designed to foster theological discussion. According to Robert Mackintosh, then of Dumfries and later Professor at Lancashire Independent College, Simon 'was the soul, and perhaps also the backbone' of the meetings of the Symposium.[98] In the same year Simon joined the Edinburgh Theological Club, of which he became a keen and valued member. To the delight of his friends he began to publish books. *The Bible an Outgrowth of Theocratic Life* appeared in 1885, to be followed by the first edition of *The Redemption of Man* (1889). Also in 1889 there appeared Simon's translation

---

[93] I therefore find it odd that Mark Johnson should say that 'As a scholar [Fairbairn] was clearly the most capable man in all of the Congregational colleges.' See *The Dissolution of Dissent*, 204. I demur when Johnson further says that Simon's going to Edinburgh 'represented a self-imposed demotion of considerable depth.' Ibid., 208. To whom did it represent a demotion? Presumably to those whose doctrine of vocation is so weak, and their hierarchical instincts so developed, that they did not find it easy to think in terms of the call which Simon undoubtedly felt it to be. How often have I heard it said of 'pulpit princes' that having arrived where they are, there is nowhere else for them to go. But there have always been small, vacant, urban and rural churches to which they could quite easily have gone. Variations in stipend sometimes seem to make things very difficult for the Holy Spirit.

[94] See A. M. Fairbairn, 'Experience in theology.'

[95] DWS, 116.

[96] Ibid.

[97] See George M'Hardy, *Historical Sketch of the Scottish Congregational Hall 1811-1911*, 7-8.

[98] For Robert Mackintosh (1858-1933) see CYB, 1934, 269; DNCBP; DTCBP; DSCHT; Alan P. F. Sell, *Robert Mackintosh, Theologian of Integrity*.

of Leonhard Stählin's *Kant, Lotze and Ritschl.* To these works I shall return in subsequent sections of this chapter. In 1890 Simon and his wife spent a few months at Stow Memorial Church, Adelaide, where he was most warmly received.[99] During the following year he spoke on 'The present direction of theological thought in the Congregational churches of Great Britain' at the first session of the International Congregational Council, and in the same year he was awarded the DD of the University of Edinburgh.

When Simon arrived in Edinburgh the Theological Hall occupied rooms in the basement of Augustine Church, but in due course, through the generosity of Miss Baxter it became possible to move into a large house in George Square. The library, too, benefited from donations by the Crawford Trust and many others. We may surmise, however, that what gave Simon the greatest satisfaction was the way in which he was able to develop the curriculum. In a paper of 1891 entitled, 'Present position and work of the Theological Hall', he recalled that whereas on his arrival in 1884 the theological course lasted for only twelve or thirteen months distributed over four years, it now extended over twenty-two or twenty-five months, making it a month shorter than in most English Congregational colleges and a month longer than the Mansfield College course. He would have welcomed the full-time services of Professor Simpson,[100] and things would be even better were a third professor to be appointed. He also hoped for further cooperation with the Free Church and United Presbyterian colleges in Edinburgh.

In 1893 Simon was once again tested in relation to a call. He received a letter dated 13 March 1893 from the Governors of Yorkshire United Independent College, Bradford, inviting him to accept the Principalship there, Principal Falding[101] having died suddenly and unexpectedly. When news of the invitation became known, Simon's best friend in Scotland, James Ross,[102] pleaded with him not to leave Edinburgh—he thought that chaos would result if he did. Others, from England, urged him to come. He had been strongly recommended to the Yorkshire Governors by Dale, C. A. Berry, H. R. Reynolds of Cheshunt College and Fairbairn who also

---

[99] See DWS, ch. 5.

[100] For Andrew Findlater Simpson (1842-1923) see SCM, 146. He was Professor of Biblical Languages and Literature from 1885 to 1920, combining this role with that of pastor in Dalkeith until 1893. On Simon's departure to Bradford in the latter year, he became full-time at the Hall. Coincidentally, he had been minister at the British and American Church, St. Petersburg (1868-72), the post to which Simon had been attracted, but declined.

[101] For Frederick John Falding (1818-1892) see CYB, 1894, 191-3; K. W. Wadsworth, *Yorkshire United Independent College*; E. Kaye, *For the Work of Ministry*. An MA, DD of Glasgow University, where he had been a Dr. Williams Scholar, he was trained at Rotherham and, following pastorates at Wellington, Salop (1845-8) and New Road, Bury (1848-51) he became Principal there in 1852. In 1888, Fairbairn of Airedale College now having left for Mansfield College, Falding became the first Principal of the Yorkshire United College. He was Chairman of the CUEW, 1888-9.

[102] For Ross (1837-1912) see CYB, 1913, 185-6; SCM, 139. He was an alumnus of the Theological Hall and, in 1905, was awarded the DD of St. Andrews University.

wrote to Simon expressing the hope that he would accept the appointment;[103] but no appeal was warmer than that of Elkanah Armitage, Professor of Apologetics, Philosophy of Religion and the History of Christian Doctrine at Yorkshire Untied College: 'Come—for we need you as a Theologian; we need you as an Evangelical Christian; we need you as a friend. We could not—even if we gave much time to it—find another man on whom we could unite as we have done on you.'[104] Both James Gregory and Ross felt that the Committee of the Theological Hall had not treated Simon well in financial terms,[105] but what prompted him to accept the invitation, by a letter of 30 March 1893, was the desire to influence a greater number of ministerial candidates than was possible in Scotland.

On arrival in Bradford Simon devoted himself to his students and his teaching, but on occasion he was required to address a wider constituency. Thus, for example, in September 1897 we find him giving an address to friends of the College at the opening of the new session. His title was, *What does Congregationalism stand for? With special reference to Doctrine.* His treatment of the subject proved controversial, as we shall see. In 1898 there appeared his full-scale discussion of *Reconciliation by Incarnation.* This drew some somewhat oscillating remarks from the reviewer in *The Expository Times*: 'Principal Simon, of Bradford, is at once acute and sound. ... Principal Simon is not always lucid, and never obvious. But he will repay study. ...' The reviewer concludes that the work 'is a sequel to that fine book, *The Redemption of Man.* Together they make a fairly complete, a sound and accurate, system of theology.'[106]

On 29 June 1899 Simon's wife died after a long and painful illness. She had never felt completely at home in England and Scotland,[107] but had faithfully supported him in all his work. She was buried at Undercliffe Cemetery, Bradford.

In 1904 Simon's book of sermons, *Twice Born*, appeared and was received, he wrote to Ross, 'in a manner that has greatly taken me aback: it is actually selling.'[108] In 1905 he tendered his resignation to the College Governors, but they persuaded him to stay on until a suitable successor could be found. They also resolved to allow him £100/0/0 per annum from College funds, and to establish a Testimonial Fund of £500/0/0. Also in 1905 Simon celebrated the Jubilee of his ministry, and the Rev. Herbert Brooke of Accrington initiated an appeal addressed to former students and friends which raised £120/0/0.[109] This was presented to Simon at

---

[103] DWS, 177. For Charles Albert Berry (1852-1899), who was Chairman of the CUEW in 1897, see CYB, 1900, 167-71.

[104] DWS, 176. For Armitage (1844-1929) see CYB, 1930, 222-3; DNCBP; K. W. Wadsworth, *Yorkshire United Independent College*; E. Kaye, *For the Work of Ministry.* He had studied under Henry Sidgwick at Cambridge University and Henry Rogers at Lancashire Independent College.

[105] Ibid., 189, 177.

[106] *The Expository Times*, X, 1898-1899, 213.

[107] See DWS, 304-5.

[108] Ibid., 252.

[109] For Brooke (1873-1925) see CYB, 1926, 159.

a meeting in the Library of the Memorial Hall, London, on 9 May. The meeting was chaired by his old friend from College days, John Brown of Bedford. In 1906 the second edition of *The Redemption of Man* appeared, shorn of its original Introduction, and with a new chapter on Paul's doctrine, which *The Expository Times* reviewer found to be 'worthy of a great book.'[110] Simon's last book, *The Making of a Preacher*, appeared in 1907.

Simon was finally released from his duties at Yorkshire College in 1907, on the appointment of Ebenezer Griffith-Jones to the Principalship.[111] During Simon's tenure ninety-three students had passed through his hands. Of these twenty-one did not complete the course—most resigned (one of whom was later readmitted), and a few were expelled. The year 1899 saw the highest number of Arts students, twenty-six, most of whom, took their course at Edinburgh University, while the largest number of Theology students, twenty-five, were registered in 1902.[112] On 19 June a Farewell Meeting was held, chaired by Robert Bruce, who had the pleasure of paying his old friend a warm tribute and presenting him with a cheque for £710/0/0—over £200/0/0 more than the Governors had hoped to raise. Simon responded appropriately, thanking the donors for removing a 'cloud of [financial] anxiety ... which otherwise would have become oppressively dark.'[113] In the course of his remarks he reflected on the fact that

> Were I an architect, or artist, or a musical composer, or a manufacturer, or a man of commerce, the results of my work would stare you and me in the face. But no one can say regarding those of us who are engaged in preparing young men for the ministry, 'If thou seekest their monument, look around.' There is nothing that attracts and fixes men's ordinary notice. ... Systematic theologians in particular are seed-sowers, and the seed is not sown on compact little farms where the crops can be seen growing and ripening; on the contrary, our seed is shown [*sic*] here, there, everywhere; it comes up too in such minute quantities, and withal so mixed up with all sorts of other seed, that no one can distinguish what is due to the one source from what is due to the other.[114]

In 1908 the Governors elected Simon Principal Emeritus.

As soon as he was officially retired Simon took steps to remove to Dresden. While he was pleased to be in Germany again, his health began to give cause for concern, so he returned to England in 1908. He stayed with members of his family until his death on 17 January 1909. His funeral service was conducted in Bradford by James Gregory on 26 January, and prayers were offered by Principal Griffith-Jones.

---

[110] *The Expository Times*, XVII, 1905-1906, 365.

[111] For Griffith-Jones (1860-1942) see CYB, 1943, 428; WWW.

[112] *Congregational College Archives. Yorkshire United Independent College*. Box 9.

[113] DWS, 259.

[114] DWS, 259-60. There is no question that this is true. It is, therefore, well that Simon died long before the advent of those latter-day scrutineers who devote themselves to the Teaching Assessment in British higher education, ever expecting definite 'input' and requiring measured 'output'.

Simon's former colleague, Dr. Duff, read the lessons, and the Revd Eric A. Lawrence gave the address,[115] which ended as follows:

> There was a beautiful simplicity in [Simon's] character and a marked absence of self-seeking. He did not care for notice or applause. He had a vivid sense of things unseen and eternal which enabled him to live in detachment from things seen and temporal. With entire devotion he gave himself to the great work to which he had been called, and they thanked God for him, for the life he had lived, and for the example he had left.[116]

Like his wife before him, Simon was buried at Undercliffe Cemetery, where the graveside service was conducted by Dr. Goodrich of Manchester and the Revd E. R. Barrett.[117]

I

Having introduced Simon I shall now proceed to an examination of his writings. I shall consider first what might be called the biblical-historical-pneumatic epistemology which was the basis of all his thought. This will entail a consideration of his approach to the Bible and his emphasis upon the spiritual. On the basis of the foundation thus laid I shall discuss his responses to the theological trends of his day, and his position on several Christian doctrines, paying particular attention, as he did himself, on the doctrine of our redemption. I shall conclude with an assessment of the man.

In the course of elucidating the biblical-historical-pneumatic foundation of Simon's thought we shall see the ways in which he sought to adjust himself to some of the intellectual currents of his time. We may set out from Simon's professor at Lancashire Independent College, Samuel Davidson. During the summer of 1844 Davidson, his wife, and two friends went to Germany. This was his first

---

[115] For Archibald Duff (1845-1934) see CYB, 1935, 272-4; A. Duff, 'A theological college professor's training in the nineteenth century'; K. W. Wadsworth, *Yorkshire United Independent College*; E. Kaye, *For the Work of Ministry*. On the appearance of the first volume of his *Old Testament Theology* (1891), Duff was accused of heresy by some. Principal Falding stood by him, and the Governors of Yorkshire College resolved that since they were untrained laymen they had no competence to adjudicate the matter, but that they had 'perfect confidence in the scholarship of our Professor,' and 'absolute trust in his Christian character. ... So we dismiss entirely the charges of heresy that have been made against him.' See A. Duff, art. cit., 313-14. A significant contrast this to the attitude of the Lancashire College Committee *vis à vis* Davidson thirty-four years earlier. For Lawrence (1830-1909) see CYB, 1910, 177-8. He trained at Spring Hill College under Simon (1871-77), and also studied at Darmstadt and Göttingen. He ministered at Square Chapel, Halifax (1883-1905) and St. Annes-on-Sea (1905-9).

[116] DWS, 293.

[117] For Albert Goodrich (1840-1919), Chairman of the CUEW in 1904, see CYB, 1920, 197-8. For Barrett (1848-1914) see CYB, 1915, 133-5.

visit to the country, and the party visited a number of academic centres. He was 'specially attracted to Halle, the seat of Prussia's leading theological university.'[118] Tholuck was among the scholars he met there. On returning to Manchester he worked on the first volume of his *Introduction to the New Testament*. It was published in 1848, with volumes two and three appearing in 1849 and 1851 respectively. On the publication of the first volume, Tholuck and his colleague Hupfeld[119] proposed that Davidson be awarded the degree of Doctor of Theology of the University of Halle and, there being no dissentient voices among the theological professoriate, the degree was duly conferred. Tholuck visited Davidson in Manchester in 1847. 'His theology,' Davidson later wrote, was rather of the *Vermittelungs* sort, stopping short of the conclusions at which a sounder criticism than his had arrived'[120] In 1852 Davidson published a two-volume work entitled, *A Treatise on Biblical Criticism*. Here the first volume was devoted to the Old Testament, the second to the New.

Davidson was asked to revise Horne's *Introduction to the Critical Study and Knowledge of the Sacred Scriptures* (1818-1821), but it quickly became apparent to him that a completely new book was required, and this is what was published in 1856 under the title, *The Text of the Old Testament Considered*. With this the storm broke around Davidson's head. As he himself put it, 'This work was fraught with momentous consequences to myself and family, since it led to our being turned out of house and home, with a name tainted and maligned.'[121] When writing the relevant section of his autobiography during the early 1870s Davidson resolved to say no more about the matter, but twenty years later he invited Allanson Picton to contribute an account of the controversy to the published version, and this appears as chapter 6, under the title, 'The College crisis.'[122] It is not to our present purpose to deal exhaustively with the controversy. Suffice it to say, by way of sample only, that Davidson argued against the Mosaic authorship of the Pentateuch,[123] and found

---

[118] A. Davidson, ed., *Autobiography and Diary*, 22.

[119] Hermann Hupfeld (1796-1866), an Orientalist and Semitic philologist, studied at Marburg and later at Halle. Following junior appointments at both universities he returned to Halle as Professor in 1843.

[120] A. Davidson, ed., *Autobiography and Diary*, 29.

[121] Ibid., 34.

[122] For James Allanson Picton (1832-1910), see ODNB; WWW 1897-1916. He studied under Davidson from 1851-56. Following pastorates at Cheetham Hill, Manchester (1857-62), Gallowtree Gate, Leicester (1862-9) and St. Thomas's Square, Hackney (1869-79), he devoted himself to literary and political work, and was Liberal MP for Leicester from 1884-6 and 1892-4. A number of writers have devoted attention to this crisis. They include Willis B. Glover, *Evangelical Nonconformists and Higher Criticism in the Nineteenth Century*; John Lea, 'The Davidson controversy'; E. Kaye, *For the Work of Ministry*; F. Roger Tomes, '"We are hardly prepared for this style of teaching yet": Samuel Davidson and Lancashire Independent College,' JURCHS, V no. 7, October 1995, 398-414.

[123] In his exemplary article, Roger Tomes rightly points out that Picton was anachronistic in stating that Davidson subscribed to an evolutionary view of the

that while a few Psalms were written by David, the majority were of a later date. All of which caused alarm to more conservative souls. They felt that Davidson was undermining the doctrine of the plenary inspiration of Scripture, and that if errors were found in the Bible here and there, why not everywhere? For good measure, Davidson was charged with denying central Christian doctrines.

At its meeting on 24 November 1856 the Lancashire College Committee heard from the Revd David Everard Ford of Richmond Chapel, Broughton, that he had received numerous letters expressing disquiet at Davidson's performance in the offending volume. Of Ford, Picton wrote that 'his warmest admirers would never have thought of setting him up as an authority on Hebrew scholarship'[124] but those whose doctrinal antennae have been assaulted have frequently been innocent of Hebrew; and that Ford felt that the enemy was at the gate is clear from his own autobiography in which he writes,

> As sure as Dr. Vaughan ... was on one side, Dr. Davidson ... would be on the other. It was not, however, suspected by anybody, not in the secret, that this spirit of antagonism would be carried into the regions of theology, and that in order to spite Dr. Vaughan's jealousy for 'the faith which was once delivered to the saints', his colleague would become the patron-general of German monstrosities.[125]

The Revd John Kelly of the Crescent Chapel, Liverpool—to Picton 'one of the ablest men in the lamentable list of perverted intellects prostrated before the idols of the sanctuary'[126]—moved that the matter be investigated, and over the next three months this was done. Davidson was invited to explain himself and he did so. The report was completed and presented to the Committee on 16 February 1857. While some doctrinal portions of the book were deemed to be unsatisfactory, the sub-committee found that in other parts of the book, and in his own oral statements, Davidson held 'all these vital truths, and regards Holy Scripture as inspired,—an unerring authority in morality and religion, and infallible in every other important matter.'[127] This hopeful stance notwithstanding, the matter rumbled on.

In May 1857 Davidson published a reaffirmation of his position, in the course of which he wrote,

> On all essential and vital matters—those constituting the evangelical system ... the volume contains unmistakable utterances of belief. Nothing in it will, in my opinion, be found to infringe on the completeness and sufficiency of Holy Scripture as an unerring rule of faith and practice, man's original depravity, regeneration by the Holy Spirit, justification by faith, the atonement made by the Divine Redeemer

---

development of the Pentateuch, since nobody subscribed view to that in 1856. See "We are hardly prepared for this style of teaching yet", 404.

124 Ibid., 42. For Ford (1797-1875) see CYB, 1876, 333-5.

125 A. Peel, 'The Autogiography of David Everard Ford,' 277.

126 J. A. Picton in *Autobiography and Diary*, 45. For Kelly (1801-1876) see CYB, 1877, 384-7; ODNB.

127 Quoted by Picton, ibid., 51.

for the sins of the world, and the application of it in redemption. ... I do not think, however, that the phraseology employed by others in enunciating and explaining them has always been happy or appropriate ... This remark applies especially to the older divines, who often presented the peculiarities of Calvinism in a repulsive aspect. ... Christ, in all his excellency and offices as the Prophet, Priest, and King of His people—the only and all-sufficient Mediator—is the precious corner-stone of the believer. May he ever be mine![128]

On 1 June 1857 the Committee met again, and Kelly proposed, and Ford seconded, a motion, which was carried, to the effect that the Committee regarded Davidson's explanations as inadequate, and that 'their confidence in him as a professor in this institution is greatly shaken, and that they view with serious apprehension the effect of his teaching and influence on the students committed to his care.'[129] They sought further clarification. The Committee adjourned for nine days, and on 10 June they learned that Davidson had made no reply to the resolution of ten days earlier. Kelly tabled a motion of no confidence in Davidson, and this was carried by twenty votes to eighteen, the Chairman, Raffles, and Vaughan being on the majority side. If the Committee expected Davidson to resign his post, their hopes were dashed. Instead, in a letter of 25 June, he invited the Committee to supply of list of the points of difficulty so that he could give due consideration to them.[130] On the same day the Committee met. R. S. Ashton moved and James Ashton seconded a motion to the effect that such a list objectionable passages and uncertainties be supplied to Davidson. Kelly moved an amendment to the effect that such action was unnecessary, and this was carried. Having no other option, Davidson resigned. Vaughan himself resigned very soon afterwards. It had become quite obvious that, in the words of John Kelly, 'We are hardly prepared for this style of teaching yet.'[131] Kelly's coadjutor, David Everard Ford, later declared that

The Lancashire Independent College was saved; but some of the men who rescued it from destruction had a heavy penalty to pay. At least, I had. The occasion cost me more than any crisis I had previously known; but never have I, for one moment, regretted it. And now, calmly looking back on the whole affair, so thoroughly am I convinced of the importance, to our churches and the world, of the interests at stake, that if during a long life I had rendered no further service to the cause of truth and righteousness than on that occasion, I should feel, on a dying bed, that I had not altogether lived in vain.[132]

---

[128] S. Davidson, *Facts, Statements, and Explanations*, quoted by J. A. Picton, *Autobiography and Diary*, 44-5.

[129] Ibid., 60.

[130] For his letter see ibid., 65.

[131] J. Kelly, *An Examination of the Facts, Statements and Explanations of the Rev. Dr. Samuel Davidson*, 25.

[132] A. Peel, 'The Autobiography of David Everard Ford,' 279.

On 13 July 1857 thirty-two former students, including Simon, Robert Bruce and William Urwick,[133] who became Professor of Hebrew at New College, London, sent a letter expressing their respect for and gratitude to Davidson, and eighteen of the then current students, including John Gwyther, did likewise.[134] In the interests of balance and accuracy it must also be said that two students, Enoch Mellor and J. Guinness Rogers published a tract entitled *Dr. Davidson, His Errors, Contradictions, and Plagiarisms*, in which they declared that whereas Davidson's views had been traditional in 1843, he had now become the 'most servile imitator' of rationalistic, German 'charlatans, whose impertinence is equalled only by their shallowness.' Moreover, Davidson's views 'are marked neither by profound thought nor original research—[he] has committed himself blindly to German leaders, not careful even to select those most deserving of confidence ...'[135]

That Davidson was not without supporters, some of them wealthy, in the Congregational constituency is clear from the fact that his friends raised £3000/0/0, which enabled him to establish a school in Hatherlow, Cheshire, to which they then sent their sons. At the time William Urwick was minister there and, indeed, Davidson had delivered the Introductory Discourse on Congregationalism at Urwick's ordination on 19 June 1851. The Davidsons later moved to London, where again he had regular contact with his old student who was by then a professor at New College. He died on 1 April 1898 and was buried in Hampstead New Cemetery on 5 April, with Urwick conducting the service.

Almost certainly the Committee members of Lancashire College were influenced by motives other than those overtly indicated. In 1847 Davidson had delivered the annual Congregational Lecture in London. His subject was *The Ecclesiastical Polity of the New Testament Unfolded*, and his book of that title appeared in 1848. A second edition was called for, and Davidson sought the opportunity to revise his work, but this was not permitted by the publisher, so the second edition of 1854

---

[133] For Urwick's reminiscences at the time of Davidson's death see ibid., 356-361.

[134] See ibid.,70-72.

[135] Mellor and Rogers, *Dr. Davidson*, quoted by John Waddington, *Congregational History 1850-1880*, 206. In his chapter on Lancashire College Rogers makes no mention of his collaboration with his great friend Mellor in the writing of this pamphlet. Now mellower, he does say of Davidson that 'The controversies of later years separated us, but they never led me to underrate the benefit I derived from his patient, painstaking, and most valuable labours. ... From him I learned how great a work was to be done in the study ...' See *J. Guinness Rogers. An Autobiography*, 70. It is interesting to contrast the opinions of Kelly expressed by Picton with those of Rogers. Picton: 'His strong, eager mind was logical in the sense of caring much more about correct syllogisms than about sound induction of premisses. ... Mr. Kelly found [his infallible authority] in the Bible, and for him the Bible spoke through Calvin's *Institutes*.' See *Autobiography and Diary*, 46. Rogers wrote of Kelly's 'uncompromising vindication of Truth,' and conceded that 'to some it seemed as though he was a hard man. But a man with tenderer soul than John Kelly never breathed.' See *J. Guinness Rogers*, 152. For Mellor (1823-1881) see CYB, 1882, 315-18. He ministered at Square Chapel, Halifax and Great George Street, Liverpool, and was Chairman of the CUEW in 1863.

replicates the first. Davidson said, 'I would have changed it to a very great extent: having convinced myself that Church government is a matter of expediency, and that it may be shaped by the spiritual consciousness of the Church, agreeably to the circumstances and exigencies of the period.'[136] To have published such an opinion would, he knew, have been brought odium upon him, for with one exception, the Congregational ministers known to him 'believed in the divine right of Congregational Independency; though they did not conform to the New Testament plan in some respects, as I carefully pointed out in the Lecture.'[137] From all we know of the more conservative members of the College Committee, they would have regarded Davidson's changing view, of which they may have had more than an inkling, as a further attack upon the authority of Scripture.

Again, it is more than likely that some of the Lancashire traditionalists felt that Davidson was giving encouragement to the home-missionary-minded Unitarianism that was making gains in the county to their distress. The Unitarian paper, *The Inquirer*, saw a new dawn for Congregationalism in Davidson's stance:

> Theological progress is one of the marked signs of the times—that progress is manifest in no one of the religious bodies more than the Congregationalists. Already many of the ordinary men of that church have in thought, if not in person, gone out to seek a better country, and now a great man has raised aloft the banner of freedom and progress. Here, from the pen of an eminent scholar, a professor in a college, strictly and designedly bound down to a Calvinistic Creed, is there a quiet but very effectual disowning of Calvinistic peculiarities.[138]

The Inquirer fails to note that the College's trust deed did not commit its students or professors to any particular view of biblical inspiration.

In other ways Davidson found 'enemies'. As Roger Tomes reminds us,[139] he opposed the Crimean War (1854-6) and the Chinese War (1857), and he was a member of the Peace Society. All of which placed him in a position contrary to that of Robert Vaughan and many others. He told a Peace Society audience that those who opposed him needed to master the rudiments of theology—a pugilistic utterance of a kind not uncharacteristic of a certain kind of pacifist, then or now. On the live issue of education Davidson argued for the minority view that the instruction given in public schools should be secular, whereas many others thought that the Bible should be taught in such institutions. To some more precisely theological straws in the wind which were among the grounds of conservative apprehensiveness I shall come in due course.

All of the considerations mentioned could sway a person against Davidson, quite apart from his specific views on the Mosaic authorship of the Pentateuch and suchlike esoteric matters. No doubt some of those who stood against him felt that

---

136 A. Davidson, ed., *Autobiography and Diary*, 24-5.

137 Ibid., 25.

138 Quoted by John Waddington, *Congregational History 1850-1880*, 205.

139 F. R. Tomes,' "We are hardly prepared for this style of teaching yet",' 404-5.

they had been vindicated for, as Picton reminds us, following his resignation, 'Davidson's critical opinions rapidly advanced in the direction of pure rationalism, though his religious feeling retained to the last its devout simplicity.'[140] W. F. Adeney later remarked, 'in the 1868 edition of his "Introduction" to the New Testament, Dr. Davidson advocated the advanced critical position of the Tübingen school, a position to which he adhered in later years even after it had been discredited.'[141] Equally, there is no doubt that others were overjoyed when at the Jubilee of Lancashire College in 1893 Davidson 'was repeatedly referred to in terms of highest admiration.'[142] In the meantime George Bubier, Davidson's most prominent supporter on the Lancashire College Committee, had served as Principal of Spring Hill College from 1864-1869, and Davidson's personal vindication reached its height, albeit after his death, when the Samuel Davidson Chair of Old Testament was established at Kings College, London—the institution from which the erstwhile Unitarian F. D. Maurice had been dismissed in 1854 because he denied the eternity of the punishment of the wicked.[143]

Whereas some in Davidson's day came to the Bible with the *a priori* presupposition that it was infallible, and hence that it was permissible—even required—to draw from its propositions deductive inferences of a dogmatic or homiletic kind, Davidson's approach, as Roger Tomes has rightly perceived, was that 'you cannot decide in advance what kind of book the Bible is but only discover that in the course of reading it.'[144] This is the point that Simon developed when he advocated the necessity of paying due heed both to biblical history on the one hand, and, against the naturalistic assumptions that more radical higher critics brought to the task, to the Bible as having a supernatural origin and as being a spiritual resource on the other. Simon's position is encapsulated in a letter to James Ward of 3 January 1870:

> If there be no God—no living personal God who cares for and trains men; who leaves none to themselves; who has sought by special means (others were fruitless, as Gentile experience shows) to recover men to Himself and to themselves—then the genius of the Jewish nation plus myth, &c., must account for the peculiarities of

---

[140] A. Davidson, ed., *Autobiography and Diary*, 67. Davidson's liberal-tending trajectory did indeed move swiftly. Robert Bruce, who left Lancashire College in 1854, testified, 'My notebooks would show how he then discussed and refuted the very errors (so-called) which he afterwards embraced and published as truths.' See *Lancashire Independent College Jubilee*, 87.

[141] W. F. Adeney, *A Century's Progress in Religious Life and Thought*, 80.

[142] Ibid.

[143] The Samuel Davidson bequest was accepted by the University of London in November 1924 (Senate Minute 481, reference UoL/ST2/2/41); the Board of Studies of Theology drew up the conditions for the Chair on 29 May 1925 (UoL/AC8/64/1/3); and Minute 659 of the Senate session 1925-6 reports that the Chair had been established (UoL/ST2/2/42). I am grateful to Richard Temple, Archivist at Senate House Library, for supplying this information.

[144] F. R. Tomes, '"We are hardly prepared for this style of preaching yet",' 406.

> the Bible. But if the objective history of the Bible be possible because we have a God such as I have described, then its peculiarities are the peculiarities of history. In this sense I object to calling the Bible a revelation, nay more, I object to calling it the record of a revelation: it is the record of the history of a nation which God was seeking to redeem, and by whose redemption he aimed to effect and prepare the redemption of mankind generally. The first question is the one I started with—Have we a living God?[145]

We now begin to see the point of the title of Simon's first book, *The Bible an Outgrowth of Theocratic Life*, which comprises lectures given at Spring Hill and in Edinburgh. In the preface he expresses his indebtedness to, among others, Rothe's *Zur Dogmatik* ('though I have drifted considerably away from some of its positions'[146]), and to his friend Tholuck's article on 'Inspiration' in Herzog's *Realencyclopaedie*; but also to F. D. Maurice's Old Testament works, 'which led me, whilst yet a student ... to realise that veritable men and women, living real human lives, lay behind the Biblical books.'[147]

Simon's investigative procedure is governed by the conviction that 'If the point of view is to be a right one, it must be determined by the subject itself; not by considerations drawn from other quarters.' Indeed, 'The bane of investigation is to take one's stand outside the subject investigated'[148]—an approach, incidentally, that is the converse of that of those latter-day analytical philosophers who regard their work as a second order linguistic enquiry. For Simon, the Bible itself must determine the method of its treatment. He traces the way in which the Bible came to be regarded as an infallible revelation, and the way in which in modern times this view was challenged by those who sought to repudiate interpretative 'monophysitism' and restore the human element in the writing and compilation of the Bible. It thus transpires that 'there is now a wide-spread disposition to maintain that whatever has no direct bearing either on the generation or the sustentation of the religious life, as such, is as human as the contents of any ordinary book ...'[149] In earlier times, he continues, some laid such emphasis upon revealed mysteries, truths above reason and prophecies of future events that the rationalistic reaction of deism was prompted in the eighteenth century. In early decades of the nineteenth century many took a more Christocentric approach to the Bible, in effect reviving Luther's view that Christ is the centre of Holy Scripture, the test of genuine canonicity, and the criterion of interpretation.

Alongside the views as sketched so far, Simon continues, another view which regards the biblical books as sources from which to derive knowledge of the life of the Hebrew nation has arisen. It is the approach exemplified by a line of writers

---

[145] Quoted in DWS, 121-2.

[146] D. W. Simon, *The Bible an Outgrowth of Theocratic Life*, viii. For Richard Rothe (1799-1867) see P. Schaff, *Germany; Its Universities, Theology and Religion*, ch. 33.

[147] Ibid.

[148] Ibid., 2.

[149] Ibid., 28.

stretching from Philo (his allegorical enthusiasms notwithstanding) through Eusebius to Spinoza and those modern critics who reduce the Bible 'to the level of ordinary literature and historical documents.'[150] In Simon's view this historical approach is the correct one, and 'Whatever peculiarity may attach to the Jewish and Christian Scriptures, considered ... simply as literature, coming into in a way analogous to that of other literatures, is *due solely to the differences between the Jewish people and its life*, and other nations and their life.'[151] Lest any should feel that he is repudiating revelation and inspiration as traditionally understood, Simon affirms his belief in both, and says that 'the application of these terms to the Scriptures is not only not excluded, but facilitated, by the adoption of the historical point of view.'[152]

Simon proceeds to argue that although we tend to think of the Bible as the presupposition of Christian faith and life, the New Testament Scriptures actually grew out of Christian faith and life, and we learn how people of past ages lived by reading the literature that gave expression to their life. But although our approach is through the literature, account must also be taken of climate, geography, surrounding nations and the general circumstances of the age. Hence the recent interest in the historical setting of the life of Jesus. We have also to beware of the fact that the results of our investigations may be controlled by *a priori* principles whether philosophical or scientific. For example,

> If a critic start with the general conviction that all early religious development was from the lower to the higher, from fetishism, animism, or what not, through polytheism to monotheism; he will be under the necessity of, to a large extent, reversing the traditional chronology of the Scriptures:—either that, or his *a priori* conviction must give way. This is the secret key to many results of the so-called higher historical criticism.[153]

For his part, 'I am writing for those who like myself believe that in the main the traditional chronology of the Scriptures is correct.'[154] Simon then reiterates his important point of principle:

> It will make all the difference in the world whether one starts with the assumption that all history on earth is the product of natural, including human, factors, without any intervention or determining action of God either on the order of nature in the form of miracles, or on the spirit of man; or, with the assumption that such extraordinary and miraculous divine interventions are possible; and in view of the

[150] Ibid., 38.
[151] Ibid., 39; his italics.
[152] Ibid., 40.
[153] Ibid., 49.
[154] Ibid., 50.

constitution of man, of the relation of man to nature, and of both to God, alike natural, probable, and fitting.[155]

Simon proceeds to discuss the human factors in the life of the Jewish people: their national socio-political circumstances and the variety of their literary activity; and then he turns to the divine factor in their national life: God gave them their national existence, their land, their institutions, their laws; he rewarded and punished them, and expressed his will for them in a variety of ways. The Jews came to conceive of themselves as witnesses for Jehovah to the whole world, and that the historical process was tending towards a final goal. They also believed that 'the condition of the well-being of the nation was obedience to the law of Jehovah.'[156]

Simon then comes in his own way to the question of inspiration. '[W]ill not a theocratic literature be also theopneustic?' he asks.[157] It is quite clear to him that if a literature 'truly and duly reflect, embody, enshrine, record, the life out of which it grew, its contents must be divine as well as human, human as well as divine.'[158] We are not true to the facts of the case if we opt for Ebionitism, or humanitarianism on the one hand, or for docetism, or deification, on the other, for 'there is a human and a divine element ... the Scripture as truly as Christ is divine-human.'[159] His positive point, against those who regard the idea of the cooperation of the Spirit of God with human agents as absurd, is that 'so far from such action of God in, with, and through a human intellect, tongue, and pen being either unworthy of God and impossible to Him, or somehow inconsistent with the freedom, independence, and dignity of man, it is normal to God and necessary to the truest intellectual activity of man.'[160] In the specific case of the Jewish nation, 'it is a question whether He who was helping to mould the individual, social, national life, in its political, moral, religious aspects, should also help to mould the literature.'[161] It is at this point that we hear the strongest echo of the voice of Richard Rothe:

[I]n the Bible it is evident that the Holy Spirit has been at work, moulding for itself a distinctively religious mode of expression out of the language of the country

---

155 Ibid., 51.

156 Ibid., 125.

157 Ibid., 128.

158 Ibid.

159 Ibid., 129. The danger in this way of putting it is that some will be tempted to add the Bible to, or regard it on the lame level as, the Trinity, with all that that entails concerning the bolstering of particular (sometimes fundamentalist) ways of reading the Bible. The question is begged, Is the Bible human and divine in the same sense in which Jesus Christ is? Simon goes on to say (p. 133), 'it is impossible to regard [the Bible's] contents as all divine,' and this is presumably because of flawed human agency. Would he wish to say that Christ's humanity is flawed? On the same page it is clear that he does not.

160 Ibid., 138.

161 Ibid., 139; cf. 142-3.

which it has chosen as its sphere, and transforming the linguistic elements which it found ready to hand, into a shape and form appropriate to itself and all its own.[162]

The question then arises as to the relation between the Bible and subsequent ages, not least our own. The first objective of the Scriptures, Simon insists, is 'to witness to the life out of which they grew.'[163] The Scriptures are a revelation *of* God, but taken as a whole they are not a revelation *from* God (a view capable of causing alarm in certain Christian quarters). But then, as if to assuage the wrath of the godly, Simon, who benefited from the higher criticism but was not uncritical of its more radical findings, continues in such a way as to clip the wings of more 'advanced' critics:

> Nature bears its own witness of God: human history in general witnesses of God: other religious literatures witness of God: but nowhere else do we find a witness to a redeeming God ... saving the world from sin and death. It testifies to God as a living Saviour, because it shows us Him in the very act of saving, whilst it also records His assurance that in Him there is no 'variableness neither the shadow of a turning.'
>
> Now such a witness-bearer or revelation the Bible would remain, even were we to concede to the critics the presence of historical and other errors, of mythical and legendary elements. ... The life reflected in the Bible, so far as its divine factor is concerned, is ... the character of God ... The primary function of the Bible is to be an abiding special witness for God.[164]

In addition to this the Bible serves as a guide to religious and moral conduct, and it has a 'scientific or philosophical purpose' in that it supplies 'materials for the construction of a view of the world as a whole.'[165]

In his concluding chapter Simon considers the condition of the discernment of the divine element in Scripture. Since the Bible has a divine-human character, those who come to it must be prepared to take account of the religious quality of the texts. Unfortunately, 'The immanence of the divine in the human, and of the human in the divine ... ordinarily escapes the observation of historians and philosophers, owing to their lack of inner fitness and preparation.'[166] Simon declares that 'The surest means of testing the truth of the Scripture testimony to God as the living Saviour is to try Him. What is needed is loyal experiment,'[167] and Scripture takes for granted God's readiness to help those who thus seek. Again, we can learn whether the moral guidance offered in the Bible is of God or not only by being ready to do God's will. When we find ourselves energized (a favourite Simon word) to do God's will which

---

[162] R. Rothe, *Zur Dogmatik*, 238. For Rothe (1799-1867), Professor at Heidelberg, see P. Schaff, *Germany; its Universities, Theology and Religion*, ch. 33.

[163] D. W. Simon, *The Bible an Outgrowth of Theocratic* Life, 176.

[164] Ibid., 178-9, 180, 181.

[165] Ibid., 182.

[166] Ibid., 189.

[167] Ibid., 191; cf. 194.

we dimly perceive, we know that the Holy Spirit is at work in us. There is a marked distinction, he concludes, 'between the certitude that could be produced by arguments before spiritual experience, and the certitude generated by spiritual experience.'[168]

Simon is, of course, aware of the objection, 'we want to know before believing', and he has sympathy with it. But he insists elsewhere that

> it is *experience* that is the condition of knowing, not *believing, in the sense of the objectors*. ... Not our knowledge of Him, but our willingness to be saved by Him on the supposition that He exists and can save ... conditions the experience out of which grows knowledge, and of which the peace of God which passeth all understanding is one of the directest, most characteristic, fruits ...[169]

The Bible an Outgrowth of Theocratic Life received high praise from a reviewer in *The British Quarterly Review*:

> The general position is that the Bible is to be approached not from the *a priori* assumption of a Divine revelation, but from an ordinary historical standpoint. ... Dr. Simon rests his acceptance of both the revelation of Divine things and the inspiration of their authors upon the intrinsic characteristics of the history. This is the method of true philosophy, and it establishes the surest conclusions. ... A more valuable and suggestive book has not recently come into our hands.[170]

Towards the end of his book Simon remarks that 'If the Bible contain the things of the Spirit of God, no man can become assured of the fact until, through the aid of the Spirit and spiritual experience, he becomes capable of spiritual discernment.'[171] This was a theme to which he regularly returned.

Before further elucidating Simon's thoughts on the matter it is important for us, who live at a time of what one might describe as rampant and sometimes self-serving spirituality, to understand that if Simon did not wish history to be divorced from things spiritual, he certainly did not wish the spiritual to be severed from the real world. He once remarked that 'When the 'spiritual' ceases to be secular it ceases also to be spiritual';[172] and John Massie recalled that 'A luscious spiritual phraseology, or what he termed, "slush", provoked him ... to an unrestrained mockery which bubbled out of a keen sense of humour and which would undoubtedly have made a matter-of-fact piety stand with it bristles erect and its mouth wide open.'[173]

Simon developed his view of the Holy Spirit in relation to the Bible reader's spiritual discernment in his article, 'The Authority of the Bible', published in *The British Quarterly Review* (1884). He challenges those Christians who seem to think

---

[168] Ibid., 200.
[169] Idem, *The Making of a Preacher*, 54-5, 60-61.
[170] *The British Quarterly Review*, CLXVI, April 1886, 487.
[171] D. W. Simon, *The Bible an Outgrowth of Theocratic Life*, 197.
[172] DWS, 360.
[173] Ibid., 127.

that 'saving faith in Christ is logically if not actually impossible to anyone who does not hold the Bible to be the inspired book of God.' They also think that the divine inspiration of the Bible can be proved to any 'candid and moderately intelligent inquirer.'[174] Even doubters and freethinkers expect this to be possible, but Simon has 'no hesitation in denying its correctness.'[175] Not, indeed, that he denies the inspiration of Scripture. On the contrary his conviction regarding the inspiration of the Bible 'is the result of prolonged experience—an experience of which the truths contained in the Scriptures and the enlightening aid of the Holy Spirit are co-operative causes. In other words, it is the product of saving faith, the product of the new life that is in and through Jesus Christ and the indwelling Spirit of God.'[176] The view that people have no right to believe until they have first convinced themselves that the Bible is inspired 'is as cruel as it is monstrous.'[177] In support of his position he invokes Calvin, John Owen and William Gurnall. Of these Owen said, 'This work of the Spirit of God, as it is distinct from, so in order of nature it is antecedent unto all divine objective evidence of the Scriptures being the Word of God.'[178] Against some in the conservative camp Simon observes that 'To plead that the Bible claims inspiration, is to make it judge and jury in its own case.'[179]

Simon returned yet again to the theme in *Some Bible Problems* (1898), the published form of lectures given at Park Congregational Church, Halifax, in the winter of 1896-97, together with a further lecture delivered at Bala Bangor Independent College in June 1897. He revisits a number of themes which have already come to our attention, but he is by now more trenchant in his opposition to the wilder biblical critics. He scorns 'the slapdash new critical position' and thunders, 'Personally, I feel bound to protest against the custom of treating the Old Testament writers and compilers, at all events some of them, as if they did not know what they were about,—and all under the pretence of being historical! Historical forsooth!'[180] He elsewhere elaborated upon this theme in the following terms:

> [I]t is now considered pre-eminently scientific or scholarly by a host of authorities to take for granted that the key to the meaning of the Biblical writers is to be found in prior and contemporary movements of thought and life. The belief that they spake and wrote as they were borne along by the Spirit of God, that they were in specially close fellowship with Him in whom are his all the treasures of wisdom and knowledge, and that consequently their writings must needs be full of a wisdom that

[174] D. W. Simon, 'The authority of the Bible,' 365.

[175] Ibid.

[176] Ibid., 366.

[177] Ibid.

[178] Ibid., 368, quoting J. Owen, 'The Reason of Faith,' in Owen's *Works*, III, 291. For Gurnall (bap. 1616, d. 1679) and Owen (1616-1683) see ODNB.

[179] Ibid., 374.

[180] Idem, *Some Bible Problems*, 155. Cf. the comment of B. J. Kidd in DWS, 191: 'I think I am right in saying that with all his free treatment of the highest subjects he ever held fast to the supernaturalism position, and regarded with deep distrust much that is put forward in the name of the Higher Criticism.'

> transcends, not only their own, but any mere human intellect, seems to be either exploded or explained away. The view I refer to is called 'historical'; it is *historical* if the special illumination of the minds of Christ's organs was not an actual fact—only then.[181]

Simon did not confine his expositions to formal lectures, but took his message to the pulpits in which he preached. The first sermon in his collection, *Twice Born*, directly addresses the role of the Holy Spirit in relation to the believer's discernment of the Word of God—indeed, the title of the collection is suggestive in this regard. The sermon, written in 1884, the year of Simon's *British Quarterly Review* article on the authority of Scripture, is on John 3:3, 'Except a man be born again, he cannot see the kingdom of God.' Simon does not set out, as might have been expected, from Nicodemus, but from Plato's cave. The inmates of the cave, facing away from the sun, can see only shadows on the walls. One prisoner is released and sees the world as it is. If he were to return and describe what he had seen to the cave-dwellers they would treat him as a victim of delusions. This, says Simon, is an anticipation of the intellectual aspect of Jesus's teaching. Those who cannot see the kingdom of God are not absolutely blind, but they see only shadows unless or until they are born again. This cannot be proved to a once-born person any more than the returned prisoner could demonstrate to the others in the cave that they were seeing only dim shadows of reality. As to the new birth, just as we cannot be physically born without physical influences, so we cannot be spiritually reborn apart from the influences of the spiritual world, of which the Holy Spirit is the agent. Just as we were in the dark before our first birth, so we were before our second. We cannot explain how the new birth happens—Jesus could not explain it to Nicodemus; but we find peace, forgiveness, courage, and confidence. The scales are removed from our eyes and we come to see that 'Christ is the key to all the problems that trouble the intellect of men.'[182] We cannot make ourselves see, for that is the work of the Holy Spirit; 'But you can co-operate; you can offer yourself; you can say to God, "We are willing."'[183]

Simon could not understand those who did not concede that the Bible could not be properly understood without spiritual discernment, and much of his writing about the Scriptures was in defence of supernaturalism and against the naturalistic excesses of the Higher Criticism. At the same time, he was sufficient of a Higher Critic himself to render himself suspect in the eyes of more conservative souls but, as Powicke remarked, 'to the scandal of the new school [he] failed to see that the method can submit to no arbitrary limits.'[184] It must also be said that where questions of biblical historicity were concerned he did not feel it necessary to—or, at least, he did not - make out a case for his acceptance of the main lines of biblical chronology, nor did he counter the critical sceptics with reasoned arguments. This may quite well have

---

181 Idem, *The Making of a Preacher*, 38-9.

182 Idem, *Twice Born*, 19.

183 Ibid., 20.

184 DWS, 157.

been because he regarded himself as what he was: a theologian adjusting himself to the intellectual currents of his time, not as a biblical scholar as such. However that may be, it is undeniable that there are some loose ends in his writings on biblical subjects, but these should not detract from the importance of his keen sense both of the importance of history and of the fact that spiritual things are spiritually discerned.

By way of a footnote, and before proceeding to more specifically theological matters, it is clear that underlying Simon's stance as just outlined, is a metaphysical-*cum*-epistemological position. He nowhere elaborated upon this, but we can see that like Payne before him and Franks after him, he believed that a viable theology would be a metaphysically sound one. In a letter to James Ross of 27 November 1903 he wrote, 'I told my colleague, Armitage, the other day that the older I get the more inseparable do the two things (Christ or Christianity and metaphysics) seem to me; and the more necessary, if I am to keep hold of the former, that I should bore my way into the latter ...'[185] It is in the Introduction to his translation of Stählin's *Kant, Lotze, and Ritschl* that he nails his colours to the mast. Disturbed by the theological position of Ritschl, Stählin found the latter indebted to Lotze, who was in turn influenced by Kant. But Kant's epistemology was unacceptable to him because he perceived it to be agnostic. That is to say, Kant held that we have knowledge only of the phenomenal realm, not of the noumenal, since the latter is not available to our senses. It followed that spiritual realities could not be known and revelation was impossible. If this were the case we should be left only with intuitions based upon religious phenomena, or inferences drawn from them, but we should have no access to objective truth. Kantianism as thus construed completely fails to satisfy Simon, and he could not agree with Ritschl that Kant's limitation of human knowledge had left the way open for morality as the foundation of dogmatic truth in such a way that notwithstanding their innocence of the noumenal realm, human beings could by the exercise of the practical reason attain the full assurance of faith.[186]

Simon follows Jacobi[187] in contending that just as our senses give us access to the material world so the supersensuous world is revealed to our reason. Our senses and our reason are both organs of perception, both yield immediate certainty, and this immediate certainty is what Jacobi understands by faith. Both, it may also be said, are varieties of experience. Hence in a passing reference elsewhere to the traditional theistic arguments Simon declares that these cannot carry us the whole way to the theistic conclusion because 'No one can properly maintain that God really is what the living Christian experience knows He is, without living Christian experience.'[188] This apparently uncontroversial remark—its circularity notwithstanding—was as

---

[185] DWS, 240.

[186] For a brief assessment of Albrecht Ritschl (1822-1889) and references to relevant literature see Alan P. F. Sell, *Theology in Turmoil*, ch. 4 and 166.

[187] For Friedrich Heinrich Jacobi (1743-1819) see L. W. Beck in *The Routledge History of Philosophy*, VI, ch. 1.

[188] D. W. Simon, 'The authority of the Bible,' 373.

fatal as a tap from an elephant's paw to what has been called the 'Paley and Old Bailey' school of Christian apologetics which, as the work of Payne and Alliott exemplifies, had held such sway among Dissenting professors, and of which Henry Rogers, Simon's predecessor at Spring Hill College and the 'safe pair of hands' to whom the Lancashire College Committee turned in the wake of the Davidson affair, was one of the last Congregational exponents.[189]

A version of what might be called spiritual realism undergirds Simon's philosophy and explains the appeal to him of Rothe and Jacobi. In his first address as Principal of Yorkshire United Independent College he underlined his conviction that systematic theology must build upon facts[190] and, in a letter to James Ward of 30 May 1870 he tersely indicated the post-Hegelian idol to which he was opposed: 'The Infinite and Absolute of philosophy is as empty as it is vague: one thing is certain, neither the Bible nor any other religion has ever known anything about an "infinite" God.'[191]

It cannot be denied that the above bristles with problems. Quite apart from the question whether Kant and others are correctly interpreted there is the problem posed by the real possibility of contradictory claims to spiritual knowledge and, on Jacobi/Simon premises, the absence of an independent court of appeal should this occur. There is also the question of the analysis of 'immediacy'. With reference to Simon, A. E. Garvie discussed the meaning of the terms 'direct spiritual communion' and 'immediate' as applied to the Spirit's action. He argued that the directness and immediacy are only apparent. There is always a process of mediation even if we are not conscious of it. He concludes that 'These adjectives cannot mean that a "self" without any faculties or activities can "commune" with a "God" without any operations or attributes; or that a "Spirit" that uses no means "acts" on a soul that is subject to no conditions.'[192]

It remains only to add that Simon dedicated *Kant, Lotze, and Ritschl* to Samuel Davidson 'as a slight token of gratitude for many kindnesses from one of his old students.'

II

As we have seen, Simon lived through changing, even at times turbulent, times as far as the approach to the Bible was concerned. As already suggested in our

---

[189] See Alan P. F. Sell, *Dissenting Thought and the Life of the Churches*, ch. 17. For the broader apologetic situation see idem, *Philosophy, Dissent and Nonconformity*, ch. 5; Dale A. Johnson, *The Changing Shape of English Nonconformity*, ch. 6; idem, 'The end of the "Evidences".'

[190] DWS, 214.

[191] DWS, 205.

[192] A. E. Garvie, *The Ritschlian Theology*, 145. For Alfred Ernest Garvie (1861-1945) see CYB, 1946, 440-1; DHT; DSCHT; ODNB; WTW; Himself, *Memories and Meanings of My Life*. He was pastor, theologian, college Principal and pioneer ecumenist.

biographical sketch by the suspicious references to 'Simon's men', the situation as regards theology was no less turbulent, as the following soundings will show.

The influence of F. D. Maurice falls first to be considered.[193] That Simon owed his conviction that the biblical characters were real, living, human beings to Maurice we have already noted. Like his mentor, Coleridge (also an erstwhile Unitarian), Maurice stood for the trustworthiness of spiritual experience, and to this extent Simon was also on his side. But he distrusted Maurice's metaphysics. Maurice believed in the essential divinity of humanity and contended that sin is the refusal to acknowledge this, while salvation is the glad recognition of it. He developed a Logos theology of the Incarnation according to which the world, far from being fallen, is already redeemed, and his denial of the eternity of punishment was prompted by his refusal to have the God-humanity continuity which lay at the heart of his theology disrupted. Simon's former student, J. Henwood Toms, speculated in a letter to Powicke of 28 November 1910 that Simon 'was never very hearty in praise of [Maurice]—I doubt if Maurice was systematic enough for the Doctor; but I think he was pleased rather than otherwise for one of his students to tell of the spiritual spell that Maurice had over him.'[194] According to Powicke, a Mauriceian cult grew up within Spring Hill College. It

> probably did more to shape our theology than the lectures of the principal, Dr. Simon. We valued these, and some of us came to see that fundamentally they were quite in accord with Maurice. But *he* did not think so. Simon was, above everything, a systematic thinker. So was Maurice. Simon, however, was always in search of the right word, and a sparing use of words, and their due logical sequence in an orderly argument. Maurice, he thought, was too careless of definition, used too many words, and often used them so as to cloud the argument. His own ever-recurring question was, 'What do you mean?'; and if, putting that question to Maurice, he got, or seemed to get, a doubtful answer, he felt impatient, and inclined to dismiss him. ... Hence, on the whole he did not encourage us to read Maurice. We had to serve, so to speak, at an altar outside the gate! Perhaps we served it the more eagerly on that account. ... When I left Spring Hill in the summer of 1877 Maurice meant far more to me than Simon, and this relation was never quite reversed, though the latter's merits as a great teacher, along with a deep sense of personal indebtedness, gave him a unique place in my affectionate reverence.[195]

---

[193] For Maurice see ODNB; J. Frederick Maurice, *The Life of Frederick Denison Maurice*; A. R. Vidler, *The Theology of F. D. Maurice*; A. M. Ramsey, *F. D. Maurice and the Conflict of Modern Theology*; O. J. Brose, *F. D. Maurice, Rebellious Conformist*; F. M. McClain, *Maurice, Man and Moralist*; T. Christensen, *The Divine Order. A Study of F. D. Maurice's Theology*.

[194] DWS, 138. Toms trained at Spring Hill College. His name does not appear in the CYB ministerial list after 1931.

[195] F. J. Powicke, 'Frederick Denison Maurice,' 171, 172.

These are the words of a disciple. I suspect that Maurice was not quite as systematic as Powicke thought he was, and I recall that Maurice himself said of his writing, 'I have laid a great many addled eggs in my time.'[196]

Before passing from the spell that Maurice cast upon a number of Congregationalists in general, and upon 'Simon's men' in particular we shall do well to ponder some words of Alexander Mackennal, which reveal the way in which powerful advocacy of some themes can so impress as to obliterate uncharitable references to other matters which the impressed hold dear:

> It is just here that we see the secret of the influence which Maurice came, afterward, to exercise on young Congregationalists. It was not because he had any sympathy with them; he displays a singular want of appreciation of their position. He repudiated their demand for the rights of the individual conscience interpreted by the individual judgment; and he was repelled even by the modified form in which Evangelical spoke of personal experience. ... His 'Kingdom of Christ' is painful reading, alike to those who love him and to those who love Congregationalism. It is dogmatic, one-sided in statement, perverse in temper. In later years the harshness became softened, but the intolerance remained. ... He did not know that many young Congregationalists were passing through a stage of sentiment like that he had experienced in youth, were tired of solitude and sectarianism; it surprised him to learn that they read his writings for the sake of the larger reaches of social, national, and spiritual fellowship which he was opening up to them, and for the sake of these could bear patiently with his severe and uncomprehending censures of much which they held dear.[197]

Brief reference may be made to two further theological excitements which upset some of the Congregational faithful—the more so because they occurred within their own ranks. In 1846 Edward White[198] published his *Life in Christ*, in which he contended that the ungodly would be annihilated and not subjected to an eternity of punishment. This was too much for *The Evangelical Magazine*, which branded White's view a 'dangerous heresy.'[199] In 1850 White further blotted his copybook in the eyes of some by rejecting infant baptism. White's friend, R. W. Dale, was among others who became persuaded of the advantages of the doctrine of annihilation—and said so in his Congregational Union Address of May 1874.[200] To White as to Dale, annihilation allowed for the divine judgment against the finally impenitent whilst at the same time avoiding the objection to the notion of the eternity of punishment, namely, that it reflected badly upon the God of all grace and

---

[196] J. Frederick Maurice (son), *The Life of Frederick Denison Maurice*, II, 631.

[197] A. Mackennal, *Sketches in the Evolution of English Congregationalism*, 198-199, 200. For Mackennal (1835-1904), Chairman of the CUEW in 1888, see CYB, 1905, 174-6; ODNB.

[198] For White (1819-1898) see CYB, 1899, 205-6; F. A. Freer, *Edward White, His Life and Work*, London: Elliot Stock, 1902.

[199] *The Evangelical Magazine*, 1846, 529.

[200] See A. W. W. Dale, *The Life of R. W. Dale of Birmingham*, 311-316.

mercy. As Samuel Davidson was eventually feted for his biblical work, so White's theological excursions, so alarming at first, did not suffice to exclude him from the Chair of the Congregational Union of England and Wales, to which he came in 1887.

The second cause of the twitching of doctrinal antennae among some Congregationalists was the publication in 1855 of *Hymns for Heart and Voice, The Rivulet*, by Thomas Toke Lynch.[201] Lynch was described as a 'thoughtful, godly and very retiring independent minister,'[202] a phrase that does not altogether capture the author of fifteen poems, more pugilistic than devotional, which he published under the title, *Songs Controversial* (1857). Lynch's *Rivulet* poems were welcomed by *The Eclectic Review* and *The Nonconformist*, but to John Grant of *The Morning Advertiser* they contained 'not one particle of vital religion or evangelical piety', and 'might have been written by a Deist, and a very large portion might be sung by a congregation of Freethinkers.' This judgment was accompanied by muttering about the 'German error'—that label so freely used by some whose primary objective was to guard the doctrinal ark.[203] John Campbell,[204] editor of *The British Banner* sallied forth with guns blazing against what he was convinced was Lynch's pantheising naturalism. Others came to Lynch's defence, among them Edward White, and gradually the storm abated.[205]

Neither of the two incidents just referred to had the potential to divide Congregationalism at large into opposing factions. The Leicester Conference of 1877, though subsequently regarded by some as a storm in a tea-cup, was, at its peak, somewhat more of a threat.[206] In this controversy Simon was an unwilling participant. The Leicester Conference on Religious Communion was held on the evening of 16 October 1877 at Wycliffe Congregational Church, Leicester, the venue in the same week of the Autumn Meetings of the Congregational Union of England and Wales. The Conference was intended for all 'who value spiritual religion', and who believe that 'agreement in theological opinion can no longer be held to be essential to Religious Communion.' The first paper was presented by James

---

[201] For Lynch (1818-1871) see CYB, 1872, 335-6; ODNB; William White, ed., *Memoirs of Thomas T. Lynch.*

[202] So H. S. Skeats and C. S. Miall, *History of the Free Churches of England*, 547.

[203] Quotations from Skeats and Miall, *History of the Free Churches of England*, 547. To the best of my knowledge *The Morning Advertiser*, founded in 1794 and still the organ of the licensed trade, does not publish reviews of devotional poems at the present time. On the day of writing, however, I find that on its website it is conducting a poll on the question, 'Would you consider hosting a stripper to boost takings?'

[204] For Campbell (1795-1867) see CYB, 1868, 259-261; ODNB.

[205] See further, Albert Peel, *These Hundred* Years, 221-230. He provides examples of Lynch's *Songs Controversial*, among them one against Campbell which begins, 'Sound the trumpets, beat the drums,/ Clash the gongs, great Magog comes.'

[206] Among accounts of the Leicester Conference are those of Mark Johnson, *The Dissolution of Dissent*, ch. 2; Mark Hopkins, *Nonconformity's Romantic Generation*, ch. 4. For the latter's refutation of the thesis of the former see p. 100.

Allanson Picton, the devotee of Samuel Davidson who had been junior to Simon at Lancashire Independent College. His subject was 'Some relations of theology to religion', and the burden of his message was that the religious feeling is largely independent of any object which inspires it, and that whereas the drive for doctrinal unity is divisive, true unity is unity in spirit. All of which was, of course, an over-reaction against scholastic Calvinism, and it was perceived by many as a pantheizing attempt to undermine evangelicalism. To *The English Independent* it was 'transcendental moonshine.'[207] F. J. Powicke, writing retrospectively, said that Picton's paper was 'of singular literary beauty combined with singular intellectual vagueness',[208] while John Waddington suspected a Unitarian movement the objective of which was to penetrate the Congregational Union.[209] In Leicester, Simon rose in rebuttal. To him, as to another opponent of the platform, Henry Allon,[210] the term 'religious communion' was imprecise, and they sought clarity on the matter. Simon asked Picton a question expecting the answer 'No':

> Is it a matter of indifference whether I conceive my God as a bundle of rags—will it have the same effect on my spiritual life as if I conceived Him as the One who revealed Himself in Jesus Christ in Judaea? ... [It] is not a matter of indifference, and never can be a matter of indifference, even if you accept his view, what object you present to the soul of our people with a view of stimulating their spiritual life. ... [T]he history of religion is, I affirm, opposed to this indifference of the object which we present for the sake of stimulating the religious life ...[211]

He reminded the audience that forty or fifty years ago both Roman Catholics and Protestants in Germany had faced the question, 'shall we have the letter or the spirit?' 'Can we', he asked, 'further the spiritual life in a higher and truer and more effective way if we cast aside this ballast of the supernatural, and simply appeal to the primary religious emotions or religious susceptibilities of human nature?'[212] Those who answer in the affirmative and opt for a spiritual liberty with no terms of communion open the door to rationalism, with the result that 'the best preachers—men frequently with great ability—preach to empty churches, whereas a poor stick of an orthodox man, who has not half the ability, if he preaches with anything like zeal, preaches to a full congregation.'[213] To Simon, as he reflected

---

[207] Quoted by M. Johnson, *The Dissolution of Dissent*, 87.

[208] DWS, 99-100.

[209] See M. Johnson, *The Dissolution of Dissent*, 87. For Waddington (1810-1880), see CYB, 1881, 398.

[210] For Allon (1818-1892) see CYB, 1893, 202-5; ODNB; Alan Argent, 'Henry Allon at Union Chapel, Islington.' Trained at Cheshunt College Allon was co-pastor at Union Chapel, Islington (1844-52) and then pastor there (1852-92). He was Chairman of the CUEW in 1864 and 1881.

[211] DWS, 99-100.

[212] Ibid., 101.

[213] Ibid.

afterwards on the Conference, 'The central point of all is Jesus Christ, the living, dying, rising Saviour of mankind.'[214]

During the course of the Leicester Conference Simon laid himself open to criticism by suggesting that it was in order for churches 'to receive inquirers, even as ministers, with the greatest tolerance and patience' but this was not a licence to those 'who deny the old faith and those who called him.'[215] The following year the Union reaffirmed its commitment to evangelical religion, and to its founding Declaration of Faith of 1833.[216]

What were Simon's reflections upon the choppy theological waters through which he had sailed? We are fortunate in having access to the concise and powerful address he delivered in London on precisely this topic at the first meeting of the International Congregational Council (1891). Before turning to his address it is worthwhile to note that the question of the present state of theology had been a recurrent one in Congregational circles. For example, in *The Eclectic Review* for 1859 an anonymous author appealed for the recovery of theology which had, he was convinced, fallen into neglect: 'Strange as it may seem, we believe that there is scarcely any study which, during the last five-and-twenty years, has been pursued with less earnestness in our Theological colleges than that from which they derive their name'[217]—an observation which hardly does justice to the contributions of, for example, John Pye Smith and George Payne, and utterly fails to reckon with the sizeable and varied list of courses with which many Dissenting professors were expected to deal.

On 15 July 1891 Simon gave his address entitled, 'The present direction of theological thought in the Congregational churches of Great Britain.' He opens in rueful vein by citing a correspondent of the Boston *Congregationalist* who, in 1871 had declared that 'In England there has been so little doctrinal preaching or theological teaching for the last forty years that the congregations have very little idea of the completeness or strength of the Calvinistic argument.' 'Now,' says Simon, 'they have no idea at all':

> What used, however, to be lack of interest has largely deepened into positive dislike, not to say contempt. When prominent ministers refer in tones of mock humility to their ignorance of Systematic Theology, or earn cheap applause by denouncing dogma and contrasting it with life; ... when leading laymen exclaim impatiently, 'We want practical preaching, not doctrine';[218] ... and when it is easier

[214] Ibid., 104-5; though Powicke's reference is incorrect.

[215] DWS, 102.

[216] See CYB, 1878, 44-5.

[217] Anon., 'Our theological colleges,' *The Eclectic Review*, January-June 1859, 100.

[218] In a less formal context he observed that 'The average layman treats a discussion on theology very much as a hungry ploughman would treat a discussion on the dietetics of bacon and cheese.' DWS, 361.

to get a thousand pounds to build a college than a hundred to provide adequate teaching—what else can one say?[219]

By way of evidence of the sorry state of theology he notes that

during the last thirty-five years only one 'Systematic Theology' has been published by British Congregationalists; that our of some 600 registered Congregational publications during, say, twenty-five years, scarcely 50 are scientifically theological; and that out of upwards of 450 discourses by Congregational ministers printed during the last five years or thereabouts in *The Christian World Pulpit*, scarcely thirty were properly doctrinal.[220]

There are three exceptions to the general rule, he continues. Interest has been shown in inspiration, the atonement and future punishment, though with 'decided signs of unreasoned sentimental conviction which is styled "finding" or "being found by" a truth.'[221] The situation is better in the field of biblical studies, and while in preaching there is an emphasis upon the ethical, there is not the direct appeal to the conscience that was evident in previous generations.

There is also an amount of nebulosity, of sentimentality, sometimes bordering on the hysterical, of tenderness towards sceptics and outsiders, conjoined with scathing severity towards assured believers and insiders, and of non-constructive criticism of orthodoxy, or what bears that name, that would make the Fathers turn in their graves.[222]

Thirty-five years ago, he says, the theological field was held by the soteriological moderate Calvinism of Pye Smith, Payne, Ralph Wardlaw, Lindsay Alexander and others—a system, 'so far as it deserves the name', which had supplanted the theocentric Puritan inheritance flowing down from Howe and Charnock. Under the influence of Coleridge, McLeod Campbell, Maurice, Bushnell, Carlyle, Tennyson and Robertson, and aided by the fact that 'like our nation generally, we are only too indifferent to philosophical or even logical consistency', we are now working towards a Christocentric system, 'or perhaps, to speak more accurately, towards one with the two foci of the Fatherhood of God and the Living personality of Christ.'[223]

We are 'all at sixes and sevens' regarding the inspiration of Scripture; the Creator-creature distinction has given way to the idea of affinity of the Fatherly, the immanent God with humanity; 'The personal Trinity seems to have been practically dropped; and we have either fallen back on a sort of Sabellianism; or into the unity of Swedenborgianism; or are trying to rest in a duality of Father and Son,—little stress is lain on the personality of the Holy Spirit, even when He has not been

[219] D. W. Simon, 'The present direction of theological thought,' 77.

[220] Ibid., 78.

[221] Ibid.

[222] Ibid.

[223] Ibid.

reduced to impersonality; and His work has been nearly merged into that of Christ.'[224] Furthermore,

> The Divine decrees and predestination have been exorcised; election has been metamorphosed; and were such subjects as irresistible grace, effectual calling, adoption, and perseverance to be seriously expounded, most people would either wonder what was meant, or silently mutter, 'Rip van Winkle.'[225]

Whereas the humanity of Christ was formerly overshadowed by his divinity, it is now in some cases supplanting it. 'The relation of the atonement to God is chiefly one of revelation: Christ propitiates man, not God. ... Conversion has been well nigh converted into decision for Christ; regeneration into a process of spiritual culture',[226] while few understand the doctrine of justification properly construed. Finally,

> On the question of man's future destiny, we are in the main divided between Universalism, the doctrine of life in Christ, the Larger Hope, and various phases of a non-committal position ... Other eschatological matters—even heaven, which preachers used to delight in depicting—awaken but languid attention. ... Those of us who ... compare the heresy-fancier of to-day with the heresy hunter of the past, will scarcely hesitate to apply the word revolution to the change that has come about. Few things, however, are more significant than the fact that Tennyson's lines, the quotation of which in my student days was almost enough to stamp a man a heretic -
>
> Our little systems have their day;
> They have their day, and cease to be;
> They are not [for *but*] broken lights of Thee,
> And Thou, O Lord, art more than they -
>
> now form part of a hymn in the 'New Congregational Hymnal.'[227]

What is the significance of the change? Simon regards the reaction against dogma as the beginning of the end of a struggle against

> one of the most grievous perversions of Christianity that have appeared during the history of the Church, namely, the transformation of the Gospel into a body of truths supernaturally revealed; with its correlate notion, that salvation hangs on the holding for true of certain saving doctrines. This is the error which found classical expression in the words of the Athanasian creed, 'Whosoever will be saved, before all things it is necessary that he hold the Catholic faith.'[228]

---

[224] Ibid., 78-9.
[225] Ibid., 79.
[226] Ibid.
[227] Ibid.
[228] Ibid.

The Independents launched a significant attack upon this view, but they still spoke in terms of saving doctrines, albeit ones contained in the Bible. The fact is, however, that

> It is not mere truths or doctrines, not even if they were guaranteed by a perpetual Divine miracle, that can generate and nourish Christian life, but the personal action of the personal God, rendered possible through Christ's work and through faith in Christ—faith conditioned by testimony, proclamation, preaching. ... [T]he error under consideration is the chief support of the ecclesiasticism, sacramentalism, and priestism which more than anything else hinder the progress of the kingdom of God.[229]

Nearing his conclusion, Simon hopes that theologians will help believers to supply a reason for their faith they already possess so that they may bear strain, witness, guide unbelievers to Christ, and give doubters a reason for believing. This hope may be delayed by the prevalence of the view that preachers should proclaim whatever seems true to them at the moment. But this is simply an updated version of the doctrine such liberals reject, namely, that what saves are truths about Christianity or God, the difference being only that whereas the truths were once believed to have been supernaturally revealed, now they are truths which each one discovers for himself, and teaches without authority. 'If this sort of thing become general,' he warns, 'I see nothing for it but relapse, of the more independent into agnosticism; for the weaker sort towards Romanism.'[230]

Simon concludes his thought-provoking paper by noting some further disquieting features of the current theological scene:

> A certain hankering after originality or novelty, which is sometimes rewarded by the discovery of mares' nests or the revival of ideas that have proved themselves unsound; in contrast thereto, a wonderful submissiveness to the behests of critical and scientific authorities, inside and outside the churches; an inclination, on the one hand, so to naturalise the supernatural, in the history of Israel, in the life of Christ, in the origin of our Scriptures, and in the rise and progress of Christian life; and, on the other hand, to supernaturalise the natural in the ethnic religions, as to bring both under the evolutionary law according to which God is supposed to be realising the cosmic idea; the advocacy of comprehension as regards membership, worship, and doctrine, which will scarcely leave anyone outside except the orthodox; a disposition to reduce prayer to a sort of spiritual gymnastic or massage; and last, not least, a tendency to co-ordinate in the work of regenerating society, all sorts of cultural agencies, with the 'Gospel, which is the power of God unto salvation', rooted more or less in the conscious conversion of Christianity, from a real spiritual dynamic, into a moral and religious regulative.[231]

---

[229] Ibid., 79-80.

[230] Ibid., 80.

[231] Ibid.

Simon believes, however, that the majority of Congregationalists will hold to the central realities of the Christian faith, and that they will in due course participate in 'the development of a theological science which will be accepted as the corner-stone of a true philosophy of the world.'[232]

I shall allude to some of the above points in the final chapter of this book, but for the moment I wish to point out that before the end of his life Simon witnessed a degree of theological activity greater than any he could have foreseen in 1891—which is not to say that all of it entranced him. Thus, for example, just ten years later, on 2 April 1901 he administered what he called 'a dose of disagreeable theology'[233] from the Chair of the Yorkshire Congregational Union. His title was, 'The Holy Spirit and His relation to the Christian ministry according to Christ.' In the course of his address he sought to redress the balance between Christ and the Spirit. As we saw, he had earlier welcomed the way in which theocentric Calvinism had been modified by a Christocentric approach which gave due place to Christ's divinity and atonement; but by now he clearly felt that Christocentrism was developing in such a way as to displace the Spirit; and, reading between the lines, it is also conceivable that he regarded the development as veering too much towards sentimentalism:

> On all hand we are being enjoined to enter into and maintain a relation to Christ not less real, conscious, varied, and influential than that held by the apostles to Him, even though He is invisible. In fact, all that Christ taught His followers, all that Christ's Church until recently taught men to expect from the Holy Spirit, is expected—to use the condemnatory language of a prominent school of theology of the present day—from a mystical relation between Christ and believers ... But Christ Himself points us to the *other Paraclete*; and surely He must have known.[234]

Six years on we find him perplexed by the New Theology propounded by R. J. Campbell.[235] This he described as 'Neo-Calvinism Hegelianised.'[236] Campbell's stance (it would be too much to call it a system) turned on a pantheizing

---

[232] Ibid.

[233] DWS, 232, quoting a letter to James Ross of 31 May 1900.

[234] Ibid., 232.

[235] For Campbell (1867-1956) see ODNB; WTW; WWW 1951-60; R. J. Campbell, 'The aim of the New Theology movement'; idem, *A Spiritual Pilgrimage*; C. T. Bateman, *R. J. Campbell, M.A., Pastor of the City* Temple; A. H. Wilkinson, *R. J. Campbell, The Man and his* Message. K. Robbins, 'The spiritual pilgrimage of the Rev. R. J. Campbell,' *Journal of Ecclesiastical History*. For the immanentist thrust in modern theology see Alan P. F. Sell, *Theology in Turmoil*, ch. 1; idem, *Philosophical Idealism and Christian Belief*. For a discussion of immanence and related concepts see idem, *Confessing and Commending the Faith*, ch. 5. The New Theology was attacked by many, among them P. T. Forsyth. Campbell subsequently departed significantly from his position, withdrew his manifesto from publication and, in 1915, returned to the Church of England, whence he had originally come.

[236] Ibid., 361.

immanentism which set its face against the Creator-creature distinction as traditionally understood by Calvinists and others, and which brought God so close that Campbell could say that God is 'the one reality I cannot get away from, for, whatever else it may be, it is myself.'[237] In a letter to Neville Jones[238] written from Dresden on 5 December 1907, Simon specified his principal difficulty with the New Theology:

> At the bottom the problem is an ethical one. But the New Theologian is, of course, shut out from dealing with the subject thus, for, logically, whatever may be his protests, his doctrine of immanence involves that God is the universal worker, that the consciousness of freedom and responsibility, &c., is an illusion, that there is no sin, that therefore little and big ragamuffins are as good as anybody else and don't deserve thrashings or being shut up—and at last they will all alike be absorbed into God and will be found to have been doing the Divine will.[239]

In a letter of 14 March 1908 to Dr. F. Linder of Rostock he lamented that

> England is being largely carried away by Rationalism and Pantheism; and, as I regard these apparently mutually exclusive *Weltanshauungen* as destructive of all higher life, I am anxious for the sake of my fellow-men, and for the sake of my Lord and Saviour Jesus Christ, to do what little I can to check their progress and to help those who are fascinated by them.[240]

For all that, in the course of his farewell speech at Yorkshire United College, he remarked,

> [T]hough I differ as radically as possible from the leading affirmations and negations of the so-called 'New Theology', I cherish the hope that its advent will prove to be in the long run a blessing. Anything is better than the cynical self-complacent indifference and carelessness about the highest problems of life and destiny, which too largely characterised our country less than a quarter of a century ago.[241]

He even found it wryly amusing that 'I used to be the best maligned theological teacher in England, *i.e.*, among Congregationalists, for heterodoxy: now I am becoming the best maligned for orthodoxy. Isn't that nice?'[242]

---

[237] R. J. Campbell, *The New Theology*, 18.

[238] He became Assistant Secretary of the London Missionary Society.

[239] DWS, 280.

[240] Ibid, 287-8.

[241] Ibid., 266.

[242] Ibid., 222, quoting a letter to James Ross of 19 October 1897.

III

Since, as is clear from the foregoing, Simon was a churchman at heart, and since he devoted the major part of his working life to the training of ministers, we shall do well to gather together his thoughts on the Church and the ministry. I say 'gather together' because Simon's utterances on these doctrines are scattered and he left no monograph on ecclesiology in general, or upon Congregational polity in particular. It is not possible to draw a comprehensive picture because he did not elaborate on the covenant concept, for example, nor did he have much to say about the sacraments.

In 1890 Simon wrote a sermon entitled, 'Not your own.' His text was I Corinthians 6: 19-20, the operative verse being the latter: 'For ye are bought with a price: therefore glorify God in your body, and in your spirit, which are God's.' He moves through a discussion of the ownership of property to God as 'the only real owner in the Universe.'[243] Our role is that of steward, and 'Property which we refuse to hold as stewards from God ceases to be our property—we become its property—it becomes our owner; we serve it whilst we think it is serving us.'[244] In a special way church members are not their own, because 'God had bought them out of the bondage into which this idea of belonging to ourselves had reduced them, and given as the price His only-begotten and well-beloved Son.'[245] The distinction between those who are of the household of faith and those who are not, is of great significance to Simon—as, indeed, the title of his collection of sermons, *Twice Born*, implies. He correctly understands that the Congregational ecclesiology turns upon this fact.

What, more particularly, does Congregationalism stand for? This was the question that Simon posed directly to himself and to his audience at the opening of the 1897-98 session at Yorkshire United Independent College. He answers it with special reference to doctrine. Congregationalism, he declares, is often represented as standing for something which 'the overwhelming majority of its adherents, both in the past and present, indignantly repudiate [namely, that Congregationalists are free to believe as they please]; or as not standing for something which the same adherents no less emphatically maintain and assert [namely, that Congregationalists hold the great evangelical doctrines].'[246] He grants that variability according to circumstances and without friction 'ought to be our glory', but 'Variation beyond certain limits denotes transmutation or revolution.'[247] Congregationalism stands, first, for 'the free, intelligent and convinced acceptance of certain great Christian verities ... held on the authority of Holy Scripture by all Protestant or Evangelical Churches'; and secondly, for a polity which accords with 'the spirit and creeds of Protestantism, not to say of the entire Christian Church, as with Biblical precedent.'[248]

---

[243] D. W. Simon, *Twice Born*, 151.
[244] Ibid., 152.
[245] Ibid., 153.
[246] Idem, *What does Congregationalism Stand For?*, 3.
[247] Ibid., 4.
[248] Ibid.

Congregationalists believe in the Trinity, the person and work of Christ, the personality and work of the Holy Spirit, eternal life as already begun in those who trust Christ as Saviour and confess him as Lord, the Scriptures as the authoritative source of Christian truth received under divine illumination. All of this is clear from their classical texts and from the history of their withdrawal from those who have denied these doctrines. Congregationalism stands for the free, intelligent and convinced holding of the above doctrines. It grants no licence to believe as one pleases—this notion is 'utterly alien' to the Congregational tradition; and feeling and sentiment must not replace rational conviction.

In reflecting upon Simon's position as here stated, we cannot but recall his insistence elsewhere that salvation is not merely a question of assenting to specified doctrines, but of answering the call of the Saviour. His plea for rational conviction regarding specific doctrines does not entail the elevation of doctrines into criteria of salvation. Rather, at a time when some were sliding into sentiment and pleading their feelings, and when the same ones, or others, were advocating a free-wheeling liberty of belief, Simon's point is that Christian freedom is freedom in, not from, the Gospel, and that those who have truly been 'twice born' will naturally find their testimony echoing that of the Christian ages. He is also concerned to warn against such 'counterfeits' as the Hegelian Trinity (a dialectical triad, not one God in three persons), the Incarnation as an ongoing process in every person, and the atonement as either an illustration of the 'die to live' motif,[249] or as what we might nowadays call a visual aid to show us something about the lengths to which divine love goes in order to reach fallen humanity.[250] All this granted, an emphasis upon commitment to Christ as Saviour and Lord would have gone some way to drawing the sting of the retort which sooner or later accompanies any given list of doctrinal essentials: Who says that these doctrines are essential, and on what grounds?

As already implied in his remarks on freedom, an attendant motif operative in Simon's thought is his concern that Congregationalism was sliding into rampant individualism, and was in danger of disintegrating. Hence his verdict that 'No communities fall to pieces so quickly as those which have no tie but sentiment, whereas communities which are welded together by convictions as well as by feelings, resist attack alike from within and without.[251] There is, however, a proper understanding of individualism, he believes, which requires to go hand in hand with the corporate idea: 'Two principles, condition sound, healthy, vigorous progress, namely, the individual or independent, and the organic or corporate. If either is exaggerated the ultimate result is stagnation, though the immediate effects, of

[249] The use made of this motif by philosophical idealist, Edward Caird, comes to mind. See further, Alan P. F. Sell, *Philosophical Idealism and Christian Belief*, 190-194.

[250] Not, indeed, that the Cross does not show this; but first, the Cross is where God's love is victoriously active for our salvation. Otherwise there is no Gospel, but only a 'Pelagian' pessimism induced by an example to whose heights we shall never rise.

[251] D. W. Simon in Anon., *Memorial of the Opening of the New and Enlarged Buildings of Lancashire College*, 91. Cf. DWS, 246-7.

course, differ.'[252] In a sermon on Matthew 23: 8, 'one is your Master, even Christ; and all ye are brethren', he develops his idea of the Church as corporate by expounding the concept of brotherhood. The brotherhood of Christians of which he conceives is not merely to be found in the local church, it is worldwide in its scope. Christ, he declares, came to reconcile God and humanity, and to establish 'an all-embracing human brotherhood, an idealised family ... the kingdom of God.'[253] He even goes so far as to say that if humanity could have attained its ideal without him, God would have been content to be like Herbert Spencer's ever-working unknowable Absolute—a very odd employment for a God of all grace who, we have been led to believe, desires fellowship with those whom he has created, and a view which implicitly returns a negative response to the old question, Would God have become incarnate in Christ had humanity not sinned?[254] Back on a more familiar track, so to speak, Simon insists that the reconciliation of humanity to God and of person to person are inseparable. He recognises that brotherhood is not always readily achieved among Christians, whose life circumstances vary so much. Although 'Even great inequalities of outward lot are easily borne, if with the increase of goods there is an increase of meekness, and sympathy, and love of Christ. ... Some contrasts violate the laws of Christian brotherhood',[255] and a church which accepts them has renounced Christ. The bond which unites this universal brotherhood is not blood, as in a human family, it is Christ himself—'One is your Master.'[256]

Simon had a place for the wider-than-local-church where questions of church discipline were concerned. 'Suppose,' he writes to James Ross,

> that an individual member of an individual Church notoriously and plainly not only entertains, but actually propagates Unitarianism ... are they to do nothing but protest? It seems to me that duty to Christ, themselves, and the erring brother, requires, first, admonition, then formal separation, either of him from the Association, or of the Association from him, *i.e.*, disfellowshipping. But you can't do this unless a certain body of doctrine is a constitutive factor of Congregationalism—which is what you seem to dispute. ... Churches owe a duty to each other in this respect. You seem to leave the whole business to the individual Church, which I call Independency gone mad.[257]

---

[252] DWS, 278.

[253] D. W. Simon, *Twice Born*, 132-3.

[254] We shall see shortly that Simon believed that had there been no sin there would have been no incarnation, for the work of the Logos throughout the cosmos would have sufficed.

[255] D. W. Simon, *Twice Born*, 138.

[256] Ibid., 139.

[257] DWS, 320-231. The letter is dated 2 June 1911. If we discount a post mortem miracle, Simon having died in 1909, we must take it that the year given is a misprint for 1900, the latter being the year of the immediately preceding and following letters in the sequence.

As to the Church's mission, Simon unburdened himself in the same letter to Ross in the following, not altogether fair, terms:

> I have long preached the doctrine that what is needed is missions to so-called Church-members rather than to outsiders. The latter are almost played out, and they minister largely to the self-complacency of those who support them. These good people who pay for, and can listen to, the inanest platitudes, provided they are well larded with certain shibboleths—eh! man, they turn my stomach inside out: I get sea-sick. They used to make me sick when I was a student, and they do still. And when, into the bargain, they are regular sweaters on a large scale, the mischief done is enormous. Personally I am convinced that unless the Churches can be made more Christian, or be extinguished, Christianity will suffer an eclipse in this country such as has never been known ...[258]

Simon left no elaborate treatise on the ministry, but in his short book, *The Making of a Preacher*, he gave some advice, expressed in homely style and with ample illustrations, from which his understanding of the ministry is easily inferred. He does not proceed through the several aspects of ministry—the nature of ministry, preaching, the conduct of worship, pastoralia and the like, but concentrates upon the intellectual aspects of ministry. He urges ministers to become expert in a particular branch of knowledge, and to study it 'at fixed times and for a fixed length of time.' Three benefits will accrue if this advice is followed:

> First, the line of study will serve a purpose analogous to that served by the string drawn through a solution of sugar—as you know, the crystals gather round it which are called sugar candy. In like manner what you read and think and observe even in other domains will more or less crystallize round the one subject, and thus place itself at your command in a way that would otherwise be impossible.[259]

Secondly, the minister's self respect will be justly heightened, and thirdly, he will enjoy the respect of others which would not otherwise come his way.[260]

He sets his face against those who, instead of thinking through biblical texts, 'treat them as pegs on which to hang truths they suppose themselves to have drawn from the study of some poet or quasi-inspired writer. They seem to regard the Bible, in fact, not as a genuine mining property which will repay working, but, to use mining phraseology, as a "claim" which has to be "salted" with extraneous ore to make it saleable.'[261] Ministers should have open minds to receive new truth, but should be ' equally loyal towards old truth. A good many seem to think that "on with the new" means "off with the old"—this may be very advisable and necessary

---

[258] Ibid., 229-230.

[259] D. W. Simon, *The Making of a Preacher*, 30-31.

[260] In English Congregationalism the ministers were invariably male until Constance Coltman was ordained in 1917.

[261] D. W. Simon, *The Making of a Preacher*, 37-8.

with sweethearts; it is neither with truth.'[262] Simon proceeds to advocate the acquisition by ministers of a system of theology. This should be done *via* the mastery of an existing system, which will yield *loci* which aid organized thought, and comparisons and contrasts between older and newer ways of thinking. Eventually they will arrive at their own system—but not all stay, or even begin, the course:

> Shall I tell you what happens to men of your vocation who never get hold of a system? They become confirmed flounderers; nay, more, they fall perpetually into self-contradictions, and all in happy ignorance of the fact—a state of things which cannot possibly contribute either to their own comfort or to the edification of their hearers—at all events of those who understand.[263]

Simon's 'bitterest pill', after having spent so many years educating men for the ministry was that

> the vast majority are going out into the ministry without any definite conviction as to the reason why they are ministers: certainly not that it is their supreme business to *convert*. At the utmost it is 'to do good'—which often means entertaining and interesting, with a little mild piety thrown in. Twenty-five years ago men *took for granted the Evangelical system* even though they might not feel strongly: men *now* scarcely take anything for granted except a sentimental Ethic with a slight admixture of Christian religion ...[264]

None of which shook Simon's own convictions concerning the ministry:

> [I]f a man preach as the oracles [*sic*] of God; if he speak as one sent by God to speak; if he let it be seen that his message for others is at the same time a message for himself; if his life illustrate his preaching and his preaching explain his life; if he have fair abilities diligently utilised; if he deliver his message in a natural, energetic, lively manner; if he be a pastor as well as a preacher; if he be pleasant, cheery, accessible, even jolly, especially in his intercourse with the young; if he see to it that public worship is bright and nothing in it too long; and if, above all, he let it be felt that when he prays he really is praying to a living God who hears; if, in addition to all this, he can give an independent theological account of himself in clear, vigorous language—that man will hold a position and wield an influence such as an archangel might envy. So he will anywhere. But woe to a man who is shilly-shally, feeble, vague, weakly sentimental; who has nothing to proclaim but what he himself has found; who lacks bone and muscle; who shrinks from personal dealing with his fellow-men; who seems, or is, too anxious about his own profit or

[262] Ibid., 39.
[263] Ibid., 44-5.
[264] DWS, 229.

ease; who, in short, is neither diligent in business nor fervent in spirit—he will be a failure.[265]

IV

Simon 'used to say (at least in his Spring Hill days) that he "revelled" in the Trinity. ... He could not think of God as personal, and, at the same time, as a solitary unit.'[266] He believed that the Trinity is 'the foundation doctrine of the Christian doctrinal system,' and that 'wherever this cardinal doctrine had either been forgotten or ignored or denied ... the system of Christian truth had crumbled to pieces.'[267] He did not, however, publish his detailed thoughts on the doctrine. To his former student Powicke, 'his treatment of the subject was, for me, too speculative and metaphysical; whereas Maurice approached it, as Paul did, from the side of experience.'[268] Be that as it may, Simon did refer to many aspects of God—his Fatherhood and his beauty, for example[269]—but his major contribution was in the field of the Christian doctrines of sin and salvation. To this we now turn.

We must set out from Simon's understanding of sin and evil. It is not that this is the only, or necessarily the best, way of approaching the heart of the Christian gospel—indeed, in due course I shall suggest that it is not; but it was Simon's way, and we must follow him here. It will become evident that, as D. L. Ritchie said, 'to [Simon] the wonder of all wonders, was the revelation of the grace of God to sinful men in the Cross of Christ. Man's sin and God's redemption were the height to which, like water to the level of its source, all his thoughts gravitated.'[270]

In a paper entitled, 'Sin and evil,' Simon reflects upon I John 3: 3, 'Sin is transgression of law.' Clearly expecting no opposition, he declares that 'There is ... no human history without sin and sinners.'[271] He further explains, in two sentences which may be taken as kernel of his position, that

---

[265] Ibid., 209. The continuing relevance of these remarks will be obvious to many, while the correct use of the subjunctive may encourage some to practise an art almost lost—even in theological writing.

[266] DWS, 340.

[267] Ibid., 219.

[268] F. J. Powicke, 'Frederick Denison Maurice,' 174.

[269] See *Twice Born*, sermons 5 and 6.

[270] DWS, 195. For David Lakie Ritchie, DD (Edinburgh), (1864-1951), see SCM, 135. Following pastorates in Dunfermline and Newcastle, he became Principal of Nottingham Congregational Institute (subsequently Paton College) (1904-19). In 1919 he became Principal of the Congregational College of Canada, Montreal, and, on the formation of the United Church of Canada he became Dean and Professor of Theology of the United Theological College, Montreal (1926-39).

[271] D. W. Simon, 'Sin and evil,' in Chas. H. Vine, ed., *The Old Faith and the New Theology*, 29.

> The Bible and Christianity take sin for granted. They conceive it as something which has intruded itself into God's world, which is opposed to His holy will, and which He seeks to eliminate by the redemptive means whose working constitutes the peculiarity of the history of Israel and is supremely embodied in the life, death, and resurrection of the Son of his love.[272]

He cautions that sin is not 'a positive or real force or power, either impersonal or personal, either virus or poison or miasma or anything else distinct from men who commit sin and are sinners.'[273] The term 'sin' denotes a quality that inheres in certain modes of behaviour, and in those who behave wrongly. In denying that sin is a positive force, Simon appears at first sight to veer towards Aquinas. Unlike Aquinas, however, he does not construe sin as a privation of good. As to other explanations of the nature of sin, he forcefully (and well nigh exhaustively) concludes that

> whether sin is the privation of being which marks the finite as compared with the infinite, or absolute; or is due to the necessity for the existence of moral evil in a world that is in any true sense morally good; or is a misleading or delusive phase of consciousness incident to development; or is traceable to the start gained by the flesh over the spirit in the growth of the individual man; or is dues to the animalism which, according to some evolutionists, lingers in humanity as an inheritance from its animal ancestry; or is referable to 'the infinite network of relations between each part and every other in the 'eternal All' or 'Universe', and is by us called evil, thought is must be really good; or is deemed explicable for [*sic*] by an original and essential personal or impersonal dualism of the universe; or, finally, has been decreed by God Himself, either for inexplicable reasons, or, as we are now being told, 'for the demonstration of the essential nature of good',—each and all of these explanations, either straight out or by roundabout ways, land us in the denial of any real difference between morality and immorality, between right and wrong, between good and evil. Accept any one of them and there is no good, there is no evil, either moral or natural.[274]

Sin, he continues, is that which ought not to be; and what ought not to be is transgression of the law. In this context 'law', for Simon, does not mean the law as understood by any particular religion, but that law which is immanent in the human being's nature, that 'invisible code of laws according to which he is meant to live.'[275] With this he comes to a brief statement of those bio-cosmological views which, as we shall see, he developed at length in *Reconciliation by Incarnation*, namely, that all living creatures accommodate themselves to their environment in ways congruent with the laws of their nature. Human beings, however, differ from all other living organisms in that they need to be aware of the demands of their 'invisible code' before they can obey them, and because they are free to obey or

---

[272] Ibid., 31.
[273] Ibid., 33.
[274] Ibid., 35-6.
[275] Ibid., 38.

disobey them. Moreover, they act, or fail to act, as members not only of humanity, but of the God-created cosmos. Hence, they are related to themselves, to others, and to God, and 'sin is committed whenever man either fails to act towards himself, or towards his fellow-man or towards God as the invisible code of his being requires; still more when he acts in direct opposition to its requirements.'[276] The light by which people may discern their duty flows partly from natural experience, partly from other human beings, but supremely from God's self-revelation in the history of Israel and in Jesus Christ. The upshot is that 'All sin is transgression of law; and as all law is from God, sin is, at its deepest, *i.e.*, most essentially, disobedience to God.'[277] What is to be done about this?

Simon's book, *The Redemption of Man* (1889) is modestly subtitled, *Discussions bearing on the Atonement*. We shall not, therefore, expect to find a complete dogmatic system here—and, indeed, Simon himself supplemented this work with his later volume, *Reconciliation by Incarnation* (1898). The former work is dedicated to Tholuck, Schöberlein[278] and Dorner, 'To whose teachings, example, and friendship I owe a greater debt than I am myself able to estimate.' In the second edition of the work (1906) the original Introduction is omitted, and a new chapter on 'Justification and the death of Christ according to the apostle Paul' is inserted. Unless otherwise stated, and because of the way in which he relates his position to that of his forebears and peers in the original Introduction, my references are to the first edition.

In the Preface Simon explains that on experiential, biblical and rational grounds, and in agreement with the Church catholic, he knows for a fact that by his death Christ has brought about the forgiveness of sins. We see immediately the reassertion of his view that spiritual facts are no less real than material ones. Given the fact, the question he has to address, he says, is, How does Christ's death achieve its result, and why was it necessary? He signals his disagreement with other writers as to the nature of forgiveness and the mode in which it was effected and, positively, he remarks that 'As forgiveness is the foundation of a right relation to God, and through that of new life and blessedness, any Christian Church that does not jealously watch over this part of its faith is either wofully [*sic*] ignorant of its duty, or else unfaithful.'[279] He proceeds to draw a distinction between orthodoxy in the sense of 'right faith'—especially 'the *credendum* that Christ shed his blood for the remission of sins',[280] and 'orthodoxy' as entailing assent to particular systematic formulations concerning God's action in Christ. In the latter sense, he somewhat pugnaciously declares, 'there is not now, and there never was any such thing, at all events in Protestantism.'[281]

---

[276] Ibid., 41.

[277] Ibid., 45.

[278] The liturgical scholar and dogmatician, Ludwig Friedrich Schöberlein (1813-1881), was professor at Göttingen (1855-81) and Heidelberg (1850-55).

[279] D. W. Simon, *The Redemption of Man, ix.*

[280] Ibid., x.

[281] Ibid.

In the Introduction he makes it clear that he presupposes throughout that Christ is 'the eternal, essential Son of God.'[282] To deny the divinity of Christ is to deny his atoning work; and to use the term 'divine' of Christ in the way in which some 'advanced' thinkers do when they claim that deity and humanity are essentially akin so that human beings may become as God, is to fall for a crypto-humanism which supposes that a mere man, even the best man, could perform a divine-human work.

Simon wishes to address three questions: How are we to understand Christ's obedience even unto the death of the Cross? What was accomplished by this death? How was Christ's obedience related to the end achieved? He notes the differences that arise among theologians over the end of Christ's work. There are objective and subjective theories of the atonement, though Simon regrets that the latter are sometimes designated 'moral', as if the former were not so in any sense of the term.

As regards objective theories, Simon sets his face against what he calls crypto-dualism, such as is found in earlier theories which suppose that a ransom for sin had to be paid to the devil, or the theory of his friend R. W. Dale, that Christ's obedience unto death was obedience to an eternal law of righteousness that existed independently of both God and humanity.[283] The alternative view, which Simon endorses and which he thinks preserves the personal God-humanity relations, is that the laws which God has to uphold are self-prescribed modes of his own being, and we cannot separate out his law from his being. Moreover, since the loss, as a consequence of sin, of every child created in his image is a loss to God, 'justice can be done to God only by the redemption of man.'[284] As for those who speak of the claims of God's justice, Simon points out that this 'is merely an abstract way of speaking of God as just.'[285] Nor is it sufficient to speak solely of the punishment of sinners as being something due to God: punishment is due to the sinners themselves; what is due to God are the sinners, 'with all their powers of body and mind'[286]—something which cannot be rendered apart from redemption. It is also to be remembered that suffering and penalty as such cannot suffice to propitiate or remove divine anger, for since God's anger is 'essentially ethical, it can only be acted upon by that which is essentially ethical, that is, by the willing sacrifice of the obedient Son, which is 'the means of establishing right relations between God and man, looked at from both sides.'[287]

---

[282] Ibid., 1.

[283] Simon traces this view back to the Cambridge Platonist Ralph Cudworth (1617-88) and the Anglican 'Arian' divine Samuel Clarke (1675-1729), for both of whom see DSCBP; ODNB. Clarke is also in DECBP. He finds the view in an article of Dale's published in the *British Quarterly* Review in 1867, but notes that in his Congregational Lecture, *The Doctrine of the Atonement* (1875) Dale modifies the position to the extent of identifying Christ with the eternal law, rather than as existing independently of it.

[284] D. W. Simon, *The Redemption of Man*, 27.

[285] Ibid., 29.

[286] Ibid., 30.

[287] Ibid., 36.

Turning to the subjective or moral theories, Simon finds that the most popular one is that which proclaims Christ's obedience unto death as 'a manifestation of divine self-sacrificing love',[288] of such a kind as will move sinners to respond to such love. More thoroughgoing is governmentalism, and this Simon finds in the writings of his fellow Congregationalists John Pye Smith, Ralph Wardlaw and (as we saw) in George Payne, who argued that while there was no personal reluctance on God's part to forgive, the demands of the law had to be satisfied by Christ before pardon was legitimated. I have already queried this dualistic view of God as moral Governor on the one hand and loving Father on the other, and Simon queries it too. It was, in Payne as we saw, and in the others mentioned, an aspect of their modification of a Calvinistic scholasticism which in the wake of the Enlightenment had come to be deemed in certain respects immoral. But when Simon branded moderate Calvinism 'Calvinism with its teeth filed but not drawn'[289] he was not altogether without excuse.

Next, Simon finds a sizeable class of manward theories (albeit with objective adhesions) which may be labelled organic or dynamic. They teach that consequent upon Christ's sacrificial obedience a vital energy has flowed down to the human race. Some views of this kind suppose that human beings are consciously appealed to by Christ's work and then make their appropriate life-changing response, while others suggest that 'the environment of humanity is ... unconsciously affected, and out of that arises the transformation of the conscious life.'[290] He classifies Schleiermacher among those who exemplify the former position, while the latter is represented by those who favour 'not a little Hegelianization of the Christian faith in general, and of the Christian atonement in particular' in such a way that 'ideas of the Hegelian philosophy are being quietly substituted for the concrete actualities accepted by the Christian Church.'[291]

At the end of his Introduction Simon reiterates his view that the fact of Christ's atonement is to be taken as given, that it is not a fact of the natural world but belongs to the moral cosmos and, accordingly, that the theory of it must submit to those moral conditions which pertain to the sphere of which God is the supreme factor. What he hopes to show is that 'the atoning work of Christ ... can only be fully and adequately justified as part of a system which embraces in its consideration the kingdom of God in its entirety, with God, creation, especially the world of intelligences, and sin.'[292]

As if in anticipation of a popular theme in the biblical theology of the 1950s and 1960s, Simon proceeds to argue that the earthly mission of Christ is 'an act or scene in the great drama of history.'[293] It is 'an episode in the relation of our Lord Jesus

---

[288] Ibid., 44.

[289] DWS, 264.

[290] D. W. Simon, *The Redemption of Man*, 55.

[291] Ibid., 63. See further Alan P. F. Sell, *Theology in Turmoil*, ch. 1; idem, *Philosophical Idealism and Christian Belief*.

[292] D. W. Simon, *The Redemption of Man*, 68.

[293] Ibid., 69.

Christ to the kingdom of God,' and if we overlook his prior relation to the system which required redemption we 'narrow his functions' and fail to appreciate the full extent of his redemptive work.[294] Because of the kingdom and Christ's place in it, he would have had a claim on humanity even if there had been no sin. Given the fact of sin, his redemptive mission was a moral necessity, 'though in form supernatural and transcending human comprehension.'[295] Not, indeed that this was a *deus ex machina* intervention. On the contrary, 'The Eternal Father, the co-equal Son, and the Holy Spirit, hold originally and naturally such a relation to the great system of things which constitutes the divine kingdom, that whatever they do is as natural and reasonable for them to do as anything that can be normally done by a human monarch within his dominions, or a human father within his family.'[296]

At this point Simon offers two explanations. He describes his approach to his theme as realistic. By this he means that he takes biblical propositions 'as denoting something real, actual.' And by the 'kingdom of God' he means 'The universe in its totality, with its innumerable intelligences.'[297] The subjects, these free intelligences, are both visible and invisible, the latter comprising deceased human beings and angels. The relations between the Monarch and his subjects are determined by unchangeable laws, the supreme law of life being 'the one laid down by Christ,' namely, 'Thou shalt love the Lord thy God, with all thy heart, and soul, and mind, and strength; and thy neighbour as thyself.'[298]

God, Simon continues, is *de jure* the universal King, but *de facto* his kingdom is disordered, with some of his subjects being in open rebellion. Sinners are not outside God's dominion, but they are not his true subjects, and need to be made so. Hence, once more, Christ's redemptive mission. He did not come to establish a new kingdom, but to rectify one in sinful disarray. His method, however, was new. It was no mere human attempt to reform existing society by remedying adverse societal symptoms. Rather, 'He came to reconcile men to God, because the alienation of God and man was the source and sustaining energy of all the other alienation, disorder, and misery that are to be found in the universe.'[299] Because of the fall, human beings 'enter the world with an inborn bias towards a rebellious relationship [with God] more or less strong.'[300] But God is still their King *de jure*, and for the sake of Christ he offers forgiveness, to which offer the due response is faith.

As for humanity, human beings are individuals though, against individualism, Simon insists that humanity as such is an organism the self-development of which is not yet complete. Accordingly, while by no means minimising those aspects of

---

[294] Ibid., 70.

[295] Ibid., 71.

[296] Ibid., 72.

[297] Ibid., 76.

[298] Ibid., 84. I shall in due course comment on the problematic phrase 'laid down by Christ.' In context (Luke 10: 27) the lawyer responded to Jesus's request for a statement of the *Jewish* law, and Jesus accepted his answer as accurate.

[299] Ibid., 91-2.

[300] Ibid., 96.

Christ's atoning work which pertain to the individual, he contends that the corporate relations of humanity to God, which are more than the sum-total of individual relations, must not be overlooked. Both individual and corporate relations are vitiated by sin, and were God incapable of anger at sin he would not be the righteous, holy God. But 'The translation of anger as predicated of God into such terms as condemnation or judicial punishment and the like, is altogether opposed to the usage of Scripture.'[301] The normal relations of both human beings and God to sin are the recognition of sin as sin, aversion to it, displeasure at it, and action to deal with it. Then comes the bold affirmation, 'The divine nature as such is clearly exalted above the possibility of injury; but the divine life—especially the affectional life of God, the heart of God, and the cosmos which has issued forth from His hand—may be prejudicially affected by man.'[302] As Simon later puts it, 'There is no such thing in the moral world as bearing a burden without feeling it to be a burden.'[303] I shall return to this point in due course.

Angered though he is by sin, God has never ceased to fulfil the conditions for the establishment of his kingdom, 'and if it be true that humanity subsists in the Logos, draws all its life from God and gives its life to God through the Logos; then it follows that all along the Logos must have been acting as the mediator for sinners, with regard alike to the relation of God to men, and the relation of men to God.'[304] With the taking on of flesh and his becoming man the Logos made manifest his work which had previously been hidden from view. At this point Simon is at pains to caution his readers:

> It is necessary not to confound two things which are often confounded, namely, the humanification of the Logos and His incarnation. The Logos did not become human when He came to earth. He is eternally manlike. It was He in whose image man was specifically made. He was, so to speak, the human in God. But He was not flesh; He became or was made flesh, as John tells us, thus manifesting what He eternally was. ... As such the Logos was in the truest sense a man of men, the Son of man, the man.[305]

The incarnation implies the self-limitation of the Logos, and led to his undergoing suffering on behalf of sinners. From the human side, 'We could not lay hold of Christ out of us, but for the Logos in us.'[306] Contrary to much Protestant teaching, Simon denies that human beings are naturally out of Christ and therefore have to be brought into connection with him. On the contrary, by virtue of the work of the Logos, they subsist in Christ, and any separation from him is the consequence of their sin. Moreover, it is because of the work of the Logos within us that we as

---

301 Ibid., 237. Cf. ch. 6.
302 Ibid., 248.
303 ibid., 360.
304 Ibid., 297.
305 Ibid., 304-5.
306 Ibid., 333.

individuals may by faith become partakers in Christ. It follows that in one sense while Christ's redeeming work is a finished work—all the conditions for reconciliation are in place, from the point of view of humanity's response to it the work is still in progress.

The apostle Paul, says Simon, construes the individual's rectified relationship with God in two ways. First, it is a matter of the forgiveness of sin: 'A forgiven man is a man who is placed in the position of one who has not sinned. ... The offences are put out of sight.'[307] Secondly, the God-human relation is now normalized; the individual is justified:

> The difference between forgiveness and justification is then this,—that whilst 'forgiveness' says 'thy once wrong relationship is now overlooked'; 'justification' says 'thy present relationship is the right one, and through it thou wilt become righteous.'[308]

According to Paul, the human response to forgiveness is repentance, while faith, itself a gift from God, is the response to justification. And all of this is the product of Christ's saving mission. He 'offers a ransom, a sacrifice, a propitiation for man to God: Christ takes man's place, and so dies on man's behalf, that man also dies with Him.'[309] All of which implies that Christ's mission is not directed to individuals alone. In Paul's view,

> Christ, in the very act of offering Himself to God, offered humanity also. Potentially the human race died in His death, was crucified in His crucifixion, and when I use the word *potentially* I do not mean merely making possible, or opening the way, or supplying the means, or moral potentiality; but potentiality in the real sense. ... The life and death of Christ as the incarnate Logos, *i.e.* as a member of the race, were and are for the whole race the potentiality of the new relation to God, which was the condition or *dikaiosune*; and faith was possible on the basis, or in virtue of, this real potence. Apart from this same potentiality, faith would have been impossible; but equally apart from faith, would the real potentiality have remained a mere potence.[310]

The concluding study in Simon's *The Redemption of Man* comprises his reflections on the influence through history of the death of Christ. It is more to our purpose, however, to proceed directly to his volume, *Reconciliation by Incarnation.* By the latter word he intends 'the entire earthly ministry of our Lord, from His conception to His ascension—the mission of which the death on the "cross" was the central, all-dominating feature.'[311]

---

[307] D. W. Simon, *The Redemption of Man*, 2nd edn, 249.
[308] Ibid., 251.
[309] Ibid., 271.
[310] Ibid., 273, 274.
[311] D. W. Simon, *The Redemption of Man*, 2nd edn, 274 n. 1.

In setting out his stall, Simon reiterates his interest in dealing with spiritual facts, realities. He defines his theory or doctrine of reconciliation as being of the personal sort; but it is personal in a way different from that in which moral influence theories are personal. The latter proceed as if there is but one person to be reconciled, namely, man to God, whereas Simon's view is that God also needs to be reconciled to man. What is most striking, and less than common, in his exposition is the way in which he locates his theory of reconciliation within a fairly fully articulated cosmology. He does this because of

> the strong conviction I entertain that the chief intellectual difficulties in the way of that fact or doctrine [of reconciliation] are rooted in a defective or false philosophical view of the rise, constitution, and history of the cosmos in general and the world in particular; and that the principles embodied in Redemption, particularly in the Reconciliation of God and man, are the same principles at a higher level that are embodied in the divine creation, sustentation, and rule, in a word, the evolution, of the world.[312]

The redemption of humanity concerns, successively, the reconciliation of God with humanity and humanity with God; liberation from sin and restoration to righteousness; and deliverance from the evils which are both the consequence and the punishment of sin and their replacement by bestowed good—'Behold I make all things new' (Revelation 21: 5). The fact of reconciliation, like all other facts, presupposes a system of kindred and correlate facts, but it would be misleading to call this system 'religious' or 'spiritual' as if these terms denoted facts that are not real in the sense in which other phenomena are real. Simon's conviction is that 'an unusually strong interaction between the divine and human factors of the great system of the universe is going on',[313] and what is required is a cosmology

> which shall do justice, alike to the facts which the science of nature has brought to light and established, on the one hand, and to the facts which may be in general designated spiritual on the other—a cosmology, in other words, among whose great momenta shall be creation and evolution, freedom and conscience. The rectification of the relations of God and man, of man and God, and of man and nature, wrought out by the Logos or Word of God, in that, through the power of the Holy Spirit, He became incarnate, taught, lived, died, rose again from the dead and ascended on high, presupposes a specific origin, constitution, and evolution of the cosmos in general, and of the earth in particular. Apart from a true rationale of the rise of the world there can be no true rationale of the redemption of the world.[314]

In these words we have the abstract of Simon's thesis. He proceeds to argue that the divine energy is the only energy, and that neither materialistic nor pantheistic

---

[312] Idem, *Reconciliaton by Incarnation*, vii-viii.

[313] Ibid., 7.

[314] Ibid., 8.

cosmologies will suffice.[315] The former tends to endow matter with qualities other than those of extension and impenetrability, while the latter tends in the direction of ascribing to the universe an all-penetrating but less than fully personal soul, which nevertheless produces effects which the free, intelligent actions of a divine being or beings alone can produce. The cosmos, Simon declares, is 'a real, though ever-varying because ever evolving, unity,' and within it 'man is essentially a somatico-psychical being.'[316] Couching his thought now in trinitarian terms, Simon writes,

> The person known as Father is in a special sense the creator of the matter out of which the cosmos is being evolved. The person known as the Holy Spirit is the intra-divine centre, and extra-divine wielder of the energy by which the cosmos is being evolved. The person known as the Logos or Word, who as incarnate is designated the Son of God, is the intra-divine centre of the activity by which the cosmic idea is formed and the extra-divine power which informs or interweaves the complex of laws or idea with the cosmic energy. Inasmuch, however, as the three persons, or, as it would be more accurate to describe them, the three personific factors of the Godhead, though distinct from each other, are yet so in each other that in a very true sense what each does all do, and what all do each does, they are therefore frequently referred to, alike in Scripture and in the thought of the Church, as if certain of their functions and activities were interchangeable.[317]

Simon concludes that only on the foundation of such a cosmology is there room for a God who is at once 'transcendent and immanent, for nature and spirit, for necessity and freedom, for law and miracle, for sin and redemption.'[318]

The next stage of the discussion concerns both the world of nature and God as being the environment in which humanity lives. On its own the material world will not meet humanity's needs, for 'A direct vital or bio-dynamic relation of God is necessary to man's normal development, growth, and life', and this spiritual energy 'is as real a form of energy as gravitation or electricity.[319] 'The material and the spiritual,' he continues, 'are much too closely interwoven, no less in the cosmos than in man, to admit of any clear and marked division.'[320]

---

[315] Simon carries the fight to both of these theories, and to a number of authors, ancient and modern, of whose views he disapproves. He is particularly, and rightly, concerned to distinguish the divine immanence from pantheism and, to the surprise no doubt of some Calvinists, he says that when Calvin asserts that 'Nothing happens but what [God] has knowingly and willingly decreed', he is, logically, a pantheist—immediately adding, 'strongly as he might resent the imputation.' See *Reconciliation by Incarnation*, 282. For reflections on immanence and related concepts see Alan P. F. Sell, *Confessing and Commending the Faith*, ch. 5; for some thoughts on pantheism see idem, *Enlightenment, Ecumenism, Evangel*, ch. 7.

[316] D. W. Simon, *Reconciliation by* Incarnation, 32, 28.

[317] Ibid., 34-5.

[318] Ibid., 35.

[319] Ibid., 50.

[320] Ibid., 65.

There follows the claim that the divine relation to humanity is conditioned by a personal or ethical relation of humanity to God which is 'self-controlled and chosen with adequate knowledge.'[321] Indeed, 'God the supreme Personality is such, and the human personality has been constituted such, that God cannot but let His supply of man's deepest needs wait on the good pleasure of man himself.'[322] Human beings would not be moral at all had they not the self-control postulated by Simon: they would not be free over against God, they would be necessitated.

The normal relations between humanity and God have been disrupted by sin, and the existing personal relations between humanity and God are such that reconciliation is required, for God's attitude towards humanity has been changed by sin, no less than that humanity's rebellion has vitiated the filial relationship. From this point of view both God and humanity are in an abnormal state. Most theologians have no difficulty in assenting to the abnormality of humanity's relationship to God, but fewer take due account of the abnormal situation in which God is found:

> To condemn the man who sins is to act righteously; to love the same man when he turns from sin is also to act righteously: but whereas the former is a relationship opposed to the purpose and mind of God, that is, it is abnormal, the latter is in full accord with the divine mind and purpose, that is, normal.[323]

Going still further, Simon declares that 'Sin has introduced, in some sense, disorder into the very life of God Himself. For ... man ... is a differentiation of divine energy, according to a divine idea. He is an immateriation or incarnation of a Logos-idea.'[324] Indeed, 'something of the nature even of a schism has been introduced into the Godhead by sin.'[325] The traditional forensic and governmental theories of the atonement are, Simon repeats, one-sided in not recognizing this two-sided situation, namely, that while humanity needs to be reconciled to God, God also needs to be reconciled to humanity.

Since human beings, as sinners, cannot themselves rectify the situation, God's Son, as the self-limited Logos, the sinless substitute, stands where sinners should stand, and suffers what they should suffer—and all this as an act of filial obedience, not as a submission to punishment. He did, however, make 'satisfaction or amends for the dishonour done to the name of God.'[326] Simon's is not a *penal* substitutionary theory of the atonement, but one in which the forensic aspect, though present since the divine law has been violated, is subsumed under the personal.

---

[321] Ibid., 79.
[322] Ibid., 91.
[323] Ibid., 170.
[324] Ibid., 303.
[325] Ibid., 304.
[326] Ibid., 367.

Externally, the risen and ascended Christ continues to approach people through the preached word of the Church and through the written word in Scripture; through the worship of the Church and 'every true embodiment and manifestation of its life;'[327] through the 'daily walk and conduct of the members'; and through its testimony to Christ. Internally, Christ acts upon people by the Holy Spirit, who enriches, energizes, guides and comforts those whose potentiality to become what they are called to be has begun to be actualized through repentance and faith. He concludes:

> Christ, by offering Himself a sacrifice to God, potentiated us to see that to offer ourselves a living sacrifice, holy and acceptable, is a reasonable service: by making it His meat and drink to do the will of God, He potentiated us to take as our highest prayer, 'Thy will be done on earth as in Heaven; and His work for the establishment of the kingdom of heaven is increasingly inspiring us to regard that as the very goal of effort, sacrifice, and aspiration.[328]

It remains to offer some observations on Simon's suggestive contribution to soteriology. First, his instinct concerning the relation of Christ's saving work to humanity at large—indeed, to the cosmos—and not simply to individuals is as true as it is biblical.[329] However, in discussing human solidarity Simon offers a hostage to fortune by invoking such verses as I Corinthians 12:12 (concerning the body of Christ and its members) and John 15:5-7 (concerning the Vine and the branches) as being applicable to the human race as a whole and not, as the contexts suggest, to the believers or disciples. I suspect that Simon is prompted in this direction by his views regarding the universal work of the Logos, in which connection, with reference to Simon, Robert Mackintosh cautioned that 'we have to be resolutely on our guard against substituting conjectures regarding the Logos for truths regarding salvation by Jesus Christ.'[330] Recognizing that some will object to his reading, Simon contends that 'Those ... who chiefly urge the narrower view of the words seem to overlook the for them perilous inferences they then warrant.'[331] It may be retorted by some that the 'perilous inference' to be drawn from Simon's words is a biblically-unwarranted universalism. The fact is, however, that human solidarity is

---

[327] Ibid., 372.

[328] Ibid., 381.

[329] The cosmological aspect of Simon's position is overlooked by T. Hywel Hughes in his brief description of Simon's work on the atonement. See T. H. Hughes, *TheAtonement. Modern Theories of the Doctrine*, London: Allen & Unwin, 1949, 287-8. For Hughes (1875-1945) see CYB, 1946, 445; SCM, 218; Robert Pope, 'Thomas Hywel Hughes.' He trained at New College, London, leaving that institution one year after Professor W. F. Adeney left it for Lancashire College, and subsequently became a DD and DLitt of London University, and a DD of Edinburgh. He, like Simon before him, and Charles Duthie after him, was Principal of the Scottish Congregational College (1922-36).

[330] R. Mackintosh, *Historic Theories of Atonement*, 278.

[331] D. W. Simon, *The Redemption of Man*, 106 n. 2.

proclaimed in other passages of Scripture, and may be inferred from still others; and since Simon elsewhere allows that while in one sense Christ's work is a finished work but that in another sense it awaits completion as regards particular individuals, there is no need to speak of 'perilous inferences' if the verses about the members of the body of Christ and Christ as the Vine and disciples as the branches are construed in their most natural and obvious way. Again, he expounds Paul's view thus: 'what he really teaches is that in the self-humiliation, the obedience, the sufferings, the death, the resurrection, and the life of Christ, humanity humbled itself, obeyed, suffered, died and rose again to newness of life.'[332] Did all of humanity do this once and for all in the past? Is it not better to say that Christ as representative human—Luther's Proper Man—humbled himself, suffered, died, rose again and ascended, and that the outworking of this once-for-all complex of acts which finds it centre in the Cross continues till now? On the next page Simon says that the 'the New Testament represents the world as already redeemed in and by Christ.'[333] That this emphasis is there cannot be denied but, as if now forestalling any universalistic construction of the fact Simon immediately adds that while in one sense forgiveness was secured by Christ's death, it has also to 'become an accomplished fact in the case of every individual man: it would therefore seem not yet to be complete', [334] and this outcome is conditional upon repentance and faith. This is consistent with his bluntly stated assertion that 'Death was and is death to men who live outside the influence of Christ.'[335] There is no cheerful universalism here. The upshot would appear to be that Simon does not always guard his flank by presenting the once-for-all-ness of Christ's atoning work alongside those teleological-eschatological considerations that are no less biblical.

Secondly, it must be granted that Simon frequently proceeds by assertion rather than by argument. In fairness to him, however, we must try to understand why this is so. It is because of his profound, realist, conviction that spiritual facts are facts like any other, that they have been borne out in his own experience, and that therefore he may advert to them as he would advert to any fact in the material realm. All of this, on his own admission, he takes as read. Standing as we nowadays do in the wake of logical positivism and of a radical empiricism which would drastically confine the territory of the factual to those matters which are susceptible of empirical investigation, we can see that Simon implicitly challenges such a stance. It would be anachronistic to expect him to have made out the case in the way we should have to do, but we may infer from his position the clue as to what needs to be done, namely, that the narrow definition of 'fact' must be shown to be inadequate, since it unwarrantably banishes ethical, aesthetic and religious experiences which, no less than the natural, contribute towards what Simon calls the environment of humanity. As G. F. Woods rightly said, 'No theory can be adequate which concludes that what

---

[332] Idem, *Reconciliation by Incarnation*, 277.

[333] Ibid., 278.

[334] Ibid.

[335] Idem, *In Memoriam, ... the Rev. Henry Simon*, 37.

happens cannot take place';[336] but an adequate theory of what Simon would call spiritual facts will have to pay particular attention to the relations of transcendence, immanence and history;[337] and, consistently with Simon's view that it is the twice born who 'see', such a theory would have the character of testimony, it would not constitute evidence of such a kind as to convince a sceptic.

Thirdly, Simon's insistence that the relations between God and humanity are personal is valuable, though it raises certain difficult questions, among them: Are God and human beings personal in the same sense, or in the same way? Nevertheless Simon rightly brings to the fore the concepts of reverence, trust and love, emphasizes humanity's dependence upon God,[338] and challenges any soteriology which majors on the forensic and legal, with the concomitant view of God as official rather than personal.[339] Thus, against Turretine, Charles and A. A. Hodge and Shedd, Simon argues that they try 'to show how an essentially personal ethical end—the appeasement of moral indignation in God—can be accomplished by legal or forensic processes. The legal is not of course unethical, still less anti-ethical; but it is a low stage of the ethical.'[340] At the same time it must be granted that if the juridical does not have its due place we may launch ourselves from the top of a slippery slope into that sentimental view of God which remembers that he is love but conveniently forgets that his love is holy, righteous, love in the presence of which sin cannot stand. Not, indeed, that Simon is in any danger here. He does not repudiate the legal relations between God and humanity, but he regards them as 'among the abnormal relations that have to be set aside,'[341] for since the normal God-humanity relation was rendered abnormal by ethical and personal conduct, normal relations can be restored only by ethical or personal conduct. That Simon's insistence upon the personal impressed one of his former students, A. R. Henderson, is clear from a letter which the latter wrote to his teacher on 24 June 1893. He wanted Simon to know, as he prepared to remove to Bradford, how greatly his work had been valued in Edinburgh. In particular,

---

[336] G. F. Woods, 'The idea of the transcendent,' 52. For the course of the debate here alluded to see Alan P. F. Sell, *The Philosophy of Religion 1875-1980*; and for an attempt to address the issue specified see idem, *Confessing and Commending the Faith*, ch. 4.

[337] For an attempt in this direction see *Confessing and Commending the Faith*, ch. 5.

[338] In an interesting (some would perhaps say, a provocative) aside, Simon observes that 'Schleiermacher would have been nearer the truth had he said that religion is rooted in absolute dependence, instead of defining it as the sense of absolute dependence. If we are absolutely dependent, then when man comes to himself he will have the sense or feeling of it; but that he cannot help. Whereas religion surely as a thing for which we are responsible—for whose lack we are blamed—must be under our free control.' See *The Redemption of Man*, 128 n. 1.

[339] Cf. D. W. Simon, *The Redemption of Man*, 276.

[340] Ibid., 419. Turretine (1623-1687) was a Reformed theologian in Geneva; the Hodges, father (1797-1878) and son (1823-1886), taught at Princeton Theological Seminary; William Greenough Thayer Shedd (1820-1894) taught at Union Theological Seminary, New York.

[341] D. W. Simon, *Reconciliation by Incarnation*, 176.

> I feel an ever-growing satisfaction in the idea of the personal relationship between God and man which you made the basis of your view of the Atonement. It is a view that will stand the wear and tear of time. Other views of our relation to God (such as the forensic) are bound, I believe, to pass into the background in the Christian's own experience as he grown in grace. These views become too mechanical to explain the life; but no such fate, I am persuaded, can overtake the view you pressed on our attention.[342]

Fourthly, the question arises whether or not, from time to time, the biological analogy usurps the personal in Simon's thinking. When his emphasis upon law and its transgression is elaborated in bio-cosmological terms which themselves seem frequently to function as argument and not simply as analogy, the question arises whether sufficient attention is paid to the ethical-filial aspects of the matter. In a word, there is a certain oscillation in his thought. He wishes to claim that his constructive theology is grounded in the *personal* relations between God and humanity; to distance himself from the biological-naturalistic thrust and the 'shilly-shally treatment' given to the question of sin by his Anglican contemporary, F. R. Tennant: 'What a beautifully soft glove the hand wears that knocks Paul on the head;'[343] whilst at the same time agreeing that his major work, *Reconciliation by Incarnation* is 'dominated' by 'the biological principle.'[344] The problem is that the more that biological laws are emphasized the closer we seem to be to necessity, and the further we seem to be from humanity's freedom to violate 'spiritual' laws, such violation, in Simon's understanding, being of the essence of sin—the very thing which makes reconciliation an urgent necessity. As so often, Robert Mackintosh poses the pertinent questions: 'is such a biological theology worthy of its theme? And is an inevitable effect the same thing as a true ethical necessity?'[345] It may be

---

[342] DWS, 181. After pastorates in Scotland and England, Alexander Roy Henderson (1862-1950) became Principal of Paton College (1931-1937) in succession to D. L. Ritchie. See CYB, 1951,512-13; SCM, 63-4.

[343] Letter of 17 November 1903 from Simon to James Ross, DWS, 238-9. Simon refers to Tennant's *The Sources of the Doctrines of the Fall and Original Sin*. Robert Mackintosh similarly rebuked Tennant for his biological naturalism, but also for his incongruous appeal to Lotze's intuitionism—'These more philosophical or more ethical positions are not harmonised with the author's biological prejudices. ... So far as it is a brute inheritance, sin is not sin. So far as sin is sinful ('exceeding sinful', quotes Dr. Tennant), it is more than a brute inheritance.' Then, with characteristic dryness, Mackintosh adds, 'You find even perversions of instinct among lower animals; yet it remains man's special achievement to have invented taverns, opium dens, and houses of ill-fame. These are no brute inheritance but things which mankind have added to God's world.' See his *Christianity and Sin*, 143, where he refers to Tennant's *The Origin and Propagation of Sin*. For Tennant (1866-1957) see DTCBP. Surprisingly, he is not in ODNB.

[344] D. W. Simon, *Reconciliation by Incarnation*, 370.

[345] R. Mackintosh, *Historic Theories of Atonement*, 277.

that Simon's best statement of the human situation appears in a more devotional work:

> if we seek [God] as befits those whose primal, deepest, all-dominating need is ethical and spiritual; if we seek Him, that is, first and foremost as sinners needing forgiveness and reconciliation; needing purification from sin and renewal of heart; needing strength to vanquish temptation and to work righteousness; needing to be quickened into trustfulness and love, into desire after goodness and hatred of evil—then, not only shall we accumulate a store of observations and experiences of God Himself as real and direct as those which we get from nature and man, but we shall be prepared for the enjoyment of the supreme privilege hinted at in the words: 'Behold, I stand at the door, and knock: if any man hear my voice, and open the door, I will come in to him, and sup with him, and he with me.[346]

Nothing could be more personal—or practical.

In the fifth place, Simon's insistence on the fact that the atonement has a Godward as well as a manward aspect is most welcome. Certainly if we proclaim only that Christ came to save human beings from their sins—still more if we think individualistically or atomistically in terms of this human being and the next, we shall find that we are preaching only half a doctrine of the atonement. In this connection Simon's critique of moral influence and governmental theories of the atonement is of importance. In some statements of the latter theory it is difficult to suppress the image of God as a divine headmaster who, even as he wields the cane, says, half apologetically, 'This is going to hurt me much more than it will hurt you.' It makes for a dualistic view of God since it drives a wedge between his love and his holiness and righteousness, and it is a point at which Simon distances himself from such earlier divines as George Payne. For Payne, as we saw, governmentalism was a stage in the tempering of a Calvinist scholasticism gone necessitarian with all that that adversely implied for the nature of God. Governmentalism is not not, finally, a stable position. But may it not be that in his own way Simon from time to time manifests dualistic tendencies? For example, he declares that while a loving God can be angered by sin, his anger cannot be attributed to his love.[347] But this is to separate the divine attributes which, although they may in the interests of convenience and clarity be expounded separately, must not be placed in opposition to one another if doctrinal confusion is to be avoided. In the present case the term 'holy love' admits of both God's righteous indignation against sin and a love which never ceases to love sinners and is victorious over the sin which alienates them from God. Although he occasionally drops his guard as I have suggested, Simon elsewhere affirms the point I wish to make. Where forgiveness is concerned, he says, sinners have to do with the personal God; and 'God does not forgive us as Sovereign, or a Ruler, or as Judge, but as God, who, as God, is Creator, Father, Ruler, Judge; and, as such, in all these aspects expects and claims

[346] D. W. Simon, *The Making of a Preacher*, 50-51.

[347] See *The Redemption of Man*, 261

the holding of all the specifically personal, normal relations, especially those which are described by such terms as reverence, trust, love.'[348] Overall Simon sees the point, but his occasional oscillations and his tendency to mistake analogy for argument may confuse the unsuspecting reader.

I turn now to some specific doctrinal points. First, Simon denies that God is immutable[349]—or, at least, he frequently writes as if this were his view. Thus, for example, he faults theologians and preachers for saying that whereas human being may change towards God, 'God can never change towards man.'[350] This view, Simon declares 'is not Biblical; the unchangeableness of God is not only compatible with, but even expresses itself in the greatest possible changeableness.[351] This means, among other things, that God can suffer. Simon does not hesitate to commend this view not only in his scholarly works but in his preaching. In a sermon of 1880 on Romans 5: 8, 'God commendeth his love toward us, in that, while we were yet sinners, Christ died for us', Simon speaks of the sacrifice God made at the Cross: 'It cost the Godhead something. Not only did the Son, or Word, suffer, but—and be not startled at what I say—the eternal Father, the Godhead also suffered.'[352] A further implication of God's ability to change is that God's affection towards humanity changes, and his feelings are coloured by humanity's attitudes towards himself. As we might expect, matters come to a head where God's anger is concerned. Simon writes, 'The divine nature as such is clearly exalted above the possibility of injury; but the divine life—especially the affectional life of God, the heart of God, and the cosmos which has issued forth from His hand—may be prejudicially affected by man.'[353] The problem here is that if the affectional life of God which is subject to injury is expressive of God's nature, as surely it must be, exactly how 'clearly' is the divine nature exalted above it? Conversely, if the affectional life of God is not revelatory of God's nature, how can we know anything at all about the latter? Does not a further dualism lurk here between God's nature and his life? Moreover, since we know God at all (insofar as we do know him) only as he makes himself known to us, how far are we competent to make assertions regarding his nature apart from such approaches? How does Simon know that 'The very being, the very nature, the very substance or essence of God cannot, of course, be prejudicially affected by human sin.'[354] The 'of course' in this sentence betrays a degree of *a priori* confidence which is not altogether becoming in a common sense realist such as Simon. This judgment is confirmed *a fortiori* when Simon pronounces that 'God varies with a

---

[348] Ibid., 286.

[349] This was a subject on which Dorner had written. See *Divine Immutability—a Critical Reconsideration*, trans. Robert R. Williams and Claude Welch; see also Robert R. Williams, 'I. A. Dorner: the ethical immutability of God.' For J. K. Mozley's summary of Simon's position on this point see *The Impassibility of God*, 143-5.

[350] D. W. Simon, *The Redemption of Man*, 116.

[351] Ibid., 116-17.

[352] Idem, *Twice Born*, 103.

[353] Ibid., 248; cf. *Reconciliation by Incarnation*, 148.

[354] Idem, *Reconciliation by Incarnation*, 147; cf. 190

variability that transcends all human calculation, but which belongs to the very essence of spirit and life.'[355] How can Simon possibly know that this is so? It seems to me that the entire Christian Gospel turns upon the truth that what God does, and how he shows himself to us genuinely comports with who he is. Were it otherwise we should not have a revelation of God. The most appropriate theology sets out from what God has been pleased to make known, and not from what he has not. The question of the divine impassibility will return when we come to T. V. Tymms and R. S. Franks, and further remarks will be required in the course of some concluding reflections.

Secondly, questions may be raised concerning some of Simon's Christological assertions. According to Simon,

> The Logos did not become human when He came to earth: He is eternally manlike. It was He in whose image man was specifically made. He was, so to speak, the human in God. But he was not flesh; He became or was made flesh ... thus manifesting to us what He eternally was. ... He individualized His eternal humanity. ... As such the Logos was in the truest sense a man of men, the Son of man, the man.[356]

So far, so traditional; but elsewhere Simon seems to qualify this position drastically:

> The person with whom we have to do is not *actualiter* Logos, the Second Person of the Trinity; for he had become flesh, He had emptied Himself of the divine form ... Nor was He man; for though ... He was essentially akin to man, He differed from man in nature, in powers, in sub-consciousness, and in intermittent consciousness, no less than in His moral and spiritual character.[357]

It would seem that whereas in the former quotation Simon rightly thinks of Jesus in terms of Luther's Proper Man, in the latter, he first denies that 'the person with whom we have to do' is man, and then states that he is akin to man, specifying distinguishing features which seem to be partly docetic (he was 'essentially akin' to man and 'differed from man in nature, in powers, in sub-consciousness, and in intermittent consciousness') and partly what one would expect of Proper Man in contrast with sinful human beings (he differed from us in 'His moral and spiritual character'). If instead of being a psychosomatic unity Jesus is simply 'akin to man' (taking 'akin' here to mean 'similar' and not 'related by blood'), do we not hear echoes, albeit distant, of the early Christian view that the Logos took the place of the human soul in Jesus? Were that the case Jesus's real humanity would be undermined and, *a fortiori*, his ability to be the representative of humanity in the saving offering of himself would be severely compromised if not entirely annulled.

Related to the above point is Simon's immediately following dismissal of the doctrine of the eternal generation of the Son (and here we may recall the view of Samuel Chandler in his controversy with John Guyse). Simon contends that the

[355] Ibid., 233.

[356] Idem, *The Redemption of Man*, 304-5.

[357] Idem, *Reconciliation by Incarnation*, 327.

Logos was designated 'Son of God' as incarnate, and the designation of God as Father and of Jesus as Son are modal or economic: that is, 'they refer to the relation which arose in consequence of the incarnation of the Logos.'[358] Accordingly, 'there is no warrant ... for designating the Logos the Son of God, and for thus representing the relationship of the Father and Son as an eternal and immanent divine relationship.'[359] All of this is asserted without argument, and it does seem to imply that to Simon the ontological Trinity comprises 'three personal or personific factors, each eternally coexistent',[360] but none of which are Father or Son. I am uncertain whether it is fair to say that adoptionism beckons because even that would seem to require more than 'personific factors'; but it is, to say the least, all very puzzling, not least because elsewhere, as we have seen, Simon does not hesitate to speak of the eternal Father, the co-equal Son and the Holy Spirit.

Thirdly, Simon is rightly critical of post-Hegelian writers whose emphasis upon the divine immanence renders it almost indistinguishable from pantheism, and those who 'reduce God's rôle in human life to that of an almighty lover who does little more than sigh and breathe and shine forth His love ... leaving men to bask in it and assimilate it.'[361] These notes, which were not infrequently sounded by the more liberal theologians and preachers of his time, made no appeal to whatsoever to Simon. Yet we can also find him saying that 'God the supreme Personality is such, and the human personality has by God been constituted as such, that God cannot but let His supply of man's deepest needs wait on the good pleasure of man himself.'[362] This seems perilously close to the equally liberal aberration (the lineage of which may be traced back at least to Luther's fiery debate with Erasmus over the bondage of the will) which, popularly, takes the form: 'God would love to save you, but he cannot do so unless you let him.' At the very least this tale of slighted love needs to be balanced by Simon's generally clear understanding of God's prevenient grace and of that 'energizing' by the Spirit which enable a person's response to God's love.

Finally, one wonders whether Simon gives due prominence to the saving act at the Cross—that is, on the stage of human history—and this despite the fact that he does not agree with those moderns who think in terms of an ideal incarnation, and who dismiss the realistic understanding of it entertained by most Christians as 'the mythical clothing of an eternal truth.'[363] This returns us to the question of starting-points for theological reflection. I hinted earlier that to set out from sin and cosmic disorder may not be the most fruitful way of approaching the atonement. The reason is that it is those who have grasped the Gospel, who have seen what it cost God to rescue a rebellious world, who begin to see what sin really is and does. One of the ways in which Simon to some extent misses the heart of the matter emerges when he specifies the two great commandments—love God, love your neighbour as

[358] Ibid., 328.
[359] Ibid., 328.
[360] Ibid., 327.
[361] Ibid., 232.
[362] Ibid., 91.
[363] Ibid., 323.

yourself—as being the 'invisible code' within all people,[364] and when he specifies these commandments as being laid down by Christ.[365] They were, of course, endorsed by Christ in answer to the lawyer's question, but the question concerned the Jewish law. Jesus's new commandment, 'love as I have loved you' more adequately drives to the heart of the Gospel, for it requires to be construed in the light of the saving act on the Cross. It is gratitude for that act which is the motivation of Christian ethics—a motivation which transcends legal requirements, important though they may be, and requires for its outworking that 'energizing' by the Holy Spirit on which Simon laid so much emphasis. That Simon is not unaware of the point I am trying to make is clear when he writes, 'before faith can be exercised not only must Christ be preached, but the Holy Spirit must open the eyes to see Him and prepare the heart to receive Him.'[366] I simply suggest that the method suggested by this insight does not play the formative role in Simon's theory of the atonement that it might have done. In one of his sermons Simon says that Christ 'brings the assurance of forgiveness through his death,' and that it is only in his presence that we gain 'an adequate idea of our sin in relation to God.'[367] That is exactly the point. In a word, the first word of the Gospel is not sin, but grace.

V

There is some justification for Robert Mackintosh's remark that as far as his style is concerned Simon 'is a shirt-sleeved and carpet-slippered philosopher. Perhaps like others he derived from Germany a preference for shapelessness over that formal neatness which so often accompanies shallow thinking. But good style need not imply slack thought, and it is a great pity when form and substance are badly matched.'[368] Certainly Simon can offer opaque sentences in his more scholarly works, and it would seem that he was not unaware of this tendency himself: 'I am thankful for my Welsh blood—that, I think, is the reason why ideas kindle in me, but it gets me into messes.'[369] In public addresses and sermons, however, he can be bluntly to the point, homely—even colloquial,[370] except when such a phrase as 'the anthropomorphistical representations of God in the Bible'[371] slips out; and he displays a facility for apt illustration the usefulness of which would never have

---

[364] Idem, 'Sin and evil,' 42.

[365] Idem, *The Redemption of Man*, 84.

[366] Ibid., 227.

[367] Simon's sermon, 'O wretched man' (Romans 7: 24, 25) in Daniel Waters, ed., *Welshmen in English Pulpits*, 265.

[368] R. Mackintosh, *Historic Theories of Atonement*, 274.

[369] DWS, 6, n. 2, in a letter of 5 February 1898 to Principal T. Witton Davies (1851-1923), Baptist minister and Semitics scholar, for whom see DWB.

[370] See, for example, *Twice Born*, 23.

[371] DWS, 130.

occurred to Richard Alliott.[372] One of his students, Charles Denman, summed up Simon's approach to preaching: 'A text of Scripture with him was a citadel to be besieged and taken and all its innermost belongings made clear and brought into immediate touch with life.'[373] Another, James Gregory, said that 'In the pulpit, as elsewhere, he would not offer that which cost him nothing, but that which cost him much thought and much prayer.'[374] Nor did Simon overlook the pastoral dimension of ministry. Among the pieces of evidence for this claim we find a series of twelve 'Letters to the perplexed' that he contributed to *The Scottish Congregationalist* in 1889. For a practical example of Simon's pastoral kindness, if not necessarily of his wisdom, consider the case of the recalcitrant minister in Bradford who took advantage of church members by pleading poverty and extorting money from them. This was reported to Simon, who received the man sternly, intending to encourage amendment of life. But the smooth talker left Simon wearing Simon's coat and shoes, and with some of his money in his pocket.[375]

As a teacher Simon gave his students not a system of theology, but a love of theologizing. Said Powicke, 'God in Christ reconciling the world to himself was the burning centre of his thought, and he succeeded in making it the centre of thought for his men.'[376] John Massie recalled that Simon would begin his lectures with the greeting, 'Fellow students', rather than 'Gentlemen', and that if he suspected that a student had never thought for himself he would say, 'I have pitched him into the mud, and it will wake him up to work himself out of it.'[377] T. W. Pinn remembered that Simon' 'reign' as Principal 'was rather of grace than of law. He trusted largely to the honour of his students, and I do not think he was often disappointed.'[378] As an administrator Simon was punctual as to engagements, and he strove to answer letters by return of post; but his colleague, Elkanah Armitage, said that Simon 'was naturally very much of a solitary, and he shrank from the duties of leadership. ... He prepared for the College meetings with unfaltering diligence, but he had not the art of presenting his matter to the Governors in a way which at once commended it to them, and he and they alike felt sometimes the strain.'[379]

As a man, Simon loved his family. The eldest of his five children, Bertha, wrote, 'I can truthfully say that it would be very, very difficult to find a man more easy to live with than he was. He never made difficulties. ... He was naturally of a bright and hopeful disposition.'[380] He delighted in the company of children,[381] and for

---

372 Robert Bruce thought that Simon excelled rather as a professor, teacher and preacher, rather than as a writer. See DWS, 141.

373 DWS, 134. For Denman (1847-1920) see CYB, 1921, 106.

374 Ibid., 225-6.

375 DWS, 299.

376 Ibid., iii.

377 Ibid., 126.

378 Ibid., 129. For Theophilus William Pinn (1846-1924) see CYB, 1925, 156-7.

379 Ibid., 115-16; 295.

380 Ibid., 305, where the full names and dates of birth of the children are given.

recreation would make things out of wood. He lived simply and, being unconventional in dress and manner, he was somewhat ill-adapted to polite society—especially, perhaps, to the more 'sniffy' parts of Edinburgh's polite society.[382] His open-mindedness was seen in his refusal to rule matters psychic (a favourite hobby of some of the intelligensia of the day) out of court, but rather to advocate the careful investigation of them;[383] and he never gave up the struggle (I choose the term advisedly, and I refer to the title of this chapter) to get to grips with the heart of the Christian faith. In his last days, writing from Dresden to his Bradford successor, Ebenezer Griffith-Jones, he says, 'I feel as if I were in some respects [note that it is still only 'in some respects'—a sign of humility] getting to see the wood as well as the trees. I think I know better than I did both what I believed and what I did not believe.'[384]

Simon, wrote A. R. Henderson, 'made a deep impression on his men by his personal character,'[385] and there is no reason to doubt this. But perhaps Charles Denman saw more deeply into his former Principal than most: 'Dr. Simon always seemed to me like a king who never came into his own, and he was always the last man to make much of himself.'[386] Alongside this remark we may place what is surely one of Simon's most touching self-assessments, made to his friend James Ross in a letter of December 1906:

> Until now I had a notion that I saw further than most of our leaders, and that if the truth as I see it were only to be set before them they would welcome, or, at any rate, take it *ad avizandum* (is that right?). But, on the contrary, most of them leave me unnoticed, and I see than I am neither fish nor flesh nor fowl nor good red herring. I have had my day, or rather—as I can't help feeling—I have missed my day. For I have always been trying to anticipate, and the people behind did not understand, whilst the people who might perhaps understand were not there: besides that I have not been iconoclastic enough in certain ways. Excuse this egoistic diagnosis—it is probably all wrong and more egoistic than diagnostic.[387]

---

[381] See his sermon on Matthew 18:10, concerning the guardian angels of children, in *Twice Born*, ch. 13.

[382] See ibid., 186-7.

[383] DWS, 309-10.

[384] Ibid., 288.

[385] Ibid., 316.

[386] Ibid., 133; cf. 191.

[387] Ibid., 255.

CHAPTER 8

Thomas Vincent Tymms (1842–1921): Apologetic Coolness and Liberal Evangelical Warmth

T. Vincent Tymms was born in London on 5 January 1842.[1] He seriously considered devoting himself to art, but under the influence of William Landels,[2] who baptized him, he changed course and in 1861 he entered Regent's Park College, London, with a view to the Baptist ministry. The Principal of the College, Joseph Angus, had been trained at Stepney College, had graduated MA (Edinburgh) in 1837, and had won the gold medal in philosophy, and fifty guineas for an essay on 'The influence of Bacon's philosophy.'[3] In 1849 he began his tenure of forty-four years as Principal, and under his guidance the College removed to Regent's Park in 1856. The institution had been affiliated with London University since 1841, and thus Tymms was able to gain the degree of MA.[4] We may surmise that from the point of view of Tymms's academic development and his induction into believing theological liberalism, the most important thing Angus did was to persuade Benjamin Davies, who had been Principal of the College from 1844 to 1847, to return to Regent's Park from his professorship at McGill University, Montreal, in 1857.[5] For Davies, a considerable Hebraist and Old Testament critic, who had studied at Bristol Baptist College, Dublin and Glasgow, had gone on to secure a PhD at Leipzig—just the kind of thing to arouse the suspicions of Baptists determined to guard the ark of conservative biblicism. We learn that in addition to biblical studies, Davies 'took his students regularly through Ignatius, Justin, and Chrysostom, as well as Ephraim Syrus and a Syrian history of Richard I's Crusade by Bar Hebraeus.'[6] Davies served

---

[1] For Tymms (1842-1921) see BH, 1922, 274; DNCBP.

[2] For Landels (1823-1899), who ministered at Regent's Park Chapel, London (1855-83) and Dublin Street, Edinburgh (1883-93) and was President of the Baptist Union of Great Britain and Ireland in 1876, see the obituary notice contributed by Tymms to BH, 1900, 224-8.

[3] See Geo. P. Gould, *The Baptist College at Regent's Park*, 68. For Angus (1816-1902) see BH, 1903, 189-193; ODNB; Ernest A. Payne, *The Great Succession*, ch. 1.

[4] For a sketch of the College during Angus's tenure see Ernest Payne, 'Nonconformist theological education,' in E. A. Payne, ed., *Studies in History and Religion*, 240-244.

[5] For Davies (1814-1875) see BH, 1876, 341-4; DWB; ODNB.

[6] E. A. Payne, 'Nonconformist theological education,' 241 n. 2.

at the College until his death in 1875, and was thus present throughout the whole of Tymms's period of training, which ended in 1865.

On leaving College Tymms entered upon his first pastorate, at Berwick, and there he remained until 1868, when he removed to Blackburn Road Baptist church, Accrington. He was remembered in Accrington for his enthusiastic chairmanship of the Young Men's Society, but 'his stay in Accrington was too short for much effective work in ministry.'[7] On 4 July 1869 he informed the church that he had accepted the call to the Downs Chapel, Clapton, London. The formation of this church was the prompt result of Landels's 1868 appeal to the London Baptist Association for a new cause in this location. The church, at the opening of which C. H. Spurgeon was the preacher, was constituted on open communion lines: 'The immersion of believers is the only ordinance taught or practised as baptism, but we make no difference in the manner or cordiality of our reception of Christ's disciples.'[8] At Clapton Tymms became 'a shining example of the missionary-minded pastor',[9] and 'one of the most thoughtful preachers in the London pulpit, exercising a powerful influence on young men.'[10] As Ernest Payne later reflected,

> Baptist life in the last quarter of the nineteenth century is sometimes described solely in Spurgeonic terms. At 'the Downs' there was something very different. Under the brilliant ministry of Vincent Tymms the gospel was presented in terms of the most liberal thought of the day and was vigorously applied to ecclesiastical and social problems.[11]

As Payne elsewhere observed, 'it was Christian apologetics of a bold and open-minded kind which drew hearers in the early decades of the [Clapton] church's history.[12]

That Tymms was more than willing to co-operate with those outside Baptist borders is clear from the fact that in 1875 the members of the Lower Clapton Congregational Church worshipped with the church at the Downs. Their minister, the Revd Frank Soden,[13] shared the preaching with Tymms, and deacons from both churches served at the Lord's table—a clear indication that the Downs was not a strict communion church. Appropriately enough, on 17 October 1875 Tymms preached a sermon at the morning service entitled, *The First Principles of Christian Union*. His text was John 17:21, where Jesus, referring to his disciples, prays 'That they all may be one ...' Tymms begins with the confident assertion that 'No prayer

---

[7] Robert J. V. Wylie, *The Baptist Churches of Accrington and District*, 158.

[8] Quoted by Ernest A. Payne, 'The rise and decline of the Downs Chapel, Clapton,' 35.

[9] R. J. V. Wylie, *The Baptist Churches of Accrington and District*, 161.

[10] W. E. Blomfield, BH, 274. William Ernest Blomfield succeeded Tymms as President of Rawdon College, Leeds, serving from 1904 to 1922. For Blomfield (1862-1934) see BH, 1935, 312-13; J. O. Barrett, *Rawdon College*, ch. 4.

[11] E. A. Payne, *The Great Succession*, 122.

[12] Ibid., 'The rise and decline of the Downs Chapel, Clapton,' 43.

[13] For Soden (1832-1895) see CYB, 1897, 218-219.

of Christ's can ultimately remain unfulfilled.'[14] He proceeds to argue that 'Christians are bound together by a common discipleship to Christ, and not by identity of opinions';[15] that 'Christians are rightly bound together by a common purpose, and not by identity of plans';[16] and that 'Union thus based on a common faith, a common purpose, and a common spiritual life, can survive and must survive all outward changes. Even death cannot separate, and the grave cannot dismember, the unity of those who grow together thus.'[17] He concludes that when the church militant becomes the church victorious all will be perfectly one in Christ. Elsewhere he rejoiced that 'To-day there is a strong yearning ... to abandon strife, to make less of differences, and to unite more widely for fraternal intercourse and common service on the ground of a common loyalty to Jesus Christ as Lord of all.'[18]

Inter-Christian cooperation—yes, but not on any terms. At the autumn assembly of the Baptist Union which gathered in Birmingham in 1889 Tymms seconded the motion of Samuel Harris Booth,[19] the Secretary of the Union, that the Union decline the invitation of the Archbishop of Canterbury to enter into talks with a view to church union on the foundation of the Lambeth Quadrilateral of 1888: the Holy Scriptures, the Apostles' and Nicene Creeds, the Sacraments of baptism and the Lord's supper, and the historic episcopate. In their reply the Baptists said that they were in favour of fraternal intercourse, practical cooperation and organic union where the absolute authority of Christ and his teaching on doctrine worship and church government were not compromised. But they could not proceed because of their commitment to non-sacerdotal religion, their view that baptism must be preceded by repentance, and their belief that the state should not be concerned in matters of church government. They also made bold to say that they already embraced the historic episcopate as defined in the New Testament. A member of the assembly asked Tymms how this reply was consistent with the fact that the Baptists themselves were divided over terms of communion. He replied that freedom of interpretation was observed in Baptist circles and thus no compromise was involved. The reply went forward.[20]

Six years later the Baptists found themselves obliged to reply to another ecclesiastical dignitary, Pope Leo XIII, who had written a 'Letter to the English People, dated April 14th, 1895.' By now Tymms was Vice-President of the Baptist Union of Great Britain and Ireland, and it was he who, on 9 October 1895, presented 'An Address to the English People regarding the Pope's letter at the autumn assembly of the Union. Following discussion of the Letter it was resolved to recast it as 'An Open Letter to Pope Leo XIII', and this was done. Although the letter is

---

[14] T. V. Tymms, *First Principles of Christian Union*, 3.
[15] Ibid., 5.
[16] Ibid., 10.
[17] Ibid., 16.
[18] Idem, *The Christian Idea of Atonement*, 5.
[19] For Booth (d. 1898) see BH, 1903, 196-200.
[20] In this paragraph I draw upon E. A. Payne, *The Baptist Union*, 145-6.

signed by the President, J. G. Greenhough[21] and the Secretary, Samuel Harris Booth, it is clear from its style, and from the fact that he presented it, that Tymms was the principal author. The Baptists 'earnestly join in prayer to the Great Head of the Church that all who are united to Him by Faith, and are thus united to each other as members of His twice-born family, may speedily be united in visible bonds of mutual love, common service, harmonious worship, and undivided testimony to the world.'[22] The words that jump out of this eirenic sentence are 'twice-born'—the declaration that the Church comprises the saints, the believers; and 'visible'—the indication that the Baptists are not in quest of an easy, 'spiritual' unity, but a union of the gathered regenerate. All of this notwithstanding, the Baptists feel obliged to speak in love concerning the grounds on which they maintain their protest against certain Roman Catholic doctrines and practices, and they briefly sketch the historical roots of their position. It is not that 'complete unity of opinion is an indispensable condition of Christian fellowship or inter-communion,[23] but reunion with the Roman Church is rendered impossible by the maintenance of beliefs and practices which we deem subversive of the first principles of Christ.'[24] Incorporating quotations from the *Decrees of the [First] Vatican* Council, they instance the claims that when the Pope speaks *ex cathedra* what he says is infallible and irreformable; that the Pope is the successor of the apostle Peter as the head of the Church militant; that the Virgin Mary and other saints are our intercessors in heaven; that images of Mary and other saints, and relics of saints, are to be given honour and veneration; that there is a purgatory; that 'Christ instituted an order of sacrificing Priests to "offer His own body and blood"'; that 'the Lord's Supper is a propitiatory sacrifice in which bread and wine become the very body of Christ and as such are offered to God'; that 'sacramental confession and penance were instituted by Christ'; that the priest acts as judge in pronouncing absolution; that the Church has the power of granting indulgences; and that 'Baptism is necessary to salvation, and that by it we are made entirely a new creature.'[25] All of these doctrines, the Baptists declare, 'are anti-Christian', and 'the Papal assertion of authority to define the doctrine of the Universal Church, and to anathematize all who think otherwise is an attempted usurpation, which only fails to excite indignation because so manifestly futile and absurd that it rather commands our compassion.'[26] They invite the Pope to 'seek unity with us in "the Liberty wherewith Christ hath made us free"', and they refer with approval to the Archbishop of Canterbury's Pastoral Letter of 30 August 1895, in which the Pope's 'narrow and schismatic' refusal to acknowledge any

---

[21] Greenhough was Principal of Midland Baptist College, Nottingham. This College was founded by the New Connexion of General Baptists in 1798.

[22] BH, 1896, 98-9.

[23] Baptists, like all other Christian communions, were in no position to argue the contrary.

[24] BH, 1896, 99.

[25] Ibid., 99-100.

[26] Ibid., 100.

Church—not least the Eastern Churches—other than the Roman is deprecated.[27] They lament the way in which the faults divisions within the Church encourage many in their unbelief, and they 'desire to unite with all our fellow Christians in praying earnestly for that Visible Unity which will be the crowning evidence of Christianity; and will usher in the ultimate desire of Christ for mankind:- "that the world may know that Thou didst send Me and lovedst them, even as Thou lovedst Me."[28]

Reverting to the 1870s, we find that on 4 April 1875 Tymms preached at Shacklewell Chapel following the death of the minister, Dr. R. K. Brewer.[29] The sermon was published in the following year, and it furnishes us with an example of Tymms's pastoral concern and evangelistic zeal. Basing his thoughts on II Corinthians 4:15 and I Corinthians 3:21-23, he declares that God understands the sorrow of the bereaved flock and wishes to turn it to joy. He hopes that in due time they will see 'the merciful and gracious meaning of what is now a heavy blow.'[30] Certainly it is no cause of sorrow for Brewer that he should be with Jesus. Death will come to all, and 'if we are Christ's, that valley path is a part of our way home.'[31] No doubt death is, in part, a curse, but blessings follow, and 'Christ, who came to deliver us from the fear of death ... has taught us to endure the death of our bodies as the final severance of our souls from sin.'[32] If his hearers belong to Christ, 'all I have said applies to you.' Otherwise 'it is not true that all things are yours; for, apart from Him, death is not yours, but you are death's';[33] and death in Scripture often means not 'the cessation of existence [but] the absence of all conscious and blessed intercourse with God.'[34] Hence Tymms's urgent appeal: 'Now is the accepted time—now is the day of salvation.'[35]

In 1876 Tymms began a long association with the Baptist Missionary Society, and in connection with this body he prepared a report some forty-six years later on the Cameroons, from which missionaries of the Society had been expelled when Germany annexed the country in 1884. Prefixed to the report are extracts from a lecture given by Sir Harry H. Johnston to the Royal Geographical Society on 24 February 1915. Johnston wrote, 'We must not forget that the civilization of the West Cameroons was entirely due to a small but remarkable band of British Baptist Missionaries, who with their West Indian colleagues between 1842 and 1855 won over to orderly ways, to fruitful commerce, the Bantu-speaking negroes of this

[27] For this Archbishop, Edward White Benson (1829-1896), see ODNB.
[28] BH, 1896, 101.
[29] For Robert K. Brewer, Mus.Doc. (1813-1875), see BH, 1876, 336-8.
[30] T. V. Tymms in *The Battle Fought*, 78.
[31] Ibid., 81.
[32] Ibid., 82.
[33] Ibid., 86.
[34] Ibid.
[35] Ibid., 88.

region.' He hoped to see British Baptist missionaries re-established in the Cameroons before he died.[36]

Tymms writes in the context of Germany's loss of the Cameroons during the First World War. He notes that 'The Cameroons Mission had its origin in the desire of many British Christians to make some reparation to the people of Africa for the wrongs inflicted upon them by the slave trade.'[37] In words which, almost a century on, it would be impossible to write, he regrets that foreigners are so slow to recognize that 'the world empire has come, and promises to remain, with England, not because of her naval and military might, but mainly because her sway means liberty of life and thought, and is founded on the willinghood and loyalty of those she rules.'[38]

In 1877 Tymms became immersed, so to speak, in the controversy over Bible translation, not least as this affected the Indian mission field. The focus of the debate was on the mode of baptism. Matters came to a head when some paedobaptist missionaries of the Calcutta auxiliary of the Bible Society who favoured sprinkling or pouring over immersionist language appealed to the Society to acknowledge their practice in the translation of βαπτιζω. When the Society responded with flexibility, the Baptist missionaries felt they had no option but to establish their own Bible Translation Society. The schism was long-lasting, with the Baptists being accused of denominational sectarianism. Eventually some among a younger generation of Baptist ministers felt that the issue had been blown up out of all proportion, but Tymms rose to defend his denomination from the charge of selfishness. He insisted on the antiquity of the immersionist construction of βαπτιζω, repudiated the Bible Society's proposal that the term be left untranslated on the ground that this would deprive the Indian populace of a standard against which to judge the teaching of the missionaries, and declared that a 'Christian union based on a conspiracy to hide a word of our Master's instructions' was not worth maintaining.[39]

In 1881 Tymms served as President of the London Baptist Association, and at the meeting of the Baptist Union in Liverpool in 1882, the last Union meeting that C. H. Spurgeon attended, he delivered an address on 'Evangelistic Work in Large Towns', in the course of which he argued that 'the spirit of the Cross was often manifested outside recognised Christian circles.' He illustrated his point by reference to the way in which British soldiers had tended to the wounds of their Egyptian enemies, and concluded, 'Truly, a little of the Nazarene was there in many a rude soldier who confessed Him not, and amidst those scenes of carnage, I read a prophecy of victory for Him who first said: "If thine enemy hunger, feed him; if he thirst, give

---

[36] For Henry Hamilton Johnston (1858-1927) see ODNB. He was an explorer and colonial administrator who, though an agnostic, valued the work of Christian missionaries as agents of evolution construed in social Darwinian terms.

[37] T.V. Tymms, *The Cameroons*, 6.

[38] Ibid., 24.

[39] *Baptist Translation Society Occasional Paper*, no II, 1877, 2, quoted by J. H. Y Briggs, *The English Baptists of the 19th Century*, to whose account of the controversy, ibid., 55-60, I am indebted.

him a drink."' We learn that 'As Mr. Spurgeon listened the tears rolled down his cheeks, and he afterwards commended the paper by describing it as "All good."'[40]

In 1885 Tymms's widely-received book, *The Mystery of God* appeared, and to this I shall return in the following section of this chapter. In 1886 his first wife died. He subsequently remarried, and he and his second wife had one son. In 1891 he accepted the call to the Presidency of Rawdon College, Leeds, and left the Downs Chapel with a thriving membership of 576, a Band of Hope, a literary society, a gymnasium, and much else besides; and a daughter church at Woodberry Down. In the same year he published *The Beauty of God*, a volume comprising the last three sermons he preached at Clapton. The first is on the theme of the book's title, and the text is Titus 2:11, 'For the grace of God that bringeth salvation hath appeared to all men.' Tymms invites his hearers to consider that the thought of beauty lies at the heart of the word 'grace', and says, 'I have striven to make men see in Christ the glory of God, the beauty of the just God and Saviour.'[41] 'From the first day I stood in this pulpit until now,' he continues,

> I have desired to burn away from every heart that obscuring veil of pagan thought which first divides a wrathful justice to the Father and a tender mercy to Christ, and then represents the Son as dying to soothe the anger and satisfy the relentless demands of the Father. Such unholy and revolting ideas are the leaven of heathenism, not the unleavened bread of Christian truth.[42]

He then introduces Paul, who represents Christ as 'Bringing salvation to all men.' Salvation is from ignorance, lies, the woes of humanity, evil passions, spiritual sorrows, and 'that dreadful looking for death and judgment which tore and rent the souls of men and sunk them down as helpless victims of priestcraft and superstition.'[43] The appearance of divine beauty in Christ educates, cultures and disciplines us, and 'God would have us all beautified with salvation';[44] but 'The beauty of the Lord can only come upon us as it came on Moses in the Mount, when we meet Him face to face.'[45]

The second sermon is on 'Religion.' Tymms reviews a number of definitions of religion, including that of Schleiermacher, 'one of the most fruitful thinkers of this century', [46] namely, that religion is a feeling of absolute dependence. In his own view, religion is 'The activity of those spiritual powers in man by which he recognises himself as related to a supreme Being (or Beings).'[47] This definition, he thinks, is broad enough to include those who are mighty in faith and those who are

---

[40] See W. Y. Fullerton, *C. H. Spurgeon*, 310. Fullerton quotes W. J. Avery in *The Baptist Union Magazine*, 1892, 61.

[41] T. V. Tymms, *The Beauty of God*, 8.

[42] Ibid., 8.

[43] Ibid., 10.

[44] Ibid., 11.

[45] Ibid., 12.

[46] Ibid., 14.

[47] Ibid., 15.

not; and it enables us to distinguish between theology and religion and morality and religion: 'Jesus did not come merely to teach theology, ... He came to correct and purify and complete man's ideas of God.'[48] Nor did he come to teach morality, but to be a quickening spirit. Everyone, Tymms says, has a religious faculty, and we are obliged to stir it up, finding help supremely from Christ. He concludes by exhorting his hearers to be like Christ, 'who, living in the form of God, took upon Him the form of a servant, and at last became obedient unto death, even the death of the Cross.'[49]

The final sermon, 'Parting words', contrasts the words of Moses in Deuteronomy 31:27 with those of Paul in Philippians 2:12-13:

> For I know thy rebellion, and thy stiff neck: behold, while I am yet alive with you this day, ye have been rebellious against the Lord; and how much more after my death?

> Wherefore, my beloved, as ye have always obeyed, not as in my presence only, but now much more in my absence, work out your own salvation with fear and trembling. For it is God which worketh in you both to will and to do of his good pleasure.

Paul, says Tymms, reverses every line of Moses's dirge as he reflects upon the faithful Christians of Philippi, who are to be emulated by the Christians of Clapton. Tymms recalls that his first sermon was on the text, 'As I was with Moses so I will be with thee; I will not fail thee nor forsake thee.' These words have strengthened and comforted him ever since.[50] But as God is working in us, so we must also work for ourselves, as Paul says. In the expectation that its members will rise to the challenge, Tymms prays God's blessing on his flock.

On leaving Clapton, Tymms and his second wife removed to Rawdon College, where, in succession to T. G. Rooke, who had died in December 1890 at the age of fifty-two,[51] he served as President until 1904, while Mrs. Tymms gave invaluable assistance in the domestic administration of the institution. Tymms was already known to the Rawdon community through his role as examiner in Apologetics, Inspiration and The Philosophy of Christian Theism.[52] The *Report of the Committee of the Northern Baptist Education Society* for 1891-92 records that Tymms was now President and Tutor in Theology. The steps taken to secure his services are described, the fact that after his election the Committee had discovered that Tymms was Rooke's hoped-for successor is noted, and the *Report* continues thus:

---

[48] Ibid., 22.

[49] Ibid., 26.

[50] Ibid., 29.

[51] For Rooke (d. 1890), see BH, 1892, 130-1.

[52] *Report of the Committee of the Northern Baptist Education Society*, 1888-19, 18-19. I am grateful to the Reverend Principal Richard Kidd of Northern Baptist College for permission to examine the Rawdon College records which are housed at the College.

> Mr. Tymms was well known as a man of great ability—in the prime of life, with a large and lengthened experience of the ministerial office, and endowed with special aptitudes for teaching and influence in dealing with young men; and it was believed that he would find in educational work a congenial sphere of consecrated Christian labour.[53]

It is further noted that Tymms's Presidential duties were to be reduced so that he could continue to maintain 'his close association with our denominational life.'[54]

One year on the Committee reported that 'Never has the presidential work of the College been more efficient or more fruitful than in the Session just ended, and the Committee heartily congratulated Mr. Tymms, and the friends of the College, upon a success which equals their most sanguine expectations.'[55] In his own first report as President Tymms said that 'My first session at Rawdon has necessarily been a time of hard and imperfect work; but it has been very happily spent. Mr. Medley has been an invaluable friend and adviser.'[56] The following year Tymms said that following a return of health he had preached on most Sundays in the year, adding that such services 'preserve a tutor's soul from becoming coldly academical, by keeping him in touch with the living church of today.'[57]

Of Tymms the President it was said that 'He was a man of powerful and independent mind, whose aim was to encourage original thought among his students rather than to prepare them for examinations.'[58] He was not unduly enamoured of the structured courses and examinations of the Senatus Academicus, which body Rawdon had joined in 1881, but the College remained in membership until the Senatus was disbanded in 1900.[59] His Rawdon colleagues were the long-serving and greatly loved William Medley, of whom it was said that 'He scarcely teaches, he reveals';[60] and David Glass, who arrived at Rawdon in 1892 from the Airdrie pastorate and remained there until 1936. He like Tymms before him, had been influenced by William Landels though in Glass's case this was during Landels's ministry at Dublin Street Church, Edinburgh.[61] Archibald Duff of the Yorkshire United Independent College, conducted senior classes in Hebrew.[62]

---

53 *Report of the Committee*, 1891-92, 2, 12.

54 Ibid., 12.

55 *Report*, 1892-3, 9.

56 Ibid., 15.

57 *Report*, 1893-94, 15.

58 J. O. Barrett, *Rawdon College*, 30.

59 See further, Alan P. F. Sell, *Philosophy, Dissent and Nonconformity*, 128-132.

60 For Medley (1837-1908), the grandson of the hymn writer, Samuel Medley, see BH, 1909, 477-9; DNCBP. Trained at Regent's Park College, he gained the London M.A. and the gold medal in philosophy, and also studied under the Old Testament specialist, Georg Heinrich August Ewald (1803-1875) in Göttingen and the Reformation historian Jean-Henri Merle d'Aubigné (1794-1872) in Geneva.

61 For Glass (1862-1942) see BH, 1943, 282.

62 For Duff see ch. 7 above, n. 114.

In 1896 Tymms was President of the Baptist Union of Great Britain and Ireland. In this connection he prepared a two-part address entitled, 'Authority: true and false.' Part One was delivered at the Spring Assembly meeting at Bloomsbury Chapel, London on 28 April; Part Two was heard by those gathered for the Autumn Assembly at Broadmead Chapel, Bristol, on 7 October. Although, as Tymms admits, there are many aspects of this large subject to which he cannot attend, his is an outstanding example of a Presidential Address, characterized by as it is by historical allusions, theological depth and evangelical passion. It is, in effect, an outline of a Christian philosophy of history. He begins by showing that despair at the apparent breakdown of society owing to the slighting of authority is nothing new: 'pessimism is an old disease';[63] and then he turns to the definition of 'authority'. Whereas 'Most writers ... are content to trace it to its Latin derivation *auctor*, which signifies the originator or creator of anything ... I venture to think that there is more light for us in the New Testament term εξουσια ... which we associate with mastery [but which] signified originally the liberty to do a thing. It ... comes to mean both ability and right to act in a given way.'[64] Thus 'true authority always includes might and right', and 'the love of liberty ... is found to spring from a consciousness of authority to judge the pretensions of all governors, coupled with a sense of power and right to live a large and full life without restraints except those imposed by righteous law.'[65] So it is that

> We Baptists repudiate the lordship of one over all, and therefore own no Pontiff on the Tiber. We reject also the lordship of a few over the many, and hence decline the pastoral sway of those Anglican Bishops who lift 'their mitred fronts' in courts and Parliament beside the Thames. But let us not deceive ourselves. We are not despisers of authority. On the contrary, we esteem it very highly, so highly that we are not prepared to relinquish it ourselves. Our claim of liberty is not a mere impatient refusal of all government, but is our assertion of personal responsibility. The very fount and spring of our Church polity lies, not in lawlessness but in the consciousness of individual authority to live each of us his own life of thought and action without any feudal superior between his soul and God.[66]

Tymms proceeds to argue that 'the primary source of man's consciousness of authority must be found in his origin as a spiritual being created in the image of God, and made expressly to have dominion over Nature.'[67] In explication of this he submits two propositions. The first is that 'the ideas of Christ directly and necessarily tend to develop the consciousness of personal authority in man.'[68] Christ's root idea, he says, is that of the Fatherhood of God with its correlative, the brotherhood of humanity: 'Am I God's Son? Does He uplift me from the dust and

[63] BH, 1897, 64.
[64] Ibid., 66.
[65] Ibid.
[66] Ibid., 66-7.
[67] Ibid., 68.
[68] Ibid.

bid me stand without quailing in His presence? Then to what man or body of men shall I cringe?'[69] The second proposition is that 'the conduct which Christ exemplified and inspires directly tends to secure authority for his disciples.'[70] We are to love and serve all, and 'Such service is the most potent weapon of conquest.'[71]

Sadly, however, 'Every great truth which Christ taught has had its counterfeit.'[72] Thus ambitious ministers have served their fellows not out of love, but from a lust for power, as may be seen from the struggles of some to gain ecclesiastical control over popular education. Conversely, throughout Christian history some Christians have first sought authority so that having gained it they may do good. Thus the story of the Roman Church, but that Church is not alone: 'Every Church which has sought or accepted political power as an instrument for the furtherance of religious plans has been a partaker of her fault, and in some measure of her plagues.' For example, the Church of England 'is weaker than she ought to be to-day, because her clergy stand to minister as privileged officials of the State.'[73]

In the second part of his address Tymms declares his confidence that 'a kingdom of Christly souls is growing up and has the promise of the world for its possession; that this authority will come as the natural crown of a loving ministry, and can never be grasped as a prize ambitiously pursued.'[74] He proceeds to offer Old and New Testament illustrations of the mingling of severity and tenderness. Jesus, for example, who said, 'My peace I leave with you,' also said, 'I came not to send peace, but a sword.' So it is that through history 'the same light of heavenly truth and love which cheers the mourner, revives the contrite, heals the wounded spirit, subdues the warlike to become like little children and which beautifies the meek with salvation, has also served to break up haughty nationalities, to shiver guilty kingdoms like a potter's vessel smitten with an iron rod.'[75] Tymms thus comes to his third proposition, 'That the ideas of Christ and the conduct he enjoins inevitably tend to shatter all selfish forms of authority among men.'[76] He illustrates his point at some length from the Bible and world history. He observes, for example, that so refined a person as Marcus Aurelius was impelled to persecute Justin Martyr because he saw that if the new religion succeeded his own authority was doomed.[77] As he develops his argument, Tymms is led to propound a frequently overlooked, paradox, namely, that 'Christian Altruism has done much to shatter despotisms and all kinds

---

[69] Ibid., 69.

[70] Ibid., 70.

[71] Ibid.

[72] Ibid., 71.

[73] Ibid., 75.

[74] Ibid., 88.

[75] Ibid., 91. Cf. idem, *The Christian Idea of Atonement*, 160, 280.

[76] Ibid., 92.

[77] Elsewhere Tymms makes the same point in more devotional style when he writes of Jesus, 'Without knowing how it happened, the sheep and the goats divided themselves at His voice. The chaff and the wheat were separated by the breath of His mouth.' *The Private Relationships of Christ*, 29.

of selfish organizations by an undesigned, but inevitable though almost undetected stimulation of Egoism.'[78] Thus, 'in making a new family of saviours, Christ inevitably raised an army of warriors against evil systems and evil men.'[79] If some adduce the French Revolution as a counter example because of the widespread lack of Christian influence in relation to it, this is only because the Huguenots had been banished before the upheaval came.

'The greatest work of the age,' Tymms declares, is 'the education of men for authority according to the method of Christ.'[80] Hence the importance of the Christian ministry, for

> that work which has the sanctification of man's spirit for its object has proved itself more practical and more potent for the improvement of man's environment than any labour expended directly on the environment itself. ... So if the men who toil in humble offices of Christian ministry were to renounce their tasks and rush into political and social struggles, as less remote from daily life, the world would soon miss their efforts. ... I am emboldened to say to my brothers, who have received a Divine ordination and human recognition as workers in Spirit, let us be doers of this one thing and never let us be drawn aside to so engage in the very best of other services to men as to subtract from wholeheartedness in this.[81]

He recognizes that 'A spiritual ministry is lightly esteemed in the world, but, next to Christ, it is God's greatest gift to man.'[82] As for God's greatest gift, to see the magnitude of that we contemplate the Cross:

> On that day everything contrary to man's liberty and progress was nailed to the cross, all evil principalities and authorities were spoiled; in that hour of shame the Victim Lamb triumphed openly, and from that cross He ascended on high, carrying captivity captive. From that day all things, and specially those which seem to be against us, have been working together to give authority on earth to men in whom Christ reigns.[83]

In 1897 Tymms published a paper on 'Christian theism', to which I shall refer shortly; and in the same year the University of St. Andrews honoured him with its DD. This drew the following expression of pleasure from the Rawdon College Committee: 'Our English Universities do not bestow the degree of Doctor of Divinity even upon the most eminent of Free Churchmen, and the fact that it is only sparingly conferred, *honoris causa*, by the Scotch Universities, enhances its value.'[84]

---

[78] BH, 1897, 97.
[79] Ibid.
[80] Ibid., 104.
[81] Ibid., 105, 106.
[82] Ibid., 107.
[83] Ibid., 108.
[84] *Report*, 1896-97, 10.

Tymms served the churches and the Yorkshire Association in ways other than by preaching, not least in arbitrating the Winton Street, Leeds, church case. We learn that 'both pastors of a divided cause had resigned and the buildings were in a dangerous state. Tymms it was who produced the solution of amalgamation with the North Street Chapel.'[85] He did not hesitate to stand up for his students when necessary. Thus, for example, in one of his annual reports he says that while the students do not preach for money, and will conduct services even if no fee is offered, they 'are not in the position of business men who preach without needing or desiring a recompense. These are very obvious truths, but they are too often overlooked.'[86]

In 1901, suffering from chronic catarrh and rheumatism, Tymms was advised to spend the winter in a warm, dry climate. He offered his resignation to the College, but this was refused, and Medley assumed charge of the College whilst Tymms and his wife went for a period to Egypt.[87] Ten years previously an attempt had been made to unite Rawdon with Manchester Baptist College, but it had failed, as did a further attempt during 1898-1899.[88] Whilst in Egypt Tymms proposed the amalgamation of the three Baptist theological colleges, Manchester, Midland and Rawdon. The latter two had already been cooperating since 1899, with Midland taking students for preliminary studies, and Tymms suggested that the amalgamated institution should be located in Manchester. Rawdon College carried a debt of £1680/0/0, and Tymms hoped that the Manchester College's original foundation on a strict communion basis no longer constitute an obstacle to union. Subsequently, however, Tymms feared that such a union would result in the curtailment of freedom in theological teaching, so he cooled towards his own idea, and sent a letter from Egypt in which he expressed his reservations.[89] In his absence the amalgamation scheme was approved, and on his return from Egypt Tymms said privately that his health would not permit his removing to Manchester, and reiterated his reservations concerning the scheme. He refused to permit his views to be discussed with the College committee or at the Annual Meeting of the College. It was, however, recorded that he had declined a Chair of Theology in the united College,[90] and that the union scheme had failed. Tymms himself reported that while he had intended to retire on his return from Egypt in order to devote himself to literary work, it had been pointed out to him that this would cause many problems now that the proposed amalgamation of colleges had foundered. Accordingly, he would remain until 2004, and would see through the centennial celebrations of the Rawdon's predecessor college, Horton, in that year.

It is impossible to isolate one cause of the failure of the colleges to unite. Diverse and mixed motives appear to have been at work. Thus, for example, it would

---

[85] Ian Sellers, ed., *Our Heritage*, 70.

[86] *Report*, 1899-1900, 12.

[87] Ibid., 1900-01, 11. 14.

[88] For a full account of attempts at union see Peter Shepherd, *The Making of a Northern Baptist College*, 130-150.

[89] See J. O. Barrett, *Rawdon College*, 32; cf. P. Shepherd, op.cit, 142.

[90] *Report*, 1902-03, 22. Cf. Charles Rignal, *Manchester Baptist College*, 230-231.

seem that while some on the Manchester side were still concerned as to whether their strict communion principles could be satisfactorily accommodated within a united college, the paramount cause of the failure to unite was a re-enactment of the Wars of the Roses in denominational terms, with those on either side of the Pennines unwilling to lose the independence of their ministerial training arrangements. In the event, the union between Manchester and Rawdon colleges did not come about until 1964.[91]

The College *Report* for 1903-04 contains the Committee's congratulations to Tymms on his appointment as Angus Lecturer at Regent's Park College,[92] as well as an expression of gratitude to Dr. and Mrs. Tymms for all that they had cone for the College over the past thirteen years.[93] In the following year Tymms was made an honorary member of the Committee.[94]

Tymms's Angus Lectures, delivered in 1903, were published under the title, *The Christian Idea of Atonement* (1904), and to these I shall return. Also in 1904 there appeared his article on 'Independents and Congregationalists' in *The Protestant Dictionary.* Three years later he published a volume of sermons on *The Private Relationships of Christ.* He focuses particularly on Jesus's family, his childhood, youth, and on to the Cross, resurrection and Pentecost and beyond. He does not hesitate to make polemical points on the basis of the texts he is considering. Thus, for example, when considering whether or not Mary had other children and Jesus had brothers, he writes,

> [I]t is contended by Romanists, and by many others, that the brethren of Jesus were the children of Joseph by a former marriage. This ... is a gratuitous assumption, and would never have been hear of but for the prevalence of a morbid asceticism which dishonours marriage, and for the superstition which magnifies Mary as the mother of God and insists upon her perpetual virginity. Apart from these vain imaginings there is no pretext for the theory that the brethren of Christ were not Mary's children.[95]

Not surprisingly, he has no patience with those 'fables, more like those of the Arabian Nights than the chaste and solemn stories of the Gospels, [which] prepared the way for that apotheosis which in Roman mythology has raised [Mary] to a throne superior to our Lord's.'[96] Less controversially, he has a word for preachers:

> Preachers of the Gospel do well to set before their hearers the brightest prospects of those who follow Christ: in depicting the believer's destiny they may dip their brush in heavenly colours; but practical, sober-minded thoughts of daily trial and

---

[91] See David Milner, 'The last days at Rawdon and the formation of Northern Baptist College.'

[92] *Report*, 1904-04, 10.

[93] Ibid., 11.

[94] Ibid., 1904-05, 13.

[95] T. V. Tymms, *The Private Relationships of Christ*, 76-7.

[96] Ibid., 174; cf. ibid., 8.

duty are as essential to the maintenance of high courage and indomitable patience as are rapturous visions of success.[97]

His reflections upon Jesus's leading of worship in the home leads Tymms to offer constructive suggestions to those who face the challenge of maintaining and leading family worship.[98] To those who suppose that it was easier for Jesus's contemporaries to respond to him that it is for those who live centuries after him, Tymms replies in Simon-like fashion, 'Flesh and blood cannot reveal the Son of God. They did not reveal Him to His brothers. The sense perceptions we crave as a help to faith were their greatest hindrance. If we believe not the written story ... neither should we have believed while as yet He was not risen from the dead, and so declared to be the Son of God.'[99] At the heart of Tymms's message is the Cross of Christ which 'has irradiated the world with light, and is filling the moral universe with songs of everlasting joy. Out of its bitterness have flowed the sweetest waters of consolation.'[100]

Tymms's last major work, *The Evolution of Infant Baptism and Related Ideas* appeared in 1913, and I shall offer an account of this shortly. Tymms's contribution as a published, if not an enduring, hymn writer merits brief mention. John Julian notes four hymns written between 1866 and 1882, which were published in the *Supplement* to the Baptist *Psalms and Hymns* and *Psalms and Hymns for School and Home*, and a fifth which appeared in *Good Words* in 1892 and in an altered version in the *Sunday School Hymnary* of 1905.[101] The *Baptist Hymn Book* of 1962 retained just one of Tymms's hymns with its first line, 'Our day of praise is ended', altered from 'Another Sabbath ended.'

Vincent Tymms died on 25 May 1921. His most appropriate memorial is surely the words of his former Rawdon students: His students wrote of him that 'He ever placed the highest ideals before us as students and preachers. He taught us to face difficulties honestly and fearlessly. We knew and loved him in the class-room as a great-minded, great-hearted and honoured friend.'[102]

I

Of Vincent Tymms it was said that 'In no sphere of theological science was he more at home than in that of apologetics. He possessed absolute candour, the impartiality of a great judge and the sympathy of a mind which had fought doubts and come out stronger.'[103] At a time when the presses were awash with agnosticism, materialism, pantheism and sundry other 'isms' that disturbed or tempted the devout, it is not

---

[97] Ibid., 18.

[98] Ibid., 84-7.

[99] Ibid., 118.

[100] Ibid., 179.

[101] J.Julian, *A Dictionary of Hymnology*, 1190, 1610.

[102] Quoted, BH, 1922, 274.

[103] BH, 1922, 274.

surprising that Tymms was by no means the only divine of his period who rose to the apologetic challenge.[104] If the Scot, Robert Flint, towered above all other exponents of the discipline in erudition, Tymms could hold his own in terms of crisp analysis and incisive wit. His most substantial work in the category under review is *The Mystery of God* (1885), which ran to a third edition. In this book he covers a wide territory, for not only does he slay the foes of materialism and pantheism to his own satisfaction, and review the cosmological and teleological arguments for the existence of God, but he also discusses the 'mystery' of evil, the 'evidences' of miracle and the fulfilment of prophecy, the reliability of the biblical texts, and concludes with chapters on the person and resurrection of Christ and the life of faith.

In approaching this book it is of more than ordinary importance that we pay heed to its subtitle, 'A Consideration of some Intellectual Hindrances to Faith', and to the Introduction, in which Tymms clearly states his objectives. We may say with confidence that Tymms's primary stimulus in writing his book is, in the words of Paul which appear on the title page and which give him his title, 'That they may know the Mystery of God, even Christ, in Whom are all the treasures of wisdom and knowledge hidden' (Colossians 2:3). Indeed, the book's origin lay in meetings which Tymms held in the winter of 1883 for a group of young men who wished 'to examine what may be called the intellectual foundations of the Christian faith.'[105] As to his method:

> It has been my endeavour to dispose at the outset of the most fundamental objections to Christianity, and thence to ascend step by step, leaving no necessary foothold unsecured, until at length objections which proceed from Theists who are 'almost Christians' are considered.[106]

But Tymms is not interested in the root and branch demolition of his intellectual foes. On the contrary, 'I have borne in mind a secret whispered to me by a distinguished Queen's Counsel, who said, "I win my cases by admissions",' and he adds, 'A full review of Christian controversy would show that more damage has been done to faith by indiscreet contentions for dubious and non-essential points than by any hostile attacks. The fate of Christianity has frequently been staked by its advocates upon the defence of certain positions which have eventually proved indefensible.'[107] This error 'has been several times repeated in our own day,' and for this reason, 'I have not contended for all that I believe, but by making occasional

---

[104] See, for example, Alan P. F. Sell, *Defending and Declaring the Faith*, which includes a chapter on Flint (1838-1910), for whom see also DNCBP; DSCHP; ODNB; WWW, 1897-1915; Donald Macmillan, *The Life of Robert Flint*, which contains a chapter by John Lindsay on Flint's theism; S. R. Obitts, *The Thought of Robert Flint*; and Alan P. F. Sell, *Philosophy, Dissent and Nonconformity*, ch. 5.

[105] T. V. Tymms, *The Mystery of God*, vii.

[106] Ibid., viii.

[107] Ibid., viii-ix.

loans to the other side, have striven to show that the Christian faith will not be injuriously affected if many current controversies are ultimately decided in a way that the majority of Christian advocates neither desire nor expect.'[108] Undeterred by the fluttering in certain Baptist dovecotes that such a stance would prompt, Tymms hopes that people will realise that 'God's gift does not hang on grammar, and that there is no valid reason why we should postpone faith in the oracles of God until every vexatious dispute about their literary vehicle has been terminated.'[109]

Tymms promises to give his reasons for thinking Christ divine, but makes it clear that 'I offer no metaphysical theory of the Incarnation, and give no theological opinions respecting the mode of His work as man's Redeemer.'[110] He further points out that the most prevalent hindrances to faith are not intellectual, they are moral; they concern the struggle between conscience and inclination. In any case, 'The life of faith is not a mere assent of the intellect to certain propositions, and it cannot therefore be produced by logic.'[111] But there cannot be a conviction-less faith, and convictions may be stated in the form of propositions which may be denied or affirmed by the reason:

> Moral hindrances can only be removed by moral suasion or discipline. Spiritual hindrances can only be removed by spiritual influences. But intellectual doubts which relate to matters of historic fact, physical possibility, or rational probability, can only be removed by appeals to the understanding. When the mind has been convinced, a man may still be destitute of personal trust in God, but a channel will be opened through which appeals to his conscience and affections may afterwards be made.[112]

Tymms's first chapter comprises his discussion of materialism. He sets outs from the words of Jesus, 'God is a spirit', a Father who seeks the reverence and love of his offspring—all of which implies that God-human relations are possible. But this is precisely what materialism denies, with its doctrine that there is no spirit, there is matter only. He admits that while 'In this dogmatic shape the creed has comparatively few professors',[113] the materialistic tendency has a history which reached back to the Bible itself. The preacher to whom we owe Ecclesiastes, for example, 'found Materialism a very gloomy creed, paralysing all endeavours after righteousness, mingling wormwood with every cup of pleasure, and throwing a cold shadow over the beauty of nature and the whole course of human life from birth to death.'[114] Tymms proceeds to sketch the course of the materialistic tendency from Greek and Roman writers to his contemporary, Professor Tyndall who, though not a professed materialist, quoted Lucretius with approval in his celebrated Belfast address

---

108 Ibid., ix.
109 Ibid.
110 Ibid., ix.
111 Ibid., x.
112 Ibid., xi.
113 Ibid., 2.
114 Ibid., 3.

delivered at a meeting of the British Association for the Advancement of Science in 1874: 'Nature is seen to do all things spontaneously of herself, without the meddling of the gods.'[115] Tymms further notes that modern materialists are necessarily necessitarians, for 'they say that all [man's] passions and thoughts are mere effects of organized substance.'[116] He finds it paradoxical that some of those who most loudly shrieked 'Liberty' during the French Revolution subscribed to views which denied freewill. His concurs so far with Herbert Spencer,[117] whom he paraphrases as holding that

> There is ... no way of accounting for a first motion, and no hope of perpetuity for the existing order of nature, apart from a self-sufficient and originative Power, undiscoverable by physical methods, but which, whether Knowable of Unknowable by other means, is a necessity of thought.[118]

But this is a confession of inability to explain the existing order of nature, and so materialism breaks down. Even if materialism could be salvaged it would provide no basis for morality, for if it be true that an organism cannot govern itself but is governed 'by the law of its material combination, ... There is no room for the word "ought" in a Materialist's vocabulary.'[119] As for those thinkers who await a complete and unbroken theory of evolution, 'it needs no prophet to predict that it will not be stated, or utterable in the terms of matter, nor exclude the operations of the Divine or the human will.'[120] Tymms concludes by observing that from the failure of materialism we may not infer the viability of Christian ideas of God. The task of establishing Christianity's credentials remains.

Having disposed of materialism to his own satisfaction, Tymms turns next to pantheism which he defines as 'a theory of the universe which regards the whole of it as God.'[121] It follows that God 'has no existence except in the system of Nature, and therefore He is not conscious, except and in so far as we and other conscious beings are parts of God.'[122] Tymms discusses specimens of pantheism as found in eastern religions and in Greek thought from Xenophanes onwards, and then argues that modern pantheism owes much of its impetus and prevalence to Spinoza and, unintentionally, to Hegel who, shunning Spinoza's originating substance as an adequate explanation of the universe, revived the notion of becoming and posited thought as the ultimate reality which conflated being and becoming. [It is somewhat surprising to note that Tymms does not refer to Kant's critical epistemology, which was transformed by Fichte, Schelling and Hegel into a metaphysic centring in a

---

[115] Ibid., 12. For John Tyndall (1820-1893) see ODNB.
[116] Ibid., 15.
[117] For Spencer (1820-1902) see ODNB.
[118] T. V. Tymms, *The Mystery of God*, 26.
[119] Ibid., 33.
[120] Ibid., 34.
[121] Ibid., 36.
[122] Ibid., 38.

posited subject-object unity—a gift to pantheists of the idealist sort]. Modern German pantheism, Tymms continues, reveals the descent of that doctrine into pessimism. This is shown in the writings of Schopenhauer, who affirms that will is the ultimate principle, or substance, of all things. Inherently unconscious, will becomes conscious as it strives for life, and it will have no peace until it renounces this will to live. Tymms's general conclusion is that 'Whether we call the whole universe Matter, or Spirit, or God, if it be all one substance, with no Being reigning over it and administering His own Will as Law, there is no moral responsibility. If we are all fragments of God, He cannot find fault with us. We are of necessity what we are, and can be no other.'[123] By contrast, Christianity 'is the only system which teaches the abiding reality and sacred worth of life, yet bids man sacrifice it cheerfully for the sake of righteousness, because to lay down life in such a cause is to gain life more abundantly. Of course, the beauty and desirability of such a faith is no sure evidence of its truth.'[124] From the fact that while raising metaphysical and ethical issues Tymms almost entirely steers clear of religious and theological ones—the personality of the divine and the importance of the Creator-creature distinction, for example—we can see that he is adhering to his policy of not introducing matters to which his opponents would turn a deaf ear on principle.[125]

Proceeding to theism, Tymms correctly observes that while 'theism' is synonymous with 'deism', the latter term is more conveniently reserved to that eighteenth-century variety of anti-Christian thought which held a personal God to be a conclusion of natural reason but repudiated the need and possibility of any revelation beyond that found in nature.[126] By 'a personal God' the theists with whom Tymms is concerned

> mean a Living Being who is not, like man, bounded by any bodily organism. ... They regard Him as uncreated, but able to originate and frame an objective universe ... They believe that to some extent this God is revealed in His works, yet is no more to be confounded with them than an architect with his building, or a father with his children. ... If these ideas be called 'anthropomorphic', that ponderous term may well be accepted by Theists as a commendation rather than a reproach.[127]

Tymms surmizes that to most minds such ideas as these seem self-evident, and he cites John Stuart Mill and David Hume as two ostensibly anti-theistic writers who

---

[123] Ibid., 57-8.

[124] Ibid., 67.

[125] Others did not hesitate to rebuke the pantheists from every conceivable angle. See, for example, Alan P. F. Sell, *Enlightenment, Ecumenism, Evangel*, ch. 7.

[126] As a general point of distinction this may be allowed, though eighteenth-century deism was more varied, and hence more interesting, than is here suggested. Unlike some nineteenth-century writers, Tymms does not foist upon his eighteenth-century predecessors the view that God was so distinct from the world as to be no longer immanent within it. See further, Alan P. F. Sell, *Enlightenment, Ecumenism, Evangel*, ch. 4.

[127] T. V. Tymms, *The Mystery of God*, 74.

could not altogether shake off the theistic possibility. The former wrote, 'It must be allowed that in the present state of our knowledge the adaptations in Nature afford a large balance of probability in favour of creation by intelligence';[128] while following the death of his mother Hume said that 'Though I throw out my speculations to entertain the learned and metaphysical world, yet in other things I do not think so differently from the rest of the world as you imagine.'[129]

Tymms discusses in turn the cosmological and teleological arguments for the existence of God, and I shall exemplify his approach by reference to his criticisms of Mill. Mill, he says, holds that within nature we observe changes which result from previous changes, and this is consistent with his view that we know only phenomena. But in the same breath he postulates 'a permanent element in nature', at which point Tymms cannot restrain himself:

> Surely this is not very lucid! In one paragraph we are told that 'changes are always the effects of previous changes', and then directly afterwards all these changes are traced up to an unchanging 'permanent element'! What would Mill have said about a village preacher who ventured to talk like that?[130]

Tymms lays further charges against Mill in order to reveal his inconsistencies and then, by way of a bridge to the arguments from design, he argues that a First Cause is a necessity of thought, and that it must possess power, will and wisdom. Indeed, 'even the language of Darwin has no meaning unless Nature is the work of One who adapts means to ends, with foresight and wisdom.'[131] He expounds the argument by reference to such standard and oft-repeated illustrations as the organs of the human body by way of showing that the way in which these are adapted to their several purposes requires a 'Divine Artificer.' And when Mill objects that the argument concludes only to a former, not a creator, of the substance of the universe, Tymms retorts that 'It was not intended to prove more. The Theist, whether Christian or not is not called upon to deny the eternity of matter.'[132] He summons the writer to the Hebrews in support: 'By faith we understand that the worlds have been *framed* by the word of God, so that what is seen hath not been made out of things that do appear' (Hebrews 11:3). 'This reply' to Mill, he says, 'is obvious.'[133] Here, it would seem, we must take Tymms as referring strictly to the teleological argument, and as being faithful to his policy of not saying all that he believes. For notwithstanding that

---

[128] Ibid., 77. Tymms quotes Mill's *Three Essays on Religion*, in *Collected Works*, X, 450. (Since Tymms does not specify the edition of the *Three Essays* that he is using, I have traced his quotations to the standard *Works*).

[129] Ibid. Tymms quotes J. H. Burton, *The Life and Correspondence of David Hume*, I, 244.

[130] Ibid., 80. Tymms refers to Mill's *Works*, X, 437. For a variety of responses to Mill's *Three Essays* see Alan P. F. Sell, ed., *Mill and Religion*; and for my own discussion of the issues see *Mill on God*.

[131] Ibid., 89.

[132] Ibid., 90-91.

[133] Ibid., 91.

some translations give 'created' for the verb just italicized, the Greek verb does mean 'adjusted' or 'set in order' rather than 'created'. But Tymms himself would surely wish to endorse the doctrine of creation *ex nihilo*, holding not only that God 'framed' matter which had existed from eternity, but that God created the matter. Be that as it may, Tymms feels that he has withstood the objections to theism levelled by some of its most powerful foes, and that 'it is tolerably evident that the fire which is to burn up faith in the Living God has not yet been kindled on the earth.'[134]

Theism as so far discussed will not, however, satisfy Jews, Christians and Muslims, all of whom declare that God has addressed humanity in a variety of ways. Tymms's question is whether 'Theism is able to justify its faith in an infinitely good and wise God, while repudiating all professed communications from Him to mankind.'[135] Since there are theists who believe in a personal God, Tymms has recourse, lexical synonymity notwithstanding, to the term 'deist' to designate those who espouse the view he is concerned to contest. He states the indictment against deists in terms of Mill's celebrated harangue against nature's cruelties.[136] How can belief in a good and loving God be sustained in the light of these? Tymms confesses that while he does not wish 'to restrict the scope of what is called Natural Theology, or to diminish the force of any argument for the Divine benevolence, ... without appealing to the whole scheme of moral culture and redemption which is inseparably identified with the revelation of God in Christ, I can find no weapon with which to repel Mill's attack.'[137]

But 'the existence of physical pain is a small thing in comparison with the existence of moral evil.'[138] As soon as a human being acted against the conviction that something ought to be done, the seed of moral evil was sown. Deists cannot say that God intended evil choices to be made and therefore made human beings accordingly, for this would be to repudiate God's goodness. But then they face the difficulty of an act of disobedience which allegedly reveals a perfect God, 'whose creation needs no remedial touch and no forth-putting of His Personal Will.'[139] Furthermore, while both Christian and deist agree that God foresaw what would happen when creating free human beings, the Christian has a theory of redemption to offer, whereas the deist 'has no revelation to fall back upon.'[140]At this point Tymms poses a version of the ancient challenge to the deist: 'If [God] could have made a better world but did not, He is not good; if he did the best he could, then He is not Almighty.'[141] The upshot is that 'The God who hears and answers the prayers of men, and is their Refuge and Strength and very present Help in trouble, is not morally the same Being as one who sets them in a world like this, and then sits

---

134 Ibid., 97.

135 Ibid., 100.

136 He quotes Mill at length on pp. 103-5, referring to Mill's *Works*, X, 385-6.

137 Ibid., 106.

138 Ibid., 107.

139 Ibid., 110-11.

140 Ibid., 111.

141 Ibid.

above the circle of the earth, and leaves them to themselves while ages multiply their sorrows and aggravate their difficulties and cares.'[142] If such were God, it would be no wonder that people would 'feel no contrition for neglecting Him who is unknown except as the Absentee Creator, the Great Neglecter of all His works.'[143]

To have shown that theism apart from revelation is incompetent to answer Mill's indictment of Nature is not to have shown that Christianity is out of the wood. What answer can Christians give to the problem of evil? Tymms eschews all reference to Satanic influence since this would shift the problem to unsearchable realms and carry no weight with Christianity's opponents, and would in any case beg the question how the tempter became evil. He does, however, insist that unlike deism, the Bible does not deny or ignore the evils to which Mill and others point. On the contrary, 'The Bible is unique ... in pointing to man's sin and God's purpose of salvation, as explanations of the pain with which the whole creation groans.'[144] Tymms fully recognizes that the crux of the matter is the apparent incompatibility of human evil with a good Creator. He cannot adopt Mill's solution, namely, that of denying God's omnipotence, but rather contends that just as Omnipotence cannot both create a world and leave it uncreated, so it cannot create a volitional being incapable of volitions. That is to say, 'We do not deny God's omnipotence, by saying that He cannot produce two contradictory and mutually exclusive things.'[145] Similarly, Tymms cannot vindicate God's goodness by denying his foreknowledge, as some writers attempt to do, for such a view 'represents God as indulging in a tremendous experiment of which he could not foresee the issue ... If he could not foresee the first sin as a fact, much less could he foresee a satisfactory method of treating it, or a termination to human misery which would redound to His own glory.'[146]

Tymms posits righteousness as 'the ultimate aim of God in creating man.'[147] Righteousness is active and progressive and has to do with determinations of the will on the part of free moral agents. He notes that the Bible does not speak of humanity's fall from a state of righteousness, but only from a state of innocence, and it sets before us

> a vision of triumph, in which Creator and creation, Master and servants, Father and children, Redeemer and redeemed, all joy and rejoice together; a vision of love purged from impurity by sacrifice, and of righteousness rendered incorruptible by the fires of a Refiner who has made a suffering world His crucible, that so the faith

---

[142] Ibid., 114.
[143] Ibid., 116.
[144] Ibid., 123.
[145] Ibid., 126.
[146] Ibid., 129.
[147] Ibid., 130.

and love of the sons of men, more precious than fine gold, may redound at last unto His own praise and glory and honour.[148]

But what of the 'dark background of future torment' which lies behind this particular aspect of the biblical witness? Tymms replies after the fashion of one influenced by modern biblical criticism: '[T]hose notions of physical torture which uses to pass current as Scriptural are gross perversions of Biblical metaphors. The combination of such incompatible things as darkness, fire, and worms proves this. Darkness cannot exist where flame it, and where flame is worms are not.'[149] Furthermore, 'The Roman Catholic torture-pit is an invention of priests, who themselves used the stake and the axe without remorse.'[150] The biblical view is that while God takes no pleasure in the death of the wicked, he will none the less separate the evil from the good; and while Christ used strong words to depict the consequences of refusing God's grace, those terms are all figurative, and designed to indicate 'the mental sufferings of those who bemoan their misused powers, lost opportunities, and rejected overtures of love.'[151] To any who might suggest that the pathway to heaven could have been made smoother, Tymms replies that 'Omnipotence could not create men with the ripe results of moral conflict in their hearts and minds prior to any actual experience.'[152] Moreover, human beings could not discern the difference between good and evil unless they were placed in an environment offering alternative courses of action attended by a diversity of consequences. Even 'The defects of the natural world, considered as an abode furnished for man's temporal comfort and convenience, are its perfections as a place or moral discipline; and, unless falsehood be sublimer than truth, the cross of Christ, followed by his exaltation to the throne, declares not only the righteousness of God in forgiving wrong, but also in permitting pain.'[153] For those who believe this the mystery of evil is 'assuredly solved'[154]—a claim which calls for my caveat that the solution is a practical one in the sense that believers are enabled to go forward in hope; it does not provide a detailed answer to the question 'Why does God permit the *righteous* suffer'—as Job discovered.

Tymms's next chapter is entitled, 'The miracle of revelation,' and here, I fear, he is not at his best. The position he wishes to defend is that 'an event is a miracle if the usual physical causation be absent, and an effect be produced inside the order of nature by a Divine act.'[155] This is the traditional view that a miracle is a breach of the natural order—a position that bristles with difficulties, among them that of determining what the natural order is, and what would count as a breach of it.

[148] Ibid., 134.
[149] Ibid., 135.
[150] Ibid., 136.
[151] Ibid.
[152] Ibid., 139.
[153] Ibid., 143.
[154] Ibid.
[155] Ibid., 148.

Tymms does not address such questions. Instead, he declares that 'the argument from physical continuity against a miraculous revelation is gone when once the will of God has been confessed to act directly on the mind of man.'[156] But the term 'confession' indicates that we are here in the realm of testimony, not of argument; and the argument against miracle is not so much 'gone' as set aside. In speaking of 'confession' Tymms all but concedes that alleged miracles do not have the status of evidence of a kind that would convince a sceptic, and hence their strictly apologetic value is thrown into question. Indeed, later in the chapter he argues that testimony can be as reliable as the evidence of our senses, and declares, begging a huge question, that 'A miracle involves no breach, even of physical continuity, if all events are thus viewed as the outworking of Divine energy'[157]—something that the sceptic is by no means willing to concede. 'On the other hand,' he continues, 'a marvellous breach of continuity is involved in the theory that God worked as the Creator by the forthputting of His will, but then straightway ceased to work at all!'[158] But (a) an unbelieving sceptic would not hold this position; and (b) there is precisely *no* breach of *natural* continuity if an alleged god, having created the world, left it to itself. It remains only to add that in the course of his remarks Tymms takes Mill and Hume to task and, in the case of Mill, seems to find him more of an ally than he really is. For while Mill does indeed say in his chapter on 'Revelation' in the *Three Essays on Religion*, that on the hypothesis that there is a Creator, modifications of the created order are not inconceivable, this is not an hypothesis with which Mill rests content—as Tymms himself admits on p. 164. Yet Mill is invoked in the chapter's conclusion where Tymms is advancing a series of 'suppositions', among them that if in spite of human sin and misery God is 'working out a plan which will bring in everlasting righteousness' it would 'remove an intellectual confusion which is fitted to paralyze man's moral endeavours, if God were to grant a special disclosure of His purpose, and were to afford, by works no human might [or?] could perform, some illustration of His own power to us-ward...' He continues,

> [I]t is submitted that ... starting, as Mill starts his in chapter, and as all Theists start, on the hypothesis of a Creator who cares for His creatures ... we do not over-estimate the value of these considerations when we say that they establish a high degree of moral and intellectual probability that such a Creator will exercise His indisputable power to enlighten His creatures concerning himself ...[159]

To repeat: the hypothesis set down by Mill was deemed improbable of establishment by him, though not by Tymms, who is willing to entertain 'suppositions' which

---

[156] Ibid., 149.
[157] Ibid., 172.
[158] Ibid.
[159] Ibid., 176.

Mill would have shunned, and to place a degree of reliance upon human testimony that both Mill and Hume would have thought quite out of place.[160]

Tymms is convinced that God is able to address humanity, and that the Bible is the locus of his revelation. In introducing this subject he declares that 'We are ... free as rational beings to acknowledge the presence of Divine oracles in the Bible, if its utterances commend themselves as from God.'[161] He proceeds to discuss the suitability of a book as a record of God's revelation over time; he indicates the variety of the Bible's contents whilst observing that there is an underlying unity of conviction concerning the nature and reality of God. That there should be such unity, given the diversity of biblical writers and the long period of time from which their writings come, renders the supposition of a presiding Higher Mind likely. Tymms discounts the 'alleged' verbal infallibility of the Bible, for it is 'obvious' that 'the Bible does not represent that all its own contents are of the same value and authority, or that every sentence is an oracle of God.'[162] Lest any of the faithful should be disquieted by this claim, he explains that 'the separation of faith, in Him of whom the Bible bears witness, from an indefensible opinion about the Bible, can scarcely fail to afford a sense of liberty and strength not previously enjoyed.'[163] Tymms is well aware of the 'slippery slope' objection, namely, that if human errors and defects are once admitted in the biblical texts, how can we be sure that it is reliable as to its major claims? He regrets that such objections have been lodged even by 'many prominent and honoured teachers of Christianity',[164] and retorts that Christians do in fact distinguish between divine and human words when reading the Bible, as when they accept the words of Jesus as from God, but not those of the tempter or the human enemies of Jesus. Errors and defects notwithstanding, the Bible is overall a credible witness. It does not set out to be a scientific treatise, its history is generally reliable, and parts of it are clearly divine, among them fulfilled prophecies, and the 'private and incommunicable persuasions' which devout readers receive. These last are not direct evidence of divine elements in the Bible, but just as those concerned with the medicinal properties of a substance will take into consideration its effects, so

> The intense conviction of Divine enlightenment, invigoration, comfort, guidance, and moral constraint which grows up in the minds of myriads of Christian men and women is a phenomenon of unparalleled character, and should command the respectful attention of all who would study the mystery of human life in a scientific spirit.[165]

---

[160] For a discussion of Mill's position see Alan P. F. Sell, *Mill on God*, 150-153.
[161] T. V. Tymms, *The Mystery of God*, 179.
[162] Ibid., 196.
[163] Ibid., 200.
[164] Ibid., 201.
[165] Ibid., 255.

In the two following chapters Tymms discusses the New Testament witness to Jesus Christ and to his resurrection (though, we recall, it is not his purpose to develop a Christology or a soteriology). As a sample of his approach we may cite the conclusion to his account of the resurrection:

> Around the grave of Christ so many marvels cluster, that if He did not rise from the dead, the facts which then call for explanation are quite as miraculous as His asserted resurrection, and, because deprived of their only moral significance, they are immeasurably more difficult to believe.[166]

As to Jesus himself,

> The scheme of moral government of which he is the centre, and of which the Bible is the exponent, is the only one which harmonizes the terrible facts of pain and moral evil with man's spiritual aspirations, and with the goodness of the Creator.[167]

While

> No force of reasoning can coerce those spiritual conditions in which Christ is discerned as the true Lord and Leader of the soul ... My aim has been to show that the severest processes of thought conduct the man of culture to the same standpoint for the contemplation of Christ's spiritual claims as is occupied by the untutored peasant or the simple child, and leave them free to yield up his nature to the influences of Christ.[168]

After all, 'A religion which comes forth from God, and is designed to deal with all men equally, must be one which places the wise and the unwise on the same level, and puts both classes to the same spiritual proof'[169]—the very 'proof' to which D. W. Simon devoted so much attention.

In his concluding chapter on 'The life of faith', Tymms argues that the Bible's demand for faith is not arbitrary, for 'without faith no intercourse with another spiritual being is possible.'[170] Yet some are reluctant to allow faith any place in their life. This may be because they fear that is once admitted, faith may be required to believe utterly fantastic 'spiritualistic phenomena'. But 'thoughtful persons who believe in the great God declared by Christ, and appreciate the nature of that kingdom which He has established on the earth, will view such phenomena with sorrowful contempt.'[171] The moral test of alleged miracles is equally effective. Some may equate faith with credulity—an error that has been fostered by 'professedly Christian

---

[166] Ibid., 316.
[167] Ibid., 317.
[168] Ibid., 321.
[169] Ibid.
[170] Ibid., 324.
[171] Ibid., 328.

bodies.'[172] The fact remains that Christ demands of all an act of private judgment, and utter commitment to himself. It follows that faith is no mere intellectual assent to the truth of certain propositions; it is a matter of personal trust. Against those who say that they would like to appropriate the spiritual benefits of Christianity whilst ignoring its historic evidences, Tymms thunders,

> The spiritual discernment of spiritual things may fairly be deemed higher and more trustworthy for religious purposes than any other kind of knowledge. It may justly be allowed to secure our assent to propositions which might otherwise be regarded as inadequately proved; and as a matter of experience, it no doubt does very often precede, and largely contribute to induce, an intellectual acceptance of the Christian evidences. But these admissions in no degree sanction the supposition that spiritual faith can be rationally entertained in defiance of a previous intellectual dissent, and in conjunction with an admission that science and philosophy have proved the most important statements in the Gospels to be absolutely incredible.[173]

Tymms concludes by enumerating the effects of Christian faith: it helps to remove the most productive causes of evil; it gives hope; it satisfies the heart and

> Finally, while faith ... is indispensable to any intelligent intercourse with God, and while the Christian faith, rightly understood, is consistent with any true philosophy, favourable to morality and satisfying to the heart, it also commends itself as giving completeness and grandeur to our intellectual conceptions of the universe.[174]

In this last clause he has in mind our relations with the animal occupants of this world and with the saints in heaven; and whereas to physical science other worlds are 'lonely islands in an untravelled ocean of ether,' to the Christian they are '"many mansions" of one great house', while the human race is 'as one of many tribes in the cosmic Israel of God, all journeying towards one Holy Hill of beatific vision...'[175]

It is clear by now that with his emphasis upon spiritual realities, Tymms ends where Simon began. While Simon gives due place to the biblical 'evidences', it is Tymms who pays more heed to traditional theistic arguments and to some, but not all, of the objections thereto, and who tackles anti-Christian 'isms' with some thoroughness. The impression thus left is that of the two Simon attaches greater weight to the experimental, Tymms to the intellectual. What is perhaps odd is that while seeking to put materialism and pantheism to flight, Tymms does not, in *The Mystery of God*, counter agnosticism. There is just a passing reference to this standpoint, so prevalent in Tymms's day, in the final chapter of the book. But four years later, in a *Contemporary Review* article, he made good the omission under the heading, 'Agnostic expositions.' To this article I now turn.

---

[172] Ibid., 331.
[173] Ibid., 340-41.
[174] Ibid., 353.
[175] Ibid., 354.

Tymms's article was occasioned by articles published by T. H. Huxley in *Nineteenth Century*.[176] Huxley's objective was 'rouse his "countrymen out of their dogmatic slumbers"'—a task for which Tymms thinks his 'admirably qualified', and in which he wishes him 'a large measure of success.'[177] There may, says Tymms, be preachers who are reluctant to acquaint their hearers with the results of biblical criticism, and there are many 'who think that ordinary congregations need and are entitled to receive a more refreshing and morally nutritious fare than critical discussions would afford'; but there is also 'a large and growing number who ardently desire that the people of this country should be fully acquainted with the actual condition of Biblical science at the present time.'[178] Tymms lays down his policy in no uncertain terms: 'By any means, and by all means, let the results of Biblical criticism be made known, and only those who are base enough to love their own opinions better than truth can fear the issue.'[179] It is appropriate to note in passing that this declaration, which at the present time would be widely regarded as a truism, must have appeared to many in Tymms's day—and not least to many of his fellow Baptists—as 'fighting talk.' For it was in October 1889, the very year in which Tymms's article appeared, that the celebrated evangelical Calvinist, C. H. Spurgeon, resigned from the Baptist Union in the aftermath of the Downgrade Controversy which had so agitated that denomination during the previous two years, with those on Spurgeon's side resenting the assaults on the inspiration of Scripture and the prevalence of doctrinal laxity which they perceived all around them.[180]

Tymms regrets that Huxley, 'the father of the Agnostic denomination',[181] should have coined the term 'agnostic' to describe his view, for even the most dogmatic Christians will agree that they have no scientific knowledge of the unseen world. The real distinction, says Tymms, is between those who believe beyond the limits of scientific evidence and those who do not. According to Huxley's definition an agnostic is a person who says 'I do not know' and who makes 'that answer a shield against all appeals for religious faith.'[182]

All of this notwithstanding, there are some points upon which Christians and agnostics agree. First, Tymms refers to Paul's assertions of the limitations of

[176] For Thomas Henry Huxley (1825-1895) see ODNB.

[177] T. V. Tymms, 'Agnostic expositions,' 692.

[178] Ibid.

[179] Ibid., 693.

[180] For a brief account of the controversy see Alan P. F. Sell, *Commemorations*, ch. 1, and references; D. Kingdon, 'C. H. Spurgeon and the Down Grade controversy'; Subsequent studies include J. H. Y. Briggs, *The English Baptists of the 19th Century*, ch. 6; Mark Hopkins, *Nonconformity's Romantic Generation*, ch. 5. For Spurgeon (1834-1892) see DEB; ODNB; R. Shindler, *From the Usher's Desk to the Tabernacle Pulpit*; John J. Ellis, *Charles Haddon Spurgeon*; W. Y. Fullerton, *C. H. Spurgeon*; J. C. Carlile, *C. H. Spurgeon*; Iain Murray, *The Forgotten Spurgeon*; P. S. Kruppa, *Charles Haddon Spurgeon*.

[181] T. V. Tymms, 'Agnostic expositions,' 694.

[182] Ibid., 695.

human knowledge, among them the claim that 'The world by its wisdom knew not God' (I Corinthians 1:21). Such a claim, says Tymms, would formerly have been regarded as an affront to human reason by those who contended that no revelation was necessary and that all light concerning God and duty could be found in nature. But now, 'Agnosticism is the slowly extorted confession ... that the ancient Biblical doctrine of man's intellectual limitations is true.'[183] Secondly, Huxley has no *a priori* objection to revelation, masking it a matter of reliable evidence alone. Thirdly, agnostics agree with Paul that to receive revelation is to take a step beyond knowledge in the strict sense of verified and demonstrable truth.'[184] Thus, for example, 'An empty sepulchre might be accepted as scientific evidence that Jesus was not there, but it could not prove that he had risen and appeared to the apostles. These things were matters of testimony.'[185]

Huxley agrees that all science 'rests upon a measure of faith', and Tymms insists that 'all faith which transcends science must also have some starting-point and foundation in reason and knowledge.'[186] In the last resort, however, 'the Christian's religion is faith in Jesus Christ as the faithful and true witness of God'[187]—at which point Tymms invokes Mill: 'To the conception of the rational sceptic it remains a possibility that Christ actually was what He supposed Himself to be.'[188]

Among Huxley's points of detail to which Tymms takes exception is the refusal to admit that Jesus died on the Cross, though he does accept Mark's account of the grave as being found empty. Huxley cannot, however, accommodate the resurrection appearances of Jesus, and, unlike Strauss, who deemed Jesus a delirious enthusiast, and Renan, to whom Jesus was a brilliant liar,[189]—both of whom Huxley cites with approval—Huxley sees no need to explain the origin of the Christian church apart from a firm faith in Christ's resurrection. To Tymms the only hypothesis consistent with Jesus's 'ordinary honesty and with the unquestioned fact that His disciples believed in his resurrection'[190] is that he was indeed raised. Tymms proceeds to show that the galaxy of 'advanced' continental theologians whom Huxley enlists in his service as if they were in harmonious accord in fact differed considerably from one another as to the 'main results' of biblical criticism. In fact, he says, Reuss[191] is the only one whose views are not obsolete, and while Tymms thinks that 'Criticism has not yet emerged from the broom and dust-pan stage of labour, and while dust is

---

183 Ibid., 696.

184 Ibid., 697.

185 Ibid., 698.

186 Ibid.

187 Ibid.

188 Ibid., quoting Mill's *Works*, X, 488.

189 For David Friedrich Strauss (1808-1874) and Joseph Ernest Renan (1823-1892) see DBI; Claude Welch, *Protestant Thought in the Nineteenth Century*.

190 T. V. Tymms, 'Agnostic expositions,' 701.

191 Edouard Guillaume Eugène Reuss (1804-1891), for whom see DBI, studied at Göttingen, Halle and Paris, and taught Biblical criticism and languages at Strasbourg, his native city.

flying from the floor in clouds, sweepers may be excused for not seeing how much more is left',[192] he does so far agree with Reuss that God's gift does not hang 'on grammar, or on proper names, on precise dates, or on a mechanical preservation of the fine gold of spiritual revelation from all human alloy', and that the Scriptures 'suffice to bring the reader into true contact with the mind of Christ and with the Spirit of God, and that this is indeed their function, and one which criticism can never take away.'[193] Those who remain concerned by biblical criticism should draw hope from the fact that whereas Strauss and Renan utterly discounted the miraculous, 'the possibility of miracles is frankly admitted by philosophy and science, and can henceforth only be disputed by those who deny the existence of God.'[194] The upshot is that criticism 'is no longer the weapon of a party, but the instrument and servant of us all.'[195]

Tymms carried this optimism into his paper on 'Christian theism' in the collection, *The Ancient Faith in Modern Light* (1897). The adjective in Tymms's title is of great significance, for it signals a change of mood, style and content. Here Tymms is no longer holding back on his deepest beliefs; he is not primarily in pursuit of alien 'isms', though he make brief reference to agnosticism and pantheism; he is theologically constructive. He touches on the doctrines of the Trinity, the Logos, the Holy Spirit, and adverse criticisms of the work of others are confined to those, notably the Unitarian James Martineau, with whom he disagrees on points of Christian doctrine. At the same time this is not merely an exercise in systematic theology. The apologetic interest remains in that Tymms's objective is to compare and contrast Old Testament and New Testament theism, 'and to point out the higher beauty and reasonableness of Christian Theism, and its greater credibility in the searchlight of modern philosophy.'[196]

Tymms argues that Hebrew theism is characterized by the conviction that God is the sole author of the cosmos; by anthropomorphic expression indicative of the belief that God is a person who enters into varied and ceaseless relations with human beings; by other expressions which represent God as invisible and inscrutable; by a belief in angelic messengers of God; by the doctrine that God is spirit; and, above all, by its essentially ethical idea of God's relations with humanity, this being supremely seen in the Decalogue with its fundamental demand of love first of God and then of neighbour.

Turning to the New Testament, Tymms concentrates upon the characteristics of Christianity which are deemed corruptions by Jews and incredible by anti-theistic writers. There is first the challenge that the theism of some of the classical creeds is incompatible with the doctrine of the unity of God. Tymms surmizes that 'it may be' that while from the desire to exclude Arianism and Sabellianism some documents were composed which are 'incurably Tritheistic in their only intelligible meaning ...

[192] T. V. Tymms, 'Agnostic expositions,' 710.
[193] Ibid., 709.
[194] Ibid., 712.
[195] Ibid.
[196] Idem, 'Christian theism,' 4.

They may conceivably, though it requires a large imagination, be reconcilable with the doctrines of the New Testament and with the religious beliefs of their own authors.'[197] In his opinion such doctrines are of historical interest only, and he is convinced that the Christian doctrine of the unity of God can be sustained from a study of the New Testament alone, to which end he cites numerous texts, not least Jesus's quotation of the ancient words, which themselves indicate Old-New Testament continuity, 'Hear O Israel! the Lord our God is one Lord' (Mark 12:29-32). Again, the Testaments concur in conceiving of God as a Person, and Tymms judges that

> Probably the most serious objection which Theists have ever had to face is that which affirms that the existence of a Sole Eternal Person is inconceivable. Many earnest thinkers when perplexed by the mysteries of Trinitarianism are inclined to flee into what is inconveniently called Unitarianism as a haven of intellectual simplicity and rest. In reality it is neither a simple nor a restful position, and is assailed by Pantheists and Agnostics with immense force.[198]

As an example of agnostic attack he cites the view of Herbert Spencer that since '"consciousness is constituted of ideas and feelings caused by objects and occurrences", ... there cannot be an Eternal Being who is both subject and object to Himself.'[199] Tymms reminds us that elsewhere he has discussed Spencer in some detail, pointing out that Spencer nowhere clearly defines 'objects' and 'occurrences' or shows how they can cause ideas and feelings, but he does at least confirm the truth that subject and object are correlative terms, and that subjects and objects cannot exist unless both exist together.[200] Tymms thus feels entitled to claim that Spencer lends 'unintended support to the position that the existence of an Infinite Mind, who is a conscious Person, is the necessary correlate to the thought of a world of "objects and occurrences", and shows that it would be more philosophical, as well as more religious, to say that the thoughts of His mind are the cause, and not the effects of those "objects and occurrences" which make up the finite universe and its historic development.'[201] For its part, pantheism denies that there can be a divine first cause of the existent universe, because apart from the objective world God could have no consciousness. Less extremely, pantheists hold that 'the Infinite One is also the manifold, and so within the Eternal Unity there is the ceaseless play of subject and object.'[202] This view, Tymms thinks, is fatal to non-Christian theism, while Christian theists must find a way of affirming the point without lapsing into pantheism.

---

[197] Ibid., 24.

[198] Ibid., 26.

[199] Ibid. Tymms quotes Spencer's 'Religion: A retrospect and prospect.' Spencer was a favourite target of nineteenth-century divines, but little that they said seemed to move him.

[200] See *The Mystery of God*, 71-3.

[201] Ibid., 73.

[202] Idem, 'Christian theism,' 27.

Enter Martineau, who is cited as one who promulgates a theism which declines any assistance from the Johannine Logos doctrine.[203] Martineau takes the Spencerian and pantheistic point that if there is no 'other-than-self' for God, the divine subject cannot exist; but he 'lamentably fails' to discover such an 'other-than-self.' The problem is that whether we think with Martineau of matter or space or eternally created 'man-like persons' as necessary conditions of God's personality, they must "'be self-existent with Him", and He is no more their Creator than they collectively are his.'[204] Martineau is thus impaled on the horns of the following dilemma:

> If God actually created all finite persons, it must be conceded that some uncreated 'other-than-self' existed with God, or within God's personal fulness of being, as the indispensable condition of His own causality. If, on the other hand, God did not create all finite persons, He is not the First Cause of the universe, and Theism disappears. Where Dr. Martineau has thus failed it is unlikely that any living or coming philosopher will succeed. He has failed where Plato and Aristotle and Zeno failed, and where all the trained hosts of metaphysicians have failed for centuries. ... The outcome of his labour is that he has virtually demonstrated the impossibility of the Unitarian position. His arguments to show that the First Cause must be One and Personal are admirable; but his attempt to render such a Being conceivable breaks down.[205]

Furthermore, since eternal creation is conceded and demanded by Martineau, 'the antiquated arguments and sneers of Arians, Socinians, and Jews against Eternal Sonship are consigned to the limbo of metaphysical antiquities.'[206]

Positively, Tymms sets out to show that 'John's "Word" can be received, not as a second God, but as the necessary and eternal self-expression of the One God, [and that] it supplies at once an objective for the Divine Mind and a manifestation of God to His creatures.'[207] He argues that both the Old and New Testaments regard God's invisibility and inscrutability as correlatives of their doctrine of revelation, and that when such a God reveals himself to us, what more appropriate than that he should do so in personal, human form? But the incarnation needs to be seen in relation to the thought that 'it is God's eternal nature to issue into knowable form, and that His self-expression is eternal. ... '[T]he Word may be conceived of as for ever saying to

---

[203] For Martineau (1805-1900) see DNCBP; ODNB; A. W. Jackson, *James* Martineau; J. Drummond and C. B. Upton, *The Life and Letters of James Martineau*; Carpenter, J. Estlin Carpenter, *James Martineau*; C. B. Upton, *Dr. Martineau's Philosophy. A Survey*; S. H. Mellone, 'James Martineau as an ethical teacher'; P. T. Forsyth, 'Dr. Martineau'; John Watson, 'James Martineau: A saint of theism'; A. M. Fairbairn, 'James Martineau'; A. S. Pringle-Pattison, 'Martineau's philosophy'; John Dickie, *Fifty Years of British Theology*, ch. 2; Ralph Waller, 'James Martineau: The development of his religious thought'; Alan P. F. Sell, *Commemorations*, chs. 1, 10.

[204] T. V. Tymms, 'Christian theism, 31.

[205] Ibid.

[206] Ibid., 33.

[207] Ibid.

the Universe, "He that hath seen me hath seen the Father ... I and my Father are one.'"[208]

At this point Tymms confesses the human inability to probe the innermost secrets of the Godhead, but he does feel entitled to claim that the 'other-than-self' for which Martineau vainly sought is the Logos, though with the proviso that

> When we speak of 'another-than-self' for God, we ... do not mean another self in the sense of a second personal God, but something which corresponds to another self in the case of finite creatures. ... His nature must contain a fulness which corresponds to at least dual personality in finite beings. ... A self-existent person cannot be dependent on His own created objects for his personality. That which corresponds to an Objective for Him must belong to His own uncreated nature. Given, therefore, such an eternal self-expression as John declares, and the First Cause stands before our thought in complete and undivided unity.[209]

Since Martineau is in Tymms's sights at this point, it is perhaps only fair to note the objection graciously levelled against Tymms by the Unitarian James Drummond:

> It may be from some inherent defect of metaphysical power, but I confess I am quite unable to assimilate the thoughts which are here presented. A personal being who is objective to God, other-than-self, must be, according to our poor thinking, a distinct person from God, and, if he be at the same time God, he must be a second God. If, in order to save the Divine unity, you deny this, and make the other-than-self really a part of the self, it becomes simply the unknown condition of an eternal self-consciousness. The argument begins with the assumption that what is needful for self-consciousness in the finite mind is also needful in the infinite, and ends by declaring that the infinite Mind is self-conscious through a condition which is absolutely different from that though which we are self-conscious. ... I am unable to soar into that rare atmosphere of speculation. ... We are surely not compelled to be either agnostics or pantheists because we think that the method of eternal self-consciousness is inscrutable, and are content to say that God has all perfection within himself, without trying to bring all the elements of that perfection within the limits of our puny reason.[210]

In attempting to adjudicate the point, I suggest that while Tymms says he does not posit a second God, and while he is right to draw attention to God's eternal work of self-revelation, he falls into the trap of inferring that the inner relations of the Godhead are analogous to subject-object relations in the human experience, and this notwithstanding his professed inability to probe the innermost secrets of the Godhead. Tymms would have done well to have been more reticent in what one might call Drummond's sense of 'godly' agnosticism. While without inner relations

---

[208] Ibid, 36, 38.

[209] Ibid., 39.

[210] J. Drummond, *Studies in Christian Doctrine*, 154-5. He does, however, grant that Tymms's general line of argument may have some force against Martineau.

within the Godhead there can be no doctrine of the Trinity, we exceed the limits of our knowledge if we liken them too closely to experiences with which we are familiar.

Tymms proceeds to discuss the powerful desire for objective forms of the divine that has characterized humanity through the ages and around the world: 'Men cannot worship Plato's Ideas or Aristotle's Mind,'[211] he declares. But he is also aware that this desire may pass over into idolatry. Can the desire be satisfied without falling into the latter pitfall? His answer is that a divine Word is the only conceivable link between the infinite and the finite, and that God takes the initiative in making himself known in the Logos made flesh, and through continuing work of the Holy Spirit. He grants that the statements in the New Testament regarding the persons of the Trinity are impossible to harmonize—the Spirit is sometimes represented as a person, at others as an almost passive influence, for example; but what is clear is that 'Christ does not reduce the Godhead into a species which consists of three individuals, with separate departmental offices, and are One God only as collective humanity is man. ... God comes to us objectively in Christ, and thus sets a living image before mankind which gives a definite and intelligible idea of Himself.'[212] From the doctrine of the Holy Spirit we learn that God is immanent as well as transcendent: 'Christ is God's self-expression, but the Spirit is His self-impartation.'[213]

In a materialistic or a pantheistic cosmos characterized by 'an endless continuity of sequences without possibility of choice within or control from above',[214] there is no moral governor, no sin, no forgiveness, no punishment, for necessity rules. Indeed, 'In such a cosmos strictly ethical problems cannot arise.'[215] Only in a personally-governed cosmos is moral agency possible. In Christianity we find the ancient moral law fulfilled in Christ's exemplary life. But how can an eternal, immutable moral order be reconciled with the idea of forgiveness for sin? Only because Christ elevates forgiveness into a supreme duty, but one conditioned by genuine repentance. Such repentance implies a change of relations with the eternal moral order, though the forgiveness bestowed does not mean that the grievous consequences of sin are immediately or totally removed. But the forgiven person is restored to fellowship with God and to service in cooperation with all who are loyal to God. Finally, Christ, as well as showing the righteousness of forgiveness, also teaches 'the mercy of severity.'[216] Thus, 'among the many rays of ethical truth which shine from the Cross, this comes to us, That God will spare no anguish to Himself or His sons, which may be necessary to conserve and solemnise the sanctity of Law:'[217]

---

211 T. V. Tymms, 'Christian theism,' 41.
212 Ibid., 47-8.
213 Ibid., 48.
214 Ibid., 50.
215 Ibid.
216 Ibid., 56.
217 Ibid.

> [T]he Cross teaches us that the Father in heaven pities His children, and takes upon Himself the burden and sacrifice of their salvation.

> The Cross is thus the living synthesis of Law and Forgiveness. it is the conciliation of the ancient paradox, 'A just God and a Saviour.' ... In loving [God], men learn to love His law, and to hate the things which grieve His Spirit and disturb the order of His world. Thus Christian Theism is not only an ethical Monotheism, but is also a regenerative force ...[218]

We are here at the threshold of what is probably Tymms's greatest work, his treatise on the atonement of Christ.

II

Of Tymms's stimulating book, *The Christian Idea of Atonement* (1904), the reviewer in *The Expository Times* wrote, 'The greatest books do not make the greatest sensation. This is the greatest modern book on the Atonement, but we know that it will be quietly received and quietly make its impression.'[219] This is high praise indeed, but I fear that the attendant prophecy remains largely unfulfilled, and this is regrettable. Tymms's volume slipped the nets of Robert Mackintosh[220] and T. Hywel Hughes,[221] both of whom surveyed then recent atonement theories. It is therefore all the more to the credit of G. B. Stevens of Yale University that he managed to include a number of references to Tymms's work in his own study, *The Christian Doctrine of Salvation* (1905), which appeared so soon afterwards; and the Anglican, J. K. Mozley, also briefly commented upon Tymms's book.[222]

In the brief Preface to his book Tymms makes a methodological point of considerable importance, especially having regard to the emphasis upon the Fatherhood of God that was so prevalent, especially in theologically liberal circles, in his day:

> I have not founded my discussion of the Atonement on the Fatherhood of God, although to my mind this expresses the most fundamental as well as the loveliest conception of God's relationship to us, and nothing at variance with it can be predicated of Him. But our Father in Heaven is also the blessed and only Potentate, the Lawgiver, Judge, and King of all the earth. Each of these analogical titles represents an aspect of the Deity which should never be ignored, and each is associated with a set of correlative terms which cannot be disused without loss, and become incongruous if intermixed. Hence it appears preferable to found our discussions on a definition of the Divine Nature rather than upon any relative term,

---

[218] Ibid., 58.

[219] ET, XV, 1903-4, 518.

[220] R. Mackintosh, *Historic Theories of Atonement*, 1920.

[221] T. H. Hughes, *The Atonement*, 1949.

[222] J. K. Mozley, *The Doctrine of the* Atonement, 175-6; idem, *The Impassibility of God*, 145-6.

however beautiful. God must always be the same in all His relations, and under all the analogical forms in which these can be partially expressed.[223]

Tymms needs no reminding that the witness of Christian history is that Christ crucified, and not any theory of the atonement, is the power of God unto salvation, but since Christianity concerns discipleship and the propagation of the faith, the cogent exposition of Christian truth is a *desideratum* of great importance. The Church's weakness in this connection is traced by some to 'the unsettling effects of the Higher Criticism', while others blame 'those who entrench themselves behind a theory of Scripture, which not only critics but thousands of illiterate people have rejected as incredible.'[224] Deeper still is the damage done by the identification of vicarious suffering with vicarious punishment—and this proclaimed as Bible truth. Even if advocates of this view shrink from saying that Christ was punished, they insist that he bore our punishment as our substitute, further explaining that if God were otherwise to stay the execution of sinners he would violate his immutable justice and nullify his threatenings. Tymms observes that 'Almost all who reject the Penal Theory of Atonement do so on ethical grounds'; many preachers maintain silence on the subject and prefer to expound semi-political, social, literary or ethical themes; and the result is that 'the gravest peril to Christian faith in the coming generation proceeds from this impression that Biblical authority and enlightened morality are in opposition.'[225] His own conviction is that 'the Christian idea of Atonement has no resemblance to the dogma commonly identified with this great word, and that the more severely the language of Scripture is examined the more vividly apparent it will be that the one is not merely a travesty, but a direct contradiction of the other.'[226]

Tymms first outlines the major approaches to the doctrine of the atonement. Those who hold the penal theory deny that 'our moral rectification was the immediate and chief end of Christ's work' and that 'this end could have been attained apart from the endurance of our punishment by Christ.'[227] Those who subscribe to the governmental theory urge that Christ's death would have been ineffective had it not both commended the King's love and upheld his authority. Devotees of these two views do not deny that the third position, the moral influence theory, rightly emphasizes the importance of the ethical appeal of the atonement, but for them this is not sufficient by itself.

Before adumbrating his positive theory, Tymms attacks the dogma that 'the Divine nature demands the inexorable and invariable punishment of all sin.'[228] While it is an axiom of Christianity that sin deserves punishment, does it follow that God's nature demands the invariable infliction of punishment? In approaching his

[223] T. V. Tymms, *The Christian Idea of Atonement*, vi-vii.
[224] Ibid., 6.
[225] Ibid., 9.
[226] Ibid., 10.
[227] Ibid., 17.
[228] Ibid., 19.

answer to this question Tymms discusses a number of patristic and medieval theories, and finds that the idea that the forgiveness of unpunished sins is unrighteous was slow to develop, and was most clearly articulated by Anselm in the twelfth century, and this in quasi-commercial terms. The penal theory cannot therefore be regarded as *the* biblical position, and hence objections to it are really objections to an 'ecclesiastical counterfeit'.[229] He proceeds to argue that none of the texts adduced in support of the doctrine actually do so. For example, however the Adam narrative is to be understood; whether the words, 'Of the tree of the knowledge of good and evil thou shalt not eat of it: for in the day that thou eatest thereof thou shalt surely die' (Genesis 2:17) are to be understood as a warning or as a threat to Adam; the fact is that while death is there connected with sin, there is 'no declaration which would be violated by an act of forgiveness after sin had been committed.'[230]

Further textual investigation leads Tymms to conclude that 'condemnation and punishment are totally different things. The one is universally necessary and cannot conceivably be dispensed with, but the other may be, and often is, remitted with beneficial effect, as every parent knows.'[231] More specifically, 'The cross of Christ is the measure not only of God's love for men, but also of His hatred of iniquity, and all who enter into living fellowship with Christ enter into His mind, and are imbued with His Spirit.'[232] Using italics for emphasis he continues, 'It was emphatically our *sin, not our punishment*, which bowed His soul in Gethsemane, and ruptured His surcharged heart at Calvary.'[233] Tymms is convinced of the necessity of distinguishing between the bearing of sin and the bearing of punishment. Furthermore, against the tenor of the penal theory, in the Old Testament as in the New, mercy is shown to be 'a fundamental quality' of God's nature, and not simply 'an attenuation of his justice,'[234] and this is amply borne out by the life and teaching of Christ, who 'elevated forgiveness into a primary moral duty.'[235] Whereas for Anselm forgiveness was 'a mere abstinence from self-avenging acts,' for Jesus it is 'a total and hearty cancelling of the offence.'[236] Finally, Tymms insists that the penal theory fails to do justice to God's utter repugnance to sin. God does not wish simply to punish sin, but to exterminate it. The only way this can be done is either by the salvation of sinners or by their extinction. Bypassing universalism and annihilationism as speculative opinions which, since they are unsupported by evidence, he cannot affirm, Tymms declares that punishment would not by itself meet God's objectives.

The measures open to God, says Tymms, are determined by God's nature, the nature of humanity, the nature of sin, and the consequences of sin. There follows a

---

[229] Ibid. 39.
[230] Ibid., 43.
[231] Ibid., 50.
[232] Ibid., 52.
[233] Ibid., 53.
[234] Ibid., 63.
[235] Ibid., 68.
[236] Ibid., 71.

discussion of God's nature as love, and an analysis of that term which accommodates both mercy and justice:

> God would not be love if He could behold His creatures perishing of sin without doing everything possible for their salvation, and this truth is written on our hearts by the cross. But it is equally true, and indeed it is part of the same truth, that God would not be love if He could behold His creatures corrupting, debauching, or in any way injuring each other without anger or without sufficient force of character to visit their transgressions with the rod. ... [Moreover] He who spared not His own Son will spare no agony or blood which may be needful for the maintenance of His Law of Love among men. The cross is God's definition of Himself. "Hereby know we love"; and in this the Divine nature is revealed.[237]

Clearly, we are here at a far remove from liberal theological sentimentalism.

As to the nature of humanity and sin, Tymms invokes Paul as teaching that every conscious transgression of God's law is sinful, but that whereas some unconscious transgressions are sinful—those of hardened and habitual sinners, for example, others—those of infants—are not. Paul was, after all, concerned with 'real moral agents, *i.e.*, persons possessed of intelligence, conscience, volition, and sufficient knowledge to allow of a choice between good and evil.'[238]

A further point which Tymms is concerned to press is that God does not arbitrarily will what is right and wrong. Indeed, 'God no more determines what is right by an act of volition as distinguishable from an act of judgment than He determines by an act of volition the necessary truths of Mathematics. Ethical duties necessarily arise with the existence of persons capable of influencing one another.'[239] It is also to be noted that the divine law is not identical with particular moral codes. For this reason (in words which we should nowadays wish to phrase differently) Tymms declares that 'God does not, and could not justly demand from the benighted heathen what He claims from those who have received the revelation of Himself in Christ.'[240] When Saul of Tarsus was persecuting the church he believed that he was doing God's will in accordance with God's law; but while what he did was objectively evil, Saul was not behaving sinfully: 'What he needed, therefore, was not punishment, but revelation, and for this cause he received that light which augmented and redirected his zeal for God's Kingdom.'[241] It is an apostolic doctrine that 'conscience is not an infallible guide to action, but is a faculty of the mind which judges our conformity, or non-conformity to whatever standard of duty we inwardly acknowledge.'[242] It further follows that 'external conformity to God's law may sometimes be sin, while external non-conformity may sometimes be sinless; and where no applicable rule of life is known, and conscience has no scope for

[237] Ibid., 99-100.
[238] Ibid., 112.
[239] Ibid., 115.
[240] Ibid., 119.
[241] Ibid., 121.
[242] Ibid., 122.

activity, there can be neither ethical obedience or disobedience, and consequently there is no sin.'[243] The theoretical distinction between evil and sin must be maintained. Tymms fully understands that from the desire to testify to God's holiness and humanity's depravity 'have come the burning words of psalmists and prophets, and of humble saints of all ages' against sin, but he regrets that 'theologians have erred chiefly in hardening these outbursts of confession and self-denunciation into cold scientific dogmas.'[244]

Tymms discusses the consequences of sin under the headings, physical, intellectual, moral and circumstantial, admitting that these distinctions are 'somewhat arbitrary, and that no such separation can be observed in the objective world of reality.'[245] In passing he draws attention to 'a striking feature of modern thought,' namely, 'the tendency to find the cause of immorality in physical conditions, and to substitute hygiene for the Gospel, and sanitation for Sanctification.'[246] More venerable is the tendency so to focus upon the ruinous moral effects of sin that 'moral responsibility was practically undermined.'[247] Within Tymms's sights at this point is the doctrine of original sin, which 'has tended to sap belief in God's Justice and to reduce men to despondent helplessness by stamping the word guilt even on attempts to pray, and discouraging endeavours after righteousness as not only vain but sinful.'[248] The upshot is that 'the Righteous Judge and Saviour must of necessity distinguish between the consequences of sin for which the individuals who suffer them are not wholly morally responsible, and those for which they are responsible either wholly or in part.'[249]

Although evil and sin are theoretically distinguishable, it does not follow that two different remedial measures are required, for evil and sin are alike contrary to God's will. The 'almost appalling truth' is that 'the cure of moral ignorance and guiltless non-conformity to God's will involves a process which often issues in the development of evil into sin. ... The coming of necessary light ... enforces on men a conscious choice of good and evil, and the choice is one which all the forces of habit, and very often the blind impulses of natural propensity and inclination, are on the side of disobedience.'[250] The coming of Christ introduces the possibility of heightened sin and deeper condemnation, for 'If Christ is not allowed to become a Saviour from both the guilt and the power of sin, the state of those who have once seen Him must of necessity be worse instead of better.'[251]

In view of the foregoing, it will not suffice to suppose that the annihilation of sinners is the cure for sin, for 'If destruction were a cure, prussic acid would be a

243 Ibid.
244 Ibid., 125.
245 Ibid., 148.
246 Ibid., 150.
247 Ibid.
248 Ibid.
249 Ibid., 154.
250 Ibid., 159.
251 Ibid., 160.

panacea for all human diseases!'[252] The only cure is one that destroys the poison and repairs the damage done in diseased moral natures. Again, eternal punishment is no remedy for it frustrates God's desire to save sinners and to exterminate sin. Yet again, the pardon of sin is not by itself a remedy, for an impetus to moral righteousness is needed. Lastly, the suppression of sin by coercion is a doomed method, since while sinners may be restrained by force they will not be changed by it; rather, it would destroy their volitional human nature—at which point Tymms makes the telling point that 'Docetism is not confined to Christology, but has often been rife in anthropology, for it inevitably enters when free-will, which is the most essential constituent of a moral agent, has been denied.'[253]

We seem now to be faced with a dilemma, Tymms continues. It is in God's nature to employ his omnipotence to exterminate sin and save sinners, but by sheer power he cannot cause people to forsake sin and live righteously. Hence—and this is the key to Tymms's atonement theory— 'The only real remedy for sin, and the only perfect satisfaction of God's nature, must consist in the reconciliation of man to a state of voluntary obedience to the Divine will.'[254] Human beings cannot do God's will without love, and 'God alone has love to give.' He must, therefore, secure his objective 'by so communicating His love as to reproduce it in [human beings] and make them partakers of His Divine nature,' and this he will do 'at any cost to Himself.'[255] In making good this claim Tymms counters the position of Augustine and Calvin that God hates sinners and loves the elect alone. Along this line, 'the difference between the reconciled and the unreconciled is not traced to the fact that the one class believes the truth about God and the other disbelieves it, but that God is friendly to the one and hostile to the other.'[256] R. W. Dale is equally at fault for he makes God's revelation of love in Christ subsidiary to penal considerations.[257]

There follows an extended discussion of biblical ideas of propitiation which leads to Tymms's assertion that the New Testament contains no propositions 'which can be tortured into a suggestion that Christ did or suffered anything whereby He made it righteous for God to remit sin.'[258] This is not to deny that redemption was a costly work: the New Testament writers reiterate the theme. For example, of Revelation 5: 9, 'Thou wast slain, and didst purchase unto God with Thy blood, men of every

---

[252] Ibid., 161.

[253] Ibid., 164; cf. 446.

[254] Ibid., 167.

[255] Ibid., 170.

[256] Ibid., 175.

[257] Ibid., 179-183.

[258] Ibid., 228. At this point Tymms takes James Denney and John Scott Lidgett to task, the latter's emphasis on the spiritual principle of the atonement notwithstanding. Cf. ibid., 453-4. He refers to Denney's *The Death of Christ*, and Lidgett's *The Spiritual Principle of the* Atonement. For Denney (1856-1917) see DHT; DSCHT; ODNB; Alan P. F. Sell, *Defending and Declaring the Faith*, ch. 9 and refs., 264; James M. Gordon, *James Denney*. For Lidgett (1854-1953) see DMGBI; ODNB; J. S. Lidgett, *My Guided Life*; Alan F. Turberfield, *John Scott Lidgett: Archbishop of Methodism?*

tribe, and tongue and people and nation, and madest them to be unto God, a kingdom and priests', Tymms writes,

> It would be difficult to frame an utterance which in letter and spirit should more forcibly contradict the idea that the blood of Christ was presented to God as the price of man's salvation. That Christ offered Himself to God is true; but He offered Himself as the self-sacrificing servant of God's redemptive purpose, and at the cost of His blood redeemed people from iniquity.[259]

How, precisely, could God reproduce his love in our hearts? This question leads Tymms to explore the theme of 'Salvation by love through faith.' The accusations of agnostics as to God's alleged tardiness in bringing all things under his sway confronts Christians with the fact that God faces an inherent difficulty in revealing and communicating his love to us. The difficulty resides in the fact that he desires the free response of sinners, and this is not readily forthcoming. As Tymms later puts it, 'Omnipotence could produce unnumbered stars and solar systems, but it would not produce a willing spirit by any coercive fiat.'[260] The New Testament affords evidence of people eager to have their physical needs met, slower to receive wisdom, and slower still to receive moral and spiritual blessing. The capacity to receive God's love is inevitably conditioned by the state of those to whom it is freely offered. If love is to be begotten, faith must be induced, and faith is the gift of God.

In turning next to the significance of Christ's death, Tymms says that he is complying with 'the demands of an enduring controversy', and is also in concurrence with the witness of the New Testament writers and of Christ himself, for 'all the interest of the gospels and the epistles centres in the cross.'[261] He at once concedes, however, that 'The death of Christ is inexplicable apart from the life which preceded and followed it.'[262] The pressing question is whether the death of Christ was an indispensable component of God's self-revelation. He sets out from the idea that social relationships as 'the condition of a mutual revelation of hearts.'[263] Christ's lowly social rank made him accessible to all and enabled him to sympathize with those for whom the experience of life was hard. Only one who lived a life of humiliation could appeal to others to deny themselves and take up his cross. By his victory over temptations he 'magnified the ideas of Law, Duty and Devotion,'[264] and by his responses to many different character types he demonstrated God's attitude towards each. All of this culminated in the cross, and Christ's death 'was directly and specifically designed to be a revelation' because 'it was allowed to be a public

---

[259] Ibid., 247.
[260] Ibid., 318.
[261] Ibid., 276.
[262] Ibid., 277.
[263] Ibid., 280.
[264] Ibid., 283

spectacle.'[265] Its effect upon those who witnessed it was integral to the revelation; this was not an atonement wrought in seclusion. Tymms submits that when Jesus on the Cross cried 'with a loud voice, saying, ... My God, my God, why hast thou forsaken me?' (Matthew 27:46), he intended the crowd to hear him quoting the opening words of the Messianic Psalm 22 which, as many of them would have known, goes on to declare, 'He hath not despised, nor abhorred the affliction of the afflicted; neither hath He hid His face from him; but when He cried unto Him, He heard' (v. 24). Thus, 'throughout the crucifixion Jesus was the object of His Father's love, ... and not only the object, but the agent of His love for men.'[266]

If this is the case, we must surely question Tymms's following assertion regarding the cry of dereliction that 'taking our Lord's words as absolutely true, they not obscurely suggest that there was a passing away of the Father from His abode in the Son of Man prior to the passing of the human spirit from the flesh which left an inanimate body on the cross.'[267] For the Father to desert one who was the object of his love throughout seems very odd, not to mention the docetic implication of the claim—an implication which is by no means skirted by Tymms's qualifying statement, 'The Father though present to His faith was not within Him as before.'[268] At this point I prefer godly agnosticism to speculation, and I am wary of any language which suggests that we may no longer say that '*God* was *in Christ* reconciling the world to himself' (II Corinthians 5:19). Certainly I should not wish to say that God was, for much or most of the time, or for all but a critical moment, in Christ reconciling the world to himself.

With Tymms's following claim that at Calvary we have God's sacrifice of his Son and Christ's sacrifice of himself it is possible to agree. But, yet again, why was the death necessary? 'Had Christ not died,' Tymms explains, 'dying men would have felt that they were passing through a valley over which He had soared with supernatural wings,'[269] and his obedience would have been untested by death. Again, 'Had Christ not died He would have been unable to reveal Resurrection in such a manner as would assure His followers of fellowship in His risen life. An ascended Christ who passed to the Throne by some process of translation would have been no pledge of revival to a race still doomed to die.'[270] Furthermore, had Christ not died he would have 'evaded the last injury which human hatred could inflict', and the cross would not have been seen as 'the climax of human wickedness.'[271] Yet again, Christ died to demonstrate God's power to forgive humanity's sins; to reveal sin's impotence against God, and God's grief at sin—and if we scruple to say that God can feel grieved, we must also deny that he can feel anger, pity, solitude, love; and then

---

265 Ibid., 285.
266 Ibid., 292.
267 Ibid., 294.
268 Ibid., 294.
269 Ibid., 287.
270 Ibid., 301.
271 Ibid., 302-3.

'the only God left to us will be the infinite iceberg of metaphysics.'[272] I shall return to the question of God's immutability and patripassionism in the Conclusion.

It is in the cross that Tymms finds the Christian answer to the problem of evil. He refers once again to John Stuart Mill's contention that the fact of evil indicates that God is less than omnipotent, and counters, 'The cross is ... precious because it reveals that God is not a mere passionless watcher of an agonising evolution, but is Himself a partaker of the universal travail, and has been constrained by love to take the chief labour on Himself.'[273] Indeed, the Cross demonstrates that omnipotence is incapable of bringing order out of moral chaos. The Cross is both the measure of God's love for humanity and of his abhorrence of sin; and it shows 'the difficulty and costliness of mercy.'[274] In fact God 'can only cease to condemn the sinner, when He has induced the sinner to condemn himself. ... Until we see the greatness of God's sacrifice to induce these eternal conditions of forgiveness in mankind, we shall never be duly affected by the moral energy of His love.'[275]

Justification by faith is the doctrine next reviewed by Tymms. Is justification simply a matter of spiritual rectification by faith, or is it a judicial act whereby God delivers believers from condemnation? Tymms thinks that the Latinized term, 'justification' is 'repellant' because it obscures Paul's association of the term with 'righteous' and 'righteousness'—an association which becomes clear in Greek. Indeed, God's righteousness, not our justification, is the paramount theme of Paul's letter to the Romans. Paul's gospel, Tymms argues, 'is the power of God unto salvation, because it is a revelation of God's righteousness, and of this in some way which is intimately connected with salvation.'[276] Individuals will be judged according to their light, and in a tribunal 'presided over and guided by Christ, there can be no injustice, no inequality, no mistake, and no respect of persons.'[277] Paul's great theme is not merely the mercy of God, but the righteousness of mercy. God's righteousness is at one with his mercy: 'there is no suggestion [in Romans] that Christ did or suffered anything which made it righteous for God to remit sin.'[278] While not denying that Paul uses forensic language, Tymms argues that Paul's 'great object was to eliminate the legal element from our conception of the believer's status before God.'[279] Indebted at this point to Thomas Erskine of Linlathen and those who follow in his wake, Tymms explains that he initially agreed with Erskine that the judicial/legal understanding of 'justification' should be repudiated; but he had since come to see that this was an error, because it was only by using 'justification'

---

272 Ibid., 312.
273 Ibid., 325; cf. 458.
274 Ibid., 331.
275 Ibid., 334-5.
276 Ibid., 346.
277 Ibid., 350.
278 Ibid., 352.
279 Ibid., 353.

in a forensic sense that Paul could meet the objections of his Jewish opponents.[280] His overriding purpose, however, is to show that if sinners were judged by strict law alone, justification would be impossible and condemnation inevitable. That it is possible is owing to the exercise of enabled faith in response God's grace; and there is no need to introduce what Tymms calls 'anti-Pauline', and what I might call 'accountancy' notions of imputation (conjured up by post-Reformation divines because of the fear that faith might be transmogrified into a 'work') in order to balance the books as between justice and mercy. This is a further point to which I shall return in the Conclusion. Meanwhile I record Tymms's confession:

> The glory of the gospel is that it proposes to place men in a position where they may lay aside all self-regarding fears and every servile feeling of obligation, and while releasing them from bondage to law, provides them with the purest possible motive to do right by inspiring them with faith in the love of God.[281]

In Tymms's view, and in that of Paul as construed by Tymms, there is no 'necessary incompatibility between fatherhood and judicial or kingly relations.'[282] In support of this view Tymms notes that in the first clauses of the Lord's Prayer 'Christ has exquisitely interfused the idea of a Heavenly Father with the reverence due to His sovereignty, and the submission due to His will.'[283] Consistently with this Tymms rightly sees that it would be fallacious 'to mentally divide the Godhead into separate departments and offices which involve different principles in the treatment of men'[284]—the very tendency which I queried in relation to the governmentalism of George Payne and others, and which Simon, like Tymms, repudiated. Tymms summarizes his position as follows:

> The word 'justify' is forensic, and the accounting faith for righteousness is on one side a judicial act. It is judicial because it releases from condemnation, but it is something infinitely deeper than forensic analogies can express, because the Judge is our Father pronouncing His own satisfaction in the faith His own goodness has begotten. By a true act of judgment therefore, man is granted an exit from the state of condemnation, but by this same act viewed under another aspect he is welcomed into a state of grace in which the terms of the law have no place. The deeper reality of this transition belongs to the realm best understood by the analogy of fatherhood ...[285]

Paul also makes it clear that as well as being a condition of justification, faith is 'a bond of union of living intercourse with the Divine Spirit. The Christian life is not

---

[280] For Erskine (1788-1870) see DEB; DSCHT; ODNB; Don Horrocks, *Laws of the Spiritual Order*.

[281] T. V. Tymms, *The Christian Idea of Atonement*, 371.

[282] Ibid., 383.

[283] Ibid.

[284] Ibid., 385.

[285] Ibid., 395.

only one of prayer and endeavour, but one of personal communion.' [286] Of this union a believer's baptism is a symbol. In Paul's thought,

> the most contradictory terms are used to represent different aspects of the same great change. As a judicial deliverance from sin it is 'justification' by faith. As a forsaking of sin it is a death. As an escape from moral decay and restoration to fellowship with God it is a resurrection. As a commencement of filial obedience it is a birth. As a deliverance from the bonds of iniquity and from a vain manner of life, effected by God at great cost, it is redemption. No one of these terms is adequate to express all the truth, and each one, if presented as complete and sufficient, becomes untrue, or at any rate implies something false.[287]

At the end of his doctrinal chapters Paul looks for the restoration of Israel to the God whose ultimate objective is not judicial punishment, but the bestowal of mercy upon all.

A life of fellowship with Christ and obedience to God is the appropriate response to the gospel—a life which is characterized by the continual renewing of the mind. It is a forgiven life, the life of an adopted son or daughter. It thus transpires that

> Atonement is an all inclusive word ... it glorifies the cross of Christ as in a pre-eminent and indeed unique sense the power of God unto salvation; but it makes that cross the central fact of history, the culmination of Divine activity on man's behalf, the sign which interprets all the ways of God, by revealing the Heart of the Everlasting Father to His ignorant and alienated sons.[288]

How does all of this stand in relation to the idea of immutable law? This is Tymms's final question. Is forgiveness a breach of order? He seeks to show that forgiveness works within the natural law, and not in opposition to it. The forgiven person may yet, in accordance with natural law, suffer the consequences of sin, the last of which is death. While death cannot harm Christ's followers the fact remains that he died for them, not instead of them. At death we shall finally be released from the ravages sin and evil. 'Nothing but atheism can theoretically exclude Divine forgiveness from the system of nature, and it does so not by insisting on the inviolability of law, but by denying God.[289] There follows an important cautionary word:

> The perfect harmony of this Christian idea of atonement with the reign of natural law by no means demonstrates the truth of our belief that God was in Christ reconciling the world unto Himself, but it leaves us free to receive into our hearts the joy of that belief without intellectual misgivings. It is an indisputable fact that

---

[286] Ibid., 399.
[287] Ibid., 402.
[288] Ibid., 419.
[289] Ibid., 430.

> a new spiritual power did come into the world with Christ, and that this power operates in ways which can be scientifically observed.[290]

At this point Tymms allows himself the optimism of supposing that 'Inside and outside the Church of Christ the love of truth and righteousness, and the appreciation of mercy, are extending; and these are the chief marks of the kingdom of Christ on the side which is visible on earth. ... [O]ld things are passing away.'[291]

He concludes:

> if we believe that Jesus lived and died and rose again that He might become the Author and Answerer of faith in the love of God; if we believe that in His Sacrifice God took upon Himself the burden of our redemption, and suffered to relieve our woe, to conquer our affections, to draw forth our trust, and to incline our hearts to keep His law, that Death becomes the pledge, not only of a personal salvation from sin, but of an everlasting purpose to glorify the race for which Christ died. Believing in this pledge we are assured that God's atoning work in Christ will never be allowed to fail ...[292]

Undeniably, Tymms's *The Christian Idea of Atonement* is profound, judicious, for the most part carefully argued, and in places moving. I have already indicated my intention of returning to the doctrines of God's immutability/impassibility, and the doctrine of imputation, in due course. It will suffice now to offer a brief general assessment of the work.

Those who find it helpful to classify theories of atonement under the headings utilized by Tymms at the beginning of his book: penal, representative, moral influence, would probably be inclined to include Tymms in the last category. Indeed, J. H. Srawley did precisely this when he said that Tymms's book represents 'an attempt to restate in a modern form the theory of atonement which has been associated with the name of Abelard,'[293] though he admits that Tymms does not mention Abelard in his historical sketch of the doctrine. However Abelard himself is to be interpreted,[294] it would not be fair to Tymms to say that what is so often said to be the Abelardian view, namely, that Christ's death is the supreme manifestation of God's love and that its purpose is to stimulate and draw forth our loving response, summarizes Tymms's position without remainder. Tymms is well aware of the sinfulness of sin; of the fact that its vanquishing is costly work entailing the sacrificial suffering and death of God's Son; that, subsequent to the Cross, God's way of redemption is difficult given his honouring of human freedom and the intransigence of human wills; and that repentance and faith are called for, and enabled. Above all, Tymms is under no illusion that something had to be done at the Cross, and not just shown and, he says, it is done by both the Father and the Son

---

290 Ibid., 433.

291 Ibid., 435.

292 Ibid., 437.

293 J. H. Srawley, Review of *The Christian Idea of Atonement*, 622.

294 See R. E. Weingart, *The Logic of Divine Love*.

each of whom makes a sacrifice. We also recall that Tymms locates the motive of divine redemption in the nature of God. This being so, I wonder whether he need have been so reticent concerning the kind of point that Simon made, namely that at the Cross something is done for God, and not just for ourselves. For surely, on Tymms's own theory, God's nature as love—indeed, as holy love, is by the victory of the Cross (juridically yet non-penally) satisfied, vindicated, and placarded before the world.

But this word 'world' points us towards the whole human race. Almost at the end of his book Tymms speaks the cross as 'the central fact of history', and of death as the pledge that God will glorify the race for which Christ died.[295] There is much more that could be said about the implications of the atonement for the human race; and if Tymms had expounded the point more fully, surely he would have needed to make much more than he does—indeed, he hardly mentions it at all—of the communal/covenant/ecclesial relationship into which, on the ground of Christ's work, the saints are in the meantime and for eternity drawn by the Spirit. In view of this lacuna, it is not surprising that his references to the union of the believer with Christ are too individualistic,[296] for to be in Christ is to be of the household of faith, a branch of the Vine, a limb of the body—all of them corporate images. Furthermore, the reference to the Spirit indicates another lacuna. As we saw—and again it comes late in the book—Tymms speaks of the Christian life as one of intercourse with the Divine Spirit;[297] but might we not have expected more concerning the role of God the Holy Spirit in what used to be called 'the application of redemption'? This is another way of saying that Tymms's language is not flavoured by trinitarian considerations to the degree that Simon's was. Finally, if there is a pneumatological deficiency, there is also a Christological one. Tymms, we recall, provided a list of the misfortunes which would have befallen humanity had Christ not died. But this begs the question, Who did he need to be in order to accomplish what he did? It is assumed throughout, and frequently stated, that Jesus is the Son of God, but the soteriological importance of his divine-human nature is not brought out; and when Tymms does come within reach of the matter we have the unfortunate statements regarding Jesus's cry of dereliction from the Cross.

Be all this as it may, there is no denying the fact that Tymms has presented us with a powerful case for the view that

> The only real remedy for sin, and the only perfect satisfaction of God's nature, must consist in the reconciliation of man to a state of voluntary obedience to the Divine will. Nothing less and nothing else can harmonise the salvation of sinners and the extermination of sin. Only thus can God and man be satisfied together, and be made perfect in one according to the prayer of Christ.[298]

---

[295] T. V. Tymms, *The Christian Idea of Atonement*, 419; 437.

[296] Ibid., 405-6, for example.

[297] Ibid., 398-9.

[298] Ibid., 167.

Lest any have a attenuated view of what this entails, and an attentuated view of what Tymms thinks it entails, I feel it safest to end this section with some words of Robert Mackintosh, Tymms's opposite number over the Pennines:

> A Christ who has no functions except Addisonian essays and gentle moral suasion, is not a Christ. The death of such a Christ has no appreciable meaning, and He will have no appreciable meaning to us when we are on our deathbeds.[299]

III

We have, on more than one occasion, seen that Tymms sometimes finds it hard to resist contrasting his views with those of Rome. Even when his concern is to resist the doctrine of imputed righteousness, he cannot forbear to say that 'Papists may be content to impute truth to ecclesiastical dogmas which are repugnant to their reason and conscience, but this sort of "assent" is not faith, and tends to destroy intellectual integrity, and thus conduces to the decay of man's moral nature.'[300] Again, 'The papistical doctrine of supererogation has no ethical or legal validity.'[301] But when we come to his last major work, *The Evolution of Infant Baptism and Related Ideas* (1913), we have not simply anti-Roman asides, but a whole book devoted to an indictment of Roman Catholic positions. He tells us that he has written the book, 'not because I attach peculiar value to any ritual act', but 'because I believe that an overestimate of baptism was one of the earliest germs of evil which gradually deformed the ancient Church, and that it always was, and still remains, a chief hindrance to an effectual Reformation.'[302]

As an open communion Baptist, Tymms further makes it clear that

> Paedobaptists who are loyal to the principle that the new birth is a purely spiritual process, will find no unsympathetic sentence in this book. The Infant Baptism of which I write is not that which is practised by modern evangelical Churches, but something altogether different which came into general use in the fifth century, and is still maintained by Churches which claim to be true historic heirs and representatives of ancient Christianity.[303]

The doctrine to which he objects is that which asserts that 'the gift of Eternal Life is bestowed, and can alone be bestowed through the administration of a material rite by human hands.' In reality, '"the word of good tidings" is the only water which can wash the human soul, the only seed by which men an be rebegotten.'[304] As if to balance matters up, he wryly remarks, 'Granting that Baptists are entitled to glory in

---

[299] R. Mackintosh, *The fact of the atonement*,' 347.

[300] T. V. Tymms, *The Christian Idea of Atonement*, 463.

[301] Ibid., 464.

[302] Idem, *The Evolution of Infant Baptism*, v.

[303] Ibid.

[304] Ibid., vi.

their adhesion to primitive doctrine and practice, there is evidently no escape from the confession that the worst corruptions of the Papacy must have had their origin in a Baptist Church!'[305]

Tymms says that the title of his book implies

> 1. That Infant Baptism is not an original institution of the Christian Church.[306]
> 2. That it was not suddenly introduced as a startling innovation, but grew up in the Church by an evolutionary process.
> 3. That it was not a mere variation of ritual, but was inseparably connected with the intellectual changes affecting the most fundamental ideas of Christianity.[307]

Tymms traces the evolution of baptismal ideas in some twenty-seven sources from Clement of Rome to Augustine, who is the key witness in the case he makes. Although 'There were greater thinkers and truer teachers' than Augustine, his influence was unrivalled in the period between Paul and Luther.[308] Tymms points out that Augustine's mother, Monica, refused her son's request for baptism from fear of post-baptismal sin—something which shows that infant baptism had not generally replaced the baptism of believers in Augustine's day. For his own part, while Augustine held to righteousness, faith and love as biblically-enjoined necessities, 'he burdened himself with the formidable task of co-ordinating sacramental and ecclesiastical conditions of salvation with those which pertain to the hidden man of the heart.'[309] In this he was 'foredoomed to failure.'[310] The upshot is that there are two systems of salvation in Augustine's works: salvation by grace and salvation by works. The first suffices for those who die on being baptized. Their baptism saves them from the condemnation consequent upon Adam's sin. The second saves those within the Church from post-baptismal sins. Thus, 'The first word of the Church to her offspring, as formulated by Augustine, is to inform them that they are no longer under grace, but under law. This new Gospel consists of an all-inclusive demand for righteousness, and it was presented in so threatening a manner that it sounded like a knell of second death over every regenerated creature, unless some new way of escape could be disclosed.'[311] This new way involved the elevation of the Church as the 'plenary representative agent of God on earth', and led

---

[305] Ibid., 17.

[306] Not being a Baptist, I consider that paedobaptism is not inconsistent with the biblical theme of covenant, to which Tymms, and more surprisingly, as we saw, the paedobaptist divines pay scant attention.

[307] T. V. Tymms, *The Evolution of Infant* baptism, 36-7.

[308] Ibid., 305.

[309] Ibid., 335.

[310] Ibid.

[311] Ibid., 359.

to the papal claim for 'supremacy in things temporal as well as spiritual.'[312] It thus came to be believed that while Christ vanquished the devil, the post-baptismal sins of Christians required the Church's priestly apparatus: confession, penance, absolution—as well as the ideas of purgatory and post-mortem salvation. Infant baptism became 'no longer a thing to be defended by argument, but an imperative duty to be enforced.'[313]

Elsewhere Tymms offers a further explanation with reference to Anselm:

> In Anselm's [atonement] theory, faith as the subjective condition or means of appropriating the benefits of Christ's death was scarcely taken into account. It left Romanists free to say that in baptism the great debt which Christ paid is cancelled once for all, but that post-baptismal sin creates a new debt, for which new and supplementary satisfactions must be made. Thus Anselm left the Roman system unsmitten, and during the centuries which followed, it became more and more corrupt, until at last the evil culminated in an unblushing sale of pardons in which the 'satisfaction' rendered was frankly commercial, and consisted solely in a money payment. This insolent defiance of common sense and conscience provoked the Protestant Revolution.[314]

In reflecting upon the evolution of infant baptism and its ecclesiastical consequences, Tymms grants that doctrinal development cannot be ruled out as intrinsically wrong, but, in good liberal fashion, he insists that we are obliged to exercise private judgment in respect of claimed doctrinal developments. As might be expected, therefore, he cannot agree with John Henry Newman (by now in his Roman Catholic phase) that it is only through 'the later utterances of the Church that we have any trustworthy knowledge of what the primordial ideas actually were.'[315] It follows that Newman, committed as he was to the Church's later teaching, could not test dogmas proclaimed as infallible by Christianity's 'primordial ideas', and hence the great fallacy in his position is that 'He proposed a rational test of doctrinal development which his principles forbade him to use.'[316]

While it is possible to query some of the details of Tymms's case, his overall argument is of continuing significance, as I shall suggest in the Conclusion to this book.

---

[312] Ibid., 365.

[313] Ibid., 411.

[314] Idem, *The Christian Idea of Atonement*, 37; cf. 441.

[315] Idem, *The Evolution of Infant Baptism*, 468. For Newman (1801-1891) see DNCBP; ODNB; Ian Ker, *John Henry Newman*; Sheridan Gilley, *Newman and His Age*. For my reflections on Newman on authority see *Commemorations*, ch. 1; for an attempt to unscramble the notion of doctrinal development see my *Enlightenment, Ecumenism, Evangel*, ch. 6.

[316] Ibid., 469.

IV

In the title of this chapter I have used the term 'liberal evangelical', and I am fully aware that I have made no attempt to define it. The term, no less than its perceived contrary, 'conservative evangelical', is slippery indeed.[317] To some it conjures up biblical reductionism, humanistic Christology, sentimental soteriology, and that unrealistic anthropology which supposes that with a few more schools and better sanitation the Kingdom will come. Of none of these was Tymms guilty—a point which is best demonstrated by a small anthology of own words which encapsulate and recapitulate the guiding principles of his thought and life:

On the Bible: 'By any means, and by all means, let the results of Biblical criticism be made known, and only those who are base enough to love their own opinions better than truth can fear the issue.'[318] '[T]he separation of faith, in Him of whom the Bible bears witness, from an indefensible opinion about the Bible, can scarcely fail to afford a sense of liberty and strength not previously enjoyed.'[319]

On apologetics: 'We are well assured that none will perish because of crude thinking, but the power of the Church to propagate her faith is largely dependent on her power to commend the great truths of the Gospel to the understanding as well as to the hearts of men.'[320]

On doctrine: 'He who spared not His own Son will spare no agony or blood which may be needful for the maintenance of His Law of Love among men. The cross is God's definition of Himself. ... It is easier to think of a change in the law of gravitation than of any variation in the moral government of God.'[321] 'As too often stated, the doctrine of election awakens painful misgivings in generous minds. The motiveless choice of individuals to obtain personal benefits and boons which are denied to others, equally needy, and not more unworthy, can never be defended.'[322] 'I have striven to make men see in Christ the glory of God, the beauty of the just God and Saviour.'[323]

On the Church: 'The very fount and spring of our [Baptist] Church polity lies, not in lawlessness but in the consciousness of individual authority to live each of us his own life of thought and action without any feudal superior between his soul and God.'[324] 'I believe in Holy Orders. I have no faith in the transmission of heavenly gifts through human bishops, whether Roman, Greek, or Anglican, but I believe that no man can fulfil the pastoral ministry without an ordination from the great Shepherd and Bishop of souls. Without His consecrating touch no man is capable of

---

317 For more on the slipperyness see Alan P. F. Sell, *Theology in Turmoil*, chs. 5, 6.

318 T. V. Tymms, 'Agnostic expositions,' 693.

319 Idem, *The Mystery of God*, 200.

320 Idem, *The Christian Idea of Atonement*, 4.

321 Ibid., 100, 443.

322 Idem, *The Private Relationships of Christ*, 187.

323 Idem, *The Beauty of God*, 8.

324 Idem, 'Authority: true and false,' BH, 1897, 67.

that high art which has living souls for its material, truth for its implement, Christ for its model, and the reproduction of His image for its aim.'[325]

Undergirding all was Tymms's love of people and love of Christ, and it is not fanciful to suppose that the heart of his faith and devotion is found in the concluding verses of his hymn, 'Let evening twilight turn to dawn.' The hymn is based upon the words in Luke 24:15, 'Jesus Himself drew near':

> So dwell in us by faith, dear Lord!
> In us by grace Thy throne uprear.
> Then of our darkest hours we'll say,
> Jesus Himself drew near.
>
> Be near us, Lord, till sense no more
> Divides from Him our souls revere:
> Be with us, Lord, till through the tomb
> To Jesus we draw near.[326]

---

[325] Ibid., 106.

[326] Carey Bonner, ed., *The Sunday School Hymnary*, no. 465.

CHAPTER 9

Walter Frederic Adeney (1849–1920): Pastor, Professor, Principal

Walter Frederic Adeney was born at Ealing on 14 March 1849.[1] His father, George John Adeney (1818-1899) was from a line of staunch Anglicans on his father's side, running back through Beatrice, daughter of Richard Adeney of Rowton, Shropshire, who was the Puritan Richard Baxter's mother. G. J. Adeney was educated at the Philological School in Marylebone, London, where the headmaster was Mr. Edwin Abbott, father of Dr. Edwin A. Abbott who, after teaching at King Edward's School, Birmingham and Clifton College, Bristol, was appointed headmaster of his *alma mater*, The City of London School, at the age of twenty-six.[2] Among G. J. Adeney's contemporaries at the Philological School was Charles Dickens. In due course Adeney's uncle William offered to support him through Oxford University if he would become a clergyman of the Church of England. But George, who had been sitting under the powerful preaching of the Congregationalist Dr. John Liefchild of Craven Chapel, Marlborough Street, London,[3] became utterly persuaded that he could not give his assent and consent to the *Book of Common Prayer* or sign the Articles of the Church of England. His New Testament taught him the propriety of the Congregational church order, and a Congregationalist he became. He later published a pamphlet entitled, *Congregationalism Scriptural; or, The Nature and Constitution of the Church of Christ as set forth in the New Testament* (1851).[4]

George Adeney found employment in Wilmot's stained glass and church furnishing business, and concurrently studied under Dr. John Harris of Cheshunt College and Dr. Robert Vaughan, minister of Horton Street Congregational Church, Kensington.[5] At the same time he was teaching in the Sunday School at Albert

---

[1] For Adeney see CYB, 1921, 102; WWW, 1916-1928; *The British Congregationalist*, 11 May 1911, 371; *East Sussex News*, 10 September 1920.

[2] For the Abbotts (1808-1882) and (1838-1926) see ODNB.

[3] For Liefchild (1780-1862) see CYB, 1863, 235-239; ODNB.

[4] Published by J. Snow of London. For G. J. Adeney see CYB, 1900, 158-9.

[5] John Harris (1802-1856) was Congregational minister at Epsom (1825-1837); theological tutor at Cheshunt College (1825-1843); and the first Principal of New College, London (1850-1856). See ODNB. Robert Vaughan (1795-1868) served at Angel Street, Worcester (1819-1825); Horton Street, Kensington (1825-1843); as Professor of Ancient and Modern History, University of London (1833-1843); and as the first

Street, London, and he began to preach for a number of evangelical bodies. In 1842 he left business on accepting the call to Ealing Congregational Church, and there he served for fourteen years. His life-work, however, was at Reigate, Surrey, where he ministered with distinction from 1856 to 1897. During the year following his arrival there the chapel was extended and new Sunday School buildings were erected.[6] He held a number of offices in the town; was active in the establishment of the church at nearby Redhill; and toured most of the English counties, as well as Ireland and the Channel Islands, on behalf of the British and Foreign Bible Society.

George Adeney's preaching was said to be 'pictorial and illustrative, his manner energetic and vivacious; the tone and spirit of his utterances were fluent, earnest, and affectionate.'[7] Never satisfied with his work, he sometimes re-wrote his sermons three or four times. He was among the first ministers to give a children's address during the Sunday morning service, and he excelled at this. He was able to marry firmness of conviction with 'the spirit of gentleness and kindness.'[8] At a valedictory meeting marking the end of his long and influential ministry Adeney 'was presented with a cheque for £300/0/0 and an album containing the signatures of the subscribers.'[9]

Walter Adeney followed his father into the Congregational ministry. His early preaching experience was gained in the country chapels associated with the Reigate church, and he never lost his love for rural England. He trained at New College, London, whose Principal was Samuel Newth. At this period the theological colleges covered arts subjects, and even some sciences, as well as theology, their students being excluded from the English universities. They entered students for the examinations of the University of London which, until it was re-constituted in 1900, was an examining body only. Degrees in theology were not available until a Faculty was constituted on 21 November 1900. Newth himself held the London BA in Mathematics, and was the first London student to earn the MA in that subject. From 1850 onwards he taught what would nowadays be regarded as the unusual combination of Mathematics and Ecclesiastical History, and when Robert Halley[10]

President of Lancashire Independent College, Manchester (1843-1857). Short pastorates at Uxbridge (1857-1860) and Torquay (1867-1868) were interspersed with literary work. See ODNB; *The Congregationalist*, VI, March 1877, 129-148; Joseph Thompson, *Lancashire Independent College, 1843-1893*, *passim*. At the opening of Lancashire College under Vaughan, Harris gave an address in which he acknowledged that while 'the preaching of some uneducated ministers had been greatly blessed', God 'did not bless on account of their ignorance, but in spite of it.' See J. Harris, *The Importance of an Educated Ministry: A Discourse preached preparatory to the Opening of the Lancashire Independent College*, 29.

[6] See John Waddington, *Surrey Congregational History*,, 285-286; Edward E. Cleal, *The Story of Congregationalism in Surrey*, 381.

[7] CYB, 1900, 159.

[8] Ibid.

[9] Edward E. Cleal, *The Story of Congregationalism in Surrey*, 382.

[10] For Halley (1796-1876) see ODNB. In the original DNB Alexander Gordon said that Halley was 'well fitted' for the post of Classical Tutor at Highbury College, where he

resigned in 1872 Newth succeeded to the Chair of New Testament Exegesis and Ecclesiastical History, whilst continuing to serve as Principal.[11]

Adeney excelled in New Testament Exegesis, and proceeded to gain high honours in the London MA (Branch III: Logic, Moral Philosophy, Political Philosophy, History of Philosophy and Political Economy).[12] A strong tradition had been established in the latter fields at Highbury College (New's predecessor) by Henry Rogers.[13] In Adeney's time Philosophy was in the hands of John Hensley Godwin, himself a student of Rogers, who later published two substantial works: *Intellectual Principles; or, Elements of Mental Science* (1884), and *Active Principles; or, Elements of Moral Science* (1885).[14]

In 1872 Adeney was called to the pastorate of Acton Congregational Church, where he remained until 1889. In June 1873 he married Miss Mary Jane Hampton, daughter of Mr. and Mrs. W. Hampton of Reigate, and they had four sons and four daughters. He was greatly appreciated for his teaching ministry, and, like his father before him, he was keenly interested in the children's work of the church. He put much effort into his classes for Sunday School teachers on Christian evidences and the Greek New Testament, and contributed to *The Sunday School Times* and Bagster's *Comprehensive Teacher's Bible* (1885). He maintained this interest to the end. In 1897 a series of three books under the title, *The Story of Christ and His People*, was published under his editorship by the Council of the Congregational Young People's Union. These are graded lessons. The First Grade volume, by Amy Pridham, contains lesson talks, questions and suggested hymns; and it includes three envelopes containing cards on which are printed illustrative line drawings in black ink. The Intermediate volume, by a Mrs. Dyson, contains talks, questions, things to do at home, and is illustrated with coloured maps. The Senior volume, by F. Herbert Stead and Adeney himself has a heavier emphasis upon biblical exegesis; there are

---

served from 1826-1839. But when, during his Manchester period (1837-1857), he supplied in that capacity at Lancashire Independent College the students took a different view. See F. J. Powicke, *David Worthington Simon*, 15; J. Thompson, *Lancashire Independent College*, 108. Halley succeeded Harris as Principal of New College in 1857, subsequently serving temporarily as Professor at Spring Hill College, Birmingham (1872-1873).

[11] For Newth (1821-1898) see CYB, 1899, 195-197; ODNB. His lecture notes are among the archives of New College, London, held at Dr. Williams's Library, London, L.9.

[12] The other two Branches were I (Classics) and II (Mathematics). I am grateful to Zoë Browne, Assistant Archivist, Senate House Library, London, for this information.

[13] For Rogers (1806-1877) see DNCBP; ODNB; Alan P. F. Sell, *Dissenting Thought and the Life of the Churches*, chs. 17, 18; idem, *Philosophy, Dissent and Nonconformity 1689-1920*, *passim*. On occasion students neglected their college theological course in favour of their MA studies. See *Dissenting Thought*, 478. Rogers lectured at Highbury until 1839, then at Spring Hill, Birmingham, until 1858, when he succeeded Vaughan as President of Lancashire Independent College.

[14] See Alan P. F. Sell, *Philosophy, Dissent and Nonconformity*, 112-114, 160-162. For Godwin (1809-1889) see CYB, 1890, 143-145; DNCBP.

questions for home study, daily Bible readings, and maps. There is material for teachers and lessons are in outline only.

Adeney worked tirelessly for the Sunday School Union, and his devotion to the cause rendered his judgment of 1900 the more telling. Sunday School methods were outmoded, he declared; they had not heeded modern biblical criticism, and they adhered to the 'old outworn system of numerous classes of all ages in a common schoolroom, amid a Babel of voices, where wholly untrained teachers' fought a losing battle.[15] Of him it was said that he 'had a keen sense of the mischief done by failing to enlighten the people, and especially the young people, as to the changed views of the inspiration of the bible effected by the results of higher critical study. In a series of articles in *The Christian* World he was very outspoken on this issue, and gave offence to some timid adherents of the antiquated conception of verbal and literal infallibility.'[16] In 1907 Adeney was among a group of eminent scholars gathered by the Sunday School Union to consider the curriculum and make practical recommendations. The convener was the Congregationalist A. E. Garvie, and the members included the Primitive Methodist, Arthur S. Peake, by now Adeney's colleague in Manchester, and the Congregationalists P. T. Forsyth and W. H. Bennett. Their proposals concerned Sunday School organization and the provision of suitably trained teachers. In the following year Adeney delivered a paper entitled, 'Sunday School reform in the use of the Bible' at the third meeting of the International Congregational Council, held in Edinburgh.[17] At the same Council Adeney caused a fluttering in the dovecotes when he raised a discussion point following a paper by the Revd. T. E. Slater of Bangalore on 'Modern theology and the missionary enterprise.' Adeney felt moved to 'utter a word of reassurance ... to those of our friends who are somehow alarmed lest newer ideas of the Bible should paralyse missionary enterprise, as some of them feared was likely to be the case in their Sunday School work.' His prescription was that 'we must not mix up fear of consequences with the pursuit of truth. If truth should lead us into a Christless wilderness, into the Christless wilderness we must go.'[18] This was too much for the Revd Thomas Lloyd of Colwyn Bay, who construed Adeney's position as an adverse judgment against those engaged in mission who took a more traditional view of Scripture. Adeney begged to offer an explanation and, following a vote, he was permitted to do this. He declared that he had no wish to imply that Lloyd was not 'a loyal follower of the truth,' but only to counter the claim that 'if certain views are

---

[15] *The Sunday School Chronicle*, 1900, 783, quoted by Philip B. Cliff, *The Rise and Development of the Sunday School Movement in England 1780-1980*, 198.

[16] Obituary, *The Christian World*, 2 September 1920, 3(i).

[17] W. F. Adeney, 'Sunday School reform in the use of the Bible,' in John Brown, ed., *Proceedings of the Third International Congregational Council*, London: Congregational Union of England and Wales, 1908, 365-372.

[18] W. F. Adeney in *Proceedings of the Third International Congregational Council*, 517.

held we could not preach the gospel, and therefore we must not hold those views because they would hinder the preaching of the gospel.'[19]

During the last two years of his pastorate Adeney gave biblical lectures at New College, and Cheshunt College, and among his first students was George Currie Martin, who later wrote,

> Accustomed to brilliant lectures at the University of Edinburgh, I was at once impressed by the clearness, honesty, and brilliance of these studies in the Theology of the Old and New Testaments. They were quite up-to-date. The lecturer knew his ground and led his men fearlessly to the sources of truth, teaching them to examine all theories, and to trust the light of reason. ... [H]is Church History lectures were vivid discussions of vital points—the dry bones being left for the study of the text-book. ... [To his students Adeney was] 'Our Chief.'[20]

In 1888 Adeney taught Church History at Hackney College. The following year saw him installed in the Chair of New Testament and Church History at New College. Like other Congregational notables, including the Old Testament Scholar, W. H. Bennett of Hackney College, the Adeneys became members of Lyndhurst Road Congregational Church, whose distinguished minister, R. F. Horton, had begun his work there in 1883, and became pastor emeritus in 1930.[21] It was not long before Bennett and Adeney began to teach classes in both Hackney and New Colleges, thereby relieving both of them of the necessity of covering the whole Bible. Bennett was later to become Adeney's successor as President of Lancashire College, Bennett's *alma mater*.[22] Adeney played his part in the affairs of the Senatus Academicus of Associated Theological colleges, British and Colonial, which had

---

[19] Ibid., 519.

[20] G. Currie Martin, 'Walter F. Adeney. An Appreciation,' *The Christian World*, 9 September 1920, 3(ii). Following a pastorate at Nairn (1890-1895), Martin (1865-1937) became G. J. Adeney's assistant at Reigate until 1903, when he became Professor of New Testament at both Yorkshire United Independent College, Bradford, and Lancashire Independent College. He was thus a colleague of Walter Adeney's until 1909, when he became joint foreign secretary of the London Missionary Society. He contributed the volumes on Proverbs, Ecclesiastes and the Song of Songs, and on Ephesians, Colossians, Philemon and Phillipians to *The Century* Bible, of which series Adeney was General Editor. From 1912 until his retirement in 1930 Martin lectured under the auspices of the National Adult School Union. Among other things, he served a term as President of the Union of Modern Free Churchmen. See CYB, 1938, 665.

[21] See Albert Peel and J. A. R. Marriott, *Ralph Forman Horton*, 145.

[22] For Bennett (1855-1920) see CYB, 1921, 103; ODNB. Bennett was at The City of London School under Dr. Abbott. From there he proceeded to the University of Manchester (BA and MA in Mathematics) and Lancashire Independent College, and thence to St. John's College, Cambridge (1st Class Hons. Theology). He taught at Rotherham Independent Academy (1884-1888) and Hackney College, London (1888-1913), before returning to Lancashire College (1913-1920). He earned the Cambridge LittD in 1902, and served as the first President of the Society for the Study of the Old Testament from 1917 until his death.

been founded in 1879 to offer degree-standard examinations in theology to those excluded from the universities,[23] and the number of his publications increased considerably. In recognition of his scholarly contribution the University of St. Andrews awarded Adeney its Honorary Doctorate in Divinity *in absentia* on 1 April 1902, at a ceremony presided over by Sir James Donaldson, Principal of the University. The biblical scholar, James Moffatt, was the other recipient of the DD on that occasion.[24]

R. F. Horton having declined the invitation of the College Governors, in 1903 Adeney followed in the wake of Caleb Scott's long Presidency of Lancashire Independent College (1869-1902).[25] The *Report* of the Lancashire College Committee for 1903 informs us that on 6 October 1903

> a public meeting was held in the College Assembly Room specially to recognise the appointment of Dr. Adeney as Principal of the College. The Rev. Thomas Cain (Chairman of the Committee) presided. The speakers were the Rev. R. F. Horton, M.A.,D.D., the Rev. R. Vaughan Pryce, M.A.,D.D. (Principal of New College, London), the Rev. A. Goodrich. D.D.,[26] Lieut.-Colonel W. W. Pilkington, J.P., Professor George Currie Martin, M.A.,B.D., and Professor Graham Taylor, of Chicago, U.S.[27]

Adeney became well known in the churches, and in 1911 delivered the Annual Sermon at the Assembly of the Lancashire Congregational Union.[28] In the following year he was Chairman of the Congregational Union of England and Wales. In one of the two addresses delivered from that Chair Adeney returned to a theme dear to his heart. While continuing to believe that it was 'God's good pleasure by the foolishness of preaching to save them that believe,' he observes that the masses were never within earshot of the preaching. He eschews the remedy proposed by those

---

[23] See further, Alan P. F. Sell, *Philosophy, Dissent and Nonconformity*, 128-132.

[24] I am grateful to Mrs. Rachel Hart, Archivist, University of St. Andrews, for this and related information. There are four references to Adeney in the Minutes of the Senatus Academicus from 14 December 1901, when his name was first proposed for the degree, and the record of its conferment. The references are at UY452/23/177; UY452/23/185; UY452/23/198; UY452/23/218.

[25] For Scott (1831-1919), himself the son of Walter Scott, the theological tutor at Airedale College (1834-1856), Yorkshire, see CYB, 1920, 112-113; J. Thompson, *Lancashire Independent College*, *passim*; Elaine Kaye, *For the Work of Ministry. A History of Northern College and its Predecessors*, *passim*.

[26] Minister of Chorlton Road Congregational Church, Manchester.

[27] *Lancashire Independent College, Whalley Range, Manchester. Report of the Committee for 1903*, 11. John Rylands University Library of Manchester: Congregational College Archives, Box 32, item 20.

[28] See W. Gordon Robinson (yet another President of Lancashire Independent College), *A History of the Lancashire Congregational Union 1856-1956*, Manchester: Lancashire Congregational Union, 1956, 175. For Robinson (1903-1977) URCYB, 1979, 265; ODNB.

who contend that if only preachers would 'fling over our philosophy and our criticism and preach the simple gospel the people would flock to hear us.' He grants that 'It will always be true that the appeal of God's love in Christ's redemption is the most potent appeal to the heart,' but points out that

> The beginning of the decline of the authority of the pulpit may be dated in the latter half of the nineteenth century. But this was the very time of Mr. Spurgeon's gospel preaching in his tabernacle, of the great Moody and Sankey missions, and of the palmy days of the Salvation Army—not to mention such pulpit giants as Liddon, Maclaren, Parker, Henry Ward Beecher, Phillips Brooks.

The question therefore presses:

> The method of exhortation proving inadequate, what other resources have we? I submit that we may do better with the method of education. This means that we must concentrate attention more assiduously on the proper objects of education and those spheres of life where it is most practicable. In other words, the main effort of the Church in preparing the way for the coming kingdom should be in the training of the young. ... This is not merely one work of the Church—one among many activities; it is *the* work in the sense that if this is done effectually the rest follows with ease, while if this fails, no amount of assiduity in other directions can ever make up for the fatal fault.[29]

Adeney's wisdom reached further afield through the exercise of his journalistic talents. Among other things he wrote a weekly column on 'The Free Churches' for the *Manchester Guardian* under the pseudonym Alpha. His first article concerned General Booth and the Salvation Army, concerning which body Adeney waxed lyrical: 'Whenever I meet a company of Salvationists in the street or on a railway platform I am struck by a combination of earnestness and cheerfulness shining through their countenances. These modern Franciscans have been fascinated by what Renan called "the sweet Galilean dream"'[30]—something which would have been news to most of them. More sternly, Adeney did not pull his punches where political matters were concerned. Writing on 'The education bill' he thought that Free Churchpeople would not favour all aspects of it, but that they would welcome the idea that state schools should be under public control, and that their teachers should not be subjected to denominational tests. Nevertheless, a

---

[29] W. F. Adeney, 'The Church for the Kingdom,' Address from the Chair of the Congregational Union of England and Wales delivered on Tuesday 15 October 1912, CYB, 1913, 54-55. In the year of Adeney's address impressive new Sunday School buildings were opened at Holmfirth, Yorkshire, while those at Hillhouse, Huddersfield; Harringay, London; Regent Street, Oldham; and Warrington were enlarged. For descriptions see CYB, 1913. Adeney wrote on changing styles of preaching in *A Century's Progress in Religious Life and Thought*, ch. 11, making clear his preference for 'simplicity, uncoventionality, naturalness' over the more florid and repetitive rhetoric of former times.

[30] *The Manchester Guardian*, 30 January 1908, 4 (vi).

> massive union of liberal forces is requisite if the bill is to be driven through Parliament; for we cannot ignore the monstrous anomaly that, in spite of a historic January 6, 1907, when Mr. Balfour received his dismissal, the dscredited ex-Premier practises a right of veto on all measures proposed by the King's Government, and that on his own responsibility alone, supported by the suffrages of a few hundred country gentlemen who happen to be born to coronets.[31]

From time to time, as we might expect, Adeney turned in his column to Sunday School affairs. He thought that the *British Weekly's* declaration that there was a gulf between the Sunday Schools and the churches indicated, if true, an appalling state of affairs. He recalled a recent address given in Salford by R. F. Horton, President of the Sunday School Union, in which he spoke of the wholesome influences propagated by Sunday Schools. This was not enough for Adeney, who sought the development of Christian character that 'in the normal course will flow along the channel of some church association.' He elevated the role of the minister as the link between church and Sunday School; he welcomed the recent development of young people's departments in the denominational centres, and while appealing for adequate teaching in Sunday Schools, he cautioned against the 'manufacture of youthful prigs.'[32] In another article he extolled Lyndhurst Road Congregational Church, Hampstead, to which he and his family had belonged during Adeney's New College days. Delightfully situated, the church 'might have become a land of lotus-eaters where it is always afternoon.' But in fact it was a model of an altruistic church. Indeed, the Methodist social gospel preacher, Hugh Price Hughes, told the members that they needed their Lyndhurst Road Mission in the poorer area of Kentish Town 'if their own souls were to be saved.' Under Horton's versatile ministry people could hear messages of the Keswick type in the mornings, and discourses on social responsibility directed to working folk in the evenings.[33] Among many other topics, Adeney wrote on children and sermons, Livingstone's centenary, and the centenary of the Wesleyan Missionary Society.[34] His last article, as retirement and departure from Manchester approached, was on the idea of a national church.[35]

In a quite different vein this lover of the countryside, of Lake District holidays and of Wordsworth, whose principal recreation was gardening, wrote pieces for *The Christian World* using the *nom-de-plume*, Romany. In one of these, on 'Our camp at Easdale', he reports that he and his family had climbed Helvellyn. From the summit they saw that 'the neighbourhood of Keswick was immersed in mist—to be dispelled, I hope, at the [Keswick] Convention.'[36] A few years later we read of the family's exploits in 'The Rhinns of Galloway.' Here they encountered an elderly landlady who, though not a Free Church of Scotland member herself, referred to the

---

[31] Ibid., 27 February 1908, 14 (ii).
[32] Ibid., 29 September 1910, 14 (iv).
[33] Ibid., 3 November 1910, 414 (iv).
[34] Ibid., 23 January 1913, 16 (iv); 20 March 1913, 14 (iv); 15 May 1910, 12 (iii).
[35] Ibid., 26 June 1913, 14 (iii).
[36] *The Christian World*, 18 July 1901, 11.

United Presbyterians, with whom the Free Church had united, in rather savage terms: 'They came out; let them stay out.'[37] Two weeks later, now on tour in Wales, the family dog went missing: 'Never more faithful dog breathed the air of England. Shall we never see him again?' Adeney begged sharp-eyed readers of *The Christian World* too keep their eyes open for a wiry Yorkshire terrier, white with black spots.[38] The following week he rejoiced in print that the lost had been found. Not for nothing did his obituarist say that Adeney 'hated being shut in, intellectually or physically, and at one time his favourite way of spending a holiday was gipsying in a caravan.'[39]

Adeney had arrived in Manchester at what was an auspicious moment for theology. With his arrival in their midst the Lancashire College Committee felt that the College 'is now in a position to take full advantage of the opportunities arising from the new Vioctoria University of Manchester, and also to contribute to the efficiency and success of the Faculty of Theology, which will shortly be established ...'[40] In 1904 the Faculty was established, a venture in which the city's theological colleges were fully involved. Adeney taught biblical subjects in Lancashire College, and was also part-time Lecturer on the History of Doctrine for the University.[41] In due course he served a term as Dean of the Faculty. Of the twelve papers gathered in the published *Inaugural Lectures*, seven were by scholars employed in the theological colleges, Lancashire College supplying those by Adeney and his colleague Robert Mackintosh.[42] In the Preface, Peake, the first Dean of the Faculty and editor of the collection, noted that 'in harmony with one of its fundamental principles the University is colour-blind to theological and denominational differences, and at every point, whether in teaching or examining, carefully protects the susceptibilities of its students from violation.'[43] Adeney's lecture was on 'Ancient schools of theology.' He sets out from the Jewish schools as grounded in the Law, itself the subject of much interpretation. He refers to the rabbis Shammai and Hillel, and then comes to Paul, the author of Hebrews, and the Johannine writings. He emphasizes the fact that the early Christian theological schools were for the training of the Church as a whole, not for a particular profession within it. In passing he commends the Society of Friends for its eagerness to provide religious education for all its members, and he expresses the hope that the new Faculty will reach out to laymen (*sic*) as well as ordinands. But the ministry does require training, and Adeney briefly notes the provision of this from Gregory of Nazianzus onwards. Originally, however, the education of the Church was through schools of catacheumens, of which those of

---

37 Ibid., 1 August 1907, 4.

38 Ibid., 15 August 1907, 11; 22 August 1907, 11.

39 Obituary, *The Christian World*, 3 (i).

40 *Report of the Committee for 1903*, 11.

41 For many years the University History of Doctrine syllabus was taught in the theological colleges by members of their staffs: this an evidence of doctrinal diplomacy.

42 For Mackintosh (1858-1933) see DNCBP, reprinted in DTCBP; ODNB; Alan P. F. Sell, *Robert Mackintosh, Theologian of Integrity*.

43 A. S. Peake, ed., *Inaugural Lectures delivered by members of the Faculty of Theology during its First Session,1904-5*, vii.

Alexandria, Caesarea, Antioch and Edessa are passed in review. With the passage of time theology became the 'Queen of the Sciences' with 'mischievous effects.'[44] But when, at the opposite pole, the University of London excluded theology altogether, this was a 'startling anomaly.'[45] He concludes that practical needs and social problems notwithstanding, 'a powerful ministry must be, if not exactly what we may venture to name "a learned ministry," still a ministry trained in a scholarship which does not shrink from the test of ordeals as rigorous as those by which candidates for the professions of law, medicine, and science, are trained.'[46]

That Walter Adeney devoted himself to the nurture of such a ministry, whilst being ever alive to the educational needs of the whole Church, I shall proceed to show as I consider in turn his contribution to biblical studies, ecclesiastical history, and doctrine, theology and apologetics.

I

The story of the reception of modern biblical criticism clearly shows that even pioneering critics of the milder sort could place their careers on the line. In Britain there was the celebrated case of William Robertson Smith, who had studied under Wellhausen, and who became Professor of Old Testament at the Free Church College, Aberdeen, in 1870. He began to introduce his students to higher critical views, but it was his articles published in 1875 in the ninth edition of *Encyclopaedia Britannica* which thrust him into the glare of ecclesiastical publicity, with the result that he was deposed from his Chair in 1881, though not dismissed from the ministry.[47] But Smith was not the first to fall foul of the authorities. As early as 1843, William Benton Clulow resigned from his post at Airedale Independent College, Bradford—despite enjoying the support of his Principal, Walter Scott—because his approach to the Bible did not commend itself to the College Committee.[48] More dramatic, as we have seen, was the resignation on 29 June 1857

---

[44] W. F. Adeney, 'Ancient schools of philosophy,' in A. S. Peake, ed., *Inaugural Lectures*, 217.

[45] Ibid. The reference is to the 'godless university' constituted in 1827, subsequently known as University College London. The Christian rejoinder to it was King's College, founded in 1829. These colleges, together with other bodies, came to comprise the University of London, which received its charter in 1836.

[46] Ibid., 218.

[47] For Smith (1846-1894) see ODNB.

[48] For Clulow (1802-1888) see CYB, 1883, 269-271; ODNB; K. W. Wadsworth, *Yorkshire United Independent College*, 113-114. Elaine Kaye, *For the Work of Ministry*, 107, gives Clulow's views on 'the Christian Sabbath' as being the cause of dissatisfaction. This, says Roger Tomes, 'does not suggest that [Clulow] was influenced specifically by biblical criticism.' See Tomes's illuminating paper, '"Learning a new technique": the reception of biblical criticism in the Nonconformist colleges,' JURCHS, VII no. 5, October 2004, 288, n. 6. But if Clulow were objecting to the biblical defences of 'the Christian sabbath' which were advanced in the *Westminster Confession* which all staff were required to sign, this could have proved a stumbling-block to those of a

of Samuel Davidson from his Chair of Biblical Language and Literature at Lancashire Independent College. By now there was a good deal of popular feeling against 'the German error', so when Davidson emerged in print as denying the Mosaic authorship of the Pentateuch, he was immediately under suspicion. He compounded his 'error' by submitting an 'explanation' to the College Committee which embodied a naturalistic view of biblical inspiration which met with open hostility. Within a month, President Robert Vaughan, who had been inclined to resign for the previous two or three years, tendered his resignation on 20 July 1857, pointing out that 'Recent events, as may be supposed, have done something towards strengthening this inclination.'[49] With hindsight Adeney observed,

> It is a remarkable testimony to the changed condition of public opinion that, at the jubilee celebration of the college [1893], Dr. Davidson was repeatedly referred to in terms of highest admiration. He lived to see the positions for which, as their pioneer, he had suffered martyrdom widely accepted by British scholarship and his own Christian character reverently honoured.[50]

This is confirmed by the remark of Elkanah Armitage, Professor of Philosophy at Rotherham Independent College on the occasion of the Jubilee: 'The victory in such struggles as these has often lain with the vanquished.'[51]

Not surprisingly, when Adeney assumed his New Testament duties at New College in 1889, he was well aware of the 'exceptionally heavy' demands laid upon any teacher in his position.[52] From reading his writings on the Bible it would seem that, temperamentally, he was ideally equipped to remove blinkers without unduly antagonising students and readers—and (which was ever a concern to college governors) without adversely affecting donations to the College; though this did not prevent him, once he was established in his post, from launching an occasional torpedo: 'It is plain that the rabbinical notion of verbal inerrancy has no longer any

---

conservative disposition. Be that as it may, Tomes cites Clulow's *Year Book* obituary to the effect that at his death in 1882 Clulow left MS notes on the Greek New Testament 'which showed that he was "abreast of the most advanced criticism."' For accounts of the general situation see Willis B. Glover, *Evangelical Nonconformists and Higher Criticism in the Nineteenth Century*; Alan P. F. Sell, *Theology in Turmoil. The Roots, Course and Significance of the Conservative-Liberal Debate in Modern Theology*, (1986), ch. 2.

[49] J. Thompson, *Lancashire Independent College*, 146. For Davidson (1806-1898) see ODNB; *The Autobiography and Diary of Samuel Davidson*, ed. by his daughter Anne J. Davidson, Edinburgh: T. & T. Clark, 1899; R. Allen, *The Presbyterian College Belfast 1853*-1953; John Lea, 'The Davidson controversy,' *Durham University Journal*, LXVIII, 1975, 15-32; F. Roger Tomes, '"We are hardly prepared for this style of teaching yet": Samuel Davidson and Lancashire Independent College,' JURCHS, V no. 7, October 1995, 398-414.

[50] W. F. Adeney, *A Century's Progress in Religious Life and Thought*, 80.

[51] *Lancashire Independent College. Jubilee 1893. Addresses delivered and Papers read*, 72. For Armitage (1844-1929) see CYB, 1930, 222-223; DNCBP.

[52] New College, London MSS. 149/1, 52.

ground to stand upon.'[53] I shall review his position on biblical criticism and introduction, and then refer to his general writings on the Bible, his exegetical work, his biblical expositions, and his New Testament theology. It will become clear that, unlike some biblical scholars, Adeney was able to write at varying degrees of technicality, and that he had a particular concern to reach ministers, people in the pews, and children.

As early as 1882 we find Adeney answering his own question, 'Why do we believe in the Bible?' His answer is to the effect that 'Our belief in the Bible can never be scientific. It must always depend on moral considerations. In other words, it must always be *faith*. Yet it may be tried by the crucial scientific test. It may be verified by experience. We try its ideas and we find they work.'[54] He spent much of the rest of his life putting flesh on these bare bones.

In 1896 Adeney published *How to Read the Bible. Hints for Sunday School Teachers and Other Bible Students*, and dedicated it to his wife, 'whose accuracy of observation, refinement of taste, and spiritual sympathies have helped in the removal of the flaws and towards the elevation of the tone and character of this little book, as of all my work.' Of this introductory work the reviewer in *The Expository* Times declared, 'It is one of the best. For Professor Adeney has made this subject almost his own.'[55] After four impressions and a Welsh translation, a revised and updated edition was published in 1905, and when that was reprinted in 1907 a total of 22,000 copies in all had been produced. So valuable was this book deemed to be that the Independent Press republished it in 1929, its text unchanged, but with a Foreword by Leyton Richards and an updated bibliography by A. J. Grieve.[56] In the Preface Adeney described the book as 'a most elementary introduction to the study of the Bible,' and explains his motivation in the following terms:

> So perverse have been the methods of popular exposition, and so long have they been pursued as of unquestionable validity, that the mention of some of the simplest rules for a right study of the Bible—rules that are accepted without question, and applied almost automatically in the case of other books—will no doubt strike some people, who are in a way very familiar with their Bibles, as a daring innovation. Thus it comes about that those principles which should be most evident, and the setting out of which in words may seem to be almost an insult to the reader's intelligence, are, in fact, the very principles which most urgently require to be insisted on.[57]

---

[53] W. F. Adeney, *A Century's Progress in Religious Life and Thought*, 88.

[54] W. F. Adeney, 'Why do we believe in the Bible?' *The Congregationalist*, XI, 1882, 896.

[55] ET, VIII, 1896-1897, 125.

[56] For Grieve (1874-1952) see CYB, 1953, 508-509; Charles E. Surman [Grieve's son-in-law], *Alexander James Grieve, MA, DD. 1874-1952*. Grieve was President of Lancashire College from 1922-1943, that is, between W. H. Bennett and W. Gordon Robinson.

[57] W. F. Adeney, *How to Read the Bible* , vii-viii.

Adeney explains that while the Bible's 'most essential truths are within the reach of the most simple reader,' the fact remains that it is a collection of ancient oriental material which is liable to be misunderstood, and has fallen prey to 'the most eccentric devices in interpretation.'[58] It has been subjected to allegorical and literalistic interpretations; later theological ideas have been read back into the text, and texts have been wrested from their contexts. Such is Adeney's diagnosis of the situation. His remedy is the application of the historical method. This entails in general the honest attempt to place ourselves in the position of the original authors,[59] so that we may determine what their intentions were. More particularly, it requires us to

> Be careful to work on a correct text;
> Endeavour to understand the exact meaning of the words and phrases studied;
> Read every passage in the light of its context;
> Note the distinctive character and purpose of each book of Scripture;
> Make a separate study of the works of each Scripture writer, and in reading any passage consider it especially with regard to the rest of the writings of its author;
> Study each part of the Bible in connection with the period when it was written, and take into account the circumstances of its origin;
> Trace the historical development of revelation;
> Study the Bible in sympathy with the spirit in which it was written;
> Use common intelligence in the reading of Scripture.[60]

Adeney proceeds to introduce the various parts of the Bible, and it will suffice us to note the way in which he handles a sample of potentially neuralgic issues. Concerning the Genesis creation narratives he declares that 'we know that the creation of the world took place in an antiquity immeasurably distant from us,' and hence, 'We have no excuse for turning to the early chapters of Genesis for instruction in astronomy, geology, or the antiquities of pre-historic man; but they are of permanent interest and authority for truths which no science can discover.'[61] Wary of those who rummage around in prophecy, Adeney reminds his readers that the prophet's 'peculiar office was to speak for God, to give God's message to the people; and that message more often concerned the present than the future.'[62]

---

[58] Ibid., 14.

[59] Adeney was, of course, fortunate in being spared the strictures of those postmodernist literary theorists who deny that this can be done (though it is tempting to speculate upon what he might have said to them).

[60] Adeney expounds each of these principles in turn. See *How to Read the Bible*, 19-50.

[61] Ibid., 56, 57.

[62] Ibid., 72.

Adeney devotes a section of his book to the Messianic prophecies in the Old Testament. In attempting to assuage the fears of those who understand historical criticism as robbing prophecies of this type of their 'peculiar value as witnesses to Christ,' he divides the Messianic prophecies into two classes: 'those that were intended from the beginning to predict the coming of the Messiah ... [or] the Messianic age; and, second, those which, though written with no such reference, nevertheless contain truths of a Messianic character.'[63] He grants that many of the prophecies to which Christians have given a Messianic interpretation do not have such a reference in their original context. To suppose that they do, 'may be ingenious; it is not exegesis.'[64] There is, however, a third option, and that is to recognize that although the prophecies in question were not Messianic in their original setting, they are, with hindsight, patient of a Messianic interpretation on the ground that they 'are perfectly realised by Christ.' In other words, 'The inspired thoughts are too great for the events with which the prophets connect them.'[65]

This is the approach that Adeney had adopted in his earlier work, *The Hebrew Utopia: A Study of Messianic Prophecy* (1879). He here summarizes his general attitude towards biblical prophecy:

> while the difficulties which repel many enquirers at the very threshold of the study of prophecy belong, for the most part, to the concrete form in which it is thrown and the objective relations which it holds with contemporary history, and do not touch the character of its ideal truths, these ideal truths constitute the sum and substance of prophecy—at least, ... they are all that is important as a Divine revelation and an introduction to the Christian faith.[66]

Along this line he is persuaded that not only prophecies regarding the anointed son of David, but also those announced in Isaiah 52, can be understood as finding their fulfilment only in Jesus Christ. He is thus led to a conclusion which owes much to the evolutionary optimism of his age which is not so easily assimilable on our side of two World Wars and subsequent horrors, namely, that the reign of Christ has been productive of much good, and that the most Christian nations (England, America and Germany) are the most progressive ones. Furthermore, Messianic prophecies concerning the admission of foreign nations to Jewish blessings are likewise fulfilled by Christ, for 'Ex-cannibals of Fiji and philosophical Hindoos, stunted Esquimaux and vigorous Kaffirs, poor peasants and great princes, little children and men of experience, reformed criminals and pure-minded saints, have been able to unite on the common ground of Christianity, and find in Christ all that will satisfy their deepest needs.'[67] This is not exactly our twenty-first century mode of speech, but undeniably everything stated has happened here and there. Towards the end of his book Adeney

---

63 Ibid., 75-76.

64 Ibid., 77.

65 Ibid., 78.

66 W. F. Adeney, *The Hebrew Utopia: A Study of Messianic Prophecy*, vii.

67 Ibid., 366.

declares that as with the Gentile, so with the Jew: the true fulfilment of prophecy is spiritual, not material, and therefore we should not 'look for the restoration of the modern Jew to Palestine as the natural accomplishment of the ends of messianic prophecy,'[68] though such an outcome may be an aspect of the deeper fulfilment. But the end is not yet, and the second advent lies before us, not because the first failed, but as the consequence and fulfilment of it.

That at least one reviewer of Adeney's book was torn between encouraging a 'young' author (Adeney was thirty-nine at the time) and cautioning against the risks taken by even the milder sort of modern biblical critic is clear from the following:

> We cordially welcome this contribution of a young theologian to the solution of a difficult problem. We think his solution far from satisfactory, and savours too much of the doctrine of Divine illusions. Still we are prepared to admit that David applied in the first instance to himself what his biographers and later prophets saw to have utterly failed of realization in him [and that] inspired prophets [may have supposed that their hopes were realized when in fact] ages had still to run before a full realization of their wondrous words could occur.[69]

There can be no question that Adeney's concern with the prophetic aspects of eschatology was recurrent throughout his life, for one of his last published papers was on 'The nature of the Advent.' He here enunciates the important general principle: 'it is not sound exegesis to explain a prophecy by what we take to be its fulfilment.' Rather, the fulfilling event must 'correspond to a conception previously formed as to the meaning of the saying in its original presentation.'[70] The principle is admirably stated, but some latter day biblical scholars would not feel as confident as Adeney that 'the meaning of the saying in its original presentation' is as easily grasped as he supposed. For all that, many to this day would agree with his conclusion, which was 'news' to many of his own time, namely, that the coming of the Kingdom and of Christ is not a physical, spatial matter (a) because they are already inwardly and spiritually present; and (b) because 'they are not subject to space conditions, to movements of location.' On the contrary, we must think of '*an effective manifestation of the presence and power of Christ and the Kingdom.*'[71]

Reverting to examples of Adeney's handling of 'awkward' biblical passages in *How to Read the Bible*, we may note his verdict upon the imprecatory Psalms: 'Nothing is more confusing to the conscience than the idea that the horrible utterances of these psalms must be justified, and even appropriated by Christians under certain circumstances, for no other reason than that they are found in the Bible.'[72] 'Read absolutely,' he continues, 'and taken as part of the sacred oracles, the imprecatory psalms attribute to God as the Divine Author of the Bible sentiments

---

[68] Ibid., 371.

[69] Anon., *The British Quarterly Review*, LXX, July and October 1879, 543.

[70] W. F. Adeney, 'The nature of the Advent,' *The Expositor*, 8th ser.. XVIII, 1919, 373.

[71] Ibid., 378, his italics.

[72] W. F. Adeney, *How to Read the Bible*, 81 .

that are quite contrary to His character.'[73] He makes no bones about the fact that while 'The wisdom literature is characterised by shrewdness rather than by depth of spiritual insight,' the book of Proverbs, taken altogether, 'makes for a sound morality.'[74] Ecclesiastes, however, is 'steeped in pessimism'; its two more cheerful concluding verses are probably a late addition; but taken as 'a study of one mournful phase of life ... it has a certain warning value.'[75] Job offers profound thoughts on the problem of evil; the Song of Songs is a collection of human love poems; Daniel, written four hundred years after the events it purports to describe, cannot be read as history; and Esther, likewise, is not history, though 'it may be founded upon a true tradition.'[76]

Turning to the New Testament, Adeney exhorts his readers to 'turn from the abstract "second Person" of the creeds and the romantic Jesus of popular ideas to the real Christ of the Gospels.'[77] He introduces the synoptic gospels and the synoptic problem, maintaining the priority of Mark. He emphasizes the fact that for all the minor discrepancies and divergencies in the gospels, 'the fundamental facts of the narratives referred to remain—Jesus was born, He left us the wonderful teachings of the famous sermon, He cured the blind, He rose from the dead and was seen by His disciples.'[78] We then come to the fourth gospel which, while it is by no means devoid of historical interest and detail, is in a different style—one which introduces us 'to the inner shrine of the glorious revelation in Christ.'[79] Indeed, Adeney elsewhere represents it as 'one of the happy results of the more recent criticism,'[80] that attention has been redirected to the history in what was formerly regarded simply as the spiritual gospel. He discusses the types of material in the gospels, paying particular attention to the teaching of Jesus, and then turns to the epistles: their authorship, dating, context and contents. Among his judgments are that 'the Epistle to the Hebrews could not have been written by St. Paul. ... [T]he genuineness of 2 Peter is very doubtful. Of St. Jude we know but little, and his epistle is not important.'[81] With an implicit eye to later doctrinal debates, he declares with regard to the illustration of Christ's work in Hebrews drawn from the Jewish sacrificial system that 'The fact of the atonement must ever be of transcendent importance; but the sacrificial imagery of the Epistle to the Hebrews need not bind the minds of Gentile Christians to one particular mode of regarding it.'[82] Finally, of Revelation he writes

---

[73] Ibid.

[74] Ibid., 85.

[75] Ibid., 87.

[76] Ibid., 90.

[77] Ibid., 93.

[78] Ibid., 97.

[79] Ibid., 101.

[80] W. F. Adeney, *The Construction of the Bible*, 86.

[81] Idem, *How to Read the Bible*, 115.

[82] Ibid., 117.

> It becomes our duty ... to inquire whether the book can be interpreted of the times when it was written, before we accept the wild theory that St. John was inspired to relate to Christians of the first century, in what to them must have been perfectly unintelligible language, the events that were to occur in succeeding centuries, apparently for no other reason than that the people who were to live in those later times might amuse themselves with an endless puzzle to which every fresh inquirer was to furnish a fresh solution.[83]

In 1899 Bennett and Adeney published their first collaborative work: *A Biblical Introduction*. Revised editions were published in 1904, 1905 and 1907. The Preface concludes with the authors' aspiration which, with its use of such code ideas as evangelical recognition, supreme authority, and interpretation and application by the Holy Spirit is as balanced as it is diplomatic:

> The authors of this volume trust that it may help readers to a truer understanding of the sacred Scriptures, and to a fuller appreciation of their unique importance; and may confirm them in the evangelical recognition of the supreme authority of the Bible as interpreted and applied by the Holy Spirit for the spiritual life.[84]

To Adeney fell the task of introducing the New Testament. As compared with the introductory works so far considered, his material here is more challenging. He refers to patristic writers and to numerous nineteenth-century British and continental scholars, and introduces untranslated Greek. Though more detailed treatment is offered, his topics are largely the same as those already discussed, as one would expect. A few soundings will indicate his conclusions, all of which follow well-argued considerations of alternative views. He thinks that the 'allusions to sayings of Christ in the Apostolic Fathers render it highly probable that Matthew, and also, though less assuredly, Luke, were used by them, and that even if that were not the case, [the sayings] are seen to be so near to our gospels as to be themselves partial confirmations of the historicity of those documents.'[85] Testimony to the antiquity of Luke's gospel is found in Marcion's recourse to it in his own gospel which, *pace* Baur (with whose conclusions Adeney is quite frequently at odds[86]), was not a Pauline gospel which Luke 'softened down to suit Catholic ideas.'[87] The fourth Gospel was most probably written by John 'the beloved disciple,' after long

---

[83] Ibid., 127-128.

[84] W. H. Bennett and W. F. Adeney, *A Biblical Introduction*, vii.

[85] Ibid., 285. It is by no means inconceivable that he had Baur in mind when he wrote, 'The wildest theories have proved themselves to be gaseous by exploding.' See his paper, 'The New Testament,' in *Faith and Criticism. Essays by Congregationalists*, 52. That Adeney continued to wrestle with issues relating to the gospels is clear from one of his last published papers, 'Synoptic variations,' *The Expository Times*, XXXI, 1919-1920, 487-491.

[86] See, *A Biblical Introduction*, 323. For Ferdinand Christian Baur (1792-1860), of Tübingen, see DBI; D. K. McKim, *Dictionary of Major Biblical Interpreters*.

[87] Ibid., 306.

meditation, though with the proviso that a disciple of his may have written the work—which would account for the signs of Greek culture within it.[88] But, as Wendt and Beyschlag have shown, 'the essential truths taught by Christ are the same in all four gospels.'[89]

A digression at this point will enable us to note Adeney's interest in extra-canonical writings. As early as 1887 we find him writing on 'The canonicity of the non-apostolic books of the New Testament.' He restricts his attention to the New Testament because the Old Testament 'has the virtual and implied attestation of Our Lord and His apostles.'[90] The question, Why are the canonical books in the New Testament while others are excluded from it' is raised afresh, he says, by such recent discoveries as 'The Teaching of the Apostles.' Should this be incorporated into the canon? Conversely, if we follow Archdeacon Farrar in denying the Petrine authorship of II Peter, should that letter be withdrawn from the New Testament? Even documents which, like the Epistle of Clement are authentic and genuine are not necessarily incorporated in the Bible. Documents have to be examined 'in the critical spirit of the scientific historian' but, unlike the Tübingen school 'which has made such havoc of the Scriptures,' we must proceed inductively and not with '*à priori* notions of what could or could not have been written by such and such an author.'[91] In the end, and formal ecclesiastical pronouncements notwithstanding, 'the body of Christian believers' comprise 'the only persons who can be expected to accept the claims to canonicity of any part of the New Testament.'[92] Adeney refers in passing to 'The Gospel according to the Hebrews,' and to this text he later devotes an entire article. He finds in it a mixture of genuine traditions not canonically preserved, unreliable legends, and re-worked passages from the synoptic gospels. Where Oscar Holtzmann preferred it to John's Gospel and Dr. George Salmon scorned it, Adeney concludes, 'Assuredly it is honestly written; and there is no reason to doubt the good faith of its author.'[93]

Returning to *A Biblical Introduction*, and to the epistles, Adeney discusses the relationship between Colossians and Ephesians in some detail. He places himself in the line of Lightfoot (thought not Baur—again) in finding the former to be genuinely the work of Paul, while the latter, understandably disputed on the grounds of its advanced Christology and the incidence of lengthy sentences and of words

---

[88] Ibid., 336.

[89] Ibid.

[90] Idem, 'The canonicity of the non-apostolic books of the New Testament,' *The Congregational Review*, I, 1887, 320-321.

[91] Ibid., 324.

[92] Ibid., 328.

[93] Idem, 'The Gospel according to the Hebrews,' *The Hibbert Journal*, III, 1904-1905, 159. Oscar Holzmann was Professor of Theology at Giessen, see DBI. For Salmon (1819-1904), mathematician and Regius Professor of Divinity at Trinity College, Dublin, whose *Introduction to the New Testament* was published in 1885, see ODNB.

which are not in Paul's normal vocabulary, is more problematic. He discusses further difficulties of attribution, and, on the ground of resemblance of Ephesians to Colossians, he concludes that both letters may have been addressed to persons with whom Paul was not personally acquainted, with Ephesians being in the form of a circular letter. That Adeney is not impressed by the subtlety of Holtzmann is clear: 'Holtzmann supposes that there was a Pauline nucleus [shared by Colossians and Ephesians], which a subsequent writer enlarged into two epistles, an elaborate theory which seems to be adopted as a counsel of despair.'[94] As for the pastoral epistles, Adeney thinks that McGiffert is closest to the mark in holding that these are 'authentic letters of Paul to Timothy and Titus, worked over and enlarged by another hand.'[95] Among Adeney's other conclusions are that the original readers of Hebrews were in Rome; that if the early date of James is sustained, James the brother of Jesus is its most likely author; there cannot be absolute certainty concerning the authorship of I Peter, though in view of its early attestation, there are 'strong reasons for believing in its authenticity'[96]; on grounds of style and contents II Peter cannot have been written by the apostle; the Johannine epistles may be attributed to the author of John's Gospel; and if John the apostle did not write Revelation, it is most likely that John the presbyter of Ephesus did.

A further example of the Bennett and Adeney collaboration[97] is the short book, *The Bible and Criticism*, undated, but published during Adeney's Manchester period. Adeney begins his New Testament section with a chapter on 'Textual and historical criticism,' and then proceeds to discuss the contents of the New Testament in roughly chronological order: the Pauline writings, the General Epistles, the Synoptic Gospels, and the Johannine writings including Revelation. He concludes with a brief chapter on the New Testament canon. Much of the material repeats that of *A Biblical Introduction*, though in abbreviated form, but there are signs of Adeney's use of developing scholarship. For example, he observes that 'scholars now refer to the collection of sayings used by Matthew and probably in part by Luke under the sign "Q" (German, *quelle*, source), although there is still a strong disposition to attribute Q [which he regards as a written source] to Matthew.'[98] Again, he now thinks that if the apostle John 'did at least furnish the traditions for the gospel that now bears his name, it is easier to think that such a very different composition as the *Apocalypse* came from John the Elder than to assign both works to one and the same author.'[99]

---

[94] Ibid., 398.

[95] Ibid., 414, quoting A. C. McGiffert, *A History of Christianity in the Apostolic Age*, 405.

[96] Ibid., 443.

[97] They also collaborated on *The Bible Story Re-told for Young* Children. Roger Tomes happily suggests that '"Bennett and Adeney" must have sounded as familiar as "Oesterley and Robinson" in a later generation'—high praise indeed. See his '"Learning a new technique": the reception of Biblical criticism in the Nonconformist colleges,' 307.

[98] W. H. Bennett and W. F. Adeney, *The Bible and Criticism*, 76.

[99] Ibid., 89.

So much for Adeney's general approach to biblical criticism and to questions of introduction, date and authorship. I now turn to the considerable effort he exerted in propagating the findings of what might be termed moderate-critical-believing scholarship far and wide. During his Manchester days Adeney revised Bagster's widely-used work, *The Comprehensive Helps to Bible Study*. It is a mine of information on the Bible, ancient manuscripts, English versions, Jewish festivals, maladies and diseases, the topography of the Holy Land, and much else besides. In addition it includes introductions to the Greek and Hebrew languages, a concordance, and maps. Again, articles by Adeney appear in both volumes of the *Dictionary of Christ and the Gospels* (1906) edited by James Hastings, and he contributed twenty longer, and a number of shorter, articles to the same editor's influential five-volume *Dictionary of the Bible*. Ever alive to the danger of reading back from later periods into the biblical text, in his article on 'Mediator, mediation' he writes:

> The OT priest killed animals and sprinkled actual blood. Christ gave His life on the cross; but the reference to His blood has no such material connexion. We must take it metaphorically for His life surrendered in death. Similarly, since he was not, like the Jewish sacrifices, an oblation laid by a priest on an altar, His sacrifice must be interpreted spiritually, and its reality found in the spiritual act of giving Himself to God in death.[100]

Of later theories he declares, 'though all of [their authors] appeal to the Bible for the justification of their positions, none of them can claim to be results of pure exegesis, or even the contents of strictly biblical theology.'[101] In his article on 'Woman' he refers to Galatians 3:28 ('There is no such thing as ... male and female; for you are all one person in Christ Jesus') and Philemon 12 ('In sending [the runaway slave, Philemon] back to you I am sending my heart'), contending with respect to both women and slavery that, 'In both cases [Paul] supported established customs for the time being while enunciating great principles which would ultimately abolish them.'[102]

Adeney wrote a number of journal articles on a variety of New Testament topics, among them one on 'The Beatitudes.' He reminds his readers that Luke's version of the Beatitudes was regarded as more primitive than Matthew's by a line of scholars flowing down from Schleiermacher. When Tholuck examined the question and opted for the priority of Matthew, he found himself standing almost alone. But others, including De Wette, sided with Tholuck, with the result that at present opinion is fairly evenly divided on the matter. After examining the evidence Adeney concludes that Luke's Beatitudes are primitive, and that Matthew gathers teachings given by Christ on other occasions and enriches his Beatitudes with them.

Under the heading of general biblical works, as now related to a popular adult readership, it remains only to add that Adeney contributed the chapter on Pilate to

---

[100] W. F. Adeney, 'Mediator, mediation,' 320(b).

[101] Ibid., 321(a).

[102] Idem, 'Woman,' 936(a).

Men of the Bible: Some Lesser-Known Characters (1904), and that he devoted a whole book to *Women of the New Testament*. This was a companion volume to R. F. Horton's on the men of the Bible. A reviewer observed that 'Professor Adeney lacks the irresponsible brilliancy of Dr. Horton's character drawing; but he has scholarship and sympathetic restraint. These are the more useful, no doubt the truer, studies of the two.'[103] Mary is here, as are Mary Magdalene, Dorcas and Phoebe, Paul's female converts, and others. Admitting that we know little of some of these, Adeney thinks that 'A halo of companionship with the Saviour encircles most of these women of the New Testament; and nearly all the others stand in the light of the afterglow that lingers throughout the apostolic period. To myself this is the fascination of the subject. I wish I could help my readers to share in it.'[104] In his concluding paragraph Adeney shows himself a child of his age—though more 'advanced' than some—when he writes:

> Irrational and unjust restrictions on the liberty of women must be resisted in the name of Christianity. Still the most modern ideas cannot destroy nature. The distinction of the sexes must remain. Woman is not man, and as she differs from man in nature so she must also differ in function. It is unnatural to demand that women shall do all that men do ... The circle of her influence may be widened with advantage from the home to the parish, from the parish to the nation; but still it must remain a circle of womanly service ...'[105]

Eighteen years later, three years before Adeney died, Constance Coltman became the first ordained woman in the English Congregational tradition of the Church.

We come now to Adeney's exegetical work. This may be exemplified first by the volumes he contributed to the *Century Bible*, of which significant series he was the General Editor. From within his own denomination he found four of the fifteen Old Testament contributors and seven of the twelve New Testament commentators. His colleague and friend, W. H. Bennett was given charge of Genesis, Exodus and the General Epistles, while Adeney himself contributed the volumes on Luke, Galatians and Thessalonians. The series was, according to taste, happily or ominously given the subtitle, 'A Modern Commentary', and it was intended for the use of a wide readership. The pattern of the volumes required general introductions to the biblical books, the printing of the text of the Authorised Version, and exegetical comments on the text of the Revised Version (with its marginal comments).

As we might by now expect, Adeney covers questions of authorship, composition[106] and date in his Introduction to Luke, and also delineates the main

---

[103] *The Expository Times*, X, 1898-1899, 178.

[104] W. F. Adeney, *Women of the New Testament*, vi.

[105] Ibid., 276.

[106] In this connection F. R. Tomes states that in the first edition of this commentary, published by T. C. and E. C. Jack in 1901, Adeney refers readers to W. F. Slater's *Century Bible* commentary on Matthew for an account of the synoptic problem. Tomes remarks, 'He could hardly have done them a greater disservice, because Slater was as confused as anybody on the subject'—a judgment which Tomes proceeds to justify. Slater was, for

characteristics of the gospel: joyousness; kindliness and liberality of spirit; sympathy with the poor; prominence of prayer and praise; the prominence of women and the interest of domestic scenes; historical relations (that is the setting of the gospel in relation to the imperial context).[107] As an example of Adeney's handling of a difficult passage we may turn to the account of the demoniac and the Gerasene swine in Luke 8: 26-39. Adeney writes:

> This incident is the strangest in the Gospels, ... The possession of a man by a host of demons, the request of the demons not to be cast into the abyss, followed by that very fate when they had entered the swine, the possession of swine by demons at all, our Lord's permission of this—these are all points difficult to understand. ... Of course, if the view that a misunderstanding of the phenomena of insanity and epilepsy will account for the belief in possession be accepted, we must conclude that the 'demoniac' was suffering from a madman's delusions. Weighty commentators have suggested that this was the case here, and that the stampede of a herd of swine at the sight and sound of the maniac's ravings gave rise to the latter part of the story. ... In a famous article on the subject ... Prof. Huxley based his rejection of historical Christianity on the presence of this narrative in the Gospels—which was attempting to rest a pyramid on its apex.[108]

This is a choice example of Adeney's desire gently to lead the blinkered towards fresh insight and to enlighten the puzzled. It also shows how difficult he found it to resist rebuking intellectual contemporaries whom he deemed wayward.

For a sample taken from an epistle, we may turn to Adeney's commentary on Galatians. He offers a thorough review of the question, Who were the Galatians? and concludes that the evidence in favour of the view that they were South Galatians, whom Paul had visited, far outweighs Lightfoot's evidence in favour of the North. To see how Adeney treats a highly significant verse we may turn to the last part of Galatians 2:20, where Paul attributed his new life to 'the Son of God, who loved me, and gave himself up for me.' Adeney explains that the phrase 'gave himself up'

---

example, 'undecided whether Mark's Gospel was the basis of Matthew and Luke or a compendium of them.' See F. R. Tomes, 'A Century of *The Century Bible*,' *The Expository Times*, CXII no. 12, September 2001,409(b). However, I can find no reference to Slater in the first edition of Adeney's *St. Luke*, Edinburgh: T. C. and E. C. Jack, [1901], nor in the later Caxton edition. Concerning Luke's sources, Adeney does produce two columns headed 'From Mark/Not from Mark', referring the reader to A. Wright, *St. Luke's Gospel in Greek*; he declines to treat the wider synoptic problem, and does not direct his readers to any authority on this matter; and he declares, 'We may take it, then, that Luke's first authority is our second gospel' (26). At the end of his Introduction he lists Plummer, Godet, Meyer, Farrar, Plumptre and Wright as his general sources. At least as early as 1897 Adeney championed the priority of Mark's Gospel; see *The Construction of the Bible*, 71: 'A careful comparison between [the synoptic gospels] leads to the conclusion that Mark was written earliest, and constituted the basis of both Matthew and Luke.'

[107] W. F. Adeney, ed., *St. Luke*, 6-16.

[108] Ibid., 223.

is 'frequently used in the gospels for the giving up of Jesus to death by God or by men (cf. Mark ix.31, x.33). Here Paul applies it to Christ's own act in surrendering himself to death.' He next offers a more detailed comment on 'for me', and it is not fanciful to suppose that later penal substitutionary theories of the atonement flit through his mind as he writes:

> **for me:** on behalf of me, for my benefit. The Greek preposition is *hyper*, which has this meaning, not *anti*, which would be used if the Apostle meant 'instead of,' in the sense that Christ gave himself to die instead of our dying. Whether Paul would have said that or not, all his language here implies is that Christ's death was for our benefit. This is according to the Apostle's invariable custom. He frequently uses the word *hyper* in this connection (e.g. Rom. 1.32, ix, 3; I Cor. 1.13, v, 7; Gal. iii.13), never *anti*.[109]

It remains to note that Adeney contributed the short commentary on Philippians to the celebrated one-volume work, *A Commentary on the Bible* (1920), edited by his Manchester colleague Arthur S. Peake. Bennett contributed I and II Samuel, while A. J. Grieve (St. Luke), Robert Mackintosh (Galatians), and H. T. Andrews—now occupying Adeney's former Chair at New College, London (I and II Thessalonians) all cited Adeney's *Century Bible* volumes.

As we should by now expect, Adeney was no mere armchair commentator. On the contrary he did much to encourage expository preaching, as his many contributions to *The Pulpit Commentary*, and his volumes in *The Expositor's Bible* demonstrate. For the former Adeney wrote numerous homilies in the volumes on Joshua, Judges, Job, Proverbs, Jeremiah, Lamentations, Ezekiel, Daniel, Matthew, Galatians, Ephesians, Philippians, Colossians and Thessalonians. From all of these I select his contribution on Job 1: 7 concerning Satan's wanderings over the earth, because it shows how the biblical critic of integrity seeks to encourage preachers to draw out the significance of a passage without destroying the faith of those who may have been raised in biblical (even dualist) literalism. Note 'perhaps' and 'necessarily' in the fourth sentence:

'*Satan's wanderings.* Here Satan appears in a very prominent and privileged position. He is the accuser rather than the tempter. At all events, he has a range of influence which suggests terrible possibilities. We must remember that we are perhaps reading a symbolical drama, and must not take every line of it with dry literal exactness, as necessarily descriptive of actual historical events. Nevertheless it suggests truths of great and lasting importance.'

> 1. Satan is at large. '[W]hen we are most off our guard he is most likely to appear.'
> 2. Satan is in motion. He leaves us, only to return to 'surprise us with novel temptations.'

---

[109] Idem, *Galatians*, 287.

> 3. Satan is watchful. 'There is no weak place in the armour that can possibly escape the vigilance of our horrible foe.'
> 4. Satan is subject to God's judgment.
> 5. Satan is restricted by Christ's victory. His 'bondage is not yet complete. But the powers of evil are cripples wherever the light of Christ shines.'
> 6. Satan's range does not extend above the earth.
> 7. Satan's range should be equalled by that of the messengers of the Gospel. 'Wherever the bite of the serpent is found, there should the healing balm be sent. Sin is world-wide, so also are the grace and power of Christ.'[110]

We may observe the way in which, while in points 5 to 7 Adeney reflects upon the Old Testament text from a Christian point of view, he does not tempt his readers into thinking that the author(s) of Job were thinking of Christ, still less of modern missionaries.

He adopts the same stance in his *Expositor's Bible* volumes on Ezra, Nehemiah and Esther and The Canticles and Lamentations. Here he has space to offer thematic expositions in which he draws liberally upon history and literature. Consider, for example, his treatment of 'The covenant' (Nehemiah 10). While not questioning Josiah's loyalty to Jehovah in imposing the Law upon the people,

> the method he followed could not lead to success. ... It was a royal reformation, not a revival of religion on the part of the people. We have an instance of a similar course of action in the English reformation under Edward VI, which was swept away in a moment when his Catholic sister succeeded to the throne, because it was a movement originating in the court and not supported by the country, as was that under Elizabeth when Mary had opened the eyed of the English nation to the character of Romanism.[111]

But now the people themselves wish voluntarily to submit to the Law: hence the covenant. Adeney explains that this was no covenant between equal parties, for people are in no position to bargain with God. Hence the use by the writers of the Septuagint of *diatheke*, not *suntheke*, for this covenant, which was 'a Divine disposition, a Divine ordinance.'[112] But, he continues, a religion of Law becomes a religion of bondage, as Paul discovered:

> As we look back to [the Jews'] position from the vantage ground of Christian liberty, we are astounded at the Jewish love of law, and we rejoice in our freedom from its irksome restraints. And yet the Christian is not an antinomian; he is not a sort of free lance, sworn to no obedience. ... He is bound to a lofty service—not to a law, indeed, but to a personal Master; not in the servitude of the letter, but, though with the freedom of the spirit, really with far higher obligations of love and fidelity than were ever recognised by the most covenant-keeping Jews. Thus he has a new

---

[110] Idem, *Job* (*The Pulpit Commentary*, 29-30.
[111] Idem, *Ezra, Nehemiah and Esther*, 307-308.
[112] Ibid., 309.

covenant, sealed in the blood of his Saviour; and his communion with his lord implies a sacramental vow of loyalty.[113]

It is clear that Adeney's expository concerns are fuelled by his theological convictions, and for him, as a Christian, these are grounded in the New Testament. In two volumes he expounded aspects of New Testament theology, and I shall look briefly at each of these in turn.

In 1894 *The Theology of the New Testament* was published. A second edition followed in 1895, and there was also a translation into Japanese. Adeney first distinguishes between biblical and systematic theology. The former, he declares, 'does not attempt to state truth absolutely: it seeks to elucidate a certain presentation of truth. ... [Its materials] are confined to the pages of the Bible; while Systematic Theology, even when relying mainly on Scripture, appeals to nature, conscience, reason, experience, etc., for the confirmation of its results, if not for the data of its arguments.'[114] Again,

> The systematic theologian undertakes to balance and harmonise the truths of religion, in order to show their organic relationship in a compact body of Divinity; the student of Biblical Theology ... proceeds to trace the development of revelation as this emerges through the successive books of Scripture, and to compare the various forms in which its ideas are conceived by the several teachers there represented. Thus it is less ambitious than Systematic Theology; but then it admits of being more exact and certain.[115]

Biblical theology, he declares, should precede systematic, for 'Here we have the stream at its fountain-head.'[116]

In these opening remarks we already see Adeney's commitment to the idea of progressive revelation, hints of which were detectable in his introductory, exegetical and expository writings. He is persuaded that Christ is the culmination of the divine revelation, and that through all the Old Testament there is movement towards him; though as a careful proponent of the historical method he is careful to observe that the development is not always smooth. In the present work he shows that within the thought of individual biblical writers there is development. This underlying conviction dictates his method of taking the New Testament books in chronological order as far as determinations of their dating will allow; and it also explains his view that 'The essential ideas of the Old Testament are presupposed in the New Testament'[117]—ideas such as monotheism, the abhorrence of nature worship, and the holiness of God. What Christianity does is to correct what is narrow and materialistic, and sets all within a spiritual context. He strikingly points out in this connection that 'Not one of the schools of theology prevalent in Palestine during our

---

113 Ibid., 310.
114 Idem, *The Theology of the New Testament*, 1.
115 Ibid., 1-2.
116 Ibid., 2.
117 Ibid., 3.

Lord's earthly life can be regarded as in any way the parent of Christianity.' The Pharisees were slaves to 'puerile rabbinical traditions; the Sadducees were materialistic; the Essenes were 'narrow, sectarian, timorous.' Hence, 'New Testament theology may be linked to Old Testament theology; but it cannot be attributed to the influences of contemporary Jewish thought.'[118] Having uttered these rather stark judgments, which some latter-day biblical scholars would wish to question or modify, Adeney does find Christianity indebted to a few of Judaism's newer ideas: the resurrection and future judgment, later Messianic ideas in relation to the Kingdom of God, and later Judaism's elevation of inspired Scripture as 'reflected in New Testament references to the law and the prophets.'[119]

Adeney sets out from John the Baptist, 'the last of the prophets.'[120] He called for repentance, he baptized, but his message was one of judgment, not of redemption. But he looked towards the Coming One who would join repentance with regeneration. For Jesus, 'The idea of the Divine kingdom was the central topic of his conversations and parables, and the realisation of it was the supreme end of His labours.'[121] Adeney detects a certain development in Jesus's teaching on the subject, from an emphasis upon the joys of the kingdom to the incorporation of the note of judgment. The kingdom is not temporal and corporeal, but eternal and spiritual. As to the person of Christ, the idea of the divinity of Christ is present in the four gospels, though it is most fully treated in John's. In particular, it is John who fastens upon the concept of Christ's pre-existence. Where the doctrine of God is concerned, in contrast with the general practice of Old Testament writers [though, one might note, entirely in accord with many late nineteenth-century liberal theologians[122]], Jesus places the Fatherhood before the awful majesty of God. The Fatherhood is, moreover, universal in its sway, and it is revealed in Christ's person and character: 'He that hath seen me hath seen the Father.'[123]

Adeney proceeds through the teaching of Jesus of forgiveness, which 'goes straight to the sin, rather than to its pains and penalties. The sin is buried in oblivion, and the penitent restores to the old status of communion with God.'[124] The reward of eternal life he finds to be normally a future hope in the synoptics, but a present reality in John. In either case the risen Christ is present with his people by the Spirit. At the heart of the Gospel is Christ's redemptive work: he comes to seek and to save the lost—at which point Adeney interposes a then topical aside: 'While the doctrine of evolution by the survival of the fittest may be a delightful creed for

---

[118] Ibid., 4-5.

[119] Ibid., 6.

[120] Ibid., 7.

[121] Ibid., 17.

[122] See further, Alan P. F. Sell, *Nonconformist Theology in the Twentieth Century*, ch. 1.

[123] W. F. Adeney, *The Theology of the New Testament*, 47, quoting John 14: 9.

[124] Ibid., 53.

the successful, it is a sentence of doom for the unfortunate.'[125] Returning to his theme he discusses Christ's healing ministry, and then faces the fact that

> It is apparent to every reader of the New Testament that the purpose of the death of Christ does not take the pre-eminence in His own teaching which it assumes in that of St. Paul. In regard to this subject more perhaps than in regard to any other we may see a development of doctrine in the New Testament. But quite apart from the fact that Christian ideas are thus introduced by degrees, it is obvious that subsequent reflections on the cross in the clear light of all its tragic circumstances are likely to be richer than anticipatory references to it in those early days when it only loomed on the horizon as a gradually emerging destiny of the future.[126]

Adeney accords a prominent place to the Lord's Supper in this connection.

Those who follow Christ are to repent, obey, and be prepared to follow Christ 'even to the gallows.'[127] They are also to follow Christ's practical guidance for living—in which connection Adeney holds that the ethical injunctions 'only admit of being embodied in the social order of any nation in proportion as the population has already become Christian. ... [They] can be put into operation just so far as the kingdom is dominant, and no farther.[128] Moreover, in following the ethical guidelines, the Christian does not behave as an individual, but as a member of a family, for, as Adeney puts it in terms familiar to his age, 'The Fatherhood of God necessarily leads to the brotherhood of man.'[129] Finally, Adeney comes to Christ's teaching on the future. According to the synoptic gospels, this is that the resurrection is not for all; it is the inheritance of the redeemed, and the impenitent wicked will lead a conscious existence after death.[130] In John's gospel 'The idea of Divine judgment is very prominent ... but with this peculiarity, that it is there generally assigned to the present age.'[131]

As he turns to the theology of the apostles, Adeney pauses to rebuke Baur and others who in a 'crude and violent' way set Peter against Paul, and Pfleiderer who, by appealing to Hellenistic ideas, landed himself 'in the extraordinary position of virtually denying that Christ is the founder of Christianity.'[132] Adeney traces a development of apostolic thought which, with the exception of echoes in James, does not set out from Jesus's teaching, but from his person, death and resurrection, these being brought into relation to 'the facts of living Christian experience.'[133] He analyses the earliest apostolic preaching, noting such disputes as that concerning the

---

[125] Ibid., 61.
[126] Ibid., 64.
[127] Ibid., 76.
[128] Ibid., 85.
[129] Ibid., 91.
[130] ibid., 104-105.
[131] Ibid., 108.
[132] Ibid., 111.
[133] Ibid., 113.

place of the Gentiles within the Church, and paying particular attention to apostolic variations upon the theme of Christ's atonement.

In the teaching of Paul, 'the great theologian of the New Testament,'[134] we find 'the logical and more external presentation of Christianity' which is 'most prominent in controversy', and 'his own spiritual experience. We may call this his mysticism.'[135] 'Jesus Christ,' he declares, 'the personal, living Redeemer and Lord, was the centre of St. Paul's religious life and thought, and the inspiring subject of all his preaching.'[136] Jesus was, to Paul, both human and divine; but

> At the same time, this ascription of greatness to our Lord goes along with a certain idea of subordination. It is not the Arian subordination of the creature who has a beginning in time. Christ is the Son, not a creature. ... Still, Christ is in a degree subject to His Father. God *sent* His Son, and the Sender must be superior to the Sent. Christ did not treat equality with God as a thing He would grasp at (Phi. 11.6) ... Moreover, St. Paul never distinguishes between the human the Divine in our Lord in such a way that anything like personality could be ascribed to the former exclusively. He thinks of one person throughout as the Son of God, who was 'formed in fashion as a man,' and afterwards exalted to the highest glory.[137]

With the letter to the Colossians we reach the high point of Paul's Christology, for there all things are said to lead up to Christ. All of which prompts Adeney's cautionary word:

> It would be a mistake, an absurd anachronism, to attempt to arrange these ideas as parts of a systematic scheme of the Trinity. St. Paul never speculated on the essential inner life of God apart from His relation to the universe. He follows our Lord's example in frequently describing God as the Father ... Jesus Christ is the Son of God. ...[The Spirit's] full Divinity is clearly taught, for the indwelling of the Holy Ghost is treated as identical with the indwelling of God ... But though the Apostle attempts no metaphysical synthesis of the doctrine of the Trinity, he certainly affirms fundamental Trinitarian ideas. Thus, for example, in the benediction he directly indicates both the Divinity and the threefold existence of Father, Son, and Holy Ghost (I Cor. xiii, 14).[138]

At the heart of Paul's message is Christ crucified, who died to save the world. He notes, as we have seen before, that Paul does not in so many words say that Christ died *instead of* us, but yet concedes that 'He died on the Cross that we might not die eternally. In this sense His dying is instead of our dying.'[139] Christians are justified (that is, declared, not made, right) by faith in the Christ with whom we are buried and with whom we rise. Henceforth they live in the Spirit, and do so as members of

---

[134] Ibid., 152.
[135] Ibid., 159-160.
[136] Ibid., 175.
[137] Ibid., 182-183.
[138] Ibid., 184.
[139] Ibid., 189.

the Church—that is, of both the whole body of Christians and the local gathering of saints. Into this body Christians are baptised, and within this body they observe the Lord's Supper 'till he come.' The resurrection is 'for those who have the gift of eternal life in Christ,'[140] though there are vague hints that the impenitent deceased may yet finally be restored.

Christology is the primary theme of the letter to the Hebrews, whose author regards Jesus Christ as both human and divine. Christ's high priestly sacrifice of himself 'never appears as the propitiation of Divine wrath. ... It is viewed ... as a purification from sin, and as a ratification of the new covenant.'[141] In the Apocalypse, too, both the divinity and humanity of Christ are asserted, but here in a context of urgent practical challenges to faith rather than of things internal and spiritual. Although the book 'often breathes a Jewish spirit ... there is not a word of commendation of the Jewish ritual. No temple is to be found in the New Jerusalem.'[142] Finally, in the Johannine writings, Jesus is both human and divine, and redemption concerns the destruction of Satan's dominion and the gift of life. For faith 'is not the reception of an idea ... but the opening up of the soul for Christ to come in; so that "he that hath the Son hath the live" (I John i, 12).'[143]

Adeney returned to *The New Testament Doctrine of Christ* (1909) in his contribution to *The Century Bible Handbooks*. 'Dr. Adeney was entitled to take for himself the greatest subject that his handbooks have to deal with. There is evidence of much independent spade work,' declared the reviewer in *The Expository Times*.[144] Once again Adeney takes the chronological approach, and much of his ground is by now familiar to us. What is new is his treatment of the Virgin Birth. He remarks that

> There are theologians who regard the virgin birth of Jesus as an essential condition of His divinity ... There is nothing in the new Testament to warrant us in giving that central and all-important position to a belief which, by the very nature of the case, is and always was incapable of proof. None of the apostolic writers ... make any reference to it. ... We may observe, however, that the virgin birth appears as explaining the way in which One whose whole life was marked with superhuman traits came into the world. ... [Even so] It is not by means of this mystery that we shall come to an understanding of the nature of Christ. There were Unitarians in the second century who accepted the virgin birth, but denied the divinity of Christ.[145]

Adeney notes that to Schleiermacher the sinlessness of Jesus was 'the most characteristic fact concerning Him.'[146] Certainly he never displayed any consciousness of guilt, nor the behaviour of a self-deluding fanatic. Moreover, his

---

140 Ibid., 215.

141 Ibid., 226.

142 Ibid., 234.

143 Ibid., 247.

144 ET, XXI, 1909-1910, 129.

145 W. F. Adeney, *The New Testament Doctrine of Christ*, 2-4.

146 Ibid., 7.

positive goodness is readily apparent. Jesus taught with authority, demanded personal loyalty, issued commands and warnings, and elevated humility. Among his many claims was that he had the right to forgive sins, and that he was Lord of the Sabbath. He was Son of Man and Son of God.

The early preachers took up the story and with their experience of the Cross and resurrection, and of their own new life, their Christological thought developed. This should not 'stagger our faith', for 'Revelation is always gradual. It was by degrees, though really not by slow degrees—for the development was very rapid—that the new testament teachers came to perceive that greatest of all truths—the truth of the Incarnation.'[147] In his treatment of Paul's teaching, Adeney makes the following important observation: 'It will always be found that meagre thoughts of the nature of Christ go with poor ideas of His redeeming work. Where, as in St. Paul, the redemption is seen to be immeasurably great in its cost and in its issues, there the Redeemer must be acknowledged as correspondingly great. It wants a divine Christ to achieve a divine redemption.'[148] With reference to the humiliation of Christ, Adeney reaffirms his view that Paul 'taught a certain subordination of the Son to the Father,' adding that the phrase in Philippians 2 to the effect that Christ did not seize a position of equality with God 'would seem to mean the opposite of aspiring to more honour; He gave up what He already possessed.' There follows the caution: 'we should remember that St. Paul was not composing a treatise of scientific theology, or drawing up a legal document every word of which must be weighed, but simply writing a friendly letter in free and fluid literary style.'[149] As for the use to which Philippians 2 has been put in kenotic theory, Adeney makes clear that Paul did not speculate on what the self-emptying of Christ might mean, and he did no distinguish, after the manner of some later theologians, between retained ethical attributes and abandoned ontological ones: 'All that he suggests is the great general truth that Christ did not come in divine majesty, but came in a humble serving life; that His dazzling glory of divinity was not simply veiled, that it was abandoned. This agrees with St. Paul's teaching of the quite actual humanity of Christ and His real death on the cross.'[150] Adeney proceeds to consider Paul's view of Christ's exaltation, and his cosmic significance. His chapter on Paul concludes thus:

> Taking the writings of St. Paul throughout, we may say that they do not justify the virtual tritheism of three exactly equal persons to be found in some clauses of the Athanasian Creed—although it is repudiated by other clauses of the same creed—nor the Sabellianism of Schleiermacher and Horace Bushnell, nor the Swedenborgian simple identification of Jesus with God. But they teach that Jesus Christ is in a unique way God's own Son, who existed in the past eternity and appeared by a great act of condescension as a man; who now lives and reigns in heaven; who, while sharing the nature of God, is in some respects subordinate to his Father; who

[147] Ibid., 65.
[148] Ibid., 92.
[149] Ibid., 104-105.
[150] Ibid., 107.

together with God is the source of redeeming grace; and who is to be trusted, served, and worshipped as our Lord and Saviour.[151]

Having reviewed the rest of the New Testament writings along the lines already described, Adeney concludes that 'There is sufficient agreement among [the New Testament writers] for us to use the expression "*The* New Testament Doctrine of Christ".'[152] He then lists the common features of their teaching—among them that Jesus is Christ; that he is truly human; and that 'He is the true Son of God in a way in which divine sonship is not affirmed of mankind generally or of Christians in particular. ... But if we cannot get beyond the practical truth of the saying of Jesus in John, "He that hath seen me hath seen the Father," we may rest satisfied, for this is really all we need.'[153]

II

If Walter Adeney had done no more than leave us his writings and edited works on the Bible, he would have bequeathed a significant legacy. But we recall that at New College he was in charge of Church History as well as New Testament studies. He contributed a number of works in the former field—indeed, his most substantial single volume falls within that field. I shall briefly review his historical writings in the chronological order of their subjects.

In 1897 Adeney published *The Early Christians. The Story of Christianity during the First Three Centuries*. This is a sixty-four-page booklet measuring 13 x 9 cm. That he was able to treat such complicated material within so small a compass is a testimony to Adeney's ability to wear his learning lightly, for the benefit of general readers. He writes of the 'missionary harvests' of apostolic times, referring to the friction between the Jewish Christians of Jerusalem and the Gentile Christians of Antioch; he draws a picture of the life of the early Church, noting the importance of the Lord's Supper and the *agape*, and taking care to observe that bishops were overseers of local churches. Then came 'Three centuries of conflict' as the Christians lived under sometimes tyrannical Roman rule. Early Christian literature is next introduced, with reference to the New Testament, the Epistles of Clement, Barnabas and others, which draw from Adeney the observation that, 'The drop from the heights of inspiration in the New Testament is tremendous.'[154] There follow the apologists, the heretics, and the Western and Eastern theologians—and all in eight small pages. The following chapter, 'Development, degeneration, and reformation', traces the transformation from Ignatius: 'Where Christ Jesus is there is the Catholic church', to Irenaeus: 'Where the church is there is the Spirit of God, and where the Spirit of God is there is all grace', and the further development of the latter view by

---

[151] Ibid., 115.
[152] Ibid., 169.
[153] Ibid., 171.
[154] Idem, *The Early Christians. The Story of Christianity during the First Three Centuries*, 40.

Cyprian.[155] In support of his view that the system now known as 'Episcopacy' 'did not exist in the earliest times,' Adeney invokes Lightfoot, Stanley, Hatch and Harnack. He sums up the situation regarding church order thus: 'the first century was congregationalist, the second episcopal, and the third sacerdotal.'[156] The last, 'so foreign to the teaching of Christ and His apostles, was chiefly elaborated by Cyprian, the bishop of Carthage, in the middle of the third century.'[157] The reforming movements led by Montanus, Marcion and Novatian did not succeed 'in winning over the main body of the church.' Adeney finds space for a concluding homily in which he cautions his contemporaries against such phrases as 'the historic episcopate', and concludes:

> We must look forward, not backward, to the golden age of Christendom when the reign of Christ shall be complete and the will of God done on earth as it is done in Heaven. But one of the first steps in progress must be the recovery of lost ground. Happy will it be for us if we can experience the glow of brotherly love and the heroism of unflinching faith that characterized the saints and martyrs of early days.[158]

While, at the beginning of the twenty-first century, we are rightly more suspicious of Christendom language than was Adeney, his running implication that the recovery of 'lost ground' will entail the removal of sectarian ecclesiological obstacles indicates a task which is to this day by no means complete, the 'ecumenical century' which has intervened between his words and ourselves notwithstanding.[159]

In one of two text books published by The Sunday School Union, *From Christ to Constantine. Christianity in the First Three Centuries* (1884), Adeney covers the ground just sketched in considerably more detail. As before, he points out that by the third century, 'We now have bishops, presbyters, and deacons. But as yet the bishop is no priest—or rather all Christians are regarded as priests. No mystical sacerdotal notion divides clergy from laity. The word "priest" first appears as an official title in the third century.'[160] He also has space to deal more fully with individual bishops, noting in particular Victor of Rome's folly in connection with the dispute over the dating of Easter, in excommunicating the Eastern churches and claiming to speak 'as the mouthpiece of Christendom ... an unheard of impertinence.'[161] Adeney further shows his hand when describing the advances in sacerdotal theory and practice which occurred during the time of Zephyrinus, bishop of Rome, who is presented as a tool of his leading official, Callistus. To Callistus 'more than to any other must be attributed the rapid advancement of sacerdotal notions in the Church. The

[155] Ibid., 50.
[156] Ibid., 53.
[157] Ibid., 54.
[158] Ibid., 63-64.
[159] See further Alan P. F. Sell, *Enlightenment, Ecumenism, Evangel*, ch. 11.
[160] W. F. Adeney, *From Christ to Constantine. Christianity in the First Three Centuries*, 101.
[161] Ibid., 103.

blasphemous claim to forgive sins, which has ever after been put forth by the Roman Catholic priesthood, was first definitely formulated by Callistus.'[162] Worship, family life and art are among other topics which come under brief review.

The second Sunday School Union text book is entitled, *From Constantine to Charles the Great. Christianity from the Third to the Eighth Century* (1888). From the time when, by the edict of Milan of 313, Constantine and Licinius granted freedom to all religions, 'We now have to deal with a Christian empire, though with one in which the vices of the earthly state are too often more visible than the graces of the Kingdom of heaven.'[163] An account follows of the Donatists, the doctrinal debates leading up to the Council of Chalcedon of 451 (with a detour to the West to accommodate Augustine, Pelagius and their successors), and its repudiation of both Nestorianism and Eutychianism. Thence to the expansion of Christianity in Western Europe and Boethius's *The Consolations of Philosophy* (524), which 'might have been produced in a heathen world which knew nothing of Christianity. It quietly ignores the Christian religion, and offers practical philosophy as the consolation for the dark troubles of the age.' It does, however, 'breathe a high tone', and its popularity 'is an awful commentary on the failure of the Church to illustrate the attractions of the gospel.'[164] Between accounts of the Monophysites and the Monothelites, the rise of Islam, and iconoclasm, is sandwiched a chapter on Gregory the Great, Augustine's mission to England, the controversy with the old British Church over the date of Easter, the coversion of Northumbria, Caedmon and Bede. The conversion of Germany, the work of Columban and Boniface, and the crowning of Charles the Great by the Pope in 800 are reported. The historical sketch complete, Adeney turns in three chapters to church government, manners and morals, and the monks. He notes particularly the advent of the doctrine of transubstantiation from the fourth century onwards, and the fact that 'The Eucharist gradually came to be regarded as a sacrifice completing or repeating the atonement of Christ.'[165] The worship of saints and the rise of Mariolatry are noted, as is the exercise of charity in hospitals and elsewhere. As for the monks,

> Surely it was a mistake for men to hope to escape from the world by fleeing into the wilderness or by retiring to the cloister, so long as the sin of the world lay coiled up like a snake in their own breasts! ... Still, cannot we discover a true though strangely perverted heroism in the awful rigour of their austerities that may well shame the pettiness and cowardice of modern lives of ease? ... Further, there can be no question that the monks conferred many inestimable boons on the world.[166]

---

[162] Ibid., 109.

[163] Idem, *From Constantine to Charles the Great. Christianity from the Third to the Eighth Century*, 3.

[164] Ibid., 78.

[165] Ibid., 151.

[166] Ibid., 173-174.

The Benedictines in particular made roads, farmed, copied precious manuscripts, taught, and cared for the poor. Despite corruptions, 'there were many bright examples of Christian goodness among the monks and nuns even in the dark days that gathered over Europe during the reigns of the successors of Charles the Great.'[167]

We come now to what I have described as Adeney's most substantial single work, *The Greek and Eastern Churches* (1908). This was his contribution to T. & T. Clark's prestigious *International Theological Library*. The first part of the book traces the history and thought of the Eastern Churches from the Apostolic age to the fall of the Byzantine Empire; the second part comprises studies of the separate churches: the modern Greek Church, the Russian Church, the Syrian and Armenian Churches, and the Coptic and Abyssinian Churches. The verdict of J. P. Whitney on the book was that while the first part might have been shortened, as being already well covered in the literature, the accounts of the Greek and Russian Churches were warmly welcomed: 'These are peculiarly difficult subjects to deal with, but the very difficulties increase the usefulness of the work to the general reader.'[168] The reviewer in *The Expository Times* was equally pleased to compliment Adeney on having presented 'difficult material with grace and reliability.'[169]

It will suffice here to note a few points of particular interest in this work of 626 pages. Adeney finds that of the Cappadocians, Gregory of Nyssa was most emphatic in following Origen's view that Christ had a real human soul, which

> was transformed under the influence of the Divine Nature after the resurrection and ascension. ... Thus we have the omnipresence of that glorified body, for the body of Christ was transmute to the flesh of God by the indwelling word. It is easy to see how readily such a theory would agree with the doctrine of transubstantiation, a doctrine which Gregory did more than anybody else of his period to advance.[170]

Unlike a number of scholars of his day—among them his Lancashire College colleague, Robert Mackintosh, who bluntly declared that 'The Christology of Chalcedon will not do'[171]—Adeney more temperately concludes that while it is not a metaphysical explanation of the person of Christ, the Formula does clearly assert Christ's humanity and divinity.

During the period of what Adeney calls 'the Monophysite troubles' the divinity of Christ became more prominent, and his humanity receded, 'so that sorrowful people who were craving for human sympathy turned from the awful Byzantine Christ to the compassionate Mary ... It is hardly too much to say that Mary became to all

---

[167] Ibid., 175.

[168] J. P. Whitney, review of Adeney's *The Greek and Eastern Churches* in *Journal of Theological Studies*, XII, 1911, 485.

[169] *The Expository Times*, XXI, 1909-1910, 209.

[170] W. F. Adeney, *The Greek and Eastern Churches*, 79.

[171] R. Mackintosh, 'Discussion' of a paper by R. S. Franks, *The Congregational Quarterly*, X, 1932, 39.

intents and purposes the incarnate Saviour, while the humanity of Christ and His incarnation were lost in the grandeur of His Divinity.'[172]

When discussing the thought of John of Damascus, Adeney summarizes his view of the principal differences between John's theological position and that of Augustine and Gregory in the West in the following terms:

> [John's] assertion of free will—a marked feature of Greek theology throughout in contradistinction from Latin; his silence as to original sin; his distinction between foreknowledge and predestination; his denial of the physical fire of hell—so prominent in the lurid horrors of the mediaeval inferno from Gregory to Dante; and his moderate views of the sacraments, which he holds to be only two—Baptism and the Lord's Supper.[173]

Two more of Adeney's opinions may be recorded. First, in a discussion of the Bogomiles, Adeney finds that while these Christians may have subscribed to doctrinal errors, their 'real offence', like that of the Albigenses in the West, 'was opposition to the sacramental materialism of the Church.'[174] Secondly, Adeney's assessment of Cyril Lucar's failed attempt to reform the Greek Church along Calvinist lines is that, his bravery notwithstanding, 'He had not displayed any intellectual originality; he had not developed reformed doctrine from within his Church; he had only tried to transplant an exotic, and it is not surprising that this would not take root in a strange soil.'[175]

The historical works by Adeney that remain to be considered take us from the Waldensians through the Separatists and Nonconformists. They include an article on toleration, and some references he made in a public address from the Chair of the Congregational Union of England and Wales. It will be better to treat these writings together rather than consecutively.

Adeney opens his lengthy article on the Waldensians with the frank recognition that 'Legend has been busy weaving fanciful impossibilities into the fabric' of the story.[176] These concern the claim that the Waldensians originated in apostolic times, or that they date from the age of Constantine, or that their founder was Claude, the eighth-century bishop of Turin. Adeney has no difficulty in repudiating such notions. Nor does it seem likely, in view of geographical difficulties and doctrinal differences, that the Waldensians owed their origins to the Albigenses on the French side of the mountains. It is more likely, says Adeney, that Peter of Bruys (1104-1125) was a precursor of the Waldensians, and that the reforming spirit of Abelard's disciple, Arnold of Brescia and Henry of Cluny lived on in them. There can be no doubt, however, about the formative role played by Peter Waldo and the Poor Men of Lyons. Indeed, 'It was his movement that gathered in the harvest of [the precursors']

---

[172] W. F. Adeney, *The Greek and Eastern Churches*, 105.

[173] Ibid., 211.

[174] Ibid., 228.

[175] Ibid., 322.

[176] Idem, 'Waldenses,' 664(a).

lives and brought about the formation of a Waldensian Church.'[177] Waldo and his followers sought to live by the teaching of the Gospels, and there is no pre-Reformation Waldensian statement of faith. Rather,

> The earlier Protestantism was partly negative, in the rejection of Roman Catholic teachings and practices which could not be justified by the NT, and, in so far as it was positive, a return to the spirituality of worship believed to have been characteristic of the primitive Church. ... [T]he Pauline theology, so emphatically and elaborately taught both by Luther and Calvin, does not appear to have been brought forward by these earlier Protestants. There was no tendency among them to elaborate a systematic theology.[178]

A number of attempts had been made to suppress the Waldensians during the thirteenth century, and in the following century their exiled followers made links with the Hussites of Bohemia and others. With the advance of the Reformation the remnant in the alpine valleys became associated with the Calvinists (though not without some internal opposition) at the Synod of Chanforan (1532), which was attended by Farel, Saunier and Olivétan. The period from 1540 to 1690 is a tale of persecutions, faithfulness, heroism, exile, and, in the latter year, of 'the Glorious Return'; and the fortunes of the Waldensians were subject to considerable fluctuations from that time onwards until full civil and religious rights were granted to them by Charles Albert in 1848. A Waldensian congregation was established at Turin, and it became home to refugee Protestants from all over Italy, some of whom resisted the traditional Waldensian church order. Hence the separation of a Free Church in 1854, and an eventual reunion by the end of the century. Adeney's article ends with a description of the then current state of the Waldensian Church, its missions and social work, and its general theological stance: 'Neither the narrower type of Calvinism nor advanced liberalism ...'[179]

Adeney has evident sympathy with the witness of the Waldensians, but in his article on 'Nonconformity' he is concerned with his own people. He defines his terms thus:

> While 'heresy' stands for opposition to ecclesiastically settled orthodoxy, 'schism' for separation from the communion of the society claiming to be the one true Church, and 'dissent' for divergence from the beliefs and doctrines maintained by the national settlement, Nonconformity consists in not carrying out the requirements of an 'Act of Uniformity,' which is a law of the State.[180]

He points out that while latter-day Nonconformists stand for 'a free Church in a free state', their Presbyterian and Congregational forebears, though not the Baptists, would have accepted varying degrees of state authorization of religion.

---

[177] Ibid., 666(b).
[178] Ibid., 668(a).
[179] Ibid., 673(b).
[180] Idem, 'Nonconformity,' 382(a).

In a chapter entitled, 'The Church in the prisons,' which he contributed to a volume commemorating the tercentenary of the martyrdoms (1593) of Greenwood, Barrow and Penry, Adeney focuses upon the witness of Barrow and Greenwood, making it clear that while the Separatist harbingers of Dissent were for the separation of Church and state, this was a consequence of their foundational belief in the separation of the Church from the world:

> They called themselves 'Separatists,' not because they were Nonconformists separated from the Church, nor because they were Free Churchmen who advocated separations of Church and State, but because their root principle was the separation of the Church from the world, and the constitution of the Church as a community of separated people—people whose confession and conduct testified to their personal godliness. Of course this principle carried with it a separation from the Church of England, because that Church included all the baptized who were not Roman Catholics or excommunicated persons, however irreligious they might be. It also involved the separation of Church and State.[181]

Having retold the story of the martyrs for general readers, Adeney is not slow to end in homiletic vein: 'If these founders of Congregationalism deemed their principles to be so momentous that they were willing to die for them, the least we can do is to inquire seriously whether it may not be our duty to live for them.'[182]

In his 'Nonconformity' article Adeney sketches the history of Nonconformity from Tudor times onwards, noting the witness of the Separatists, and paying particular attention to the Cromwellian period and to the penalties enacted against Nonconformists following the Restoration of the monarchy in 1660—notably the Act of Uniformity of 1662, which required all clergymen (and schoolmasters) to give their 'unfeigned assent and consent' to the contents of the *Book of Common Prayer* of the Church of England, or forfeit their livings. Hence the Ejectment of nearly two thousand ministers, and their precarious, and sometimes dangerous, position over the following decades. In his Spring Address from the Chair of the Congregational Union in 1913, Adeney recalled the great impression the bicentenary celebrations of the Ejectment had made upon him:

> For my own part, looking back across these long fifty years, I can say with confidence that that celebration stands out as the one national event which impressed my boyhood, and to my father's lecture at Reigate on that occasion I trace an indelible consciousness of the necessity of Nonconformity and of the duty of maintaining those great truths and duties that were illustrated in the heroic conduct of the ejected ministers. I mention this autobiographical fact because I

---

[181] Idem, 'The Church in the prisons,' 11.
[182] Ibid., 22.

> gather from it the inference that we can hardly begin too soon the training of young people in the history of the Free Churches.[183]

Of the Act of Uniformity itself Adeney declares that it 'did not even aim at uniformity—in any large and national application of the idea. It was frankly and brutally separatist; it was meant to be so.'[184] He invokes the Anglican historian, Gwatkin, in support of this contention.

Following the accession of William and Mary, the Toleration Act of 1689 was passed. No earlier adverse acts were repealed but, says Adeney, Nonconformists were granted exemption from their penalties, though he does not in this article explain that toleration was granted to *Trinitarian* Protestants only. This omission is made good in Adeney's fuller encyclopaedia article on 'Toleration', in which he sets out from Greece and Rome. He points out that

> The word 'toleration' in its legal, ecclesiastical and doctrinal application has a peculiarly limited signification. It connotes a refraining from prohibition and persecution. ... Toleration is not equivalent to religious liberty, and it falls far short of religious equality. It assumes the existence of an authority which might have been coercive, but which for reasons of its own is not pushed to extremes. It implies a voluntary inaction, a politic leniency. ... The very practice of it involves an exalted position of power enjoyed by the people who tolerate as opposed to an inferior position in which the tolerated are living.[185]

For all its inadequacies, the tolerated Nonconformists were given some scope for worship and witness. By the end of the seventeenth century 2418 licences for places of worship had been issued, though many socio-political barriers remained in place against them. There follows Adeney's account of the fluctuating fortunes of Nonconformity down to his own time—a time when Nonconformist membership reached its peak, educational disabilities still rankled, and the National Council of Evangelical Free Churches (including now the Methodists) was founded in 1892. Adeney concludes with a section on Welsh Nonconformity, the greatest distinction between the situation in Wales being the small percentage of (Arminian) Methodists and the high proportion of post-Evangelical Revival Calvinistic Methodists (Welsh Presbyterians from 1811 onwards).

Adeney, writing in a time of Anglo-Catholic ascendency, was in no doubt that the Free Church witness on behalf of liberty, and of union with Christ the sole Mediator as being the criterion of church membership was, if anything, more urgently needed than hitherto:

---

[183] Idem, 'The more excellent way,' CYB, 1913, 36. I have a strong suspicion that, for a variety of reasons, this history is infrequently taught to young people today. See further, Alan P. F. Sell, *Testimony and Tradition*, ch. 11.

[184] Ibid., 37.

[185] Idem, 'Toleration,' 360(b), 365(a).

> In face of Laudian notions of Church authority, Apostolical succession, priest and sacraments, rites and ceremonies, the ideas of liberty and spirituality need to be re-asserted to-day. The sons of the Puritans, who were driven out of the Church of the Stuarts because they would not admit such perversions of the original spiritual faith of Christ as they understood it, should not be easily tempted back to a communion three-fourths of which is far more sacerdotal and ritualistic than the Church which expelled their ancestors was in the age of the Act of Uniformity.[186]

These ecclesiological reflections entice us forward to Adeney's more doctrinal and theological and apologetic writings.

III

Adeney left no fully-fledged systematic theology, but in the course of his writings he touched upon a number of major Christian doctrines. Of *The Christian Conception of God* (1909) a reviewer wrote, 'Only a man of Dr. Adeney's knowledge could write so simply. Only a man of Dr. Adeney's experience could write so humbly.'[187] Adeney takes his bearings from the Johannine writings. I John opens with an appeal to personal experience, and running through John's Gospel we find testimonies to the source of the author's knowledge of God: 'He saw God in Christ, and what he saw of God in Christ was love incarnate.'[188] Reflecting upon this, Adeney declares that

> We cannot have a greater or clearer idea of God than the character of Jesus. The supreme greatness of God is not His infinity, His almighty power, His perfect knowledge, His unfailing wisdom. Moral attributes are greater than physical energies, and even greater than intellectual capacities. The crowning glory of God is His character. ... [I]t is reasonable to think of God as possessing the very real goodness which we see manifested in the life and doings of Jesus Christ.[189]

Jesus is not simply the founder of Christianity, 'He is its centre, and that because of what He was and did and suffered. ... [T]he life, death, and resurrection of Christ are all stages in His revelation of God.'[190] The testimony of Christ's early disciples is confirmed by Christian history: 'The proof of redemption is that Christ redeems.'[191]

In setting out from Christ, Adeney does not wish to imply that other means of knowing God are of no value. By elevating God-consciousness 'Schleiermacher opened the way for more vital spiritual thinking,'[192] but in their extreme reaction against eighteenth-century natural theology and their elevation of the historic Christ

---

186 Idem, 'The more excellent way,' 42.

187 ET, XXI, 1909-1910, 276.

188 W. F. Adeney, *The Christian Conception of God*, 7.

189 Ibid., 8, 9.

190 Ibid., 14, 15.

191 Ibid., 16.

192 Ibid., 20.

the more rigorous Ritschlians erred in what Adeney describes as a Marcionite direction. In fact the Old Testament is neither to be repudiated nor deemed to be 'of the same rank with the New Testament in the scale of revelation.'[193] Moreover, Christianity does not deny knowledge of God beyond the bounds of the Christian faith. The metaphysical theistic arguments, for example, seek to demonstrate the infinite and the absolute, and their deliverances are neither neutralized nor invalidated by revelation. However,

> These are not the phases of Divinity manifested in the Incarnation. Yet they are implied in the Christian idea of God. That He is the Infinite One inhabiting eternity cannot be seen from the manifestation of perfect goodness in our Lord's life on earth. Yet the Incarnation would not be what it is to us unless He were that. Thus the basal theism comes into the Christian conception of God and is presupposed by it.[194]

Elsewhere Adeney cites Jesus's words, 'Believe in God, believe also in me' (John14:1) in support of this position. 'Here,' he says, 'are the two spheres of faith represented respectively by Theism and Christianity.'[195]

In the Old Testament Adeney finds a God who is sovereign, holy, righteous, merciful and compassionate. He also finds in later Jewish writings an exaggerated understanding of the divine transcendence. This leads him into an excursus on mysticism, and to the conclusion that for all the mystic's interiority, 'the mystic knowledge of God has to rest on the revelation of God in Christ if it is to be a Christian knowledge of God.'[196]

Turning towards the New Testament, Adeney expresses his surprise that in their books Samuel Harris, James Orr and John Caird proceed from theism to the Trinity, bypassing the question of the nature of the God revealed in Jesus Christ. Adeney does not deny the doctrine of the Trinity, but he does regard it as a development of the New Testament witness and avers, 'no impartial student of the life and teachings of Christ will come to the conclusion that when He reveals God to us that revelation consists in the doctrine of the Trinity'[197]—which is not to deny that the roots of the doctrine are in the New Testament. When we turn to Christ's actual teaching on the nature of God we find that central to it is the idea of the divine Fatherhood: 'The whole idea of the gospel springs from that conception of God's love to lost and sinful men which is just an outcome of His fatherly heart.'[198] He is particularly concerned to point out that when Paul contrasts the status of every human being as a child of God with Paul's understanding of the saints as adopted sons (and daughters)

---

[193] Ibid., 23.
[194] Ibid., 28.
[195] Idem, *Faith To-day*, 7-8.
[196] Idem, *The Christian Conception of God*, 47; cf. 262-266.
[197] Ibid., 51.
[198] Ibid., 57.

of God, this implied no restriction upon God's universal Fatherhood. Adeney cordially agrees that

> With many of us the redemption of the world by the incarnation, life, death, resurrection, and eternal work of the ever-living Christ is the peculiar core and pith of the gospel. But then the root of that is God's fatherly relation and disposition towards mankind. It is just because God is our Father that He sent Christ to be our Redeemer.[199]

He further notes that whereas the order of human experience follows that of Paul's benediction: 'The grace of the Lord Jesus Christ and the love of God ...', in the order the divine action God's fatherly love comes first. It is 'the source and spring of the Christian gospel.'[200]

Adeney is well aware of the challenge (possibly as posed by his Congregational contemporary, P. T. Forsyth?[201]) that alongside God's Fatherhood must be set his holiness, righteousness and justice; and he is no advocate of sentimentalized notions of God's fatherly love. But he thinks that the qualities specified, and others, are included within the concept of Fatherhood: 'For can any one be perfect even as a father unless he is of perfect character?'[202] On the way to this conclusion he finds it possible to commend the Unitarian, Theodore Parker, for teaching that 'God combines in His nature and in His relation to us motherhood together with fatherhood. Since He is our sole Supreme Parent we might think of Him as our Father and Mother in one.'[203] He does not, however, pursue this point in relation to the Trinity, the creeds, the worship of the Church or the devotions of the individual believer.

Instead he points out that although the truth of God's Fatherhood is the greatest truth, it is not the only one. While grateful for the work of Erskine of Linlathen, McLeod Campbell, F. D. Maurice and George Macdonald in demolishing the old idea that while God was a 'terror', Jesus was winsome,[204] there is more to the gospel than God's Fatherhood. At the heart of Christianity is Christ himself. Not surprisingly, therefore, 'the theological discussion of the Church in the third, fourth, fifth, and sixth centuries ... chiefly turned on the old question, "What think ye of Christ?"'[205] Nevertheless, 'Christ is what He is to us in order that He may restore to us the happy consciousness of sonship so that we may live in the light of God our Father.'[206]

---

199 Ibid., 64.

200 Ibid., 65.

201 See Alan P. F. Sell, *Testimony and Tradition*, ch. 7.

202 W. F. Adeney, *The Christian Conception of God*, 77.

203 Ibid., 71.

204 For these and other seminal thinkers see W. F. Adeney, *A Century's Progress in Religious Life and Thought*, ch. 2.

205 Ibid., 84.

206 Ibid, 85.

Adeney proceeds to a discussion of the personality of God, arguing that 'If you are to banish the idea of feeling from your conception of the Divine Being you must give up the thought of personality.'[207] He conducts a running critique of materialism, naturalism and pantheism, observing that if the latter is denied and God is other than that which he has created, this implies a certain limitation in God. For all that, God is 'the supreme moral Personality.'[208] As for 'infinity' and 'the absolute', Adeney finds nothing in them that he can call divine or regard as worthy of worship: 'Not starting with any philosophical definition of God as the Infinite or the Absolute into which our religious ideas are to be fitted, we may be prepared to accept just such an idea of God as we receive in the revelation of Christ.'[209]

Turning next to the themes of immanence and transcendence, Adeney insists that notwithstanding all of Jesus's teaching concerning God's watchful care for the things he has made, there is no metaphysics, and hence no doctrine of immanence, in the gospels. It does not follow, however that 'the whole discussion [rife in Adeney's day] with reference to the immanence of God is alien to the spirit of Christianity.'[210] He argues that the emphasis upon immanence was a reaction against that upon transcendence urged by the eighteenth-century deists; and he is a pains to make clear that immanence is not synonymous with pantheism, for God's personality and human will-power and responsibility are preserved. Indeed, 'When you affirm identity your deny immanence. Pantheism is a negation of the idea of the immanence of God.'[211] Again, the idea of divine immanence coheres with that of evolution in so far as God may be understood as being in the process at every stage. If this is so, the older understanding of miracles as breaches of the natural order cannot be sustained, for 'If God is always working in nature through its normal operations, He cannot be regarded as stepping in or interfering when anything happens apart from the normal.'[212] But this does not preclude miracles altogether. After all, 'Christ Himself is the greatest of miracles; the resurrection of Christ is the best attested of miracles.'[213] The idea of divine immanence is, however, limited in two ways: first by human free will: God respects the independence he has given us and does not dominate us; and the sense of alienation we feel when we are guilty of sin, while it may be prompted by 'the touch of the immanent God',[214] is distinct from it. The second limitation derives from the divine transcendence: 'It is just because God is transcendently good that He has shown Himself immanently gracious.'[215]

---

[207] Ibid., 93.

[208] Ibid., 109.

[209] Ibid., 119. See further, Alan P. F. Sell, *Philosophical Idealism and Christian Belief*.

[210] Ibid., 124.

[211] Ibid., 140.

[212] Idem, *A Century's Progress in Religious Life and Thought*, 107.

[213] Idem, *The Christian Conception of God*, 131.

[214] Ibid., 146.

[215] Ibid., 151.

As to the person of Christ, Adeney contends that 'The fact of the Incarnation is the foundation of the Christian faith,' and that this 'involves the doctrine of the Divinity of Christ in conjunction with that of his humanity.'[216] In his view, 'One of the happiest products of recent theological thought has been its recovery of the genuine humanity of Jesus.'[217] Those who accept the authority of Scripture have no difficulty in accepting the divinity of Christ. But is it necessary first to vindicate scriptural authority before we can proceed to demonstrate Christ's divinity? 'Such a requirement,' he laments, 'opens up to us a dreary vista of argumentation.'[218] But there is no need to take this route. Consistently with his approach in more specifically biblical studies, Adeney recommends that we go straight to the witness of the gospels, and there we shall find more than sufficient evidence of Christ's divinity. Thus in a paper on 'The divinity of Christ' he sets down the seven lines of thought which lead him to his conclusion:

> [Christ's] assured sinlessness; His incomparable claims; His consciousness of unique Sonship ('He never joined Himself with us when speaking of the Fatherhood of God')[219]; His resurrection; the impression He made on those who knew Him best; His work throughout the centuries; the experience of His people.[220]

We have already seen how he goes about such a task, but it is worth briefly noting a number of additional points here. First, Adeney shuns the sentimental liberal view that we could all be Christ-like if we would, for this 'is to beg the question, for the very fact of difference is that Christ's will agrees with God's will, while ours does not.'[221] Secondly, what we have in Jesus is an incarnation, not an inspiration, as is proposed by those who construe the incarnation in terms of immanentism. Thirdly, by reason of his divinity, Jesus 'is the one true Man the world has ever seen.'[222] Fourthly, Jesus's human limitations of power and knowledge may be accounted for by the great act of condescension which the incarnation involved. Some have construed this in terms of *kenosis*; others, with Irenaeus and Dorner, in terms of a gradual process such that there was more and more of God in Christ as he progressed through life. On the latter suggestion Adeney cautiously (or elusively) remarks, '*Possibly* some of us *may* think this view more acceptable than the Kenotic theory.'[223] Finally, as before, Adeney elevates the resurrection, 'one of the best attested facts of history',[224] in support of Christ's divinity.

---

[216] Ibid., 153, 155.

[217] Ibid., 156.

[218] Ibid., 158.

[219] Idem, 'The divinity of Christ,' in Chas. H. Vine, ed., *The Old Faith and the New Theology*, 96.

[220] Ibid., 90.

[221] Idem, *The Christian Conception of God*, 164; cf. 161-162.

[222] Ibid., 177.

[223] Ibid., 183. My italics.

[224] Ibid., 160. Cf., idem, 'The divinity of Christ,' 98-100. Adeney faulted Carl Weizsäcker for paying inadequate attention to the historicity of the resurrection in his

In a paper on 'The resurrection' he contends that whereas the 'centre of gravity of faith' from the fourth century to the present in Catholic circles was the incarnation; and whereas in Protestantism it has traditionally been the atonement, in apostolic times it was the resurrection.[225] He grants that nowadays 'We do not believe that He is the Christ because God raised Him from the dead. ... It would be more correct to say that we are able to accept the ancient testimony to this great marvel because we are already convinced of His unique nature and mission as the Son of God and Saviour of the world.'[226] Nevertheless the resurrection is crucially important. It signifies that Jesus 'lived after death'; that he 'remained essentially unchanged in nature and character'; that he is still our 'brother man'; that 'Jesus returned to this world after His death'; and that 'this continual life of Jesus is active.'[227] The 'fundamental proof' of the resurrection is 'the resurrection of the Church.'[228] Hence, we are not left with Renan's 'sweet Galilean dream.' Rather, for us the Easter message is the basis of the Easter faith, as it was for the first disciples.

In the course of reviewing *The Christian Conception of God*, a writer waxed panegyric: 'The chapter on the Holy Spirit is itself unmistakable evidence of the Spirit's grace and power.'[229] 'Whatever else the Holy Spirit may be for us,' Adeney writes, 'the immediate fact is that we use the name for the agency of God's immediate working in our spirits.'[230] He proceeds to show from Scripture that 'most, if not all, of our knowledge of the subject, and the language and imagery with which we discuss it, are derived from the Bible; and ... the Spirit has come on the Church with especial fulness through Christ.'[231] There follows a discussion of the Spirit in relation to immanence, and Adeney distinguishes the latter from the former in the following way:

> There is ... a distinctive experience associated with the gift of the Holy Spirit which is not found in the idea of immanence. The latter is universal and independent of our personal conditions, not so the former. The Christian teaching is that there are specific endowments of the Holy Spirit given through Christ to those who are in a fit state to receive them, and withheld from others; and this teaching is confirmed by experience. There have been men filled with the Spirit, doing great deeds for God in the might of this endowment; but that cannot be said of all men.[232]

He immediately concedes the possibility that this ability may be the result of a particular manifestation of God's immanence, and that this is what occurs when we

---

book, *Das Apostolische Zeitalter der Christlichen Kirche*. See W. F. Adeney, 'Weiszäcker on the resurrection,' *The Expositor*, 4th ser. VIII, 1893, 137-146.

225 W. F. Adeney, 'The resurrection,' 231.

226 Ibid., 233.

227 Ibid., 240-241.

228 Ibid., 245-246.

229 ET, XXI, 1909-1910, 276.

230 W. F. Adeney, *The Christian Conception of God*, 186.

231 Ibid., 190.

232 Ibid., 212.

speak of the Spirit's outpouring. Moreover, when it is said that the Holy Spirit is not simply personal, but a Person, the reference is to something other than immanence, and it points towards the doctrine of the Trinity.

To Adeney, the doctrine of the Trinity is 'essentially Christian', by which he means that it 'springs out of genuine Christian facts and truths,' and 'It is not merely a Church doctrine, and therefore Christian in the wider, looser sense of the term.'[233] It is unique to Christianity, and what are adduced as Platonic and Hindu parallels 'cannot be compared to [*sic*] the Christian threefold existence, in which there is no illusion, and yet which is essentially monotheistic.'[234] The doctrine cannot satisfactorily be deduced *a priori*, and a philosophically-based Trinity such as Hegel's 'is not the Christian Trinity, because it does not involve the idea of a personal God.'[235] Whereas the doctrine of the Trinity is not promulgated in the New Testament, the facts upon which it depends are to be found there, and the doctrine 'has grown up as the least inadequate conception of the Godhead consistent with those facts.'[236] The facts are that God is one; that Christ is divine; and that the Holy Spirit is within us—or, as he more popularly puts it, 'the Father above us, the Brother by our side, the Spirit within us.'[237]

When considering the objection that divisions within the Godhead imply that God is less that perfect, Adeney warns us against materialistic assumptions, and observes that God need not be a simple monad. Moreover, God has revealed himself in the way declared in trinitarian doctrine. He reminds us that 'person' in the traditional trinitarian formula did not mean a distinct individual, but nor may we espouse Sabellian emanations, for they do not accord with 'the very marked distinctions of the Scripture language.'[238] Equally, we must not succumb to Arianism with its subordinate, creaturely Christ, or tritheism. The idea of the equality of the Persons, suggested by the Athanasian Creed, 'is simply unintelligible, a collection of phrases, each marvellously clear in itself; a triumph of concise statements; but in its totality hopelessly self-contradictory.'[239] For a certain subordination (though not an Arian one, since the Son is not said to be a creature) is evident in the Father's sending of the Son, and the Son's sending of the Spirit: 'The Sender is superior to the Sent.'[240]

---

233 Ibid., 216.

234 Ibid., 218.

235 Ibid., 222.

236 Ibid., 227.

237 Idem, 'The Trinity,' in *Studies in Christian Evidences*. Series I, 128. The appellation 'Brother', beloved of liberal theologians of the day, would cause more distress if we did not know that Adeney thinks that Christ is much more than that. Consider his cautionary word: 'Unitarianism—or the denial of the trinity in theology—always goes with humanitarianism, or the denial of the divinity of Christ in Christology.' Ibid., 126.

238 Idem, *The Christian Conception of God*, 245.

239 Idem, 'The Trinity,' 133.

240 Ibid. Or, more happily, 'logically prior to'? Cf. *The Theology of the New Testament*, 182-183, to which reference has already been made.

Among the questions Adeney addresses is this: Why are there *three* persons? He answers, 'I do not affirm that God only exists and acts in Trinity, I venture to set no limits to the possibilities of the Godhead.' We affirm the Trinity because God 'has come to us in a threefold way.'[241]

Adeney insists throughout that 'the Christian idea of God in itself is not based on speculative grounds.'[242] We do, however have to acknowledge that the given revelations are partial, and we cannot confine our attention to Jesus's person and character, for

> He did not only reveal His nature and character by His utterances; He made them more evident by His life and deeds. Therefore if we are to see God in Christ, this will be by contemplating His whole life-course. But that life-course was crowned and consummated by His death and resurrection.[243]

From this position he never departed.

Adeney was in no doubt that Christianity is a social, not an individualistic, religion, and hence he recognized the inescapability of the Church. This is nothing less than we should expect from one steeped in the Congregational tradition. This is underscored in his historical works, backed by his biblical studies, which assured him that by 'Church' is to be understood both the one Church in heaven and on earth and the local gatherings of saints; and that those who are 'in Christ' are not simply children, but sons and daughters of God (this without prejudice to God's universal Fatherhood). His attitude towards the Church's formal witness to the faith of the ages combines the grateful with the cautious. Thus, for example, of the Nicene Creed he writes that

> it brings before us the Fatherhood of God, the combined Divinity and Humanity of Christ, and the living power of the Holy Spirit. I am not sure that there is much advantage in our making public use of this venerable document of all Church literature. It is so metaphysical, so antique, and at the same time so crisp and clear and positive, where some of us must confess to great wonderment and a sense of profound mystery. But I am convinced that most of the theologies that deny its central ideas are further from the truth of God revealed to us by Christ.[244]

In my account of his biblical studies the importance Adeney attached to a (non-sacerdotal) practice of the Lord's Supper became apparent. As to baptism, he contributed a pamphlet on this to a series of *Faith and Conduct Papers for Young People*. He describes the sacrament as 'the initial rite of Christianity.'[245] He proceeds to rule out baptism as the essential condition of salvation, observing that Mark 16:16, 'He that believeth and is baptized shall be saved; he that believeth not shall

---

[241] Ibid., 136.

[242] Idem, *The Christian Conception of God*, 248.

[243] Ibid., 253.

[244] Ibid., 272-273.

[245] Idem, *Baptism its Nature and Privileges*, 71.

be damned', is a later addition to the gospel; and that although Jesus tells Nicodemus that baptism by water and the spirit is necessary (John 3:5), in the ensuing conversation there is further reference to the Spirit, but none to water. Furthermore, John the Baptist's baptism was a water baptism unto repentance, but Christ gives the regenerating Spirit. Again, Jesus opposed 'all trust in forms and ceremonies,'[246] and Paul baptized nobody, and emphasized the 'new creature' not the baptized person (Galatians 6:15). Hence the 'idea of salvation by baptism is an error ... a very deplorable one.'[247] As to paedobaptism, Adeney finds that while there is no conclusive statement in the New Testament that this occurred, 'we have good reason for believing that when a man was converted and baptized, his family was also baptized.'[248] Moreover, Christ himself welcomed children into his company.

Positively, 'baptism is enrolment in the school of Christ', and the Church undertakes 'to see that [children] are taught His truth and trained as His disciples.'[249] Parents should understand this, and if they do not, they should be taught the meaning of the rite, for both the Church and they themselves assume certain responsibilities when a child is baptized:

> The act of baptism is the Church's recognition that Christ has a claim on the child; it is the Church's declaration that all the blessings of Christ's gospel are awaiting this child for his soul's welfare and destiny in life; it is the Church's acceptance of the child for Christian teaching. For this reason the command is to baptize, not to be baptized, a command to Christ's followers to accept disciples and train them for Him, not to converts to seek baptism.[250]

Baptism gives 'the Church visitor, minister, or teacher a valid reason, indeed a clear duty, for visiting the home ...'[251] Baptized children also have responsibilities, for while their lives were dedicated to God at their baptism, 'To make them also *consecrated* lives rests with [their] own choice and decision.'[252] Adeney does not dwell on believer baptism in this pamphlet.

In the two addresses he delivered from the Chair of the Congregational Union of England and Wales, Adeney both justifies his Nonconformity and also makes clear the Church's obligation to serve the wider society. As to the former, he writes,

> We have no desire to be graciously permitted to return to the Established Church, either as her whipped children creeping in at a back door, or even as respectable exiles welcomed home with generous admissions that we should never have been ostracised. These 250 years have not been lived in vain. We have come to see the utter unchristianity of the control of Church affairs by the arm of the State, to see

[246] Ibid., 73.
[247] Ibid.
[248] Ibid., 75.
[249] Ibid., 77.
[250] Ibid., 78.
[251] Ibid., 79.
[252] Ibid.

> that it is a usurpation of the rights of Christ and a dishonour to His body that not one line of the obligatory Book of Prayer can be altered without the consent of Parliament, and that the chief places in the pastoral office should be filled at the dictation of the First Lord of the treasury—even though we might imagine a time when that Minister of State should happen to be a Baptist. ...
>
> I should be only too glad to unite in Christian fellowship with my friends of the Church of England if they would let me be myself, would recognise me not only as a Christian brother, but also as already a member of a Christian Church, and as a Christian minister requiring no fresh ordination. But union by submission I respectfully decline.[253]

Where the social calling of the Church is concerned, Adeney is trenchant:

> The object of the existence of the Church of Christ is the establishment of the Kingdom of Heaven. Therefore the Church must be missionary, or it will cease to exist. It must be furthering Christ's reconstruction of society, or it will be no longer the body of Christ. ...
>
> I visit prosperous Churches in the manufacturing towns of Lancashire and Yorkshire and learn that here they are building a new organ, and there they are furnishing a parlour. It is well, and the gifts mean some sacrifice on the part of the givers. But I observe that while the manufacturers live in stately mansions and have fine paintings on their walls, and drive to their offices in swift motor-cars, their workpeople are huddled together in back-to-back houses that double the infant mortality, and I ask myself, would not these Churches be more true to the mind of the Master if they helped to bring about equable conditions in the communities among which they are planted, even at the cost of a third manual to the new organ, or a Turkey carpet in the church parlour?
>
> Or I visit one of our charming villages in the south country, with its mossy thatch and rose-clad porches, and though I know that the little old chapel can do no more than make a brave fight for existence, I wonder whether the greater resources of the Churches in stronger centres might not be forthcoming to secure for the agricultural labourer a living wage and a home that is a habitable cottage, and not merely a picturesque ruin—the greatest economic requirement of England to-day.[254]

Important though all of this is, however, 'these things will not in themselves constitute the Kingdom of God, for that kingdom is not meat and drink.'[255] Nor do secular social reformers have the answer, for they overlook the 'ignorance, stupidity, obstinacy, selfishness, passion, sin' of human nature. Where they can but formulate

---

[253] Idem, 'The more excellent way,' 45, 47.

[254] 'The Church for the Kingdom,' 50, 51. Despite these examples of 'blindness', in ch. 10 of *A Century's Progress in Religious Life and Thought*, Adeney chronicles the way in which the older, individualistic, understanding of salvation has been tempered by growing concern for its social implications.

[255] Ibid., 55.

a demand, it is Christ who makes the 'new creatures' who can realise humanity's deepest hopes.[256] Hence, 'It is the mission of the Church to bear witness to the spiritual world and its eternal verities. If it ceases to do that, its candlestick is removed and its light has gone out, even though it is bubbling with social activities from the billiard-room in the basement to the gymnasium in the roof. I believe in the Institutional Church ... when there is a real live Church to be institutional, but not in an institute that has absorbed and assimilated its Church.'[257]

Turning to the last of the traditional 'departments' of systematic theology, eschatology, we find that Adeney has relatively little to offer in this field. That he was alive to the challenge of addressing such themes in the context of naturalistic evolutionary thought is clear from his paper on 'Evolution and immortality.' His thesis is that 'The evidence in favour of the theory of the evolution of physical nature moves along an entirely different road from that on which the proof of the immortality of the soul travels.'[258] It is quite clear to him that while immortality cannot be established 'from a consideration of the analogies of nature,'[259] such analogies may be of assistance in removing some objections to it. After all, 'If Nature is silent in regard to immortality, we are not to be surprised that the exclusive study of nature should leave the idea of immortality shadowy and doubtful. But it will be a great point to have come to see that nature has nothing to say against the immortality of that which is above the range of material structure.'[260] We can then study the evidence for immortality from 'the moral nature of man, the Fatherly government of God, the words, life, and resurrection of Christ. In particular, it is very significant that though our Lord revealed few details of the future life, His language in affirming the existence of that life was unmistakably clear and unhesitatingly positive.'[261]

Adeney was well aware that notwithstanding Jesus's reticence upon the subject, others had subsequently made much of it. In his review of nineteenth-century theology he devotes a chapter to 'The future', which reveals his general stance on matters eschatological. He notes that at the turn of the eighteenth century 'it was common to set forth hope of the ineffable bliss of Heaven, and fear of the unutterable woe of Hell, as the supreme attracting and repelling forces in religion.'[262] Gradually, however, it came to be perceived that this involved 'a selfish conception of the aims of religion.'[263] Again, whereas John Pye Smith expounded the eternity of punishment in his *First Lines of Christian Theology*[264] the views of F. D.

---

[256] Ibid., 55.

[257] Ibid., 56.

[258] Idem, 'Evolution and immortality,' 111.

[259] Ibid., 125.

[260] Ibid., 127.

[261] Ibid., 128.

[262] Idem, *A Century's Progress in Religious Life and Thought*, 151.

[263] Ibid.

[264] These lectures, published posthumously in 1854, had been used by Pye Smith from the beginning of the century. For Pye Smith (1774-1851) see ODNB.

Maurice and others did much to erode this position. He proceeds to review conditional immortality as held by a line of thinkers from Arnobius through Locke to Isaac Watts, and notes the stir caused by Edward White's advocacy of the doctrine in his *Life in Christ* (1875), in which the natural immortality of the soul is declared to be an extra-biblical doctrine. In the New Testament immortality is 'a supernatural gift bestowed through Jesus Christ.'[265] White argues that in the Bible 'the punishment of sin is nearly always described as "death" and "destruction" rather than as pain and torment, and the blessing of salvation as "life" rather than happiness. Thus the doom of the lost is not everlasting torment, but extinction of being, a fate that comes about simply by leaving the guilty to the course of nature.'[266] White was attacked by H. P. Liddon for denying everlasting punishment, and by the liberal Congregationalist, J. Baldwin Brown, for denying natural immortality. R. W. Dale, however, gave his blessing to White's approach. Some, however, were concerned for 'the great multitude of the heathen world' who had not heard of Christ; hence the proposal that the destruction might be gradual, with probationary possibilities preceding final extinction of the wicked—an approach which travelled under the name of the 'larger hope'.

Adeney observes that while the doctrine of conditional immortality is not without difficulties, the discussion surrounding it has prompted a more sensitive and less gruesome discussion of immortality: 'We shall never return to the harshness and horror of the old position.'[267] He reaches a similar, typically cautious, conclusion in respect of the last judgment—and one, equally characteristically, in which children are present to his mind. Referring to former presentations of the doctrine which envisaged the rising of the dead at the sound of a trumpet and judgments before an actual white throne—a notion popularized in a 'once popular book entitled *Peep of Day*, on which so many young people were brought up,' with the result that 'to nervous little boys and girls the rumbling of thunder, the sight of a red sunset, and even the crowing of a cock were signs that the Judge was at the door,' he writes,

> It is a happy thing for children that these terrors have been swept away. It will not be a happy thing for the world if with them the very notion of judgment is abandoned as a superstition of the world's childhood. That would be both a flat denial of the spirit as well as the letter of Scripture, and also a violent contradiction of the instinct of justice, deep-rooted in the conscience of mankind. But people

---

[265] W. F. Adeney, *A Century's Progress in Religious Life and Thought*, 158.

[266] Ibid., 158-159. For Edward White (1819-1898), Congregational minister, see CYB, 1899, 205-207; Frederick Ash Freer, *Edward White*. In October 1887 White delivered the inaugural lecture of the Winter session at New College, London, on 'The influence of spiritual states upon biblical criticism.' He contended that 'A literary criticism, springing from a secret hostility of men to the supernatural and divine in their souls, is necessarily fatal to fair dealing with the Bible,' and that apart from divine illumination we become 'blind guides' and 'lose all power of leading the people in the way everlasting.' See *The Congregational Review*, I, 1887, 999-1000.

[267] Ibid., 161.

have been led to see that the pictorial language of the Bible must not be interpreted literally ...[268]

Judgment is generally regarded either as taking place at the moment of death, or as being an ongoing process through life, or as a spiritual event which will occur *post mortem*. Similarly, resurrection is no longer generally regarded as a matter of the reconstitution of entombed and decomposed bodies, 'though it is not denied that this future life may have some kind of bodily clothing.'[269]

I have already outlined the way in which Adeney, in apologetic fashion, reflected upon immortality in relation to the then prevalent evolutionary thought. But, while his stance on apologetic method is readily detectable throughout his writings, towards the end of his life, Adeney further reflected upon the apologetic task. That this more sustained reflection was occasioned by the First World War should not surprise us. But first, let us gather some general hints from his earlier writings. Adeney opens his book, *The Christian Conception of God*, with these words:

The question of supreme importance for all of us in not 'Is there a God?' but 'What is God?' You may demonstrate to me the necessity of what you are pleased to call 'a First Cause' and leave me cold and untouched. ... You may go further, and prove the existence of an infinite and eternal Being, and still I am unmoved if I am left to think of Him in the Epicurean way as outside the circle of my own experience. But immediately you speak of One in whom I live and move and have my being, it becomes supremely important for me to know what His nature and character are.[270]

On the last page of the same book he writes,

The Christian conception of God is that idea of His nature and character which we derive from Christ. ... It cannot be evolved by abstract speculation. It is not to be arrived at by a contemplation of the physical universe and an induction of facts of Nature. Whatever we may learn of the Divine by means of ontological or cosmological methods—and some may think much or little—our peculiarly Christian knowledge of God as our Father, whose highest attribute is perfect love, comes to us from what we see in Christ, and depends for its fulness and its assurance on the extent to which He has won our soul's confidence and captures our heart's devotion.[271]

All of this implies the viability of Adeney's appeal to the facts of the case. These facts comprise, as we have already seen, the biblical witness to Christ's life, death, resurrection and continuing work by the Spirit, and also the impact of all of these upon believers. Well aware that 'The word "fact" has a tempting sound for the

---

[268] Ibid., 165.
[269] Ibid., 167.
[270] Idem, *The Christian Conception of God*, 1.
[271] Ibid., 273.

Englishman of Philistine proclivities,' Adeney nevertheless asserts that facticity need not be confined

> to what is visible or tangible, to mere matters of sense perception; inward experiences such as joy, hope, love, fear, are also legitimately reckoned facts. But here we are concerned with a region above and beyond all experience. The life and death of the Saviour we take to be facts; the recovery of men and women from lives of shame and folly as far as this can be observed may also be set down in the category of facts.[272]

But if Adeney is unpersuaded that the classical theistic arguments can take us very far if we seek not merely an undifferentiated theism, but God, he is equally sceptical that evidentialist appeals will fare any better. He poured scorn upon the reissued rationalist book, *Supernatural Religion* (1902). On its first appearance thirty years before, he says, it created a stir. The fact that by contrast it is now seen to be outmoded is a tribute to the degree to which biblical criticism has been accepted: 'Today that terrible book comes back to us as an anachronism. Although its author informs us that it has been carefully revised, its spirit and tone and temper are unchanged, and they are the spirit and tone and temper of an effete Philistine Anti-Christian Crusade.'[273] The author continues in the line of Paley when he writes, 'It is admitted that miracles alone can attest the reality of divine revelation'; at which Adeney expostulates, 'what an old-world flavour that clause has for us today!'[274] The entire book 'represents the special pleading of a debater.'[275]

The inadequacy of the evidences was the subject of what, as far as I have been able to discover, was Adeney's last published (posthumous) paper: 'Miracle and prophecy,' which opens thus:

> The present generation has witnessed a revolution in Christian Apologetics. All down the ages until the later part of the nineteenth century the main defence of the truth of Christianity rested on the two pillars, miracle and prophecy. Paley's *Evidences* carried the old method down to our own times by being used as a University examination text-book—a soul-destroying futility.[276]

Whereas in earlier centuries precedence was given to prophecy,

> When we turn to the eighteenth century, that golden age of English apologetic theology, we find that the centre of gravity shifted from prophecy to miracle. If only Hume can succeed in destroying belief in the physical marvels of the Bible, the citadel of the faith would seem to be lost. On the other hand, if Paley can so

[272] W. F. Adeney, *The Atonement in Modern Religious Thought*, 144.
[273] Idem, review of *Supernatural Religion*, 391-392.
[274] Ibid., 392.
[275] Ibid., 394.
[276] Idem, 'Miracle and prophecy,' 133.

> marshal the evidence as to convince a British jury that they actually happened, Christianity is to be accepted as a revelation from Heaven.[277]

Such approaches have been driven from the field as the definition of miracle as a breach of the laws of nature has been queried because of the unproven assumption it contains; and also because in philosophy the sharp dichotomy between the physical and the spiritual has broken down. To rest faith on miracles is to behave in a *quasi*-materialistic way; to rest on the supposed fulfilment of foretold events is to fail to understand that 'the most characteristic feature of the prophetic mind was the gift of insight rather than that of foresight.'[278] It was not so much that the great prophets spoke of what Jesus would in fact do; it is rather that 'He endorsed the great ideas of the prophets, and moulded His course of action upon the programme with which they furnished Him ... selecting those prophecies with which He was most in sympathy and working on the lines which they had laid down.'[279] In this way 'Christ is seen to be realising the brightest dreams of the world's greatest seers.'[280]

On the basis of the aforementioned apologetic method, what has Adeney to say in the midst of the agonies of war? For the answer we must turn to his short book, *Faith To-day*. The reviewer in *The Expository* Times was not incorrect in judging that 'the deepest impression' made by Adeney's book of 1901, *A Century's Progress in Religious Life and Thought*, was 'that the world is actually making progress in moral and mental as well as in material things.'[281] A decade and a half later, such a claim seemed to many quite impossible to substantiate. Not surprisingly given the circumstances, Adeney takes up the themes of suffering and the providence of God. He points out that while the present calamity is quantitatively greater than any previously encountered, faith has always been challenged by, and has been the believer's mainstay in, times of disaster. Voltaire was behaving like an 'arrant sentimentalist', not a rationalist, when he allowed himself to be turned from deism by the Lisbon earthquake, for this tragedy 'supplied him with no new kind of substantial evidence against the idea of Providence.'[282] While calamitous events may be the direct consequence of misconduct, it does not follow that the events were 'planned, purposed, and produced by God.'[283] The old idea of an occasionally-interfering God who is normally transcendent in the sense of remote from the world has been rejected; it 'never was in the teaching of Christ; it is evidently excluded by St. Paul's ... great aphorism, "In Him we live, and move, and have our being."'[284] God, being good, cannot will evil.

---

[277] Ibid., 134.
[278] Ibid., 140.
[279] Ibid., 141.
[280] Ibid., 142.
[281] ET, XII, 1900-1901, 409.
[282] W. F. Adeney, *Faith To-day*, 15.
[283] Ibid., 18.
[284] Ibid., 20.

Why, then, does God not prevent evil? Adeney thinks it absurd to speak of the good God as permitting evil; and he returns the challenge to the questioner by asking, 'What sort of prevention do you think of?'[285] In his view, 'we may imagine one of two things either of which certainly would have prevented this present world calamity and all other world calamities. The first is never to have created such a world as that in which we live, the second to have stayed its course immediately it was about to go wrong.'[286] The hurtful things we experience in time of war are caused by the wrong use of human faculties. If the results were to be nullified, so would the faculties be.

Adeney argues that 'The possibility of good involves the possibility of evil,' and God 'values the glad, willing choice of the way of goodness.'[287] Mechanistic determinists dispute this point, but their own view 'cuts away the foundations of ethics and leaves us no ground for moral judgments.'[288] The divine Parent witnesses human folly; but the Christian gospel presents him as 'offering us graciously all needful help for rescue and recovery, but not at the price of depriving us of freedom and personality, those properties of Divine sonship which mark us off from the brute creation as made in His own image.'[289]

Adeney recognizes that while the foregoing line of argument may clear God of complicity in evil, this is a negative result. What, positively, can be said for the divine providence? It is his conviction that 'History is a record of Providence. Again and again we see how human frailty, folly, and wickedness have been frustrated and God's good purposes effected in spite of the mischief they were making.'[290] It is hard for us in calamitous circumstances to accept this, 'but afterwards, looking back, we have been able to perceive how wisely, how securely we have been led.'[291] This, however, will not convince the doubter. Even at a time when agnosticism and materialism are being superseded by 'a spiritual conception of the universe' the fact remains that 'neither science nor philosophy can prove' God's providential governance to us.[292] Hence,

> we cannot arrive at a sound faith in God's providence along the way of induction, based on the facts of life. It must be admitted that the awful evils that surround us to-day quite block that road. But then we may see that it never was the right road. Only a superficial, selective, and sentimental style of thinking could ever have proposed it. The rough facts of life declare it futile. There remains the path of Christian faith.[293]

---

[285] Ibid., 29.
[286] Ibid., 30.
[287] Ibid., 32, 33.
[288] Ibid., 34.
[289] Ibid., 37.
[290] Ibid., 40.
[291] Ibid., 45.
[292] Ibid., 48.
[293] Ibid., 49.

So to the facts of the faith. He considers Christ's teaching concerning God's care of all he has made; he discusses Jesus's apocalyptic teaching—'Until recently this has been almost ignored by most exponents of Christ's teaching'[294]—and he makes it quite clear that far from ascribing present evils to God's providential order, Jesus regarded them as 'deplorable facts' to be finally abolished.[295] Turning more closely to the events of Jesus's life, Adeney shows that the 'spirit of love shines out from the life and character of Jesus in all that He is and all that He does. But can it be imagined that God is not so good as Christ?'[296] He recalls that 'crabbed theology which once passed for evangelicalism' according to which Jesus was 'the Mediator assuaging the wrath of an angry Divinity and in a way persuading God to show kindness to His erring creatures. But that shocking conception, never set forth in the Bible, involved hopeless contradictions. The only harmonious view is that which sees Christ's lovingkindness as springing from the lovingkindness of God, since Christ's first being springs from the being of God.'[297]

The Christian gospel, Adeney continues, comes to us not only as information, but as redemptive power, notwithstanding that this seems to be discredited by the fact that 'The greater part of Christendom is now torn with internecine strife.'[298] It is particularly lamentable that 'we have read of strange [militaristic] utterances by Teutonic theological professors, some of whom we had been accustomed to admire as our teachers.'[299] Science, abused, has made warfare ever more devastating. Socialism never 'got beyond the brotherhood of the workers' with the result that the chasm between capital and labour is now wider than ever before. In such circumstances we are, in Paul's words, shut up to Christ.[300] Jesus predicted division rather than peace in face of the world's evil, but he also 'looked forward to final victory, and to that He encouraged us to look forward.'[301]

In his concluding chapter Adeney grants that Christianity repudiates war, yet their very religion is urging people to enlist in war:

> They join in war to counteract war. Of course this will not satisfy the Tolstoyan pacifist. But it seems to me that that impracticable person is worse than a literalist; he is really under the influence of a materialistic view of life. There are worse things than bodily pain and physical death ... [I]f life may be given to save a good cause, it may be necessary to take life for the same reason.[302]

At the same time, Adeney has admiration for those Quakers who refuse to enlist. They are not latter-day priests and levites; 'Theirs is the beautiful part of the Good

---

[294] Ibid., 57.
[295] Ibid., 58.
[296] Ibid., 67.
[297] Ibid., 69.
[298] Ibid., 71.
[299] Ibid., 79.
[300] Ibid., 83.
[301] Ibid., 84.
[302] Ibid., 87.

Samaritan—binding up bleeding wounds.'[303] He looks forward to the challenge of reconstruction the renewal of relationships which surely will face the Church after peace is declared; but further than that, he contemplates John's vision of the heavenly city built by Christ, the coming of which is even more sure.

IV

What shall be our verdict upon Adeney's contribution to Christian thought and communication? In the first place he showed competence across a broad field of theological enquiry. He was at home in biblical scholarship, Church history and doctrine, theology, and apologetics. Secondly, he could treat all of these fields at all levels from the professional journal to the Sunday School lesson notes. Few in his time, or since, have been as broadly adept as he.

As to his specific contributions: Adeney was among those 'believing biblical critics'—a company including Westcott and Hort among the Anglicans and Peake and Adeney's colleague, W. H. Bennett, among Nonconformists, who harvested the fruits of modern biblical criticism in such a way that only the most suspicious conservative evangelicals would think of accusing them of undermining Scripture. A. E. Garvie wrote nothing less than the truth when, in a tribute to Bennett, he bracketed him with his friend and said of them both, 'He and his colleague, Dr. Adeney, were among the pioneers in making accessible to the general reader the methods and results of the more modern biblical scholarship. This difficult task was discharged by them with such "sweet reasonableness" as to disarm prejudice, unless the most inveterate.'[304] In addition to his biblical introductions, Adeney served all the churches through his editorship of *The Century Bible*; he was generous in his contributions to the dictionaries of others; and he was as concerned to expound the Bible as undertake the patient task of exegesis.

Adeney's major historical work, *The Greek and Eastern Churches*, is ambitious in its scope, dealing as it does with all the Christian centuries and all of the major Orthodox churches. Doctrinal thickets are patiently and lucidly explored. At certain points one cannot but feel that subsequent scholarship has moved on, but this is only to be expected; and occasionally Adeney does not follow through as we might have expected him to do. For example, it is a little surprising, in view of his conviction expressed elsewhere that the creeds 'are not summaries of full-orbed theology. They are bulwarks against certain threatened attacks to the citadel of faith,'[305] that when describing the Chalcedonian Formula, Adeney did not make more of the 'four famous adverbs' which affirm that Christ's two natures coexist 'without confusion, change, division, separation', and were intended to block off the exits to those heresies—Arianism, Nestorianism, Eutychianism—which it had been the task

---

[303] Ibid., 90.

[304] A. E. Garvie, 'Principal Bennett,' *The British Weekly*, 9 September 1920, 442 col. 5.

[305] W. F. Adeney, *The Christian Conception of God*, 32.

of many decades to repudiate.[306] But whatever latter day scholars may wish to make of some of Adeney's findings and observations, it cannot be denied that in his study of the Greek and Eastern Churches he broke new ground in territory which had at the time been little explored—least of all by Nonconformists.[307] The remainder of Adeney's historical works reveal his sympathy for the underdogs of the Christian story: the Waldensians, the Separatists and the Nonconformists. Nor was it surprising that James Hastings invited him to write on 'Toleration' in the *Encyclopaedia of Religion and Ethics*.

Turning finally to Adeney's doctrinal, theological and apologetic writings we may first applaud the careful distinction he draws between God's immanence and pantheism. We may further note his commitment to the doctrine of the Trinity, whilst observing also that unlike some latter-day theologians, Adeney, ever the textually-based thinker, does not extrapolate, or draw analogies, from the inferred inner fellowship of the members of the 'social' Trinity to the fellowship of Church. This is consistent with his view that 'Speculation about God always plunges us into darkness. Man cannot by searching find out God.'[308] Analogously, he applies his method of textual recourse to Christology and, in the course of some generally appreciative remarks on A. M. Fairbairn's 'supremely important work', *The Place of Christ in Modern Theology*, he questions the latter's approach:

> By a curious process of reasoning, which reminds us of patristic logic, Dr. Fairbairn finds arguments for the divine nature of our Lord in His own revelation of God. If God by His essence is love, He must by nature be social; and His very Fatherhood implies Sonship. Thus the nature of God revealed by Christ testifies to the eternal pre-existence of the Son of God. To many people, no doubt, such deductive reasoning will not appear satisfactory.[309]

As to the doctrine of the Church, Adeney is surely correct in asserting that in the New Testament 'church' refers either to the whole Christian community or to local gatherings of saints. He does not draw out the implications of this for the denominational juggernauts which were at the height of their power in his day, and he could not have foreseen the way in which the majority of those in the English and English-speaking Welsh Congregational fold would come to be persuaded that, given the fractured state of the Church, and as a 'temporary' expedient, a churchly understanding of a denomination as such might be acceptable: hence the national

---

[306] See idem, *The Greek and Eastern Churches*, 100-101.

[307] We recall that D. W. Simon's doctoral thesis on 'The Dissenting Sects of Russia' was equally virgin territory for an English Dissenter.

[308] W. F. Adeney, *The Christian Conception of God*, 248. It is, no doubt, an unsanctified thought, but one sometimes feels that some present-day theologians think that they know as much about the inner working of the Trinity as some older Calvinist divines thought they knew about God's *inscrutable* will.

[309] Idem, 'Andrew Martin Fairbairn, D.D., LL.D,' ET, V, 1893-1894, 445. For Fairbairn (1838-1912) see ODNB; Alan P. F. Sell, *Dissenting Thought and the Life of the Churches*, ch. 19; E. Kaye, *Mansfield College*; idem, *For the Work of Ministry*.

covenant transformed the Congregational Union of England and Wales into the Congregational Church in England and Wales (1966).[310] Indeed, it is odd that when writing of Congregationalism in general, and of baptism in particular, Adeney, as a biblical scholar, did not have recourse to the concept of covenant, so important in that tradition.[311] In connection with the relations of Nonconformity and the Anglican establishment, however, Adeney does well to remind us, sometimes quite bluntly, of theological issues concerning the 'matter' of the Church and Christ's sole Lordship over the Church which, despite all the ecumenical co-operation and many levels which has occurred since his day, to this day have hardly been adequately discussed, still less resolved.[312]

For all his insight, learning and determination to be faithful to Scripture, I cannot help but detect a certain playing down of the Cross which runs through all Adeney's work. This is the more surprising because of his regular reiteration of the centrality of the Cross and resurrection in the Christian Gospel. We recall, for example, his insistence that we attend not only to Jesus's sayings, but to his 'whole life course' which was 'crowned and consummated by His death and resurrection.'[313] Elsewhere he declares that

> in all ages the winning power of the Gospel has gone with a passionate preaching of redemption through the Cross of Christ. The Fatherhood of God, the Brotherhood of Jesus, the ethics of the Sermon of the Mount, our Lord's magnificent conception of the kingdom of heaven—great truths that have come to the front in our own day, ... have none of them evinced the missionary energy, the evangelising efficacy, that have been found to accompany the preaching of salvation through the Cross. We are told to look at facts. This is a fact the significance of which cannot be gainsaid.[314]

Again, he contends that 'the *subjective* effect of the Atonement is found to be most pronounced just in proportion as there is faith in its previous *objective* efficacy.'[315] But all of these assertions raise the question, What has Christ *done* at the Cross to effect our redemption? Adeney seems so to elevate the resurrection as the supreme fact in the Christian Gospel as to play down the fact, clearly attested to by the apostles, that the Cross, not the empty tomb, is the site of the victory over sin and death, while the resurrection is the confirmation of it. Thus, when Adeney informs us that 'Christ is what He is to us in order that he may restore us to the happy consciousness of sonship so that we may live in the light of God our Father,'[316] he begs the question, What are the salvific prerequisites of this happy outcome? There

[310] See further, Alan P. F. Sell, *Saints: Visible, Orderly and Catholic. The Congregational Idea of the Church*, ch. 6; idem, *Testimony and Tradition*, ch. 12.

[311] See further, idem, *Dissenting Thought and the Life of the Churches*, ch. 1.

[312] See further, idem, *Testimony and Tradition*, ch. 11.

[313] W. F. Adeney, *The Christian Conception of God*, 253.

[314] Idem, *The Atonement in Modern Religious Thought*, 146-147.

[315] Ibid., 150.

[316] Idem, *The Christian Conception of God*, 85.

seems to be a significant attenuation here and elsewhere—above all, perhaps, in his war-time apologetic, *Faith To-day*. He here writes of Jesus that 'He did not expect the golden age till the powers of evil were worsted. But he looked forward to final victory, and to that He encourages us to look forward.'[317] How different from the declaration of P. T. Forsyth in his war-time theodicy, *The Justification of God*, published in the same year as Adeney's book, in which the note of victory already won at the Cross is resoundingly struck.[318]

Is it possible to hazard an explanation of Adeney's reticence concerning the Cross? It seems to me that he is caught in a pincer movement. From the one side, while his central focus upon the life and teaching of Jesus is the proper starting-point for access to the Christian Gospel, his developmental understanding of revelation seems to militate against his correct insight that more than the teaching and character of Christ have to be taken into account. He is thus inclined to treat the witness of Paul and others as somewhat less than original, despite his assertion that 'richer' ideas of the Cross developed after the crucifixion and resurrection.[319] My question is thus, Does Adeney do sufficient justice to the insight that the Gospel is not adequately (it can never be fully) grasped—indeed, is not graspable at all—until after the victory has been won; and that it is to the eternal credit of Peter, Paul and others that they elevated both the Cross and the resurrection, where Adeney lays much greater weight upon the latter than the former?

From the other side, Adeney is on the outward swing of the anti-Calvinist pendulum, and because of the perceived abuses they had caused, it seems characteristic of Adeney's temperament that, despite his recognition that fact cannot be separated from theory, he should shy away from atonement theories. He rightly finds some older ways of articulating the atonement—for example, the suggestion that God could not be gracious until Christ had died—thoroughly objectionable. Again, he writes, 'the way in which imputed sin and imputed righteousness were set forth is suggestive of scheming ingenuity. It lacks moral breadth and a sense of reality, not to say veracity.'[320] He was by no means the only Nonconformist to question his tradition's Calvinistic heritage. Indeed, as early as 1887 Adeney felt able to speak of 'the expulsion of the old bones from a formerly prevalent theology, the extraction of the very skeleton about which that theology was built up.'[321] It must be said, however, that some of the complaints were one-sided, and frequently turned upon an unfortunate and unnecessary confusion of predestination *qua* religious doctrine with philosophical determinism (something towards which some

---

[317] Idem, *Faith To-day*, 84.

[318] See P. T. Forsyth, *The Justification of God*, (1916).

[319] See W. F. Adeney, *The Theology of the New Testament*, 64, to which reference was made above.

[320] Idem, *A Century's Progress in Religious Life and Thought*, 147.

[321] Idem, in *The Congregational Review*, I, 1887, 1059.

theologians were tempted by Calvin*ists* themselves).[322] For his part, Adeney was 'confident in the assurance that the change which has taken place has not involved any departure from the evangelical faith.'[323] Yet, to repeat, he says little concerning the saving act of Christ at the Cross, surely the heart of evangelical testimony. This is perhaps compatible with his elevation of God's Fatherhood as the supreme divine attribute, and his reluctance to have it qualified by such terms as holiness and righteousness, contending that these are included within perfect Fatherhood. But if, as he acknowledges, Fatherhood can be construed sentimentally, is there any harm, and may there not be real benefit, in holding together in our thought, speech and writing: holy Fatherhood; righteous and merciful Father?

Finally, I commend Adeney for his willingness to tackle some of the big apologetic questions regarding providence and evil. His thought was adventurous, and in his practice he was true to his conviction that 'I do not believe that any sincere soul has ever been lost by thinking—no, not even when sounding a dim and perilous way on unknown seas of thought. But many a poor, starved spirit has been smothered in the feather-bed of mental torpor.'[324] I also think that he was correct in seeing that whatever the classical theistic arguments may yield, they yield but a characterless Being, not the God in whom Christians believe. If we would learn of God and have communion with him, we need to approach him through Christ his Son as revealed in Scripture.[325] This conviction dictated Adeney's method and, for the most part, he followed it out scrupulously. But there is one place where he seems to esteem too highly one who took a different line. In his article on A. M. Fairbairn he correctly observes that the first part of Fairbairn's *Christ in Modern Theology* is historical while the second part is speculative and constructive. In the first part Fairbairn 'brought out ... the humiliating truth that the main current of the thinking of the ages has been anything but a normal development in the direction of a more and more correct perception of the facts of the spiritual universe.' While many valuable insights have been bequeathed, 'their immediate result has been to make the stream more turbid rather than to clarify it.'[326] From this point of view the book 'is the most powerful reply that has yet appeared to the root idea of Newman's

---

[322] Idem, *A Century's Progress in Religious Life and Thought*, chs 7, 8. See further Alan P. F. Sell, *Nonconformist Theology in the Twentieth Century*, ch. 1; cf. idem, *Enlightenment, Ecumenism, Evangel*, ch. 5, and 325-338.

[323] Idem, *The Congregational Review*, I, 1887, 1059.

[324] W. F. Adeney, 'The more excellent way,' 41.

[325] Thereby hangs a lengthy tale concerning viable Christian apologetic method, its subjects, its objectives, its starting-point, its presuppositions, its relation to other aspects of thought. I have sought to tell this tale in *Confessing and Commending the Faith. Historic Witness and Apologetic Method.*

[326] From this it would appear that Fairbairn's attitude where matters intellectual are concerned is not dissimilar to Joseph Priestley's attitude regarding matters ecclesiastical. See the latter's *An History of the Corruptions of Christianity*, (1782), in J. T. Rutt, ed., *The Theological and Miscellaneous Works of Joseph Priestley*, (1817-1832), V. See further, Alan P. F. Sell, *Enlightenment, Ecumenism, Evangel*, ch. 6.

Essay on Development.' Hence the value of the current return to Christ; hence also the justification of Fairbairn's severance of history from speculation and construction.[327] Undoubtedly, 'back to Christ' is a prominent motivation of Adeney's entire corpus. But his very advocacy of modern biblical criticism, for example, implies that he knows very well—and, indeed, makes the point himself[328]—that there can be no severance of history from theory and interpretation, no biblical restorationism abstracted from the witness of subsequent Christian history and scholarship. For good or ill we do not read the Bible exactly as our forebears in the faith did. They had their presuppositions, we have ours, and Fairbairn most decidedly had his. Adeney could not 'return to the Bible' as if Tholuck, Lightfoot—and even the dreaded Baur—had not lived; nor did he do so. Can it be that what is operative here is 'My high personal regard for the Principal of Mansfield College, and my admiring interest in his aims and labours, [which] will necessarily condition what I have to say ...?'[329]

V

The Adeneys having retired to Southover, Lewes, Sussex, Walter's lust for travel came to the fore. He and his wife embarked upon an extended world tour, during which Mrs. Adeney regularly sent home circular letters to their children. These were collected and published in 1919 under the title, *Following the Sun: Letters to my Children during a Two Year's Journey around the World*.[330] They set off on 27 June 1913 and returned home on 6 June 1915. Their itinerary is marked by the chapter headings: Canada, The South Seas, New Zealand, Tasmania, Australia, Java, Malay Peninsula, Siam, Burma, India. During the tour they visited many Congregational churches and institutions, and Adeney frequently delivered sermons and lectures. The volume contains both a General Index and a two-page Index of Birds.

Walter Frederic Adeney died at Lewes, Sussex, on 1 September 1920, within days of the death of his great friend and successor in Manchester, W. H. Bennett. He had suffered indifferent health following an operation two years earlier, but had managed nevertheless to maintain his series of lessons published in *The Sunday School Times*. He also showed himself a staunch advocate of the League of Nations. In the last letter he wrote to his former student, George Currie Martin, he said, 'Button-hole everybody about it—that is the only way!'[331] On the day following his death *The Christian World* carried an obituary which included the following judgment: 'An

[327] W. F. Adeney, 'Andrew Martin Fairbairn, D.D., LL.D.,' 443.

[328] Idem, *The Atonement in Modern Religious Thought*, 144: 'The life and death of the Saviour we take to be facts; the recovery of men and women from lives of shame and folly as far as this can be observed may also be set down in the category of facts. But the connection between these two series traverses a vast expanse of theory.'

[329] Ibid., 442. For further reflections upon Fairbairn see Alan P. F. Sell, *Dissenting Thought and the Life of the Churches*, ch. 19.

[330] Published by James Clarke of London.

[331] G. Currie Martin, 'Walter F. Adeney. An Appreciation,' 3(iii).

amiable, stimulating, and charming personality, Dr. Adeney will be missed by a host of friends;'[332] while G. Currie Martin declared that 'His old students are in every land, and there was not one of them but loved him. ... It would be difficult to exaggerate the greatness of the service that Dr. Adeney rendered in his generation to progressive religious thought.'[333]

On 6 September 1920 the General Committee of Lancashire Independent College met at the Congregational Church House, Manchester. The Committee recorded its sorrow at the loss of Principal W. H. Bennett, Professor G. Lyon Turner, and Principal Adeney. Gratitude to God for all of them was expressed, and the Colleges sympathy with their widows was conveyed. Dr. F. J. Powicke, seconded by Gerard N. Ford moved the resolution concerning Adeney, and 'paid a worthy tribute to one with whose work at the College they had been closely acquainted, and in whom they had found a personal friend.'[334]

Adeney's funeral service took place at the graveside at Lewes Cemetery, where his friend and former minister, R. F. Horton, delivered the address. Edwyn Holt, J.P. represented Lancashire Independent College and the Manchester Congregational Board at the service. On the following Sunday the minister of Lewes Congregational Church, the Revd E. W. Bremner, preached on II Chronicles 26:5, which tells of the boy king Uzziah's eagerness to seek guidance from Zechariah, who 'instructed him in the fear of the Lord.' It is not difficult to guess the direction taken by Mr. Bremner in his sermon, for of Adeney it was said that 'he would have loved to be remembered more as the friend of young people than for any other reason.'[335]

---

[332] *The Christian World*, 2 September 1920, 3(i).

[333] G. Currie Martin, 'Walter F. Adeney. An Appreciation,' 3ii, iii.

[334] *Minutes of the General Committee of Lancashire Independent College*, John Rylands University Library of Manchester, Congregational College Archives, Box 33, Lancashire Independent College Book of Proceedings no. 10.

[335] CYB, 1921, 102. For Eustace William Bremner (1863-1946) see CYB, 1949, 496-497. He served at Lewes from 1917 to 1924, proceeding thence to Newquay, Cornwall, where the church was burnt down on the night of his induction. My interest in Adeney was stimulated not least by the recollection that the Revd George Sydney Morgan (1879-1960), my minister at the time I left home to prepare for the ministry, to whose memory I dedicated my pamphlet, *Congregationalism at Worplesdon 1822-1972*, and to whom I have referred in *Testimony and Tradition*, 321, was a student during Adeney's Presidency of Lancashire Independent College. He was ordained at Centenary Congregational Church, Lancaster, in 1912, serving as assistant to J. A. Tait. Tait took part in the ordination service, together with Adeney, Benjamin Nightingale and F. G. Tizzard. For G. S. Morgan's obituary see CYB, 1962, 446-447.

Part IV

In the Wake of Theological Liberalism

Charles Sim Duthie (1911–1981)

CHAPTER 10

Robert Sleightholme Franks (1871–1964): Experience, History and Reason

Robert Franks was born in the Congregational manse at Redcar on 1 April 1871.[1] His father, the Revd William James Franks served the Redcar church for the whole of his ministry, from 1865 until 1902.[2] William was born at Leppington, near Malton, on 6 July 1838, and trained for the ministry at the Cotton End Academy, Bedfordshire. At Redcar 'he exercised a remarkable influence, based, not so much upon special pulpit power, as upon force of character. Shrewdness, invincible uprightness, and the gift of sympathy were notably marked in him.'[3] His wife, Ann Eliza, was the daughter of Robert Sleightholme of Whitby. On a stipend of £200 p.a. they raised a sizeable family. Robert was the eldest of four sons, all of whom went into the Congregational ministry following training at Mansfield College, Oxford.[4] Like his brothers, Robert attended William Turner's Grammar School,[5] but as the school could not keep pace with his mathematical prowess, his father arranged

---

[1] For Franks see CYB, 1964-65, 439-40; DHT; ODNB; WTW; WWW, 1961-70; *The Times*, 21 January 1964, 12; Elaine.Kaye, *Mansfield College*; idem, *For the Work of Ministry*.

[2] For W. J. Franks see CYB, 1929, 215.

[3] Ibid. He died at Bakewell on 21 October 1927.

[4] For John Edwin (1872-1951) see CYB, 1952, 512. He read Classics at Cambridge, but ill health prevented his completing the Mansfield course. He taught for some years, but eventually entered the ministry until he was forced by ill health to retire in 1929. For Ernest William (1874-1953) see CYB, 1954, 510-11. He became MA of Edinburgh University prior to his Mansfield course. He served with the London Missionary Society in India until his wife's ill health compelled their return. A series of pastorates followed, combined with service to the LMS Board and Committees. For Richard Lister (1876-1948) see CYB, 1949, 499. A Dr. Williams Arts Scholar, he graduated MA of Glasgow University, where he was influenced by the philosopher Henry Jones and the preacher John Hunter. Following his Mansfield course he served a number of churches, including Gosport, where he succeeded his brother Ernest. He retired through ill health in 1934. He was unmarried, and for over forty years his sister, Mary A. C. Franks shared his home and his ministry, and cared for him in sickness.

[5] William Turner (1615-1692), born at Kirkleatham, had been involved in the rebuilding of London after the fire of 1666. He left a fortune of some £6m., a portion to be used to found a school. The original school failed, but a fresh start was made in 1868.

for him to lodge with a minister in Somerset so that he might receive additional coaching. This stood him in good stead, and he proceeded to St. John's College, Cambridge as an exhibitioner in mathematics, to which subject he devoted himself from 1889 to 1892. Some of the Redcar deacons also assisted him financially. It had been expected that he would be a wrangler, but prior to the tripos examinations he became ill, and was awarded the *aegrotat*. Years later, on the death of his principal tutor in mathematics he wrote,

> Will you permit a tribute to the memory of a great teacher from a former pupil, who, though his Cambridge career came to a somewhat inglorious end with an *aegrotat* degree, has nevertheless always felt the warmest gratitude to the University and in particular to R[obert] R. Webb for a mental discipline which has since proved serviceable in other spheres than mathematics? ... [W]hat a 'guide, philosopher, and friend' R. R. Webb was to the mathematical aspirant! He inspired both confidence in himself and interest in the subject. He was an absolute prestidgitator with mathematical symbols, and he enlivened his teaching with what was very much like a conjuror's patter. ... The story went round that he had refused to coach Miss Philippa Fawcett, because 'he considered that the presence of a lady in his class would prevent that freedom of language necessary for teaching mathematics.' ... An offence once brought down on the misdemeanants the threat, 'I'll never forgive you, no, not even if I live for a geological period.' ... [N]ext time we met, all was forgiven and forgotten.[6]

After Cambridge Franks spent a year in Yorkshire, and then went to Mansfield College, Oxford, to train for the ministry under A. M. Fairbairn.[7] His other teachers were George Buchanan Gray, the Old Testament scholar; the classicist and New Testament textual critic, John Massie; and the historian, J. Vernon Bartlet.[8] At the end of the theological course Franks remained a further year at Mansfield during which time he prepared a thesis, 'The theories of the Atonement of Anselm and Grotius', which earned him the degree of BLitt.[9] With this thesis he set the direction for his future scholarly work. Not, indeed, that he became a medievalist of the narrow sort, but to Anselm and Abelard he returned time and again, and his depth of knowledge of the theology and philosophy of the Middle Ages was as impressive as it was unusual in Congregational ministers of the period.

---

[6] R. S. Franks, 'Mr. Robert Webb,' *The Times*, 5 August 1936, 14.

[7] For Fairbairn (1938-1912) see CYB, 1913, 165-6; DNCBP; DSCHT; ODNB; WTW; W. B. Selbie, *The Life of Andrew Martin Fairbairn*; K. W. Wadsworth, *Yorkshire United Independent College*; E. Kaye, *Mansfield College*; idem, *For the Work of Ministry*; Alan P. F. Sell, *Dissenting Thought and the Life of the Churches*, ch. 19.

[8] For Gray (1865-1922) see CYB, 1923, 107; ODNB; WTW. For Massie see ch. 7 n. 78 above. As we saw, Massie had worked with Simon at Spring Hill College. For Bartlet (1863-1940) see CYB, 1941, 392-3; ODNB; WTW. For all three see E. Kaye, *Mansfield College*.

[9] Franks, being a Nonconformist, was not eligible to submit for the BD.

From 1898 to 1900 Franks was a tutor at Mansfield, and in the latter year he was called to the pastorate of Prenton Congregational church. Prenton was a rapidly expanding community between Rock Ferry and Birkenhead. Services led by the Revd James Wishart[10] had begun in a hired pavilion in 1887, and the infant cause was supported by the County Union. Wishart worked in an honorary capacity until ill health forced his withdrawal. Nevertheless 'On Friday, April 18, 1890, a "school-chapel, at once substantial and picturesque, and capable of seating 220 people," was opened by Dr. Mackennal.'[11] There was further encouragement in the return to health of Wishart, who continued to build up the cause at no cost to the church. In 1892 the Revd Stanley Lamb[12] succeeded Wishart and progress was gradually made. Lamb removed to Burslem in 1900, and Franks was called to Prenton. By 1902 the members were contemplating the erection of a new chapel. In January 1904 they 'withdrew from the aided list',[13] and their new premises were opened that year. In September of the same year Franks, having accepted the post of tutor at The Friends' Settlement for Religious and Social Study at Woodbrooke, Birmingham, resigned his pastorate. In the meantime, in 1902, he had married a Quaker, Katherine (1872-1971), daughter of Joseph Shewell, an engineer and iron bridge builder of Redcar. One of their sons, Oliver, a philosopher and public servant, became Baron Franks;[14] and there were in addition another son and two daughters. Of the Franks' home it has been said that

> A mettlesome air of intellectual enquiry pervaded the entire household. Oliver and his sisters and brother were expected to think—think hard—for themselves. Mealtimes were feasts of conversation. Robert Franks did not read the newspaper at breakfast; the family talked—talked about everything from the flowers in the fields to the Channel Fleet. They weighed words and knew their meaning. They analysed articles in *The Times*. On Sundays they dissected the sermon they had heard. The opinions were sensible, but the talk was unrestrained. This was a liberal household in more senses than one.[15]

Whilst at Woodbrooke Franks collected his 'Bible Notes' published in *The British Friend* under the titles, *The Life of Paul* (1909) and *The Writings of Paul* (1910); and

---

[10] For Wishart (1822-1904) see CYB, 1905, 193-4. Educated at St. Andrews and Aberdeen, he ministered at Thurso (1849-54), Swanland, Yorkshire (1854-65), Toxteth, Liverpool (1865-81) and Prenton (1889-93. He was out of pastoral charge from 1881 to 1889.

[11] F. J. Powicke, *A History of the Cheshire Union of Congregational Churches*, 253.

[12] For Walter Stanley Lamb (1870-1952) see CYB, 1954, 514-15. Trained at Cheshunt College, he served at Prenton (1892-1900), Burslem (1900-09), Plaistow (1909-1914), and then became secretary of the British and Foreign Sailors Society. He returned to pastoral charge at Copeland Street, Stoke-on-Trent (1920-25), Wollerton, Salop (1915-31) and Berkeley, Glos. (1931-35).

[13] F. J. Powicke, op.cit., 254.

[14] For Oliver Franks (1905-1992) see ODNB; Noel Annan, *The Dons*, 270-274.

[15] 'Oliver Franks' in ODNB by Alex Danchev.

he contributed a paper on 'The idea of salvation in the theology of the Eastern Church: a study in the history of religion' to Fairbairn's seventieth birthday *festschrift*. In the latter he argues that while there are points of contact between Greek soteriology and the New Testament, the former differs markedly from the latter because 'there is a great hiatus between the natural theology characteristic of the Greek Fathers, and their doctrine of redemption.'[16] In summary,

> We have ... as the characteristic elements in the Greek doctrine of salvation: (1) the rationalistic moral scheme [which supposes that Christ, the Logos, illuminates human beings whose intellect has been darkened by the fall] which hardly allows a place for a doctrine of redemption at all; (2) the breaking through of this by the doctrine of redemption from the devil; and (3) still more by the doctrine of deification.[17]

It thus transpires that the focus in the Greek doctrine of salvation is upon redemption from death, corruption and the power of the devil, rather than upon the Pauline ideas of redemption from sin and guilt. Even fallen humanity remains morally free according to Greek thought, and hence a physical and not an ethical redemption is required. Franks proceeds to argue that 'the three characteristic lines of the Greek Christian doctrine of salvation correspond exactly to the three principal lines along which the subject of salvation was regarded in ancient Greek religion.'[18] The first line echoes the Olympian religion with its anthropomorphic gods patterned after human rulers; the second echoes the Chthonian element in Greek religion with its 'dark deities of the underworld and the spirits of the dead';[19] the third echoes Dionysian religion, at the heart of which was 'the deification of the worshippers, who in the ecstasy of the Bacchic dance believed themselves to become god-possessed.'[20] When Dionysian religion came to be blended with Chthonian religion in the Orphic mysteries, the idea was added that human beings have an element in the soul which is higher than ecstasy. It is essentially divine, craves the return to its source, but is impeded by the body. Hence Orphic asceticism 'as a means of promoting the return of the soul to God.'[21] In the writings of Origen the foregoing lines of thought are recognizable: for example, in his beliefs that Christ died to rescue us from evil spirits, and that Christ died as a ransom to the devil whose just claim is recognized. Franks concludes that

> the Greek Christian doctrine of salvation, while a Christian doctrine of salvation, for it testifies with no uncertain voice that salvation is in Christ, is yet shaped through and through by the spirit of the ancient Greek religion. 'The eye brings

[16] R. S. Franks, 'The idea of salvation in the theology of the Eastern Church,' 251.
[17] Ibid., 253.
[18] Ibid., 257.
[19] Ibid., 260.
[20] Ibid., 261.
[21] Ibid.

with it what it sees'; and the Greeks found in Christ that for which their former religion had trained them to look.[22]

According to the Minutes of the General Committee of Western College, on 28 September 1909 Principal Charles Chapman of Western College tendered his resignation.[23] He had entered the College fifty-eight years before, and had been Principal for thirty-three years. The Committee appointed a special sub-committee to take steps regarding a successor. On 8 December the Committee resolved to honour Chapman with the title, Principal Emeritus, and to make him an allowance of £200/0/0 p.a. Then the Revd W. K. Burford moved and the Revd Charles Williams seconded a motion to invite Arnold Thomas of the prominent Highbury church, Bristol, to become Principal.[24] Mr. G. H. Wicks asked whether in view of Thomas's indisposition it was fair to approach him and remove him from his present sphere of influence in Church and society. Following discussion it was resolved that the Committee would rebaptize itself a Council, invite Thomas to be its President, and seek a Principal from elsewhere.

The sub-committee charged with the responsibility of the succession circulated a number of names of possible candidates to members of the Council, and on 7 March 1910 it was reported that the Bristol members Council had interviewed the two who had been short-listed: R. S. Franks, who was recommended by Dr. Rendel Harris, Principal W. B. Selbie of Mansfield College, and the Revd J. H. Jowett;[25] and E. H.

---

[22] Ibid., 264. For some reflections on Orthodox views in relation both to patristic writers and to more recent Orthodox theologians see Alan P. F. Sell, *Confessing and Commending the Faith*, 70-79.

[23] *Western College Minute Book from the time of the amalgamation of Western College, Plymouth, with the Bristol Theological Institute. 1891*.For Chapman (1828-1922) see CYB, 1923, 102-3; J. Charteris Johnstone, 'The story of Western College,' 105; E. Kaye, *For the Work of Ministry*. He trained at Western College under Richard Alliott, and gained the London MA. He was co-pastor at Queen Street, Chester (1856-64), and minister of Percy, Bath (1864-71). He was then in Montreal (1871-76), where he combined pastoral work with lecturing at McGill University, of which he became an Honorary LLD. He was Principal of Western College from 1876-1910. Until his death he held the title Principal Emeritus. Johnstone describes him as 'the grand old man of Western Congregationalism, who, unlike many, is only more a *persona grata* the older he grows.' Art.cit., 105.

[24] For William Knibb Burford (1863-1944) see CYB, 1945, 426. He served at Wicker, Sheffield (1888-1901), Sherwell, Plymouth (1901-11), and Tower Road, Hindhead (1913-39). For Henry Arnold Thomas (1848-1924) see CYB, 1925, 161-2; WTW; N. Micklem, ed., *Arnold Thomas of Bristol*. An MA of London and Cambridge, he served at Burnt Ash, Lee (1873-4), Ealing (1874-6) and Highbury, Bristol (1876-1923). Bristol University conferred its Hon.LLD upon him.

[25] For James Rendel Harris (1852-1941), biblical scholar and palaeographer, see ODNB. He transferred his allegiance from Congregationalism to Quakerism. The Minutes incorrectly render his name, Rendall. For William Boothby Selbie (1862-1944) see CYB, 1941, 445; ODNB; WTW; E. Kaye, *Mansfield College*. For Walter F. Adeney see ch. 9 above. For John Henry Jowett (1863-1923) see CYB, 1925, 152-3; ODNB; WTW; Frank

Titchmarsh, who was recommended by Principal Adeney and Principal Clemens[26] of Ranmoor Methodist College, Sheffield.[27] After 'careful and prayerful consideration' they had unanimously recommended Franks. Franks's letter of acceptance was read out, and in it he agreed to a salary of £350 p.a. increasing to £400 p.a. on Chapman's death or after five years; together with occupancy of the Principal's house free of rent and rates. Professor Macey, who taught Hebrew and Logic, then asked that his salary might be increased, but this was deemed unaffordable.[28]

Thus began Franks's distinguished principalship of twenty-nine years. A shy man, he played little part in denominational affairs, but locally he did chair the Governors of Redland High School for Girls, and gave lectures through the Workers Educational Association. His primary focus, however, was upon his students, and his wider recognition came through scholarship and publication. I shall discuss his major writings shortly, but the following notes will at least partially illuminate to his Bristol years.

It fell to Franks to lead the College during the First World War until the temporary closure of the College in 1917. On 15 September 1914, at a special meeting of the Bristol members of the Council, the Principal was asked to write to all students, not to urge them to enlist, but to say that if any 'felt it their duty to do so, every reasonable facility would be afforded them.' The Congregational Union of England and Wales published a series of pamphlets under the title, 'The War and our Faith. Papers by Congregationalists.' To this series Franks contributed *The Cross and the War*. He sets out from J. H. Newman's sermon title, 'The Cross the measure of the world,' and asks whether this is really what is believed: 'We have set [the Cross] high above our churches; we have graven it upon our altars. But often it has become no more than an ornament and a decoration, and its real significance has

---

Morison, *J. H. Jowett*; A. Porritt, *John Henry Jowett*. Trained at Airedale and Mansfield, he was CH and MA, DD (Edinburgh). He ministered at St. James, Newcastle-upon-Tyne (1889-95), Carrs Lane, Birmingham (1895-1911), Fifth Avenue Presbyterian Church, New York (1911-18) and Westminster Chapel, London (1918-22). He was Chairman of the CUEW (1906-7), and President of the National Free Church Council (1910-11).

[26] The Minutes incorrectly give 'Clements'.

[27] For Edward Harper Titchmarsh, MA, ATS, (1862-1935) see CYB, 1936, 664. He trained at New College, London, and held pastorates at Erith; Newbury; Nether, Sheffield; and Halstead. He was Chairman of the Yorkshire Congregational Union and a temporary tutor at Lancashire Independent College (1920-21). For John S. Clemens (1857-1920) see G. G. Hornby, 'Victoria Park and Ranmoor Colleges', 153-4; Henry Smith, John E. Swallow and William Treffry, eds, *The Story of the United Methodist Church*, 87, 141 and *passim*. He was Principal of Ranmoor College from 1898 to 1913. A BA of London and BD (St. Andrews), he was awarded the latter's DD in 1912. He was President of the last Methodist New Connexion Conference prior to the union of that body with the Free Methodists and the Bible Christians in 1907.

[28] An alumnus of Western College, Plymouth, Thomas Stenner Macey served at Wiveliscombe (1880-86) and then, from 1886 to 1924, he taught first in Plymouth and then in Bristol.

passed out of sight.'[29] The War brings us face to face with the meaning of the Cross; it helps us to understand the suffering involved in the Cross; it calls our attention to Christ's victory over the evil in the world; and it awakens us from complacency in the world. Christ, he continues, consecrates human suffering by accepting it, but Franks proceeds to make it clear that Christ tasted death not for one nation, but for everyone. All true sacrifice, he declares, will have the reward of furthering God's kingdom on earth. He concludes by saying that 'If the War can teach us in some fresh way to understand the reality of the Cross, the Cross can teach us how, as Christians, we may bear the War, and in what spirit we are to interpret the terrible sufferings and sacrifices of the time.'[30]

That Franks did not always get his way with the Council's Education Committee is evident from a minute of 27 September 1915. Franks moved that W. Gordon Hatcher, who had narrowly failed re-sit examinations, be allowed to remain as a student because he was well liked in the churches and could become 'a useful minister of Jesus Christ.' The motion failed. There was much satisfaction in the Western College community when, in 1919, Franks received the Oxford DLitt degree for his major study of *A History of the Doctrine of the Work of Christ*, published in 1918 and dedicated to his father. When in 1922 his predecessor at the College, Charles Chapman, died at the age of ninety-four, Franks moved a gracious memorial resolution at the Highbury church.[31]

In his annual Report to the subscribers for 1926 Franks disclosed his educational method:

> It is too often forgotten that the ideal of ministerial education is not to send a man out with some knowledge of every subject he will afterwards find useful. It is to send him out with a mind that can tackle with success any subject as need arises. The opposite leads to self-confident shallowness.

On 26 September 1927 the Council noted the acceptance of the first woman student, Miss N. Leaton. She scored 480 in the entrance examination, whereas F. Bentley mustered 211 and H. G. Davis, 212.[32] Sadly, however, we read in the Minutes for 5 October 1933, that 'On the motion of the Bursar, seconded by the Principal it was resolved that this College has not the facilities for the training of

---

[29] R. S. Franks, *The Cross and the War*, 3.

[30] Ibid., 12.

[31] For the text of the resolution see CYB, 1923, 103.

[32] For Nellie Leaton (1888-1964) see CYB, 1964-65, 443.Before entering the College she had served as a deaconess in the United Methodist Church. She graduated BA and was ordained in 1932. She served at Oulton Broad (1932-38), King's Cliffe (1938-39), Oundle (1938-41), Bolton Villas, Bradford (1942), Elloughton (1943-46), Garston and Bricket Wood, Watford (1946-48), Bromsgrove (1948-50), and Boxford (1954-56). Her later years were marked by ill health. She was 'a most faithful pastor and friend.' For Herbert George Davis (1904-1974) see URCYB, 294-5. He served at Halstead (1933-41), Baddow Road, Chelmsford (1941-46), Heaton Moor, Stockport (1947-51), Over, Winsford (1951-56) Newbury (1956-69) and Angel Street, Worcester (oversight) (1969-73).

Women Students and that it therefore discontinues its practice of receiving applications from Women Candidates.' In the following year A. J. Bowen headed the list of twelve candidates with scores of 78 (Mathematics), 65 (History), 70 (Essay), 70 (Scripture), 81 (Latin), and 95 (Greek); a total of 459.[33] Meanwhile, in 1929 Franks had been awarded the Honorary LLD of Bristol University.

In 1936 Franks contributed a paper entitled, 'Christian worship in the Middle Ages' to the volume, *Christian Worship*, which was edited by Nathaniel Micklem, Principal of Mansfield College.[34] He sets out from the generally recognized position that the worship of the early Church was a eucharist comprising two elements: the liturgy of the catechumens—the inheritance from Judaism, and the Lord's Supper. By the fourth century 'the simple worship of the primitive Eucharist had grown up into an imposing structure of ritual, in which the daily office may be regarded as an extension of the first part of the Eucharist service.'[35] In the medieval period the Byzantine liturgy became dominant, though it existed in three different forms: the liturgies of Chrysostom, Basil and the Presanctified. In the West the Roman mass ultimately superseded the Mozarabic and Gallican rites, though there were local variations of it. In both East and West, however, the eucharist remained the primary service of the Church. The service was susceptible to a variety of interpretations:

> Thus the liturgy of St. Basil prays that the Holy Spirit may descend upon the offered gifts, and bless and sanctify them, and 'show' them to be the body and blood of the Lord; while the Liturgy of St. John Chrysostom asks that the Spirit may 'change' the elements and 'make' them Christ's body and blood. It is practically the same difference that we have in the West between the Augustinian spiritualistic doctrine of the sacrament, and the Ambrosian realistic doctrine which issued finally in the Medieval dogma of transubstantiation.[36]

Again, in the West the dominant idea is of the eucharist as a renewed presentation of Christ's sacrifice on Calvary understood as a propitiation for the sins of the world, whereas in the Byzantine liturgy the older idea of the sacrifice as 'an oblation of the gifts of the Church is still uppermost.'[37] Thus, 'in the Eastern rite what is offered is the gifts of the worshippers to be consecrated by the Spirit for sacramental use, whereas in the Mass it is the body and blood of Christ that are offered as a sacrifice after the consecration has taken place.'[38]

Franks concludes by enquiring whether the Middle Ages solved the problem of Christian worship—an important question at a time 'when medieval ideas of worship

---

[33] For Arthur James Bowen (d. 1990) see URCYB, 1990-91, 194. He ministered at Nailsworth (1940-46), in the Guildford district churches (1946-9), and at Wimborne (1949-81), with oversight of Sturminster Marshall and Ferndown (1967-81).

[34] For Micklem (1888-1976) see CYB, 1977, 266; ODNB; WTW; N. Micklem, *The Box and the Puppets*; E. Kaye, *Mansfield College*.

[35] R. S. Franks, 'Christian worship in the Middle Ages,' 100.

[36] Ibid., 112-13.

[37] Ibid., 114.

[38] Ibid., 115.

are influencing even the Evangelical Free Churches.'[39] Resorting to italics for emphasis, Franks insists that '*The problem of Christian worship is really a theological problem.*'[40] To summarize his argument in his own words:

> The Ancient Church and the Middle Ages had a natural theology or rational doctrine of God, upon which was superimposed a doctrine of redemption, which the East conceived essentially as the sanctification and deification of humanity through the Incarnation, while the West thought mainly of a propitiation offered to God by Christ. ... The Reformation, by returning to the original sources of the Christian religion in the Scriptures brought about a better understanding of God and of His relation to man and of salvation through Christ. ... The central doctrine of the Reformation was that of God's grace as free favour shown to man in Christ and accepted in faith or trust. Such an approach was bound to transform worship, even when old forms were retained. There was no longer room for the distinction of a preliminary worship of prayer, praise, and instruction from the more perfect worship of the sacramental rite: nor, again, was the conception of the Eucharistic worship either as mystery or as propitiatory sacrifice any longer tenable. Evangelical worship in all its parts is communion with a God already known to be gracious. ... [T]he sermon, which preaches [God's grace] afresh comes to have an importance quite beyond that accorded it in the Middle Ages: to call it 'instruction' is altogether to minimize its value as a proclamation of the Gospel. ... [We can but recognize] the ultimate incompatibility of medieval worship and Evangelical faith.[41]

In addition to his books and articles, Franks published a considerable number of reviews, notably in *The Congregational Quarterly*. In due course I shall refer to some of these that bear upon his major themes, but in order to indicate the range of his interests and competence I shall now refer to some others in which Franks's criticisms, positive and negative, reveal his own standpoints.

In *The Gnosis or Ancient Wisdom in the Christian Scriptures* William Kingsland sets out to show that according to the New Testament, Christianity, like other religions ancient and modern, teaches that God is the ineffable absolute, and that the soul descends from, and returns to this deity, who can be described only in negative terms. This, says Franks, is a renewal of Neoplatonism. He does not deny that Christian thinkers have allied themselves sometimes slightly, sometimes extremely, with Neoplatonist thought, and he concedes that the Logos doctrine of Paul, *Hebrews* and John 'has undoubted affinities with Neoplatonism.'[42] Kingsland attacks what he calls the anthropomorphic Jahweh of the Old Testament. Further, he says that Jesus used the term 'Father' of the One only as a concession to the ability of his hearers to grasp his meaning. 'But we have not so learned Christ,' Franks thunders:

---

[39] Ibid.

[40] Ibid., 116.

[41] Ibid., 116-17.

[42] CQ, XV no. 4, October 1937, 517.

> Jesus Himself stood in the line of the *O.T.* Prophets, in the same personal communion with a personal God, as they did. It is an adherence to the prophets in the *O.T. and to the Synoptic Jesus in the* N.T. as the very bases of our religion that must prevent us from ever allowing Pauline or Johannine Christianity from being transformed into a Neoplatonic Gnosis. ... When a similar doctrine was propounded by Schelling, Hegel justly compared it to the night in which all cows are grey. To be quite plain and definite—if God is truly to be Light and not darkness, He must be Love, and Love is essentially personal.[43]

Turning from largely adverse criticism, we may note the warm welcome accorded by Franks to Burton Scott Easton's translation of, and introduction to, *The Apostolic Tradition of Hippolytus*, the schismatic bishop of the third century.[44] Easton has taken a subject which 'is both fascinating and important in a very high degree.' The work brings before us

> the atmosphere of Roman Christianity in the days of its persecution by the State. The canvas is crowded with bishops, presbyters, deacons and confessors, widows, and lay Christians. We see how the various ordinations took place; how baptism, the Eucharist, and the *Agape* were celebrated; on what terms members were admitted to the Christian Church, and how they were expected to comport themselves when in it; we see especially what instruction they had and what hours of prayer they had to observe. Exorcism appears as a very real thing: the demons are all too close at hand and must perpetually be banned.[45]

Franks does not, however, content himself with this lively description of the work. Characteristically, he continues,

> It is immensely important for Free Churchmen to realize how order was introduced into the Early Church by taking over *Old Testament* ideas: the bishop is a high priest, and as such must propitiate God: the ordination prayers appeal to the example of the *O.T.* to show how God from the days of Moses established princes and priests. It is clear that the governing idea throughout was that the new Israel must resemble the old Israel in all important details.[46]

E. R. Dodds's edition of Proclus's *The Elements of Theology* was received by Franks with equal excitement, for here we have expounded the Neoplatonic system which underlies the better known and miscellaneous *Enneads* of Plotinus. Theological students in particular should be interested in Proclus because

> Neoplatonism has bitten deep into Christian theology: one need only mention St. Augustine and St. Thomas Aquinas as examples of its influence on the general development of Christian thought; while in our own country we have the Cambridge

---

[43] Ibid., 517, 518.
[44] CQ, XII no. 4, October 1934, 460-61.
[45] Ibid., 460.
[46] Ibid., 460-61.

Platonists and in the present time Dean Inge, who has written a great book on Plotinus and recommends Neoplatonism as the only satisfactory basis for a modern theology.[47]

Moreover, with this book, Franks continues, we can go behind the negative theology and hierarchical schematism of Dionysius the Areopagite, from whose hives Aquinas drew much of his honey.

In the following year Franks had the opportunity to return to Neoplatonism, this time in connection with Nesca A. Robb's work, *Neoplatonism of the Italian Renaissance*. Robb shows that with the Renaissance the intellectual influence of Aristotle waned, and there was a return to Plato, but to a Plato viewed through Neoplatonic eyes and synthesized with the humanism of the times. All of which was foreshadowed in Petrarch and completed by Marsilio Ficino and Pico of Mirandola. Franks draws particular attention to Robb's conclusion, in which she compares and contrasts Renaissance Neoplatonism with early nineteenth-century Romanticism: 'Both viewed the world as spiritual and believed in the dignity of man, and especially of the artist, as its interpreter. But the men of the Renaissance were only conscious of man's power and spontaniety [*sic*]: the Romantics were also keenly aware of the way in which his power and freedom were everywhere thwarted.'[48]

It may as first glance seem a huge leap from William of Ockham to Emil Brunner, but Franks accomplishes it in his review of Ernest Moody's book, *The Logic of William of Ockham*. Simple apprehension is at the root of Ockham's logical system: the mind directly apprehends substance and quality. For example, 'I must apprehend the substance through the term *wall* and the quality through the term *white*, before I can form the proposition, *The wall is white*.'[49] In Ockham's view the objective of science is to ascertain 'what necessary affirmations and denials can be made about things by means of terms.'[50] To this end he sharply distinguishes science from metaphysics, for 'The metaphysical existence of things is not something to be scientifically explained; but is on the contrary a presupposition of all science.'[51] In all of this Moody finds Ockham to be not, as has been alleged, a precursor of Locke, but rather a disciple of Aristotle who opposes Platonism's understanding of all things as developments from the Idea of the Universe. While granting that Ockham did not intend it, Franks nevertheless avers that his science-metaphysics disjunction did open up the way 'for Locke's partial, and finally for Hume's total, contempt of metaphysics.'[52] When Ockham's position is applied to theology, that discipline is said to be concerned, like all other science, with terms and propositions. Since we cannot apprehend God in his proper nature, revelation

---

[47] CQ, XII no. 1, January 1934, 111.
[48] CQ, XIII no. 4, October 1935, 483.
[49] CQ, XIV no. 2.April 1936, 235.
[50] Ibid., 236.
[51] Ibid.
[52] Ibid.

imparts the terms and relations of the knowledge of God—at which point Franks discloses his hand as an opponent of the so-called theology of the Word:

> In a word, the proper knowledge of God is altogether beyond us, except in so far as it is miraculously produced in the mind by the direct action of God Himself. This notion of the entirely arbitrary character of all theological knowledge had bitten deep into the history of later Christian thought; nor is it dead to-day—it is precisely what Brunner means, when he says: *Gott kann nur durche erkannt werden.*'[53]

Franks's review of Clement Webb's *The Historical Element in Religion* ends in confessional mode. Webb rightly dissents from the view that the findings of historical criticism are irrelevant to the use of the Bible as a spiritual resource, and maintains that there is a core of fact in the Bible to which Christianity's essential character is inescapably bound. Webb argues that 'the individual member of a religious community can so share its common life as to have experiences which have evidential value as regards the nature of its past.'[54] This, declares Franks,

> is substantially the position on which Schleiermacher's famous work, *The Christian Faith*, is based; by accepting it Prof. Webb paces himself in the great modern development of theology that comes down from that master. The writer, who is an ardent admirer of Schleiermacher, is glad to observe in *The Historical Element of* [*sic*] *Religion* an evidence of his continued influence at the present time.[55]

Franks did not write at length on ecclesiology, but he reviewed two books by his fellow Congregationalist, Daniel T. Jenkins, on that subject.[56] Far from needing to infer the reviewer's own position, he positively placards it. The first book is entitled, *The Nature of Catholicity*. Jenkins approaches the subject as a dogmatic theologian who regrets that too many expend most of their energy on biblical criticism or questions of church order. The Church exists to proclaim the Gospel, which is Jesus Christ as testified to by the apostles in the New Testament—a testimony that is correctly interpreted by the Chalcedonian definition of one person in two natures. This definition, Jenkins explains, means that Jesus Christ is not 'a man' but is 'man', universal humanity, the Second Adam. The task of dogmatic theology is continually 'to bring the Church under the judgment of the Word of God revealed in Jesus Christ and testified to in the Scriptures. The Liturgy of the Church has a similar office of judgment: its purpose is to bring the worshippers to repentance and reformation according to the Word of God.'[57] All of this, Franks

---

[53] Ibid. For Franks's review of N. Micklem, *Reason and Revelation: A Question from Duns Scotus*, see CQ, XXXI no. 4, October 1953, 365-6.

[54] CQ, XIII no. 4, October 1935, 482.

[55] Ibid.

[56] For Jenkins (1914-2002) see ODNB; URCYB, 2003, 326; WTW.

[57] CQ, XX no. 4, October 1942, 362.

observes, reveals Jenkins as a follower of Barth. But while Jenkins 'sees quite rightly the cardinal importance of a theological foundation and constitution of the Christian Church and its worship',[58] his position is vulnerable and five points.

First, Jenkins's reliance upon the testimony of the apostles implies a 'devastating scepticism' concerning the historical Jesus, 'to whom we are told we cannot get back. If we cannot, what becomes of the Incarnation beyond a doctrine or a myth? ... [A] historical religion founded on a history that is ambiguous and uncertain is in a parlous case.' Secondly, Jenkins overlooks the fact that the testimony of the apostles has an apologetic as well as a dogmatic aspect: Christ is preached 'in the language and in terms of the thought of the First Century. To treat the Apostolic preaching as if it had been formed in a hermetically sealed chamber without contact with the *Zeitgeist* is unhistorical and altogether impossible.' Thirdly, to say that Jesus was not 'a man' is once again to deny the Incarnation and to repudiate the apostolic testimony. Fourthly, while agreeing that 'the divisions of the Christian Church are contrary to its proper nature', Franks regrets that Jenkins combines this insight with an attack upon democracy as a form of Church polity: 'he seems to leave it quite hazy how the unity of the Church is to be assured in practice.'[59] Finally, Franks rebukes Jenkins for the slighting way he treats those whose theological opinions differ from his own. For example, he says that it is 'preposterous' to regard Dr. C. J. Cadoux as a representative of Congregationalism. To this Franks replies:

> Dr. Cadoux does represent with great energy and great learning, though perhaps in an extreme form, one important type of Congregationalist thought, the liberal Evangelicalism which is by no means as dead as Mr. Jenkins thinks it is. It is a pity that so able a book as *The Nature of Catholicism* should be marred by personal attacks of so provocative a character.[60]

In fairness I ought to point out with regard to Franks's fourth critical point, that Jenkins's protest against democratic process in church government arises from his view that the Church is not an institution whose government turns upon one person, one vote, and government by the majority. Rather the Church acknowledges the sole Lordship of Christ and seeks, not majority rule, but unanimity in him; and it does this by prayer, discussion and consensus (for in this context 'unanimity' does not mean 100% agreement; it means that individuals who have manageable reservations concerning a particular issue will not break fellowship). But the more important point concerns the person of Christ. Franks is right to protest that if Jesus is not 'a man' the Christian faith is undermined and theology is utterly vitiated. But we need not allow Jenkins's unfortunate predilection for the strong disjunction to obliterate

---

[58] Ibid. 363.

[59] The quotations thus far in this paragraph are found at ibid., 363.

[60] Ibid., 364. For Cadoux (1883-1947) see CYB, 1948, 489-90; ODNB; WTW; E. Kaye, *C. J. Cadoux: Theologian, Scholar, Pacifist*, Edinburgh: Edinburgh University Press, 1988; idem, *Mansfield College*; Alan P. F. Sell, *Nonconformist Theology in the Twentieth Century*.

the thought that Jesus is also Luther's Proper Man, the representative man, the one who at the Cross stands for all humanity before God and, indeed, presents humanity faultless before him. Here is a prime instance of the need for a 'both ... and', of which construction Franks generally approves, as we shall see in a moment.

Jenkins's second book is entitled, *The Gift of Ministry*.[61] Both giving and taking away, Franks begins his review thus: 'The outstanding excellence of this book must be recognized even by those who altogether disagree with its theology.'[62] Jenkins says that the minister speaks with the authority of the Word of God, and Franks at once retorts:

> Just here ... we come to the controversial aspect of the book. If by the Word of God Mr. Jenkins merely meant the essential message of the Bible, those whose theology differs from his could agree with him in the way he puts the matter. But by the Word of God he means the Barthian theology, a romanticized Calvinism, Calvinism itself being a systematized Paulinism. No proof has ever been given by Barth that the Word of God and his theology are equivalent, but his whole position rests upon the sheer assumption that it is so: the Word of God is what he defines it to be an nothing else.
>
> Mr. Jenkins says that the critics of Barth either represent his theology as a useful emphasis on one aspect of Christian truth, or as wrong altogether. The reviewer would substitute for this 'Either-or' the 'Both-and', so detested by the Barthians. Barthanism does rightly emphasize the demand made by the Christian Gospel for a decision for God in the actual situation of the moment. But this emphasis can stand with an altogether different interpretation of Christianity, *viz*. that its essence is the revelation of God's love in the human sacrificial love of the historical Jesus Christ, a love which of its very nature at once judges and pardons, and so is the saving power of God.[63]

Jenkins proceeds to claim 'that Barthianism is more modern that Liberalism because it more truly recognizes the chaotic nature of the present.' To which Franks replies that it actually looks back to Calvin with the same kind of nostalgia that Newman looked back to the ancient Catholic Church. As 'a life-long Congregationalist with Puritanism in my blood' Franks can appreciate Jenkins's nostalgic appeal to John Owen. The fact remains, however, that neither Newman's nor Barth's attack on liberalism will succeed, for

> neither of them faces the questions of the modern world in a rational way, but only on the basis of a great assumption, certainly in each case a different one: the very difference itself at once raises the question whether either assumption is right.

---

[61] Not, *The Gift of the Ministry*, as at the head of Franks's review in CQ, XXV no. 4, October 1947, 366-7.

[62] Ibid., 366.

[63] Ibid.

> As to the argument that the abandonment of Calvinism (or alternatively of Catholicism) in favour of Liberalism is condemned by its fruits, *viz*. the two World Wars and the confusion ensuing from them, this *post hoc ergo propter hoc* is no better than the pagan reasoning that the fall of Rome was due to the abandonment of paganism for Christianity, an opinion which Augustine trounced so thoroughly in his *City of God*.[64]

It is clear that as well as showing something of the range of Franks's interests, the selection of reviews considered are very revealing of his own stances on a number of substantive issues. They thus provide us with some background before we approach his major works.

Reverting now to the Minutes of the Council of Western College, we find that on 16 June 1930 W. J. F. Huxtable was accepted as a probationer. He scored 90 in the Scripture examination, but sat no other papers because of school examinations. As a pastor, Principal of New College, London, Minister-Secretary of the Congregational Union/Church in England and Wales, and Joint Secretary of the United Reformed Church Huxtable exercised a considerable influence within and beyond his own denomination. He was always grateful that he was 'one of Franks's men', and in his autobiography he has some revealing things to say about his teacher:

> The story told about him, probably true, was that one day when he was in the midst of putting on or taking off one of his garments, he enquired of his wife, 'Kitty, my dear, am I getting up or going to bed?'
>
> I recall a meeting held in a room in Clifton. It was of academics, teachers of philosophy, clerics and a few undergraduates. Franks had been asked to describe the philosophy of Hegel. This he did in a paper of about 50 minutes. As we were dispersing after the discussion, G. C. Field,[65] the Professor of Philosophy in Bristol, walked so far along the road with me. 'You are one of Franks' men, aren't you?' 'Yes.' 'Well I hope you're proud of him. I don't know anyone anywhere who could do what he has done this evening with such fairness and competence.'
>
> Franks used to say that it is better to read big books, even if you disagreed with them, than clutter your minds with pious little books which are like hayforks: they pitch you up and toss things about and land you where you were before.
>
> He was responsible for what we were taught about sermon preparation, how to cope with the chores of ministerial life and how to order our devotional life.[66]

When Huxtable was preparing to proceed to Mansfield College after Bristol, he was interviewed by Principal Nathaniel Micklem. Micklem's first question was, 'Why do you want to come here? You've had Franks—we haven't anyone like him here.'[67]

---

[64] Ibid., 367.

[65] For Field (1887-1955) see WWW 1941-50.

[66] J. Huxtable, *As it Seemed to Me*, 9, 10, 11. For Huxtable (1912-1990) see also URCYB, 1991-92, 229; ODNB; WTW.

In 1939 Dr. and Mrs. Franks retired to Winscombe, where they attended the Quaker meeting. Robert continued to write and publish. He died on 20 January 1964, leaving an unpublished work, 'Enigma', on the relations between science and theology. Like his father before him, he was remembered as being a righteous man, and one with a lively wit and a love of music.

I

It is not perversity which prompts me to introduce Franks's discussion of the theology of his former Principal before coming to his own works. From a consideration of his paper, 'The theology of Andrew Martin Fairbairn', we shall derive first, an indication of the degree to which Franks's evangelical liberalism was indebted to, and differed from, that of his mentor; and secondly, it will become clear that Franks's insistence upon the importance of the metaphysical underpinnings of theology was a direct inheritance from Fairbairn, and one which suggests the most appropriate way of classifying his writings.

Franks shows that the underlying motive in Fairbairn's thought is that reason is serviceable to faith. In his dogmatic work, *Christ in Modern Theology*, reason, 'by a critical process dealing with the history of the Christian religion, discovers the consciousness of Christ as the true Christian authority,' while in *The Philosophy of the Christian Religion* reason 'justifies this authority and exhibits its deliverances as harmonizing with a true understanding of the world and of human history.'[68] There follows a lengthy quotation from the latter book, the kernel of which is as follows:

> The only condition on which reason could have nothing to do with our religion is that religion should have nothing to do with truth. For in every controversy concerning what is or what is not truth, reason and not authority is the supreme arbiter; the authority that decides against reason commits itself to a conflict which is certain to issue in its defeat. ... The man who despises or distrusts reason, despises the God who gave it, and the most efficient of all the servants He has bidden work within and upon man in behalf of truth.[69]

Fairbairn was alive to, and grateful for, modern historical criticism because 'if a Christian theology means a theology of Christ, at once concerning Him and derived from Him, then to construct one ought, because of our greater knowledge of His and His history, to be more possible to-day than at any previous moment.'[70] Whereas, formerly, says Fairbairn, the way of correcting the bias of Greek philosophy and Roman law in Christian theology was by appeal to the teaching of Paul, now we have better access to the historic Christ and his consciousness, and at the root of that consciousness is the affirmation of God's Fatherhood. Redressing the balance in

---

[67] Ibid., 9.
[68] R. S. Franks, 'The theology of Andrew Martin Fairbairn,' 141.
[69] Ibid., 142, quoting *The Philosophy of the Christian Religion*, 18-19.
[70] Ibid., 144, quoting *Christ in Modern Theology*, 297.

received Calvinism, Fairbairn insists that while God is indeed sovereign, he is first Father: his is a Fatherly Sovereignty. Moreover, 'The revelation of God's Fatherhood is bound up with the Sonship of Christ, through whom we too learn a filial trust in God, and that in spite of the sin which everywhere exists through the misuse of human freedom, except only in Jesus Himself, whose moral transcendence marks Him out from all others and exhibits Him as the perfect Son of God.'[71] In a word, Franks concludes, the reasoning of the two books under review 'turns on the identification of the Divine Logos with the Son of God,' and 'the manifestation of the Divine Logos or Reason culminates in the Incarnation, the result of which is Jesus, the Christ, the Son of God, and the Revealer of the Father.'[72]

Franks then addresses the question, Why, when Fairbairn's books made such a great impression in his own time, are they no longer a living force now? First, he thinks, it is because the alliance of reason and faith and the emphasis upon the Fatherhood of God are nowadays taken for granted. Writing in 1939, in the aftermath of World War I, as the tensions leading to World War II were building, and as the works of Barth were becoming known in Britain, Franks says, 'The influence of Fairbairn is still to be seen in the Liberal Evangelicalism that he fostered in his pupils, and that still, in spite of so many changes, continues as a powerful religious and theological current among us to-day.'[73] Not, indeed that Fairbairn can be taken just as he stands. Franks finds his mentor's work inadequate in that his approach to the Old Testament is pre-Wellhausen, and he fails to distinguish sufficiently between the synoptic and Johannine traditions in the New Testament.

Secondly, and more seriously, Fairbairn's work is mediating theology in the bad sense of the term. While all theology must mediate between the revelation in Scripture and the interpreters of it, Fairbairn's is a theology 'that blurs its outlines by taking two different ways at once.' Thus,

> [I]n the working out of the details of his theology he uses traditional Trinitarian and Christological conceptions, while at times he throws doubts on their validity: moreover, in the interpretation of Scripture, and especially of St. Paul, he often reads his own meaning into the passage and modernizes it in a way that is impossible as sound exegesis. If there is one thing that I hope we may have learned since Fairbairn's time it is that in giving the sense of Scripture we must give the historical sense, whether we like it or not: it is another question altogether what weight we give to the passage in question in theological construction.[74]

Thirdly, like his contemporary Ritschl, Fairbairn, for all his emphasis upon the consciousness of Jesus, neglects the eschatological element in it: 'Fairbairn interprets the Kingdom of God simply as a religious-ethical society.' In this respect

---

[71] Ibid., 145.
[72] Ibid., 146.
[73] Ibid., 147.
[74] Ibid.

he and Ritschl were 'children of their own age.'[75] In the wake of War this will no longer suffice. We now have 'on the one hand, a return to the theology of Calvin, with its emphasis on the Divine Sovereignty; on the other hand, there came about a certain scepticism as to the Gospel history'[76]—the former associated with Rudolf Otto and Karl Barth, the latter with the form-critical approach of Martin Franz Dibelius.[77]

Franks readily admits that the liberal emphasis upon the Fatherhood of God did in some cases lead 'to a shallow and easy-going optimism';[78] but Fairbairn was not to blame for this, nor did he endorse it, and 'There really is no ground whatever for the calumny that to accept God's Fatherhood *ex animo* is to think lightly of sin.'[79] With clear reference to Barth's 'wholly other' God Franks sets his face against the most prominent currently available alternative to evangelical liberalism:

> I cannot believe that a theology founded on sheer authority and upon the absolute unlikeness of God and man will ever permanently satisfy the human mind; nor does it make much difference here whether we say that what authority reveals is the Trinitarianism and Christology of the creeds, or over and above this the whole body of Reformation doctrine contained in Calvin's *Institutes*. Moreover, I think that Fairbairn was absolutely right when he made the consciousness of Christ the norm of Christian thought. It is said to-day ... that the Person of Christ and His redeeming acts are more than His teaching; and this is true. But surely it is equally true that His teaching must be the canon by which to test the soundness of any theological development that seeks to interpret the Person and the acts. ... Jesus must be the prime interpreter of His own Person and work.[80]

Franks concludes that Fairbairn's principles must be developed with greater accuracy that he himself displayed, and that 'It would be a task worthy of the efforts of any British theologian to complete the work of Fairbairn in this way.'[81]

In this paper on Fairbairn, then, we have the confirmation of the hints already dropped in the introductory section to this chapter. The War, Barth, Otto and the form critics notwithstanding, Franks remains a liberal evangelical. No doubt he wishes to recast Fairbairn's theological liberalism in the light of subsequent scholarship and world events, and he will have nothing to do with doctrinal sentimentalism or facile optimism; but, equally, he will shun the wholly other God and doggedly uphold the relationship between reason and faith, philosophy and

---

75 Ibid., 148.

76 Ibid.

77 Franks cites Otto's *The Idea of the Holy* (1917); Barth's *The Epistle to the Romans* (ET 1932); and Dibelius's *From Tradition to Gospel* (1919). For Otto (1869-1937) see Lindsay Jones, ed., *Encyclopedia of Religion*; for Barth (1886-1968) and Dibelius (1883-1947) see Donald K. McKim, ed., *Dictionary of Major Biblical Interpreters*.

78 Art.cit., 148.

79 Ibid., 149.

80 Ibid.

81 Ibid., 150.

theology, finding the locus of theological authority in the consciousness of Christ. From these positive points I draw the method of the rest of this chapter. I shall first introduce Franks's more philosophical writings and then turn to his doctrinal works.

II

In the last sentence of his review of W. G. De Burgh's, *Towards a Religious Philosophy*, we have a clear statement of Franks's desideratum. He hopes that De Burgh's book 'may serve to promote that reconciliation of faith and reason which it one of the interests I have most at heart.'[82] But none knew better than he that in face of a logical positivism which was if not hostile to, at least dismissive of, the faith; and of the theology of the Word which, from its side, suspected reason and lived within a circle of revelation, converts to his view would not be easily won. Nevertheless, as he elsewhere insisted, 'What is Christian and what is rational can never be really opposed—if they appear to be so, it is our business to think further till we see their harmony.'[83] What Franks brought to this task was a well-grounded competence in philosophical analysis and metaphysical enquiry. By 'well grounded' I mean that his mathematical training gave him a bridge to logical studies, while his understanding of the course of Christian thought, in its philosophical as well as its doctrinal aspects, enabled him to see current trends in historical perspective.

Consider, for example, the conciseness and precision of the opening sentences of his review of Suzanne K. Langer's, *An Introduction to Symbolic Logic*:

> 'Logic,' said William of Ockham, 'is the aptest instrument of all the arts, without which no science can be had in perfection.' But how many different things Logic has meant in the course of the ages! That was true even in its Aristotelian form, as can be seen from Prantl's enormous *History of Logic*, which brings the subject down to medieval times, where Ockham's own great contribution to the subject is included. But modern Logic has been even more multiform. Kant distinguished Formal Logic, as the science of mere thinking, irrespective of what is thought, and Transcendental Logic, as the science of knowledge in regard to its proper objects and its possibilities. Hegel converted the latter type of Logic into Metaphysic in his great *Science of Logic*, whose subject-matter he himself described as 'the kingdom of shadows, or God as He was in Himself, before the creation of the world', while Bradley later characterized it as 'the bloodless ballet of the categories'. Bradley's own famous *Principles of Logic* is itself epistemological, though it prepares for the metaphysic of *Appearance and Reality*. But, in opposition to all such modern developments of Logic towards epistemology and metaphysics, Mrs. Langer's book is restricted absolutely to the formal structure of thinking. She describes the logical task in words which strangely recall those of Ockham, six hundred years ago:

---

[82] Idem, CQ, XVI no. 1, January 1938, 100. For De Burgh (1866-1943) see DTCBP.

[83] CQ, XVI no. 1, January 1938, 98.

> What mathematics is to the natural sciences, logic, the more general study of forms, is to philosophy, the more general understanding of the world.[84]

Franks proceeds to explain that Boole, a pioneering symbolic logician, sought to reduce forms of thought, abstracted from content, to symbolism in a manner analogous to algebra. His calculus of classes developed into a calculus of propositions in such a way as to show their mutual implications. But this approach ran aground to some extent, and it was left to Russell and Whitehead, in *Principia Mathematica*, to set out from the calculus of propositions and derive the calculus of classes from it. It is this development which Mrs. Langer expertly traces.

Franks inclines to think that the advocates of symbolic logic claim too much for it, but he does welcome two of its contributions in particular. The more important is the recognition that there are logical relations over and above the subject-predicate relations of traditional logic. The less important is the way in which symbolic logic enables those of a mathematical turn of mind to express complicated processes of reasoning in forms which facilitate their assessment. As to the value of symbolic logic for epistemology and metaphysics, Franks declares that 'the real activity of thought falls outside the calculus of relations: it attaches itself rather to the complementary function of denotation.' Hence, 'Oxford continues to study Bradley, supplemented by Cook Wilson; and Oxford is not invariably a home of lost causes.'[85]

We may note in passing that one year later we find Franks discussing a work on logic which could hardly be more different from the foregoing: Dewey's *Logic. The Theory of Enquiry*. Dewey sets his face against the theory of induction and deduction as found in Aristotelian logic, and insists that logic is never merely formal: it concerns form-in-matter. Explanations of events come by way of the testing of hypotheses, and causality is a teleological matter of seeking means towards ends. Dewey's fundamental principle is 'inquiry', that is, 'a determination of an indeterminate situation.' The key to such determination is pragmatic, by which he means, 'the function of consequences as necessary tests of the validity of the propositions, provided these consequences are operationally brought about and are such as to resolve the special problem evoking the operations.'[86] From this standpoint Dewey discusses many topics in logic and Franks, somewhat guardedly, welcomes the book as 'a mine of information on the different parts of logical theory, as they are to be understood from its special point of view.'[87]

Returning to the sphere of denotation as distinct from the calculus of relations, Franks accords a warm welcome to Gilbert Ryle's *Philosophical Arguments*. It is, he declares, 'a brilliant piece of work.'[88] Ryle observes that people make concrete propositions concerning matters of fact, and these are verifiable by observation. But

---

[84] Ibid.

[85] Ibid., 101.

[86] CQ, XVII no. 3, July 1939, 377.

[87] Ibid., 378.

[88] CQ, XXIV no. 2, April 1946, 180.

we also assert non-verifiable abstract propositions. Since these may be doubted or denied by others, the question arises, How far are such assertions tenable? Philosophy is concerned to investigate the implications of propositions and concepts, and then turns to the coherence or incoherence of the implications themselves. The objective is to systematize non-absurd propositions and to clarify their use. All of which, thinks Franks, is an accurate account of the nature and method of philosophy.

Are we to understand Franks as meaning that there is nothing more to philosophy that this? He gives this impression in his review, but it surely cannot be so. His entire enquiry into the metaphysical underpinnings of religion would fail if it were. It would seem that he has not fully taken the measure of Ryle's anti-metaphysical, ordinary language, stance. Thus, for example, Ryle elsewhere wrote that

> there is ... a sense in which we can properly enquire and even say 'what it really means to say so and so.' For we can ask what is the real form of the fact recorded when this is concealed or disguised and not duly exhibited by the expression in question. And we can often succeed in stating this fact in a new form of words which does exhibit what the other failed to exhibit. And I am for the present inclined to believe that this is what philosophical analysis is, and that this is the sole and whole function of philosophy.[89]

Ryle immediately 'confesses' that he would prefer 'to allot to philosophy a sublimer role', but that philosophy is 'at least' a matter of 'the detection of the sources in linguistic idioms of recurrent misconstructions and absurd theories,' he cannot seriously doubt.[90] Moreover, Ryle was famously opposed to 'isms' in philosophy, an argument he made in a paper entitled, 'Taking sides in philosophy.' 'There is no place for "isms" in philosophy,' he declared; 'to be affiliated to a recognizable party is to be the slave of a non-philosophic prejudice in favour of a (usually non-philosophic) article of belief.'[91] All the more ironic, therefore, that he fell foul to the accusation of having fallen for behaviour*ism* in his celebrated work, *The Concept of Mind*. The fact remains that his therapeutic, even curative, approach in philosophy remained consistent through all his writings, and Franks's practice shows that to him this work, though important, does not exhaust the philosopher's task.[92]

Hence Franks's continued interest in other philosophical approaches that were being explored at Oxford and elsewhere. In 1938 he reviewed *Critical Realism* by G. Dawes Hicks, a volume the realism of which he found akin to that of Samuel Alexander's *Space, Time and Deity*. The world of nature, Hicks argues, comprises both quantitative and qualitative features that are apprehended through sense

---

[89] Gilbert Ryle, 'Systematically misleading expressions,' 36. Cf. idem, 'Ordinary language,' 186.

[90] Ibid.

[91] Idem, 'Taking sides in philosophy,' 317.

[92] For an account of approaches to philosophy *vis à vis* the philosophy of religion see Alan P. F. Sell, *The Philosophy of Religion 1875-1980*.

perception. Nature contains both colours, sounds and temperatures as well as what is denoted by such terms as force, energy, strain and stress. None of these are entirely subjective phenomena. Mind is 'that activity of discrimination by which we recognize the existence of all these elements of nature.'[93] Hicks strongly denies the existence of *sensa* between mind and nature. Every act of awareness is contained by, and is inseparable from, its object. He repudiates Kant's doctrine that our knowledge is conditioned by a transcendental mental factor that guarantees its objectivity: the mind remains an empirical self, a unity of acts of discrimination. Franks thinks that Hicks has advanced pertinent criticisms of many epistemologies, and that he has shown that epistemology is indispensable to philosophy, but the question remains, How do we know that a subjective act of awareness—say of a red object—guarantees that red is an intrinsic natural quality. Moreover, our awareness of objects depends upon nerve processes, and a colour-blind person who cannot distinguish between red and green would seem to testify against the claim that 'the awareness of an object is *ipso facto* the revelation of the object.'[94]

Two years later Franks turned from realism to idealism in his review of Brand Blanshard's substantial work, *The Nature of Thought*.[95] Here the idealism in question is not Berkeley's subjective idealism or Kant's critical idealism, but that objective idealism which, under the inspiration of Hegel, had flowed into such British writers as Green, Caird, Bosanquet and Bradley, and into the American philosopher, Royce. For Blanshard, coherence is the test of truth. The transcendent aim of thought is to know reality, the immanent aim is to produce a mentally satisfying, coherent, system. Well aware of empiricist scepticism and of the challenge of those epistemologists who embrace the correspondence theory of truth, Blandshard nevertheless holds that the immanent objective is congruent with the transcendent aim, and that as we advance in systematization so our understanding of reality increases. Blandshard concedes that there is no absolute proof of the coherence theory of truth, but he argues that the only alternative to it is scepticism.

Later in the same year, 1940, Franks turned his attention to R. G. Collingwood's, *An Essay on Metaphysics*. Collingwood, he says, calls for a thoroughgoing reform of metaphysics. Whereas metaphysicians characteristically seek to identify the ultimate presuppositions of science and culture, which they then construe as propositions requiring proof, Collingwood thinks that this a forlorn task, for these propositions can never be proved. Were it otherwise, this would simply show that the proposition in question rested upon other presuppositions, and thus they would be no longer ultimate, but relative. The proper task of metaphysics is historical, Collingwood declares. It analyses the ultimate presuppositions upon which existing science and culture depend. It follows that since science and culture are subject to change over time, these presuppositions cannot be absolute, and thus metaphysics will change with changing times. Scientists who revolt against

[93] CQ, XVI no. 3, July 1938, 365.

[94] Ibid., 366.

[95] CQ, XVIII no. 2, April 1940, 213-214.

metaphysics, he continues, are revolting against the false metaphysics of professional philosophers; in asserting their ultimate presuppositions against these the scientists themselves become amateur metaphysicians. Psychologists and logical positivists can, for different reasons render no help to science in its battle with the professional metaphysicians, because science depends upon ultimate presuppositions—the very things whose existence is denied by psychologists and logical positivists. The psychologists hold that all mental states are equal, and hence nothing can be more ultimate than anything else; the logical positivists declare that ultimate presuppositions cannot be justified by empirical generalizations—the only proof the positivists will allow. Franks judges that Collingwood's is 'a most bracing production', but he doubts whether 'the explanation of metaphysics as a historical science will stand.'[96] One could wish that he had allowed a glimpse of his grounds for this judgment.

Franks finds that Whitehead's *Process and Reality* has affinities with Bergson on the one hand and Alexander on the other. It is a new realist work. Franks summarizes what is a complicated work replete with novel terminology, and I shall not attempt further to précis his account. Rather, I wish to state and remark upon Franks's reaction to the work as a whole:

> The greatest problem of theology to-day is that of religion and science, God and nature. Every philosophy which helps to interpret the stark entities of science in a way that makes a bridge from God and religion to the world and science is a good friend to the theologian. It is not likely that Christian theists will accept Whitehead's doctrines *en bloc*—his doctrine of God forbids that. Whitehead is himself perfectly conscious of its difference from orthodox theism. But his thought will act as a powerful solvent upon some of our most difficult theological problems, and is likely to leave us infinitely grateful to him.[97]

Once again, it would be interesting to know in what respects Franks thought that *Process and Reality* would help to bridge the alleged gap between God and religion on the one hand and the world of science on the other; but perhaps it is asking too much of the author of a brief review to attempt this task. At the very least one who warmly welcomed Ryle's account of philosophy's therapeutic value might have dropped a passing remark to the effect that Whitehead's writing provides ample scope for such activity. I recall that Susan Stebbing called Whitehead's way of speaking both of God's 'non-temporal actuality and of his role as 'the poet of the world, with tender patience leading it by his vision of truth, beauty and goodness' as 'indefensible' and 'nothing short of scandalous.'[98] Seven years later Franks does not seem to be quite so sure of the benefits of Whitehead's approach. In a review of A. P. Ushenko's book, *The Philosophy of Relativity*, he concludes that its merit is that

---

[96] CQ, XVIII no. 3, July 1940, 325.

[97] CQ, VIII, 1930, 228.

[98] L. S. Stebbing, Review of *Process and Reality*, 475. For further reflections see Alan P. F. Sell, *The Philosophy of Religion*, 68-73.

'it reviews and will introduce the reader to a number of modern tentative efforts (by Whitehead, Russell, etc.) at describing a universe which is being daily transformed before our eyes by the advance of modern physics; but it does not appear that these efforts have as yet attained any great degree of success.'[99] A sentence like this makes one regret all the more that Franks's 'Enigma' was never published.

That Franks knew full well that there were more and less satisfactory ways of regarding the religion-science relation is clear from his review of *Contemporary American Philosophy*. Having considered the papers in this collection he concludes that the realistic philosophy of Dewey is paramount. He therefore quotes two of Dewey's sentences and then adds his own comment:

> The objective biological approach of the Jamesian psychology led straight to the perception of the importance of distinctive social categories, especially communication and participation. It is my conviction that a great deal of our philosophizing needs to be done over again from this point of view, and that there will ultimately result an integrated synthesis in a philosophy congruous with modern science and relation to actual needs in education, morals and religion.

We must say: *Non tali auxilio*. The aim is admirable, but an "objective biological approach" can never lead to the absolute values with which alone morals and religion can be satisfied.[100]

No account of Franks's adjustments to the philosophical thought of his day would be complete without reference to the three Roman Catholic thinkers, Gilson, Maritain and Marcel, of whom the first two were devoted neo-Thomists while the latter, though he repudiated the label 'existentialist', nevertheless addressed from a Christian point of view questions posed by existentialists. In 1939 Franks welcomed Gilson's book, *The Unity of Philosophical Experience* for its sturdy defence of metaphysics. Although sceptics have repeatedly attacked metaphysics, the latter 'always buries its undertakers.'[101] Whenever the place of metaphysics is usurped, whether by Logic (Abelard), mathematics (Descartes), or sociology (Comte), scepticism follows. At the present time, says Gilson, pragmatism, humanism and agnosticism are all varieties of scepticism. The remedy is to return to Aquinas's fundamental principle, Being. This principle contains the axioms of identity, contradiction and causality, and these apply universally and all scientific work rests upon them. I quote Franks's verdict, which clearly reveals his stance *vis á vis* the revival of Thomism in his day:[102]

---

[99] CQ, XV no. 3, July 1937, 388.

[100] CQ, VIII, 1930, 364. Shades of D. W. Simon's tendency to mistake the biological analogy for a biological argument.

[101] CQ, XVII no. 2, April 1939, 246.

[102] In passing we may note that Franks was not as excited by more traditional expressions of Thomism, such as that of R. P. Phillips in his *Modern Thomistic Philosophy*. Holding that science deals only with appearance, not with reality, Phillips

This sounds all very abstract and very remote from actuality. But M. Gilson means by it something very practical—and also something very debatable. He means that Thought must follow Being; as he puts it, how can that which is only a part of Being ever adequately survey it? The enemy intended is Idealism, which proclaims the identity of Thought and Being, which in fact holds Being itself to be of the nature of Thought. M. Gilson's is a brave challenge; but the matter needs much consideration. The way we decide settles all our philosophy: we stand at the watershed and dividing line of systems. The question to ask ourselves before we side with M. Gilson is, whether it is so certain after all that Thought is only a part of Being? If it is, how can the part transcend itself and apprehend the whole? But Thought must apprehend Being, if a science of Being is to be possible: the category of whole and part does not seem therefore fitly to describe the mutual relations of being and Thought.[103]

In 1940 Maritain's *A Preface to Metaphysics* came to Franks's attention.[104] It is a work which concerns pure Being. Franks reminds us that Hegel meditated on pure being until it dissolved into Nothing, and from that, by utilizing his method of thesis, antithesis and synthesis he deduced his system of thought, nature and spirit. Maritain is not so bold. What metaphysicians require is intuition into Being. This enables them to see Being whole, that is, not as bare identity, but as a rich complex which contains the opposition of essence and existence, and which shows itself as the One, the true and the good. It also includes the principles of identity, sufficient reason and causation. Franks welcomes the exposition, and in particular he values the way in which Maritain relates his position to Bergson's intuitionism and Heidegger's existentialism.

In the first volume of *The Mystery of Being*, Marcel had argued that the philosophical quest begins from actual bodily existence in a particular situation, the uneasiness of which is experienced as the call of Being. Primary reflection, he claimed, reveals to us the broken world in which we live—a world in which the individual is a thing among things; whereas secondary reflection is synthetic. By it we are restored to a life in which others are not objects, but presences. Thus we reach the mystery of Being. In volume two, *Faith and Reality*, which Franks reviews here, Marcel argues that we may transcend the world around us by heeding the call of Being. For this we require faith, which is not faith *that* such and such is, or is not, the case, but it is a belief *in* something: 'I am free when I receive the call of Being

---

shuns it and claims that it is Aristotelian metaphysics which puts us in touch with reality. Franks retorts that 'The attitude of *Modern Thomistic Philosophy* to modern science reminds one too much of that of the Medieval Church to Galileo; and one still thinks to hear the latter saying, "*e pur si muover*."' See CQ. XIII no. 2, April 1935, 245. That Franks did not consider that idealism was necessarily a panacea in this connection is clear from the way he also faulted the post-Hegelian absolute idealism of F. H. Cleobury for its lack of attention to natural science. See his review of Cleobury's *God, Man and the Absolute* in CQXXV no. 3, July 1947, 275.

[103] CQ, XVII no. 2, April 1939, 246.

[104] CQ, XVIII no. 2, April 1940, 212-13.

as a gift of grace to which I respond.'[105] Faith includes hope and love: hope is faith transcending death; love, intersubjectivity as such, is the ontological basis of faith. Franks concludes, 'Substitute for the fall of Adam M. Marcel's broken world, and for idolatry his mechanization and socialization, and we have the ancient philosophy, clothed in modern language and adapted to meet our present situation in a most masterly way.'[106]

Franks welcomed W. F. Lofthouse's study of *F. H. Bradley*. Following a careful exposition of Bradley's thought Lofthouse faults him for his agnosticism regarding the origin of appearances from or in the absolute. Lofthouse considers that the deficiency may be supplied only by a theistic construction developed by means of the analogy of organism. This, Franks rightly says, is no longer Bradley; though he agrees with Lofthouse that

> it is unsatisfactory to say to say that we know for certain that all but the Absolute is appearance, but yet we do not know how appearances arise. This peculiar blend of knowledge and ignorance is necessarily unstable, and must develop one way or the other, either to the positivism abhorred alike by Bradley and his expositor, or else to a Theism which the latter represents. But the questing mind of man cannot be expected, permanently to accept the 'thus far shalt thou go and no further' of positivism; and therefore in the end the advance to Theism seems inevitable.[107]

This reference to theism prompts me to introduce a handful of works on natural theology to which Franks adjusted himself. In 1940 Franks gave a cordial welcome to D. L. Scudder's book, *Tennant's Philosophical Theology*. Tennant is dissatisfied with those philosophies of religion (like Simon's) that set out from religious experience. In his opinion such experience is of secondary importance, since 'it depends upon an objective idea of God independently obtained.'[108] Accordingly he insists that natural theology is of primary importance because if we have no assured knowledge of God we cannot accept a putative revelation as being in fact from God. He further argues that sensation and introspection are the building blocks of natural theology, but the objects thus yielded are in the first instance private. We then compare our perceptions with those of others, in reliance upon analogical inference. Even then the objects, now publicly shared, do no more than represent reality, but from them we infer the metaphysical reality that has caused them. By analogical reasoning from the metaphysical objects that are our own selves and those of others, we proceed to the Creator God. Tennant grants that these analogical inferences are probable only, and that we never have objective certainty where God is concerned. Scudder's criticism of Tennant is, first, that analogical inference does not suffice to counter solipsism; and secondly, apart from an intuition of other selves and of God we cannot reach them: analogical inference will not by itself carry us to the desired

---

[105] CQ, XXIX no. 4, October 1951, 361.

[106] Ibid., 362.

[107] CQ, XXVII no. 4, October 1949, 364.

[108] CQ, XVIII no. 4, October 1940, 427.

destination. In particular analogical inference cannot carry us to the Creator God because the idea of creation *ex nihilo* is not present in the non-religious experience we have. Scudder does, however, value Tennant's approach of arguing from elements in our non-religious experience provided that this be regarded as a supplement to the argument from religious experience. In agreement with Scudder, Franks concludes:

> what rational arguments for the Divine existence reach is always an abstraction, only religious experience can give concreteness and real content to this abstraction. [Cf. Simon's emphasis upon the importance of regeneration by the Spirit in order that we may 'see']. On the other hand, the abstraction is useful as pointing to the place where religious experience comes in; and it can serve as a standard of criticism by which genuine religious experience may be distinguished from the many counterfeits which claim the name.[109]

Austin Farrer's *Finite and Infinite* is regarded by Franks as a 'great book'. Farrer thinks that in the field of rational theology the Thomists ask the right questions, and have the appropriate analogical means of answering them, but he finds it necessary to break the hold of Aristotelianism upon Thomism. Accordingly, he does not argue from the universe to God, but thinks first of the relation between God and the universe on the assumption that God exists. He understands that finite being can never prove the infinite, but all our arguments must nevertheless proceed by analogy from observed distinctions within finite being. Central to his case is his construal of substance as activity. The substance we know best is the self, at the heart of which is will, which can transcend its physical limitations and reach towards higher purposes. We know the rest of finite being only by analogy with the self. We may argue to God both from the self and from finite being at large; from the former we are led to the idea of Absolute Perfection, from the latter, to Absolute Being. Franks suspects that some may feel that, like others, Farrer has not given due place to natural science. In fact, however, he has clearly shown the place of science within his world view: science 'is a study of abstractions, which, however widely it expands, and however useful it may be, can never be a substitute for a metaphysic that asks and attempts to answer the ultimate questions.'[110]

I am very well aware that I have not fully expounded the works to which brief allusion has been made. My objective has been to show how Franks understood the contents of the books he reviewed, and to see through his remarks upon them how he adjusted himself to the several positions adopted. We have seen so far that he wishes natural science to receive its due in any intellectual construction; that reason and experience must be held together against idealists on the one hand and empiricists on the other; and that the traditional theistic proofs yield an abstraction only. Above all, Franks's running refrain has been that in theology we may not repudiate metaphysics in favour of revelation. In the concluding paragraph of his review of Farrer's book he clearly states his position in summary form:

---

[109] Ibid., 428.

[110] CQ, XXI no. 4, October 1943, 372.

> Particularly valuable in Mr. Farrer's work is his contention that the metaphysical conception of God is implicit in our religious utterances about Him. The metaphysic is not to be rejected in favour of the doctrine of a Living God known only by revelation.[111] It is simply drawing out in logical form what is meant when we say 'God', and understand what we say. To reject the metaphysical conception of God is simply to take up with something that is not God: in other words, it is to put an idol in His place. It is the place of metaphysics to remind us of the limitations of our anthropomorphisms and so save us from idolatry.[112]

We may with some justification take Franks's assertion that 'the complete exclusion of metaphysic from the mind means the suffocation of reason'[113] as the key to his approach. It is the ground on which he stands when confronted by 'Christian thinkers who would do well to return from the present obsession with Kierkegaard and Barth.'[114] Among these he finds H. A. Hodges, author of *Christianity and the Modern World View*. If Franks thought that some thinkers were paying insufficient attention to natural science, Hodges is concerned by the domination of it. He seeks to address the challenge which the scientific mind-set poses to Christianity. He first observes that all world views turn upon presuppositions which cannot be proved. Modern science presupposes 'the uniformity of nature as governed by the Law of Causality; over against this stands the religious presupposition which traces everything back to God; between the two is the metaphysical presupposition which may be described as a depersonalization of the presupposition of Religion. Only the religious presupposition can sufficiently explain the universe in the truest sense.'[115] The great obstacle before this presupposition is the problem of evil in the world; but theism 'does more to meet it than any other explanation of the world, since it shows God revealing Himself redemptively to meet this very difficulty.'[116] However, because of the requirement of obedience to God that entails a denial of natural instincts, human beings find it hard to accept the religious presupposition. Indeed, it cannot be accepted apart from divine help—grace. But even when enabled by grace we still live in a paradox, for Christianity turns the world upside down. In characterizing religion as a paradox, Franks thinks that Hodges concedes too much to 'this latest fashion':

---

[111] See Franks's approval of W. M. Urban's book, *Humanity and Deity*; CQ, XXX no. 2, April 1952, 169.

[112] CQ, XXI no. 4, October 1943, 372..

[113] CQ, XXXIII no. 5, July 1953, 269.

[114] CQ, XXVIII no. 2, April 1950, 177. I think that Franks is unfair to Kierkegaard at this point, for the latter was not opposed to metaphysics as such, but only to the Hegelian version of it, which he deemed pernicious. See further J. Heywood Thomas, 'Kierkegaard's alternative metaphysical theology,' *History of European Ideas*, XII no. 1, 1990, especially p. 61: 'Kierkegaard showed the fundamental flaw in Hegelian theology, its transformation into some abstract principle.'

[115] CQ, XXVIII no. 2, April 1950.

[116] Ibid.

> A paradox can never be a place to rest in, but is only a halt on the way to further explanation. Professor Hodges himself suggests the way out of the paradox in one place where he speaks of metaphysics as a bridge between science and religion. He thinks of it indeed only subjectively as a stage of thought to be passed through. But a more persistent pursuance of this idea might reveal metaphysic as possessed of objective value, and as the likeliest healer of the open breach with which he leaves us.[117]

Elsewhere, in a review of Campbell N. Moody's book, *Christ for us and Christ in Us*, Franks returns to this point. The invocation of paradox, he declares, 'is a favourite method in much modern theology. But to rest in a paradox can never really be satisfactory. An apparent paradox is just a call to think further and more deeply ...'[118] Certainly, to rest too soon upon paradox may simply betoken laziness of thought, but, I ask, can paradox altogether be avoided? Did not Franks himself also write, 'The paradox, but also the glory of, Christianity is this: "The Word became flesh and dwelt among us"'?[119] Did he not also speak of 'that peculiar modification of religious experience which we know as Christian, with its strange paradox that the personality of Jesus has become absolutely infused with the experience of God'?[120] And is there any way of extruding 'Not I, but Christ' from Christian experience, or of disregarding it when pondering the ethical challenges of the Christian life?

No author received a warmer welcome from Franks that W. G. De Burgh, Hodges's predecessor in the Chair of Philosophy at the University of Reading. In *Towards a Religious Philosophy* De Burgh sets himself the task of developing what he called 'a speculative outlook on the world and on life which as philosophy is grounded on reason and as religion is centred in God.'[121] He resolutely opposes any notion of a 'double truth' and observes that religion develops a total world view, while reason takes the whole world for its parish. 'Either one must entirely destroy the other, or else they must come to perceive that in the end they are approaching the same Reality from different angles.'[122] De Burgh adopts the latter view, and argues that 'just as there is a rational element in faith which works out as theology, so there is an element of faith in reason in so far as it is never mere ratiocination but always includes an intuition of first principles.'[123] Moreover, metaphysical knowledge is abstract, while religious knowledge is personal. In De Burgh's view (so different from that of Ryle, for example), 'Philosophy seeks synthesis of the universal and particular moments in experience by developing impersonal knowledge

---

[117] Ibid., 177. Though it was something for the Professor of Philosophy of a secular university (Reading) to write in this vein at all in the heyday of ordinary language, empiricist philosophy.

[118] CQ, XIV no. 1, January 1936, 111.

[119] R. S. Franks, 'The person of Christ in modern scholarship,' 36.

[120] Idem, 'The fullness of God: Father, Son, and Holy Spirit,' 550.

[121] CQ, XVI no. 1, January 1938, 98.

[122] Ibid., 99.

[123] Ibid.

of the former; religion by developing personal knowledge of the latter.'[124] He proceeds to delineate the contents of a religious philosophy, and concludes that God's transcendence notwithstanding, we may affirm, univocally, that God is Love. Franks says how pleased he is to find the endorsement of many of the conclusions which he himself had reached in his Dale Lectures on the atonement: 'It has been with [me] as it was with Bunyan in the experience he describes in *Grace Abounding*, where he tells of the joy he found in reading Luther's Commentary on *Galatians* and in discovering that another had passed along the same road as himself.[125] Franks never came closer to eulogistic abandon than that.

Against the background now presented, and as Christian doctrine comes ever more closely into view, I shall introduce Frank's two major contributions to the discussion of the relations between philosophy and theology and religion. In 1927 he contributed a paper entitled, 'The present relations between philosophy and theology' to James Marchant's symposium, *The Future of Christianity*. Taking his cue from Troeltsch,[126] who said that historians of Christian theology should take account of the traditional ideas of the religion as well as of the philosophical notions which become attached to them; but above all they should reflect upon the relations between faith and reason, Franks declares that 'the question how they can exist together is the cardinal question of theology, so far as it is theology, and not simply confession of faith.'[127] His thesis is that 'Christian experience is the necessary foundation of Christian theology, and ... that *such appeal to experience does not make us independent of philosophy, but is rather the modern form of relating theology to philosophy*.'[128] The appeal to experience is one which implies that the experience has an objective reference, and the justification of that reference is the task of philosophy. Were there no objective reference theology 'would become simply a branch of empirical psychology, and its best stated doctrines would be (to borrow a happy illustration from St. Anselm) like pictures painted on air.'[129]

Franks argues that although the relations between philosophy and theology through history were never absolutely harmonious, the degree of alliance there had been was shattered by Kant, who regarded religion as but an appendix to morals. At this point I quote two sentences from Franks's review of *The Pain of This World*, by M. C. D'Arcy which sum up his adverse criticism of the scholastic philosophy which he believed Kant to have made redundant: 'The reason of the schoolman is a reason which argues rigorously within certain presuppositions. Chief of these is the axiom that the rational idea of God is *ipso facto* different from that contained in the Christian faith.'[130] In Kant's wake there developed exact scientific research into the biblical texts such that the unity of the biblical revelation was lost; and there was no

---

[124] Ibid.

[125] Ibid.

[126] Ernst Troeltsch (1865-1923), German theologian and philosopher.

[127] R. S. Franks, 'The present relations between philosophy and theology,' 49.

[128] Ibid.,50, his italics.

[129] Ibid.

[130] CQ, XVI no. 1, January 1936, 112.

longer 'the presupposition of a firmly established metaphysic.'[131] Kant had (to his own satisfaction and in the opinion of many) demolished the traditional theistic arguments, and had replaced them with the postulates of morality: God, freedom and immortality.

I here interject the thought that at this point there is an important missing link in Franks's exposition. He does not refer to Kant's epistemology, according to which we have knowledge of phenomena but not of noumena, the things in themselves. Apart from this explanation it is impossible to understand Franks's immediately following reference to 'the negative aspect of Kantianism' which has discarded religion. It has done so because of the conviction that we have no knowledge of the noumenal realm. In other words, on this side Kant is a father of nineteenth-century agnosticism; and morality, in the alleged absence of grounds for thinking in terms of absolute obligation, becomes utilitarian in character. The opposite result flowing down from Kant is the attempt, supremely made by Hegel, to restore the relations between nature and spirit, with the result that religion is all but turned into a metaphysic.

In Franks's opinion the key to the most appropriate response to Kant's work of demolition is to be found in both the theology and the philosophy—too often overlooked—of Schleiermacher. He maintained the independence of religious experience, but did not understand it in such a way as to divorce religion from philosophy. His appeal to experience was rooted in the principles expounded in his *Dialectic* and *Outline of Philosophical Ethics*. In the former work Schleiermacher argues that both science and morality are social products: they turn upon agreement that science is in touch with ultimate reality, and that moral law is absolute. In religion we experience a deeply-felt unity with 'the reality that underlies alike the physical and the moral world.'[132] In his *Speeches on Religion* Schleiermacher argues that religion is not a matter of knowledge or action, but of intuition and feeling; in *The Christian Faith* he says that religion is the feeling of absolute dependence. While there is this conviction regarding the absolute in Schleiermacher's theory, this is not on a par with the approach of that development from Kant which yielded Hegelian absolutism, for, as Franks elsewhere points out, Schleiermacher 'was not prepared like Fichte and others to sublimate the historical element in Christianity into metaphysical truth.[133] In Schleiermacher's theory the absolute functions as a criterion for evaluating empirical knowledge. Moreover, in his system religion has an independent place; indeed, without religion 'there is no ultimate solution of the philosophical problem.'[134]

Franks sides with those who find Schleiermacher's understanding of religious experience as unduly pantheistic, and he notes Ritschl's criticism that it is 'too aesthetic: it is too little distinguishable from the sense of beauty as the harmony of the cosmos. Hence Ritschl's emphasis upon God as the supreme moral personality

---

[131] R. S. Franks, 'The present relations between philosophy and theology,' 53.

[132] Ibid., 56.

[133] R. S. Franks, *he Doctrine of the Trinity*, 164.

[134] Idem, 'The present relations between philosophy and theology,' 57.

and, as he puts it, 'In religion the thought of God is given.'[135] Consistent with this is Otto's insistence that in religion we know God, the *mysterium tremendum et fascinans* as the 'Entirely Other.' In reflecting thus far, Franks says that

> The above criticisms and developments of Schleiermacher's doctrine of religion to not essentially affect its value. They are rather directed to ensure its central idea, viz., the independence of religion in relation to all other modes of psychic activity. This can be secured only if religious feeling is sufficiently distinguished from aesthetic feeling, and if the uniqueness of the object of religion is adequately brought out.[136]

Franks proceeds to argue that 'Schleiermacher's philosophy need not fear comparison either with Positivism or with Hegelianism.'[137] Neither positivism nor naturalism yield an adequate doctrine of religion:

> If our knowledge is limited to the physical sciences and our morality to utilitarianism, no religion worthy of the name is possible. A religion such as Comte's is only a glorified ethic. The best that positivism can do for religion (and it is a poor best) is to be seen in the agnosticism of Spencer. But it is on the side of its ethics that positivism especially breaks down. A utilitarian morality can never explain the sense of absolute obligation which it the very foundation of true morality. Thus we have to go back to Kant to obtain a firm basis for ethics, and if we go back to Kant we must necessarily go forward again to Schleiermacher.[138]

As for the development from Kant for which Hegel is primarily responsible: while metaphysic and religion both deal with the absolute, the former 'reaches out to it along the line of pure knowledge as far as that will take it. But the other seeks it along the line of personal devotion and communion.'[139]

Franks turns next to the cleavage between the natural sciences and the philosophy of the spirit. While not denying that the values of the spirit are 'produced upon the basis of nature. They do not, nevertheless, cease to be spiritual values altogether different from the principles of nature. ... Truth, Beauty, Goodness—these supreme values transcend all their temporary embodiments and draw on the soul of man to higher and ever higher and nobler aspiration and effort.'[140] Supreme among the values, however, is the holy. Religion affords

> an experience of union with God who is the True, the Good and the Beautiful in One, and who, beyond all that, is the Holy, enhancing those noble values with a supernatural power and grace. The fullest conception of such a union with God is

[135] Ibid., 58. Franks quotes A. Ritschl, *Justification and Reconciliation*, I, 17.

[136] Ibid., 59.

[137] Ibid.

[138] Ibid., 59-60. See further on Comte's religion of humanity and utilitarianism, Alan P. F. Sell, *Mill on God*, ch. 3.

[139] Ibid., 60-61.

[140] Ibid., 62-3, 66.

> seen in the Christian idea of the Kingdom of God, which is that of a life abidingly true and real, ethically good and satisfyingly harmonious, entirely sustained by the grace of God.[141]

It thus appears that religion intuitively has already attained the unity which philosophy is perpetually seeking. Whereas the natural sciences deal with aspects of the whole, religion affords an imaginative view of the world which interprets the whole. Theology, which 'begins as an analysis of religious experience, ... widens out into a view of the world.'[142] Theology sets out from the sphere of religion, philosophy from that of science, and sometimes their paths do not cross. But 'when partial knowledge gives place to perfect knowledge ... their alliance [will be] absolutely firm and sure.'[143]

A few reflections are in order at this point. First, Franks does well to underline the fact that when Schleiermacher defines religion as the feeling of absolute dependence, he is not thinking in terms of subjective emotion only, still less of 'cosy glows.' It is experience with an objective ground: it is an experience *of* God.[144] Secondly, it is clear that Franks retains what, at the time he was writing, was being regarded as the 'older' view of the nature of philosophy and its relations to religion. He is some way from regarding philosophy as simply the 'humble' task of investigating the informal logic or ordinary language, for example, though, as we have seen, he is appreciative of that activity; it is just that he thinks that philosophy has a wider brief than that. Thirdly, I wonder whether there is not a contradiction in Franks's hostility to all things Barthian on the one hand, and his desire to carve out an utterly independent place for religion *vis à vis* 'all other modes of psychic activity'[145] on the other? He certainly seems uncritically to adopt Otto's view of God's 'Wholly other-ness'—the very thing he objects to in Barth.

In May 1928 Franks delivered three lectures at King's College, London. In the following year these were published under the title, *The Metaphysical Justification of Religion*.[146] He here recapitulates and expands many of the ideas to which I have already drawn attention. In the first lecture he once again contends for the necessity of a metaphysic of religion that justifies the practice of developing theology on the basis of religious experience. He argues that 'religious experience is a particular form of experience in general.'[147] Experience, he says, implies the subject-object relation, and it yields 'a form of knowledge [which is] not yet related to the ultimate grounds of thought and being.'[148] He follows C. H. Weisse[149] in holding that the only way

---

[141] Ibid., 67.

[142] Ibid., 69.

[143] Ibid., 70.

[144] See further Alan P. F. Sell, *Confessing and Commending the Faith*, 337-341; idem, *Theology in Turmoil*, 15-20.

[145] R. S. Franks, 'The present relations between philosophy and theology,' 59.

[146] Idem, 'Towards a metaphysic of religion' is a foretaste of this book.

[147] Idem, *The Metaphysical Justification of Religion*, 5.

[148] Ibid., 11.

in which conflicts over the meaning of religious experience can be overcome is by proceeding from descriptive psychology to epistemology and metaphysics. This is the lesson of Weisse's master, Hegel, namely, that 'experience only truly furnishes us with knowledge, when it can be included in a system.'[150] For all the help it offers, the psychological account of religious experience is too subjective. As soon as we raise the question of the validity of acquired knowledge we cannot but face the question of the objective reality of its content. Psychology itself cannot fail to notice that 'the claim to possess objective knowledge is very vital to religion.'[151] Franks introduces Karl Heim as one who, in face of Feuerbach's view that religion is no more than a projection of human ideals, has seen the need to move beyond psychology to epistemology and the metaphysical justification of religion. Indeed, says Franks, we ought to hear much more of him in Britain, for 'His theology would do us much more good than the Barthianism, which is now so loudly proclaimed upon the housetops.'[152] In the line of Weisse and Heim, Franks concludes his first lecture with the recommendation that

> To get on to solid ground we must have recourse to metaphysics, to first principles of thought, which are also first principles of being. Our epistemology of religion must end either in utter scepticism or in a metaphysic of religion, which will assure us of the objective ground of religious knowledge, and thus finally deliver us from the circle of mere subjectivity.[153]

Franks opens his second lecture with the claim that in the wake of Schleiermacher psychology took a wrong course in supposing that it was self-sufficient. This was not Schleiermacher's own view. On the contrary, as we have already seen, Schleiermacher's position was grounded in metaphysics, and Franks reiterates the point. He now adds that in his *Ethics* Schleiermacher applies his scheme to concrete experience:

> The notion which has now become dominant is that of the highest good, or, in other words, the view of the world has become *teleological*. The notion of the universe as the unity implied by knowledge and action and discerned in religious feeling, gives place to the idea of the world as an ever developing unity of Nature and Reason. Nature means the development, so far as it has gone. Reason points the way of further development towards the end, which is the highest good.[154]

The end may be described in a variety of ways, but 'the highest notion of all is that of the Kingdom of God, as including ... both complete knowledge and complete mastery of the world, but realizing both through the full development of individual

---

149 Christian Hermann Weisse (1801-1866), German philosopher-theologian.
150 R. S. Franks, *The Metaphysical Justification of Religion*, 18.
151 Ibid., 36.
152 Ibid., 38. Karl Heim (1874-1958), German theologian.
153 Ibid., 40.
154 Ibid., 55.

spirits.'[155] Unlike Weisse and Heim, Ritschl, Kaftan[156] and James[157] uprooted psychology from its metaphysical background, and

> When Ritschl and the Ritschlians proclaimed the watchword, "Theology without metaphysics," they were in fact side-tracking religion, though it was the last thing they meant to do. When James sought to substitute for theology a psychology of the religious experience, and for a metaphysical apologetic of religion a justification of it by the pragmatic test, he also was turning religion into a side-track.[158]

In the absence of an epistemology and a metaphysic, Franks insists, we have no defence against the charge of psychologism, that is, the view that religion is illusion.

There follows a discussion of the True, the Good, the Beautiful and the Holy in the context of a teleological view of the world, his case being that

> religion, when metaphysically understood, is a synthesis of the True and the Good, not only in their common Ground, which is the Holy or Divine, but also in their resulting harmony, which, in and for itself, is the Beautiful, but, as it appears in religion, is subordinated to the Holy, just as are the True and the Good.[159]

Although giving great credence to Schleiermacher's view of religion as the feeling of absolute dependence, Franks introduces an important qualification, thus:

> religion is never merely a feeling of absolute dependence. It includes also a moment of knowledge and a moment of activity, subordinated to the feeling and bound together by it. There is in religion, not only a belief in the reality of God, but also a longing for His salvation, which, even if it be satisfied in part, strains beyond all present enjoyment to a satisfaction still fuller and richer, to a pure joy in God and in the final harmony of His universe. ... The movement of the world as a whole is from God as Source to God as Salvation. It is just because we are finite and imperfect, that we cannot yet see the whole motion of the tremendous process.[160]

In his concluding lecture Franks sums up his argument, and sees to defend his position against objectors. Some, for example, might ask whether his speculation bears any relation to the facts of nature and history. This, he replies, 'is a demand for the shifting of the court of appeal from the *a priori* to the *a posteriori*,' and such confirmation can have only a secondary importance, for 'A metaphysic can never merely rest upon facts, but *only upon facts as valued*.'[161] Moreover, 'There is no

---

[155] Ibid., 55-6.
[156] Julius Wilhelm Kaftan (1848-1926), German theologian.
[157] William James (1842-1910), American philosopher.
[158] R. S. Franks, *The Metaphysical Justification of Religion*, 57.
[159] Ibid., 79.
[160] Ibid., 82-3, 84.
[161] Ibid., 93.

sufficient solution of the practical problem of life apart from that of the theoretical problem of the unity of the Values.'[162] In the course of demonstrating that unity Franks once again doffs his cap to Otto's 'Altogether Other.'[163] He believes that 'Our metaphysic serves to bind experience together in the closest possible way. Not only is individual experience universalized through its participation in the Values, but the Values themselves are universalized by participation in the Holy.'[164] His final point is that 'the ultimate Unity of the Universe has its nearest analogy in the ultimate unity of our own personality.'[165] This, he thinks, is the point to which Schleiermacher ought to have been led, but his strong focus upon religion as implying a feeling of absolute dependence precluded this. In the first edition of his *Speeches*, however, he did come within reach of the point when he described religion 'as a feeling and intuition of the Whole. In this original expression of his view it comes out clearly, that the religious attitude is not simply feeling, but is a unique union of the theoretic and the emotional attitudes.'[166] After all, 'Dependence implies more than feeling, it implies *trust*, a form of experience in which the votive element is included.'[167] Taking a further step, he suggests that 'the unity of our own being, which we seem to realize in our moments of religious insight, is a true reflection of the Unity of the Universe.'[168] If this is so 'religion is justified in holding that God is personal, even though we have to admit, that there is an infinite difference between personality in Him and in us.'[169] This insight comes through faith, or trust. As Luther said, '"These two belong together, faith and God." They belong together, because faith unifies and achieves our personality by its *rapport* with the Personality, that unifies the Universe.'[170]

I sum up Franks's philosophical position by referring to two more of his reviews. The first reference will recapitulate Franks's stance in relation to faith, reason and metaphysics; the second will indicate his indebtedness, as a liberal evangelical theologian, to modern biblical criticism, and will lead us into his doctrinal writings.

While welcoming the way in which John Baillie, in his book, *Our Knowledge of God*, distances himself from Barth and Brunner by maintaining that in humanity the *imago dei* is not utterly defaced; and while agreeing that we have an immediate knowledge of God 'in the moral religion which is the true religion',[171] Franks questions the absence of metaphysical justification in Baillie's book. 'Even the

---

[162] Ibid., 101.
[163] Ibid., 105.
[164] Ibid., 112.
[165] Ibid., 124-5.
[166] Ibid., 125.
[167] Ibid., 126.
[168] Ibid., 127.
[169] Ibid., 127-8.
[170] Ibid., 128. Franks quotes Luther's *Greater Catechism*, Exposition of the First Commandment, 3.
[171] CQ, XXVIII no. 1, January 1940, 98.

profound experience of religion needs to be related to the rest of experience before the mind can be satisfied,'[172] he declares. Indeed, 'the religious man is truly religious when he seeks for the intellectual justification of what he most assuredly believes. The search for such justification is one form of the service of God, Who gave man not only a heart that feels, but also a mind that thinks.'[173]

In *The Glass of Vision*, Austin Farrer argues that the knowledge of God is partly by means of analogies drawn from natural phenomena, but in its highest form it is supernatural, and is conveyed to human being through biblical imagery. Franks enters one caveat into his generally positive review of this book: 'I cannot accept the ban put upon the criticism of [the Bible's] images on the plea that they are supernaturally given. ... At a conference in Oxford many years ago a speaker made an indelible impression on my mind by suggesting that the right thing to do with a creed was not to reflect upon it, but to *sing* it! Dr. Farrer does not go to that length; but I am afraid that his argument tends in the same direction.'[174]

I suspect that we are now sufficiently apprised of Franks's general philosophical stance as it bears upon questions of reason, faith, experience and metaphysics; and perhaps also sufficiently alerted to some of his intellectual foes, to be able to approach his more theological writings with some confidence.

III

It is no exaggeration to say that the predominant theme which runs throughout Franks's theological writings is that of the atonement, the work of Christ. I have already shown that his theological work was underpinned by considerable philosophical reflection, and I now claim that, to a degree not always found in systematic theologians, his constructive doctrinal work was firmly grounded in biblical studies. Thus in 1908 he contributed the volume on *The New Testament Doctrines of Man, Sin and Salvation* to the series of *Century Bible Handbooks* edited by Walter F. Adeney. Franks's book is a model of lucid compression. As befits the series in which it appears, the emphasis is upon description rather than detailed textual analysis, but Franks shows himself remarkably *au fait* with what at the time were regarded as the positive results of biblical criticism, and he is particularly indebted to R. H. Charles's article on 'Eschatology' in the *Encyclopaedia Biblica*, as well as to a number of German scholars. His title notwithstanding, he wisely and entirely appropriately opens with chapters on the Old Testament and later Jewish reflections on his themes, and then proceeds from the teaching of Jesus in the synoptic gospels, through the speeches of Peter in Acts, the epistles and Revelation, concluding with the gospel and epistles of John. He pays particular attention to future or eschatological salvation, because of the prominence of this emphasis in

---

172 Ibid.

173 Ibid.

174 CQ, XXVII no. 2, April 1949, 171.

later doctrinal developments, and because this was the route by which the approach to the doctrine came to be spiritualized.

The social—Israel, the Church—and the personal aspects of salvation are in view throughout, and Franks shows how they are united in the teaching of Jesus, in whose mind the idea of salvation is inseparable from the ideas of the Fatherhood and kingdom of God. God's righteousness is brought within Jesus's understanding of God's Fatherhood, and 'God's omnipotence is at the disposal of His fatherly nature, and carries out its ends.'[175] Franks does not doubt that Jesus thought of himself as the Messiah and of the kingdom of God as not only future, but as present. Indeed, the idea of present salvation is 'the peculiar jewel in the teaching of Jesus.'[176] The correlate of the divine Fatherhood is the sonship of those who 'repent and believe the good news'—a quotation from Mark 1: 11 which Franks does not hesitate to say is 'Not strictly accurate. Faith is not with Jesus a condition of salvation, but rather the subjective realisation of salvation, whether of future salvation as hope, or of present salvation as experience.'[177] Righteousness, a matter of the heart and motive and not simply of external obedience, is likewise a condition of entry to the kingdom—not in the sense of Jewish legalistic thought according to which the kingdom is earned by righteousness—the kingdom is always God's gift; but in the sense that the kingdom is one of righteousness, and 'righteousness is a chief blessing of the kingdom.'[178] Jesus's attitude to sin is practical rather than theoretical, and his teaching contains no doctrine of original sin. He has no illusions as to the seriousness of sin, the forgiveness of which is among the chief blessings of the kingdom. Although in one place (Matthew 15: 24) Jesus appears to limit his mission to his own people, there is an implicit universalism in much of what he says, and this becomes explicit as when he declares that salvation is for Jews and Gentiles alike (Luke 13: 29). Whether in relation to present or future salvation, 'There is no entrance to the kingdom apart from Jesus.'[179] Moreover, 'Jesus ... views his whole life as one of service, the climax of which is his death.'[180] He gives his live 'a ransom for many', by which Franks understands that by his death Jesus atones 'for all the members of the kingdom of God.'[181] Lest this appear an unduly restrictive interpretation, given that I John 1: 2 speaks of Jesus's death as a propitiation for the sins of the whole world, Franks explains that

> Since Jesus offers His death, not for a definite number like Eleazar,[182] but for the indefinite 'many', who become members of the kingdom of God, it is clear that the

[175] R. S. Franks, *Man, Sin and Salvation*, 44.
[176] Ibid., 47.
[177] Ibid., 49-50; cf. 117-18.
[178] Ibid., 53.
[179] Ibid., 69.
[180] Ibid.
[181] Ibid., 73.
[182] Cf. ibid., 38, where the reference is to II Maccabees 7:37, 38; IV Maccabees 6:28, 17:20-28.

merely external idea of substitutionary sacrifice, such as we find in Maccabees, is transcended. If Christ's atonement avails only for those who are brought into the kingdom ... then it is evident that there must be some deep-lying connection between the atonement and the personal influence of the Saviour.[183]

In Franks's view, Mark's account of the Last Supper[184] is 'perhaps the richest of all presentations of the efficacy of the death of Jesus,'[185] containing as it does the ideas of covenant, communion, and the thought that 'the salvation which Jeremiah prophesied as future is now realised as present, being mediated by the sacrifice of Christ, which establishes the kingdom of God, as the sacrifice of Moses established God's first covenant with Israel.'[186] All of which underlines the point that 'the external idea of substitution requires to be transcended, before we arrive at Christ's own view of His death as an atonement', and that 'subjective conditions required to be fulfilled before the death of Jesus is efficacious as an atonement.'[187]

Although the speeches of Peter in the Acts of the Apostles make it clear that forgiveness may be enjoyed in the present, the emphasis is upon that future salvation which is assured through the death and resurrection of Jesus. With Paul, salvation is at once the work of God and of Jesus, as it was in the teaching of Jesus himself. While Paul has a good deal to say about future salvation, it is in connection with present salvation that his 'originality especially appears.'[188] Present salvation is not 'an *anticipation* of future', but 'future salvation tends to be regarded as the *completion* of present salvation.'[189] Concerning this life,

It is ... the antithesis of sin and salvation which, in its various forms, gives its peculiar stamp to Paul's thought. ... [I]n the Epistle to the Romans [Paul] balances all that he says of salvation with antithetic teaching on sin, and, what is more, does this in such a way that the doctrine of sin comes first and the doctrine of salvation follows. [Hence] we recognise in Paul the precursor of the usual method of Christian theology, whether Catholic or Protestant.[190]

In Paul's writings Franks finds both a theory of sin that derives it from Adam's fall, and a philosophical or experimental theory, which derives it from the inherent sinfulness of the flesh. He proceeds to outline Paul's position on the law and punishment, and then turns in more detail to the apostle's view of present salvation. Paul opposes justification by works to justification by grace (albeit the term 'justification' is not found in Colossians and Ephesians), and Franks regards the term 'justification by faith' as 'simply a pregnant expression describing the mode of

---

183 Ibid., 74.
184 Mark 14:22-25.
185 R. S. Franks, *Man, Sin and Salvation*, 75.
186 Ibid., 76.
187 Ibid., 77.
188 Ibid., 82.
189 Ibid., 98.
190 Ibid., 99.

justification by grace.'[191] Paul regards both the death and the resurrection of Christ as events which include the death and resurrection Christians. Christ, says Paul (Romans 4:24), was 'raised for our justification.' This, Franks concludes, 'finally makes impossible the identification of Paul's view of the atonement with the transactional view, according to which the atonement consists simply in the payment of the debt of sin by Christ's death.'[192] This is not to deny that the death was an expiation for sin, but rather means that 'in His death and resurrection He was inclusive of His people, and that His resurrection was equally necessary with His death to our justification.'[193] Paul's understanding of salvation includes the idea of the believer's deliverance from both the guilt and the power of sin, and this by virtue of the believer's union with Christ, and the work of the Holy Spirit. Paul's teaching that the Spirit is 'the abiding power of Christian character, whose fruits were the virtues, the chief of which was love ... is one of Paul's greatest achievements ...'[194] Present justification notwithstanding, the final judgment is not done away; on the contrary, Christian are urged to be ready to meet it. In Colossians and Ephesians the power of the law is represented as that of hostile angels, while Christ's death, though it is called a sacrifice in Ephesians, is not a propitiatory sacrifice, but a freewill offering accepted because of the love which motivated it. Again, in Ephesians the social aspect of salvation is emphasised: 'It is the Church as a whole for which Christ sacrifices Himself ... [and] to which the Spirit is given. In a word, it is the Church as a whole that is the sphere of salvation, and individuals are saved by membership of it.[195]

In the Pastoral Epistles the place which 'faith' occupies in Pauline thought is taken by 'godliness', while in I Peter eschatology is to the fore and, in place of the mystical union of the believer with Christ, we have faith conceived as a belief in God's promises which is sustained by a living hope grounded in Christ's resurrection. The Letter to the Hebrews brings to the fore the conviction that Christians in this world are already 'partakers of the Messianic salvation',[196] and the worth to God of Christ's sacrifice is said to consist in the Son's obedience. In Revelation, salvation in its future aspect is almost entirely dominant, while in the Letter of James there is no reference to Christ's work. Both Jude and II Peter emphasise the Parousia, when mercy and eternal life will be granted to believers, while the ungodly will be adversely judged. According the II Peter the Parousia is delayed in order to allow more time for repentance. Finally, in the Johannine writings present salvation is regarded as sonship, though, unlike Paul, John does not use the term 'adoption'. To a greater degree than Paul, John thinks of salvation as being union with God. It is, moreover, a union the reality of which is to be shown through the ethical fruit of those who claim it. Both John and Paul agree that 'the

---

[191] Ibid., 118.
[192] Ibid., 121-2.
[193] Ibid., 122.
[194] Ibid., 124.
[195] Ibid., 135.
[196] Ibid., 149.

ground of salvation is the love of God.'[197] John emphasises Christ's role as light and life—indeed, he communicates the life of God to people. As with Paul, so here: the importance of faith is demonstrated, though John generally used the term 'belief', and, in harmony with the synoptic gospels, it is faith in the sense of trust that John has in mind.

There is much more in Franks's densely-packed handbook, but enough has been said to indicate his general approach. We might also note that in his more technical theological works Franks does not hesitate to refer to conclusions reached in this volume which was intended for a general readership.

Before coming to those more detailed studies of the work of Christ it will be advantageous to turn to introduce Franks's paper on 'The person of Christ in the light of modern scholarship', which he read in Manchester during the centenary meetings of the Congregational Union of England and Wales on 7 October 1931. The reason for this apparent digression is that this paper will remind us of Franks's liberal evangelical approach to the Bible, especially as that concerns the person of the one to whose work he devoted such a large part of his life. He begins from the assertion that whereas our relation to God is the foundation of Christianity, 'it is Jesus Christ Who brings us into communion with God; and what we actually have in Him is all bound up most intimately with what we find in Jesus.'[198] By modern scholarship Franks means, 'the principle of free critical investigation'[199]—something which neither the fundamentalist who stands on the authority of the Bible nor the Catholic who stands on the authority of the Church will permit.

According to the ancient creeds Christ's human nature is impersonal, for 'the personality of the Incarnate Word is that of the Eternal Word who became incarnate.'[200] Modern theology, however, distinguishes between the Jesus of history and the Christ of faith. This distinction has its roots in the separation of the gospels from the epistles which was effected by the English deists—a separation that prompts us not to read back into the gospels from the epistles. There is the distinction between the synoptic gospels and that of John which, while by no means devoid of history, is predominantly theological whereas the synoptics contain 'a nucleus of irreducible fact; and the synoptic source analysis and the method of form-history, which forbid us to think that we can derive a consecutive life of Jesus from the four gospels, singly or in combination. Rudolf Bultmann, 'probably the most outstanding representative of the new school',[201] holds that there are two irreducible facts which modern criticism yields, and a third which is more doubtful. The two are Jesus's ethic and his eschatological expectation; the third is his Messianic claim. Franks has no hesitation in including the third as an 'irreducible and stubborn' fact in Jesus's life. The ethic is an irreducible fact because of its originality and uniqueness; the eschatology because when the Christian Church faced the problem that the world

[197] Ibid., 172.

[198] Idem, 'The person of Christ in the light of modern scholarship,' 27.

[199] Ibid.

[200] Ibid., 28.

[201] Ibid., 31. Rudolf Bultmann (1884-1976) German biblical scholar and theologian.

had no speedily ended, as had been expected, only the memory that Christ had uttered his eschatological sayings could have kept them in the gospels. As to the Messianic claim: no doubt as Jesus construed this his view was at odds with that current among the Jews, but this claim 'is the only reasonable explanation of His execution'[202] [though elsewhere Franks says that it was persistence in the loving service of men that brought death upon the Messiah'—surely an insufficient view of the matter.[203]]

The upshot is that 'the Christology of the creeds ... is not consistent with what we know of the Jesus of History.' In passing, it is interesting to note that Franks immediately adds, 'I do not think that that need trouble Congregationalists, who have continually urged their independence of a creed. We need not feel secretly bound to the Creeds, whose authority we do not openly acknowledge.'[204] The point of conflict between modern scholarship and the creeds is the genuine humanity of Jesus, for

> The correct logical consequence of the doctrine of the Creeds [with their idea that the Logos assumed an impersonal human nature], is that Jesus was omniscient and well as omnipotent. ... This ... is precisely the Fundamentalist notion of Jesus ... which is bound to put some artificial explanation upon His unfulfilled prophecies of the speedy advent of the Kingdom.[205]

Franks is at pains to point out that to abandon the creeds is not necessarily to abandon the doctrine of the divinity of Christ. He is 'the perfect and complete Revelation of God within humanity.' His divinity does not involve an abridgment of his humanity: he is 'Divine in the peculiar *quality* and *content* of His humanity, which distinguishes it from the humanity of the rest of us sinful men.'[206] We should be grateful for the way in which the creeds have preserved the doctrine of Christ's divinity throughout the ages, but if their propositions are not longer tenable as they stand, can we modernize 'the primitive Christian conception of the Messiahship of Jesus?'[207]

If we are to bring together the Christ of history and the Christ of faith we need an explanation of how the historical Jesus became the object of the Church's faith, but one which does not uproot the faith from history. Franks thinks that the best way to proceed is to take

> a firm hold upon the earliest and most original confession of the Christian Church: *Jesus is the Messiah*. ... The Messiahship of Jesus means that He is the earthly representative of God and God's plenipotentiary in His Kingdom. The meaning of Messiahship is developed in the two great complementary titles, *Son of God* and *Son of Man*. The first name ascribes to Jesus a unique and perfect filial

---

202 Ibid., 32.
203 CQ, XVI no. 1, January 1938, 101-102.
204 R. S. Franks, 'The person of Christ in the light of modern scholarship,' 33.
205 Ibid.
206 Ibid., 34.
207 Ibid., 36.

> consciousness. The second describes Him as the Ideal Man, Who is the Divinely appointed head of Humanity. ... Jesus is the Perfect and Ideal Man Who all throughout His life yielded Himself absolutely in obedience to God in such a way that His whole thought an feeling were one with the Spirit of God, and that He became the human organ of God's saving manifestation in the world. As such a human representative of God He is eternally one with God and now dwells among us through the Spirit of God, which is His Spirit also. Jesus does not hide God from us, or come between us and God. We see God in Him. We know God as Our Father, because His Fatherhood is reflected in the Sonship of Jesus, the Christ. ... Jesus is Divine because we find God uniquely in Him.[208]

Clearly, we are intended to understand the concluding sentence as referring to the ground of our testimony, not to the cause of Christ's divinity.

Having thus considered who Franks thinks the Saviour is, we may now turn to his studies of Christ's work. The principal items for consideration are the two-volume book, *A History of the Doctrine of the Work of Christ* (1918) and the Dale Lectures for 1933, *The Atonement* (1934). I shall supplement these with references to other papers and reviews by Franks. Clearly, I cannot proceed through the two large volumes in any exhaustive way, nor is this necessary. My objective is to focus upon Franks's thought rather than upon that of others. I am helped by the fact that in the preface to *The Atonement* Franks informs his readers that the major influences upon his thought have been Alexander of Hales (c.1186-1245), Schleiermacher, C. H. Weisse, Ritschl, Harnack, Troeltsch and Karl Heim. With regard to two of these he testifies thus:

> Brought up in the older evangelicalism, supported as it was by the doctrine of the infallibility of the Bible, I experienced as a theological student the full force of modern Biblical criticism, and had to cast about for a fresh foundation and new statement of the Christian faith. At this stage two books came into my hands, Ritschl's *Justification and Reconciliation*, and Harnack's *History of Dogma*. Mutually supporting each other, together they came to me as a revelation ... I found in Ritschl's *Justification and Reconciliation* the key to Holy Scripture, which Calvin's *Institutes* had been to my evangelical forefathers. ... I still think that Ritschl's great work is the most useful key to the Scriptures for the Christian ministry [though he came to regret Ritschl's divorce of theology from metaphysics].[209]

My plan in introducing Franks's *magnum opus* will be focus primarily upon his conclusions regarding the Eastern, Medieval, Reformation and Modern soteriologies, and to indicate as appropriate the ways in which he has found some of the authors just named to be of assistance in the development of his own position on the atonement.

---

[208] Ibid. 36, 37, 38.

[209] Idem, *The Atonement*, vii-viii.

Franks's major work is considerably more than a textbook blow-by-blow account of a particular Christian doctrine. He has a thesis which he wishes demonstrate, namely, that 'the modern doctrine of the work of Christ ... in its most typical form, as developed by Scheliermacher and Ritschl, is no arbitrary opinion on the subject, but that the whole course of doctrinal development has led to it by an immanent necessity.'[210] Under the rubric of 'the work of Christ' he includes 'the saving effects of Christ's Incarnation, Life, Passion, Death, and Resurrection.'[211] Having already sketched the biblical background to the doctrine in *The New Testament Doctrines of Man, Sin and Salvation*, he confines himself here to the ecclesiastical development of his chosen doctrine (or complex of doctrines). Moreover, he concentrates his attention upon those authors who have sought 'to reduce the doctrine to systematic unity'[212] and to analyse the various methods they have employed to achieve this. He is further guided by the conviction that the particular doctrine must be studied from the point of view of the total organism of Christian doctrine—a lesson learned from Harnack's *History of Dogma*.[213] In addition to Harnack, Franks expresses his indebtedness to the works of Weisse, Kaftan and Heim.

Of particular interest in Franks's discussion of Eastern theology is his observation that while Irenaeus's doctrine of recapitulation is Pauline in origin (Ephesians 1: 10), 'It is ... a development which carries us beyond Pauline doctrine, when Irenaeus goes back behind Christ's death and resurrection and views salvation as already given in the Incarnation.'[214] The idea, says Franks, is 'fundamentally Johannine' (John 1: 1-18; I John 1: 1-4), except that whereas 'John interprets the idea through an intellectualist mysticism, [John 17: 3], Irenaeus, while not without this interpretation, in the main like Paul in Rom. VI. 1 ff., is realistic. The Incarnation is thought of as a ferment in humanity which leavens it with incorruption and immortality.'[215] Athanasius follows suit, and so, in the West, does Bernard of Clairvaux—except that with Bernard, God's saving entrance in humanity is not conceived physically, as it was by the Greek thinkers who emphasized life and incorruption, but more subjectively and psychologically: God's coming in patience and love inspires similar attitudes in us. [216]

I may here remark that in Irenaeus's teaching at this point we have a stimulus to a theological emphasis which, when it percolates through modern idealism in its more pantheistic expressions designed to side-step adverse historical criticism, can have the effect of uprooting the Cross from history and transmogrifying the complex of atonement doctrines with which Franks is concerned into a set of ideas for which

---

[210] Idem, *A History of the Doctrine of the Work of Christ*, I, vii.

[211] Ibid., 1.

[212] Ibid., 3.

[213] Adolf Carl Gustav Adolf Von Harnack (1851-1930), German theologian.

[214] R. S. Franks, *A History of the Doctrine of the Work of Christ*, I, 45. Irenaeus (c.130-c.200), Bishop of Lyons.

[215] Ibid.

[216] Ibid., 193. Bernard (1090-1153), Abbot of Clairvaux.

universality is claimed. His indebtedness to Ritschl's emphasis on history cautioned Franks at this point.

Indications of a further line of thought which echoes to the present day, albeit after modern humanism has banished the Incarnate Logos, are found in Clement of Alexandria's view that 'The Incarnate Logos is for us a teacher and an example only.'[217] Other Greek positions were fuller than this, but having reviewed authors from Origen[218] to John of Damascus[219] Franks finds that the Greeks arrived at no final theoretical synthesis:

> On the one hand salvation is regarded as the direct result of the Incarnation (a) as a Divine revelation, (b) as (along with the death and resurrection of Christ) a communication of life to mankind. ... On the other hand salvation is viewed as following from a certain negative pre-condition, either that of a sacrifice to God or of a price paid to the devil, a pre-condition the accomplishment of which removes the obstacles which stand in the way of God's desire to save men.[220]

Turning to the West, Franks finds a distinctly different view of the matter in the writings of Ambrose,[221] in whose thought the death of Christ is central. Indeed, 'In no Western theologian before or after is there a greater emphasis on the cross.'[222] But it is in Augustine's *Enchiridion* that we find a position which contrasts sharply with that of Greek theology:

> We breathe a different atmosphere. The presuppositions and the conclusions are alike different. The central points are no longer the physical corruption wrought by the Fall, and the Incarnation as in principle the destruction of death and the deification of humanity; but instead we have original sin, justification by grace, and the reconciliation of God by the sacrifice of Christ. The Western type of thought here asserts itself in a fundamental and most striking form.[223]

In Anselm's view human beings are made for eternal bliss, but they cannot attain this unless their sins are remitted. Justice demands that sin be punished; satisfaction must be made to God's honour relative to the weight of the sin; human beings are incompetent to render such satisfaction; hence the incarnation and the work of Christ. Anselm, says Franks,

> sets aside altogether the doctrine of redemption from the devil, though he retains in a subordinate place that of Christ's victory over him. The recapitulatory and moral theories he regards as void, unless some more solid theory can serve as a basis for

[217] Ibid., 51.

[218] Origen (c.185-c.254), Alexandrian biblical scholar and theologian.

[219] John of Damascus (c.655-c.750), Greek theologian.

[220] R. S. Franks, *A History of the Doctrine of the Work of* Christ, I, 95-6. It must therefore be a slip when on p. 260 and elsewhere Franks refers to the Greek synthesis.

[221] Ambrose (c.339-c.397), Bishop of Milan.

[222] Ibid., 109.

[223] Ibid., 125. Augustine (354-430), Bishop of Hippo Regius.

them. This solid basis Anselm finds in the doctrine that Christ made satisfaction for sin and merited salvation. This is the essence of His work, the necessity of which may be seen *a priori*. It is not unimportant, however, that Christ gave us an example: by following this we are qualified to share in His merit.[224]

Franks describes Anselm's doctrine of satisfaction and merit as 'epoch-making', and he uses the same term of Anselm's application 'to the work of Christ [of] the legal conceptions proper to the ecclesiastical penance.'[225] In summary, Anselm turns his back on the mystical idea, found in Gregory of Nyssa,[226] John of Damascus and Augustine, to the effect that the death and resurrection of Christ act as a ferment in humanity in such a way that sin and death are destroyed and righteousness and immortality are imparted. In Anselm's view Christ's death is the gift of his life to God, and it brings salvation by virtue of God's gracious acceptance of the gift. This, says Franks, 'means a theological revolution.'[227]

By contrast with Anselm, Abelard's contribution is to have 'reduced the whole process of redemption to one single clear principle, viz. the manifestation of God's love to us in Christ, which awakens an answering love in us. Our of this principle Abelard endeavours to explain all other points of view.'[228]

Since Franks himself was a convinced Abelardian, I pause here to note his later admission that in his Dale Lectures he commented upon the apparently casual and unsystematic way in which Abelard introduced his atonement doctrine. But when reviewing J. R. McCallum's translation of Abelard's *Ethics*, the alternative title of which is *Know Thyself*, he came to see that Abelard did not think merely 'in brilliant flashes of insight, but in an entirely coherent and connected way.'[229] In particular,

Abelard quarrels with the traditional Augustinian notion that man is so ruined by the fall that he has lost all power of moral choice, except in so far as a new nature is supernaturally imparted to him by grace. ... Abelard believed that whatever evil consequences the fall of Adam might have brought upon man, it had destroyed neither his reason nor his power of moral choice; so that he can still respond to the overtures of the Divine love in Christ and use the grace thus manifested in his case....

The second title, *Know Thyself*, is itself chosen to call attention to Abelard's fundamental belief that the principle of man's action is always truly in himself, and never in any power external to his own personality. Abelard here anticipates Kant and Dr. Oman. He stood in complete opposition to the Realism of his master,

[224] Ibid., 174-5.
[225] Ibid., 176. Anselm (c.1033-1109), Archbishop of Canterbury.
[226] Gregory (c.330-c.395), Bishop of Nyssa.
[227] R. S. Franks, *A History of the Doctrine of the Work of Christ*, I, 185.
[228] Ibid., 189. Peter Abelard (1079-1142/3), philosopher and theologian.
[229] CQ, XIII no. 2, April 1935, 244.

> William of Champeaux, who held that individual men were no more than accidental forms of the one true essence, man or humanity.[230]

It remains to add that while neither Anselm nor Abelard give any credence to the notion that humanity's redemption was from the devil, Abelard does formally subordinate Christ's work to the Augustinian doctrine of predestination: 'Only the elect are the objects of Christ's redeeming work; its scope is limited beforehand by the Divine decree.'[231]

Bernard of Clairvaux, though by no means unaware of the subjective aspects of Christ's work, thought (not altogether accurately) that Abelard had laid too exclusive an emphasis upon it. In Bernard's summary statement regarding the work of Christ he makes it clear that he is not in favour of a subjectivism which has no objective foundation:

> Three principal things I perceive in this work of our salvation: the pattern of humility, in which God emptied Himself: the measure of love, which He stretched even unto death, and that the death of the cross: the mystery of redemption, in which He underwent the death, which He bore. The two former of these without the last are like a picture on the void.[232]

While Bernard's objective view included the untenable notion of a ransom paid to the devil, this does not detract from the importance of the fact that his dispute with Abelard set the stage for subsequent discussions of subjectivist *versus* objectivist doctrines of the atonement. Also of importance is Bernard's conviction that it was not Christ's death as such, but the fact that he freely willed it, that pleased God—though, like Augustine and others, he does not think that the incarnation was absolutely necessary for God, though it was so from the point of view of humanity.

In contrast to the Greeks, the theologians of the West did work their way towards a theoretical synthesis concerning Christ's work, and Franks finds that Alexander of Hales was the first to present this in some detail. Alexander holds that subject to the divine predestination there was a necessity for Christ's incarnation and passion. The latter was necessitated by sin. Christ's love merited grace from his conception onwards, but his loving acts merited it in a different way. The infusion of this grace enables our good works which in turn merit salvation. But grace is also the remedy for sin, and this Christ merited by his passion alone. This, together with the resurrection, awakens faith, and the resurrection is the source of Christ's judicial power. Alongside Christ's procurement of grace is the revelation of the law, which is most fully expressed in the New Testament, and is accompanied by the dominical sacraments which convey grace to the faithful. Finally, Alexander has a place (hinted at by Athanasius) for the passion and resurrection of Christ as 'awakening faith and

---

[230] Ibid. William of Champeaux (c.1070-1131), scholastic philosopher.

[231] Idem, *A History of the Doctrine of the Work of Christ*, 192.

[232] Ibid., 199. Franks quotes Bernard's *Tractatus contra quaedam capitula errorum Abaelardi*, IX. 25.

love and stimulating to virtue.'[233] Franks concludes his summary of early Franciscan theology by remarking that in the Western scheme the sacraments are said supernaturally to convey grace, and so, in virtue of its natural psychological influence, does the incarnation as such. This leaves the following problem, namely, that

> The same thing, viz. love as the principle of action is viewed as being produced both by a supernatural and a natural cause; and therefore, inevitably, on the principle of the parsimony of reason, the one view must ultimately be reduced to the other. There remains here in fact a problem for subsequent theology, to determine which view is to predominate.[234]

What was it about Alexander of Hales that so attracted Franks? He gives his own answer in his contribution to *Amicitiae Corolla*, the *festschrift* presented to James Rendel Harris on his eightieth birthday. 'The theology of Alexander,' he declares, 'is of real interest as a theology of Christian experience before either Schleiermacher or the "Library of Constructive Theology".'[235] While Alexander found a disciple in Bonaventure, he continues, the latter was more philosophically inclined. From the time when Aquinas's less mystical and more rational system began to hold the stage, 'the experimentalism of Alexander lived on in the main outside the central stream of Christian thought among such people as the Mystics, the Anabaptists, the Quakers, the Pietists, and the Moravians, until the time of Schleiermacher ...'[236] In particular Alexander emphasises the fact that

> Theology originates by an assimilation to the Holy Spirit, who is Goodness. It is directed by the Spirit through an information from the Spirit. It leads to God by no abstract reasoning, but by the principles of fear and love and by faith in the justice and mercy of God.
>
> It is astonishing to read all these things in thirteenth-century theology. The experimental basis of theology is here. The principle of value-judgments is also present: there is the true as true and the true as the good, i.e., the truth in its moral reference. There is even Ritschl's distinction between moral value-judgments and religious value-judgments; there is the true as the moral good and the true as the good graciously given by God, or in other words, the true in its religious reference.[237]

---

[233] Ibid., 261. Athanasius (c.296-373), Bishop of Alexandria.

[234] Ibid.

[235] Idem, 'The interpretation of Holy Scripture in the theological system of Alexander of Hales,' 83.

[236] Ibid., 84.

[237] Ibid., 94-5. It is interesting to read these remarks alongside Franks's paper, 'The Christian good: its constitutive principle and validity.' In the course of this discussion (p. 501) he affirms both that God is the highest good, and yet that there are other forms of good. He then asks, 'Does the introduction of God into the notion of the Good rob them

In his concluding paragraph Franks cannot resist a further sally against Barth. In Alexander,

> The thirteenth century and the nineteenth century join hands across the intervening ages. At this moment a strong attack is being delivered by Barth and his school upon the principles of experience and of value, which are characterized as expressions of modern subjectivity. Whether the principles are right or wrong is not a matter for this essay, but the study of Alexander of Hales certainly prevents their being dismissed as an expression of *modern* subjectivity.[238]

Reverting now to the historical development of the doctrine of Christ's work, Franks observes that whereas Alexander of Hales 'hesitated between the view that the doctrines of natural theology were the antecedents and the doctrines of revelation the consequences of the intuition of God as the first truth, and the view that the doctrines of revelation were fresh truths not to be deduced by human reason from the first truth,'[239] Aquinas opted for the latter view and carefully demarcated the spheres of natural and revealed theology. Unlike Alexander, Aquinas says that by virtue of sacramental grace human beings are deified—a stance which brings him close to the Greek idea, except that he explains that the deification bestowed by Christ as God is purchased by the merit of Christ as man. In Franks's opinion the main advances made by Aquinas upon Alexander are that the former is more thorough in his use of the Bible; in his soteriology he pays greater attention to the Gospel history; and his criticisms of patristic doctrines are more thorough. He has high praise for the reason-revelation synthesis achieved by Aquinas.

Franks proceeds through the rest of the Middle Ages to the Renaissance, and then comes to the Reformation theologians. Here he finds that Calvin synthesized the thought of his contemporaries as no one else did. The most I can do here is to present Franks's succinct conclusion in his own words:

> On the one hand [Calvin] has eliminated the mediaeval element from Luther's doctrine of the sacraments [that concerning the real presence of Christ at the eucharist]; while on the other hand he has conserved Luther's religious view of the sacrament as a Gospel in act, and has not followed the merely ethical doctrine of Zwingli on this point. Again, Calvin has realized the synthetic character of Protestantism, as intended by Luther, better than Melanchthon. His view of the application of the benefits of Christ is less analytic than that of Melanchthon: the gift of the Spirit, faith, justification, and sanctification are seen to be all moments in an indivisible process, in which each implies the other. Similarly Calvin's view of Christianity as a whole is more synthetic than that of Melanchthon: law and gospel are, while distinct, realized by him as a unity as they are not by

---

of all value? Is the only true form of religion that which negates the finite? A powerful Continental school does indeed exactly tell us so.' Which 'powerful Continental school' can he possibly have had in mind?

238 Ibid., 95.

239 Idem, *A History of the Doctrine of the Work of Christ*, 263.

> Melanchthon. At this point, however, it is to be observed that Calvin, influenced by Zwingli, conceives the unity with a leaning towards making law the dominant idea, instead of following Luther's suggestion that the law is God's *opus alienum*, and another form of the Gospel. What, however, concerns us most of all in Calvin's theology, is the emergence of a new doctrine of the work of Christ, distinct from either the patristic or the mediaeval, viz. the doctrine of the threefold office [of prophet, priest and king]. This doctrine, the really characteristic Protestant doctrine of the work of Christ, is highly synthetic in character. It has not merely the value of presenting the whole work of Christ in a single view, but also of presenting it in such a manner that it shows how it terminates in the production of faith (*fiducia*) through the Gospel. It is thus of an eminently practical character: the objective aspect of the work of Christ is here duly completed by the subjective aspect.[240]

Franks admits that while in Calvin's *Institutes* the scholastic way of interspersing systematic with historical elements persists, there is also the earnest of a new conceptual unity. There is also in Calvin's writings the Greek scheme of revelation by the Logos and the destruction of sin and death by the incarnation. But this, Franks thinks, can be taken up into the historical *cum* systematic synthesis which Alexander of Hales and Aquinas began, and which Calvin carried further. Thus, 'The Protestant synthesis of the threefold office ... includes the advantages of both prior great stages of the doctrine of the work of Christ. It is worthy of note that it is altogether Calvin's own, even within Protestantism.'[241]

Franks opens Volume II of his *magnum opus* with an account of the development of Protestant scholasticism. He observes that in their doctrine of the work of Christ the Protestant divines generally accepted the idea of the passive obedience of Christ's sufferings and death and the active obedience of his life as specified in the Formula of Concord of 1580, and viewed the entire doctrine through the lens of the threefold office. The emphasis thus falls on Christ's states of humiliation and exaltation, rather than upon his saving work as such. These developments took place in the seventeenth century, and the results are sometimes disparaged under the term 'Protestant scholasticism.' Franks concedes that there was a return to scholastic methods, though Aristotle's influence was, by comparison with the medieval period, reduced; but although a greater degree of formalism followed the freer trends of the sixteenth century, Franks thinks that there is 'a real advance in the thinking out and systematizing of the theological principles of the Reformation.[242] In particular,

> The *schema* of the threefold office successfully expresses in the one doctrine of the work of Christ the whole of Christianity, and that as neither the Greek fathers nor the medieval schoolmen were able to do. For in the view of the Greek Church the work of Christ needed to be supplemented by our works; and in the mediaeval view, though it procured sacramental grace which made our works possible, it still

240 Ibid., 440-441.
241 Ibid., 443-4.
242 Ibid., II, 2.

> ultimately needed the same supplement. But in Protestantism Christ is all and does all; and the doctrine of the threefold office succeeds in so stating the work of Christ as to show this. His work as Prophet, Priest, and King is complete, and leaves no room for anything which is not simply itself in another form.[243]

In this doctrine, he continues, Protestant theology reaches a relative conclusion—not a final conclusion because medieval ideas of satisfaction are incorporated into the expression of the doctrine, and further refinements are needed.

These refinements came with the passage of time, and in particular as challenges of one kind or another had to be faced and met. These challenges included Socinianism and rationalistic Arminianism.[244] A landmark was reached when, as Franks wrote elsewhere, Grotius abandoned 'all attempts to prove any *quantitative* equivalence between what men should have suffered as punishment and what Christ actually bore'[245]—an idea which was, as we have seen, to have a significant influence upon George Payne, even though the characteristic early nineteenth-century way of accommodating the insight was not altogether satisfactory in that is tended towards a dualistic view of God's character: now as Saviour, now as Judge.

Leaving the continent for England, Franks discusses the contributions to soteriology of Richard Hooker and John Owen, than the latter of whom no seventeenth-century Congregationalist divine was more rigorous an advocate of the satisfaction theory of the atonement and particular redemption. Moving on, Franks correctly states that Locke held that the confession of Christ's Messiahship was the indispensable minimum of belief, though (a) he does not make it clear that Locke thought that this minimum belief sufficed to qualify one as a Christian: he did not think that this was all that it was necessary for Christians to believe; and (b) Franks does not in *The Atonement* explicitly state that in Locke's understanding of 'Jesus is the Messiah' a number of other doctrines coalesce, so that the phrase is of the umbrella kind, though this may be inferred from Franks's exposition.[246] In his later work, *The Doctrine of the Trinity*, he explicitly acknowledges that for Locke the term 'Messiah' includes 'as its concomitants belief in [Christ's] resurrection, rule and coming to judgment.'[247] He rightly sees that Locke's view of different stages in New Testament expressions of doctrine we have a harbinger of modern biblical criticism. It is also noteworthy that when writing of Thomas Chubb the deist, Franks brings to the fore that moral protest against the ways in which some Christian doctrines, especially that of the work of Christ, had come to be expressed: 'Socinus and Chubb,' he writes, 'agree in repudiating the orthodox doctrine [that

---

[243] Ibid., 5.

[244] The adjective will sufficiently distinguish this form of Arminianism—the Arminianism of the head, from Wesley's Arminianism of the heart, for which, in relation to Calvinism, see Alan P. F. Sell, *The Great Debate*.

[245] CQ, XVIII no. 2, July 1940, 215.

[246] See further Alan P. F. Sell, *John Locke and the Eighteenth-Century Divines*, 286-201.

[247] R. S. Franks, *The Doctrine of the Trinity*, 147.

Christ rendered satisfaction to God by being punished in our stead]. But their reasons are different. Instead of referring to the legal impossibilities, which Socinus finds in the orthodox theory, Chubb rests his case solely on its moral incompatibility with the idea of God's mercy.'[248] This latter idea was to play an increasingly significant part in the renovation of Christian doctrine.

Passing over interesting discussions of Butler and Jonathan Edwards, and noticing that whereas present-day Methodist scholars (especially American ones) are eager for us to see in John Wesley a theologian of some weight, Franks does not find it necessary to mention that worthy anywhere in the book, we come to the nineteenth century. Franks thinks that 'Speaking generally, we may say that German theology alone in this modern period is fully systematic', whereas that of Britain and America is largely 'monographic.'[249] The result is that to the Germans, especially to Schleiermacher and Ritschl, we owe 'the fourth great doctrinal synthesis', the modern synthesis, which succeeds those of the Greeks, the medieval period and the seventeenth-century Protestants. In the modern synthesis are taken up the evangelical experience of the Reformers, Socinian and Enlightenment criticisms, and 'the new philosophy of self-consciousness' which appeared 'first in the form of the Kantian criticism.'[250]

Fundamental to the new synthesis, as is transparently clear in the writings of Schleiermacher and Ritschl, is 'the experience of communion with God in Christ.'[251] Compared with the earlier syntheses, the Bible is not generally allegorized or plundered for proof texts, but is rather viewed in the light of 'the principles of the Biblical religion.'[252] Not, indeed, that the views of the contributors to the modern synthesis are entirely homogeneous. On the contrary, Schleiermacher, Franks reminds us, has a metaphysical basis to his theology where Ritschl does not. In particular, 'Ritschl's statement that religious truth is given in the form of value judgments is unsatisfactory, unless it be added that in these judgments we touch reality.'[253] For his part, however, Ritschl, in his doctrine of God draws much more upon the New Testament idea than does Schleiermacher, whose doctrine of God begins independently of the intuition of God in Christ. Moreover Ritschl makes an advance upon Schleiermacher by bringing the Kingdom of God to the fore in his theology.[254] The two are at one, however, in taking the turn to experience, and where the work of Christ is concerned this is of importance for whereas the older juristic theological method 'considered punishment in abstraction from its relation to

---

[248] Idem, *A History of the Doctrine of the Work of Christ*, II, 173. I have elsewhere argued that this moral protest is a significant gift of the Enlightenment (so frequently despised by certain theologians) to theology. See Alan P. F. Sell, *Enlightenment, Ecumenism, Evangel*, ch. 3.

[249] Ibid., 208.

[250] Ibid., 365.

[251] Ibid., 366.

[252] Ibid.

[253] Ibid.

[254] Cf. idem, *The Doctrine of the Trinity*, 171.

consciousness', now 'it is only in the consciousness of guilt that evils appear as penal.'[255] Franks welcomes the way in which Ritschl subordinates the category of representation to that of revelation in his account of the work of Christ: 'It is from the standpoint of fellowship with God, implying His revelation to us in Christ, that we think of Christ as our Representative and Substitute'—a position with which Schleiermacher is in substantial agreement.

Franks's second volume ends with brief chapters on a number of British writers and the American theologian, Bushnell. The briefest flavour of their soteriologies as construed by Franks must here suffice. Coleridge, like Schleiermacher, places redemption by Christ as the centre of Christianity, and understands redemption as regeneration. Both Thomas Erskine of Linlathen and F. D. Maurice eschew substitutionary theories of the atonement in favour of the idea of Christ as our representative, with the difference that Erskine says that in his incarnation Christ accepted God's condemnation of sin, whereas Maurice emphasises Christ's surrender to God as revelatory of 'the true sinless root of humanity.'[256] Both Schleiermacher and McLeod Campbell think of salvation in terms of fellowship with God, but whereas the former thinks in terms of the impartation of God-consciousness, 'Campbell, like Ritschl, is more Scriptural, in that he conceives God as the Father, and fellowship with Him as the life of sonship.'[257] Both Schleiermacher and Ritschl rejected Thomasius's idea of Christ's vicarious penitence as violating the idea of Christ's personal innocence—the sinless one has no need to [even logically cannot] repent—but Campbell made this a distinctive aspect of his doctrine.

In Franks's opinion, 'Bushnell has perhaps more than any other modern theologian reproduced the spirit of Abelard's doctrine of the work of Christ.'[258] Furthermore, he takes account of Christ's total life history in expounding the doctrine of his work. Like Ritschl he emphasises the way in which Christ fulfils the demand of the moral law, and is 'more "teleological" and less "aesthetic" in his view of the work of Christ than Schleiermacher.'[259] The focus in R. W. Dale's Congregational Lecture on *The Atonement* is upon the death of Christ as the objective ground on which human beings are absolved from sin and delivered from hell, and upon the love of the Father for the Son which gives unique value to Christ's work. Christ's death vindicates the divine righteousness. According to Dale, says Franks, 'We have not ... here to do with a pardon of sin compensated by the punishment of an innocent man: it is God Himself in Christ who endures the suffering instead of inflicting it.'[260] In this saving work Christ stands as humanity's representative. Franks notes that although Dale defends penal substitution, he does it without venturing into ideas of equivalence of substituted punishment, and is thus, perhaps, closer to the position of Ralph Wardlaw and George Payne than he realizes.

---

[255] Idem, *A History of the Doctrine of the Work of Christ*, II, 368.

[256] Ibid., 391.

[257] Ibid., 400.

[258] Ibid., 402.

[259] Ibid., 414.

[260] Ibid., 419.

In his criticism of Dale we begin to see more clearly how Franks himself would proceed with the doctrine of the atonement. He thinks that in Dale's account one idea, namely Christ's substitutionary death, predominates over all others. Hence,

> There remains the question, how the idea is modified, when it is associated with and controlled by, other ideas, and above all the question, as to which idea is to dominate all the rest. If, for example, the idea of the Fatherhood of God, or, again, that of the Kingdom of God, is to be supreme, then all that Dale says of the New Testament may be true, and yet in the ultimate construction of Christianity as a religion the idea of substitutionary sacrifice may emerge radically modified by the wider context into which it is brought.[261]

The volume concludes with short notices of the positions of two Anglicans: Westcott, whom Franks finds to be in the line of Erskine and Maurice, and Moberly, who follows McLeod Campbell to some extent, and denies that there is anything properly penal in Christ's vicarious sacrifice. He does, however, tone down Campbell's view of Christ as a human being distinct from all others by processing his thought through an Hegelianism which enables Moberly to hold that Jesus is 'as an inclusive and pervasive Spirit.'[262] The upshot is that 'in Moberly's reversion to the Catholic tradition the realistic mysticism of the typical Greek theology is replaced by an idealistic mysticism.'[263] Franks concludes with a fourteen-line 'Retrospect' in which he feels sure that those who have followed the sometimes tedious way he has led them 'will discover that there has been and is progress in theology.'[264]

Thus thought Franks when he laid down his pen in 1918. We have already had hints of the fact that subsequently he would have hard things to say concerning what he deemed the Barthian regress in theology. To that subject I shall return in due course. First, however, I wish to bridge the gap between 1918 and Frank's *The Atonement* (1934) by selecting for notice three of Franks's reviews on the subject.

I choose the review of N. P. Williams's *The Ideas of the Fall and of Original Sin*—'a work of very great learning'[265]—because in it Franks compares the author's position with that of F. R. Tennant, and reaches his own conclusion. He reminds us that Tennant published *The Origin and Propagation of Sin*, *The Sources of the Fall and Original Sin*, and *The Concept of Sin*. Tennant and Williams agree in dispensing with Augustine's teaching on concupiscence as being a sin, and they opt for the Scotist view that it is merely '"the kindling-matter of sin" (*fomes peccati*).'[266] The Anglo-Catholic Williams, however, pays more heed to Church tradition and the Eastern fathers than does Tennant. He seeks a way between Scylla and Charybdis of

---

261 Ibid., 423.
262 Ibid., 436.
263 Ibid.
264 Ibid., 437.
265 CQ, V no. 4, October 1927, 488.
266 Ibid.

Augustinianism and Pelagianism, and thinks that Tennant sails too close to the latter. Williams builds on Tennant's demonstration that Paul derived his doctrine of the Fall from later Judaism, where in the first instance it concerned not Adam and Eve but angels who fell owing to their marriage with mortals. Hence, according to Williams as summarized by Franks, 'the Scriptural doctrine of the fall of Adam can in no way be treated as the foundation of the doctrine of original sin, ... all the evidence goes to show that what came first was a moral and spiritual experience which sought more than one form in which to clothe itself in Biblical times, and which may now fitly reclothe itself in other forms to meet modern needs.'[267] But what is most interesting of all is the fact, according to Franks's analysis, that

> Dr. Tennant comes to the question of original sin from the standpoint of evolution and seen in it the dominant survival of instincts and customs that ought to be been superseded in the advance of moral progress—the general background theory of evolution is regarded by him as being in itself a sufficient explanation of such survivals. Dr. Williams founds his doctrine of original sin on moral and religious experience, but seeks a speculative explanation why there should be a domination of the lower instincts and the baser customs in place of an advance to higher things. He revives for this purpose Origen's theory of a fall before the present existence of the sinner, diverging from the great Greek theologian in regarding as the primary subject of the fall not the individual sinner himself, but rather a World Spirit or principle of cosmic existence, through whose decline from goodness it comes about that not only man but nature itself is affected with an inherited moral disease.[268]

Franks prefers Tennant's agnosticism concerning original sin to Williams's 'speculative "Origenism".'

From Franks's substantial review of F. C. N. Hicks's *The Fullness of Sacrifice* I draw two points, one positive, one negative. First, Franks welcomes Hicks's demonstration of the fact that Paul never thinks of the death of Christ apart from his resurrection. With reference to his Congregational colleague he continues, 'Dr. Forsyth's emphasis on the "Cruciality of the Cross" is right; yet it is not to be understood in the sense that the Cross can be separated from its whole context in the total sacrifice of Christ, which includes His Incarnation, His Passion, His Resurrection, and His heavenly Intercession all in one.'[269] Secondly, Franks cannot endorse Hicks's elevation of the numinous over the ethical, and of the priestly over the prophetic:[270]

---

[267] Ibid.

[268] Ibid., 487-8.

[269] CQ, VIII, 1930, 506. I have pointed out that in Forsyth's writings 'Cross' connotes such factors as those which Franks rightly specifies. See Alan P. F. Sell, *Testimony and Tradition*, 149, 161.

[270] In his later review of W. J. Phythian-Adams, *The People and the Presence*, Franks detected the same approach and commented: 'If the premiss of the supremacy of the numinous over the ethical is once accepted, the argument from that basis must be judged coherent and excellent; but those who entirely reject the premiss, as does the reviewer,

> This is the fundamental issue for a Protestant in dealing with all Catholic theories. It is clearly stated in Luther's assertion that grace is not a quality of the soul, infused or imparted, but is the free favour of God accepted and responded to by faith.
>
> If we substitute the Protestant for the Catholic idea of grace in the Bishop's theory, the change will be revolutionary. We shall come nearer to that moral theory whose austerity he admires in Rashdall's book on the Atonement, but which is far from being, when properly stated, a theory of moral example only. It is a theory of the revelation of the love of God through Christ's whole life and work indeed, but focused once for all in his great act of self-surrender on the Cross. The effect of this love, the true grace that stoops to the sinner, is first the experience of forgiveness and peace of conscience and then an answering love that is kindle by it in the soul....
>
> Not life but *love* is the supreme word in Christianity.[271]

The third review is that of Gustaf Aulén's *Christus Victor*. Aulén's case is that what Franks calls the 'ding-dong battle' between exponents of the 'objective' satisfaction theory of the atonement and those who stand for "subjective" theories is ineffectual. Accordingly, he recalls combatants to a third type of theory, the patristic, which 'he calls by the question-begging name of "classical".'[272] This theory as developed by the early theologians is that 'Christ through the Incarnation, the Cross, and the Resurrection, breaks the power of Death, Sin, and the Devil. Luther adds to the list of defeated enemies also the Law and the Wrath of God.'[273] To Aulén this is in no sense mythological: 'the world is *really* reconciled to God.'[274] Franks cannot believe that current debate concerning the atonement is to be resolved by returning to the patristic view. He does not deny that it has a basis in the New Testament, but so have the other theories, and all three theories may be found in Luther's writings. If all three theories 'correspond to something in Christian experience, the fundamental problem is to find the central point of view, whence the different elements of experience can be seen in their true proportions.'[275] It is Franks's conviction that

> That central point of view must be found in the revelation of the Divine love in the Cross. The worth of the satisfaction theory is that it emphasizes the element of cost in the Atonement. The patristic theory can only be of value if the victory of Christ over the opposing powers is treated not as something dramatically staged for our contemplation, but as a conquest really and truly won in our hearts. The return upon the patristic theory may have one good effect. It may remind us that the current way of speaking of the relation of God's redeeming love in Christ as something

---

will continue to prefer Jeremiah to Ezekiel and Abelard's doctrine of the Atonement to that of the Greek Fathers.' CQ, XXI no. 2, April 1943, 174.

[271] Ibid., 507, 508.

[272] CQ, X, 1932, 112.

[273] Ibid.

[274] Ibid.

[275] Ibid.,

'subjective' is altogether unfounded. Christ, His Cross, the love of God, are all *objective*. It took all the objectivity of our Lord's Passion and Death to win a victory over the hardness of the human heart.[276]

This is the position that Franks expounded more fully in his Dale Lectures, *The Atonement*, published in 1934 and dedicated to his wife.

As I have already said, in the Preface to *The Atonement* Franks specifies those theologians to whom he feels most indebted; but he also distinguishes the position he proposes to advance and defend from that of Hastings Rashdall and F. C. N. Hicks. He is in agreement with the former as to the supremacy of the Abelardian theory of the atonement, but whereas Rashdall maintains that God suffers, Franks cannot allow this. Franks's view of Hicks's *Fullness of Sacrifice* has been noted, but now we must understand that Franks's objective is not merely to repudiate the 'Catholic' presuppositions on the basis of which Hicks works out his doctrine of the atonement, but to prove 'an altogether different theory of the Atonement ... and to point out the connexion of that theory with the modern Protestant view of the Christian religion, which is also defended in the lectures.'[277] Franks cannot accept the idea that 'the Eucharist is a presentation of Christ's sacrifice to God: we have rather to say that His sacrifice is presented to us under the figures of the broken bread and out-poured wine, in order to kindle in us faith, hope, and love.'[278] But Franks's principal objection to Hick's approach is that it is biological rather than ethical in that grace is regarded as a divinely infused or imparted quality of the soul rather than as God's free favour.

In one sentence Franks encapsulates the Abelardian doctrine that he endorses: 'It is the doctrine that Christ reconciles men to God by revealing the love of God in His life and still more in His death, so bringing them to trust and love Him in return.'[279] This doctrine, he declares, is unjustly designated the moral theory of the atonement, for it is a religious theory which has primarily to do with God's grace, and secondarily with human moral freedom. It has also been 'very unfairly labelled subjective, because it involves the subjectivity of the human response to the Divine love: it is in truth fundamentally objective, inasmuch as God, Christ, His Cross, and the Divine love are all the objects of human trust and responsive love. It would be more correct to speak of the *experiential* theory; since the term experience implies both object and subject and the relation between them.'[280]

The question which 'greatly troubled' Franks for many years was whether the Abelardian theory could accommodate such themes as the fulfilment of the moral law, the punishment of sin and the possibility of forgiveness—all issues arising within the New Testament, and all issues central to Dale's major work on the doctrine. Eventually 'Light came from a most unexpected quarter'—from none other

---

[276] Ibid., 113.

[277] Idem, *The Atonement*, xiv.

[278] Ibid.

[279] Ibid., 2.

[280] Ibid., 4.

than Anselm, whose theory of the atonement was 'almost directly opposed to that of Abelard.'[281] As Franks explains,

> I found in Anselm's *Cur Deus Homo* the idea of a central point of view in theology from which its different problems are seen in their due proportion. It occurred to me that by utilizing the method of Anselm, the proof of the Abelardian theory, hitherto lacking in me, might be possible. As an example of method in Christian thinking the *Cur Deus Homo* has never been surpassed.[282]

Anselm's objective is to show why the incarnation was necessary. To this end he presents a chain of argument in which the key idea is that of satisfaction. Moreover his case has an eye to both the articulation and the defence of the faith, that is, to both dogmatics and apologetics. 'What this means,' says Franks, 'is that all theology comes under the head of the reconciliation of authority and reason', and 'the modern method of experience is simply a new way of solving the ancient question of authority and reason.'[283] This is the first thing we learn from Anselm. The second is that notwithstanding the fact that Anselm is regarded by present-day theologians as a bulwark of orthodoxy, he was in fact a devastating critic of traditional ideas, notably that concerning redemption from the devil. The moral is that 'A living theology must perpetually renew itself by change.'[284] The third lesson from Anselm is that if it is to be both dogmatic and apologetic in character, 'theology must find a standing ground justifiable by reason.'[285] At this point Anselm was opposed by those who recalled that no less a person than Augustine had denied that human reason could show that the incarnation was absolutely necessary.

The debate over the relation of faith and reason occupied thinkers from Alexander of Hales to Ockham. The medieval Franciscans distinguished between belief upon divine authority and trust in the God who is truth. Alexander oscillated between these two options. However, by the time we reach Ockham, we find that his nominalism has led him to the view that the subject matter of theology rests upon authority alone. Franks finds Ockham *redivivus* in Barth's *Deus dixit*, and suggests that Calvin with his doctrine of the divine sovereignty is the bridge between the two of them. Barth and Brunner 'so emphasize the transcendence of God as to make a trust based on insight into His character impossible.'[286] Teetering on the brink of a concession, Franks says, 'Let us try to be fair to Barth and Brunner.'[287] They have fastened upon the important religious principle, advanced by Otto, concerning the element of awe in religions and God's wholly otherness. But, against them, Franks

---

[281] Ibid., 6.

[282] Ibid. It seems to me that Tymms followed this method, though without discoursing on the method as such.

[283] R. S. Franks, *The Atonement*, 12-13.

[284] Ibid., 15.

[285] Ibid.

[286] Ibid., 20.

[287] Ibid., 21.

invokes John Oman, who, in *The Natural and the Supernatural*, points out that 'the "awesome holy" is not the highest idea of God. Taken alone, it leads back to primitive superstition. It gives us a God without moral character ...'[288]

The fourth lesson to be drawn from Anselm is that theology requires a metaphysical basis:

> We must first find the true central standpoint whence a real insight can be gained into the character of God and the saving work of Christ. Then, in the light of this supreme revelation, we must survey all the difference modes and ways of Christian thought and relate them in due gradation, so as to understand the manifold wisdom of God which meets different human conditions by many degrees of adaptation and accommodation to their needs.[289]

To do this will be to do as Anselm did in his time; but we must do it for our time. For us the central point of reference must be the experiential rather than the satisfaction doctrine with its suggestion that in a *quasi*-commercial transaction the Son willingly rendered his life to the Father—something that could not have been required of him since he was sinless—thereby discharging the debt of the whole of humanity. Indeed, Franks continues, Anselm himself detected a weakness in his position, namely, that the doctrine of satisfaction proclaims only the possibility of forgiveness; he therefore Anselm supplemented it with considerations respecting Christ's example and merit: 'God rewards the merit of Christ by bestowing eternal beatitude on the imitators of Jesus. ... It is of enormous importance that Anselm, the great protagonist of a purely objective doctrine of the Atonement, can do nothing with it until the objective work of Christ is shown to produce a subjective response.'[290] The moral is that 'if law is made fundamental, any operation of grace is made impossible. We must seek another foundation for theology than Anselm's: what can it be but the love of God?'[291]

Consistently with Anselm's method, Franks proceeds from authority to reason by first discussing relevant biblical material and then turning to the historic theories of the atonement. His accounts of these matters have already been presented, but if we are to understand his doctrine of the atonement aright, we must see how, in a systematic way, he locates it within an overarching doctrine of the Kingdom of God. At this point his concise and lucid paper on 'The atonement' comes to our aid. The centre of the Christian Gospel, he declares is reconciliation with God. This, however,

> is not the whole of the Gospel. Jesus came preaching the Kingdom of God: the Gospel of the Divine Kingdom is the Christian Gospel in all its height and depth and breadth and length. But the Gospel of Reconciliation is the burning centre

---

288 Ibid., 21.
289 Ibid., 23.
290 Ibid., 25.
291 Ibid., 26.

> where the Divine Love comes to a focus in the Cross of Christ. ... To establish His Kingdom is God's saving purpose for man in its widest scope.[292]

Given the fact of sin, which is rebellion against the rule of God with social as well as individual consequences, 'The Gospel of the Kingdom attains its full measure as a Gospel for the sinner.'[293] By his work Jesus 'advances the Kingdom of God and destroys the kingdom of sin.'[294] This line of thought, Franks declares, has only recently come to full clarity in 'the greatest of all books on Atonement, Ritschl's work, *The Christian Doctrine of Justification and Reconciliation*. The fundamental thoughts of this book are: (1) that salvation is entrance into the Kingdom of God; and (2) that the way of salvation is personal reconciliation to God through Jesus Christ.'[295]

Reverting to *The Atonement*, we are now in a position to see how Franks works the method of Anselm, the vantage point of Abelard, and the biblical principles just specified into a Christian metaphysic. He first points out that although his method coincides formally with that of Anselm, 'in concrete actuality it is different from his.' This is because 'The map of the universe has expanded since the early Middle Ages; and the problem of bringing Authority and Reason together has become more complicated than it was for Anselm.'[296] The three principles on which Anselm constructed his theory were that God is metaphysically inviolable; that he cannot let sin go unpunished; and that he requires satisfaction for injury done to his honour. Whereas Anselm uncritically identifies these three with one another, Franks finds that they are mutually inconsistent: for example, the latter two are incompatible with the first. The remedy is to replace the metaphysic of law with that of love. Thus Franks argues that 'Reason leads us to the conclusion that the love of God is the foundation of the universe.'[297]

The unacceptable details of his theory notwithstanding, Anselm, by advancing the ontological argument did, in Franks's opinion, provide a firm foundation for a Christian metaphysic, for 'the ontological argument is at bottom an expression of the finite reason's confidence in Reason itself.'[298]

I assume that by this Franks means that Anselm's is a *reductio ad absurdum* argument designed to show the self-contradictory position we should be in were we to deny the existence of the one than whom no greater (or more perfect) can be conceived. As Anselm put it in *Proslogion* chapter 3:

> Thou so truly art, then, O Lord my God, that thou canst not even be thought of as not existing. And this is right. For if some mind could think of something better

[292] Idem, 'The atonement,' 195.
[293] Ibid., 197.
[294] Ibid.
[295] Ibid., 201.
[296] Idem, *The Atonement*, 102.
[297] Ibid., 104.
[298] Ibid., 105.

than thou, the creature would rise above the Creator and judge its Creator: but this is altogether absurd. And indeed, whatever is, except thyself alone, can be thought of as not existing.[299]

Thomas Aquinas constructed an influential counter argument, the nub of which is that

granted that everyone understands that by this name God is signified something than which nothing greater can be thought, nevertheless, it does not therefore follow that he understands that what the name signifies exists actually, but only that it exists mentally. Nor can it be admitted that there actually exists something than which nothing greater can be thought; and this precisely is not admitted by those who hold that God does not exist.[300]

As for Kant, although his attention was directed against Descartes's restatement of the ontological argument, his adverse conclusion is no less firm than Aquinas's. Kant distinguishes between analytic propositions, in which the concept of the predicate is already contained within the concept of the subject; and synthetic propositions in which the concept of the predicate is not contained in the concept of the subject, and hence further enquiry is require to substantiate or falsify them. On this basis Kant asks whether a proposition asserting existence is analytic or synthetic:

If it is analytic, the assertion of the existence of the thing adds nothing to the thought of the thing [that is to say, existence is not a predicate]; but in that case either the thought, which is in us, is the thing itself, or we have presupposed an existence as belonging to the real or the possible, and have then, on that pretext, inferred its existence from its internal possibility—which is nothing but a miserable tautology. ... But if, on the other hand, we admit, as every reasonable person must, that all existential propositions are synthetic, how can we profess to maintain that the predicate of existence cannot be rejected without contradiction? This is a feature which is found only in analytic propositions, and is indeed precisely what constitutes their analytic character.[301]

Not surprisingly, discussion of the ontological argument has continued in a number of interesting directions since Kant's day, but my purpose here has simply been to state the positions of Anselm, Aquinas and Kant in order to show that the repudiation of the ontological argument by the latter two was not less determined than Anselm's advocacy of it.

Although he recognizes that both Aquinas and Kant formally rejected the ontological argument, Franks thinks that it nevertheless accords with the spirit of their work. For while Aquinas's rejected the argument because an idea cannot

[299] For the extended argument see Anselm in *A Scholastic Miscellany: Anselm to Ockham*, 73-5.

[300] Aquinas, *Summa Theologica*, Q. 2. art. 1. Reply Obj. 2.

[301] I. Kant, *Critique of Pure Reason*, 504.

guarantee its own reality, he also held that God's essence involves his existence. As for Kant, while he, too, formally repudiated the argument because of his conviction that we may know only phenomena, Franks's reading of the *Critique of Pure Reason* leads him to the view that Kant's final word is not that 'nothing is real except the measurable', but that 'nothing is real unless it is immanently rational.' Indeed, 'The very science of measurement is a rational science', and it is reason that gives meaning to the rational concepts of substance and cause.[302] Turning to Kant's *Critique of Practical Reason* Franks remarks, 'When Kant insists on the primacy of the Practical reason, what is this but a new articulation of the ontological argument?'[303] Franks thus argues that although Kant intended to abolish metaphysics, he actually set metaphysics upon new lines: 'It is as impossible to get away from metaphysic as it is to escape from one's own shadow.'[304] The ontological argument can still suffice, says Franks, for it can be recast in such a way as to allow for the development of an independent science of nature since Anselm's day.

In the light of the foregoing discussion Franks declares that 'The agreement of Authority and Reason which we seek is established, when we identify the Good Will ... with the Divine Love as it is revealed in Jesus Christ. That fixes the principle of the experiential doctrine of the Atonement as at the same time the basis of a Christian metaphysic.'[305] This, he continues, 'is in direct pursuance of the line taken by Christian theology from the first, in so far as Christianity was declared to be the revelation of the Logos. ... [T]he great identification of Jesus with the Logos ... must still be the inspiring principle of Christian theology.'[306] The Christian metaphysic is neither a legalism, nor a pure supernaturalism, but an ethical supernaturalism in which the good will is identified with the love of God. But how does the love of God which sustains the universe come to bear upon the individual? The answer is, through God's revelation in Christ. Drawing once again upon insights from Schleiermacher, Franks contends that against the supernaturalistic Scotist notion of the pure unintelligibility of Christianity 'we must set that of an intuition of God as Love, an insight into His character as the highest ethical ideal, and a feeling of complete dependence upon Him for the realization not only of the ethical ideal, but also of all accompanying blessings that our composite nature requires.'[307] There is, he continues,

> moral power in the story of Jesus: it is the story of a love to man which is nothing other than the love of God, operative through the love of Jesus for God. The religious dependence of Jesus upon the Father involves the moral unity of Jesus with the Father; so that faith in Jesus is faith in God, and love to Jesus is love to God. ... The personality of Jesus is the true revelation of God. ... [and] The Spirit of

---

[302] R. S. Franks, *The Atonement*, 110.
[303] Ibid., 115.
[304] Ibid.
[305] Ibid., 119.
[306] Ibid.
[307] Ibid., 131-2.

God must be understood, not as sheer supernatural and inexplicable power, but as God's personal love felt in the heart.[308]

Through the revelation of God in Christ the Kingdom of God is realized among human beings; 'God's love transforms human nature into its own likeness: it energizes in and through the Church.'[309] This, however, is the ideal picture. In reality, 'It is the fact of sin that turns the doctrine of the Revelation of God's love through Christ into a doctrine of Atonement, and that changes the doctrine of the Church from one of a fellowship of saints into one of a fellowship of pardoned sinners called to be saints.'[310] Sin is the rejection of God's love; hence to know what sin is we must first know what the love of God is.[311] Forgiveness is the judgment that annuls the guilt of sin: '[T]he sense of forgiveness and the sense of guilt cannot live together in the same breast, any more than light and darkness can coexist in the same room.'[312] Forgiveness is more than the remission of a penalty, it is a restoration of the sinner to communion with God, and in it the initiative lies with God, whose Son lays down his life for the sheep, and whose active love seeks us in the far places to which our sin has brought us:

Christian theology has been guided by a sure instinct in connecting the Atonement with the sufferings, and especially with the death of Jesus. Where it has gone astray has been in thinking that it was the sufferings and death themselves that saved us; whereas the saving power was in the love that carried Our Lord into them, and bore them. Their value is not purificatory, or expiatory, or satisfactory: it is revelatory.[313]

It follows that the Church is primarily 'a company of those who have sinned, and have received forgiveness through the final revelation of God's love on the Cross.'[314]

In a later review of Vincent Taylor's book, *Forgiveness and Reconciliation*, Franks expresses his concern that Taylor veers in the direction of a new

---

[308] Ibid., 138, 146.

[309] Ibid., 151.

[310] Ibid., 151. At this point I demur, since the implication of what Franks says is that the church members are not saints yet. But they are. According to Romans 1: 7 they are 'saints by calling'—that is, they are saints because they have been called. This is the foundation of the doctrine of the Church as a divine institution. As is all too clearly manifest, it does not preclude the corollary that the saints are also sinners, as Franks goes on to say.

[311] Here is a principle fundamental to good homiletic procedure (as opposed to fifty-five minutes of sin and five minutes of Gospel-as-escape-hatch).

[312] R. S. Franks, 'The atonement,' 206.

[313] Idem, *The Atonement*, 166. Four years after *The Atonement* was published Franks reviewed W. J. Sparrow Simpson's book, *The Redeemer*. The author understands Jesus's sacrifice as reparation, but Franks rightly points out that this 'leaves no place for forgiveness; for where a debt is paid no forgiveness is required.' See CQ, XVI no. 1, January 1938, 102.

[314] Ibid., 171.

scholasticism because of his undue reliance upon pure exegesis which 'presupposes a theological precision in the New Testament which simply does not exist.'[315] Franks holds that reconciliation is 'forgiveness or justification *become effective*.'[316] This being so, and against Taylor's exegetically-inspired presumption,

> There will be no room for the removal of an obstacle presented by sin, which is temporarily or even logically *prior* to restoration to fellowship with God: the removal of the obstacle and restoration to fellowship will be one and the same thing. Instead, therefore, of saying that Christ's sacrifice is the offering of a perfect penitence[317] as a preliminary to our reconciliation by His revelation of the Divine Love, we shall say that by the sacrifice of a perfect obedience He presented to God the means of fully revealing His forgiving love to sinners, and so of restoring them to fellowship with Him and to the pursuit of holiness.[318]

This is what Franks means when, in *The Atonement*, he recommends that 'Instead of attempting to interpret the Atonement through ancient ideas of sacrifice, we reinterpret the idea of sacrifice through it: we baptize it into Christ, and so perfect the meaning of the word.'[319] As he elsewhere put it,

> There is a central point of view from which the whole Christian Gospel becomes intelligible, clear, and evident. ... This inner point of view is taken when we find the centre of the Christian Gospel in Atonement as Reconciliation to God. It is lost when we begin to explain Atonement by notions of ransom and sacrifice. It is possible to explain the use of these terms in the New Testament when we occupy the standpoint of Reconciliation; but if we start from them Reconciliation becomes inexplicable. ... In the Cross God's love so finds us that the most formidable obstacle to His gracious purpose in the establishment of His Kingdom is overcome. The grace of the Cross is a continuation of the grace of the Kingdom, but it exceeds it. It is grace upon grace, a miracle of grace. ... Within this sphere ... it is still possible to give a deep and true sense to the language of sacrifice and ransom. They speak to us of the *cost*, of all that Jesus endured. ... We can say that He offered Himself up on the Cross, that He might become the willing instrument of God's

---

[315] CQ, XX no. 1, January 1942, 83.

[316] Ibid.

[317] Surely Christ needed to offer no penitence at all since he had not sinned—as Franks declares, analogously, in *The Atonement*, 184: 'When McLeod Campbell teaches that Christ made a vicarious confession of sin on behalf of humanity, we can only say that the conception violates the fundamental principles of moral personality. A confession of sin on behalf of others has something unreal in it. ... The vicarious penitence which Moberly substitutes for McLeod Campbell's vicarious confession of sin, is no improvement on Campbell's theory.' The reference is to R. C. Moberly, *Atonement and Personality*, 118-124.

[318] CQ, XX no. 1, January 1942, 83.

[319] R. S. Franks, *The Atonement*, 191.

> effectual revelation of pardoning love. ... The Cross is ... the foundation of our hope, and is the power of Atonement.[320]

I now pass over some remarks of Franks to which I shall return shortly, in order to say that *The Atonement* concludes with the practical considerations which are implied in his theory. To Franks these are more important than the theory itself. The primary question is does the theology establish a gospel that can be preached? He considers the rebuke to modern theology that 'it has no effective gospel with which to replace the simple old gospel, that Jesus paid in full the price of sin, and turned away the wrath of God; so that all that we have to do is to trust in His finished work.'[321] In response Franks points out that 'What is simple depends upon the presuppositions from which we start,'[322] and he notes that to Bernard of Clairvaux the simple gospel was that by his death Jesus paid a price to the devil for his captives—and 'If Aulén thinks [this position] can be renewed, it is because he thinks dualism can be restored also.'[323] Similarly, the doctrine of penal substitution rests upon a dualism of justice and mercy. For those who believe this

> it will be easy to say:
>
> In my place condemned He stood;
> Sealed my pardon with His blood.
>
> But if an analogy with the state has ceased to guide our thinking about God, then the presuppositions for the older evangelism have disappeared.[324]

The old doctrine 'had a message for the awakened sinner, guilty, trembling, doubting, fearing. But it had no message for the man really *dead* in trespasses and sins. ... But the problem today is far deeper. It is with the man who feels no sense of sin at all.'[325] Accordingly, while we do not have to propound the experiential doctrine of the atonement in every sermon,

> We have to preach in the *spirit* of the Atonement; so that the Cross not only shines by its own light, but illuminates everything else. Above all we have to live in the spirit of the Atonement. Whatever be the case with other doctrines of the Atonement, the gospel of the love of God in Christ can only be preached effectively by those who prove the truth of their preaching by exhibiting the power of that love in their lives.[326]

I do not think it can be denied that Franks devoted more years and more thought to the doctrine of the Atonement than any other English theologian of the twentieth

---

320 Idem, 'The atonement,' 199-200, 205, 211, 213.
321 Idem, *The Atonement*, 193
322 Ibid.
323 Ibid., 194.
324 Ibid.
325 Ibid., 196.
326 197.

century, or that to that reflection he brought scholarship at least as wide-ranging as that of any other writer. He sought and found his systematic vantage point in the Abelardian theory of the atonement, cleared it from opposition on grounds of undue subjectivity, and defended it against contenders for other theories. He saw, too, that the question of reason and authority lies beneath dogmatics and apologetics, and that metaphysics could not be banished. In view of his high praise for Calvin's exposition of the threefold office of Christ, it is arguable that Franks might have expounded the Saviour's priestly office more fully for its own sake, and not simply as a challenge to 'catholic' views of the matter. I have noted a number of points of detail in Franks's exposition which I shall resume in relation to others of the ten divines in the Conclusion.[327] For the present I wish simply to raise a point of technical scholarship, a semantic point, a philosophical query, a philosophico-theological point, and a theological consideration.

The point of scholarship concerns Franks's medieval hero, Alexander of Hales. Until about 1882 Alexander's authorship of the *Summa Theologica* was largely unquestioned, though Roger Bacon had described it as 'that great summa, heavier than a horse, that was not done by him but by others.'[328] But then the works of Bonaventure appeared in a critical edition, and Pierre Mandonnet and others argued that some sections of Alexander's *Summa* seemed to have been written by Bonaventure. Up to the early nineteen-twenties a number of scholars espoused the view that the *Summa* was a compilation, although when the first three volumes of

[327] Franks's theory of the atonement was largely to the liking of the liberal evangelical Congregationalist, C. J. Cadoux, though he wished that Franks had devoted more attention to the suffering brought upon God by human sin. Rightly or wrongly (and this is a point to which I shall return in the Conclusion), Franks denied that God could suffer, so he was not likely to meet Cadoux's first request. Secondly, Cadoux would have welcomed more on 'the close dependence of Jesus' suffering on his moral character (through its effect on his enemies).' Thirdly, he would have liked to hear that 'the presence of the same Divinely-redemptive power [is] in *all* self-sacrificing love as was supremely present in the self-sacrificing love of Jesus.' Whereupon Cadoux quotes W. N. Clarke, *Outline of Christian Theology*, 359: 'Union with Christ delivers a man from that selfish isolation in which the sins and burdens of his human brothers are nothing to him, and *brings him into the fellowship of saviourhood.*' (Cadoux's italics). At this point sentiment seems to place us on a slippery slope whose terminus is the dangerous—even blasphemous, view, not that we are Christians, but that we are little Christs. See C. J. Cadoux, *The Case for Evangelical Modernism*, 149 n. For Cadoux (1883-1947) see CYB, 1948, 489-90; ODNB; WTW; E. Kaye, *C. J. Cadoux: Theologian, Scholar, Pacifist*; idem, *Mansfield* College. The Congregationalist T. Hywel Hughes also entered the lists against Franks. I cannot here deal exhaustively with him. Suffice it to say that he misunderstands Franks at a number of points. For example, he treats Franks as a subjectivist, as if Franks had not taken great pains to deny that interpretation of the Aberlardian view by showing its objective foundation. See T. Hywel Hughes, *The Atonement*, 216-223.

[328] Quoted by Gordon Leff, *Medieval Theology*, 247. It should be remembered that the scholarly but irascible Bacon (c.1214 or c.1220-1292 or later) was keen to elevate theology above all other knowledge, rather than to synthesize reason and revelation.

the critical edition of it appeared from 1924, the editors, oddly, did not discuss the matter.[329] Franks does not appear to have been aware of this scholarly debate, but we should be cautioned that at least some parts of the *Summa* do not appear to have been written by Alexander himself, but by other Franciscans. It does not follow, of course, that the interpolations are incompatible with his thinking, or that he was not the primary shaper of the work.[330]

The semantic point concerns the slippery term 'feeling', so prominent in Schleiermacher's definition of religion, so integral to Franks's experientialism, and so apt to mislead the unsuspecting. As we have seen, Franks rightly insists that for Schleiermacher the objective dimension of the experience is crucial, as it is for his own theory. Even so, I should have welcomed a fuller account of 'feeling' that would have pointed out that in the eighteenth century the term connoted more than 'having an emotion.' Thus, if I may quote myself:

> Rupert Davies has explained that 'When Charles Wesley wrote, "My God, I know, I feel Thee mine", he meant by the second verb that he was aware of the nearness and fatherly love of God in the whole of his being, not in his emotions alone', and, moreover that the important things was not that he and other had the experience, but that God had wrought it in them.[331] ... [Accordingly] G. D. Hicks is wide of the mark when he writes, 'In speaking of a "feeling of *dependence*" Schleiermacher had, in fact given his case away. Mere feeling could not proclaim its own nature.'[332] Schleiermacher is not concerned with 'mere feeling' in Hicks's sense [and neither is Franks].[333]

The philosophical point concerns Franks's discussion of Aquinas and Kant as tacit upholders of the ontological argument for God's existence, despite his recognition of their formal repudiation of it. There is much that could be said here, but I must be brief. Leaving on one side the accuracy or otherwise of Franks's interpretation of Aquinas and Kant, it seems to me misleading to say, as Franks does,[334] that they set forth an ontological *argument* when they so manifestly, to their own satisfaction, demolished it. It would be better to say, though it would need fuller demonstration that Franks here provides, that Aquinas and Kant proceed on the basis of an ontological intuition (which has always been the basis of the ontological argument, and which is not necessarily to be despised because the argument as such fails). Thus, for example, 'When Kant insists on the primacy of the Practical Reason,' he is not, as Franks says, advancing 'a new articulation of the ontological argument,'[335] for God, freedom and immortality are in Kant's view postulates, or

[329] See Ignatius Brady, 'The *Summa Theologica* of Alexander of Hales.'
[330] For the authorship question see Kenan B. Osborne, 'Alexander of Hales,' 6-7; 13-16.
[331] Rupert Davies, 'The people called Methodists. 1. Our Doctrines', 149.
[332] G. Dawes Hicks, *The Philosophical Bases of Theism*, 106.
[333] Alan P. F. Sell, *Confessing and Commending the Faith*, 328.
[334] R. S. Franks, *The Atonement*, 107, 108, 115, 116.
[335] Ibid., 115.

conditions of thought, of the practical reason; they are precisely not said to be demonstrably proved. It does not seem to me that Franks has conclusively shown that, or how, the ontological *argument* can be recast in such a way as to allow for the development of an independent science of nature since Anselm's day.

The philosophico-theological point concerns Franks's claim that 'The Kantian metaphysic still stands as the basis of modern Christian theology.'[336] It is not churlish to remind readers that, as noted above, the Kantian epistemology also still stands as the fountain-head of modern agnosticism,[337] Be that as it may, it must be noted that in *The Doctrine of the Trinity* Franks says enough to show that in his view the 'basis' supplied by Kant's metaphysic was not an absolutely copper-bottomed one:

> The two Critiques of Pure and Practical Reason may be regarded as the two halves of a new Logos doctrine. In ancient philosophy Logos (or Reason) was immanent both in the world and in the mind of man. In Kant's system Reason (or Logos) is immanent as Pure Reason in the principles of our knowledge of the world, man included; while as Practical Reason it is immanent in man's mind in the moral law, which is under God the organizing principle of His Kingdom in the world. The similarity with the old Logos doctrine is plain, but so also is the difference. What in ancient philosophy was one, is now in two parts. Reason appears to be divided against itself ...
>
> In the third Critique, the *Critique of Judgment*, Kant did something towards restoring the unity of reason. He found in the absoluteness of Beauty as symbol of the controls of the sphere of sense by the moral law, and he also found a teleology in nature which foreshadows the moral teleology of the Kingdom of God.
>
> On the other hand in his book *Religion within the bounds of Pure Reason*, Kant found a new and worse breach between reason and sense than anything previously found. Here reason takes the breach into itself by making inclination and not duty the maxim of conduct. Instead of the ideal of the Kingdom of God we have a radical evil in the will as the reality in human existence. This is what Christianity calls sin, but at the same time has a gospel of redemption. So in his own way has Kant. His philosophical principle that what ought to be must be, allowed him to speak of salvation by faith in the moral ideal as realized, which he said might be described in a figure as 'the Son of God come down from heaven.' At the same time he recognized the value of Jesus as a moral example. On the other hand his cool and severe moral judgment mistrusted as fanatical all dependence upon the Holy Spirit, and he regards the doctrine of the Trinity as of no practical value. By his Critiques Kant made an end of the Aufklärung, and yet in religion he got little further than the Aufklärung.

---

[336] Ibid., 116.

[337] There was a burgeoning of discussion of the theistic arguments by philosophers of religion from about 1965 onwards, for which see Alan P. F. Sell, *The Philosophy of Religion 1875-1980*, 215-227. Franks died in 1964.

> He was like Moses, who led the children of Israel through the wilderness, but never entered the promised land.[338]

In Franks's opinion two things were needed: a more satisfactory unification of Kant's Logos doctrine than he himself had accomplished; and greater justice for religion and Christianity. Advances were made in the former quest by Fichte, Schelling and Hegel, and in the latter by Schleiermacher and Ritschl.

The theological point concerns Franks's preference for the experiential vantage point over the patristic and satisfaction ones, and this in relation to a lacuna in, or at least an under-emphasized aspect of, Franks's atonement theory. In a review of *The Doctrine of the Work of Christ* by Sydney Cave, his Congregational opposite number at New College, London, Franks says that he differs from Cave in that he would 'interpret the patristic theory by means of Abelard's, and not *vice versa*.'[339] Like Franks, Cave seeks to synthesize the truth in all three theories, but, influenced by Aulén, he gives precedence to the patristic view. Franks quotes him thus:

> Men speak to-day of the Cross that lies always on the heart of God, but if we so speak we have to do so as those who see in the Cross the symbol not of suffering only but of triumph. Christ's work for men was not only a revelation of God's love. It was that love in decisive and victorious action.[340]

Franks questions the distinction between revelation and action. To him they are 'one and the same thing ... [Christ] acts by melting [men's] hard hearts, and by moving them to penitence and trust.'[341] Cave would not have disagreed with this; but Franks's opposition of revelation and action misses Cave's point which is, precisely, that sentimental ideas of the Cross will not suffice. Something is *done* at the Cross, not simply shown (we recall that Cave, though well qualified to do so, did not study at Oxbridge, but at Hackney College under P. T. Forsyth). To put it in homely terms, the Cross is not simply a visual aid designed to show us the depths of suffering to which God in Christ goes for us; it is the place where, on the stage of human history, the decisive act is done, the victory is won. Clearly Franks is correct in saying that we need not endorse the God-devil dualism of the patristic period, but it may be suggested that he does not derive all he might have done from the theme of the victory of the Cross.

This impression is reinforced when Franks appears too dismissive of the cosmic significance of Christ's work. In his review of *The Cross and the Eternal Order* by yet another Congregationalist, Henry W. Clark,[342] Franks contests the author's view that what took place at the Cross affected humanity as a whole. Such a view, he

---

[338] R. S. Franks, *The Doctrine of the Trinity*, 158-9.

[339] CQ, XV no. 3, July 1937, 386.

[340] Ibid., quoting Cave, *The Work of Christ*, 267. For Cave (1883-1953) see CYB, 1954, 506-7; DHT; ODNB; WTW; WWW 1951-60; Ronald Bocking, 'Sydney Cave.'

[341] Ibid.

[342] For Clark (1869-1949) see CYB, 1950, 508.

declares, turns upon the Greek philosophical doctrine of the reality of universals, and we can no longer subscribe to that. He admits that the doctrine harmonizes with Paul's world view, and he can understand how the Greek fathers felt at home with it. But we cannot nowadays espouse it: 'The notion of a "cosmic" redemption prior to the actual redemption of individual men, must be given up as meaningless. While a philosophic theology is a prime necessity for the Church today, Paul's cosmic thought cannot be made the basis of it.'[343] No doubt; but from the fact that we can no longer endorse the philosophical underpinnings of Pauls's view it does not follow that there is no 'cosmic' dimension to Christ's work. After all, we do not jettison Genesis 1 and 2 because we no longer find the notion of a three-tier universe tenable. It therefore seems to me that Franks is not fully consistent at this point with his policy of viewing matters through an Abelardian lens but at the same time drawing upon other theories as appropriate. It is true that in *The Atonement* he says in a passing phrase, 'When ... Christ's saving acts are spoken of as "cosmic acts", as is not uncommon at the present time, we can welcome the phrase as glorifying their universal scope, provided only that we supply mentally the qualification that they work religiously and morally';[344] but there is room for much more adumbration at this point, which might well have begun with the analysis of the term 'cosmic act'. On an analogous matter: while Franks is utterly convinced of the sinfulness of sin, and thinks of the sinner as a rebel against God's love, he does not major upon the idea of sin as violating God's holy love. It may therefore be suggested that he does not draw all he might have done from the satisfaction theory of the atonement. In explanation of this it is not unreasonable to trace the deficiency to his stout denial that God can suffer—a matter to which I shall return in the Conclusion.

To return to Franks's remarks in *The Atonement* which I passed over: he reiterates his view that the experiential theory of the atonement entails the abandonment of the impersonal humanity of Christ as advanced in the Greek Christology; but, equally, he thinks that Brunner's notion that Jesus could not have a human personality because that would mean that he was sinful, must also firmly be rejected. Indeed, 'The possibility and actuality of a sinless human personality in Jesus must be unflinchingly maintained.'[345] A reconstructed Christology must begin from this point, he continues, and it will have to be worked out through a firmly monotheistic doctrine of the Trinity:

> There must be maintained indeed the immanent distinctions of the Persons, established by the eternal generation of the Logos and the eternal procession of the Spirit. But the tempting social analogy must be avoided, which interprets the Godhead as though it were a company of human individuals. All this ... will be in steady pursuit of the tendency of the best Latin theology.[346]

---

[343] CQ, XXII no. 2, April 1944, 174.
[344] R. S. Franks, *The Atonement*, 181.
[345] R. S. Franks, *The Atonement*, 193.
[346] Ibid.

To the agenda here specified Franks himself turned in his last published book, *The Doctrine of the Trinity*, to which work I now turn.

IV

In 1953, at the age of eighty-two, Franks published *The Doctrine of the Trinity*. Running to only 201 pages, it is a marvel of lucid compression, in which he proceeds through the New Testament, the patristic period, the Middle Ages, the Reformation and on through Schleiermacher and Ritschl to Leonard Hodgson's book of the same title as his own, which had been published in 1943. Not surprisingly, Franks repeats a number of themes with which we have already become familiar. I shall therefore not attempt a full summary of the book, but shall rather indicate some particularly significant points, and then offer some reflections on Franks's position as a whole.

On the very first page Franks sets his face against any who would take intellectual refuge in the thought that the doctrine of the Trinity is a mystery.[347] On the contrary, he declares, the doctrine 'is the result of a rational and intelligible process, and its value can only be appreciated through a study of this process.'[348] Indeed, 'The formation of the doctrine of the Trinity will appear as an argument from history to a metaphysic as the solid basis that gives meaning to the history.'[349] Here, once again, we see the metaphysics-history-theology relationship which figured so prominently in Franks's work throughout his writing and teaching career. In the development of the doctrine we also see how authority, reason and experience played their parts in varying permutations.

The New Testament is, to Franks, 'the matrix within which the doctrine of the Trinity begins to be formed,' though 'Passages of a directly Trinitarian complexion are ... few in number.'[350] He shows how the seeds of trinitarian doctrine are present in Peter's first speech (Acts 2: 14-36, 38, 39), in which Father, Son and Holy Spirit are present together, and in the title 'Lord' as now ascribed to Jesus. Father and Son, though distinguished, both have a saving function. Paul's objective was to universalize Christianity, and to the primitive *kerygma* of Peter's speeches he added the clause that 'Christ died for our sins according to the Scriptures' (I Corinthians 2: 2), which 'became the very centre of the Apostle's preaching.'[351] By his use of the terms, 'Lord' and 'Son of God' Paul reinterpreted what a Jew would have understood by 'Messiah' for the benefit of the Gentile mind. A further aspect of Paul's Christology is that concerning Christ as the pre-existent Son of God, who is identified with the cosmic Wisdom or Logos—the latter a term which Paul never uses. As for the Holy Spirit, to Paul he is 'a permanent regenerating influence

---

[347] He elaborates upon this point with particular reference to J. H. Newman, in 'The fullness of God, Father, Son, and Holy Spirit,' 551-2.

[348] R. S. Franks, *The Doctrine of the Trinity*, 1.

[349] Ibid., 2.

[350] Ibid., 4.

[351] Ibid., 25.

received by faith and baptism.'[352] In Franks's opinion, 'Paul's transformation of the original *kerygma* in order to universalize it is the greatest turning point in Christian theology.'[353] The importance of the Letter to the Hebrews, he continues, is that its author discerns that Christianity implies a metaphysic, and that he emphasizes the true humanity of Christ. In the Johannine writings we find the synoptic story retold in terms of a Logos Christology, which is a development of, not a departure from, the primitive *kerygma*. Moreover, in these writings due place is accorded to the Holy Spirit, who proceeds from the Father and will be sent by the Son. The term 'Father' is almost invariably used of the God-Jesus relation, and God is said to be Spirit, Light and Love (John 4: 24; I Jn. 1: 5; I Jn. 4: 8). What Franks finds in the New Testament is a unity of attitude towards Jesus as Saviour and Lord, though not of doctrine—that is developing.[354]

The questions which subsequently began to press upon those who wrestled with Christian doctrine were, 'Could monotheism be preserved? and, Could justice be done to the humanity of Christ?'[355] Since neither question could be answered without attending to Christology it is not surprising that in the patristic period authority and reason predominated over experience where doctrinal matters were concerned. In face of the Gnostics the New Testament was established as an authority additional to the Old, and in the West the baptismal confession and the Rule of Faith, the confession of the church in Rome of about A.D. 150, came to prominence, as did the disciplinary role of the bishops. In the East there was less credal precision and greater recourse to the Scriptures.

The contributions of the Apostolic Fathers and the Apologists are discussed, and then Franks continues through the major thinkers. He refers to Tertullian as being the first to use the term *trinitas*; and he commends Origen for providing 'the first complete Christian theology,'[356] while noting that his doctrine of the Trinity was subordinationist both as regards the Son and the Spirit. Thence to the Arian controversy and Athanasius, and on to the Cappadocian Fathers and John of Damascus, to whom I shall return in the Conclusion. It is Augustine who comes closest to thinking of the Trinity in terms of the living God of the Old Testament, thereby uniting Christian doctrine with the earlier emphasis upon the divine unity. Thomas Aquinas restates Augustine's position in terms of the double procession of intellect and will in God—in other words, he employs psychological analogies in relation to the persons of the Trinity. Franks expounds Aquinas thus:

> The Divine Intellect, which is One with the Divine Essence, produces an Image of itself, which being Divine is consubstantial and co-equal with itself. Thus is

---

[352] Ibid., 34.

[353] Ibid., 37.

[354] See ibid., 4, 49, for Franks's 'strong' dissent from Oscar Cullmann's 'purely arbitrary' view, set forth in *Christ and Time* (1946), that there is no Hellenism in the Johannine writings or Hebrews.

[355] Ibid.

[356] Ibid., 88.

> explained the Father's begetting of the Son. But upon this first internal process in God there follows a second, which is that of the Divine Will (also one with the Divine Essence), directed towards the Image conceived by the Intellect. This process is not a begetting as in the former case: its result is Love, which being a living impulse is properly called Spirit.[357]

At the Reformation Luther went back to Paul for the view that grace is God's free favour, and that to be justified was to be accounted righteous and have one's sins forgiven: this on the ground of trust in God as revealed in Christ. In other words, 'the principle of experience, which had previously found expression in medieval mysticism, was associated by Luther with his gospel of justification by faith.'[358] For all of this the Bible alone was the authority, and the experience of the Christian, coupled with the testimony of the Holy Spirit, was brought to the fore. The emphasis upon the theology of the Cross at first drove the doctrines of the incarnation and the Trinity into the background. Calvin's restriction of 'the testimony of the Holy Spirit' to the authorizing of Scripture, the ensuing development of Protestant scholasticism, and the challenge of anti-trinitarianism turned attention once more to authority and reason once more. Socinianism, Arminianism, deism and latitudinarianism all come under brief review, and then in the wake of the English Quakers and the continental Pietists come Schleiermacher and Ritschl. The new emphasis upon experience and the fact of historical criticism of the Bible altered the face of theology and, when coupled with the Kantian understanding of rationality, render it truly 'modern'. Schleiermacher's understanding of the Trinity is focused upon God's self-revelation; he does not go behind that to the eternal being of God. He is monotheistic, and gives due place to the humanity of Christ. With his kenotic theory of the incarnation, Thomasius of Erlangen holds that Christ held in abeyance his divine attributes of omnipotence, omniscience and omnipresence, whilst retaining those of absolute power, freedom, holiness, truth and love. In this way he seeks 'to secure the full humanity of Christ without leaving the ground of the orthodox doctrine of the Incarnation.'[359] By the time we come to Ritschl, the return to Kant is in progress, and renewed emphasis upon the Jesus of the synoptics is evident. These ideas meet in Ritschl's exposition of the Kingdom of God. Not all were satisfied by Ritschl's position, however. Kähler contrasted the Jesus of history with the Christ of the Bible, while Ritschl's son-in-law, Weiss, argued that Jesus understood the Kingdom in terms of Jewish apocalyptic ideas, as did Schweitzer in *The Quest of the Historical Jesus*. It remained for Otto and C. H. Dodd to temper the radical eschatology of Weiss and Schweitzer with the view that 'Jesus, preaching the Kingdom of God, was already the eschatological event realized in history.'[360]

---

[357] Ibid., 134.
[358] Ibid., 153.
[359] Ibid., 175.
[360] Ibid., 177.

Under the influence of Kierkegaard's existentialism, Barth turned from the liberal theology of his teacher, Herrmann, and in the aftermath of World War I proposed a renewed understanding of the divine transcendence. A summarized by Franks, Barth holds that

> Apart from Revelation God is hidden and unknown [hence Barth's emphasis upon the Word]. Analysis of what is included in Revelation yields (1) the Revealer, (2) the act of Revelation, (3) the state of Revelation [*Offenbarer*, *Offenbarung*, *Offenbarsein*]. These distinctions correspond to Father, Son and Holy Spirit in Scripture ...
>
> To see how this is so, Barth interprets transcendence as God's Freedom. God reveals Himself in His Freedom as Sovereign Lord (*Herr*) and as Absolute Will. ... Even in the historical Jesus God preserves His sovereignty. In Him God is still present *incognito*. Only as God's revelation to the individual creates faith is Jesus known as Lord.[361]

Thus we see that whereas 'Schleiermacher and Ritschl began with the historical Jesus and find God immanent in Him, Barth begins with God in the form of revelation, God the Word. ... [I]n Jesus Christ the Word is the subject and humanity is the predicate.'[362]

Franks goes on to argue that Barth has more in common with Schleiermacher and Ritschl than is sometimes supposed. He finds Barth's philosophy of revelation to be a variant of Schleiermacher's, though with a greater emphasis upon God's transcendence. If, to the latter God transcends nature and spirit and is known in religious feeling, to the former God is so transcendent that he touches humanity in at one point only, in Jesus Christ. But, says Franks,

> it is to be observed that this doctrine of transcendence requires the Kantian philosophy of the autonomous ego, or some variant of it such as Hegelianism, to act as a foil to itself. Without the autonomous reason which it challenges, it would float free in the ether of the Absolute, making no contact with earth anywhere. In other words, transcendence could not become revelation.[363]

Barth differs from Schleiermacher and Ritschl in thinking that

> faith should express itself, not only in the testimony of prophets and apostles, but also in the patristic creeds and the Reformed Theology. This is the most debatable point of his system. If we agree, as we must, that we have in Scripture the classical and normative expression of the Christian faith, there still seems no reason that faith to-day must express itself in the same language, let alone that it should further be bound by the traditional exegesis of Scripture. Historical criticism, which Barth accepts, must play upon Scriptural modes of thought as well as upon Scripture

---

[361] Ibid., 181.
[362] Ibid., 182.
[363] Ibid., 183.

records of history. As a matter of fact Barth does so allow it to play when he identifies Father, Son and Holy Spirit with the 'moments' of revelation, its Subject, its Form and its Contingency. The Scripture names, he says, are only analogical.[364]

Franks thus concludes that Barth is more of a 'modernist' than he admits. Be that as it may, it is clear that Franks himself remains faithful to liberal evangelicalism. His book concludes with a sketch of some English writers on the Trinity. Most space is accorded to Leonard Hodgson's book, *The Doctrine of the Trinity*, because in it Hodgson propounds a social doctrine of the Trinity which Franks is quite unable to accept. I shall return to this discussion in the Conclusion.

In a brief 'Postscript' Franks retraces his steps, and reaffirms his view that 'since all subsequent theologies stand as an interpretation of the *kerygma*, it is by their faithfulness to the *kerygma* that they must be judged.'[365] This reduces to the questions from which he set out: Do they assert monotheism? Do they uphold the real humanity of Christ? 'Theology,' he says, 'may, and indeed must, go beyond the *kerygma* in interpreting it, but it must not contradict it.'[366] What will a doctrine of the Trinity look like which meets this objective? Franks may give his own answer:

> Schleiermacher's doctrine of the Trinity is not as satisfactory as his Christology. The reason is not far to seek. It is in his unsatisfactory doctrine of God. Because he thought of God as the Identity of Nature and Spirit, he explained the 'Persons' in the Trinity as phases of Divine manifestation which do not touch the Divine essence. To rectify the situation, firstly, we have to assert with Ritschl the truth that God is Spirit, the Creator both of Nature and of finite spirits; secondly, we have to affirm the principle stated by Barth in substantial agreement with John of Damascus and Calvin, that God is as He reveals Himself, or in other words, He is eternally what He is in time. The doctrine of the Trinity must therefore carry back what we learn through the Divine revelation into the eternal Being of God.[367]

Hence his conclusion which 'can be stated in a sentence: the Christology of Schleiermacher must be combined with the Trinitarianism of Aquinas as reinterpreted by Barth.'[368]

J. G. Riddell wrote a generally favourable review of Franks's book. While agreeing with Franks that a full exposition of his own position would have required

---

[364] Ibid., 183-4.

[365] Ibid., 195.

[366] Ibid., 186.

[367] Ibid., 198. Elsewhere Franks speaks of three different lines of God's manifestation in the world: his universal immanence; his special manifestation in Christ; his saving presence as the Holy Spirit. He then observes that 'Since all things temporal have their grounds in eternity [thereby hangs a metaphysic], these three modes of manifestation have to be traced back to their roots in the being of God. Accordingly, a doctrine of the Trinity in Unity will be, not the presupposition, but the conclusion of the whole dogma.' See his 'Dogma in Protestant scholasticism,' 141.

[368] Ibid., 199.

a further, long, book, he nevertheless says that many readers would have welcomed 'a clearer indication of it'; indeed, that, in the absence of further elucidation, the words I have quoted at the end of the last paragraph are 'tantalizing'.[369] It is difficult not to endorse this remark as an observation upon this particular volume; but when we place the elusive sentence against the background of Franks's entire *corpus* it is not so difficult to grasp Franks's overall position. Riddell further wishes that Franks had had more to say on the 'comparative silence of theology regarding the place of the Holy Spirit in Trinitarian theology.'[370] It may be that the inference to be drawn is that under the impress of authority and reason the Spirit took a back seat along with experience, or even that at certain times and in certain places charismatic excesses disinclined theologians to dwell too much on the Spirit. However these things may be, it would have been interesting to have heard Franks upon them.

The fact remains that Franks's book clearly shows that theologians could not avoid going beyond the *kerygma*. As soon as they found themselves addressing a Greek view of the world; as soon as they found it necessary to repudiate perceived heresies, they had to rebaptize terms and develop their arguments. Moreover since, unsurprisingly, the person of Christ was so often the central point at issue, Franks could not avoid making Christology the centre-piece of his history of the development of trinitarian doctrine. His insight that the crucial matter was to maintain monotheism whilst doing justice to the true humanity of Christ is entirely justified.

Reserving the social Trinity to my Conclusion, one thing remains to be queried. Franks sees the need to hold together authority, reason and experience. Although he understands why, in the urgency to maintain discipline within the Church and to rebut its foes from without, experience often gave place to authority and reason; and although he welcomes the recovery of experience by various pre-Reformation groups, but supremely at the Reformation, his own characterization of experience seems frequently to be more intellectualist, or cerebral, than existential, or as having to do with trust, *fiducia*. Thus, for example, on the second page of *The Doctrine of the Trinity* he says that 'The ultimate aim of the doctrine [of the Trinity] was to show how God could be both One and Three.'[371] This seems to make the doctrine an answer to an intellectual puzzle. On the penultimate page of the same book he writes in summary of his own view, that 'as the Divine grace filled Christ's human consciousness and completely dominated it, He remained a man like other men, and was yet the Word of God made flesh, who through the communication of His consciousness of God to others in the Spirit is the Saviour of the world.'[372] But Christ's being the Saviour of the world has to do with sin, forgiveness, reconciliation, as Franks's exposition of the legitimate development of the *kerygma* in the New Testament makes clear,[373] and as his own book on *The Atonement*

[369] J. G. Riddell in *The Expository Times*, LXIV, 1952-3, 329.
[370] Ibid.
[371] Ibid., 2.
[372] Ibid., 200.
[373] See, for example, ibid., 58-9, 238.

abundantly bears witness, and not simply with the 'communication of his consciousness of God to others.' The same point applies to a statement in Franks's earlier article on the Trinity, in which he says that Origen's valuable ideas may be brought 'into correspondence with that fundamental Christian experience which we are making the starting-point of our theology. Let us say that we depend upon God the Father Himself for our very being and all that may sustain and develop it. We depend upon God revealed in Jesus Christ for our ideal of personal character, and we depend upon the Holy Spirit for the power to realize that ideal.'[374] It is the Christological sentence here which seems to represent a significant attenuation: we depend upon Christ for far more than is here specified. Indeed, I would claim that, having regard to the monotheism of Judaism and the philosophy of the Greek world, the impetus to Christological and trinitarian debate was such questions as, Who is this that forgives sin? We have found reconciliation, new life, new light, a new way, salvation in Christ; but God alone can save: who, then, must he be? How, but by the Spirit whom he sent, can we account for his post-ascension presence with us? These considerations do not seem, at crucial points, to have influenced Franks's language in his writings on the Trinity as much as they might have done, his regret at the paucity of experiential considerations from the second century to the Reformation notwithstanding. Except that, at least on occasion, Franks does not like the word, we might almost call it a 'paradox' that one who builds so strongly upon the experiential should at times have had such a thin way of specifying that experience.

V

The metaphysical basis of theology; the marriage of authority, reason and experience; the Abelardian vantage-point (not construed in ultra-subjectivist fashion) in theology; and the reasonableness of trinitarian doctrine: these are the great themes to which Franks constantly returned, and which he adumbrated in conversation with both Scripture and doctrinal tradition. Not, indeed that he lived in the past. Responses to the thought, both secular and religious, of his own day, flowed readily from his pen, and his integrity as a liberal evangelical is displayed in the fact that neither the horrors of World War I nor Barth and all his works could deflect him from that theological stance. I shall conclude this chapter by reference to some of his judgments on the theological environment in which he lived.

First, for all his interest in the thought of Thomas Aquinas, and his respect for his critical method, Franks did not think that Aquinas's system was watertight. Not surprisingly, therefore, he found fault with that neo-Thomism which was coming to out of the seminaries and on to the broader stage of philosophical discussion from

[374] Idem, 'The fullness of God, Father, Son and Holy Spirit,' 554.

about 1925 onwards.[375] Consider, for example, in his review of H. S. Box's book, *The World and God*:

> It may be willingly conceded that a patient study of St. Thomas will do all philosophers and all theologians good. But it seems to us that Dr. Box overstates his case. He uses Thomas very much as Thomas himself used Aristotle: in the *Summa contra Gentiles* and the *Summa Theologica* Aristotle is *philosophus*, and other thinkers are mentioned only to be corrected: just so, in *The World and God* St. Thomas is always right, and everyone else—Descartes, Kant, Hegel, and the rest—wrong. ... The merit of Thomism is its completeness as a survey of the field; but considered as a system it is full of loose joints, and its imperfection has been brought to view over and over again by the subsequent development of philosophy. It is hopeless advice to bid us to return to the thirteenth century and wash out everything that has happened since in philosophy, except only the neo-scholasticism which makes some attempt to revise the relation of St. Thomas to modern science.[376]

Lest this seem the partisan judgment of a bigoted Nonconformist, let it also be clearly understood that Franks had little patience with those who sought to regurgitate un-reformed Reformed scholasticism. He fully understood that '[T]he Protestant doctors were compelled by the antithesis of Roman Catholicism to formulate the doctrine of Holy Scripture with great care and fullness. It is one of the most original parts of their work';[377] but he did not for one moment imagine that matters could be left as they had left them. In particular, in the wake of modern biblical criticism, we can no longer maintain their doctrine of verbal inspiration. Of course, the 'can' in that last sentence is a logical 'can'. In terms of will and ability B. B. Warfield found no difficulty whatsoever in reproducing the older view. While recognizing his great and up-to-date learning, Franks, when reviewing *Christology and Criticism*, nevertheless brands Warfield 'the prince of Fundamentalists, but he is a Fundamentalist.'[378] Elsewhere, in his review of Warfield's *Biblical Doctrines*, Franks writes,

> It is not likely ... that all [Warfield's] scholarship or his polemical energy will hinder the progress of modern thought. 'So fight I,' said St. Paul, 'as one not beating the air.' But that is just what Dr. Warfield does: he beats the air. He is like a soldier, thinking to repel an advancing cloud of gas by means of vigorous bayonet-thrusts or blows of the clubbed rifle. If his pre-suppositions were secure, his polemic might be successful. But it is just those pre-suppositions that the ineluctable movement of thought has rendered uncertain.

---

[375] See further, Alan P. F. Sell, *The Philosophy of Religion 1875-1980*, 84-92, 155-6.

[376] CQ, XIII no. 1, January 1935, 116.

[377] R. S. Franks, 'Dogma in Protestant scholasticism,' 118.

[378] CQ, VIII, no. 3, July 1930, 372.

> Dr. Warfield treats the Bible as a book of revealed knowledge, in itself certain and sufficient, quite apart from any interpretation through experience. All that is necessary is to make out the surface-meaning of the Biblical text, using indeed one part to explain another. The historical method simply does not exist for Dr. Warfield.[379]

While valuing Barth's insistence that God is as he reveals himself, Franks, as we have seen on a number of occasions, weighed the Swiss and found him wanting. In his opinion, like that of Adeney, the most general description of the Barthian theology is that 'it is a reaction to Calvin after a period in which men rejoiced to have emancipated themselves from his influence.'[380] But this attempt is doomed to failure: 'What would John Calvin have made of a Calvinism without religion and without History? The Barthian movement, at any rate in its present form, seems, in spite of much sound and fury, to lead no whither.'[381] Franks particularly resents Barth's way of castigating liberal theology for its commitment to a metaphysical basis for theology. As for the claim that liberal theology is dead, it still survives, and it cannot but survive, because

> *the causes which produced it still exist.* The dominance of the scientific view becomes ever greater; and the problems raised by historical criticism become ever more and more acute. Also, the philosophical instinct towards a unification of knowledge remains strong in the human mind; and it is not enough simply to condemn reason and send it into a corner as a naughty boy. Reason has a way of coming out of the corner and behaving as an *enfant terrible*, whether we like it or not.[382]

Franks further notes that Calvin was not against reason to the degree that Barth is; hence we may return to Calvin and still have a natural theology:

> I do not think that Barth will in the end be able to suppress reason. He says in his *Church Dogmatic* that there are fundamentally only two types of Christian theology, the Pauline and the Apologist of the second century. Paul founded his theology on the inspiration of the Holy Spirit, the Apologists sought to equate Christianity and Logos or Reason. But in view of *Rom.* 1 and 2 it is erroneous to say that Paul did not respect reason: these chapters are the starting-point of all natural theology in the Christian Church ever since. And the Apologists began a work which is necessary if Christianity is to live and work in the world. I myself believe in a Logos theology, and think that the future of Christianity lies that way.

---

379 CQ, VIII no. 1, January 1930, 99.
380 R. S. Franks, 'Trends in recent theology,' 19.
381 Idem, 'Books that have influenced our epoch,' 107.
382 Idem, 'Trends in recent theology,' 27.

> I regard Barth as a great spellbinder, but I believe that the Church will presently free itself from the spell and return to saner ways of thought.[383]

One of Franks's mentors, Troeltsch, pronounced the following verdict, with which Franks was in entire sympathy:

> The Orthodox Theology did not originate from the pure desire for knowledge, nor yet from the ideal of merely fixing the content of faith or the consciousness of the Church—these are modern conceptions on the nature of Dogmatic Theology, upon which a retreat has been made after the discovery of the invincible difficulties of its proper task. It rather originated, like all Dogmatic and like the ancient Dogma itself, from the apologetic need of an orientation between the positive religious ideas and the other knowledge of a civilized people.[384]

We can almost hear Franks's rueful response to the latter sentence: This is precisely what Barth forbids, and what the self-fossilized Warfield prevents himself from undertaking.

As he surveyed the systematic theologies of the centuries, Franks singled out Origen's *On First Principles*, Aquinas's *Summa Theologica*, Calvin's *Institutes*,[385] Schleiermacher's *The Christian Faith*, and Ritschl's *Justification and Reconciliation* as being the most important. He further declared that 'no Protestant theologian of comparable calibre with Ritschl has appeared since his time. ... [A]ll the fundamental questions of Christian theology have been answered by the last great doctor of the Protestant Church.'[386] The omission of Augustine and Barth from Franks's list is all too evident. The inference is that he did not think that Augustine, with his occasional writings and his articulation of contradictory 'evangelical'-Pauline and ecclesiastical-sacramentarian views was sufficiently systematic; or that Barth saw matters intellectual sufficiently 'whole' in view of his denigration of metaphysics, his arbitrary restriction of the sphere of influence of the Word, and his lack of interest in apologetics. Support for this analysis is found in Franks's conviction that the systematic theologian must ever work with three elements: 'The first is a direct experience of God and blessedness. The second is the connexion of this experience with a definite history, which may be summed up under the three heads of Jesus Christ, the Bible, and the Church. The third is the rational element, the endeavour to assimilate experience and history alike by the help of universal reason.'[387] It may fairly be said that Robert Franks held all three elements together

---

[383] Ibid., 29. Sixty-three years later at the time of writing, Franks's prophecy awaits fulfilment. For other Nonconformist reactions to Barth see Alan P. F. Sell, *Nonconformist Theology in the Twentieth Century*, 25-32.

[384] R. S. Franks, 'Dogma in Protestant scholasticism,' 131. Franks quotes E. Troeltsch, *Vernunft und Offenbarung bei Johann Gerhard und Melanchthon*, 1.

[385] In 'Trends in recent theology,' 20, Franks judges that 'Calvin is without doubt the greatest theologian produced by the Reformation.'

[386] R. S. Franks, 'Books that have influenced our epoch,' 104, 107.

[387] Ibid, 105.

with a greater degree of consistency than many of his theological contemporaries and forebears who regarded that approach as viable.

By gathering together all of his published books, most of his articles, and many of his reviews, we have been able to gain an insight into the thought of Franks, who was, in terms of philosophy, the history of Christian thought and systematic theology, the most learned of all the divines treated in this book. More than that, he was the most learned Nonconformist divine of the twentieth century. No other twentieth-century Nonconformist systematic theologian ranged so widely over the subject, or brought a sharper critical mind to bear upon it than did Franks.

At the end of *The Doctrine of the Trinity* Franks invokes Richard of St. Victor:

> 'What if it be not granted me to arrive at my destination? What if I fail in the race? Yet will I rejoice in seeking the face of my Lord, to have run, toiled and sweated as I have had strength.' Though I have come to a conclusion different from his, I have unity with him in endeavour.[388]

'The Christian Church', wrote Franks, 'will ... never be able to dispense with theological systems, and the great theologians, though not honoured always as much as they ought to be, have been among her most faithful servants.'[389] No one was a more faithful theological servant of the Church than Robert Franks.

---

[388] Idem, *The Doctrine of the Trinity*, 201. He quotes Richard's *De Trinitate*, III.1. Richard propounded a version of the social Trinity, hence Franks's 'different conclusion'.

[389] Idem, 'Books that have influenced our epoch,' 105.

CHAPTER 11

Charles Sim Duthie (1911–1981): The Gospel, the Church and the World

Charles Duthie, known to his friends (and to his students) as Charlie, was born at Rosehearty, Aberdeenshire, on 6 January 1911.[1] For the early influences upon him we may turn to his own words:

> 'Thy salt is lodged for ever in my blood.' Thus the poet-tramp W. H. Davies. I was born less than one hundred yards from a point where the North Sea breaks angrily on a rocky shore in Aberdeenshire. From early beginnings I seem to have been aware of two things, the precariousness of life and the reality of God.
>
> The precariousness of life was brought home to me by the loss of men at sea and by the grim struggle for food and a living in the twenties. ... The First World War reinforced the lesson. My two much older cousins who visited me when on leave did not return from the great slaughter of 1917. In the same year my father was invalided out from the Navy. It took him several years to recover a reasonable measure of health. Some of my friends were killed by a mine on the seashore. I barely escaped drowning myself. I think there is a significance in the fact that when I preached my first full sermon in my home church, the theme should be 'The problem of suffering.' Even then the Cross seemed to me to be the only truly luminous point in the dark ocean of human pain.
>
> How did the awareness of God come? The majesty and mystery of the sea was a fitting background for its birth. My religious heritage was important. It had two sides, each complementary to the other. My mother's family belonged to the old United Free Church. There was an unspoken emphasis on character and kindliness. The deed counted more than wordy profession, but the great Gospel was always in mind. On the other side, the tradition was firmly and warmly evangelical. It summed itself up in my grandfather and grandmother, two profoundly religious people. Although they died before I was eleven they left an indelible imprint on my life.

---

[1] For Duthie see SCM; his MS Memoirs and *curriculum vitae*, which were entrusted to me by Dr. Duthie with a view to my writing an account of his life and work; James M. Calder, 'Our President-elect'; D. S., 'Principal Duthie's latest honour'; J. H. L. Burns, 'Tribute to whom tribute is due'; Anon., *1811-1961*; R. Waters, 'He is alive.' I am grateful to The Revd Dr. William D. McNaughton for supplying photocopies from Scottish magazines.

> They belonged to the local meeting of the Open Brethren, from which my father broke free to join the Congregational Church. My grandfather was a fisherman who had acted as a pupil teacher for two years after leaving school. He was accounted a remarkable man by those who knew him—extremely well read in the Bible, wise and full of the saving salt of humour. He took a large view of the Church and criticised his own meeting or assembly for standing aside from the North-East revivals and then proceeding to pick up the converts. ... He said to me more than once, 'Boy, you carry on my work after me'—his work as a preacher and teacher he meant. I would like to think than in some measure I have done that and that he was and indeed is large-hearted enough to recognise it.[2]

Duthie was greatly influenced by the evangelical preaching of Thomas Johnstone, a Yorkshireman[3] who was minister at Mid Street Congregational Church, Fraserburgh; and he later 'became convinced that [Mrs. Johnstone] had prayed me into the ministry. It was as if she had heard the call of God before I did.'[4] It was at a two-week mission conducted by a Scottish evangelist that Duthie committed himself to Christ, and then swiftly discovered that 'when assurance came, it came not only as joy in the HOLY GHOST but as an illumination of life and a great provocation to the mind.'[5] Far from regarding his decision as a terminus, Duthie valued the teaching of Johnstone that 'Christian discipleship is a continuous growth in obedience and outgoing love, as Christ takes a firmer and firmer grip upon our lives.'[6]

At school Duthie's intense love of football had for a time threatened to compromise his studies, but he now devoted himself to his books. In 1928 he left Fraserburgh Academy as Equal Dux—a Classical Prizeman and an English Prizeman. He proceeded at once to Aberdeen University, which at that time had a student body of thirteen hundred.

> My course started on a humourous note. Because I dared to wear a bow tie I was taken with twelve others, syruped and painted and feathered, and made to march through the streets, bowing to statues. They had the decency to give us a hot bath at the end, but not before we had consented to sing a verse of
>
> We are but little children weak,
> Nor born to any high estate.[7]

---

[2] C. Duthie, Memoirs, 1-2.

[3] Thus the Memoirs; but Johnstone (1861-1938), of Scottish descent, was born at Runcorn, Cheshire, and brought up on Tyneside. He trained for the ministry at Paton College, and served at Knottingley (1886-91), and then in Scotland: Annan (1891-6), Panmure Street, Dundee (1896-1907), and Fraserburgh (1907-1938). He was President of the Scottish Congregational Union (1936-7), and his preaching prowess took him to many countries in Europe and to the United States and Canada. See CYB, 1939, 728.

[4] C. S. Duthie, Memoirs, 2.

[5] Ibid., 3.

[6] Ibid., 4.

[7] Ibid., 5.

At the end of his first year Duthie transferred from Classics and English to Philosophy. In his 'Memoirs' he attributes this transfer to the negative influence of a worthy, but intensely boring, Professor of Greek; but later he wrote that the lecture which John Macmurray gave at the Student Christian Movement Quadrennial at Liverpool in 1929 'started off a process in my mind which led me just over a year later to transfer my chief interest from English literature and the classical languages to philosophy.'[8] Concurrently he felt an undeniable call to the ministry. The teacher who most influenced him was the Regius Professor of Moral Philosophy, John Laird, who 'imparted to me a horror of shoddy thinking which I trust I have not entirely lost.'[9] Whilst at university, Duthie participated in the activities of the Student Christian Movement, and valued the ecumenical emphasis and the intellectual challenge supplied by the Movement. He spent his eighteenth birthday at the SCM's Liverpool Quadrennial. But his commitment to mission was fulfilled in the Student Campaign Movement. Under the auspices of this body denominationally diverse campaigns were organized every year at Easter and in September. In this context he met Ronald Gregor Smith, Matthew Black, John Graham, and F. F. Bruce, all of whom subsequently attained university chairs.[10] Like James S. Stewart, G. T. Thomson and Leslie Weatherhead, Duthie came under the influence of the Oxford Group Movement.[11] While he valued the emphasis on the devotional life, surrender to God, and the sharing of one's experience, he later came to disagree with the methods of the Movement. Duthie was politically committed but not active in political societies. He did, however, join a group which visited prisoners at Craiginches Prison every Sunday.

In 1932 Duthie graduated with First Class Honours in Philosophy. Along the way he had become the Fullerton Moir and Gray Scholar in Philosophy, and he also won the Ferguson Scholarship in Philosophy, which was open to students from the four Scottish universities. Encouraged by some to proceed to Oxford to pursue further studies in philosophy, Duthie, by now set upon the ministry, went instead to the Scottish Congregational College, and also attended some classes in the Faculty of Theology of Edinburgh University at New College. From his College Principal, T. Hywel Hughes, he learned that 'psychology, wisely applied, has much to contribute to the cure of souls.'[12] His main interest, however, was theological, and at the time the 'new theology' was that of Karl Barth. Duthie read Barth, but found Emil Brunner more congenial. He owed most, theologically, to Professor Hugh

---

[8] Idem, 'Religion and reality,' 9.

[9] Idem, Memoirs, 5. For Laird (1887-1946) see DTCBP; ODNB.

[10] For Smith (1913-1968) see DSCHT. For Black (1908-1994) see ODNB; D. K. McKim, *Dictionary of Major Biblical Interpreters*. For Bruce (1910-1990) see DSCHT; ODNB; F. F. Bruce, *In Retrospect*; D. K. McKim, *Dictionary of Major Biblical Interpreters*.

[11] For Stewart (1896-1900) see DSCHT; ODNB. For Thomson (1887-1958) see DSCHT; WWW 1951-60. For Weatherhead (1893-1976) see DMBI; ODNB; WTW; J. Travell, *Doctor of Souls*.

[12] C. S. Duthie, Memoirs, 7. For Hughes see ch. 7, n. 327 above.

Ross Mackintosh, 'a splendid and wonderfully kind Highlander, a Christian gentleman to the fingertips.'[13] Duthie heard as lectures most of Mackintosh's book, *Types of Modern Theology*, and he felt that every theological student ought to read Mackintosh's *The Christian Experience of Forgiveness*—an opinion in which I heartily concur. But the man who influenced him above all others was the pastoral theologian at the Congregational College, George S. Stewart, 'a strong, humourous [*sic*], utterly dedicated man, whose approach to theology was truly catholic, and whose emphasis upon the importance of prayer has ever remained with me.'[14]

In 1934 Duthie was a Dr. Williams Divinity Scholar and Prizeman, and the following year he graduated BD (Aberdeen) with distinction in Theology. He also won the Baxter Scholarship for study abroad and, at Mackintosh's suggestion, he went for a year to Tübingen University, where he sat under the Reformation historian, Hans Rückert (1901-1974) and the systematician Karl Heim by whom, we recall, Robert Franks was also favourably impressed. Mackintosh had said to Duthie, 'You will have to wrestle with Barth all your life. Better hear someone else', and Duthie was profoundly grateful for his Tübingen experience. Whilst there he heard the anti-Nazi Martin Niemöller preach, he attended a secret meeting of Church leaders, and he felt the tension building towards war as he spoke to students, visited a Jewish family, and lodged in a German household.

Duthie had hoped to spend a second year on the continent, either in Germany or France, but an urgent call came from Paton [Congregational] College, Nottingham, which institution was seeking its first Resident Tutor. The subjects to be taught were Logic, English and Greek. Duthie accepted the call and moved to Nottingham. John Brown Paton, the founder of the Nottingham Institute, which was later renamed in his honour, had inaugurated a scheme of ministerial training designed to equip candidates for work in the burgeoning industrial society. The curriculum included the traditional theological disciplines as well as law, social studies and health. In 1920 Paton became the first theological college to host a Chair of Psychology and Social Science. This post was financed by a gift of £10,000 from the Nottingham chemist, Jesse Boot.[15] Duthie testified that this approach 'convinced me at an early age that theology is not theology unless in the end it bears powerfully on life.'[16]

Duthie was ordained in Edinburgh and inducted at Castle Gate Church, Nottingham, where the Alliotts had ministered, on 2 October 1936. On 5 October a welcoming party was held at the College. Of his colleagues Duthie wrote,

> How fortunate is every young minister who finds wise older men as friends and guides! Dr. Sanders was a quiet genial scholar whom we all loved. Dr. Henderson, the Principal, was a charming giant of a man, with steel beneath the charm. The personality of the College was the Professor of Psychology and Social Science, Dr.

---

[13] Ibid. For Mackintosh (1870-1936) see DSCHT; ODNB.

[14] Ibid. For Stewart (1866-1945) see SCM.

[15] For Paton College see R. R. Turner and Ian H. Wallace, *Serve Through Love*. For Duthie see ibid., 47.

[16] C. S. Duthie, Memoirs, 10.

> J. G McKenzie. What a man he was! He had left school at 11 to work in a factory. He went back at 22, prepared for University in Aberdeen, took his MA, BD, and within seven years had taken the newly-founded Chair at Paton. I had heard him once in Aberdeen, when two or three of us almost fell out of the front seat of the gallery laughing at his inimitable children's address. My interest in psychology entered upon a new phase through my friendship with him; for he was a practising psychotherapist, with brilliant gifts of diagnosis and an extraordinary capacity to put people on the road to recovery. I had the privilege of accompanying him on several occasions to his clinic and of discussing personality disorders with him. Later when he returned to Scotland in 1951 our association became even closer. It is largely owing to his help that the teaching of pastoral counselling is a staple part of ministerial training in Scotland.[17]

Duthie recalled that among his Paton students was the efficient Senior Student, Douglas Smith, who ended his ministry as Moderator of the Wessex Province of the United Reformed Church.[18] As he taught Greek, explored Form Criticism, and studied C. H. Dodd's *Romans* Duthie became convinced that 'the Biblical scholar has a magnificent contribution to make but that systematic theology is needed in order to interpret and communicate the Bible and its message in a world whose presuppositions are not those of the first century.'[19]

At this point I interrupt the biographical narrative to underline the importance to Duthie of the pastoral-*cum*-psychological dimension of ministry. As we shall see, there are hints of this in his dealings with people and in a number of his writings, but it is perhaps in some of his sermons that the emphasis most clearly apparent. Thus, for example, in a sermon entitled, 'Five ways of dealing with temptation', Duthie grounds in the Bible, and develops his practical points with reference to psychological insights. His text is I Corinthians 10: 13: 'There hath no temptation taken you but such as is common to man: but God is faithful, who will not suffer you to be tempted above that ye are able; but will with the temptation also make a way to escape.' Duthie grabs his hearers' attention at once:

---

[17] C. S. Duthie, Memoirs, 10. For Harold Freer Sanders (d. 1956 aged 88) see CYB, 1957, 522-3. An alumnus of Lancashire College, he served at Newtown, St. Helens (1895-8), and for the next forty years taught Old Testament, philosophy and psychology at Paton College. In retirement he served the church at Lynton (1938-1944). For Henderson see ch. 7, n. 342 above. He had trained under D. W. Simon at the Scottish Congregational College. He was Chairman of the CUEW, 1922-3, and an Hon. DD of Edinburgh University.

[18] For Douglas Andrew Smith (1911-1998) see URCYB, 2000, 306. He served at the John Howard Church, Bedford (1938-59), as CUEW Executive Secretary for Lay Preaching and Maintenance of the Ministry (1959-66), as Moderator of the Southern Province of the Congregational Church in England and Wales (1966-72) and of the Wessex Province of the United Reformed Church (1972-6).

[19] C. S. Duthie, Memoirs, 11. For Charles Henry Dodd (1884-1973), Congregational minister and distinguished biblical scholar, see ODNB; URCYB, 1975, 294; WTW; F. W. Dillistone, *C. H. Dodd, Interpreter of the New Testament*; D. K. McKim, *Dictionary of Major Biblical Interpreters*.

> There is an old saying that while you cannot prevent the crows from flying over your head, you can see to it that they do not build their nests in your hair. That is deeply true of the moral struggle in which we are all engaged. Temptation, whatever form it takes, is quite inescapable because we are moral beings exposed to the prompting of both good and evil. But temptation is not sin ...

There follows the diagnosis:

> There are generally three stages in any fall—the stage of desire when our mind alights on the coveted object or course of action, the stage of delight when we contemplate or anticipate the pleasure of possession, and finally the stage of consent, when our defences crumble and the will gives in. But it is always open to us to arrest the downward movement at the first or second stage.

The five ways of dealing with temptation are as follows:

> 1. The first thing ... is that *we can do very much to settle the issue beforehand.* ... We can follow the example of Jesus by so steeping ourselves in the thought and language of the Bible that the great affirmations and promises of Scripture come crashing through to drown the voice of the tempter. We can so set our hearts on God that we are antiseptic to evil. We can forge the weapons of victory in the secret places of prayer. If we come at our temptations victoriously we are much more likely to emerge from them victoriously.
>
> 2. Then *we can draw strength from the brotherhood of temptation.* ... Paul with his thorn in the flesh, Bunyan wrestling with his voices, Livingstone in the African jungle, Bonhoeffer striving to maintain his faith in a Nazi prison. More inspiriting still is the fact that Christ is brother to us in our temptations....
>
> 3. ... It is sometimes when we count ourselves beyond all lure of certain temptations that a sudden crisis finds us without defence. Whether we are young or old, *we have but one safe course with many temptations—we must put the greatest possible distance between them and us in the shortest possible time.*
>
> 4. Yet we cannot runaway from *all* our temptations. In nine cases out of ten *we must fight the battle out like men, under the eye of God and with the help of God.* ... In the moral struggle there are not two factors only—myself and my temptations: there are three: myself, my temptations and God.
>
> 5. But *the best of all ways of coming through the moral struggle victoriously is to make the very agony of temptation a moment of redemption for those who are much more sorely tempted than we are.* Our trouble often is that we concentrate selfishly on saving ourselves. So long as we are fighting and even praying about our temptations, we allow them to occupy the centre of the stage and thus to continue to exercise their spell upon us. ... At the end as at the beginning [Jesus] was asked to abandon the way of suffering love ... How did He meet it? He began to pray immediately for those who had crucified Him and were now taunting Him ... [O]ur

> temptations, by the marvel of intercessory prayer, can become ladders by which others may be helped to climb into the presence of God.[20]

It is difficult to conceive of a more practical, sermon-length, approach to the problem of temptation. But it is equally clear that undergirding the pastoral approach is intense Bible study, theological acumen, and psychological insight—not least that concerning the psychological law of reversed effort, which is especially evident in remedies 1 and 5.

Although it would have been possible for Duthie to remain at Paton, and although he enjoyed his work there, he felt that he ought to experience ministry for himself. Accordingly, in 1938 he took the difficult decision to leave the College and accept the pastorate at Bathgate. It was a church with a tradition of strong ministry: both A. M. Fairbairn and John Short had begun their ministries there.[21] Owing to the advent of World War II Duthie actually served for just under two years at Bathgate, though he was officially the minister there until 1944. During his initial period the premises were redecorated, a cine-projector was installed for educational purposes, and the procedures for the training and reception of members were revised. There was a monthly Sunday evening sermon-lecture, followed by discussion and a social. United services with other churches were held during Holy Week, and a system of school chaplaincies was brought in. At the outset of the war Duthie offered himself as a chaplain to the forces. He was now twenty-eight, and as the only single minister in the town he felt this to be an appropriate response to the dire situation. In January 1940 he reported to Salisbury, where he met the Senior Chaplain, Dr. Yelverton, a regular soldier, scholar and Doctor of Divinity. Because of his dapper appearance he was known as Flash Alf. Three week later Duthie was sent to the 17th General Hospital near Boulogne, where the padres beat the doctors at football 4-0. The Baptist minister who kept goal later became the Mayor of Colchester. Then the casualties began to flood in. Duthie and others reached Dover a few days before Dunkirk, and he was next posted to Leeds, Hatfield and the East coast of England. During this period, in 1941, he married Nancy, and after a week-long honeymoon they parted for the next three years. In due course they had a son and a daughter. Duthie was sent to the Egyptian Delta, and was involved in the sad retreat to Alamein and the ensuing Western advance. A short posting to Palestine was followed by a return to Egypt, where he coached candidates for the ministry and was joint-minister of a Baptist-Congregational church that met at the Nile Mission Press.

With hindsight Duthie reflected that while it had been necessary to fight the war, Britain, by not acting sooner, was partly to blame for the way in which the dire situation had developed. The war reinforced his conviction that the Church must 'identify itself with human need. War strips away the pretences';[22] and proximity to

---

[20] C. S. Duthie, 'Five ways of dealing with temptation,' 282-3.

[21] For Fairbairn see ch. 7, n. 91 above. Short went on later to Richmond Hill church, Bournemouth, before leaving for Canada.

[22] C. S. Duthie, Memoirs, 16.

masses to whom Christ was a stranger was a motivating factor in his subsequent evangelistic activities. As he contemplated the problem of evil, which was thrown into relief by the war, Duthie

> could find only one answer. The Cross is the symbol of the divine descent into the cauldron of man's sin. God suffers with his world because he is our Father. Although there is no teaching about this in John Oman, I went back to him during the war, and with the light of the rediscovered Gospel, read more into him than perhaps was legitimate. But here was a theology of God's personal dealing with man as man, in his strange contradictory nature, that to me made sense. I am not and never could be a follower of Oman; but here is a theology that while insisting on grace as preeminent and prevenient, sees that grace is for personality, which it makes and redeems in Christ.[23]

In 1945 Duthie published *The Church and Our Ex-servicemen*, and fifteen years later there appeared a sermon for Remembrance Sunday. His text was Matthew 5: 9, 'Blessed are the peacemakers: for they shall be called the children of God.' In the course of his remarks he recalled those who had

> set themselves to fight—a business which they hated—not as starry-eyed crusaders but as those who, in their splendid understatement, 'had a job of work to do.' We do well to remember them.
>
> If not all were peacemakers by intention, all were peacemakers by necessity. ... 'What we need after the war,' a tank sergeant said to me a few days before he died, 'is a flat-out effort to win the peace on a level with our present effort to win the war.' How right he was! ...
>
> Like those whom we recall, [Christ] died to give the world peace. ... In His will is not only our peace but the peace of the world.[24]

In 1944 Duthie was called back to Edinburgh to become Principal of the Scottish Congregational College, taking his place in a succession which included W. Lindsay Alexander, D. W. Simon and H. F. Lovell Cocks, and there he remained until 1964. In 1946 he was appointed lecturer in the Postgraduate School of Theology of the University of Edinburgh. Duthie's immediate predecessor as Principal was the systematic theologian David Russell Scott.[25] The College had, since 1930, been

---

[23] Ibid. For Oman (1860-1939) see DHT; DSCHT; DTCBP; ODNB; WWW 1929-40; F. G. Healey, *Religion and Reality*; S. Bevans, *John Oman and his Doctrine of God*; Adam Hood, *Baillie, Oman and Macmurray*.

[24] Idem, 'Making peace,' 25, 26.

[25] For Scott (1870-1954) see SCM. A BA of Oxford and MA of Edinburgh, he held the PhD of St. Andrews and was honoured with its DD in 1938. Following pastorates in Wick (1897-1904), Baltic Street, Montrose (1904-18) and Castle Street, Dundee (1918-20) he took up the Chair of Systematic Theology. In addition he had charge of the

operated jointly with that of the United Free Church, and Duthie's relations with his UF colleagues was most cordial. Indeed, G. S Stewart, the Professor who had so greatly influenced him during his student days, belonged to the UF Church. Stewart had retired from his post in 1937, and he completed eight years as an Honorary Professor at the end of Duthie's first year as Principal. Allan Barr of the UF Church had been Professor of New Testament since the colleges had come together in 1930, and he remained in that post until 1970. David Frank Philip taught Elocution from 1936 until 1949, when he was succeeded by Thomas Hall Bissett. James Wood held the Chair of Biblical Languages, Criticism and Exegesis from 1947 to 1997, assuming in addition the Principalship on Duthie's departure for London in 1964. William G. Baker of the Churches of Christ taught Practical Theology and Church History from 1960 to 1970.[26]

In addition to his teaching duties Duthie threw himself into numerous other activities. He inaugurated the Friends of the Congregational College, reconstructed the chapel, revised the curriculum and brought in J. G. McKenzie, his former Paton College colleague, to teach Pastoral Theology. The College's finances were stabilized, and retreats for staff and students were held. From 1946 to 1959 Duthie led teams of thirty to forty students on inter-Church evangelistic campaigns—the first Principal ever to have done such a thing; he served as President of the Edinburgh Student Christian Movement; and was involved with the Tell Scotland mission movement almost from its beginning in 1952.[27] Between 1953 and 1971 he regularly contributed articles to *The British Weekly*, and some twenty of his sermons were published in *The Expository Times*.

Duthie's service to his denomination included chairing the Forward Movement Committee (1946-8), writing the bulk of a *Statement of Belief* (1949), and serving as President of the Union (1952-3). In 1952 Aberdeen University, his *alma mater*, honoured him with its DD. Between 1959 and 1964 he was joint-chairman of the committee that conducted conversations between Scottish Congregationalists and the Church of Scotland. He was a founder and first President of the Scottish Pastoral

Congregational church at Dalkieth (1922-36). He was President of the Congregational Union of Scotland in 1928.

[26] For Barr (1893-1988), Philip (1892-1949), Bissett (1901-1992), Wood (1906-1991) and Baker (1917-1944) see SCM; and for Baker see also URCYB, 1996, 258. Barr, a DD of Glasgow University, was Moderator of the General Assembly of the UF Church in 1939 and 1940. Wood, MA, BD (Oxon), MA (Manchester) was President of the Congregational Union of Scotland, 1958-9. Following pastorates in Macclesfield (1933-43) and Belmont, Aberdeen (1943-7) he was Lecturer in Biblical Criticism in the University of Aberdeen from 1945 to 1946, when he assumed his Chair at the College. Baker had studied at the Universities of Birmingham and Leeds, and at Butler and Harvard Universities in the United States. He was awarded the DD of Christian Theological Seminary, Indianapolis, in 1963. He chaired the Scottish Committee of Churches of Christ (1956-74), and served on the Faith and Order/Mission and Unity department of the British Council of Churches (1962-74).

[27] Most of the information in this paragraph and the next is extracted and ordered from Duthie's *curriculum vitae*.

Association, whose members were ministers and persons from other caring professions. Further afield, he participated in the meetings of the International Congregational Council in 1949 (Wellesley, Massachusetts), 1953 (St. Andrews) and 1962 (Rotterdam); and under the auspices of that body he visited Holland, Switzerland, Sweden, Finland and Germany. Whilst in the United States in 1949 he investigated theological education, evangelism and the work of the laity; and in 1957 he was similarly engaged there, and also spent six weeks in Canada at the invitation of the United Church of Canada, which was sponsoring a Mission to the Nation. Duthie preached, gave lectures, and conducted short missions. Meanwhile, at the invitation of the Congregational Union of England and Wales, he had published the Lent book for 1955, *God in His World*.

As he reflected upon his twenty years as Principal in Edinburgh, Duthie concluded that three main concerns had dominated his thought and practice:

> 1. To find a form of theology which would be true to the central message of the Bible and the main tradition of the Church while remaining open to new light and truth. You might call that the concern for the Gospel.
>
> 2. To affirm the unity among Christians which transcends all their differences and hold them together despite the divisions which come either from the past or from the present. You might call this the concern for the Church.
>
> 3. To take part in a form of continuing engagement with men and women in the interest of the Gospel which had both to be declared and to be demonstrated. You might call this the concern for the world.
>
> I see this threefold concern for Gospel, Church and World as constituting one of the basic Christian triangles.[28]

He goes on to say that this concern

> explains my preoccupation during those years with the thought of Blaise Pascal. He combined passionate loyalty to the Gospel with a sort of existentialist analysis of the human condition, believing that men might come to the point in exploring their own mysterious natures where, unable to explain themselves or to deliver themselves from evil, they were ready to listen to a word from beyond, God's word in Jesus Christ 'in whom is all our virtue and all our happiness.'[29]

The more formal fruit of Duthie's preoccupation with Pascal is to be found in two places. First, in 1948 he published a substantial review of Emile Cailliet's book, *Pascal: Genius in the Light of Scripture*. 'Pascal,' he writes approvingly, 'is proving a powerful ally to those who are eager to show that a Bible-centred and impenitently supernaturalist Christianity surprises but does not outrage the reason of

---

[28] C. S. Duthie, Memoirs, 17. Hence the sub-title of this chapter.

[29] Ibid., 18.

man, if reason be understood not as a separable faculty of the personality but as the whole man gathered to the pitch and point of decisive personal quest for the ultimate.'[30] Pascal's thinking, he declares, 'never rests in speculation or even contemplation. It passes over into proclamation, persuasion, evangelism. Because he has seen God, he wants others to see God.'[31] Secondly, Duthie published a paper entitled, 'Pascal's Apology.' He here reviews recent Pascal scholarship, one benefit of which is that we may no longer think of Pascal as one who opposed the heart to the reason: 'he did not leave his scientific habits of thought behind him' when he turned to consider religion.[32] He did, however, begin from the human predicament in all its wretchedness and contradictoriness. The only acceptable explanation of this situation, says Pascal, is that provided by Christianity, namely, that humanity, made in the image of God, has fallen. In God alone are hope and happiness to be found. Duthie then turns to the famous wager: 'If you bet for God, you gain all if God exists: if you bet for God, you lose nothing if God does not exist.'[33] The freethinker, whom Pascal is addressing, still cannot believe. He cannot see that there are things beyond reason's reach. As reported by Duthie, Pascal's prescription is that 'We ought not to resort to metaphysical proofs for the existence of God but to recognise that it is through Jesus Christ and in Him alone that we know God.'[34] Pascal proceeds to support this latter contention by reference to the Bible. He grants that miracles and prophecies 'are not in themselves absolutely convincing. They speak only to the seeking heart which God inclines by His grace.'[35] In Duthie's opinion, by setting out from humanity's plight, by seeking to force the issue with the wager, and by showing the truth and reasonableness of the Christian religion, Pascal has completed 'a pioneer endeavour to make a dramatic literary form the vehicle of an intelligent Christian evangelism.'[36] The *Apology*, he continues, is not, then, an exercise in natural theology; the contrast on which it turns is not that between reason and faith but that between '"man without God" and "man with God".'[37] Duthie concludes by suggesting that the world's present predicament 'places us in a good position to value his message.'[38]

In a more popular context Duthie returned to Pascal eight years later. He had received two requests to write on existentialism in his series of articles in *The British Weekly*. He does not claim that Pascal directly influenced later existentialists, but he suggests that he was a precursor of them insofar as he anticipated many of their concerns:

[30] Idem, Review of E. Cailliet, *Pascal.*, 98.
[31] Ibid., 103.
[32] Idem, 'Pascal's Apology,' 130.
[33] Ibid., 137.
[34] Ibid., 138.
[35] Ibid., 139.
[36] Ibid., 140.
[37] Ibid.
[38] Ibid., 141.

> He was preoccupied with man in his mingled 'greatness' and 'wretchedness.' He felt the strangeness of existence—why am I here rather than there? He saw man as the only being endowed with the capacity to stand off from himself and his world. He plumbed the meaning of estrangement and guilt. He rejected the more of scholastic philosophy. He called for the individual to choose.

Pascal also knew that 'In [Jesus Christ] is all our virtue and all our happiness. Apart from Him there is only vice, misery, error, darkness, death, despair.'[39]

So much for Duthie's thoughts as he reflected on his Edinburgh Principalship, and for the development of his ideas on Pascal. The question remains, What did his Edinburgh students think of him? I have canvassed opinion on this matter, and I find that he is remembered as one who was 'precise and gracious, an immense intellect, with a huge range of interests and enthusiasms. He had a warm personality and enjoyed nothing better than walks in the College garden with individual students. In the College Chapel, he was the gentlest of critics in the sermon class.' The same correspondent recalls that Duthie

> was a superb teacher, always clear, always analytical, always positive. He introduced us to the 'greats' of the day—Barth and Brunner (and to the dispute between them). He was himself very attracted to the 'third great', Tillich, who was seeking to move the faith into new areas and new understandings. He was not so keen on the demythologising project of Bultmann. He did speak much of Bonhoeffer, especially interpreting his theology in the light of his extraordinary life. But he did not neglect some of the more *avant garde* theology of the day—van Buren and the 'death of God' writers. I always felt, however, that he had a particular soft spot for the 'personalist' theologies of people like Farmer, Oldham and Donald Baillie insofar and they reflected his own understanding of God as constantly gracious. In the same way, he introduced us to a writer who was not at all well-known—von Hügel who, as I remember, wrote out of a warm pastoral concern.

The writer further remembers the way in which in class Duthie shared his insights into such writers as Jung and Fromm; and also introduced the reading of *The Cocktail Party* and other modern plays into his courses. My correspondent also valued talks given by the preacher, Bill Martin, the missionary, Bernard Thorogood (himself an alumnus of the College) and the theologian Nels Ferré, who came to the College at Duthie's invitation. All of my correspondents recall the evangelistic missions, evenings spent at the Duthies' home, and the way in which Nancy supported Charles and went out of her way to befriend the students. Some express much gratitude for the pastoral care they received from the Principal. One grants that 'He had ... a blind spot—he was very severe on bad behaviour by students, especially of a sexual nature.' In this connection the comment of another former student is instructive: 'I remember well how he was criticised when a student erred in getting his girl friend pregnant and Charlie expelled him. The decision caused him much grief—and I think he was not uninvolved in the acceptance of the man by the Church

---

[39] Idem, 'Existentialism,' 9.

of Scotland ministry!' The same writer may sum matters up: 'He was a superb preacher, biblical, personal, authoritative and was an evangelical without being in the least a fundamentalist. He led the College very well, commanding respect from colleagues and students alike, a Principal of principle.' None of the former student correspondents confirmed or denied the following observation which appeared in print in 1952: of Duthie it is written that 'His only known vice is that he is much given to Alpine yodelling.'[40] I have no evidence to suggest that this adversely affected his theology, and I strongly suspect that in this predilection Duthie is unique among the ten divines studied in this book.

In 1964 Duthie accepted the Principalship of New College, London. When his predecessor there, John Huxtable, went to Edinburgh to enquire whether he would be open to the call, Duthie 'fell silent; then he looked up, and said, "I only want to do what is right."'[41] To London he and Nancy went, exchanging Edinburgh snobbery for English superiority and London Anglican pretensions, and they soon found themselves welcomed by students and churches alike. As in Edinburgh they opened their home to students and others, and one tutor remembers Mrs. Duthie's accomplished playing of the piano. In 1968 Duthie published his *Outline of Christian Belief*, a lucid work comprising articles (some expanded) from *The British Weekly*, which had been written with laypersons especially in mind. He attended the University of London theological seminar, and contributed a paper to the volume, *Providence*, which was published under its auspices in 1969. In 1971-2 he served as President of the Congregational Church in England and Wales, the latter year being that in which the union of English Presbyterians and the majority of English and English-speaking Welsh Congregationalists came together in The United Reformed Church. He played his part in the administration of Theology in the University of London, and was Chairman of the Board of Studies in Theology from 1974 to 1976. He served as an examiner, and was a member of Boards concerned with the appointment of Professors.[42] In 1979 he edited a selection of Drew Lectures on Immortality under the title, *Resurrection and Immortality*. The concluding lecture in the volume is his own Drew Lecture, 'Ultimate triumph.'

Duthie's longest-serving colleague at New College was the church historian, Geoffrey Nuttall, who once said that he felt that he had served '*under* Cave, *with* Huxtable, and *over* Duthie.'[43] Certainly it fell to him to acquaint his new colleague with the unfamiliar ways of the University of London: his was a shepherding role, and it does seem that Duthie could on occasion find himself all at sea in the metropolis. A former student writes, 'I don't think he found living in London easy: it was too big and busy for him, and he really needed looking after, even to get down

---

[40] D.S. 'Principal Duthie's latest honour,' 85.

[41] Geoffrey F. Nuttall, 'Charles Sim Duthie, DD,' 2. For Huxtable (1912-1990) see ODNB; URCYB, 1991-92, 229; WTW; J. Huxtable, *As It Seemed to Me*.

[42] I use the capital P by way of indicating that in Britain these are senior posts.

[43] See Alan P. F. Sell, 'Conversations with Geoffrey Nuttall.' For Geoffrey Fillingham Nuttall (1911-2007) see also URCYB, 2008, 302-3. For Sydney Cave see ch. 10, n. 340 above.

to King's. There was always the slight air of the absent-minded professor about him.' Another recalls the Principal's consternation one morning when he looked out of his window and saw that his car was not in its usual place. He called the police and expressed his distress to Nancy, 'who reminded him that he had gone out in the car the previous night but actually had come back by public transport.'

It is to Nuttall that we owe a glimpse of Duthie at business meetings:

> If in the conduct of a meeting he could appear oblivious of the purpose of a minute, as indicated an accepted decision, an agreed policy or an undertaking to *do* something, it was, I think, because he was more concerned with the opportunity of the minute in the other sense of the word, to do what was called for *now*. And if he sometimes seemed to be moving about in worlds not realized, or to be leading on through a Scotch mist, it was often because he was responding to higher lights, which to the rest of us were not visible or were no more than will-o'-the-wisps.[44]

Nuttall recalled that of the three Principals with whom he had served, Cave was the most remote, he agreed most with Duthie, but, despite their significant differences over ecumenism and churchmanship, he got on best with Huxtable. He felt that Duthie was sometimes hard to pin down, and that he could be understanding of student difficulties to the point of undue leniency.[45] If this is the opinion of one who could be principled to the point of pernickety, it is also the opinion of one who was unusually skilled at perceiving the motives of others:

> The late 1960s were ... a time of student unrest, from which the College was not exempt. The Principal's way of meeting this was his own and no one else's. Though often anxious and sometimes hurt, he would, wherever possible, defuse, interpret and reconcile. If at times he seemed incapable of standing up to the awkward squad, or of holding them to agreements previously reached, he held to *them*; and, whatever might appear to be lost meantime in customs or even standards, he in the end *won them*. Some of those who had been most difficult were, in fact, to be among the most deeply attached to him. This was his secret: his secret weapon—for he did not talk about it—and the secret of his achievement. 'We must allow a man his freedom', he would say. ... [I]f he could not *persuade* them to cooperate, then he would wait.[46]

This speaks volumes concerning Duthie's respect for the other, and it calls to mind an observation of Robert Waters, who studied under Duthie in Edinburgh, concerning Duthie's evangelistic activities:

> [T]o be recognised by the world as an Evangelist requires something more than Charles Duthie had: it requires a kind of killer instinct, a readiness to press home

---

[44] G. F. Nuttall, 'Charles Sim Duthie, DD,' 5.

[45] See Alan P. F. Sell, 'Conversations with Geoffrey Nuttall.'

[46] Ibid., 4, 5.

> the final advantage with a disregard for the individual as such—though always in his own interest of course! I think Charlie was too gentle when it came to that point.[47]

Duthie knew better than most that while people may be loved to Christ they cannot be forced to him, and that if students or others proved a disappointment, they were to be loved all the more. It is entirely conceivable that where persons are concerned patient waiting, which may to some appear as indecisiveness, will in the end produce more lasting fruit than the 'killer instinct'. Above all, I think, Duthie knew that this was the method of God himself. As he wrote, 'the omnipotence of God is the omnipotence of Grace, by which He inclines and constrains, but never overpowers. If I may so put it, God's love *begets* an answering love in us, it does not *produce* it. His action is vital, not mechanical.'[48] As he said in a sermon: 'God's patience is the patience of almighty love and is a sign not of His weakness but of His strength. Only the strong can be patient.'[49]

As for students in pastoral need,

> *[A]ny* student in trouble could turn to [Duthie] for sympathy and wise advice, and often did so; and *all* students, however tiresome, were equally welcomed in his home. He was not one for standing on ceremony, least of all in his home. He simply assumed that you too were *at home*, as *he* was: happy, safe, and at peace, because Mrs. Duthie was there. Without her behind him all through, he could never have achieved what he did.[50]

Among Nancy Duthie's many services to the College was playing the piano for chapel services; improving the piano technique of some students; hosting student tea parties in The Lodge; and graciously offering support to students in a variety of ways. In once case she assisted the finances of a newly-wedded student by employing his wife in domestic duties. A former student writes that the Duthies 'were generous in their hospitality and kindness to the student community, even inviting individuals occasionally to live in The Lodge if they required extra coaching or support.' The helpfulness was not all in one direction. Duthie, ever the ardent soccer fan, was delighted when a student was able to obtain tickets for the 1966 World Cup. He did not confine his attendance to top-flight games but went to College matches as well: 'One vivid memory I have,' writes a former student-footballer, 'is of a member of a team we were playing—when being told that our college Principal was with us, thought that the rather sedate man on the touchline was CSD when it was a fellow student. That the Principal should be running the touchline and shouting coaching tips to the players was outside the other college's experience!'

The same writer continues,

---

[47] R. Waters, 'He is alive.'

[48] C. S. Duthie, 'A God of action,' 9.

[49] Idem, 'God is still at work,' 382.

[50] G. F. Nuttall, 'Charles Sim Duthie, DD,' 5.

> My particular memories of Charlie (as the students usually referred to him) are of someone whose mind was usually operating on a higher plane than the rest of us. He had a photographic memory and could locate quotations with ease as he roamed through his vast collection of books. However he often forgot the correct names for household objects, and sometimes people, and was nearly always at odds with anything mechanical. Driving with him could be a memorable experience. He was a scholarly evangelical who encouraged engagement in mission. I think of him as saintly.

According to another student, 'Billy Graham was in London sometime between 1964 and 1966. Duthie on at least one occasion shared a platform with him.' Then, with reference to John Huxtable, she muses (almost certainly accurately), 'I don't think Hux would have done that.'[51] A correspondent whose New College course saw both the departure of Huxtable and the arrival of Duthie writes,

> We may have been wary at the start of this reserved—I will not say 'dour'—Scot, and comparison was inevitable with the affability of John Huxtable. But just as John, though affable, brooked no presumption in his care for discipline and order, so Charles, though restrained, showed in his kindly smile and open approach a warm and mellow disposition. I think of him as a true example of 'meekness' in what I understand to be the Biblical sense of that word—a man possessed of the inner strength that shows itself in greatness.

The same writer continues, 'What I remember of his teaching was that he had an excellent grasp of systematic theology and a clear manner of putting it across backed up by carefully prepared and detailed scripts. By his introduction to many modern theologians he educated students whose BD course might have led them to believe that theological thinking ended with Calvin.' Another draws a further contrast between Duthie and Huxtable: 'Hux knew where he stood on matters academic and theological, and made this known to his students. Duthie considered every possible point of view, and invited us to learn from them all. I think it was Duthie who expounded the principle that it is always good to listen to what another positively affirms, but not to take too much notice of what they deny.' That this very breadth was disquieting to at least one student is clear from the following:

> [Duthie's teaching] was wide-ranging, though we did seem to come back to Tillich and Barth a great deal (there was something of an unworthy sense of relief around when these great worthies died, as though this would somehow put them beyond quotation). Sometimes the breadth was puzzling: one exasperated student once asked, 'Dr. Duthie, whose theology do you really espouse?' and received the answer [from the diminutive Principal], 'I'm too big a man to put in anyone's pocket.'

Through visits from such scholars as Nels Ferré and Helmut Thielicke, and the presence of foreign students, Duthie brought the world to the College. He also

---

[51] Huxtable did, perhaps somewhat cheekily, borrow Graham's slogan, 'The Bible says' as the title of a book in which he exploded conservative approaches to Scripture.

encouraged some students to proceed on graduation to the United States for further study.

Duthie did not cease to care for his students onnce they had left the College. On the contrary he maintained contact with them and encouraged them in their ministries. One *alumnus* recalls that Duthie 'bullied me into doing an MPhil—and indeed came down from Scotland to be one of the assessors ... when I presented it: I think his last trip away from home.'

Unlike The Scottish Congregational College, New College was residential, and its occupants included both theological students (by now the minority) and hostel students who were studying a wide variety of University subjects. Among the latter was David Peel, then reading chemistry. When Duthie learned through another student that the chemist was contemplating the ministry and pondering the connections between the worlds of science and religion, Duthie directed him to books by Tielhard de Chardin, Tillich and Norman Pittenger.[52] Dr. Peel writes of Duthie, 'He was particularly impressed by Tillich and, especially, Nels Ferré. ... I found him very open to new ideas. ... Charles was very supportive when I applied to study in the USA on a W[orld] C[ouncil of] C[hurches] scholarship ... not least because I wanted to study "under" Schubert Ogden. ... I got the impression that Charles had more standing as a theologian in the USA than in the UK, but I might be wrong on that score.'

On 16 June 1977 the closing service of New College was held, with H. F. Lovell Cocks, the last surviving student of P. T. Forsyth, giving the address. The College was a casualty of the falling number of ministerial candidates and the desire of the United Reformed Church to rationalize its provision of theological education. Within the University of London the College's position had been weakened by the closure of Richmond (Methodist) College and by the decision of King's College, London, to cease training ministerial candidates.

Nancy and Charles Duthie retired to Portobello on the shore of the Firth of Forth, where from 1978 to 1979 he had charge of the Congregational church. By now, however, his health was failing and he died on 11 January 1981. The simple funeral service, conducted by the Portobello minister, Archie Small, included an address by Robert Waters, a former student and at the time General Secretary of the Congregational Union of Scotland.[53] At a Service of Thanksgiving held in London

---

[52] Following pastorates in Geddington and Kettering (1976-81) and Stockton on Tees (1981-6), David Peel became Tutor (1988-93) and then Principal (1993-2003) of Northern College, Manchester, the successor institution to Western College, where Payne, Alliott and Franks were Principals; Yorkshire United College, of which Simon was Principal; Lancashire College, where Simon trained and Adeney taught; and Paton College, where Duthie briefly taught. Dr. Peel was Moderator of the General Assembly of the United Reformed Church (2005-06), and is currently Education and Training Officer in the Northern Synod of that Church.

[53] For Archibald Amos Small (1913-1992) see SCM. He ministered at United Free churches until coming to Portobello (1980-83), and was Moderator of the UF General Assembly in 1977-8). For Robert Waters (1930—) see SCM. He had embarked upon a

on 19 February 1981 addresses were given by another former student, Bernard Thorogood,[54] and by Geoffrey Nuttall.

I

Turning now to Duthie's thought, I shall first consider his appraisals of contemporary theological writers and movements; then, taking the themes of Gospel, Church and World, I shall present his understanding of the Christian faith, of the Church, and of those intellectual trends and ethical currents in the world to which he felt bound to respond.

Some theologians who were contemporary with Karl Barth, or who have followed in his wake, have been largely persuaded by his theological stance, and a few appear to have been almost consumed by it. Others have found it possible to continue ploughing their theological furrow without reference to Barth. Some have nodded in Barth';s direction, almost as if they have felt that to have ignored him completely would have been an act of theological cowardice. Yet others, Franks among them, have had serious reservations concerning Barth's project: in Franks's case primarily on the ground that Barth unwarrantably disjoined dogmatics and apologetics. Duthie was among those who found it necessary to tackle sections of Barth's *corpus* from time to time. In his paper, 'Providence in the theology of Karl Barth' his general view of Barth's work becomes clear. Duthie carefully expounds Barth's understanding of providence, and in the course of so doing he make a number of adversely critical points. Barth writes,

> What is the value of all our thought and talk about Christ and His resurrection, about grace ... if in face of the simple demand to acknowledge God as the One who does all in all we are suddenly gripped by anxiety, as though perhaps we were ascribing too much to God and too little to the creature, as though perhaps we were encroaching too far on the particularity and autonomy of creaturely activity and especially on human freedom and responsibility? As if there could be any sense in sheltering from such a demand under the safe cover of a crude or subtle synergism![55]

Duthie wonders whether Barth 'has not such an anxiety-complex with regard to synergism that he fails to do justice to the reality and freedom of man.'[56] It is not

---

career in coal mining but, converted at one of Duthie's student campaigns in Musselburgh, he proceeded to the ministry. He held pastorates at East Kilbride (1962-8), and Augustine Bristo, Edinburgh (1968-71). He was Chairman of the Congregational Union of Scotland, 1970-71, and in the latter year became its General Secretary.

[54] For Bernard Thorogood (1927—) see SCM; WTW. He served in the South Pacific from 1953-70; from 1970-80 he was first Deputy Director (1970-71) and then Director of the Congregational Council for World Mission/Council for World Mission; and finally General Secretary of the United Reformed Church (1980-92).

[55] C. S. Duthie, 'Providence in the theology of Karl Barth,' 69. Duthie quotes Barth's *Church Dogmatics*, III.iii.147.

[56] Ibid., 68.

that Barth is unaware of 'the coincidence of divine and human action'; on the contrary, he repeatedly affirms it; but 'he leaves his statements on the level of generalization and does not show how this coincidence works out in practice in daily life.'[57]

Duthie's diagnosis of the cause Barth's 'anxiety-complex' is that he is so concerned to uphold the ultimate Lordship of God that he is reluctant 'to employ the concept of "cause" when dealing with God's activity and his relation to natural or creaturely happenings lest God and his freedom be made subordinate and subservient to "causality".'[58] Barth sidesteps the issue by saying, for example, that 'We have to understand the activity of God and that of the creature as a single action.'[59] Duthie questions whether this 'naked assertion' has a biblical basis; but his main point is that Barth 'simply puts the two things together and affirms their unity while holding fast to the transcendent character of the activity of God. The junction between God's action and man's is mysterious and unfathomable. What else can we expect if God be God?'[60] Duthie feels that at this point we come up against 'the issue that meets us in almost every aspect of Barth's theological system,'[61] and supremely in connection with the doctrine of reconciliation:

> Granted that there is a danger of falling into synergism, of thinking that man is the co-saviour of himself along with God, must we not take full measure of the fact that, although man is not the author of his own salvation, he is involved as a person in that salvation, responding as well as receiving, indeed responding in so far as he does receive?'[62]

Even if it be replied that the human response is itself of God's grace, it may still be held that Barth does not 'do justice to the human element in the "paradox of grace", the "yet not I but Christ". If faith is both the gift of God and my free act, then, as H. R. Machintosh used to urge, we must guard against the one-sided interpretation for which faith is nothing more than the Holy Spirit bending back upon himself *through me*.'[63] Duthie agrees with Barth that 'God does not need the creature but the creature has absolute need of God,' but argues that

> it is also true that God respects the being of those whom he has created in his own image. Barth does not take proper acount [*sic*] of what may be called the tensional because truly personal relationship between God and man. It is a relationship which by its very nature gives to man the opportunity either to co-operate or to resist.[64]

---

[57] Ibid., 69.
[58] Ibid., 72.
[59] Ibid., quoting *Church Dogmatics* III.iii.113.
[60] Ibid.
[61] Ibid., 73.
[62] Ibid.
[63] Ibid., 74.
[64] Ibid.

Here we see the combined influence of the biblical witness, theological discussions ancient and modern regarding 'who does what?' in the matter of human salvation, and the influence of a strain of theological personalism for which Duthie was indebted to H. H. Farmer, John Macmurray and others, as we shall see. More than this, however, as regards the impersonal natural order, Duthie does not think that Barth allows the world its 'relative independence'—a phrase of H. H. Farmer's. Barth appears to be 'haunted by the fear of making God "the author of evil".' Duthie accepts the fact of evil in the world, but goes on to ask, 'what if God accepts the responsibility for creating a world in which evil is first a possibility and then a reality? To maintain this is not creaturely impertinence or irreverence, for we know that God has involved himself at great cost in the life, death, and resurrection of Jesus Christ. This is the measure of his acceptance of responsibility for giving man life and freedom.'[65]

The upshot is that Barth's treatment of providence is disappointing because it precludes a reasoned and reasonable apologetic. It contains too many 'confident assertions which are not properly grounded', and 'We do not see much in it that throws light on the vexing problem of "the absence of God".'[66] All of this notwithstanding, Duthie thinks that we can learn from Barth, (a) 'that the Christian view of providence can only be constructed from within the circle of Christian faith'; (b) that the God whose providence we trust is the God made known in Jesus Christ; and (c) that we must find a way of combining the idea of God's universal Lordship over all with that of his transcendence. Having diagnosed the weaknesses in Barth's position, Duthie concludes by prescribing the remedy:

> What is needed to correct and amplify Barth's teaching is the reminder that once we have seen God in Jesus we know that this grace is not only condescending and undeserved, it is persuasive and accommodating. Because he is Love, God lays himself alongside his world and the personal beings he has created. He seeks to win without dominating. The application of this idea to Barth's theology as a whole would compel some modification not only in his teaching on providence but on much else.[67]

As early as 1966 Duthie was found regretting a tendency 'to dismiss [Emil] Brunner as a theologian of yesterday or to consider him as almost negligible when compared with his contemporaries, Barth and Tillich.'[68] Duthie seeks to redress the balance. He notes that from the publication in 1929 of Brunner's book, *The Theology of Crisis*, he has made a significant impact upon the theology of English-speaking countries. Although he outgrew the Religious Socialism movement by which he had been influenced, he never ceased to relate the Gospel to life. Indeed, 'His large work *The Divine Imperative* was the first full-scale attempt by a Reformed

---

[65] Ibid., 75.

[66] Ibid.

[67] Ibid., 76.

[68] Idem, 'Towards the Cross,' 9.

theologian for a number of years to write on Christian ethics,'[69] and it was followed by *Justice and the Social Order*. In the wake of World War I, and inspired by his reading of Luther and Kierkegaard, Brunner became critical of Schleiermacher's theology and of the liberal theology flowing down from it. With Barth, says Duthie, Brunner became 'the exponent of a theology of the Word that created faith, of Christianity as the vehicle of a unique revelation, of man as a sinner cast utterly for his salvation upon the divine mercy.'[70] Then came the breach with Barth over the question whether God's image in human beings was utterly destroyed by sin or not. Brunner, against Barth, contended that there remained a point of contact between sinners and God:

> This was the conclusion of Brunner the pastor and evangelist. He had already learnt from Pascal that an offensive Christian 'apology' is possible in which ... you start off from man in order to reach God, not by deducing God from man's situation but by showing man that he can neither save nor explain himself until he is willing to listen to ... the voice of God in Jesus Christ.[71]

Pascal's insight greatly influenced Brunner's anthropology. It also prompted his move away from that theological objectivism which not only distinguishes humanity from God but places them in stark opposition to each other. Hence Brunner's admission, in *The Divine-Human Encounter*, that the pietistic form of subjectivism had been wrongly traduced, and his new emphasis upon religious experience understood always in relation to the God who grants it. [We may suppose that Franks would have welcomed this 'conversion']. God always takes precedence in the relationship, and humanity is always *Man in Revolt*, called by God to repent, respond and obey.

Unlike Barth, Brunner does not place the 'speculative doctrine' of the Trinity at the front of his system, but elevates the biblical kerygma. Again, when others in burgeoning ecumenical times were elevating the institutional Church, Brunner published *The Misunderstanding of the Church*. He was concerned lest the institution—he referred to the 'Catholic structure'—should swamp the 'fellowship of persons' which is the true nature of the New Testament church. At this point Duthie demurs on the ground that while the danger to which Brunner points must be avoided, the Church (on earth) cannot but have a shape in the world if it is to be recognizable. Duthie concludes a masterly summary as follows:

> Brunner's Christian thought is a stream that broadens from its source to include the experience of the individual, the life of the family, the order of the state, the march of civilisations. Like Tillich and Ferré he finds no sphere of life beyond the relevance of the Christian faith. The source of the stream itself is never in doubt. It is that original, fontal, creative outgoing of God towards man which meets us and

---

[69] Ibid.

[70] Ibid.

[71] Ibid.

claims us in Jesus Christ, the 'self-movement of God.' This is the theme of *The Mediator*.

It is a long time now since I read this stabbing sentence in the preface. 'The fundamental reason for the impotence of the Church is her ignorance of the power of Christ.' That is a typical sentence of Emil Brunner. The Church's only hope lies in being joined to that centre.[72]

As more than one of his former students remarked to me, Duthie regularly returned to the thought of Paul Tillich and Nels Ferré, and he did so, too, in his *British Weekly* articles. He himself wrote, 'It must be obvious ... that I owe a special debt to certain thinkers. If I make mention of Paul Tillich and Nels Ferré, it is not because I agree with all the main positions they occupy but because I feel deeply that they are concerned to fashion a living theology for our own time, a theology which is faithful to the "given" Gospel in terms of man's predicament to-day.'[73] It is not, therefore surprising that to Tillich Duthie accorded space on three successive weeks, and this in addition to single articles on other occasions. By the time he wrote his series of three articles all three volumes of Tillich's *Systematic Theology* were to hand.[74] Duthie carefully recounts the main lines of Tillich's thought. He reminds us that Tillich distinguishes between a kerygmatic theology the main purpose of which is to announce the Gospel, and an apologetic or 'answering' theology designed to interpret life from the vantage-point of central Christian affirmations.[75] God is not *a* being—even the greatest being in the world, God is the ground of all being, being itself. At this point Duthie corrects J. A. T. Robinson, whose book, *Honest to God*, had caused a stir when it was published in 1963. Robinson had borrowed ideas from Tillich and others, and had waged war on spatial metaphors: God is not *up* there or *out* there. But, says Duthie, Tillich had no problem with the use of spatial metaphors and, indeed, thought that such useage was unavoidable:

---

[72] Ibid. On the death of Brunner, Edwin Robertson published a tribute to him in *The British Weekly*, see 'Brunner, the great,' 6. He notes how easily the English took Brunner to their hearts and then remarks, 'I think Barth has always been more popular in Scotland, which only goes to show how much more serious the Scots are in theology than the English.' This is not universally true. Moreover, it might equally show that the Scots are more imprisoned in a disjunctive mind-set than the English—and this is not universally true either. At the end of what is generally a kindly tribute, Robertson surmizes that 'Brunner will not long remain second to Barth ...'

[73] C. S. Duthie, *God in His World*, 8.

[74] Duthie's set of Tillich's *Systematic Theology* is now in my possession. There are many underlinings and numerous marginal annotations. The latter include queries to Tillich, observations such as 'Very Pascalian', and instructions to himself to 'Think this out.'

[75] For my brief observations on Tillich's method see *The Philosophy of Religion 1875-1980*, 170-175; *Enlightenment, Ecumenism, Evangel*, 303-6.

> The question whether God could be *located* was for [Tillich] a senseless question. The real question was whether God was the ultimate, whether we draw a circle called the world and put God in it or draw a circle called God and put the world in it. Tillich was sure the second mode of thinking was the proper Christian procedure. ... This view is often called pantheism [*sic*: read 'panentheism'[76]] ('everything in God') ..[77]

Tillich analyses the human situation, Duthie continues, and finds that we are estranged from God, ourselves and others. How does Tillich think we may be re-united with God?

> The possibility of such re-union has been effected by Jesus the Christ, in whom the New Being had appeared in the world, changing history for ever. In Him God Himself participates in our human life, entering into our estrangement and conquering it from within.[78]

In his third volume Tillich discusses the spiritual presence, eternal life and the kingdom of God.

In his second article on Tillich, Duthie draws attention to the way in which Tillich devises his own terminology, and draws language from such fields as psychology, sociology and philosophy. Tillich insists that biblical theology permeates his system, but his objective is to reach people for whom traditional language has become irrelevant. To this end, the risk, in Tillich's words, that 'the substance of the Christian message may be lost' must be taken. In Duthie's opinion Tillich builds on a sound foundation: eternal or 'unambiguous' life if a gift of God, and auto-soterism is ruled out. The several Christian Churches live in an ambiguous situation. They are related to the new being in Christ as a spiritual community, but at the same time they are unholy, divided and non-universal. Hence, 'While the Spiritual Presence is in them, because Christ is, [the Churches] must always point beyond themselves to Him.'[79]

The third article on Tillich concerns 'The final destiny', and includes Duthie's assessment of Tillich's system as a whole. For Tillich the kingdom of God means that 'saving power breaks into history, works through history, but is not created by history.'[80] The centre of history is the appearance of the new being as Christ. The Churches point to the kingdom, but they are not the kingdom as such. On the contrary, 'Tillich seems to rise to something like hot indignation as he contemplates the arrogance with which Churches make claims for their own life in the face of such gross distortions as exclusivism, persecution and wrongful alliance with the secular

---

[76] This error was corrected at the foot of the following week's article.

[77] C. S. Duthie, 'Theologian significant,' 9. I have myself suggested that when spatial metaphors are used of God they are most appropriately construed in moral terms. See *Confessing and Commending the Faith*, 126-8.

[78] C. D. Duthie, 'Theologian significant,' 9.

[79] Idem, 'The spiritual presence,' 9.

[80] Idem, 'The final destiny,' 9.

power.'[81] This is an articulation of Tillich's Protestant principle derived from Luther, who opposed a false Church in the interests of a true Church 'submissive to the Word of the Gospel and the power of the Spirit.'[82] As to the last things, Tillich says that we may maintain agnosticism in face of God's inexpressible glory; or we may interpret New Testament passages concerning the Second Coming literally; or, as Duthie phrases it, 'We may say that the Kingdom of God as the end of history means that nothing created will be lost: it will be lifted up into the life of God.'[83] Tillich holds to the third alternative, and understands eternal life as not simply future, but as now, because God is. Alive to the challenge to universalism of the biblical teaching concerning heaven and hell, Tillich says that 'We can take for granted neither "the security of the return to God" nor the baselessness of "the threat of eternal death". ... It is his belief, however, that in the end the finite centres we call men will pass from the state of estrangement into that of "essentialisation" which is fulfilment through reunion with God, the Ground of Being and Father of our Lord Jesus Christ.[84]

How does Duthie evaluate Tillich's system? First, he welcomes the powerful assertion of the Protestant principle. Secondly, he thinks that Tillich succeeds in correlating Christian answers with questions posed by the challenges of life. Thirdly, there is a 'grandeur that liberates in Tillich's sustained endeavour to pass beyond unsatisfying traditional theologies to a more compelling view of God's relation to our estrangement ...'[85] But there are also 'inescapable questions and doubts.' We have to work from the Gospel to the human situation and not only *vice versa*, for we must not only address human questions but 'submit them to God's questioning.' Again, 'it is doubtful whether Tillich's idea that nothing is lost to the divine life rises to the full height of a Biblical-Christian doctrine of eternal life.' Duthie therefore thinks that there is 'some point in reading Tillich with Barth in hand. The reverse procedure has also much to be said for it!'[86] But it is in his first *British Weekly* article that Duthie confronts the underlying issue regarding Tillich's method, and what he says is worth quoting in full:

> [W]e cannot *use* Tillich without raising the question of the truth of his system. The attempt to build a system is not to be condemned in itself: Christianity is a philosophy of life as well as a way of life springing from the Gospel. And we can acknowledge gladly that Tillich's whole endeavour to think things together as a whole is based upon his conviction that the world has *some* kind of unity founded on the unity of God, despite the disintegrating effect of sin and estrangement. What is not clear is whether the starting-point for his synthesis [is] in the philosophy of Being Itself or the revelation of God in Christ as the New Being or an uneasy combination of both. Very often it appears to be the philosophy of Being itself;

[81] Ibid.
[82] Idem, 'Saint Martin Luther?' 9.
[83] Idem, 'The final destiny,' 9.
[84] Ibid.
[85] Ibid.
[86] Ibid.

and then one feels that the realities of the Christian faith have to be fitted into this framework.[87] At other times the impression is given that Tillich is trying to subdue himself and his thought to the reality of God in Christ. At still other times he looks like a man driving two horses that find it almost impossible to pull together.

My own judgment is that Tillich is a man from whom we can learn but hardly a man to follow all the way.[88]

In another *British Weekly* article Duthie was prompted to reflect further upon what he thought was missing in Tillich's writings. A friend who had read his series wondered whether he had capitulated to Tillich's theology. In reply Duthie admitted that his emphasis had been rather upon appreciation than upon criticism, but he then said,

There is undoubtedly something big missing in Tillich's theology. ... [It is] the note of doxology, of exulatation in what God has done for the human race in Christ. There is much about the love of God but there is not enough about the grace of God. This missing element becomes apparent when I lay Tillich alongside another theologian who has meant and still means much to me. I mean Peter Taylor Forsyth.[89]

He proceeds to testify that 'One page of Forsyth can do more to stir the conscience and inflame the heart than a dozen pages of some thinkers of quite high repute.'[90] Having found the missing note in Forsyth, and while granting that a major reinterpretation of the Christian message was now required, Duthie cautioned that

The peril of all re-interpretation is that in our concern to make the Gospel understandable, we may so accommodate it to the Zeitgeist that it loses its convincing and converting power. We may gain what looks like a larger faith only to find that it is a less effective faith.

It is because this is true that in the final issue I find myself, like many others, closer to Forsyth than to Tillich.[91]

Towards the end of his article Duthie, ever the theologian-evangelist, poses two questions which are as pertinent now as they were when he articulated them:

---

[87] This is a function of Tillich's underlying, and self-confessed, indebtedness to philosophical idealism. He wrote, 'I am an idealist if idealism means the assertion of the identity of thinking and being as the principle of truth.' See *The Interpretation of History*, 60. For other examples of idealist 'fitting in' of Christian truth see Alan P. F. Sell, *Defending and Declaring the Faith*, ch. 4; idem, *Philosophical Idealism and Christian Belief*.

[88] C. S. Duthie, 'A prophet or a heretic?' 9.

[89] Idem, 'Fireworks in a fog?', 9.

[90] Ibid.

[91] Ibid.

> Is our trouble today in the Church that we have no substitute for evangelical conversion and are endeavouring to get men and women to pursue the Christian goals without the Christian dynamic? Is there any alternative to the radical change by which Christ makes men [and women, as we should nowadays rightly say] new creatures, filled with thankfulness to God and eager to do His will?[92]

Duthie had a particular affection for Nels Ferré and, as already indicated, he was in not uncritical sympathy with his theological stance. In one of his articles he introduces Ferré's book, *The Living God of Nowhere and Nothing*. The author's idea is that God is ultimate; we cannot put him into our space or time. Similarly, the term 'theism' is redundant because it implies the philosophy of substance; but God cannot be even the greatest substance for that would make him a being. Ferré stands with Tillich in holding that God is not *a* Being. But he does not subscribe to Tillich's panentheism. In Duthie's words of explanation:

> When 'Being itself' is the description of God, the personal living God of the Bible disappears. Nor can [Ferré] accept any theology which seeks to interpret God in terms of 'process', the favoured word of his teacher, A. N. Whitehead. 'Process thinking in its deepest impulses is rather Buddhist than Christian.' God and the world are not co-equally eternal. God alone is final and the world is dependent on Him.[93]

How, then, are we to speak of God? Ferré expounds the biblical terms, 'Spirit', 'Life', and 'Love' as being decisive. While Ferré has always understood love to be the primary characteristic of God, we need the word 'Spirit' 'to express His ultimate, transcendent and mysterious character.'[94] He even supposes that God 'can withdraw as personal Spirit while yet remaining present as sustaining Spirit'—a proposition to which Duthie, like I myself, can assign no clear meaning. We are on more familiar ground when Ferré contends that the living God who is Spirit and Love, has become incarnate in Christ. However, in opposition to the basis of the World Council of Churches, namely, that Jesus is 'God and Saviour', Ferré says that 'My main contention is that the affirmation that Jesus is God is a myth while the confession that Jesus is the Son of God is sober truth.' Duthie finds this use of the term 'myth' unhelpful, whilst granting that the point being made coheres with the New Testament and the classical creeds. His questions notwithstanding, Duthie commends the book as one which 'breathes a spirit of adventure and hopefulness.'[95]

Duthie does not confine his attention to exotic theologians. He also writes on English, Scottish and Welsh thinkers. Consider first John Oman, of whom, as noted earlier, Duthie said that while he found value in his personalism, he was not and never could be a follower. Why was this so? The answer comes in a tightly-packed paragraph as follows:

---

[92] Ibid.

[93] C. S. Duthie, 'The God of nowhere and nothing,' 9.

[94] Ibid.

[95] Ibid.

> There have been Christian thinkers in our century who have felt uncomfortable with the thought that God comes to dwell within. F. R. Tennant and John Oman were among them. Oman was afraid that we might construe God's grace as mechanical and irresistible. Grace, he kept saying, is just God being gracious and this gracious God always acts in a fatherly way, respecting the freedom He has given us. He interpreted God's grace chiefly as God's mercy. Oman's thought is a welcome correction of all Christian systems which talk of God acting upon us as a physical force acts upon another physical force; but he missed something very big in the New Testament. God does indeed respect man's freedom and never treats us as less than personal; but He knows that our freedom is not complete and has been marred by our wrongdoing. Man may be God's child but he is God's erring and sinful child; and his condition is such that he needs to be forgiven, delivered, enlightened and empowered. That broad emancipation is something that happens 'within the soul.'
>
> We can agree with Oman that the gracious God acts in relation to us both in accordance with His own nature and the nature He has given to us and then go on to see how broad and deep this renewing action is.[96]

In Duthie's opinion, Oman's student, H. H. Farmer,[97] made good the deficiency with his version of encounter theology. He commends Farmer for his witness to the fact that 'Christianity is a life to be lived as well as a faith to be held,' and for propounding 'a theology that can be preached.'[98] Farmer, he continues, is indebted to Oman for the emphasis upon reverence, freedom and sincerity, and also for the idea that in religion the supernatural means the personal. To Farmer, as Duthie expounds him,

> In the Christian faith we have to deal with 'the world of persons'; but a consistent 'personalism' is not simply a philosophy of inter-personal relationships on the horizontal plane; it is rooted in the ultimate-personal, God, who stands over against the world of men as Father and Lord.[99]

Another influence upon Farmer is the 'I-Thou' philosophy of Martin Buber, Karl Heim and E. Griesbach. As Duthie correctly judges, this 'is really another form of the same basic [personalist] conception.'[100] Thus

> *The Servant of the Word* is a fine exposition of the conviction that in the personal encounter between preacher and hearer God lays his inescapable claim upon the worshipping congregation. Farmer uses this idea of 'claim' quite often. But God's

---

[96] Idem, 'A God of action,' 9.

[97] For Farmer (1892-1981) see DHT; DTCBP; ODNB; WTW; WWW, 1981-90; Healey, F. G., *Prospect for Theology.Essays in Honour of H. H. Farmer*; C. H. Partridge, *H. H. Farmer's Theological Interpretation of Religions.*

[98] Idem, 'Darkness and light,' 9.

[99] Ibid.

[100] Ibid.

> relation to us is not merely that of claim. He comes to us at once in 'absolute demand' and in 'final succour'. If He asks all, He gives all.[101]

God's supreme giving is at the Cross, where light shines out of darkness, but does not banish it. Hence Farmer's turn away from the classical proofs of the existence of God which, in his view, presuppose a clearer understanding of things than we have, in favour of an emphasis upon the reasonableness of belief in God. In Farmer's view, religious conviction comprises

> the coercive, the pragmatic and the reflective. Belief in God speaks persuasively to what is deepest in us; it proves itself in the business of living; and it offers a more satisfying view of our mysterious world than any alternative faith of philosophy can put forward.[102]

While Christians must render the Gospel intelligible and relevant, sceptics must approach the Christian faith seriously and expectantly.[103]

Providence is among the themes upon which Farmer wrote widely:

> He believes that we must somehow hold together the idea of the 'relative independence of the world', with its order given to it by God, and God's sovereign rule over the world. If we have room only for the first, God becomes powerless. If we make the second completely regulative, then we may fall into a dangerous monism in which every action is God's and the end it complete determinism.[104]

Duthie finds that Farmer correctly notes 'the paradox of the religious perception that all events whatsoever lies within the providential ordering of God, yet without ceasing to be the result of intramundane activities, including the activities of free moral agents,' but he queries the suggestion that Farmer borrows from Heim that 'what seems impossible within one "dimension" may be quite possible when considered from the viewpoint of a "superior" dimension.'[105]

At this point I think that Duthie lets Farmer off too lightly, though I grant that in an article of one thousand words on an author's *corpus* the main emphasis must be upon exposition rather than adverse criticism. But it does seem that the purely speculative invocation of more than one 'dimension' is redundant given that proper agnosticism which Farmer thinks we are necessarily obliged to affirm in a world in which light shines in the darkness and we see only 'puzzling reflections in a mirror' (II Corinthians 13:12). Again, when Duthie concurs with Farmer in maintaining that 'Christianity as the religion of the unique revelation comes not only in judgment to

---

[101] Ibid.

[102] Ibid.

[103] The best agnostics and atheists have always done this—and had a sound grasp of the claims of Christianity. From reading some currently well-marketed writers I suspect that in these respects we nowadays need a better class of atheist and agnostic.

[104] C. S. Duthie, 'Darkness and light,' 9.

[105] Ibid.

other faiths but in fulfilment of any truth they may possess,' we seem to hear an echo of that pyramid view of religions which was espoused by A. M. Fairbairn and many others in the late nineteenth century (and which was at least an improvement upon the dismissal of all non-Christian religion as heathenish), according to which all the religions have something of worth, but Christianity has most. As it stands the proposition seems too exclusively orientated towards truths claimed by religions, whereas Christianity supremely emphasises something that has been *done* at the Cross and not just taught; and it overlooks the fact that the first thing the 'unique revelation' judges is the Church. Finally—and, again, I may be asking for too much—I miss any recognition of the fact that by the time Duthie wrote his article, the encounter theology, and especially the idea of a self-authenticating experience, had come under attack from such philosophers as C. B. Martin and Ronald Hepburn, and that Farmer's pupil, John Hick, had risen in his defence. I cannot here treat the matter in detail, but at the heart of it are the views that from the having of an experience we may not argue to an object which has prompted the experience: we may simply be reporting on the state of our psyche; and that since we can be mistaken when we think that we are experiencing other human beings as they really are, how much more so with claims to experience God? Hick properly reminds the opponents that Farmer actually thinks that the theistic arguments are religiously improper and philosophically untenable and that, accordingly, Farmer was not erecting a theistic argument on the basis on human experience. Rather, he was attempting to show that Christian belief was a coherent possibility, by relating religious experience both to lived confirmation of it and to rational reflection upon it. He was not simply appealing to a self-certifying experience of encounter with God.[106]

As we saw, Duthie was impressed by the personalism of John Macmurray from his undergraduate days onwards.[107] Not, indeed, that this was the only aspect of Macmurray's thought which appealed to him. He valued those writings of Macmurray that encouraged thought on communism and the place of Russia in the world; and he was grateful for Macmurray's discussion of chastity in *Reason and Emotion*, which analyzed the concept not only in relation to things extra-marital but to marriage itself. He welcomed Macmurray's distinction between a society founded on cultural, economic and political considerations and 'a community which is founded upon concern for the neighbour'[108]—a distinction which cannot, presumably, devolve into a strong disjunction. In his Gifford Lectures, *The Self as Agent* and *Persons in Relation* Macumurray discussed the organic relation of action

[106] I have developed these points somewhat in *Confessing and Commending the Faith*, 342-4. The relevant works are C. B. Martin, 'A religious way of knowing'; Ronald W. Hepburn, *Christianity and Paradox*; and John Hick, 'A philosopher criticizes theology.'

[107] For Macmurray (1891-1976) see DTCBP; ODNB; SDCHT; J. E. Costello, *John Macmurray*; A. Hood, *Baillie, Oman and Macmurray*; D. Fergusson and N. Dower, eds, *John Macmurray: Critical Perspectives*.

[108] C. S. Duthie, 'Religion and reality,' 9.

and thought, and the unavoidably communal character of life. Duthie rightly says that 'John Macmurray has been a philosopher who considered the study of life more important than the study of the history of philosophy'—a fact, I may add, which did not commend him to those philosophers who eschewed the role of prophet and 'public intellectual', which represented a sea-change in attitude from that of his predecessor in the Chair of Moral Philosophy at Edinburgh University, A. E. Taylor. As for religion, Macmurray thought that 'the distinction between real and unreal religion is more important than that between true and false.'[109] This is consistent with the view he expressed following his reception into the Religious Society of Friends, namely, 'The central conviction which distinguishes the Society of Friends is that Christianity cannot be defined in terms of doctrinal beliefs; that what makes us Christians is an attitude of mind and a way of life; and that these are compatible with wide variations and with changes in beliefs and opinions.'[110] Here, I think, is a doctrine-life disjunction that Duthie might well have questioned. An 'attitude of the mind' towards whom? A 'way of life' in the company of whom? Granted that people are not made Christians by assenting to what Quakers would call 'notions', but would it be a rational act—or, since Christians are supposed to love God *inter alia* with all their mind, a Christian act—to repose one's 'trust and confidence', (which Macmurray opposes to intellectual assent) in one of whom they knew nothing—not even that he were worth following?[111] Furthermore, would it accord with Macmurray's view that action (and presumably the act of faith-commitment) is not *ad hoc*, but has a teleological dimension and is grounded in reasons? I think not, and therefore I suggest that doctrine is not so readily expungeable as Macmurray proposes.[112] When Macmurray goes on to argue that, in Duthie's words, 'the Churches should recognise each other as Christian and work for the kind of cohesion which will include a variety of belief, ritual and organisation,'[113] he concedes the point concerning the non-excludability of doctrine; and we might note that 'ritual' and '(church) organisation' are frequently rooted in doctrinal considerations: for example, How are we to understand the sacraments? What is the nature of the Church?

The Welshman Duthie introduced to readers of his *British Weekly* articles is Keri Evans.[114] Evans's book, *My Spiritual Pilgrimage. From Philosophy to Faith* was

---

[109] Ibid.

[110] Ibid. Duthie quotes from Macmurray's *Search for Reality in Religion*, 70.

[111] In his *Outline of Christian Belief*, 14, Duthie declares that faith 'is not an act of the intellect: it is what Brunner calls the totality-act of the personality.' But is not the intellect implicated in this? Thirteen lines later, Duthie restores the balance: 'We cannot believe "in" God without believing something about God.'

[112] See further Alan P. F. Sell, 'Friends and philosophy,' 114.

[113] C. S. Duthie, 'Religion and reality,' 9.

[114] For Evan Keri Evans (1860-1941) see his autobiography; CYB, 1942, 435; Robert Ellis, *Living Echoes of the Welsh Revival*, ch. 8. The CYB obituary is careful to state, 'Not associated so much with the emotional and popular side of the revival, [Evans] was instrumental in guiding the awakening into deeper and more permanent channels.'

sent to Duthie by a reader of his articles, and he was sufficiently impressed by it to devote an article to its author. Evans, like Payne and Alliott before him, had studied philosophy at Glasgow, in his case under Edward Caird. In 1888 he achieved first class honours in Philosophy and, like Duthie, he was awarded a Ferguson Scholarship, on the strength of which he went to Leipzig University. In 1891 he became Professor of Philosophy at Bangor University College, and held that position until 1895 when, constrained by a call to the ministry, he went for training to the Prebsyterian College, Carmarthen. He then served as a Congregational minister at Hawen, Cardigan (1897-1900) and Priory South Church, Carmarthen (1900-1938). From 1900 to 1907 he combined his Carmarthen ministerial duties with a Professorship at the Presbyterian College there. Duthie reports that from the philosophical idealist Edward Caird Evans learned 'the meaning of "dying to live." The same lesson was given at greater depth by Henry Drummond,' whose sermons Evans heard in Glasgow: 'Christ was brought from the past and from the clouds,' wrote Evans, 'to be a living person in the present and our companion on life's way.'[115] This experience was intensified during the Welsh Revival of 1904. Evans afterwards reflected that insofar as they were both connected with the person of Christ, the experiences he had had under Drummond's preaching and during the Welsh Revival were connected. But the latter was 'more highly-objective for the simple reason that it was more deeply-subjective, and at the same time broader and many-sided.'[116] For all their depth, Evans did not allow his religious experiences to blunt the edge of his reason. On the contrary, he recognized the danger in times of revival that the spiritual may, wrongly, be elevated above the moral.

On all of this Duthie offers two observations. First, that the sub-title of Evans's book is not accurate, for he was a person of faith whilst he was a professional philosopher. Secondly, Evans's book

> compels us to look twice at what we mean by 'religious *experience*.' It is a good word when it reminds us of the immediacy of our contact with God. But faith is more than 'experience'. It has a continuing life which *includes* experiences of many kinds. Most importantly and especially for the Christian, experience must never be separated from its object [Schleiermacher and Franks say 'Amen!']. The Christ we experience is greater by far than our experience of Him; and He creates our experience as he creates the experience of all Christians.[117]

The first proposition in the concluding sentence here is a truism; the second would bear further elucidation as regards the manner whereby Christ does what he is here said to do.

By seeing how Duthie adjusted his thinking in his *British Weekly* articles to that of some of his philosophico-theological contemporaries we now have a fuller understanding of his own vantage-point. If we continue to be uncertain of his general

---

[115] C. S. Duthie, 'Spiritual pilgrimage,' 9.
[116] Ibid.
[117] Ibid.

stance, a paragraph from his Memoirs, written at the end of his Edinburgh Principalship, will come to our aid:

> It is ... [the] interest in the nexus between theology and life, theory and practice that explains, I believe, my alignments and affinities, my distastes and revulsions in theology. Having been brought up with an open-minded evangelical faith I could not be satisfied with liberalism, although I trust I learned from the Fosdicks of this world. But I never felt entirely at home with the neo-orthodoxy that stemmed from Barth. It was too intransigent, too contemptuous of experience, too sure that it had the final truth about God in its pocket. I am forced to smile when I find that the radical theologies of today often betray the same intransigence. It is one thing to be sure, quite another to be cocksure. It has been my habit during the last fifteen years—long before Robinson popularised Tillich—to immerse students in Barth and Tillich as two of the major theologians of our century. In simple terms Barth is the man who recalled the Church to the Gospel. Tillich is the man who recalled the church to the task of interpreting the Gospel. I see a certain complementariness between these two theologians.[118]

To this we might add that Duthie brought to his theological criticism a strong conviction drawn from the personalist philosophical theologies of the first half of the twentieth century. Against this background I shall now turn to Duthie's understanding of the Gospel—in the sense of the principal doctrines of the Christian faith.

II

Like Paul, Augustine, P. T. Forsyth and others, Duthie has not left us a fully-rounded theological system. As is the case with his illustrious forebears, most of his writings are occasional. This, in a sense, is what we should expect, given his practical-*cum*-pastoral interests in rapidly-changing times, and his particular gift of addressing the concerns of lay persons in lucid and far from shallow articles. It is, however, possible to order his scattered doctrinal convictions, and this is what I shall now attempt to do. By way of preface, I should note that in Duthie's view faith is much more than doctrinal assent. It

> consists essentially in a life of fellowship with an obedience to God, issuing in the practical service of love towards the neighbour. ... [It] may come into being and continue at a fairly low level of intellectual comprehension. Nevertheless ... faith by its very nature seeks to understand ... God, His relation to man, the meaning of history, the world, the goal to which creation is moving. All Christians are theologians in the sense that they wish to live by a faith which understands as far as it is possible to understand.[119]

[118] Idem, Memoirs, 19.

[119] Idem, *Outline of Christian Belief*, 8.

The motivation in all of this is the conviction of the reasonableness of belief—a conviction 'based upon the experience of the trustworthiness of God in Christ. Where understanding cannot penetrate, we can still trust Him—and obey.'[120] Characteristically, he adds, 'the thought which shapes belief and true belief that bears fruit in action must be under-girded by prayer. Belief finds its place within the whole of the full-orbed Christian life.'[121] With these considerations in mind, let us hear Duthie on some basic Christian doctrines.

In one of his *British Weekly* articles Duthie replies to a woman correspondent who feels baffled by the Trinity. He first affirms that difficulties concerning the Trinity are not to be dismissed as unreal: 'We must know what we believe about the God we worship and seek to obey.'[122] Moreover, we should respect a doctrine which has played such a large part in the Church's history, especially given that the doctrine developed from the strict monotheism of Israel: 'If Christians in the first period of the Church's life were inexorably driven towards the doctrine of the Trinity, it surely must have been for good and sufficient reasons.'[123] It entailed a profound revision of inherited ideas about God which was stimulated by the impact which Jesus had made. Christians came to believe, with Paul, that 'God was in Christ reconciling the world to himself' (II Corinthians 5: 19), and that at Pentecost 'The Spirit of the Christlike God came in power.'[124] Duthie grants that a full doctrine of the Trinity cannot be obtained from Scripture, but he claims that the materials for the doctrine are there: 'Jesus spoke of God as Father. He also promised that the Spirit would come. Paul's letter to the Romans, especially in its 8th chapter, shows one early attempt to put the ideas of Father, Son and Spirit together.'[125]

These ideas, Duthie continues, 'belong together in the unity of Christian experience. We may say that the Father comes to us in the Son, that we come to the Father through the Son and that our new life is life "in the Spirit".'[126] He proceeds to consider Brunner's view that the doctrine of the Trinity, while it derives from biblical thought, is also indebted to philosophical ideas which are remote from that thought. Duthie agrees that there are dangers in giving priority to theological reflection over Christian experience, but he reiterates his view that the early theologians 'were right when they concluded from experience and from thought that God is triune.'[127] Hence Barth's placing of the doctrine among the Prolegomena to his *Church Dogmatics*. His reasoning was that 'God is as He has revealed Himself to be. And if we can discern Father, Son and Holy Spirit in that revelation by the process of reflection, then Father, Son and Holy Spirit are real elements, real

---

[120] Ibid., 9.
[121] Ibid., 19.
[122] Idem, 'Baffled by the Trinity,' 9.
[123] Ibid.
[124] Ibid.
[125] Ibid.
[126] Ibid.
[127] Ibid.

"persons" as we say in God's being.'[128] Duthie finds help in Leonard Hodgson's distinction between mathematical unity on the one hand and constitutive or organic unity on the other. The Trinity is a unity of the latter type, and it yields the social interpretation of the Trinity. However, in his attempt to ensure that the persons of the Trinity are understood as equals—this with a view to ensuring that the Son and Spirit are not conceived of as divine in a secondary sense—Hodgson himself veers in the direction of a mathematical-quantitative unity which is problematic. We recall that Franks was also concerned by Hodgson's account of the social Trinity, and I reiterate my promise to return to this matter in the Conclusion to this book.

His concern to avoid tritheism notwithstanding, Duthie nevertheless says, 'Provided we do not think of God as a triad of inter-related personal beings, it is not wrong to thing of a "fellowship" within the divine Being. The fact that the human person has a social as well as a solitary aspect may be part of what we mean by man's being made in the image of God.'[129] I suspect that we should need to emphasize the 'may' in the sentence just quoted, and Duthie would seem to be aware of this when elsewhere he quotes and comments upon Jesus's words in John's Gospel, 17: 5:

> 'And now, Father, glorify me in thine own presence with the glory which I had with thee before the world began.' ... These words point to the reality of eternal fellowship in God. In order to be in a personal relationship we need 'the other': God has 'the other' within Himself. From Augustine onwards Christian thinkers have striven hard to picture the 'inner life of the Trinity.' When we begin to talk of 'procession' and 'co-inherence' and even 'co-equality we soon find ourselves in the realm of conjecture.[130]

Duthie's next point is that the order of the words, Father, Son and Spirit, is important, for in God Fatherhood has a certain, albeit non-chronological, priority: 'We speak naturally and rightly of God as Father, we think of Christ as revealing the Father, we pray mostly to God as our Father, as Jesus Himself taught us. Any theology which does not take these facts into account is defective.'[131] Furthermore, in *God and His World* Duthie declares, against Hodgson' view of the equality of the persons on the Trinity, that when Paul contemplates Christ's final victory he says that 'when all things shall be subdued unto him, then shall the Son also himself be subject unto him that put all things under him, that God may be all in all' (I Corinthians 15: 24-8). This, to Duthie, indicates that 'within the being of God the Father has a determinative position.'[132] But none of this, he repeats, should be so interpreted as to question the full divinity of the Son and the Spirit. Our 'frequent

---

[128] Ibid.
[129] Ibid.
[130] Idem, *Outline of Christian Belief*, 37.
[131] Idem., 'Baffled by the Trinity,' 9.
[132] Idem, *God in His World*, 45.

failures' in construing the Trinity 'remind us that even when He makes Himself known to us God retains the mysterious character of His being.'[133]

On the relation between the Son and the Spirit, Duthie has this to say:

> It was only when the revelation of God had been completed in the life, death, resurrection and ascension of His Son that men could know what God was, and therefore what His Spirit was. The Holy Spirit is the Spirit of the God whose character shines out in the man Christ Jesus. ... A distinction does exist which can probably best be expressed by saying that while the Spirit is the cause or the agent of the divine indwelling, Christ is the substance or the content of that indwelling.[134]

As so often, Duthie ends on a practical note:

> For the practical business of life it is enough to know that Christ has revealed God to us and that through Him we have access to the Father: that the Father cares for us His children and longs that all men shall know that He cares: that the Spirit is God himself in action through Christ in human life, whether in the Church or beyond it. ... Jesus told his men that it is not saying 'Lord, Lord' that counts, but doing the will of the heavenly Father. We may add that it is not saying 'Father, Son and Spirit' that has primary importance, but acting out our obedience to God, however faulty our understanding of him.[135]

The missing notes that one might have expected to have heard struck, even in a short article on the Trinity, are (a) the experience of the early Christians of Christ as Saviour which, since they believed that God alone can save, threw the Christological question into relief; and (b) the way in which the doctrine of the Trinity was forged and refined as mission took the Church into non-Jewish worlds of thought, and as 'heretics' presented doctrinal challenges which required clear answers.

Turning now to God as creator, we find that Duthie anchors the doctrine not, in the first place, in the early chapters of Genesis, because ancient cosmology will not suffice; nor in scientific theories about the 'origin' of the universe, because science as such has nothing to offer concerning creation by God; but in the prologue to John's Gospel, for 'Christ is the key to the greatness of God as He is to the heart of God.'[136] In Duthie's view God created the world by the word of his power; his creation is good; and humanity is the crown of it. If all this is granted, we may then turn to science for insights concerning the world as given. For example, 'Science can ... help us to understand how God works on a vast time-scale to bring forth a being like man. We revere God the more and not the less when we understand His patience'[137]—there, once more, is the idea of the patience of God, to which Duthie

[133] Idem, 'Baffled by the Trinity,' 9.
[134] Idem, *God in His World*, 183, 184.
[135] Ibid.
[136] Idem, *Outline of Christian Belief*, 44.
[137] Ibid., 45.

so often returns. Above all, the doctrine of creation proclaims that God, not the world, is ultimate. The world is not co-equal, co-eternal or identical with God; nor is God an 'emerging God who is virtually a prisoner in the universe ... God is sovereign.'[138] Hence God, who has a purpose for the world, can bring his work to its fulfilment. Of this 'Christ, the agent of creation, continuance and consummation is the sure pledge.'[139]

In a number of places Duthie discusses the relations between God and the world, especially as these bear upon the problem of evil and suffering. His fundamental conviction is that if God is as revealed in Christ, then he cannot be separate from the world, but must be involved in it. Indeed, 'the longer we look at Jesus and the more we trust the insight of Christian faith, the stronger becomes the urge to think of God as the Father who lays Himself alongside His children and enters sufferingly—yes, sufferingly, into their condition.'[140] In the absence of this conviction, what could Christians say about the suffering and evil in the world? First, they could say that 'the very existence of a world suitable for the life of personal beings, gifted with freedom, carries with it the possibility of evil.'[141] Even if human beings had lived impeccable lives from the first they could not have avoided such natural evils as storm and flood, earthquake and forest fire. Moreover, there is the fact of moral and personal evil—of sin. In Duthie's opinion, 'We are reluctant to state roundly that God committed the world to an adventure so worthwhile that the inescapable risk of evil is justified.'[142] While it is true that at the consummation the entire created order will be transformed, he continues, this does not entitle us to say that natural evil is somehow the consequence of human sin. In any case, 'That creation may bring evil in its train is only abhorrent so long as God is envisaged as entirely separate from it. If God is involved, the perspective is at once changed.'[143] As for sin, which Duthie defines as 'disobedience against God, a wounding of the divine heart, a rejection of the Father's love,'[144] he again follows Farmer in asserting that human beings are persons, which means that they can respond to God or refuse God. Yet at the same time, he declares, we must also say that 'when men abuse the freedom God has given them ... God somehow comes down into the hell they have brought upon themselves and others, and Himself bears the weight of their sin.' 'Somehow'? Surely Duthie could have been a little more specific here. To those who contend that come the *eschaton* all will be explained, Duthie replies that this will not suffice, for we live in the here and now, and 'If we are to live by God and with God in such a

---

[138] Ibid., 46.

[139] Ibid.

[140] Idem, 'God in his world,' 17. This is Duthie's [C. J.] Cadoux Lecture, which was delivered on 8 May 1952.

[141] Ibid., 18.

[142] Ibid.

[143] Ibid., 19.

[144] Idem, *Outline of Christian Belief*, 56.

world, surely it must be with a God who is fully involved as our Companion in the way.'[145]

God's involvement is supremely seen in the reconciling work of Christ:

> In Jesus Christ God himself takes the initiative for our redemption. The parabola of the outgoing and downcoming love of God is a movement of grace from the beginning to the end of the life of Jesus. The nadir, the lowest point, of that movement is the Cross; but the Cross only expresses in its character as climax the inner meaning of the movement as a whole. ... God spending, giving, sharing, humbling, pouring Himself out on our behalf. ... [I]t is a movement both of incarnation and atonement, two ideas which cannot be separated from each other.[146]

Duthie has further things to say concerning the suffering of God, and these will be among the agenda of my Conclusion. For the present we must pass to his general understanding of God's relation to the world. The world, he says, may be understood in one of three ways. There is the way of the pantheist, who holds that the world is God and *vice versa*. In this connection Duthie recalls his teacher, John Laird, who taught that pantheism may be distributive: 'each several thing in the world may be divine'; or totalitarian: the world taken as a whole may be divine. According to Duthie, pantheism witnesses in a defective way to the all-inclusive character of God, but it fails to understand God as personal.[147] Secondly, it may be said that God is utterly independent of the world. This view upholds God's transcendence but at the cost of separating him from the world. Influenced by Whitehead, Hartshorne and Ferré have criticized this understanding of transcendence, and while Duthie does not adopt their position *in toto*, he does endorse their view that 'the absoluteness of God does not consist in His standing outside all relations but is compatible with His standing in relation to everything and everyone in the world.'[148] Duthie himself inclines to the third view, which is that of S. L. Frank, Hartshorne and Tillich, namely, that all things have their being in God, for which doctrine the label is 'panentheism'. While not necessarily committed to all the ramifications of this position, Duthie thinks that this central affirmation accords with the Gospel: 'Because the world and the men in it are rooted in the being of God, both world and men have a reference to God, a Godward-pointing metaphysical status, established from the side of God, which can be denied but not destroyed.'[149] As he puts it elsewhere, 'If I may coin a word, God is circum-ambient. He is the ocean in which we swim, the element by which we are upborne, the God in whom "we live, and

---

[145] Idem, 'God in his world,' 20.

[146] Ibid., 21. Duthie more than once borrows the image of the parabola from Emil Brunner.

[147] This is, of course, a very concise description and critique. For some philosophical, ethical and religious criticisms of pantheism see Alan P. F. Sell, *Enlightenment, Ecumenism, Evangel*, ch. 7.

[148] C. S. Duthie, 'God in his world,', 23.

[149] Ibid., 24.

move and have our being".'[150] If this is so, 'we can put our trust in a God who is dynamically present in the onward moving history of the world.'[151] We may claim that while the biblical writers do not set out a metaphysic of God's relation to the world, the heart of panentheism accords with biblical trust, and that 'a Christian doctrine of God can be based on the Bible without being bounded by the Bible.'[152]

Duthie does recognize the peril in the panentheist position, namely, that

> If God is the all-inclusive reality, then evil would have to be regarded as lying within or even belonging to that reality. We should then have to maintain the precarious position that, although evil has its place within the being of God, it cannot be predicated of God. I content myself with saying that this position may not be so indefensible as at first sight appears.[153]

I wish that Duthie had not contented himself with this somewhat lukewarm apologetic. Can we, for example, say that in God's taking sin, evil and death to himself at the Cross so as to vanquish it, we have the paradigm case of what he is continually doing 'between the times'? It remains only to add that, practical as ever, Duthie concludes by saying that we shall attain to a firmer grasp of God's relation to the world if we ourselves embark upon costly involvement in the needs and sins of the world. For then 'God catches us up into His own redemptive action'[154]—though lest we are tempted to think of ourselves as little saviours, I should prefer to say that God empowers the witness we make and the service we offer in gratitude for his redeeming grace.

This grace is supremely active at the Cross, and with this thought we come to the person of the Saviour and his work. Duthie nowhere expounds a Christology at length, but he does make plain where he stands on the subject. He thinks that the Gospels are broadly trustworthy; that at the heart of Christianity is the person of Jesus; and that the heart of the Church's witness is that 'Jesus is the One through whom we are reconciled to God and enabled to lead a new life as His children.'[155] Whatever may be the truth of the references to the Virgin Birth—a question on which Duthie suspends judgment—Jesus Christ, the Son of God, took our manhood upon him, and was at the same time one in whom 'the complete being of the Godhead dwells embodied' (Colossians 2: 9);[156] he lived, died and was raised. Duthie advocates a moderate theory of Christ's self-emptying (*kenosis*)—a topic to which I shall return in the Conclusion. While the Cross is central, the whole course of his obedience may not be overlooked, and by his ascension he becomes the cosmic

---

[150] Idem, *Outline of Christian Belief*, 40.
[151] Idem, 'God in his world,' 26.
[152] Ibid.
[153] Ibid., 27.
[154] Ibid.
[155] Idem, *Outline of Christian Belief*, 21.
[156] Ibid., 29.

Christ. Following Teilhard de Chardin, Duthie speaks of a 'Christ-suffused view of the universe.'[157]

To Duthie, 'The Cross is the final and clinching extension of the principle that operates through all the ministry of Jesus. It is the principle of urgently concerned and self-sacrificing love.'[158] The Cross, he surmizes in Abelardian tones, has become the central symbol in Christianity because 'the early Christians saw in the dying of Jesus evidence that amazed them of the length to which God had gone in order to reclaim men.'[159] As we think about the Cross we are constrained by a double necessity: 'We must give [Christ's] death the significance which the New Testament writers assign to it and we must never isolate it from the life which leads to it nor from the continuing life which supervened upon it through the resurrection.'[160]

Duthie's first answer to the question, Why did Jesus die? is that there were those—people in many ways like ourselves—who wanted him killed. Not, indeed, that Jesus waited for death to come to him: he chose to go out to meet it. The second answer to the question is that it was necessary for Jesus to be born, to live, and to die as we do if he were to be both our Brother and our Redeemer. Thirdly, 'Christ's death is the focus of the reconciling action by which God seeks to bring men and indeed a world back to Himself. ... [I]n His death an action took place which was not only demonstrative but emancipatory. It not only showed men what God's heart was like: it revealed the strength of His arm.'[161] Here Duthie seems to be departing from a narrowly-construed Abelardianism. Indeed he proceeds to contrast what he (as I, with Franks, think), reduces by calling it Abelard's view of the death of Christ as 'a simple expression of God's love for man which moves man to answering love',[162] with the view which sees an element of substitution or satisfaction in the atonement. He attempts to balance matters out thus:

> The first lays the accent where it must first fall, on the fact that God does not need to be prevailed upon to be gracious, that He is gracious and that atonement flows from His grace. But the second reminds us, if sometimes in quite inadequate language, that reconciliation is not a cheap and easy business. Like forgiveness, which is part of it, it is very costly.[163]

Duthie's phrasing of the second view is not, in my judgment, as robust as it might have been, given the violation of God's holiness by human sin and rebellion. Certainly God does not have to be somehow bribed by a death to be gracious, but his holy love (note the conjunction of divine attributes) requires to be vindicated. The other side of the coin, as Duthie elsewhere expresses it, is that 'while [Christ] was

---

157 Ibid.

158 Idem, *God in His World*, 28.

159 Idem, 'The meaning of the Cross,' 9.

160 Ibid.

161 Idem, 'Why did Jesus die?' 13.

162 Ibid.

163 Ibid.

not punished by the Father for our sins, He so entered into the alienation and the darkness which sin brings with it that He can be described as the sin-bearer. God has made Him, who knew no sin, to be sin for us (II Corinthians 3:21).'[164]

How, then, does what was done at the Cross bear upon succeeding ages? Duthie answers that 'the Cross can only be contemporary if what happened at Calvary shows us what is always happening—man rejecting the God who seeks him, God in Christ meeting that rejection with patient [there is that word again] love.'[165] But Duthie wisely recognizes that

> Any idea of a continuing suffering of Christ and of God in Christ must be held in conjunction with at least three other ideas—(1) What Christ has done and suffered in His life on earth is 'finished' in the sense that it is completely adequate. But the love that gave itself to death goes on. (2) Crucifixion was followed by resurrection and victory. If there is a continuing crucifixion in any real sense it is within the victorious life of God, one element in His infinite blessedness [a sentence, this, to which it is difficult to assign a clear meaning]. (3) While it may be true that by our greed and thoughtlessness and self-concern and lack of compassion we continue to reject God who surrounds us by refusing to respond to His various appreaches [*sic*] in such a way that we can be said to crucify Christ, *we are only able to think of things in this way because we have already pondered the meaning of the historical crucifixion.* In other words, a theology of our relation to the ground of being [Tillich] is dependent on a theology of God's historic deed of saving love in Christ.[166]

Duthie's answer to the question, How shall people be brought face to face with the Cross today? is that this happens 'as they hear the declaration of God's love in the Gospel and meet the demonstration of that love in the lives of ordinary Christians.'[167]

Deeply concerned though he was with the response to the Gospel and the challenge of evil and suffering in the here and now, Duthie was no less keen to reflect upon the eschatological dimension of Christ's work. Hence his Drew Lecture on Immortality, 'Ultimate triumph,' in which he addresses the question, 'Will all who have been fashioned in the image of god be united with him within the redeemed community? Or will some persist obstinately for ever in the repudiation of his grace, self-excluded from heaven?'[168] Duthie reports that in discussing these questions with Christians, even those most concerned to give due weight to such words as 'Depart from me' (Matthew 25: 41) have almost invariably said that they hope that none will be finally lost. Such testimonies, as Duthie recognizes, are not conclusive, but 'what the Christian heart feels in this and in other matters must have

---

[164] Idem, *God in His World*, 33.
[165] Idem, 'Continuing Cross?' 9.
[166] Ibid.
[167] Idem, 'Four questions,' 9.
[168] Idem, 'Ultimate triumph,' 192.

some importance, since it is itself in some measure shaped by the Spirit of God.'[169] We are thus confronted not with outright universalism, but with 'the tension between the universalistic element and another weighty factor within the Christian consciousness,'[170] and by biblical passages which suggest universal restoration and others which do not. Over and above particular biblical texts, Duthie points to the emphasis, current in the biblical theology of his day, upon 'the cosmic sweep of Christ's ultimate triumph.'[171]

Duthie enters upon an examination of relevant biblical passages, and finds that in the New Testament, while there are inclinations towards universalism, these are 'set within the dominant New Testament pattern of two opposed destinies between which men must choose.'[172] The tension thus exposed 'increases when the argument passes beyond the examination of proof-texts and passages to the consideration of the character of God as holy love, his reconciling action towards man in Christ and the scope of his final triumph.'[173]

Against the biblical background thus provided Duthie introduces H. H. Farmer and Karl Barth with a view to showing that although their views of the God-humanity relation—in particular their understanding of human freedom—by no means coincide, they both tend in the direction of universalism without positively affirming it. Farmer reaches this point by emphasizing the character of God and the ultimate irresitibility of his grace, while Barth's notion that election in Christ is already decided by God and is universal brings him to the brink of universalism, where he calls a halt. Despite their differences the theologies of Farmer and Barth 'have one massive emphasis in common. *It is the stress on the outgoing, world-embracing, utterly faithful, endlessly self-spending grace of God towards mankind.*'[174]

As he draws towards his conclusion Duthie suspects that many Christians think in terms of abiding consequences of unrepented sin and then suppose that the duration of those consequences is limited in the after-life. Such Christians, Duthie declares, are crypto-universalists. This and much else Duthie takes as indication that there is a movement in Christian thought towards universal salvation; indeed, 'Our thought cannot help travelling in the direction in which God is going.'[175] At this point I must demur. From the fact that (some elements of) Christian thought are moving in a certain direction, it cannot automatically be assumed that this is the direction in which God is going. A more discriminating case needs to be made, not least because Christian thought can be, and sometimes is, apostate. Moreover, there is an *ad hominem* flavour to Duthie's remark which suggests that if we do not concede his point as to the strength of the pro-universalism movement our thought

---

[169] Ibid., 193.
[170] Ibid., 194.
[171] Ibid.
[172] Ibid., 197.
[173] Ibid., 198.
[174] Ibid., 206.
[175] Ibid., 208.

is not travelling in the direction in which God is going—and how is that direction to be determined with any great precision? Is there an analogy here with 'Church assembly politics'—that attitude on the part of the 'platform' to annex the Holy Spirit and to imply that all in the constituency who cannot concur with the officers are either dim or wayward?

Happily, Duthie immediately introduces some necessary qualifications. First, practical as ever, he insists that 'we have no right at all to envisage or speak of a world redemption unless we ourselves are working for it with our dedicated powers', though he does not stop to explain what it means to be 'caught up in the redemptive passion of God.'[176] Secondly, he says that notwithstanding the 'inescapable movement of the Christian mind towards the idea of universal salvation,' 'we cannot banish from our minds the strong words of our Lord about fire, about darkness, about it [*sic*] being better for a man never to have been born.' For this reason

> The appeal to our awful human responsibility remains. Thus the hope which Christians cannot but cherish that God in his great love will find his way ultimately to the throne of every human heart, cannot become the subject of preaching in the form of a dogma or cannot enter into preaching in a way that would diminish by one iota the answerability of the hearer as he listens to the Word of Life. But it can inform preaching as a dynamic, giving to it an insistent and urgent note of wooing that is in accord with the very spirit of the Gospel.[177]

Least of all, Duthie cautions, may we take our own future state for granted. God's love 'is not a cushion on which we can rest but a spur that drives us to obedient action.'[178] He concludes by observing that

> If the Christian hope is fulfilled in God's long future it will surely be not because God has beaten down all resistance but because with the ingenuity of his tireless grace he has found a means whereby to bring about the glad and free surrender of all. Whatever new forms it may assume that means will still be what we Christians call the way of the Cross.[179]

This completes my attempt to gather together Duthie's thoughts on some of the major Christian doctrines. He himself draws many of the doctrinal strands together in an article entitled, 'Is the Gospel simple?' What follows is a brief summary of it. The Gospel is good news about God which is only discovered and understood in Jesus Christ, who was himself utterly confident in his Father, who is loving, gracious, holy and good. In his life and teaching Jesus showed us God, and claimed to be the Son of God. God was personally present in him as in no other, and through him God seeks people out: 'The Cross is the final, clinching extension of the

---

[176] Ibid.

[177] Ibid.

[178] Ibid., 209-10.

[179] Ibid., 210. For related themes see C. S. Duthie, *Outline of Christian Belief*, ch. 9.

principle that operates through all the ministry of Jesus.'[180] It reveals God as in Christ 'reaching out in love and bearing man's sin upon His own heart.'[181] This essential core of the Gospel is not difficult to understand; its simplicity 'springs from its pre-occupation with the personal. It is concerned with God and man and with the relation between God and man.'[182] However, the Gospel's simplicity 'is not the simplicity of that which is completely comprehensible to man but of something mysterious and subduing.'[183] Again, the Gospel is not simple in the sense that it concerns the individual alone: it has a bearing on relationships in the world. Nor is it simple in the sense that once it has been understood a positive response is inevitable: 'There is that in the gospel which is a stumbling-block to the "natural man".'[184] The Church should refrain from creating fresh stumbling-blocks, and Christians should 'be so possessed ourselves of the gospel, so mastered by the love of God that we ourselves become bearers of the Good News to our fellows.'[185]

With this we come to Duthie's understanding of the nature and mission of the Church.

III

At a time when so many Christians despaired of the Church as an institution, Duthie is concerned that we understand the Church in its relation to God and his purpose. While in a sense the Church began at Pentecost, we may not overlook the people of God of in the Old Testament. But even beyond that is the idea that 'The Church is grounded in God's original purpose for mankind.'[186] Both the Church and its mission come from beyond itself and, the historic divisions of the Church notwithstanding, there is but one Church of the Lord Jesus Christ. It is because the Church is God's creation that no forces can finally destroy it.

The Church, he continues, is the Church of Christ because it is in Christ that God meets us. With reference to the persons of the Trinity the Church may be called God's family, the body of Christ and the fellowship of the Holy Spirit. It derives from the personal relation of God with his people: 'It is the community of human persons who have been reconciled by the Divine Person.'[187] The Church is the servant and, despite its faults, it is the first instalment of the kingdom of God, which is understood as God's reign and rule. The Church is not, however, co-terminus with the kingdom. There is, further, a distinction between the Church and the state, the latter being 'a providential means of protecting society against destructive forces and

[180] Idem, 'The Mind of Christ. III. Is the Gospel simple?', 239.

[181] Ibid.

[182] Ibid.

[183] Ibid., 240.

[184] Ibid.

[185] Ibid.

[186] Idem, *Outline of Christian Belief*, 64.

[187] Ibid., 66.

of fostering a decent life.'[188] Again, the Church is distinguished from the human community at large by its worship and by its undergoing of persecution. At this point I detect an attenuation which is surprising on the part on one so committed both to evangelism and to the Congregational church order. Does not the Church, as Simon insisted, comprise the 'twice-born', Christians, saints, believers; and is not this a distinction of both temporal and eternal significance? That Duthie elsewhere makes good the deficiency, at least implicitly, is clear from his concern lest within the Church nurture take precedence over conversion, baptism over a person's personal response of faith to God's approach in Christ.[189]

Duthie proceeds to observe that over the course of history the Church has sometimes been personified, notably as Mother—a term suggestive of 'love, warmth, faithfulness, security.'[190] But this should not be pressed to the extent of supposing that the Church is sinless, or that the Church forgives sin: 'only Christ is sinless, only God in Christ can forgive sin.'[191] Again, the Church has been thought of in institutional terms. Primarily it is a fellowship of persons, but such a fellowship cannot exist in a non-embodied state: some institutional shape is inescapable. The question then arises whether there is one particular church order given once for all that must be adhered to? The Roman Catholic Church answers in the affirmative in the *Decree on Ecumenism* of the Second Vatican Council: '"Christ entrusted the office of teaching, government and sanctification to the college made up of the Twelve", with Peter and his successors in a position of supreme authority.'[192] In other circles 'there is less eagerness to make extravagant claims for any one form of polity and a greater willingness to see whether the values of episcopal, presbyteral and congregational systems can be united in a single Church or in Churches.'[193] Yet again, the Church must not be absolutized, and Duthie welcomes a qualification, which he italicizes, in the *Decree on Ecumenism*: 'Only through the Catholic Church of Christ ... can the means of salvation be reached *in all their fullness*.'[194] Duthie's point is that 'while salvation in its fullness is found in the Church and the Church has its visible aspect, we cannot tell where the frontier of the Church is to be drawn.'[195] Because Jesus identified himself with the whole of humanity and not only with the Church, Duthie cannot agree with those who understand the Church as an extension of the incarnation. In my opinion, however, the crucial objection to this view is that urged by P. T. Forsyth, to whom Duthie so frequently refers, but

---

[188] Ibid., 67.

[189] See idem, 'Have we abandoned conversion?' Cf. 'Responding to the Gospel,' 245-6.

[190] Idem, *Outline of Christian Belief*, 68.

[191] Ibid.

[192] Ibid., 69. Duthie quotes the *Decree on Ecumenism* I: 2. See Austin Flannery, *Vatican Council II*, 454.

[193] Ibid.

[194] Ibid., 70.

[195] Ibid.

not in this context: 'That which owes itself to a rebirth cannot be the prolongation of the ever sinless.'[196]

In his address to the Sixth International Congregational Council meeting at Wellesley in 1949 Duthie turned his attention to the purpose and order of the Church:

> The Church in this century has rediscovered the Church because it has rediscovered God and His purpose with men. ... Because [God] is love, He willed the Church into being as the community of love. The grand objective of God's design is a society of persons rooted in adoring dependence upon Himself and exhibiting in the order and in the personal relationships of its whole life a movement of free, self-giving and reciprocal love which mirrors the ultimate movement of the divine life from which it derives. ... On the one hand the Church is both constrained and commissioned to be a herald of the good news that God cares. On the other hand, a necessity is laid upon the Church to become herself a part of the good news as the caring community.[197]

In Duthie's view the ecumenical movement's concern with Church order is owing to the increasing realization that a church's order is justified only insofar as it allows Christ his due place among his people and facilitates the communication of his Gospel. At the heart of Congregational order lies the principle that 'the Church is constituted ... by the presence of Christ in His kingly rule among His people.'[198] Christ's place is not to be usurped by the state, and the ground of Congregational catholicity is that 'To be in Christ is to be in His Body and therefore to be indivisibly one.'[199] Hence, 'We hail Christians everywhere, without a shadow of hesitation, as our brethren in Christ.'[200] Duthie has no place for what has been called 'granular Independency'. On the contrary, 'The authority of Christ in the local Church and the authority of Christ in a group of Churches is not two authorities but one, for Christ is one.'[201]

Central to the Congregational order is the Church Meeting, on which subject Duthie quotes Daniel Jenkins, who contends that the Church Meeting 'is a solemn assembly of the people of God in a particular place, who meet together before God, to consider together, in the light of the Word which is preached and on the basis of their sacramental fellowship with Christ, how they may discern and obey the Lord's will for themselves and His people in that place.[202] This prompts Duthie to remark that a local church ought never to be allowed to exceed a certain size, lest the sense of intimate fellowship or community be lost and pastoral care be undermined. The

---

[196] P. T. Forsyth, *The Church and the Sacraments*, 82-3.

[197] C. S. Duthie, 'The Gospel, the Church and Church order,' 78-9.

[198] Ibid., 80.

[199] Ibid., 81.

[200] Ibid.

[201] Ibid., 82.

[202] Idem, *God in His World*, 83. Duthie quotes D. Jenkins, *Congregationalism: A Restatement*, 46-7.

rueful thought occurs that this is not a problem that currently afflicts the English and Welsh heirs of Congregationalism at the present time. Duthie does note that while the danger of becoming what he calls 'separate and Pharisee' must be avoided, 'A constant effort must be made to ensure that every congregation of "saints" is distinctively marked off from the world by the Christian quality of its living.'[203] He does not, however, pursue the point into the territory of the well-nigh lost art of church discipline; yet the polity turns upon our knowing who the professed and covenanted saints are.[204] On the other hand, Duthie is quite clear that where Christian nurture is concerned, 'The goal is still the personal confession of faith in Jesus Christ as Saviour and Lord. ... Affirming our faith in the company of others is itself an experience of the reality of the Church. We belong to Christ, it is true, as individuals; but we belong to him *with others* in His Body.'[205]

What, next, of the faith of the Church as it has developed over time? In an article on 'Affirmations of faith' Duthie argues that pressure from more than one quarter prompts a fresh consideration of this issue. What are we to make of the classical interpretations of the faith in creed and confession? Are they fixed for all time or are they subject to amendment? Or is the Church under obligation to write fresh affirmations for each successive age? How are we to understand the Bible as the supreme and decisive standard? To these questions which derive from the Church's history may be added pressure from the ecumenical movement which requires attention by the several Christian traditions to their inherited standpoints; and the pressure arising from the obligation to communicate the Gospel effectively 'in the presence of religions, movements and philosophies which put forward rival affirmations concerning God or man or both.'[206]

Traditionally, Duthie continues, creeds have been understood as bearing witness to Christ who is above and within the Church, and is the source of its life. They have served as bonds of unity, and they have marked off the Church from the unbelieving world. With the passage of time the creeds as affirmations of faith came to be regarded as definitions of the faith, and assent to creeds came to regulate the understanding of faith. In Duthie's view, 'Faith as man's trustful response to God may bring forth a creedal affirmation: it cannot be equated with assent to that affirmation.'[207] If that equation is made, the unity which the creed symbolizes becomes an external, not a truly personal unity. Then, instead of serving as the frontier between the Church and the world, the creeds become frontiers between Christians. The creeds must be scrutinized in the light of Scripture; they are subject to correction and amplification; and they are not the only means by which the

---

[203] Ibid., 85. The inverted commas around 'saints' are redundant (which is to make both a biblical and an ecumenical point).

[204] For some ruminations on this see Alan P. F. Sell, *Enlightenment, Ecumenism, Evangel*, 238-42; 339-55.

[205] C. S. Duthie, 'Responding to the Gospel,' 247.

[206] C. S. Duthie, 'Affirmations of faith,' 2.

[207] Ibid., 3.

Church confesses the faith: proclamation, life, service, suffering—these are all ways in which this is done.

As for the confessions of faith flowing down from the Reformation: in the earlier ones in particular the polemical element is marked. Some are more theological, others more practical; and 'mildly surprising' though it be, they all honour the ancient creeds. As contrasted with the latter, the Reformation confessions elevate Scripture and emphasize soteriology. In recent centuries, Duthie declares, loyalty to the Reformed confessions has waned, and in three sentences he attempts a sweep of three centuries which compels me to insert equally crisp observations in square brackets:

> The eighteenth century brought with it a battle against rationalism in which Protestantism, having itself submitted to the ordering powers of reason, was not too well equipped to fight. [But from 1700 to 1850 a good deal of fighting went on: this was the heyday of modern (but now outmoded) apologetics]. Protestant vitality was saved by pietism on the Continent and by the Evangelical Revival in Britain [these were a mixed blessing in that they fostered an ecclesiology-damaging individualism, and in some quarters the emphasis upon conversion adversely affected ideas of baptism and nurture]; but the resurgence of a deeply personal religion relies more on the Bible than on creed. The nineteenth century saw a partial revulsion from both creed and confession under the influence of romanticism, scholarship and liberalizing tendencies in thought [if some of this went too far, at best the attempt was made to communicate the Gospel in terms that the age could assimilate—something of which Duthie approves]. In the twentieth century the movement which stems from Karl Barth revived interest in the Bible and its message and sent Protestant teachers, at least, back to the Reformers [the way this was done was too often at the cost of the apologetic task]. But the confessions could not regain their former place ...[208]

Turning to the Reformed tradition in Scotland, Duthie observes that the Congregationalists have regarded statements of faith as testimonies rather than as tests of faith; that is, they 'have been anxious to distinguish the living act of faith from assent to a declaration of the Church's belief and have been against subscription'[209] [especially, one might add, against legally required subscription: it is not the prerogative of the monarch or government to prescribe the faith of the Church]. For their part, the Presbyterians 'have been greatly concerned to make the point that it is the truth of the Gospel, the objective grace of God that creates faith or Christian experience and have consequently seen the need for sound doctrine.'[210] [It must be said that, their Moderates notwithstanding, the Scots generally fared better in this respect than the English Presbyterians, the majority of whom had, by the end

---

[208] Ibid., 5.
[209] Ibid., 6.
[210] Ibid.

of the eighteenth century, become either Congregationalists or Unitarians.[211] It would appear that creeds and confessions may witness to the faith if it is held; but if it is not, they (like bishops in other traditions) cannot force assent, though they may gently prod the consciences of erstwhile subscribers who do not suffer from confessional amnesia]. The Presbyterians do, however, permit a reasonable liberty of interpretation, 'springing, I would take it, from the conviction shared with Congregationalists and others that creedal fundamentalism is as open to objection as biblical.'[212] At this point Duthie makes a complimentary reference to *A Declaration of Faith* published by the Congregational Church in England and Wales in 1967.[213] He welcomes 'the atmosphere of humble and wondering Christian assurance which pervades' it, judging that this 'seems to me to be very appropriate to a faith which knows that it sees through a glass darkly. Our certainties do not shine any the less brightly for acknowledging that there is twilight and cloud and sometimes darkness about us. ... [W]e must rule out intransigent dogmatism about creedal statements and abjure a strictly compulsive use of them.'[214] He ends by reiterating his point that the Church's verbal assertions 'are abstract and thin without the concrete substance of self-giving, service, mission.'[215]

Duthie did not write at length on the sacraments, though he does refer to them from time to time. The roots of the dominical sacraments, he reminds us, are in pre-Christian Jewish history, but

> they receive their significance from Christ. ... They use familiar elements of life to convey spiritual reality—water, bread, wine. They remind us that faith has to do with the workaday world ... Both speak to man's deep need of forgiveness. Broadly regarded, Baptism may be seen as the sacrament of reception, the Supper as the sacrament of renewal.'[216]

Although the Quakers and the Salvation Army do not observe the sacraments as such, Duthie continues, 'we believe that the spiritual reality to which they point is nevertheless present. God is not bound by the sacraments.'[217] At the same time, there are 'dangers' in appealing to our religious experience as having no need of sacramental 'crutches'. At once, and consistently with his understanding of catholicity, Duthie adds

---

[211] For this intriguing and complicated tale see Alan P. F. Sell, *Dissenting Thought and the Life of the Churches*, ch. 5.

[212] C. S. Duthie, 'Affirmations of Faith,' 7.

[213] See further on this *Declaration*, Alan P. F. Sell, *Nonconformist Theology in the Twentieth Century*, 84-9. On the general topic see idem, 'Confessing the faith and confessions of faith.'

[214] C. S. Duthie, 'Affirmations of faith,'' 7.

[215] Ibid., 8.

[216] Idem, *Outline of Christian Belief*, 77-8.

[217] Ibid., 78.

> On the other hand, it is equally dangerous to regard [the sacraments] as automatically and almost magically effective or to connect them with a doctrine of ministerial succession which excludes Christians of another sort from participating. When a Church, for instance, cannot bid Christians from another Church welcome to the Table which the Lord has given it, we may well ask ourselves whether it can legitimately be called the Lord's Table.'[218]

As he elsewhere expressed the point with reference to Congregationalists, 'If we have not always given due place to the Sacraments, it was often because our hearts told us that where others were making these holy gifts of Christ a cause of division, instead of an instrument of reconciliation and unity, it was necessary to go behind although not beyond the Sacraments to Him to whom the Sacraments bear witness.'[219] I suspect that the strength of Duthie's conviction that Christians are united by virtue of their being 'in Christ' informs his view that 'While baptism is solidly present and clearly enjoined in the New Testament, I am not entirely happy about the present habit of finding the major point of Christian unity in baptism.'[220]

Not, indeed, that divisions over things sacramental are restricted to Protestant-Catholic relations. Duthie is well aware of the gulf within Protestantism between paedobaptists and believer baptists, and he is open to the possibility that both modes of baptism might find a place within a single church order. He grants that whatever may be deduced from the New Testament on the subject, it is undeniable that in the course of Christian history

> meanings became attached to the baptism of infants which can only be applied to that of adults, or, to put the matter more precisely, to adult *believers*. For instance, ... renunciation of evil and profession of faith in Christ—cannot be directly assigned to a child a few weeks old. On the other hand, the Baptist protest against Infant Baptism as contrary to New Testament practice and as opening the way to superstitious beliefs came, by its very stance of opposition, to lay so much emphasis upon the individual's response to God in faith that this response was not clearly enough connected with the divine initiative in which it is rooted and by which it may even be said to be created.[221]

Nevertheless both traditions of baptism have preserved important truths of the Gospel:

> The tradition of Infant Baptism has pointed throughout history to the prevenience of God's act of grace in Christ, to the responsibility of the Church and parents in Christian nurture, to the process of growth towards full Christian faith. The tradition of Believers' Baptism has borne needed witness to the fact that this faith is not something automatically produced by the Church as an institution but the most personal of all happenings in which the individual gives his answer to God, in

---

[218] Ibid.

[219] Idem, 'The Gospel, the Church and Church order,' 81.

[220] Idem, 'Responding to the Gospel,' 246.

[221] Idem, 'Baptism—infant or believers'? 9.

acknowledgment of His grace, thus at one stroke being joined to Christ and to his people.[222]

While the sacraments are instruments in God's hands, says Duthie, we must not forget that 'God's finest means for touching our lives are not instruments but agents, not things, but persons. When God reached out to us in the fulfilling stage of His purpose, He did it through a man. We can say that Jesus Christ is the sacrament of God. Through Christ Christians can become sacramental to each other.'[223]

It is hardly surprising that one who spent thirty years of his life training ministers should have some clear thoughts on the nature and purpose of the Christian ministry. Two themes emerge strongly from Duthie's writings on this subject. The first is that Jesus Christ is *the* minister, who sets the pattern of humble service to which all ministry should conform. The second is that ministry is the task of the people of God as a whole (it is more than each individual Christian making his or her contribution here or there); and that both clericalism and laicism are to be shunned. With reference to Congregationalism's traditional unease over the term 'lay', he points out that the minister, no less than anyone else, is of the *laos*, the people of God, and that to affirm this is not denigrate the ministry, which is God's gift to the Church.[224] Entirely content with the idea of lay preaching, Duthie makes what is to my mind an unanswerable point when he declares that 'It is difficult, if not impossible, to find a Protestant theological justification of lay preaching which is not also a justification of lay administration of the sacraments.'[225] I have often marvelled at what appears to be an inconsistency in this connection. Both Word and sacrament testify to the Gospel, and the latter is 'dumb' without the preached word. Yet some drive a wedge between these two which the liturgiologists say belong together, by allowing almost anyone to preach and being very opposed to the lay 'administration' (ugly word) of the sacraments. There is also the further incongruity in the Church at large when the sacrament of baptism is recognised if performed with water and in the name of the Trinity, whereas the Lord's Supper is 'defective', 'irregular' or even 'not a sacrament' if presided over by one not in the approved clerical order.

Two things are necessary, says Duthie. The first is to address the question, 'Has the Church any right to expect an apostolic ministry unless she takes steps to clarify the priorities and set her ministers free to preach, to counsel, to pray with people and to pursue with love those who have no Christian faith?'[226] The second is to heed the caution that 'A great deal of our past Christian thinking has been based on the assumption that a minister's chief job is to look after his congregation. It is rather

---

[222] Ibid.

[223] C. S. Duthie, *Outline of Christian Belief*, 78.

[224] On the foregoing points see idem, 'The ministry of the whole Church,' 9.

[225] C. S. Duthie, *God in His World*, 91.

[226] Idem, 'Changing patterns,' 9.

the job of both minister and congregation to look after the men and women for whom Christ died and rose again.'[227]

As to preaching, Duthie insists that this mode of proclaiming the Gospel must be allied with 'a determined effort to convey the Gospel that is proclaimed through fellowship, service and various forms of Christian action.'[228] True preaching is empowered by the Holy Spirit, and it 'meets our deepest need by exposing to our view and conveying to our hearts the reality of God Himself.'[229] Unfortunately, Duthie does not here specify what our 'deepest need' is, or what God does to meet it. Although he frequently refers to, and quotes, P. T. Forsyth, he sometimes stops short of the Cross in a way that the latter never did, emphasizing caring love and inter-personal relationships more than God's judging, forgiving and renewing grace. Nevertheless he stoutly affirms that 'the day of preaching is not done because its theme is the supreme dialogue, the dialogue between man and God in Jesus Christ. Preaching will endure so long as there is a Gospel to preach and man [*sic*] and women who need that Gospel.'[230]

Duthie did not hesitate to commend the ministry to young 'men' (though we must assume that he included young women in this, since he trained some of them):

> There is no higher honour that could be conferred on a young man than to be summoned by God to be a servant of His servants ... [I]f any youth today is looking for a task in which there are no Trade Union hours, a task in which he will have to give and give and still give himself when strength seems utterly spent, a task which will call for every ounce of manhood he possesses and the extra manhood that God will have to give him, then I commend to him the Christian ministry.[231]

As for those whom Duthie trained for ministry, we may suppose that, however they may have responded to it, they all heard his message: 'While theological education must deal faithfully with the Biblical foundation of the faith, the worship and life and thought of the Church through the centuries, and the challenges which face Christianity in the modern world, it must also engender a passion to spread the Good News.'[232]

Duthie takes a broad view of the Church's mission of spreading Good News:

---

227 Ibid.

228 Idem, *God in His World*, 76.

229 Ibid.

230 Idem, 'Responding to the Gospel,' 246.

231 Idem, *God in His World*, 177. Fifty years on, we find a minority of ministers advocating the unionization of the ministry: a cause which, since it has to do with 'conditions of service' and the 'rights' of 'employees' *vis à vis* 'employers' would seem to turn the doctrine of vocation on its head. See further on the ministerial vocation, Alan P. F. Sell, *Aspects of Christian Integrity*, 137-142; idem, *Testimony and Tradition*, 14-15, 41-42, 46.

232 C. S. Duthie, 'Responding to the Gospel,' 248.

> No single Christian activity exhausts the scope of that mission. It includes preaching and personal witness, pubic service and prophetic criticism, protest against evil things, and quiet prayer—and, by no means least, suffering for the sake of Christ. ... [The Church] cannot be loyal to the generous love of God towards all men without seeking to become the champion of humanity. It must speak for the hungry, the dispossessed, the victims of racial persecution. It must work for justice and freedom. It must plead the cause of poor nations. The political dimension of the Gospel is unavoidable.[233]

He fears, however, that one aspect of mission is too easily overlooked or neglected: 'The Church is charged by God and constrained by His love to claim the uncommitted or wrongly committed heart of man for Jesus Christ.'[234] Duthie therefore elevates evangelism as an inescapable obligation upon the Church and, interestingly, he does this in a contribution to the *Festschrift* for Erik Wickberg, General of the Salvation Army—a body noted for its passion both to evangelize and to enter with zeal into the socio-political context in which it is placed. Of course, evangelism must be undertaken intelligently, persuasively, and in such a way as to respect the personality of those to whom would reach: 'The Gospel of Christ must be communicated in the spirit of Christ.'[235] Moreover, as the Church undertakes its mission 'It is enabled to do so with joyful confidence because it does not depend on its own resources. In the mission it undertakes Christ precedes it by His presence, accompanies it as Encourager and follows it with His blessing.'[236]

I here give notice that in the Conclusion to this book I shall consider Duthie's two articles on Mary the mother of Jesus in relation to Tymms's case against Roman Catholicism and the current ecumenical situation. Now, however, I wish to turn to some of Duthie's writings in which he seeks to tackle issues raised by the world in which the Church is set, and into which it ventures in mission.

IV

The first thing to be said is that when Duthie thinks of 'the world' he is not thinking simply of 'the world around us'. His thought has a cosmic dimension. He sums up his stance in one sentence uttered in the course of his concluding sermon delivered in Rotterdam on Thursday 12 July 1962 at the Ninth Assembly of the International Congregational Council: 'We need to learn again that the first reality is not the world but God.'[237] He goes on to observe that many are re-learning this lesson from the scientist-philosopher Teilhard de Chardin, at the centre of whose thought is the adoring vision of God. To Teilhard's thought Duthie returns on more

---

[233] Idem, 'Responding to the Gospel,' 243-4.

[234] Ibid., 244.

[235] Ibid. For further references to the principles and practice of evangelism see C. S. Duthie, *God in His World*, 36-7, 68-9, 102, 107-13, 141-160; idem, *Faith in a Time of Doubt*, 10-17.

[236] C. S. Duthie, 'Responding to the Gospel,' 249.

[237] Idem, 'The Communion sermon,' 162.

than one occasion. He surmizes that Teilhard's thought appeals to scientists who realize that their discipline does not have the final clue to human life, and to Christians who wish to integrate their faith with the remarkable advances in science. Teilhard's vision is of the evolutionary sort, and within the process there are certain critical points: the 'cellular revolution' and the advent of humanity among them. The goal, or Omega point, of the entire process and the principle on which advance is made, is love. In Duthie's view, 'If we take the personalism of de Chardin seriously, I think we must equate Omega with Christ, with God Himself since only God could be the power that creates, sustains, unites and finally consummates the converging universe.'[238] Duthie (more easily than some of Teilhard's readers) finds it possible to end his initial survey on a positive note:

> Although de Chardin is hardly what we to-day call a 'Biblical theologian', ... his thought shows ... affinity with that of St. Paul. There is the same sense of a world in process of travail towards the manifestation of the sons of God and the same overmastering conviction that Christ is the agent of creation, the one in whom all things cohere and, finally the Consummator who will being that process to a head—not *its* head but to Himself, the Head.[239]

Teilhard was persuaded that all things are animated by the Spirit, but human beings alone can love and work in union with the Spirit. God is in all things and we are never apart from him. Our calling is not to isolation from the world but to working within it for God's sake. In all of this, says Duthie, Teilhard was pre-empting Bonhoeffer's subsequently-expounded idea of 'holy worldiness'. Duthie further recognizes that Teilhard was accused by some of having succumbed to pantheism, but he agrees with those who acquit him of the charge in view of Teilhard's convictions that submersion in the All would render communion impossible, and that pantheism may foster contempt for the material world. Duthie wonders whether Teilhard accords a sufficient place to sin and redemption, and concludes that Teilhard's recognition that evil is an inevitable feature of the route towards Omega resembles Paul's view of the world created by god yet subject to temporary frustration. But 'The universal defect of a journeying world is matched by the redemptive power of a cosmic Christ.'[240] Teilhard's world process is one in which the Cross of suffering and victory is evident, and his vision is that ultimately all with be 'Christified'.

Duthie has a number of questions to pose to Teilhard:

> Is our knowledge both of earth and what lies beyond it such that we can speak with his confidence of world-evolution? Is his own reconstruction of the story of life on earth acceptable? Does he fail to mark the depth of the human plight? What relation

[238] Idem, 'The scientific revolution,' 9.
[239] Ibid.
[240] Idem, 'Everything will be "Christed",' 9.

> does his 'system' bear to the traditionally cherished doctrines of the Christian faith?[241]

Following his customary policy of seeking first to learn from others, Duthie concludes that whatever may be the answers to these questions, Teilhard 'compels us to ask whether our thoughts of God are really big enough.'[242]

In an article entitled 'The predicament of man', Duthie interestingly compares Teilhard with his hero, Pascal. They were born within a few miles of one another in the Auvergne region of France; they were both scientists, intensely religious, and loyal to, yet at odds with, their Church. They both focus upon humanity and its place in the universe:

> Pascal saw man as the creature who alone among other creatures is able to stand back and understand his world and himself by the power of thought. Against the background of a world travelling forwards in God to Point Omega de Chardin understands 'the phenomenon of man' as the appearance of the major clue to the purpose for which the world exists. Man is the arrow which discloses the direction is which the world is moving—consciousness, complexity, coherence in the *mileu divin*, in fact the Church which is the Body of Christ.[243]

There are also differences between Pascal and Teilhard. Pascal was much concerned with space in his relatively small world, whereas Teilhard, indebted to Bergson and to evolutionary thought, pondered time and the long ages of human and cosmic history. Pascal is sensitive to the individual's predicament, Teilhard thinks in terms of human solidarity. Pascal's writing on the suffering Redeemer is almost pessimistic, whereas Teilhard envisages the transformation of all things by Christ the cosmic victor. Underlying the writings of both, however, is 'a complete devotion to God and a deeply compassionate love for man.'[244] Duthie detects an irony in the fact that whereas Pascal, though not himself a Jansenist, defended Jansenists against the Jesuits, Teilhard, a Jesuit, now carries the Pascalian torch forward.

While Duthie was properly optimistic that God's purposes would finally be fulfilled, his was no unthinking or facile optimism. He had known the agonies of war; he knew the threat of armaments in peacetime; he had deep sympathy with the suffering and the hope-less; and in the wake of the death of God theology, secularization, biblical criticism, and the continuing influence of sometimes vociferous communism and humanism, no theological Principal who was warm and breathing could have been unaware of the challenges to the Christian faith from within and without the Church. Accordingly, we may suppose that his choice of a theme for his address as President of the Congregational Church in England and Wales in 1971 was by no means accidental: *Faith in a Time of Doubt*.

---

241 Ibid.

242 Ibid. See also Duthie's later article, 'The earth is my altar.'

243 Idem, 'The predicament of man,' 9.

244 Ibid.

Duthie begins by observing that Christians are not immune to 'the battle of faith [which] often becomes a battle *for* faith.'[245] He further notes that the Church's action is weakened if the faith that nourishes it is feeble or dying. But he does not wish his hearers to react hysterically to the situation in which they are placed. We should neither fail to wrestle with doubt nor 'allow ourselves to be swayed by those who make out that it is much harder to believe than it really is.'[246] Indeed, 'the rivals and substitutes for the Christian faith are not succeeding everywhere in winning the whole-hearted allegiance of men.'[247]

Among the rivals and substitutes in vogue at the time Duthie was speaking was humanism. It received a good deal of attention in the media, and was for a time a preoccupation of many members of what has come to be known as the chattering classes. Duthie devoted a *British Weekly* article to this subject. He quotes the humanist Margaret Knight, whose broadcast talks had generated much discussion: 'The essence of humanism is that it is non-supernatural. It is concerned with man rather than God, and with this life rather than the next.'[248] In Duthie's words, humanism 'affirms man and his worth and denies the existence of God.'[249] He further explains that whether the noun 'humanism' is qualified by the adjectives 'secular', 'ethical', 'scientific', or 'naturalistic', the fundamental idea is that 'man's worth is not dependent on his having his source in the supernatural.'[250] He concedes that there are those, like Maritain, who speak of Christian humanism, but in common usage humanism is 'definitely non-Christian and may even be anti-Christian.'[251] While Christians may welcome the high value that humanism places upon the human person, and while they should co-operate with humanists in humanitarian concerns, knowing that God's Spirit works even where he is not acknowledged, they cannot endorse the humanist denial of God. 'In the Christian faith,' says Duthie, 'man is defined by his relation to God with such words as "creature", "sinner", "son", and his destiny is both in this world and beyond it. For Humanism, man emerges in the long process of evolution but requires no personal God beyond and within the process to give him value.'[252] 'Christianity is full of hope for man', he continues, but it does not' hope in man.'[253] Hence,

> The ultimate difference between Humanism and Christianity is Jesus Christ and the faith which He evokes. We believe that in Him God has come to meet us in a human life. This gives man a very high value indeed. It means, for one thing, that if human nature can become the dwelling-place of God or, ... if God can invest Himself with

---

[245] Idem, *Faith in a Time of Doubt*, 6.

[246] Ibid., 7.

[247] Ibid.

[248] Idem, 'Humanism,' 11. Duthie quotes from *Morals Without Religion*.

[249] Ibid.

[250] Ibid.

[251] Ibid.

[252] Ibid.

[253] Ibid.

human nature, then that nature must have some affinity with God's. This is what we mean by saying that man is made in God's image. But it means something else. If God has gone to such lengths for man in Jesus Christ, then man both needs to be saved and is worth saving.

Humanism is man telling himself how much he is worth and acting upon that belief. Christianity is God not only telling man but *showing* man how much he is worth and, as a result, man rising to the height of the new status God has given him.[254]

Returning now to Duthie's Presidential Address, we find him saying that in addition to the fact that alternative world views are not amassing numerous converts, there is the encouraging fact of the continuity of the life of faith in the succession of believers among whom there is much 'unheralded faithfulness.'[255] Furthermore there is the gain of half a century of New Testament scholarship which reassures us that the picture given of Jesus is substantially reliable. We are confronted by

God savingly present within our humanity. His death upon the Cross throws upon the darkness of the world's sin and suffering the light of a love that draws our folly and our foulness into its own great heart and consumes them in the fire of its agony. It is cheering to find that many of our younger theologians are coming to see that the Resurrection is the very foundation on which our faith rests.[256]

In terms that we have already noted, Duthie proceeds to call the Church to its evangelistic task, urging that as well as a concern with the world around them, Christians should never 'restrict [their] horizons to the present life and ... allow [their] hopes of the life everlasting to fade.'[257] In the meantime the Church must continue to let its light shine in proclamation, witness and service, because darkness and strife are still present. In such a world, 'Faithfulness is always possible because God remains faithful and because we have the hope that through the power of the Spirit our lesser lights, however fitfully they burn, will point to Him who is indeed the Light of the World.'[258]

As Duthie knew only too well, faithfulness is not simply a matter of articulating the faith in face of contrary belief systems, or of proclaiming the faith to the unevangelized. It is also a matter of godly living. In this connection, in 1970 and 1971 he published two articles: 'Morality, Old and new', and 'The Christian understanding of sexuality.' To those who have memories of 'the new morality' and 'the permissive society' it will come as no surprise that a theologian as concerned as Duthie was to relate faith and life should have spilled some ink on these themes.

Consistently with his remarks upon humanism, Duthie maintains that those who do not subscribe to belief in a Supreme Being can and do have a sense of moral

---

254 Ibid.

255 Idem, *Faith in a Time of Doubt*, 8.

256 Ibid., 8-9.

257 Ibid., 18.

258 Ibid., 22.

obligation. Religion is not a *sine qua non* of morality. Christians and humanists may hold certain values in common and join in concerted action on moral issues; and, indeed, sometimes the dividing line in ethics is not between Christian and humanist but between Christian and Christian, humanist and humanist. In Duthie's opinion (which I endorse) we may not seek an explanation of the common ground that exists between Christian and humanist by invoking John Baillie's idea that people may deny God with the top of their minds whilst believing in him in the bottom of their hearts. This saying may indicate a possibility, but (a) we may not split the human personality in the way posited; and (b) 'an unbeliever or a non-believer ... is not a believer who is unaware of the fact that he believes. The fact and problem of genuine unbelief must be taken quite seriously.'[259]

That moral attitudes and customs vary around the world is undeniable, but Duthie nevertheless contends that it is a necessary condition of human life that people are aware of the sense of obligation. Furthermore, 'God reaches out to man through the moral order but it is open to the individual either to recognise His presence there or to deny it.'[260] Despite the common ground between Christian and secular morality the latter is, from the Christian standpoint, inadequate for three reasons. First, it does not see humanity in the context of the divine reality; secondly it does not sound the depth of the human predicament; and thirdly, 'by its rejection of God it forfeits that spiritual reinforcement which is needed to sustain the moral life in full vigour.'[261]

Duthie discusses three issues in turn. The first is what he calls the revolt against traditional morality. In part this is a protest against legalism, in part it entails the elevation of love as the supreme criterion of morality. Thus, in his book, *Situation Ethics*, Joseph Fletcher declares that love is only thing that is intrinsically good, and that right and wrong are always relative to the situation in which we find ourselves. In each situation we must determine what is the loving thing to do. Duthie agrees that

> The Christian life in its essence is a life of concern for others which is rooted in the concern of god made manifest and effective in Jesus Christ. It springs from gratitude for what God has done. Action from a new spirit, a new motivation rather than obedience to a set of laws and rules is its chief characteristic. ... But this does not mean that there is no place for the notions of duty, law, principle and rule in a Christian ethic.[262]

Religion, he argues, contains the complementary principles of gift and demand. Moreover, love is not a sufficient guide for conduct: it requires to be exercised in

[259] Idem, 'Morality, old and new,' 339.
[260] Ibid., 340.
[261] Ibid.
[262] Ibid., 342-3.

relation to guiding rules and principles, among them the principle of justice. To deny people such guidance 'might be contrary to the principle of love.'[263]

Secondly, Duthie considers the stance of permissiveness, according to which 'Moral rules and standards are not objective and universally binding but [are] simply conventional constructs which enable men to get on with the business of living without excessive friction or conflict.'[264] In response, Duthie argues that Christianity reminds us that, if unchecked, permissiveness 'will sap and may eventually destroy the moral health of the nation;'[265] and

> More importantly, [Christianity] can show us that a return to responsible and mature manhood may depend on our recovering a high sense of stewardship for the life which is given to us. ... It makes a profound difference to the way in which you live if you are convinced that your deepest gratitude and responsibility is owed not to yourself, nor to others, nor to society but to God.[266]

Thirdly, Duthie considers the distinction which is frequently drawn between public and private morality—a distinction often employed to legitimate behaviour behind closed doors, so to speak. He prefers to follow Basil Mitchell in distinguishing between public and private behaviour, 'each of which may be good or bad, right or wrong.'[267] But is there an agreed public morality? Duthie thinks that a measure of common moral agreement is necessary to the proper functioning of a society; that such agreements are enshrined in such institutions as marriage and in the law of the land; and that established morality is susceptible to change in the light of developing moral insight: 'To quote only one example, it has taken centuries for Christianity to give woman her true worth and the process is by no means complete.'[268] Law and order have traditionally been spoken of as 'the strange work of Christ', designed 'to preserve and enhance the framework within which a decent human life may be possible.'[269] But this, says Duthie in conclusion, 'needs to be supplemented by His "proper work" which is to reconcile men to God, to put a new spirit in them and to give them a new concern for the neighbour wherever he may be found.'[270]

In 'The Christian understanding of sexuality' Duthie says that intimate sexual relationships, the very stuff of life, are an inseparable part of the wider life-relationship between two people. At its best Christianity has blended reverence and realism in its attitude towards sexuality; at its worst, for fifteen centuries sexuality

---

[263] Ibid., 343. Duthie might also have noted that were it not for moral rules—and even the constraint of the law of the land—some of us some of the time and some of us most of the time would find the demands of love too great and simply fail to do the right thing.

[264] Ibid., 344.

[265] Ibid., 345.

[266] Ibid.

[267] Ibid., 346. Duthie refers to Mitchell's book, *Law, Morality and Religion.*

[268] Ibid.

[269] Ibid.

[270] Ibid., 347.

was regarded as shameful. Believing as he does that marriage is the appropriate context for the expression of sexual relations, Duthie makes four points concerning marriage. First, 'it is a commitment for life based upon love and fidelity;'; secondly, 'by a necessity more than natural marriage is completed by the coming of children' [at which point one could wish that he had uttered a pastoral word to those married couples who, through no fault of their own, cannot have children]; thirdly, 'marriage is a matter of concern not only for the individuals involved in it but for the society in which they live. As a focus of community on a small scale it is a stabilising factor. A large-scale breakdown of marriage affects the health of the larger unity'; fourthly, owing to human weakness, selfishness and waywardness, marriages can fail.[271]

Duthie stoutly advocates 'chastity on the way to marriage, chastity within marriage and chastity where marriage is unlikely or impossible.'[272] He justifies the use of contraception within marriage on the ground that sexual intercourse is relational as well as procreational. He thinks that the unmarried, whether heterosexual or homosexual should likewise be guided by the standard of chastity. Duthie does not wish to be understood as saying that there can be no fulfilled or happy life outside the relationship of marriage: 'one can choose to be and to remain unmarried just as one can choose to be married. Nevertheless there are many who do not have the opportunity to marry and whose condition is one of relative unhappiness in the absence of other forms of fulfilment.'[273] He concludes by saying that in these matters Christians must be prepared to be different; they must expound their understanding of sexuality; and they must point to the Gospel which 'holds us to what is highest and best and at the same time provides the inspiration and the resources to live in the light of high ideals without being driven to despair by them and to achieve what we could not have achieved without God.'[274]

By the time Duthie was writing no one living in Britain—especially in urban Britain—could have been unaware of the influx of immigrants from various parts of the world. While some of these were Christians, others brought the world religions to the land as never before. These religions, therefore, were now an important part of the 'world' with which Christians had to reckon in the name of the Gospel, and Duthie did not shirk the obligation to reflect upon this aspect of the missionary situation. In an article entitled, 'The challenge of other faiths' he sets out from an earlier work of the Dutch missiologist, Hendrik Kraemer, *The Christian Message in a Non-Christian World.* Kraemer here represents the faiths of the world as being intransigently opposed to the Christian Church, whereas the Christian revelation, far from fulfilling whatever truth the other religions may have, stands over against them in judgment. More moderate is H. H. Farmer's view that Christ both judges and fulfils the glimpses of truth possessed by, other religions; and in Kraemer's later

---

[271] Idem, 'The Christian understanding of sexuality,' 4-5.
[272] Ibid., 5.
[273] Ibid., 6.
[274] Ibid., 9.

works, *Religion and the Christian Faith* and *World Cultures and World Religions*, he too advocates dialogue and cooperation between the several world religions.

Duthie proceeds to discuss two books in greater detail. The first is *No Other Name* by W. A. Visser 't Hooft, the then General Secretary of the World Council of Churches. He argues that while from the point of view of other religions Christianity is also a religion, from its own point of view it is not one religion among others, but is God's adequate and definitive revelation in history. He opposes the syncretistic notion that there are many route to the divine reality and that all of them are variously deficient; and points out that even if a new religion could be devised from parts of all the existing religions, this religion would then claim superiority—the very thing for which Christianity is currently rebuked. There is, however, a proper Christian universalism which derives from Christ who is the centre from which we may draw a circle which embraces the cosmos. This universalism, Duthie explains, is one 'which leaves the road open for so-operation between men of differing faiths, which accommodates its message to the life-situation of other cultures without adulterating it and which calls for a manifestation of unity among Christians adequate to its wide sweep. ... [I]t is a universalism which demands a real dialogue between Christians and non-Christians of other religions.'[275] Dialogue entails both talking and listening, but also witnessing in a humble and respectful manner.

The second book under consideration is Tillich's, *Christianity and the Encounter of the World Religions*. For Tillich, religion is the state of being grasped by an ultimate concern, and this concern is characteristic not only of religions as such, but also of such '*quasi*-religions' as communism and secularism. With other religions Christianity is in a dialectical union of rejection and acceptance. In the course of its history Christianity has absorbed and assimilated much whilst retaining its inherent universalism. For this reason it should be possible for Christianity to enter into dialogue with other religions and *quasi*-religions. But when Tillich specifies the objective as 'Not conversion but dialogue', Duthie the dedicated theologian-evangelist calls a halt: 'We miss the clear emphasis on the Christian testimony to Christ. It may be that Tillich cannot give its due place to such testimony because it seems to savour too much of conquering the false religion. Much more seriously, however, it may be because his view of Christ is not big enough'[276]—a serious judgment for which some further justification might have been offered.

From the two books Duthie draws the following lessons:

> First, that Christianity is firmly anchored in a particular history. It lives by its faith that, in Christ, God himself has come into our life and ushered in the new age of the Kingdom.

---

[275] Idem, 'The challenge of other faiths,' 9.

[276] Ibid.

> Second, that because the God who has drawn near in Christ is the God of the whole earth and the Lord of all men Christianity must search diligently to find traces of the working of his Spirit outside 'the history of God's people' ...
>
> Third, that we who come to men of other faiths with the Gospel of redemption come without any sense of superiority but as men without excuse who stand under the same grace and judgment as they do.
>
> There is only one stance from which to proclaim the Crucified. That is under the Cross, which is their hope and ours.[277]

Lest the advocated talking, listening and witnessing should seem, from the article just discussed, to be less problematic than it is, I should point out that elsewhere Duthie was alive to the fact that there are serious doctrinal differences between the world religions. For example, in an article on reincarnation he writes,

> The difficulties raised by the doctrine of re-incarnation seem to me to be very great.
>
> (1) If my soul existed before my present life, then either it has existed from eternity or it came into being by the decree of God at a specific time in the past. In the first alternative I seem to be co-eternal with God and other souls. In the second alternative I am in the realm of time and there is no reason to prefer 'then' to 'now'.
>
> (2) Re-incarnation seems to imply an identity of person throughout my various existences without enabling me to establish that identity and thus profiting from the fact that all this is happening to me for a purpose. ...
>
> (3) The idea of working out destiny in a series of existences tends to move in the direction of a final absorption in the All or God. In the end I hope that I shall not be separated from God but united with Him; but in order to be united I must retain my distinctiveness.[278]

It seems to me that it is necessary to add that underlying the difference between Christianity and those religions which teach reincarnation are profoundly different understandings of history: the teleological, consummation-orientated view of Christianity as distinguished from a cyclic view of history. But on the general point I believe that Tillich is right to say that an inter-faith dialogue loses its integrity if any of its participants forget that the dialogue room is not a mission hall and make an attempt to convert others; and that Duthie is right to emphasise the importance of testimony in the dialogue situation, for if any participants feel, or are made to feel, that they may not testify to their sincerely-held beliefs—which will inevitably include points of agreement and disagreement with others—the integrity of the dialogue is, once again, lost.[279]

---

[277] Ibid.

[278] Idem, 'Re-incarnation,' 9.

[279] Cf. Alan P. F. Sell, *Enlightenment, Ecumenism, Evangel*, 386.

V

Unlike some of the divines discussed in this book, Charles Duthie did not bequeath a learned tome with which contemporary scholars and future ages would need to reckon. He fulfilled a role more akin to that of Thomas Ridgley, whose *Body of Divinity*, though it would stagger some present-day theological students, was written for the edification of church members. In Duthie's time this objective was achieved principally by the challenging and time-consuming discipline of maintaining a weekly column in *The British Weekly* over a period of years. There can be no question that he was ideally suited to this work, which almost certainly made him the most widely-read of all those discussed herein. It takes a particular skill to drive to the heart of a Tillich, a Teilhard, a Ferré, and to present a reasoned account of their thought together with cogent reflections upon it—and all within one thousand words and in such terms that he who runs may read.

Again, where Abraham Taylor would peddle a Calvinistic party line in defiance of all comers, Duthie was open to a wide range of theological thought, and his primary impetus was always to learn before he adversely criticized. Neither a way-out liberal nor an unreconstructed conservative in theology, he was open to biblical scholarship[280] and, although he did not write a fully-rounded systematic theology, the consistent standpoint from which he viewed the Church and the world was that of the caring, patient love of God supremely manifested in Jesus Christ—a theme which he developed in the spirit of Pascal and with the aid of insights drawn especially from personalist philosophy. He was not a theological 'party man'. He did not sign up to either of the theological giants of his day—Barth and Tillich—but drew from them what he found to be of benefit, challenged them where he saw fit; and, above all, understood, as did Payne and Franks, that due place is to be given to both dogmatics and apologetics. In his writings Duthie covered 'The Gospel, the Church and the world' more comprehensively than any other divine treated in this book.

James Calder aptly applied to Duthie the words he had read on a memorial tablet to a minister in a Sussex church: 'By nature a man of talent, by education a man of learning, by Grace a man of God.'[281] Loved and trusted by students, colleagues, the folk in the churches and readers far and wide, he was, indeed, an 'all round' minister.

Above all, like Richard Alliott before him, Duthie was an evangelist—notwithstanding his patience-*cum*-persuasion-inspired lack of the 'killer instinct'. As he wrote of his beloved Pascal, 'Because he has seen God, he wants others to see God.'[282] This deep desire was the inspiration of Duthie's witness and service too, and for further confirmation of this we may heed the words of his former student, Robert Waters: 'the one reality on which his life was built is that of the Christ encounter. You approached Charles Sim Duthie and you met Jesus. I can pay him no higher tribute.'[283]

---

[280] See, for example, C. S. Duthie, 'Biblical conservatism,' 9.
[281] J. M. Calder, 'The Rev. Principal Charles S. Duthie.'
[282] C. S. Duthie, Review of E. Cailliet, *Pascal*, 103.
[283] Robert Waters, 'He is alive.'

When Charles Duthie died suddenly on 11 January 1981 many Christians in Scotland, England and across the world felt that they had lost a true friend. That, at any rate, was their immediate feeling, I am sure. But then they would pull themselves up and remember that the one of whom they were thinking had lived in the light of the resurrection; had written a moving Drew Lecture on 'Ultimate triumph'; and was, in fact, a victor. On more than one occasion Charles said, and wrote, that of the trio, faith, hope and love, it was hope that needed renewed emphasis. Certainly, his own lively hope in God's final consummation did not fade. There can be no question but that he took to heart the text of his sermon entitled, 'Our Christian hope', in terms both of the injunction it contains and the manner of proceeding it prescribes: 'Always be prepared to make a defence to anyone who calls you to account for the hope that is in you, yet do it with gentleness and reverence' (I Peter 3:15):

> With gentleness and reverence! because in the very act of giving it we know that we are unworthy of a privilege which is sheer grace, because the men to whom we speak must not be bludgeoned into believing but persuasively wooed and won, and, most of all, because this is the only fitting way to present to the world the Christ whose humble approach to His human brothers was the way of the cradle and the Cross.[284]

[284] C. S. Duthie, 'Our Christian hope,' 219.

Part V

Conclusion

CHAPTER 12

Conclusion

I have now introduced the ten hinterland theologians, and discussed their writings. Chandler was a Presbyterian, Tymms was a Baptist, and the rest were Congregationalists. We should almost certainly have known if Ridgley were a son of the manse; of the remainder, all except Tymms and Duthie had fathers in the ministry. Ridgley, presumably Taylor, and certainly Tymms and Adeney were born in London, while Chandler and Payne came from the West Country, Alliott from the East Midlands, Simon was born in Cheshire and raised in Derbyshire, Franks was from the North-East, and Duthie was a Scot. All of them studied for the ministry in Dissenting academies or Nonconformist colleges. Payne and Alliott were also alumni of Glasgow University, Tymms and Adeney earned the degrees of London University, Franks was at both Cambridge and Oxford, and Duthie graduated from Aberdeen. Simon, Franks and Duthie also studied in Germany. Between them the four ancient Scottish universities honoured all our hinterland divines except Franks. All had experience of full-time pastoral charge, though that of Franks and Duthie was brief. With the exception of Chandler, they were all involved in the theological education of ministerial candidates, believing that rigorous preparation was required for so exacting a vocation. Whereas Alliott, Simon, Adeney, Franks and Duthie urged students to think for themselves and reach their own conclusions, Taylor was more interested in tying students to the high Calvinist (but not antinomian) party line. Alliott, Duthie and Tymms displayed more overt evangelistic zeal than the others, though Tymms's was of the liberal-*cum*-Social Gospel variety. Payne had a particular gift for reaching young men, while children's work was Adeney's greatest love. If Payne, Alliott, Tymms, Adeney and Duthie held high ecclesiastical office, Simon and Franks shunned it.

In a variety of ways they all sought to take the measure of their times. Ridgley and Chandler were exercised by the confessional debates of their day, and if Chandler found it necessary to hammer the deists (not least because liberals like himself were frequently accused of being of that flock), Taylor manifested a particular zeal for policing the doctrinal utterances of his fellow Dissenters, whether they were antinomians, Arminians or Arians. Ridgley did much the same, but in a more measured way. Payne was often found in pursuit of Unitarians, Tymms of Roman Catholics, as well as pantheists, materialists and agnostics; and Adeney was disinclined to concede much to surviving Calvinists. Chandler was the supreme man of affairs, a preacher of integrity who would not say what he did not believe, and one who, on (good) doctrinal grounds resisted the blandishments of the Church of England. Adeney ranged over the greatest number of theological disciplines, and could as easily reach scholars as little children, whereas Alliott 'was remarkable rather for thoroughness and depth, than for wideness and range.'[1] Duthie excelled in communicating difficult contemporary theological ideas to a wide public, and commented perceptively upon numerous issues current in the mid-twentieth-century. Payne, Alliott and Franks ploughed narrower scholarly furrows, but did so with considerable skill and, in Frank's case especially, with great learning. The ten divines display a wide variety of writing styles. Where Chandler piles authority upon authority, his contemporary Ridgley does not; where Alliott adds qualification to qualification in tightly-written prose devoid of illustration, Simon oscillates between throwing off the homely phrase or anecdote and perpetrating almost impenetrable prose.

Adeney and Tymms seem to have been blessed with the most outgoing temperaments; in Payne, Simon, Franks and Duthie there was warmth and kindness beneath a certain reserve; Ridgely and Chandler evinced concern for the needy; but in terms of personality the opposites in this group are Abraham Taylor, whom I described as 'a volatile theological meteor' and Richard Alliott, of whom it was said that 'He was not a blazing meteor that flashed athwart the sky and speedily disappeared; but the calm steady light which constantly and gently shone, and told whence all its lustre was derived.'[2] As I have come to know these divines better, I have found myself wondering which of them I like best. I can only conclude that they have all become friends and that, as with one's living friends, I like them all for different reasons.

With a view both to recapitulating fresh theological departures and to detecting intellectual time-lags I shall next consider the ten theologians in relation to the chronological periods within which I set them. That done, the rest of this chapter will comprise a review of some of the themes discussed in the study as a whole by way of indicating the topics on which the hinterland theologians may stimulate the ongoing theological conversation. I shall first reflect upon some of the doctrinal changes that were prompted by the dilution of Calvinism in English Dissenting circles.[3] There will follow reflections upon two running themes: the question of the methods and starting-points in theological endeavour, and the relations between philosophy and theology. That done, I shall reintroduce a selection of doctrinal topics raised by the hinterland divines that seem to me to merit, and in some cases are receiving, continuing attention; and I shall follow this with a miscellany of more general 'matters arising' from the foregoing discussions. A concluding paragraph will encapsulate my verdict on the whole.

---

[1] C. Clemance, *Funeral Services for the Rev. R. Alliott, LL.D*, 6-7.

[2] Ibid., 6.

[3] See Alan P. F. Sell, *Enlightenment, Ecumenism, Evangel*, ch. 5.

I

I introduced the ten theologians in the chronological order of their birth, and I placed each in the wake of a significant landmark: the so-called Toleration Act of 1689,[4] the Enlightenment and the Evangelical Revival, the rise of modern biblical criticism, and the phenomenon of liberal theology. It has become clear that there was doctrinal change ('development' is too loaded a term[5]), and that there were fresh theological approaches following each of the four landmarks but, as I hinted in the Introduction, we have also become aware of certain time-lags in the varieties of theologico-philosophical thought with which we have been especially concerned. Thus, for example, it might have been expected that the Toleration Act of 1689 would have encouraged a degree of freedom of theological thought and expression hitherto unknown; and certainly people like Samuel Chandler were controversial on certain neuralgic theological issues if reticent, and therefore suspect, on others, but no more so than those seventeenth-century Dissenters who, in accordance with their several predilections, went in vociferous pursuit of such tribes as the Calvinists, Arminians, antinomians, and neonomians.[6] In a word, the passing of the Act was not necessary to the fomenting of doctrinal strife, but neither did it cause such strife to cease. Throughout the eighteenth century numerous doctrinal controversies arose, some of which put Dissenters at risk, as when, ostensibly in the interests of Church and state, the Trinity became a stick with which to beat the still-officially-non-tolerated Unitarian, Joseph Priestley, during the Birmingham riots of 1791.[7] Conversely, it would have taken more than a Toleration Act to have deflected Abraham Taylor from his staunch Calvinism: he was clearly in continuity with much that had gone before, as was the less pugilistic Thomas Ridgley. Ridgley's exposition of the *Westminster Larger Catechism* is in a line of Puritan catechetical tomes that includes that of the Presbyterian divine, Thomas Watson, who died three years before the Act of 1689.[8]

There can be little doubt that the Evangelical Revival of the eighteenth century constrained some Calvinists to revise a number of their received doctrines, notably the embargo against freely offering the Gospel to all hearers; or that from the side of the Enlightenment there issued a moral challenge to the way in which Calvinistic doctrines had come to be expressed which prompted George Payne in a governmentalist direction. I shall return in more detail to these points shortly. For the present I simply add that on the apologetic front Payne was not so forward-

---

[4] 'So-called' because the term 'Toleration' occurs neither in the official title nor in the text of the Act.

[5] See Alan P. F. Sell, *Enlightenment, Ecumenism, Evangel*, ch. 6.

[6] See further idem, *The Great Debate*, ch. 2.

[7] See further David L. Wykes, '"A finished monster of the true Birmingham breed": Birmingham, Unitarians and the 1791 Priesley Riots,' 46. For Priestley (1733-1804) see DEGBP; ODNB; Robert E. Schofield, *The Enlightenment of Joseph Priestley*; Isabel Rivers and David L. Wykes, eds, *Joseph Priestley, Scientist, Philosopher, and Theologian*.

[8] For Watson (d. 1686) see ODNB. His style is considerably pithier and hence more memorable than that of Ridgley.

looking—though he was typical of his age—insofar as he persisted with the traditional theistic arguments as if Hume and Kant had not spoken. Twenty years on, however, Richard Alliott was early in making the turn to experience in the wake of Schleiermacher.

A further shaking of the theological foundations was occasioned by the impact of modern biblical criticism from the mid-nineteenth century onwards. As with other landmarks, there had been harbingers of this, not least in Locke's method of paraphrasing New Testament epistles—a method which entailed a departure from piecemeal proof-texting and a concern 'to read the same Epistle over and over, and over again, till I came to discover, as appeared to me, what was the Drift and Aim of it, and by what Steps and Arguments *St. Paul* prosecuted his Purpose.'[9] But in Britain, from about the 1850s onwards, 'the German problem', coupled with the rise of modern historiography, led to close textual analysis, source criticism and, on the part of many, the determination to approach the Bible in the manner in which they would approach any other ancient text. Payne and Alliott were at the threshold of this development, but the rapidity with which their hermeneutic was overtaken is surprising: Samuel Davidson, we recall, passed from being a troubler of Israel to being regarded by Adeney as espousing outmoded ideas within the space of some thirty years. Even Simon, who sought, somewhat inconsistently, to place the buffers behind the advance at the place he thought appropriate was suspect in the eyes of some, and it is small wonder that many Christians wondered what Tymms and Adeney were doing to the assumed biblical foundations of the faith once delivered to the saints.[10] Not least of the casualties, from the conservative point of view, was the undermining of the apologetic 'evidences' of miracle and prophecy. This, together with the by now more widely recognised failure of the classical proofs of the existence of God, stimulated (except in such a case as that of B. B. Warfield—as ever, there were time-lags) a fresh approach in apologetics, motivated by the turn to experience—or to spiritual realities as in Simon's case, the defence of which required the attempted slaying of such foes as pantheism, materialism and agnosticism. Furthermore it takes no great imagination to suppose that the glee with which Adeney celebrated the decline of Calvinism was as distressing to conservative spirits as were his unbiblical grounds, his inadequate specification of the underlying principles of Calvinism and his premature conclusion:

> Calvinism is the aristocratic temper in religion; the essence of it is privilege. But ... the modern democratic temper is in direct antagonism to the underlying principles of Calvinism. ... 'Liberty, equality, fraternity', sound the death-knell of Calvinism as well as of feudalism.[11]

---

[9] J. Locke, *A Paraphrase and Notes on the Epistles of St. Paul*, I, 110. See further Alan P. F. Sell, *John Locke and the Eighteenth-Century Divines*, 92-107.

[10] See further, Willis B. Glover, *Evangelical Nonconformists and Higher Criticism in the Nineteenth Century*.

[11] W. F. Adeney, *A Century's Progress in Religious Life and Thought*, 123.

The response to the liberal evangelical theology that Tymms and Adeney represented was, once again, diverse. If some became enamoured of Barth's theology of the Word, for example, many did not. Franks began and remained a liberal evangelical theologian throughout his long life, notwithstanding two World Wars and Barth, because he was persuaded that the causes that had ushered in theological liberalism were still operative, notably the necessity of giving an account of the faith rooted in up-to-date scholarship and alive to contemporary intellectual challenges. For his part Duthie, strongly influenced by experiential considerations and by personalist philosophy, perceptively reviewed the theologians and issues of his day, learned from all, and was bowled over by none. He assumed the viability of the then widespread approach in biblical theology and, in striking contrast to Taylor, for example, his method of reasoning was not strongly disjunctive, but was discriminating, more given to 'on the one hand ... on the other' than to 'it is this ... it is not that.' Above all, like Alliott and Tymms before him, he was an evangelist who sought patiently to introduce people to Jesus Christ.

As I view the three centuries together, I gain the distinct impression that of the several landmarks—Toleration, the Enlightenment and the Evangelical Revival, the advent of modern biblical criticism, and liberal theology—it was the coalescence of modern biblical criticism with demise of former apologetic methods that marked the greatest discontinuity between what had gone before and what followed. This is not to deny that following every fresh departure there were those who remained in the 'old paths', nor is it to dispute the fact that throughout the centuries under review there have been important continuities of thought, their diverse modes of expression and their various intellectual opponents notwithstanding. All of the ten hinterland divines were trinitarians, for example; they all reflected deeply on the person and work of Christ; and all of them accorded a high place to the Church as a divine institution. Interestingly, none of the three theologians, Simon, Tymms and Adeney, who had to adjust their thought to fresh developments in biblical studies, had much to say about the other considerable boulder thrown into post 1850s theology: evolution. This suggests how quickly evolution came to be regarded, in much of mainstream Anglicanism and Nonconformity, as a theme rather than as a purely scientific theory. It came to be construed by many theologians as indicating the way in which God went about his work of creation, and some used the idea of evolution to support their attempts to cash Christian thought in terms of post-Hegelian immanence.[12]

This account of doctrinal change and intellectual time-lags has thrown into relief the running question of the viability of Calvinism.[13] For this reason I shall now offer some further reflections on this matter, leaving other doctrinal themes to subsequent sections of this chapter.

---

[12] See further Alan P. F. Sell, *Theology in Turmoil*, ch. 3; idem, *Philosophical Idealism and Christian Belief*, *passim*.

[13] See further idem, *Enlightenment, Ecumenism, Evangel*, ch. 5.

II

Joseph Hussey, whose spiritual pilgrimage included his transformation from anti-Calvinist Presbyterianism to high Calvinist Congregationalism, was among those who taught that since the elect alone could receive the Gospel, any notion that the Gospel might be freely offered to all wrongly presupposed the ability of fallen persons to accept it. 'By offers of grace, tenders and proffers of salvation,' he declared, 'it is evident, men do thereby imply that free grace and full salvation is propounded, tendered, and offered to all sinners within the sound ... Is not this a piece of robbery against the Holy Spirit' who works 'His grace on sinner's hearts that sinners may believe, repent, and be saved?'[14] That the Evangelical Revival did not completely eradicate this view is clear from the fact that John Skepp, John Gill and John Brine, among others, stoutly maintained it, and it lingers to this day. But as early as 1742, in the infancy of the Revival, so staunch a high Calvinist as Abraham Taylor repudiated the position in his *Address to Young Students in Divinity*, and in his pamphlet on *The Modern Question*. He declared that sinners had a duty to repent and believe, and therefore enjoined preachers freely to offer the Gospel—this without in any way denying that sinners would be brought to faith only by the agency of the Holy Spirit. With all of this George Payne and Richard Alliott were, in the wake of the Revival, in full accord and, as we saw, Alliott gave Christ's evangelical command precedence over human doctrinal reasonings.[15] For an interesting insight into the challenges posed at the grassroots by the question of the free offer we may turn to Charles Duthie's home church, Mid Street, Fraserburgh, whose minister from 1818 to 1840 was Alexander Begg.[16] Begg was succeeded by Archibald Duff, whose son of the same name was the Old Testament scholar at Yorkshire United Independent College who taught senior Hebrew to Tymms's Rawdon students. The latter wrote of Begg that his father's predecessor, Mr. Begg,

> had been wont to preach in the morning service—where the well-to-do folk attended—the high old-fashioned notion that God loved and saved through Jesus only a selected few of us poor human folk whilst in the evening service—where the masses attended—Mr. Begg told out freely and grandly the unlimited love of the great 'Jesus' heart of the Creator. ... Mr. Duff said at once he must preach the same great message to the morning hearers as to the evening crowds. But the former dissented from such a faith in the size and bounds of God's care, and ere long the young enthusiast and apostle had to leave the old building. A great church meeting of members only, of course, decided that God's heart was of the smaller size. So, on

---

[14] See J. Hussey, *God's Operations of Grace but no Offers of Grace*, 21. 23. For Hussey (1659-1726) see G. F. Nuttall, 'Northamptonshire and the Modern Question,' 111-114; idem, 'Cambridge Nonconformity 1660-1710: From Holcroft to Hussey'; Alan P. F. Sell, *The Great Debate*, ch. 2.

[15] R. Alliott, *The Christian Ministry*, 12.

[16] For Begg (1787-1840) see SCM. This was his sole pastorate.

January 2nd, 1845, 59 men and women and the pastor, threescore in all, joined in fellowship in forming a new church.[17]

Returning to the eighteenth century, we find that Calvinistic doctrines were challenged on moral grounds by deists and 'Arian' divines alike.[18] Hence Ridgley's determination to show in *A Body of Divinity* that the doctrines of election, particular redemption and efficacious grace were not 'inconsistent with the moral perfections of the divine nature.'[19] As Franks reminded us, Thomas Chubb the deist lodged a moral complaint against such doctrines as that God could not forgive unless his Son were punished for the sins of humanity. This was not likely to carry much weight with Ridgley, who wrote of the deists that 'Though they express not a due veneration for the divine Majesty, they profess not to be Atheists, that they may not be excluded from the society of mankind, who have some degree of abhorrence of Atheism impressed on their nature. They talk, indeed, of God, and of natural religion, but make revealed religion the subject of their scorn and ridicule.'[20] Abraham Taylor thought likewise, and Samuel Chandler was particularly keen not to give the high Calvinists any excuse for labelling him a deist. As for the eighteenth-century Arians, the Presbyterian, Henry Grove, was among many who took strong exception to the doctrine of God's eternal decrees, which, like not a few scholastic upholders of the decrees, he construed in terms of a philosophical determinism which denied genuine freedom to human beings and from eternity consigned them to heaven or hell:

> Whatever principles destroy the very notion of moral good and evil, i.e. of virtue and vice, holiness and sin, and all distinction between them, have a plain tendency to banish virtue or holiness itself from the earth; for, if once a man believes that all actions are alike indifferent, as to any moral good or evil that is in them, any praise or blame they deserve, there can be no room for conscience, which always supposes an intrinsick immutable difference in actions, and applauds or reproaches men according as they observe or neglect this difference in the conduct of their lives. ... [A]ccording to [high Calvinists] the supreme Being conducts all his proceedings by mere arbitrary will and pleasure. ... [I]f all things (actions as well as events) are in pursuance of absolute decrees, it is certain that men are not free agents; and if men are not free, so as to have a power to do good or evil, they cannot be obliged to do the one, and to forbear the other; nor can anything they do be properly good or

---

[17] William D. McNaughton, *Early Congregational Independency in the Highlands and Islands*, 399, quoting Robert Duthie, *A Northern Light*, 15-16. For Duff senior (1810-1883) see SCM.

[18] On this one occasion I place the noun within inverted commas by way of reminding readers that most of the eighteenth-century Arian divines were not consciously disciples of Arius, and, when they were charged as such, a number of them denied all knowledge of him: they said they simply read their Bibles.

[19] T. Ridgley, *A Body of Divinity*, I, vii.

[20] T. Ridgley, *A Body of Divinity*, I, 637.

> evil, in a moral sense, being the pure effect of necessity. ... God ... would not be a proper object of our imitation, having no moral perfections for us to imitate ...'[21]

Clearly, Thomas Ridgley's assurance that God was not the author of sin, which he decreed to permit though not to effect;[22] that God did not decree to damn a large part of humanity without foresight of sin; that the decree does not remove human free will, or 'obstruct the preaching of the gospel, or the proclaiming of the glad tidings of salvation, to those who sit under the Christian ministry'[23] did not avail with deists and Arians.

Where predestinating decrees were concerned the Calvinists found themselves caught in a pincer movement between deists and Arians on the one side and evangelical Arminians, headed by John Wesley, on the other. Wesley took strong exception to the decree of reprobation, regarding it 'as being utterly irreconcilable to the whole scope and tenor both of the Old and New Testament.'[24] He was quite unmoved by Calvinistic defences to the effect that preterition, passing by, was not the same as a positive decree of reprobation. Nor was Richard Alliott's father inclined to appeal to that subterfuge: to him the decree of reprobation was not found in the Bible, and it was not essential to Calvinism.[25] In the wake of the Revival, and with reference to Enlightenment challenges, George Payne had recourse, with mixed results, to governmentalism which was intended to justify God's wrath without impugning his grace, but which involved the problematic distinction between God's public and private characters according to which God's saving intention as sovereign is general, whereas his intention as ruler is particular. Nevertheless, Payne endorsed Edward Williams's description of 'Calvin's ill-digested reprobating decree,'[26] whilst resisting what he took to be Erskine of Linlathen's reduction of the doctrine of the atonement to a matter of the demonstration of God's love with a view to winning the sinner and curing his or her moral disease, and this at the expense of the honouring of God's justice. Wishing to hold that whatever God intends he achieves, Payne concluded that while God as moral governor would save those disposed to repent and believe—that is, the elect—alone, Christ's atonement was in fact sufficient for all. (Franks is not correct, then, in saying that on the view of Payne and others, 'by the death of Christ no one is saved, but all may be.'[27]) Similarly, Christ's heavenly intercession is on behalf of the elect alone. Through it all, Payne strove to find a way between what he called ultra Calvinism on the one hand and Arminianism on the other.

---

[21] H. Grove, *Ethical and Theological Writings*, IV, 216-17 n.

[22] T. Ridgley, *A Body of Divinity*, I, 258.

[23] Ibid., I, 254.

[24] J. Wesley, *The Works of the Rev. John Wesley, MA*, X, 211. For further examples of eighteenth-century doctrinal squabbles see Alan P. F. Sell, *Dissenting Thought and the Life of the Churches*, ch. 7; idem, *Enlightenment, Ecumenism, Evangel*, ch. 3; PNT II.

[25] R. Alliott (Sr.), *An Apology for Calvin and Calvinism*, 20.

[26] G. Payne, *Lectures on Divine Sovereignty*, 425.

[27] R. S. Franks, *A History of the Doctrine of the Work of Christ*, II, 393.

A further bone of contention among Calvinists and between them and others concerned the relations of doctrine and ethics. If we place our hinterland theologians in sequence we can readily detect both ethical continuity and discontinuity over the centuries. In the Puritan tradition, making the assumptions of Christendom, and with their predilection for bodies of doctrinal and practical divinity, it would not have occurred to Ridgley or Taylor to drive a wedge between doctrine and ethics. They strongly held that right action flowed from right belief; Ridgley lamented the way in which doctrines were discounted and 'the work and glory of the Holy Ghost is traduced, or deem'd unnecessary to the promoting of practical Godliness'[28]; and Taylor, with a passing blow against 'the Socinians who skulked in Poland',[29] argued that doctrinal declension was followed by the corruption of manners. Rather surprisingly, Adeney was so far in the wake of the Puritans as to hold that Christ's practical guidance 'only admits of being embodied in the social order of any nation in proportion as the population has already become Christian'[30]—a position which would seem to preclude any interpretation of natural law, and any recourse to common ethical ground as between believers and others. Samuel Chandler took the view that human beings were conscious of a sense of obligation deriving from the nature of things which is, however, 'strengthen'd by the express Authority of God himself.'[31] Chandler further declared that the eternal difference between moral good and evil is 'intirely independent of the Will of God',[32] thereby bringing down the wrath of John Gill upon his head on the (mistaken) ground that Chandler was divorcing morality from God and opening the gates to polytheism, deism, antinomianism and libertinism. What in fact Chandler was doing was to raise an ethical issue which was by then already venerable: Does God command what is right, or is what is right that which God commands? George Payne came down strongly in favour of the former clause, for if actions became right only because God commanded them they would have no rectitude in themselves, and God might capriciously command now what he had previously prohibited, and *vice versa*.[33] With this Franks was in entire agreement. He thought it important 'to avoid the Scotist notion that right and wrong depend simply upon the arbitrary *fiat* of God. Surely it is better to maintain moral autonomy, and then to say with Dale: 'In God the law is *alive*, it reigns on His throne.'[34] Franks urged the same point against Emil Brunner who, 'In his recent great book, *The Divine Imperative* ... maintains the old heresy that the good is the good simply because God wills it and for no other reason—which means in the end founding Christianity upon the arbitrary and absolute Sovereignty of God.

[28] T. Ridgley, *The Advantage of Falling into the Hand of God rather than Man*, 4.
[29] A. Taylor, *Of Spiritual Declensions*, 28.
[30] W. F. Adeney, *The Theology of the New Testament*, 85.
[31] S. Chandler, *Benevolence and Integrity Essentials of Christianity*, 13.
[32] Idem, *The Necessary and Immutable Difference between Moral Good and Evil*, 9.
[33] See G. Payne, *Elements of Mental and Moral Science*, 344-5.
[34] R. S. Franks, Review of *The Christian Answer*, 176.

Surely Anselm was right when he opposed this doctrine of pure Sovereignty, saying that unless God is just, He is not God.'[35]

In his substantial volume on ethics, George Payne sounded Puritan-like from time to time, as when he wrote that 'Godliness is an essential part of morality ... to be destitute of godliness and to be destitute of morality, are convertible terms.'[36] For the most part, however, his book has a distinctly different flavour from that of the older bodies of practical divinity. Payne was only tangentially concerned with godly living, for example, and is much more concerned than his Puritan forebears to enquire into ethical theory as dissociated from doctrinal or systematic considerations. He wished to investigate the implications of mental science for ethical statement. Hence, for example, in criticism of Butler he writes,

> An ethical system which does not attempt to explain the nature, either of conscience or virtue, or which satisfied itself with a statement which really explains nothing—*viz*., that conscience is that which approves virtue and virtue that which is approved by conscience—must, surely, be allowed to be imperfect; and on a point, too, where we might have expected to find it most full and explicit.[37]

In a word, by the time Payne was writing on ethics, that discipline had been divorced from doctrinal and systematic theology, no least in the curriculum of the Dissenting academy—of which change Henry Grove of the academy at Taunton was, as far as I have been able to discover, was the pioneer.[38] Since that time ethics has gone its separate way and is nowadays, in the West, a largely secular discipline, sometimes intensely analytical, sometimes issue-driven; and one, furthermore, with which latter-day systems of theological ethics such as that of Brunner, and even other varieties of Christian ethics, in my opinion, have all too little contact.

In other places Payne did discuss doctrines which have a bearing upon ethics, notably in *The Doctrine of Original Sin*. Here he dealt at some length with the position promulgated over a century before by the Arian Presbyterian, John Taylor of Norwich, whose book, *The Scripture-Doctrine of Original Sin* (1740) drew responses from as far afield as Jonathan Edwards in America. Taylor's position is encapsulated in his comment upon John 3: 6, 'That which is born of the flesh is flesh; and that which is born of the spirit is spirit':

> The natural birth produceth the mere Parts and Powers of a Man: The Spiritual Birth produceth a Man sanctified into the right Use and Application of those Powers in a Life of true Holiness. This I take to be the true Sense of the Text: but do not see that it either affirms or implies, that we derive from Adam, by natural Generation, a Nature quite indisposed, and disabled to all spiritual Good. Certainly that cannot be concluded from the Force of the Text; which, on the contrary, supposeth that we

---

[35] Idem, Review of *Grace and Nature*, 98.

[36] G. Payne, *Elements of Mental and Moral Science*, 428.

[37] Ibid., 370.

[38] See Alan P. F. Sell, *Dissenting Thought and the Life of the Churches*, ch. 6.

> have a Nature susceptible of the best kind of habits, and capable of being born of the Spirit.[39]

Against this view Payne urged that

> as an expression of his abhorrence of sin—a sin so peculiarly atrocious as was the transgression of Adam—the great and blessed God withdrew the sovereign gift of his Spirit from man ... so that every member of the human family is born destitute of original righteousness—mere flesh, with undiminished animal propensities ... and all those inferior principles of action, which, thought they ought to be in subjection to reason and conscience, have never, in point of fact, been held in control by anything but the love of God. The result of this deprivation of primitive holiness is, that the inferior and animal principles, given to be servants, become absolute masters of the heart; principles of action merely become principles of evil action, and the entire race 'go astray from the womb speaking lies.'[40]

Here we seem to have total depravity, where 'total' is construed intensively—there remains no good in human beings; 'natural man' can do nothing pleasing to God, and is God's enemy. But if, as I believe, 'total' in total depravity is best understood extensively—as meaning that (owing to mixed motives and our propensity to sin) nothing that we do is wholly good, then I find myself at this point with Brunner who, as Duthie reminded us, departed from Barth in part because of Barth's insistence that there is no point of contact between sinners and God. Brunner thought that, despite sin, a point of contact remained. Indeed, were it otherwise any approach of God would be a further instance of divine sovereignty gone arbitrary; it would be far removed from the loving, personal, approach of a heavenly Father to whom a free, albeit graciously enabled, response is due.[41]

Released, as they felt themselves to be, from the clutches of Calvinism, Simon, Tymms and Adeney did not reflect much on 'Calvinistic'[42] doctrines *vis à vis* ethics, though Tymms made some remarks about Augustinianism which are analogous to those of Franks *contra* Barth:

> Augustinianism is necessarily a form of Docetism because it affirms an apparent, but only an apparent, action of the human will, both in the reprobate who transgress because delivered to do evil, and in the elect who obey, or appear to obey, but only because dominated by irresistible grace, *i.e.*, by a grace which is dynamical and not ethical in its operations.[43]

---

[39] J. Taylor, *The Scripture-Doctrine of Original Sin*, 144-5. For Taylor (1694-1761) see DECBP; ODNB; Alan P. F. Sell, *Dissenting Thought and the Life of the Churches*, ch. 7; G. T. Eddy, *Dr. Taylor of Norwich*.

[40] G. Payne, *The Doctrine of Original Sin*, p. 309.

[41] See further, Alan P. F. Sell, *Confessing and Commending the Faith*, 267-279.

[42] I place the term in inverted commas by way of suggesting that Calvinists of a non-sectarian kind would simply regard the doctrines as being biblical.

[43] T. V. Tymms, *The Christian Idea of Atonement*, 446.

More generally, the three liberal evangelicals welcomed the way in which the increased sense of social responsibility was tempering older individualistic attitudes in the churches. Alive to societal issues, they lived in the hey-day of those large institutional churches in growing industrial towns that offered everything from soup to sermons, temperance to tennis. Far from needing to advocate such activity, they felt that a cautionary word was needed. Thus Simon was concerned lest Christianity be converted 'from a real spiritual dynamic, into a moral and religious regulative';[44] Tymms queried the tendency on the part of some 'to find the cause of immorality in physical conditions, and to substitute hygiene for the Gospel, and sanitation for Sanctification;'[45] and Adeney testified, 'I believe in the Institutional Church ... when there is a real live Church to be institutional, but not in an institute that has absorbed and assimilated its Church.'[46] No doubt they could without difficulty supply doctrinal grounds for the Church's socio-ethical witness—human beings as children of God, the realization of the kingdom of God, for example; but the terms in which they did so modified and supplemented the more strictly confessional terms of a Ridgley, a Taylor, or even a Payne.

A generation on from Payne, D. W. Simon was able to welcome what he called the 'wider, more rational and more merciful views of religious truth'[47] that had come into view through the efforts of F. D. Maurice and others, and he could refer to the earlier moderate Calvinism as 'Calvinism with its teeth filed but not drawn.'[48] At the same time, he lamented the way in which, with the decline of Calvinism, doctrinal preaching had become a rarity, and many members of congregations had not appreciation whatsoever of the strengths of Calvinism. For his part he would not repudiate the juridical aspects of the atonement in favour of love gone sentimental. Adeney, however, though willing to regret the loss of the 'virile energy' of the 'sturdy Puritan theology', nevertheless rejoiced that the fight with a discredited complex of doctrines was over: 'Calvinism, that was fought during the first half of the [nineteenth] century as though it were some fierce dragon with a terrible abundance of life in it, is not as quietly studied as if it had no more power to hurt than the fossil skeleton of an antediluvian dinosaur.'[49] Neither Franks nor Duthie found it necessary either to endorse or to repudiate the more angular expressions of Calvinistic doctrine.

I choose the words of that last phrase carefully, for I hold that we can still have fruitful conversation with Calvinism, as with other earlier formulations of the faith. No doubt it is easier to do this now that the genuine relief which many, and above all Adeney, felt at the releasing of a crippling burden of belief, has subsided. For example, I think it quite possible to find good news in predestination, provided that it be unscrambled from philosophical determinism, and construed in what I take to

---

[44] D. W. Simon, 'The present direction of theological thought,' 80.

[45] T. V. Tymms, *The Christian Idea of Atonement*, 150.

[46] W. F. Adeney, 'The Church for the Kingdom,' 56.

[47] Quoted by F. J. Powicke, *David Worthington Simon*, 17.

[48] Ibid., 264.

[49] W. F. Adeney, *A Century's Progress in Religious Life and Thought*, 120.

be the original Pauline sense, namely, as the retrospective, grateful recognition by the believer that, to put it crudely, 'I did not get here under my own steam.' In other words, it is a testimony to God's prevenient grace; and from propositions asserting this as applied to ourselves we are ill advised to draw negative implications regarding anyone else.[50] If my stance as here expressed should be deemed heretical by some high Calvinists, I can only reply (though this is not by itself a sufficient justification) that it is an heresy which enables me to sleep at night.

III

Inextricably interwoven with the adjustments to Calvinism is the question of the methods and starting-points for theological construction—my first running theme to emerge from this study. It is fair to say that whereas, of our ten theologians, Adeney was as much a polymath as might reasonably have been expected by the turn of the nineteenth century, Ridgley and Payne came closest to covering all the traditional 'departments' of systematic theology—from creation to eschatology; but all of them saw the value—indeed, the necessity and urgency—of the systematic presentation of Christian truth. D. W. Simon, we recall, advised ministers to master a system of theology as a means of disciplining their thoughts *en route* to the formulation of their own systems, adding the warning that those who fail in this task 'become confirmed flounderers';[51] while Thomas Ridgley was convinced that in a time of doctrinal declension 'the society of Catechumens who attend on the Lecture in the Old-Jewry' needed nothing so much as a firm grasp of 'the Excellent Composure of the Reverend Assembly of Divines at Westminster.'[52] But as between the system expounded by Ridgley and the systematic presentations of theologians from Payne onwards, there is a great gulf fixed. Ridgley adopted and expounded a given, corporately-devised, catechism; Payne and his successors had greater liberty in choosing the doctrinal starting-points of their more personal productions. Thus, for example, in one place Payne says the doctrine of original sin is 'the first stone in the great evangelical system',[53] and Franks observed that in placing sin before salvation Paul was 'the precursor of the usual method of Christian theology, whether Catholic or Protestant.'[54] Elsewhere, however, and somewhat more cheerfully, Payne says that 'the doctrinal and experimental and practical branches of our holy religion form one beautiful and consistent whole, of which the atonement of Christ is at once the centre and support. It would be absurd, says an excellent writer, to affirm that there is a single lane in the country which does not lead to the metropolis, as to suppose that there is a single doctrine, promise or precept in the word of God which is not connected directly or indirectly with the Cross.'[55] Of Simon it was said that 'Man's

---

[50] See further, Alan P. F. Sell, *Enlightenment, Ecumenism, Evangel*, 325-338.
[51] D. W. Simon, *The Making of a Preacher*, 44-5.
[52] T. Ridgley, *The Advantage of Falling into the Hand of God rather than Man*, 4-5.
[53] G. Payne, *The Doctrine of Original Sin*, 2.
[54] R. S. Franks, *Man, Sin and Salvation*, 99.
[55] G. Payne, *Lectures on Christian Theology*, II, 497.

sin and God's redemption were the height to which ... all his thoughts gravitated'[56] and, with only occasional departures, he generally followed the Pauline way of proceeding from humanity's sin to God's saving remedy. Franks, however, seeking a vantage-point from which to view the whole system of Christian truth, found it in the love of God, revealed supremely at the Cross, which calls forth our loving response, and held that we do not really understand what sin is until we know God's love, for sin is the rejection of that love. I have much sympathy with this view, believing as I do that the first word of the Gospel is grace, not sin, and that we do not truly grasp the exceeding sinfulness of sin until the message of what it cost God to vanquish it has been brought home to us.

One way of drawing the contrast between the theological climate in which Ridgley, Taylor and, with reservations, Chandler worked and that of their successors is to say that the former was more formally confessional, the latter much less so. Chandler stood for doctrinal integrity and liberty of conscience; to him the imposition of confessions of faith as tests of orthodoxy was 'a thing unreasonable in itself, as it hath proved of infinite ill consequence in the Church of God',[57] and consequently he opposed the notion of formal subscription to creeds and confessions. One of the standard Dissenting objections to subscription was the view that one should not bind oneself to the words of men, and that God the Holy Spirit may have further doctrinal light to shed upon the churches in due course. Whether as a result of divine light or of sinful declension, there was certainly confessional change within the tradition to which Ridgley and Taylor were committed. In 1833 the infant Congregational Union of England and Wales adopted a *Declaration of Faith* which is moderate Calvinist in tone and contents. The 'Preliminary Notes' explain that subscription is not in view and that liberty of conscience is not at risk In the 'Principles of Religion' which follow, The covenant of grace is mentioned, that of works is not; the term 'predestination' nowhere appears, and 'preterition' is itself passed by.[58] All of which would, no doubt, have appealed to Samuel Chandler.

While there is much to be said for churches' setting down the things commonly believed among them, it cannot be denied that confessional literature, whether in the form of declarations of faith or catechisms, is always, and rightly, of its time. Confessions are acts of confessing, and catechisms are confessionally-grounded aids to education. Given the religious context in which they were called upon to confess the faith, it is not surprising that those who framed the classical Reformed confessions and catechisms paid great heed to the Bible, and to justification by grace through faith. On the other hand, for example, they said comparatively little about creation, the right stewardship of which is of such concern today; and their anathemas against the anabaptists, and the suggestion that the Pope is the antichrist are impossible to justify biblically and are not particularly ecumenically helpful.

---

[56] F. J. Powicke, *David Worthington Simon*, 195, quoting David Ritchie.

[57] S. Chandler, *The History of Persecution*, 377.

[58] For this *Declaration* see Williston Walker, *The Creeds and Platforms of Congregationalism*, 542-552. See further, Alan P. F. Sell, *Dissenting Thought and the Life of the Churches*, 51-3; idem, *Enlightenment, Ecumenism, Evangel*, 152-3.

Whilst acknowledging the context in which they witnessed, it may be argued that the *Westminster Larger Catechism*, which oscillates between the being and attributes of God and Scripture, and does not reach the Trinity until Question IX and the Gospel until much later, is not putting first things first. Yet again, there is always the danger—and it is one that has fuelled sectarian strife—that the impression will be given, or the alleged 'fact' will be insisted upon, that we are saved by assenting to specific doctrinal formulations: of which a slightly blinkered Simon declared that 'there never was any such thing, at all events in Protestantism.'[59] Duthie was standing in a long line of testimony when he rightly said that 'Faith as man's trustful response to God may bring forth a creedal affirmation: it cannot be equated with assent to that affirmation.'[60]

A further dimension is added to the discussion of theological starting-points by Richard Alliott, that theologian between the times, who was early among the English in commenting on Schleiermacher's theology, and was aware of the turn to experience in theological method. He drew a contrast between the older, objective, theology—that of Ridgley, Taylor and their peers, and the newer theology which was subjective. His question was, Are we to rely upon truths objectively revealed by God, or upon an inward light given by God? He pleaded for balance, arguing that it is only by reference to the objective that we can evaluate the subjective, and concluded that 'The true way to escape spiritual deadness is not by a rejection or a neglect of truth, but by a warm, hearty, living reception of it.'[61] Feeling, though integral to, is not the whole essence of, religion, which also concerns knowledge and the exercise of the will. On this point Franks was in full accord with Alliott,[62] and among Franks's and Duthie's objections to Barth was the latter's denigration of experience. To Franks, far from its being the case that the appeal to experience renders us independent of philosophy, the appeal is 'rather the modern form of relating theology to philosophy.'[63] He consistently maintained this position, with the proviso that religion is 'never merely a feeling of absolute dependence. It includes also a moment of knowledge and a moment of activity, subordinated to the feeling and bound together by it.'[64] The question arises, Which comes first: Do we first know and then have the experience, or does the latter lead to the former? Simon was familiar with those who wished to know before they made a faith commitment, but he argued that 'it is *experience* that is the condition of knowing. ... Not our knowledge of him, but our willingness to be saved by Him on the supposition that He exists and can save ... conditions the experience out of which grows

[59] D. W. Simon, *The Redemption of Man*, x. Cf. idem, 'The present direction of theological thought,' 79.

[60] C. S. Duthie, 'Affirmations of faith,' 3. Cf. idem, *Outline of Christian Belief*, 14. For further reflections upon the matters briefly raised in this paragraph see Alan P. F. Sell, 'Confessing the faith and confessions of faith.'

[61] R. Alliott, 'Address' on the old and the new theology, 9.

[62] R. S. Franks, *The Metaphysical Justification of Religion*, 82-4; 126.

[63] Ibid., 50.

[64] Ibid., 82-3.

knowledge.'[65] The only way that I can make sense of this pronouncement is by unravelling the ambiguity of 'knowledge' as here used. The saved 'know' God, albeit not exhaustively, in the sense that they experience a (sometimes fluctuating) personal relationship with him: we might call this clamant knowledge; but would they have a prior willingness to be saved unless they knew that there was a God of the saving type, and would they behave rationally if they committed themselves to one of whom they knew nothing? At this point we may recall Abraham Taylor's tendentious description of Samuel Chandler's view that religion is more about loving God than about knowing him as 'Nonsense dropping from him unawares', since we cannot worship one of whose existence we are uncertain.[66]

A final observation concerns the position of the Bible in theological construction. In the confessional period the Bible was appealed to as the perfect rule of faith and obedience because, as Ridgley said, 'The scriptures of the Old and new Testaments contain a revelation of the whole mind and will of God' as far as human beings are capable of assimilating it;[67] and confessional and catechetical arguments were bolstered by the kind of proof-texting which in the wake of modern biblical criticism and historical method is unavailable to many of those who stand in the tradition of Ridgley and Taylor (though biblical inerrantists are still to be found in some parts of the Reformed family). Again, Ridgley, in good confessional (and polemical) fashion, made it clear that the negative implication of the elevation of Scripture was that Roman Tradition was no authority at all. Scripture stands in opposition to 'the popish doctrine of human traditions, which are pretended to be of equal authority with the word of God.'[68] Not the least interesting feature of the inner-Dissenting theological controversies of the eighteenth century is that both high Calvinists like Ridgley and Taylor and more liberal divines like Chandler appealed to the principle of the sufficiency of Scripture. To Chandler, no less than to Ridgley, the Bible was a revelation from God, and the rule of faith and morals.[69] It has become clear that the common appeal to Scripture sufficiency did not prevent the divines from reading texts in mutually contradictory ways.

As far as our ten divines are concerned, Alliott, who lived at the threshold of modern biblical criticism, was the last who could with some justification uphold the idea of the plenary inspiration of the Bible (though, as we saw, Franks rebuked Warfield, who died in 1921, for continuing to accomplish the feat). Simon, who suffered a degree of guilt by association over modern attitudes towards the Bible, himself was open to critical methods provided that they did not go too far, but he made it very clear that people do not have to espouse a particular view of Scripture before they can have faith in the Saviour. The idea that people have no right to believe until they have convinced themselves that the Bible is inspired, he thundered,

---

65 D. W. Simon, *The Making of a Preacher*, 54-5, 60-61.

66 A. Taylor, *A Letter to a Friend*, 10.

67 T. Ridgley, *A Body of Divinity*, I, 28; cf I, viii.

68 Ibid., I, 30.

69 S. Chandler, *The Case of Subscription*, 40.

'is as cruel as it is monstrous;'[70] and he rebutted the argument that the Bible claims inspiration for itself by saying that this 'is to make it judge and jury in its own case.'[71] He also insisted upon the role of the Holy Spirit in illuminating the Bible and bringing its truths home to reverent readers. In Tymms's judgment, 'the gravest peril to Christian faith in the coming generation proceeds from [the] impression that Biblical authority and enlightened morality are in opposition.'[72] By the time we come to Franks, who upheld 'the principle of free critical investigation'[73] of the Bible, the Jesus of history, who is also the Christ of faith, the one to whom the Bible witnesses, is the *locus* of authority rather than the texts as such; while for Duthie the witness which begins in the Bible and is continued by the Church is that 'Jesus is the One through whom we are reconciled to God and enabled to lead a new life as His children. ... At the centre of the New Testament message stands the reconciling power of God in Christ.'[74] Here, as it seems to me, we have the due balance of objectivity and subjectivity: at the Cross the reconciling act has been performed, and to this believers have, by enabling grace, joyfully responded.

IV

My second running theme concerns the relations between philosophy and theology. In our own time Barth has been represented as querying whether there can, or ought, to be any relations between these two disciplines, and he was challenged by Robert Franks on the ground that Barth remained with dogmatics (dogmatically) and ruled out apologetics. By contrast, Franks maintained that any satisfactory theological system would accord due place to what I have called confessing and commending the faith (not least *vis à vis* alternative theories and views of the world),[75] and because of Barth's deficiency in the latter respect Franks felt unable to place his work among the major theological systems of the Christian Church. As Franks himself put the point:

> Dogmatic and Apologetic are not two distinct branches of Theology. They are aspects of the one theological science ... Dogmatic is the inner face of theology which is turned to the Church, Apologetic the outer face which is turned to the world. ... [T]he two coincide everywhere. There is no dogma into which Apologetic considerations do not enter. There is no Apologetic which does not look towards an end in the Dogma.[76]

---

[70] D. W. Simon, 'The authority of the Bible,' 366.

[71] Idem, *The Bible an Outgrowth of Theocratic Life*, 374.

[72] T. V. Tymms, *The Christian Idea of Atonement*, 9.

[73] R. S. Franks, 'The person of Christ in the light of modern scholarship,' 27.

[74] C. S. Duthie, *Outline of Christian Belief*, 21, 25.

[75] See my trilogy, *John Locke and the Eighteenth-Century Divines*, *Philosophical Idealism and Christian Belief*, and *Confessing and Commending the Faith*.

[76] R. S. Franks, *The Atonement*, 12.

None of Franks's hinterland predecessors would have dissented from his view, and neither did his successor, Duthie, hence the latter's way of placing Barth and Tillich side by side with a view to benefiting from both and succumbing completely to neither. Simon, too, was in no doubt that an assemblage of biblical teaching was insufficient, and that the Christian faith must be vindicated against its opponents.[77] He further wished that church members took more interest in 'the rational justification of their faith.'[78]

To differing degrees a number of our divines turned their attention to the classical theistic arguments for the existence of God, and/or the 'evidences' of miracle and prophecy. Ridgley, like Simon and others, saw the necessity of the Christian's giving a reason for his or her belief and, furthermore, he argued that it will not suffice to receive the doctrine of God by tradition, or because others believe in it. Although weakened by apostacy, our reasoning powers 'are not wholly obliterated,' he declared, and hence we can know God apart from special revelation.[79] In a manner characteristic of eighteenth-century thinkers Ridgley advanced a cosmological argument for God's existence, the argument from universal assent, and adverted to the evidences of miracles and prophecy. He did not, however, suppose that reason by itself could bring us to God: 'the strongest Reasons, and clearest Evidences cannot comfort; 'tis Sovereign Grace that refreshes, as well as quickens and enlivens.'[80] To the same effect, though couched in language framed in the aftermath of the turn to experience, was Simon's conviction that the theistic arguments fall short because 'No one can properly maintain that God really is what the living Christian experience knows He is, without living Christian experience.'[81] Tymms was equally insistent that 'The life of faith is not a mere assent of the intellect to certain propositions, and it cannot therefore be produced by logic.'[82] Nevertheless, he added, 'When the mind has been convinced, a man may still be destitute of personal trust in God, but a channel will be opened through which appeals to his conscience and affections may afterwards be made.'[83]

In the wake of the Enlightenment, and notwithstanding the adverse criticisms of Hume, George Payne was still found advancing the cosmological argument for God's existence, whereas Adeney, half a century on, took a different line. He contended that the theistic arguments, seeking as they do to demonstrate the infinite and the absolute are neither neutralized not validated by revelation. This does not, however, render theism redundant, for although they are not manifested in the Incarnation, these theistic ideas are implied in the Christian idea of God. 'Thus,' he concludes, 'the basal theism comes into the Christian conception of God and is presupposed by

---

[77] D. W. Simon in Anon, *Memorial of the Opening of the New and Enlarged Buildings*, 86.

[78] Idem in Anon, *Mansfield College*, 193-4.

[79] T. Ridgley, *A Body of Divinity*, I, 10.

[80] Idem, *A Funeral Sermon Preached ... on the Decease of Mrs. Gertrud Clarkson*, 99.

[81] D. W. Simon, 'The authority of the Bible,' 373.

[82] T. V. Tymms, *The Mystery of God*, x.

[83] Ibid., xi.

it,'[84] though its contribution is surpassed by the revelation in Christ of God as perfect love.[85] In different terms Franks reached much the same conclusion:

> what rational arguments for the Divine existence reach is always an abstraction, only religious experience can give concreteness and real content to this abstraction. On the other hand, the abstraction ... can serve as a standard of criticism by which genuine religious experience may be distinguished from the many counterfeits which claim the name.[86]

We have seen that in addition to the classical theistic arguments, a number of the hinterland theologians appealed to the traditional evidences of miracle and prophecy. Samuel Chandler, for example, defended the miraculous against the freethinker, Anthony Collins, with passing rebukes to Locke; and he repudiated Collins's view that the prophecies of the Old Testament have reference only to those who first heard them, contending that they were fulfilled in Christ. For his part, Richard Alliott, writing in answer to Hume's critique of miracles, argued that only by the unwarrantable restriction of experience to ordinary human experience could the appeal to miracles as supernatural occurrences be ruled out. By the time we come to Adeney, the evidences were rapidly being dismantled, both on the ground that biblical scholars were increasingly understanding miracles as signs to believers rather than as evidence capable of convincing sceptics, and because the theological construction of evolutionary thought in terms of God's immanence undermined the notion that miracles were breaches of the natural order, because 'If God is always working in nature through its normal operations, He cannot be regarded as stepping in or interfering when anything happens apart from the normal.'[87] As for prophecy, Adeney underlined the importance of the newer insight that 'the most characteristic feature of the prophetic mind was the gift of insight rather than that of foresight.'[88]

In the interests of moving the battle onto the territory of his intellectual opponents, Tymms did not, in his apolgetic writings, contend for all he believed. In this respect he is reminiscent of Joseph Butler who, in his *Analogy*, sought to discomfit the deists by standing as far as possible upon their own ground. 'I have argued', he wrote, 'upon the principles of others, not my own; and have omitted what I think true, and of the utmost importance, because by others thought unintelligible, or not true.'[89] This, once again, raises the question of starting-points. Consistently with his overriding interest in systematic theology, Simon, here in the line of Abraham Taylor, who insisted that spiritual things were 'spiritually

---

[84] W. F. Adeney, *The Christian Conception of God*, 28.

[85] Ibid., 273.

[86] CQ, XVIII no. 4, October 1940, 428.

[87] W. F. Adeney, *A Century's Progress in Religious Life and Thought*, 107.

[88] Idem, 'Miracle and prophecy,' 140.

[89] J. Butler, *The Analogy of Religion*, 192. For Butler (1692-1752) see DECBP; ODNB; C. Cunliffe, ed., *Joseph Butler's Moral and Religious Thought*; A. Duncan-Jones, *Butler's Moral Philosophy*;

T. Penelhum, *Butler*.

discerned',[90] took a quite different approach. He elevated those spiritual realities that objectors to Christianity were overlooking, while subjecting the actual positions of adverse critics to relatively little close analysis.'[91] The questions arise, on the one hand, how far it suffices to engage with the intellectual foes of Christianity by concentrating upon what they discount *ab initio*, and on what, on Simon's view, can be grasped only by the 'twice-born'; and, on the other hand, how successfully have we commended Christianity if we bracket some of its fundamental claims? If we take apologetics to be a matter of *Christianity Defensively Stated*, to quote the subtitle of A. B. Bruce's well-known work,[92] we may find that by having intellectual opponents constantly in view we shall be working with one hand tied behind our back as far as reasoned apology (which may well incorporate the lively slaughtering on intellectual foes *en passant*) is concerned. I believe that a strong case can be made for apologetics which first commend the faith (and closely examine the presuppositions of doing this), and in the process enter into dialogue with alternative theories and world views.[93] 'Defence in the context of construction' seems a more appealing way than 'The defensive followed by the offensive' (which, in another sense, some apologetic offerings sadly are[94])

Underlying the apologetic questions is that of the general relations between theology and philosophy. Ridgley, Taylor and Chandler were habituated to the scholastic method of argumentation, though Ridgley was wary of scholastic term 'used by metaphysicians and schoolmen [that] have done little service to the cause of Christ.'[95] To Payne it was unthinkable that theologians could neglect metaphysical issues, not least in their ethical enquiries, which presupposed a position on the nature of mind as framer of ethical judgments; and Alliott thought that philosophy was of great benefit to theological students because since, unlike theology, it involved no appeal to authority, it developed students' intellectual powers in reliance upon their own observation and reasoning abilities. No all varieties of metaphysics appealed to the divines under review, however. For example, Simon was suspicious of the 'Hegelianization of the Christian faith,' and felt that 'deal of the Hegelian philosophy are quietly being substituted for the concrete actualities accepted by the Christian Church.'[96] Similarly, Adeney denied that the Hegelian trinity was the

---

[90] A. Taylor, *The Insufficience of natural Religion*, 33.

[91] For this reason he is not to be found among the apologists discussed in ch. 5 of my *Philosophy, Dissent and Nonconformity*.

[92] See A. B. Bruce, *Apologetics; or, Christianity Defensively Stated*. For Bruce (1831-1899) see DBI; DHT; DSCHT; ODNB; WWW, 1897-1916; Donald K. McKim, *Dictionary of Major Biblical Interpreters*; Alan P. F. Sell, *Defending and Declaring the Faith*, ch. 5.

[93] See Alan P.F. Sell, *Confessing and Commending the Faith*; idem, 'Confessing the faith in the intellectual environment.'

[94] I saw a shelf in a Christian bookshop labelled, 'Apologetics: Roman Catholicism and Other False Religions.'

[95] T. Ridgley, *A Body of Divinity*, viii.

[96] D. W. Simon, *The Redemption of Man*, 63.

Christian Trinity, 'because it does not involve the idea of a personal God.'[97] This properly cautions us against casually reading off theological meanings from philosophical assertions—notably those concerning the absolute. It is essential that theologians remember that if they seek to utilize the terms of a prevalent philosophical 'ism' they are functioning as anabaptists, not poachers.[98] That is to say, they are engaged in an analogical task, and analogies can be both positive and negative: the absolute of philosophy is not altogether identical with God conceived as the Absolute. Franks, we recall, regretted Ritschl's avoidance of metaphysics on the ground that the claim that religious truth was given in the form of value judgments was unsatisfactory unless it could be shown that those judgments brought us into touch with reality. Unless this could be shown, he was convinced that we could not rebut the charge of psychologism. Franks had learned from Anselm that if theology is to be both dogmatic and apologetic, it 'must find a standing ground justifiable by reason.'[99] More generally, he applauded Austin Farrer for recognizing that metaphysics is not to be repudiated in favour of revelation, for it is metaphysics that enables us to 'draw out in logical form what is meant when we say "God", and understand what we say.'[100] Furthermore, as he elsewhere observed, in the absence of a metaphysic and an epistemology believers have no defence against the charge of psychologism. Hence Franks's concern at the 'obsession' with Barth. He was convinced that Barth's repudiation of the apologetic task, and hence of philosophy, entailed the view that the character of theological knowledge was 'entirely arbitrary' because 'proper knowledge of God' was 'altogether beyond us, except in so far as it [was] miraculously produced in the mind by the direct action of God Himself.'[101] As if this were not enough, it was Barth's unjustified account of what the Word of God was that was to be received. It is at this point that Duthie's procedure of bringing Barth and Tillich together comes into its own, his criticisms of both notwithstanding. That is to say, Duthie understood the necessity of both confessing and commending the faith, and saw that the latter cannot be done in innocence of, or neglect or repudiation of, the general intellectual and philosophical environment in which the task must be undertaken. As I might myself illustrate the point: Barth assumes that something, namely God, exists over against us. But this is a metaphysical assertion that deserves to be explored. Duthie, for example, approaches an answer to this question in terms of panentheism: 'Because the world and the men in it are rooted in the being of God, both world and men have a reference to God, a Godward-pointing metaphysical status, established from the side of God, which can be denied but cannot be destroyed.'[102] I think that an analogous argument—and one

[97] W. F. Adeney, *The Christian Conception of God*, 222.
[98] See further, Alan P. F. Sell, *Philosophical Idealism and Christian Belief*, 118-124.
[99] R. S. Franks, *The Atonement*, 15.
[100] R. S. Franks, CQ, XXI no. 4, October 1943, 372.
[101] Idem, CQ, XIV no. 2, April 1936, 236.
[102] C. S. Duthie, 'God in his world,' 24. In 'A God of action',9, Duthie says that 'We are not particles of divinity but we are rooted in God by a kind of metaphysical necessity.'

that does not have to face the problem of conceiving of the world's evil as somehow being 'in God'—may be developed in terms of the *imago dei*.[103]

Again, those theologians who wish to major on religious experience generally reflect carefully upon the question whether the religious consciousness can lead a person astray. As Richard Alliott pointed out, if people equate the deliverances of their religious feelings with the voice of God they cannot consistently question them, for they have become their authority. If they do question them their reason has usurped their authority. But if people believe that their religious feelings may lead them astray they will employ their mental powers to discover the truth and will examine all relevant evidence. Along this route further metaphysical questions are raised. Moreover, in our own time some of those theologians who have resorted to a distinct religious faculty or experience (Alliott denied the former, and Franks inconsistently asserted the latter) have felt it necessary to offer an answer to those anti-metaphysical philosophers who would restrict 'experience' to sense experience. It seems to me quite important that theologians should be willing to address the challenge of logical positivism and its successors, in order to show, in Ewing's words, that 'the denial of the possibility of asserting transcendental facts is an assumption for which, once we have admitted that the verification principle is not true, no evidence can be produced.'[104] If this were not the case then, for example, Simon's assertions regarding spiritual realities would be reduced to hot air. With many of the intellectual opponents of the faith it is well to investigate the degree to which their presuppositions are allowing them to mark out, and constrict, the territory of the meaningful, justifiable or rational, with the result that they discount important *facts* of human experience.

It is not, of course, being argued that an individual's faith is at risk unless the believer can provide metaphysical justification for it. In that sense religion does not depend upon metaphysics, least of all upon particular metaphysical systems, which are subject to flaws and, indeed, to redundancy. But if religious claims are made, metaphysical stances are presupposed by them, and it will be the task of theologians to pay heed to these if theology is not to become encapsulated within an intellectual ghetto. So one might go on; but enough has been said to suggest that the policy of driving a wedge between theological affirmation and metaphysics is, sooner or later, shown to be self-defeating. As Franks said, the mutual adjustment of authority and reason is a perennial theological task, and 'it is not enough simply to condemn reason and send it into a corner as a naughty boy. Reason has a way of coming out of the corner and behaving as an *enfant terrible*, whether we like it or not.'[105]

---

[103] See Alan P. F. Sell, *Confessing and Commending the Faith*, 70-79.
[104] A. C. Ewing, 'The necessity of metaphysics,' 147-8.
[105] Idem, 'Trends in recent theology,' 27.

V

I turn now to a selection of doctrinal matters on which the ten hinterland theologians stimulate ongoing theological conversation. In broad terms we may say that they would all have agreed with Thomas Ridgley's observation, 'That which is in itself incomprehensible, cannot be so revealed that we should be able fully to comprehend it; though that which is possible, or at least necessary, to be known of God, is clearly revealed to us.'[106] So far in agreement, Abraham Taylor cautioned that we must not believe anything that our reason tells us is false on the ground that it is a mystery, because that is the tactic of 'the papists who impose that monstrous absurdity of transubstantiation.'[107] None of this, however, prevented sometimes quite violent disagreements among the divines as to what had in fact been revealed and how it was to be understood.

Unsurprisingly, the ten theologians had much to say concerning the doctrine of God. Samuel Chandler, for example, discoursed upon the providence of God, conceding that while extraordinary events may be susceptible to naturalistic explanation this did not preclude their being intended by God; while in view of God's all-embracing providence, George Payne denied that there was an essential difference between 'every-day events and miracles.'[108] But the aspect of the doctrine of God which I wish to focus upon is that concerning God as holy Trinity. In the wake of the Salters' Hall controversy Taylor pursued Isaac Watts on this subject, rebuking him for seeking clear and distinct ideas where none could be had, and he lambasted Arians ancient and modern for 'tricking and disguise, for insincerity and double dealing.'[109] Taylor was convinced that the authors of *The Savoy Declaration of Faith and Order* were correct in saying that 'The doctrine of the Trinity is the foundation of all our communion with God, and comfortable dependence on him.'[110] Against the high Calvinist John Guyse, Samuel Chandler invoked the general point expressed above and applied it to the doctrine of the Trinity. He declined to speculate upon the precise distinctions between the Father, Son and Spirit, for this was 'of very little importance for us to know, because 'tis incomprehensible and cannot be understood and known by us. And I am more persuaded of this, because you gentlemen, who set up for the direct preacher of Christ, and to be the only sound men in the doctrine of the Trinity, differ greatly yourselves about it.'[111] As for the abstruse terms in which the doctrine was classically expounded, Chandler could not think that what was expressed was 'either plain or important doctrines of the gospel.'[112]

George Payne was convinced that 'The doctrine of the Trinity ...lies at the foundation of the entire economy of salvation,'[113] though he could not explain the

[106] T. Ridgley, *A Body of Divinity*, I, 28.
[107] A. Taylor, *The True Scripture Doctrine of the ... Trinity*, 8.
[108] G. Payne, *Lectures on Christian Theology*, II, 282.
[109] A. Taylor, *The True Scripture Doctrine of the ... Trinity*, ii.
[110] Ibid., 13 n.
[111] S. Chandler, *A Letter to the Reverend Mr. John Guyse*, 28.
[112] Idem, *The History of Persecution*, 366.
[113] G. Payne, *Lectures on Christian Theology*, I, 222.

manner or the mode of the unity and plurality of the persons. He thought that in trinitarian doctrine we were concerned with something analogous to personality, 'though what that something is we are totally unable to explain;'[114] and the attempts of the early Church to explain it were 'worse than useless.'[115] In Payne's view, with which I have much sympathy, 'the object of Divine revelation' was 'not to show what God is in himself, but what he is in relation to us.'[116] I believe that while the Christian faith depends upon God's being as he has revealed himself to be in Christ, we are not obliged to say that this is all there is to be known of the inner relations of the Godhead, nor should we encourage wanton speculation on this matter.

D. W. Simon 'revelled' in the Trinity as being 'the foundation doctrine of the Christian doctrinal system,'[117] and he regretted that

> The personal Trinity seems to have been practically dropped; and we have either fallen back on a sort of Sabellianism; or into the unity of Swedenborgianism; or we are trying to rest in a duality of Father and Son,—little stress is laid on the personality of the Holy Spirit, even where he has not been reduced to impersonality; and His work has been nearly merged in that of Christ.[118]

Simon did not, however, offer a detailed discussion of the doctrine. Vincent Tymms, presumably with cruder versions of the social doctrine of the Trinity in his sights, did lay it down that 'Christ does not reduce the Godhead into a species which consists of three individuals, with separate departmental offices, and are One God only as collective humanity is man;'[119] but in his critique of Martineau he tied himself in knots over the inner personal relations of the Trinity. Small wonder that James Drummond, Martineau's Unitarian defender, sighed, 'I am unable to soar into that rare atmosphere of speculation.'[120] On the basis of his biblical studies, W. F. Adeney supposed that 'no impartial student of the life and teachings of Christ will come to the conclusion that when He reveals God to us that revelation consists in the doctrine of the Trinity.'[121] As for Paul, while he 'attempts no metaphysical synthesis of the doctrine of the Trinity, he certainly affirms fundamental Trinitarian ideas',[122] but his writings 'do not justify the virtual tritheism of three exactly equal persons to be found in some clauses of the Athanasian Creed—although it is repudiated by other clauses of the same creed ...'[123]

---

[114] Ibid., 224; cf. 273-4.

[115] Ibid., 245.

[116] Ibid., 248.

[117] F. J. Powicke, *David Worthington Simon*, 219.

[118] D. W. Simon, 'The present direction of theological thought in the Congregational churches of Britain,' 79.

[119] T. V. Tymms, 'Christian Theism', 47.

[120] J. Drummond, *Studies in Christian Doctrine*, 155.

[121] W. F. Adeney, *The Christian Conception of God*, 51.

[122] Idem., *The Theology of the New Testament*, 184.

[123] Idem, *The New Testament Doctrine of Christ*, 115.

Tymms and Adeney repudiated the foundations of the social Trinity, as did R. S. Franks. Franks found an anticipation of the theory in the writings of Richard of St. Victor, who held that God as absolute love must have another to love and a third to enjoy the bliss of their mutual love. By contrast, Aquinas maintained that God is entirely self-sufficient, needing no other to complete his happiness. But in Franks's day is was the Anglican Leonard Hodgson who strongly advocated the social Trinity. Hodgson, whose underlying philosophy was empiricist rather than idealist, argued that the Trinity was first experienced as social; that is to say, through the experience of adoption believers shared the relation of the Son to the Father through possession by the Spirit. As Franks put it, 'It is the Trinity that we know, the Unity that thought strains towards', and he points out that 'this is the exact opposite of the position of John of Damascus, who says most decidedly that the Unity is the first point in our knowledge of God, and that the knowledge of the hypostases is subordinate to it.'[124] He realised, of course, that Hodgson was fully aware of the peril of tritheism, but felt that his language of three self-conscious personalities tended in a tritheistic direction. He objected to the social Trinity on three grounds: Authority, where he invokes the support of John of Damascus, Aquinas and Augustine; Reason, for the social Trinity 'leaves us with no intelligible conception of God. What it offers is too much like the unknown emergent of the future ... ;[125] and Experience: 'It must be denied that Christian experience is an experience of three distinct Divine Personalities. It is an experience of the One God through Christ in the Spirit. Theology can analyse out of the experience the mediation of Christ and the power of the Spirit, but in the actual experience all is fused into communion with God.'[126]

On this I should like to make two comments. First, I think that Hodgson is correct in saying that the experience of the early Christians prompted their thinking in a trinitarian direction: they had found Christ to be Saviour, but God alone could save; they knew the presence of the risen Lord and that his Spirit was with them, as he had promised. But, now more on Franks's side: it was all a profound reconstruction of the way they experienced and expressed their monotheism. The divine unity was not to be sought (how?) above and beyond the three persons. As Franks himself put it, 'There must be maintained indeed the immanent distinctions of the Persons, ... But the tempting social analogy must be avoided, which interprets the Godhead as though it were a company of human individuals.[127] Hence Franks's judgment that 'The formation of the doctrine of the Trinity will appear as an argument from history to a metaphysic as the solid basis that gives meaning to the history.'[128]

Charles Duthie was somewhat more sympathetic to the idea of the social Trinity, provided that the unity of the Godhead were conceived in accordance with Hodgson's distinction between a mathematical unity and a constitutive or organic one; but he

---

124 R. S. Franks, *The Doctrine of the Trinity*, 188.

125 Ibid., 196.

126 Ibid.

127 Idem, *The Atonement*, 193.

128 Idem, *The Doctrine of the Trinity*, 2.

felt that despite his intentions, Hodgson himself, in his concern to uphold coequality lest the Son and Spirit were regarded as only secondarily divine, had tended in the direction of a mathematical unity. Duthie nevertheless concluded that 'within the being of God the Father has a determinative position.'[129] As for the Son-Spirit relationship, Duthie maintained that 'The Holy Spirit is the Spirit of the God whose character shines out in the man Christ Jesus. ... [W]hile the Spirit is the cause or the agent of the divine indwelling, Christ is the substance or the content of that indwelling.'[130]

That these issues are still current in theological discussion is clear from the fact that there is a revival of commitment to the social Trinity on the part of a number of theologians. This leads me to my second comment on Franks's case against Hodgson. It concerns his appeal to authorities. Clearly Franks selected those that suit his case; he did not, for example, select Richard of St. Victor, whom others might cite as an authority in this connection. In a word, as Franks must surely have known, the argument from authority always raises the further question of the competence or otherwise of the specified authority to pronounce an acceptable judgment. Divines like Abraham Taylor and Samuel Chandler were past masters in piling up authorities designed to knock down those set up by their opponents. There is the further question of the correct interpretation of authorities. In recent years supporters of the social Trinity, Colin Gunton among them, have appealed for support to the Cappadocian Fathers. The question arises whether this is justifiable. Franks was well aware that the Cappadocians had frequently been represented as perpetrating a 'veiled tritheism', and he welcomed G. L. Prestige's book, *God in Patristic Thought*, as a corrective to this view. Prestige showed from a close analysis of the Greek texts that in to the Cappadocians, God was 'one object in Himself and three objects to Himself', that is, that 'in God there are three divine organs of God-consciousness, but one centre of Divine self-consciousness. As seen and thought He is three; as seeing and thinking, He is one.'[131] It was the Latins, says Prestige, who converted the three objects of the Greek Trinity into three subjects, and thus the Cappadocians appeared to advocate tritheism. Further puzzlement arises when supporters of the social Trinity, adverting to the 'sociality' of the three persons, say such things as, 'The Church is called to be the kind of reality at a finite level that God is in eternity.'[132] While the empirical evidence all around us makes it fairly safe to guess that the calibre of the Church's fellowship is at some remove from that internal to the Godhead, our knowledge of the latter is, as it seems to me, so slight as to render the challenge meaningless.[133]

---

[129] C. S. Duthie, *God in His World*, 45.

[130] Ibid., 183, 184.

[131] Quoted by R. S. Franks, Review of *God in Patristic Thought*, 110.

[132] Colin E. Gunton, *On Being the Church*, 78.

[133] See Alan P. F. Sell, *Nonconformist Theology in the Twentieth Century*, 176-7. My good friend, the late Colin Gunton, was fully aware of the perils of tritheism and three pages later he cautioned against drawing logical inferences from the inner relations of the Trinity on the ground that we do not have 'detailed knowledge of the inner constitution of

VI

I come now to some stimuli to reflection upon the person of Christ that are supplied by the hinterland divines. None of them denied the divinity of Christ or his full humanity, though some of them couched their expositions in more traditional language than others. Ridgley followed the *Westminster Larger Catechism* closely in his exposition of these doctrines, and also in treating at some length the threefold office of Christ as prophet, priest and king. George Payne also elaborated upon the threefold office, while Franks, regarding the this doctrine as Protestantism's characteristic teaching on the work of Christ, valued it as bringing together the objective and subjective aspects of the atonement. Adeney was typical of the liberal evangelical scholars of his day in adducing the following evidence of Chrst's divinity: his sinlessness, personal claims, consciousness of unique Sonship, resurrection, influence on those who knew him best, his work through the centuries and the experience of his people.

From the many Chistological lines of thought pursued by the hinterland divines I select as an examples of the way in which they continue to stimulate the theological conversation that doctrine of the eternal generation of the Son, and the kenotic theory of the person of Christ. Perhaps surprisingly, for so confessional a writer, Thomas Ridgley opposed the doctrine of the eternal Sonship, largely because he thought that the term 'eternal generation' provided an entrée to Arians who wished to contend that the communication of the divine essence or personality to the Son and the Spirit implied their subordination to the Father, whereas Ridgley held that the divine essence and personality are communicated necessarily and from all eternity to the Son (which is precisely what Athanasius meant by 'generation'). For his part, Abraham Taylor had no qualms about robustly calling the doctrine of the eternal Sonship by its name, while Samuel Chandler challenged John Guyse to adduce biblical evidence in its favour even as he covered his back by professing belief in the deity of Jesus Christ. George Payne followed Ridgley, quoting copiously from him, in arguing that the terms 'Son' and 'eternally begotten' refer only to the incarnate Christ as Mediator. Neither he nor Ridgley denied the eternal pre-existence of the second person of the Trinity, but this person was Son 'in intention and appointment, though not in act and accomplishment' until his 'miraculous incarnation.'[134] Simon concurs, bluntly affirming that 'there is no warrant ... for designating the Logos the Son of God, and thus representing the relationship of the Father and Son as an eternal and immanent divine relationship.'[135] In a different vein Adeney found wanting Fairbairn's argument that since God's essence is love his nature must be

---

the Godhead.' The social Trinity is not the only aspect of Trinitarian doctrine currently under review. I need only mention the protest of some feminist, anti-patriarchalist, theologians against the use of 'Father' language of God. Our hinterland divines were spared this important (because it drives to the heart of the Gospel), if sometimes rather shrill, debate.

[134] G. Payne, *Lectures on Christian Theology*, I, 268.

[135] D. W. Simon, *Reconciliation by Incarnation*, 328.

social, his Fatherhood implies Sonship, and hence the Son is eternally pre-existent. 'To many people,' declared Adeney, 'such deductive reasoning will appear unsatisfactory.'[136] I think this is too swift a dismissal of Fairbairn, for there is biblical witness to the eternal presence of the Son with the Father (II Corinthians 8: 9; Philippians 2: 5-7); it is difficult to conceive of a Father without a Son 'except one in intention and appointment'; and it is not for nothing that the Logos was, as has been said, 'bowed out of the creeds.'

This echo of Payne's words leads me to a further point. Payne belonged to a generation of theologians who could write on Christology without reference to kenotic theories. In defence of his view that Christ was not eternally Son he argued that had the opposite been the case it would be 'utterly impossible to say of the Son [what the gospels do say of him] that he knows not the hour of judgment, that he increased in wisdom as well as in stature, without surrendering the omniscience of the Saviour in whom we have put our trust.'[137] Once kenotic theories came into view a fresh stage of Christological debate was inaugurated. Whereas Ridgley's catechetical exposition had given due place to Christ's humiliation and subsequent exaltation,[138] it now became fashionable in some quarters to think in greater detail about the Son's voluntary self-limitation in becoming incarnate. By common consent the New Testament does not offer a kenotic *theory* any more than it offers a fully-fledged doctrine of the Trinity. Adeney reminded us that what Paul wrote to the Philippians was not a theological treatise or a legal document, but a friendly letter, and that he did not distinguish between ethical attributes which later theologians said Christ retained, and ontological ones which, they said, he relinquished: 'All that he suggests is the great general truth that Christ did not come in divine majesty, but came in a humble, serving life; that His dazzling glory of divinity was not simply veiled, that it was abandoned.'[139] Furthermore, if it be said that Paul's words in Philippians 2 concerning Christ's emptying of himself on becoming incarnate are but a slender basis upon which to erect a significant kenotic theory, the reply is that careful study of the gospels reveals a Christ who humbled, limited, and sacrificed himself—in other words, who did all the things Paul said he did. Indeed, it was the growing interest in the historical Jesus which fuelled the development of kenotic ideas from the mid-nineteenth century onwards and, as if in answer to Payne, Thomasius and others argued that in the interests of his full incarnate humanity, the divine Son renounced such incommunicable attributes as omnipotence, omnipresence and omniscience (the attribute Payne was anxious to defend). By the same token the modern kenoticists would never have veered in the direction of docetism as did some

[136] W. F. Adeney, 'Andrew Martin Fairbairn, D.D., LL.D,' 445.

[137] G. Payne, I, 266.

[138] John M. Wilson, Ridgley's editor, takes Ridgley to task for saying that Christ 'emptied himself of his glory.' This, says Wilson, is to go beyond Paul. It is, however, what is stated in the answer in the *Westminster Larger Catechism* to Question XLVI. See T. Ridgley, *A Body of Divinity*, 593 n. 3, 577.

[139] W. F. Adeney, *The New Testament Doctrine of Christ*, 107. We must be careful to understand that it was the 'dazzling glory' that was abandoned, not the divinity itself.

early theologians by saying that Jesus did not really feel hunger pangs: he only appeared to do so by way of sympathising with hungry people; the kenotic Jesus got hungry. Furthermore, he was genuinely tempted, not knowing beforehand (since the human-divine Jesus was not actively omniscient, so to speak, whilst on earth) that he would survive the temptations. As might expected, not all kenotic theories were equally successful, and many came to feel that the somewhat arbitrary stripping off of divine attributes threatened Christ's divinity, especially if it were also maintained that the divine self-consciousness and will were also surrendered. Hence the view that the attributes were voluntarily held in abeyance, or reduced to potentiality, by the Son, who remained divine whilst living under the conditions and constraints of temporality.

Of our ten hinterland divines, it was the most recent, Charles Duthie, who was the beneficiary of a long line of kenotic exposition. He reflected interestingly but, in not stating the positions of some of those he was discussing, tantalizingly, upon it.[140] I shall therefore fill out the argument, beginning with H. R. Mackintosh, Duthie's teacher, whom he does not mention in this context. Mackintosh clearly specified the alternatives thus:

> [O]nce it has been made clear that Christ is God—since redemption is as typically a Divine work as creation—the possible alternatives are few. It may be said that [Jesus Christ] acquired Godhead, which is pagan. Or that He carried eternal deity unmodified into the sphere of time—which it unhistoric. Exclude these options, andit only remains to say that in Christ we are face to face with God, who in one of the distinguishable constituents of His being came amongst us by a great act of self-abnegation. But there is no possibility of forming a precise scientific conception of what took place ...[141]

The moderate kenoticism of Mackintosh was criticised by William Temple (whom Duthie does refer to), who found 'intolerable difficulties' with it, among them, 'What was happening to the rest of the universe during the period of our Lord's earthly life?'[142] Donald Baillie borrowed Temple's words in his own critique of kenoticism,[143] and Duthie quite rightly rebukes him for not having considered O. C. Quick's reply to Temple (which Duthie does not reproduce), namely, all that the kenotic theory demands is 'a limitation of consciousness rather than of actual being.'[144] When Baillie further charges that the kenoticists teach that 'He who formally was God changed himself temporarily into a man, of exchanged His divinity for humanity,'[145] Duthie retorts, accurately enough, 'It is striking ... that he does not quote any responsible [or, indeed any irresponsible] Kenoticist as having

---

[140] See C. S. Duthie, *God in His World*, 29-33.

[141] H. R. Mackintosh, *The Doctrine of the Person of Jesus Christ*, 470-471.

[142] W. Temple, *Christus Veritas*, 142.

[143] D. M. Baillie, *God was in Christ*, 96.

[144] O. C. Quick, *The Doctrines of the Creed*, 145.

[145] D. M. Baillie, op.cit., 96.

made a statement to this effect.'[146] Again, Baillie represents kenoticism as asserting that Christ was successively God, then man, then God again, and that this vitiates the classical doctrine of the permanent manhood of Christ. Duthie replies that kenotic theologians are very much concerned (as I have already indicated) to defend the full manhood of Jesus, and that they would say that 'the only satisfactory way of doing this is to show first that He really was a man while on earth.'[147] Finally, Baillie develops

> a more general notion of Kenosis in which God limits Himself in creation and shares our suffering in redemption. But from what source can we derive such a general notion save that of the Incarnate Life? Is Dr. Baillie not in danger of by-passing Jesus Christ? If there is anything like a self-emptying or self-limitation on the part of God we can only discover it or deduce it from a scrutiny of His self-disclosure in His Son.[148]

It remains only to note that Duthie regrets that Baillie did not refer to P. T. Forsyth's *The Person and Place of Jesus Christ*, in which the idea of kenosis is balanced 'with the equally Scriptural idea of a Plerosis, that is, of a gradual fulfilment progressively realized through the very process of self-humbling.'[149]

To come full circle, and to add a point of some importance, Temple expresses his own view in these terms:

> If God the Son lived the Life recorded in the Gospels, then in that Life we see, set forth in terms of human experience, the very reality of God the Son. The limitations of knowledge and power are conditions of the revelation, without which there would be no revelation *to us* at all; but the Person who lives under these limitations is the Eternal Son in whom the life of the Eternal Father goes forth in creative activity and returns in filial love.[150]

I cannot see that there is an hairsbreadth of difference of principle between this statement and that of H. R. Mackintosh from which I set out.

VII

Turning now to the work of Christ I shall first briefly indicate some themes of importance which arise from the hinterland writings, and then discuss in somewhat more detail the doctrines of imputation and divine impassibility/passibility. First, I do not think that any of the ten hinterland divines would have dissented from Calvin's view that the work of Christ concerns 'the whole course of his

---

[146] C. S. Duthie, *God in His World*, 30.
[147] Ibid., 31.
[148] Ibid.
[149] Ibid., 30.
[150] W. Temple, *Christus Veritas*, 132.

obedience',[151] and not only his death upon the Cross. Although George Payne testified that 'The obedience of Christ, and the sufferings of his life ... enter ... into the very essence of the atonement,'[152] I detect a stronger insistence upon this point in the later, rather than the earlier theologians. I attribute this to the increasing interest in the historical Jesus from about 1860 onwards, and also, perhaps, to disenchantment with more grotesque, 'divine orientated', homiletic or published expositions of the atonement.[153] Be that as it may, Tymms spoke for his liberal evangelical contemporaries when he wrote that 'The death of Christ is inexplicable apart from the life which preceded and followed it.'[154] Adeney concurred. Jesus, he wrote,

> did not only reveal His nature and character by His utterances; He made them more evident by His life and deeds. Therefore if we are to see God in Christ, this will be by contemplating His whole life-course. But that life-course was crowned and consummated by His death and resurrection.[155]

In agreement with this, Franks referred to his Congregational colleague, P. T. Forsyth: 'Dr. Forsyth's emphasis on the "Cruciality of the Cross" is right; yet it is not to be understood in the sense that the Cross can be separated from its whole context in the total sacrifice of Christ, which includes His Incarnation, His Passion, His Resurrection, and His heavenly Intercession all in one.'[156] In similar vein Duthie urged that 'We must give [Christ's] death the significance which the New Testament writers assign to it and we must never isolate it from the life which leads to it nor from the continuing life which supervened upon it through the resurrection.'[157] Adeney also stated the obvious in answer to those who were presenting Jesus as the supremely good teacher, implying and sometimes declaring that Paul and others subsequently muddied the waters with their emphasis upon the Cross:

> It is apparent to every reader of the New Testament that the purpose of the death of Christ does not take the pre-eminence in His own teaching which it assumed in that of St. Paul. ... [I]t is obvious that subsequent reflections on the cross in the clear

---

[151] J. Calvin, *Institutes*, II.xvi.5.

[152] G. Payne, *Lectures on Divine Sovereignty*, 174; cf. ibid., 178.

[153] It is even conceivable that some—possibly Tymms more than the others—would have queried Roman Catholic devotions centring in the wounds of Christ.

[154] T. V. Tymms, *The Christian Idea of Atonement*, 277.

[155] W. F. Adeney, *The Christian Conception of God*, 253.

[156] R. S. Franks, CQ, VIII, 1930, 506. Forsyth concurred: 'To preach only the atonement, the death apart from the life, or only the person of Christ, His words apart from His life, may all be equally one-sided, and extreme to falsity.' Again, 'You cannot sever the death of Christ from the life of Christ.' See, respectively, *The Cruciality of the* Cross, 42; *The Work of* Christ, 153. I have myself concluded that in Forsyth's writings the term 'Cross' is frequently used as an umbrella term embracing a cluster of convictions. See *Testimony and Tradition*, 161, 181.

[157] C. S. Duthie, 'The meaning of the Cross,' 9.

> light of all its tragic circumstances are likely to be richer than anticipatory references to it in those early days when it only loomed on the horizon as a gradually emerging destiny of the future.[158]

To Franks, 'The fundamental question in Christian theology is whether Jesus is to be interpreted through Paul and the Apostles, or whether Paul and the Apostles are to be interpreted through Jesus, as we know Him mind in the Synoptic Gospels.'[159] My own view is that while we do not have the Gospel in its fullness until after the resurrection, any more than we have the *Lord's* Supper before it; and while it was the genius of Paul and others to see the point of the life, death and resurrection of Jesus in a way that would have been impossible prior to the resurrection, all subsequent interpretations must be read and, if need be, corrected in the light of Jesus's words and deeds—and supremely the deed at the Cross.

Secondly, the ten divines could not bypass the question, In what sense is Christ our substitute? Ridgley and Taylor would have agreed that when we say that Christ died for us we mean 'that he died in our room and stead, or that he bore that for us which the justice of God demanded, as a debt primarily due from us, and that he did so as an expedient for taking away the guilt of sin, and delivering us from his wrath to which we were liable.'[160] Richard Alliott explained that God provided his Son as a substitute for sinners who could not otherwise, consistently with divine justice, receive God's blessing; Christ bore 'the penal consequences of their guilt.'[161] To Simon, Jesus was the sinless substitute who, because suffered as an act of filial obedience, not as a recipient of punishment, made 'satisfaction or amends for the dishonour done to the name of God.'[162] None was more eager than Adeney to resist the corollary attached to Christ's substitutionary work by the 'crabbed theology which once passed for evangelicalism', namely, that a death was required to assuage God's wrath and persuade him to show kindness to sinners. On the contrary, 'The only harmonious view is that which sees Christ's lovingkindness as springing from the lovingkindness of God, since Christ's first being springs from the being of God.'[163]

Thirdly, to differing degrees the ten theologians saw the importance of upholding both the subjective and the objective aspects of the atonement. George Payne, for example, thought that Thomas Erskine of Linlathen had veered too much in the subjective direction. Payne denied that Christ's death was necessary 'not so much to render the exercise of forgiveness consistent with the claims of truth, justice, and holiness, but to afford a display of love so overpowering as to win back the alienated hearts of sinners to God, that is, to cure their moral disease.'[164] Few were as careful

---

[158] W. F. Adeney, *The Theology of the New Testament*, 64.
[159] R. S. Franks, CQ, XVI no. 3, July 1939, 376.
[160] T. Ridgley, *A Body of Divinity*, I, 513.
[161] R. Alliott, 'Address' on the old and the new theology', 15.
[162] D. W. Simon, *Reconciliation by Incarnation*, 367.
[163] W. F. Adeney, *Faith To-day*, 69.
[164] G. Payne, *Lectures on Divine Sovereignty*, 325.

to hold the balance in this matter as Alliott. He summarized the position held by Ridgley as quoted in the preceding paragraph, namely that the purpose of Christ's death was to enable God to pardon sinners consistently with his law and moral government, and faulted it because no reference was made to the effects of the transaction on sinners' hearts: 'This ultimate subjective end of the atonement has been by some too lightly regarded', he said.[165] On the other hand, he continued, some have bypassed the objective end and have supposed that 'the first and only direct object of the atonement of Christ was to manifest Divine love, and thus draw the sinner back to God.'[166] While essential to atonement theory, this theme was insufficient by itself because it was the objective end which produced the subjective effect, and the ultimate effect of the atonement was not simply upon sinners, but upon 'the universe of intelligent creation—an effect which could not be produced except by means of the objective end.'[167] Adeney expressed the matter as concisely as any: 'the subjective effect of the Atonement is found to be most pronounced just in proportion as there is faith in its previous objective efficacy.'[168] But it was Franks who set the discussion firmly in the context of the history of doctrine, especially with his welcoming of Abelard's insight and his concessions to Anselm. He was thus able to conclude that

> Christ reconciles men to God by revealing the love of God in His life and still more in His death, so bringing them to trust and love Him in return. ... [This doctrine has been] very unfairly labelled subjective, because it involves the subjectivity of the human response to the Divine love: it is in truth fundamentally objective, inasmuch as God, Christ, His Cross, and the Divine love are all the objects of human trust and responsive love. It would be more correct to speak of the *experiential* theory; since the term experience implies both object and subject and the relation between them.[169]

Fourthly, of the modern theologians we have introduced, it was D. W. Simon who emphasised most strongly the fact that Christ's atoning work does something for God and not just for sinners. Thomas Ridgley had made the point much earlier. It accords with God's nature as righteous and holy, and not simply with his will, 'that he is obliged to punish all sin, even that which he designs to pardon. But this could not have been done without a demand of satisfaction to be given, by a surety, in the sinner's behalf; which plainly evinces the necessity of satisfaction.'[170] As he surveyed the theological scene towards the end of the nineteenth century, Simon regretted that this emphasis had been lost, and that 'The relation of the atonement to God is [now] chiefly one of revelation: Christ propitiates man, not God.'[171] He

[165] R. Alliott, 'Address' on the old and the new theology, 12.

[166] Ibid.

[167] Ibid., 13.

[168] W. F. Adeney, *The Atonement in Modern Religious Thought*, 150.

[169] R. S. Franks, *The Atonement*, 4.

[170] T. Ridgley, *A Body of Divinity*, I, 509.

[171] D. W. Simon, 'The present direction of theological thought,' 79.

would therefore have found Franks's summary statement onesided and insufficient: 'Christ reconciles men to God by revealing the love of god in His life, and still more in His death, so bringing them to trust and love Him in return.'[172] By contrast, Simon insisted that God needed to be propitiated, for 'Sin has introduced ... disorder into the very life of God Himself.'[173] At the Cross God's holy love is vindicated, and sin and death are vanquished. If we proclaim only the latter half this sentence, I believe that we have no more than half a doctrine of atonement.

Fifthly, the ten divines had to come to terms with the concept of punishment as it relates to Christ's atoning work, and especially as it bears upon the question of substitution. Thomas Ridgley wrote that Jesus Christ bears 'those griefs, sorrows, or punishments which were due to us for sin,'[174] but he does not say that the sinless Christ was himself punished by God, though in some writings and sermons that impression was given is not always explicitly stated. As we might expect, Samuel Chandler was zealous to guard against any such doctrine: Christ, he said was not punished by God, but bore the punishment due to us on account of our sins.[175] George Payne was equally concerned to make the same point:

> Punishment is, properly speaking, the infliction upon an individual of evil, *i.e.* pain, or suffering, in consequence of a moral offence, and an offence committed by himself. ... Our blessed Lord endured the death of the cross in consequence of the sin of man; but that which would have been punishment to us was, in correct thought, mere suffering to him.[176]

Payne also repudiated any notion that Christ endured 'the precise amount of punishment, which must otherwise have fallen upon the elect,'[177] for this language of pecuniary debt was incompatible with that of pardoning grace, and it also limited 'the sufficiency of the atonement to the elect.'[178]

Against any theories which supposed that a wrathful God had to be bought off by a death, or punish the innocent, before he could be merciful—caricatures of the truth which are to this day represented by some as standard Christian teaching so that they can rebut them[179]—Richard Alliott finely said,

> It is not ... taught by the doctrine of the atonement that God needed to be stirred up by his Son to exercise a mercy to which he was indisposed, much less to be bought

---

[172] R. S. Franks, *The Atonement*, 2.
[173] D. W. Simon, *Reconciliation by Incarnation*, 303.
[174] T. Ridgley, *A Body of Divinity*, I, 516.
[175] S. Chandler, *Sermons*, IV, 390-391.
[176] G. Payne, *The Doctrine of Original Sin*, 32.
[177] Idem, *Lectures on Christian Theology*, II, 143.
[178] Ibid., 144.
[179] For some examples (among them the idea that God is a child-batterer) see Alan P. F. Sell, *Enlightenment, Ecumenism, Evangel*, 288-9; 381-2. They all drive a wedge between the Father and the Son, and overlook Paul's declaration that '*God* was *in Christ* reconciling the world to himself' (II Corinthians 5: 19).

> over to exercise it. He himself was predisposed to its exercise, and, hence, of his own love provided the sacrifice whereby he could exercise it without inflicting a moral injury on the rest of his intelligent creatures. Christianity, I conceive, teaches no other doctrine in reference to the atonement than this; and it cannot be fairly represented as implying that he is cruel, vindictive, and delighting in suffering and blood.[180]

A generation later P. T. Forsyth said that 'The atonement did not procure grace, it flowed from grace. ... We must renounce the idea that [Christ] was punished by the God who was ever well pleased with His beloved Son.'[181] Tymms concurred in no uncertain terms. As he left his London pastorate he told the congregation that

> I have desired to burn away from every heart that obscuring veil of pagan thought which first divides a wrathful justice to the Father and a tender mercy to Christ, and then represents the Son as dying to soothe the anger and satisfy the relentless demands of the Father. Such unholy and revolting ideas are the leaven of heathenism, not the unleavened bread of Christian truth.[182]

Tymms strongly denied that the New Testament contained any propositions which could be 'tortured into a suggestion that Christ did or suffered anything whereby He made it righteous for God to remit sin.'[183]

The following words of Robert Mackintosh are pertinent at this point:

> [W]e must apprehend the moral necessity of our Lord's death before it can produce its moral influence in our hearts. ... but we are not bound to explain moral necessity as arising out of penal law. On the contrary; if we do so, we can never legitimately advance to the moral influences of Christ upon ourselves. The doctrine of substitution is intent upon a quantum of suffering, or a quantum of merit; Christ's moral influence is personal. Having begun with the law, we cannot end in the Spirit. If we start with a mechanical conception of the procuring of grace, we must end with a mechanical conception of the application of grace.[184]

On the specific issue of punishment, Tymms elsewhere asserted that 'It was emphatically our sin, not our punishment, which bowed [Christ's] soul in Gethsemene, and ruptured His surcharged heart at Calvary.'[185] As Charles Duthie later put it, 'there is an unmistakable sense that while [the Son] was not punished by the Father for our sins, He so entered into the alienation and darkness which sin brings with it that He can be described as the sin-bearer. God has made Him, who knew no sin, to be sin for us (2 Cor., 3, 21).'[186]

---

[180] R. Alliott, *Psychology and Theology*, 246-7.

[181] P. T. Forsyth, *The Cruciality of the Cross*, 41.

[182] T. V. Tymms, *The Beauty of God*, 12.

[183] Idem, *The Christian Idea of Atonement*, 228.

[184] R. Mackintosh, *Essays Towards a New Theology*, 428.

[185] Idem, *The Christian Idea of Atonement*, 53.

[186] C. S. Duthie, *God in His World*, 33.

VIII

This quotation leads us directly to the doctrine of imputation. A review of what the ten hinterland theologians thought about this will reveal considerable change over the centuries. Lying behind the relevant clauses of the *Westminster Larger Catechism* are Calvin's interpretations of biblical teaching. At once we see that we are concerned both with the imputation of Adam's sin to the human race, and the imputation of Christ's righteousness to sinners. As to the former, Calvin writes, 'Adam, by sinning, not only took upon himself misfortune and ruin but also plunged our nature into like destruction. This was not due to the guilt of himself alone, which would not pertain to us at all, but was because he infected all his posterity with that corruption into which he had fallen.'[187] As to the latter, in one of his more succinct statements Calvin says that 'we explain justification simply as the acceptance with which God receives us into his favor as righteous men. And we say that it consists in the remission of sins and the imputation of Christ's righteousness.'[188] In the *Westminster Larger Catechism* these ideas are transmitted through the lens of federal theology. Thus, 'The covenant being made with Adam, as a public person, not for himself only but for his posterity, all mankind descending from him by ordinary generation, sinned in him, and fell with him in that first transgression.'[189] Again, 'Justification is an act of God's free grace unto sinners, in which he pardoneth all their sins, accepteth and accounteth their persons righteous in his sight; not for any thing wrought in them, or done by them, but only for the perfect obedience and full satisfaction of Christ, by God imputed to them, and received by faith alone.'[190]

In exposition of Adam's status, Ridgley said that Adam was more than our common parent; he was 'constituted as the head of his posterity in a federal was, by an act of God's sovereign will; and so must be regarded as their representative, as well as their common parent.'[191] Ridgley was well aware that 'It is objected, that what is done by one man, cannot be imputed to another, as being contrary to the divine perfections, to the law of nature, and the express words of scripture.'[192] He replies:

> Now, when we speak of persons being punished for a crime committed by another as being imputed to them, we understand the word 'imputation' in a forensic sense; and we do not suppose that there is a wrong judgment passed on persons or things, as though the crime were reckoned to have been committed by them. Accordingly, we do not say, that we committed that sin which was more immediately committed by Adam. In him it was actual sin; it is ours as imputed to us, or as we are punished for it, according to the demerit of the offence, and the tenor of the covenant in which

---

[187] Ibid., II.i.6.

[188] J. Calvin, *Institutes*, III.xi.2; cf. III.xi.23, IV.xvii.2.

[189] Answer to Question XXII.

[190] Answer to Question LXX.

[191] T. Ridgley, *A Body of Divinity*, I, 400.

[192] Ibid., 403.

> we are included. Moreover, it is not contrary to the law of nature or nations, for the iniquity of some public persons to be punished in many others, so that whole cities and nations suffer on their account. As to scripture instances of this, we often read of whole families and nations suffering for the crimes of those who have been public persons, and exemplary in sinning.[193]

With none of this was Samuel Chandler satisfied. He denied that the guilt of Adam is imputed to their heirs and contended that what Adam and Eve did typifies what all human beings have actually done and do. This debate raged throughout the remainder of the eighteenth century, with John Gill *versus* John Taylor of Norwich, John Wesley and Jonathan Edwards *versus* John Taylor, and Joseph Priestley *versus* all Anselmic-*cum*-Calvinistic-comers,[194] and its flames flicker spasmodically to this day. The burden of the anti-Calvinist position was that the doctrine of imputed sin and guilt removed freedom and responsibility from human beings, and assaulted the principle that one individual may not be responsible for the actions of another, with the consequence that the divine equity and justice were called into question.

On imputed righteousness Ridgley had this to say:

> our Lord Jesus Christ has wrought out this righteousness for us, as our surety, by performing active and passive obedience; which is imputed to us for our justification. ... [W]hat Christ did and suffered in our room and stead, is as much placed to our account as if we had done and suffered it ourselves; so that we are, in consequence, discharged from condemnation. ... It was a very great display of grace in our Saviour that he was pleased to consent to perform this work for us.[195]

Abraham Taylor was convinced that at the root of all spiritual declensions through history and in his own time was the 'attempt to obscure the great and glorious doctrine of justification by Christ's imputed righteousness.'[196]

George Payne affirmed the doctrine of Christ's imputed righteousness in his letter of application to the Dissenting academy at Hoxton,[197] and later found himself attempting to chart a course between the Scylla of Socinianism (Adam was the father of the human race, but his descendants were not adversely affected by his actions) and the Charybdis of high Calvinism (Adam's guilt was imputed to his heirs). He argued that while Adam's sin was imputed to his heirs, his guilt was not. Accordingly, we are not punished for Adam's sin, but only for our own.[198] As for Christ's righteousness, this is imputed to believers, but his sufferings upon the Cross were not a punishment, for he had committed no offence. Payne was opposed to the high Calvinist way, exemplified by Tobias Crisp, of a literal (*quasi*-mechanical) transfer

---

[193] Ibid.

[194] See Alan P. F. Sell, *Dissenting Thought and the Life of the* Churches, 245-9; idem, *Enlightenment, Ecumenism, Evangel*, 98-101.

[195] T. Ridgley, *A Body of Divinity*, II, 88, 92, 94-5.

[196] A. Taylor, *Of Spiritual Declensions*, 24.

[197] See J. Pyer, 'Memoir,' xxv.

[198] See G. Payne, *The Doctrine of Original Sin*, 90-91.

of Christ's righteousness, preferring to think that Christ's righteousness is regarded as if it were the sinner's own;[199] but he also took Andrew Fuller to task for thinking of the accounting sinner's righteous and treating them as such as two distinct operations rather than as aspects of one act.[200] In other words, he denied that Christ's righteousness 'actually passes over to the believer, or literally becomes him; or, that it is legally counted to the believer, that is, if by that phraseology be meant anything distinct from, and previous to, his being treated as a just man, for the sake or in reward of the righteousness of Immanuel.'[201] Richard Alliott felt called upon to rebut a different anti-imputation argument, namely, that if Christ's righteousness were imputed to sinners they would have received an unearned reward, and the ethical motive supplied by reward and punishment would be annulled. On the contrary, Alliott replied, the doctrine 'is ... calculated to excite love in the case of sinful beings previously destitute of the principle, by showing a provision made for them, at a vast expense, of blessings wholly undeserved; thus inducing in them a desire to please God, not indeed with the view of purchasing his favour, but yet because the love stirred up within them moves them to regard pleasing him as pleasurable, and grieving him as painful, to themselves.'[202]

Thirty-five years on, D. W. Simon was anxious to draw attention to the practical implications of the doctrine of imputation:

> [W]hat Christ accomplished on men's behalf ... cannot avail them unless it carry them with it. He cannot be our substitute in such a manner that He is righteous and so forth for us, whilst we can remain unrighteous and yet be freed from penalty and inherit heaven. He came to save us, to redeem us unto Himself a [peculiar people, zealous of good works, not merely to set aside the penalties of sin; He came to reconcile us to God, not merely to save us from torment. Whatever He has accomplished is supposed to be ours, though it is His work. This true principle lies at the back of the doctrine of imputed righteousness, though as ordinarily presented that doctrine takes into consideration solely the active righteousness of Christ or His obedience, and not His passive righteousness, or suffering.[203]

Vincent Tymms was more concerned to clear Paul of responsibility for some of the misconceptions that had become attached to his teaching over the centuries. Thus, for example, in II Corinthians 5: 11 to 6: 2, we have

> a sustained effort to bring the love of God in Christ to bear upon the hearts and lives of the Corinthians. Paul traces all that Christ did and suffered to the grace of God, who 'was in Christ reconciling the world unto Himself; not imputing unto them their trespasses'; but he does not say 'imputing their trespasses to Christ', nor

199 See idem, *Lectures on Divine Sovereignty*, 251-4.
200 See idem, *The Doctrine of Original Sin*, 99 n.
201 Idem, *Lectures on Divine Sovereignty*, 257; cf. 314-315.
202 R. Alliott, *Psychology and Theology*, 250.
203 D. W. Simon, *The Redemption of Man*, 340-341.

> could he have said this without teaching the absurd contradiction that God imputed these trespasses to Himself, because He was actually 'in Christ.'[204]

Tymms further objected to the Reformers' 'correction' of Paul's affirmation that God reckons faith for righteousness: 'They were afraid that, by adhering to the unadulterated language of Scripture, they would be raising faith to the level of a "good work", and to avoid this Pauline heresy they manufactured a doctrine of imputed righteousness which is utterly foreign to Paul's thought and fatal to the ethical purity and spiritual simplicity of the gospel.'[205] We are here at a considerable remove from Ridgley and Taylor, and even from Payne and Alliott, not to mention the *Westminster Confession* chapter 11. Tymms reiterated Paul's assertion that the believer's faith is 'reckoned to him for righteousness', and continues:

> in the face of this statement the *Westminster Confession* ... ventures to categorically deny that God justifies men 'by imputing faith itself, the act of believing, or any other evangelical obedience to them as their righteousness'. Having thus denied the apostle's doctrine it goes on to substitute another, viz., that God justifies 'by imputing the obedience and satisfaction of Christ unto them.'[206]

Properly understood, Tymms adds, there is nothing artificial in Paul's doctrine of the imputed righteousness of Christ. He admits that 'justify' is a forensic term, and that the accounting of faith for righteousness is to that extent a judicial act insofar as it releases from condemnation, 'but it is something infinitely deeper than forensic analogies can express, because the Judge is our Father pronouncing His satisfaction in the faith His own goodness has begotten. ... [M]an is granted an exit from the state of condemnation ... [and] welcomed into a state of grace in which the terms of law have no place.'[207] At one particular point Tymms presses his argument too far:

> In the more modern form of the dogma that Christ's righteousness is imputed to the believer, it is confessed that God cannot really think that we are other than we are; but, it is held, that without thinking erroneously, He treats us as if we were, or as if He thought we were, as righteous as Christ. This modified Calvinism avoids an imputation of false judgment to God, but ascribes to Him what is even worse—viz., a determination to divorce action from judgment, and to maintain a permanent discord between deeds and thoughts.[208]

I do not think that Tymms fairly represents the moderate Calvinists, none of whom, as far as I know, held that believers were 'as righteous as Christ.' In my view, in its most wholesome interpretation, the doctrine of Christ's imputed righteousness means that by grace believers are accounted righteous on the ground of the Son's

---

[204] T. V. Tymms, *The Christian Idea of Atonement*, 55.
[205] Ibid., 362.
[206] Ibid., 362.
[207] Ibid., 395.
[208] Ibid., 465.

saving work. There is thus no 'permanent discord between [the Father's] deeds and thoughts', but rather the fulfilment of his redemptive intention.

In a more general sense Tymms is open to criticism. When he agrees with Paul that the believer's faith is 'reckoned to him for righteousness', he brackets the fact that this faith, though the believer's own, is also, in a logically prior way, a gift of God, so that none may conceive of faith as a 'work' to be rewarded, or boast as if it were a personal achievement (Ephesians 2:9). With this gift comes the accounting righteous of the believer for the Saviour's sake; the believer is 'in Christ', united with Christ, and the 'benefits' of Christ, his righteousness among them, are his or hers. I find support for my case in other assertions of Paul, notably Philippians 3: 9, '[I find] myself in union with [Christ], with no righteousness of my own based on the law, nothing but the righteousness which comes from faith in Christ, given by God in response to faith.' Tymms traces the use of the verb *logizomai*, to reckon or impute, and finds that it 'never represents a merely formal or nominal, much less a fictitious attribution to things or persons, of some quality which is not actually recognised as theirs. In particular, it is never used in any sentence which suggests the ascription to one person of any merit or demerit which actually belongs to someone else.'[209] Taking this at face value, it is nevertheless pedantic, for what Paul says in Philippians 3: 9 seems compatible with a doctrine of imputation which recognizes that the heart of the Gospel is the amazing fact that God judges, accounts, *sinners* righteous now that by grace through faith they are in Christ, and this in contrast to righteousness earned under the law. Again, at Romans 5: 17 Paul contrasts the old life in Adam with the new life in Christ: If, by the wrongdoing of one man, death established its reign through that one man, much more shall those who in far greater measure receive grace and the gift of righteousness live and reign through the one man, Jesus Christ.' On this verse Tymms's contemporaries, Sanday and Headlam comment:

> Every term here points to that gift of righteousness here described as something objective and external to the man himself, not wrought within him but coming to him, imputed not infused. It has its source in the overflow of God's free favour; it is a gift which man *receives*.[210]

It seems clear that the reason for Tymms's attenuation here was his desire to discount any mechanical-transactional understanding of imputation—a motive with which I am in entire sympathy; but a broader reading of Paul's thought on this issue would surely have modified his charge that the Reformers 'manufactured' the doctrine of the imputation of Christ's righteousness, albeit their formulations of the doctrine, and those of some of their successors, tempted some into unfortunate, *quasi*-commercial, understandings of it. Such a broader reading may even justify Joseph Hart's high Calvinist elision of Ephesians 6: 11-13 on the whole (that is, the

---

[209] Ibid., 363.

[210] W. Sanday and A. C. Headlam, *A Critical and Exegetical Comentary on the Epistle to the Romans*, 141.

complete) armour of God with the expression of a doctrinal technicality beloved of high Calvinists:

> Righteousness within thee rooted
> May appear to take thy part;
> But let righteousness imputed
> Be the breastplate of thy heart.[211]

Adeney, as we might expect, was critical of the terms in which the doctrine of imputation had been couched in the past. It was, he thought 'suggestive of scheming ingenuity. It lacks moral breadth and a sense of reality, not to say veracity.'[212] Although he introduced many historical expressions of the doctrine, Franks did not himself treat it constructively on his own account. In his biblical theology, however, he did, for example, remark that the narrative of the Fall 'exercised no influence on the Old Testament in general. It is only after the completion of the Old Testament that the narrative begins to exercise the very potent influence, which it has ever since maintained, over the doctrine of sin;'[213] and he found two theories of the origin of sin in Paul's writings: 'the historical theory which derives it from the fall of Adam, and the philosophical, or perhaps we may now call it the experimental theory, which derives it from the inherent sinfulness of the flesh.'[214] Whereas in ecclesiastical doctrine the latter is deemed the consequence of the former, Paul himself makes no such claim. He does however construe reconciliation in terms of the non-imputation of sins: 'The Pauline conception of reconciliation, while negatively equivalent to the forgiveness of sins, or the laying aside of God's wrath against the sinner, is also positively the bringing of the sinner into communion with God by removal of the sinner's enmity towards Him.'[215]

From this survey of the fortunes of the doctrine of imputation as understood by the ten hinterland divines, it would seem that from the first the doctrine met with objections, as is clear from Thomas Ridgley's attempts to clear it of them; Samuel

---

[211] From the hymn, 'Gird thy loins up, Christian soldier,' in J. Hart, *Hymns Composed on Various Subjects*, pp. 175-6. For Hart (1712-1768) see DEB; ODNB; WW, III, 343-7; J. Julian, *Dictionary of Hymnology*; T. Wright, *The Life of Joseph Hart*; J. A. Jones, *Bunhill* Memorials, 80-81; A. W. Light, *Bunhill Fields*, I, 203-9. Hart was Congregational minister at Jewin Street, London from 1760 until his death. Walter Wilson wrote that his hymns, 'though entirely destitute of poetical merit, have been much esteemed on account of the store of Christian experience which they contain.' Op.cit., 347. This notwithstanding, Hart's 'Come, Holy Spirit, come', 'Come, ye sinners, poor and wretched', and 'This God is the God we adore', are to be found in mainline hymnals to this day.

[212] W. F. Adeney, *A Century's Progress in Religious Life and Thought*, 147.

[213] R. S. Franks, *The New Testament Doctrine of Man, Sin and Salvation*, 24-5.

[214] Ibid., 104.

[215] For an attempt to treat imputation and related terms in a devotional context see Alan P. F. Sell, *The Spirit Our Life*, ch. 3.

Chandler adopted an attenuated version of it; in the wake of the eighteenth-century moral challenges to Calvinistic doctrine George Payne denied that Adam's guilt was imputed to his heirs; and the post 1850 theologians dwelt more upon the imputation of Christ's righteousness than upon Adam's sin, and for the most part repudiated any *quasi*-commercial expression of the former. Unlike their earlier co-religionists they did not assume the historicity of Adam. Tymms was most strongly opposed to any transactional view of the imputation of Christ's righteousness, and in this cause he offered an attenuated version of the doctrine. As applies throughout this study, the ten divines may be take as representative of significant strands of Dissenting thought; which is not to say that one cannot to this day find some writers who rest content with seventeenth-century statements of the doctrine of imputation.

IX

Not far beneath the surface of many discussions of the work of Christ there lies the question whether or not God can suffer. This question may be regarded as having reference to the broader issue of the divine immutability. By the latter term is meant that God cannot change; he is ever what he is. The terms stands for his reliability, his trustworthiness, his truthfulness to his own character as a moral God of holy love.[216] The idea is found in Malachi 3: 6, 'I, the Lord, do not change', and in James 1: 17, 'With [God] there is no variation.' By contrast with the Greek notion that 'Being as perfect as he can be, every god, it seems, remains simply and for ever in his own form',[217] the Hebrew of the text, 'I am who I am' (Exodus 3: 14) suggests the divine activity, as does, 'I am the living God' (Jeremiah 10: 10). In his exposition of the *Westminster Larger Catechism*, Thomas Ridgley declares that God is immutable in his being, knowledge and will, and that it is well for us that this is so:

> Any changeableness in the will of God, would render the condition of the best men, in some respects, very uncomfortable. They might be one day the object of his love, and the next of his hatred; and those blessings which accompany salvation might be bestowed at one time, and taken away at another. ... [T]here is ... nothing in him that, in the least degree, can lead him to change his will, or determination, with respect to events.[218]

With this George Payne was in agreement. God's immutability was to him a great source of comfort, for it 'forbids the fear that our imperfections and sins, distressing as they are to us, will cause him to withdraw his love from us.'[219]

---

[216] T. V. Tymms wrote, 'It is easier to think of a change in the law of gravitation than of any variation in the moral government of God.' See *The Christian Idea of Atonement*, 443 n. 11.

[217] Plato, *The Republic*, 70-71.

[218] T. Ridgley, *A Body of Divinity*, 90.

[219] G. Payne, *Lectures on Christian Theology*, I, 43-4.

As an implication of the doctrine of God's immutability, some divines have held that God cannot suffer, for to suffer is to change; while others have held that God's moral and affective constancy entails change, for he must be able to be angry at sin and lovingly merciful when sinners repent. Matters come to a head when we ask whether the Father suffered in the Son at the crucifixion. George Payne bluntly declared that 'it was only [the Son's] human nature that could suffer'[220]—a venerable line of thought, indeed, but one which surely tends in a docetic direction. He further argued that since grief was incompatible with God's blessedness and repentance with his infallible foreknowledge, God was 'said to do both in accommodation to the weakness of our capacities.'[221] It is not easy to regard this as anything other than a theological subterfuge. To D. W. Simon, 'The divine nature as such is clearly exalted above the possibility of injury; but the divine life—especially the affectional life of God, the heart of God, and the cosmos which has issued forth from his hand—may be prejudicially affected by man.'[222] One wonders just how 'clearly' the divine nature is exalted above the possibility of injury, and how it may be disentangled from the life. Simon seems to drive a wedge between God as he has made himself known—with all changes of feeling and attitude consistent with his character as holy love, and an 'God' of speculation and inference (of whom we know nothing) who exists somewhere beyond the God of revelation. Again, Simon wrote, 'The very being, the very nature, the very substance or essence of God cannot, of course, be prejudicially affected by human sin.'[223] This is a very confident 'of course'; but, again, how does he know this? Is he not postulating a possible uncomfortable dichotomy between God as he had made himself known, and God as he is in himself (of whom we know nothing). It would seem that if Payne veers towards docetism, Simon tends in the direction of gnosticism.

As if to qualify the views of Payne and Simon, Adeney argued that 'If you are to banish the idea of feeling from you conception of the Divine nature you must give up the thought of personality.' [224] Tymms was even more forceful:

> If we scruple to think of God [*sic*] being grieved we must go on to deny that He can be angry or pleased, that He can feel pity or solicitude or love. Indeed, as the logical issue of our fastidiousness we shall be committed to a denial of all relations, and then the only God left to us will be the infinite iceberg of metaphysics. ... The question is not, May we, like the ancient Patripassians, identify the Father and the Son? But does the Son truly represent the Father? If we are forbidden to find in Christ's sorrow a sacramental sign of something in God which is thus expressed to human minds, then we must discard the idea that Christ reveals the Love of God, or His Righteousness, His Holiness, His hatred of sin. Indeed, once started on this road of critical negation we must renounce the gospel; and denying the very

---

[220] Idem, *Lectures on Divine Sovereignty*, 174.

[221] Idem, *Lectures on Christian Theology*, I, 39.

[222] D. W. Simon, *The Redemption of Man*, 2nd edn, 271.

[223] Idem, *Reconciliation by Incarnation*, 147; cf. 190.

[224] W. F. Adeney, *The Christian Conception of God*, 93.

> possibility of divine self-revelation, we must retreat into Agnosticism, and live as best we can without God.[225]

Positively, Tymms held that 'He who spared not His own Son will spare no agony of blood which may be needful for the maintenance of His Law of Love among men. The cross is God's definition of Himself.'[226]

For all the attention he paid to the doctrine of the work of Christ in Scripture and in history, and to the doctrine of the Trinity, Robert Franks could not allow that God suffered:

> I do not say that the suffering of Christ is the suffering of God, any more than I say that God died: the suffering and death belong to the human revelation of the Divine Love, which Jesus came to make. But I do say that the same love, which in Jesus found expression in suffering and death, is the very love of the Father: it is the power of the Divine forgiveness, the grace that saves to the uttermost.[227]

As he elsewhere expressed the point more technically, the 'deep question' is

> whether the life of God is in time; or is, as the medieval theologians believed, a *totum simul*, a *punctum stans*, *i.e.*, is altogether beyond and above time as is eternal, as distinguished from everlasting. If this is the right conception of the Divine Life, then it is possible to admit that there are elements in it which would be elements of suffering, if that Life were lived in time. But as elements of the Eternal Life of God they are taken up into a larger whole, whose nature is joy and bliss. In the Eternal Life of God all that in itself would cause suffering is overcome and transmuted; so that it does not mar the perfect bliss of God.
>
> Suffering as such belongs to the time process; it was as man that Christ suffered, so revealing to us who live in time the Eternal Love of God. Suffering is not in itself good, nor is it Divine. But it is the form taken by the revelation of the Divine Love in a world of sin.[228]

On this matter T. Hywel Hughes weighed Franks and found him wanting. He found an inherent contradiction between two basic principles in Franks's writings: First that God cannot suffer; secondly, that love is the fundamental fact in the universe because God is love. Hughes continues, 'It is impossible to reconcile these two principles, for if God is love, it must be possible for him to suffer. Love carries with it the possibility of the most poignant suffering.'[229] This line of thought has

---

[225] T. V. Tymms, *The Christian Idea of Atonement*, 312, 313.

[226] Ibid., 100; cf. idem, 'Christian theism,' 56.

[227] R. S. Franks, *The Atonement*, 169.

[228] Idem, CQ, XVIII no. 1, January 1940, 95. Franks was pleased to find W. G. De Burgh in accord with him on this matter. See CQ, XVI no. 1, January 1938, 99. He also construed H. Wheeler Robinson as having 'combined Abelardianism with the doctrine of the Divine passibility.' See CQ, XX no. 3, July 1942, 266.

[229] T. H. Hughes, *The Atonement*, 223.

become increasingly prominent since Hughes wrote. Added impetus was given to it by such sayings of Dietrich Bonhoeffer as that 'The Bible ... directs [humanity] to the powerlessness and suffering of God; only a suffering God can help.'[230]

Charles Duthie who, we recall, had seen war service, was in this line:

> [W]hile the idea of the impassible God, which affected the thought of the creed-making period, bears a sort of negative testimony to the continuing and inviolable beatitude of God, it must be challenged and corrected by the picture Jesus gave us of a caring Father and by what Tillich calls God's participation through Christ in man's estrangement. Bonhoeffer's 'Only a suffering God can help' is a truth heavily underlined by the events of the twentieth century.[231]

Again, he wrote, 'the longer we look at Jesus and the more we trust the insight of Christian faith, the stronger becomes the urge to think of God as the Father who lays Himself alongside His children and enters sufferingly—yes, sufferingly, into their condition.'[232] On this basis Duthie took exception to von Hügel's advice that we should settle for God's sympathy and Christ's suffering:

> Observe the price von Hügel pays for denying the possibiity of suffering within the life of God. To say that Christ suffers as human and cannot suffer as divine is to split the personality of our Lord into two separate parts [as George Payne did earlier]. Von Hügel was prepared to go to this length because he was convinced that since suffering must always contain an element of evil it cannot be allowed an entrance within the infinite blessedness of the divine being.'[233]

Hence the view of some that Jesus is near, God is distant—which meant that 'Somehow God had become de-christianised.'[234]

Elsewhere Duthie spoke of 'what can only be called a demand for a God who suffers'; but he immediately added that we also 'cry for a God who suffers and triumphs through suffering. That is what we have in the Christian faith.'[235] Because of this latter fact, and because God knows all things from the beginning, I do not think we need to fear that God's passibility ultimately interferes with his eternal bliss; on the contrary, it is his chosen route towards the securing of his own and his people's ultimate happiness. *Pace* Franks, God lives in the incarnate Son under the conditions of time. To suppose that there is an impassible God-beyond-God is, it seems to me a revelation-side-stepping-claim that we are too ignorant to make, and one that is, in any case, countered by what God has been pleased to make known to us. It is one thing to claim that there are depths in the Godhead which we cannot fathom—and it is a true claim; it would be quite another to assert that the Godhead is

---

[230] D. Bonhoeffer, *Letters and Papers from Prison*, 122.

[231] C. S. Duthie, 'Affirmations of faith,' 3.

[232] Idem, 'God in his world,' 17; cf. idem, 'Continuing Cross?, 9.

[233] Ibid., 21-22.

[234] Ibid., 22.

[235] Idem, *Outline of Christian Belief*, 28-9.

utterly different from what has been made known to us. This would be tantamount to saying either that there had been no true revelation at all, or that while there had been a revelation, the Revealer were not a God of truth, but of deception. The upshot is that God the Son suffers: on this there is widespread agreement; but if the Father is not suffering alongside him, how can we any longer maintain that in a deep sense each person of the Trinity is involved in the acts of all? I find it odd that Franks, so reticent as to the inner workings of the Trinity, should be so decided (and, so moved by the kind of considerations that, for example, Augustine drew from Plotinus) on the matter of God's alleged impassibility, which is similarly non-demonstrable and has the character of an *a priori* assumption.[236]

Circa 1520 *The Trinity*, a large altarpiece, was commissioned by Jakub Debinski for the church of Debno, Poland. The largest figure is that of the Father. He is seated, front-facing, and looking out towards the viewers. The much smaller blood-stained figure of the Son is nailed to the Cross, his back to the Father. The Holy Spirit, represented by a dove, hovers above Christ's head. Christ's hands are nailed to an out-of-scale cross-beam suggestive of weight, and the Father's large, cupped, hands, are at either end of the heavy cross-beam from behind. The Father at once supports the weight, holds the Son close to his heart, and appears to offer him to the world. Angels are on either side of the picture, and at the foot of the Cross, conventionally enough, we see the Debinski males on one side the picture, the females on the other. It would be churlish to complain that the three individuals—a man-like God, Jesus and a dove—suggest tritheism. This striking picture says with extreme clarity that the Father is actively involved in the sacrifice of the Cross: he is not remote from it or untouched by it; no wedge is driven between the allegedly tyrannical Father and the allegedly docile Son; the Father is not punishing the Son, but on the contrary he takes the weight and offers Christ to the world, with the promised Comforter standing by. There is no unmoved, impassible, God anywhere else whose eternal bliss is untouched by the event.[237]

X

For my last example of a particular doctrine on which the ten hinterland divines may stimulate our thought I turn to the doctrine of the Church. Thomas Ridgley argued that the Church comprises those who were called; but he went on to explain that there was an external call whereby persons belong to the Church visible on profession of faith, and an internal call, heard by the elect alone who comprise the Church invisible. By contrast, embracing what high Calvinists would have regarded as a weaker position, Samuel Chandler, in protest against what he regarded as

[236] The helpfulness of J. K. Mozley's book of 1926, *The Impassibility of God*, remains undiminished, not least because of his concluding discussion of the motives on either side of the argument, and the 'six necessary questions' he poses to participants in the debate.

[237] For an excellent reproduction of *The Trinity*, photographed by Andrea Pistolesi, see Grzegorz Rudziński, *The Golden Book of Cracow*, 47.

Bellarmine's usurpation of the Church by the priesthood, declared that the marks of the Church are the adherence of the called members to Christ as Lord and Saviour, and their resultant holy lives; and he stoutly objected to the annexation of the Church by the Roman priesthood. To George Payne the Church comprised both the sanctified who would meet in heaven and the members of particular congregations 'meeting statedly for religious purposes on earth.'[238] From this view none of the ten hinterland theologians would have dissented, though they did not always make it clear that what one was called into was the Church catholic in one of its local expressions.

Given the socio-political context in which the Separatists and Dissenters hammered out their understanding of the Church, it is not surprising that a number of those we have studied paid attention to the church order that they found most consonant with Scripture. What I find surprising, given the prevalence of local church covenants until about 1830, is that Ridgley and his contemporaries did not make more explicit reference to the covenant idea in their accounts of Congregationalism. George Payne, anxious to counter latitudinarianism whilst avoiding bigotry, was convinced that the New Testament idea of the Church did not sanction 'a heterogeneous mixture of the pious and the profane',[239] but he does not have explicit recourse to the covenant idea either. He does, however, affirm that 'Real congregationalism is not democracy'; rather, pastors rule the church by executing Christ's laws 'with the concurrence of the church.'[240] Running throughout is the distinction that Richard Alliott assumed between the church and the congregation at large—an idea which Simon was later to expound in terms of the 'twice-born'—that is, that the Church comprises the regenerate. Drawing upon a theme which was not so greatly emphasised by his predecessors, Alliott extolled Congregationalism for its commitment of responsibility to every member, each of whom stands under the 'direct kingly authority of our Lord Jesus Christ.'[241] At the same time he cautioned against that spurious Independency which claimed freedom from both human and divine control. Vincent Tymms expressed to Pope Leo XIII the hope that all who are united to Christ by faith and therefore 'to each other as members of His *twice-born* family, may speedily be united in bonds of mutual love ...'[242] He, like Alliott before him, elevated the individual's personal responsibility 'to live each of us his own life of thought and action without any feudal superior between his soul and God.'[243]

As might be expected, Adeney, a Congregational biblical scholar, did discuss the covenant idea in the Bible, but he did not elaborate upon it in his advocacy of Congregationalism. Even more surprising are some remarks he made on Payne's *Lectures of Divine Sovereignty*:

---

[238] G. Payne, *The Church of Christ considered*, 2.
[239] Ibid., x.
[240] Ibid., 80.
[241] *Bi-Centenary of Castle Gate Meeting*, 30.
[242] BH, 1896, 98-9. My italics.
[243] BH, 1897, 67.

> Dr Payne, after beginning with the Divine sovereignty, proceeds to devote six lectures of his not very bulky volume [it comprises 454 pages] to the doctrine of election. Can we imagine any influential theological writer proceeding on these lines to-day? In point of fact, we have ceased to be interested in the doctrine of election at all. It is no longer within the region of living questions; the fierce fires of controversy that once raged about it are reduced to grey ashes.[244]

Admittedly, the much abused doctrine of predestination was in Adeney's sights, but it is nevertheless odd that a Congregational biblical scholar would write in such unqualified terms. Does the Church not comprise those who are, in Paul's words, 'saints by calling' (Romans 1:7)? Are they not the election of grace? Are they not, in Simon's words, the 'twice-born'? Is there not a distinction of eternal significance between those who are 'in Christ' and those who are not? The Congregational polity turns upon affirmative answers to these questions. It is the more puzzling because Adeney understood that the witness of the Separatists was not in the first place against the Church of England, but against 'the world'.

This separation did, however, imply separation from the Church of England, as Adeney rightly observes, 'because that Church included all the baptized who were not Roman Catholics or excommunicated persons, however irreligious they might be. It also involved the separation of Church and State.'[245] Here are themes which, again, run right through the history.[246] To Ridgley the Church of England was founded on the laws of men, not those of Christ.[247] Chandler was equally opposed to the establishment, though he was wooed by it. His particular objection concerned doctrinal subscription which, he was convinced, encroached upon 'that liberty wherewith Christ hath made [Englishmen] free.'[248] Here was territory from which the civil magistrate was properly excluded. For his part, Payne lamented that the Church of England was the spouse of the state, not solely of Christ, and he advocated the divorce of the Church from the state. The same position is implied in Alliott's definition of the Church: 'A Christian church is a society of professing Christians united, under the authority of Christ, for the observation of his ordinances, mutual edification, and the conversion of sinners. Of such a society Christ is the only head, and his word the only statute book.'[249] Adeney was more specific: 'We have come to see the utter unchristianity of the control of Church affairs by the arm of the State, to see that it is a usurpation of the rights of Christ and a dishonour to His body that not one line of the obligatory Book of Prayer can be altered without the consent of parliament, and that the chief places in the pastoral office should be filled at the dictation of the First Lord of the Treasury. ...[250]

---

[244] W. F. Adeney, *A Century's Progress in Religious Life and Thought*, 120.
[245] Idem, 'The Church in the prisons,' 11.
[246] For a survey of this history see Alan P. F. Sell, *Testimony and Tradition*, ch. 11.
[247] T. Ridgley, *A Body of Divinity*, II, 25.
[248] S. Chandler, *The Case of Subscription*, 39.
[249] R. Alliott, *The Union of the Convert with the Visible Church*, 83.
[250] W. F. Adeney, 'The more excellent way,' 45.

So much for the state control of church affairs. But what of discipline within the churches? Thomas Ridgley maintained that any who denied fundamental Christian doctrines were to be excluded from communion, though he made it clear that such exclusion was 'design'd to reclaim him who is thus dealt with, as well as to assert the honour of Christ.'[251] Moreover, disciplinary action should be characterized by love and meekness, not malice and revenge, and he made it clear that pastors and elders 'have no power to act without the consent of the church, in receiving members into or excluding them from its communion.'[252] It was George Payne's opinion that lack of attention to church discipline led to the disastrous consequences that the influence of the Holy Spirit was withdrawn from the lax church, and sinners would not be converted in it. D. W. Simon took a dim view of the 'advocacy of comprehension as regards membership, worship, and doctrine, which will scarcely leave anyone outside except the orthodox.'[253]

Turning now to the dominical sacraments, we recall Ridgley's view that God is the author of both baptism and the Lord's Supper; that both sacraments signify the benefits of Christ; that both are to be 'dispensed' only by ministers of the Gospel; and both are to continue until Christ comes again. The sacraments as such have no power to effect salvation or to confer grace, and their efficacy is 'not derived from the piety or intention of those by whom they are administered.'[254] The succeeding nine divines under review would have agreed with most of this though, from the middle of the nineteenth century onwards Congregational lay persons appointed by the Church Meeting were permitted on occasion to preside at the Lord's table—this on the ground of the priesthood of all believers (construed individualistically), and in reaction against the sacerdotalism of Anglican ritualists which they viewed with dismay if not abhorrence.[255]

Our ten hinterland divines did not write extensively on the Lord's Supper, though Ridgley and Taylor inveighed against the doctrine of transubstantiation; Chandler insisted that 'the Lord's Supper is only a memorial of Christ's death, and not a propitiatory sacrifice either for the living or the dead';[256] and Tymms was never slow to rebuke Rome on the subject. Ridgley argued that children, though members of the church in the sense that their parents have brought them within its orbit, are not qualified to receive communion until, in God's own time and way, they are able to make their profession of faith. Their eternal salvation is not adversely affected by their absence from the Lord's table. As to the meaning of the Supper, Ridgley argued that while it was instituted in commemoration of Christ's death, we should have in mind not only the crucifixion but the whole course of Christ's obedience. The words

---

[251] T. Ridgley, *An Essay concerning Truth and Charity*, 30-31.

[252] Idem, *A Body of Divinity*, II, 31.

[253] D. W. Simon, 'The present direction of theological thought,' 80. For further reflections upon church discipline see Alan P. F. Sell, *Enlightenment, Ecumenism, Evangel*, 238-242, 339-355.

[254] T. Ridgley, *A Body of Divinity*, II, 487.

[255] See Alan P. F. Sell, *Testimony and Tradition*, 24-6.

[256] S. Chandler, *The Notes of the Church Considered*, 23.

of institution are to be taken metaphorically: Christ, though omnipresent, is not corporeally present; and those who partake 'are to have communion with one another, and thereby to express our love as members of Christ's mystical body ...'[257] Ridgley has much to say on the Christian's self-examination prior to approaching the Lord's table, though with pastoral sensitivity he observes that those who have doubts as to their worthiness to approach may be mistaken in this judgment; and he opposes those who contend that unless persons are able to specify the time of their conversion they should not be welcomed at the table. In Robert Franks's opinion Mark's account of the Last Supper was 'perhaps the richest of all presentations of the efficacy of the death of Jesus, for it contained the ideas of covenant and communion, and the thought that 'the salvation which Jeremiah prophesied as future is now realised as present, being mediated by the sacrifice of Christ, which establishes the kingdom of God, as the sacrifice of Moses established God's first covenant with Israel.'[258] The relation of the Lord's Supper to the preached word; the eschatological dimension—'till he come'; and the unfortunate use of the sacrament as a stick with which to penalize the undisciplined, are among matters on which our selected divines have little if any light to shed.

As to baptism, Ridgley, like Abraham Taylor, contended that candidates may be believing adults or children of believing parents. Edmund Calamy exhorted Chandler and his colleagues at their ordination in the following terms: 'When you baptize infants, take the Opportunity of making the Parents sensible of their Neglect, if they come not to the Lord's Table,' and, clearly indicating that paedobaptism marks the beginning of a process of Christian initiation, he continued, 'Stick not at taking Pains with such as are passing out of the State of Infant into that of Adult Church Members, that so you may bring 'em to renew their Baptismal Covenant, in the holy Eucharist, understandably, deliberately, and sincerely.'[259] However reticent some high Calvinists may have found Chandler on some doctrinal points, he did not hesitate to write in his Catechism that baptism is to be performed in the name of the Father, Son and Holy Spirit, 'as a standing Memorial in the Christian Church, of that Relation which all Christians have to the Father as their Creator, the Son and their Redeemer, and the Holy Spirit of God as their Sanctifier and Comforter.'[260] Never slow to contrast biblical teaching with that which he found deficient, Ridgley stoutly denied the 'absurd notion' that in paedobaptism the guilt of original sin is washed away, for this 'puts a saving and sanctifying virtue into that which is no more than an outward and ordinary means of grace.'[261] Baptism is a 'sign and seal of the covenant of grace,' but it does not itself confer the grace of the covenant, 'as the Papists pretend.'[262] On this point Payne was even more blunt. He regarded the doctrine of baptismal regeneration as 'so manifestly absurd it might be left to perish

---

[257] T. Ridgley, *A Body of Divinity*, II, 524.

[258] R. S. Franks, *Man, Sin and Salvation*, 75, 76.

[259] E. Calamy, *The Principles and Practice of Moderate Nonconformists*, 34.

[260] S. Chandler, *A Short and Plain Catechism*, 26.

[261] T. Ridgley, *A Body of Divinity*, II, 487-8.

[262] Ibid., 495.

by its own folly.'[263] Ridgley further objected to the provision of godparents, not because the church as a covenant family stood by child and parents, but for fear of diminishing the role of parents, and because godparents may not live up to their responsibilities.

When Richard Alliott was contemplating the requirements for uniting converts with the Church he specified a credible profession of faith; church association with believers; and communion with believers at the Lord's table. Interestingly, baptism is not on his list. Perhaps he could make the assumption more easily than we can today that converts would have been baptized as infants; more likely, he was under the sway of the Evangelical Revival with its emphasis upon conversion as being the way into the Church of the twice-born;[264] possibly he did not wish to indulge in polemics against baptismal regeneration. What is clear is that he was living in a period in which new local church covenants were rarer than hitherto and, as we have seen, the link between paedobaptism and the church as God's covenant people was not always explicitly made, even by those who were concerned to regard children as being, in a qualified sense, members of the Church.

Walter Adeney brought modern biblical criticism to bear upon the question of baptism. Agreeing that it is 'the initial rite of Christianity',[265] he denied that salvation depended upon it; distinguished Christian baptism from that of John the Baptist; and noted that Paul did not practice the rite. While he could find no conclusive New Testament evidence that infants were baptized, Adeney thought it probable that if the father of the family was baptized the other members would follow suit. He adds that Christ welcomed children into his company.[266] By the time that Charles Duthie was writing about baptism the modern ecumenical movement was well under way. He was concerned that baptism should not be emphasised above a person's individual response of faith to God's approach in Christ and, consistently with his view that 'the Church is constituted ... by the presence of Christ in His kingly rule among His people,'[267] he said, 'I am not entirely happy about the present habit of finding the major point of Christian unity in baptism.'[268] Neither am I; and

---

[263] G. Payne, *Lectures on Divine Sovereignty*, 452.

[264] See further David M. Thompson, *Baptism, Church and Society in Modern Britain*, ch. 2.

[265] W. F. Adeney, *Baptism its Nature and Privileges*, 71.

[266] Indeed, he did; but from the way in which, in pastoral contexts, irate grandparents have quoted the text 'Suffer the little children to come unto me, and forbid them not' at godly ministers who are endeavouring to honour the 'children of the covenant' motif, I have sometimes been tempted to wish that Jesus had not said this. To receive parents as church members and to baptize their child at one and the same service—now that would indicate that the evangelical opportunity, which is what requests for infant baptism are often said to present, had really been taken. The offending text is, of course, an ideal motto for Sunday Schools; it is its association with paedobaptism that is problematic to the point of pastorally dangerous.

[267] C. S. Duthie, 'The Gospel, the Church and Church order,' 80.

[268] Idem, 'Responding to the Gospel,' 246.

my way of expressing the point is to say that the Church is constituted by the grace of God in the Gospel, and that the Word and sacraments bear witness to this grace. By infant baptism persons are incorporated into the family of the Church as catechumens, their process of Christian initiation is begun; but to suppose that baptism is the major point of Christian unity would imply that regeneration invariably accompanies, or is even somehow caused by, it. For this view I find no biblical support. It is, of course, a cause of sorrow that there are so many thousands of uncompleted initiations across the land. Duthie further found deficiencies in the way in which paedobaptism and believer baptism were thought of: the former came to incorporate ideas such as the renunciation of evil which cannot be applied to infants; the latter sometimes laid so much emphasis upon the individual's response to God that God's prevenient grace was thrown into the shade. He was, however, convinced that both traditions had preserved important Gospel truths: the prevenience of God's grace on the one hand; the personal acknowledgment of that grace on the other.

At this juncture I would observe that where baptism is regarded as a moment in a process of Christian initiation which culminates in profession of faith it is not impossible to have both modes of baptism within one church order—as, indeed, is provided for in the constitution of The United Reformed Church among others.[269] The pastoral proviso is always to be noted, however, that where it is expected or hoped that the dedication of infants will be followed in due course by believer baptism, the choice before parents is not between infant dedication and infant baptism with water in the name of the Trinity, but between infant baptism and believer baptism. To put it otherwise: infant baptism is an alternative to believer baptism, not to infant dedication.

As might be expected, Vincent Tymms, consistently with his view that baptism should be preceded by repentance, upheld believer baptism, though he did not discuss it at length. On the contrary, he devoted a substantial book to infant baptism, not as currently understood by his contemporary Free Church paedobaptists, but as the practice of it had developed during the first five centuries of the Christian era. In the event, and long before the season of international bilateral dialogues between the several Christian world communions overtook us, he produced an argument that has lain like an unexploded bomb under a number of dialogues in which Roman Catholics have participated with those of other Christian traditions.

Tymms charted the rise of a priest-driven ecclesiastical apparatus that rebranded catholicism Roman—that is, it transformed it into a sect. The question turned on the status and fate of those deemed to be regenerate because they had been baptized, who thereafter sinned. The solution proposed by Augustine was that the priesthood could absolve post-baptismal sins, and it came gradually to be believed that through their ordination priests had a judicial power (*potestas*) to do this.[270] As we travel down the

---

[269] See also the recommendations of the international Baptist-Reformed dialogue: *Baptists and Reformed in Dialogue*, Geneva: World Alliance of Reformed Churches, 1984; cf. Alan P. F. Sell, *A Reformed, Evangelical, Catholic Theology*, 142-6.

[270] See further David F. Wright, *Infant Baptism in Historical Perspective*, ch. 6.

centuries the view was taken that only those who are in communion with the Bishop of Rome have this power, and hence the ministries and sacraments of others are irregular, invalid—if, indeed, they are truly ministries and sacraments at all. In popular speech, if a person asks a question to which the answer is obvious, the jocular retort may come, 'Is the Pope a Catholic?'—a question expecting the answer 'Yes'. But I think it is a serious question whether the Pope (I do not refer specifically to the present incumbent of Peter's chair but to Popes in general) is a Catholic—a Roman, certainly.[271] I say this because of my understanding of catholicity:

> On the ground of the finished work of Christ the Son, the Father graciously and freely calls out by the Spirit a people for his praise and service; he enables their confession of Christ's lordship, and in drawing them to himself, he gives them to one another in a fellowship in which all barriers of race, sex, and class have been broken down; this people, whose membership encompasses heaven and earth, we call the Church catholic.[272]

However much of this affirmation Roman Catholics may endorse, it is clearly not sufficient for them. It is not that my understanding of catholicity refers only to the remote (and convenient) Church invisible. On the contrary, mine is a realistic ecclesiology which turns upon the visibility of the saints. When I think of the Church as being given in and with the Gospel I mean that those called into visible fellowship, wherever they are, comprise the Church, and that what they are called into is the one Church catholic in one of its local expressions: one cannot be a Christian in general; to be a Christian is to be of the people of God. When Roman Catholics think of the Church as being given in and with the Gospel, they have in mind their own institution with its hierarchical and sacerdotal arrangements, with papal primacy at its apex.

Before proceeding further I wish to enter two caveats. First, it is not my intention to launch into old-fashioned anti-Roman polemics. On the contrary, I write as one who was intimately involved in the second phase of the Reformed-Roman Catholic international dialogue. A few sentences from the 1991 report of that phase of the dialogue will make clear the genuineness of the desire on both sides to find common ground, whilst not papering over the cracks of equally genuine disagreement:

> [T]he nature of ordination still causes difficulty between us. Is the laying-on of hands a sending on a mission, a passing on of a power, or an incorporation into an order? ...

---

[271] Samuel Chandler, more bluntly than I, judged Bellarmine's claim that the Roman Church was catholic to be 'direct nonsense, because the catholick church is nothing but the collection of all true Christians and particular churches in the world.' See *The Notes of the Church Considered*, 18.

[272] Alan P. F. Sell, *Enlightenment, Ecumenism, Evangel*, 282. I should now add the following to the penultimate clause: 'and empowers them for his mission in the world.'

> Reformed Churches take the view that, precisely because Christ himself is the host at the table, the Church must not impose any obstacles. All those who have received baptism and love the Lord Jesus Christ are invited to the lord's [*sic*] Supper...
>
> The Roman Catholic Church, on the other hand, is convinced that the celebration of the Eucharist is of itself a profession of faith in which the whole Church recognizes and expresses itself. Sharing the Eucharist therefore presupposes agreement with the faith of the Church which celebrates the Eucharist.[273]

Secondly, it would be quite wrong to suggest that one Christian tradition alone is capable of evincing the sectarian spirit, by which I mean the attitude that says, Unless and until you see things exactly as we do, and do things in our way, we cannot have full fellowship with you. It is always a double-edged sword, because it impacts both on those without and those within the sectarian fold. That is to say, on the one hand it attempts to guard the ark (thereby usurping the role of God the Holy Spirit); on the other hand it drives dissent underground—or out.[274] As I have elsewhere argued,[275] there are conservative evangelicals who insist that they cannot engage in ecumenical endeavour because unity is in the truth (by which they can only mean their interpretation of the truth); and I take no comfort whatsoever in the knowledge that a certain brand of Presbyterianism is sending out missionaries of the most fundamentalist kind, whose Gospel will not equip those to whom they go to face up to intellectual challenge, and whose sectarian spirit will further harm the body of Christ.

Returning to the main issue, it is because of the doctrinal development which flowed from the baptismal situation which Tymms so carefully discussed, that the Roman Church cannot but think of the true Church as subsisting in itself. Roman Catholics cannot consistently say, as Samuel Chandler did, that 'All who receive [the Scriptures] as the Rule of their Faith, and live by them as the Rule of their Morals, I own so far as sound Members of Christ's Body, I embrace them as my Brethren, I will gladly communicate with them, and will never bar them from my Communion.'[276] They cannot, with Charles Duthie, 'hail Christians everywhere, *without a shadow of hesitation*, as our brethren in Christ.'[277] It is a logical 'cannot' which derives from the fact that from the Roman Catholic point of view non-Roman Christians do not meet all the criteria for full fellowship. Hence the notorious words of *Dominus Iesus*, an official document with which the Roman Church greeted the

---

[273] *Towards a Common Understanding of the Church*, 49, 55.

[274] I take no pleasure whatsoever from being told by Roman Catholic scholars in the corridors between dialogue sessions that on certain neuralgic points they agree with me, but if they said so they would no longer be permitted to teach. In recent decades we have learned of a number of such scholars who have felt unable to maintain silence, and have suffered the consequences.

[275] In *Enlightenment, Ecumenism, Evangel*, 286-8.

[276] S. Chandler, *The Case of Subscription*, 39.

[277] C. S. Duthie, 'The Gospel, the Church and Church order,' 81.

new millennium: 'the ecclesial communities which have not preserved the valid episcopate and the genuine integral substance of the eucharistic mystery are not churches in the proper sense (*sensu proprio Ecclesiae non sunt*); however, those who are baptized in these communities are, by baptism, incorporated in Christ and thus are in a certain Communion, albeit imperfect.'[278] In July 2007 the Vatican clarified its position and this was queried by Setri Nyomi, General Secretary of the World Alliance of Reformed Churches in a letter written to Cardinal Walter Kasper, President of the Pontifical Council for Christian Unity. The Vatican statement read,

> These [Reformed] ecclesial Communities which, specifically because of the absence of the sacramental priesthood, have not preserved the genuine and integral substance of the Eucharistic Mystery cannot, according to Catholic doctrine, be called 'Churches' in the proper sense.[279]

Pouring petrol on troubled waters, Kasper simply reiterated the point in his reply:

> A thorough reading of the text makes clear that the document does not say the Protestant churches are not churches but that they are not churches in the proper sense, i.e., they are not churches in the sense in which the Catholic Church understands itself as such.[280]

All of which prompts the sigh, 'What a blessing!' For the Roman Church has come to believe two things in particular which can only be regarded as highly problematic. In the first place, there is in place a doctrine of development which, when associated with the sacerdotal structure of the Church (itself the product of development), has, since the First Vatican Council (1870), come to legitimate those utterances of the Pope which (however much they may be derived from long and prayerful discussion) are delivered *ex cathedra* as infallible.[281] A prominent example is that concerning Marian dogma. Charles Duthie wrote a careful and sensitive article on this, in which he traced the course of Marian dogma from the Council of Ephesus which met in 430 to the 1960s. At Ephesus Mary was declared to be the 'mother of God'; in 1854 the doctrine of Mary's immaculate conception was promulgated on the ground that 'she whom God chose to be the mother of the Redeemer and who humbly consented to do His will should be grounded in holiness from the first moment of her existence.'[282] In 1950, the 'Marian Year', Mary's bodily assumption was proclaimed to underline the fact that Mary's imperishable body is with her Son; and in the course of the Second Vatican Council 'the position of Mary as "mother of

---

[278] *Dominus Iesus*, para. 17. For further discussion see Alan P. F. Sell, *Testimony and Tradition*, 338-340.

[279] Quoted by Anon. in *WARC Update*, September 2007, 10.

[280] Ibid.

[281] For a discussion of various ways in which doctrinal development has been understood—whether as something beneficial or disastrous—see Alan P. F. Sell, *Enlightenment, Ecumenism, Evangel*, ch. 6.

[282] C. S. Duthie, 'The elevation of Mary,' 13.

the Church" and indeed "mother of men" has been given formal expression while the controversial titles of mediatrix and co-redemptrix have moved closer to the centre.'[283] Duthie commented as follows:

> In bringing Mary into closest relation with God, Christ and the Church the Second Vatican Council is developing the logic implicit in the historical development. *The Dogmatic Constitution on the* Church ... makes the forthright statement 'It is right that Mary should have from the Church the honour of a special cult. She has been raised by God's grace to a position second to her Son above all angels and men; she is the most holy Mother of God and has been involved in the mysteries of Christ.'[284] Protestant thought can no longer treat Roman teaching about Mary as an aberration that does not touch the substance of Roman faith. Mary's place in the whole structure of dogma is now too secure for that. Roman Catholicism stands or falls with Mary.[285]

Duthie recognised that charitable discussion of this position is required, but so is dissent from it. He argued that 'veneration of Mary is founded upon a very insecure interpretation of Scripture.' He cited the Vulgate's rendering of Luke 1: 28, 'Hail Mary, full of grace' as 'the starting-point for a theology of co-operation, merit and the "glories of Mary", whereas a more accurate rendering of the Greek is, 'most favoured one.'[286] Again, more is made of Mary's involvement in the ministry of Jesus than can be found in the gospels. From a psychological perspective, the way in which in Marian devotions Mary has become the focus of infantile tendencies is disquieting. But the most important objections are theological. Duthie wrote,

> [W]hile Roman theology makes a distinction between the veneration due to Mary and the reverence to be given to God and to Christ, it is plain that devotion can be *diverted* to Mary, that he function as mediatrix requires a very sophisticated theology to justify it and that the pre-eminence of Jesus Christ is seriously threatened. *De Ecclesia* contains the sentence 'While she is the subject of preaching and attention, she is calling believers to her Son, to his sacrifice, and to the Father's love.'[287] That may be the *intention* of the deepest strain in Roman Catholicism, but can it be denied that both in theology and in practice Mary also *draws attention to herself* and in such a way as to upset the very balance of which Rome speaks? What causes deepest disquiet about this whole development is that Mary like us was a creature, a human being, a sinner redeemed by her Son who was also her Saviour. Roman Catholic faith has made so much of her that it is not unjust to say that she appears to be leaving the creaturely sphere and to be on the verge of the triune Being of God.

---

283 Ibid.

284 See A. Flannery, *Vatican Council II*, 421, where the order of the two quoted sentences is reversed.

285 C. S. Duthie, 'The elevaton of Mary,' 13.

286 Ibid.

287 See A. Flannery, op. cit., 420-21.

> The elevation of Mary cannot perhaps be separated from the central tendency of Roman Catholic theology to give to humanity and to co-operation with God a status that is unwarranted. We ought to make the most of Mary's humble and beautiful submission to God; but to enthrone her with her humanity as the Roman Church has done and to make her co-operation with God a source of merit is to imperil the reality of grace and to incur the risk of idolatry.[288]

Secondly, there is the fact that, quite apart from problems posed by specific doctrines, infallibility carries with it the unalterability of doctrines deemed to be infallible. This places the Roman Church in the unfortunate position (from my point of view) of making important tracts of its teaching non-reformable by the Holy Spirit. This is precisely the point made by the British Baptists in their reply to Leo XIII, and it called forth Tymms's criticism of J. H. Newman, who 'proposed a rational test of doctrinal development which his principles forbade him to use.'[289]

At this point the issue of papal primacy comes into view. There are certain non-Roman Catholic ecumenists of a genial sort who say, 'If you are to have a global Church it needs a representative figure-head, so why not a Pope?' This pragmatism seems to regard the Pope as if he were an administrative or fellowship-fostering convenience. In fact the Pope is the apex of a sacerdotal, sectarian institution in whose name he promulgates infallible and hence unreformable dogma. The Church has boxed itself into a corner; it logically cannot admit mistakes over infallibly-proclaimed truths; it may therefore be isolating itself from the continuing guidance of God the Holy Spirit. This is a most serious position for a Church to be in. In a more recent, and more eirenic, paper Walter Kasper has said that

> beyond differences ... we do not lose sight of what we have in common, of which there is so much, and which is more important. ... Jesus Christ is ... salvifically present in a saving way in the churches and ecclesial communities that are divided from us. That is really no small thing. A few decades ago such a statement would have been totally unthinkable, and I am not sure that all our ecumenical partners would say it of us. ... [Nevertheless] Since we are not as one in our understanding of the Church, and, to a great extent, the eucharist, we cannot gather at the one table of the Lord and eat the one eucharistic bread or drink from the one eucharistic sup. This is offensive and, for many, a heavy burden. But it does not help to conceal wounds; we need to leave them open, even where there is pain; only then can we treat them and, with God's help, heal them.[290]

---

[288] C. S. Duthie, 'The elevation of Mary,' 13. In his article, 'Unique motherhood', Duthie eschewed Mariolatry but urged that Mary be given her due place in Christian thought as the one who was given the unique role of mother of Jesus; who learned to be subject to her Son; and who became a believer and a witness. Articles on Mary from a variety of standpoints may be found in Carl E. Braaten and Robert W. Jenson, eds., *Mary, Mother of God*.

[289] T. V. Tymms, *The Evolution of Infant Baptism*, 469.

[290] W. Kasper, 'The light of Christ and the Church,' 352, 353.

This, it will be noted, is a mirror image of conservative Protestant biblicism: until we all look up the same periscope on *x* we may not do *y*. It seems to me that only when this log jam is broken will the healing desired by Kasper and myself be possible. How can it be done? Only, I believe, by an exercise of lateral thinking where we start not from the specific ecclesiastical and sacramental positions we hold, but from a fresh examination of the question, What has happened? What has God done? As indicated earlier I believe that in Christ the Father has called out one people for his praise and service. There is but one Church. The unity is already given, it is not to be created, but it is to be manifested. Whatever prevents that manifestation of unity—supremely at the table of the Lord—is a strong indicator that something sectarian is afoot. To wait until we agree upon all points of doctrine and practice is to slight what God has already done. This was the burden of my paper delivered at an international ecumenical consultation at the Monastery of Bose, Italy, 14-20 2002. Cardinal Kasper was among those in attendance and I have lived to tell the story. In my paper I wrote the following:

> [A] significant ecumenical step forward would be taken if the Pope and his theological advisers could bring themselves to consider the possibility that in their hands the Church's true catholicity may be under threat, and that there are biblically appropriate ways of manifesting the unity which God has given in Christ by the Spirit which do not require any to embrace the sectarianism of others. All that is required is the joyful recognition of what the gracious God has done for us all in the Cross-Resurrection, and the celebration of this together at the table of the Lord. To the degree that our theory prohibits such celebration we need, in the light of Scripture, to modify or reject it. Failure at this point communicates itself to others as arrogance, and protestations to the effect that despite our lack of episcopacy we of the Reformed family, for example, 'are, by Baptism, incorporated in Christ and are thus in a certain communion, albeit imperfect, with the Church', however well-intentioned, come across as patronizing nonsense (or invite the slang response, big deal!), for to be 'incorporated into Christ' by God's sovereign grace is precisely and exclusively what suffices for full Christian fellowship. Accordingly, the sooner the ecclesiastical obstacles to such fellowship are removed, the better. If my language seems strong at this point it is not primarily because many of my own tradition feel hurt, despair or irritation ... It is because the qualification in the last phrase quoted seems to minimize what God the Holy Spirit has done in calling our his Church. We may not deal in percentages with the grace of God. ... [W]e should do well to ponder one of the most sobering injunctions in the whole of Scripture, 'Do not grieve the Holy Spirit of God' (Ephesians 4:30).[291]

I do not see the end of this road. I simply note that there are yet seven thousand who have not bowed the knee to sectarianism. Among them are some ardently committed ecumenists who are deeply saddened by biblically and theologically

[291] Alan P. F. Sell, *Enlightenment, Ecumenism, Evangel*, 293-4, 298. All of the papers delivered at the Bose consultation are in D. Donnelly, A. Denaux and J. Famerée, *The Holy Spirit, the Church, and Christian Unity*.

groundless ecclesiaticisms which perpetuate, and even require, the division at the Lord's table of those whom God has already made one in Christ by the Spirit. I do not wish kindly Roman priests to wink at their church discipline ('Just toddle up to the altar, old chap: his nibs [namely, the bishop] won't know'). I wish my Roman Catholic friends (and, for that matter, my Anglo-Catholic ones) to consider the possibility that their theory and practice may require revision in the light of the Gospel; this in obedience to Christ's invitation to his table; in the interests of the Church catholic; and with a view to the fuller manifestation of the already given unity of the one Church. If this were done (and it would be difficult, and the temptation to save face would need to be overcome) we could then think of the several expressions of Christian ministry in a fresh light. We should then have a context in which we might profitably pursue the suggestion made by John Paul II in connection with papal primacy: 'I insistently pray to the Holy Spirit to shine his light upon us, enlightening all the Pastors and theologians of our Churches, that we may seek—together, of course—the forms in which this ministry may accomplish a service of love recognized by all concerned.'[292] It would, of course, need to be made clear that there would be no suggestion that the route to the fuller expression of catholicity lies along the sectarian path.

XI

From among the many general matters arising from our study of the ten hinterland theologians, I select four for brief reflection. My purpose is simply to indicate both topics currently under review on which our divines have a contribution to make, and currently neglected themes to which they may prompt us to return.

First, it has been said that up to and including the eighteenth century an educated person could know more or less all that there was to be known. This can no longer be said. As a consequence of the continuing explosion of knowledge polymaths have gone the way of dinosaurs. Even as late as the beginning of the twentieth century Walter Adeney could range over biblical studies, history and theology in a way which some current specialists of the present day would regard as pretentious or 'not serious'. But before we become too precious concerning our own corner of the intellectual vineyard we should recognize the disadvantages which flow from the fact that the 'departmentalizing' of the theological disciplines has led to the compartmentalizing of them, with the result that there has been a sundering of things which ideally belong together. Thus, if one may gently tease on so important an issue, it is alleged that there are Christian Old Testament scholars who, when they see a theological idea approaching over the horizon, rush off to some desert place and start digging for pots ('Tell it not in Gath'). There are New Testament specialists who, when pressed on a theological point will reply, 'This is out of my

[292] John Paul II, *Ut Unam Sint*, 107.

territory, I'm a philologist.'[293] Conversely, there are systematicians who proceed in innocence of the findings of the biblical scholars (which, admittedly, are sometimes mutually contradictory); and dogmaticians, of whom Barth is the supreme example, who eschew the apologetic task—to the dismay of Franks and Duthie, who believed that the patient commendation of the faith to those with doubts about it or aversions to it was integral to the theological task, and that dogmatic assertion was insufficient. Not, indeed, that the older apologetics can altogether satisfy us today. We cannot have straightforward recourse to the classical theistic arguments and to the 'evidences' of miracle and prophecy; and while it may be necessary to challenge alien world views as Vincent Tymms did, this, I suggest, is best done not simply as a defensive activity, but in the context of the intellectual commendation of the faith—a task which, in turn, requires that the several possible starting-points—the Bible, revelation, experience—receive fresh examination, and that the positions of Barth, the logical positivists and some postmodernists who deny that the task can or should be done at all, are addressed.[294]

Some theologians are averse to metaphysics, a position which in their different ways, all of the ten hinterland divines would have repudiated, and none of them would have understood some of the prevalent courses in clinical pastoral counselling in which the underlying anthropologies of sundry psychotherapeutical gurus are seldom analysed in the headlong rush towards 'techniques'. They would have insisted that the first thing about pastoral theology is that it is theology. This prompts reference to a further bifurcation. Whereas in the broadly confessional times in which Ridgley and others lived the pattern of the Decalogue and of Paul's letter to the Romans was largely followed: this is what is to be believed; this, then is how you should live—in other words doctrine and ethics were deemed integral to one another, as the hefty *Bodies of Doctrinal and Practical Divinity* amply prove; from the eighteenth century, when, for example, Henry Grove of the Dissenting academy at Taunton divorced ethics from dogmatics in his curriculum, Christian ethics has blossomed in a variety of directions, and in some of its more issue-orientated manifestations it is nowadays as remote from theological underpinnings as it is from

---

[293] The words of Leslie Houlden, a biblical scholar, are to the point here: 'If I thought that ... learned and intelligent Christians, had really come to terms ... with their founding documents and their implications, I should be less worried when [New Testament scholars] diversified into the many lush fields now open to them. But at least in the life of the churches, there is a terrible failure to deal with the basic interpretative issues in the handling of Scripture. Most of our current problems spring from easy literalism on the one had or crass modernity on the other.' See L. Houlden, 'Education in theology,' 176. On reading this I am emboldened to admit to an unsanctified thought which, no doubt, only a philosopher-theologian would entertain, namely, that it would seem that in the case of some biblical scholars the 'crass modernity' of which Houlden speaks is a useful refuge from exegesis that can be indulged in with little reference to ancient languages.

[294] See my trilogy on Christian apologetic method: *John Locke and the Eighteenth-Century Divines*; *Philosophical Idealism and Christian Belief*; *Confessing and Commending the Faith.*

the analytical questions posed by moral philosophy. George Payne could make the assumptions of Christendom when writing on ethics, and regarded God as the source of all morality (so that an atheist could not be a moral person), but Christian ethicists who today meet with humanists and others on multi-disciplinary committees investigating specific issues, would not normally be expected to lay out their theological presuppositions at any great length. How, one wonders, would they reply to the question implicit in Payne's rebuke to Butler: 'An ethical system which does not attempt to explain the nature, either of conscience or of virtue, or which satisfies itself with a statement which really explains nothing—*viz.*, that conscience is that which approves virtue and virtue is that which is approved by conscience—must, surely, be allowed to be imperfect; and on a point, too, where we might have expected to find it most full and explicit'?[295] On the general point raised in this paragraph, we might ask ourselves how far is it possible today to act upon Payne's charge to an ordinand that he exhibit the entire Christian system because 'The doctrinal and experimental and practical branches of our holy religion form one beautiful and consistent whole, of which the atonement of Christ is at once the centre and support.'[296]

XII

Secondly, we must ask, What are the implications of the foregoing for theological education? With the exception of Samuel Chandler, the theologians whose work we have reviewed were all engaged in the theological education of intending ministers, but Chandler, no less than the others, had a deep concern for the ministry as such. Their ordination charges are revelatory of their understanding of the ministerial role. For example, Taylor supplied an ordinand with a formidable list of doctrinal subjects to be treated from the pulpit; Chandler emphasized the preacher's integrity; Alliott underlined the ministers' accountability before God for the saints who had called them; and Duthie contended that Christ is the one minister, in whose work not only the pastor but all the members corporately share. But how should such persons be trained? Alliott insisted that students should study classics, mathematics and philosophy before approaching theology, and Payne's and Simon's list of subjects to be studied, some of them more naturally to be found in an Arts faculty today, were lengthy indeed. Many more subjects could now be added to their lists, for during the twentieth century many 'genitive' subjects have come into their own: psychology of religion, sociology of religion, history of religions, as well as a range of new specialisms such as ecumenical theology, feminist theology, and liberation theology. In addition, pastoralia had developed in ways hitherto undreamt of, while homiletics, liturgics, missiology and even church administration appear in the 'course offerings' of more comprehensively-minded theological colleges and seminaries. All of which raises the question, how much of this can satisfactorily be

---

[295] G. Payne, *Elements of Mental and Moral Science*, 370.

[296] Idem, *Lectures on Christian Theology*, II, 497.

treated in a three- or four-year course? If students are expected to become acquainted something of everything, is there not the danger that we shall merely inoculate them against certain disciplines for life, by giving them so little that they never really master subjects, or stay long enough with them to enjoy them? How shall we do justice to subjects which require cumulative attention over a lengthy period? How successful have we been if, in the final year of the course, students are still taking courses entitled, 'A survey of this' and 'An introduction to that'? Robert Franks's words echo down the years with increasing relevance: 'the ideal of ministerial education is not to send a man out with some knowledge of every subject he will afterwards find useful. It is to send him out with a mind that can tackle with success any subject as need arises. The opposite leads to self-confident shallowness.'[297]

This, however, begs the question, What, then, should we ensure that theological students destined for Christian ministry receive? No doubt I reveal my bias (but I also advert to what I have found to be of great benefit in ministry) if I suggest that, consistently with my idea that systematic and constructive theology are a conversation with the past in relation to the present, a firm grounding in the Bible (and not simply in a few 'set texts') and in Christian thought through the ages (which includes, but is not restricted to, historical theology) should be mandatory. Otherwise I do not see how the conversation can be continued with any depth, or how ministers can be encouraged to see all the work they do in their pastorates in a theological perspective. At which point Richard Alliott's perceptive words come to mind, 'If we bring out and strengthen the intellectual faculties of our students, teach them to think for themselves—fit them to investigate truth, we do far more for their future power and usefulness that if we were to store their memories with all the divinity found in the works of our most eminent theologians'[298]—or, one might add, the most voluminous post-lecture 'handouts'.

It goes without saying that, the curriculum apart, the circumstances in which theological education is now offered to ministerial candidates is light years away even from that with which Duthie was familiar until his retirement in 1976. It is a matter of simple observation that during the past thirty years a revolution has taken place in the circumstances of theological education for the ministry. Most mainline denominations in Britain now have a preponderance of second career persons among their candidates, many of these are married with family commitments, and they commute to college for perhaps one or two days per week only. Moreover when they get there, they may be dispatched into the community for substantial periods of time in the interests of the 'action-reflection-action' method of theological education.[299] Antediluvian though it may seem in come circles, I persist in thinking that for the sake of future theological leadership in the churches we need to encourage our able younger candidates who will have the time to develop into those leaders to immerse

---

[297] R. S. Franks, Annual Report, 1926.

[298] R. Alliott, 'Our Colleges,' 5.

[299] I have engaged in a cheerful discussion with Dr. David Peel on this question. See his 'So last century?—Review article,' and my response in JURCHS, VIII no. 1, January 2008, 49-59.

themselves in the most rigorous theological education available. We should be careful lest, in the interests of economics, or of uncritical commitment to a 'one size fits all' approach to theological education, we deprive such younger persons of the education that may best enable them to be good stewards of the gifts they have been given.[300]

I am very well aware that the formation of ministerial candidates is no less important than the informing of them,[301] and there is some evidence to suggest that a reconsideration of the doctrine of vocation would not come amiss. Anyone wishing to embark upon such a task might consider placing Abraham Taylor's words to John Hurrion at his ordination: 'you are tied to [the people] in a near and close relation, bear them much on your heart ...',[302] against such increasingly common talk of ministerial 'job-hunting', 'career patterns' and even 'the hiring and firing of pastors.'[303] The difference in tone would seem to betoken a significant difference in theology—possibly even the absence of theology in the latter case. It is not surprising that where there is general confusion as to the nature of the vocation ministerial candidates should be less than clear on the matter. Long ago, and after many years in ministerial education, Simon lamented that 'the vast majority are going out into the ministry without any definite conviction as to the reason why they are ministers: certainly not that it is their supreme business to *convert*. At the utmost it is 'to do good'—which often means entertaining and interesting, with a little mild piety thrown in.'[304] I have lost count of the number of times, when asked in my presence, Why do you wish to become a minister? ministerial candidates have replied, Because I want to help people. To this the response can only be, But medical practitioners, social workers, lawyers and many others help people—why do you wish to become a *minister*? Is there no call? Is there no Gospel to be proclaimed? Are there no saints to be cared for—and was not Richard Alliott right when he said that ministers are accountable before God for the souls of the saints who have called them?

---

[300] In this connection I should like to reiterate a concern that I have expressed elsewhere, namely, that in many fields of study what I call the seed-corn disciplines are in peril. We find, for example, art courses devoid of draughtsmanship, acting courses devoid of voice production and, dare one say it, English courses devoid of grammar. As to the theological fields, few students come to theology with a background in classics (nowadays almost entirely the preserve of public—that is, independent fee-paying—schools), or logic, or historical method. Faithful to my conviction that where the education of ministers is concerned it is not the case that 'one size fits all', I nevertheless wish that more could be given the rigorous preparatory training that they deserve so that in due course they may become the well-grounded theological resource persons that the churches will need.

[301] See further Alan P. F. Sell, *Testimony and Tradition*, 8-10.

[302] A. Taylor, *Exhortation* to John Hurrion in *Of the Difficult Work and Happy End of Faithful Ministers*, 37.

[303] See further, Alan P. F. Sell, *Aspects of Christian Integrity*, 137-143; idem, *Testimony and Tradition*, 14-15, 41-42, 46.

[304] F. J. Powicke, *David Worthington Simon*, 229.

There is then the further question, Why do you wish to be a minister in this particular tradition of the Church? In an increasingly consumerist society, in which people choose their 'church home' for a variety of reasons, many of them quite unconnected with the heritages of specific denominations, it becomes increasingly difficult to elicit an adequate answer to this question. When I sought entry to the theological college I was required, on the basis of a prescribed reading list, to sit examinations on the history and principles of Congregationalism. Current intelligence suggests that such papers are rarely taken nowadays. The justification for the change, 'We now live in ecumenical times', is too easy. It is precisely because we live in ecumenical times and have more opportunities than ever before of sharing what God has given with other members of his flock that we need to know our history and principles. Were the Dissenters wrong to devise their church order in such a way as to show that Christ alone (and not Christ plus the monarch and Parliament) is Lord of the Church? Were they mistaken when they taught that the Church comprises the saints, and that the only way to be a member of the Church catholic is to be gathered with the saints locally, for one cannot be a 'Christian in general'? Are we ill advised to protest to this day against that sectarianism which divides at the Lord's table those whom the Holy Spirit has called and made one in Christ? So one might go on. All of these questions are of ecumenical, not simply narrowly-denominational, significance; they are derived from a lengthy history of prayerful reflection upon Scripture; and too many saints have died and suffered for the principles they enshrine for us to cast them aside in cavalier fashion.

XIII

A third way in which the ten hinterland divines can challenge us is concerning doctrines on which there is widespread reticence. Ridgley, we recall, was concerned that church members should be acquainted with the principal Christian doctrines, though not with the technical language in which they were frequently discussed. Payne regretted that the fundamentals of the faith were studied by so few Christians, and feared that 'if a moral deluge were to sweep away our accustomed words and phraseology on religious subjects, it would not, in very numerous instances, leave many ideas behind it.'[305] Half a century on, Simon listed some of the doctrines of which little was heard in Congregational circles at the end of the nineteenth century:

> Scarcely even a passing reference is now made to the theme of the Divine sovereignty on which our fathers used to touch with such awe ... election has been metamorphosed; and were such subjects as irresistible grace, effectual calling, adoption, and perseverance to be seriously expounded, most people would either wonder what was meant, or silently mutter, 'Rip Van Winkle.'[306]

[305] G. Payne, *Lectures on Divine Sovereignty*, vi.
[306] D. W. Simon, 'The present direction of theological thought,' 79.

To these lacunae we might add the doctrine of the eternal generation of the Son, which, as we saw, exercised some our divines through the entire period under review, or the doctrine of assurance which Abraham Taylor expounded with such clarity and pastoral sensitivity.

Adeney, we recall, was quite undisturbed by the silence on traditional Calvinist modes of doctrinal talk. But he was too much 'in recovery' from hard-line scholasticism to approach the some of these themes with scholarly impartiality. I have already referred to his unbalanced treatment of election, but from Simon's list I might pick the term 'adoption' which is crucial to the Gospel, and by which I understand that Christians are, by God's free grace, adopted as his sons and daughters. They are then 'in Christ', to use Paul's phrase; they 'abide in Christ', to use John's. I do not see how we can cease to use the term 'adoption' without cutting out the heart of the Gospel. I cannot remember hearing a sermon on the theme, apart from those of my own making (though I am quite often exhorted to be on the side of peace, justice and the planet in a threatened and unequal world); and this I find disturbing. It seems to me that our present situation is more serious than that which George Payne faced. He was worried that if the customary religious terms and phrases were swept away there would be few ideas left. I suspect that notwithstanding more than a century of public education in which religious knowledge has been communicated, and not to mention the considerable labours of Sunday School teachers, we are to a large extent in that situation: we have lost the language and with it the ideas. I have elsewhere sought to diagnose this situation in more detail; the remedy, in part at least, is to redouble our efforts to acculturate children and church members in the Gospel and the teachings of the Bible.[307] As to the teachings of the Bible, I specify these in addition to the Gospel because the Gospel comes first; to confine ourselves to the teachings of the Bible may mean that we leave people with a miscellany of unconnected episodes (and pictures of them)—Noah in the ark; Daniel in the lion's den; Jesus on the Cross; Paul in prison); and, moreover, if these are treated in a pre-critical way it is small wonder that people sooner or later relegate them to childhood memories. At this point we do well to recall the stern judgment of Vincent Tymms: 'By any means, and by all means, let the results of Biblical criticism be made known, and only those who are base enough to love their own opinions better than truth can fear the issue.'[308] To this end, as we saw, Adeney devoted a large part of his life, writing guides for adults and children alike.

Underlying the remarks in the preceding paragraph is the question of theological and ministerial integrity. This greatly exercised Samuel Chandler:

> If [a minister] preaches what he doth not believe, he deals falsely with God and man, and deserved to be doubly abhorred for his hypocrisy, and vice. He forfeits all claim

---

[307] See further, Alan P. F. Sell, *Nonconformist Theology in the Twentieth Century*, 164-170.

[308] T. V. Tymms, 'Agnostic expositions,' 693.

> to respect and honour from men, and hath a double condemnation to expect from God.[309]

I suppose that ministers might refrain from articulating certain doctrines because they feel insecure in them; or because they do not believe them; or because they fear the consequences of doing so. In all such cases they may be tempted to divert their attention to current affairs or current crusades. Tymms, we recall, regretted the way in which some preachers steered clear of the atonement, preferring to concentrate upon semi-political, social, literary or ethical themes. Similarly, Simon detected 'a tendency to co-ordinate in the work of regenerating society, all sorts of cultural agencies, with the "Gospel, which is the power of God unto salvation", rooted more or less in the conscious conversion of Christianity, from a real spiritual dynamic, into a moral and religious regulative,'[310] and this motive is not entirely inoperative to this day. Difficult issues arise here. It might seem straightforward to agree with Samuel Chandler it would betoken a serious lack of integrity if ministers proclaimed what they did not believe—the very point Abraham Taylor made in relation to those who formally subscribed to confessions of faith whilst disbelieving some of their contents. True to his conviction, Chandler's reticence on certain points rendered him suspect in some quarters. He was not, of course, alone. As we saw, he praised his deceased contemporary, George Smyth, because he did not 'express himself in such an ambiguous Manner, that he might appear to be what some call Sound, when conscious to himself that he was not so.'[311]

However, there is also integrity *vis á vis* the church which issued the minister's call. When Thomas Belsham faced insuperable personal difficulties over the doctrine of the Trinity he resigned his teaching post at Daventy academy in 1789 and removed to the more liberal Hackney academy. This was the honourable thing to do. It reveals his integrity; but it also implies his understanding that the constituency served by Daventry academy had a right to hear trinitarian doctrine from those who believed it.[312] The minister is, after all, the leader of *the people's* worship, not the censor of it. In this connection we might nowadays ask ourselves whether those ministers who rightly complain of patriarchal abuses of power are not themselves guilty of an abuse of power if they edit out of worship, and even out of the trinitarian formula, references to God as Father.[313] Perhaps some issues are best handled in discussion groups rather than in public worship where the main thrust should be in the direction of praise, affirmation and rededication, rather than in the discussion of technicalities whether exegetical, theological or ideological. This is not to say that the saints need to be patronized. It is a matter of knowing what the primary purpose is at certain given times, and of deciding whether or not we have the right to decline, on behalf of

---

[309] S. Chandler, *The Character and Reward of a Christian Bishop*, 19.

[310] D. W. Simon, 'The present direction of theological thought,' 80.

[311] S. Chandler, *Christ the Pattern of the Christian's Future Glory*, 27.

[312] See further Alan P. F. Sell, *Enlightenment, Ecumenism, Evangel*, 374.

[313] See further, ibid., 365-375; *Nonconformist Theology in the Twentieth Century*, 168-170.

(frequently non-consulted) church members, Jesus's invitation to call his Father our Father, or to opt them out of the broad tradition of Christian testimony without so much as a by your leave.

XIV

Fourthly, in addition to particular doctrines which seem to be relatively little heeded there are numerous broader themes on which more work is needed. Of these I shall simply note four. First, Simon in particular, but also Franks and others, encourage us to think again about the supernatural. Simon insists that

> It will make all the difference in the world whether one starts with the assumption that all history on earth is the product of natural, including human, factors, without any intervention or determining action of God either on the order of nature in the form of miracles, or on the spirit of man or, with the assumption that such extraordinary and miraculous divine interventions are possible; and in view of the constitution of man, of the relations of man to nature, and of both to God, alike natural, probable, and fitting.[314]

It seems to me that Simon's heart is in the right place, namely, that serious objections may be levelled against naturalism—not least that implicit in A. C. Ewing's pronouncement that 'the denial of the possibility of asserting trans-empirical facts is an assumption for which, once we have admitted that the verification principle is not true, no evidence can be produced.'[315] But Simon's concern to protect 'extraordinary and divine interventions' raises the spectre of the arguments against miracles construed as breaches of the natural order and, if extended to the 'mechanics' of salvation, it may appear to license magical rather than ethical behaviour on God's part. This, at least, was the burden of Robert Mackintosh's cautionary word:

> In order to safeguard the doctrine of God's grace in Christ, men have thought necessary to represent saving grace as a peculiar supernatural department of human experience, hermetically sealed against all others. ... [On the contrary] as [God's] providence runs through all creation,—it seems natural rather to assume that God's grace is the flowering and consummation of His ordinary providence,—that all agencies in the world, Christian or heathen, which have a trace of moral goodness in them, are worked up into Christ's purpose, and that saving grace is not a special magical gift, but a thing spiritual and moral.[316]

I agree that saving grace is not a special magical gift but we may take Mackintosh's point without eschewing the supernatural. As I have elsewhere written, 'I understand the saving act to be supernatural in two respects: first, its provision is not from

---

[314] D. W. Simon, *The Bible an Outgrowth of Theocratic life*, 51.

[315] A. C. Ewing, 'The necessity of metaphysics,' 147-8.

[316] R. Mackintosh, *Essays Towards a New Theology*, 442.

nature, least of all from human beings, but from the holy God of all grace. Secondly, it has to restore nature, especially ours.'[317]

But this leads us to a second theme which calls for careful study: the claim that Christ's work is of cosmic significance and the relation of that work to history. In this connection Simon appeared somewhat muddled. On the one hand he contended that according to the New Testament the world is already redeemed by Christ; on the other hand he declared that the individual's salvation is conditional upon the person's repentance and faith. Franks argued that talk of a cosmic act turned upon the Greek view of the reality of universals, and he could not understand how there could be salvation prior to the salvation of individuals. Elsewhere he did concede that we could speak of Christ's 'cosmic acts' by way of indicating their universal scope and with the proviso that they work religiously and morally, and I suggested that a closer analysis of the term 'cosmic act' was desirable. To this I now add the consideration that to a much greater degree than even in Duthie's time, it is now necessary to consider this question in relation to the realities of a pluralist society, remembering that while the Cross may well be an offence to many, Christians should not be offensive. Moreover, if Christians wish to claim that in some sense Christ is the centre of history they need carefully to distinguish the Christ of whom they speak from the Church they represent—at which point Duthie's comment on Tillich returns to the mind: 'Tillich seems to rise to something like hot indignation as he contemplates such gross distortions as exclusivism, persecution and wrongful alliance with the secular power.'[318] While we may rightly rejoice in the triumph of the Cross,[319] we should never be triumphalist concerning the earthen vessel which communicates God's Gospel from age to age—something of which Chandler and Tymms in particular were only too aware. When Duthie, in further exposition of Tillich, adds that 'We may say that the Kingdom of God as the end of history means that nothing created will be lost: it will be lifted up into the life of God'[320] we may once again, and at the risk of being accused of a lack of poetic imagination, enquire what precisely this means. As for the interim, may we derive any assistance from Tymms's doctrine of history? The Jesus who promises peace also came not to send peace but a sword, he reminded us, adding that 'the same light of heavenly truth and love which cheers the mourner, revives the contrite, heals the wounded spirit, subdues the warlike to become like little children and which beautifies the meek with salvation, has also served to break up haughty nationalities, to shiver guilty kingdoms like a potter's vessel smitten with an iron rod.'[321] On the one hand the claim of Christ does require a decision for or against him. On the other hand we should do well to recognize that the 'light of heavenly truth and love' that is said to have broken up haughty nationalities and shivered guilty kingdoms like a potters vessel smitten with an iron rod, has too often been aided and abetted by sometimes

---

317 Alan P. F. Sell, *Confessing and Commending the Faith*, 180.

318 C. S. Duthie, 'The final destiny,' 9.

319 See further Alan P. F. Sell, *Enlightenment, Ecumenism, Evangel*, ch. 13.

320 Ibid.

321 T. V. Tymms, BH, 1897, 75.

far from charitable Christian warriors. The moral is that any attempted Christian philosophy of history will need to be characterized by a high degree of rigour and sensitivity.

Thirdly, a number of the ten divines recall us to the spiritual dimension of life. It would seem from the plethora of retreats, quiet days, and workshops, and also from the proliferation of tomes and tracts on spirituality, that many are heeding the call. The range of 'pathways' on offer is almost bewildering: from what is alleged to be Celtic spirituality through medieval mysticism to Puritan devotions and charismatic experience—not to mention the eastern and the ecological turns—the options are many. In some Christian or post-Christian circles, whereas the slogan used to be 'Not doctrine but life', the slogan now is 'not doctrine but spirituality'; and I have even seen it written that (doctrinally innocent) spirituality is the new ecumenism. This, as it seems to me, is an echo of the paper delivered by James Allanson Picton at the Leicester Conference in 1877, in which he argued, to Simon's regret, that the drive for doctrinal unity is divisive and that true unity is unity in the spirit. It is by no means my purpose to dampen or disparage the spiritual quest of any, but it may be appropriate to make a few points from a Christian standpoint. Here some of our divines will help us. Abraham Taylor made his point with characteristic bluntness: 'They are wretchedly infatuated, who pretend to elevated communion with God, in the perfection of a contemplative life, or in internal prayer, or inward martyrdom, or whatever swelling words of vanity they invent, and at the same time neglect Christ, by whom, only we can have communion with God.'[322] Over two hundred years later, in his review of the Anglo-Catholic E. L. Mascall's book, *Christ, the Christian and the Church*, Robert Franks likewise emphasised the centrality of Christ to Christian spirituality, albeit in more technical and less provocative terms: 'I am not convinced that the *via negationis*, despite its correction of anthropomorphism, is an advance on what might be termed the *via Incarnationis* in prayer.'[323] Against an anthropocentric understanding of spirituality Simon asked a question expecting the answer No: 'Can we further the spiritual life in a higher and truer and more effective way if we cast aside this ballast of the supernatural, and simply appeal to the primary religious emotions or religious susceptibilities of human nature?'[324] He was equally concerned that people should have a personal, and not simply an 'official' relationship with God.[325] Out of his concern to root Christian spirituality in the soil of credible biblical interpretation, Tymms uttered an important cautionary word:

> The spiritual discernment of spiritual things may fairly be deemed higher and more trustworthy for religious purposes than any other kind of knowledge. It may justly be allowed to secure our assent to propositions which might otherwise be regarded as inadequately proved; and as a matter of experience, it no doubt does very often precede, and largely contribute to induce, an intellectual acceptance of the Christian

---

[322] A. Taylor, *Of Assurance of God's Love*, 40-41.
[323] R. S. Franks, CQ, XXV no. 1, January 1947, 76.
[324] Quoted by F. J. Powicke, *David Worthington Simon*, 101.
[325] D. W. Simon, *The Redemption of Man*, 287-290.

> evidences. But these admissions in no degree sanction the supposition that spiritual faith can be rationally entertained in defiance of a previous intellectual dissent, and in conjunction with an admission that science and philosophy have proved the most important statement in the Gospels to be absolutely incredible.[326]

Much more might be said,[327] but I conclude this paragraph by suggesting the importance of something which is overlooked every time I am told by spiritual enthusiasts that we are all on a journey, seeking our individual 'pathway' to wherever it is. The problem here is twofold. First, it makes a great difference whether I am on a journey *towards* faith, or *of* faith. Secondly, the latter journey is not simply an individual, but a decidedly corporate one. The same J. Guinness Rogers who as a young minister rebuked his former professor, Samuel Davidson, later, on having become an ecclesiastical statesman wrote that Congregationalism's 'ideal Church is a body of spiritual men [and women] converted by the grace of God, and living by faith in the Lord Jesus Christ. This is something radically different from a society of truth-seekers, resolved to live up to their light and to wait in hope that more light will come.'[328] The challenge is to advance ever more closely towards the ideal.

Finally some of the ten divines, notably Payne, Alliott, Tymms and Duthie, recall us to the privilege of evangelism. Richard Alliott lived at a time when the 'new measures'—the anxious bench and the penitent's stool among them, adopted but not invented by the American evangelical Oberlin perfectionist, Charles Grandison Finney, were becoming known in England. Alliott judiciously found a place for both the ordinary and the extraordinary means of grace, and he urged that the objectives of the ministry are 'the conversion of sinners and the edification of the Church.'[329] My impression is that today many in the mainline churches are not so sanguine. 'Evangelism' is a term not frequently heard in some circles, and too tub-thumpingly heard in others. We may thank God that we are not like other men, or even as those tele-evangelists, but we do not have much else to say about evangelism; in fact, we do not know what to do about it. 'Is our trouble today,' Charles Duthie asked, 'that we have no substitute for evangelical conversion and are endeavouring to get men and women to pursue the Christian goals without the Christian dynamic?'[330] It is entirely conceivable that the most effective form of evangelism occurs when one person tells God's good news to another and when the other detects sincerity in the evangelist. This, of course, presupposes that the evangelist knows broadly what the Gospel is, can articulate it lovingly, and actually reveals its grace in daily life. I say 'broadly' because our words never capture the

---

[326] T. V. Tymms, *The Mystery of God*, 340-41.

[327] For further reflections on spirituality see Alan P. F. Sell, *Enlightenment, Ecumenism, Evangel*, ch. 8.

[328] J. Guinness Rogers, *The Church Systems of England in the Nineteenth Century*, 644.

[329] R. Alliott, *The Christian Ministry*, 12.

[330] C. S. Duthie, 'Fireworks in a fog?' 9.

Gospel in all its fulness, and in any case the ultimate convincer of another is not ourselves but God the Holy Spirit, who removes scales from people's eyes. But there are also customary services of worship and special occasions of evangelistic outreach. Here Robert Franks, probably the last person one would have expected to see at an evangelistic mission, comes to our aid by reminding us of the need to be alert to the context in which we speak. The old doctrine, he said, 'had a message for the man really *dead* in trespasses and sins. ... But the problem today is far deeper. It is with the man who feels no sense of sin at all.'[331] Hence,

> We have to preach in the *spirit* of the Atonement; so that the Cross not only shines by its own light, but illuminates everything else. Above all we have to live in the spirit of the Atonement. ... [T]he love of God in Christ can only be preached effectively by those who prove the truth of their preaching by exhibiting the power of that love in their lives.[332]

However we go about it, the fact remains, as Duthie insisted, 'The Church is charged by God and constrained by His love to claim the uncommitted or wrongly committed heart of man for Jesus Christ. ... The Gospel of Christ must be communicated in the spirit of Christ.'[333] The motivation is implicit in Duthie's words concerning Pascal: 'Because he has seen God, he wants others to see God',[334] and explicit in the words attributed to Jesus, 'Go therefore to all nations and make them my disciples ... ' (Matthew 28: 19). The power to go is supplied by the only agent of conversion, God the Holy Spirit. There is an urgent need of a thoroughgoing theology of evangelism which will arouse the slumbering and remind any who may need to be reminded that there is more to it than the invocation and application of marketing techniques.

XV

The book is ended, but there is much more to be learned and done. The theological conversation continues. As it does so, one may hope that the voices of hinterland theologians, past and present, shall be heard for, as has been shown, what they have to say is frequently constructive, occasionally provocative, and variously stimulating. They have pertinent observations to share on our current theological agenda, and they challenge us by reminding us of some themes which we may have been inclined to overlook. The hard work of recovering their witness, which has entailed reading and analysing as much as I could find of what they wrote; reading what they read; reading what others said about them; attempting to set them in their several contexts and relating their thought worlds to our own, may turn out to have been a holiday as compared with the hard work required to carry the theological conversation forward. Robert Franks was right:

---

[331] R. S. Franks, *The Atonement*, 196.
[332] Ibid., 197.
[333] C. S. Duthie, 'Responding to the Gospel,' 244.
[334] Idem, Review of E. Cailliet, *Pascal*, 103.

> Inestimable ... have been the benefits conferred upon the Church by those who in any age have enabled it to know its own mind and to handle with certainty and mastery the deposit of truth committed to it by the past, so as successfully to meet its own present needs.[335]

I trust that it has become clear that a not insignificant contribution to this task has been made and can been made by hinterland theologians.

[335] R. S. Franks, *A History of the Doctrine of the Work of Christ*, I, 4.

Appendix

Readers whose appetites have been whetted by the studies in this book may be interested in other British hinterland philosophers and divines on whose behalf the author has arranged mini-resurrections. Numerous other hinterland persons appear in such books as *John Locke and the Eighteenth-Century Divines*, *Confessing and Commending the Faith*, *Philosophy, Dissent and Nonconformity*, and *Nonconformist Theology in the Twentieth Century*. The following abbreviations are supplementary to those listed in the front pages.

BDTCP: *Biographical Dictionary of Twentieth-Century Philosophers*, eds Stuart Brown, Diané Collinson and Robert Wilkinson, London: Routledge, 1996.

ERF: *Encyclopedia of the Reformed Faith*, ed. Donald K. McKim, Louisville: Westminster/John Knox Press, 1992.

Alexander, William Lindsay (1808-1884), DNCBP.
Alliott, Richard (1804-1863), DNCBP.
Allon, Henry (1818-1892), DNCBP.
Armitage, Elkanah (1844-1929), DNCBP.
Aspland, Robert (1782-1845).
Balfour, Arthur James (1848-1930), BDTCP.
Barclay, Robert (1649-1690), DSCBP; *Commemorations*, ch. 6.
Batchelor, Henry (1823-1903), DNCBP.
Bennett, James (1774-1866), DNCBP.
Bennett, William Henry (1855-1920), ODNB.
Best, Thomas (d. 1821), *Dissenting Thought and the Life of the Churches*, ch. 13.
Bourn, Samuel (1689-1754), ODNB; *Dissenting Thought and the Life of the Churches*, ch. 7.
Bourn, Samuel (1714-1796), ODNB.
Bowen, Thomas (1766-1852), *Dissenting Thought and the Life of the Churches*, ch. 16.
Browne, Robert (c. 1550-c. 1633), ERF.
Bruce, Alexnder Balmain (1831-1899), DHT; *Defending and Declaring the Faith*, ch. 5.
Burder, George (1752-1832), *Dissenting Thought and the Life of the Churches*, ch. 10.
Cadoux, Cecil John (1883-1947), WTW.
Caird, Edward (1835-1908), *Philosophical Idealism and Christian Belief*.
Caird, John (1820-1898), ERF; *Defending and Declaring the Faith*, ch. 4.
Campbell, Thomas (1763-1854), *Enlightenment, Ecumenism, Evangel*, ch. 6.
Cave, Sydney (1883-1953), DHT; *Testimony and Tradition*, ch. 9.

Chater, John (fl. 1752-1773), *Dissenting Thought and the Life of the Churches*, ch. 4.
Clarke, Samuel (1675-1729), *Dissenting Thought and the Life of the Churches*, ch. 4.
Cocks, Harry Francis Lovell (1894-1983), ODNB; WTW; *Commemorations*, ch. 13.
Conder, Eustace Rogers (1820-1892), DNCBP.
Courtney, William Leonard (1850-1928), DNCBP.
Dean, Peter (1849-1905), *Dissenting Thought and the Life of the Churches*, ch. 16.
De Burgh, William George (1866-1943), DTCBP.
Denney, James (1856-1917), *Defending and Declaring the Faith*, ch. 9.
Dods, Marcus (1834-1909), DBI.
Dye, Alfred (1851-1930), *Alfred Dye, Minister of the Gospel.*
Erskine, Ebenezer (1680-1754), *Commemorations*, ch. 7.
Erskine, Ralph (1685-1752), *Commemorations*, ch. 7.
Eucken, Rudolf Christoph (1846-1926), BDTCP.
Fairbairn, Andrew Martin (1838-1912), DNCBP; ODNB; *Dissenting Thought and the Life of the Churches*, ch. 19.
Flint, Robert (1838-1910), DNCBP; ERF; ODNB; *Defending and Declaring the Faith*, ch. 3.
Forrest, David William (1856-1918), DSCHT; *Defending and Declaring the Faith*, ch. 8.
Franks, Robert Sleightholme (1872-1964), DHT.
Fraser, Alexander Campbell (1819-1914), DSCHT; *Commemorations*, ch. 10.
Fraser, James (1700-1769), of Alness, ODNB; *Dissenting Thought and the Life of the Churches*, ch. 8.
Fuller, Andrew (1754-1815), *Testimony and Tradition*, ch. 6; *Enlightenment, Ecumenism, Evangel*, ch. 4.
Godwin, John Hensley (1809-1889), DNCBP.
Goodall, Norman (1896-1985), WTW.
Goodwin, John (c.1594-1665), DSCBP.
Gratton, John (1641/2-1712), *Enlightenment, Ecumenism, Evangel*, ch. 2.
Gray, Joshua Taylor (1809-1854), DNCBP.
Green, Thomas Hill (1836-1882), *Philosophical Idealism and Christian Belief.*
Grove, Henry (1684-1738), DECBP; *Dissenting Thought and the Life of the Churches*, ch. 6; *Testimony and Tradition*, ch. 5.
Haldane, Robert (1764-1842), *Commemorations*, ch. 8.
Heywood Thomas, John (1926-), DTCBP.
Hodgson, James Muscutt (1841-1923), DNCBP.
Howe, John (1630-1705), DSCPB; *Dissenting Thought and the Life of the Churches*, ch. 3.
Huxtable, William John Fairchild (1912-1990), ODNB.
Illingworth, John Richardson (1848-1915), *Philosophical Idealism and Christian Belief.*

Iverach, James (1839-1922), DNCBP; DSCHT; *Defending and Declaring the Faith*, ch. 6; *Enlightenment, Ecumenism, Evangel*, ch. 7.
Jones, Henry (1852-1922), *Philosophical Idealism and Christian Belief.*
Jones, Noah (1725-1785), *Dissenting Thought and the Life of the Churches*, ch. 12.
Kennedy, John (1819-1884), DSCHT; ODNB; *Defending and Declaring the Faith*, ch. 2.
Lardner, Nathaniel (1684-1768), ODNB.
Lindsay, James (1852-1923), DNCBP.
McAll, Samuel (1807-1888), DNCBP.
Mackintosh, Hugh Ross (1870-1936), DSCHT.
Mackintosh, Robert (1858-1933), DNCBP; DSCHT; DTCBP; ERF; ODNB; *Robert Mackintosh, Theologian of Integrity*; *Testimony and Tradition*, ch. 9.
Macquarrie, John (1919-2007), BDTCP.
Martineau, James (1805-1900), *Commemorations*, chs 1, 10.
Mascall, Eric Lionel (1905-1993), BDTCP
Matthews, Walter Robert (1881-1973), DTCBP.
Miall, Edward (1809-1881), DNCBP.
Mitchell, Basil George (1917 -), BDTCP.
Myers, Edward (1830-1897), *Dissenting Thought and the Life of the Churches*, ch. 16.
Newman, John Henry (1801-1890), *Commemorations*, ch. 1; *Enlightenment, Ecumenism, Evangel*, ch. 6.
Nye, Philip (c.1596-1672), DSCBP.
Oman, John (1860-1939), BDTCP; ERF.
Orr, James (1844-1913), DBI; *Defending and Declaring the Faith*, ch. 7.
Owen, Huw Parri (1926-1996), DTCBP.
Parry, William (1754-1819), DNCBP.
Payne, George (1781-1848), DNCBP; *Testimony and Tradition*, ch. 9.
Peake, Arthur Samuel (1865-1929), DBI.
Penelhum, Terence (1929-), BDTCP.
Pope, William Burt (1822-1903), *Dissenting Thought and the Life of the Churches*, ch. 19.
Powicke, Frederick James (1854-1935), DTCBP; *Enlightenment, Ecumenism, Evangel*, ch. 1.
Priestley, Joseph (1733-1804), *Enlightenment, Ecumenism, Evangel*, ch. 6.
Pringle-Pattison, Andrew Seth (1856-1931), *Philosophical Idealism and Christian Belief.*
Redford, George (1785-1860), DNCBP.
Reynolds, John (1668-1721), ODNB.
Robinson, Norman Hamilton Galloway (1912-1978), DTCBP; 'Clarity, precision, and on towards comprehension: the intellectual legacy of N. H. G. Robinson (1912-1978), in U. van der Heyden and A. Feldtkeller, eds, *Border Crossings. Explorations of an Interdisciplinary Historian. Festschrift for Irving Hexham*, Wiesbaden: Steiner, 2008, 267-285.

Robinson, William Gordon (1903-1977), ODNB.

Rogers, Henry (1806-1877), DNCBP; *Dissenting Thought and the Life of the Churches*, chs 17, 18.

Rooker, James (1728/9-1780), *Dissenting Thought and the Life of the Churches*, ch. 11.

Rowe, Thomas (c.1657-1705), DSCBP.

Selbie, William Boothby (1862-1944), WTW.

Smart, Roderick Ninian (1927-2001), BDTCP.

Smith, John Pye (1774-1851), *Commemorations*, ch. 8.

Sortain, Joseph (1809-1860), DNCBP.

Spalding, Samuel (1807-1843), DNCBP.

Stanley, Howard Spencer (1901-1975), WTW.

Stoughton, John (1807-1897), DNCBP.

Taylor, Alfred Ernest (1869-1945), *Philosophical Idealism and Christian Belief.*

Taylor, John (1694-1761), DECBP; ODNB; *Dissenting Thought and the Life of the Churches*, ch. 7.

Thomson, John Radford (d. 1918), DNCBP.

Toplady, Augustus Montague (1740-1778), ERF.

Towgood, Micaijah (1700-1792), *Dissenting Thought and the Life of the Churches*, ch. 7.

Travers, Robert (fl. 1692-1747), *Dissenting Thought and the Life of the Churches*, ch. 9.

Vaughan, Robert (1795-1868), DNCBP; *Enlightenment, Ecumenism, Evangel*, ch. 6.

Wardlaw, Gilbert (1798-1873), DNCBP.

Wardlaw, Ralph (1779-1853), DNCBP.

Warren, Matthew (c.1642-1706), DSCBP.

Watts, Robert (1820-1895), *Dissenting Thought and the Life of the Churches*, ch. 19.

Webb, Clement Charles Julian (1865-1954), *Philosophical Idealism and Christian Belief.*

Whale, John Seldon (1896-1997), ODNB.

Bibliography
of Works Referred to in the Text and/or Notes

Manuscript Sources

Re: Thomas Ridgley

Testimonial to David Jennings by Ridgley and others, Dr. Williams's Library, London, MS. 38.97.1.

Re: Abraham Taylor

Lectures on Natural and Revealed Theology. Delivered in the Academy, at Deptford. By Abraham Taylor, D.D., 1739. Congregational Library MS at Dr. Williams's Library, London, 1.d.24.

An Introductory Discourse concerning the Various Ways in which it pleased God to make a Revelation of his Mind and Will under the Old Testament [together with] *A Discourse concerning the Various Ways, and Methods in which it pleas'd God to make a Revelation of his Mind and Will under the New Testament*, Congregational Library MS at Dr. Williams's Library, London, 1.d.25.

An Introduction to Logick, with a few Lectures, on Perception, the first part of that Science, Dr. Williams's Library, London, MS 69.24. Also in the Congregational Library MSS, 1.d.25.

Re: Samuel Chandler

An Account of the Presbyterian and Independent Ministers in London about the year 1730, by a gentleman who had removed thither from Northampton, Walter Wilson MSS, II, at Dr. Williams's Library, London.

On Edward Harwood: Walter Wilson MSS A8.61.62, at Dr. Williams's Library, London.

Re: George Payne

The Congregational College Archives, Lancashire Independent College Box 32, at John Rylands University Library of Manchester.

Re: Richard Alliott

'Tutors in the College at Plymouth 1845,' in *Western College Register*, 1861; The Congregational College Archives, Western College, Bristol, Box 45, at John Rylands University Library of Manchester.

Re: D. W. Simon

Minute Book of the Spring Hill College Committee of management and Mansfield College Council 1866-1916, Mansfield College Archives.

The Congregational College Archives. Yorkshire United Independent College. Box 9, at John Rylands University Library of Manchester.

Senate House, University of London, Archives. Senate Minute 481 (UoL/ST2/2/41); UoL/AC8/64/1/3; Minute 659 (UoL/ST2/2/42).

Re: Walter F. Adeney

Minutes of the Senatus Academicus of the University of St. Andrews: UY452/23/177; UY452/23/185; UY452/23/198; UY452/23/218.

New College, London, MSS at Dr. Williams's Library, London: 149/1; L.9.

Congregational College Archives, at the John Rylands University Library of Manchester: Lancashire Independent College, Boxes 23, 32.

Re: Robert S. Franks

Western College Minute Book from the time of the amalgamation of Western College, Plymouth, with the Bristol Theological Institute. 1891. The Congregational College Archives at the John Rylands University Library of Manchester: Western College, Bristol, Box 45.

Re: Charles S. Duthie

Memoirs and *Curriculum Vitae*; Thanksgiving Addresses by Geoffrey F. Nuttall and Bernard Thorogood; in the author's possession.

Miscellaneous

W. Wilson MSS A8.61.62, at Dr. Williams's Library, London.

Websites

Re: Abraham Taylor

www.devon.gov.uk/etched?_IXP_=1&_IXR=100159

Re: Mary Chandler

http://condor.depaul.edu/~cchaden/bath/Chandler/html

Re: Bernard of Clairvaux

Tractatus contra quaedam capitula errorum Abaelardi, in *Opera Omni*, at http:www.binetti.ru/bernardus/21.shtml

Books and Articles by the Ten Theologians

Adeney, Walter F., *The Hebrew Utopia: A Study of Messianic Prophecy*, London: Hodder and Stoughton, 1879.

—, 'Why do we believe in the Bible?' *The Congregationalist*, XI, 1882, 887-897.

—, *From Christ to Constantine. Christianity in the First Three Centuries*, London: The Sunday School Union, [1884].

—, 'The canonicity of the non-apostolic books of the New Testament,' *The Congregational Review*, I, 1887, 320-328.

—, 'Evolution and immortality,' in Frederick Hastings and A. F. Muir, eds, *Christianity and Eveolution*, London: Nisbet, 1887.

—, *From Constantine to Charles the Great. Christianity from the Third to the Eighth Century*, London: The Sunday School Union, [1888].

—, 'Job' in H. D. M. Spence and Joseph S. Exell, eds, *The Pulpit Commentary*, London: Kegan Paul, Trench, Trübner, 1891.

—, 'The Church in the prisons,' in Alexander Mackennal, ed., *Early Independents. Six Tracts written to commemorate the Tercentenary of the Martyrdoms of Greenwood, Barrowe, and Penry in 1593*, London: Congregational Union of England and Wales, 1893.

—, 'The New Testament,' in *Faith and Criticism. Essays by Congregationalists*, 2nd edn, London: Sampson Low Marston, 1893.

—, 'Andrew Martin Fairbairn, D.D., LL.D.,' *The Expository Times*, V, 1893-1894, 442-446.

—, 'Weiszäcker on the resurrection,' *The Expositor*, 4th ser. VIII, 1893, 137-146.

—, *The Theology of the New Testament*, London: Hodder and Stoughton, 2nd edn 1895.

—, 'The atonement in modern religious thought,' in the book of the same title, London: James Clarke, 1900.

—, *Baptism, its Nature and Privileges*, (*Faith and Conduct Papers for Young People*, V), London: Congregational Union of England and Wales, n.d.

—, 'The Trinity,' in *Studies in Christian Evidences*, Series I, London: Charles H. Kelly, n.d.

—, *How to Read the Bible. Hints for Sunday School Teachers and Other Bible Students*, London: James Clarke, 1896; revised edn, 1907.

—, *Women of the New Testament*, London: Nisbet, 1899.

—, *The Early Christians. The Story of Christianity during the First Three Centuries*, London: Congregational Union of England and Wales, 1897.

—, *The Construction of the Bible*, London: The Sunday School Union, [1897].

—, *St. Luke* (Century Bible), Edinburgh: T. C. and E. C. Jack, n.d.
—, 'Mediator, mediation,' in J. Hastings, ed, *A Dictionary of the Bible*, q.v., III, 1900, 311-321.
—, *A Century's Progress in Religious Life and Thought*, London: James Clarke, 1901.
—, Revision of *The Comprehensive Helps to Bible Study*, London: Samuel Bagster, n.d.
—, Review of *Supernatural Religion* in *The Hibbert Journal*, I, 1902-1903, 391-392.
—, 'Woman' in J. Hastings, ed., *A Dictionary of the Bible*, q.v., IV, 933-936.
—, 'Pilate,' in G. Milligan *et* al., *Men of the Bible, Some Lesser-Known Characters,* Manchester, 1904.
—, 'The Gospel according to the Hebrews,' *The Hibbert Journal*, III, 1904-1905, 139-159.
—, 'Ancient schools of philosophy,' in A. S. Peake, ed., *Inaugural Lectures*, q.v., 1905.
—, *Ezra, Nehemiah and Esther*, in W. Robertson Nicoll, ed., *The Expositor's Bible*, London: Hodder and Stoughton, 2nd edn 1906.
—, 'The divinity of Christ,' in Charles H. Vine, ed., *The Old Faith and the New Theology*, London: Sampson Low, Marston, 1907.
—, 'The resurrection,' in F. W. Ward Orde, ed., *Lux Hominem. Studies of the Living Christ in the World of To-day*, London: Francis Griffiths, 1907.
—, *The Greek and Eastern Churches*, Edinburgh: T. & T. Clark, 1908.
—, 'Sunday School reform in the use of the Bible,' in John Brown, ed., *Proceedings of the Third International Congregational Council*, London: Congregational Union of England and Wales, 1908, 365-372.
—, *The Christian Conception of God*, London: Thomas Law, 1909.
—, *The New Testament Doctrine of Christ*, London: T. C. and E. C. Jack, 1909.
—, *Thessalonians and Galatians* (Century Bible), London: Caxton Publishing Company, n.d.
—, 'The more excellent way,' CYB, 1913, 35-48.
—, 'The Church for the Kingdom,' CYB, 1913, 49-62.
—, *Faith To-day*, London: James Clarke, [1916].
—, 'Nonconformity,' in James Hastings, ed., *Encyclopaedia of Religion and Ethics*, Edinburgh: T. & T. Clark, IX, 1917.
—, 'Then nature of the Advent,' *The Expositor*, 8th ser. XVIII, 1919, 371-379.
—, 'Synoptic variations,' *The Expository Times*, XXXI, 1919-1920, 487-491.
—, 'Philippians,' in A. S. Peake, ed., *A Commentary on the Bible*, London: T. C. and E. C. Jack, 920.
—, 'Miracle and prophecy,' *The Hibbert Journal*, XIX, 1920-1921, 133-142.
—, 'Toleration,' in James Hastings, ed., *Encyclopaedia of Religion and Ethics*, Edinburgh: T. & T. Clark, XII, 1921, 360-365.
—, 'Waldenses,' in James Hastings, ed., *Encyclopaedia of Religion and Ethics*, Edinburgh: T. & T. Clark, XII, 1921, 663-673.

—, See also under Bennett, W. H. and Walter F. Adeney; and Stead, F. Herbert and Walter F. Adeney.

Alliott, Richard (1804-1863), *The Christian Ministry. A Sermon, delivered on entering into the duties of that important work, at the Independent Chapel, Castle Gate, Nottingham, on Sabbath evening, Aug. 10, 1828*, Nottingham: Thomas Kirk, [1828].

—, *The Christian Rewarded according to his Works. A Sermon preached in James Street Chapel, Nottingham, March 16, 1837, before the Nottinghamshire Association of Independent Ministers and Churches*, London: Jackson and Walford, 1837.

—, *The Doctrine of Apostolical Succession tested by Scripture. A Sermon delivered in Castle Gate Meeting, Nottingham, January 23rd, 1842*, London: Dinnis, 1842.

—, *The Union of the Convert with the Visible Church*, 7th in a course of sermons on the life of a Christian delivered at York Road Chapel, Lambeth, 1843-4. This lecture and the following item only are at the British Library, and no bibliographical details are given on them.

—, *The Christian Working for God. A Sermon, preached on Sunday Evening, January 28, 1844 ... at York Road Chapel, Lambeth*. This is the 10th sermon in the series noted in the preceding item.

—, *On the Evidences of Christianity. A Discourse, delivered on Sunday Evening, November 17, 1844 ... at York Road Chapel, Lambeth*, London: James Paul, 1844.

—, *Lecture on the Moral Evidence of Christianity*, London: Hamilton, Adams, [1845].

—, *Seven Lectures to Young Men*, 1846. Lecture 3 only, *On the varied Mental Constitution of Young men, and the Peculiar Temptations to which their Mental Constitutions expose them. Delivered at York road Chapel,. on Sunday evening, February 1, 1846*, is at the British Library.

—, *The Duty of a Christian Church to its Pastor*, 1848.

—, *Mutual Recognition in Heaven. A Discourse delivered in York Road Chapel, Lambeth, by the Rev. R. Alliott, LL.D*, Lambeth: Miller and Field, 1848.

—, *Lectures on the History of the Children of Israel*,[1849]. Incomplete copy at the British Library.

—, *Psychology and Theology: or, Psychology applied to the Investigation of Questions relating to Religion, Natural Theology, and Revelation*, London: Jackson and Walford, 1855.

—, 'Address' on the old and the new theology, *The Congregational Year Book*, 1859, 5-18.

—, 'Address' on revivals, *The Congregational Year Book*, 1859, 38-52.

—, *The Funeral Sermon for the late Rev. Joseph Sortain, A.B., preached on Sunday Morning, July 29, 1860, in North Street Chapel, Brighton*, Brighton: John Smith, [1860].

—, 'Our Colleges. An Inaugural lecture, delivered at Spring Hill College, September 21st, 1860, ... on his entering on the Office of Professor of Theology and Philosophy,' reprinted from the *Evangelical Magazine*, November-December 1860.

Chandler, Samuel, *A Vindication of the Christian Religion. In Two Parts. I. A Discourse on the Nature and Use of Miracles. II. An Answer to a Late Book entituled, A Discourse of the Grounds and Reasons, &c.*, London: S. Chandler, 1725.

—, *Reflections on the Conduct of the Modern Deists, in their late Writings against Christianity: Occasioned chiefly by two Books, entitled, A Discourse of the Grounds and Reasons, &c. and The Scheme of Literal prophecy considered. With a Preface containing some Remarks on Dr. Rogers's Preface to his Eight Sermons*, London: John Chandler, 1727, reprinted London: Routledge/Thoemmes Press, 1995.

—, *A Vindication of the Antiquity and Authority of Daniel's Prophecies, and their Application to Jesus Christ: in Answer to the Objections of the Author of the Scheme of Literal Prophecy Consider'd*, London: John Gray, 1728.

—, *Plain Reasons for being a Christian*, London: J. Roberts, 1730.

—, *A Letter to the Reverend Mr. John Guyse, Occasioned by his Two Lecture Preached at St. Helens, on Acts ix.20. In which the Scripture-Notion of Preaching Christ is stated and defended: An Mr. Guyse's Charges against his Brethren are Considered, and proved Groundless*, London: John Gray, 1730.

—, *A Second Letter to the Reverend Mr. John Guyse: in which Mr. Guyse's latitude and Restrictive ways of preaching Christ are proved to be entirely the same: The Notion of preaching Christ's person is examined. The Scripture Account of preaching Christ is farther cleared and defended. The Charge against his of demeaning his Brethren, is maintained and supported; and his solemn Arts in Controversy are considered and exposed*, London: John Gray, 1730.

—, *The History of the Inquisition* [by Philippus van Limborch] *translated into English by S. Chandler. ... To which is prefixed, a large Introduction, concerning the Rise and Progress of Persecution*, London: 2 vols 1731.

—, *The Dispute better adjusted about the Proper Time of applying for a Repeal of the Corporation and Test Acts*, London: J. Roberts, 1732.

—, *An Answer to the Brief Remarks of William Berriman, D.D. Rector of St. Andrew's Undershaft, and Fellow of Eton College: On Mr. Chandler's Introduction to the History of the Inquisition. In a Letter to the said Doctor*, London: John Gray, 1733.

—, *A Second Letter to William Berriman, D.D., Rector of St. Andrew's Undershaft, and Fellow of Eton College, in which His Review of his Remarks on the Introduction to The History of the Inquisition is considered, and the Characters of St. Athanasius and Martyr Laud are farther stated and supported*, London: John Gray, 1733.

—, *A Vindication of a Passage of the Right Reverend the Lord Bishop of London's Second Pastoral Letter, against the misrepresentations of William Berriman, D.D. In a Letter to his Lordship*, London: J. Roberts, 1734.

—, *The Notes of the Church Considered: in a Sermon On I Tim. iii. 14, 15. Preached at Salters-Hall, January 16, 1734-5*, London: T. Cox, R. Ford, R. Hett and J. Gray, 1735.

—, *A Second Treatise on the Notes of the Church: As a Supplement to the Sermon preach'd at Salters-Hall, January 16, 1734. Being the Substance of two Sermons preach'd at the Wednesday Lecture at the Old Jury* [*sic*], *Jan. 22, and 29*, London: T. Cox, R. Ford, R. Hett and J. Gray, 1735.

—, *An Account of the Conference held in Nicholas-Lane, February 13th 1734-5. Between Two Romish Priests, and some Protestant Divines. With some Remarks on a Pamphlet, entitled, The Two Conferences, &c. truly stated*, London: J. Gray, 1735.

—, *Plain Reasons for being a Protestant: A Sequel to Plain Reasons for being a Christian*, London: T. Cooper, [1735?].

—, *A Paraphrase and Critical Commentary on the Prophecy of Joel*, London: J. Noon, 1735.

—, *Benevolence and Integrity Essentials of Christianity. A Sermon preach'd at the Old Jury [sic], March 3, 1735-6. To the Society for Relief of the Widows and Children of Dissenting Ministers*, London, 1736.

—, *The Case of the Protestant Dissenters with Reference to the Corporation and Test Acts*, London, 1736.

—, *The History of Persecution, in Four Parts. Viz. I. Among the Heathens. II. Under the Christian Emperors. III. Under the Papacy and Inquisition. IV. Amongst Protestants. With a Preface, containing Remarks on Dr. Rogers's Vindication of the Civil Establishment of Religion*, London: J. Gray, 1736. The edition used herein is that of Charles Atmore, Hull: Atmore and J. Craggs, 1813.

—, *Knowledge and Practice necessary to Happiness. A Sermon Preached in the Old Jury* [*sic*], *on Wednesday, March, 1727/8, At the Conclusion of the Lecture for the last Winter Season*, London: J. Gray, 1738.

—, *A Letter to the Right Hon. the Lord Mayor, occasioned by his Lordship's nomination of five Persons, disqualified by Act of Parliament, as fit and proper Persons to serve the Office of Sherrifs, in which the Nature and Design of the Corporation Act is impartially considered and stated*, London: J. Roberts, 1738.

—, *The Necessary and Immutable Difference between Moral Good and Evil, asserted and explained, in a Sermon preached to the Societies for Reformation of Manners, at Salters Hall, September the 25th. 1738*, London: J. Oswald, 1738.

—, *Death the Wages of Sin, and eternal life the Gift of God by Christ represented in a Sermon preached at Peckham in Surrey, March 8, 1741. On Occasion of the Death of the late Reverend Thomas Hadfield, M.D., who died February 21, 1741, in the 46th Year of his Age*, London, 1741.

—, *A Short and Plain Catechism. Being an Explication of the Creed, the Ten Commandments, and the Lord's Prayer. By way of Question and Answer*, London: J. Noon, 1741.

—, *A Vindication of the History of the Old Testament, in Answer to the Misrepresentations and Calumnies of Thomas Morgan, M.D. and Moral Philosopher*, London: J. Noon, R. Hett and J. Davidson, 1741 (Part I) and 1743 (combined volume).

—, *The Witnesses of the Resurrection of Jesus Christ re-examined: and their Testimony proved entirely Consistent*, London: J. Noon and R. Hett, [1744].

—, *Great-Britain's Memorial against the Pretender and Popery*, London: J. Roberts, [1745].

—, *The Danger and Duty of Good Men, under the present unnatural invasion. A Sermon Preach'd at the Old-Jewry, September 29th. 1745*, London: J. Noon, 1745.

—, *Christ the Pattern of the Christian's Future Glory. A Sermon Occasioned by the Death of the late Reverend Mr. George Smyth, A.M. Who departed this Life, May 8, 1746. Aged 57. Preached May 18, at Hackney*, London: J. Noon and Joseph Highmore, [1746].

—, *National Deliverances just reasons for Publick Gratitude and Joy. A Sermon preached at the Old-Jewry, October 9, 1746, Being the Day appointed by His Majesty for a General Thanksgiving, on account of the Suppression of the late Unnatural Rebellion*, London: J. Noon and J. Highmore, 1746.

—, *The Case of Subscription to Explanatory Articles of Faith, as a Qualification for Admission into the Christian Ministry, Calmly and Impartially Review'd: In Answerto I. A Late Pamphlet intitled The Church of England Vindicated in requiring Subscription from the Clergy to the xxxix Articles. II. The Rev. Mr. John White's Appendix to his Third letter to a Dissenting Gentleman. To which is added the Speech of the Rev. John Alphonso Turretine, previous to the Abolition of all Subscriptions at Geneva, translated from a MSS in French*, London: J. Noon and Jos. Davidson,1748.

—, For Chandler's Funeral Oration at I. Watts's interment see, D. Jennings, *A Sermon.*

—, *The Scripture Account of the Causes and Intention of Earthquakes. in a Sermon Preached at the Old-Jury* [sic], *March 11, 1749-50, on Occasion of two Shocks of an Earthquake, the first on February 8, the other on March 8*, London: John Noon, 1750.

—, *The Character and Reward of a Christian Bishop. A Sermon Occasioned by the Death of the late Reverend Mr. Moses Lowman, Who departed this Life, May 3, 1752. Preached at Clapham, June 14*, London: John Noon, 1752.

—, *Preaching the Gospel a more effectual Method of Salvation, than human Wisdom and Philosophy. A Sermon preached at the ordination of the Reverend Mr. Thomas Wright, at Lewin's-Mead, Bristol, May 31, 1759*, [1759].

—, *The Character of a great and good King Full of Days, Riches and Honour. A Sermon Preached on Occasion of the Death of his late Majesty King George II of*

glorious and blessed Memory, in the Old Jewry, November the 9th 1760, London: J. Noon and A. Millar, 1760.
—, *A Review of the History of the Man after God's own Heart, in which the falsehoods and misrepresentations of the historian are exposed and corrected*, London: J. Noon, 1762.
—, For Chandler's Charge to Harwood and Davis see, T. Amory, *The Motives and Obligations to Love and good Works*.
—, *A Critical History of the Life of David: in which the Principal Events are arranged in the order of Time: the chief objections of Mr. Bayle, and others, against the Character of this Prince, and the Scripture account of him, and the Occurrences of his Reign, are Examined and Refuted; and the Psalms which refer to him Explained*, London: J. Buckland and J. Coote, 2 vols. 1766.
—, *Sermons*, 4 vols, London: Printed for Sam. Chandler by the Author's Widow, 1768.

Duthie, Charles Sim, *The Church and Our Ex-servicemen*, 1945.
—, Review of Emile Cailliet, *Pascal: Genius in the Light of Scripture*, in *The Scottish Journal of Theology*, I no. 1, June 1948, 97-103.
—, 'The Gospel, the Church and Church order,' *Proceedings of the Sixth International Congregational Council*, ed. Frederick L. Fagley, Boston and Chicago: The Pilgrim Press and London: Independent Press, 1949, 78-83.
—, 'The mind of Christ. III. Is the Gospel simple?' *The Expository Times*, LXII, 1950-51, 238-240.
—, 'God in his world,' *The Congregational Quarterly*, XXX no. 1, January 1953, 16-27.
—, *God in His World*, London: Independent Press, 1955.
—, 'Pascal's Apology,' *The Congregational Quarterly*, XXXIV no. 2, April 1956, 128-141.
—, 'Five ways of dealing with temptation,' *The Expository Times*, LXIX no. 9, June 1958, 282-3.
—, 'Our Christian hope,' ibid., LXX no. 7, April 1959, 218-219.
—, 'Making peace,' ibid, LXXII no. 1, October 1960, 25-6.
—, 'God is still at work,' ibid., LXXII no. 12, September 1961, 381-2.
—, 'The Communion sermon,' in *Proceedings of the Ninth Assembly of the International Congregational Council*, London: Independent Press, 1962, 161-4.
—, 'A prophet or a heretic?' *The British Weekly*, 15 August 1963, 9.
—, 'Have we abandoned conversion?' ibid., 3 October 1963, 9.
—, 'The scientific revolution,' ibid., 17 October 1963, 9.
—, 'Everything will be "Christed",' ibid., 14 October 1963, 9.
—, 'Humanism,' ibid., 14 November 1963, 11.
—, 'The challenge of other faiths,' ibid., 12 December 1963, 9.
—, 'The ministry of the whole Church,' ibid., 9 January 1964, 9.
—, 'Changing patterns,' ibid., 16 January 1964, 9.
—, 'Biblical conservatism,' ibid., 2 April 1964, 9.

—, 'Baptism—Infant or Believers'? ibid., 4 June 1964, 9.
—, 'Existentialism,' ibid., 10 September 1964, 9.
—, 'A God of action,' ibid., 8 October 1964, 9.
—, 'Theologian significant,' ibid., 15 October 1964, 9.
—, 'The Spiritual Presence,' ibid., 22 October 1964, 9.
—, 'The final destiny,' ibid., 19 October 1964, 9.
—, 'Fireworks in a fog?' ibid., 17 December 1964, 9.
—, 'The earth is my altar,' ibid., 25 February 1965.
—, 'The meaning of the Cross,' ibid., 1 April 1965, 9.
—, 'Why did Jesus die?' ibid., 8 April 1965, 13.
—, 'Continuing Cross,' ibid., 15 April 1965, 9.
—, 'Four questions,' ibid., 29 April 1965, 9.
—, 'The elevation of Mary,' ibid., 20 May 1965, 13.
—, 'Unique Motherhood,' ibid., 27 May 1965, 9.
—, 'Religion and Reality,' ibid., 3 June 1965, 9.
—, 'Spiritual Pilgrimage,' ibid., 10 June 1965, 9.
—, 'Baffled by the Trinity,' ibid., 29 July 1965, 9.
—, 'The predicament of man,' ibid., 26 August 1965, 9.
—, 'Saint Martin Luther?' ibid., 4 November 1965, 9.
—, 'Darkness and Light,' ibid., 20 January 1966, 9.
—, 'Re-incarnation,' ibid., 10 February 1966, 9.
—, 'Towards the Cross,' ibid., 24 March 1966, 9.
—, 'The God of nowhere and nothing,' ibid., 18 August 1966, 9.
—, 'Affirmations of faith,' *Bulletin of the Department of Theology of the World Alliance of Reformed Churches and the World Presbyterian Alliance*, VII no. 3, Spring 1967, 1-8.
—, *Outline of Christian Belief*, London: Lutterworth, 1968.
—, 'Providence,' in M. Wiles, ed., *Providence*, q.v., 62-76.
—, 'Morality, old and new,' *The Baptist Quarterly*, XXIII no. 8, October 1970, 338-347.
—, 'The Christian understanding of sexuality,' ibid., XXIV no. 1, January 1971, 2-9.
—, *Faith in a Time of Doubt*, London: The Congregational Church in England and Wales, 1971.
—, 'Responding to the Gospel,' in J. W. Winterhager and A. Brown, *Vocation and Victory*, q.v., 243-9.
Duthie, Charles S., ed., *Resurrection and Immortality. Aspects of Twentieth-Century Christian Belief*, London: Bagster, 1979.

Franks, Robert Sleightholme, *The Life of Paul*, Croydon, 1909.
—, *The Writings of Paul*, Croydon, 1910.
—, *The New Testament Doctrines of Man, Sin and Salvation*, London: T.C. & E.C. Jack, 1908.

—, 'The idea of salvation in the theology of the Eastern Church: A study in the history of religion,' in *Mansfield College Essays presented to The Reverend Andrew Martin Fairbairn, D.D. on the Occasion of his Seventieth Birthday November 4, 1908. With a Bibliography*, London: Hodder and Stoughton, 1909, 249-264.
—, *The Cross and the War*, London: Congregational Union of England and Wales, n.d.
—, *A History of the Doctrine of the Work of Christ in its Ecclesiastical Development*, London: Hodder and Stoughton, 2 vols, [1918]; republished in one volume as *The Work of Christ. A Historical Study of Christian Doctrine*, London: Nelson, 1962.
—, 'The present relations between philosophy and theology,' in James Marchant, ed., *The Future of Christianity*, 48-70.
—, 'Towards a metaphysic of religion,' *The Congregational Quarterly*, IV no. 4, October 1927, 523-530.
—, 'Books that have influenced our epoch: Ritschl's "Justification and Reconciliation",' *The Expository Times*, XL, 1928-1929, 103-8.
—, *The Metaphysical Justification of Religion*, London: University of London Press, 1929.
—, 'Dogma in Protestant scholasticism,' in *Dogma in History and Thought. Studies by Various Writers*, London: Nisbet, 1929, 111-141.
—, 'The fullness of God, Father, Son, and Holy Spirit,' *The Congregational Quarterly*, VII, October 1929, 549-556.
—, Review of A. N. Whitehead, *Process and Reality. An Essay in Cosmology*, in *The Congregational Quarterly*, VII no. 3, 1930, 226-8.
—, Review of Benjamin B. Warfield, *Biblical Doctrines*, in *The Congregational Quarterly*, VIII, 1930, 98-99.
—, Review of George P. Adams and Wm. P. Montague, eds, *Contemporary American Philosophy*, in *The Congregational Quarterly*, VIII no3, July 1930, 363-4.
—, Review of Benjamin B. Warfield, *Christology and Criticism*, in ibid., 372.
—, Review of F. C. N. Hicks, *The Fullness of Sacrifice*, *The Congregational Quarterly*, VIII no. 4, October 1930, 505-508.
—, 'The atonement,' in Albert Peel, ed., *Essays Congregational and Catholic issued in Commemoration of the Centenary of the Congregational Union of England and Wales*, London: Congregational Union of England and Wales, [1931], 193-213.
—, 'The Christian good: its constitutive principle and validity,' *The Congregational Quarterly*, IX no. 4, October 1931, 498-505.
—, 'The Person of Christ in the light of modern scholarship,' *The Congregational Quarterly*, X, 1932, 27-38.
—, Review of G. Aulén, *Christus Victor*, in ibid., 112-13.
—, 'The interpretation of holy Scripture in the theological system of Alexander of Hales,' in *Amicitiae Corolla. A Volume of Essays Presented to James Rendel*

Harris, D.Litt. on the Occasion of His Eightieth Birthday, ed., H. G. Wood, London: University of London Press, 1933.
—, *The Atonement. The Dale Lectures for 1933*, London: OUP, 1934.
—, Review of E. R. Dodds, *Proclus, The Elements of Theology*, in *The Congregational Quarterly*, XII no. 1, January 1934, 111-112.
—, Review of Hubert S. Box, *The World and God*, in *The Congregational Quarterly*, XIII no. 1, January 1935, 115-116.
—, Review of *The Apostolic Tradition of Hippolytus*, trans. and intro. by Burton Scott Easton, in *The Congregational Quarterly*, XII no. 4, October 1934, 460-461.
—, Review of J. R. McCallum, *Abailard's Ethics*, in *The Congregational Quarterly*, XIII no. 2, April 1935, 244-5.
—, Review of R. P. Phillips, *Modern Thomistic Philosophy*, in ibid., 245.
—, Review of Clement C. J. Webb, *The Historical Element in Religion*, in *The Congregational Quarterly*, XIII no. 4, October 1935, 482.
—, Review of Nesca A. Robb, *Neoplationism of the Italian Renaissance*, in ibid., 483.
—, 'Christian worship in the Middle Ages,' in Nathaniel Micklem, ed., *Christian Worship. Studies in its History and meaning by Members of Mansfield College*, London: OUP, 1936, 100-118.
—, Review of M. C. D'Arcy, *The Pain of This World*, in *The Congregational Quarterly*, XIV no. 1, January 1936, 111-112.
—, Review of Ernest Moody, *The Logic of William of Ockham*, in *The Congregational Quarterly*, XIV no. 2, April 1936, 235-6.
—, Review of Campbell N. Moody, *Christ for Us and Christ in Us* in *The Congregational Quarterly*, XIV no. 1, January 1936, 110-112.
—, Review of G. L. Prestige, *God in Patristic Thought*, in *The Congregational Quarterly*, XV no. 1, January 1937.
—, Review of Sydney Cave, *The Doctrine of the Work of Christ*, in *The Congregational Quarterly*, XV no. 3, July 1937, 385-6
—, Review of A. P. Ushenko, *The Philosophy of Relativity*, in ibid., 386-8.
—, Review of William Kingsland, *The Gnosis or Ancient Wisdom in the Christian Scriptures*, in *The Congregational Quarterly*, XV no. 4, October 1937, 517-18.
—, Review of A. G. Hebert, *Grace and Nature*, in *The Congregational Quarterly* XVI no. 1, January 1938, 97-8.
—, Review of W. G. De Burgh, *Towards a Religious Philosophy*, in *The Congregational Quarterly*, ibid., 98-100.
—, Review of Suzanne K. Langer, *An Introduction to Symbolic Logic*, in ibid., 100-101.
—, Review of W. J. Sparrow Simpson, *The Redeemer*, in ibid., 101-102.
—, Review of G. Dawes Hicks, *Critical Realism: Studies in the Philosophy of Mind and Nature*, in *The Congregational Quarterly*, XVI no. 3, July 1938, 364-6.

—, 'The theology of Andrew Martin Fairbairn,' *Transactions of the Congregational Historical Society*, XIII, April 1939, 140-150.
—, Review of E. Gilson, *The Unity of Philosophical Experience*, in *The Congregational Quarterly*, XVII no. 2, April 1939, 245-6.
—, Review of Felix R. Cirlot, *The Early Eucharist*, London: SPCK, 1939.
—, Review of John Dewey, *Logic. The Theory of Enquiry*, in ibid., 377-8.
—, Review of F. W. Lewis, *The Work of Christ*, in *The Congregational Quarterly*, XVIII no. 1, January 1940, 94-5.
—, Review of John Baillie, *Our Knowledge of God*, in ibid., 95, 97-8.
—, Review of Jacques Maritain, *A Preface to Metaphysics*, in *The Congregational Quarterly*, XVIII no. 2, April 1940, 212-13.
—, Review of Brand Blanshard, *The Nature of Thought*, in ibid., 213-14.
—, Review of Alexander McCrea, *The Work of Jesus in Christian Thought*, in ibid., 214-215.
—, Review of R. G. Collingwood, *An Essay on Metaphysics*, in *The Congregational Quarterly*, XVIII no. 3, July 1940. 324-5.
—, Review of D. L. Scudder, *Tennant's Philosophical Theology*, in *The Congregational Quarterly*, XVIII no. 4, October 1940, 246-8.
—, Review of Vincent Taylor, *Forgiveness and Reconciliation. A Study in New Testament Theology*, in *The Congregational Quarterly*, XX no. 1, January 1942, 82-3.
—, Review of H. W. Robinson, *Redemption and Revelation*, in *The Congregational Quarterly*, XX no. 3, July 1942, 263-6.
—, Review of Austin Farrer, *Finite and Infinite*, in *The Congregational Quarterly*, XXI no. 4, October 1943, 371-2.
—, Review of W. J. Phythian-Adams, *The People and the Presence. A Study of the Atonement*, in *The Congregational Quarterly*, XXI no. 2, April 1943, 174-5.
—, Review of Henry W. Clark, *The Cross and the Eternal order. A Study of the Atonement in its Cosmic Significance*, in *The Congregational Quarterly*, XXII no. 2, April 1944, 172-4.
—, 'Trends in recent theology,' *The Congregational Quarterly*, XXIII no. 1, January 1945, 19-29.
—, Review of Gilbert Ryle, *Philosophical Arguments*, in *The Congregational Quarterly*, XXIV no. 2, April 1946, 180-181.
—, Review of E. L. Mascall, *Christ, the Christian and the Church*, in *The Congregational Quarterly*, XXV no. 1, January 1947, 76.
—, Review of Henry P. Van Dusen, ed., *The Christian Answer*, in *The Congregational Quarterly*, XXV no. 2, April 1947, 176.
—, Review of F. H. Cleobury, *God, Man and the Absolute*, in *The Congregational Quarterly*, XXV no. 3, July 1947, 274-5.
—, Review of Austin Farrer, *The Glass of Vision*, in *The Congregational Quarterly*, XXVII no. 2, April 1949, 171.
—, Review of W. F. Lofthouse, *F. H. Bradley*, in *The Congregational Quarterly*, XXVII no. 4, October 1949, 363-4

—, Review of H. A. Hodges, *Christianity and the Modern World View*, in *The Congregational Quarterly*, XXVIII no. 2, April 1950, 176-7.
—, Review of Gabriel Marcel, *The Mystery of Being*, in *The Congregational Quarterly*, XXIX no. 4, October 1951, 361-2.
—, Review of W. M. Urban, *Humanity and Deity*, in *The Congregational Quarterly*, XXX no. 2, April 1952, 169-70.
—, *The Doctrine of the Trinity*, London: Duckworth, 1953.
—, Review of H. W. Cassirer, *Kant's First Critique*, in *The Congregational Quarterly*, XXXIII no. 3, July 1955, 268-9.

Payne, George, *Youth Admonished to Submit to the Guidance of God. A Sermon. Preached at the Chapel, in Fish-Street, Kingston-upon-Hull, January 8, 1809*, Hull: J. Ferraby, 1809.
—, *Britain's Danger and Security, or the Conduct of Jehosophat Considered and Recommended. A Sermon Preached at the Chapel in Fish-Street, Kingston-upon-Hull, February 5, 1812*, Hull: J. Perkins, 1812.
—, *An Exposition of Romans, chap. ix. 6-24, Designed to Illustrate the Doctrine of Divine Sovereignty*, Edinburgh, 1816.
—, *A Collection of Psalm and Hymn Tunes, In a great variety of Metres; Particularly adapted to Ewing and Payne's Hymn Book; Selected from the Best Authors by George Payne, A.M. Minister of Albany Street Chapel, Edinburgh*, Edinburgh: W. Whyte and A. Black, [1818].
—, *Remarks on the Moral Influence of the Gospel upon Believers, and on the Scriptural manner of ascertaining our State before God; to which are added Observations on the Radical Error of the Glassite or Sandemanian System, and on the Doctrine of Divine Influence*, Edinburgh, 1820.
—, *On the Instrumentality of Divine Truth in the Sanctification of the Souls of Men. A Discourse on John xvii. 17*, Edinburgh, 1823.
—, *Elements of Mental and Moral Science*, (1828), London: John Snow, 4th edn, 1856.
—, *The Separation of Church and State calmly considered, in reference to its probable Influence upon the Cause and Progress of Evangelical Truth in this Country*, Exeter, 1834.
—, *Facts and Statements in reference to the Bible-Printing Monopoly*, n.d.
—, *The Operation of the Voluntary Principle in America: an Extract from the recent Work of Drs. Reed and Matheson*, [1836].
—, *Lectures on Divine Sovereignty, Election, the Atonement, Justification, and Regeneration. To which are appended Strictures upon Recent Publications by Dr. Marshall and Mr. Haldane, on the Atonement; and upon the Statements of Dr. Jenkyn on the Influences of the Holy Spirit*, (1836), London: John Gladding, 3rd enlarged edn, 1846.
—, *The Response of the Church to the Promise of the Second Coming of our Lord. Discourse on the Death of the late Mr. Heudebourck*, Exeter, 1837.

—, *A Funeral Discourse occasioned by the Death of the late Rev. Joseph Buck of Wiveliscombe*, Exeter, 1837.

—, *The Church of Christ considered in reference to its Members, Objects, Duties, Officers, Government, and Discipline*, London: Hamilton, Adams, 1837.

—, *A Letter to the Editor of The American Biblical Repository, containing Remarks upon a paper in that work, by Professor Stuart, on Original Sin*, London: James Dinnis, 1839.

—, *A Manual Explanatory of Congregational Principles*, London: J. Dinnis, 1842.

—, *The Question: 'Is it the Duty of the Government to Provide the means of Education for the People?' Examined*, London: John Gladding, 1843.

—, *Elements of Language, and General Grammar*, London: John Gladding, 1843.

—, *Remarks upon a Pamphlet entitled, 'The Doctrine of the Universal Atonement Examined' ascribed to The Rev. David Thomas of Mauchline*, Glasgow: James Maclehose, 1844.

—, *The Doctrine of Original Sin; or, the Native State and Character of Man unfolded*, London: Jackson and Walford, 1845.

—, *The Nature and Means of Religious Revivals, exhibited in a Discourse delivered before the Members of the South Devon Congregational Union, at their Annual Meeting, at Stonehouse, April the 28th, 1846*, Plymouth, 1846.

—, 'Consolation for Christian mourners,' *Evangelical Magazine*, 1846, 680-686.

—, 'Assurance of salvation,' *Evangelical Magazine*, 1848, 398-402.

—, *Lectures on Christian Theology*, ed. Evan Davies, 2 vols, London: John Snow, 1850.

Ridgley, Thomas, *A Funeral Sermon Preached (and since enlarged) on the Decease of Mrs. Gertrud Clarkson (Daughter of the Late Reverend & Excellent Divine, Mr. David Clarkson) Who Departed this Life, the 23d. of April, 1701*. London: N. Hiller, 1701.

—, *The Abuse of feastings and Recreations Consider'd in a Sermon preach'd at the Evening Lecture in Jewen-street, London, December 26, 1717. To which is added A Discourse concerning the Origin and Superstitious Observance of Religious Festivals*, London: John Clark, 1718.

—, *The Advantage of Falling into the Hand of God rather than Man*, London, 1719.

—, *The Unreasonableness of the Charge of Imposition exhibited against several Dissenting Ministers in and about London, consider'd. And the Difference between Creed-Making as practis'd in former Ages, and Their late Conduct in declaring their Faith in the Doctrine of the Blessed Trinity, Stated and Argued*, London: John Clark, 1719.

—, *An Essay concerning Truth and Charity in Two Parts. Containing 1. An Enquiry concerning Fundamental Articles of Faith, and the Necessity of adhering to them, in order to Church-Communion. 2. Some Historical Remarks on the Behaviour of the Jews and Primitive Christians, towards those who had either departed from the Faith, or by any other Offences render'd themselves liable to*

Excommunication. Shewing also what is that Uncharitableness which discovers itself in the Conduct of men towards one another, London: John Clark, 1721.
—, *The Doctrine of Original Sin Considered. Being the Substance of Two Sermons preached at Pinners Hall. With a Postscript, Explaining, Correcting, or Vindicating some Passages therein*, London: John Clark and Richard Hett, 1725.
—, *A Sermon Occasioned by the Death of the Reverend Mr. Thomas Tingey, Who departed this Life November 1, 1729. Preached at the Church of which he was Pastor, Nov. 9*, London: Aaron Ward, Richard Hett and John Oswald, 1729.
—, *A Body of Divinity: wherein the Doctrines of the Christian Religion are Explained and Defended. Being the Substance of Several Lectures on the Assembly's LargerCatechism*, (1731), New York: Robert Carter, 2 vols. 1855.
—, *A Sermon Occasioned by the Death of the Reverend Mr. John Hurrion, Who departed this Life December 31st 1731. The Substance whereof was preached to the Church of which he was Pastor, the 9th of January following*, London: Daniel Midwinter, Aaron Ward, John Oswald and Richard Hett, 1732.
—, *A Sermon occasion'd by the Death of the Reverend Mr. John Sladen, Who Departed this Life Octob. 19, 1733. The Substance whereof was preached to the Church of which he was Pastor, October 28*, London: Aaron Ward, John Oswald and Richard Hett, 1733.

Simon, D. W., *The Dissenting Sects of Russia*, unpublished doctoral thesis, Tübingen University, 1863.
—, *Historical Christianity and the Spiritual Life. An Address delivered at the Anniversary Meeting of Spring Hill College, held June 21, 1870*, Birmingham: Hudson, 1870.
—, *A New Year's Address to Sunday School Teachers and Members of the Birmingham Sunday School Union*, Birmingham: White and Pike, [1872].
—, 'The authority of the Bible,' *The British Quarterly Review*, LXXX, July and October 1884, 364-377.
—, *The Bible an Outgrowth of Theocratic Life*, Edinburgh: T. & T. Clark, 1886.
—, *The Redemption of Man. Discussions bearing on the Atonement*, Edinburgh: T. & T. Clark, 1889.
—, 'The present direction of theological thought in the Congregational churches of Great Britain,' *The International Congregational Council, London, 1891. Authorised Record of Proceedings*, London: James Clarke, 1891, 77-85.
—, 'Present position and work of the Theological Hall,' *The Scottish Congregationalist*, July 1891, 204-207.
—, *In Memoriam. Addresses and Sermons delivered in connection with the Funeral of the Rev. Henry Simon, (Late Pastor of Harecourt Chapel, Canonbury), by the Rev. Principal D. W. Simon, D.D. and Rev. Edward White. August 1892*, London: James Clarke, 1892.
—, *What does Congregationalism Stand For? With Special Reference to Doctrine*, Edinburgh: Turnbull & Spears, 1897.

—, *Reconciliation by Incarnation. The Reconciliation of God and Man by the Incarnation of the Divine Word*, Edinburgh: T. & T. Clark, 1898.

—, 'O wretched man,' in Daniel Waters, ed., *Welshmen in English Pulpits, or Sermons by English Congregational Ministers from Wales*, London: Alexander and Shepheard, 1898.

—, *Twice Born and Other Sermons*, London: Melrose, 1904.

—, *The Making of a Preacher*, London: Andrew Melrose, 1907.

—, 'Sin and evil,' in Chas. H. Vine, ed., *The Old Faith and the New Theology*, q.v., ch. 3.

[Taylor, Abraham], *The Scripture Doctrine of the Trinity Vindicated. In Opposition to Mr. Watts's Scheme of One Divine Person and Two Divine Powers*, London: J. Roberts, 1726.

[Taylor, Abraham], *A Letter to a Friend: Occasioned by a Rhapsody, Delivered in Old Jewry; by A Reverend Bookseller in London; At the shutting-up of his Evening Entertainment, for the last Winter Season*, London: James Roberts, 1729.

[Taylor, Abraham], *The Modern Question concerning Repentance and Faith, Examined with Candour. In Four Dialogues; between Zelotes and Bathynous on one Side, and Purodoxus and Sophronius on the other. In which the Arguments on both Sides are fairly stated and discussed; and Repentance unto Life, and Faith unto Salvation, are proved at large to be the Duties of Sinners*, London: James Brackstone, 1742.

Taylor, Abraham, Preface to *The Doctrine of the Trinity, asserted from the Sacred Scriptures by Charles Mastertown, M.A. With a Recommendatory Preface and Greek Notes by A. Taylor*, Belfast: Francis Joy, 4th edn, 1745.

Taylor, Abraham, *The Scripture Doctrine of the Trinity Vindicated in Opposition to Mr. Watts's Scheme of One Divine Person and Two Divine Powers*, London: J. Roberts, 1726.

—, *The True Scripture-Doctrine of the Holy and Ever-Blessed Trinity, Stated and Defended, in Opposition to the Arian Scheme*, 2 vols. London: John Clark and Richard Hett, 1727.

—, *Of Assurance of God's Love. A Sermon preach'd at Deptford in Kent*, London: John Clark and Richard Hett, 1728.

—, *A Practical Treatise of Saving Faith in Three Parts*, London: Richard Hett, 1730.

—, *Of the Instability of Earthly Monarchies, and of the Nature and Stability of Christ's Kingdom. A Sermon preach'd on the Fifth of November, by Abraham Taylor*, London: Richard Hett, 1730.

—, *A Letter to the Author of an Enquiry into the Causes of the Decay of the Dissenting Interest. Containing an Apology for some of his Inconsistencies; with a Plea for the Dissenters and the Liberty of the People*, London: J. Roberts, 1730.

—, *Of the Work of Ministers, and the Respect due to them from their People. A Sermon preached at Deptford in Kent, on New Years Day 1731. At the*

Ordination of Mr. Abraham Taylor; with a Charge deliver'd on that occasion by John Hurrion. To which is added Mr. Taylor's Confession of Faith, London: Richard Hett, 1731.

—, *Of the Happiness of Believers in their Death. A Sermon occasion'd by the Death of the late Reverend Mr. John Beaumont, Minister of the Gospel; Preached at Deptford in Kent, November the Fourth 1730*, London: Richard Hett, 1731.

—, *Of Spiritual Declensions, and the Danger of being Insensible under them. A Sermon preached in Harecourt, in Aldersgate-Street, January 6 1731/32*, London: A. Ward, 1732.

—, *Of the Difficult Work and Happy End of Faithful Ministers. A Discourse Occasioned by the Death of the late Reverend and Learned, Mr. John Hurrion. To which is added, An Exhortation to Mr. John Hurrion; delivered at his Ordination, at Gosport, May 3, 1732*, London: R. Hett and J. Oswald, 1733.

—, *A Sermon preach'd at the Ordination of the Reverend Mr. William Johnson; October 6 1736. At Ryegate in Surrey. By John Guyse, D.D. To which are added Mr. Johnson's Confession of Faith, and An Exhortation to him by Abraham Taylor, D.D.*, London: J. Oswald, 1736.

—, *A Sermon preached at the ordination of the Reverend Mr. Benjamin Vowell, April 19, 1738, at Colchester, in Essex, by Peter Goodwin; together with Mr. Vowell's Confession of Faith, and an Exhortation to him, by Abraham Taylor, D.D.*, London: J. Oswald and J. King, 1738.

—, *An Address to Young Students in Divinity, By way of a Caution against some Paradoxes, Which lead to Doctrinal Antinominaism*, London: J. Oswald, 1739.

—, *The Insufficience of Natural Religion: A Discourse preached by Mr. Abraham Taylor at the Lecture in Lyme-Street, London: Reprinted on the Occasion of Dr. Mayhew's later Sermons. With a Preface by Andrew Croswell, V.D.M.*, Boston: J. Draper, 1755.

—, Two sermons on the above theme in *A Defence of some Important Doctrines of the Gospel, in Twenty-Six Sermons. Most of which were Preached at Lime-Street Lecture. By several eminent Ministers*, 2 vols., Glasgow: William Smith, 2nd edn, 1773. Vol. 2 contains Taylor's sermons, *A Vindication of the Evangelical Doctrine of Man's Salvation by the Free Grace of God from the Charge of Promoting Licentiousness*, and *A Humble and Impartial Enquiry into the Causes of the Decay of Practical Religion; or into the True Grounds of the Declensions, as to the Life and Power of Godliness, Visible in such as Profess it in the Present Day.*

Tymms, T. Vincent, *First Principles of Christian Union. A Sermon preached at The Downs Chapel, Clapton, on Sunday morning, October 17, 1875*, London: Yates and Alexander, 1875.

—, 'Death is yours. A Sermon preached at Shacklewell Chapel, Sunday Evening April 4th 1875, after the Death of Dr. R. K. Brewer, Pastor of the Church,' in *The Battle Fought: or, A Short Memoir of the Rev. Dr. R. K. Brewer*, London: Hamilton Adams, 1876, 71-88.

—, *The Mystery of God. A Consideration of some Intellectual Hindrances to Faith*, London: Eliot Stock, 1885.

—, 'Agnostic expositions,' *The Contemporary Review*, May 1889, 692-712.

—, *The Beauty of God and Other Sermons*, London: James Clarke, 1891.

—, 'An Open Letter to Pope Leo XIII, respecting his Letter to the English People, dated April 14th, 1895, *The Baptist Handbook*, London: Clarke, 1896, 98-101.

—, 'Authority: true and false,' *The Baptist Handbook*, London: Veale, Chifferiel, 1897, 63-77, 87-109.

—, 'Christian Theism,' in *The Ancient Faith in Modern Light. A Series of Essays*, Edinburgh: T. & T. Clark, 1897, ch. 1.

—, Obituary of William Landels, *The Baptist Handbook*, London: Baptist Union of Great Britain and Ireland, 1900, 224-228.

—, *The Christian Idea of Atonement. Lectures delivered at Regent's Park College, London, in 1903*, London: Macmillan, 1904.

—, 'Independents or Congregationalists,' in C. H. H. Wright and C. Neil, eds, *The Protestant Dictionary, Containing Articles on the History, Doctrines and Practices of the Christian Church*, London: Hodder and Stoughton, 1904.

—, *The Private Relationships of Christ*, London: James Clarke, 1907.

—, *The Evolution of Infant Baptism and Related Ideas*, London: The Kingsgate Press, [1912].

—, *The Cameroons (West Africa). A Historical Review ... With Extracts from Recent Statements by Sir Harry H. Johnston, G.C.M.G., K.C.B. Also Letters from the Rev. R. Wright Hay and the Rev. Thomas Lewis, formerly Missionaries in the Cameroons*, London: The Carey Press, [1921/2].

Books and Articles by Others

Abelard, *Abailard's Ethics*, trans. and introd., J. Ramsey McCallum, Oxford: Blackwell, 1935.

Abram, William Alexander, *A Century of Independency in Blackburn, 1778-1878. An Historical Sketch prepared for the Centenary of Chapel-Street Congregational Church, Blackburn, in October 1878*, Blackburn, 1878.

Adams, George P. and Wm. P. Montague, *Contemporary American Philosophy. Personal Statements*, London: Allen & Unwin, 2 vols, 1930.

Adeney, George J., *Congregationalism Scriptural; or, The Nature and Constitution of the Church of Christ as set forth in the New Testament*, London: J. Snow, 1851.

Adeney, J., *Following the Sun. Letters to my Children during a Two Year's Journey around the World*, London: James Clarke, 1919.

Alexander, Samuel, *Space, Time and Deity*, London: Macmillan, 1920.

Alexander, W. L., *Memoir of the Life and Writings of Ralph Wardlaw*, Edinburgh: Adam and Charles Black, 1856.

Allen, R., *The Presbyterian College Belfast 1853-1953*, Belfast: Mullan, 1954.

Alliott, Richard (1769-1840), *The Danger and Duty of our Country. A Discourse addressed to Three United Congregations of Protestant Dissenters in Nottingham, on the day of the late General Fast*, Nottingham: J. Dunn, 1803.

—, *Jesus of Nazareth the Son of God. The Credibility of the Miraculous Conception of the Lord Jesus Christ Vindicated. Reply to a Sermon, preached at Belper, in Derbyshire, on Christmas Day, 1808, and entitled 'Jesus of Nazareth the Son of Joseph'*, Nottingham: J. Dunn, 1809.

—, *Christian Union; the substance of a Sermon preached at Loughborough, on Monday, June 19th, 1815, at the Formation of a Sunday-School Union Society*, Nottingham: J. Dunn, 1815.

—, *An Apology for Calvin and Calvinism, in Two Letters, to the Vicar of St. Mary's, Nottingham*, Nottingham: J. Dunn, 1823.

—, *The Nature and Obligations of Christian Liberality, and the Influence of these Obligations on the Support of Christian Missions. A Sermon delivered be3fore the London Missionary Society at their thirty-fourth Anniversary, at Surrey Chapel, May 14, 1828*, London: Frederick Westley and A. H. Davies, 1828.

Alliott, Richard (1839-1899), *The Attitude of the Church Toward the Young*, London: Watson and Hazell, 1875.

—, *The Supply of Christian Ministry: An Address delivered at the Twelfth Annual Conference of the Hertfordshire Congregational Association, held at Great Berkhamstead, October 30th and 31st, 1876*, Bishops Stortford: Arthur Boardman, [1876].

Alliott, William, *What is Popery? The Substance of a Discourse on the Leading Features and Essential Principles of Popery, delivered at Howard Chapel, Bedford, on Sabbath Evening, December 1st, 1850*, London: Allen, [1850].

—, *Christianity a Religion of Consolations, and Life in Christ. Two Discourses delivered at Howard Chapel, on Lord's-Day mornings, Nov. 28th and Dec. 5th, 1858*, Bedford: John G. Nall, 1858.

Amory, Thomas, 'Account' of Henry Grove prefixed to *The Works of Henry Grove, containing all the Sermons, Discourses and Tracts published in his Life Time*, 4 vols, 1747.

—, *The Motives and Obligations to Love and good Works, represented in a Sermon preached at the Ordination of the Reverend Mr. Edward Harwood, of Bristol, and the Reverend Mr. Benjamin David, of Marlborough, October the 16th, 1765, in the Old Jewry, London* [to which S. Chandler's *Charge* is appended], [1765].

—, *Dying in Faith explained, and the Happiness attending it, represented in a Sermon on Heb. xi.13. Preached at the Old Jewry, May 18, 1766; on occasion of the Death of the Rev. Sam. Chandler, D.D. and F.R. and A.S.S. Who died May 8, in his seventy-third Year. To which is added the Speech at his Interment, and a Catalogue of his Works*, London: J. Buckland and T. Becket, [1766].

—, Preface to S. Chandler's *Sermons*, 1768, q.v.

Anderson, P. J., *Fasti academiae Mariscallanae Aberdonensis*, Aberdeen: New Spalding Club, 1898.

Annan, Noel, *The Dons. Mentors, Eccentrics and Geniuses*, London: HarperCollins, 2000.

Anon., *An Authentick Account of Several Things Done and Agreed upon by the Dissenting Ministers lately Assembled at Salters-Hall*, London, 1719.

—, *A True Relation of some Proceedings at Salters-Hall by those Ministers who sign'd The First Article of the Church of England, and the Answers to the Fifth and Sixth Questions in the Assemblies Shorter Catechism, March 3. 1719*, London, 1719.

—, *A Letter to the Author of The Doctrine of the Trinity Vindicated: Pretended to be written by a Dissenting Country Gentleman; Wherein his false and abusive Representations of the Reverend Mr. Watts are plainly exposed*, London: John Chandler, 1727

—, *A Letter from a Friend to Samuel Chandler, Occasion'd by his Sermon against Popery, Preach'd at Salters-Hall, Jan. 16. 1734-5. By a Countryman, and a Lover of Truth*, London: T. Wilford, 1735.

—, 'Biography of the Life of the Rev. Samuel Chandler, D.D., F.R. and A.S.,' *The Protestant Dissenter's Magazine*, I, 1794, 217-223, 257-264.

—, 'Memoir of the late Rev. George Lambert, of Kingston-upon-Hull,' *The London Christian Instructor, or Congregational Magazine*, III, 1820, 521-6, 577-581, 633-8.

—, *Discourses delivered at the Ordination of the Rev. Hugh M'Kay, over the Independent Church and Congregation at Liskeard, Cornwall, on Tuesday, September 29th, 1846. ... The Introductory Discourse, by the Rev. George Payne, LL.D., of the Western College ...* , London: John Snow, [1846].

—, 'R', *A Letter in Answer to Dr. Payne's work on Original Sin*, Nottingham, n.d.

—, *Bi-Centenary of Castle Gate Meeting. An Historical Account of the Congregational Church worshipping in Castle Gate Meeting House, Nottingham; to which are prefixed Two Sermons preaches October 7, 1855, by the Rev. Richard Alliott, LL.D., Principal of the Western College, Plymouth, and the Rev. Samuel McAll, Minister of Castle Gate Meeting, in Commemoration of the Bi-Centenary of the Church*, London: Ward, 1856.

—, Two Graduates [i.e. Enoch Mellor and J. Guinness Rogers], *Dr. Davidson, his Errors, Contradictions, and Plagiarisms*, London, 1857.

—, 'Our theological colleges,' *The Eclectic Review*, January-June 1859.

—, *Funeral Services for the Rev. R. Alliott, LL.D. Address delivered at the General Cemetery, Nottingham, December 28, 1863, by the Rev. C. Clemance, B.A. Sermon delivered at Acock's Green, January 3, 1864, with Sketch by the Rev. G. B. Johnson*, London: Hamilton, Adams, [1864].

—, 'Dr. Robert Vaughan,' *The Congregationalist*, VI, March 1877, 129-148.

—, *Memorial of the Opening of the New and Enlarged Buildings of Lancashire Independent College*, Manchester: Tubbs and Brook, 1878.

—, Review of D. W. Simon, *The Bible an Outgrowth of Theocratic Life*, in *The British Quarterly Review*, CLCVI, April 1886, 487.

—, *Reports of the Committee of the Northern Baptist Education Society*, Bradford: M. Field, 1888-1905.

—, *Mansfield College, Oxford: Its Origin and Opening. October 14-16, 1889*, London: James Clarke, 1890.

—, *Lancashire Independent College. Jubilee 1893. Addresses delivered and Papers read*, Manchester: J. E. Cornish, 1893.

—, Review of W. F. Adeney, *How to Read the Bible*, in *The Expository Times*, VIII, 1896-1897, 125.

—, Review of D. W. Simon, *Reconciliation by Incarnation*, in *The Expository Times*, X, 1898-1899, 178.

—, Review of W. F. Adeney, *A Century's Progress in Religious Life and Thought*, in *The Expository Times*, XII, 1900-1901, 409.

—, *Supernatural Religion. An Inquiry into the Reality of Divine Revelation*, London: Watts, 1902.

—, Review of T. V. Tymms, *The Idea of Atonement*, *The Expository Times*, XV, 1903-4, 518.

—, *Lancashire Independent College, Whalley Range, Manchester. Report of the Committee for 1903*, Manchester: Richard Gill, 1904.

—, Review of D. W. Simon, *The Redemption of man*, 2nd edn, in *The Expository Times*, XVII, 1905-1906, 365.

—, 'London Congregational Board,' CHST, II, 1905-1906, 50-60.

—, *Memorable Unitarians. Being a Series of Brief Biographical Sketches*, London: British and Foreign Unitarian Association, 1906.

—, Review of W. F. Adeney, *The New Testament Doctrine of Christ*, in *The Expository Times*, XXIm 1909-1910, 129.

—, Review of W. F. Adeney, *The Greek and Eastern Churches*, in *The Expository Times*, XXI, 1909-1910, 209.

—, Review of W. F. Adeney, *The Christian Conception of God*, in *The Expository Times*, XXI, 1909-1910, 276.

—, *Faith To-day*, London: James Clarke, [1916].

—, *Bristol Baptist College. 250 Years 1679-1929*, published by the College, [1929].

—, *Statement of Belief*, Glasgow: Congregational Union of Scotland, 1949.

—, *1811-1961. Triple Jubilee. The Scottish Congregational College*, Edinburgh, 1961.

—, *A Declaration of Faith*, London: Congregational Church in England and Wales, 1967; reprinted in David M. Thompson, ed., *Stating the Gospel: Formulations and Declarations of Faith from the heritage of the United Reformed Church*, Edinburgh: T. & T. Clark, 1990.

—, *Towards a common understanding of the Church. Reformed-Roman Catholic International Dialogue: Second Phase 1984-1990*, Geneva: World Alliance of Reformed Churches, 1991.

—, 'WARC questions Vatican statement on status of Reformed Churches,' *WARC Update*, September 2007, 10.

Anselm, *Cur Deus Homo?* trans. and intro. Edward S. Prout, London: Religious Tract Society, n.d.

—, *Proslogion* in *A Scholastic Miscellany*, ed. and trans. Eugene R. Fairweather, London: SCM Press, 1956, 73-75.

Aquinas, see Thomas Aquinas.

Argent, Alan, 'Henry Allon at Union Chapel, Islington,' *Congregational History Circle Magazine*, I no. 3, 1993, 12-31.

Atmore, Charles, ed., S. Chandler's *The History of Persecution from the Patriarchal Age to the Reign of George II*, Hull: John Perkins, 1813.

Augustine, *The Enchiridion of Augustine*, London: Religious Tract Society, n.d.—, *The City of God*, ed. Ernest Rhys, London: J. M. Dent, 2 vols, 1945.

Aulén, Gustaf, *Christus Victor. An Historical Study of the Three Main Types of the Idea of the Atonement*, London: SPCK, 1931.

Baillie, Donald M., *God was in Christ. An Essay on Incarnation and Atonement*, London: Faber and Faber, 1961.

Baillie, John, *Our Knowledge of God*, London: OUP, 1939.

Barrett, John O., *Rawdon College (Northern Baptist Education Society) 1804-1954. A Short History*, London: The Carey Kingsgate Press, 1954.

Barth, Karl, *The Epistle to the Romans*, trans. from the 6th edn by Edwyn C. Hoskyns, London: OUP, 1933.

—, *Church Dogmatics*, III. *The Doctrine of Creation*, Parts 1-4, Edinburgh: T. & T. Clark, 1958.

Bartlet, J. Vernon, Obituary of John Massie, *Mansfield College Magazine*, XII no. 9, December 1925, 219-225.

Bateman, C. T., *R. J. Campbell, M.A., Pastor of the City Temple, London*, London: S. W. Partridge, 1903.

Beck, Lewis White, in *The Routledge History of Philosophy*, eds R. C. Solomon and Kathleen Higgins, VI, ch. 1, London: Routledge, 1993.

Bennett, W. H. and Walter F. Adeney, *The Bible Story Re-told for Children*, London: James Clarke, 1899.

—, *The Bible and Criticism*, London: T. C. and E. C. Jack, n.d.

—, *A Biblical Introduction*, 4th rev. edn, New York: Thomas Whitaker, 1907.

Berriman, William, *The Authority of Civil Powers in Matters of Religion asserted and vindicated. A Sermon Preached before the Right Honourable the Lord Mayor, the Court of Aldermen, and Liveries of the Several Companies of London, in the Parish Church of St. Lawrence Jewry, on Saturday Sept, 29, 1722. Being the Day of Election of a Lord Mayor for the Year ensuing*, London: J. Bettenham for T. Payne, 1722.

—, *Some Brief Remarks on Mr. Chandler's Introduction to the History of the Inquisition: so far as it relates to the Cause of Arianism, and the Two First General Councils: in which His gross Misrepresentations of Fact are detected and exposed. Together with a Reply to his Calumnies against Archbishop Laud*, London: T. Ward and A. Wicksteed, 1733.

—, *A Review of the Remarks on Mr. Chandler's Introduction to the History of the Inquisition: in which His Answer to the said Remarks is consider'd; His Misrepresentations of Fact are farther laid open; and his Prevarications in Defence of them exposed*, London: T. Ward and E. Wicksteed, 1733.

Bevans, S., *John Oman and his Doctrine of God*, Cambridge: CUP, 1992.

Binfield, Clyde, 'Chapels in crisis. Men and issues in Victorian Eastern England,' CHST, XX no. 8, October 1968, 237-254.

—, *So Down to Prayers. Studies in English Nonconformity 1780-1920*, London: J. M. Dent, 1977.

—, ed., *The Cross and the City. Essays in Commemoration of Robert William Dale 1829-1895*, Supplement to JURCHS, VI (Supplement 2) and *The Congregational History Circle Magazine*, IV (Supplement no. 1), Spring 1999.

Blanshard, Brand, *The Nature of Thought*, London: Allen & Unwin, 1939.

Blaxill, E. Alec, *History of Lion Walk Congregational Church, Colchester 1642-1937*, privately printed, 1938.

Blomfield, W. E., 'Memorial' of T. V. Tymms, *Baptist Handbook*, London: The Baptist Union Publication Department, 1922, 274.

Bocking, Ronald, 'Sydney Cave (1883-1953)—Missionary, Principal, Theologian,' *The Journal of the United Reformed Church History Society*, VII no. 1, October 2002, 36-44.

Boethius, *The Consolations of Philosophy*, numerous editions, 524.

Bogue, David and James Bennett, *History of Dissenters from the Revolution in 1688, to the year 1808*, 2nd edn, 2 vols, London: F. Westley and A. H. Davis, 1833.

Bolam, C. Gordon, Jeremy Goring, H. L. Short and Roger Thomas, *The English Presbyterians from Elizabethan Puritanism to Modern Unitarianism*, London: Allen & Unwin, 1968.

Bonhoeffer, Dietrich, *Letters and Papers from Prison*, London: Collins Fontana, 1959.

Bonner, Carey, ed., *The Sunday School Hymnary*, London: The National Sunday School Union, 1905.

Bourn, Samuel, *A Letter to the Revd. Samuel Chandler, D.D. concerning the Christian Doctrine of Future Punishment*, London: R. Griffiths, 1759.

Box, Hubert S., *The World and God*, London: SPCK, 1934.

Braaten, Carl E. and Robert W. Jenson, eds, *Mary, Mother of God*, Grand Rapids: Eerdmans, 2004.

Bradley, F. H. *Principles of Logic*, (1883), London: OUP, 1922.

—, *Appearance and Reality. A Metaphysical Essay*, (1893), Oxford: Clarendon Press, 1930.

Brady, Ignatius, 'The *Summa Theologica* of Alexander of Hales (1924-1948),' *Archivum Franciscanum Historicum*, LXX, 1977, 437-447.

Brewer, J., *A Discourse on The Nature of a Christian Church, by the Rev. J. Brewer; A Charge by the Rev. G. Burder; and a Sermon by the Rev. G. Gill; with the Confession of Faith, &c. Delivered April 8, 1795, at the Public*

Separation of the Rev. Richard Alliott, to the Pastoral Office, in the Independent Church, Castle-Gate, Nottingham, Coventry: M. Luckman, [1795].

Briggs, J. H. Y., *The English Baptists of the 19th Century*, Didcot: The Baptist Historical Society, *1994*.

Brine, John, *A Refutation of Arminian Principles, Delivered in a Pamphlet, intitled, the Modern Question concerning Repentance and Faith, examined with Candour, &c. In a Letter to a Friend*, London: A. Ward, 1743.

Brodrick, James, *The Life and Works of Blessed Francis Robert cardinal Bellarmine, S.J., 1542-1621*, London: Burns, Oates and Washbourne, 2 vols, 1928.

—, *Robert Bellarmine, Saint and Scholar*, London: The Catholic Book Club, 1961.

O. J. Brose, *F. D. Maurice, Rebellious Conformist*, Athens, OH: Ohio University Press, 1971.

Brown, Stuart, ed., *Dictionary of Twentieth-Century British Philosophers*, Bristol: Thoemmes Press, 2005.

Browne, John, *History of Congregationalism and Memorials of the Churches in Norfolk and Suffolk*, London: Jarrold, 1877.

Bruce, A. B., *Apologetics; or, Christianity Defensively Stated*, Edinburgh: T. & T. Clark, 1892.

Bruce, F. F., *In Retrospect: Remembrance of Things Past*, (1980), London: Marshall Pickering, rev. edn., 1993.

Brunner, Emil, *The Theology of Crisis*, New York: Scribners, 1929.

—, *The Mediator*, London: Lutterworth, 1934.

—, *The Divine Imperative*, London: Lutterworth, 1937.

—, *Man in Revolt. A Christian Anthropology*, London: Lutterworth, 1939.

—, *The Divine-Human Encounter*, London: SCM Press, 1944.

—, *Justice and the Social Order*, London: Lutterworth, 1945.

—, *The Misunderstanding of the Church*, London: Lutterworth, 1952.

Burder, Henry Forster, *Memoir of the Rev. George Burder*, London: F. Westley and A. H. Davis, 1833.

—, 'Address at the Interment of the Rev. George Payne, LL.D,' in G. Payne, *Lectures on Christian Theology*, q.v., cxxv-cxxix; reprinted in *Evangelical Magazine*, 1848, 415-416.

Burton, John Hill, *The Life and Correspondence of David Hume*, 2 vols, Edinburgh: William Tait, 1846.

Butler, Joseph, *The Analogy of Religion to the Constitution and Course of Nature*, (1736), London: Ward, Lock, n.d.

Cadoux, C. J., *The Case for Evangelical Modernism*, London: Hodder & Stoughton, 1938.

Cailliet, Emile, *Pascal: Genius in the Light of Scripture*, Philadelphia: Westminster Press, 1945.

Calamy, Edmund, *The Principles and Practice of Moderate Nonconformists with Respect to Ordination, Exemplified: In a Sermon preach'd at the Ordination of Mr. John Munckley, January the 19th. 1717. And a Charge given to Mr. James Read, Mr. Henry Read, Mr. Richard Biscoe, Mr. George Smyth, and Mr. S.*

Chandler, after their being Ordain'd, Dec. 19th. 1716. To which is added, A Letter to a Divine in Germany, giving a brief but true Account of the Protestant Dissenters in England, London: John Clark, 1717.

—, *An Historical Account of My Own Life, with some Reflections on the Times in which I have Lived*, ed. J. T. Rutt, 2 vols., London: H. Colburn and R. Bentley, 1829.

Calder, James M., 'Our President-elect. The Rev. Principal Charles S. Duthie, MA, BD,' *The Scottish Congregationalist*, June 1951.

Calvin, John, *Institutes*, trans. Ford Lewis Battles, ed. J. T. McNeil, Philadelphia: Westminster Press, 2 vols, 1961.

Cameron, Nigel M. deS., ed., *Dictionary of Scottish Church History and Theology*, Edinburgh: T. & T. Clark, 1993.

Campbell, John McLeod, *The Nature of the Atonement and its relation to Remission of Sins and Eternal Life*, London: Macmillan, 2nd edn, 1867.

Campbell, R. J., 'The aim of the New Theology movement,' *The Hibbert Journal*, V, 1907, 481-493.

Carlile, J. C., *C. H. Spurgeon*, London: Kingsgate, 1933.

—, *A Spiritual Pilgrimage*, London: Williams and Norgate, 1916.

Carpenter, J. Estlin, *James Martineau, Theologian and Teacher*, London: Green, 1905.

Cassirer, H. W., *Kant's First Critique. An Appraisal of the Permanent Significance of Kant's Critique of Pure Reason*, London: Allen & Unwin, 1954.

Cave, Sydney, *The Doctrine of the Work of Christ*, London: University of London Press, 1937.

Chandler, Mary, *A Description of Bath. A Poem. With Several other Poems*, 6th edn, London: James Leake, 1744.

Charles, R. H., 'Eschatology,' in *Encyclopaedia Biblica*, eds T. K. Cheyne and J. Sutherland Black, London: A. and C. Black, 1899, II, cols 1335-1390.

Charnock, Stephen, *Several Discourses on the Existence and Attributes of God*, London, 1682. Reprinted Grand Rapids: Sovereign Grace Publishers, 1971.

T. Christensen, *The Divine Order. A Study in F. D. Maurice's Theology*, Leiden: Brill, 1973.

Clark, Henry W., *The Cross and the Eternal Order. A Study of the Atonement in its Cosmic Significance*, London: Lutterworth, 1943.

Clark, Joseph, *A Full and Particular Reply to Mr. Chandler's Case of Subscription to Explanatory Articles of Faith*, London: W. Innys, 1749.

Cleal, Edward E., *The Story of Congregationalism in Surrey*, London: James Clarke, 1908.

Clemance, Clement, *Funeral Services for the Rev. R. Alliott ... Address delivered at the General Cemetery, Nottingham, December 28, 1863, by the Rev. C. Clemance ... Sermon delivered ... January 3, 1864, with a Sketch, by the Rev. G. B. Johnson*, London: Hamilton, Adams, [1864].

Clements, Keith, Review of Alan P. F. Sell, *Nonconformist Theology in the Twentieth Century*, in *The Ecumenical Review*, LXI no. 4, October 2007, 564-5.

Cleobury, F. H., *God, Man and the Absolute*, London: Hutchinson, 1947.

Cliff, Philip B., *The Rise and Development of the Sunday School Movement in England 1780-1980*, Nutfield, Surrey: Christian Education Council, 1986.

Collingwood, R. G., *An Essay on Metaphysics*, Oxford: Clarendon Press, 1940.

Collins, Anthony, *A Discourse of the Grounds and Reasons of the Christian Religion*, London, 1724.

—, *The Scheme of Literal Prophecy Considered; in view of the Controversy, occasion'd by a Late book, intitled, A Discourse of the Grounds and Reasons of the Christian Religion. Vol. 1*, London, 1726.

Columbanus, *Sancti Columbani Opera*, trans. G. S. M. Walker, Dublin: Institute for Advanced Studies, 1957.

Cone, Carl B., *Torchbearer of Freedom. The Influence of Richard Price on Eighteenth-Century Thought*, Lexington, KY: University of Kentucky Press, 1952.

Costello, John E., *John Macmurray: A Biography*, Edinburgh: Floris, 2002.

Coster, George Thomas, *Pastors and People: A Centenary Memorial of Fish-Street Congregational Church, Hull*, London: Hodder and Stoughton, [1869].

Cullmann, Oscar, *Christ and Time. The Primitive Christian Conception of Time and History*, London: SCM Press, 1951.

Cunliffe, Christopher, ed., *Joseph Butler's Moral and Religious Thought*, Oxford: Clarendon Press, 1992.

Cunningham, William, *Historical Theology. A Review of the Principal Doctrinal Discussion in the Christian Church since the Apostolic Age*, (1862), 2 vols, London: The Banner of Truth Trust, 1960.

D. S., 'Principal Duthie's latest honour,' *The Scottish Congregationalist*, April 1952, 85.

Dale, A. W. W., *The Life of R. W. Dale of Birmingham*, London: Hodder and Stoughton, 1899.

Dale, R. W., *The Doctrine of the Atonement*, London: Hodder and Stoughton, 1875.

—, 'Memoir' of Henry Rogers prefixed to the 8th edn on the latter's *The Superhuman Origin of the Bible*, London: Hodder and Stoughton, 1893.

Dalgarno, Melvin T. and Eric Matthews, eds., *The Philosophy of Thomas Reid*, Dordrecht: Kluwer, 1989.

Daniel, Curt, 'John Gill and Calvinistic Antinomianism,' in Michael A. G. Haykin, ed., *The Life and Thought of John Gill (1697-1771). A Tercentennial Appreciation*, Leiden: Brill, 1997, 171-190.

D'Arcy, M. C., *The Pain of This World and the Providence of God*, London: Longmans, Green, 1935.

Darwent, C. E., *The Story of Fish Street Church, Hull*, London: William Andrews, 1899.

Davidson, Anne J., ed., *The Autobiography and Diary of Samuel Davidson*, Edinburgh: T. & T. Clark, 1899.

Davidson, Samuel, *An Introduction to the New Testament; containing an examination of the most important questions relations to the authority, interpretation, and integrity of the canonical books, with reference to the latest enquiries*, 3 vols, London: Samuel Bagster, 1848-51. Reprinted in two vols by Longmans Green in 1882, and by Kegan Paul, Trench, Trübner, 1894.

—, *The Text of the Old Testament considered; with a Treatise on Sacred Interpretation, and a brief Introduction to the Old Testament Books and the Apocrypha*, London: Longmans, Brown, Green, Longmans & Roberts, 1856.

—, *Facts, Statements, and Explanations*, London: Longman, Brown, Green, Longmans & Roberts, 1857.

Davies, Benjamin, *Israel's Testament. A Sermon preached at Haberdashers' Hall, London, on account of the much lamented Death of The Rev. Thomas Gibbons, D.D. Who departed this Life Feb. 22. 1785. By B. Davies*, London, 1785.

Davies, David, *Jesus of Nazareth the Son of Joseph. A Sermon preached on Christmas Day, 1808, at the Unitarian Chapel, Belper, Derbyshire*, Belper: S. Mason, 1809.

—, *Letters on the Miraculous Conception. A Vindication of the Doctrine maintained in a Sermon, preached at Belper, in Derbyshire; in Answer to the Rev. Mr. Alliott, and the Rev. Mr. Taylor*, Belper: S. Mason, 1809.

Davies, Rupert, 'The people called Methodists. 1. Our doctrines,' in Rupert Davies and Gordon Rupp, eds, *A History of the Methodist Church in Great Britain*, London: Epworth Press, 1965, 145-179.

Davies, William, *The Tewkesbury Academy with Sketches of its Tutor and Students*, Tewkesbury: W. J. Gardner, n.d.

Davis, Arthur Paul, *Isaac Watts, His Life and Works*, London: Independent Press, 1943.

De Burgh, W. G., *Towards a Religious Philosophy*, London: Macdonald & Evans, 1937.

Denney, James, *The Death of Christ*, London: Hodder and Stoughton, 1902.

Dewey, John, *Logic. The Theory of Enquiry*, London: Allen & Unwin, 1938.

Dibelius, M. F., *From Tradition to Gospel*, London: Ivor Nicholson and Watson, 1934.

Dickie, John, *Fifty Years of British Theology*, Edinburgh: T. & T. Clark, 1937, ch. 2.

Dillistone, F. W., *C. H. Dodd, Interpreter of the New Testament*, London: Hodder and Stoughton, 1977.

Dix, Kenneth, *Strict and Particular. English Strict and Particular Baptists in the Nineteenth Century*, Didcot: The Baptist Historical Society for the Strict Baptist Historical Society, 2001.

[Doddridge, Philip], *Free Thoughts on the Most Probable Means of Reviving the Dissenting Interest. Occasion'd by the late Enquiry into the Causes of its Decay.*

Addressed to the Author of that Enquiry. By a Minister in the Country, London: Richard Hett, 1730.

Dodds, E. R., *Proclus, The Elements of Theology*, London: OUP, 1963.

Donnelly, D., A. Denaux and J. Famerée, *The Holy Spirit, the Church, and Christian Unity. Proceedings of the Consultation held at the Monastery of Bose, Italy (14-20 October 2002)*, Leuven: Peeters, 2005.

Dorner, I. A., *History of the Development of the Doctrine of the Person of Christ*, trans. J. L. Alexander and D. W. Simon, 5 vols., Edinburgh: Clark, 1859, etc.

—, *Divine Immutability—A Critical Reconsideration*, trans. Robert R. Williams and Claude Welch, Minneapolis: Fortress Press, 1994.

Drummond, James, *Studies in Christian Doctrine*, London: Philip Green, 1908.

Drummond, James and Upton, C.B., *The Life and Letters of James Martineau*, 2 vols, London: Nisbet, 1902.

Drysdale, A. H., *History of the Presbyterians in England*, London: Publications Committee of the Presbyterian Church of England, 1889.

Duff, Archibald, 'A theological college professor's training in the nineteenth century,' *The Congregational Quarterly*, XIV, 1936, 302-314.

Duncan-Jones, Austin, *Butler's Moral Philosophy*, Harmondsworth: Penguin Books, 1952.

Duthie, Robert, *A Northern Light. The Story of the Mid Street Congregational Church in Fraserburgh*, Banff, 1947.

Dyson, Mrs., *The Story of Christ and His People*, I, London: Council of the Congregational Young People's Union, 1897.

Easton, Burton Scott, *The Apostolic Tradition of Hippolytus*, Cambridge: CUP, 1934.

Eddy, G. T., *Dr. Taylor of Norwich. Wesley's Arch-heretic*, Peterborough: Epworth Press, 2003.

Ella, George M., *John Gill and the Cause of God and Truth*, Eggleston, Co. Durham: Go Publications, 1995.

Ellis, John J., *Charles Haddon Spurgeon*, London: Nisbet, n.d.

Ellis, Robert, *Living Echoes of the Welsh Revival 1904-5*, London: The Delyn Press, n.d.

Evans, E. Keri, *My Spiritual Pilgrimage*, London: James Clarke, 1961.

Evans, George Eyre, *Vestiges of Protestant Dissent. Being Lists of Ministers, Sacramental Plate, Registers, Antiquities, and other Matters pertaining to most of the Churches (and a few others) included in the National Conference of Unitarian, Liberal Christian, Free Christian, Presbyterian, and other Non-subscribing or Kindred Congregations*, Liverpool: F. & E. Gibbons, 1897.

Ewing, A. C., 'The necessity of Metaphysics,' in H. D. Lewis, ed., *Contemporary British Philosophy. Personal Statements*, London: Allen & Unwin, 1956, 141-164.

Ewing, Greville and George Payne, *A Collection of Hymns from the Best Authors, Adapted both for Public and Family Worship*, Glasgow: The University Press, 1814.

Fairbairn, *The Place of Christ in Modern Theology*, London: Hodder and Stoughton, 1893.
—, 'James Martineau,' *The Contemporary Review*, LXXXIII, 1903, 1-10.
—, *The Philosophy of the Christian Religion*, London: Hodder and Stoughton, 1902.
Farmer, H. H., *The Servant of the Word*, London: Nisbet, 1941.
Farrer, Austin M., *Finite and Infinite. A Philosophical Essay*, London: Dacre Press, 1943.
—, *The Glass of Vision*, London: Dacre Press, 1948.
Fergusson, David A. S., *John Macmurray: The Idea of the Personal*, Edinburgh: The Handsel Press, 1992.
Fergusson, David A. S. and Nigel Dower, eds, *John Macmurray: Critical Perspectives*, New York: Peter Lang, 2002.
Ferré, Nels F. S., *The Living God of Nowhere and Nothing*, London: Epworth, 1966.
Flannery, Austin, *Vatican Council II. The Conciliar and Post Conciliar Documents*, Collegeville, MN: Liturgical Press, 1975.
Fletcher, Joseph, Jr., *The Select Works and Memoirs of the Late Rev. Joseph Fletcher, D.D.*, 3 vols, London: John Snow, 1846.
Fletcher, Joseph, *Situation Ethics: The New Morality*, London: SCM Press, 1966.
Flint, Robert, *History of the Philosophy of History*, Edinburgh: Blackwood, 1893.
Forsyth, P. T., 'Dr. Martineau,' *The London Quarterly Review*, XCIII, 1900, 214-250.
—, *The Cruciality of the Cross*, (1909), London: Independent Press, 1948.
—, *The Work of Christ*, (1910), London: Independent Press, 1958.
—, *The Justification of God*, (1916), London: Independent Press, 1953.
—, *The Person and Place of Jesus Christ*, (1909), London: Independent Press, 1961.
—, *The Church and the Sacraments*, (1917), London: Independent Press, 1947.
Fraser, A. Campbell, *Thomas Reid*, Edinburgh: Oliphant Anderson and Ferrier, 1898.
Freer, Frederick Ash, *Edward White*, London: Elliot Stock, 1902.
Fuller, Andrew, *The Gospel Worthy of all Acceptation*, Northampton: T. Dicey, 1785.
Fullerton, W. Y., *C. H. Spurgeon. A Biography*, London: Williams & Norgate, 1923.
Garrett, Stephen M., Review of Alan P. F. Sell, *Nonconformist Theology in the Twentieth Century*, in *Reviews in Religion and Theology*, XIV no. 4, September 2007, 602-5.
Garvie, A. E., *The Ritschlian Theology Critical and Constructive. An Exposition and an Estimate*, Edinburgh: T. & T. Clark, 1899.
—, 'Principal Bennett,' *The British Weekly*, 9 September 1920, 442.
—, *Memories and Meanings of My Life*, London: Allen and Unwin, 1938.
Gilbert, J., *Memoir of the Life and Writings of the late Edward Williams, D.D.*, London, 1825.

Gill, John, *The Doctrines of God's Everlasting Love to his Elect, and their Eternal Union with Christ; Together with some other Truths, Stated and Defended, in a Letter to Dr. Abraham Taylor*, in *Sermons and Tracts*, 6 vols (1814), reprinted Choteau, MT: Old Paths Gospel Press, 1997, V, 1-62.

—, *The Cause of God and Truth*, (1735-8), Grand Rapids: Sovereign Grace Publishers, 1971.

—, *The Necessity of Good Works unto Salvation consider'd: Occasioned by some Reflections and Misrepresentations of Mr. (alias Dr.) Abraham Taylor, in a Pamphlet of his lately published, called, An Address to young Students in Divinity, by way of Caution against some Paradoxes which lead to Doctrinal Antinominaism*, London: A. Ward, 1739.

—, *A Body of Divinity*, 2 vols (1769), 1795 edn reprinted Grand Rapids: Baker Book House,1978.

—, *A Dissertation concerning the Eternal Sonship of Christ; shewing by whom it has been Denied and Opposed, and by whom Asserted and Defended in all Ages of Christianity*, in *Sermons and Tracts*, 6 vols (1814), reprinted Choteau, MT: Old Paths Gospel Press, 1997, VI, 178-222.

—, *The Moral Nature and Fitness of Things Considered. Occasioned by some Passages in the Rev. Mr. Samuel Chandler's Sermon, lately preached to the Societiesfor the Reformation of Manners*, in *Sermons and Tracts*, VI, 129-156.

Gilley, Sheridan, *Newman and His Age*, London: Darton, Longman and Todd, 1990.

Gilson, Etienne, *The Unity of Philosophical Experience*, London: Sheed & Ward, 1937.

Glover, Willis B., *Evangelical Nonconformists and Higher Criticism in the Nineteenth Century*, London: Independent Press, 1954.

Godwin, J. H., *Intellectual Principles; or, Elements of mental Science*, London: James Clarke, 1884.

—, *Active Principles; or, Elements of Moral Science*, London: James Clarke, 1885.

Gordon, Alexander, *Freedom After Ejection. A Review (1690-1692) of Presbyterian and Congregational Nonconformity in England and Wales*, Manchester: Manchester University Press, 1917.

—, *Addresses Biographical and Historical*, London: Lindsey Press, 1922.

Gordon, James M., *James Denney (1856-1917). An Intellectual and Contextual Biography*, Milton Keynes: Paternoster, 2006.

Goring, Jeremy, 'The break-up of the Old Dissent,' in C, Gordon Bolam, Jeremy Goring, H. L. Short and Roger Thomas, *The English Presbyterians from Elizabethan Puritanism to Modern Unitarianism*, London: Allen & Unwin, 1968, 175-218.

[Gough, Strickland], *An Enquiry into the Causes of the Decay of the Dissenting Interest. In a Letter to a Dissenting Minister*, London: J. Roberts, 1730.

Gould, Geo. P., *The Baptist College at Regent's Park (Founded at Stepney, 1810). A Centenary Record*, London: The Kingsgate Press for private circulation, 1910.

Grass, Tim, *Gathering to His Name. The Story of the Open Brethren in Britain and Ireland*, Milton Keynes: Paternoster, 2006.

Grave, S. A., *The Scottish Philosophy of Common Sense*, Oxford: Clarendon Press, 1960.

[Grey, Zachary], *English Presbyterian Eloquence, &c. In a Collection of remarkable Flowers of Rhetorick. Humbly inscribed to those two celebrated Historiasters, Mr. Oldmixon, Auth or of the History of the Royal House of Stuart, &c. &c. &c. and Mr. Samuel Chandler, Author of the late History of Persecution. Cum Notis variorum. By an Admirer of Monarchy, and Episcopacy*, London: J. Roberts, 1736.

Grove, Henry, *Ethical and Theological Writings*, ed. and intro., Alan P. F. Sell, Bristol: Thoemmes Press, 6 vols, 2000.

Guyse, John, *Christ, the Son of God, the great subject of a Gospel Ministry, opened and recommended. In Two Sermons Preached at St. Hellen's April 17th and 24th, 1729*, London: Richard Hett, 1729.

—, *The Scripture-notion of preaching Christ further clear'd and vindicated: In a letter to the Reverend Mr. Samuel Chandler, in Answer to one from him to the author. In which Mr. Chandler's charitable Temper, his Treatment of sacred Things, his Misrepresentations, his Notion of preaching Christ, and hi Charge of Uncharitableness, &c. are consider'd*, London: Richard Hett and John Oswald, 1730.

—, *The Reasonableness of believers dying, and the greater advantage they will have by Jesus Christ, as the resurrection and the life, than if they were not to die; with the importance of believing this. Consider'd in a Sermon on John xi. 25, 26. Occasioned by the Death of the late Revd. Mr. John Asty, January 20, 1729/30, aetat. 57. Preached February the 8th, to the Church in Ropemakers-Alley, of which he was Pastor, in answer to his and their desire, and published at their request; with an enlargement which relates to his life and character. To which is added, A Postscript relating to the Reverend Mr. Samuel Chandler's second letter to the author about Preaching Christ, &c.*, London: Richard Hett and John Oswald, 1730.

Haldane, Alexander, *The Lives of Robert and James Haldane*, (1852), Edinburgh: The Banner of Truth Trust, 1990.

Haldane, J. A., *The Doctrine of the Atonement, with Strictures on the Recent Publications of Drs. Wardlaw and Jenkyn. To this edition is added an Appendix containing a Reply to Dr. Payne's Arguments on the Subject*, 2nd edn, Edinburgh, 1847.

Halley, Robert, *Lancashire, Its Puritanism and Nonconformity*, 2 vols, London: Tubbs and Brook, 1896

Hardy, Daniel W. and Colin E. Gunton, *On Being the Church. Essays on the Christian Community*, Edinburgh: T. & T. Clark, 1989.

Harnack, A., *History of Dogma*, London: Williams & Norgate, 7 vols, 1894-1899.

Harris, John, *The Importance of an Educated Ministry: A Discourse preached preparatory to the Opening of Lancashire Independent College*, [1843].

Harrison, F. M. W., *The Life and Thought of the Baptists of Nottinghamshire. With special reference to the period 1770-1914*, unpublished MPhil thesis, University of Nottingham, 1972.

Hart, Joseph, *Hymns Composed on Various Subjects, with the Author's Experience, the Supplement and Appendix*, Cranbrook: J. T. Dennett, 1871.

Hart, Trevor, ed., *Justice the True and Only Mercy. Essays on the Life and Thought of P. T. Forsyth*, Edinburgh: T. & T. Clark, 1995.

—, *The Dictionary of Historical Theology*, Carlisle: Paternoster, 2000.

Harvest, George, *A Letter to Mr. Samuel Chandler: Being a Defense of the Church of England's requiring Subscription to Explanatory Articles of Faith*, London: M. Cooper, 2nd edn [1748].

Hastings, James, *Dictionary of the Bible*, 5 vols. Edinburgh: T. & T. Clark, 1898-1904.

—, *Dictionary of Christ and the Gospels*, 2 vols., Edinburgh: T. & T. Clark, 1906.

Hayden, Roger, 'The contribution of Bernard Foskett,' in William H. Brackney and Paul S. Fiddes, eds, *Pilgrim Pathways. Essays in Baptist History in Honour of B. R. White*, Macon, GA: Mercer University Press, 1999, 189-206.

—, *Continuity and Change. Evangelical Calvinism among Eighteenth-century Baptist Ministers trained at Bristol Academy, 1690-1791*, Chipping Norton: Nigel Lynn for the author and the Baptist Historical Society, 2006.

Hayes, John H., ed., *Dictionary of Biblical Interpretation*, Nashville: Abingdon, 1999.

Haykin, Michael A. G., *At the Pure Fountain of Thy Word. Andrew Fuller as an Apologist*, Carlisle: Paternoster, 2004.

Hazlitt, William, *A Sermon on Human Immortality, preached at Marshfield, Gloucestershire, the 18th of May 1766. Occasioned by the much lamented Death of the late Reverend and Learned Samuel Chandler, D.D. Who departed this Life the 8th of May, 1766, in the 72d Year of his Age*, Bristol: T. Cadell, [1766].

Healey, F. G., *Religion and Reality: The Theology of John Oman*, Edinburgh: Oliver & Boyd, 1965.

Healey, F. G., ed., *Prospect for Theology. Essays in Honour of H. H. Farmer*, Welwyn: Nisbet, 1966.

Hebert, A. G., *Grace and Nature*, London: Church Literature Association, 1937.

Hegel, G. W. F., *The Science of Logic*, trans. A. V. Miller, Amherst, NY: Humanity Books, 1999.

Henderson, A. R., *History of Castle Gate Congregational Church Nottingham, 1655-1905*, London: James Clarke, 1905.

Hepburn, Ronald W., *Christianity and Paradox*, London: Watts, 1958.

Herzog, Johann Jakob, *Realencyklopädie für protestantische Theologie und Kirche*, Hamburg: R. Besser, 1854-68.

Heywood Thomas, John, 'Kierkegaard's alternative metaphysical theology,' *History of European Ideas*, XII no. 1, 1990, 53-63.

Hick, John, 'A philosopher criticizes theology,' *The London Quarterly and Holborn Review*, 1962, 103-110.

Hicks, F. C. N., *The Fullness of Sacrifice: An Essay in Reconciliation*, London: Macmillan, 1930.

Hicks, G. Dawes, *The Philosophical Bases of Theism*, London: Allen & Unwin, 1937.

—, *Critical Realism. Studies in the Philosophy of Mind and Nature*, London: Macmillan, 1938.

Hodges, H. A., *Christianity and the Modern World View*, London: SCM Press, 1949.

Holtby, R. T., *Daniel Waterland, 1683-1740. A Study in Eighteenth-Century Orthodoxy*, Carlisle: Charles Thurman, 1966.

Hood, Adam, *Baillie, Oman and Macmurray: Experience and Religious Belief*, Aldershot: Ashgate, 2003.

Hopkins, Mark, *Nonconformity's Romantic Generation. Evangelical and Liberal Theologies in Victorian England*, Milton Keynes: Paternoster, 2004.

Hornby, G. G., 'Victoria Park and Ranmoor Colleges, in W. Bardsley Brash, *The Story of Our Colleges 1835-1935. A Centenary Record of Ministerial Training in the Methodist Church*, London: Epworth Press, 1935, ch.12.

Horne, T. H., *An Introduction to the Critical Study and Knowledge of the Sacred Scriptures*, 3 vols, London 1818-1821.

Horrocks, Don, *Laws of the Spiritual Order. Innovation and Reconstruction in the Soteriology of Thomas Erskine of Linlathen*, Carlisle: Paternoster, 2004.

Houlden, Leslie, 'Education in theology: story and prospects,' *Theology*, CXI no. 861, May-June 2008, 170-177.

Howe, John, *The Works of John Howe, M.A., Sometime Fellow of Magdalen College, Oxon*, ed. Henry Rogers, London: The Religious Tract Society, 1862-3.

Hughes, T. Hywel, *The Atonement. Modern Theories of the Doctrine*, London: Allen & Unwin, 1949.

Hurrion, John, *The Scripture Doctrine of the proper Divinity of Christ, real Personality, and the external and extraordinary Works of the Holy Spirit*, 1734.

Hussey, Joseph, *God's Operations of Grace but no Offers of Grace*, 91707), Elon College, NC: Primitive Publications, [1973].

Huxtable, John, *The Bible Says*, London: SMP Press, 1962.

—, *As it Seemed to Me*, London: The United Reformed Church, 1990.

Jackson, A. W., *James Martineau. A Biography and Study*, London: Longmans, Green, 1900.

James, T. S., *The History of the Litigation and Legislation respecting Presbyterian Chapels and Charities in England and Ireland*, London: Hamilton Adams, 1867.

Jenkins, Daniel T., *The Nature of Catholicity*, London: Faber & Faber, 1942.

—, *The Gift of Ministry*, London: Faber & Faber, 1947.

—, *Congregationalism: A Restatement*, London: Faber & Faber, 1954.

Jennings, David, *An Introduction to the use of the Globes and the Orrery: With the Application of Astronomy to Chronology*, London, 1739.

—, *A Sermon Occasioned by the Death of the late Reverend Isaac Watts, D.D. Preached to the Church of which he was Pastor. December 11, 1748. ... To which is added the Funeral Oration at his Interment. By Samuel Chandler*, London: J. Oswald, W. Dilly, J. Buckland and E. Gardner, 2nd edn 1769.

—, *Jewish Antiquities: or a Course of Lectures on the Three First Books of Godwin's Moses and Aaron. To which is annexed, a Dissertation on the Hebrew Language*, [ed. P. Furneaux], London: 2 vols, 1766.

Jeremy, Walter D., *The Presbyterian Fund and Dr. Daniel Williams's Trust: with Biographical Notes of the Trustees, and some Account of their Academies, Scholarships and Schools*, London: Williams and Norgate, 1885.

John Paul II, *Ut Unum Sint. Encyclical Letter of the Holy Father ... on Commitment to Ecumenism*, London: Catholic Truth Society, 1995.

Johnson, Dale A., 'The end of the "Evidences": a study in Nonconformist theological transition,' *The Journal of the United Reformed Church History Society*, II no. 3, April 1979, 62-72.

—, *The Changing Shape* of *English Nonconformity 1825-1925*, New York: OUP, 1999.

Johnson, G. B. 'Sketch' of Alliott, see under Clemance, Clement.

Johnson, Mark D., *The Dissolution of Dissent, 1850-1918*, New York: Garland Publishing, 1987.

Johnstone, J. Charteris, 'The story of the Western College,' *Congregational Historical Society Transactions*, VII, 1916-1918, 98-109.

Jones, J. A., ed., *Bunhill Memorials. Sacred Reminiscences of Three Hundred Ministers and other Persons of Note, Who are Buried in Bunhill Fields, of every Denomination*, London: James Paul, 1849.

Jones, Lindsay, ed., *Encyclopedia of Religion*, 2nd edn, Detroit, MI: Thomson Gale, 2005.

Jones, William, *Memoirs of the Life, Studies, and Writings of George Horne, late Bishop of Norwich*, London, 1809.

Julian, John, ed., *A Dictionary of Hymnology*, revised edn with Supplement, London: John Murray, 1907.

Kant, I., *Critique of Pure Reason*, trans. Norman Kemp Smith, (1929), London: Macmillan, 1976.

—, *Religion within the Limits of reason Alone*, trans. and intro. Theodore M. Greene and Hoyt H. Hudson, Chicago: Open Court, 1934.

—, *Critique of Judgment*, trans. and intro. by Werner S. Pluhar, Indianapolis: Hackett, 1987.

—, *Critique of Practical Reason*, trans. and ed. Werner S. Pluhar, Indianapolis: Hackett, 2002.

Kasper, Walter, 'The light of Christ and the Church,' *Irish Theological Quarterly*, LXXII no. 4, 2007, 350-355.

Kaye, Elaine, *C. J. Cadoux: Theologian, Scholar, Pacifist*, Edinburgh: Edinburgh University Press, 1988.

—, *Mansfield College Oxford. Its Origin, History and Significance*, Oxford: OUP, 1996.

—, *For the Work of Ministry. A History of Northern College and its Predecessors*, Edinburgh: T. & T. Clark, 1999.

Kelly, John, *An Examination of the Facts, Statements and Explanations of the Rev. Dr. Samuel Davidson*, London, 1857.

Ker, Ian, *John Henry Newman: A Biography*, Oxford: Clarendon Press, 1988.

D. Kingdon, 'C. H. Spurgeon and the Down Grade controversy,' in *The Good Fight of Faith*, London: Westminster Conference and Evangelical Press, 1971.

Kingsland, William, *The Gnosis or Ancient Wisdom in the Christian Scriptures*, London: Allen & Unwin, 1937.

Kirk, Brian, *The Taunton Dissenting Academy*, Taunton: Somerset Archaeological and Natural History Society, 2005.

Knight, Margaret, *Morals Without Religion, and Other Essays*, London: Dobson, 1951.

Kraemer, Hendrik, *The Christian Message in a Non-Christian World*, London: Edinburgh House Press, 1938.

—, *Religion and the Christian Faith*, London: Lutterworth, 1956.

—, *World Cultures and World Religions: The Coming Dialogue*, London: Lutterworth, 1962.

Kruppa, Patricia Stallings, *Charles Haddon Spurgeon: A Preacher's Progress*, New York: Garland, 1982.

Langer, Suzanne K., *An Introduction to Symbolic Logic*, London: Allen & Unwin 1937.

Larsen, Timothy, 'Honorary doctorates and the Nonconformist ministry in nineteenth-century England,' in David Bebbington and Timothy Larsen, eds, *Modern Christianity and Cultural Aspirations*, London: Sheffield Academic Press, 2003, 139-156.

Lavington, John, *An Humble Enquiry into the Nature of the Gospel-Offer, Faith, and Assurance, Occasioned by some late Writings on these Subjects*, London, 1759.

Lea, John, 'The Davidson controversy,' *Durham University Journal*, LXVIII, 1975, 15-32.

Leff, Gordon, *Medieval Thought. St. Augustine to Ockham*, Harmondsworth: Penguin, 1958.

Lehrer, K., *Thomas Reid*, London: Routledge, 1989.

Leland, John, *A View of the Principal Deistical Writers that have Appeared in England in the last and present Century; with Observations upon them, and some Account of the Answers that have been published against them. In several Letters to a Friend*, (1754), London: R. and J. Dodsley; T. Longman, 1766.

Lewis, F. Warburton, *The Work of Christ*, London: Epworth Press, 1942.

Lidgett, John Scott, *The Spiritual Principle of the Atonement as a Satisfaction made to God for the Sins of the World*, London: Charles H. Kelly, 1897.

—, *My Guided Life*, London: Methuen, 1936.

Light, A. W., *Bunhill Fields*, London: C. J. Farncombe, 2 vols., 1913, 1933.

Locke, John, *An Essay concerning Human Understanding*, ed. Peter H. Nidditch, Oxford: Clarendon Press, 1975.
—, *A Paraphrase and Notes on the Epistles of St. Paul*, ed. and intro., Arthur W. Wainwright, Oxford: Clarendon Press, 2 vols, 1987.
Lofthouse, W. F., *F. H. Bradley*, London: Epworth Press, 1949.
Lusty, F. C., *Walgrave Baptist Church 1700-1950*, Northampton: Billingham, 1950.
Lynch, Thomas T., *Hymns for Heart and Voice: The Rivulet. A Contribution to Sacred Song*, London: Longman, Brown, Green and Longmans, 1856
McCurdy, Leslie, 'P. T. Forsyth bibliography,' in Trevor Hart, ed., *Justice the True and Only Mercy*, q.v.
McGiffert, A. C., *A History of Christianity in the Apostolic Age*, Edinburgh: T. & T. Clark, 1897.
M'Hardy, George, *Historical Sketch of the Scottish Congregational Theological Hall 1811-1911*, Edinburgh: Morrison and Gibb, 1911.
Mackennal, Alexander, *Early Independents. Six Tracts written to commemorate the Tercentenary of the Martyrdoms of Greenwood, Barrowe, and Penry in 1593*, London: Congregational Union of England and Wales, 1893.
—, *Sketches in the Evolution of Congregationalism*, London: Nisbet, 1901.
McKim, Donald K., ed., *Dictionary of Major Biblical Interpreters*, Downers Grove, IL: InterVarsity Press, 2007.
Mackintosh, H. R., *The Doctrine of the Person of Jesus Christ*, Edinburgh: T. & T. Clark, 1912.
—, *The Christian Experience of Forgiveness*, London: Nisbet, 1927.
—, *Types of Modern Theology*, London: Nisbet, 1937.
Mackintosh, Robert, *Essays Towards a New Theology*, Glasgow: Maclehose, 1889.
—, 'The fact of the atonement,' *The Expository Times*, XIV, 1902-3, 344-350.
—, *Christianity and Sin*, London: Duckworth, 1913.
—, *Historic Theories of Atonement with Comments*, London: Hodder and Stoughton, 1920.
—, Discussion of a paper by R. S. Franks on 'The Person of Christ,' *The Congregational Quarterly*, X, 1932, 38-42.
McLachlan, Herbert, *English Education under the Test Acts*, Manchester: Manchester University Press, 1931.
—, 'Bridgwater Academy, 1688-1756?' UHST, III, 1945, 93-6.
—, *Essays and Addresses*, Manchester: Manchester University Press, 1950.
Macmillan, Donald, *The Life of Robert Flint*, London: Hodder and Stoughton, 1914.
Macmurray, John, *Search for Reality in Religion*, London: Quaker Home Service, 1965.
—, *The Self as Agent*, London: Faber, 1969.
—, *Persons in Relation*, London: Faber, 1970.
McNaughton, William D., *The Scottish Congregational Ministry 1794-1993*, Glasgow: The Congregational Union of Scotland, 1993.

—, *Early Congregational Independency in the Highlands and Islands and the North-East of Scotland*, Tiree: The Trustees of Ruaig Congregational Church, 2003.

—, *Early Congregational Independency in Lowland Scotland*, Glasgow: The Congregational Federation in Scotland, 2 vols, 2005, 2007.

McCrea, Alexander, *The Work of Jesus in Christian Thought*, London: Epworth Press, 1939.

Mander, William J. and Alan P. F. Sell, eds, *Dictionary of Nineteenth-Century British Philosophers*, Bristol: Thoemmes Press, 2002.

Manning, Bernard Lord, *Essays in Orthodox Dissent*, (1939), London: Independent Press, 1953.

Marcel, Gabriel, *The Mystery of Being*, vol. 2: *Faith and Reality*, London: Harvill Press, 1951.

Marchant, James, ed., *The Future of Christianity*, London: John Murray, 1927.

Marck, Johannes (Markius), *Christianae theologiae medulla*, Amsterdam, 1721.

Maritain, Jacques, *A Preface to Metaphysics*, London: Sheed & Ward, 1939.

Marsh, John B., *The Story of Harecourt. Being the History of an Independent Church*, London: Strahan, 1871.

Martin C. B., 'A religious way of knowing,' in A. G. N. Flew and A. MacIntrye, eds, *New Essays in Philosophical Theology*, London: SCM Press, 1955, 76-95.

Martin, George Currie, 'Walter F. Adeney. An appreciation,' *The Christian World*, 9 September 1920, 3.

Matthews, A. G., *Calamy Revised. Being a Revision of Edmund Calamy's* Account *of the Ministers and Others Ejected and Silences, 1660-2*, (1934), Oxford: Clarendon Press, 1988.

Maurice, J. Frederick, ed., *The Life of Frederick Denison Maurice, Chiefly Told in His Own Letters*, 2 vols, London: Macmillan 1884.

Medway, John, *Memoirs of the Life and Writings of John Pye Smith*, London, 1853.

Mellone, S. H., 'James Martineau as an ethical teacher,' *International Journal of Ethics*, X, 1899-1900, 380-386.

Miall, James G., *Congregationalism in Yorkshire. A Chapter of Modern Church History*, London: John Snow, 1868.

Micklem, Nathaniel, *Reason and Revelation: A Question from Duns Scotus*, London: Nelson, 1953.

—, *The Box and the Puppets*, London: Geoffrey Bles, 1957.

Micklem, Nathaniel, ed., *Arnold Thomas of Bristol. Collected Papers and Addresses. With a Memoir by Nathaniel Micklem*, London: Allen & Unwin, 1925.

Mill, John Stuart, *Three Essays on Religion*, in *Collected Works of John Stuart Mill*, X, *Essays on Ethics, Religion and Society*, ed. J. M. Robson, Toronto: University of Toronto Press, and London: Routledge & Kegan Paul, 1969.

Millar, David, *Useful and Important Answers freely given, to Useful and Important Questions, Concerning Jesus the Son of God, Freely propos'd: or, A Vindication of the Co-essential Sonship of the Second Person of the Trinity; with an Answer to the learned Roel, Dr. Ridgley, Dr. Anderson, &c.*, London: R. Hett and J. Ward, 1751.

Milner, David, 'The last days at Rawdon and the formation of Northern Baptist College,' in J. H. Y. Briggs, ed., *Bible, Church and World. A Supplement to The Baptist Quarterly published in Honour of Dr. D. S. Russell, Principal of Rawdon College, 1953-64, Joint Principal, Northern College, 1964-67, General Secretary, Baptist Union of Great Britain and Ireland, 1967-82*, London: Baptist Historical Society, 1989.

Mitchell, Basil, *Law, Morality and Religion in a Secular Society*, London: OUP, 1967.

Moberly, R. C., *Atonement and Personality*, London: John Murray, 1907.

Moody, Campbell N., *Christ for Us and Christ in Us*, London: Allen & Unwin, 1935.

Moody, Ernest, *The Logic of William of Ockham*, London: Sheed & Ward, 1935.

Moon, Norman, *Education for ministry. Bristol Baptist College 1679-1979*, published by the College, 1979.

Morden, Peter J., *Offering Christ to the World. Andrew Fuller (1754-1815) and the Revival of Eighteenth-Century Baptist Life*, Carlisle: Paternoster Press, 2003.

Morell, J. D., *Historical and Critical View of the Speculative Philosophy of Europe in the Nineteenth Century*, 2 vols, London, 1846.

Morgan, Thomas, *The Moral Philosopher*, (1743), London:Routledge/Thoemmes, 1995.

—, *A Vindication of the Moral Philosopher; against the False Accusations, Insults, and Personal Abuses, of Samuel Chandler, Late Bookseller, and Minister of the Gospel*, London: T. Cox, 1741.

Morgan, William, *Memoirs of the Life of the Rev. Richard Price, D.D., F.R.S.*, London, 1815.

Morison, Frank, *J. H. Jowett, M.A.,D.D., A Character Study*, London: James Clarke, 1911.

Mozley, J. K., *The Doctrine of the Atonement*, London: Duckworth, 1915.

—, *The Impassibility of God. A Survey of Christian Thought*, Cambridge: CUP, 1926.

Muller, Richard A., *Dictionary of Greek and Latin Theological Terms Drawn Principally from Protestant Scholastic Theology*, Grand Rapids: Baker Book House, 1985.

Murch, Jerom, *A History of the Presbyterian and General Baptist Churches in the West of England; with Memoirs of some of their Pastors*, London: R. Hunter, 1835.

Murray, Iain, *The Forgotten Spurgeon*, London: The Banner of Truth Trust, 1966.

Nettles, Tom J., 'John Gill and the Evangelical Awakening,' in Michael A. G. Haykin, ed., *The Life and Thought of John Gill (1697-1771). A Tercentenary Appreciation*, Leiden: Brill, 1997, ch. 6.

Nightingale, Benjamin, *Lancashire Nonconformity; or, Sketches, Historical & Descriptive, of the Congregational and Old Presbyterian Churches in the*

Country. [II] *The Churches of the Blackburn District*, Manchester: John Heywood, n.d.

—, *The Story of the Lancashire Congregational Union 1806-1906*, Manchester: John Heywood, [1906].

Noake, John, *Worcester Sects; or A History of the Roman Catholics & Dissenters of Worcester*, London: Longman, 1861.

[Noorthouck, John], *The History of the Man after God's own Heart*, London: R. Freeman, 1762.

Nowell-Smith, P. H., *Ethics*, Harmondsworth: Penguin, 1954.

Nuttall, Geoffrey F., 'Northamptonshire and *The Modern Question*: A turning-point in eighteenth-century Dissent,' *The Journal of Theological Studies*, NS XVI, 1965, 101-123.

—, 'Cambridge Nonconformity 1660-1710: from Holcroft to Hussey,' *The Journal of the United Reformed Church History Society*, I no. 9, 1977, 242-258.

—, 'Chandler, Doddridge, and the Archbishop: a study in eighteenth-century ecumenism,' *The Journal of the United Reformed Church History Society*, I no. 2, November 1973, 42-56.

Nuttall, Geoffrey F., ed., *Calendar of the Correspondence of Philip Doddridge DD (1702-1751)*, London: HMSO, 1979.

Obitts, S. R., *The Thought of Robert Flint*, unpublished doctoral dissertation, University of Edinburgh, 1962.

O'Higgins, James, *Anthony Collins, the Man and his Works*, The Hague: Martinus Nijhoff, 1970.

Osborne, Kenan B., 'Alexander of Hales,' in K. B. Osborne, ed., *The History of Franciscan Theology*, St. Bonaventure, NY: The Franciscan Institute, St. Bonaventure University, 1994, 1-38.

Otto, Rudolf, *The Idea of the Holy*, London: OUP, 1924.

Owen, John, *The Works of John Owen*, ed. William H. Goold, (1850-1853), 16 vols., London: The Banner of Truth Trust, 1968.

Owen, W. T., *Edward Williams, D.D.*, Cardiff: University of Wales Press, 1963.

Paley, William, *A View of the Evidences of Christianity*, numerous editions from 1794.

—, *Natural Theology, or. Evidences of the Existence and Attributes of the Deity collected from the Appearances of Nature*, numerous editions from 1802.

Partridge, Christopher H., *H. H. Farmer's Theological Interpretation of Religions*, Lampeter: Edwin Mellen, 1998.

Paul, S. F., *Historical Sketch of the Gospel Standard Baptists*, (1945), London: Gospel Standard Publications, 1961.

Payne, Ernest A., *The Great Succession. Leaders of the Baptist Missionary Society during the Nineteenth Century*, London: Carey Press, 1946.

—, *The Baptist Union. A Short History*, London: The Carey Kingsgate Press, 1958.

—, 'The rise and decline of the Downs Chapel, Clapton,' *The Baptist Quarterly*, XXVII, 1977-8, 34-44.

—, ed., *Studies in History and Religion Presented to Dr. H. Wheeler Robinson, M.A., on his Seventieth Birthday*, London: Lutterworth, 1942.

Peach, W. B. and D. O. Thomas, eds, *The Correspondence of Richard Price*, Cardiff: University of Wales Press, 3 vols, 1983-94.

Peake, A. S., ed., *Inaugural Lectures delivered by Members of the Faculty of Theology during its First Session, 1904-5*, Manchester: Manchester University Press, 1905.

Peel, Albert, *These Hundred Years. A History of the Congregational Union of England and Wales, 1831-1931*, London: Congregational Union of England and Wales, 1931.

—, 'The Autobiography of David Everard Ford,' *Congregational Historical Society Transactions*, XI no. 6, September 1932, 265-279.

Peel, Albert and J. A. R. Marriott, *Ralph Forman Horton*, London: Allen & Unwin, 1937.

Peel, David, 'So last century?—Review article,' *The Journal of the United Reformed History Society*, VIII no. 1, January 2008, 49-54.

Peirce, James, *Plain Christianity Defended. Being an Answer to a Pamphlet lately printed at Exon, intitled Arius Detected and Confuted*, London: J. Noon, 1719.

—, *The Evil and Cure of Divisions. A Sermon preach'd at Exon at the Opening of a New Meeting House, March 15 1718/19, being the first Lord's Day after the Ejectment of the Miinisters*, London: John Clark, 1719.

Peirce, Sarah, *An Account of Mr. Thomas Ridgley, an Independent Minister and Preacher at the Three Cranes in Thames Street, [his] wilful and malicious blaspheming the Work of the Spirit of God in a Member of that Church; and how he and Mr. Peter Pindar, and Mr. Robert Hancock, have labour'd to drive her to Distraction and Despair ... and also how the Sufferer declar'd all this to his Face at Pinners-Hall, before the Ministers, and he did not contradict one word she said*, London: Printed for the Sufferer, 1700.

Penelhum, Terence, *Butler*, London: Routledge & Kegan Paul, 1985.

Pfizenmaier, T. C., *The Trinitarian Theology of Samuel Clarke*, Leiden: Brill, 1997.

Phillips, R. P., *Modern Thomistic Philosophy*, London: Burns, Oates, 1934.

Philpot, J. H., *The True, Proper, and Eternal Sonship of the Lord Jesus Christ, the Only Begotten Son of God*, (1861), Harpenden: Gospel Standard Baptist Trust, 1962.

'Philochristus', *A Letter to the Reverend Mr. Samuel Chandler, Occasioned by his late Discourse, entitled, The Case of Subscription ... impartially considered. Proving that the Qualification for Admission into the Christian Ministry among the Dissenters from the Church of England, and in those Foreign Protestant Churches, who have abolished all Subscriptions, lays the Persons to be ordained, under the same Difficulties and Restraints, as the Subscribing to explanatory Articles of Faith in the Church of England. With some Observations on the ancient Creeds cited by Mr. Chandler*, London: W. Owen, 1748.

Phythian-Adams, W. J., *The People and the Presence. A Study of the Atonement*, London: OUP, 1942.

Plato, *The Republic*, trans. and introd. by F. M. Cornford, Oxford: Clarendon Press, 1941.

Pope, Robert, 'Thomas Hywel Hughes (1875-1945): a forgotten theologian,' *The Journal of Welsh Religious History*, NS V, 2005, 9-35.

Pope, W. B. *The Person of Christ: Dogmatic, Scriptural, Historical*, London: Wesleyan Methodist Book Room, 1885.

Porritt, Arthur, *John Henry Jowett*, London: Hodder and Stoughton, 1924.

Powicke, F. J., *A History of the Cheshire County Union of Congregational Churches. Prepared (to commemorate its Centenary, 1806-1906) at the request of the Executive Committee*, Manchester: Thomas Griffiths, 1907.

—, *David Worthington Simon*, London: Hodder and Stoughton, 1912.

—, 'The Salters' Hall controversy,' CHST, VII no. 2, 1916, 110-124.

—, 'Frederick Denison Maurice (1805-1872), *The Congregational Quarterly*, VIII, 1930, 169-184.

Prantl, Carl, *Geschichte der Logik im Abenlande*, Leipzig, 1855-70.

Prestige, G. L., *God in Patristic Thought*, London: Heinemann, 1936.

Price, Ernest J., 'Dr. Fairbairn and Airedale College: the hour and the man,' *Transactions of the Congregational Historical Society*, XIII no. 3, April 1939, 131-139.

Price, Richard, *A Review of the principal Questions of Morals*, (1758), 3rd edn, 1787, ed. D. Daiches Raphael, Oxford: Clarendon Press, 1948.

Pridham, Amy, *The Story of Christ and His People*, London: Council of the Congregational Young People's Union, 1897.

Priest, Gerald L., 'Andrew Fuller, hyper-Calvinism and the Modern Question,' in Michael A. G. Haykin, ed., *'At the Pure Fountain of Thy Word'. Andrew Fuller as an Apologist*, Carlisle: Paternoster, 2004, 43-73.

Priestley, Joseph, *An History of the Corruptions of Christianity*, (1782), in J. T. Rutt, ed., *The Theological and Miscellaneous Works of Joseph Priestley*, (1817-1832), Bristol: Thoemmes Press, 1999, V.

Pringle-Pattison, A. S., 'Martineau's philosophy,' in idem, *The Philosophical Radicals and Other Essays*, Edinburgh: Blackwood, 1907, 78-107.

—, *The Idea of God in the Light of Recent Philosophy*, New York: OUP, 2nd edn revised, 1920.

Pyer, John, 'Memoir of the Rev. George Payne, LL.D. with notices of his writings,' prefixed to G. Payne, *Lecures on Christian Theology*, q.v., xvii-cxxiv. For Pyer's brief 'Memoir' of Payne prefaced by notes of H. F. Burder's funeral sermon see *Evangelical Magazine*, 1848, 393-398.

Pyle, Andrew, ed., *Dictionary of Seventeenth-Century British Philosophers*, Bristol: Thoemmes Press, 2000.

Quick, Oliver C., *Doctrines of the Creed*, (1938), London: Collins Fontana, 1963.

Raffles, Thomas Stamford, *Memoirs of the Life and Ministry of ... Thomas Raffles*, London, 1864.

Ramsey, A. M., *F. D. Maurice and the Conflict of Modern Theology*, Cambridge: CUP, 1951.

Reed, Andrew, the Elder, and James Matheson, *A Narrative of the Visit to the American Churches by the Deputation from the Congregational Union of England and Wales*, 2 vols, London, 1835.

Rees, David, *Infant Baptism no Institution of Christ; and the Rejection of it justified from Scripture and Antiquity. In Answer to Mr. Fowler Walker's Book, entituled, A Defence of infant Baptism, &c. To which are annex'd Animadversions on the Reverend Dr. Thomas Ridgley's Dissertation on Infant Baptism*, London: Aaron Ward, John Noon, H. Whitridge and Samuel Rogers, 1734.

Reynolds sisters, *Henry Robert Reynolds, D.D. His Life and Letters Edited by his Sisters, with Portraits*, London: Hodder and Stoughton, 1898.

Richard of St. Victor, *La Trinité*, intro., trans. and notes, Gaston Salet, Paris: Éditions du Cerf, 1999.

Riddell, J. G., Review of R. S. Franks, *The Doctrine of the Trinity*, in *The Expository Times*, LXIV, 1952-3, 329.

Rignal, Charles, *Manchester Baptist College 1866-1916. Jubilee Memorial Volume*, Bradford and London: William Byles, [1916].

Ritschl, Albrecht, *The Christian Doctrine of Justification and Reconciliation*, trans. H. R. Mackintosh and A. B. Macaulay, Edinburgh: T. & T. Clark, 1900.

Rivers, Isabel and David L. Wykes, eds, *Joseph Priestley, Scientist, Philosopher, and Theologian*, Oxford: OUP, 2008.

Robb, Nesca A., *Neoplatonism of the Italian Renaissance*, London: Allen & Unwin, 1935.

Robertson, Edwin, 'Brunner, the great,' *The British Weekly*, 14 April 1966, 6.

Robbins, Keith, 'The spiritual pilgrimage of R. J. Campbell,' *Journal of Ecclesiastical History*, XXX, 1979, 261-76.

Robinson, H. Wheeler, *Redemption and Revelation in the Actuality of History*, London: Nisbet, 1942.

Robinson, J. A. T., *Honest to God*, London: SCM Press, 1960.

Robinson, W. Gordon, *A History of the Lancashire Congregational Union 1856-1956*, Manchester: Lancashire Congregational Union, 1956.

Rogers, J. Guinness, *The Church Systems of England in the Nineteenth Century*, London: Hodder and Stoughton, 1881.

—, *J. Guinness Rogers. An Autobiography*, London: James Clarke, 1903.

Rothe, Richard, *Zur Dogmatik*, Gotha, 1863.

Russell, K. P., *Memoirs of the Rev. John Pyer*, London: John Snow, 1865.

Ryle, Gilbert, 'Systematically misleading expressions,' *Proceedings of the Aristotelian Society*, XXXI, 1931, reprinted in A. G. N. Flew, ed., *Logic and Language. First Series*, ch. 2.

—, 'Taking sides in philosophy,' *Philosophy*, XII, July 1937, 317-322.

—, *Philosophical Arguments*, Oxford: Clarendon Press, 1945.

—, *The Concept of Mind*, London: Hutchinson, 1949.

—, 'Ordinary Language,' *The Philosophical Review*, 1953, 167-186.

Sanday, William and Arthur C. Headlam, *A Critical and Exegetical Commentary on the Epistle to the Romans*, Edinburgh: T. & T. Clark, 1895.
Schaff, Philip, *Germany; Its Universities, Theology and Religion*, Philadelphia: Lindsay and Blakiston, 1857.
Schleiermacher, F. D. E., *On Religion. Speeches to its Cultured Despisers*, trans. John Oman, New York: Harper & Row, 1958.
—, *The Christian Faith*, trans. and ed., H. R. Mackintosh and J. S. Stewart, Edinburgh: T. & T. Clark, 1960.
—, *Dialectic, or, The Art of Doing Philosophy: A Study of the 1811 Notes*, trans. and intro. by Terrence N. Tice, Atlanta, GA: Scholars Press, c.1996.
—, *Lectures on Philosophical Ethics*, ed. Robert B. Louden, trans. Louise Adey Huish, Cambridge: CUP, 2002.
Schofield, Robert E., *The Englightenment of Joseph Priestley. A Study of his Life and Work from 1733 to 1773*, University Park, PA: Pennsylvania State University Press, 1997.
—, *The Enlightened Joseph Priestley. A Study of his Life and Work from 1773 to 1804*, University Park, PA: Pennsylvania Statue University Press, 2001.
Schweitzer, Albert, *The Quest of the Historical Jesus. A Critical Study of its Progress from Reimarus to Wrede*, London: Black, 1910.
Scudder, Delton Lewis, *Tennant's Philosophical Theology*, New Haven: Yale University Press and Oxford University Press, 1940.
Selbie, W. B. *The Life of Andrew Martin Fairbairn, DD, DLitt, LL.D, FBA, Etc., First Principal of Mansfield College, Oxford*, London: Hodder and Stoughton, 1914.
Sell, Alan P. F., *Congregationalism at Worplesdon*, privately printed, 1972.
—, 'Friends and Philosophy,' *The Friends' Quarterly*, XVIII nos 2 and 2, April and July 1973, 72-82, 111-122.
—, *Alfred Dye, Minister of the Gospel*, London: The Fauconberg Press, 1974.
—, *Robert Mackintosh, Theologian of Integrity*, Bern: Peter Lang, 1977.
—, *The Great Debate. Calvinism, Arminianism and Salvation*, (1982), reprinted Eugene, OR: Wipf & Stock, 1998.
—, *Church Planting. A Study of Westmorland Nonconformity*, (1986), Eugene, OR: Wipf & Stock, 1998.
—, *Saints: Visible, Orderly and Catholic. The Congregational Idea of the Church*, Geneva: World Alliance of Reformed Churches and Eugene, OR: Wipf & Stock, 1986.
—, *Theology in Turmoil. The Roots, Course and Significance of the Conservative-Liberal Debate in Modern Theology*, (1986), Eugene, OR: Wipf & Stock, 1998.
—, *The Philosophy of Religion 1875-1980*, London: Croom Helm, 1988, reprinted Bristol: Thoemmes Press, 1996.
—, *Dissenting Thought and the Life of the Churches. Studies in an English Tradition*, Lewiston, NY: Edwin Mellen, 1990.
—, Review of M. D. Johnson, *The Dissolution of Dissent*, in *The Baptist Quarterly*, XXXIII no. 5, January 1990, 243-6.

—, *A Reformed, Evangelical, Catholic Theology. The Contribution of the World Alliance of Reformed Churches 1875-1982*, (1991), Eugene, OR: Wipf & Stock, 1998.
—, *Commemorations. Studies in Christian Thought and History*, (1993), reprinted Eugene, OR: Wipf & Stock, 1998.
—, *Philosophical Idealism and Christian Belief*, Cardiff: University of Wales Press and New York: St. Martin's Press, 1995; reprinted Eugene, OR: Wipf & Stock, 2006.
—, Review of T. C. Pfizenmaier, *The Trinitarian Theology of Samuel Clarke*, in *Enlightenment and Dissent*, XVIII, 1999, 270-275.
—, *The Spirit Our Life*, Shippensburg, PA: Ragged Edge Press, 2000.
—, *John Locke and the Eighteenth-Century Divines*, Cardiff: University of Wales Press, 1997; reprinted Eugene, OR: Wipf & Stock, 2006.
—, *Confessing and Commending the Faith. Historic Witness and Apologetic Method*, Cardiff: University of Wales Press, 2002; reprinted Eugene, OR: Wipf & Stock, 2006.
—, *Mill on God. The Pervasiveness and Elusiveness of Mill's Religious Thought*, Aldershot: Ashgate, 2004.
—, *Philosophy, Dissent and Nonconformity 1689-1920*, Cambridge: James Clarke, 2004.
—, *Enlightenment, Ecumenism, Evangel. Theological Themes and Thinkers 1550-2000*, Milton Keynes: Paternoster, 2005.
—, *Testimony and Tradition. Studies in Reformed and Dissenting Thought*, Aldershot: Ashgate, 2005.
—, *Nonconformist Theology in the Twentieth Century*, Milton Keynes: Paternoster, 2006.
—, Review of M. Hopkins, *Nonconformity's Romantic Generation*, in *The Journal of Ecclesiastical History*, LVII no. 4, October 2006, 791-2.
—, 'Confessing the faith in the intellectual context,' *Journal of Reformed Theology*, I no. 2, 2007, 132-152.
—, 'Confessing the faith and confessions of faith,' in Eduardus Van der Borght, ed., *Christian Identity*, q.v., 151-167.
—, 'So last century?—A response,' *The Journal of the United Reformed Church History Society*, VIII no. 1, January 2008, 55-59.
—, 'Conversations with Geoffrey Nuttall,' *The Journal of the United Reformed Church History Society*, forthcoming.
Sell, Alan P. F., ed., *Protestant Nonconformists and the West Midlands of England*, Keele: Keele University Press, 1996.
—, ed., *Mill on God. Contemporary Responses to Three Essays on Religion*, Bristol: Thoemmes Press, 1997.
—, ed., *P. T. Forsyth: Theologian for a New Millennium*, London: The United Reformed Church, 2000.
—, ed. and intro., H. Grove, *Ethical and Theological Writings*, q.v.

Sell, Alan P. F., David J. Hall and Ian Sellers, eds, *Protestant Nonconformist Texts. II. The Eighteenth Century*, Aldershot: Ashgate, 2006.

Sellers, Ian, ed., *Our Heritage. The Baptists of Yorkshire, Lancashire and Cheshire 1647-1987*, Leeds: The Yorkshire and The Lancashire and Cheshire Baptist Associations, 1987.

Shepherd, Peter, *The Making of a Northern Baptist College*, Manchester: Northern Baptist College, 2004.

Shindler, R., *From the Usher's Desk to the Tabernacle Pulpit: The Life and Labours of Pastor C. H. Spurgeon*, London: Passmore and Alabaster, 1892.

Sibree, John and M. Caston, *Independency in Warwickshire; A Brief History of the Independent or Congregational Churches in that County; containing Biographical Notices of their Pastors; with an Illustrative Map and Vignette Engravings*, Coventry: G. and F. King, 1855.

Simms, T. H., *Homerton College 1695-1978. From Dissenting Academy to Approved Society in the University of Cambridge*, Cambridge: The Trustees of Homerton College, 1979.

Skeats, Herbert S. and Charles S. Miall, *History of the Free Churches of England 1688-1891*, London: Alexander & Shepheard and James Clarke, [1891].

Slate, R., *A Brief History of the Rise and Progress of the Lancashire Congregational Union; and of the Blackburn Independent Academy*, London: Hamilton, Adams, 1840.

Slater, W. F., *Matthew* (Century Bible), Edinburgh: Blackwood, 1901.

Smith, Henry, John E. Swallow, and William Treffry, eds, *The Story of the United Methodist Church*, London: Henry Hooks, [1932].

Smith, John Pye, *First Lines of Christian Theology*, London, 1854.

Sortain, B. M., *Memorials of Joseph Sortain*, London: Nisbet, 1861.

Sortain, Joseph, *A Lecture Introductory to the Study of Philosophy, Delivered in Cheshunt College, Herts., November 14, 1838*, London, [1839].

—, *The Life of Francis, Lord Bacon*, London, [1851].

Sparrow-Simpson, W. J., *The Redeemer*, London: Longmans, Green, 1937.

Spencer, Herbert, 'Religion: A retrospect and prospect,' *The Nineteenth Century*, XV, January-June 1884, 1-12.

Srawley, J. H., Review of T. V. Tymms, *The Christian Idea of Atonement*, in *The Journal of Theological Studies*, VI, 1905, 622-624.

Stählin, Leonhard, *Kant, Lotze and Ritschl. A Critical Examination*, Edinburgh: T. & T. Clark, 1889.

Stead, F. Herbert and Walter F. Adeney, *The Story of Christ and His People*, II, London: Council of the Congregational Young People's Union, 1897.

Stell, Christopher, *An Inventory of Nonconformist Chapels and Meeting-houses in Central England*, London: HMSO, 1986.

Stephens, John, 'Samuel Chandler and the *Regium Donum*,' *Enlightenment and Dissent*, IV, 1996, 57-70.

Stevens, George Barker, *The Christian Doctrine of Salvation*, Edinburgh: T. & T. Clark, 1905.

Stevenson, Peter K., *God in Our Nature. The Incarnational Theology of John McLeod Campbell*, Carlisle: Paternoster, 2004.

Stewart, H. F. *Pascal's Apology, extracted from the Pensées*, Cambridge: CUP, 1948.

Summers, W. H., *History of the Congregational Churches in the Berks, South Oxon and South Bucks Association, with Notes on the Earlier Nonconformist History of the District*, London: Publication Department, Memorial Hall, 1905.

Surman, Charles E., *Alexander James Grieve, MA, DD. 1874-1952*, Manchester: Lancashire Independent College, 1953.

Taylor, John, *The Scripture-Doctrine of Original Sin proposed to Free and Candid Examination*, London, 1740.

—, *A Narrative of Mr. Joseph Rawson's Case: or, an Account of several Occurrences relating to the Affair of his being excluded from Communion with the Congregational Church in Nottingham. With a Preface in Defence of the Common Rights of Christians*, [1737], 2nd edn 1742.

Taylor, John H., *The Congregational Fund Board 1695-1995*, a Supplement to *The Congregational History Circle Magazine*, *The Journal of the United Reformed Church History Society*, and *Y Cofiadur, Cylchgrawn Cymdeithas Hanes Annibynwyr Cymru*, 1995.

Taylor, John H. and Clyde Binfield, *Who They Were in the Reformed Churches of England and Wales 1901-2000*, Donington: Shaun Tyas, 2007

Taylor, Richard, *A History of the Union between the Presbyterian and Congregational Ministers in an a round London, and the Causes of the Breach of it*, London, 1698.

—, *A Discourse of Christ as He is a Rock of Salvation*, London, 1701.

—, *The true Scripture Doctrine of Justification, Explained and Vindicated*, London: J. Clark and R. Hett, 1727.

Taylor, Vincent, *Forgiveness and Reconciliation. A Study in New Testament Theology*, London: Macmillan,. 1941.

Temple, William, *Christus Veritas*, London: Macmillan, 1930.

F. R. Tennant, *The Origin and Propagation of Sin*, Cambridge: CUP, 1902.

—, *The Sources of the Doctrines of the Fall and Original Sin*, Cambridge: CUP, 1903.

—, *The Concept of Sin*, Cambridge: CUP, 1912.

Tholuck, F. A., 'Inspiration' in J. J. Herzog, *Realencyclopädie*, q.v.

Thomas Aquinas, *Summa Theologica*, Part I, in Anton C. Pegis, *Basic Writings of Saint Thomas Aquinas*, I, New York: Random House, 2 vols, 1945.

Thomas, D. O., *Richard Price 1723-1791*, Cardiff: University of Wales Press, 1976.

—, *The Honest Mind. The Thought and Work of Richard Price*, Oxford: Clarendon Press, 1977.

Thomas, D. O., ed. and Introduction, William Morgan's *Memoirs*, q.v., in *Enlightenment and Dissent*, XXII, 2003.

Thomas, D. O., John Stephens and P. A. L. Jones, *A Bibliography of the Works of Richard Price*, Aldershot: Scolar, 1993.

Thomas, Roger, 'The non-subscription controversy amongst Dissenters in 1719,' *Journal of Ecclesiastical History*, IV, 1953, 162-186.

Thomas, Roland, *Richard Price, Philosopher and Apostle of Liberty*, London: OUP, 1924.

—, 'Presbyterians in transition,' in C. G. Bolam, *et al*, q.v., ch. 4.

Thompson, David M., *Stating the Gospel: Formulations and Declarations of Faith from the Heritage of The United Reformed Church*, Edinburgh: T. & T. Clark, 1990.

—, *Baptism, Church and Society in Modern Britain. From the Evangelical Revival to Baptism, Eucharist and Ministry*, Milton Keynes: Paternoster, 2005.

Thompson, John Handby, *A History of the Coward Trust. The First Two Hundred and Fifty Years 1738-1988*, Supplement no. 1 to the *Journal of the United Reformed Church History Society*; Supplement no. 2 to *The Congregational History Circle Magazine*, May 1998.

Thompson, Joseph, *The Owens College: Its Foundation and Growth; and its Connection with the Victoria University, Manchester*, Manchester: J. E. Cornish, 1886.

—, *Lancashire Independent College, 1843-1893. Jubilee Memorial Volume*, Manchester: J. E. Cornish, 1893.

[Thorpe, A. F.], *Gusetwick-Briston 1652-1952*, privately printed, [1952].

Tibbutt, H. G., *Bunyan Meeting Bedford 1650-1950*, Bedford: The Trustees of Bunyan Meeting, n.d.

Tillich, Paul, *The Interpretation of History*, New York: Scribners, 1936.

—, *Systematic Theology*, Chicago: Chicago University Press, 3 vols, 1951, 1957, 1963.

—, *Christianity and the Encounter of the World Religions*, New York: Columbia University Press, 1963.

Timpson, Thomas, *Church History in Kent from the Earliest Period to the Year MDCCCLVIII*, London: Ward, 1859.

Tomes, F. Roger, '"We are hardly prepared for this kind of teaching yet": Samuel Davidson and Lancashire Independent College,' *Journal of the United Reformed Church History Society*, V no. 7, October 1995, 398-414.

—, 'A Century of *The Century Bible*,' *The Expository Times*, CXII no. 12, September 2001, 408-412.

—, '"Learning a new technique": the reception of biblical criticism in the Nonconformist colleges,' *Journal of the United Reformed Church History Society*, VIII no. 5, October 2004, 288-314.

Torrance, J. B., 'The contribution of McLeod Campbell to Scottish theology,' *The Scottish Journal of Theology*, XXVI, 1973, 295-311.

Travell, John, *Doctor of Souls. Leslie D. Weatherhead, 1893-1976*, London: Lutterworth, 1999.

Troeltsch, Ernst, *Vernunft und Offenbarung bei Johann Gerhard und Melanchthon*, Göttingen, 1891.

Turberfield, Alan F. *John Scott Lidgett: Archbishop of Methodism?* London: Epworth Press, 2003.

Turner, R. R. and Ian H. Wallace, *Serve Through Love. Per Caritatem Servite. A History of Paton Congregational College, Nottingham*, privately printed, [1984].

Tuttle, George M., *So Rich a Soil. John McLeod Campbell on Christian Atonement*, Edinburgh: The Handsel Press, 1986.

Upton, C. B., *Dr. Martineau's Philosophy. A Survey*, London: Nisbet, 1905.

Urban, W. M., *Humanity and Deity*, London: Allen & Unwin, 1951.

Urwick, William, *Nonconformity in Worcester*, London: Simkin, Marshall, Hamilton, Kent, 1897.

Ushenko, A. P., *The Philosophy of Relativity*, London: Allen & Unwin, 1937.

Van der Borght, Eduardus, ed., *Christian Identity*, (*Studies in Reformed Theology*, XVI), Leiden: Brill, 2008.

Van Dusen, Henry P., ed., *The Christian Answer*, London: Nisbet, 1946.

Vaughan, Robert, *Congregationalism: or the Polity of Independent Churches, viewed in relation to the State and Tendencies of Modern Society*, 2nd edn revised and enlarged, 1842.

Vickers, John A.,ed., *A Dictionary of Methodism in Britain and Ireland*, Peterborough: Epworth Press, 2000.

Vidler, A. R., *The Theology of F. D. Maurice*, London: SCM Press, 1948.

Vine, Chas. H., ed., *The Old Faith and the New Theology. A Series of Sermons and Essays on some of the Truths held by Evangelical Christians, and the Difficulties of accepting much of what is called the 'New Theology'*, London: Sampson Low, Marston, 1907.

Visser 't Hooft, W. A., *No Other Name*, London: SCM Press, 1963.

Waddington, John, *Congregational History, 1700-1800, in relation to Contemporaneous Events, Education, the Eclipse of Faith, Revivals, and Christian Missions*, London: Longmans Green, 1876.

—, *Congregational History 1800-1850*, London: Longmans Green, 1878.

—, *Surrey Congregational History*, London: Jackson, Walford, and Hodder, 1866.

Wadsworth, K. W., *Yorkshire United Independent College*, London: Independent Press, 1954.

Walker, Williston, *The Creeds and Platforms of Congregationalism*, (1893), Boston: Pilgrim Press, 1960.

Waller, Ralph, 'James Martineau: The development of his religious thought,' in Barbara Smith ed., *Truth, Liberty and Religion. Essays celebrating Two Hundred Years of Manchester College*, Oxford: Manchester College, 1986.

Wardlaw, Ralph, 'Reminiscences of the late Rev. George Payne, LL.D.,' in G. Payne, *Lectures on Christian Theology*, q.v., I, cxxxiii-cli.

Warfield, Benjamin B., *Biblical Doctrines*, New York: OUP, 1929.

—, *Christology and Criticism*, New York: OUP, 1929.

Waterland, Daniel, *A Vindication of Christ's Divinity, being a Defense of some Queries relating to Dr. Clarke's Scheme of the Holy Trinity, in Answer to a Clergyman in the Country*, Cambridge, 1719.

Waters, Robert, 'He is alive,' *The Outlook*, March 1981.

Watson, John, 'James Martineau: A saint of theism,' *The Hibbert Journal*, I, 1902-1903, 253-271.

Watson, Thomas, *A Body of Divinity*, (1692), London: The Banner of Truth Trust, 1975.

Watts, Isaac, *The Christian Doctrine of the Trinity: or, Father, Son and Spirit, three Persons and one God, asserted and proved, with their Divine Rights and Honours vindicated by plain Evidence of Scripture, without Aid or Incumbrance of Human Schemes, Written chiefly for the use of private Christians*, London, 1722.

Weingart, Richard E., *The Logic of Divine Love: A Critical Analysis of the Soteriology of Peter Abelard*, Oxford: Clarendon Press, 1970.

Webb, C. C. J., *The Historical Element in Religion*, London: Allen & Unwin, 1935.

Welch, Claude, *Protestant Thought in the Nineteenth Century*, New Haven and London: Yale University Press, 1971.

Wesley, John, *The Works of the Rev. John Wesley, A.M.*, ed. Thomas Jackson, London: John Mason, 14 vols, 1829-31.

White, Edward, *Life in Christ. Four Discourses upon the Scripture Doctrine that Immortality is the Peculiar Privilege of the Regenerate*, London, 1846.

—, *Life in Christ. A Study of the Scripture Doctrine on the Nature of Man, the Object of Divine Incarnation, and the Conditions of Human Immortality*, London, 1875.

—, 'The influence of spiritual states upon biblical criticism,' *The Congregational Review*, I, 1887, 982-1000.

White, John, *A Letter to Mr. Samuel Chandler; Being a Vindication of some Passages in the Three Letters to a Gentleman Dissenting from the Church of England ... Against his Reflections in his late Book, entitled, The Case of Subscription ... With some Considerations upon the Speech (therein published) of John Alphonso Turretine, previous to the Abolition of all Subscriptions in Geneva*, London: C. Davis and Ipswich: W. Craighton, 1749.

White, William, ed., *Memoirs of Thomas T. Lynch*, London: Ibister, 1874.

Whitehead, A. N., *Process and Reality. An Essay in Cosmology*, Cambridge: CUP, 1929.

Whitehead, A. N. and Bertrand Russell, *Principia Mathematica*, Cambridge: CUP, 1910-1913.

Wiles, Maurice, ed., *Providence*, London: SPCK, 1969.

Wilkerson, Albert H., *R. J. Campbell, The Man and His Message*, London: Francis Griffiths, 1907.

Williams, N. P., *The Ideas of the Fall and of Original Sin*, London: Longmans, Green, 1927.

Williams, Robert R., 'I. A. Dorner: the ethical immutability of God,' *Journal of the American Academy of Religion*, LIV no. 4, Winter 1986, 721-739.

[Wilson, Walter], 'Some account of Mr. Samuel Jones,' *Monthly Repository*, IV, 1809, 651-7.

Wilson, Walter, *History and Antiquities of Dissenting Churches and Meeting-houses in London, Westminster and Southwark*, London: W. Button, 4 vols., 1808-1812.

Winterhager, J. W. and Arnold Brown, eds, *Vocation and Victory. An International Symposium presented in Honour of Erik Wickberg, LL.D.*, Basel: Brunner, 1974.

Woods, G. F., 'The idea of the transcendent,' in A. R. Vidler, ed., *Soundings. Essays concerning Christian Understanding*, Cambridge: CUP, 1963, 43-65.

Wright, Arthur, *A Synopsis of the Gospels in Greek*, London: Macmillan, 1896.

Wright, David F., *Infant Baptism in Historical Perspective. Collected Studies*, Milton Keynes: Paternoster, 2007.

Wright, Thomas, *The Life of Joseph Hart*, London: Farncombe, 1910.

Wykes, David L., '"A finished monster of the true Birmingham breed": Birmingham, Unitarians and the 1791 Priestley Riots,' in Alan P. F. Sell, ed., *Protestant Nonconformists and the West Midlands of England*, q.v., 43-69.

Wylie, Robert J. V., *The Baptist Churches of Accrington and District. Their Formation & Gradual Development with Numerous Character Sketches of Baptist Worthies*, Accrington: W. Shuttleworth, Wellington Press, 1923.

Yolton, John W., J. V. Price and J. Stephens, eds, *Dictionary of Eighteenth-Century British Philosophers*, Bristol: Thoemmes Press, 1999.

Index of Persons

Index of Place, Churches and Educational Establishments

Select Index of Subjects

Studies in Christian History and Thought

(All titles uniform with this volume)
Dates in bold are of projected publication

David Bebbington
Holiness in Nineteenth-Century England

David Bebbington stresses the relationship of movements of spirituality to changes in their cultural setting, especially the legacies of the Enlightenment and Romanticism. He shows that these broad shifts in ideological mood had a profound effect on the ways in which piety was conceptualized and practised. Holiness was intimately bound up with the spirit of the age.

2000 / 0-85364-981-2 / viii + 98pp

J. William Black
Reformation Pastors
Richard Baxter and the Ideal of the Reformed Pastor

This work examines Richard Baxter's *Gildas Salvianus, The Reformed Pastor* (1656) and explores each aspect of his pastoral strategy in light of his own concern for 'reformation' and in the broader context of Edwardian, Elizabethan and early Stuart pastoral ideals and practice.

2003 / 1-84227-190-3 / xxii + 308pp

James Bruce
Prophecy, Miracles, Angels, *and* Heavenly Light?
The Eschatology, Pneumatology and Missiology of Adomnán's Life of Columba

This book surveys approaches to the marvellous in hagiography, providing the first critique of Plummer's hypothesis of Irish saga origin. It then analyses the uniquely systematized phenomena in the *Life of Columba* from Adomnán's seventh-century theological perspective, identifying the coming of the eschatological Kingdom as the key to understanding.

2004 / 1-84227-227-6 / xviii + 286pp

Colin J. Bulley
The Priesthood of Some Believers
Developments from the General to the Special Priesthood in the Christian Literature of the First Three Centuries

The first in-depth treatment of early Christian texts on the priesthood of all believers shows that the developing priesthood of the ordained related closely to the division between laity and clergy and had deleterious effects on the practice of the general priesthood.

2000 / 1-84227-034-6 / xii + 336pp

Anthony R. Cross (ed.)
Ecumenism and History
Studies in Honour of John H.Y. Briggs

This collection of essays examines the inter-relationships between the two fields in which Professor Briggs has contributed so much: history—particularly Baptist and Nonconformist—and the ecumenical movement. With contributions from colleagues and former research students from Britain, Europe and North America, *Ecumenism and History* provides wide-ranging studies in important aspects of Christian history, theology and ecumenical studies.

2002 / 1-84227-135-0 / xx + 362pp

Maggi Dawn
Confessions of an Inquiring Spirit
Form as Constitutive of Meaning in S.T. Coleridge's Theological Writing

This study of Coleridge's *Confessions* focuses on its confessional, epistolary and fragmentary form, suggesting that attention to these features significantly affects its interpretation. Bringing a close study of these three literary forms, the author suggests ways in which they nuance the text with particular understandings of the Trinity, and of a kenotic christology. Some parallels are drawn between Romantic and postmodern dilemmas concerning the authority of the biblical text.

***2006** / 1-84227-255-1 / approx. 224 pp*

Ruth Gouldbourne
The Flesh and the Feminine
Gender and Theology in the Writings of Caspar Schwenckfeld

Caspar Schwenckfeld and his movement exemplify one of the radical communities of the sixteenth century. Challenging theological and liturgical norms, they also found themselves challenging social and particularly gender assumptions. In this book, the issues of the relationship between radical theology and the understanding of gender are considered.

***2005** / 1-84227-048-6 / approx. 304pp*

Crawford Gribben
Puritan Millennialism
Literature and Theology, 1550–1682

Puritan Millennialism surveys the growth, impact and eventual decline of puritan millennialism throughout England, Scotland and Ireland, arguing that it was much more diverse than has frequently been suggested. This Paternoster edition is revised and extended from the original 2000 text.

***2007** / 1-84227-372-8 / approx. 320pp*

Galen K. Johnson

Prisoner of Conscience

John Bunyan on Self, Community and Christian Faith

This is an interdisciplinary study of John Bunyan's understanding of conscience across his autobiographical, theological and fictional writings, investigating whether conscience always deserves fidelity, and how Bunyan's view of conscience affects his relationship both to modern Western individualism and historic Christianity.

2003 / 1-84227-223-3 / xvi + 236pp

R.T. Kendall

Calvin and English Calvinism to 1649

The author's thesis is that those who formed the Westminster Confession of Faith, which is regarded as Calvinism, in fact departed from John Calvin on two points: (1) the extent of the atonement and (2) the ground of assurance of salvation.

1997 / 0-85364-827-1 / xii + 264pp

Timothy Larsen

Friends of Religious Equality

Nonconformist Politics in Mid-Victorian England

During the middle decades of the nineteenth century the English Nonconformist community developed a coherent political philosophy of its own, of which a central tenet was the principle of religious equality (in contrast to the stereotype of Evangelical Dissenters). The Dissenting community fought for the civil rights of Roman Catholics, non-Christians and even atheists on an issue of principle which had its flowering in the enthusiastic and undivided support which Nonconformity gave to the campaign for Jewish emancipation. This reissued study examines the political efforts and ideas of English Nonconformists during the period, covering the whole range of national issues raised, from state education to the Crimean War. It offers a case study of a theologically conservative group defending religious pluralism in the civic sphere, showing that the concept of religious equality was a grand vision at the centre of the political philosophy of the Dissenters.

2007 */ 1-84227-402-3 / x + 300pp*

Byung-Ho Moon

Christ the Mediator of the Law

Calvin's Christological Understanding of the Law as the Rule of Living and Life-Giving

This book explores the coherence between Christology and soteriology in Calvin's theology of the law, examining its intellectual origins and his position on the concept and extent of Christ's mediation of the law. A comparative study between Calvin and contemporary Reformers—Luther, Bucer, Melancthon and Bullinger—and his opponent Michael Servetus is made for the purpose of pointing out the unique feature of Calvin's Christological understanding of the law.

***2005** / 1-84227-318-3 / approx. 370pp*

John Eifion Morgan-Wynne

Holy Spirit and Religious Experience in Christian Writings, c.AD 90–200

This study examines how far Christians in the third to fifth generations (c.AD 90–200) attributed their sense of encounter with the divine presence, their sense of illumination in the truth or guidance in decision-making, and their sense of ethical empowerment to the activity of the Holy Spirit in their lives.

***2005** / 1-84227-319-1 / approx. 350pp*

James I. Packer

The Redemption and Restoration of Man in the Thought of Richard Baxter

James I. Packer provides a full and sympathetic exposition of Richard Baxter's doctrine of humanity, created and fallen; its redemption by Christ Jesus; and its restoration in the image of God through the obedience of faith by the power of the Holy Spirit.

2002 / 1-84227-147-4 / 432pp

Andrew Partington,

Church and State

The Contribution of the Church of England Bishops to the House of Lords during the Thatcher Years

In *Church and State*, Andrew Partington argues that the contribution of the Church of England bishops to the House of Lords during the Thatcher years was overwhelmingly critical of the government; failed to have a significant influence in the public realm; was inefficient, being undertaken by a minority of those eligible to sit on the Bench of Bishops; and was insufficiently moral and spiritual in its content to be distinctive. On the basis of this, and the likely reduction of the number of places available for Church of England bishops in a fully reformed Second Chamber, the author argues for an evolution in the Church of England's approach to the service of its bishops in the House of Lords. He proposes the Church of England works to overcome the genuine obstacles which hinder busy diocesan bishops from contributing to the debates of the House of Lords and to its life more informally.

***2005** / 1-84227-334-5 / approx. 324pp*

Michael Pasquarello III

God's Ploughman

Hugh Latimer: A 'Preaching Life' (1490–1555)

This construction of a 'preaching life' situates Hugh Latimer within the larger religious, political and intellectual world of late medieval England. Neither biography, intellectual history, nor analysis of discrete sermon texts, this book is a work of homiletic history which draws from the details of Latimer's milieu to construct an interpretive framework for the preaching performances that formed the core of his identity as a religious reformer. Its goal is to illumine the practical wisdom embodied in the content, form and style of Latimer's preaching, and to recapture a sense of its overarching purpose, movement, and transforming force during the reform of sixteenth-century England.

***2006** / 1-84227-336-1 / approx. 250pp*

Alan P.F. Sell

Enlightenment, Ecumenism, Evangel

Theological Themes and Thinkers 1550–2000

This book consists of papers in which such interlocking topics as the Enlightenment, the problem of authority, the development of doctrine, spirituality, ecumenism, theological method and the heart of the gospel are discussed. Issues of significance to the church at large are explored with special reference to writers from the Reformed and Dissenting traditions.

2005 / 1-84227-330-2 / xviii + 422pp

Alan P.F. Sell

Hinterland Theology

Some Reformed and Dissenting Adjustments

Many books have been written on theology's 'giants' and significant trends, but what of those lesser-known writers who adjusted to them? In this book some hinterland theologians of the British Reformed and Dissenting traditions, who followed in the wake of toleration, the Evangelical Revival, the rise of modern biblical criticism and Karl Barth, are allowed to have their say. They include Thomas Ridgley, Ralph Wardlaw, T.V. Tymms and N.H.G. Robinson.

***2006** / 1-84227-331-0 / approx. 350pp*

Alan P.F. Sell and Anthony R. Cross (eds)

Protestant Nonconformity in the Twentieth Century

In this collection of essays scholars representative of a number of Nonconformist traditions reflect thematically on Nonconformists' life and witness during the twentieth century. Among the subjects reviewed are biblical studies, theology, worship, evangelism and spirituality, and ecumenism. Over and above its immediate interest, this collection provides a marker to future scholars and others wishing to know how some of their forebears assessed Nonconformity's contribution to a variety of fields during the century leading up to Christianity's third millennium.

2003 / 1-84227-221-7 / x + 398pp

Mark Smith

Religion in Industrial Society

Oldham and Saddleworth 1740–1865

This book analyses the way British churches sought to meet the challenge of industrialization and urbanization during the period 1740–1865. Working from a case-study of Oldham and Saddleworth, Mark Smith challenges the received view that the Anglican Church in the eighteenth century was characterized by complacency and inertia, and reveals Anglicanism's vigorous and creative response to the new conditions. He reassesses the significance of the centrally directed church reforms of the mid-nineteenth century, and emphasizes the importance of local energy and enthusiasm. Charting the growth of denominational pluralism in Oldham and Saddleworth, Dr Smith compares the strengths and weaknesses of the various Anglican and Nonconformist approaches to promoting church growth. He also demonstrates the extent to which all the churches participated in a common culture shaped by the influence of evangelicalism, and shows that active co-operation between the churches rather than denominational conflict dominated. This revised and updated edition of Dr Smith's challenging and original study makes an important contribution both to the social history of religion and to urban studies.

***2006** / 1-84227-335-3 / approx. 300pp*

Martin Sutherland

Peace, Toleration and Decay

The Ecclesiology of Later Stuart Dissent

This fresh analysis brings to light the complexity and fragility of the later Stuart Nonconformist consensus. Recent findings on wider seventeenth-century thought are incorporated into a new picture of the dynamics of Dissent and the roots of evangelicalism.

2003 / 1-84227-152-0 / xxii + 216pp

G. Michael Thomas

The Extent of the Atonement

A Dilemma for Reformed Theology from Calvin to the Consensus

A study of the way Reformed theology addressed the question, 'Did Christ die for all, or for the elect only?', commencing with John Calvin, and including debates with Lutheranism, the Synod of Dort and the teaching of Moïse Amyraut.

1997 / 0-85364-828-X / x + 278pp

David M. Thompson

Baptism, Church and Society in Britain from the Evangelical Revival to *Baptism, Eucharist and Ministry*

The theology and practice of baptism have not received the attention they deserve. How important is faith? What does baptismal regeneration mean? Is baptism a bond of unity between Christians? This book discusses the theology of baptism and popular belief and practice in England and Wales from the Evangelical Revival to the publication of the World Council of Churches' consensus statement on *Baptism, Eucharist and Ministry* (1982).

***2005** / 1-84227-393-0 / approx. 224pp*

Mark D. Thompson

A Sure Ground on Which to Stand

The Relation of Authority and Interpretive Method of Luther's Approach to Scripture

The best interpreter of Luther is Luther himself. Unfortunately many modern studies have superimposed contemporary agendas upon this sixteenth-century Reformer's writings. This fresh study examines Luther's own words to find an explanation for his robust confidence in the Scriptures, a confidence that generated the famous 'stand' at Worms in 1521.

2004 / 1-84227-145-8 / xvi + 322pp

Carl R. Trueman and R.S. Clark (eds)

Protestant Scholasticism

Essays in Reassessment

Traditionally Protestant theology, between Luther's early reforming career and the dawn of the Enlightenment, has been seen in terms of decline and fall into the wastelands of rationalism and scholastic speculation. In this volume a number of scholars question such an interpretation. The editors argue that the development of post-Reformation Protestantism can only be understood when a proper historical model of doctrinal change is adopted. This historical concern underlies the subsequent studies of theologians such as Calvin, Beza, Olevian, Baxter, and the two Turrentini. The result is a significantly different reading of the development of Protestant Orthodoxy, one which both challenges the older scholarly interpretations and clichés about the relationship of Protestantism to, among other things, scholasticism and rationalism, and which demonstrates the fruitfulness of the new, historical approach.

1999 / 0-85364-853-0 / xx + 344pp

Shawn D. Wright

Our Sovereign Refuge

The Pastoral Theology of Theodore Beza

Our Sovereign Refuge is a study of the pastoral theology of the Protestant reformer who inherited the mantle of leadership in the Reformed church from John Calvin. Countering a common view of Beza as supremely a 'scholastic' theologian who deviated from Calvin's biblical focus, Wright uncovers a new portrait. He was not a cold and rigid academic theologian obsessed with probing the eternal decrees of God. Rather, by placing him in his pastoral context and by noting his concerns in his pastoral and biblical treatises, Wright shows that Beza was fundamentally a committed Christian who was troubled by the vicissitudes of life in the second half of the sixteenth century. He believed that the biblical truth of the supreme sovereignty of God alone could support Christians on their earthly pilgrimage to heaven. This pastoral and personal portrait forms the heart of Wright's argument.

2004 / 1-84227-252-7 / xviii + 308pp

Paternoster: thinking faith

Paternoster

9 Holdom Avenue,

Bletchley,

Milton Keynes MK1 1QR,

United Kingdom

Web: www.authenticmedia.co.uk/paternoster

July 2005